Encyclopedia of World Cultures

Volume VIII

MIDDLE AMERICA

AND THE

CARIBBEAN

ENCYCLOPEDIA OF WORLD CULTURES

David Levinson
Editor in Chief

North America
Oceania
South Asia
Europe (Central, Western, and Southeastern Europe)
East and Southeast Asia
Russia and Eurasia / China
South America
Middle America and the Caribbean
Africa and the Middle East
Index

The Encyclopedia of World Cultures was prepared under the auspices and with the support of the Human Relations Area Files at Yale University. HRAF, the foremost international research organization in the field of cultural anthropology, is a not-for-profit consortium of twenty-three sponsoring members and 300 participating member institutions in twenty-five countries. The HRAF archive, established in 1949, contains nearly one million pages of information on the cultures of the world.

Encyclopedia of World Cultures
Volume VIII
MIDDLE AMERICA
AND THE
CARIBBEAN

James W. Dow
Volume Editor

Robert Van Kemper
Associate Volume Editor

G.K. Hall & Co.
Boston, Massachusetts

MEASUREMENT CONVERSIONS

When You Know	Multiply By	To Find
LENGTH		
inches	2.54	centimeters
feet	30	centimeters
yards	0.9	meters
miles	1.6	kilometers
millimeters	0.04	inches
centimeters	0.4	inches
meters	3.3	feet
meters	1.1	yards
kilometers	0.6	miles
AREA		
square feet	0.09	square meters
square yards	0.8	square meters
square miles	2.6	square kilometers
acres	0.4	hectares
hectares	2.5	acres
square meters	1.2	square yards
square kilometers	0.4	square miles

TEMPERATURE

$°C = (°F - 32) \div 1.8$

$°F = (°C \times 1.8) + 32$

© 1995 by the Human Relations Area Files, Inc.

First published 1995
by G.K. Hall & Co., an imprint of Macmillan Inc.
866 Third Avenue
New York, NY 10022

10   9   8   7   6   5   4   3   2   1

Library of Congress Cataloging-in-Publication Data
(Revised for volume 8)
Encyclopedia of world cultures.
    Includes bibliographical references, filmographies, and indexes.
    Contents: v. 1. North America / Timothy J. O'Leary,
David Levinson, volume editors—   —[etc.] — v. 5.
East and Southeast Asia / Paul Hockings, volume editor—
        —v. 8. Middle America and the Caribbean / James
W. Dow, volume editor.
    1. Ethnology—Encyclopedias. I. Levinson, David,
1947-   .
GN307.E53   1991   306   90-49123
ISBN 0-8168-1840-X (set : alk. paper)
ISBN 0-8161-1808-6 (v. 1 : alk. paper)
ISBN 0-8161-1812-4 (v. 3 : alk. paper)
ISBN 0-8161-1814-0 (v. 5 : alk. paper)
ISBN 0-8161-1816-7 (v. 8 : alk. paper)

The paper used in this publication meets the minimum requirements of American National Standard for Information Sciences—Permanence of Paper for Printed Library Materials. ANSI Z39.48-1992.   ∞™

MANUFACTURED IN THE UNITED STATES OF AMERICA

Contents

Project Staff   vi

Contributors   vii

Preface   xv

Introduction   xxi

Maps

    1. Central America and the Caribbean   xxxv

    2. Cultures of Northern Mexico   xxxvi

    3. Cultures of Southern Mexico   xxxvii

    4. Cultures of Central America   xxxviii

    5. The Caribbean   xxxix

Cultures of Middle America and the Caribbean   1

Glossary   319

Filmography   325

    Index to Filmography   326

Ethnonym Index   327

The Editors   330

90541

Contributors

Janis Alcorn
Chevy Chase, Maryland
United States

Wasteko

William Lee Alexander
Department of Anthropology
University of Arizona
Tucson, Arizona
United States

Tepehuan of Chihuahua;
Tepehuan of Durango

Luc Alofs
Aruba
Netherlands Antilles

Arubans

Vered Amit-Talai
Department of Sociology/Anthropology
Concordia University
Montréal, Québec
Canada

Cayman Islanders

Marina Anguiano
Academia de Educación Indígena
Universidad Pedogógica Nacional
México, D.F.
Mexico

Cora

Kathlene Barber
Rochester, Michigan
United States

Awakateko

Riva Berleant-Schiller
University of Connecticut
Torrington, Connecticut
United States

Montserratians

John R. Bort
Department of Sociology and Anthropology
East Carolina University
Greenville, North Carolina
United States

Ngawbe

Thomas Bowen
Department of Anthropology
California State University—Fresno
Fresno, California
United States

Seri

María Eugenia Bozzoli de Wille   ***Boruca, Bribri, and Cabécar; Costa Ricans***
Vice Rectory for Research
University of Costa Rica
San José
Costa Rica

Pete Brown   ***Tzotzil and Tzeltal of Pantelhó***
Department of Anthropology
Lawrence University
Appleton, Wisconsin
United States

Katherine E. Browne   ***Martiniquais***
Department of Anthropology
Colorado State University
Fort Collins, Colorado
United States

C. H. Browner   ***Chinantec***
Departments of Psychiatry and Behavioral Science
University of California, Los Angeles
Los Angeles, California
United States

Anne Browning   ***Pima Bajo***
Department of Anthropology
University of Arizona
Tucson, Arizona
United States

Robert S. Carlsen   ***Tz'utujil***
University of Denver
Denver, Colorado
United States

Barry Chevannes   ***Rastafarians***
Institute of Social Studies
The Hague
The Netherlands

N. Ross Crumrine   ***Cahita***
Department of Anthropology
University of Victoria
Victoria, B.C.
Canada

James W. Dow   ***Otomí of the Sierra; Tepehua***
Department of Sociology and Anthropology
Oakland University
Rochester, Michigan
United States

Barbara Edmonson   ***Wasteko***
Department of Anthropology
Tulane University
New Orleans, Lousiana
United States

María de la Paloma Escalante Gonzalbo   ***Ladinos***
Division de Estudios de Posgrado
Escuela Nacional de Antropología e Historia
Instituto Nacional de Antropología e Historia
México, D.F.
Mexico

Susan J. Fernández   **_Cubans_**
St. Petersburg, Florida
United States

José Abraham Franco Ozuna   **_Guarijío_**
Departamento de Sociología
Universidad de Sonora
Hermosillo, Sonora
Mexico

Víctor Manuel Franco Pellotier   **_Amuzgo_**
Centro de Investigaciones y Estudios Superiores en
   Antropología Social
Tlalpán, México D.F.
Mexico

Douglas P. Fry   **_Zapotec_**
Department of Anthropology
Eckerd College
St. Petersburg, Florida
United States

Carlos Garma Navarro   **_Totonac_**
Departamento de Antropología
Universidad Autónoma Metropolitana—Iztapalapa
Iztapalapa, D.F.
Mexico

José González Rodrigo   **_Nahua of the State of Mexico_**
Departamento de Antropología
Universidad Autónoma Metropolitana—Iztapalapa
Iztapalapa, D.F.
Mexico

Nancie L. Gonzalez   **_Garifuna_**
Annapolis, Maryland
United States

Kenneth J. Goodman   **_Dominicans_**
Department of Anthropology
University of South Florida
Tampa, Florida
United States

Edmund T. Gordon   **_Creoles of Nicaragua_**
Department of Anthropology
University of Texas, Austin
Austin, Texas
United States

James B. Greenberg   **_Chatino_**
Bureau of Applied Research
Department of Anthropology
University of Arizona
Tucson, Arizona
United States

David Griffith   **_Puerto Ricans_**
Department of Anthropology
Institute for Coastal and Marine Resources
East Carolina University
Greenville, North Carolina
United States

Paul Grifhorst
Utrecht
The Netherlands

W. Penn Handwerker
Department of Anthropology
University of Connecticut
Storrs, Connecticut
United States

Mary W. Helms
Department of Anthropology
University of North Carolina—Greensboro
Greensboro, North Carolina
United States

Peter H. Herlihy
Department of Geography
University of Kansas
Lawrence, Kansas
United States

Christine G. T. Ho
Department of Anthropology
University of South Florida
Tampa, Florida
United States

Charles Andrew Hofling
Department of Anthropology
McMicken College of Arts and Sciences
University of Cincinnati
Cincinnati, Ohio
United States

Nicholas A. Hopkins
Department of Anthropology
Florida State University
Talahassee, Florida
United States

César Huerta Ríos

Robert C. Hunt
Department of Anthropology
Brandeis University
Waltham, Massachusetts
United States

Rose Jones
Department of Anthropology
Southern Methodist University
Dallas, Texas
United States

Morton Klass
Department of Anthropology
Barnard College
Columbia University
New York, New York
United States

Curaçao

Barbadians

Miskito

Emberá and Wounan; Sumu

Chinese in the English-Speaking Caribbean

Itza'

Ch'ol

Triquis

Cuicatec

Saint Lucians

East Indians in Trinadad

Susan M. Knowles-Berry
Vancouver, Washington
United States

Chontal of Tabasco

Robert Lawless
Department of Anthropology
Wichita State University
Wichita, Kansas
United States

Haitians

Anthony Layng
Department of Anthropology
Elmira College
Elmira, New York
United States

Carib of Dominica

Mindie Lazarus-Black
Department of Criminal Justice
University of Illinois
Chicago, Illinois
United States

Antiguans and Barbudans

Moisés Leon
San José
Costa Rica

Chinese of Costa Rica

Frank J. Lipp
Bronx, New York
United States

Mixe

Miguel Lisbona Guillen
Instituto Chiapaneco de Cultura
Tuxtla Guitérrez, Chiapas
Mexico

Zoque

James H. McDonald
Department of Sociology, Anthropology, and Social Work
University of Michigan—Flint
Flint, Michigan
United States

Italian Mexicans

Ian Mast
Department of Anthropology
Southern Methodist University
Dallas, Texas
United States

K'iche'; Lenca; Pame; Poqomam

Judith M. Maxwell
Department of Anthropology
Tulane University
New Orleans, Louisiana
United States

Chuj

William L. Merrill
National Museum of Natural History
Smithsonian Institution
Washington, D.C.
United States

Tarahumara

José Luis Moctezuma Zamarrón
Tucson, Arizona
United States

Kikapu

John Monaghan
Department of Anthropology
Vanderbilt University
Nashville, Tennesee
United States

Mixtec

Mary Beck Moser
Summer Institute of Linguistics
Tucson, Arizona
United States

Seri

Cristina Oehmichen Bazán
Instituto Nacional Indigenista
México, D.F.
Mexico

Otomí of the Valley of Mezquital

María Eugenia Olavarría
Universidad Autónoma Metropolitana—Iztapalapa
Iztapalapa, D.F.
Mexico

Yaqui

Enriqueta M. Olguin
México, D.F.
Mexico

Cora

Charlotte Swanson Otterbein
Williamsville, New York
United States

Bahamians

Keith F. Otterbein
Department of Anthropology
University at Buffalo
State University of New York
Buffalo, New York
United States

Bahamians

Maya Lorena Pérez Ruíz
Departamento de Etnografía e Antropología Social
Instituto Nacional de Antropología e Historia
México, D.F.
Mexico

Mazahua

María Ana Portal Ariosa
Departamento de Antropología
Universidad Autónoma Metropolitana—Iztapalapa
Iztapalapa, D.F.
Mexico

Mazatec

Norbert Roβ
Institut für Völkerkunde
University of Freiburg
Freiburg im Breisgau
Germany

Tzotzil of San Andrés Larrainzar

Brenda Rosenbaum
Albany, New York
United States

Tzotzil of Chamula

Andrew Roth-Seneff
Department of Anthropology
Southern Methodist University
Dallas, Texas
United States

Tarascans

Arthur J. Rubel
Medical Center
University of California, Irvine
Irvine, California
United States

Chinantec

Mario Humberto Ruz
Centro de Investigaciones y Estudios Superiores en
  Antropología Social
Tlalpán, México D.F.
Mexico

Tojolab'al

Michael Salovesh
Department of Anthropology
Northern Illinois University
DeKalb, Illinois
United States

Tzotzil of San Bartolomé de los Llanos

Alan R. Sandstrom
Department of Sociology and Anthropology
Indiana/Purdue University
Fort Wayne, Indiana
Unites States

Nahua of the Huasteca

Stacy B. Schaefer
Department of Psychology and Anthropology
University of Texas—Pan American
Edinburg, Texas
United States

Huichol

Frans J. Schryer
Department of Sociology and Anthropology
University of Guelph
Guelph, Ontario
Canada

Cattle Ranchers of the Huasteca

Norman B. Schwartz
Department of Anthropology
University of Delaware
Newark, Delaware
United States

Itza'

Daniel A. Segal
Department of Anthropology
Pitzer College
Claremont, California
United States

Trinidadians and Tobagonians

John R. Sosa
Department of Sociology-Anthropology
State University College at Cortland
Cortland, New York
United States

Yukateko

James M. Taggart
Franklin and Marshall College
Lancaster, Pennsylvania
United States

Nahuat of the Sierra de Puebla

Karin E. Tice
Ann Arbor, Michigan
United States

Kuna

Amy Todd
Department of Anthropology
Brandeis University
Waltham, Massachusetts
United States

Cuicatec

Evon Z. Vogt
Department of Anthropology
Peabody Museum
Harvard University
Cambridge, Massachusetts
United States

Tzotzil of Zinacantan

John M. Watanabe
Department of Anthropology
Dartmouth College
Hanover, New Hampshire
United States

Mam

Thomas Weaver
Department of Anthropology
University of Arizona
Tucson, Arizona
United States

Pima Bajo; Tepehuan of Chihuahua;
Tepehuan of Durango

William Wedenoja
Department of Sociology, Anthropology, and Social Work
Southwest Missouri State University
Springfield, Missouri
United States

Jamaicans

Linda M. Whiteford
Department of Anthropology
University of South Florida
Tampa, Florida
United States

Dominicans

Philip D. Young
Department of Anthropology
University of Oregon
Eugene, Oregon
United States

Bugle; Ngawbe

Preface

This project began in 1987 with the goal of assembling a basic reference source that provides accurate, clear, and concise descriptions of the cultures of the world. We wanted to be as comprehensive and authoritative as possible: comprehensive, by providing descriptions of all the cultures of each region of the world or by describing a representative sample of cultures for regions where full coverage is impossible, and authoritative by providing accurate descriptions of the cultures for both the past and the present.

The publication of the *Encyclopedia of World Cultures* in the last decade of the twentieth century is especially timely. The political, economic, and social changes of the past fifty years have produced a world more complex and fluid than at any time in human history. Three sweeping transformations of the worldwide cultural landscape are especially significant.

First is what some social scientists are calling the "New Diaspora"—the dispersal of cultural groups to new locations across the world. This dispersal affects all nations and takes a wide variety of forms: in East African nations, the formation of new towns inhabited by people from dozens of different ethnic groups; in Micronesia and Polynesia, the movement of islanders to cities in New Zealand and the United States; in North America, the replacement by Asians and Latin Americans of Europeans as the most numerous immigrants; in Europe, the increased reliance on workers from the Middle East and North Africa; and so on.

Second, and related to this dispersal, is the internal division of what were once single, unified cultural groups into two or more relatively distinct groups. This pattern of internal division is most dramatic among indigenous or third or fourth world cultures whose traditional ways of life have been altered by contact with the outside world. Underlying this division are both the population dispersion mentioned above and sustained contact with the economically developed world. The result is that groups who at one time saw themselves and were seen by others as single cultural groups have been transformed into two or more distinct groups. Thus, in many cultural groups, we find deep and probably permanent divisions between those who live in the country and those who live in cities, those who follow the traditional religion and those who have converted to Christianity, those who live inland and those who live on the seacoast, and those who live by means of a subsistence economy and those now enmeshed in a cash economy.

The third important transformation of the worldwide cultural landscape is the revival of ethnic nationalism, with many peoples claiming and fighting for political freedom and territorial integrity on the basis of ethnic solidarity and ethnic-based claims to their traditional homeland. Although most attention has focused recently on ethnic nationalism in Eastern Europe and the former Soviet Union, the trend is nonetheless a worldwide phenomenon involving, for example, American Indian cultures in North and South America, the Basques in Spain and France, the Tamil and Sinhalese in Sri Lanka, and the Tutsi and Hutu in Burundi, among others.

To be informed citizens of our rapidly changing multicultural world we must understand the ways of life of people from cultures different from our own. "We" is used here in the broadest sense, to include not just scholars who study the cultures of the world and businesspeople and government officials who work in the world community but also the average citizen who reads or hears about multicultural events in the news every day and young people who are growing up in this complex cultural world. For all of these people—which means all of us—there is a pressing need for information on the cultures of the world. This encyclopedia provides this information in two ways. First, its descriptions of the traditional ways of life of the world's cultures can serve as a baseline against which cultural change can be measured and understood. Second, it acquaints the reader with the contemporary ways of life throughout the world.

We are able to provide this information largely through the efforts of the volume editors and the nearly one thousand contributors who wrote the cultural summaries that are the heart of the book. The contributors are social scientists (anthropologists, sociologists, historians, and geographers) as well as educators, government officials, and missionaries who usually have firsthand research-based knowledge of the cultures they write about. In many cases they are the major expert or one of the leading experts on the culture, and some are themselves members of the cultures. As experts, they are able to provide accurate, up-to-date information. This is crucial for many parts of the world where indigenous cultures may be overlooked by official information seekers such as government census takers. These experts have often lived among the people they write about, conducting participant-observations with them and speaking their language. Thus they are able to provide integrated, holistic descriptions of the cultures, not just a list of facts. Their portraits of the cultures leave the reader with a real sense of what it means to be a "Taos" or a "Rom" or a "Sicilian."

Those summaries not written by an expert on the culture have usually been written by a researcher at the Human Relations Area Files, Inc., working from primary source materials. The Human Relations Area Files, an international educational and research institute, is recognized by professionals in the social and behavioral sciences, humanities, and medical sciences as a major source of information on the cultures of the world.

Uses of the Encyclopedia

This encyclopedia is meant to be used by a variety of people for a variety of purposes. It can be used both to gain a general understanding of a culture and to find a specific piece of information by looking it up under the relevant subheading in a summary. It can also be used to learn about a particular region or subregion of the world and the social, economic, and political forces that have shaped the cultures in that region. The encyclopedia is also a resource guide that leads readers who want a deeper understanding of particular cultures to additional sources of information. Resource guides in the encyclopedia include ethnonyms listed in each summary, which can be used as entry points into the social science literature where the culture may sometimes be identified by a different name; a bibliography at the end of each summary, which lists books and articles about the culture; and a filmography at the end of each volume, which lists films and videos on many of the cultures.

Beyond being a basic reference resource, the encyclopedia also serves readers with more focused needs. For researchers interested in comparing cultures, the encyclopedia serves as the most complete and up-to-date sampling frame from which to select cultures for further study. For those interested in international studies, the encyclopedia leads one quickly into the relevant social science literature as well as providing a state-of-the-art assessment of our knowledge of the cultures of a particular region. For curriculum developers and teachers seeking to internationalize their curriculum, the encyclopedia is itself a basic reference and educational resource as well as a directory to other materials. For government officials, it is a repository of information not likely to be available in any other single publication or, in some cases, not available at all. For students, from high school through graduate school, it provides background and bibliographic information for term papers and class projects. And for travelers, it provides an introduction into the ways of life of the indigenous peoples in the area of the world they will be visiting.

Format of the Encyclopedia

The encyclopedia comprises ten volumes, ordered by geographical regions of the world. The order of publication is not meant to represent any sort of priority. Volumes 1 through 9 contain a total of about fifteen hundred summaries along with maps, glossaries, and indexes of alternate names for the cultural groups. The tenth and final volume contains cumulative lists of the cultures of the world, their alternate names, and a bibliography of selected publications pertaining to those groups.

North America covers the cultures of Canada, Greenland, and the United States of America.
Oceania covers the cultures of Australia, New Zealand, Melanesia, Micronesia, and Polynesia.
South Asia covers the cultures of Bangladesh, India, Pakistan, Sri Lanka and other South Asian islands and the Himalayan states.
Europe covers the cultures of Europe.

East and Southeast Asia covers the cultures of Japan, Korea, mainland and insular Southeast Asia, and Taiwan.
Russia and Eurasia / China covers the cultures of Mongolia, the People's Republic of China, and the former Union of Soviet Socialist Republics.
South America covers the cultures of South America.
Middle America and the Caribbean covers the cultures of Central America, Mexico, and the Caribbean islands.
Africa and the Middle East covers the cultures of Madagascar and sub-Saharan Africa, North Africa, the Middle East, and south-central Asia.

Format of the Volumes

Each volume contains this preface, an introductory essay by the volume editor, the cultural summaries ranging from a few lines to several pages each, maps pinpointing the location of the cultures, a filmography, an ethnonym index of alternate names for the cultures, and a glossary of scientific and technical terms. All entries are listed in alphabetical order and are extensively cross-referenced.

Cultures Covered

A central issue in selecting cultures for coverage in the encyclopedia has been how to define what we mean by a cultural group. The questions of what a culture is and what criteria can be used to classify a particular social group (such as a religious group, ethnic group, nationality, or territorial group) as a cultural group have long perplexed social scientists and have yet to be answered to everyone's satisfaction. Two realities account for why the questions cannot be answered definitively. First, a wide variety of different types of cultures exist around the world. Among common types are national cultures, regional cultures, ethnic groups, indigenous societies, religious groups, and unassimilated immigrant groups. No single criterion or marker of cultural uniqueness can consistently distinguish among the hundreds of cultures that fit into these general types. Second, as noted above, single cultures or what were at one time identified as single cultures can and do vary internally over time and place. Thus a marker that may identify a specific group as a culture in one location or at one time may not work for that culture in another place or at another time. For example, use of the Yiddish language would have been a marker of Jewish cultural identity in Eastern Europe in the nineteenth century, but it would not serve as a marker for Jews in the twentieth-century United States, where most speak English. Similarly, residence on one of the Cook Islands in Polynesia would have been a marker of Cook Islander identity in the eighteenth century, but not in the twentieth century when two-thirds of Cook Islanders live in New Zealand and elsewhere.

Given these considerations, no attempt has been made to develop and use a single definition of a cultural unit or to develop and use a fixed list of criteria for identifying cultural units. Instead, the task of selecting cultures was left to the volume editors, and the criteria and procedures they used are discussed in their introductory essays. In general, however, six criteria were used, sometimes alone and sometimes in combination to classify social groups as cultural groups: (1) geographical localization, (2) identification in the social science literature as a distinct group, (3) distinct language, (4) shared traditions, religion, folklore, or values, (5) maintenance of group identity in the face of strong assimilative pressures, and (6) previous listing in an inventory of the world's cultures such as _Ethnographic Atlas_ (Murdock 1967) or the _Outline of World Cultures_ (Murdock 1983).

In general, we have been "lumpers" rather than "splitters" in writing the summaries. That is, if there is some question about whether a particular group is really one culture or two related cultures, we have more often than not treated it as a single culture, with internal differences noted in the summary. Similarly, we have sometimes chosen to describe a number of very similar cultures in a single summary rather than in a series of summaries that would be mostly redundant. There is, however, some variation from one region to another in this approach, and the rationale for each region is discussed in the volume editor's essay.

Two categories of cultures are usually not covered in the encyclopedia. First, extinct cultures, especially those that have not existed as distinct cultural units for some time, are usually not described. Cultural extinction is often, though certainly not always, indicated by the disappearance of the culture's language. So, for example, the Aztec are not covered, although living descendants of the Aztec, the Nahuatl-speakers of central Mexico, are described.

Second, the ways of life of immigrant groups are usually not described in much detail, unless there is a long history of resistance to assimilation and the group has maintained its distinct identity, as have the Amish in North America. These cultures are, however, described in the location where they traditionally lived and, for the most part, continue to live, and migration patterns are noted. For example, the Hmong in Laos are described in the Southeast Asia volume, but the refugee communities in the United States and Canada are covered only in the general summaries on Southeast Asians in those two countries in the North America volume. Although it would be ideal to provide descriptions of all the immigrant cultures or communities of the world, that is an undertaking well beyond the scope of this encyclopedia, for there are probably more than five thousand such communities in the world.

Finally, it should be noted that not all nationalities are covered, only those that are also distinct cultures as well as political entities. For example, the Vietnamese and Burmese are included but Indians (citizens of the Republic of India) are not, because the latter is a political entity made up of a great mix of cultural groups. In the case of nations whose populations include a number of different, relatively unassimilated groups or cultural regions, each of the groups is described separately. For example, there is no summary for Italians as such in the Europe volume, but there are summaries for the regional cultures of Italy, such as the Tuscans, Sicilians, and Tirolians, and other cultures such as the Sinti Piemontese.

Cultural Summaries

The heart of this encyclopedia is the descriptive summaries of the cultures, which range from a few lines to five or six pages in length. They provide a mix of demographic, historical, social, economic, political, and religious information on the cultures. Their emphasis or flavor is cultural; that is, they focus on the ways of life of the people—both past and present—and the factors that have caused the culture to change over time and place.

A key issue has been how to decide which cultures should be described by longer summaries and which by shorter ones. This decision was made by the volume editors, who had to balance a number of intellectual and practical considerations. Again, the rationale for these decisions is discussed in their essays. But among the factors that were considered by all the editors were the total number of cultures in their region, the availability of experts to write summaries, the availability of information on the cultures, the degree of similarity between cultures, and the importance of a culture in a scientific or political sense.

The summary authors followed a standardized outline so that each summary provides information on a core list of topics. The authors, however, had some leeway in deciding how much attention was to be given each topic and whether additional information should be included. Summaries usually provide information on the following topics:

CULTURE NAME: The name used most often in the social science literature to refer to the culture or the name the group uses for itself.

ETHNONYMS: Alternate names for the culture including names used by outsiders, the self-name, and alternate spellings, within reasonable limits.

ORIENTATION
Identification. Location of the culture and the derivation of its name and ethnonyms.
Location. Where the culture is located and a description of the physical environment.
Demography. Population history and the most recent reliable population figures or estimates.
Linguistic Affiliation. The name of the language spoken and/or written by the culture, its place in an international language classification system, and internal variation in language use.

HISTORY AND CULTURAL RELATIONS: A tracing of the origins and history of the culture and the past and current nature of relationships with other groups.

SETTLEMENTS: The location of settlements, types of settlements, types of structures, housing design and materials.

ECONOMY
Subsistence and Commercial Activities. The primary methods of obtaining, consuming, and distributing money, food, and other necessities.
Industrial Arts. Implements and objects produced by the culture either for its own use or for sale or trade.
Trade. Products traded and patterns of trade with other groups.
Division of Labor. How basic economic tasks are assigned by age, sex, ability, occupational specialization, or status.
Land Tenure. Rules and practices concerning the allocation of land and land-use rights to members of the culture and to outsiders.

KINSHIP
Kin Groups and Descent. Rules and practices concerning kin-based features of social organization such as lineages and clans and alliances between these groups.
Kinship Terminology. Classification of the kinship terminological system on the basis of either cousin terms or genera-

tion, and information about any unique aspects of kinship terminology.

MARRIAGE AND FAMILY

Marriage. Rules and practices concerning reasons for marriage, types of marriage, economic aspects of marriage, postmarital residence, divorce, and remarriage.

Domestic Unit. Description of the basic household unit including type, size, and composition.

Inheritance. Rules and practices concerning the inheritance of property.

Socialization. Rules and practices concerning child rearing including caretakers, values inculcated, child-rearing methods, initiation rites, and education.

SOCIOPOLITICAL ORGANIZATION

Social Organization. Rules and practices concerning the internal organization of the culture, including social status, primary and secondary groups, and social stratification.

Political Organization. Rules and practices concerning leadership, politics, governmental organizations, and decision making.

Social Control. The sources of conflict within the culture and informal and formal social control mechanisms.

Conflict. The sources of conflict with other groups and informal and formal means of resolving conflicts.

RELIGION AND EXPRESSIVE CULTURE

Religious Beliefs. The nature of religious beliefs including beliefs in supernatural entities, traditional beliefs, and the effects of major religions.

Religious Practitioners. The types, sources of power, and activities of religious specialists such as shamans and priests.

Ceremonies. The nature, type, and frequency of religious and other ceremonies and rites.

Arts. The nature, types, and characteristics of artistic activities including literature, music, dance, carving, and so on.

Medicine. The nature of traditional medical beliefs and practices and the influence of scientific medicine.

Death and Afterlife. The nature of beliefs and practices concerning death, the deceased, funerals, and the afterlife.

BIBLIOGRAPHY: A selected list of publications about the culture. The list usually includes publications that describe both the traditional and the contemporary culture.

AUTHOR'S NAME: The name of the summary author.

Maps

Each regional volume contains maps pinpointing the current location of the cultures described in that volume. The first map in each volume is usually an overview, showing the countries in that region. The other maps provide more detail by marking the locations of the cultures in four or five subregions.

Filmography

Each volume contains a list of films and videos about cultures covered in that volume. This list is provided as a service and in no way indicates an endorsement by the editor, the volume editor, or the summary authors. Addresses of distributors are provided so that information about availability and prices can be readily obtained.

Ethnonym Index

Each volume contains an ethnonym index for the cultures covered in that volume. As mentioned above, ethnonyms are alternative names for the culture—that is, names different from those used here as the summary headings. Ethnonyms may be alternative spellings of the culture name, a totally different name used by outsiders, a name used in the past but no longer used, or the name in another language. It is not unusual that some ethnonyms are considered degrading and insulting by the people to whom they refer. These names may nevertheless be included here because they do identify the group and may help some users locate the summary or additional information on the culture in other sources. Ethnonyms are cross-referenced to the culture name in the index.

Glossary

Each volume contains a glossary of technical and scientific terms found in the summaries. Both general social science terms and region-specific terms are included.

Special Considerations

In a project of this magnitude, decisions had to be made about the handling of some information that cannot easily be standardized for all areas of the world. The two most troublesome matters concerned population figures and units of measure.

Population Figures

We have tried to be as up-to-date and as accurate as possible in reporting population figures. This is no easy task, as some groups are not counted in official government censuses, some groups are very likely undercounted, and in some cases the definition of a cultural group used by the census takers differs from the definition we have used. In general, we have relied on population figures supplied by the summary authors. When other population data sources have been used in a volume, they are so noted by the volume editor. If the reported figure is from an earlier date—say, the 1970s—it is usually because it is the most accurate figure that could be found.

Units of Measure

In an international encyclopedia, editors encounter the problem of how to report distances, units of space, and temperature. In much of the world, the metric system is used, but scientists prefer the International System of Units (similar to the metric system), and in Great Britain and North America the English system is usually used. We decided to use English measures in the North America volume and metric measures in the other volumes. Each volume contains a conversion table.

Acknowledgments

In a project of this size, there are many people to acknowledge and thank for their contributions. In its planning stages, members of the research staff of the Human Relations Area Files provided many useful ideas. These included Timothy J. O'Leary, Marlene Martin, John Beierle, Gerald Reid, Delores Walters, Richard Wagner, and Christopher Latham. The advisory editors, of course, also played a major role in planning the project, and not just for their own volumes but also for the project as a whole. Timothy O'Leary, Terence Hays, and Paul Hockings deserve special thanks for their comments on this preface and the glossary, as does Melvin Ember, president of the Human Relations Area Files. Members of the office and technical staff also must be thanked for so quickly and carefully attending to the many tasks a project of this size inevitably generates. They are Erlinda Maramba, Abraham Maramba, Victoria Crocco, Nancy Gratton, and Douglas Black. At Macmillan and G. K. Hall, the encyclopedia has benefited from the wise and careful editorial management of Elly Dickason, Elizabeth Kubik, and Elizabeth Holthaus, and the editorial and production management of Ara Salibian.

Finally, I would like to thank Melvin Ember and the board of directors of the Human Relations Area Files for their administrative and intellectual support for this project.

DAVID LEVINSON

References

Murdock, George Peter (1967). _Ethnographic Atlas_. Pittsburgh: University of Pittsburgh Press.

Murdock, George Peter (1983). _Outline of World Cultures._ 6th rev. ed. New Haven: Human Relations Area Files.

Introduction

The Culture Area

Over 153 million people live in the Middle American and Caribbean culture areas, which are divided primarily between the Middle American mainland cultures and the Caribbean cultures of the West Indian islands and Bermuda.

Middle America is the region south of the United States and north of South America. It includes Mexico and Central America. A subarea of Middle America in which stratified societies, settled agricultural communities, and urban centers had evolved before contact with Europeans, has been labeled "Mesoamerica." Paul Kirchhoff (1943) first used the term "Mesoamerica" to describe this region of high civilization. The precise boundaries of Mesoamerica have never been fixed because it is a cultural concept rather than a geographical one. The approximate location of Mesoamerica is shown in fig. 1.

Bermuda is considered part of the Caribbean culture area, despite its geographic location outside the West Indies, because its cultural connections are with the Caribbean. The Caribbean culture area covers the West Indies and Bermuda. Bermuda has been included because it is culturally connected to the Caribbean, although it is geographically outside the West Indies. The main island groups in the West Indies are the Bahamas, the Greater Antilles, and the Lesser Antilles. The largest populations are found in Cuba, the Dominican Republic, Haiti, Puerto Rico, Jamaica, and Trinidad.

Cultural Patterns

Before the European Conquest, early in the sixteenth century, the cultures of Middle America and the Caribbean were evolving in response to natural environments and to contact with each other. The first people in Middle America came from Asia, across the Bering Strait land bridge, a connection between Asia and North America that allowed passage sometime between 28,000 and 10,000 years ago. Later cultures of Middle America were highly influenced by the evolving civilizations of the Mesoamerican heartland, including the Olmec, Teotihuacán, Zapotec, Maya, and Aztec. In the Caribbean area native cultures were influenced by people migrating northward from the coast of South America. The diffusion of culture traits in pre-Hispanic times was slow. Besides evolving in different contexts, the Middle American and Caribbean cultures had different histories of contact with the Europeans. Therefore, it is often necessary to treat them separately.

Middle America, with a surface area of 433,784 square kilometers, is the larger area of the two areas. It had a population of 122,656,331 in 1992.

A major cultural division within Middle America today is between the rural and the urban cultures. The rural cultures are quite varied. Most are derived from the native cultures, as affected by the Conquest. Others are the result of expanding commercial economies or the mixing of native and immigrant groups. Urban cultures had a gradual beginning in the Preclassic period, long before the Spanish Conquest in 1521. In the latter half of the twentieth century, urban centers have grown rapidly as a result of rural-to-urban migration. Metropolitan Mexico City, already one of the largest urban areas in the world, will have a population of at least 20 million by the end of the century.

In the rural areas of Middle America, one often finds two opposing cultural systems: a subsistence-oriented culture that may have Indian origins and a commercially oriented culture. The latter is often labeled "mestizo" or "Ladino." The term "mestizo" is used north of the Isthmus of Tehuantepec and is more of a social-scientific than a vernacular term. A common phrase that people use to describe mestizos is *gente de razón* (educated, thinking people), a phrase that is clearly derogatory to Native Americans. The term "Ladino" is used south of the Isthmus of Tehuantepec and carries with it the connotation of Indians who have learned to speak Spanish and who interact with the educated segment of society. Often there is a blurring of the distinction between Indian and mestizo cultures, particularly in areas where most of the native population lived on commercial haciendas in the nineteenth century, such as in parts of Morelos, Michoacán, and Hidalgo. Throughout Middle America, however, these subsistence-oriented cultures exhibit such features of the material basis of the original Indian independent villages as maize, tortillas, chilies, grinding stones, and adobe houses with straw roofs.

In many cases, the Indian origin of the subsistence-oriented cultures is clear, especially when a native language is spoken. Because the dominant political powers are involved in the spread of modern capitalism and its ideology, the native cultures are often portrayed as unfortunate backward remnants of a vanished era. Anthropological studies have shown, however, that they are viable long-lived cultures with a Native American base. They have

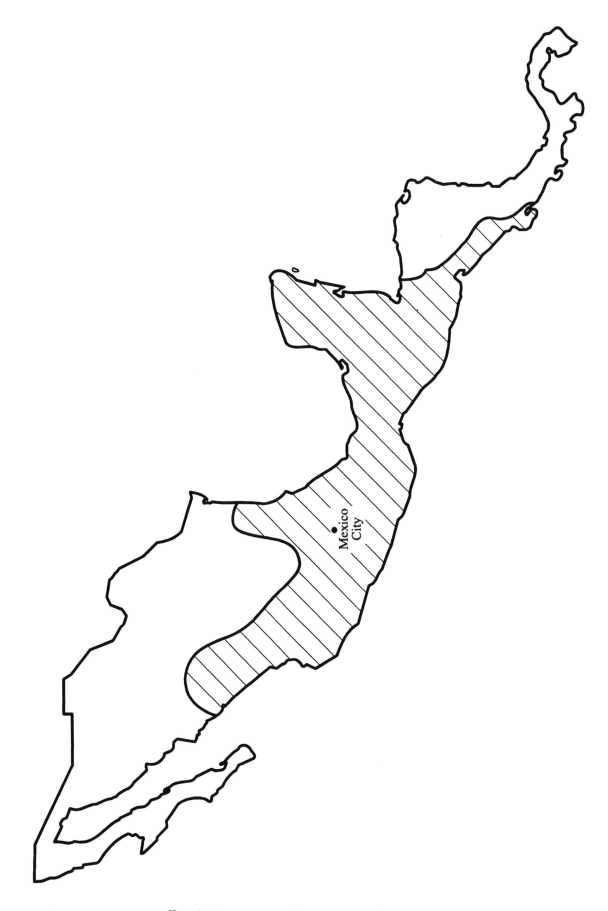

Fig. 1 *Mesoamerica within Middle America*

survived hundreds of years of colonialism and continue to survive the expansion of modern industry. They do constitute a problem for "progressive" economically oriented national governments because they do survive so well without being integrated into a market-oriented economy, which often seeks their land to exploit and thereby denigrates their cultural heritage.

The rural commercially oriented cultures are usually ethnically mestizo or Ladino., Not all people who are labeled "mestizo" or "Ladino," however, are involved in the commercially oriented culture. Sometimes poor peasants who do not speak an Indian language are called "mestizo" because they lack many definitive Indian cultural traits. These are still subsistence-oriented cultures, and some may have had a European origin. Apparently, as in the United States, Europeans who acculturated to Indian culture, "going the wrong way," so to speak, have been somewhat ignored by historians because they were not "progressive."

The Caribbean cultures have had a different history. No division between Indian and mestizo exists there. The modern Caribbean cultures had their origins in the plantation system of the of the seventeenth, eighteenth, and nineteenth centuries. After being freed from plantation work, the various rural workers of African, Hispanic, and Asian ancestry established subsistence-oriented cultures there.

In both areas, the political systems are intertwined with economics and religion. The general shift from pre-Hispanic times to the present followed Steward's (1955) general pattern of sociocultural evolution. The first change was from theocratic rule to militaristic rule (Wolf 1959), but the theocratic principles were never eliminated. An important pattern observable in the nineteenth and twentieth centuries in Middle America has been the resort to theocratic rule (civil-religious hierarchies) in reaction to abusive centralized power.

In modern Middle America and the Caribbean, nation-states have been established with constitutions modeled along Western lines. The United States constitution has been a model for some mainland countries, whereas English, Dutch, and French governments have been models for the Caribbean islands. Although constitutions have provided ideal models of government and civil rights, many de facto dictatorial regimes heavily influenced by Spanish-colonial traditions can be found on the mainland. In Latin America, constitutions act as guidelines for government and not necessarily as enforceable law. National law in Middle America has followed the Napoleonic tradition rather than the English tradition.

Natural Environment and Cultural Evolution

Middle America

Middle America lies between 8° and 32° N. Most of it is mountainous, and a large part of it is in the torrid zone, the region between the Tropic of Cancer and the Tropic of Capricorn. In the torrid zone, the range between average monthly high and low temperatures is small: in Mexico City it is only 7° C; however, the mountains create differences in climate by varying temperature with elevation and

by concentrating rainfall on the windward slopes. As theelevation rises, the temperature drops. Some mountains are so high that they are snow covered the year-round.

Two north-south mountain ranges, the Sierra Madre Occidental and the Sierra Madre Oriental, converge in central Mexico to form a plateau region called the Mesa Central. On the Mesa Central, cool climates prevail in the high intermontaine valleys. Alpine forests cover the higher levels. One valley—the Valley of Mexico, in the Mesa Central—has been an important center of cultural development for millennia. The climate in the Valley of Mexico, at 2,350 meters in elevation, is comfortable: the mean daily high temperature is 22° C, and the mean daily low around 10° C. Agriculture is productive, and lake resources provided extra food, which facilitated the development of human civilization (Niederberger 1979).

Elevations in other parts of Middle America vary between sea level and 5,747 meters, creating a wide range of temperatures. Rainfall also varies widely. Steady easterly trade winds blowing across the Gulf of Mexico deposit large amounts of rain against the eastern escarpment of the Mesa Central. Tropical rainforest environments exist there. Interior rain shadows in other parts of Middle America, such as the northcentral plateau of Mexico, produce desert environments.

The north of Mexico is dry; in the past, it supported only low population densities. Although agriculture is difficult, the aboriginal inhabitants cleverly adapted it to these dry environments by making use of what rain runoff there was in the valleys and by using river water for irrigation. Modern irrigation from the river systems of northern Mexico has greatly improved agricultural productivity. Much produce is intended for export to the United States. Mining and industry have greatly increased the urban populations of northern Mexico.

South of the Mesa Central, the land is lower. It continues to be mountainous until one reaches the Isthmus of Tehuantepec, a low plain connecting the Atlantic and Pacific coasts. The area between the Mesa Central and the Isthmus of Tehuantepec contains two important aboriginal cultural regions: Morelos, where temperature and climate favored commercial agriculture in the nineteenth century, particularly sugarcane, and Oaxaca, with less rainfall, a warmer temperature, and a large modern Indian population. South of the Isthmus of Tehuantepec mountains rise again. The Central American highlands arise in the Mexican state of Chiapas and extend southward in a chain to the next lowlying region, the Isthmus of Panama, just west of the border with Columbia, in South America. The Central American highlands have been the home of many important native cultures. The best known of these is the Maya, living today in the Chiapan and Guatemalan highlands, the folded limestone hills of the Petén to the north, and the Yucatán Peninsula farther north. This Mayan region includes parts of modern Belize and Honduras.

Commercially oriented farming people are found in Central America as well, particularly along the Pacific coast. Farther south, the tropical forests of Costa Rica and Panama have been cut back to create fields for cattle grazing. Cattle are also an important source of income along the Atlantic coast of Mexico. Cattle raising in the tropical coastal regions of the Mexican state of Veracruz has led to the development of rural commercialfarming cultures.

The Atlantic coasts of Honduras, Nicaragua, and Panama have a swampy riverine environment. Transportation has always been, and still is, by boat. There the cultures were influenced by contact with the water. Fish, sea turtles, and other marine resources provided food. Cultural influences resulted from contact with Caribbean maritime traders. These cultures resisted influences from the central and Pacific coast regions of Central America.

The Caribbean

The ring of islands making up the Antilles was created by mountain-building geological forces. Consequently, most have a central mountain range. The climate of the West Indian islands is moderated by the ocean. Steady trade winds blow from the northeast. Temperatures average 27° C. Rainfall averages 165 centimeters annually and tends to fall on the windward slopes of the mountains.

The level and fertile land provided a good resource for tropical agriculture. Hillsides provided forest resources. As is the case with most island cultures, the sea also provided abundant resources. The warm climate was attractive to Europeans as a place for tropical plantation agriculture. Under colonial rule, the economies were developed to produce sugarcane, cotton, tobacco, bananas, and spices for export. Native populations and cultures were destroyed in all but a few places. Contemporary cultures derive from immigrants to the islands. Because most of them were workers and slaves for the colonial enterprises, modern cultures of the West Indies generally have African, European, and Asian origins. There was some colonial advantage to island geography. It was harder for the slaves to get away and merge with native populations than it was on the mainland of Middle America, where imported slaves were not a large commercial success. Nevertheless, Caribbean slaves did escape or revolt in numerous places. Many independent Afro-American communities were founded by runaway slaves. Haiti is an entire country founded by rebellting slaves. Eventually, slavery was abandoned throughout the West Indies.

History

Pre-Hispanic History

Mesoamerica spawned its own variant of civilization. There is evidence of some pre-Columbian transoceanic contact, but so far no one has shown that culture brought from Europe, Asia, or Africa before the Spanish Conquest had any significant impact on the evolution of civilized cultures in Mesoamerica.

The cultures of Mesoamerica passed through several prehistoric periods: the Preclassic period (2500 B.C. to A.D. 300), during which settled villages expanded to form urbanized stratified societies; the Classic period (A.D. 300 to 900), during which centralized state power grew and produced glorious works of art and architecture; and the Postclassic period (A.D. 900 to 1521), during which both trade

and population expanded under the control of numerous states. During the Postclassic period, people placed less emphasis on the arts and more on warfare. These "period" designations are rough time marks in a diverse florescence of native cultures in what was clearly the heartland of native North America. The cultural influence of Mesoamerica was felt as far north as the Great Lakes and as far south as El Salvador.

The pre-Columbian history of the West Indies shows a more moderate cultural development. Archaeological evidence indicates that the islands were settled in several waves by people moving northward from South America. The first inhabitants, the Ciboney, were foragers who relied on fishing, hunting, and gathering. Later arrivals from the south, the Arawak, formed more permanent settlements between A.D. 300 and 1000. They relied on agriculture. Hereditary chiefs ruled over Arawak villages with ceremonial architecture such as ball courts and plazas. Ceremonial systems were well developed and supported chiefly rule.

The arrival of the Arawak from the south is confirmed by the presence of many traits, including language cognates still spoken on the South American mainland. These connections are confirmed even though Cuba, in the north, is only 200 kilometers from Florida. No influences moved south. A lesser contact with Mesoamerica does seem to be evident in the ball courts and stone "collars" made by the Arawak. Ball courts were found throughout Mesoamerica during the Classic period, and the Mesoamerican Gulf Coast cultures made stone ceremonial devices similar to the "collars." These devices were modeled after the ball player's garb. Authorities differ on whether or not this contact was "significant," but it was clearly not the main line of cultural diffusion.

The last wave of settlers from South America were the Carib Indians (A.D. 1000 to 1500), who seized the small islands of the Lesser Antilles from the Arawak. The Arawak remained in the Greater Antilles, the Bahamas, and Trinidad. The Carib had a simpler social organization than the Arawak and were more warlike.

Post-Conquest Cultural Development

Middle America. The Conquest by the Spanish in Middle America—and later by the English, French, and Dutch in the Caribbean—affected cultural development. The native peoples were ravaged by European diseases, to which they had no resistance. Contact destroyed over 90 percent of the native population; because it occurred at different times in different places, further populations were exposed to the infections as the Europeans advanced. Smallpox was the primary killer in the first years of contact.

Besides suffering from the diseases, the natives were also subjected to virtual enslavement through various Spanish schemes. On the one hand, the Spaniards purported to advance the welfare, mostly spiritual, of the Indians; on the other hand, their intent was to provide labor for various agricultural and mining enterprises designed to bring wealth to the colonists. The Indians did not take well to these schemes. They died from stress or disease, or they fled to defensive villages, away from the colonists.

Middle America was a Spanish domain. The Spanish arrived first and established a firm foothold in the colonies from Florida to South America. The only area of Middle America that the Spanish did not control completely was the Caribbean coast from Belize to Panama.

After the Conquest, tributary districts (_encomiendas_), were assigned to Spanish colonists. An encomienda was a Crown grant of Indian tribute to a Spaniard. The encomienda system allowed colonists to use Indian labor and property in setting up agricultural and mining enterprises. The Spanish Catholic church took on the task of Christianizing and "protecting" the Indians. Indians isolated themselves by speaking only their own language, seeking the protection of the Catholic church, setting up political systems that resisted control from the outside, and/or fiercely defending their land. Nevertheless, the colonists took most of the best agricultural land.

Land became commercial property in the nineteenth century. The sale of Mexican Indian land to wealthy Mexicans and to foreigners created a new hacienda system. Nineteenth-century haciendas were commercial farms growing crops for sale. The government declared Indian communal land "unused" and sold it for commercial development. The Ley Lerdo initiated by President Miguel Lerdo de Tejada in 1856 forced the sale of land owned by the Catholic church as well. The taking of land for commercial agriculture reached a peak under the dictator Porfirio Díaz, who was president between 1876 and 1910. The government kept the money from the sales and suppressed Indian revolts. Land-poor natives were forced to work for wages on the haciendas being created from property that was once theirs.

The hacienda system fragmented Mesoamerican native cultures. Independent Indian villages became culturally defensive and closed. Outsiders in these communities were regarded with great suspicion. A wealthy class of _hacendados_ (hacienda owners) was created. They maintained their dominant position through a police state that ruled the countryside. Displaced Indians and increasing numbers of poor mestizos became attached to the haciendas through debt peonage: debts for goods bought at the hacienda store (_tienda de raya_) kept the workers legally bound to their work. These hacienda workers usually lived in their own communities on hacienda lands. This system of exploitation destroyed many native communities. Some regions lost their connections to their Indian past, but, in others, Indian cultures survived in independent villages that resisted control by the hacienda system.

The hacienda system eventually collapsed because it rewarded so few and ruined so many. In the early part of the twentieth century, reactions led to the Mexican Revolution, which eventually replaced the Díaz dictatorship with the present constitutional republic, the United Mexican States (Estados Unidos Mexicanos). During the Revolution, the hero Emiliano Zapata restored land to the Indians. Many hacienda workers returned to nearby Indian villages, which reclaimed land or, in many instances, established their own claims to hacienda land as independent communities.

In the 1930s the postrevolutionary Mexican government began to restore lands to subsistence-oriented people. The restored lands,e known as _ejidos_, were unalienable. Article 27 of the Mexican constitution of 1917 allowed the government to seize land without arguing its title and to grant use of that land to landless families. In the 1930s and thereafter, rural subsistence-oriented cultures throughout Mexico had a new land base to support their continued existence.

The struggle between peasants and commercial farmers over land continues. To make agriculture more productive in a market economy, President Carlos Salinas in 1992 pushed through a revision to Article 27 of the Mexican constitution that would allow the workers of ejido land to own that land under a commercial title. On 3 January 1992, Article 27 was amended to allow ejidos to be sold. The principles for which Zapata had fought were compromised to encourage further commercialization in agriculture. Titles could be individual or communal. The decisions about the title are made by new peasant corporations formed from the ejido. The utopian capitalist philosophy of this move harks back to the times before the reign of Díaz, when it was thought that free enterprise would make the country, not just a few people, wealthy. Fearing a new type of disenfranchisement, peasants reacted once again under the banner of Emiliano Zapata. Peasant protests increased in 1993. In 1994 Tzeltal Indians launched an armed uprising in the Mexican state of Chiapas. They named their movement the Zapatista Army of National Liberation. In Guatemala, natives fought over similar issues throughout the 1970s and 1980s.

The commercially oriented rural cultures also arose out of this struggle for land. The new spirit of commercial enterprise brought by the Spanish established a European-like culture in the rural areas. At first, tribute and the mining of silver and gold were the objectives of the colonists. Then, as Indian populations declined and mixed-race and Spanish populations increased, commercial ventures were started to replace lost revenues from mining and tribute. A new rural class interested in profit and commerce arose. In the colonial world, with its rigid caste divisions, the average person could not engage in much commerce; however, after independence from Spain in 1821, which resulted in a gweakening of the racial barriers, people of poor Spanish and mixed Spanish-Indian heritage could follow in the footsteps of the colonists and develop profitable businesses. There arose a rural class that lived by investing in commercial agriculture and commerce. This commercial class is a rural upper class today, in the sense that its average income is greater than that of the subsistence-oriented, peasant people. Culturally, they are described as mestizo or Ladino.

The Caribbean. Practically all the Caribbean cultures have emerged from a colonial past that began with the arrival of the Spanish. Within the first 100 years of the Spanish occupation, the natives of the West Indies were practically all decimated by slavery and disease. There are now but a few remnants, which have intermingled with escaped slaves (see "Carib of Dominica").

The first Spanish settlements did not prosper. Most of the Spanish inhabitants left to seek greater fortunes on the mainland; however, the Spanish Crown retained control of certain port towns in order to refurbish and protect the valuable shipments to Spain. Thus, the ports of San Juan in Puerto Rico, Santo Domingo in Hispaniola, and Santiago and Havana in Cuba became heavily fortified outposts of the Spanish Empire. What the Spanish feared were raids by the northern European powers—the English, Dutch, and French—who had become interested in exploiting colonies in this area of the world. Concentrating their hold on the larger islands, the Spanish left the Lesser Antilles open to colonization by the northern European countries.

The remnants of the Spanish population on the islands of the Greater Antilles tried small-scale plantation agriculture, but the heavy-handed royal administration of Spain left little room for free enterprise. Their northern European rivals looked on their colonies in a different way. They granted charters to commercial companies and allowed them to colonize and rule the new land. The companies had greater freedom to decide how the land and people would be exploited. To exploit new colonies in the Lesser Antilles, the British, Dutch, and French hit on the idea of plantation agriculture, but there was a shortage of labor. Natives disappeared soon after contact. Laborers from Europe were unwilling to face the rigors of the tropics and, furthermore, became independent after their indenture. Therefore, the colonial companies turned to the only remaining source of labor for the new plantations—African slaves. In the seventeenth and eighteenth centuries the Lesser Antilles were given over to slave-based plantation agriculture. It was quite profitable for the European investors. The main crop was sugar, although other tropical crops such as tobacco, indigo, and ginger were tried at times.

After the slaves were freed over the course of the nineteenth century, workers were brought from India and China. In the twentieth century the European plantations declined in profitability, and the two large Spanish islands, Cuba and Puerto Rico, became involved with the United States, Cuba, as a client state and Puerto Rico as a territory. In Cuba, undemocratic governments led to political unrest; rural laborers in the sugar industry brought about a socialist revolution in 1959. Puerto Rico was able to demand democratic government by more peaceful means.

Middle America Today

The modern cultures of Middle America can be divided into four categories: rural subsistence-oriented cultures, rural commercially oriented cultures, immigrant cultures, and urban cultures.

Rural Subsistence-Oriented Cultures. Most of the rural subsistence-oriented cultures in Middle America that have been studied by anthropologists have their origins in the native traditions of the area.

Ethnic Identification. Anthropologists designate a Mesoamerican culture "Indian" if it uses an Indian language, produces native crafts, relies on native tools, possesses a heritage of plant genetic material in the form of plants and seeds and knowledge of how to cultivate carefully and con-

serve local lands, practices a native religion affected by Spanish Catholicism, and adheres to a worldview appropriate to subsistence farming.

Although they represent only about 7.9 percent of the population of Mexico (Instituto Nacional Indigenista 1994, 18) and about 44 percent of the population of Guatemala, the pure Indian cultures of Mesoamerica have been the main focus of traditional anthropological studies of Middle America. These cultures are important in a wider sense because they are the basis for most of the rural cultures of Mesoamerica, and they have spread to urban areas through migration. They are important symbolically because national education programs have made Mexico's Indian heritage part of its national identity.

The native cultures of Mesoamerica share many common traits, including subsistence agriculture based on maize, beans, and squashes; the worship of community religious images; open-air weekly markets; and characteristic styles of clothing. Yet, the widespread diffusion of cultural features has not resulted in homogeneity. Thousands of small variations in language, customs, and technology maintain ethnic distinctiveness. Perhaps the most puzzling of these is language. Indigenous dialects of the same language can be almost unintelligible over distances as small as 20 kilometers. These linguistic variations can be attributed to the fact that they are the result of thousands of years of cultural evolution in the same location and that for contact and commerce the people have always used the language of their conquerors (e.g., Aztec, Spanish).

Today Mesoamerican natives identify with their village or *municipio* more than with any "tribal" group because, after the Conquest, the larger society did not value their Indian identity, and they turned inward, toward the village, to avoid contact with a predatory colonial system. Early Catholic missionaries and the Spanish Crown supported this defensive response. This is changing, however. The participation of Indians in the Mexican Revolution raised their political status, and they have been recognized by the postrevolutionary Mexican governments as distinct regional ethnic groups. Although they are still politically neglected, considering their numbers, a rising sense of being Indian is bringing them further into the mainstream of political life in Mexico and Guatemala.

The classification of native villages into larger "ethnic" units is today done primarily on the basis of language. Language indicates common awareness and understanding; however, the linguistic classifications do not correspond precisely to the earlier political units that were destroyed by the Conquest, nor to earlier ethnic units based on common origin myths. Neither do linguistic classifications necessarily reflect a modern sense of unity among the speakers.

Economic Activities. The native economies revolve around subsistence agriculture, which is typically based on the co-cropping of maize, beans, and squashes in fields known as milpas. The cultigens exist in countless varieties developed over the centuries to fit the various environments in which people live. Wild plants, which are encouraged but not cultivated in the milpas, are also important contributors to subsistence. In mountainous terrain, people cultivate the land with a *coa* (traditional spade). On flatter land, draft animals—cows and horses—pull lightweight wooden plows. Irrigation has been used for millennia in many areas. Some irrigation techniques depend on terracing and the control of rainwater. Others make use of canals. Some raise the fields over a wetland area.

Each ecological zone in Middle America, of which there are many, has its own sequence of planting, cultivation, and harvest. Year after year, natives select the best seeds for each microecological zone, resulting in a rich wealth of plant genetic material. A group that occupies a number of ecological zones will have different seeds and techniques for exploiting these different zones. Planting, cultivating, and harvesting are timed to take advantage of seasonal rains.

Although the economic foundation of these cultures is subsistence farming, they are involved in the cash economy as much as possible. The subsistence foundation is a support on which they lean when cash opportunities fail, as they often do. Commercial farms have stimulated subsistence farmers to raise cattle and to grow cash crops like sugarcane and coffee. Men also leave their home villages to seek wage-paying jobs on large commercial farms, in and around cities, and in the United States. A little cash can go a long way toward supporting life in a subsistence-oriented village.

The native people also produce items such as pottery and clothing. Although these productive activities can draw them into the cash economy, people still have a strong sense of being peasant, subsistence farmers. Sometimes the few successful entrepreneurs in the cash economy will wear native garb and live humbly like the others to avoid envy.

Market networks are part of indigenous culture. Customary traders buy in one market, transport their goods, and sell at a higher price in another market. Transportation may be by truck, but, in the more remote regions, traders still carry their wares on their backs or on beasts of burden. The major buyers and sellers, who link the rural markets to the larger cash economy, often belong to rural commercially oriented (mestizo) groups.thus

The opportunities for wage labor have increased greatly since 1940. Migrants from native communities first went to parts of Middle America where commercial agriculture was developing, for example, to the coffee plantations in the Pacific piedmont of Guatemala or to the market farms east of Mexico City. Later migrations took Indians across the border to the United States, where they have contributed to commercial farming and food-processing industries.

Politics and Religion. A politically stratified society developed in the Late Preclassic period (400 B.C. to A.D. 300). What led to the emergence of a stratified society is still not understood completely. It does not seem to be simply the result of population pressure (Brumfield 1976). By the beginning of the Classic period (A.D. 300), most of the Indians of Mesoamerica apparently lived in politically stratified societies.

Today the rural, subsistence-oriented communities are organized internally by religious groups, peasant organizations, and political parties. The anthropologist confronts a dilemma in trying to separate politics from religion in Middle America. This seems to be possible only in the case of the rural commercially oriented and urban cultures, indicating that such a separation is linked to the market economy. In the subsistence-oriented native cultures, religion is intimately associated with local politics and cannot be separated from it.

In the nineteenth century a politico-religious system called civil-religious hierarchy (Carrasco 1961; Dewalt 1975) appeared in many subsistence-oriented communities (Chance and Taylor 1985). A civil-religious hierarchy is a system for ranking families. It may encompass a single village or a collection of villages organized within a municipio. The family's rank confers political power on the male family head.

A civil-religious hierarchy depends on a fiesta system, a system of traditional religious celebrations. By paying for the fiestas and performing the rituals, the families sacrifice their wealth in order to accumulate prestige in the community. There is often a ladder system on which men move from less to more prestigious offices. These ritual offices, which obligate the families to sponsor the fiestas are called *cargos* and are usually assumed for a year or two. Between offices, a man and his family will rest for several years. The office is assigned to the male head of a family, but his wife may have an accompanying title as well and is usually also a ritual actor. As prestige is accumulated, men assume civil posts in the local government appropriate to their rank. After an older man has filled the highest offices, he graduates from the system to become an elder (*anciano, pasado*). The elders are the most respected and the most politically powerful men in a community.

Middle America has suffered protracted civil wars, and many rural areas have been in states of relative anarchy for decades. Civil-religious hierarchies were in many cases democratic reactions to powerful military leaders who filled power vacuums. At times, however, civil-religious hierarchies have become oppressive or have fallen under the control of undemocratic leaders.

Since civil-religious hierarchies favor a redistributive economy in which wealth is funneled though fiestas from the relatively rich to everybody else, they do not fit well within a capitalist economy that favors the accumulation and investment of capital. Since World War II, the industrial economies of Middle America have been growing rapidly and have created new sources of wealth, including labor opportunities for the people in the subsistence-oriented cultures.

The most widespread response to new economic values has been the spread of Protestantism. People are attracted by the Protestant cults that favor economic individualism and familism. Middle America is an area of rapid Protestant expansion. For example, both Guatemala and the Mexican state of Chiapas have experienced very rapid rises in the number of rural Protestant churches in the second half of the twentieth century. Evangelical Protestantism is a successful politico-religious ideology for rejecting the power of civil-religious hierarchies. Fundamentalist Protestant doctrines reject superior human authority, particularly any incorporating Catholic ideas, by saying that any literate person who can read the Bible can become his own religious authority. Thus, the authority of the elders of a village, derived from their ritual performance, is negated by the new Protestant doctrines.

Where civil-religious hierarchies have become undemocratic, reactions have occurred. For example, in Chamula, a Tzotzil village in Chiapas, evangelical Protestantism has been a means of opposing an unpopular political elite (see "Tzotzil of Chamula"). Thus, civil-religious hierarchies, although they redistribute the wealth of the rich, are not perfect democratic institutions. Civil-religious hierarchies are subject to their own forms of corruption.

In the twentieth century political parties and peasant organizations have increasingly been new means of political organization within the subsistence-oriented rural communities, and they have replaced civil-religious hierarchies in many instances (see "Tzotzil of San Bartolomé de los Llanos"). Indian consciousness, which began to emerge in the 1990s, promises to be a greater political force in the future.

Religious Ideas. Outside religious concepts have entered Indian communities in various ways. In pre-Hispanic times, the people added the gods of conquering Indian states to their local pantheons. Afterward, the Spanish introduced new gods, which were also added to the local pantheons. Spanish missionaries established religious brotherhoods (*cofradías*), which helped the Indians organize their societies under colonial domination. Thus, the native religions have always changed to meet the political pressures that were placed on them, but they have done so in a syncretic way, maintaining something of the past while adding something new.

Some common elements in the native religions do not come from Christianity. For example the Zoque of Chiapas believe in a female goddess associated with the water, who has the power to seduce men. Identical beliefs can be found among the Otomí, Nahua, and Tepehua, 600 kilometers to the north, along the Gulf coast. The Sun, Moon, Earth, and an old fire god appear in many native religions. Accretions to belief have been slow, and many of the old ideas remain.

Rural Commercially Oriented Cultures: Mestizos and Ladinos. Middle America exhibits many regional rural cultures labeled "mestizo" and "Ladino" to the south. In this introduction, they are all referred to as "mestizo." They do not have an overt indigenous aspect, and the people actively reject any connection with Indians; however, many of their features, such as dress, food habits, or religious customs, may have unrecognized indigenous origins. These regional cultures have resulted both from the acculturation of indigenous peoples to a national culture and from the acculturation of colonists to a rural native culture. The variations in these commercially oriented cultures are complex and have not been fully analyzed by anthropologists.

The majority of mestizo cultures seem to have resulted from a frontierlike cultural contact between entrepreneurs and natives. The entrepreneurs sought new opportunities to profit from trade and agriculture in rural areas. The natives were utilized as a lower laboring class for the entrepreneurial activities. As a result of their frontier origins, often related to cattle ranching or mining, mestizo cultures have some common features: their economies are oriented toward commercial farming and trade in the national economy; they engage in commercial enterprises such as trucking, selling fertilizer, and owning stores; they maintain social ties to people in towns and cities; they are socially stratified; they speak only Spanish; they declare themselves to be entirely distinct from Indians and look down on Indians; they tend to be active in politics and usually control the political links to state and national government wherever Indians are present; they have large extended families that cooperate in running their businesses; and they value work highly.

The status of a mestizo family is often based on the time of arrival of that family in a "frontier" region. Mestizos place a high value on defending this status. This is sometimes conceptualized in the idea of *machismo*, manliness. Men are expected to defend their family's honor; however, to those who recognize the established hierarchy, much friendliness can be shown. Loyalty to the family is very important.

Regional mestizo cultures have their own arts and symbolic expressions. For example, the culture of the cattle ranchers of the Gulf Coast of Mexico includes a type of music with humorous lyrics called Huasteca, as well as beer drinking, horse racing, cock fighting, and the consumption of kidney soup. Many of the elements in mestizo cultures derive from a cattle-ranching background.

Mestizos gain their superior wealth from the control of land, which they use for commercial farming, including cattle raising, and from the control of markets. Mestizo landownership developed during the nineteenth century, when there was a strong effort to commercialize land and take it out of the subsistence sector. One obstacle to land reform is that each member of a extended mestizo family legally owns a fraction of a large landholding (*latifundio*) that is less than the maximum that identifies the land as a latifundio, subject to land reform. Because they have the greatest political influence in rural areas, mestizos have been able to maintain governments that favor their style of rural economy.

Mestizos also control trade in rural areas. Trade between the modern industrial economy and a local subsistence economy can be quite profitable (Dow 1973). Dendritic marketing systems that do not provide alternative markets for the sale of local products also allow considerable profits to be made in trade (Smith 1977). Political and commercial links with other towns and cities assist mestizo business owners in maintaining these dominant trade positions.

Mestizo cultures are changing as the economic conditions that gave rise to them change. Education is becoming one of the important pathways to economic mobility. Mestizo families seek the best education for their children, often sending them to cities to attend better schools. Children aspire to more middle-class urban occupations than managing the rural enterprises that originally brought wealth to their families.

Religion. Religious affiliation varies across Middle America. Catholicism is the dominant religion. Women attend church more frequently than do men. Protestantism is very strong in some areas. In Guatemala, evangelical Protestantism is a significant religion in rural areas; however, the rural areas do not have the complex mix of new religions that are found in the urban areas.

Politics. Mexico has judicial and legislative branches of both state and national governments; however, vestiges of the violence of its civil wars are still close to the surface, and practically all the real power is in the executive branch of the government. The Mexican municipio is the executive unit directly below the office of state governor. Each municipio has a powerful executive known as the _presidente municipal,_ who distributes funds received from the state and is expected to respond to the needs of the community. Because there is little oversight, those who hold this office are often accused, rightly or wrongly, of misappropriating and benefiting from these public funds.

Political opposition often takes the form of new party affiliations in the local elections. Candidates opposing the incumbents will campaign under the banner of one of the numerous opposition parties. If the opposition is serious, these candidates can be co-opted by the dominant party and reappear as their candidates. Lying behind the political system of the Mexican rural commercially oriented cultures is a web of deals forming a pyramid of patronage that holds the structure together. Each time a political deal is made, there are promises that go with it: to deliver votes, to receive money, to support someone else, and so on. If all works out well, everyone, including the people on the bottom, receives something.

If things do not work out well, however, as is often the case, a series of seemingly bizarre events can ensue. An elected official can be removed from office without another election, elected people can change parties, the presidente municipal can be driven from the community by an angry mob, the municipio office building can be occupied for months by protesters, people can be assassinated, the state police can intervene, and so forth.

Immigrant Cultures.   Some immigrants to Middle America have settled in the cities, but others have established their own villages in rural zones. There are villages of Italian and Spanish farmers in Mexico. Chinese immigrant communities are found in Mexico, Costa Rica, and Panama. German immigrants have made significant intellectual contributions to Middle American culture. Communities of retired U.S. and Canadian citizens exist in Mexico and Costa Rica. Middle Eastern immigrants are shop owners throughout Middle America.

Afro-American cultures are found along the Pacific coast and along the Caribbean coasts of Belize, Honduras, and Nicaragua. Some Afro-American communities of Pacific Mexico remain culturally distinct. A prejudice toward them is expressed by local mestizos.

The majority of the people of Belize are descendants of African slaves. The Garifuna, or Black Carib, of Belize originally came from the island of Saint Vincent. Because of their resistance to the British on Saint Vincent, they were deported to Roatán. Various migrations finally took them to Belize. Their unique culture has its roots both in the African culture of escaped West Indian slaves and the culture of the island Indians.

Urban Cultures.   An urban settlement is something more than a large town. A city is a center of power, and its occupants are nonagricultural specialists who maintain the political order and the economy. A growth in the size of settlements took place in Mesoamerica the Preclassic per-iod. Although the archaeological evidence for the Preclassic period is not clear, it may be assumed that some of these settlements contained nonagricultural populations and reached the point of dominating the political and economic life of the countryside, to the extent that they could be called small cities. Clear evidence of large-scale craft production and political power can be found in the archaeological remains of Teotihuacán, near Mexico City, dating to the beginning of the Classic period. Thus, urban cultures in Middle America predated the Spanish Conquest by more than a thousand years.

Rapid urbanization took place in many parts of Middle America after World War II. The urban migration was a way in which peasants could participate as laborers in the industrializing economies. The subsistence economies produced only a minimal food supply and required considerable work. The lowest wages earned from work in the city seem attractive when one can buy housing and food with wages from less work than it would take to produce the same on one's own land. If one has little land, migration is imperative. Today Middle America is home to millions of urbanized people working for low wages. The hourly wage of a worker in the Ford plant in Cuautitlán near Mexico City in 1987 was U.S.$1.45 an hour. Many urban factory workers earn less than the minimum wage, which was around U.S.$1.15 an hour in 1994.

Urban cultures in Middle America are highly stratified. There are distinct residential areas for the lower, middle, and upper classes. Oscar Lewis (1961) coined the term "culture of poverty" to describe the lower-class culture of modern Mexico City, the largest city in Middle America.. What Lewis meant to convey was that modern cities generate a rock-bottom poverty culture that has more similarities than differences from city to city. The culture of poverty in Mexico City is an optimistic culture; people have migrated from the countryside and are seeking to improve their standard of living through wage employment. The new immigrants live in sanitary conditions no better than they experienced in the countryside, but they have new wage-labor and educational opportunities. Dwellings are one-room rented family units, often with a single bathroom shared among half a dozen families. Indian languages and customs are respected only in the home. Kinship ties among urban immigrants are stronger than in the countryside and form a safety network that helps them cope with the transition to the urban environment. The urban immigrants also maintain close contact with their home villages and return often.

Life in Mexico City for the lower classes is not costly. The Mexican government has subsidized food and transportation. Lower-class men and women may have laboring and service jobs. Piecework may be taken home by children to add to the family income. Small manufacturing businesses thrive on the availability of cheap labor.

The city also has its middle and upper classes. The middle class can be defined as the owners of small businesses, higher-salaried workers, and professionals catering to middle-class needs. Examples of small businesses are operating a taxicab, a dry-cleaning store, a furniture store, a factory making paper bags, a toy shop, and the like. As the businesses make more profits, the owners rise in the hierarchy of economic stratification.

The upper classes consist of the owners of the larger businesses, the professionals catering to them, and wealthy politicians. Much of the wealth is invested in land or other stable forms not subject to inflation. Children of the upper classes attend private schools. The urban upper classes socialize primarily within their own group. The few studies of this group indicate that there is often a breakdown of family ties and that they suffer quite a bit of psychological stress. In many cases a family's wealth has been generated rapidly within one generation, and managing it wisely is very stressful for the family.

Culture Areas of Middle America

Culture Areas within Mesoamerica

The high plateau region around Mexico City has been a melting pot of cultures for millennia. When the Spanish arrived in 1519, they found a rich civilization, ruled by the Aztecs. The Aztecs were master politicians who had managed to weld the numerous ethnic groups in central Mexico together into a complex alliance. The interweaving of these groups into a feudal state will probably never be completely understood. Lords governed tributary districts, some of which were defined by ancient kinship rights and others by conquest of peripheral domains. Self-reproducing peasant villages with their own customs were at the lowest tier of the system.

Today the remnant cultures of these various allied groups continue to inhabit the central plateau. Some of the Indian groups that were involved in the Aztec alliance, such as the Otomí and Mazahua, live close to Mexico City.

The largest group left over from the Aztec Empire are the modern Nahua, the cultural descendants of the Aztecs. The Nahua are also called "Mexicanos" in many places. This labels them as the ex-rulers of Mexicayotl, the Mexica domain. Their cultural ancestors are called "Aztecs" because, according to an origin myth, they came from a place called Aztlán, but when Hernán Cortés arrived, they were known as "Colhua Mexica." Today their linguistic descendants are known as "Nahua," after the dialects of the language that they speak.

Another system of alliances, that of the Tarascans, existed to the west in the state of Michoacán. The Tarascans were not part of the Aztec Empire. Today they are a separate ethnic group, preferring to call themselves the "Purépecha." Like other areas, the Tarascan region suffered from the Spanish Conquest. Its recovery was somewhat unusual. Bishop Vasco de Quiroga, who led a group of humanist friars, instituted a reorganization of Indian society between 1538 and 1565. The people were congregated in towns and reorganized in a utopian order. The effect of this reorganization is not well understood. By the time anthropologists began to study the culture, at the beginning of the twentieth century, the people had gone through many periods of cultural change, including the devastating effects of the nineteenth-century hacienda system. The modern Purépecha fit into the general Central Mexican native cultural pattern. Lake Pátzcuaro has provided resources for specialized craft production. The region has an extensive network of markets. Farther to the west, the modern Cora and

Huichol are located where the states of Jalisco and Nayarit meet. The Huichol are further to the east than the Cora. Both are mountain people who escaped the brunt of the Conquest. They have relatively dispersed settlement patterns, and authority is granted to shamans as well as to community elders.

Other linguistic groups, such as the Totonac and Tepehua, live along the Gulf coast. The Otomí and Wasteko live on the north-central Gulf coast, and Popoluca and Zoque live in the south. The Gulf coast was an important center of power in pre-Hispanic times. Today it is an agricultural region, producing many tropical crops. The coastal plain supports many mestizo cattle ranchers. It is also the region where most of the petroleum is produced. Moderate-sized cities are found here: Veracruz is a major Atlantic port, and Poza Rica and Coatzacoalcos are centers for the petroleum industry.

The natives of Oaxaca are the remnants of a densely populated center of civilization that rivaled that of Central Mexico. The main languages spoken today are Zapotec, Mixtec, Chatino, Cuicatec, and Mazatec. To the west of Oaxaca live a group of Nahua speakers in the Mexican state of Guerrero.

Mayan speakers are the largest native linguistic group in Mesoamerica. The homes of the Maya-speaking natives are the Yucatán Peninsula, the folded limestone hills to the south, and the Central American highlands. The larger Maya groups are the Yukateko of the Yucatán Peninsula; the Mopan Maya of the Belize hills; the Tzeltal, Tzotzil, Ch'ol, Lakandon, and Tojolab'al of Chiapas; and the K'iche', Kaqchikel, Mam, Ixil, and other highland Maya in Guatemala.

Culture Areas beyond the Frontiers of Mesoamerica

A number of native groups the cultures of which survived the Conquest live in the hills of northwestern Mexico. The Northern Tepehuan live in rugged mountains in southern Chihuahua. The Tarahumara live north of them, in the mountains around the Copper Canyon. Cahita groups, such as the Mayo, are found farther west. All these people practice rainfall agriculture and, in the past, supplemented agriculture with hunting.

The hunter-gatherer cultures of northern Mexico have disappeared, but in the northern desert region of Baja California live some rather isolated groups such as the Cocopa, Digueño, Kiliwi, and Pai Pai. Their subsistence is based on desert farming, cattle, and wage labor.

The natives of the Atlantic coast of Central America traded with the English, supported colonies of escaped slaves and pirates, and generally failed to integrate well with the Spanish-speaking colonial governments on the Pacific side of Central America. Descendants of Indians and fleeing Africans, the modern Miskito people live along the coasts and rivers of Atlantic Honduras and Nicaragua. The name is probably derived from "musket." They were armed by English traders, who regularly visited the coast in the last two centuries. Representing an enclave of Anglophone influence in Central America, the Miskito were employed in the twentieth century by the United States against the Sandinista government of Nicaragua; however, the post-

Sandinista government is now bringing them peacefully into Nicaraguan national life for the first time.

Other Central American natives such as the Emberá and the Kuna in Panama are well removed from Meso-american influences. Kuna became politically active in seeking native rights for themselves and other Middle American Indians. Their way of life depends on fishing, hunting, farming, handicrafts, and seeking work in the cities. The lesser known native groups of Central America are the Bokotá, Boruca, Cabecar, Catio, Chorotega, Guaymí, Jicaque, Lenca, Matagalpa, Monimbo, Paya, Sub-tiaba, Sumu, Teribe, and Wounaan. Some of these natives no longer speak their aboriginal language, and many of them are described in this volume.

The Caribbean Today

The modern Caribbean cultures show the impact of slavery, plantation capitalism, and export-oriented colonialism to a far greater extent than the cultures of Middle America, which were impacted by these institutions in a more complex way. What remains on the Caribbean islands are cultures evolved from the cultures of freed slaves and other plantation workers. Modern cultures in the Caribbean now have class structures that have resulted from the breakdown of a colonial system in which the White European colonists were at the top and slaves and debt peons were at the bottom. The island of Cuba, containing the largest number of people in the Caribbean group, has moved the furthest toward breaking down the colonial class structure. The other islands support a class structure in which wealth has replaced race as the generator of status.

The original Amerindian cultures of the Caribbean have disappeared or, in a few cases, have merged with the cultures of freed slaves to produce a new amalgam. A similar process occurred on the Atlantic Coast of Central America, the cultures of which resemble those of the Caribbean. (See the articles on the Blacks of Costa Rica, the Garifuna, and the Miskito.) A circum-Caribbean culture area has been proposed by Steward (1944), who based his idea more on the pre-Hispanic situation than on the modern distribution of cultures. A circum-Caribbean concept would be difficult to justify in a contemporary ethnological perspective. Nevertheless, the Gulf- and Atlantic-coast societies of Mexico and Central America share some traits with the Caribbean island groups.

One of the things common to Caribbean cultures is the existence of fishing villages, a natural result of contact with the sea. There is a difference between villages involved in fishing and those involved in farming. Often the fish are traded locally, and the two types of villages form a dependent association.

Another important aspect of modern Caribbean cultures is migration. Industry on the islands suffers from high transportation costs. Industrialization has moved slowly, if at all. On the smaller islands, the most important "natural resources" that can be commercialized seem to be sun and sand, attractions for tourists. Men often leave the smaller islands to find work on larger islands, such as Trinidad and Jamaica, or in North America and Europe. Cultural enclaves of migrants exist in many North American and European cities. This migration has been facilitated by the willingness of some of the islands to retain a dependency or commonwealth status with one of the ex-colonial powers.

Anthropological Investigations

The Middle American and Caribbean region has been and continues to be one of the most anthropologically studied areas of the world. Hundreds of articles and dozens of books are published every year and are reviewed in summary publications such as the *Annual Review of Anthropology* and the *Handbook of Latin American Studies*. In the brief note on anthropological research below, I just skim the surface of what has been done and can not do justice to the volume of research that has come forth. Leads to this research can be found in the bibliographies attached to the articles.

In Mexico, the gap between archaeology and modern ethnography has been bridged by excellent ethnohistorical research. Some ethnographic texts were written by Native Americans (e.g., Chimalpahin Cuauhtlehuanitzin [1978], Alvaro Tezozomoc [1944], and Don Fernando de Alva Ixtlilxochitl [1985]). Authorship of the *Annals of Cuauhtitlán* is unknown. Some of the early missionaries, such as Fray Bernardino de Sahagún and Fray Alonso de Motolonia, also contributed to the early ethnographic literature on native cultures. Reports by the conquistadors, such as Hernán Cortés and Bernal Días del Castillo are historically important but ethnographically naive. All of these historical sources have inspired important ethnohistorical research in Mexico. The ethnohistorical approach to modern Mesoamerica continues today with scholars from around the world actively interpreting and reinterpreting currents in Mesoamerican culture history. Historical analysis today takes into account both the symbolic systems and the material conditions of previous Middle Americans (Carmack, Gasco, and Gossen 1996).

As well as inspiring a world-renowned school of Meso-american ethnohistory, Mexican anthropologists have studied modern ethnic groups. Manuel Gamio investigated the cultures in the Teotihuacán Valley in the 1920s. A post-revolutionary movement, Indigenismo, led by Gamio, sought to integrate the Indian cultures into national life. Gamio became the first director of the Instituto Indigenista Interamericano (III) in 1942. The III supports research and publishes the anthropological journal *América Indígena*. In 1948 Mexico created a government agency, the Instituto Nacional Indigenista (INI) that looks after the welfare of native groups in Mexico. Part of the work done by INI has been to continue the study of native cultures and to propagate an appreciation of them. Universities and many other research organizations in Middle American countries have also contributed to cultural-anthropological research.

At the turn of the twentieth century, U.S. cultural-anthropological study of Middle America was little more than well-written traveler's reports. Later, the new empirical approach to anthropology began to make itself felt in studies of northwestern Mexican Indians. Mesoamerica was also a prime object of study for a "Chicago" school of anthropology started by Robert Redfield with his study of a central Mexican village, Tepotztlan (1941). Traveler's reports of Mayan ruins published in the nineteenth century also stimulated anthropological interest in Mesoamerica. In the early part of the twentieth century, the Carnegie Institution of Washington sponsored archaeological research in the Mayan area that eventually spun off more cultural research. In the 1930s Sol Tax investigated the Maya of Guatemala. Later, U. S. anthropologists contributed to the understanding of many native cultures throughout Middle America. An important early summary volume was edited by Sol Tax (1952).

Robert Redfield's work made peasant cultures a legitimate object of study in cultural anthropology, which previously had been identified mostly with the study of tribal cultures. The nature of Mesoamerican peasant character was an important question closely connected to the American school of psychological anthropology in the 1940s and 1950s. The question was never finally answered because it was difficult to measure the variables involved, as was the case with other culture and personality studies.

Later research by anthropologists from Mexico and other countries focused on economics and religion. The body of work did much to reveal how economic decisions were made in rural villages. This work coincided with a shift in anthropology away from a concern with symbolic expressions and toward a concern with economic and material factors. Anthropologists explored the connection between the religious-fiesta systems and economics. The topic was opened up for the anthropological study of Middle America by Frank Cancian (1965). Fiestas leveled some wealth differences and promoted native egalitarian values, yet they maintained a village society that was stratified both in political power and wealth. Those who sponsored the fiestas traded wealth for power and prestige but did not destroy the differential economic bases generating wealth in the peasant communities.

Another issue that is still being debated today is the extent to which native cultures are carrying on pre-Columbian traditions. Are they modern forms of an ancient Indian tradition, or have they been molded extensively by contact with the colonial and postcolonial power holders? Most cultural anthropologists today accept the idea that contact with external cultures has profoundly influenced the development of native villages since the Conquest.

Work in cultural anthropology in the 1980s and into the 1990s has reflected the general concerns of anthropologists. Some of the latest anthropological research is represented in this volume. Middle America has received particular attention in the areas of women's studies, economic anthropology, medical anthropology, and ethnic relations. A concern with the symbolic elements in culture continues. These more symbolic approaches have enlivened the interpretations of the symbolic meaning of cultural forms and have added a humanistic element to the descriptions of culture. For example, the meaning of Mayan speech and myth has been explored extensively (Berlin, Breedlove, and Raven 1974; Colby and Colby 1981; Gossen 1974; Tedlock 1982).

Various efforts have been made to provide conceptual overviews of the cultures of Middle America and the Caribbean. The culture-area concerns of the early twentieth century led Paul Kirchhoff to formulate the concept of the Mesoamerica area previously mentioned. Robert Redfield (1956) developed the notion of the folk-urban continuum; his hypothesis was that all Mesoamerican cultures lay along a range of cultural forms, from the independent rural subsistence-oriented community to the large city. He also introduced the concept of the peasant community.

The idea of the peasant community put forward by Redfield was so broad and multidimensional that a better one was needed. This was provided by Eric Wolf (1957, 1986), who defined the "closed corporate peasant community" to describe Mesoamerican and other native peasant societies. This concept defines some of the important social characteristics of rural subsistence-oriented communities in Middle America, particularly their defensive posture toward outsiders. Wolf (1955) also noted the more proletarian and open characteristic of the Caribbean villages. Fernando Cámara (1952) classified Middle American peasant villages as either centripetal, inward looking, or centrifugal, outward looking. It was another way of looking at the difference between closed subsistence-oriented cultures vs. more open commercially oriented cultures.

Others emphasize Middle America's history of colonialism and capitalism as the predominant element in the development of its cultural patterns. Gonzalo Aguirre Beltrán (1973, 1979) developed the idea that most native cultures were formed as refuge regions created by a predatory colonialism. The investigation of the formative effects of colonialism and capitalism on Middle American cultures has been carried forward by Rudolfo Stavenhagen (1968, 1975), Arturo Warman (1980), and many others.

The Writing of This Volume

The writing of this volume has been a collaborative work. I would like to thank David Levinson, the editor in chief, and Robert V. Kemper, the associate editor, for their editorial help. Also important to the production of the volume was the work of Ruth Gubler, who did most of the translations. I thank Arnulfo Embriz and Norberto Zamora of the Instituto Nacional Indigenista, Mexico, for their help with the maps. Above all, I would like to thank the many contributors who gave freely of their time and without whom this volume would not be possible.

It was apparent when I took over editorship of this volume that it could not possibly do justice to every culture within its scope within the time allotted. My response to this situation was to concentrate on the areas where new and unique data could be presented. We sought out authors who had studied a culture extensively, preferably in the field, and could write new and insightful works. These works were given the greatest space. In the other cases, articles were based on the latest published sources. Bibliographical information had been added to allow the reader to explore what is currently known about a culture in more depth. Thus, Volume 8 is not merely a summary of published work on Middle America and the Caribbean, it is a source of new information that cannot be obtained elsewhere.

It is unfortunate that some of the Mayan cultures could not be covered in more depth. Anthropological work in this area has been disrupted by civil war. Many Mayanist anthropologists have been extensively involved in presenting the native side of these conflicts. At the time the volume was being prepared, a rebellion had broken out in the Mexican state of Chiapas. A large number of the experts in this area did not have time to write in time to meet what became a rather tight publication schedule. Some of the Mayan cultures in the volume are covered by short entries; however, the longer entries represent new sources of information on Mayan cultures that have been poorly documented in the past.

The spelling of native words is governed by different traditions. Each language has developed, or is developing its own orthography. In many cases there are several competing orthographies. The International Phonetic Alphabet (IPA) has not been used much in creating these new orthographies because the characters are not easy to reproduce, few people can read it, and the coding of allophones still could be idiosyncratic. In this volume we have followed the traditions that have developed for each culture, which have utilized mostly Roman characters and diacritical marks. The use of the straight apostrophe (') rather than the IPA character ʔ to indicate a glottal stop is common in all the orthographies. Also, underlining is a common way of indicating the nasalization of vowels. Because a glottal stop and a glottalized consonant seldom appear together in Mayan words, the straight apostrophe after a consonant in Mayan languages indicates that the consonant is glottalized and does not indicate a glottal stop. The spelling of the Maya language names follows the standards laid down by the Academia de Lenguas Mayas.

Bibliography

Aguirre Beltrán, Gonzalo (1973). _Regiones de refugio: El desarrollo de la comunidad y el proceso dominical en mestizo América._ Mexico City: Instituto Nacional Indigenista.

Aguirre Beltrán, Gonzalo (1979). _Regions of Refuge._ Washington: Society for Applied Anthropology.

Alva Ixtlilxochitl, Fernando de (1985). _Historia de la nación chichimeca._ Madrid: German Vazquez.

Alvarado Tezozomoc, Fernando (1944). _Crónica mexicana._ Mexico City: Secretería de Educación Pública.

Berlin, Brent, Dennis E. Breedlove, and Peter H. Raven (1974). _Principles of Tzeltal Plant Classification: An Introduction to the Botanical Ethnography of a Mayan-Speaking People of Highland Chiapas._ New York: Academic Press.

Brumfield, Elizabeth (1976). "Regional Growth in the Eastern Valley of Mexico: A Test of the 'Population Pressure' Hypothesis." In _The Early Mesoamerican Village,_ edited by Kent V. Flannery, 234–249. New York: Academic Press.

Cámara, Fernando (1952). "Religious and Political Organization." In _Heritage of Conquest,_ edited by Sol Tax, 142–173. Glencoe, Ill.: Free Press.

Cancian, Frank (1965). _Economics and Prestige in a Maya Community: The Religious Cargo System in Zinacantan._ Stanford, Calif.: Stanford University Press.

Carmack, Robert M., Janine Gasco, Gary H. Gossen, et al. (1996). _The Legacy of Mesoamerica: History and Culture of a Native American Civilization._ Upper Saddle River, N.J.: Prentice Hall.

Carrasco, Pedro (1961). "The Civil-Religious Hierarchy in Mesoamerican Communities: Pre-Spanish Background and Colonial Development." _American Anthropologist_ 63:483–497.

Chance, John, and William Taylor (1985). "Cofradías and Cargos: An Historical Perspective on the Mesoamerican Civil-Religious Hierarchy." _American Ethnologist_ 12(1): 1–26.

Chimalpahin Cuauhtlehuanitzin, Domingo Francisco de San Anton Muñón (1978). _Historia mexicana: A Short History of Ancient Mexico._ Lincoln Center, Mass.: Conemex Associates.

Colby, Benjamin N., and Lore M. Colby (1981). _The Daykeeper: The Life and Discourse of an Ixil Diviner._ Cambridge: Harvard University Press.

DeWalt, Billie R. (1975). "Changes in the Cargo Systems of Mesoamerica." _Anthropological Quarterly_ 48:87–105.

Dow, James (1973). "Models of Middlemen: Some Issues Concerning the Economic Exploitation of Modern Peasants." _Human Organization_ 32(4): 397–406.

Gossen, Gary (1974). _Chamulas in the World of the Sun: Time and Space in Maya Oral Tradition._ Cambridge: Harvard University Press.

Instituto Nacional Indigenista (1994). _Instituto Nacional Indigenista, 1989-1994._ Mexico City: Instituto Nacional Indigenista.

Kirchhoff, Paul (1943). "Mesoamérica." _Acta Americana_ 1:92–107.

Lewis, Oscar (1961). _The Children of Sanchez: Autobiography of a Mexican Family._ New York: Random House.

Niederberger, C. (1979). "Early Sedentary Economy in the Basin of Mexico." _Science_ 203:131–142.

Redfield, Robert (1941). _Tepoztlan, a Mexican Village: A Study of Folk Life._ Chicago: University of Chicago Press.

Redfield, Robert (1956). _Peasant Society and Culture._ Chicago: University of Chicago Press.

Rouse, Irving (1948). "The West Indies." In _Handbook of South American Indians._ Vol. 4, _The Circum-Caribbean Tribes,_ edited by Julian H. Steward, 495–565. Washington, D.C.: Bureau of American Ethnology.

Smith, Carol A. (1977). "How Marketing Systems Affect

Economic Opportunities in Agrarian Societies." In *Peasant Livelihood: Studies in Economic Anthropology*, edited by Rhoda Halperin and James Dow. New York: St. Martin's Press.

Stavenhagen, Rodolfo (1968). *Clases, colonialismo y aculturación: Ensayo sobre un sistema de relaciones interetnicas en Mesoamérica*. Guatemala City: Editorial J. de Pineda Ibarra; Ministerio de Educación.

Stavenhagen, Rodolfo (1975). *Social Classes in Agrarian Societies*. Garden City, N.Y.: Anchor Press.

Steward, Julian H. (1947) "American Culture History in the Light of South America." *Southwestern Journal of Anthropology* 3:85–107.

Steward, Julian H. (1955). *Theory of Culture Change*. Urbana: University of Illinois Press.

Tax, Sol (1952). *Heritage of Conquest*. Glencoe, N.Y.: Free Press.

Tedlock, Barbara (1982). *Time and the Highland Maya*. Albuquerque: University of New Mexico Press.

Warman, Arturo (1980). *Ensayos sobre el campesinado en México*. Mexico City: Editorial Nueva Imagen.

Wauchope, Robert, gen. ed. (1964-1976). *Handbook of Middle American Indians*. 16 vols. Austin: University of Texas Press.

West, Robert C., and John P. Augelli (1989). *Middle America: Its Lands and Peoples*. Englewood Cliffs, N.J.: Prentice Hall.

Wolf, Eric R. (1955). "Types of Latin-American Peasantry: A Preliminary Discussion." *American Anthropologist* 57:452–471.

Wolf, Eric R. (1957). "Closed Corporate Peasant Communities in Mesoamerica and Java." *Southwestern Journal of Anthropology* 13:1–18.

Wolf, Eric R. (1959). *Sons of the Shaking Earth*. Chicago: University of Chicago Press.

Wolf, Eric R. (1986). "The Vicissitudes of the Closed Corporate Peasant Community." *American Ethnologist* 13:325–329.

JAMES W. DOW

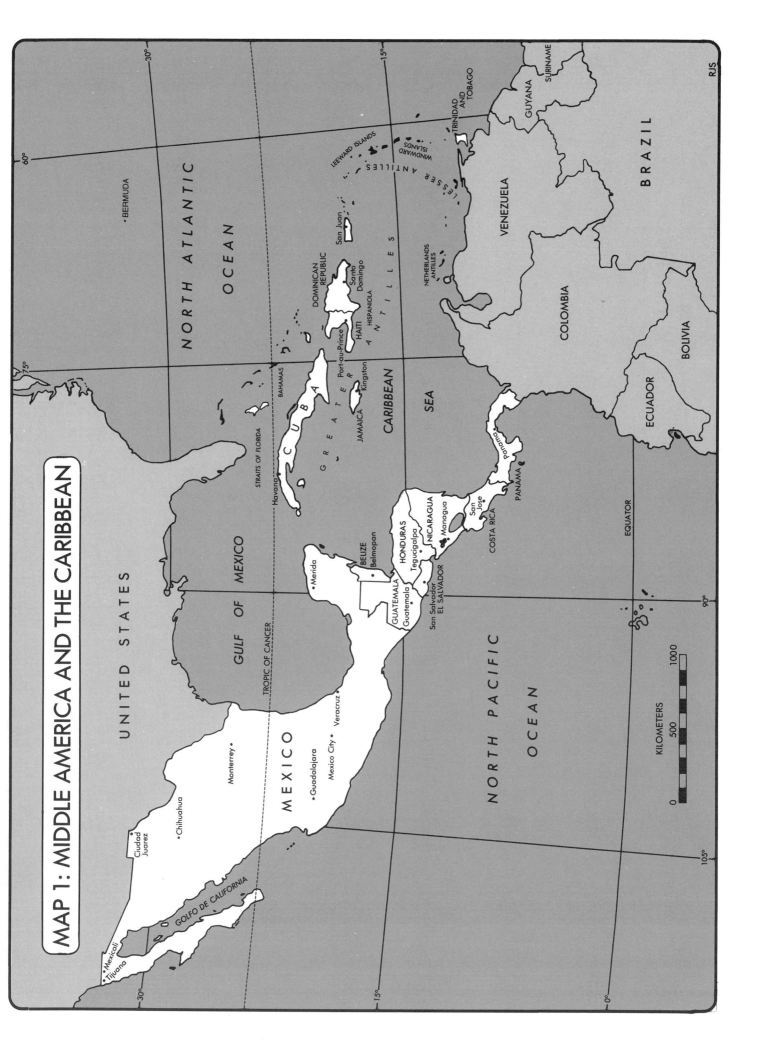

MAP 1: MIDDLE AMERICA AND THE CARIBBEAN

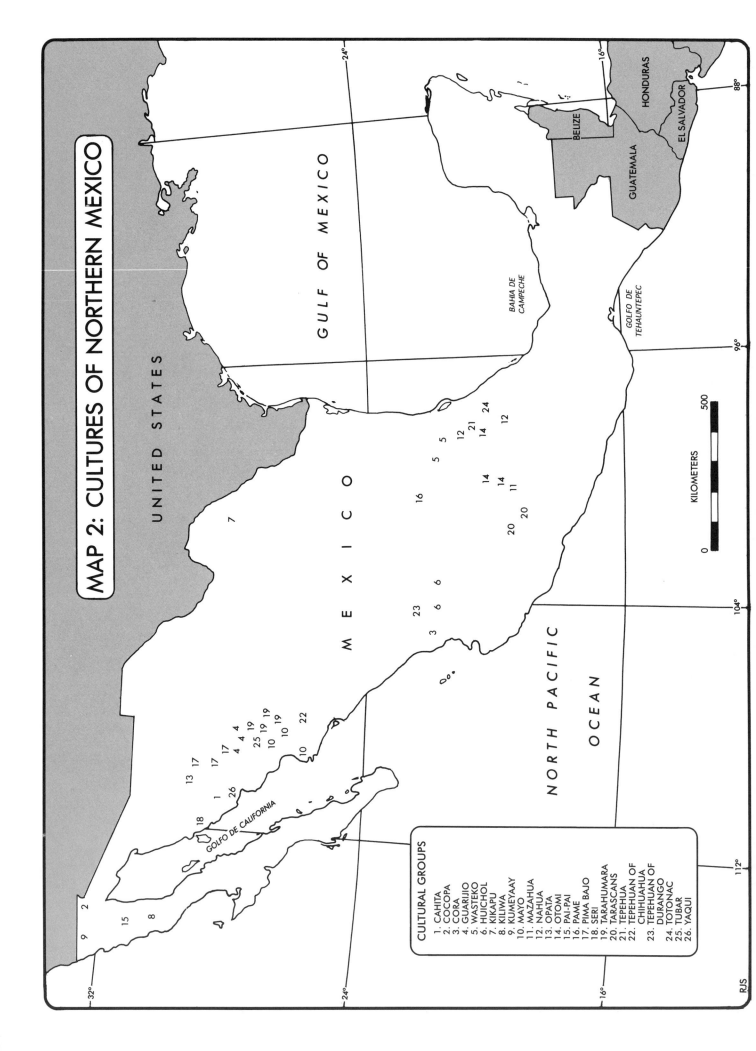

MAP 2: CULTURES OF NORTHERN MEXICO

UNITED STATES

MEXICO

GULF OF MEXICO

BAHIA DE
CAMPECHE

GOLFO DE
TEHAUNTEPEC

BELIZE

GUATEMALA

HONDURAS

EL SALVADOR

NORTH PACIFIC

OCEAN

GOLFO DE CALIFORNIA

CULTURAL GROUPS
1. CAHITA
2. COCOPA
3. CORA
4. GUARIJIO
5. WASTEKO
6. HUICHOL
7. KIKAPU
8. KILIWA
9. KUMEYAAY
10. MAYO
11. MAZAHUA
12. NAHUA
13. OPATA
14. OTOMI
15. PAI-PAI
16. PAME
17. PIMA BAJO
18. SERI
19. TARAHUMARA
20. TARASCANS
21. TEPEHUA
22. TEPEHUAN OF
    CHIHUAHUA
23. TEPEHUAN OF
    DURANGO
24. TOTONAC
25. TUBAR
26. YAQUI

KILOMETERS
0   500

RJS

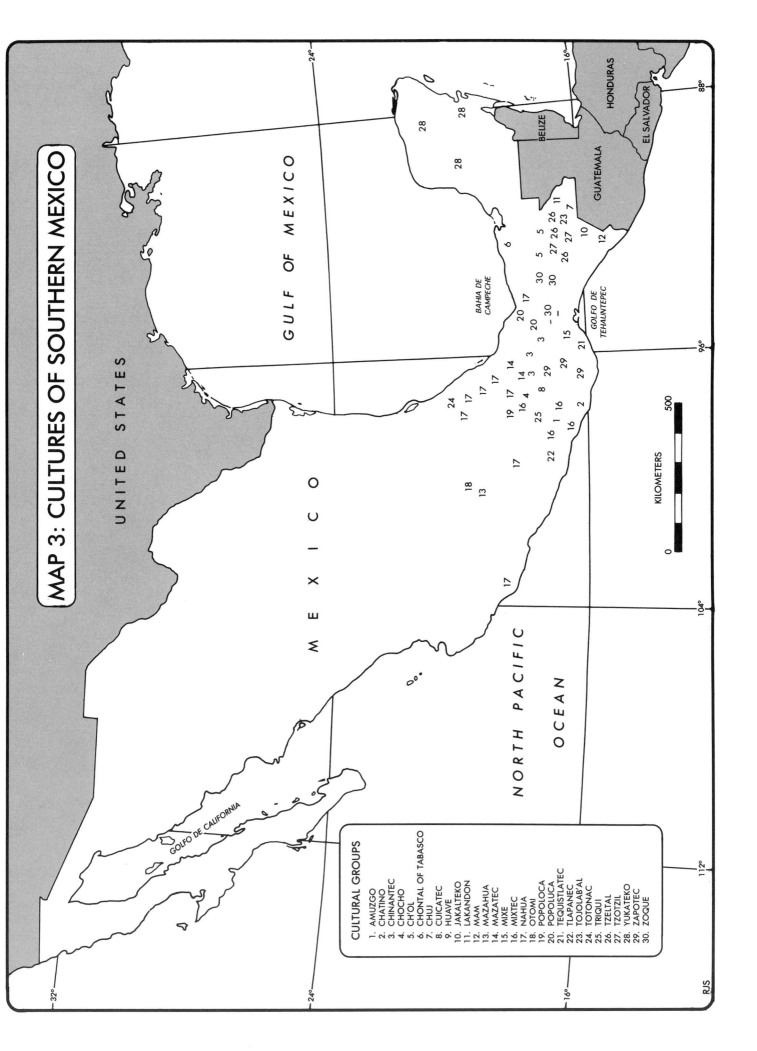

MAP 3: CULTURES OF SOUTHERN MEXICO

UNITED STATES

M E X I C O

GULF OF MEXICO

BAHIA DE CAMPECHE

GULFO DE TEHAUNTEPEC

NORTH PACIFIC OCEAN

GOLFO DE CALIFORNIA

BELIZE

GUATEMALA

HONDURAS

EL SALVADOR

CULTURAL GROUPS
1. AMUZGO
2. CHATINO
3. CHINANTEC
4. CHOCHO
5. CH'OL
6. CHONTAL OF TABASCO
7. CHUJ
8. CUICATEC
9. HUAVE
10. JAKALTEKO
11. LAKANDON
12. MAM
13. MAZAHUA
14. MAZATEC
15. MIXE
16. MIXTEC
17. NAHUA
18. OTOMI
19. POPOLOCA
20. POPOLUCA
21. TEQUISTLATEC
22. TLAPANEC
23. TOJOLAB'AL
24. TOTONAC
25. TRIQUI
26. TZELTAL
27. TZOTZIL
28. YUKATEKO
29. ZAPOTEC
30. ZOQUE

KILOMETERS
0   500

RJS

32°
24°
16°

112°
104°
96°
88°

24°
16°

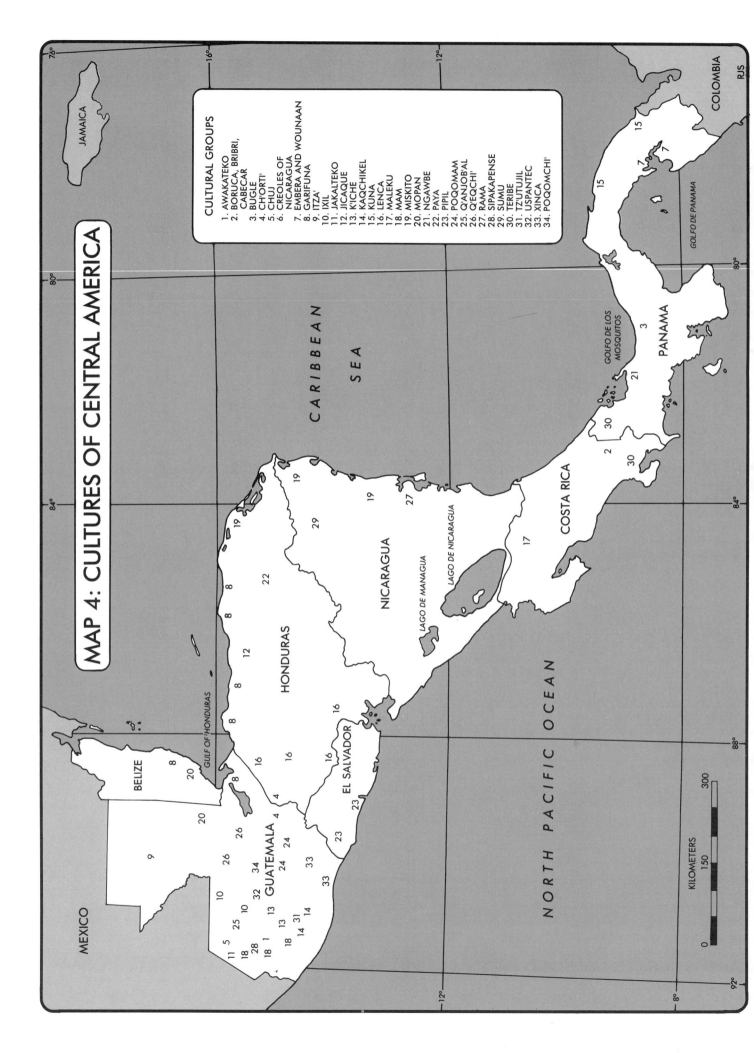

MAP 4: CULTURES OF CENTRAL AMERICA

CULTURAL GROUPS

1. AWAKATEKO
2. BORUCA, BRIBRI, CABECAR
3. BUGLE
4. CHORTI'
5. CHUJ
6. CREOLES OF NICARAGUA
7. EMBERA AND WOUNAAN
8. GARIFUNA
9. ITZA'
10. IXIL
11. JAKALTEKO
12. JICAQUE
13. K'ICHE
14. KAQCHIKEL
15. KUNA
16. LENCA
17. MALEKU
18. MAM
19. MISKITO
20. MOPAN
21. NGAWBE
22. PAYA
23. PIPIL
24. POQOMAM
25. Q'ANJOB'AL
26. Q'EQCHI'
27. RAMA
28. SIPAKAPENSE
29. SUMU
30. TERIBE
31. TZ'UTUJIL
32. USPANTEC
33. XINCA
34. POQOMCHI'

MEXICO

JAMAICA

BELIZE

GUATEMALA

HONDURAS

EL SALVADOR

NICARAGUA

LAGO DE MANAGUA

LAGO DE NICARAGUA

COSTA RICA

PANAMA

COLOMBIA

CARIBBEAN SEA

GULF OF HONDURAS

GOLFO DE LOS MOSQUITOS

GOLFO DE PANAMA

NORTH PACIFIC OCEAN

KILOMETERS
0   150   300

RJS

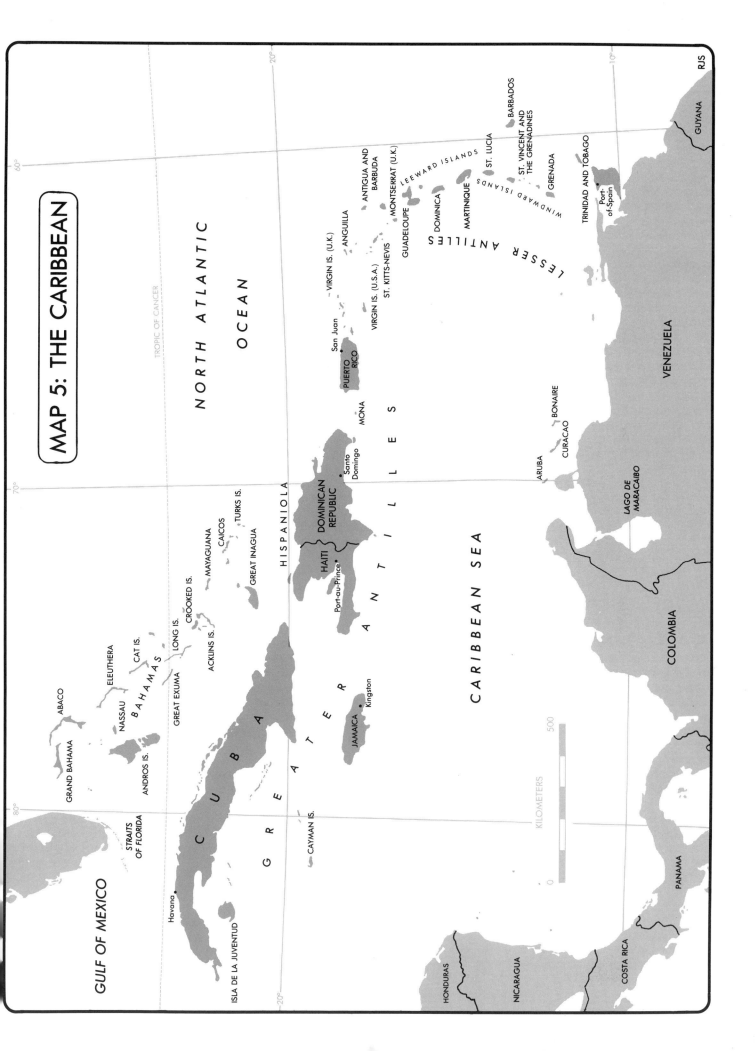

Encyclopedia of World Cultures

Volume VIII

MIDDLE AMERICA

AND THE

CARIBBEAN

African Mexicans

Coniff, Michael, and Thomas J. Davis (1994). *Africans in the Americas.* New York: St. Martin's Press.

ETHNONYMS: none

As in the rest of the New World, the majority of Africans who settled in Mexico came as slaves. Mexico was the first mainland nation to receive large numbers of slaves; from 1528 to 1620 perhaps as many as a thousand slaves per year arrived from West Africa in Veracruz, on the Gulf Coast. African slaves were imported mainly because the local Indian populations were not deemed suitable by the Spanish as workers in Spanish enterprises. Thus, Africans were forced to work refining silver and on ranches in northern Mexico; as household workers, on public construction projects, and in textile factories in cities; in sugar fields and refineries near Veracruz, Morelos, and Puebla; and as gold miners on the Pacific coast. Because the Pacific-coast region was relatively lightly populated by Spanish settlers and physically isolated from central Mexico, it became a haven for runaway slaves (called *cimarrones*), who intermarried with Indians and mestizos there and established communities that grew in size and were eventually, with Spanish consent, incorporated as towns.

Today there are some sixteen African Mexican towns in the Pacific Costa Chica. Although the residents of these communities see themselves as Mexican, rather than as African or Indian, there has been a revival of interest in their African heritage, as indicated by public displays of African-based music, dance, and folklore. Other African Mexican communities are located near Veracruz; the towns of Mata Clara and Coyolillo are the best known. It is estimated that about 3 percent of the Mexican population is of partial African ancestry (Coniff and Davis 1994, 272).

Bibliography

Aguirre Beltrán, Gonzalo (1972). *La población negra de Mexico: Estudio etnohistorico.* 2nd ed. Mexico City: Fondo de Cultura Económica.

Aguirre Beltrán, Gonzalo (1989). *Cuijla: Esbozo etnográfico de un puebla negro.* Mexico City: Universidad Veracruzana; Instituto Nacional Indigenista; Gobierno del Estado de Veracruz; Fondo de Cultura Económica.

Amuzgo

ETHNONYMS: none

Orientation

Identification. The name "Amuzgo" comes from a Nahuatl word to which various interpretations have been given. According to one version, the term derives from *amoxtli*, "place of books or papers"; another version—perhaps a more plausible one—translates the word *amoxko* to mean "place of clouded water" (the greenish slime floating on the surface of rivers). There is no known general self-designation for the group, although one form of ethnic self-recognition is evident in their reference to those who speak *hñonda*, a term that is difficult to translate but that expresses the idea of "word [language] of water"; other languages are referred to as *kñosko*, "word [language] of leaves."

Location. The Amuzgo live near the Pacific Ocean, in the lower portions of the Sierra Madre del Sur, along the coasts of the Mexican states of Guerrero and Oaxaca (known as La Costa Chica). The area they occupy, located between 16° and 17° N and between 98° and 99° W, has an average elevation of 500 meters and a semihumid climate. The main Amuzgo settlements in the state of Guerrero are the *municipios* of Xochistlahuaca, Tlacoachistlahuaca, and Ometepec. In Oaxaca, the main settlements are San Pedro Amuzgos and Santa María Ipalapa.

Demography. In 1990 the number of Amuzgo speakers was calculated at 32,637: 27,629 in the state of Guerrero and 5,008 in Oaxaca. These figures include children under 5 years of age with Amuzgo-speaking parents. The actual number of Amuzgo could be higher, however, because it is difficult to count people living in small and dispersed settlements. The 1990 census counted temporary migrants at their location of migration rather than in their home communities. The Amuzgo area is also the home of mestizo, Afro-Mexican, Mixtec, and Nahua populations.

Linguistic Affiliation. The Amuzgo language is classified as an independent branch of the Otomanguean Language Family. Amuzgo shows dialectal differences but maintains relative mutual intelligibility. It is marked by enough diversity that people who know the language can identify the home territory of a speaker. In the Amuzgo area of Guerrero, monolingualism reaches 50 percent, and in Oaxaca, 20 percent. Bilingualism is the result of migration, schooling, and contact with mestizos in the capitals of the municipios.

History and Cultural Relations

Information on the history of the Amuzgo is very scarce, although some data can be reconstructed from tangential sources. From Mixtec codices it is known that around the year A.D. 1000 the Mixtec king Eight Deer was recognized as a Mixtec ruler in a ceremony that took place in Jicayan, a place near the eastern Amuzgo region and the boundary of the Tututepec domain. This leads one to deduce that Amuzgo pueblos must have existed since that time. In the second half of the fifteenth century, the western part of the Amuzgo area, in the present state of Guerrero, including centers of Amuzgo populations like Ayotzinapa (which has no Amuzgo population today) and Xochistlahuaca, an area controlled by the province of Ayacastla and inhabited mainly by Ometepec and Igualapa, was under Aztec domination. Around the Amuzgo area, besides Mixtec, there were Chatina-, Ayacatzec-, Nahua-, Cahuatec-, Tzintec-, and Tlapanec-speaking pueblos. On two Mixtec *lienzos* (painted deerskins), those of Zacatepec and Jicayan (dated 1550), wherein boundaries are described, there appears a glyph with the name of the town of Amuzgos: a ball ending in an element resembling threads, as it were a cotton seed, with the Mixtec name *ñuñama*, "town of the cotton ball." The Relación de Xalapa, Cintla, and Acatlán of 1580 shows several capitals dependent on the *alcaldía mayor* (area governed by an *alcalde mayor*), which included *estancias* (towns) where Amuzgo was spoken: Xicayan de Tovar, Ayocinapa, Ometepec, Suchistlahuaca, and Ihualapa. Many of these towns were devastated by the Spanish invasion and epidemics related to it. Pedro de Alvarado began the conquest of the southern coast, and the conquistador Tristán de Luna y Arellano, under the Perpetual Estate of the Marshall of Castile, developed one of the largest landed estates of the area, which included part of Amuzgo territory. The estate disintegrated during the first half of the nineteenth century because of disputes over succession. After haciendas were established in the area, the indigenous population suffered the consequences of new economic activities: cattle raising led to the destruction of cultivable land, and a system of forced labor was imposed in conjunction with the production of sugarcane and cochineal.

Settlements

The Amuzgo settled in various towns: Ayotzinapa, Ometepec, Xochistlahuaca, Igualapa, Cozoyoapa, Tlacoachistlahuaca, Huajintepec, Quetzalapa, Chalapa, and Amuzgos.

Xochistlahuaca ("Vale of Flowers") was made the capital (*cabecera*) of the Amuzgo region in 1563. Of the towns that survived epidemics and colonization, those that still exist today are Cozoyapan, Huehuetonoc, Minas, San Cristóbal, Tlacoachistlahuaca, Cochoapa, Huajintepec, Huixtepec, and Zacualpan in Guerrero and the territories of Amuzgos and Ipalapa in Oaxaca. When the state of Guerrero was formed in 1849, the Amuzgo found themselves divided between two states, a division that was detrimental to intercommunity relations between Amuzgo towns. Besides these towns, there is a large population dispersed in smaller *cuadrillas* or *parajes* (hamlets), in which people live temporarily or permanently, in order to be nearer their cultivable land and their *encierros* (fenced pastures). Amuzgo settlements were exposed to the cultural influence of the coastal Black population, as is evident by the construction of round houses, known as *redondos*, made of mud, plaited lightweight cane, and *otate*-cane wood. Later the dominant form was the square adobe house with a two-eaved tile roof. Settlements in cabeceras (principal towns/administrative centers) or large towns are agglutinative; in the hamlets or cuadrillas they are dispersed. In a cabecera, the mestizo population generally lives in the center and the indigenous population on the periphery.

Economy

Subsistence and Commercial Activities. Nowadays the economy of Amuzgo communities is based on agriculture. The main cultigen is maize, the foodstuff that forms the basis of the indigenous population's daily diet. Beans, squashes, chilies, cacao, coffee, various fruits, and poultry complement the indigenous diet. *Panela* (raw-sugar loaves) and *aguardiente* (white rum) are made from sugarcane, which is still pressed in the animal-powered sugar presses introduced during the colonial era. Given the area's soil quality and the hilly nature of the land, the system of agriculture is slash and burn. Implements include the machete, *tarecua* (a weeding tool), *coa* (native spade), and *enduyo* (a planting tool). The amount of seed sown is measured in *maquillas* (units of weight) or *cajones* (boxes). Only very few indigenous families can afford to maintain cattle. The Amuzgo complement crop and livestock production by producing handicrafts, mainly weaving and embroidery.

Trade. Indigenous products formerly played a major part in commercial exchange, but, in the hands of the mestizo population, trade has turned toward modern goods and increasingly less toward local handicrafts. Commercial activity increases during the festivities in the various pueblos of the area, but the majority of the merchants who come to sell at the fairs are from outside the area.

Migration. There has been a rapid increase in migration. The migratory flow is within the surrounding area, to the capital, to nearby cities, to Mexico City, and to the United States.

Division of Labor. Men generally work in the fields, and women in the home; however, in some cases women help the men with agricultural labor or tending herds and flocks. Handicrafts generally fall within the domain of women.

Land Tenure. In Amuzgo communities, landownership is in the form of *ejidos* (federal land grants to peasant farmers), communal lands, and smallholdings. Landownership has been a constant struggle for the Amuzgo, as they have had to contend with mestizos recurrently buying up land. Given the system of slash-and-burn cultivation, it is necessary for plots of land to lie fallow. Access to ejido and communal land guarantees the use of _monte_ (hillside land) for planting, pasture, gathering, and hunting. Private property is mainly in the form of encierros—fenced plots of land wherein cattle are grazed—and cultivated land, which only the owner can use.

Kinship

Kin Groups and Descent. Nowadays there are no lineage or descent groups, but some patrilineal practices survive in rules of residence and inheritance. In some Amuzgo towns, a social differentiation based on attachment to paternal or maternal groups is still evident, for example, when a child is considered to belong to the family of the mother's father. Kinship unity is strengthened by coresidence in a single household, which unites child-rearing, economic, and kinship functions. Patrilocal residence is the form preferred by newlywed couples, although matrilocal residence also occurs; neolocal residence is infrequent.

Kinship Terminology. Amuzgo terminology has different kinship terms for parents and their siblings and a differentiation based on sex (the Eskimo model). A subdivision by age provides terms denoting older and younger; for example, in cases where Ego is older, a parent's brother will be called "sibling's son," and the reciprocal term "parent's brother" will be used to refer to Ego. The system does not differentiate between the sexes of descendants below Ego's generation.

Marriage and Family

Marriage. In more traditional communities, it is still the custom to ask for the bride's hand: the young man requests that his father act as intermediary. The marriage ritual begins with the mediation of a _pedidor_ (negotiator), who presents himself at the home of the bride's parents and makes known the groom's family's intention. After several visits, the proposal is usually accepted. The process continues with a ritual called the _quedamento_, during which the engagement is publicly announced, as well as the day that the Catholic wedding rite will be performed. This tradition, which was the norm prior to the 1970s, has gradually lost force as couples face an ever increasing process of modernization. A big marriage fiesta—a good _fandango_—will be indicative of a good marriage. Ideally, baptismal godparents will be chosen to act as marriage godparents.

Inheritance. The Amuzgo do not have precise guidelines for the inheritance of goods, rights, or obligations. There is a slight tendency to prefer the oldest son of the first formally married wife to inherit the headship of the family.

Socialization. Women are in charge of introducing girls and boys into the social order. When nearing adolescence, girls assume practically all domestic functions, and boys begin to work more closely with their fathers in agriculture, fishing, and hunting.

Sociopolitical Organization

Social Organization. The social life of Amuzgo communities is based on the relationship between land organization, agriculture, the family, marriage, social traditions, _compadrazgo_ (ritual coparenthood), the _cargo_ system, and the ritual cycle of religious festivals.

Political Organization. Since the seventeenth century, when _macehuales_ (members of the peasant class) became local authorities in _cabildos_ (village governments) and other governing bodies, an internal social hierarchy has determined the rules for ascent in status through a long chain of political and religious offices (cargos). Such a system persists among the Amuzgo and is linked to national political structures. The cargo system requires a young man coming of age to perform certain community work, called _fajina_ in Guerrero and _tequio_ in Oaxaca. Later on, he undertakes cargos such as those of _topil_ (messenger), _policía de machete_ (policeman armed only with a machete), _policía urbano_ (policeman not armed with a machete), and _cabo, sargento,_ and _comandante_ (chiefs of groups of police). Still later, he will acquire higher status with cargos like _juez de barrio_ (barrio judge), member of the _sociedad de padres de familia_ (school advisory board), _presidente de bienes comunales_ (overseer of community property), _comandante de arma,_ member of the _junta patriótica, alcalde segundo,_ or _presidente municipal_ (chief executive officer of a municipio). The highest rung of the hierarchy is reached by an individual of advanced age who becomes a _principal_ and member of the _consejo de ancianos_ (council of elders). _Mayordomías_ (stewardships) during religious festivals are usually the cargos by means of which individuals acquire prestige. The names and the particular functions of cargos vary from one community to the next. The introduction of political models from outside the community through opportunities for greater social mobility have created conflicts between the cargo system and political forms from outside.

Social Control. The maintenance of internal social order involves elements of the cargo system, magicoreligious beliefs (_nahualism_), and even blood vengeance. Local indigenous authorities are in charge of resolving disputes arising from accusations of harm caused by nahualism or witchcraft, animals entering milpas, theft, unsanctioned sexual relations, and debt payment, usually by mediation during negotiations between the two parties. Only seldom are conflicts—even serious ones—transferred to higher legal authorities.

Conflict. The most common social conflicts arise from political arguments and situations involving land tenure or rivalry between individuals. In some Amuzgo communities, especially during the latter part of the 1970s, agrarian movements caused conflict between the indigenous population and mestizo landholders. Conflicts over local political control can crop up because of the way positions of authority are distributed between the indigenous and mestizo populations. In some areas, powerful caciques or factional competition between political parties create conflict. Violence is a frequent resort in personal disputes; justice is sought through vengeance, and homicide is often the result.

Religion and Cultural Expression

Religious Beliefs.   The dominant religion is Catholicism, although Protestant groups are also active. Magical beliefs associated with supernatural elements constitute part of Amuzgo wisdom regarding daily activities; for example, the timing of economic and symbolic activities may depend on the phases of the moon. It is thought that children will die during an eclipse of the moon, adults during an eclipse of the sun. There is a strong belief in nahualism, the power of certain persons to cause others harm by utilizing their animal spirit, or nahual.

Religious Practictioners.   Besides Catholic clergy and cargo holders, there are a number of other specialized religious practitoners who participate in rituals at church and in homes. Singers and prayer makers are needed for various rituals. There are also specialists in calendrical divination, who cure and prognosticate during public rituals. In large and small communities, *mayordomos* take the chief responsibility for staging religious fiestas. Catholic churches are generally served by a parish priest who travels constantly to perform religious rites. Among Protestant groups, pastors reside within the communities; they practice locally but there is also intercommunity exchange.

Ceremonies.   Fiestas are held according to the Catholic ritual calendar: Carnival, Holy Week, Todos Santos (the Days of the Dead during and after the Catholic All Saints' Day), and festivals for the town's patron saints. Ceremonies associated with civic and school events are organized annually. With variations from pueblo to pueblo, almost every community has a mayordomía for some patron saint. An essential element of festivals and mayordomías are the dance performances, among which "Las Mascaritas," "Chilolos," "Macho Mula," "Tortuga," "Tigre," "Conquista," "Los Doce Pares de Francia," "Diablos," "Chareo," "Las Mojigatas," "Cebolleras," "Toritos," "Pan De Panela," "Tlaminques," "Malinches," "Moros y Cristianos," "Apaches y Gachupines," and "Pichiques" are most notable. These dances may be accompanied, for example, by a flute and a drum or by band music. "Chilena" music from the Costa Chica has also penetrated the Amuzgo region. There are propitiatory rituals for rain, performed on plots of land being cultivated; stone figurines are used and animal blood is offered.

Art and Technology.   Basically, the Amuzgo make their own tools and utensils for the home. Their culture is reflected in the classificatory nature of the language used to describe the numerous instruments and utensils they make. Clay, as well as plants and wood have multiple functions; they are used to make houses, corrals, and tools. As regards handicrafts, there is much spinning and weaving, and *huipiles* (the dresses of indigenous women) are made on strap looms; formerly, this clothing was of cotton.

Medicine.   Sickness and misfortune are generally believed to have been caused by some enemy using nahuales. In some aspects, nahualism is also linked to curing practices. Some of the misfortune or illnesses attributed to supernatural forces are *espanto* (sudden fright), *mal de ojo* (the evil eye), *coraje* (anger), attack by nahuales, and attack by a shade (*sombra*). Sorcerers have various diagnostic and therapeutic techniques such as *ver la sangre* (consulting the blood) and *pulsear* (taking the pulse) as well as techniques for curing, like *limpiar* (cleansing/ridding the patient of evil influences), *enfriar* (cooling off), and *curar de espanto* (curing fright). A large number of plants are used in curing.

Death and Afterlife.   Beliefs regarding life after death are a combination of Catholic and traditional elements. Deceased who had been married are buried with their heads facing west, single people and children with their heads facing east. A light casket, which will allow for easy decomposition of the body into the earth, is preferred. A distinction is drawn between the soul and the shade: the soul leaves the body immediately after death; the shade leaves it after nine days. If, during the nine days—while the grave cross is prepared—the deceased is not satisfied with the offerings that have been made, his or her shade may refuse to leave and will not rest in peace. The spirits of the dead return for Todos Santos at the end of October.

Bibliography

Acuña, René, ed. (1984a). "Relación de Justlahuaca." *Relaciones geográficas del siglo XVI; Antequera.* Vol. 2, Part 2, 279–324. Mexico City: Universidad Nacional Autónoma de México.

Acuña, René, ed. (1984b). "Relación de Xalapa, Cintla, y Acatlán." *Relaciones geográficas del siglo XVI; Antequera.* Vol. 3, Part 2, 277–294. Mexico City: Universidad Nacional Autónoma de México.

Caso, Alfonso (1966). *Interpretación del Códice colombino.* Mexico City: Sociedad Mexicana de Antropología.

Castro Domingo, Pablo (1994). "El sistema de cargos en una comunidad amuzga de Guerrero." Licenciatura Thesis in Social Anthropology, Escuela Nacional de Antropología, Mexico City.

Cervantes Delgado, Roberto (1993). "Los amuzgos." In *Así somos . . . , organo quincenal de información cultural.* Chilapa, Guerrero, Mexico: Centro de Investigación y Cultura de la Zona de la Montaña.

Cruz Hernández, Modesta (1993). *N'oan nan kobijnd'ue n'an tzjon noan: Los usos de la madera entre los amuzgos.* Mexico City: Centro de Investigaciones y Estudios Superiores en Antropología Social.

Cuevas Suárez, Susana (1985). *Ornitología amuzga: Un análisis etnosemántico.* Mexico City: Instituto Nacional de Antropología e Historia.

Egli, Walter (1982). *San Pedro Amuzgos: Ein mexicansisches Dorf Kämpft um sein Land: Agrargeschichte der Costa Oaxaca von der Kolonialzeit bis sur Gegenvart.* Zurich: Limmat Verlag Genossenschaft.

Ravicz, Robert, and A. Kimball Romney (1969). "The Amuzgo." In *The Handbook of Middle American Indians,* edited by Robert Wauchope. Vol. 7, *Ethnology, Part One,* edited by Evon Z. Vogt, 417–433. Austin: University of Texas Press.

Tapia García, Fermín (1985). _Las plantas curativas y su conocimiento entre los amuzgos, árboles grandes y arbustos._ Mexico City: Centro de Investigaciones y Estudios Superiores en Antropología Social.

VÍCTOR MANUEL FRANCO PELLOTIER

Anguillans

ETHNONYMS: none

The name "Anguilla" refers to a 96-square-kilometer dependent island territory of the United Kingdom, located in the northeast Caribbean at 18°03′ N, 63°04′ W. Anguillans speak English and are mostly of African descent. The population was approximately 6,900 in 1992. "Anguilla," the Spanish word for "eel," refers to the shape of the island, which originated as a coral formation.

The earliest inhabitants of the island were Saladoid Indians, who arrived sometime around 1300 B.C.; they grew cassava and built several large villages. In the tenth century A.D., post-Saladoid Indians came to the island and established a theocracy. British enslavement of the Indians and European diseases killed all the Anguillan Indians by the 1600s. Anguilla was colonized by the British in 1650, although the Carib and French both attacked the colony in the seventeenth and eighteenth centuries, respectively. Anguilla was later to become a part of the Saint Kitts-Nevis-Anguilla colony. As Saint Kitts gradually gained more independence from the U.K., Anguilla moved toward independence from the Saint Kitts government, and in 1980 it separated from Saint Kitts and Nevis to become a British Dependent Territory, drafting its own constitution in 1982. The Valley, capital of Anguilla, is home to the governor (the Crown representative), an elected seven-member executive council, and an elected eleven-member legislature known as the House of Assembly.

The economy of Anguilla is presently booming because of the tourist trade and the location there of offshore banks. Prior to 1985, however, high unemployment and emigration were common. The island has few natural resources (salt and lobsters), poorly developed agriculture (pigeon peas, maize, and sweet potatoes), and little manufacturing (boat building).

Bibliography

Douglas, Nik, ed. (1987). _Review, 1981–1985._ The Valley, Anguilla: Archaeological and Historical Society.

Petty, Colville L., and Nat Hodge (1987). _Anguilla's Battle for Freedom._ Anguilla: PETNAT Publishing Co.

Westlake, Donald E. (1972). _Under an English Heaven._ New York: Simon & Schuster.

Antiguans and Barbudans

ETHNONYMS: none

Orientation

Identification. The country Antigua and Barbuda includes two of the Leeward Islands located in the eastern Caribbean Sea. Settled by English colonists in the seventeenth century, the islands have a history of slavery and British colonial rule. Antigua and Barbuda won independence in 1981. The national motto is "Each endeavouring, all achieving."

Location. Antigua measures 281 square kilometers in area, and Barbuda 161 square kilometers. A third island, uninhabited Redonda (3.25 square kilometers), is a dependency of the state. Volcanic and comprised of limestone, Antigua is generally flat, except for the southwestern section, which is the site of the highest point, Boggy Peak (403 meters). The coastline has many fine white sandy beaches, some protected by dense bush, and many natural harbors. Antigua's vegetation is evergreen and deciduous forest and evergreen woodland. Most of the country's government buildings are located in the capital, Saint John's, together with a central market, schools, banks, shops and restaurants, a deep-water harbor, and, since the late 1980s, a modern tourist complex.

Relatively isolated Barbuda lies some 50 kilometers to the northeast. It is a coral island covered with open scrub. Cattle, deer, guinea fowl, and hogs roam freely through the bush. Barbuda's unsafe harbors have contributed to its isolation over the centuries; regular air service from Antigua began only in 1961. Almost all of Barbuda's 1,200 residents live in historic Codrington Village. The island has a few shops, some resort hotels where people find seasonal work, an elementary school, a health clinic, and several churches.

Demography. Antigua and Barbuda's population, according to the 1991 census, was 60,840 persons (29,638 men and 31,202 women, a ratio of 105 females for every 100 males); of these, only 2 percent lived on Barbuda. The vast majority of Antiguans and Barbudans, 60,148 persons, live in private households. Most of the islanders are African Caribbean people, their ancestors having been brought as slaves in the seventeenth and eighteenth centuries. Other groups include a few remaining descendants of British colonists, the progeny of Portuguese indentured servants who came in the mid-nineteenth century under planter-inspired schemes to find field laborers, and the children of Syrian and Lebanese traders who arrived at the turn of the twentieth century. West Indians from other islands and a small group of expatriates from the United States, Canada, and England reside in Antigua as well.

Linguistic Affiliation.   Antiguans and Barbudans speak English, although there is a creole dialect most commonly heard in the countryside. Most citizens are literate.

History and Cultural Relations

Antigua and Barbuda's first indigenous people included Siboney and later Arawak Indians. These were hunting and fishing peoples whose settlements have been located at several sites on both islands. From their villages in Dominica and Saint Kitts, Carib Indians raided the Arawak and later the European colonists on Antigua and Barbuda. The first English colonists arrived in Antigua in 1632. They were led by Sir Thomas Warner, who had earlier headed an expedition to Saint Christopher (now Saint Kitts). These colonists and their indentured servants grew tobacco, cotton, and subsistence crops and defended themselves against the Carib and the French. Within a few years, they had devised a regular system of government, complete with elected assemblies, governors' councils, parish vestries, and a hierarchy of courts. By the early eighteenth century the colonists had adjusted their legal codes to the exigencies of managing an economy devoted to sugar and organized around plantation slavery (Lazarus-Black 1994). Gaspar estimates that 60,820 African slaves were imported to Antigua between 1671 and 1763 (1985, 75). Slaves accounted for 41.6 percent of the population in 1672; 80.5 percent in 1711; and 93.5 percent in 1774 (p. 83).

Unlike Antigua, Barbuda never developed sugar estates. Early attempts by English settlers to farm the island were unsuccessful, and the Carib proved a constant menace. In 1685 the Crown leased Barbuda to the Codrington family for a payment "unto her Majesty yearly and every year one Fat Sheep if demanded" (Hall 1971, 59). The Codringtons used the island as a supply depot, manufacturing center, and slave "seasoning" area. Until 1898, when the Antiguan legislature assumed responsibility for its government, the islanders, most of them descendants of Codrington's slaves, were without political representation or social services.

Slavery was abolished in 1834, but much of the political, social, and economic organization of these islands remained largely unchanged over the next century. Barbudans continued to reside in Codrington Village, working subsistence gardens, fishing, and hunting. In Antigua, there was little land available for purchase and few jobs beyond those offered on the estates. Workers remained in very impoverished conditions and most continued to plant and harvest sugarcane under the terms of the infamous Contract Act. Reform began with the legalization of trade unions in 1940, higher wages, and the extension of political representation in the 1950s and 1960s.

Settlements

The largest town, Saint Johns, is on the northwestern coast of Antigua. It is the hub of island activity. Beyond Saint Johns, villages dot the rural Antiguan landscape. Many of these were founded immediately after Emancipation and adopted names such as "Liberta" and "Freetown." The freedmen built wattle-and-daub (wood frame and straw) houses for their families in preference to residing on the sugar estates. Churches became centers of religious and social life in these villages. Today the villages of Parham, Bolans, All Saints, and English Harbour are large enough to serve as centers for schools, police stations, courts, post offices, and other government services. Barbudans mostly reside in Codrington Village. Despite opposition from the government in Antigua, they continue to insist upon communal ownership of the land beyond the village.

Economy

Subsistence and Commercial Activities.   Antigua's economy remained almost singularly devoted to sugarcane for more than two centuries. The last sugar factory closed in 1972, but there are periodic attempts to revive that industry. Agricultural production is moving toward greater diversification, which includes fruits, vegetables, and grains (World Bank 1985, 15–16).

Tourism began to develop haltingly in the early 1960s; by the 1980s it had become the single most important economic activity in Antigua. Its direct value now accounts for approximately 21 percent of the gross domestic product, and at least 12 percent of the labor force is directly employed in this sector (World Bank 1985, 24). Other economic sectors include the personal-service industries, distributive trades, construction, transport, agriculture, and fishing. The government employs some 30 percent of the total work force (p. 4). Unemployment remained at around 20 percent through the first half of the 1980s.

Industrial Arts.   Industrial activity includes processing local agricultural produce; some manufacturing of clothing, furniture, and household goods; and production of rum and other beverages. In 1983 manufactured exports represented about 85 percent of total domestic exports (World Bank 1985, 20). A handful of firms produce more than half of the output and employ at least half of the industrial work force. Crude oil, machinery, automobiles, luxury consumer items, and clothing are imported.

Trade.   Antigua exports cotton, pineapples, live animals, rum, tobacco, and animal and vegetable products. Provision crops are consumed locally, with surpluses passed on to family and friends or sold for extra cash. The middle class depends heavily on imported foods and consumer items. People travel abroad specifically to shop for retail goods.

Division of Labor.   Holding multiple jobs and sharing jobs are common in Antigua and Barbuda. For example, a man may work as a carpenter, keep cows, and rent a house. The growth of tourism has enabled many more people, particularly women, to enter the labor force. For the most part, however, household chores, tending gardens and domestic animals, and child care remain women's work even if they hold full-time jobs.

Land Tenure.   The government owns nearly 60 percent of the available land in Antigua. The practice of offering short-term leases to individuals has not proved particularly conducive to land improvement. Barbudans individually own their homes in Codrington Village, but they hold in common lands beyond the village.

Kinship

Kin Groups and Descent. Antiguans and Barbudans trace family relationships bilaterally through blood and law. Family is very important, both to one's social identity and for social, economic, and political support. A woman is said to have a child "for" a man, a way of noting that children create new social bonds and alliances. Marriage is the preferred form of union, but many persons marry later in life after their families have been established. Families are generally large, and they may include legitimate ("inside") as well as illegitimate ("outside") children who are socially acknowledged. Because of the small populations of these islands, people have extensive knowledge about kinship ties and histories.

Kinship Terminology. Antiguans and Barbudans inherited the kinship terminology of the British colonists who settled these islands, but they do not make a linguistic distinction between "half" and "whole" siblings. "Aunty" and "uncle" may be used as terms of respect for elders. Another departure from English tradition is that men and women who have lived together for some time may refer to each other as "wife" or "husband" even though the couple is not legally married.

Marriage and Family

Marriage and Family Structure. Scholars have gone to great lengths to try to explain the high rates of illegitimacy, the prevalence and popularity of three different conjugal forms (visiting unions, concubinage, and legal marriage), and the pervasiveness of female-headed households in the English-speaking Caribbean. Early efforts to explain these patterns centered on slavery; historians argued that bondage made marriage and a stable family life impossible. An alternative perspective suggested that slaves retained vestiges of African polygamy and matrilineal kinship practices. Others have attributed West Indian kinship and household organization to economic factors, particularly persistent poverty, male migration, and other social and demographic factors.

Historical investigations suggest there was never a single type of slave family form in the Caribbean (Higman 1984). As was true throughout the region, Antiguan slaves toiled in different socioeconomic contexts, and these influenced the content and forms of their conjugal and reproductive practices. Slaves on large estates, for example, might have experienced relative stability in their day-to-day lives and had access to a pool of potential conjugal partners on their own and nearby estates. Slaves who labored in towns, in contrast, were more likely to live in mother-child households than were field laborers (pp. 373, 371). The record shows a pattern in which most slaves had a number of partners early in life and later settled into long-term unions with single partners. Certain men of unusual talent, wit, or charisma, however, maintained multiple unions.

Religion and law exerted important influences on the marriage and kinship practices of Antiguans. By the end of the slave trade in 1807, for example, the missions claimed to have converted about 28 percent of the Black and Colored population in Antigua, Saint Kitts, Montserrat, Nevis, and the British Virgin Islands (based on Goveia 1965, 307). Early in the nineteenth century, free colonists, including free persons of color, married in the Anglican church in Saint Johns (Lazarus-Black 1994).

For much of Antigua's early history, there were three separate marriage laws, each corresponding directly to a person's role in the island's division of labor. Free Antiguans, for example, were married by Anglican ministers. These men generally married women of their own social standing in the community, but some also entered into nonlegal unions with women of color. In contrast, "respectable" free women married and refrained from extramarital affairs. Ministers were forbidden by law, however, from performing marriages for slaves or indentured servants unless the latter had permission from their masters. After 1798, a special marriage law, only partially resembling that pertaining to free persons, governed the unions of slaves. A child of a slave marriage was not allowed to take the father's surname or inherit property. The law did provide for a public declaration of a couple's intention to live together, monetary awards from masters for marrying, and a brief ceremony in which the marriage was officially recorded in the estate records. After slavery ended in 1834, there was a single marriage code. Nevertheless, the establishment of families without formal legal confirmation remained commonplace across the social classes.

Domestic Unit. Married couples prefer to live in their own households, although needy relatives and friends are welcomed. If a couple is unmarried and the man is "visiting," the children usually reside with their mother. Kinship and the domestic unit are not coterminous; many children live away from their biological parents, and some children grow up in several different households. Parents make choices about where a child should reside, considering the economy of the household, people's work patterns, the need to care for the elderly, educational opportunities, and the simple fact that a relative may ask for a child to keep from being lonely.

Inheritance. Since 1987 it has been illegal to discriminate against a person because of birth status; a child born out of wedlock may readily be legally acknowledged by his or her father, and any child so recognized can inherit from the father's estate. The islanders usually divide inheritances equally among their children. A married man often remembers his illegitimate children in his will or with a gift made during his lifetime.

Socialization. Children are desired by both men and women, although women have primary responsibility for children's early care. In the past, many children were cared for by female relatives or older siblings. Today day-care centers and preschools are an option. Nevertheless, the extended family remains crucially important in children's socialization.

Sociopolitical Organization

Social Organization. The contemporary social structure consists of a small socioeconomic elite and two broad classes, middle and lower. The elite includes high-ranking political officials, local businessmen, major landholders, senior attorneys, and a few foreign entrepreneurs and expatriates who play important roles in the economy but who are noticeably absent from the official political proce̶ The homes, cars, leisure activities, and family life of elite are virtually indistinguishable from those of peopl Antigua's middle class. The middle class includes young lawyers, landowners, teachers, clergymen, retailers, members of the civil service, and the few industrialists. The upper strata of the lower class consists of a petite bourgeoisie who own some productive resources and who may be self-employed. The large working class includes agricultural workers, fishermen, domestics, hotel workers, and common laborers. Barbudans are relatively homogeneous in terms of their homes and life-style; most are working class.

Political Organization.   Few Antiguans could meet the property qualifications for voting, much less running for office, until well into the twentieth century. Planters controlled local politics until labor unrest heralded a movement for political reform. Adult suffrage was granted in 1951. Shortly thereafter, election rules were changed to allow greater participation among the working people. Independence occurred through a series of stages that Henry (1985) refers to as "constitutional decolonization." In 1969 the islands became associated states, gaining control of their internal affairs. Since 1981, Antigua and Barbuda has become a parliamentary democracy with a bicameral legislature and an elected prime minister. The governor-general is the representative of the British Crown. The government has proclaimed a nonaligned foreign policy but maintains its strongest political and economic ties with Britain, Canada, and the United States. There are two major political parties, the Antigua Labour party and the United Progressive party. The former, led by V. C. Bird, Sr., has been politically dominant since 1946.

Social Control.   Antiguans and Barbudans pride themselves on being a law-abiding people; the crime rate remains low. A police force and a four-tiered court system presently serve the islands. The first tier consists of the magistrates' courts, which decide some family cases, disputes between persons over small property claims, personal grievances, traffic matters, and minor assaults. The High Court settles major civil and criminal cases. The Appellate Division of the Supreme Court of the Eastern Caribbean meets intermittently. Because Antigua and Barbuda is a member of the Commonwealth, cases decided by the Supreme Court may be appealed to the Privy Council in England.

Religion and Expressive Culture

Religious Beliefs.   There have been two major waves of missionary activity in Antigua. The first occurred at the end of the eighteenth century, spurred by the arrival of Methodist and Moravian ministers on the island. The second wave of proselytizing began around World War I and gained momentum during the years of the Great Depression. Today the Anglican church has the largest following. Other large congregations include the Moravian, Methodist, Catholic, Seventh Day Adventist, Pilgrim Holiness, and Pentecostal churches. Churches have historically played a very important role in the lives of Antiguans and

Barbudans, and they remain very important today. Despite ̶ small size, more than half a dozen churches find ̶ns.

̶ people also believe in a body of knowledge and set of rites called obeah. Deriving from Africa, obeah can be used for a variety of purposes including healing, causing sickness or other physical harm, determining who has been guilty of theft, "fixing" a court case, and ensuring that a loved one will remain faithful. It is illegal, but practitioners are mainly ignored by police.

Religious Practitioners.   Ministers are accorded high prestige in the community. In addition to their roles as spiritual leaders, they provide psychological counseling and often mediate in conflicts among their parishioners.

Ceremonies.   Antiguans and Barbudans celebrate with friends and relatives a child's birth, baptism, and marriage. Weddings and funerals are very important and elaborate events. Independence Day is celebrated on 1 November.

Arts.   Cricket is the national sport. Antiguans and Barbudans also take great pride in their music. Calypso and steelbands are very popular, and there are annual competitions at Carnival at the end of July to determine the best songs, singers, and bands. During Carnival, troupes march in colorful costumes in the street and excited viewers "jump-up" enthusiastically to urge the revelers on. Visitors to Antigua can see an overview of the country's history at the Museum of Antigua and Barbuda in Saint Johns. Choral and theatrical groups perform occasionally.

Bibliography

Gaspar, David Barry (1985). *Bondmen and Rebels: A Study of Master-Slave Relations in Antigua*. Baltimore: Johns Hopkins University Press.

Goveia, Elsa V. (1965). *Slave Society in the British Leeward Islands at the End of the Eighteenth Century*. New Haven: Yale University Press.

Hall, Douglas (1971). *Five of the Leewards, 1834–1870*. Saint Lawrence, Barbados: Caribbean Universities Press.

Henry, Paget (1985). *Peripheral Capitalism and Underdevelopment in Antigua*. New Brunswick, N.J.: Transaction Books.

Higman, B. W. (1984). *Slave Populations of the British Caribbean 1807–1834*. Baltimore: Johns Hopkins University Press.

Lazarus-Black, Mindie (1994). *Legitimate Acts and Illegal Encounters: Law and Society in Antigua and Barbuda*. Washington, D.C.: Smithsonian Institution Press.

World Bank (1985). *Antigua and Barbuda Economic Report*. Washington, D.C.

MINDIE LAZARUS-BLACK

Arubans

ETHNONYMS: none; historical names for the island, of pre-Colombian or Spanish origin: Oirubae ("companion," that is, to Curaçao), Ora Oubao ("shell island"), Oro Ubo ("once there was gold")

Orientation

Identification. Aruba is a multicultural island society with both Caribbean and Latin American features in its culture and social structure. Its people have been strongly influenced by the globalization of world culture.

Location. Aruba is the most southeastern island of the Caribbean archipelago. It is located 27 kilometers off the coast of the Venezuelean peninsula of Paraguana and 90 kilometers west of Curaçao. Together with Curaçao and Bonaire, it forms the Dutch Leeward Islands. Aruba's area is 193 square kilometers. The climate is tropical, with an average temperature of 28° C. The main rainy season is from October to January. Yearly rainfall usually does not exceed 50 centimeters.

Demography. The population and housing census of 1991 showed that 66,687 people live on Aruba, not including an estimated 2,500 to 5,000 illegal aliens. Compared to the period 1972–1981, during which the population increased 4.2 percent, the growth rate climbed to 10.6 percent between 1981 and 1991, mostly owing to immigration after 1987. The proportion of foreign-born inhabitants has risen from 18.5 percent in 1981 to 23.9 percent in 1991.

Linguistic Orientation. The traditional language of Aruba is Papiamento (Talk), a creole language that is also spoken on Curaçao and Bonaire. The origins of Papiamento are much debated. Two points of view dominate the discussion. According to one, it originated as a lingua franca, based on Portuguese and West African languages, during the seventeenth-century slave trade. Others maintain that it developed during the interaction between the Spanish and the Dutch. Indian names of plants and places are included in its lexicon. Owing to 350 years of colonial domination, Dutch is the official language in education and public affairs. The oil industry, tourism, and subsequent migration brought English and Spanish to the island, which are the second- and thirdmost spoken languages. Most Arubans are multilingual.

History and Cultural Relations

Prior to European discovery, Aruba was inhabited by Indian populations. From 2000 to 1000 B.C. the island was populated by preceramic Indians. Around 1000 B.C. Arawak from the east of Venezuela migrated to Aruba, introducing pottery and agriculture.

Aruba was discovered by the Spanish around 1499. Because of the absence of precious metals, Aruba, Bonaire, and Curaçao were declared *islas inutiles* (useless islands). In 1515 their inhabitants were deported to Hispaniola to work in the mines. After an unsuccessful effort toward colonization by Juan de Ampíes (1526–1533) the islands were abandoned to their fate. Other Indians later migrated to Aruba, and Spanish priests from the Falcón region of Venezuela undertook to Christianize them.

The Dutch West India Company (WIC) took possession of Aruba in 1636, two years after the conquest of Curaçao. Colonization of the island was forbidden until 1754; the island was used to breed cattle for trade and to supply food for the residents of Curaçao. After the dissolution of the WIC (1792) and the English interregnum (1810–1816), colonization started on a more serious footing. A short-lived trade upheaval and, in 1824, the discovery of gold and the introduction of more liberal regulations of administration favored colonization. Although gold mining and (after 1879) phosphate mining temporarily supported economic growth, the elite were mainly active in commercial agriculture and (illegal) trade with the South American mainland. The Aruban peasantry remained dependant on small-scale agriculture, fishing, and labor migration to the mainland and the Cuban sugar estates. Slavery was marginal; colonists and Indians intermixed and formed the traditional Aruban population. Between 1816 and 1924 the population increased from 1,732 to 9,021.

The arrival of the oil industry in the 1920s resulted in rapid modernization and massive immigration of thousands of industrial laborers, merchants, and civil servants from the Caribbean, Europe, and the Americas. Aruba became a pluralistic society consisting of over forty nationalities. The Eagle Oil Refining Company (a Royal Dutch/Shell affiliate) ceased its activities in 1953. The Lago Oil and Transport Company changed hands several times and became part of the Standard Oil concern (later Exxon) in 1932. Lago began to automate in 1952 and closed its gates in 1985. Since then, tourism, which was first initiated in the 1950s, has strongly expanded, becoming the main source of income and employment. The need for labor resulted in a new wave of migration from the Caribbean, South America, and the Netherlands. In 1988 the Coastal Oil Company was established on the island.

As a relatively wealthy island, Aruba has strived for separation from the former colony of the Netherlands Antilles since 1933. Insular nationalism was and is strengthened by cultural and racial differences with Curaçao. In the 1970s this sense of nationalism resulted in a heightened cultural self-esteem and increased political participation on the part of the traditional Aruban population. In 1986 Aruba became an autonomous entity within the Dutch kingdom. The mass media and tourism are the agents of rapid change in Aruban cultural identity. Growing concern about this issue inclines some Arubans toward cultural conservatism.

Settlements

The capital, Oranjestad, is situated on the west part of the southern coast. San Nicolas, on the east side of the southern coast, is the second-largest town and the locus of the oil industry. Townships are spread over the rest of the island. The most important villages are Noord (located near the tourism area), Santa Cruz, and Savaneta. The hilly northeastern part and the rocky northern coast are uninhabited. Aruba has a population density of 354.7 (legal) inhabitants per square kilometer.

Economy

Subsistence and Tourism. Having scant natural resources of its own, Aruba has relied on oil refining and tourism as its main sources of income throughout the twentieth century. The government, the single largest employer on the island, has a payroll of approximately 5,000 persons. After the closure of the Lago refinery in 1985, the number of hotel rooms was more than doubled; a tripling is under way. The trade and construction sectors have expanded but are strongly dependent on tourism. The unemployment rate rose to nearly twenty percent after the closing of the refinery, but was less than 1 percent in the early 1990s. Of the total employed population of 29,220 persons in 1991, 10,604 worked in hotels, restaurants, and wholesale and retail companies. The construction and manufacturing sectors had 2,975 and 1,717 employees respectively.

The gross domestic product more than doubled between 1987 and 1992. Despite the economic recovery, serious concerns have arisen because of inflation and strains on the labor market, infrastructure, and the natural environment. Furthermore, the worsening competitive position in tourism, possible future claims on government guarantees of stalled hotel projects, and a recession in the United States add to the concern about future economic prospects.

Efforts to attract industry in the 1960s proved largely unsuccesful. After the closure of the Lago refinery in 1985, Coastal Oil Corporation renovated the remains of the old refinery and started operations in 1988. Oil transsshipment is handled by Wickland Oil Company. Other industrial efforts are of minor importance. The construction sector, which largely depends on tourism and the need for housing and business offices, is booming.

Trade. Apart from oil refining and transshipment, trade is mainly directed toward tourism and local consumption. A free zone is becoming increasingly important because of revenues related to port charges and services. Some nine offshore companies have been established on Aruba.

Division of Labor. Labor participation of men and women between 20 and 54 is respectively 89.8 and 66.0 percent. All through the economy men possess the more important positions. An important division of labor is based on ethnicity. Naturalized citizens and permanent residents of Lebanese, Madeirean, Chinese, and Jewish descent focus mainly on trade. Post-1985 migrants from the Philippines, Colombia, and Venezuela, whose residency may be temporary, hold the lower positions in tourism. Women from Santo Domingo, Colombia, and Jamaica work as live-in maids with upper- and middle-class families. Young Dutch migrants work mostly in business, especially in bars and restaurants. Civil servants are drawn mostly from traditional Arubans and migrants who arrived during the oil-boom years.

Land Tenure. Since the decline of agriculture after the arrival of the oil industry in the 1920s, land tenure has been most important to the population for the construction of houses. Three types of land tenure occur: regular landed property, hereditary tenure or long lease, and the renting of government grounds. For economic purposes, es- pecialy in the oil and tourism industries, government grounds are given in long, renewable leases of sixty years.

Kinship

Kin Groups and Descent. Until the beginning of the twentieth century, the extended family and the conjugal nuclear-family household were the centers of kinship organization. Traditionally, as a result of patri- or matrilocal settlement, groups of brothers and/or sisters and their spouses lived near each other on family grounds. Marriage between close kin was common. Incest prohibition applied to the *primo carnal* (bilateral first cousin). Geographical and genealogical propinquity therefore were virtualy synonymous. A shortage of land and urbanization caused a decrease in patri- and matrilocal settlement and the weakening of the traditional type of kinship organization. Descent rules are bilateral.

Kinship Terminology. Kinship terminology parallels that of Catholic canon law. The term *yui mayó* (oldest child) refers to the eldest offspring's special position as the first successor to the parents. Kinship terminology is also used to address oneself to nonrelatives, the terms *ruman* (brother), *primo* (cousin), and *swa* (brother-in-law) meaning "friend." Ritual kinship focuses around the godparents, the *padrino* and *madrina*, who each have clearly defined obligations regarding the godchild's baptism, first holy communion, and marriage.

Marriage and Family

Marriage. Monogamy and legal marriage are the norm, but extramarital and premarital relations are common. Concubinage doubled between 1981 and 1991. Teenage pregnancy is a growing concern. Intraethnic marriages are favored, but the census of 1991 showed that in 1990 and 1991, 45.2 percent of Aruban-born men married foreign spouses and 24.8 percent of Aruban women married non-Arubans. One cause of this is the great number of marriages of convenience ("fake marriages"). By marrying Arubans, foreigners can obtain the much-desired Dutch nationality.

Domestic Unit. The conjugal nuclear family is the most favored domestic unit. Nevertheless, one-person households, extended-family or composite households, and consensual nuclear-family households are socially accepted. The traditional household can be characterized as matricentric. The everyday authority lies with the mother, the ultimate authority with the father. In family affairs, the oldest child (yui mayó), who has special influence in situations of decision making and conflict.

Inheritance. Inheritance, like descent, is bilateral; normally, all children receive a share.

Socialization. Socialization generally takes place within the family and social organizations as well as at school. Within the nuclear family, it is predominantly the mother who takes care of the children. A growing number of children attend day-care centers before going to school. The educational system is based on the Dutch model. At the age of 4, children attend kindergarten, and after age 6 primary school. They enroll in secondary or lower vocational school after age 12. Higher education is provided by a pedagogical institute, and the study of law or economics may be pursued at the University of Aruba. A hotel school is designed after the U.S. system. Many students leave for the Netherlands or the United States to attend institutions of higher education. Adult education is very popular and is provided by Enseñanza pa Empleo (Education for Employment), a development project cofinanced by the Aruban and the Dutch governments and a great number of for-profit institutes.

Social organizations are important loci of socialization and social participation for all age groups and classes. The most important organizations are sports and service clubs, scouting associations, community centers, and religious and professional organizations. Ethnic clubs were extremely important between approximately 1945 and 1970 but have lost their impact on later generations.

Sociopolitical Organization

Social Organization. Aruba is divided along class, ethnic, and geographical lines, which in part overlap. Although the gap between rich and poor is significant, class lines are loosely defined. Anthropological research has devoted much attention to ethnic relations. Ethnic boundaries are not as rigid as in typical Caribbean plural societies such as those of Suriname or Trinidad but can be seen between (descendants of) traditional Arubans and Afro-Arubans. Trade groups, such as the Chinese and the Portuguese from Madeira, and the traditional elite hold their own position. Recent migration has created new boundaries between newcomers and older ethnic groups. Ethnic and geographical divisions can be seen in labor specialization, patterns of marriage and settlement, choice of language, and political affiliations.

Political Organization. Aruba has been an autonomous part of the Dutch kingdom since 1986. The *gouvernor* is the local representative of the Dutch monarch and the head of the Aruban government. The kingdom's Council of Ministers consists of the complete Dutch cabinet and two ministers plenipotentiary, one representing Aruba and the other the Netherlands Antilles. It is in charge of joint foreign policy, defense, and justice and the safeguarding of fundamental rights and freedoms. Political autonomy in internal affairs is almost complete. Although it was decided in 1983 that Aruba would become independent and leave the Dutch kingdom in 1996, this is now being changed and Aruba will maintain its autonomous status within the kingdom. Execution of this resolution, however, is contingent on restructuring of the governmental apparatus, enhancing the quality of administration, and reducing public expenditures.

Aruba is a parliamentary democracy with a multiparty system. Elections are held every four years. Since achieving the Status Aparte, government has been dependent on coalitions between one of the two bigger parties and the smaller ones. The biggest parties are the Christian-democratic Arubaanse Volkspartij (People's party of Aruba) and the social-democratic Movimento Electoral di Pueblo (People's Electoral Movement). Democracy functions with a certain degree of patronage and nationalistic rhetoric. Political parties carefully select candidates from different regional and ethnic backgrounds.

National festive days are the Day of the National Anthem and the Flag on 18 March and Queen's Day on 30 April. The first stresses Aruba's political autonomy, the second the partnership with the Dutch kingdom. Aruba's former political leader François Gilberto "Betico" Croes (1938–1986) is commemorated on his birthday, 25 January. Croes is the personification of Aruba's struggle for separation from the Netherlands Antilles. He was seriously injured in a car crash, a few hours before the proclamation of the Status Aparte, on New Year's Eve 1985. He died in November 1986.

Social Control. The small scale of the society allows gossip to be an effective means of social control. Newspapers, of which Aruba has four in Papiamento, two in Dutch, and three in English, also function as such. Legal forms of social control are provided by the juridical system. Aruba has its own legislative powers but shares a Common Court of Justice with the Netherlands Antilles. The Supreme Court is situated in the Netherlands.

Conflict. Most public conflicts on the island arise from political and ethnic differences. Some labor conflict occurs but has virtually never led to serious threats to peace in the workplace or to economic stability. Massive migration and a shortage of adequate housing cause much social tension and resentment. The rise in criminality is often ascribed to the growing number of immigrants. Informants state that the kin group is the most important locus of social interaction but also the biggest source of social conflict.

Religion and Expressive Culture

Religious Beliefs. Catholicism is the prevalent religion on Aruba. In 1991, 85 percent of the population claimed to be Catholic. Church attendance is much lower. The first chapel on Aruba was built in 1750. Protestantism, the religion of the traditional elite, is embraced by less than 3 percent of the population. The Protestant Church of Aruba was founded by Lutherans and Reformed in 1822, who both had been without ministers or churches until then; Lutheran and Reformed communities ceased to exist as separate entities. Although, officially, it has no specific denomination, its present identity can be described as "Calvinistic." Twentieth-century migration led to the appearance of other groups such as Jehovah's Witnesses, Methodists, and evangelical sects (one having emigrated from Suriname during the oil-boom years, another originating in the United States), each comprising 2 percent or less of the population; as well as small communities of Anglicans, Adventists, Jews, Muslims, and Confucianists. Nearly 3 percent of the population claims to have no religion. The number of and participation in new religious sects and movements is increasing.

Traditional popular assumptions about the supernatural are called *brua*. Although the term probably originates from the Spanish word *bruja* (witch), brua is not to be equated with witchcraft. It includes magic, fortune-telling, healing, and assumptions about both good and evil. Magic is conducted by a *hacido di brua* (practitioner of brua) and can be applied for both beneficently and maliciously. As a counterpoint to Christian belief, the evil spirit is called *spirito malu*. Belief in brua is often not confirmed because of the low social esteem attached to it.

Ceremonies.   Traditional (semi-)religious ceremonies have a Catholic origin or orientation. On New Year's Eve, best wishes are delivered at homes by small bands singing a serenade called Dandé. Saint John's Day (24 June) is celebrated with bonfires and the ceremony of Dera Gai (the burying of the rooster). Traditionally, a rooster was buried, leaving its head under a calabash above the ground. At present the ceremony is carried out without the rooster. Blindfolded dancers from the audience try to hit the calabash with a stick while a small band plays and sings the traditional song of San Juan. Carnival was introduced on Aruba by Caribbean migrants but has become the preeminent festival of the entire population. Easter Monday is called Black Monday; at present people camp for up to a week at the beach in tents and shacks, but the custom originates from the yearly picnic held by Afro-Caribbean Methodists. Of special importance are the celebrations of an individual's fifteenth, fiftieth, and seventy-fifth birthdays.

Arts.   Of the fine arts, music, poetry, singing, theater, dance, painting, and other visual arts are the most important. Aruban artistic production can be divided into two spheres, one noncommercial and the other directed at tourism and local recreation. Numerous artists are active in both. Many noncommercial artists are inspired by Aruba's history, tradition, and natural landscape, reworking these in a modern form. A lack of funds and clear governmental policy results in tension between the commercialization of art for the benefit of tourism and the professionalization of local talent for noncommercial purposes. Aruba hosts an annual jazz and Latin music festival and biennial dance and theater festivals.

Medicine.   Most family doctors and specialists have been educated in the Netherlands, the United States, or South America. The Doctor Horacio Oduber Hospital has 350 beds. Traditional healing methods (Papiamento: *remedi di tera*) make use of herbs, amulets, and so on, and are practiced by a *curadó* or *curioso* (healer), who often also acts as hacido di brua. Some of the methods are legally forbidden. Modern natural healing methods seem to be growing in popularity.

Death and Afterlife.   Opinions on death and the afterlife are in accord with Christian doctrine. The traditional wake is called Ocho Dia—"eight days," the duration of the customary mourning period. In a carefully closed room, prayer and singing around a small altar continue for those eight days. The wake is concluded by a ceremony in which close kin and friends participate: at the last evening of mourning, the altar is taken apart, and chairs are turned upside down. The windows are opened to make sure the spirit of the deceased is able to leave the house. The ceremony ends with a meal and storytelling. The wake, which has a medieval Spanish origin, is losing popularity in the course of modernization.

Bibliography

Alofs, Luc, and Leontine Merkies (1990). *Ken ta arubiano?: Sociale integratie en natievorming op Aruba* (Who is Aruban?: Social integration and nation building on Aruba). Antillen Working Papers, 15. Leiden: Koninklijk Instituut voor Taal, Land- en Volkenkunde, Caraïbische Afdeling.

Eelens, Frank C. H. (1993). *The Population of Aruba: A Demographic Profile*. Aruba: Central Bureau of Statistics.

Green, Vera (1974). *Migrants in Aruba*. Assen: Van Gorcum.

Kalm, Florence (1975). *The Dispersive and Reintegrating Nature of Population Segments of a Third World Society: Aruba, Netherlands Antilles*. Ann Arbor, Mich.: University Microfilms.

Koulen, Ingrid, and Gert Oostindie, with Peter Verton and Rosemarijn Hoefte (1987). *The Netherlands Antilles and Aruba: A Research Guide*. Royal Institute of Linguistics and Anthropology, Caribbean Series, no. 7. Dordrecht and Providence, R.I.: Foris Publications.

Phalen, John Harvey (1977). "Kinship, Color, and Ethnicity: Integrative Ideologies in Aruba, Netherlands Antilles." Ph.D. thesis, State University of New York at Stony Brook.

LUC ALOFS

Awakateko

ETHNONYMS: Aguacateco, Aguateca, Awaketeco, Balamiha

Orientation

Identification.   The Awakateko are an indigenous Mayan ethnic group residing in the *municipio* of Aguacatan in the northwestern highlands of Guatemala.

Location.   The traditional home of the Awakateko is the southeastern corner of the base of the Cuchumatan Mountains, a volcanic range parallel to the Guatemalan coast, in a lush valley along the Río Buca. The township of Aguacatan is located in the department of Huehuetenango. Elevations range from 1,500 to 3,000 meters, and the annual precipitation averages from 80 to 100 centimeters. Conditions in northern Aguacatan extending into the high Cuchumatans are humid, whereas in the south, conditions are subhumid. Aguacatan falls into an ecological zone known as the Intermediate Highlands, which is characterized by areas that range from wet to dry; it is heavily forested with pines and oaks at the lower elevations, rain forest at the higher.

Demography.   Extending over about 300 square kilometers, Aguacatan, the fifth-largest municipio in Guatemala, is divided into twenty-six *aldeas* (hamlets). Rural Indians constitute 87 percent of the population and Spanish-speaking non-Indians the other 13 percent. Four distinctive ethnic groups—the Awakateko Easterners, the Awakateko Westerners, the Ladinos, and the K'iche'—make up 99 percent of the population of Aguacatan. Both the Easterners and the Westerners are found in southern Aguacatan; the K'iche' live in the north, and the Ladinos populate towns and hamlets that adjoin the other groups. A census conducted in 1973 of individual ethnic groups indicated that, of the 2,964 households that were interviewed, 41 percent were Easterners, 31 percent K'iche', 14 percent Westerners, and 13 percent Ladinos; an additional 1 percent were Mam Indians (Brintnall 1979).

Linguistic Affiliation.   The four distinctive ethnic groups speak four distinctive languages: the Ladinos speak Spanish, the K'iche' speak the K'iche' language, and the Easterners and Westerners use different dialects of Aguacateca, collectively called *kayol*. Differences in grammar and vocabulary linguistically fragment each ethnic group.

History and Cultural Relations

The Maya civilization flourished in the lowlands of the Petén and the Yucatán during the first millennium. Famous for their ceremonial centers and hieroglyphic system, the Mayan civilization collapsed mysteriously and suddenly. At the time of the Spanish Conquest in the sixteenth century, the Classic Maya had passed their peak, and Maya had settled in the municipio of Aguacatan in the western Guatemalan highlands. The Awakateko were subjugated by a rising elite class of Ladinos, which exerted political, economic, and cultural domination over the Indians and treated them as a lower class in a social structure similar to a caste system.

This system was perpetuated into the first half of the twentieth century. The Ladinos formed a local government headed by an *intendente,* who had dictatorial power over the Indians. Traditional Aguacatan began to dissolve in 1944, when a general strike forced the dictator Jorge Ubico to resign, and an effort to reinstate the military dictatorship failed. Political parties were formed, and a new constitution was drafted. Repressive national labor laws and the intendente system, according to which local government officials carried out the direct orders of Ubico, were scrapped. Between 1954 and 1964, the civil-religious hierarchy system collapsed. A shift of power from the elders to a younger group allowed the younger Awakateko to assert leadership, gain independence from the Ladinos, and develop pride in their communities. After the 1968 election of a Ladino alcalde, the Eastern Indians took control of the local Christian Democratic party. Gonzolo Raymundo, named as the Indian party's candidate, took office in 1970 as head of the local Aguacatan government and swept out the Ladinos. Tensions mounted in Aguacatan as the federal government suspended the constitution and took power away from the Indians and gave it to Ladino officials. In 1971 the Guatemalan military sent troops to Aguacatan because of an Indian uprising protesting Ladino intervention. Arrests and imprisonment of the Indians continued for a week. Ladinos continued to occupy government positions until the 1974 election, when a higher voter turnout resulted in a victory for the Indian Christian Democratic party. A Peasant League united the four ethnic

groups, addressed issues, and gained political force within the community. In 1974 a Western Awakateko candidate from the National Liberation party eventually became the alcalde of Aguacatan after a fraudulent negation of election results at the national level.

Settlements

Awakateko settlements have focused on open central plazas, where trade and exchange take place. The pueblo of Aguacatan consists of houses scattered around agricultural plots, as well as houses in and around the central town. The Aguacatan market is the center for socializing and a place for local merchants to gather on weekends, especially Sundays.

Awakateko farmers live in family homesteads located in the countryside on less than two hectares of land. A typical homestead has a rectangular, one-roomed dwelling of adobe (mud brick) with an orange-tiled roof. Characteristic of Aguacatan houses are the long, extended porches where the family gathers and women weave. Almost all the homes are devoid of furniture, with the exception of a bed constructed of planks. A *chuj* (sauna), where the Awakateko bathe, is located near the house.

Economy

Subsistence and Commercial Activities.   As a labor-intensive society, the Awakateko practice subsistence agriculture and livestock raising, employing the use of the hoe, plow, draft animals, irrigation, and the digging stick. Sheep and goats are utilized for organic fertilizer and wool. Small livestock consists of chickens, turkeys, pigs, and goats. Cows and horses are draft animals. The diet is based on maize, the most important staple food. Maize tortillas, *atole* (maize gruel), and tamales are just a few examples of foods made with maize. As a source of protein, the Awakateko most commonly consume pork and poultry.

Different varieties of vegetables and fruits—such as squashes, beans, bananas, and mangoes—contribute to the diet. Coffee plantations in the coastal lands have had a great impact on the economy. Coffee emerged in the late nineteenth century as the major national export crop, and, as a result, the population and coffee production grew hand in hand. Through coerced labor operating under strict national labor laws enforced by the Ladino government, and through seasonal migration, the Indians were taken away from their own subsistence plots, resulting in a cycle of low yields and debt. The cash cropping of garlic and onions, the irrigation of new lands, and the abolition of forced labor on the coffee plantations allowed local native farming to become productive. With the profits from irrigated agriculture, Indians were able to buy back land from Ladinos and irrigate more of it.

Industrial Arts.   The Awakateko create original handwoven clothing, pottery, and embroidery work, for which there is a large market in the United States. Intricately designed sashes and skirts are also produced.

Trade.   Most Awakateko trade takes place in the market held in the central plaza of the pueblo. Here, numerous buyers and sellers, mainly women, exchange eggs, fruit, and vegetables for baskets, pottery, and clothes in the center of the plaza, while the men remain on the outside, bartering for potatoes, maize, beans, and animals.

Division of Labor. Cooking, washing, tending the animals, caring for the children, and collecting firewood are all responsibilities of Awakateko women. Children are taught skills by sharing the duties of the household, daughters helping their mothers and sons helping their fathers. Farming and raising cattle and horses are male activities, although in times of need, women work beside the men in the fields. Traditionally, men have played the dominant roles in Awakateko society.

Land Tenure. Land is kept within the family and passed on patrilineally. Those Awakateko possessing 30 *cuerdas* (57 hectares) are considered extremely wealthy. Aguacatán males who do not own their own land must rent it, work as laborers, or live with their fathers-in-law, which is looked upon by other Indians as a sign of poverty.

Kinship

Kin Groups and Descent. About two-thirds of Awakateko households are nuclear, and one-third are extended. The most common extended family is formed by incorporating married sons.

Kinship Terminology. Awakateko kinship terminology is bilateral. Cousins all have the same term of reference and are not equated with siblings. Children of cousins are referred to by the same name as the cousins (*wajwutz*). Terms of reference for brothers depend on the sex of the speaker and recognize relative age. Nephews and nieces are referred to by the same term.

Marriage and Family

Marriage. Marriage is monogamous. Young men of 15 begin to save money; girls of 15 prepare for courtship by taking interest in their appearance. Either personally or through a representative, an Aguacatán boy will approach the female he admires. Negotiations begin between the two families, with the future bride's father setting a bride-price. Sometimes the price is too high, and the couple runs off together. Under patrilineal rules, a girl must convert her religious beliefs to conform with those of her husband. The marriage ceremony involves family, friends, and shamans: it is called *quicyuj,* meaning "cacao beans," which in ancient times were used as money for the payment of the bride-price. The heavy influence of missionary activity has emphasized church and civil ceremonies. After the marriage, the bride lives with her parents and receives nightly visits from her husband. In two to three weeks, the couple moves to the husband's household. Sons live on or near their parents' land, whereas daughters always leave their parental homes. Fidelity is highly valued, and divorce is not common, for it is said that unfaithfulness angers the dead. Mixed marriages with other ethnic groups are sensitive.

Domestic Unit. The two basic domestic units in Awakateko society are nuclear and extended families. The most common is the nuclear family consisting of a father, mother, and two or three children. A few family-based households include widowed or divorced parents. Households that are not nuclear or extended are mostly centered on women—widows or divorcées living alone or with their children. Men almost never live apart from women.

Inheritance. Land is inherited patrilineally by male children through a patrilocal-residence pattern. Inherited land is classified by soil quality, irrigability, rockiness, etc., and inheritance can be a difficult decision for the father. At times, wives will create animosity among the brothers over the inheritance. Through gradual installments over a period of time, the father will issue the land to his sons, retaining his power and role as the patriarch.

Socialization. Children are raised to perform adult tasks and to help with feeding the animals and other farming tasks. Fathers take control over their sons, and mothers, over their daughters. Obedience and respect are instilled at a very early age, but threats of physical punishment are not employed.

Sociopolitical Organization

Social and Political Organization. Prior to 1964, each ethnic group had its own political organization, based on a civil-religious hierarchy that supported the power of the elderly. A group of male elders were leaders of all the people. Age-graded positions in Awakateko society were like a ladder upon which the younger males ascended toward a higher level of respect, honor, and authority. A range of age barriers controlled the passing from one political rank to another, enabling the Awakateko male society to postpone the transfer of political power to younger males. The duties of the elders included organizing fiestas and supplying the shamans with goods, food, and services.

After the civil-religious hierarchies lost their power in the early 1960s, national political institutions became the focus of local politics. At first, Ladinos dominated the local political parties and won the elections, but Indians began to wrest control from the Ladino minority. Indian-controlled local wings of national political parties became the important organizers of political power in the municipio in the 1970s. Mild Easterner-Westerner ethnic opposition has emerged in this context.

Social Control and Conflict. Language and isolation are utilized by the Ladinos as a means of controlling the Indian groups. Within the Awakateko groups, authority and punishment are exercised by the elders and shamans of the community.

Religion and Expressive Culture

Religious Beliefs. Present Awakateko religion is a mix of Catholicism, Protestant religions, native elements, and ancestor worship. In addition, there are many gods representing natural features, such as mountains and springs, that are sites for their supernatural owners. Celestial bodies are gods in themselves. Traditional (but disappearing) ancestor worship (the cult of the dead) acknowledges power beyond the grave. Deceased parents and grandparents continue to play an active part in the lives of the living, helping when the Awakateko have resided harmoniously and punishing when animosity and jealousy occur. The dead communicate with the living through the divination of shamans and through daily natural occurrences that are taken as messages from the dead. The dead influence Awakateko public ritual life. When an Awakateko is mistreated by another, a shaman is hired to contact the dead ancestor of the offended individual and to file a complaint. The dead elders send a close dead relative of a wrongdoer to a "jail." The jailed, suffering ancestor then sends a *mantar* (punishment) to the living wrongdoer. To rid themselves of this punishment, the Awakateko call upon a shaman to free the ancestor by paying fines to the ancestor elders.

Religious Practitioners. Shamans lead both magical and public rituals (*costumbres*). They question the dead ancestors and relay the conversations back to the families. Spiritual cleansing is achieved by scattering beans on the ground and picking them up while reciting the days of the week from the ancient Mayan calendar. Mediums are also involved in conversations with the dead.

Ceremonies. Prior to 1960, regular festivals called *k'ej* (fiestas) lasted seven days and involved parades, music, dancing, and much drinking. During these festivals, shamans performed ceremonies and rites. There were three ritual-dance groups—two Eastern (Tz'Unum and Muztec) and one Western (Moros). Dance obligations were inherited from father to son and from mother to daughter; minor rituals were the duties of certain families.

Medicine. In the traditional religion, dead ancestors play a prominent role in illness and curing. The dead may heal through shamanic intervention. Shamans are hired to call upon the dead for spiritual consultation, healing, and advice. Morality is mixed with medicine in Awakateko society. Wellness or health may depend upon the actions and behavior of the individual.

Death and Afterlife. The Awakateko do not conceive of the afterlife as a heaven or a hell, but a place where the dead ancestors reside and are active in the lives of the living. The afterlife once had such a strong hold on the people that their daily lives were consumed by ancestor worship.

Religious Change. The traditional Awakateko practice of ancestor worship was supplanted by new religions in the 1950s, when Protestant and Catholic missionaries came to Aguacatan and offered the Indians a secularized alternative to their religious system. As a result, the Eastern Indians were the first to abandon the political-ritual system; the Westerners followed suit shortly thereafter. Missionary involvement drastically changed Awakateko society. Young Indians who based their prestige on the new religious organizations emerged as the new community leaders. Internal unity in each ethnic group was destroyed, as some were converted and others retained the traditionalist practice.

Bibliography

Brintnall, Douglas E. (1979). *Revolt against the Dead: The Modernization of a Mayan Community in the Highlands of Guatemala.* New York: Gordon & Breach.

KATHLENE BARBER

Bahamians

ETHNONYMS: none

Orientation

Identification. The name "Bahamas" derives from *baja mar* (Spanish: shallow water). The best-known islands in the Bahamas island chain, from northwest to southeast, are Grand Bahama, the Abacos, the Biminis, New Providence, Eleuthera, Andros, Cat, San Salvador, the Exumas, Long, Crooked, Acklins, Mayaguana, and Inagua. Turks and Caicos, at the southeast end of the island chain, are a British crown colony; the two islands were separated from the Bahamas in 1848.

Location. The Bahama Islands, a chain of islands, reefs, and cays lying southeast off the Florida coast of North America, extend over 942 kilometers from 20°56' to 27°22' N and between 72°40' and 79°20' W. Depending upon the count, there are twenty-nine islands and 661 cays. The total land area is approximately 14,000 square

kilometers. (These measurements and figures do not include the Turks and Caicos.) The largest islands in the group are rimmed with sandy beaches and coconut groves. Low-lying hills, seldom exceeding a height of 30 meters, run the length of these islands. Pine forests grow on many of the ridges. The Bahamas have a subtropical climate, with an annual mean daily temperature of 25° C; the mean for the coldest month, February, is 22° C, and for the warmest, August, 28° C. Rainfall, concentrated in the late-summer months, averages about 125 centimeters per year.

Demography. The population was estimated at 268,726 in July 1993. The official census of 1980 placed the population at 209,505. Of the thirty inhabited islands and cays, the most densely populated is New Providence, with 171,502 residents (almost 70 percent of the total population) in an area of only 208 square kilometers. Andros, the largest island, with an area of 5,980 square kilometers, had a population of 8,155. Approximately 85 percent of the population is of African origin. Of the Whites, some 25,000 are native Bahamians; the rest are largely British, American, and Canadian expatriates. Most White Bahamians live on New Providence, the Abacos, and Grand Bahama.

Linguistic Affiliation. Standard English is the official language of the Bahamas. Creolized English, termed "Bahamian dialect," is the language of working-class Bahamians. Many White Bahamians and middle-class Bahamians of African ancestry speak varieties of English that fall between Standard and creolized English. All Bahamians understand standard English, and many can converse in several dialects.

History and Cultural Relations

The Bahamas were discovered by Europeans in 1492, when Columbus made his first landing in the West Indies on San Salvador, or Watlings Island. The Spaniards transported the aboriginal population of Lucayan Indians to Hispaniola and Cuba to work in mines, and within twenty-five years of Columbus's arrival the islands were depopulated. During the latter half of the seventeenth century the islands were colonized by English settlers, who brought along their slaves. By 1773 the population, which totaled approximately 4,000, had an equal number of Europeans and people of African origin. Between 1783 and 1785 many Loyalists who had been expelled from the American colonies immigrated to the islands with their slaves. These slaves, or their parents, had originally been transported to the New World from West Africa during the eighteenth century to work on cotton plantations. This influx to the Bahamas increased the number of Whites to approximately 3,000 and the number of slaves of African ancestry to approximately 6,000. Most of the slave plantations established by the Loyalists in the Bahamas were on the "Cotton Islands"—Cat Island, the Exumas, Long Island, Crooked Island, San Salvador, and Rum Cay. At first they were successful economic enterprises; after 1800, however, the production of cotton declined because the slash-and-burn technique used to prepare the fields for planting depleted the soil. Following the emancipation of slaves in the British Empire in 1838, some departing plantation owners gave their land to their former slaves, and many of these freed slaves adopted the names of their former owners in gratitude. At the time of Emancipation the English captured a number of Spanish ships transporting slaves taken in the Congo, the primary site of slave-trade activity after 1800, and brought their human cargo to special village settlements on New Providence and some of the other islands, including Long Island. The newly freed Congo slaves who went to the Exumas and Long Island intermarried with former slaves who were tilling the soil of the abandoned plantations. With the increased number of occupants on already depleted land, many were forced to migrate and Long Island and the Exumas experienced a decline in population after 1861. From the middle of the nineteenth century onward, Bahamians sought ways to bring prosperity to the islands. During the U.S. Civil War they engaged in blockade-running and gunrunning from New Providence to the southern states. Later attempts at large-scale export of agricultural products, such as pineapple and sisal, failed as more successful growers emerged elsewhere. Sponge gathering flourished early in the twentieth century but suffered a severe setback with the advent of a widespread sponge disease in the 1930s. Rum-running to the United States, a lucrative enterprise, ended with the repeal of Prohibition. World War II created a demand for migrant agricultural laborers to fill jobs abandoned by Americans newly recruited into industry and the military, and Bahamians seized the opportunity to "go on the contract" on the U.S. mainland. The most enduring prosperity for the Bahamas has come from tourism; New Providence has evolved from a wintering place for the very wealthy, as it was in the nineteenth century, to the center of a massive tourist industry that it is today.

Settlements

A rimless, many-spoked wheel superimposed upon the islands depicts the relationship of New Providence, where the capital, Nassau, is located, to the other islands (out islands, or the Family Islands, as the government prefers to call them); it also depicts the isolation of the individual islands. Nassau is a magnet for people from the out islands who seek both residence and employment. The second-largest city is Freeport, on the island of Grand Bahama (population: 41,035); like Nassau, it is a tourist center. The third-largest settlement is Marsh Harbor on Abaco Island. Most settlements are villages of scattered houses located near the shore (e.g., the settlement of Long Bay Cays consists of villages spread out over a distance of 11 kilometers). Nucleated villages are found on offshore cays such as Green Turtle Cay and Abaco. Mail boats, which also carry supplies and passengers, link the settlements to Nassau but not directly to one another.

Economy

Subsistence and Commercial Activities. The Bahamian economy is based mostly on tourism and offshore banking. The commercial-agriculture and industrial sectors are comparatively small. From 1981 to 1990, tourist arrivals increased an average 8.5 percent per year, owing to an almost threefold increase in the number of cruise-ship visitors. In 1990, 3,628,372 tourists visited the islands; half of them arrived by sea and 1,561,600 stayed twenty-four hours or more. U.S. citizens comprise 85 percent of the tourist population. Expenditures by tourists totaled $369.1 million in 1981 and $1.26 billion in 1990. (The Bahamian dollar is kept equivalent to the U.S. dollar.) The government is promoting agricultural development to fill the gaps left by exploitive foreign companies that have pulled out of the Bahamas. Subsistence farming has been carried on in the out islands since the first settlements. Two important crops are Indian maize, used for grits, and pigeon peas, which are added to imported rice to make the national dish, peas and rice. Some men in the out islands fish for their families and sell extra fish to neighbors.

Industrial Arts. Industry is scarcely developed. Two major exports are the spiny lobster and crude salt. Beer and rum are produced for local consumption and for export.

Trade. Nearly everything that Bahamians need is imported, from automobiles to food. Indeed, over half of the government's revenue is derived from general import taxes. Total revenues exceed $600 million.

Division of Labor. The government is the number-one provider of employment. Hotels and resorts, as a group, are a major employer, and banks are primarily operated by Bahamians. In the out islands, men and women perform many of the same jobs. Most men are farmers and fishermen; their wives, housekeepers and farmers. To earn the cash needed to purchase groceries, clothes, and household furnishings, men and women must perform wage labor. Since there are few paying jobs in the out islands, most Bahamians go off to seek jobs in Nassau and Freeport, often leaving their children in the care of grandparents.

Kinship

Kin Groups and Descent. A person's kindred includes all known consanguineal relatives. In most areas of the Bahamas, a man will not marry a female member of his kindred. A person's descendants form an unrestricted descent group or a descending kindred. Land held in common by the descent group is called "generation property." Unilineal descent groups are absent.

Kinship Terminology. Bahamian kinship terminology is of the Eskimo type, the same as that in use in England and the United States.

Marriage and Family

Marriage. Unlike many of the peoples of the Caribbean, Bahamians have a mating system characterized by marriage and extraresidential unions but not consensual unions. A double standard of sexual morality regulates the behavior of men and women. A man is expected to have both premarital and extramarital affairs; a woman is not. Seldom do an unmarried man and woman live together. One-third of the children born in the 1960s were "outside," that is, illegitimate, and the percentage of illegitimate births has risen steadily.

Domestic Unit. The nuclear-family household is the ideal norm. With the migration of adults to Nassau and Freeport, households headed by one or both grandparents are common in the out islands. Single-parent and single-person households are also found.

Inheritance. Bahamians frequently follow the rule of primogeniture, a legacy of British colonialism. For most people, their home is the only item of value. On the death of the husband, the home becomes his wife's, to be used by her until her death, at which time it is inherited by the oldest son. Property may also be received by will.

Socialization. The primary caretaker for most children is either the mother or grandmother. The caretaker not only provides for immediate needs but also acts as the chief disciplinarian. Women who fear the supernatural are more likely to use corporal punishment than those who view the supernatural as benevolent. The punishment itself does not seem to prevent the establishment of strong bonds of loyalty. Adult children frequently give gifts (often money) to their mothers, sometimes to help the older women raise their grandchildren. In the past, children in the out islands attended local schools for eight years, then went to Nassau for secondary education. Since independence, secondary schools, drawing from several settlements, have been introduced in many out islands where there had been only primary schools. These schools are staffed by teachers from other parts of the British Commonwealth as well as Bahamians.

Sociopolitical Organization

Social Organization. Social organization is based primarily on kinship. The members of one's kindred provide both emotional and material support. The unrestricted descent group may even provide a building lot for a man. Growing up in the same settlement is likely to lead to lifelong friendships, but school attendance fosters friendships among children from different settlements. The social-class system of the Bahamas prior to about 1960 can be characterized as a three-tiered pyramid, with Bahamians of African ancestry at the base, Bahamian Whites (known as "Conchs" or pejoratively as "Conchy Joes") in the middle, and the British official class, including wealthy expatriates, at the top. Many Bahamian Whites, particularly those residing in Nassau, have some African ancestry. Today the British are gone, many members of the business class are of African ancestry, and the Progressive Liberal party (PLP), the ruling party from 1968 to 1982, largely draws its membership from among Bahamians of African ancestry. The former opposition political party, the Free National Movement (FNM), draws its membership from both the White community and that of African ancestry.

Political Organization. The Bahamas has a parliamentary government inherited from the British. From independence (10 July 1973) until August 19, 1992, the PLP controlled the forty-nine-seat House of Assembly. Sir Lynden Pindling, leader of the PLP, was the prime minister for this entire period. The FNM defeated the PLP on 19 August 1992 by obtaining thirty-two seats in the House of Assembly. Hubert Alexander Ingraham, leader of the FNM, became prime minister and Orville Alton Turnquest the deputy prime minister. In addition to the leadership, there are thirteen cabinet ministers. The Senate has sixteen members, with nine appointed by the governor-general on the advice of the prime minister, four on the advice of the leader of the opposition, and three on the advice of the prime minister after consultation with the leader of the opposition. The governor-general represents the British monarch, who is the titular head of government.

Social Control. A well-developed legal structure was inherited from the British; English common law and much of English statute law were adopted almost word for word. The basic structure is entrenched in the constitution of the Bahamas. Three main functions are generally distributed under the authority of the law of the constitution: the executive function is entrusted to the prime minister and his cabinet, the legislative function is entrusted to parliament, and the judicial function is entrusted to the courts. The independent judiciary includes magistrates courts, the Supreme Court with a chief justice and five other justices, and a three-judge Court of Appeal; the constitution grants the right to appeal to the Judicial Committee of the Privy Council in England. In the out islands commissioners can act as magistrates. The administration of justice properly includes law enforcement (i.e., police functions) and lawful prosecutions (the sphere of the attorney general's office). Informal social control, particularly in the out islands, is based on fear of developing a bad reputation and fear of obeah, the practice of harmful magic.

Conflict.   Except for the very early years (before 1718) when Nassau was a center for pirates, the Bahamas was a peaceful country for much of its history; there were no slave uprisings. The riots of 1942 were sparked by wage inequities. Verbal public confrontations, although common, seldom escalated into violence, and homicides were rare. In recent times, however, drug trafficking has brought crime and violence to the country.

Religion and Expressive Culture

Religious Beliefs.   Three realms of the supernatural can be identified. Most Bahamians belong to a Christian church and frequently attend their own church as well as others. Most people believe God helps the faithful and punishes the wicked. The spirit of a person who dies "in Christ" goes to rest and can help the living; if an ungodly person dies, the spirit wanders about frightening and hurting people. Obeah is practiced to harm rivals, to protect one's property and person, and to raise the spirits of the dead.

Religious Practitioners.   Ministers and priests head the Christian churches. In the out islands local men, and sometimes women, serve part-time as preachers. Specialists in the practice of obeah are called obeah men; although never common, obeah practitioners are becoming even less numerous as young people turn away from old practices and embrace the modern world.

Ceremonies.   Junkanoo, once widespread in the Caribbean, is a cultural event similar to New Orleans's Mardi Gras. Its roots lie in pre-Emancipation days, when slaves were allowed a special Christmas holiday. The culmination of Junkanoo is a costumed parade with floats and bands, which takes place along Nassau's Bay Street on Boxing Day (26 December) and New Year's Day.

Arts.   Goombay is the calypso-style music of the Bahamas. In the out islands, local bands using guitars, goatskin-headed drums, and saws entertain at dances and weddings. The major decorative art is straw work. Women in the out islands plait "straw" from palm fronds into long strips, which are then sewn together to form hats, baskets, and purses. Raffia paper and seashells are typically sewn to the straw work in decorative patterns.

Medicine.   Modern medicine is provided at the Princess Margaret Hospital in Nassau. In 1992 the out islands were served by 107 clinics; the seriously ill are flown to Princess Margaret Hospital. Many Bahamians, particularly those in the out islands, often rely on "bush" medicine; parts of selected plants are commonly boiled in liquid, and the resulting "bush tea" is then drunk. Love-vine (*Cuscuta americana*), for example, is said to produce a tea that gives a man "courage."

Bibliography

Collingwood, Dean W. (1989). *The Bahamas between Worlds*. Decatur, Ill.: White Sound Press.

Collingwood, Dean W., and Steve Dodge, eds. (1989).

Modern Bahamian Society. Parkesburg, Iowa: Caribbean Books.

Craton, Michael (1986). *A History of the Bahamas*. 3rd ed. Waterloo, Ont.: San Salvador Press.

Craton, Michael, and Gail Saunders (1992). *Islanders in the Stream: A History of the Bahamian People*. Vol. 1, *From Aboriginal Times to the End of Slavery*. Athens: University of Georgia Press.

Dupuch, S. P., editorial director (1991). *Bahamas Handbook and Businessman's Annual, 1992*. Nassau: Etienne Dupuch, Jr. Publications.

Holm, John A., with Alison Watt Shilling (1982). *Dictionary of Bahamian English*. Cold Spring, N.Y.: Lexik House Publishers.

Hughes, Colin A. (1981). *Race and Politics in the Bahamas*. New York: St. Martin's Press.

LaFlamme, Alan G. (1985). *Green Turtle Cay: An Island in the Bahamas*. Prospect Heights, Ill.: Waveland Press.

Otterbein, Charlotte Swanson, and Keith F. Otterbein (1973). "Believers and Beaters: A Case Study of Supernatural Beliefs and Child Rearing in the Bahama Islands." *American Anthropologist* 75:1670–1681.

Otterbein, Keith F. (1966). *The Andros Islanders: A Study of Family Organization in the Bahamas*. Lawrence: University of Kansas Press.

Otterbein, Keith F. (1978). "Transportation and Settlement Pattern: A Longitudinal Study of South Andros." *Anthropology* 2(2): 35–45.

KEITH F. OTTERBEIN AND
CHARLOTTE SWANSON OTTERBEIN

Barbadians

ETHNONYM: Bajans

Orientation

Identification.   Barbadians are people born on the island of Barbados and people born elsewhere who have at least one Barbadian parent who maintains cultural ties to this island nation. Barbadian communities in Canada, the United Kingdom, the United States, and Guyana maintain active ties with their kin and friends in the West Indies.

Location. Barbados, a coral limestone outcropping of the South American continental shelf, is located at 13° 10' N, 59° 33' W. Barbados thus lies in the western Atlantic Ocean, 150 kilometers east of the island of Saint Vincent and the geological fault line along which most of the Caribbean islands have emerged, and 275 kilometers north of Trinidad and the northern coast of South America. The island's shape resembles a leg of lamb 40 kilometers long. The north (shank) of the island exhibits a width of about 10 kilometers, the south a width of about 25 kilometers. In contrast with most West Indian islands of volcanic origin, which rise dramatically from the sea to elevations of more than 1,000 meters within a kilometer or so of the shore, Barbados has low, rolling hills that rise no higher than 300 meters, and, in the north and south portions of the island, extensive areas of relatively level ground. Nonetheless, like nearly all West Indian islands, Barbados exhibits significant microclimate variation. Rainfall averages more than 125 centimeters annually across the central portion of the island, but levels are higher on the windward (eastern) coast and the hilly interior, and lower on the leeward (western) coast. The northeast corner of the island, however, exhibits a semidesert biome. The southern portions of the island, characterized by little topographic variation, receive little rainfall, although more than the northeast corner. Barbados averages more than 3,000 hours of sunlight annually. Northeast trade winds blow year-round and significantly moderate a mean daytime temperature of around 27° C, which fluctuates little over the course of the year. Sugarcane and tourism have brought prosperity to Barbados, even in the face of occasional droughts, hurricanes, and world recessions.

Demography. More than 260,000 people now live on this small island of some 443 square kilometers. Only Hong Kong, Singapore, and Bangladesh surpass Barbados's national population density of 586 persons per square kilometer. As early as 1680, the island was home to 70,000 people. Barbadians who couldn't find land on the island emigrated to other New World locations, including South Carolina, Antigua, and Jamaica. Whereas other island populations dwindled or grew slowly during the 1800s, Barbados sent more than 50,000 of its citizens elsewhere (especially to Guyana and Trinidad) and still experienced an extraordinary annual growth rate of about 1.2 percent between Emancipation in 1806 and the first years of the twentieth century.

Until 1960, high birth and death rates prevailed. The island's population consisted mostly of young people; Barbadians emigrated in large numbers to the United Kingdom and in smaller numbers to the United States and, later, to Canada. Barbados began demographic transition about 1960, reached replacement-level fertility in 1980, and fell to below-replacement levels quickly thereafter. Aided by continuing emigration of the young and a new stream of elderly immigrants, the population of Barbados aged rapidly in the succeeding decade. The population of elderly (aged 60 and over) grew 15 percent during the 1980s and comprised 15.3 percent of the total population by 1990. Barbadian projections suggest that, by the year 2050, the proportion of the population aged 65 and over will range between 25 and 33 percent of the total population.

Linguistic Affiliation. Barbadians speak a dialect of English with tonal qualities that reflect the West African heritage of the vast majority of its people, and an English-West African pidgin called Bajan. The number of native Bajan speakers has declined precipitously since 1950.

History and Cultural Relations

Barbados was colonized by the English early in the seventeenth century. The English found the island uninhabited when they landed in 1625, although archeological findings document prior habitation by both Carib and Arawak Native Americans. By 1650, Barbados was transformed by the plantation system and slavery into the first major monocropping sugar producer of the emerging British Empire, and its fortunes were tied to sugar and to England for the next 310 years. In 1651, Barbados won from England most of the freedoms the United States gained only by revolution 100 years later, and established what was to become the oldest continuing parliamentary democracy in the world outside England. This significant degree of autonomy encouraged Barbadian planters to remain on the island rather than, as was typical elsewhere in the English and French West Indies, to return to Europe when their fortunes improved. Barbados continues to be distinguished in the West Indies by an unusually high proportion of population with a largely European ancestry. When West Indian sugar plantations disappeared elsewhere over the course of the 1800s, Barbadian plantations remained competitive. The improvement in living standards that had marked the nineteenth century was brought to an end by the creation of a merchant-planter oligopoly in the early twentieth century. The Great Depression precipitated massive labor disturbances. Subsequent investigations of living conditions, particularly the Moyne Commission Report, established grounds for fundamental political change. The franchise, which until the late nineteenth century had been restricted to propertied, White males, was made universal in 1943. By the 1950s, the descendants of former African slaves controlled the Barbadian Assembly and set in motion a series of actions that fundamentally transformed the island. Barbados opted for full independence in 1966, but it remains a member of the British Commonwealth.

Settlements

Bridgetown, founded early in the seventeenth century on the southern leeward (western) coast, is the island's capital and only city. Small towns exist at Holetown, 5 kilometers north of Bridgetown; Speightstown, 6 kilometers north of Holetown; and Oistens, 10 kilometers south of Bridgetown. Holetown, Speightstown, and Oistens, along with numerous other small communities along the leeward coast, now form one long megalopolis containing about 70 percent of the island's population. About 50 percent of the island's residents live in or south of Bridgetown. The southeastern region, formerly planted in cane, now has another 10 percent of the island's population and may be best described as a dispersed bedroom community for Bridgetown. The remaining 20 percent of the population lives amongst plantations and small farms in settlements that vary from dispersed homes to small, nucleated villages.

Economy

The Barbadian economy stems from a diverse population, which is one of the world's most highly educated, with a literacy rate very close to 100 percent. The currency is the Barbados dollar, which is linked to the U.S. dollar at a rate of BDS$2.00 to U.S.$1.00. Excellent public and private bus and taxi services take advantage of nearly 1,300 kilometers of roads and make it possible to move easily and quickly, and relatively cheaply, from any spot on the island to any other. Barbados supports one of the three campuses of the University of the West Indies (the others are in Jamaica and Trinidad and Tobago). The local campus (Cave Hill) offers degrees in the physical, biological, and social sciences, in the humanities, and in law and medicine. Barbados Community College was modeled along lines originally established by the California community-college system; it offers a wide variety of courses in technical fields and the liberal arts. Advanced education is also available through a teacher-training college, a polytechnic college, the Extra Mural Centre of the University of the West Indies (which has branch campuses on all eastern Caribbean islands), and a hotel school. A large number of private and public primary and secondary schools offer educational programs modeled on those in the United Kingdom.

The year 1960 initiated a structural change in the Barbadian economy marked by decline in sugar production and the growth of industrial manufacturing and tourism. By 1980, the sugar industry contributed only about 6 percent of domestic output and accounted for less than 10 percent of employment and 10 percent of foreign-exchange earnings. At the same time, manufacturing and tourism contributed respectively about 11 percent and 12 percent of domestic output and about 18 percent and 41 percent of foreign-exchange earnings. These proportions remained about the same a decade later. Sugar plantations were turned into manufacturing sites, subdivided for new housing sites or small agricultural plots, or converted to the production of vegetables for a growing domestic market for food. Manufactured goods include garments, furniture, ceramics, pharmaceuticals, phonograph records and tapes, processed wood, paints, structural components for construction, industrial gases, refined petroleum, paper products, and solar-energy units. Data processing and assembly of electronics components also figure in the ecconomic array. Barbados served as a tourist destination as early as the 1600s; it advertises that George Washington was one of its more illustrious early visitors. The growth of tourism on Barbados, however, as throughout the world, depended on the rise of cheap, global transportation and rising proportions of discretionary income. Small numbers of tourists come from South America and other islands in the Caribbean. A significant stream of tourists come from northwestern Europe, primarily the U.K. Most tourists, however, come from the United States and Canada, which send many flights to the island daily, and, during the height of the tourist season, cruise ships call almost daily. Long known in the Caribbean as "Little England," many Barbadians now claim that the island's increasingly important ties to the United States have transformed it into "Little America."

Kinship

Barbadians trace descent and inheritance through both their father and their mother. They recognize no organized, corporate groups of kin. Barbadians use the Eskimo cousin terminology common to the United Kingdom, Canada, and the United States. Biological fathers and mothers are sharply distinguished from other adults who may serve various caregiving and economic-support functions for children.

Marriage and Family

A Barbadian household may consist of a single man or woman or of a mixed-gender group of as many as fifteen people. Barbadians idealize a household that consists of a married couple and their children, which characterizes about 45 percent of all households on the island. Around 35 percent of Barbadian households are organized around a mother and her children. These households occasionally encompass three generations of women; they may include brothers, uncles, sons, and the sexual partners of members of the core family unit.

Historically, in Barbados as elsewhere in the West Indies, sexual activity usually began at an early age. Women traded sex for economic support and children (called "visiting" or "keeper" relationships). Visiting unions gave way to common-law unions that, when a couple was older, a church ceremony might legitimate. Young people, however, were not the only ones who had visiting relationships. Historically, West Indian islands have been job-poor. Men left the islands in large numbers to look for work, which left significantly more women than men at nearly all ages. As a result, many women could not legally marry. Lower-class men might never marry. Moreover, no relationship implied men's sexual fidelity. Lower-class men commonly drifted from one temporary sexual partner to another. Married men in the middle and upper classes commonly engaged in a series of visiting relationships with "outside" women. Barbadian fathers, consequently, often were not husbands; even those who were frequently did not live with the mother and her children. When they did, they might contribute little to domestic life. Men often were not home. They spent time instead with girlfriends or other men, often in rum shops, which remain popular among older men. What they contributed, other than a house and money, all too often was violence directed at the mother and children.

Women, for their part, usually drilled into the children not only how much they sacrificed and how hard they had to work to raise them properly, but also that their labors were that much more arduous because they had no companion to help them. It was easy to explain family hardships. Men were irresponsible and abusive. Understandably, fathers could expect domestic help from their sons and daughters only incidentally, and the weak filial obligations that existed applied only to biological fathers. By contrast, childbearing was an investment activity for Barbadian women. In a woman's youth, children legitimated her claims on income from men, although establishing those claims required her subservience. As she moved toward middle age, daughters took over nearly all household chores, and sons provided financial support that could make her independent of spousal support and reduce or eliminate her subservience to an autocratic male. In her old age, financial and domestic support from children meant the difference between abject poverty and a moderate, or even comfortable, level of living. Indeed, these phases often transformed gender relations. Because men could expect support from their children only if they had maintained a relationship with their children's mother, the women dependent on men in their youth found men dependent on them by late middle age. Gender power relationships thus were contingent on historical conditions that made women dependent on men in their youth, and on their male children during and after middle age.

Since 1960, however, Barbadian kin relations have undergone a revolution that reflects global leveling processes that were set into motion by the Industrial Revolution in England 200 years ago. Growth in the world economy, spurred by the Industrial Revolution, was marked by increasing numbers of resource-access channels. Large numbers of resource-access channels imply high levels of competition. High levels of both international and regional competition offer selective advantages to technical skills and competencies and reduce power differentials both between nations and within societies. Gender and skin color have become less important determinants of social position.

Barbadian women experienced a conjunction of good job opportunities and increased educational levels that ushered in a revolution in the relations between generations and between genders. The West Indian marriage pattern of visiting, common-law, and legal unions persists, but empowered women enjoy more domestic help, emotional support, and affectionate behavior than women who are not empowered, and they experience little or no family violence. Women freed from dependency on childbearing have fewer children. Women freed from dependency on men have markedly better relationships with their partners. The incidence of family violence on Barbados fell dramatically in just one generation.

Sociopolitical Organization

Social Organization. Prior to 1960, Barbadian society was characterized by a small merchant-planter elite of largely European ancestry; a slightly larger class of accountants, lawyers, medical personnel, journalists, and teachers of diverse ancestry; and a huge lower class of field laborers and domestic servants with a largely African ancestry. The elite remains about the same size but has grown much more diverse in heritage. The lower class has all but disappeared. In its place, there now exists a huge middle class that encompasses skilled blue-collar workers employed in manufacturing firms and hotels, and a wide range of white-collar, professional, and managerial occupational groups employed directly or, in the case of public employees, indirectly in the manufacturing and tourist sectors of the economy.

Political Organization. Barbados is organized as an independent parliamentary democracy within the British Commonwealth. For administrative purposes, the island is divided into the city of Bridgetown and eleven parishes: Saint Lucy, Saint Peter, Saint Andrew, Saint James, Saint Joseph, Saint Thomas, Saint John, Saint Philip, Saint George, Saint Michael, and Christ Church. The monarch of England is recognized as the head of state, and the highest court of appeals is the Supreme Court of the United Kingdom. The monarch appoints a governor-general, selected from among nominees put forth by the majority and minority political parties. Two principal political parties, the Barbados Labour party and the Democratic Labour party, compete for seats in the House of Assembly; members of the Senate are appointed by the governor-general. The leader of the majority party in the Assembly serves as prime minister. A cabinet appointed from among majority-party members of the Assembly assists the prime minister in carrying out executive functions of government. The judiciary consists of a national police force and three tiers of courts. Magistrates oversee Lower Courts, which adjudicate minor cases and hear preliminary evidence for major ones. Judges who sit in the Assizes hear cases involving allegations of major crimes. Barbados's chief justice heads a group of three judges who hear cases in the Court of Appeals. The last court of appeals is the Privy Council in England.

Religion and Expressive Culture

Religious Beliefs. More than 80 percent of the population claims adherence to one or another Christian denomination or sect. More than half of these belong to the Church of England and attend appropriate parish churches; Methodists, Roman Catholics, and Seventh Day Adventists constitute most of the remainder. A small East Indian community includes some Hindus, and a small number of people of diverse backgrounds practice Islam. A growing, albeit still small, number of people embrace Rastafarianism. A small Jewish community with Sephardic roots attends services in a synagogue originally built in A.D. 1640.

Medicine. Barbadians use two bodies of knowledge to prevent and treat illness. They rely heavily on a biomedical system organized on a Western model. The health-care system consists of physicians and other staff who practice in public, government-run hospitals, clinics, halfway houses, and long-term care facilities of various kinds, and physicians and other health-care workers who practice in a private system of hospitals, clinics, nursing homes, and private offices. Individual health-care providers frequently participate in both formal systems.

Barbadians also rely heavily on an indigenous ethnomedical system that makes use of "bush" teas and "home remedies." Around 70 percent of the population uses home remedies at rates that vary from daily to once or twice a year. Most of those who use this indigenous medicine regard it as an alternative to biomedical care; the remainder use indigenous medicine to supplement care available through the biomedical system.

When Barbadian economic development began in the 1950s, the island's health-care needs arose from high rates of acute infectious disease. Accordingly, the government of Barbados built an outstanding health-care delivery system directed at these problems. The medical school at the University of the West Indies is located at a 600-bed facility for acute care, Queen Elizabeth Hospital. Separate geriatric and psychiatric hospitals provide specialized care for the elderly and mentally ill. Smaller facilities are available for younger mentally and physically handicapped patients. Public clinics, located in nearly every parish, and private clinics, concentrated in the heavily populated parishes of Saint Michael and Christ Church, serve primary health-care needs. The accomplishments of this system included a reduction in infant-mortality rates from more than 150 per 1,000 in the early 1950s to around 15 per 1,000 in the early 1990s, and control over other infectious diseases, rivaling the developed regions of Europe, North America, and Asia.

Today, however, large numbers of Barbadians suffer from arthritis, hypertension, adult-onset diabetes and its complications, cancer, and heart disease. Often, these diseases remain untreated even after diagnosis. Disabilities grow more common and more serious with aging; the vast majority of disabilities can be traced to arthritis and to diabetes and its complications. Significant proportions of disabled Barbadians experience unmet needs for physical aids that bear on the most fundamental human needs— seeing, eating, and walking.

Barbadians tend to equate mental illness with being "crazy" and, therefore, deny they experience emotional disorders even in the presence of significant symptoms. Almost no one who displays symptoms of depression and anxiety seeks treatment. By creating intense emotional pain, family violence in particular leads to high-risk sexual behavior and the spread of sexually transmitted diseases like HIV/AIDS. Although the incidence of family violence has declined, much interpersonal violence still is within families. Still more violence comes from outside the family. The island suffers from an increasing use of crack cocaine and its accompanying patterns of violence.

Bibliography

Brathwaite, Farley, ed. (1986). *The Elderly in Barbados.* Bridgetown: Carib Research and Publications.

Dann, Graham (1984). *The Quality of Life in Barbados.* London: Macmillan.

Greenfield, Sidney (1966). *English Rustics in Black Skin.* New Haven: College and Universities Press.

Handler, Jerome S. (1974). *The Unappropriated People: Freedmen in the Slave Society of Barbados.* Baltimore: Johns Hopkins University Press.

Handwerker, W. Penn (1989). *Women's Power and Social Revolution.* Newbury Park, Calif.: Sage Publications.

Handwerker, W. Penn (1993). "Gender Power Differences between Parents and High-Risk Sexual Behavior by Their Children." *Journal of Women's Health* 2:301–306.

Karch, Cecilia A. (1979). *The Transformation and Consolidation of the Corporate Plantation Economy in Barbados: 1860–1977.* Ann Arbor: University Microfilms.

Massiah, Joycelin (1984). *Employed Women in Barbados.* Institute of Social and Economic Research (Eastern Caribbean) Occasional Paper no. 8. Cave Hill, Barbados: University of the West Indies.

Richardson, Bonham C. (1985). *Panama Money in Barbados, 1900–1920.* Knoxville: University of Tennessee Press.

Worrell, DeLisle, ed. (1982). *The Economy of Barbados, 1946–1980.* Bridgetown: Central Bank of Barbados.

W. PENN HANDWERKER

Bermudians

ETHNONYMS: none

Bermuda is a self-governing British dependency located in the southern North Atlantic Ocean at 32°18′ N, 64°47′ W. It is an archipelago of approximately 150 islands, which have a total land area of 53 square kilometers. Geologically, it is a limestone formation that lies above an extinct volcano. The ground is very porous, and so the people must depend upon rainwater collected from their roofs.

The majority (61 percent) of the 58,337 (1990) Bermudians are Black, 38 percent are White (English, Portuguese, Canadian, and other European), and the remaining 1 percent are Chinese and East Indian. The people speak English. The most popular religion is Anglicanism (37 percent), followed by Catholicism (14 percent), African Methodist Episcopalianism (10 percent), Methodism (6 percent), and Seventh Day Adventistism (5 percent); the remaining 28 percent are of other faiths.

The history of Bermuda is unusual. There were no aboriginal inhabitants for the Spanish explorers to discover in the early sixteenth century. The Spanish did not colonize it, but the British did after some English colonists bound for Virginia plantations were shipwrecked there in 1609. An enterprise called the "Bermuda Company" sent colonists to begin a plantation; however, the soil was so thin and poor that the crops failed; even today less than 1 percent of the land is arable. The colonists responded by turning to the sea, and in ships made of Bermudian cedar they transported goods and traded all up and down the eastern seaboard of the United States and as far south as Barbados. They also collected salt, fished, and whaled. During the eighteenth and nineteenth centuries, many of the colonists profited as privateers and pirates. A few slaves were imported, but there was little need for them. Most of the colony's Black population originated from immigration from the West Indies. Despite the poor soil, the colonists persisted in trying to farm, even importing Portuguese laborers for that purpose in the nineteenth century, at about the time that steamships were undermining the Bermudian maritime industry.

Racial relations have long been contentious. The small White population controls most of the economy and government, a situation that led to racial riots in 1972, 1973, and 1977.

The Bermudians established a constitution in 1968. Their government consists of a governor appointed in London, a cabinet appointed by the governor, and a bicameral legislature comprised of an appointed Senate and an elected House of Assembly. There is also a Bermudian court system with a supreme court. Political patronage is a central feature of the government. Moneys and favors circulate within the large extended families of the colony. Whites often keep Blacks politically and economically indebted to them, and Blacks repay their debts by buying from their benefactors and by voting for them in elections. Anger caused by this system manifests itself infrequently because the leaders make sure that all Bermudians have food and housing. Nevertheless, the benefactors can fire Blacks from their jobs, raise their rents, deny them credit or promotions, or cancel their mortgages, making most Blacks very dependent on the White elite.

The Bermudian economy is strong, with virtually no unemployment. The mainstay of the economy is tourist dollars, most of which come from the United States. Another bright point in the economic picture is the offshore industries, of which there are more than 6,200, including many insurance corporations. Many of the offshore corporations are in Bermuda to escape the political uncertainties found in Hong Kong and Panama.

Despite the full employment and growing economy, there are economic problems in Bermuda. The shortage of land has created a shortage of housing, which has led to very high prices. The prices of nearly all consumer goods are also extremely high owing to the fact that they must all be imported. Farming, never very productive in the first place, has declined as more attention has been devoted to tourism. Fishing is now mostly for sport, and manufacturing never was important. The colony has strong right-to-work laws, which have greatly weakened whatever power the unions have been able to create; wages have therefore remained low. The government has paid scant attention to the social needs of the poor.

Bibliography

Critchley, David (1989). *Shackles of the Past*. Bermuda: Engravers.

Manning, Frank E. (1973). *Black Clubs in Bermuda: Ethnography of a Play World*. Ithaca, N.Y.: Cornell University Press.

Manning, Frank E. (1978). *Bermudian Politics in Transition: Race, Voting, and Public Opinion*. Hamilton, Bermuda: Island Press.

Blacks of Costa Rica

ETHNONYMS: none

Blacks constitute 3 percent of the population of Costa Rica, but nearly 24 percent of the population of the province of Limón, on the Atlantic coast. The ancestors of most Costa Rican Blacks did not arrive in Costa Rica to work as slaves on plantations, as in other parts of the Americas and the Caribbean; they came much later, as free people in search of employment. They came primarily from the British West Indies, and especially from Jamaica, in the late nineteenth century to build a railroad that was needed to transport coffee from the interior highlands to Puerto Limón. Once the railroad was completed, Blacks found work principally in the banana plantations of the United Fruit Company. Costa Rican Blacks, even those born in the country, did not have citizenship at this time. By the 1930s, worsening economic conditions led to popular political pressure for employers to hire Costa Rican citizens preferentially, and in 1936 a congressional act to that effect was passed, leaving many Blacks unemployed. In the same year, president Leon Cortés forbade Blacks from entering the almost purely White highlands by prohibiting Blacks from traveling past the city of Turrialba in the direction of the highlands. This policy extended even to railroad employees who were Black; they had to disembark the train at Turrialba and be replaced by White workers when the train traveled away from the coast. The United Fruit Company pulled up stakes in eastern Costa Rica in the early 1940s to move its operations to western Costa Rica. Blacks, by virtue of the presidential order, could not follow the company, and many were left without employment. During the 1948 civil war, some Blacks supported José "Pepe" Figueres, the leader of the group that won. Figueres, in return for this support, offered Blacks Costa Rican citizenship and paid some heed to their needs in later elections. Blacks accepted this offer, even though citizenship carried with it a requirement that children attend Spanish-language schools and learn Spanish, something the English-speaking Blacks did not find attractive. English of the Jamaican dialect continues to be spoken, however, despite the Spanish-language requirement.

Prior to 1950, the Black community was almost completely endogamous. By 1978, however, 6.5 percent of marriages in a sample of 218 households were racially mixed, and 45 percent of Black people in those households viewed marriage to people of Spanish origin as desirable. There has long been a preference among many Costa Rican Blacks for light skin, which they believe brings social rewards such as status, wealth, and power, and this is one reason for increased intermarriage.

Most Costa Rican Blacks today still live in the province of Limón, an area that produces the majority of Costa Rica's bananas and cacao and that boasts the country's principal commerical port. The people there are mostly working-class poor, and the region is not densely populated. Nevertheless, in the 1980s and 1990s, many Blacks have moved away from the rural areas for better jobs in Costa Rican cities and in the United States.

Bibliography

Lefever, Harry G. (1992). *Turtle Bogue: Afro-Caribbean Life and Culture in a Costa Rican Village*. Selinsgrove, Pa.: Susquehanna University Press.

Melendez Chaverri, Carlos, and Quince Duncan (1981). *El negro en Costa Rica*. San José: Editorial Costa Rica.

Purcell, Trevor (1993). *Banana Fallout: Class, Color, and Culture among West Indians in Costa Rica*. Los Angeles: University of California, Los Angeles, Center for Afro-American Studies.

Boruca, Bribri, and Cabécar

ETHNONYMS: For the Boruca ("village within the ashes"): Brunca, Brunka (name of the tribal group and the language, which also refers to ash); for the Bribri: Talamanca, Viceita, Se'ie ("like ourselves"), Bribriwak ("owners of mountainous territory"); for the Cabécar: Bianco, Talamanca, Kabekirwak ("owners of kbek," the quetzal bird).

Orientation

Identification. The three groups are located in southeastern Costa Rica—the Boruca on the slopes of the Brunqueña Mountain range, along the valley of the Río Diquís; the Bribri and Cabécar on the Atlantic and Pacific watersheds of the Talamanca Mountain range.

Location. The Boruca live in the township (*cantón*) of Buenos Aires (in the villages of Boruca, Curré, Maíz, Bijagual, Cañablancal, Cajón, Mano de Tigre, Lagarto, Chánguina, and Puerto Nuevo) and in the township of Osa. The Boruca-Térraba Reservation was established in 1945, later divided into Térraba (for the Teribe Indians) and Boruca and Curré (for the Boruca). The Bribri and Cabécar are in the townships Buenos Aires, Turrialba, Matina, and Talamanca. There are four Bribri reservations: Talamanca Bribri and Këköldi on the Atlantic watershed, Salitre and Cabagra on the Pacific watershed. There are six Cabécar reservations: on the Atlantic, Nairi-Awari, Chirripo, Tayni, Telire, and Talamanca-Cebécar; on the Pacific side, Ujarrás. Some Cabécar live among the Bribri, and some Bribri live among the Cabécar; a few Boruca males reside with the other two groups, because of migration and intermarriage. Non-Indians also live in the reservations of the three groups.

Demography. In 1990 the Boruca on reserved land numbered 2,660; the Bribri on reserved land had a population of 6,700; the Cabécar, 8,300. All three groups have some members living outside the reservations, in neighboring rural areas and towns. Allowing for population increase and the families outside reserved lands, the three groups may have accounted for a population of about 19,000 in 1994.

Linguistic Affiliation. The languages of the three groups belong to the same division of Chibchan languages. The most recent classification (Constenla 1992) places them in the Isthmic Subdivision of the Paya-Chibcha Stock (which also includes Paya, Votic, and Magdalenic). The Isthmic Subdivision includes Teribe, Viceitic (Bribri-Cabécar), Boruca, Guaimiic, Coracic, and Kuna. The Bribri and Cabécar are mostly bilingual, speaking their language and Spanish; very few are monolingual in their native language, and there is a trend toward becoming monolingual in Spanish. In the 1980s the Brunka language was spoken by eleven people and forty understood it.

History and Cultural Relations

The earliest date for the acquaintance of these groups with the Spaniards is 1502, when Columbus landed in Limón on his fourth voyage. There were Spanish expeditions in 1519, 1522, 1523, 1526, 1539, 1540, and 1560, but more precise early information stems from the Spanish conquistador Juan Vásquez de Coronado. He met with officials of the three language groups in 1563–1564. At the time of Conquest, these and the other Costa Rican Indians were organized into chiefdoms. Those of the Boruca and their neighbors were destroyed in 1563; the Indians began to be reassigned into colonial social units, such as missions and *ecomienda*. The Talamanca on the other side of the mountain range managed to retain traits of the chiefdom type of social organization up to the first three decades of the twentieth century. The Boruca were considered pacified in 1608. A village was founded with that name in 1629. The site was a stop for the mule trains going from the Spanish capital Cartago toward Portobelo in Panama. During the seventeenth century, Boruca was the only village in the south Pacific region to become organized for colonial functions. By the end of the century, it consisted of a town hall (*cabildo*), the community hall (*casa comunal*), a shelter for travelers, and twelve huts. Up to the eighteenth century, the Indians that remained from neighboring disappearing groups were integrated into the village. In 1770 twenty-five huts and 155 Indians of both sexes were counted, and by 1801 there were 250 people in the village. When Costa Rica was granted independence, in 1821, the colonial impact included diminished population, change in settlement pattern (to this nucleated village and scattered homesteads), Catholicism, iron tools, pigs, chickens, and cattle. The first non-Indian settlers arrived in 1848, 1865, and 1875, from Chiriquí and from the Central Valley of Costa Rica. Between 1860 and 1940 the area remained sparsely populated and isolated, but the building of the Pan-American Highway opened up the region between 1945 and 1963 to massive immigration of non-Indians from the central part of the country. Ethnic conflict arose because of competition for land and other resources, which in some ways is observable even today. At the legal department of the National Commission of Indian Affairs (CONAI), there are cases of farms or lots claimed by both Indians and Whites. Other cases involve boundary disputes. Expressions of resentment over the presence of one or the other group can still be heard. The municipal council has never been pleased about the existence of Indian reserves in the cantón.

The early Spanish recognized the other two linguistic groups, Bribri and Cabécar, but treated them as a single nation because of their very close similarities in language and institutions. Both groups managed to retain a high degree of independence and isolation from European influence well into the twentieth century. A major revolt against Spanish colonial rule occurred in 1610. Following another such uprising in 1709, missions and non-Indian settlements were prohibited until 1882. Since 1882, there has been a gradual penetration, which became especially intensive after 1940, with the establishment of primary schools and the expansion of the Costa Rican non-Indian farming population into the Talamanca area. The traditional clan hierarchy of the Talamancans was observed until about 1920. Today it is delineated in stories and held in memory. Political, ritual, and other specialties were hereditary along clan lines. During the latter part of the nineteenth century, in matters concerning community threats (such as war, hostility on the part of foreigners, epidemics, natural catastrophes, famine, and crop failures), the Bribri and Cabécar clans were commanded by the _useköl_ or _kpa_, the highest-ranking chief, who resided in Upper Coen (San José Cabécar), to observe periods of fasting and abstinence. Regarded as sacred, the kpa could not be touched, looked at directly, or spoken to directly. The next rank was held by the _blu'_, called _rey_ ("king") in Spanish, an executive chief who conducted war and foreign relations. The last king died in 1910. In the early 1990s the aboriginal culture is rapidly disappearing, but one can still find individuals, families, or hamlets that have maintained tradition rather extensively.

Settlements

The main village of the Boruca is a town by the same name. It is located 240 kilometers east and south from San José. The Diquís, or Grande de Térraba River, borders the village 10 kilometers to the southeast. All the Borucan hamlets are bordered by this river or lie close to it. The Pan-American Highway passes through some of the villages and hamlets and near the others. The roads that branch off from the highway are unpaved, rough, and difficult to traverse during the rainy season. Houses have been built over the hills, separated by grassy or cultivated areas. Some of them are in the traditional style: huts with steeply peaked roofs thatched with savanna grasses, their dark brown walls made of broad, horizontally placed wood boards. Frame houses with metal roofs, in the style of rural Costa Rica, are more frequent today, however. All other buildings (stores, churches, schools, medical facilities, jails, storage places, dance halls, and community centers) have metal roofs and are constructed of painted, sawed boards or of cement. The houses are usually built near creeks or small rivers flowing into the main river. Those located near the nucleus of church, community center, stores, and school have running water, showers, and sinks inside; electricity is available, and there are telephone booths in the

villages or hamlets. The Bribri and the Cabécar traditionally preferred a more dispersed pattern of homesteads than did the Boruca. Until the 1970s, they did not really have a "village" because they distanced their homes from schools, chapels, and other public buildings. Traditionally, they built rectangular and oval thatched-roof huts. The conical hut of the nineteenth century has been revived as a gesture of cultural revitalization, but given that it is a major undertaking to build such a hut, only three of them have been erected, as community centers. It was this type of house, however, that better reflected the cosmological views of the Talamanca; fortunately, this symbolism is now known. The thatched-roof houses, large and raised on stilts on the Talamanca plain, are also being replaced by the painted frame houses of rural Costa Rica. Today, with the increase in population and the shortage of land for cultivation, as well as the reduction of the forests, the patterns of Bribri and Cabécar settlements more and more resemble those of the Spanish towns. There is a central plaza surrounded by public buildings; nearby are homes with access to running water and electricity.

Economy

Subsistence and Commercial Activities. All three groups were agriculturists, depending primarily on maize, beans, manioc, sweet potatoes and other root crops, pumpkins, peach palms, and cocoa. From colonial times onward, they completely incorporated several kinds of plantains and bananas, rice, and, later, coffee. Native and old-world fruit trees have been common on the farms. Since World War II Indian farmers have joined governmental and nongovernmental programs to improve seeds and introduce new crops. Since the late 1940s, the cultivation of garden vegetables has been taught at the grade schools. On the Atlantic side, the Bribri and the Cabécar have depended more on cocoa and plantains as a cash crop; on the Pacific side, these two groups and the Boruca have depended more on the sale of maize and beans. Income from agriculture, however, has always been very limited. The Indians have a marginal economy. As communications improve, they are also able to sell oranges, peach-palm fruits (_pejibayes_), hearts of palm, and other crops. Hunting and river fishing have always supplemented agriculture. Today these activities are either restricted or absent, because of the reduction in forests and the increase in population. Wild plants still provide foods, medicines, and materials for building and for crafts. Indians have always worked for non-Indians as manual laborers and continue to do so. In the villages, Indians also have government jobs as teachers, health assistants, policemen, and guards. Those who have learned other professions (agronomists, and electricians, for instance) have left the villages but usually help their families. Domestic animals are kept in the farms and village households and also sold to non-Indian traders who come regularly to buy pigs, chickens, turkeys, and ducks. Cattle raising is important for a few families only, and most Indians do not own horses. Those who do may get some income from renting them.

Industrial Arts. The tradition of making cotton thread has been maintained and is practiced by a few families in all three groups. Additionally, in the village of Boruca, in the 1960s, one family knew how to weave bags, belts, and material for skirts on the traditional hand loom. This ability was encouraged by the schools and promoted for sale to tourists, which has allowed the craft to prosper. The Boruca have retained the knowledge of natural dyes, but today they also use commercial ones. Some Boruca sell masks made of *Ochroma* wood. In all three groups, a few artisans sell baskets, cord bags, hammocks, decorated gourds, drums, and bows and arrows made of pejibaye (*Bactris gassipaes*) wood. Government and private projects have encouraged artisans to fashion traditional objects for sale. Most men know how to make canoes and build huts and modern dwellings. Some women are seamstresses; they own sewing machines and buy material in the larger towns.

Trade. Trade has always been important. Until the early part of the twentieth century, the Bribri and Cabécar came to the village of Boruca to exchange items such as bows and arrows, cord bags, baskets made from vines, and some forest products. The foreign party remained on the outskirts of the village. The Boruca brought out dyed woven material and salt, among other things. Afterward, the outside traders would be asked to come into the village. It was a rule for first visitors (usually youngsters) not to ask any questions about what they saw or heard; they could ask and comment after they were back home. Trade patterns among all Costa Rican Indians have been traced back to colonial and pre-Conquest times. Today they sell their products to non-Indians either at their homes or on the roads that lead to their settlements. They then buy foods and manufactured goods in local stores, which are usually owned by non-Indians, or travel to the larger urban towns to do their shopping.

Division of Labor. Men clear the land and raise livestock. Women participate with men in planting, harvesting, and transporting crops. Women may still be seen carrying loads while men walk ahead carrying a machete. When nontraditional occupations are available, they may be held by either sex. In Talamanca, some women still plant their own maize fields in the traditional manner, although their husbands may help, and wives may help in their husbands' fields. Animals (pigs, chickens) raised by women are theirs, and men have to raise their own.

Land Tenure. Land formerly was owned by families, but individual ownership, fostered by government administration of the reservations and Costa Rican laws, has become the norm. On the Pacific side, from colonial times to about the 1950s, there were communally owned pastures and maize fields for the church and the school. Reservation land is legally held in trust by the Indian development associations, but individual property rights of Indians and non-Indians are recognized. Keeping land in Indian hands has been a very complex and conflictive issue.

Kinship

The native kinship system is either followed or remembered. The degree to which the kinship rules are enforced is conditioned by the degree of transculturation of the group. The Boruca had the Hawaiian type of sibling-cousin terminology, but today they mostly follow Spanish rules and terminology. The Bribri and Cabécar largely maintain

their matrilineal clan system. Bribri kinship terminology is bifurcate merging for the first ascending generation; sibling-cousin terminology is of the Iroquoian type; second ascending generation and second descending generation use reciprocal terms that distinguish Ego's mother's side from Ego's father side, and sex. Siblings address each other by the same term when the sex is the same (sister to sister or brother to brother) but vary the term when addressing siblings of the opposite sex. The Cabécar use the same terms as the Bribri, with only slightly different pronunciation, in Ego's generation. They differ with the Bribri in that terms applying to the male's first ascending generation are bifurcate collateral among the Cabécar. Their terminology is cognate with the Bribri one, except for the terms for father, father's brother and father's sister. The Talamanca have preferred to practice bilateral cross-cousin marriage; about half of them follow the custom. Formerly, the practice of sororal polygyny was widespread—and more acceptable than the occasional occurrences of it today.

Marriage and Family

Marriage. Among the Boruca, marriages take place in the Catholic church, but common-law unions are very frequent. Monogamy is the rule, but separations are also frequent. Legal divorce is rare, not shameful, but not expected. A young man who wants to get married speaks to his—and the girl's—parents. The two sets of parents decide whether the couple should be married by the Church or live in a common-law union. Neolocal residence is preferred.

The Bribri-Cabécar tend to follow native custom, but some marry in the Catholic or Protestant churches to which they belong. In native custom, although the couple may have agreed to the marriage on their own, outwardly the two sets of parents decide, the male taking the matter to them. Mothers or grandmothers of the girl may have a great deal of influence on the decision. The son-in-law comes to live with the bride's parents for some time; neolocality may follow the initial matrilocal or uxorilocal residence. Sororal polygyny may still be observed. Separations are easy. In all three groups, either parent, or a relative of either parent, may take care of the children in case of a separation. If there is a custody conflict or child-support claim, the matter may be referred to the Costa Rican courts.

Domestic Unit. In the Boruca language, the word for family corresponds to the household. Nuclear families are common; other arrangements are the extended, one-parent, and brother-sister households. Many families include unmarried grown daughters with offspring. Among the Bribri-Cabécar, extended households, with people related through the female line are common, but other arrangements, especially nuclear ones, are also observed. In all three groups, older people are generally invited into the households if they are not able to support themselves.

Inheritance. Women's possessions are usually passed on to daughters or uterine nieces and men's possessions to sons (among the Boruca) or to sons and uterine nephews (among the Bribri-Cabécar). Borucan women do not usually inherit land; it is transferred to the husband when the woman marries. In the 1970s, in the main village of Boruca, in six out of seventy-nine households, women had inherited land from their mothers. Female inheritance of land was expected to become more common. Among the Bribri-Cabécar, in the traditional system, women and men inherited from mothers and mother's bothers. It is becoming more common for males to leave property to their children and not to their sisters' children. Disputes taken to courts are solved according to Costa Rican inheritance laws.

Socialization. The Boruca often prefer male children to girls. By age 4, girls may begin to take care of younger sisters when their mothers or grandmothers are not present. Girls will be reprimanded if they leave their sisters alone. When a girl reaches the age of 11 to 14, and she wants to be with boys and not with her little sister, a family problem arises, but parents are not harsh; they expect the girl to become more mature as time goes by. The older son always takes care of his younger brother. Brothers are usually cordial to each other. Children are instructed in sex from the age of 6, when they are told not to let anyone touch them in the genital area. When children are alone, they sometimes experiment with each other, in a playful manner. The majority of newborn children are baptized when the priest arrives at the villages. When people are older, they are usually called by nicknames. At age 6 or 7, the child is considered responsible enough to go to the store on errands. Children learn songs from age 3 onward and play different games. Guidance is given in regard to toilet training, manners, dressing, and responsibility to the family.

Bribri-Cabécar children are welcome, and children of relatives are easily adopted, but, as with the Boruca, the traditional preference may have been for small families. The three groups have knowledge of methods to provoke miscarriage or to prevent pregnancy for defined periods. In the Bribri-Cabécar culture, children were not formally named. The mother assigned nicknames for family use; outsiders referred to people by clan names and kinship terms. Brother-sister avoidance rules are still enforced. From about the 1940s to the 1970s, the people learned to follow Spanish rules for first and last names and to register the newborn according to Costa Rican law. Children's birthdays are celebrated. They are given duties at early ages. Most of their games are imitations of adult roles. Children of the three groups can attend grade schools from age 7 until six grades have been completed, but some drop out. There are scholarship programs that benefit some of the youngsters who go on to high schools or to the universities; others are supported by their own families for these later studies. Adults often attend short training courses in agriculture, crafts, health, community development, and so forth.

Sociopolitical Organization

Social Organization. The Boruca lack traditional governing structures; they organize locally as non-Indian rural communities. The elderly, however, continue to be highly respected. It is also common for individual community leaders to exercise a great deal of influence through local communities and projects. Nationally and internationally, the Boruca have held prominent positions in Indian movements. Constant change, deliberate adoption of—and ad-

aptation of—outside influences is a norm; however, the identity of an indigenous group is retained, and people feel they share a common Indian ancestry. The Bribri and Cabécar respect shamans and, generally, the elders of both sexes. Informally, or more formally at meetings, the shamans and elders make known what younger leaders they support for community projects or representation. Churches, schools, and local committees usually take the initiative for community activities.

Political Organization. Governing structures are those of Costa Rican national administration. Each village has a Rural Police office with one or two officers. Policemen may be from the specific area or assigned to it. There are district committees and elected individuals linked to the township municipality, whose concerns are road maintenance, welfare, and coordination with the national government. Until the 1930s, the villages of Boruca had the structure of a colonial corporate community, featuring an elders' council and _mayordomos_. The Bribri and Cabécar partially kept the hierarchical clan structure into the twentieth century. All reservations have a development association which, in accordance with the national Indian Law, must resolve land issues and undertake socioeconomic improvements. They appoint representatives to the National Commission of Indian Affairs. Every village has several voluntary committees that work to improve health and education and organize sporting and cultural events. About three national Indian associations exert some influence, depending on the issues. A national group, organized between 1993 and 1994, is made up of women. The national political parties have committees in the Indian villages.

Social Control. The Rural Police is one means of maintaining order and conformity. Other control mechanisms are religious teachings and family norms. Prohibited are such things as bodily harm to another person, not helping seniors, theft, murder, embezzlement, and impoliteness. The most elderly insist on the prohibition of incest. All three groups tell traditional myths in which punishments for incest are elaborated. Gossip and avoidance of interaction with people who violate prohibitions are informal sanctions. There is some fear of witchcraft. People may be accused by neighbors or the local police before outside agencies of the Costa Rican judicial system.

Conflict. Factionalism is ever present. It manifests itself in clan or family rivalries; among adherents of opposing national political parties; and over any issue in which a traditional custom or attitude is confronted by another labeled "modern" or "progressive," the acceptance or nonacceptance of non-Indians, and religious affiliation—given that there are Catholics, different Protestant groups, Baha'i, and those who prefer the traditional Indian beliefs (the latter among the Bribri-Cabécar). Internally, families may be greatly divided by problems relating to land distribution, alcoholism, or marital disputes.

Religion and Expressive Culture

Religious Beliefs. Most Boruca are nominally Catholic. Nearly every house has at least one religious picture. A catechism class is conducted for the younger children; mass is said when a priest is available, and people attend services such as the rosary. Legends and myths are told but are considered things of the past.

The Bribri-Cabécar belong to the Catholic church, to different Protestant denominations, and to the Baha'i faith. A few have revitalized the traditional system of belief, which includes a single creator with whom people relate through the shamans but not through individual supplication. All social norms are said to have come from him. Spiritual beings related to nature are important in this cosmology.

Religious Practitioners.   Among the Boruca, the mayordomos, or *delegados de la palabra,* who assist the Catholic priests, have been instrumental in tending religious buildings, teaching the faith, and leading prayers. In the Protestant denominations, there are Boruca, Bribri, and Cabécar pastors. Among the Indian cultures that remained in Costa Rica after the eighteenth century, the Bribri-Cabécar culture has the most elaborate patterns for dealing with disease, birth, and death. On both sides of the Talamanca range, native shamans and trained buriers officiate on these occasions. Not all the Talamanca utilize these traditional services or believe in their efficacy, but all respect them.

Ceremonies and Arts.   The three groups celebrate Costa Rica's national holidays with activities organized by the schools. Public Catholic ceremonies such as those commemorating patron saints, Christmas, and Holy Week are also major events. The Boruca have retained two colonial celebrations. Día de los Negritos, celebrated 6 through 8 December, commemorates the coming of the Spaniards and their repulse by the Boruca. Seven to ten players make forays against a carved horse head carried by the master of ceremony. The horse head symbolizes the Spanish; it is lassoed and symbolically burned. During this dance-game, players must slur their words, replace phonemes in them, and change sentence order. Drum and flute are played. Jokes are told and a spirit of merrymaking prevails. Día de los Diablitos is celebrated from 31 December to 2 January. The master of ceremony is the principal devil. Players wear carved masks of light wood and a gunnysacklike dress. Voice and language are disguised, and the native language may be used. A skin drum and a reed flute are sounded. A player, representing the Spanish conquistador, carries a carved bull face and cloth frame. The bull chases the little devils (representing the Borucan) round the village. The latter steal little things from the houses and do other mischief to neighbors. Stolen things are distributed to players on the last day. The bull kills the principal devil and the second devil first, then the remaining diablitos. Women, represented by men, are killed last. The bull hides, but the dead diablitos revive and look for him. When the bull is located, it is dragged to the center of the village and symbolically burned. Thus the Spaniards are destroyed. The three groups practice the *chichada,* an occasion for drinking a beer made of maize. This celebration often brings together dispersed relatives and neighbors for recreation and as repayment for farm or communal labor. During this event, the more traditional Bribri and Cabécar perform an aboriginal dance (symbolic of relationships with forest animals) derived from their stories of origin.

Medicine.   The three groups normally rely on Western medicine. Health posts are located in the villages or nearby. Traditional medical practices are conducted in homes or on the advice of native specialists. The Boruca have female herb healers. In times of need, they resort to herbal drugs for specific purposes: to bring about love, hatred, marriage, divorce, pregnancy, amnesia; to prevent pregnancy, labor pains, frustration; to cure snake bite and other ills. A few believe that a drug could change a human to an animal. Traditionally, Bribri-Cabécar shamans and non-Indian witchcraft practitioners in Buenos Aires and the Central Valley of Costa Rica were consulted. For the Bribri and Cabécar, the native medical system and Western medicine are complementary. Bribri-Cabécar shamans treat illness by means of fasts, herbal and other kinds of medicines, and esoteric chants. They consult spirit beings by means of crystals.

Death and Afterlife.   Among the Boruca, if there is no priest in the village when a death occurs, a mayordomo goes to the church and rings the bells. The corpse lies in state at the home of the deceased or that of a relative or friend. There must be adequate space for people to sit and view the body, which is covered with a white sheet. Candles are placed at the head and feet and religious pictures or sculptures complete the scene. Meat (pork, chicken), tamales, and beverages are served. The mayordomo—or someone else—recites prayers at intervals during the wake. People may bring money to help pay for the funeral expenses, candles, coffee, rice, and other foods. If the priest is available, a Mass will be held before burial, which is usually attended by most villagers. If not, the mayordomo leads prayers. Prayer sessions or Masses are attended for the next nine days. At the ninth, or Last Rosary, food is served at the house where all have come to pray.

Among the Bribri and the Cabécar, for those who are Catholic, the proceedings are about the same, except that religious pictures or sculptures are uncommon. Regardless of religious affiliation, these people prefer to bring in the buriers to handle the body. Visitors must not talk to the parents of the deceased for a specified period. They—and anybody who had contact with the burial proceedings—must be ritually cleansed by the main burier or a shaman. The native death ceremony requires ritual cooking and ritual distribution of food. Death procedures address a proper return of the soul to the underworld so that the reproduction of the deceased's clan is assured on earth.

Bibliography

Bozzoli de Wille, María Eugenia (1975a). "Birth and Death in the Belief System of the Bribri Indians of Costa Rica." Ph.D. dissertation, University of Georgia. Translated as *El nacimiento y la muerte entre los bribris.* 1979. San José: Editorial de la Universidad de Costa Rica.

Bozzoli de Wille, María Eugenia (1975b). *Localidades indígenas costarricenses.* San José: Editorial Universitaria Centroamericana (EDUCA).

Chapin, Mac (1992). *Indigenous Populations: The Coexistence of Indigenous Peoples and the Natural Environment of*

Central America. Research and Exploration. Washington, D.C.: National Geographic Society.

Constenala Umaña, Adolfo (1991). _Las lenguas del Area Intermermedia_. San José: Editorial de la Universidad de Costa Rica.

Constenla Umaña, Adolfo (1992). "Sobre el estudio diacrónico de las lenguas chibchas y su contribución al conocimiento del pasado de sus hablantes." Paper presented at the Sixth Congress of Anthropology, University of Los Andes, Colombia.

Stone, Doris Z. (1949). _The Boruca of Costa Rica_. Cambridge: Harvard University Printing Office.

Williams, Arya Rod (1976). "Boruca Borucac: An Indian Village of Costa Rica." B.A. dissertation, Pitzer College, Claremont, Calif.

MARÍA EUGENIA BOZZOLI DE WILLE

Bugle

ETHNONYMS: Bogotá, Bokotá, Buglere, Bukueta, Guaymí-Sabanero, Muri, Murire, Sabanero

Orientation

Identification. The Bugle (pronounced "boo-glay") are a small, little-known Native American group who live in the interior of northwestern Panama. The meaning of the term "Bugle" is not known. Better known in the literature as "Bokotá" or "Bogotá" and often considered a subcultural group of the Ngawbe (Guaymí), the "Bugle," as they prefer to call themselves, insist on their cultural distinctiveness from the Ngawbe. It is important to note that the Ngawbe also consider the Bugle to be a culturally distinct (but politically affiliated) group. Their views on their cultural distinctiveness reflect the contemporary political importance of ethnic-identity issues for the indigenous populations in Panama.

Location. The Bugle proper occupy a small area in the easternmost portion of Bocas del Toro Province and the westernmost portion of northern Veraguas Province, between the drainages of the Río Chucará to the west and the Río Calovébora to the east, and between the Caribbean coastal plain to the north and the continental divide to the south. Most of them live within the _corregimiento_ (municipality) of Santa Catalina, district of Bastimento, province of Bocas del Toro.

Demography. There are an estimated 7,000 speakers of Buglere and Murire (Guaymí-Sabanero); however, many fewer—perhaps only 1,200 to 1,500—claim Bugle as their ethnic identity.

Linguistic Affiliation. Buglere is a dialect of Murire (Guaymí-Sabanero), a language of the Chibchan Family and one of several Chibchan languages that are spoken in Panama and elsewhere in Central America.

History and Cultural Relations

The closest cultural affiliations of the Bugle are with the Muri (Sabanero) branch of the Ngawbe (Guaymí). Their precise historical relationships are uncertain. Numerous cultural similarities to the Ngawbe, especially to the eastern Murire speakers, suggest ancient historical connections, although some specific practices are explicitly considered by the Bugle to be recent borrowings from the Ngawbe. The Bugle themselves locate their ancestors to the south, on the Pacific slopes of the central cordillera, an area that is still occupied by the remaining Muri. According to legend, the Bugle once had wings like birds and could fly anywhere they liked. One day they crossed the cordillera and arrived at their present location. Soon they engaged in improper behavior, and the consequence was that they lost their ability to fly, so they remained where they are. The area occupied by the Bugle is part of a more extensive area in the provinces of Chiriquí, Bocas del Toro, and Veraguas, one that the Ngawbe have for several years been attempting—without success—to persuade the government of Panama to declare an official reserve for the Ngawbe-Bugle.

Settlements

The Bugle, much like the Ngawbe, live in a highly dispersed pattern, in individual houses and in small hamlets (called _caseríos_) consisting of two or three houses occupied by consanguineously and affinally related individuals. Bugle dwellings are located mostly along or near rivers and streams. Traditional houses were round, with conical roofs of straw or palm leaves, low walls of sticks or cane, earthen floors raised a few centimeters above the surrounding ground, and, generally, with two entrances but with no particular orientation. This house type was widespread among the indigenous peoples of western Panama and eastern Costa Rica (which are sometimes known as "Talamancan" cultures). The traditional houses measured up to 10 meters in diameter and 7 or 8 meters from the floor to the apex of the roof. This type of dwelling was noted as being the most common during the visit of Erland Nordenskiöld in 1927. By 1964, however, rectangular houses made of the same materials—some with earthen floors and others raised above the ground on posts—were more common, apparently as a result of influence from the nonindigenous coastal cultures. The change is attributed by the Bugle to greater ease of construction. The traditional circular houses never contained interior partitions; the rectangular houses sometimes do. Each type of house has an interior platform under the roof, accessed by a notched-log ladder, that serves as a storage area for agricultural products and personal belongings. The cooking fire is usually located in the center of the floor—on a prepared clay base, in the case of houses elevated on posts.

Economy

Subsistence and Commercial Activities. The Bugle practice swidden-based subsistence agriculture as the main source of their livelihood. Their most important crops for daily consumption are maize, rice, and bananas, the latter harvested green and then boiled. Other crops include plantains; beans; root crops such as *otoe* (taro/*Xanthosoma spp.*), *ñampi* (yams/*Dioscorea spp.*), and sweet manioc; peach palms (*Guilielma gasipaes*); cacao (*Theobroma cacao*); avocados; mangoes; chayotes (*Scisyos edulis*); sugarcane; pineapples; calabashes; and chili peppers. Almost all of these crops are grown for household use, but rice is regularly produced in surplus and taken to the coast to be sold. Chickens, ducks, and pigs are raised for home consumption, but they are also sold to obtain the cash needed to purchase the manufactured items to which the Bugle have become accustomed. Cattle are raised on a very limited basis and are usually sold. The Bugle told Herrera and González in 1964 that they used to raise more cattle, but that the numbers had been greatly reduced owing to a plague that had also affected other domestic animals and children (71). The hunting of deer, wild pigs, and other small animals with bows and arrows, traps, and rifles (which are not common now and were not available in Nordenskiöld's time) supplements agriculture and animal husbandry, as does fishing with hook and line, harpoons, nets, and at least three types of plant poisons. Some wild plants are gathered as food and others as medicine.

Industrial Arts. The manufacture of sturdy baskets of various sizes—well made but not aesthetic in quality—is traditional. Fashioning net bags out of plant fibers is also a traditional handicraft of the Bugle. Various sizes of bags are made, using a technique of knotless netting. Some of these net bags are crude and strictly utilitarian, but others are of fine artistic quality. Although most are made for home use, many are sold. According to tradition, the Bugle manufactured ceramic vessels in the past, but they have now lost the knowledge of this craft. Nordenskiöld collected a single pottery vessel in 1927. Pottery is now nonexistent except for ocarinas and small whistles, usually zoomorphic in form. The Bugle also make flutes of bamboo and bone. Woven hats, representing a craft of recent introduction (some time prior to the 1950s), are of very fine quality and are offered for sale as well as being used at home. There is a ready market for these hats in the towns of Veraguas Province. Beaded collars, introduced in the twentieth century through contact with the Ngawbe, are made by and for men and are supposedly broader than the typical Ngawbe collar. Clothing was traditionally made of bark cloth. Its use for clothing is now rare, but it is still made and has other uses, such as sacks and blankets. The Bugle are the only indigenous group in Panama that still makes and uses at least some bark cloth for clothing. Strings of beads, now of commercial glass but formerly of vegetable substances, are used as necklaces by women and children.

Trade. Trade occurs with nonindigenous communities on the Caribbean coast, with people in southern Veraguas, and with itinerant merchants who travel through the Bugle area. Rice, sometimes maize and domestic animals, and the two principal handicrafts, straw hats and net bags, are exchanged for Western manufactured goods such as metal cooking pots, cloth, and machetes.

Division of Labor. According to Nordenskiöld, men cleared the land, and women cultivated it. Today, although men still clear the land, men, women, and sometimes children perform other tasks in the agricultural cycle—planting, weeding, and harvesting. Women do most of the food preparation and assume most of the child care in the household. Men hunt and fish, and women do most of the gathering. Men make the fine woven hats for which the Bugle are noted, and women make the net bags.

Land Tenure. Land is owned by kin groups rather than by individuals. Individuals, both women and men, inherit use rights to the lands owned by their kin groups. Fallow land remains the property of the kin group whose members originally cleared it. Disputes may occur when others appropriate and use such fallow land, but such disputes are reported to be unusual and infrequent.

Kinship

Descent is presumably cognatic, as among the Ngawbe. No clans, lineages, or other unilineal descent groups are reported for the Bugle. The universal unit of production and consumption is the nuclear family. There are some laterally and lineally extended family households, as well as polygynous households. Larger groups cooperate in various agricultural tasks and house building through the mechanism of the cooperative labor party, or *junta*. Such labor groups consist of kin and nearby neighbors (who are usually kin as well). Juntas operate on the principle of balanced reciprocity: the host owes equivalent labor to each of those who has helped him.

Marriage and Family

Marriage. Monogamy is the most common form of marriage, although polygyny is permitted and does sometimes occur. The low incidence of polygyny was attributed by the Bugle to a shortage of women. Intermarriage has occurred with the Ngawbe, usually between Ngawbe women and Bugle men—again, supposedly because of a shortage of Bugle women. In remote areas it is reported that there are many families of Bugle with no history of intermarriage with other groups. There is no formal marriage ceremony, and none was remembered by the elderly people who were interviewed by Herrera and González in 1964. Women often marry at the age of 12 or 13, whereas young men often must remain unmarried for several additional years. Marriage is by common agreement between a man and a woman. Women may accept or refuse offers of marriage. The custom of parents giving a prepubescent girl to her future husband to be raised by his family was said by the Bugle in 1964 to be no longer practiced, although Herrera and González documented two cases in their brief ethnographic survey (75). Herrera and González also report several instances of cousin marriage, but they note that their Bugle guide and chief informant considered such marriages to be immoral (76). Residence after marriage may be neolocal or patrilocal; the choice seems to depend on whether the young couple is prepared to be economically independent of the man's family.

Domestic Unit. The nuclear family is the most common unit of production and consumption, but extended-family households occur and may have been more common in the past. Fathers have traditionally exercised authority over their married sons, especially under conditions of patrilocal residence.

Inheritance. Some personal items are buried with their owner. A house in which a person dies is abandoned. Nordenskiöld reported that all of the personal belongings that are not buried with the deceased are abandoned, along with the house. Use rights to land are inherited by both men and women.

Socialization. Young children are allowed to run freely through the house and are treated with considerable tolerance. Their play mimics adult activities of the appropriate sex. Children of both sexes begin to learn early by observation and by assisting their parents in the tasks for which they will be responsible as adults. A puberty ceremony for a girl at her first menses signals her transition to adulthood and her eligibility for marriage. No puberty ceremony is reported for males. It is reported that school attendance is enthusiastic wherever schools have been established and that formal education has become highly valued among the Bugle.

Sociopolitical Organization

Social Organization. Little is known about the relative status of women and men among the Bugle. Men meet outside their own homes for social purposes, whereas it is reported that women as a group do not do so. Men are dominant in the public arena, but evidence suggests that in the domestic arena men and women are equal partners in household decisions and that women (as well as men) own and control their own personal property, including crops and domestic animals. Social stratification does not exist, but some individuals (usually elder males) are more highly respected than others for their wisdom and decision-making abilities or for their control of special bodies of knowledge, such as traditional medicine.

Political Organization. Nothing is known about traditional forms of political organization among the Bugle. Political authority was probably kin-group based, as among the Ngawbe. During the nineteenth century and the early part of the twentieth, it is reported that the Bugle accepted the authority of the Ngawbe governors, but it should be noted that the system of governors was originally a system imposed upon the Ngawbe by outside authorities. Since about the early 1970s, the Bugle have allied themselves with the Ngawbe chief of Veraguas Province, particularly with reference to relations with the national government. Local civil authorities called *corregidores*, who are appointed by the national government, are responsible for keeping order and settling local disputes. Corregidores frequently appoint subalterns, called *comisarios*, whose responsibilities are to keep order in their own hamlets.

Social Control. Adultery and robbery are punishable offenses among the Bugle. Until about the middle of the twentieth century, wooden stocks (presumably of colonial origin) were used as the common form of punishment. In disputes between individuals or kin groups, the protagonists meet, along with other members of the community, and attempt to settle the quarrel, with the local comisario serving as arbitrator. If a satisfactory resolution is not achieved, a similar meeting will be held with the corregidor serving as arbitrator. Individual skills and accumulated respect are better determiners of success in disputes that are arbitrated by corregidores and comisarios than is the force of authority that is attached to these positions.

Conflict. At the national level, there has been a long-standing and continuing conflict between the national government and the Bugle and Ngawbe regarding legal recognition of their lands as a reserve. Disputes between kin groups may also occur over land. Conflicts between individuals arise for a variety of reasons, and others become involved, in alignment with their kin (see "Social Control").

Religion and Expressive Culture

Religious Beliefs. Today the Bugle accept aspects of Christianity, but the few details of myths and ceremonies that are available hint at a still-existing set of non-Christian beliefs. The Bugle accept the existence of a high god, whom they refer to as Shubé or Chubé in their language, as well as an opposing evil force referred to by the Spanish term for devil, *diablo*. The ceremony that is held to protect a new house attests to a belief in a deity of lightning. According to one myth, the maize goddess initially brought the Bugle many varieties of the grain, but when the iguana and the river bird angered her one day as she was making *chicha* (a beer prepared from maize), she returned to the sky, taking with her the large-grained maize and leaving only the small-grained maize for the Bugle. From the sky, she continues to call to the maize, which accounts for why there are sometimes ears with no grains and ears with bare tips.

Religious Practitioners. The traditional religious practitioner among the Bugle until shortly before the 1960s was the *sukia* (shaman). Sukias apparently effected cures through communication with the spirit world. A child who was predestined to become a sukia, it was believed, refused to accept breast milk and was therefore fed chocolate water made from the first harvest of cacao or from wild cacao. Such a child was isolated and placed in the care of old women. Sukias could use their powers for both good and evil. The literature does not specify whether sukias could be women as well as men.

Ceremonies. A ceremony to insure a bountiful harvest is conducted, generally four days before planting, at which time large quantities of chocolate drink (made of hot water and unsweetened cocoa beans from the first harvest, ground into a paste) are drunk. *Chicherías*, ceremonies at which *chicha* and food are consumed in large quantities, are commonly held on a variety of occasions. They are generally interpreted as social gatherings, but they probably have some deeper social and religious significance, as they do among the Ngawbe. One type of chichería traditionally takes place eight days after the birth of a child. Singing, dancing, and the playing of traditional musical instruments occur during chicherías and also during the female puberty ceremonies. Some form of funeral ceremony occurs, but no details are available. The *balsería*, or stick game, is played among the Bugle, but there is some disagreement as to whether it is a traditional ceremony or a result of recent Ngawbe influence. After the construction of a new house, a ceremony is held to propitiate the god of lightning, in order to protect the house from lightning bolts. During the ceremony, a designated person perforates the ear lobes of the participants with a stingray spine and collects the blood as an offering. Women are not permitted in the house during this ceremony, but they do attend the chichería that immediately follows, at which there is much eating, drinking, and dancing.

Arts.   Traditionally, face painting by both men and women was common, but it is now reported to be infrequent except among young men. Simple horizontal lines across the cheeks were the most common forms of decoration, with red and black the preferred colors. Straw hats and net bags are decorated with geometric designs. Some of the designs on the net bags are said to represent birds and animals.

Medicine.   *Curanderos*, traditional specialists who cure with the use of plant medicines (but never through interaction with the spirit world), are still common among the Bugle. Numerous plant substances are used in curing. The curandero shows the family of a sick person how to process and administer the specific plants that are needed for a particular cure. Some plant medicines are taken internally; others are boiled in water and used to bathe the patient. Natural waters, sometimes from thermal springs, are also prescribed.

Death and Afterlife.   Details of any belief in an afterlife other than the Christian heaven are unknown. The fact that individuals are buried with some of their personal belongings may be indicative of a belief that utilitarian items will be needed in an afterworld.

See also Ngawbe

Bibliography

Herrera, Francisco A., and Raúl González (1964). "Informe sobre una investigación etnográfica entre los indios bogotá de Bocas del Toro." *Hombre y Cultura* 1(3): 56–81.

Torres de Araúz, Reina (1980). "Bokotas (Buglere)." In *Panamá indígena*, 295–311. Panama City: Instituto Nacional de Cultura, Patrimonio Histórico.

Wassén, S. Henry (1952). "Some Remarks on the Divisions of the Guaymí Indians." In *Indian Tribes of Aboriginal America: Selected Papers of the Twenty-Ninth International Congress of Americanists*, edited by Sol Tax, 271–280. Chicago: University of Chicago Press.

Wassén, S. Henry (1966). "Notas sobre la colección etnográfica de los indios bogotá (bukueta) de Panamá, existente en le Museo Etnográfico de Gotemburgo, Suecia." *Hombre y Cultura* 1(5): 3–26.

Young, Philip D. (1965). "Nota sobre afinidades lingüísticas entre bogotá y guaymí sabanero. *Hombre y Cultura* 1(4): 20–25.

PHILIP D. YOUNG

Cahita

THNOMYMS: Haqui, Mayo, Tehueco, Yaqui

Orientation

Identification.   "Cahita" refers to Cahitan speakers, members of the three modern ethnic or "tribal" groups in southern Sonora and northern Sinaloa, Mexico. The people themselves would not recognize this term but use "Yoreme" (Yaqui: Yoeme, indigenous peoples) to designate themselves and the term "Yori" to mark mestizos (non-Indian Mexicans). The terms "Yaqui" and "Mayo" appear to have been drawn from the river valleys of the same names. The Spanish mistakenly applied the native term *kahita* (nothing) to the indigenous language. Apparently, when the local people were asked the name of the language they spoke, they replied "kaita," meaning "nothing" or "it has no name."

Location.   Located around 27° N and 109° W, the modern Cahitans include: the Yaqui, inhabiting the central coast of the state of Sonora in northwest Mexico; the Mayo, living south of the Yaqui along the southern coast of Sonora and the northern coast of Sinaloa; and other smaller dialect groups such as the Tehueco, who have been mainly absorbed by the Mayo. Many Yaqui inhabit a special reservation area, whereas Mayo live interspersed with mestizos. Lack of archaeological research in the area makes it difficult to delineate a precontact Cahitan territory, although since Spanish contact Mayo-Yaqui territory has remained stable, with the exception of the gradual reduction in control over the territory. Modern Cahitan territory reflects a dramatic contrast between the fertile Yaqui, Mayo, and Fuerte irrigation areas, with their fantastic agricultural production and high population density, and the sparsely settled thorn-forest desert areas, with abundant wild fruits, woods, and fauna. This hot coastal area is characterized by long periods of dry weather broken by heavy summer thundershowers and more sustained lighter winter rains producing between 40 to 80 centimeters of precipitation per year.

Demography. At the time of Spanish contact, there were over 100,000 Cahitans, with the Yaqui and the Mayo accounting for 60,000 of the total; the 1950 census lists slightly over 30,000 Mayo speakers, and the Yaqui numbered about 15,000 in the 1940s. The 1970 census lists almost 28,000 Mayo speakers. These figures could well be doubled, however, because of the present dispersal of these peoples throughout Sonora and southern Arizona and the difficulty in identifying them as separate populations.

Linguistic Affiliation. The Mayo, Tehueco, and Yaqui dialects constitute the Cahitan Subfamily of the Uto-Aztecan Stock. The Mayo and the Yaqui have no difficulty communicating with each other, as the dialects are similar, and Tehueco is even closer to Mayo than is Yaqui. Today the Mayo write in Mayo, although in the precontact period, Cahitan does not seem to have been a written language.

History and Cultural Relations

Gaps in the information available and changes through time have produced shifting Cahitan natural, social, and cultural boundaries, the histories of which are not completely clear. Today Mayo-speaking peoples are concentrated along the lower Mayo and Fuerte river valleys, with the Tehueco in the higher Río Fuerte area and the Yaqui concentrated in the lower Río Yaqui area. Throughout this Cahitan area (chiefly the coastal plain of southern Sonora and of northern Sinaloa, embracing the three river valleys), Cahitan social and cultural boundaries are marked primarily by dialect spoken and social and ceremonial labor and exchange.

Within this general area, considerable family movement exists, with numbers of modern Mayo families living in Yaqui territory and vice versa, and Río Mayo living in the Fuerte area and vice versa. Cahitan individuals participate in Mexican institutions such as schools, _ejidos_ (land-holding units established by the government after the 1910 Revolution), markets, the army, and the Institutional Revolutionary party (PRI), simply as peasant farmers. With little hope of upward mobility in the Mexican system, many Cahitans prefer to seek prestige within their traditional culture and society. The Cahitans have either reestablished old associations, as in the case of the traditional "Eight Yaqui Pueblos," or are adapting and revitalizing others, as in the case of the new Mayo religious movements, which continue to appear in the 1990s.

Settlements

Modern Cahitan culture is that of embedded groups. Precontact Cahitans, however, lived in loose clusters of buildings (rancherías) usually housing fewer than 300 related individuals, although a few may have reached 1,000 persons. During the missionization, the Jesuits concentrated Cahitans into seven or eight Mayo and an equal number of Yaqui church towns of some 2,000 to 3,000 persons. Today many Yaquis live on the reservation, although Mayo family settlements are characterized by several patterns: several hundred scattered rancherías, more than forty small villages of one to several hundred people, urban districts in the four larger Mexican towns, and ejido communities.

Economy

Precontact Cahitans relied on river flooding to water crops of maize, beans, and squashes, but modern farmers irrigate their fields of cotton, wheat, and safflower. Even today Cahitans still use the remaining wild desert areas to supply some variety in their diet—deer, small game, fish, shellfish, fruits of numerous cacti, beans of the mesquite, agave, and many other seed- and fruit-producing plants. Working as small-scale farmers, wage laborers, and fishermen, they borrow money from banks, request irrigation water from the hydro commission, and plant the recommended commercial crops. With cash or credit from the sale of their crops or fish, the Mayo and the Yaqui purchase much of their food, clothing, and household items in the local mestizo markets. The Cahitan concept of wealth itself is dual in nature: land, farm produce, and modern Mexican material goods stand opposed to respect and Holy Flowers. One should give freely of the productivity of one's fields in support of Cahitan ceremonialism and thus achieve respect in this world and heavenly rewards after death.

Subsistence and Commercial Activities. Modern Cahitan technology and subsistence focus upon farming, fishing, and wage labor. Before the Conquest, Cahitans raised two food crops per year, fished, and collected wild foods that constituted perhaps up to 40 percent of their diet. Jesuit missionaries introduced sheep, goats, and cattle as well as wheat and irrigation agriculture but did not basically change the Cahitan economy. Modern irrigation and farming technology, however, have dramatically modified Cahitan subsistence.

Industrial Arts. Most families own a _jacal_ (mud thatch) or adobe dwelling with a separate cooking room, a table, chairs, folding cots or wooden beds, a set of enamel or glass bowls and cups and enamel spoons, and a wooden trunk for pictures, valuables, and documents. A few individuals, chiefly among the Mayo, still weave blankets and _petates_ (split-cane mats), make pottery, and carve ceremonial masks and wooden utensils.

Trade. Besides farming, most households raise chickens and some keep pigs, turkeys, and cows. The pigs are generally sold, but the cows are often butchered for fiesta contributions and ceremonial exchanges.

Division of Labor. Age and sex provide the major dimensions in the division of labor. The major production roles are carried out by young adults within households, which are the major production and consumption units. Among the adults, labor was divided along gender lines, with women collecting wild foods and caring for household production while men hunted and farmed. This division of labor still exists, although both adult men and women will work for wages in the fields when such work is available. A few of the women are trained as weavers and _cantoras_ (singers who accompany the _maestros_), and a few men fill the roles of maestro (chanter and lay minister) and *maso* (deer) dancer and *paskola* (ceremonial) dancer and musician. A healthy household with a larger percentage of young adults will grow in wealth and influence. In general, however, no long-term, wealth-based stratification system has developed to separate households and provide the basis for a more complex division of labor.

Land Tenure.   About three-fourths of the rural families hold small parcels of land, either as private holdings or as ejido members. In the larger villages and towns, however, often as many as one-half or more of the families in the community hold no lands at all. Ejido membership (*socio*) and rights to land carried by membership are inherited and can be passed to a wife or a daughter as well as to a son, as stipulated by the socio.

Kinship

Kin Groups and Descent.   Traditional and modern Cahitan kin-group organization is based upon the nuclear family, the extended family, the household, the ceremonial kin group, and ceremonial-center membership. It has been suggested (Spicer 1969, 839) that the precontact social organization was characterized by bilateral descent, bifurcate-collateral with Hawaiian cousin kinship terminology, local-group (ranchería) exogamy, suprarranchería political organization only during periods of warfare, and a council of ranchería elders in peacetime. Spicer finds no evidence of precontact unilineal descent groups among the Yaqui.

Kinship Terminology.   Although the traditional kinship terminology probably was bifurcate collateral with an emphases on the relative age of ones parents' and one's own siblings, today many families utilize a modified Mexican kinship terminology, lineal and Eskimo, with Cahitan terms applied to parents, siblings, and children and Spanish terms for aunts, uncles, cousins, and in-laws.

Ceremonial kinship is still extremely important, with godparents selected at times of birth, marriage, and ceremonial participation. Cahitan terms are used for godparents and godchildren. Groups of coparents become crucial cooperative units, especially in ceremonial contexts.

Marriage and Family

Marriage.   In the past a wedding was an elaborate household ritual, although more recently it has become simpler or is omitted either when a couple elopes or at the time of a second or third union, when the couple simply begins living together. No clear postmarital residence rules have been discovered, although many Mayo express strong matrilocal preferences—"Our daughter should stay at home." In fact, this is not a clear social pattern, as couples often opt for a pragmatic solution. Formal divorce is unusual among the Cahita, owing to earlier years of high death rates and revolution, but many individuals have experienced the death of a first spouse and eventually begin living with a second or third spouse. Others simply run away and begin living with someone else. There is much joking and gossip about those who have multiple spouses. Although this practice is not permissible within the formal Catholic church, multiple women living in the household of an especially well-known individual have been observed. This suggests that polygyny was an accepted pattern in precontact times.

Domestic Unit.   The household, consisting of related nuclear and extended families, is the basic domestic unit. Related individuals living in a room or rooms around a common cooking area constitute the household. The household was traditionally the scene of the major passage rituals of birth, marriage, and death as well as that of socialization of the children and the major work area of the mature women.

Inheritance.   With very little except lands and a household plot to inherit, inheritance is very informal. The few items of material culture are shared among the closest relatives, especially the members of the household.

Socialization.   Initial socialization takes place within the household, the children being raised by parents, kin, and then as they mature, by siblings. As children approach 6 years of age, they not only enter school but also dance as Matachines (a church dance sodality) and take part in the Lenten processions and Easter-week rituals. In the household, children are taught honesty, truthfulness, and the value of fulfilling promises. "Good words" are much preferred over physical punishment, which is rarely administered.

Sociopolitical Organization

Social Organization.   Cahitan society is organized according to age and gender. The elderly are perceived as powerful and highly respected. The division of labor tends to separate young and middle-aged adults along gender lines, with women having a status equal to but different from that of men. This contrasts sharply with the typical Latin machismo complex.

These principles provide the bases of family organization, which is articulated with the local ceremonial center through a range of political and ceremonial sodalities.

Political Organization.   Goh Naike Pueblo Juracionim (the eight pueblo jurisdictions) exist among both the Mayo and the Yaqui, although in the latter case the pueblos are autonomous units. The Mexican government provides services, schools, roads, an irrigation system and water, health clinics, and so forth. The Jesuit missionaries emphasized membership in certain ceremonial sodalities and introduced a more complex pattern of village government. The Yaqui have elaborated and conserved this political system. Mayo village government has been absorbed by the modern Mayo church-ceremonial center organization: Mayo political organization was disrupted by the Revolution to the extent that, by the 1960s, no secular Mayo government existed; the Mayo had turned to their religious system as a way of organizing their society beyond the level of the family (see "Religious Beliefs").

Social Control.   For the Cahita, social control is shared between the Mexican institutions and the more traditional village government. The modern Yaqui town organization is based on five integrated realms of authority: civil, church, military, fiesta, and Holy Week customs, each with its own set of ranked officers. Decisions are made at open meetings of this town council.

Conflict. Conflict is either repressed or resolved by the church-center government or by the Mexican authorities, such as the local sheriff.

Religion and Expressive Culture

Religious Beliefs. Contemporary Cahitan beliefs are a unique and complex fusion of indigenous traditions, Jesuit teachings, and nineteenth- and twentieth-century Mexican culture. The Yaqui pueblo political organization is tightly integrated with the ceremonial and mythical systems. The modern Mayo church-pueblo organization consists of several sodalities: five church governors and five helpers; the lay ministers; the Matachini dance sodality; the Parisero sodality (the Lenten masked male society); and the Paskome (*fiesteros*), who promise to serve the patron saint of the church.

The realms of nature and the supernatural are also organized as a family, with God (Our Father) identified with the sun, the Virgin (Our Mother) equated with the moon, and Jesus (the Child of Our Father and Our Mother). The animals of the forest are the Children of the Old Man of the Forest, and the fish are the Children of the Old Woman of the Sea.

Religious Practitioners. The Cahitan religious organization requires several part-time specialists, such as the maestro, or lay minister, who "prays for the dead"; cantora or female chanting assistant to the maestro; deer and paskola dancers and musicians, who entertain at the fiestas; Matachinim, church dancers and their musicians; Pahkome and Parisero sodality members, who maintain the yearly and Lenten ritual cycles; and *yorem medikom* (curers), who mediate between humans and the gods.

Ceremonies. Among the Cahitans, saints'-day fiestas or ceremonies are celebrated with prayer, feasting, fireworks, and the entertainment of masked paskola and deer dancers and musicians. Especially elaborate are the Lenten and Holy Week ceremonies, which are characterized by masked Pariseros who crucify Jesus and ultimately are destroyed by the power of God as Christ returns to the church from the land of the dead. In the Mayo-Yaqui ceremonial cycle, the Easter ceremonial is followed by village ceremonies for the Holy Cross, the Holy Spirit and Holy Trinity, Saint John, the Virgin of Guadalupe and, early in November, for the returning dead (Animam Velaroa).

Arts. A range of art forms is still dynamic among modern Cahitans, including paskola and deer dancing, deer and secular songs, *alabanzas* (various Mayo, Spanish, and Latin hymns) sung by maestros and cantoras, the decoration of altars and the images of saints, and weaving styles and designs.

Medicine. Social Security clinics and hospitals for ejido members, private doctors, and yorem medikom provide assistance to ill Cahitans. Medicines are available in clinics and from drugstores, market herbalists, and the thorn forest. Illnesses are attributed to natural causes; fright; problems with God, the saints, the dead, and bad wishers (witches); and violation of the hot/cold principles.

Death and Afterlife. The funeral rituals are the most important life-cycle events. Cahitans have a dual set of societal rituals associated with death and the dead: 1 and 2

November (All Souls' and All Saints' days, Animam Velaroa) and Lent. For the Mayo, there is a very close relationship between the family, the ritual for the dead early in November, and the form, structure, and meaning of the Lenten ritual. Rooted in this model, the Mayo continue to experience visitations of Our Father and Our Mother and, to avoid the wrath, punishment, and destruction promised by Our Father, who is angry with the secular state of the modern world, continue to innovate ceremonies in honor of God and the saints.

See also Yaqui

Bibliography

Beals, Ralph L. (1945). *The Contemporary Culture of the Cáhita Indians.* Bureau of American Ethnology Bulletin 142. Washington, D.C.: Smithsonian Institution.

Crumrine, N. Ross (1988). *The Mayo Indians of Sonora, Mexico: A People Who Refuse to Die.* Reissued with a new postscript and references. Prospect Heights, Ill.: Waveland Press.

Spicer, Edward H. (1969). "The Yaqui and Mayo." In *Handbook of Middle American Indians,* edited by Robert Wauchope. Vol. 8, *Ethnology, Part Two,* edited by Evon Z. Vogt, 830–845. Austin: University of Texas Press.

Spicer, Edward H. (1980). *The Yaquis: A Cultural History.* Tucson: University of Arizona Press.

N. ROSS CRUMRINE

Carib of Dominica

ETHNONYMS: Carifuna, Garifuna, Island Carib

Orientation

Identification. The Carib of Dominica constitute much of what remains of the Native American occupants of the Lesser Antilles at the time of Columbus. Having migrated from the South American mainland, they were in the process of replacing the Arawak when European interference ended their Caribbean expansion. Presently living within the Carib Territory (formerly the Carib Reserve), the Dominican Carib constitute a distinct ethnic minority within the largely Creole population of this West Indian island. Dominican Carib are a mixed-race population, as are many other Dominicans. "Carib" are those Dominicans who have at least one Carib parent and are affiliated with a Carib Territory residence.

Location. The Carib Territory, with an area of less than 16 square kilometers, is located on the east coast of Dominica. Prior to the coming of English and French settlers to the region, this mountainous island was not considered particularly attractive as a Carib home base. As Carib were displaced from other islands, they found a haven in the rugged topography of Dominica, where very few Whites had settled. The Carib sought to avoid detection and attack by European soldiers by establishing settlements and gardens on the isolated windward coast. As a result, the Carib Territory contains no flat land nor any of the island's several rivers and bays, and its shoreline consists mostly of cliffs. By 1900 Dominica was the only island containing a significant number of Carib, and a reservation was established by the English governor at that time to protect this declining ethnic enclave.

Demography. The 1992 population of Dominican Carib was approximately 3,000. They are generally in good health and expanding rapidly, having increased from less than 2,000 in 1975. In the 1930s only about 400 people occupied the Carib Reserve. At the beginning of the twentieth century, there may have been as few as twenty Carib families in all of Dominica. The Carib have been increasing in numbers far more rapidly than has the predominantly Creole population of Dominica.

Linguistic Affiliation. The traditional language, Carifuna or Garifuna, has been retained by Carib populations in Venezuela and by Black Carib in Belize, Honduras, and Guatemala, but in Dominica only a few words have been retained by some individuals or reintroduced. There have been no Dominican speakers of the native language since about 1920. All but a few of the oldest residents of the Carib Territory now speak English, and nearly everyone speaks both English and a creole French patois. The usual pattern is that children first learn what is locally called "broken French" and in school learn English, the language of instruction. The French patois, generally understood throughout rural Dominica, is also commonly spoken in the neighboring French islands of Martinique and Guadeloupe.

History and Cultural Relations

Prior to European domination of the Caribbean, the Carib frequently captured Arawak women, who retained much of their own language and culture as Carib wives. With the importation of slaves into the region, many Africans were incorporated into island Carib populations. French Catholic missionaries lived with the Carib beginning in the seventeenth century but claimed very few converts. In this same period, Carib raiding parties from Dominica attacked early White settlements on other islands, in some cases inflicting heavy casualties. Spanish slavers captured some Carib, and European soldiers attempted to exterminate Carib populations on various islands, including Dominica. Eventually, the Carib either died out on other islands, were transported elsewhere, or resettled in Dominica. In the late 1700s, after two centuries of hostile relations with Europeans, the small remnant Carib population on Dominica was generally ignored by the planters who had settled on the west coast. There was far more interaction between the Carib and African Maroons who lived in the interior. By 1850 Carib culture was generally similar to that of other rural Dominicans. Today Carib language and life-

style are nearly indistinguishable from that of their Creole neighbors.

Settlements

A few families were living in thatch houses in the mid-1980s, but now all structures within the Carib Territory are typical of those found throughout the island, including many that are largely of hand-cut lumber and, increasingly, of concrete. Houses tend to be a bit more scattered than is the case elsewhere, many preferring to live some distance from any neighbors. There are no Carib villages, only single residences and clusters of houses, located near the main road or reachable only by footpath.

Economy

Subsistence and Commercial Activities. The major source of income for most residents of the Carib Territory is banana farming. Some subsistence crops continue to be raised by most households, but since the 1970s there has been a growing trend to purchase more and more of the food consumed. A very few Carib have steady employment that frees them from having to farm. Several others are self-employed as truck drivers, shopkeepers, carpenters, and masons. The Carib council established a food shop, an auto-repair shop, and a concrete-block making operation in the 1980s, and a few Carib own and run small stores as family businesses.

Industrial Arts. Some Carib work part-time making canoes and baskets for sale to outsiders, and a few continue to make canoes and baskets for their own use, but both practices are declining. These canoes are used for fishing in the sea, but only in calm weather, and most fishing expeditions merely acquire enough for the households of the fishermen and perhaps a few relatives. Surpluses are sold to any who gather on the beach at the end of the day. Until 1980 or so, most males were experienced at cutting lumber from local trees and constructing homes. Today, however, more and more new homes are being built of concrete and imported lumber.

Trade. Aside from selling farm goods to outside merchants, some households trade baskets and a few canoes, the only other important exchange items.

Division of Labor. In the past, Carib culture was characterized by a clear sexual hierarchy and a strict division of labor, women having exclusive responsibility for cultivating, harvesting, and processing food. Today women are less politically dependent, and men share fully in agricultural production. Until the mid-1960s, men still relied on friends to help them clear new gardens in the forest and perform other heavy labor such as house building, but modern houses now last much longer and chemical fertilizer enables today's farmers to cultivate the same garden plot for many years before it becomes necessary to clear new land. Young women and adolescent girls are expected to do laundry, carry water, perform kitchen chores, clean house, and care for younger siblings and other close relatives. In contrast, young men and adolescent boys have much leisure for games and idleness. They work very hard at specific tasks, but they are not kept nearly as busy as their female counterparts.

Land Tenure. The Carib have consistently resisted privatizing landholdings. Even though gardens and house sites are considered "owned" by individuals, no deeds or legal titles exist for such holdings within the Carib Territory. Prior to the independence of Dominica in 1978, this land was a reservation, but collective title is now held by the Carib council. Because of a lack of surveys, there are frequent internal boundary disputes between farmers who cultivate adjoining gardens.

Kinship

Kin Groups and Descent. Social networks of friends and selected relatives structure personal relationships far more than do any exclusive kin-based groups. Which relatives an individual turns to for assistance of any sort depends on personal preferences and calculations rather than any standardized kinship roles. Most children are given the father's surname, and most maintain far stronger ties to the mother than to the father, but the Carib kinship system is bilateral. Godparent/godchild relationships are common and usually considered binding. The only corporate kin-based groups are households.

Kinship Terminology. Carib kinship terminology differs little from that found throughout the English-speaking Western Hemisphere. Common-law spouses are usually identified as "boyfriend" and "girlfriend" rather than by kin terms. The term "mother" may be used by a child in reference to anyone given major responsibility for that child's care, whether she is a birth parent's sister or mother or even an otherwise unrelated female.

Marriage and Family

Marriage. Roughly two-thirds of all Carib infants are born to unwed mothers and are referred to by their parents as "illegitimate." Sexual relationships before marriage are expected and accepted. Those that may eventually lead to marriage begin casually, long before a couple establishes a common residence. Formal marriage usually is initiated only after a couple has had one or more children and has lived together for some time. Where each couple establishes a new home depends more on economic calculations than on any kinship-based rule of residence; however, married Carib show a slight preference for locating near the husband's kin. Because most Carib marry individuals from their own neighborhood, couples usually live near relatives of both partners.

Domestic Unit. Household composition is highly variable and shifts over time. Most domestic units contain one (but only one) couple, married or consensually cohabiting, one child or more, and at least one additional relative such as a grandparent.

Inheritance. Property inherited from a parent or other relative is usually divided among children, males and females alike, sometimes while the owner is still living. Much confusion and disputing attend inheritance, since wills are the exception. One sibling may inherit a piece of land and another may inherit the fruit or coconut trees that grow on that land. Houses are usually left to the couple residing there at the time of the owner's death.

Socialization. The care and instruction of a young child is a responsibility shared by many. A mother, grandmother, or other relative may be designated as the primary caretaker of a given child, but others, especially older siblings, are likely to play an active supporting role. If one's mother is very young or employed elsewhere, a more mature aunt or a grandmother may assume the role of mother. On days when the mother is in the hills gardening or on shopping trips to the city, a child is likely to be left in the care of an older sister, half-sister, or cousin. Girls are expected to be interested in schoolwork but willing to skip school to care for preschoolers. Young boys are considered less inclined to take an active interest in school, and very few domestic demands are made on them, in contrast to their sisters. When they are about 8 years old, parental permissiveness declines sharply, and they are likely to receive a great deal of teasing and arbitrary chastisement as well as physical bullying from older brothers. Either parent may administer corporal punishment for any action considered disrespectful, but discipline in young boys is neither anticipated nor highly valued, and adolescent boys are considered too old to be advised by their elders. All children are enrolled in school, but attendance is irregular, standards and expectations are low, and most drop out by age 15.

Sociopolitical Organization

Social Organization. Voluntary organizations such as adult sports teams, Boy Scout troops, commercial cooperatives, and church congregations provide some structure to social activities, but most of these are short-lived and involve relatively few individuals. Even though adults who live together do not usually pool their belongings, households structure much of the economic activities of members. Dyadic ties between friends are perhaps far more instrumental in shaping the daily activities of most adults, however, especially those of men.

Political Organization. The elected Carib council and Carib chief symbolically represent the Carib people to outsiders, but they have limited power and influence within the territory. There are named neighborhoods within the territory but no corporate communities. The Carib have had a representative in the national parliament since 1975. Political parties vie for Carib loyalties before national elections, but the Carib are neither well represented nor well organized as a political force. At times when the special political status of the Carib Territory was considered to be under attack, however, the residents have shown that they have the capacity to coalesce and act in unison. Presently, there is much consensus that less interference and more funding by the national government would be welcome.

Social Control. Until the mid-twentieth century, a strong ethos of egalitarianism was generally accepted by all Carib, but this attitude has been compromised by an unevenly rising standard of living within the territory. Although jealousy and accusations of witchcraft continue to operate as social-control mechanisms that encourage more sharing of individual wealth, these controls are now least effective when directed at relatively rich Carib. A national police post was established in the Carib Reserve in 1930; these police had little to do in the past, but today a sharp rise in reports of theft keeps them busy.

Conflict. The Carib chief is often described as being responsible for settling disputes among the people, but his role in this regard is very limited. Increasingly, individuals turn to the Dominican court system for addressing grievances with other Carib. Adults often gossip viciously about offending neighbors, and fights sometimes break out between drunken men or jealous women. Bystanders are likely to consider such behavior a great source of entertainment. Many Carib believe that neighbors who live too close to each other are more likely to have disputes, and there are many examples illustrative of such conflicts.

Religion and Expressive Culture

Religious Beliefs. Carib beliefs in supernatural forces involve some retention of traditional elements, a long history of Catholic influence, more recent Christian missionary endeavors, and generalized West Indian folklore. Most Carib consider themselves Catholics and continue to have babies baptized by the local priest, but they express little interest in Catholic theology. A growing number have become affiliated with U.S.-based Protestant fundamentalists. Numerous maladies continue to be attributed to witches, but fear of witchcraft is diminishing. The Carib believe that Creoles are the most dangerous witches. Children are told stories about the wondrous magical powers of their Indian ancestors. In the mid-twentieth century, the Carib still relied on magic to protect their gardens from theft, but such remedies are no longer considered effective.

Ceremonies. Religious rituals are performed in churches, but most Carib seldom attend a church service. The Baptists sometimes have a public baptism to initiate new members; these, however, attract very few participants or spectators.

Arts. Traditional drumming has all but died out because the Carib now prefer the music they hear on the radio. Some of the baskets they make, especially those for sale, are aesthetically enhanced by coloring, and some attempts have been made to produce additional arts and crafts for the tourist trade. As art supplies and photographic equipment have become more obtainable, some interest in painting and photography has begun to emerge.

Medicine. The availability of modern medicine has eroded faith in magical cures. The last remaining medicine woman has died, but many still experiment with herbal cures, and some older residents insist that certain formulas are particularly reliable. Many, especially pregnant women and women with babies, take advantage of the services of a local public-health nurse and clinics staffed by a visiting doctor. Maladies that fail to respond to modern medical treatment are likely to be attributed to witchcraft.

Death and Afterlife. When someone dies at home, as is usually the case, the body is laid out and neighbors are encouraged to drop in. Funerals, at which the corpse is buried in a cemetery, are modest; but wakes are far more elaborate, involving a large number of family, friends, and even strangers who may wish to come by if only for food, drink, and games. There is general agreement that the dead have an afterlife, but there seems to be no clear picture of what such an existence entails.

Bibliography

Johnson, Tim (1990). "Carib Gallery." *Northeast Indian Quarterly* 7(3).

Layng, Anthony (1979). "Religion among the Caribs." *Caribbean Review* 8(2).

Layng, Anthony (1980). "Ethnic Identity, Population Growth, and Economic Security on a West Indian Reservation." *Revista/Review Interamericana* 9(4).

Layng, Anthony (1983). *The Carib Reserve: Identity and Security in the West Indies*. Lanham, Md.: University Press of America.

Layng, Anthony (1985). "The Caribs of Dominica: Prospects for Structural Assimilation of a Territorial Minority." *Ethnic Groups* 6(2-3): 209-221.

Owen, Nancy (1975). "Land, Politics, and Ethnicity in a Carib Indian Community." *Ethnology* 14(4): 385-393.

ANTHONY LAYNG

Cattle Ranchers of the Huasteca

ETHNONYMS: mestizo rancheros, pequeños proprietarios, rancheros

Orientation

Identification and Location. The Spanish conquerors who landed in Mexico in the sixteenth century introduced new domesticated animals such as horses, donkeys, and cows. The spread of these Old World species, along with the arrival of colonists and colonizers, led to the emergence of new cultural patterns throughout the Americas. One such pattern is the cowboy complex, with its ranches, frontier mentality, and a cult celebrating male valor. The type of ranching and social relations among ranch owners, cowhands, and aboriginal peoples, however, vary from region to region. This discussion focuses on the cattle ranchers who live on the coastal plain of the Gulf of Mexico, especially in the Huasteca region.

The Huasteca consists of parts of the Mexican states of Hidalgo, Veracruz, Tamaulipas, and San Luis Potosí. Cattle raising is the mainstay of this predominantly rural region. There is very little industry or mining, and the only major urban centers are the port city of Tampico (in Tamaulipas) and Ciudad Valles (in San Luis Potosí). Although various agricultural activities are undertaken, the production of cattle is not only preeminent, but the one best known to outsiders. Moreover, for at least a hundred years, the cattle producers of this region, known as *rancheros*, have constituted a dominant group in terms of both economic power and political control. Their worldview and values reflect and help to maintain their hegemony over this geographical and cultural region where most other people, even those who do not own or necessarily work in cattle ranches, identify with or try to emulate the life-style of the rancheros.

This entire Gulf coast region is characterized by a high degree of intermingling of cultures and races, yet ethnic boundaries persist. Almost all the rancheros are mestizos (Spanish speakers of racially mixed descent). Identifying themselves as *gente de razón* (lit., "people with reason"), these rancheros differentiate themselves from their more agriculturally oriented indigenous (Amerindian) neighbors. Some rancheros—especially those descended from recent European immigrants—add the designation "White." Nevertheless, rancheros have almost the same customs, eating habits, and material culture as both Spanish-speaking and indigenous (Nahua and Huastec) peasants in the region.

Most of the Huasteca, which is traversed by the tributaries of several rivers, was once cut off from the rest of Mexico. Until the 1970s there were few passable roads, and travel was by foot or on horseback. The topography consists of the narrow coastal plain and the foothills and lower valleys of the Sierra Madre. This region used to be covered with lush forest. Since the time of the Conquest, however, cattle production has gradually transformed the landscape into a vast expanse of grassland used for grazing. These pastures were created as a result of the clearing of trees through slash-and-burn cultivation. Today, the remaining tree cover is heavier along the inland mountain fringe. Precipitation is distributed over two rainy seasons (one in the late spring and another in the fall), and the average level of ground moisture gradually declines as one travels from south to north. Much of the area is extremely hot and humid, especially between April and October.

Demography. The Huasteca has long been seen as a frontier, with untapped resources and few people. This image still fits reality to some extent since the overall population density is much lower than that of central Mexico. For example, the Huasteca average in 1970 was around 40 inhabitants per square kilometer, compared to over 120 for the state of Morelos. There are large internal discrepancies as well: the flatter, northwestern portion has the lowest population densities; the more mountainous southeastern rim more closely approximates the population profile of central Mexico. In the latter subregion, Spanish-speaking cattle ranchers interact with the indigenous peasant population on almost a daily basis. It is impossible to calculate exactly how many rancheros live on the Gulf coast. Based on the extrapolation of figures included in a Huasteca regional study carried out in the late 1970s, one can arrive at a very rough estimate of 30,000 rancheros (counting only heads of ranchero households), assuming that each ranchero had about fifty head of cattle. If one further assumes an average of 6 persons per household, members of ranchero households represented 10 percent of a total population of close to 2 million people at that time. This estimate does not include the many relatives of rancheros

working as cowhands or engaged full time in other occupations.

Linguistic Affiliation. The mother tongue of ranchers in the Huasteca is the local version of Mexican Spanish. Depending on their degree of contact with indigenous peasants, mestizo rancheros may also be bilingual, as a result of having learned a second, native language (Nahuatl, Huasteco, Otomí, or Totonaco). Which language is used in daily intercourse depends on the context of ethnic relations, which ranges from coexistence to open conflict.

History and Cultural Relations

Cattle ranching in the Huasteca dates from the Conquest—specifically from the arrival of Nuño de Guzmán, a rival of Ferdinand Cortes. The first Spanish newcomers, who encountered a large native population along the coast and river valleys, captured numerous natives for slave labor in the West Indies and elsewhere. The rest of the indigenous population succumbed to new diseases or fled into the hills. In order to facilitate the collection of tribute, taxes, and corvée labor, the Spanish Crown later forced this dispersed native population to congregate into the remaining native towns and villages. At the same time that it recognized the boundaries of native corporate communities as delimitations of "Indian republics," the Spanish Crown granted large tracts of land left vacant to people of Spanish descent. The resulting privately owned estates specialized in extensive cattle production, and the incursion of wandering cows and horses onto the agricultural domain of native peasant communities became a source of bitter disputes. The introduction of sugarcane, locally processed in small-scale animal-powered mills called *trapiches*, stimulated the development of smaller rural enterprises known as *ranchos*. Such ranchos were located both within the boundaries of colonial cattle estates and on sections of communally owned land rented from native communities.

The fragile coexistence of cattle estates, ranchos, and native communities continued throughout the colonial era. During the early part of the nineteenth century (when Mexico became independent), the Huasteca attracted immigrants from the central-plateau region of Mexico and abroad. This influx brought about additional encroachment on Indian land as well as the subdivision of huge estates into the smaller, privately run ranchos. The newcomers introduced commercial crops (e.g., coffee and tobacco) and engaged in commerce and the production of sugar loaf (*pilón* or *piloncillo*). Almost all these entrepreneurs also established cattle ranches, resulting in the development of a ranchero culture. These rancheros gradually obtained more political control, which was consolidated during and after the Mexican Revolution (1910–1917). Mestizo cattle ranchers, who already controlled many smaller counties on the fringes of the Huasteca, ousted the remaining owners of larger cattle estates (haciendas), many of whom did not even live in the region.

Settlements

A unique pattern evolved during the period of frontier settlement and increasing contact between native peasants and mestizo newcomers. Newcomers originally built houses and corrals on their own land, resulting in a dispersed settlement pattern. These rancheros, however, many of whom often started off as merchants or artisans, usually kept a second house in a nearby town (*pueblo*), especially if such a town served as an important market center or the administrative center (*cabecera*) of a *municipio*. A new generation of rancheros born in the Huasteca countryside often bought town houses where they could stay when they made numerous trips on horseback to attend to business or to political affairs.

In areas with a large indigenous population, many ranchos were founded close to native communities (*comunidades*). In such cases, cattle ranchers demarcated the boundaries of their ranchos by means of fences. Nevertheless, the rancho's main house might well become part of the outskirts of an expanding native settlement. This form of shared settlement was especially likely to occur if the rancho was located inside the original communal boundaries of native villages, whose poorer inhabitants ended up working for the rancheros. Such close proximity led to the virtual transformation of larger native villages into mestizo towns, as the owners of ranchos set up business and started building houses in existing native centers. In more remote areas, rancheros allowed both Spanish-speaking newcomers and native peasants to build huts and cultivate corn plots (*milpas*) on their privately owned land, in return for seasonal help in running the ranch. Although technically tenants or sharecroppers, such part-time rural laborers developed de facto settlements of their own within the boundaries of many larger ranchos. A ranchero's trusted employee (often a poor relative) might eventually establish his own rancho and obtain a separate land title. Overtime and part-time workers as well as poor relatives of such new, independent rancheros might in turn create additional rural settlements or hamlets (*rancherías*). Such hamlets—some of which could again evolve into quite large villages—did not look that different from subordinate settlements within the communal lands under the jurisdiction of native towns. Even in the late twentieth century both mestizo and indigenous rancherías lack street plans; the houses are strung out along the side of a hill or on both sides of a stream.

Economy

The rancheros, whether nouveau-riche peasants or descendants of families who once owned large estates, are personally involved in a variety of productive and commercial activities. Even the most prosperous rancheros tend some of their own cattle, and they can all ride horseback. Although they participate in hard physical labor on occasion, the rancheros rely on day laborers or sharecroppers to clear their land and likewise employ wage laborers for most agricultural tasks and to operate trapiches. Small stills and stores owned by the rancheros are managed by their immediate relatives.

Subsistence and Commercial Activities. Even poor rancheros rent land to landless or land-poor peasants for the slash-and-burn cultivation of maize. Such farmers (who may also work as part-time cowhands) turn over part of their harvest to the landowner. In this way, the rancheros obtain maize for their own household consumption, for an-

imal fodder, or as a means of payment to part-time day laborers who cannot produce enough maize on their own. Such slash-and-burn cultivation of maize created most of the natural and cultivated pastures found in the Huasteca today. In more remote areas, rancheros used to drive their cattle into the fields of stubble after the maize harvest. Throughout the Huasteca, even in the late twentieth century, rancheros also make their own milpas, albeit with the "help" of day laborers. The harvested maize is dried and stored in bins or under the roof until it is ready to be ground into tortillas, just as in other parts of rural Mexico. Unlike native peasant farmers, however, rancheros—some of whom specialize in slaughtering cattle—produce their own meat (part of which is dried) and dairy products.

Although rancheros are largely self-sufficient in meat, cattle are kept mainly for commercial purposes. The finishing (fattening) of cattle is more prevalent on the lowland plain, whereas the breeding (raising) of cattle—together with limited dairy production—is concentrated in the foothills and mountain valleys. In both subregions, cattle are left in open pastures (as opposed to stables and barns), and commercial agriculture or growing oranges is a secondary source of profits. The introduction of new techniques, beginning in the 1940s, has led to greater productivity. Leading ranchers have introduced new breeds of cattle (especially the tick-resistant Cebu variety) and rotate their grazing cattle between sections of fenced-in pastures planted with special grasses. Such pastures still need occasional weeding (*chapoleo*), which is carried out by seasonal workers; however, the more specialized ranchero economy has overall become less labor intensive.

Industrial Arts. There is little specialization in industrial arts, although most rancheros used to run small-scale sugar mills (*trapiches*); these have only survived in native regions. Some rancheros also used to combine ranching with such crafts as shoe repair or blacksmithing. Huasteca ranchero families of Italian descent used to specialize in making the copper vats and other equipment required to convert sugar loaf (*pilón*) into *aguardiente* (a potent brandy). Wealthy rancheros, who also bought up pilón from native producers, once monopolized this activity.

Trade. The buying, selling, and transporting of both local agricultural produce and manufactured goods produced outside the region has long been an important sideline for the rancheros. Some eventually became almost full-time merchants, leaving the management of ranchos in the hands of other family members. Most rancheros began their careers in commerce working as independent mule drivers until they could hire others to take care of transportation. Ranchero merchants still bring in most of the luxury goods for sale at local marketplaces, but they tend to specialize in buying coffee and pilón produced by small indigenous enterprises. Such commercial activities are often based on the extension of informal credit; some wealthy rancheros became notorious usurers. In the late twentieth century these ranchero merchants are more likely to own and operate trucks, which, when not fully loaded, also carry passengers as standees.

Division of Labor. The rancho is characterized by the traditional sexual division of labor. Women therefore tend the cattle, and they still do most of the milking and cheese making. Some ranchero women also operate stores and small restaurants, and widows often manage entire cattle ranches on their own. School-aged children from ranchero families used to work part time side by side with ranch peons to learn all aspects of rural production, although nowadays they are more likely to attend agricultural schools. It is not unusual for poor relatives of powerful rancheros to specialize in mule driving, horse taming, or bringing cattle to distant markets. The more educated offspring of rancheros might become physicians or lawyers, yet still get involved in cattle raising as a sideline.

Land Tenure. Rancheros see their ranchos as small, privately owned rural properties. They refer to themselves as *pequeños proprietarios* (small property holders), although the actual amount of land under the control of a single person may vary from a dozen to well over a thousand hectares. The legal aspects of land tenure are more complicated, however. Owners of very small ranchos often do not have proper titles because they cannot afford to pay land taxes or the legal fees to obtain proper documentation. In some cases, their ranches may even be located in what are de jure communal lands associated with Nahua or Huastec villages. On the other hand, much of the legally registered private rural property in the Huasteca used to be part of much larger estates owned jointly by numerous ranchero families in a form of corporate ownership known as *condueñazgo*.

Kinship

As in many agrarian societies, landownership, politics, and kinship are closely interconnected.

Kin Groups, Descent, and Kinship Terminology. Strictly speaking, mestizo rancheros do not have corporate kinship groups. Nevertheless, their large extended families, many of whom may enter into joint business ventures, often function as political "clans." A good example is the influential Santos family, which ruled the San Luis Potosí portion of the Huasteca for several generations. As in other parts of Latin America, Spanish surnames are passed on through the male line, although both men and women obtain the paternal surname of their mother as well. Officially, all property is inherited through both the male and female lines, but the male offspring are more likely to gain access to the family estate.

As with other Spanish-speaking Mexicans, kinship terminology is of the lineal or Eskimo type (as is the case for most speakers of European languages). People in the Huasteca, however, distinguish between close, usually first, cousins (*primos hermanos*) and more distant primos. This emphasis on differing degrees of proximity is consistent with the large size of extended families and the even more extensive network of in-laws and relatives.

Ties with both distant relatives and friends or neighbors can be strengthened by the well-known Latin American institution of *compadrazgo* (coparenthood). This is a form of fictive kinship whereby one couple promises to help another after becoming godparents of their child or sponsoring another ritual for them. Rancheros can become compadres to other rancheros as well as to economic subordinates.

Marriage and Family

Marriage and Domestic Unit. The level of formality of marriage ceremonies reflects the political and economic importance of the respective partners. Poorer rancheros often practice common-law marriage. Moreover, it is not unusual or considered improper for wealthy ranchero men to form consensual unions with additional women even if the man is already legally married. Such de facto polygamy results in multiple households, either in the same settlement or in different localities, but never under a single roof or even close to one another. The norm is that a man should only engage in such multiple marriages if he can afford to maintain more than one family. Mestizo rancheros may select indigenous women as second wives.

Inheritance. Technically, all legitimate children have the right to inherit land from their parents; however, although grown children often build houses and set up households on the family estate, the land is rarely divided until after the original patriarch passes away. For this reason, young couples interested in setting up their own ranchos usually have to buy land elsewhere. Given the strong intrafamily competition over eventual inheritance of large ranchos, there is often rivalry among brothers and close cousins. For men, marriage with women who come from the same class of rancheros could mean greater access to land. By the same token, it is not to the advantage of these men to have their own sisters married to men who could become additional claimants to the family estate.

Socialization. Until about the mid-1940s, children learned most of their life skills at home and at work. For boys, in particular, this included exposure to cowboy techniques, shooting, and an attitude of paternalism and racial superiority vis-à-vis the native population. At the same time, ranchero children used to interact daily with both native and mestizo workers, with whom they shared many cultural traits. Rancheros usually received at least some formal education in rural one-room schools, but with the expansion of the modern school system and opportunities to study outside of the region, a younger generation of rancheros is becoming increasingly urban and cosmopolitan in terms of values, linguistic usage, and identity. Consequently, many ranchero families have moved permanently into town and only visit their rustic homes on rare occasions, leaving the management of their properties in the hands of a manager to whom they might not even be related. This absenteeism is leading to a growing social gap between the rancheros and their ranch hands or other economic subordinates living on their ranchos.

Sociopolitical Organization

Mestizo rancheros have always maintained strong links with the national society while preserving a separate regional identity. Although formally integrated into the national system, rancheros kept effective control over the Huasteca through an informal power structure known as *caciquismo* (strong-boss rule). This form of organization is also associated with other regions of Mexico but—together with the use of violence to eliminate political opponents—has been especially strong in the Huasteca. A personalistic form of politics, involving the activation of patron-client bonds by rival power holders, goes hand-in-hand with a high level of competition among leading families. Nevertheless, despite the periodic outbreaks of factional violence, the rancheros present a common front vis-à-vis outsiders, the Mexican state, and any threat to their class interests from below. Since the 1960s such social-class bonds have become institutionalized through a powerful regional cattlemen's association.

Social Control.   The ranchero way of life is rapidly being incorporated into mainstream Mexican culture. Nevertheless, social control on the local level can still be exercised by means of the threat of violence. An infamous figure in the Huasteca is the gunslinger (*pistolero*) who specializes in intimidation or assassination, usually at the behest of informal power holders. A high level of violence and the prevalence of cattle rustling and banditry in the past (especially in the period following the Mexican Revolution) put a premium on centralized control at both the municipal and regional level. While guaranteeing a minimum level of security for merchants and ranchers, as well as the public in general, the ranchero strong-bosses (caciques) of the Huasteca still had to use hired gunmen to implement their orders. Such caciques, even if they were working together with the government to "impose order," were prone to the abuse of authority. For example, ranchero politicians used to mobilize the peasant population into communal work parties to perform labor for the personal benefit of the cacique or to repair roads and put up buildings in mestizo centers, thus reducing the costs of local administration. More subtle forms of control were exercised through a ranchero value system that glorified machismo, strong leadership, and a disdain for more polite, urbane forms of social interaction.

Conflict.   Prior to the 1970s, family vendettas were the predominant form of social conflict. Such interfamily feuding is an expression of tensions associated with difficulties in finding economically suitable marriage partners and rivalry over potential common-law partners; open confrontations were more prevalent among young, unmarried men brought up in a culture that emphasized valor and manliness (machismo). Barroom-type brawls and open gun battles over "skirts and land" were a frequent occurrence. Since about 1970, open class confrontations between rancheros and poor peasant cultivators have become more prevalent, especially in more densely populated areas. Such class conflict developed at a time of increasing economic inequalities and growing differentiation of life-styles between the ranchero elite and their economic subordinates. Ironically, violent confrontations involving land invasions by angry peasants (or cowboys) started to occur at a time when town-based rancheros were becoming more educated and "civilized." In this situation, old-style pistoleros again had an opportunity to make a living by fighting on both sides.

Religion and Expressive Culture

Religious Beliefs.   Almost all Huasteca rancheros are nominally Roman Catholic, although some are quite anticlerical while others are devout. There is no tradition of some sons becoming priests, however, so there are few ranchero priests (compared to many ranchero teachers or doc-

tors). In terms of personal beliefs and practices, especially those concerning healing, traditional rancheros have a lot in common with the rest of the population. For example, rancheros are just as likely to consult native healers. Some rancheros also participate in the same religious ceremonies as mestizo and Nahua or Huastec peasants. Mestizo rancheros also celebrate the Huastec version of the Day of the Dead, as do other people from the region.

Arts.   Male rancheros in the Huasteca developed their own country-music tradition, consisting of improvisational vocal singing (*sones*) accompanied by a violin and a four-string and a five-string guitar. Verses sung with a high falsetto were ripe with sarcasm, satire, and humor. Several musical groups (*trios*) whose members came from ranchero families achieved national and even international fame. This music was played at all dances held in ranchos and rancherías throughout the Huasteca until about the mid-1970s. With the invasion of new, externally created styles of music and ballroom-style dancing, the traditional *huapango* dances fell into decline, to be performed for occasional folklore or school displays. This decline of ranchero-style music is another indication of the rapid ebbing of ranchero hegemony.

See also Nahua of the Huasteca

Bibliography

Falcón, Romana (1984). *Revolución y caciquismo: San Luis Potosí, 1910–1940.* Mexico City: El Colegio de México.

Feder, Ernest (n.d., ca. 1977). "Lean Cows, Fat Ranchers: The International Ramification of Mexico's Beef Cattle Industry." Preliminary chapter of a proposed book to appear in Spanish. Research Institute of the Berghof Institute for Conflict Research, Berlin.

Harnapp, Vern (n.d., ca. 1972). "The Huasteca Region Ranch Development Program." Unpublished report.

Harnapp, Vern (1978). "Landsat Imagery: A Tool for Updating Land Use in the Gulf Coast, Mexico." *Journal of Geography* 77:141–144.

Lomnitz-Adler, Claudio (1992). *Exits from the Labyrinth.* Berkeley and Los Angeles: University of California Press.

Meade, Joaquín (1962). *La Huasteca veracruzana.* Veracruz: Editorial Citlaltepetl.

Ortiz Wadgymar, Arturo (1977). "Ensayo sobre la ganadería huasteca." In *Las huastecas en le desarrollo regional de México,* edited by Angel Bassol Batalla et al., 145–206. Mexico: Editorial Trillas.

Schryer, Frans J. (1980). *The Rancheros of Pisaflores.* Toronto: University of Toronto Press.

Schryer, Frans J. (1990). *Ethnicity and Class Conflict in Rural Mexico.* Princeton, N.J.: Princeton University Press.

FRANS J. SCHRYER

Cayman Islanders

ETHNONYMS: none

Orientation

The Cayman Islands are an English-speaking British crown colony situated in the northwest Caribbean. Its three small islands lie between 19°15′ and 19°45′ N and 79°40′ and 81°30′ W. The largest and most populated of the islands is Grand Cayman, which is located about 240 kilometers south of Cuba, 740 kilometers south of Miami, and 290 kilometers northwest of Jamaica. Grand Cayman is 35 kilometers long and has a total land area of 197 square kilometers. Cayman Brac, the second-largest island, is located 142 kilometers away. It is 19 kilometers long and has a total land surface of 36 square kilometers. The island of Little Cayman completes the group. It lies about 10 kilometers from Cayman Brac and is 16 kilometers long, with a land area of 26 square kilometers.

According to the last census, in 1989, the total population of the Cayman Islands was 25,355, indicating a tripling of the population in the preceding thirty years. A provisional estimate, by the Economics and Statistics Office, of 31,150 by the end of 1993 suggests that the population has continued to increase. Ninety-four percent of this population reside on Grand Cayman, which has been the major site of tourist and financial development since the late 1960s. The population of the "sister islands" together numbered only 1,474 in 1989, with the majority residing on Cayman Brac. There were only 33 residents on Little Cayman. Unlike that of Grand Cayman, the population size of the sister islands has remained relatively stable, alternately rising and then declining between 1960 and 1989.

History and Cultural Relations

Ethnographic and historical depictions of the Caribbean have been dominated by the impact of the plantation systems that drove the colonization of this region. The Caymanian experience, however, diverges considerably from the elements that are usually associated with this form of historical development. With limited arable land and scarce fresh water supplies, the Cayman Islands were never able to support large-scale plantations. The islands do not appear to have ever been inhabited by Amerindians, and although the first White settlers owned slaves, the numbers were very small compared to the large plantation work forces of other Caribbean societies. In 1802 the total population was 933, of whom 551 were slaves. Agriculture, therefore, was small scale and largely oriented toward local consumption; the wide variety of crops included maize, cassava, yams, and potatoes.

Seafaring formed the true backbone of the Caymanian economy until the late twentieth century. From the early stopovers of European ships during the 1600s, and well into the 1900s, turtling constituted an important marine enterprise. Indeed, it was the abundance of large sea turtles on the shores and in the local waters of the Caymans that first attracted Europeans to the islands. As local sup-

plies became exhausted, Caymanians, in search of turtles, voyaged further afield, to the south coast of Cuba and later to the keys off Nicaragua. This voyaging was reflected in the small-scale shipbuilding that occurred throughout the islands. Among the personal recollections of the early twentieth century gathered for the Cayman Islands Memory Bank, ship launches are recounted as an exciting and important social occasion, drawing people from other districts and providing a special opportunity for interaction and communal celebration.

During the twentieth century, turtling came to be rivaled and then surpassed by another form of seafaring. Caymanian men put their maritime skills to use in service on merchant ships belonging to the United States, Honduras, and Panama. Their labor infused otherwise scarce cash into the local economy and soon became its mainstay as the proportions of men away at sea increased. It was very difficult for the men to arrange time off or passage back to Cayman, and they were often away from their families for months, or even years. Facing such obstacles, many seamen settled in the United States, contributing to the steady stream of emigration that characterized the Cayman Islands from the mid-nineteenth until the mid-twentieth century.

Unlike the plantation systems of other Caribbean territories, the limited agriculture and maritime enterprises of the Caymanian economy could not support a class of leisured landowners. The elite consisted of a small number of merchant families who based their wealth and influence on mercantile trade and ship ownership rather than on land. Apart from this small elite, however, class differences were limited. Until the development of the 1970s and 1980s, most Caymanians, of whatever racial background, had quite meager incomes and modest life-styles. This economic convergence also served to mute the impact of racial differences. Although the wealthy merchant families were White, many White islanders lived in much the same circumstances as their Black counterparts. For most of the history of the Cayman Islands, interracial conjugal unions have been very common. Thus, unlike the tendency in plantation societies toward polarization between a small White elite and a large Black proletariat, in the Cayman Islands the majority of residents were of mixed racial background and were publicly recognized as such.

Settlements

When slavery was abolished in the British Empire in 1834, there was enough uninhabited land in the Cayman Islands for the former slaves to establish their own freeholds. This broad access to land became very important when the price of real estate started to rise dramatically in the late 1960s, allowing many Caymanians to turn a profit on land that formerly had little commercial value. Many of the former slaves settled in the North Side District, one of five districts in Grand Cayman (the others being West Bay, George Town, Bodden Town, and East End).

The original capital of Grand Cayman was Bodden Town, which is located in the central part of the island. Bodden Town was eventually replaced by George Town, which today is the most populous district of Grand Cayman. The development of tourism, banking, and commerce that transformed the Cayman Islands has been largely concentrated in George Town. The city of George Town is the seat of government and the center for social and medical services, finance, and duty-free shops. The landing for cruise ships is located in the city, and the international airport is situated in the George Town District, as are most of the major hotels and restaurants. Given this centralization, it is perhaps not surprising that in 1989, 12,921 people, or about half of the total Cayman Islands population, resided in this district. In addition, many residents of the two adjoining districts, West Bay and Bodden Town, commute to workplaces in George Town.

This commuting is made possible by a modern road network that now connects settlements in all five districts. Before World War II, there were few roads, and internal transport and communication was very difficult, especially for the isolated outer districts of North Side and East Side, and even more so for the sister islands. Settlements were self-sufficient, and interaction between them was very limited. As a result, a strong sense of local-district identity developed, juxtaposed with far-flung international contacts through seafaring and emigration. To some extent, that juxtaposition persists in spite of the contemporary ease of access and communication between the settlements and their integration into a centralized island economy and infrastructure. People who travel frequently out of the country, deal regularly with tourists and expatriate workers, wear the latest Western fashions, drive cars made in the United States or Japan, and find fax machines indispensable can nonetheless be very reluctant to move from the district in which they grew up to another district only 10 or 20 minutes away by car.

Economy

Driving past the luxury condominiums, hotels, restaurants, and shops on West Bay Road or the duty-free shops and office towers of George Town, it is difficult to imagine the seafaring and agricultural communities of the Grand Cayman of the 1950s and 1960s. Today one is far more likely to encounter turtles or crops in the managed breeding pools of the Turtle Farm in West Bay or the Smith Road demonstration farm than in the districts or shores of Cayman. The Cayman Islands currently meets virtually all the consumption needs of residents and visitors through imports, and its economy is almost entirely based on tourism and finance. In 1990 there was a total of 614,870 visitors, and the number continues to increase: in 1994, Cayman received 503,000 visitors in the first six months alone. Encouraged by the absence of any direct taxation of companies and individuals or of inheritance taxes and estate duties, an extensive professional and financial infrastructure has evolved. The climate of confidentiality, backed by legislation and sophisticated communications, has induced some 546 banks and trust companies from over sixty countries, 24,000 companies, and approximately 500 mutual funds to locate or register in the Cayman Islands. In addition, Cayman has become one of the world's most popular centers for offshore captive insurance, (insurance companies owned by other companies that thereby acquire business insurance at rates lower than they could get from independent insurers), with 367 such companies operating in 1992.

Several developments appear to have facilitated this dramatic transformation. The construction of the George Town airport in 1953 and an airstrip in Cayman Brac in 1954 made the islands more easily accessible to visitors. During the early 1960s, the mosquitoes that infested the Caymans and made life very uncomfortable were finally brought under control. This made the islands much more appealing to tourists. The most important development, however, was probably the 1962 decision of Caymanians not to follow Jamaica into independence from Britain.

The status of the Cayman Islands had, for most of its history, been linked with Jamaica. From 1863 until 1959, the Cayman Islands were formally a dependency of Jamaica. From 1957 until 1962, both the Cayman Islands and Jamaica were members of the Federation of the West Indies. Nonetheless, in 1962, when the majority of Jamaicans voted to leave the federation and to seek independence from the United Kingdom, the Cayman Islands did not follow suit, opting instead to remain a British colony. The continuity of colony status has been perceived by investors and visitors as a potent symbol of the Cayman Islands' political stability in the face of the more turbulent political upheavals that have marked recent years in Jamaica and other parts of the Caribbean.

The reputation of the Cayman Islands as a stable, peaceful spot in which outsiders can safely vacation and invest has been both its greatest asset and its Achilles' heel. It has helped to make Caymanians very prosperous. The Cayman Islands' per capita income is very high, comparing most favorably with that of Western industrialized societies. There is little unemployment or poverty, and, during the 1980s and early 1990s, the gross national product enjoyed impressive rates of annual growth. That prosperity has, however, involved a very high and rather precarious dependence on outsiders with little vested interest in the Cayman people themselves. That dependence extends to labor as well as capital.

The rapid and dramatic expansion of the Caymanian economy has created a shortage of labor at all levels of the economy. The Cayman Islands responded by importing labor from all over the world but in particular from other parts of the Caribbean, North America, Britain, and Ireland. Expatriate workers are employed in the civil service, financial industries, cultural organizations, hotels, restaurants, shops, water-sports outlets, and construction and as doctors, accountants, lawyers, and architects. In short, foreign workers have become a critical mainstay for the Caymanian economy, and their presence has been an important contributor to Cayman's recent population expansion. In 1989 these workers and their families accounted for 32 percent of the total population. Most come to Cayman on temporary work permits (Gainful Occupation Licenses) granted to their prospective employers and subsequently renewed only on the condition that there are no suitable local workers who can fill the position. This transitory status does not do much to encourage foreign workers to make long-term investments in the Cayman Islands, a situation that can evoke resentments among both locals and expatriates.

Kinship, Marriage, and Family

Contemporary households tend to be occupied by nuclear rather than extended families. This pattern appears to be long-standing and not a recent development. Hannerz (1973, 1974) found that in 1970 most households at all levels of the social hierarchy were made up of nuclear families. At about the same time, in a study of households in East End, a community then still dependent on seafaring, Goldberg (1976) found that, to be considered a full adult, a man was expected to set up his own household, marry, and have children.

The composition of households may not have changed, but the roles of its members have. One of the most significant shifts has been the entry of women into the paid labor force. Until the 1960s, economic opportunities for women were extremely limited. One of the few sources of cash income for women used to be the sale of ropes that they wove from the fronds of the thatch palm (Goldberg 1976a, 117). In contrast, in 1989, out of a total of 10,125 women over the age of 15, 7,513 (74 percent) were employed outside the home. In most contemporary Caymanian families therefore, both parents are now employed outside the home. This shift has raised concerns about the welfare of youngsters who may come home from school to an empty house—the "latchkey children," as they are called. Initially, there were few organized responses to this situation. In 1994, however, the Ministry for Community Development announced plans to set up after-school programs at churches in every district.

There is concern about the impact of rapid development on the institutions of Caymanian society. The extended Caymanian family, some people fear, is breaking down, with unwelcome consequences for child rearing and social order. Although Caymanian families have certainly had to adjust to a changing economic and social climate, kinship links continue to be extensive and valued. Most native-born Caymanians are the descendants of a small group of early settlers. As a result, certain surnames are extremely common. Although a shared surname does not necessarily indicate an active or even traceable kinship link, most Caymanians can count many known and recognized kin within their local community. In fact, the improvement of internal and external transportation has made it easier to maintain contact with kin both off and on the islands. As a result of the extensive emigration from the Cayman Islands, many Caymanians have relatives in other countries, with whom contact has been greatly facilitated by modern communications and air travel.

Sociopolitical Organization

The Constitution Order of 1972 provided for much of the current government framework, vesting legislative power in the Legislative Assembly and executive power in an executive council and governor. During the early 1990s, the constitution was subjected to a lengthy process of review and subsequent amendment. The Legislative Assembly is now made up of fifteen members who are elected every four years by voters in the six political districts of the Cayman Islands. These elected members in turn elect the Speaker of the Assembly. An additional three "Official Members" of the Legislative Assembly—the financial secretary, the attorney general, and the chief secretary—are appointed by the governor. The executive council comprises five elected ministers and the three "official" appointees and is chaired by the governor. Although the Cayman Islands have achieved a fair amount of internal self-government, the final say still rests with the governor, who is appointed by—and is subject to—the authority of the British Crown. The Crown also has the power to disallow laws passed by the Cayman legislature, and the Judicial Committee of the British Privy Council is the final domestic court of appeals for the Cayman Islands. In considering the issue of a constitutional amendment, the National Team government, elected in 1992, pointed out that the changes they recommended were minor and did not "advance" the constitution at all; that is, the changes did not move the Cayman Islands any closer to full internal self-government or independence.

It has been more difficult to assert control over crime and, even more significantly, fear of crime. Although crime rates remain generally low, violent crime being rare, residents who were accustomed to leaving their homes and cars unlocked, now have a growing perception and concomitant fear that Cayman is not quite as safe as it once was. A good deal of newspaper print and policing effort is devoted to the "war against drugs." It is commonly believed that the Cayman Islands are used as a warehouse for drugs en route to the United States, although most arrests are for simple possession. Among inmates in Northward Prison, 85 percent were jailed for drug-related offenses. In 1994 a new ministry was created, devoted to health, drug-abuse prevention, and rehabilitation.

Religion and Expressive Culture

Churches play an extremely significant role in Caymanian society. The majority of native Caymanians are regular churchgoers, but, as the government proposal for church-based after-school programs indicates, the churches are far more than religious centers; they are also key community centers. Churches serve as the basis for a variety of voluntary associations and activities. They sponsor programs, including Bible schools, for children, and full-time private schools are usually affiliated with a particular church or religious movement. The United Church of Jamaica and Grand Cayman has the largest membership, but the Baptist movement dominates in Cayman Brac. There are a number of other Christian denominations, but other religions do not, as yet, have institutional representation, although they do have some adherents.

In the 1980s there was an efflorescence of new organizations concerned with recording, preserving, and promoting Cayman's cultural and historical heritage. One such organization is the Caymanian Cultural Foundation, which mounts plays in—and administers—the Harquail Theatre. The foundation also has a broader mandate: to promote appreciation for and expression of a range of fine arts, with a particular concern for traditional crafts and folk art. The National Trust has gradually honed down an initially broad mandate to preserve natural environments and places of historic significance. The National Museum was initially mandated by legislation in 1979 but only opened to the public in 1990 when the Old Courts Building in George Town was renovated for its use. The National

Archive is a repository for historical archives and government records. It has also become the home for the Cayman Islands Memory Bank which, inspired by the Jamaican Memory Bank, aims to harvest an oral history of the Cayman Islands through interviews with elderly Caymanians. The proliferation of these cultural organizations reflects a growing sense of urgency, in certain quarters, that unique elements of Cayman's environment, history, and culture must be salvaged before they are entirely eradicated by economic development.

Bibliography

Buchler, I. R. (1962). "Caymanian Folk Racial Categories." *Man* 62:185–186.

Buchler, I. R. (1963). "Shifting Cultivation in the Cayman Islands." *Antropologica* 12:1–5.

Davies, Elizabeth (1989). *The Legal System of the Cayman Islands.* Oxford: Law Reports International.

Doran, Edwin (1953). "A Physical and Cultural Geography of the Cayman Islands." Ph.D. dissertation, University of California, Berkeley.

Goldberg, Richard S. (1976a). "The Concept of Household in East End, Grand Cayman." *Ethnos* 41(1–4): 116–132.

Goldberg, Richard S. (1976b). "East End: A Caribbean Community under Stress." Ph.D. dissertation, University of Texas at Austin.

Hannerz, Ulf (1973). "Managerial Entrepreneurship and Economic Change in the Cayman Islands." *Ethnos* 38 (1–4): 102–112.

Hannerz, Ulf (1974). *Caymanian Politics: Structure and Style in a Changing Island Society.* Studies in Social Anthropology, 1. Stockholm: University of Stockholm, Department of Social Anthropology.

Hirst, George S. (1910). *Notes on the History of the Cayman Islands.* Kingston, Jamaica: P.A. Benjamin Manf. Co. Reprint. 1967. Grand Cayman: Caribbean Colour.

Hughes, H. B. L. (1946). "Notes on the Cayman Islands." *Jamaican Historical Review* 1(2): 154–158.

McLaughlin, Heather R. (1991). *Cayman Yesterdays: An Album of Childhood Memories.* Grand Cayman: Cayman Islands National Archive.

Martins, Dave, ed. (1992). *Cayman Islands: Who's Who & Business Guide.* Grand Cayman: Star Communications.

Williams, Neville (1970). *A History of the Cayman Islands.* Grand Cayman: Government of the Cayman Islands.

VERED AMIT-TALAI

Chatino

ETHNONYMS: Chatino, Cha'tnǫ

Orientation

Identification.   The Chatino are an indigenous group of the state of Oaxaca, Mexico. The term "Chatino" is a Spanish rendering of the word *cha'tnǫ*, which glosses literally as "words work." The Chatino use this word to refer both to their language and themselves. As a group, they distinguish themselves from neighboring Zapotec who speak *cha'mstye,* "crazy words," and from the bordering Mixtec who speak *cha'puta,* "whore's words."

Location.   There are some fifty Chatino communities along the Pacific coast of Oaxaca from 16°00′ to 16°36′ N and from 97°30′ to 97°34′ W. The majority of these communities are in eight *municipios* in the district of Juquila—San Juan Lachao, San Juan Quiahije, San Miguel Panixtlahuaca, Santa Catarina Juquila, Santa Maria Temaxcaltepec, Santos Reyes Nopala, Tataltepec de Valdéz, and Santiago Yaitepec. The rest are in the municipio of Santa Cruz Zenzontepec in the district of Sola de Vaga. The area is mountainous. From a narrow coastal plain, the Sierra Madre del Sur, which transects the region from east to west, rises to over 2,500 meters. Numerous rivers and streams have carved narrow valleys and deep gorges into the landscape. Ecologically, three zones may be distinguished: tropical lowlands; a temperate zone above 800 meters of deciduous oak-climax forests; and coniferous, cold country above 1,600 meters. There are two seasons: rainy and dry. The former extends from mid-May through October. The region receives between 100 and 200 centimeters of precipitation annually.

Demography.   There are approximately 30,000 Chatino speakers. National census figures for the region, however, are notoriously poor, and, if anything, tend to underestimate the populations of their communities, particularly the percentage of Chatino speakers. Where careful demographic studies have been made, they indicate that Chatino populations are young and growing rapidly. Birthrates run 40 to 50 per 1,000, compared, for instance, with the national average of 29 in 1993. Even so, infant-mortality rates, which run more than 65 deaths per 1,000 live births, are more than twice the national average, regardless of various methods of measurement. Death rates, which average 25 per 1,000, are likewise nearly five times the national figures. As a result, compared with 68 for males and 76 for females nationally, Chatino life expectancy is in the 40s and 50s. Such disparities are symptoms of the greater poverty and malnutrition and relative lack of medical services that this indigenous population copes with in its daily struggles to survive.

Linguistic Affiliation.   Chatino belongs to the Macro-Mayan Phylum of languages, to the Oaxacan Subphylum, and the Zapotecan Family. There are at least three distinct dialects of Chatino, with centers in Yaitepec, Tataltepec, and Zenzontepec.

History and Cultural Relations

What little is known of Chatino origins is rooted in linguistic and archaeological studies. Lexostatistical evidence suggests that Chatino diverged from the Zapotecan Family some time between 4000 B.C. and A.D. 200. Archeological evidence suggests that the Chatino broke politically and culturally from the Zapotecs of Monte Albán around the time of Christ. The Chatino enter the historical record in the Mixtec codices. During the reign of Eight-Deer Tiger Claw, (A.D. 1011–1063), the Chatino rulers of Juquila appear to have formed an alliance with Eight-Deer, the Mixtec king who had extended his dominion from Tilantongo in the Mixteca Alta to the coastal kingdom of Tututepec. When the Spanish conquistador Pedro de Alvarado conquered Tututepec in 1522, the Chatino were still its tributary subjects. As they did everywhere, the conquistadors placed themselves at the apex of pre-Hispanic states by exploiting well-developed native institutions such as tribute, slavery, and indirect rule. Although the Conquest brought new masters, a new god, and heavier tribute, these were minor consequences compared with the decimation of the population by European diseases. The precontact population of Tututepec's empire may have been 250,000. By 1544, after two epidemics, its population had fallen to 7,000 tributaries, about 35,000 people, and continued to plummet for the next 100 years. The transformation of the economy went far beyond taking control of the aboriginal tribute system; it also involved the introduction of European mercantile capitalism, as a result of which land and labor became cash commodities. Moreover, trade policies effectively geared the economy of New Spain to the requirements of the mother country. In this planned economy, the Spanish and the Indians basically specialized in different types of production. The Spanish plantations along the Oaxacan coast initially produced native crops (cacao, maize, and cotton), but as the native population declined, causing chronic labor shortages, the Spanish turned to large-scale cattle ranching, which required much less labor. Although the Chatino continued to plant their subsistence crops in order to meet their tribute obligations, they took their place in this planned economy as producers of cochineal, an insect dyestuff that was second only to silver in value among New Spain's exports. Cochineal was obtained from the Chatino through _repartimentos de comercio_—a system of forced sales repaid with cochineal. Because _alcaldes mayores_, who administered Indian districts, were required to post substantial bonds, they typically formed a partnerships with rich Mexico City merchants, who not only posted the bond, but provided trade goods or cash to be distributed among the indigenous population. These commodities were forcibly sold on credit to Indians in the district at inflated prices. Because the Chatino needed money to pay their tribute, they had little choice but to accept such "sales" and cash advances. Although the Crown repeatedly tried to outlaw this practice, such prohibitions were routinely ignored, and repartimentos de comercio continued to finance the cochineal trade throughout the colonial period. After the Mexican War of Independence (1810–1821), the Spanish, who had dominated and financed the marketing of cochineal withdrew their capital, leaving the new republic in an economic shambles. The cochineal market was in the doldrums. Although some production continued, the introduction of cheap aniline dyes in the late 1850s drove down prices to new lows and soon destroyed the cochineal market. To solve Mexico's financial problems, church and native lands came under scrutiny. Between 1856 and 1859 the Liberal government passed legislation designed to confiscate the church's estates, the largest landholdings in Mexico. Because the laws were framed to include all corporate bodies, countless native villages lost their lands. In the district of Juquila, the initial expropriations were not immense. Nevertheless, Tataltepec, Tepenixtlahuaca, and Zenzontepec lost their best lands. These early abuses of the Liberal reform laws were minor compared to the damage done by their cynical application during the Porfiriato (i.e., the dictatorship of Porfirio Díaz, 1884–1911). After 1880 what had been a trickle of coffee growers became a torrent as the floodgates of the landgrab were opened. Whereas small coffee plantations of 25 hectares had been established in the 1870s, the new wave of land speculators carved plantations of up to 2,200 hectares out of the communal lands of Chatino communities. The Chatino reacted to these expropriations of their lands by launching an insurrection in 1896, "the War of the Pants," in which they tried to wipe out the literate mestizos (the new landowners and merchants), whom they identified as "wearing pants" rather than native dress. Although the War of the Pants was quickly and brutally suppressed by Federal troops, it was symptomatic of the tensions that eventually made the Revolution of 1910 inevitable. Although the Revolution is credited with bringing about sweeping reforms in land tenure and social structure, few of the tensions were resolved in the Chatino region. The promised land reform never took place. Between the mid-1930s and 1950, Chatino peasants were induced by offers of credit and higher prices to plant coffee on their communal lands. Planting coffee, however, led to de facto privatization of communal lands, engendering conflicts and blood feuds in many Chatino communities. During the 1980s, a strange new cash crop made its way into the Chatino region—marijuana—the advent of which promises to renew the bloody violence of the past.

Settlements

Chatino communities are organized administratively into municipios and are classified as _rancherías, agencias municipales, cabeceras municipales._ Chatino settlement patterns reflect this municipio organization in that the cabeceras (county seats) are surrounded by smaller subordinate communities that typically arise so that peasant farmers may be closer to their fields. Rancherías typically are small (100 to 300 inhabitants) but lack formal representation in the municipal system. Agencias or townships have their own civil authorities and typically range from 300 to 1,500 residents. Cabeceras in the region range from 1,500 to 6,000 residents. Larger communities are usually divided into two barrios (neighborhoods), which have their own civil officials. Spatially, most communities are from one to six hours' walk from their nearest neighbor. Chatino villages usually have a small nucleated civic center consisting of a plaza, town hall, church, school, and small stores. Ringing the civic center, houses—standing amid fenced maize fields, gardens, and fruit trees—are dispersed, giving villages a decidedly rural flavor. These residences often consist of a cluster of several houses built around a common patio and occupied by closely related kin. Surrounding a village are its fields. Where fields are distant from the village, their owners build a makeshift structure as protection from the elements and a place to cook and sleep while performing field labor. Chatino houses were traditionally single-room structures built of wattle and daub or of bamboo cane with a peaked roof of thatch and a dirt floor. Although a few such houses can still be found, adobe-walled houses with tile roofs have replaced most of them. In those villages connected to roads, adobe houses are being replaced with brick homes with concrete floors and corrugated or cement roofs. Some two-story homes have even appeared since the 1970s. Increasingly, houses have electric power and sport television antennas.

Economy

Subsistence and Commercial Activities.   Although large coffee plantations exist in the region, the Chatino are smallholders. In this mountainous area, swidden techniques are used to grow traditional crops—maize, beans, and squash. Rapid population growth, however, has cut fallow periods to as short as three years, which in combination with overcultivation, has led to the severe erosion of large areas on mountainsides. Coffee—the primary cash crop—is grown with bananas or under canopy trees. Chatino maize fields and coffee plantings typically are less than 5 hectares. Cultivation is carried out with very simple implements—digging sticks, hoes, and machetes. In the few level areas that exist, metal-tipped wood plows may be drawn by oxen. Aside from crops, most households have a few chickens or turkeys. Wealthier households may have a few head of cattle, horses, mules, or donkeys. The Chatino also supplement their diet by hunting deer, iguanas, *javalinas* (peccaries), and various birds. Villagers obtain additional vegetables and fruits from kitchen gardens and trees surrounding their homes (e.g., tomatoes, chilies, guavas, lemons, oranges, and mangoes). As a general rule, the Chatino try first to guarantee their subsistence base of maize, dedicating any excess land to cash crops. Thus, the larger the holding, the greater the percentage planted in coffee. Even so, few households possess enough land to make ends meet from their smallholdings alone. Most are forced to work seasonally on large coffee plantations, do daily wage work, or produce crafts for sale in the market. Out-migration is increasing, especially to Oaxaca and Mexico City. Census figures indicate some 10 percent of Chatino speakers live outside of the region.

Industrial Arts.   Although there are few full-time specialists, the Chatino produce a number of crafts, including pottery, mats, baskets, tumplines, ropes, hammocks, wood saddles for mules and donkeys, and ritual masks. Carpenters make beds, tables, chests, and chairs. Local blacksmiths fashion machetes, horseshoes, and branding irons. "Traditional" dress is maintained, although it is worn less commonly than in the past. Women embroider elaborate blouses, make men's shirts and trousers, and weave belts, girdles, and tortilla bags.

Trade.   The Chatino have been part of commodity chains and market system integrated into a global economy since the sixteenth century, and the local expressions of these relations are visible in the regional market systems. The major periodic markets within the region are held in Juquila and Nopala. These commercial centers have the stores and shops carrying the industrial merchandise the Chatino want, and their weekly markets attract Chatino from the surrounding communities. Each Chatino community tends to specialize by selling certain crafts and produce. For example, Amialtepec is known for its pottery, Ixtapan for its net bags and hammocks, Tataltepec for its chilies, Tepenixtlahuaca for brown sugar, Zenzontepec for goats, and Cuixtla for cattle. In addition to these regular markets, during fiestas, especially for the village's patron saint, fairs are held in Chatino communities. The largest of these, held for the Virgin of Juquila on 8 December, attracts some 200,000 pilgrims to its monthlong fair.

Division of Labor.   There is a sexual division of labor for a number of tasks. Although women may help in the fields, most heavy labor is done by men. Similarly, hunting and fishing are male domains. Tending livestock also is a predominantly male activity. Women's work includes most domestic chores such as cooking, cleaning, and the burden of most child care, as well as tending kitchen gardens, domestic fowl and pigs, and gathering wild foods. In their households, women also do much of the craftwork, such as pottery, weaving, embroidery, and basketry. Women usually do the greatest share of marketing and shopping for the household.

Land Tenure.   In the Chatino region, both communal and private property exist. Parcels of privately owned land, such as large and small coffee plantations or house lots, are commodities that are freely bought and sold. All Chatino communities also have communal lands. In theory, these belong to the community, and decisions about how they are to be allocated or reallocated are made by town officials. If any unclaimed land exists, villagers in need of land may petition village officials for usufruct rights. In practice, these rights to most arable land are held by individual households and are not only inheritable, but such lands may be bought and sold as long as sales are made to "native" members of the community. Areas such as pastures are considered common lands. Some of the land-poor communities also "rent" lands either from the communal-lands commissions of neighboring communities or on large private estates.

Kinship

Kin Groups and Descent.   The basic kin group among the Chatino is the family. Kinship is cognatic: an individual recognizes a circle of relatives related to him or her by blood and marriage through both mother and father. Although descent is bilateral, postmarital residence is usually virolocal. As a result, groups of male kin often live in close proximity.

Kinship Terminology.   Chatino kinship terminology resembles the Eskimo pattern in that a clear distinction is drawn between lineal ascendants and descendants and collateral relatives. All collateral relatives are referred to as *ta'a*.

Marriage and Family

Marriage. The Chatino are monogamous. Technically, the Chatino practice two types of marriage: civil-religious and common-law. The latter is a marriage not performed by a priest nor legally recorded. This is not to say that such unions do not involve religious rituals or that they are not recognized socially. A civil-religious wedding is a union sanctioned by the state, and the civil wedding is a legal prerequisite for an optional church ceremony. Both civil-religious and common-law marriages involve periods of sexual abstinence, rites of bathing, lighting candles, planting crosses, presenting rosaries, ritual blessings, prayers, and feasting. Making marriage arrangements involves initiating a complex set of social and economic exchanges between the families of the bride and groom. Marriages are generally arranged at a young man's request. Usually, these arrangements are initiated by a go-between, an older relative of the groom. If the girl's parents agree, a series of formal visits commences. The prospective groom comes bearing gifts—baskets of bread, chocolate, mescal, wine, cigarettes, beans, maize, firewood, and money. After these initial visits, the groom may do a year of bride-service. Each day, the young man is expected to bring gifts for his prospective in-laws and help his father-in-law in the fields. Wedding feasts themselves usually last three to four days. After the rituals of the first day, the feast turns into an ordinary fiesta, with the emphasis on drinking and dancing.

Domestic Unit. Because postmarital residence tends to be virolocal, Chatino households are frequently composed of a three-generation extended family. Even where nuclear households are formed, couples often live in close proximity to the husband's family and may even live in the same compound.

Inheritance. Among the Chatino, inheritance is bilateral and partible, and sons and daughters are supposed to receive equal shares of the property to be divided.

Socialization. Chatino children grow up surrounded by an extended family. Parents, although loving, are strict disciplinarians and demand obedience. Deviations from the norm are taken seriously. Children are often disciplined physically and severely, not only by their parents but also by older siblings. Children begin learning and doing chores at an early age. Babies as young as 1 year old are given dull machetes to play with. By the age of 5, boys are fetching firewood and helping their fathers in the fields, and girls are helping their mothers make tortillas. As children approach puberty, parents worry about their son's drinking, fighting, or keeping bad company, and about their daughter's moral conduct. The authoritarian stance of parents must be understood in the context of households that often live at the economic margin. Mistakes can be costly, and poor decisions may have dire consequences.

Sociopolitical Organization

Social Organization. The Chatino are an ethnic group within a nation-state organized along the lines of race and class. As Indians and peasants, they are marginalized to the lowest rungs on the nation's social totem pole. That said, within their communities, family, residence, status, and wealth provide the foundations of social organization. In their agrarian communities, because of virolocal residence, related males tend to occupy clusters of households. Within the community, a family's status derives from men's service in a hierarchy of civil and religious offices that organize age-grades. All men in the course of their lifetime are expected to serve in offices at each level of the age-grade until they ultimately become elders of the community. As officeholders must pay the costs of their service themselves, the status they achieve reflects not only their age-grade level, but their wealth. Because the wealthy can afford the costs of the more prestigious offices, they tend to have more distinguished careers and higher status than the poor. A man's service requires that his wife join his efforts, and her status therefore usually mirrors that of her husband.

Political Organization. Civil and religious hierarchies organize most Chatino communities. These hierarchies consist of two ladders with four to five rungs of civil and religious offices. Most civil posts are mandated by the state constitution (e.g., *presidente*, alcaldes, *regidores, tesorero*, secretary, chief of police); however, their numbers and their ranking in the hierarchy are local traditions and thus subject to local definition, as are those of subsidiary offices (e.g., *tequitlatos, topiles*). Religious offices (e.g., *mayordomos*) derive from the Chatino relationship with the Catholic church. Mayordomos, for instance, pay for the costs of fiestas held for the saints. Because the community requires all men to serve, willingly or not, in civil and religious posts, "elections" are based on the previous offices men have held and the number of years that have passed since their last period of service. Men who refuse to serve may be jailed until they accept the post to which they have been elected. After serving in the highest level of offices, men become members of a council of elders who are consulted on important matters. Although the national political parties have attempted to influence local affairs, these efforts have met with only limited success in communities in which civil-religious hierarchies are still intact.

Social Control. Children are socialized from an early age into the norms of proper conduct. They are taught that the gods will punish misbehavior with disease, catastrophe, and death. Moreover, individuals who violate social norms face both informal and formal sanctions. Usually gossip and ostracism are enough to control improper behavior; however, serious violations may bring the matter to the attention of local authorities. Within Chatino communities, local authorities usually attempt to mediate the disputes brought before them. If their attempts are unsuccessful, they may pass the case to state police or the district courts.

Conflict. Although conflicts existed between communities and large plantations, especially over land, until the adoption of coffee as a cash crop by Chatino communities, internal conflicts were rare. Beginning in the 1930s and intensifying in the 1950s, the Chatino began to plant coffee trees on their communal lands. As this process in essence privatized communal lands, conflicts internal to these communities over access to land sent homicide rates soaring as blood feuds divided many communities. Since 1950, homicide rates in Chatino communities have ranged from 284 to 511 per 100,000 or 16 to 29 times the national average.

Religion and Expressive Culture

Religious Beliefs.   Chatino religion is a blend of Catholicism and a system of pre-Hispanic beliefs, rituals, and cosmology. The Chatino cosmos is conceived of as an ecological system in which human beings, animals, spirits, ancestors, deities, and saints interact with one another to maintain the universe in equilibrium. The world, floating in the midst of a sea, is envisioned as being connected by "doors" to a series of layered heavens and underworlds. Through these doors, various spirits and deities pass between the layers of the cosmos. Such doors are entrances to "houses." As "house" and body are equated, the Chatino pantheon is mapped onto nature. Gods and spirits have houses on mountaintops, in caves, and in rivers. Thus, the mountaintop that is said to be the "house" of the rain god is also said to be the rain god.

Religious Practioners.   Among the Chatino, native priests and curers are called *ne' ho'o*—literally, "person saints" (and therefore, holy people). They are consulted not only after a birth to determine a child's *tona* ("animal-spirit companion"), but also regarding marriages and to determine the cause of illnesses; they may be called in for any important undertaking.

Ceremonies.   The Chatino perform both calendrical and noncalendrical ceremonies and rituals. The latter include rites of passage at birth, marriage, and death. The former, Catholic fiestas, are demarcated by periods of sexual abstinence, remnants of a pre-Columbian ritual calendar of 260 days that interlocked with a calendar of 18 months of 20 days, plus 5 "evil" days (Greenberg 1981, 114). Although the fiestas celebrated vary from community to community, most celebrate New Year, Santa Cruz, the Virgin de Rosario, and Todo Santos (All Saints' Day).

Arts.   Music and dance are important elements of Chatino culture and are part of most ritual celebrations. Traditional music is played with flutes, drums, and rattles. Church and popular music is sung in Spanish and is accompanied by guitars, violins, and brass and woodwind instruments. The popular music of the region—the "Chilena"—is a form supposed to have originated with Chilean sailors visiting the coast of Oaxaca during the nineteenth century.

Medicine.   The *curandero* or ne' ho'o, as part of his or her ritual, eats *ho'o kwiya'* (sacred mushrooms) that enable a curer to assume animal form and send his or her *nagual* or *ho'o kwichi* (animal companion spirit) to determine who may be bewitching a patient or what offense the latter may have given to one of the gods or saints. Aside from curanderos, the Chatino also consult other medical practitioners, such as herbalists and midwives. Native practitioners continue to have wide followings despite increasing access to medical services provided by the National Indian Institute's doctors and nurses.

Death and Afterlife.   Funerals are fairly elaborate affairs that reflect a person's age and marital status. The deceased is bathed. A wake is held, and the person is buried the next day. The burial is followed by a novena—nine days of prayers. A second novena is held a year later, when a permanent cross is erected. The dead are thought to take a path with nine stops or (steps) that leads to the underworld. They are said to live in a village that is much like their own and to return each year to this world to visit their homes and families during Todo Santos.

Bibliography

Bartolomé, Miguel A., and Alicia M. Barabas (1982). *Tierra de la palabra: Historia etnografía de los Chatinos de Oaxaca*. Centro Regional de Oaxaca, Etnología, Colección Científica, 108. Mexico City: Instituto Nacional de Antropología e Historia.

Cordero Avendaño de Duran, Carmen (1986). *Stina jo'o kucha, el santo padre sol: Contribución al conocimiento socio-religioso del grupo étnico Chatino*. Oaxaca: Biblioteca Pública de Oaxaca, Cultura y Recreación.

Greenberg, James B. (1981). *Santiago's Sword: Chatino Peasant Religion and Economics*. Berkeley and Los Angeles: University of California Press.

Greenberg, James B. (1989). *Blood Ties: Life and Violence in Rural Mexico*. Tucson: University of Arizona Press.

JAMES B. GREENBERG

Chinantec

ETHNONYMS: The Chinantec are subdivided by dialect, habitat, and culture into at least four main groups. "Hu-hmei," "Wa-hmi," and "Dzah-hmi" are the ethnonyms used by groups inhabiting central, eastern, and western subregions, respectively. No ethnonyms are reported for northern and northwestern groups.

Orientation

Identification.   The name "Chinantla" derives from the Nahuatl word *chinamitl*, meaning "enclosed space" or "near the canes." There is no Chinantec term to describe this region. The unity of the contemporary Chinantec derives from the group's self-differentiation from neighboring non-Chinantec communities rather than from any internal political or social cohesion. A paucity of research, particularly comparative work, makes it difficult to determine what is shared Chinantec culture and what is peculiar to a particular village or hamlet. Few data exist on pre-Conquest Chinantec culture. The terms "traditionally" and "in the past" here refer to the period between the Spanish Conquest and the mid-1950s.

Location. The Chinantec reside, as their ancestors did aboriginally, in northern Oaxaca, Mexico, within the Papaloapan River Basin, generally to the south and east of the Santo Domingo and Valle Nacional rivers, which join near the city of Tuxtepec. Today there are fourteen Chinantec townships, each with several lesser dependent communities. The area is very mountainous and characterized by high humidity and extremely heavy rainfall.

Linguistic Affiliation. Chinantec is a branch of the Otomanguean Language Family. Its closest linguistic relations are with Amuzgan and Popolocan, but Chinantec has been separated from them for about 3,500 years. Fourteen dialects are recognized.

Demography. There were 12,000 Chinantec speakers in 1876, the date of the earliest population estimate. The 1980 census reports an estimated 67,000 Chinantec speakers, 17,000 of whom speak no Spanish.

History and Cultural Relations

The origin of the Chinantec is unknown. It is possible that they migrated from the west near the Tehuacán Valley to their present location as recently as A.D. 1000. By the fifteenth century Chinantec settlements were concentrated in the well-watered, fertile lowland valleys near present-day Valle Nacional. The Chinantla was successfully invaded in 1454–1455 by Nahuatl speakers and then again in the early sixteenth century by the Spanish. Three closely spaced epidemics of European-introduced diseases soon decimated an estimated 80 percent of the Chinantec population, and by the 1570s many Chinantec lived in dispersed hamlets of eleven to fifteen persons. To facilitate political control and religious conversion, colonial authorities forcibly congregated these Chinantec in concentrated communities in the highlands. A great simplification in social structure was one result. Most of the Chinantec region was not held in *encomienda* but instead administered directly by the crown. Although the Spaniards had hoped to find vast deposits of gold there, the area came instead to be valued for cotton and cochineal. By the nineteenth century the best lands had been taken by foreign companies, and many lowland Chinantec were again displaced. Even after the 1910 Mexican Revolution, coffee, banana, and tobacco production remained in foreign hands. Development programs instituted since 1947 by the Papaloapan River Commission displaced other lowland Chinantec.

The Chinantec region is contiguous with Zapotec communities to the south and those of the Cuicatec to the west, Mazatec to the north, and Mixe to the southeast.

Settlements

History and variable terrain have contributed to the diversity of Chinantec settlement patterns—notably, congregated, semicongregated, and dispersed. Each town has a number of smaller, dependent hamlets, which are abandoned when their soil becomes exhausted. Settlements range in size from town centers of about 1,000 to hamlets of just one nuclear family. Some larger communities are subdivided into corporate, exogamic barrios that control lands, milling machinery, and religious chapels. Only in

the lowlands do towns follow the standard Spanish grid pattern. Although most highland houses possess an adjoining garden plot, they lack obstructing hedges or fences. Lowland houses are rectangular and windowless, with doors at both ends, wooden posts, and thatched or tin roofs. Highland houses are also rectangular but have windows. They are generally adobe with tile or tin roofs, although some are concrete.

Economy

Subsistence and Commercial Activities. Traditionally, the Chinantec used digging sticks to cultivate maize, beans, and squashes. Forced displacement into the upper-mountain regions brought about adoption of the European bull-drawn plow. The Chinantec cultivate these same three crops today, supplemented by raising fowl and pigs and some wild and cultivated fruits and nuts. Today, as in the past, slash-and-burn gardening is most common. There still is no irrigation, and few farmers use fertilizer. Fishing continues to be important in the lowlands. Coffee is of increasing significance as a cash crop. During the nineteenth century many Chinantec subsistence farmers also worked as peons on local, foreign-owned plantations in the riverside regions. Today many Chinantec of both sexes are temporary or permanent labor migrants to Mexican cities and the United States.

Industrial Arts. The Chinantec have few technological activities other than farming. Since at least the 1950s, most items have been purchased. Only limited domestic production of fiber bags and baskets, fishing nets, pottery, and *huipiles* (handwoven women's garments) persisted into the present.

Trade. In the past the subsistence crops were neither exported nor traded. All other products were obtained from resident merchants or itinerant peddlers, who were usually Cuicatec in the lowlands and Zapotec in the highlands. Coffee export to the national market dates at least to 1900. At various historical periods, native markets were found in highland communities, but they often had to be suspended owing to intercommunity tension. These trade patterns persist, although the advent of a highway, connecting roads, and motor transport enables the Chinantec to leave their communities to make purchases in Oaxaca, Tuxtepec, and Valle Nacional.

Division of Labor. Women and men both engage in agriculture, although the nature and extent of women's participation varies by community. Women are also responsible for all domestic tasks, including care of pigs and fowl. These contemporary patterns appear to have historical precedent. Today both sexes also engage in cash-generating activities. Children traditionally participated in agricultural activities from about the age of 7. They continue to do so today as classes permit.

Land Tenure. Most townships have communally owned tracts, with members permitted indefinite occupancy and use, although the land cannot be alienated. In the past, corporate groups such as barrios or age grades also controlled limited communal lands. In addition, communities may have smallholder plots. In riverside communities plantations were expropriated from foreign companies by the federal agrarian reform program and awarded to Chinantec peasants who cultivate and govern them as *ejidos*.

Kinship

Kin Groups and Descent.   Descent is strictly bilateral. There is no evidence of lineages or other extended kinship groups, nor of kinship units owning specific pieces of land.

Kinship Terminology.   Chinantec kinship fits George P. Murdock's general definition of the Hawaiian classification, but in classifying the parental generation and descending lineal generations it approaches Type b, European, in the Lowie-Kirchhoff scheme.

Marriage and Family

Marriage.   Marriage was traditionally arranged by the groom's parents, directly or through an intermediary. This custom continues in attenuated form. Female virginity was, and still is, not essential. In some areas short periods of bride- or groom-service were formerly expected; elopements were frequent, in part because ritual gifts and other aspects of the wedding were so expensive. Polygyny was apparently practiced prior to the Spanish Conquest and, to a limited extent, thereafter. Today, as in the past, divorce is not permitted, but marital separations sometimes occur, in which case the abandoning partner is fined.

Domestic Unit.   The conjugal pair, their minor children, and sometimes a surviving parent are the most common domestic unit. Sons, or occasionally daughters, may live with their parents for a short time following marriage. Single-person households are rare.

Inheritance.   Customs vary by locality, and in communities where most lands are communal, there may be little other than the house and house site to inherit. In general, sons inherit more often than daughters and receive equal shares. The house is typically inherited by the youngest son (or daughter), who is expected to care for the elderly parents until their death.

Socialization.   The mother, along with older siblings, carries out most child socialization. There are no specific children's games but rather ones improvised with natural products like earth or flowers. Children are given responsibilities at a young age. Communities vary greatly in their attitudes toward formal schooling, from those that place great stock in it to those that are indifferent. In the past, only boys were formally educated, but now girls also attend school.

Sociopolitical Organization

Social Organization.   Although considerable variation is seen among communities, the core of all Chinantec social organization is the nuclear family, with a tendency toward extension through Catholic *compadrazgo*, or godparent sponsorship. In the past, many Chinantec communities were organized around corporate groups, such as barrios, age grades, and status groups (e.g., widows). In some communities, barrio structures were elaborate and could include socio-ritual organizations and marriage prohibitions. Today barrios are of small importance. Age grades formerly contributed to men's status; after successfully fulfilling a series of ranked community responsibilities, they became respected elders, or *ancianos*. Such individuals were viewed as collectively responsible for the community's welfare. Today, as in the past, women in most communities do not participate in formal political activities, but they are not submissive to men and enjoy high social status.

Political Organization.   Chinantec political organization, as throughout rural Mesoamerica, consists of a civil-religious hierarchy (*cargo* system). In most communities the post-Conquest pattern survives: all married men are obliged to serve in unremunerated public office; men living in outlying hamlets usually must serve in the center. All matters affecting community welfare are discussed in public assemblies composed of all men under age 50. A council of elders, which survives in conservative communities, is an extraconstitutional body responsible for protecting the community from internal dissension and the threat of supernatural forces. Although the elders cannot override the municipal president, no major decision is made without consulting them. In the past, the collectivity of ancianos appointed officeholders and had the authority to sanction those who refused to serve. Today state law requires that town officers be elected by universal suffrage. In less conservative communities, the president and elected authorities are now counseled by groups of bilingual, middle-aged married men.

Social Control.   Traditional discipline was not harsh and rewards and punishments for both children and adults were generally verbal, with the exception of the public execution of witches accused of causing epidemics (e.g., of whooping cough). The chief concern of the police was to prevent quarrels, fires, or other damage caused by excessive alcohol consumption. Today, punishment is still lenient. The ritual elders, in conjunction with municipal authorities, are responsible for maintaining the public peace. Gossip and fear of witchcraft are the main means of social control.

Conflict.   The Chinantec were not and are not today violently competitive; particularly in the highlands, homicide and even physical fighting are rare. Nevertheless, long-standing friction between neighboring Chinantec communities, between head towns and dependent hamlets, and even between barrios continues to be common. In communities where both Chinantec and mestizos reside, intergroup relations are fraught with conflict.

Religion and Expressive Culture

Religious Beliefs.   Chinantec religion after the Spanish/Catholic Conquest had many syncretic elements (e.g., a bisexual "Father and Mother of Maize"). Chinantec cosmology posited two worlds, day and night, in eternal struggle. Creation myths varied but most were based on humans descending from monkeys or monkeys as the ancients. Deference, respect, and gratitude are shown to prominent features of the natural environment and the creatures inhabiting it; failure to do this is punished by sickness. Although the Chinantec are still nominally Catholic, there have been Protestant inroads in some communities.

The best evidence of pre-Christian expressive culture is the sizable Chinantec collection of folklore about the sun and moon, animal "tricksters," and "owners" or "kings" of animal and fish species, prominent mountain peaks, the earth, and other natural phenomena. There are divining specialists who gain access to the supernatural world by using hallucinogenic psilocybin mushrooms or seeds of the _Rivea corymbosa_ vine. Use of these substances is not restricted to specialists.

Religious Practitioners. Most Chinantec communities are served by parish priests who visit once or twice a year on major holidays. These visits are supplemented by another priest contracted to celebrate Mass on other important fiesta days. In the absence of a resident priest, communities rely on trained laypeople to perform rosaries. Particularly in the highlands, there is a long history of fractious relations with local priests; many of these conflicts persist to this day. Traditional, divination specialists still exist in some communities.

Ceremonies. Differential disposal of male and female placentas continues in some communities: a girl's is buried under the family hearth, and a boy's is hung on a nearby tree branch. Chinantec rites to assure the harvest, once common, persist in places in attenuated form. One or more elders may still undertake an annual pilgrimage to churches in neighboring villages or major towns in the Oaxaca Valley in an effort to assure the village welfare. The principal festivals are the annual pre-Lenten carnivals, organized by bachelors, which reenact the arrival of the Spanish conquerors. Also important are the annual fiestas that honor each community's patron saint and the New Year's Day ceremony marking the investiture of new officials.

Arts. No evidence of traditional Chinantec arts, crafts, drama, or other aesthetic expression has been found. In some highland communities, a well-developed complex of dances is performed for carnival. Village bands play at all ceremonial occasions.

Medicine. A rich tradition of medicinal-herb use predates the Spanish Conquest. Today, curing is by herbal, spiritual, and mechanical techniques. There are few indigenous Chinantec healers, and people are reluctant to go to either physicians or specialized curers; most health care is administered by women at home.

Death and Afterlife. A person is born with several souls. Death can be caused by kidnapping one of them. All souls leave the body at death. Among the Chinantec there is no fear of a soul or a ghost returning to haunt the living. Although never elaborate, death rites varied. The cadaver was usually rolled in a straw mat or a sheet or placed in a wooden box. In the lowlands, objects (e.g., clothing, flowers, food) were often buried along with the corpse. There was generally some form of ritual purification after burial. In the highlands, there were no grave objects or ritual purification. Today graves are prepared by municipal officials, and the body is accompanied to the cemetery by municipal musicians.

Bibliography

Bevan, Bernard (1938). _The Chinantec: Report on the Central and South-Eastern Chinantec Region._ Vol. 1, _The Chinantec and Their Habitat._ Publication 24. Mexico City: Instituto Panamericano de Geografia Historia.

Hopkins, Nicholas (1984). "Otomanguean Linguistic Prehistory." In _Essays in Otomanguean Culture History,_ edited by J. Kathryn Josserand, Marcus Winter, and Nicholas Hopkins, 25–64. Publication no. 31. Nashville: Vanderbilt University Publications in Anthropology.

Weitlaner, Roberto J., and Howard F. Cline (1969). "The Chinantec." In _Handbook of Middle American Indians,_ edited by Robert Wauchope. Vol. 7, _Ethnology, Part One,_ edited by Evon Z. Vogt, 523–552. Austin: University of Texas Press.

C. H. BROWNER AND ARTHUR J. RUBEL

We wish to thank Sarah L. Cline for graciously providing access to the field notes and papers of her late father, Howard F. Cline.

Chinese in the English-Speaking Caribbean

ETHNONYMS: Chinee Royal, "Colored" Chinese, Creole Chinese

Orientation

Identification. Conventional wisdom has it that the overseas Chinese cling to their ancestral traditions and reject the forces of acculturation. Research suggests that Caribbean Chinese may be exceptions to this rule in that they have been creolized. The Creole culture forged in the Caribbean, over a period of five centuries, combines primarily elements from Europe and Africa, the cultures with the longest history in the region. Creolization, then, is the process by which peoples who are neither African nor European become enculturated in Euro-African culture.

Location. Between 1853 and 1879, 14,000 Chinese laborers were imported to the British Caribbean as part of a larger system of contract labor bound for the sugar plantations. The majority of indentured laborers—almost half a million—came from India. There were also several thousand Portuguese from the Madeira Islands. Most of the laborers were destined for British Guiana (Guyana), taken from the Dutch in the Napoleonic Wars, and Trinidad, captured from Spain in 1797 (these two new colonies were underpopulated and underdeveloped compared to Jamaica). The sugar planters of British Guiana and Trinidad were attempting to rival Jamaica during the nineteenth century.

Demography. Most of the Chinese laborers initially went to British Guiana; however, importation ended in 1879, and the population declined steadily, mostly from out-migration to Trinidad and Suriname. In the 1960s the Chinese comprised 0.6 percent (i.e., about 4,800) of the Guyanese population of 800,000, 0.65 percent (i.e., about

14,462) of the Jamaican population of 2,225,000, and 1 percent (i.e., about 10,000) of the Trinidadian population of 1,000,000. Although the sex ratio and the proportion of racially mixed to "pure" is unclear, the vast majority were born locally. The issue of "racial purity" is a thorny one because racial mixing is a cultural ideal in Creole society, except among the upper class, and because census figures are based on self-identification. Hence, at least some of those who identify themselves as Chinese are racially mixed. Many racially mixed Chinese also identify themselves as "mixed," a census category that, in Trinidad in 1990, comprised 207,558. The population census of 1990 in Trinidad and Tobago revealed 4,314 Chinese out of a total population of 1,125,128, males numbering 2,317 and females 1,997. The dramatic population decline is mainly the result of tremendous out-migration, mostly to North America.

Linguistic Affiliation.　Chinese, as a language, is virtually extinct. Generally speaking, Chinese in the English-speaking Caribbean speak Creole English.

History and Cultural Relations

Chinese migrated to the British Caribbean in two phases. The first was part of a larger population movement from China to all of the Americas. In the mid-nineteenth century, as other Chinese journeyed to North America, one-quarter of a million Chinese (45 percent of Chinese immigrants to the Western Hemisphere) were heading for other parts of the Americas: 125,000 (48 percent) went to Cuba, 100,000 (38 percent) to Peru; but only 18,000 (8 percent) reached the former British West Indies (Jamaica, Trinidad, and British Guiana, now Guyana). The remaining 6 percent moved in small streams to the part of Colombia that became Panama in 1903, to Costa Rica, the Dutch and French West Indies, Brazil, and even to Chile.

The second phase of Chinese migration to the British Caribbean took place within a larger context of general immigration to the region after 1834, the year that the Emancipation of African slaves took effect. Sugar cultivation had been the cornerstone of the British West Indian economy since the middle of the seventeenth century. Together with the Atlantic slave trade, plantation slavery satisfied the labor requirements of this system of agricultural production. Even before 1834, however, the sugar planters clamored to import indentured laborers, arguing that the profitability of the plantation system hinged on the presence of an abundant and cheap labor force; they were outraged at the thought of losing their slaves.

The foundations of Caribbean Creole society were laid down in the days of plantation slavery. Over the course of four centuries it evolved into a three-tiered pyramidal structure—a "pigmentocracy," permeated by color bias. Small in numbers, the light-skinned elite, at the top, consisted mostly of planters and government officials. In the middle was the darker-colored middle class, produced by miscegenation between European masters and slave women. Their intermediate status derived from the special privileges given them: education, occupational skills, and the right to own property at a time when the slave majority was still defined by law as property. These racial hybrids not only identified with the ruling class, but also emulated

them by attempting to distance themselves from the lower class in ways other than physical, devoting their lives to the pursuit of respectability. For instance, the middle class chose to adopt religious faiths linked to European orthodoxy such as those of the Catholic, Anglican, or Methodist churches, whereas the lower class preferred more exuberant (and African-inspired) forms of worship such as those of the Shango, Spiritual Baptists, Pukkumina, and the like.

It was not until the mid-nineteenth century that other racial and cultural groups, including the Chinese, entered the picture, by which time the basic structure had long been established. The task of the newcomers was to grasp the nature of the Caribbean power structure and find their places within this hierarchical arrangement. In pursuit of upward mobility, the Chinese understood the need to comprehend and master Creole culture.

Settlements

Imported as a contract labor force from China, Chinese settled in three main locations: Jamaica, Trinidad, and British Guiana, initially working on the sugar plantations. In British Guiana, however, they stayed on the plantations much longer because other occupational outlets such as retail trade and market gardening were monopolized by the Portuguese and were thus closed to Chinese. In Trinidad and Jamaica, they promptly deserted the plantations.

Economy

Subsistence and Commercial Activities.　There are differences in the historical development of economic activities among the Chinese in the three different locations. In British Guiana, the planter class allowed the Portuguese to develop a monopoly on retail trade, which the Chinese were not able to enter until the turn of the twentieth century. The Chinese population dwindled rapidly as migrants sought better opportunities in Trinidad, Suriname, and Jamaica. Those who remained practiced a wide range of occupations; many joined the civil service. There was also a corresponding range in wealth and subtle class divisions. In Trinidad, after abandoning the plantations, most Chinese went into the rurally dispersed retail trade, although some had become major merchants themselves by 1896, expanding into wholesale trade, direct importation, and investment in the then-budding petroleum industry. Most important, the retail trade in Trinidad was shared among the Chinese, the East Indians, and the Portuguese. Thus, although shopkeeping in general was regarded as exploitative, animosity was never directed exclusively at the Chinese.

Trade.　The Chinese dominated the retail grocery trade in Jamaica beginning in the 1890s. Indeed, a Chinatown developed in Kingston and radiated into the countryside. In the Jamaican case, the preponderance of Hakka over Cantonese promoted subcultural solidarity, in contrast to the Chinese community in Trinidad, which was segmented according to region of origin and language. In fact, Hakka commercial success in Jamaica was bitterly resented (particularly by historically older groups of Chinese immigrants who were less successful in achieving upward mobility), to the extent that Hakka became the targets of violence in riots in 1918, 1938, and 1965. The 1930s in the English-speaking Caribbean was a time of tremendous political and economic turmoil: general strikes and rioting ensued from the global depression, and the region's trade-union movement was born.

Division of Labor. Observations of the Chinese community in British Guiana in 1956 revealed a cleavage between those born in China and those born in the Caribbean. The former were primarily small merchants and shopkeepers, many of whom corresponded with their families and sent remittances to them in China. Sometimes they were also active in family affairs. They saved money either to return to China themselves or to recruit kin to work in the family business. This included importing brides from China who would then work in the small shops alongside their husbands. Added to the shopkeeping work of these wives were household duties, as well as child-care responsibilities. Some of the men born in China had wives and children there, as well as in British Guiana. The men's cultural identification was definitely oriented toward China.

In contrast, those born locally cared little about China. Having been creolized, they identified with Guyanese culture and considered themselves Guyanese. They were described as having a foreigner's ignorance of China and no appreciation of Chinese history; their knowledge of the past being limited to the accounts of the lives of their personal ancestors. They were neither literate in written Chinese, nor could they speak any Chinese dialect. The women, in particular, rejected marriage opportunities to men born in China, complaining that these men did not have Guyanese friends, did not know how to dance or party, and did not know how to have a good time, furthermore, they spoke English poorly and had great difficulty communicating with locally born women who spoke only Creole English. Men born in China, in turn, complained that locally born women were too Westernized: they were not frugal, industrious, or self-sacrificing and wanted too many comforts. A similar situation prevailed in Trinidad.

Kinship

The Chinese in Guyana have been described as "scarcely Chinese" in matters of culture. In the realm of kinship, for instance, although a broad range of kin ties was recognized and kin were scattered throughout the colony in separate households, there were no clans, no attempt to trace lineages or to keep genealogies, no ancestral tablets or ancestor worship, and no common burial ground. There was no Chinese newspaper, nor were there Chinese schools to teach Chinese language and culture or to provide other features of a formal Chinese education. There was no Chinatown nor a concentration of Chinese businesses. There were very few voluntary associations and only one or two recreational clubs. Given the absence of descent groups, it follows that there is now no corresponding kin terminology based on principles of descent. Chinese in the English-speaking Caribbean use English terms of reference and terms of address that reflect the kindred principle such as "aunt," "uncle," "cousin," and so forth.

Marriage and Family

Marriage. Given the shortage of Chinese women in the Americas during the nineteenth century, Chinese men were willing to marry Black women, especially those who were shopkeepers in the countryside. Although many of these unions were common-law marriages, some were official. The motivation was partly to develop rapport with their Black clientele, but also to engage their trust. In the early twentieth century, some men born in China continued to arrive in the Caribbean for commercial purposes and imported China-born wives. Since the end of World War II, however, with the creolization of second, third, and fourth generations, traditional arranged marriages only take place among the few born in China and, hence, are rare. The marriage norm clearly favors a Chinese spouse (locally born, however), although marriage to Euro-Americans and Europeans is acceptable. Marriage to East Indians and Blacks is explicitly frowned upon, but the existence of many racially mixed Chinese is evidence that such unions are not infrequent. In Jamaica, the racially mixed are called "Chinee Royal."

Domestic Unit. The traditional Chinese patriarchal family is virtually nonexistent. The basic household unit is the nuclear family in which women work, have an equal voice in family affairs, and are often very influential in business matters. It is important to note, however, that nuclear-family households are strongly linked to extended kin with whom they interact frequently and exchange personal services such as child care. Among the less affluent, there is also a pooling of income and other resources.

Socialization. Intimate relationships with Creole women encouraged the creolization of Chinese men, which enhanced their acceptance by the Creole people who surrounded them. Knowing only Creole culture themselves, Creole wives were powerful agents of creolization of their children, which ensured the creolization of subsequent generations. Furthermore, Chinese immigrants were willing to learn Creole languages, which included both Creole English and Creole French, called _patois,_ and adopted English and French surnames. For instance, there are Chinese families in Trinidad with surnames like Scott and McLean. Subsequent generations not only moved away from the Chinese language as the main channel of communication but adopted Western values and styles of dress; however, even the children of mixed-race unions developed dual identities (i.e., Chinese and Euro-African).

Sociopolitical Organization

Social Organization. A study of the Chinese in Jamaica suggested that their economic success was made possible by the replication of Chinese social institutions. The most important of these, of course, was the rotating-credit association, which enabled many to accumulate enough capital to underwrite business ventures. The creation of the Chinese Benevolent Society served to disseminate information about rules and regulations governing commerce, later it became the hub of social life. There were also secret societies, or tongs. In response to the political unrest of the 1930s, when they were denounced for not supporting the then-budding labor movement, the Chinese formed merchant associations to protect their businesses. Other institutions included a Chinese alms house, a Chinese home for the aged, a Chinese sanatorium, a Chinese funeral home, and a Chinese cemetery. In matters of culture, they established a Chinese newspaper (the *Chinese Public News*); a Chinese library; a literary society promoting Chinese music and drama and featuring lectures on China; and a Chinese public school to teach their children Chinese history and language. By means of these institutions the Chinese in Jamaica cultivated their cultural (Hakka) distinctiveness and perpetuated their social isolation from Creole society.

In contrast, the Chinese in Trinidad were divided along lines of social class, expressed not only in residence patterns but in membership in district associations. The well-to-do lived in high-status, fashionable Creole neighborhoods, separated from other Chinese shopkeepers who lived above their shops in depressed neighborhoods or in the country. This upper class belonged to a literary society, the China Society, where they discussed things such as horse breeding, foreign travel, good marriages, sending their children to good universities in Britain and North America, and fears of Communism.

A handful of district associations in Trinidad were formed on the basis of region of origin in China, and their membership embraced mostly small shopkeepers, restaurant owners, and laundry owners. Often located in dilapidated buildings in run-down, commercial parts of town, these associations, in the early days, were reputed to be gambling houses, then later became centers for sports and recreation. They also housed banquet halls to celebrate festivals such as "double-ten" (i.e., 10 October), the date of the birth of the Republic in China in 1911, and ceremonies like weddings, during which Chinese food would be served, to be followed by Creole-style dancing to Creole-style music played by Creole orchestras.

Political Organization. The Chinese in the English-speaking Caribbean are governed by the national Governments of Jamaica, Trinidad, and Guyana. It is interesting to note that one of early governors-general of independent Guyana, Sir Arthur Chung, was part Chinese, and the first governor-general of independent Trinidad and Tobago, Sir Solomon Hochoy, was also Chinese. Patterson (1975) has observed that this could not have happened in Jamaica, where Chinese encapsulation fueled an image of them being far-removed from nation building.

Religion and Expressive Culture

Religious Beliefs. The Chinese, including those born in China, were quick to convert to Christianity. By 1891, a majority had become Anglican, and many had become Catholic, the two major denominations, whereas a few became Presbyterians, Methodists, and so on. Clearly, the Chinese recognized that upward mobility had to be on Creole terms, requiring not only entrance into the Western colonial education system but also nominal adherence to one of the Western religions, which were sponsors of many of the better schools. Hence, Chinese moved to urban areas to give their children access to better schools. School, then, became the main socializing agent, bringing Chinese children into contact with other races and cultures in Creole society. Indeed, a high illiteracy rate among East Indians in the Caribbean was the price paid for not converting from Hinduism and Islam to Christianity until World War II.

Food, Sports, and Recreation. Chinese food is very popular, and there are many Chinese restaurants in Caribbean cities, which illustrates Chinese success in popularizing their own cuisine in Creole society. At the same time, however, it has been creolized in the sense that it has incorporated many local ingredients, for example, Shaddo Benie, a potent spice resembling cilantro. Another distinctive characteristic of Carribean Chinese cuisine is the use of parboiled rice, which has a slightly different flavor from the rice of mainland China. The Chinese were also successful in popularizing their gambling games: Whe whe (pronounced "way-way") is a numbers game played by many in Trinidad, and in 1994 it became a nationally televised numbers game called "Play Whe" that is almost as popular as the national lottery. With regard to sports, the Chinese avidly adopted Western games such as cricket, soccer, tennis, and badminton. According to Look Lai (1993), a Chinese New Year street parade was held only in nineteenth-century British Guiana.

Arts. There are several prominent artists among the Trinidad Chinese who are well-known for their paintings; for instance, Carlysle Chan and Sibyl Atteck are virtual household names. There are also Chinese designers of Carnival costumes, as well as leaders of masquerade bands in the Trinidad Carnival, such as Stephen Lee Heung and Max Awon. The Carnival celebration is an important national event including music competitons and dancing. Trinidadian calypsonian "Crazy," whose real name is Edwin Ayoung, is Creole Chinese. Ever-popular, he has produced many calypso hits since 1978. In Jamaica, Byron Lee is a Creole Chinese bandleader whose party music has thrilled audiences for decades. He has fans not only in the Caribbean, but also throughout the Caribbean diaspora.

Medicine. Chinese herbal medicines are sold by Chinese shopkeepers in the Caribbean. These medicines, although marketed for a Chinese—yet Westernized clientele—to treat common ailments such as colds, arthritis, and stomach upsets, are also used by Creole people.

Bibliography

Bentley, Gerald, and Frances Henry (1969). "Some Preliminary Observations on the Chinese in Trinidad." In *McGill Studies in Caribbean Anthropology*, edited by Frances Henry, 19–33. Montreal: McGill University, Centre for Developing-Area Studies.

Fried, Morton H. (1956). "Some Observations on the Chinese in British Guiana." *Social and Economic Studies* 5(1): 54–73.

Ho, Christine G. T. (1989). "Hold the Chow Mein, Gimme Soca: Creolization of the Chinese in Guyana, Trinidad, and Jamaica." *Amerasia Journal* 15(2): 3–25.

Johnson, Howard (1987). "The Chinese in Trinidad in the

Late Nineteenth Century." *Ethnic and Racial Studies* 10(1): 82–95.

Lee, Russell Dwight (1979). "The Perils of Ethnic Success: The Rise and Flight of the Chinese Traders in Jamaica." Ph.D. dissertation, Harvard University.

Look Lai, Walton (1993). *Indentured Labor, Caribbean Sugar: Chinese and Indian Migrants to the British West Indies, 1838–1918.* Baltimore: Johns Hopkins University Press.

Nettleford, Rex (1970). *Mirror, Mirror: Identity, Race, and Protest in Jamaica.* Kingston: Collins & Sangster.

Patterson, Orlando (1975). "Context and Choice in Ethnic Allegiance: A Theoretical Framework and Caribbean Case Study." In *Ethnicity: Theory and Experience,* edited by Nathan Glazer and Daniel P. Moynihan, 305–349. Cambridge: Harvard University Press.

CHRISTINE G. T. HO

Chinese of Costa Rica

ETHNONYMS: la Colonia China (the Chinese colony), los Cantoneses (the Cantonese), los Chinos (the Chinese)

Orientation

Identification. The Chinese of Costa Rica constitute a small ethnic community of immigrants from southern China (Guangdong Province) and their descendants. The migrants, who began to arrive in the second half of the nineteenth century, worked as indentured servants in farm labor, domestic service, and the construction of the railroad to the Atlantic coast. Since then, other immigrants from the same districts in southern China, who are directly and indirectly related to the first groups, have continued to migrate in small numbers to Costa Rica.

The immigrants and their descendants rapidly turned to commercial activities for subsistence, coming to dominate the economy of some communities throughout the country. At present, they constitute an important part of Costa Rican society, with a strong presence in the commercial sector and increasing participation in professional fields and politics.

Location. The first and second generations of immigrants settled mostly in and around the country's two main ports on the Pacific and Atlantic coasts. From 1883 through 1973, (except the year 1892) the largest numbers were found in towns and villages throughout the Atlantic coast, where immigrants who had arrived in 1873 had been engaged in the construction of the railroad.

The Pacific port of Pantarenas was the port of entry for most immigrants, and thus became another focus of settlement. From that port, immigrants moved into the northwestern region of the country, the dry, tropical Pacific province of Guanacaste, following agricultural settlement of that area. By the time of the 1892 census, their presence was common in the main cities of the Central Valley: San José, Cartago, Heredia, and Alajuela. In 1927 the largest immigrant populations were found on the Atlantic coast and in the provinces of Pantarenas and Guanacaste, in that order.

A significant settlement pattern emerged in the first stages of migration, when immigrants clearly chose to settle away from the centers of power, accepting small-volume commercial opportunities provided by towns and villages in rural areas, possibly in exchange for limited competition and a low profile. Another pattern is that settlement radiated out from the two main ports: Pantarenas on the Pacific coast and Limón on the Atlantic side.

Demography. In 1864 only 3 Chinese immigrants were reported by the less-than-adequate census, despite the fact that nine years earlier, 73 Chinese had entered the country legally, albeit under unknown terms. The following census, that of 1883, reports 219 Chinese, only ten years after 653 had entered the country under contract to the railroad company. In both instances, the census probably failed to register all Chinese; immigrants, in turn, were probably not eager to be recorded in the census because they were subject to repatriation when their contracts expired or were canceled. Underreporting and unorthodox means of entry and registration have since affected the quality of information on the immigrants.

The largest number of immigrants from southern China living in Costa Rica at any point in time is the 933 (0.001 percent of the population) reported in 1950. In 1963 the census reported 666 China-born residents, but only 271 (41 percent) claimed Chinese nationality, an important shift toward greater assimilation, which began after the Communist Revolution of 1949 in China and is clearly recorded over the next two decades after 1963. Another significant trend is that by 1984 the southern Chinese represented only 6 percent of the Chinese in Costa Rica. Others are from Taiwan and Hong Kong, with the Taiwanese representing 83.4 percent of those who are Chinese by birth. At present, the numbers of Taiwanese continue to increase, whereas the immigration of southern Chinese has virtually stopped. The largest concentrations of Asian immigrants are found in the cities of the Central Valley and in the ports, much as in the past. No data are available on the number of individuals of mixed Costa Rican-Chinese culture.

Linguistic Affiliation. Two main Cantonese dialects were spoken by the immigrants, depending on their place of origin: the dialect spoken in the area of Zhong shan, place of origin of those who settled in the Pacific and northwestern region, and the dialect, and variants thereof, spoken in the district of En ping, where most settlers of the Atlantic region originated. A very small number of immigrants spoke the Haaka dialect and other dialects of southern China. Presently, only the eldest and the most recent immigrants speak Chinese dialects. Among the descendants, both pure and mixed, little value is attached to knowing the Chinese language, although other cultural values are held in high regard. In fact, Chinese cultural values related to family structure, roles and traditions, and social values and ethics persist among immigrants and descendants.

History and Cultural Relations

In 1855 two groups totaling 73 Chinese immigrants arrived in the port of Pantarenas, Costa Rica, from Panama, where they had probably been engaged in the construction of the transisthmian railroad completed that year, to work as domestic servants and farm hands in the large haciendas of general José Cañas and the German baron von Bulow on the Pacific coast of Costa Rica. Little is known about them and their descendants.

A second and more important group of 653 contract workers arrived in 1873 from Macao to work in the construction of the railroad to the Atlantic coast. The government later approved the railroad company's request for additional Chinese laborers, but there is no clear evidence that any others entered the country under subsequent railroad contracts. A number of studies have focused on this second group, those who joined them later, and their descendants.

The background of these other migrations to the Americas is found in the growing poverty and political unrest experienced by China in the eighteenth and nineteenth centuries, particularly in the provinces of Guangdong, Fujian, Jiangsu, and Hunan. The need for a large number of cheap laborers to replace African slaves after Abolition constituted the main attracting factor of the Americas. The colonial presence of Portugal in Macao and the British in Hong Kong facilitated the emigration of large numbers of Chinese who participated as indentured workers in the construction of railroads in Peru, Panama, the Caribbean, the United States, and Mexico. They also provided labor for the plantations of the Caribbean region and for the excavation of the Panama Canal.

After 1873, when railroad contacts began facilitating Chinese immigration, the first immigrants to Costa Rica were joined by near and distant kin, real and nominal, who arrived in small numbers. Steadily, however, they increased the size of the immigrant community and also replaced elder members who were retiring to their ancestral homes in China. The immigrant community also grew through intermarriage with Hispanic women, and, very exceptionally, Hispanic men, such unions creating cross-cultural individuals, the *cruzados*, who were, and continue to be, a very important link to the local Hispanic community. Although primarily socialized within Hispanic culture, the cruzados retain an appreciative understanding of their forefathers' culture and a deep regard for the immigrant's historical experience, and thus they have been able to act as cultural and social brokers between the immigrant community and Costa Rica society.

Since 1950, Taiwanese immigrants have been migrating to Costa Rica in large numbers; by 1984 they outnumbered the mainland Chinese by 14 to 1. Although the Hispanic community perceives the two groups as one and the same, in fact the two differ markedly in their origins, their social, economic, and demographic characteristics, and in their reasons for migrating to Costa Rica.

Immigrants from Hong Kong have also been entering the country since the early 1950s, and, like the Taiwanese, they constitute a separate subculture of Chinese culture in Costa Rica.

Economy

The original immigrants left their contract jobs within a short period of time. Of the 653 who had entered under the railroad contract of 1873, only 236 remained with the railroad project a year later. Departure from the railroad was facilitated by the purchase of their contracts by private citizens, for whom the immigrants performed domestic services and farm labor. Once freed from their contractual obligations, a few sold vegetables, poultry, and household merchandise in the streets of the port towns, but most set up small grocery stores (*pulperías*), eateries (*fondas*), and drinking establishments. To finance these enterprises, they counted on the small savings obtained while under contract, and on loans from their previous patrons and other Chinese immigrants. The credit societies they established once they had begun to accumulate capital became a very important—often the only—source of credit, especially among newcomers.

By 1902, immigrants had become dominant in the economy of the port of Limón, where they owned the largest proportion of commercial establishments that catered to railroad and banana-plantation workers. They were also dominant in the economy of the town of Cañas, in the northwestern region, and had a very strong economic presence in the port of Puntarenas, on the Pacific, and in Nicoya, on the peninsula of the same name. In other parts of the country, although not as prevalent, the store or restaurant of "el Chino" was a popular feature.

The relative economic and social independence provided by involvement in commercial activities allowed immigrants to maintain their cultural orientation toward the motherland and to supply a steady stream of monetary remittances that significantly bolstered the economies of their hometowns in China.

Eventually, a number of immigrants established businesses that flourished and permitted expansion into other economic areas, such as agricultural production, while allowing them to provide credit to young immigrants who were just getting started. Among them were veritable tycoons such as José Chen Apuy, who established the well-known general store "Man chong sing" in Puntarenas and who helped many of his countrymen with the process of immigration and settlement; Juan José León Yee, a successful merchant, agricultural producer, and common-cause politician on the city council of the port of Limón, who was a well-regarded benefactor of that city; and Luís Wa Chong, one of the first cattlemen in the northern Atlantic plains and among the first coffee producers in the southern Pacific region of Coto Brus. He later became Costa Rican ambassador-at-large to the community of Asian nations.

Since the 1950s, many Chinese merchants have diversified their investments; from the traditional small and large grocery stores and restaurants, which are still the most visible enterprises, they have branched out into farming (rice, cattle), agro-industry (processing agricultural products, such as cocoa, for export), and small local industry (dried foods, pastries, rubber thongs).

Marriage and Family

The first groups of immigrants were composed of young unskilled men, many of whom established consensual unions with local Hispanic women of low socioeconomic status and rural background. Immigrants of solid economic status brought brides from China or from immigrant colonies in neighboring countries, such as Panama and Colombia. Otherwise, an undetermined number of immigrants, and later their descendants, traveled to China to find consorts.

As unions between Chinese immigrants and Hispanic women produced offspring, the growing population of cruzados provided marriageable partners to an immigrant community that was chronically faced with a scarcity of females.

In an effort to strengthen Chinese cultural values, immigrants who could afford to sent their older children to special schools for immigrants' children in southern China, (Hong Kong, Zhong shan) and encouraged them to marry preselected Chinese brides.

The family structure prevalent among Costa Rican Chinese today can be safely assumed to represent patterns common in southern China, first practiced by the early immigrants, mixed with those of local Hispanic society, as introduced by Hispanic consorts and by the descendants raised and educated in Costa Rica. The structure was based on a clearly defined hierarchy of positions of authority and roles, in which gender and age were the most important factors. The oldest males in the family —grandfather, father, and his brothers—held the highest position of authority and respect, followed by male children in descending order. Kinship terminology emphasized the rank of males in the structure and clan membership as defined through the father's line of descent. Under traditional rules of inheritance, older males likewise, had more rights, and females were practically excluded.

Although the family structure valued by traditional local Hispanic society is similar in principle to that of the immigrants, Hispanic women play a more important role in the family hierarchy and in decision making; the incorporation of Hispanic women tended to introduce changes in the immigrant household leading to a stronger role, and increased recognition, for females. The functionality of the structure is attested by the stability of immigrant households: divorces, separations, and broken families are rare.

However, despite the father's important role in emphasizing Chinese cultural values, and despite the strength of the family structure and the economic power that helped retain descendants within the immigrant family and community, cruzado children gravitated toward the culture of their Hispanic mothers. Moreover, for both cruzado and full-blooded Chinese children, the local public-school system strengthened the process of assimilation to local Hispanic society. Today, 140 years after the arrival of the first immigrants from southern China, only the eldest members of the community, immigrants who arrived after the 1920s, retain a strong Chinese cultural identity. Their descendants, although favoring aspects of Chinese culture, are predominantly culturally Hispanic.

Sociopolitical Organization

Social Organization.   Different forms of organization evolved among the immigrants in their efforts to assist each other and needy newcomers. Orientation to the culture and community, temporary room and board, and training and financial assistance were provided by each household to its immigrating kin, followed by employment along kinship lines and the establishment of credit societies (not necessarily among kin) among those who were permanently settled in a locality. The credit system, primarily run by well-established older men in the community, replicated credit systems based on games of chance common in southern China; it continues to play an important role in the economy of the community.

Immigrant groups on the Atlantic coast region also established kinship group organizations (family or clan associations), which owned "clan houses." Thus, members of the kin group arriving from China were first housed in these clan houses, often remaining for a period of time in such quarters, while working under contract to repay their kin for the cost of transportation overseas and other services.

As the immigrant community increased in size, Chinese community clubs, which grew out of the informal meetings of the merchants in a community, were established to provide assistance and formal representation to all members of the immigrant community. For this purpose, through the financial contributions pledged by each of its members, the community bought a house in which cultural symbols were kept and traditional Chinese festivities and holidays were celebrated, along with private celebrations such as birthdays and other recreational activities. With the establishment of a club, other organizations were formed.

The elders, an informal group vested with the maximum authority on community matters, continue to meet at the club to discuss community issues, especially those that require arbitration, without involving the local Hispanic community and authorities.

As the number of women in the immigrant community increased, they formed organizations that helped them adapt to the culture, learn the language, and organize social activities for their children. Women also formed recreational groups to which the game mah-jongg was central. The clubs are still present in the larger communities, although their social functions are beginning to wane. The Atlantic coast Colony Club remains socially very active, although some of the original Chinese celebrations held there are no longer practiced.

The family or clan houses run by each family on the Atlantic coast lost part of their original purpose once the club was established, yet, as the number of immigrants of advanced age increased, such houses became retirement centers for the elders of each family who did not retire to China.

At least one community, the port of Limón, set up a

"Chinese School" in the late 1940s, for full-blooded and cruzado children; spoken and written Cantonese was taught, along with geography, history, and culture. This effort ended owing to a high dropout rate among the cruzado children, who could not be assisted by both parents in learning the language. Moreover, the bulk of students came under the competing demands of the Hispanic high school system in the late 1960s.

Political Organization. Two immigrant political organizations allowed them some degree of involvement in the political life of China: the Guomindang and the Chicuntong. The first organization had club houses in Pantarenas, San José, and Limón, where political meetings were held to rally economic support for the Chiang Kai-shek government in Taiwan. Through such support, Guomindang chapters in the Americas helped significantly in the military defense of the island.

The Chicuntong association was a less popular, Atlantic coast political organization, which opposed the Guomindang but was not categorically in favor of the Chinese Communist government. It functioned like a brotherhood, or "lodge," for the poor, and had a large membership on the coast.

Religion and Expressive Culture

Immigrants practiced forms of traditional or "popular" Buddhism, sometimes mixed with Daoist elements, common in southern China, but over the years many have become practicing Catholics.

Among the celebrations shared by the immigrants at the Colony Club were ceremonies paying homage to traditional Chinese figures and symbols; to this day traditional symbols of Chinese culture and representations of Buddhist and Confucian thought are found decorating immigrants' businesses and homes.

Fundamental in the system of beliefs of Chinese immigrants is the "cult" of the ancestors, based on reverence and emphasized in family history and structure. Rituals and gifts are presented in an annual ceremony (attended only by the men) at the tomb of the ancestors. Although an elaborate tradition in the homeland, without its social context, it became a simple ritual.

Other beliefs and practices relate to traditional superstitions common in Chinese culture dealing with natural justice (e.g., "filial piety brings its own rewards"), honesty, respect, sharing, and matters of luck, the latter being a very prevalent concern, involving games of chance.

Some of the Chinese traditions formerly celebrated by the immigrants are remembered only by the oldest members of the community because, through the years, they have been replaced by local Hispanic customs. The traditional Chinese symbols, the lions, no longer dance at the celebrations and ceremonies held by the immigrant community, but the Chinese dragon is a common feature in the Carnivals of the Caribbean coast and, occasionally, in other Hispanic festivities.

Bibliography

Chang, Sen-dou (1968). "The Distribution and Occupations of Overseas Chinese." *Geographical Review* 58(1): 89–107.

Chang-Rodriquez, E. (1958). "Chinese Labor Migration into Latin America in the Nineteenth Century." *Revista de Historia de las Américas* 46:375–397.

Fonseca, Zaida M. (1979). "Los Chinos en Costa Rica en el Siglo XIX." Thesis for the degree of Licentiate, History Department, University of Costa Rica.

León, Moisés G. (1987). "Chinese Immigrants on the Atlantic Coast of Costa Rica: The Economic Adaptation of an Asian Minority in a Pluralistic Society." Ph.D. dissertation, Tulane University, New Orleans.

Lind, Andrew W. (1958). "Adjustment Patterns among the Jamaican Chinese." *Social and Economic Studies* 7:144–164.

Pérez de la Riva, Juan (1978). *El barracón: Esclavitud y capitalismo en Cuba.* Barcelona: Grijalbo.

Stewart, Watt (1961). *Chinese Bondage in Perú.* Chapel Hill, N.C.: Duke University Press.

Stewart, Watt (1967). *Keith y Costa Rica.* San José: Editorial Costa Rica.

Sung, Betty Lee (1967). *The Story of the Chinese in America.* New York: Collier.

MOISÉS G. LEÓN

Chocho

ETHNONYMS: Chochol, Chocholteca, Chochón, Chocho-Popolocan, Chochoteco, Chono, Chucho, Chuchón, Hochón, Ixcatec-Chocho

The 1,200 or so Chocho Indians live in the Mixteca Alta region of northern Oaxaca, Mexico. Their language and customs are closely related to the nearby Popoloca of southern Puebla. The two groups have often been confused and looked on as one ethnic entity; however, many anthropologists regard them as two distinct groups (Jäcklein 1974). The Chocho language belongs to the Oto-Manguean Stock and is called Popoloca by the Chocho people, further compounding the confusion. Both *popoloca* and *chocho* were derogatory terms applied to allegedly barbaric and uncivilized races, the former by the Aztec and the latter by the Spanish. Thus the words were originally used indiscriminately and have only recently come to be attached, albeit in a rather confused way, to distinct cultural groups.

The terrain inhabited by the Chocho is largely mountainous. Rainfall is rare, summertime temperatures are very high, and wintertime temperatures fall below freezing. There is little natural flora or fauna in the region. The people live in villages that are further divided into barrios named after saints or local geographic features. Some barrios have elected officials who assign people to work on projects benefiting the entire community and who act as truant officers for the schools. All barrios have a _mayordomo_ who hosts a fiesta for the barrio's patron saint on the saint's day; in most cases, the mayordomo must bear the cost of the fiesta.

The staple of the Choco diet is maize, although they also eat beans, chiles, peaches, apples, tomatoes, quinces, oranges, lemons, plantains, and white _zapote_ fruits. Meat, usually goat meat, is eaten on Sundays, although fiestas generally call for chicken or turkey dishes.

The traditional Chocho house has a wooden frame and walls of _quiote_ (the stem of the maguey plant). It is eight to 10 meters in length and 3 to 4 meters wide. Roofs are made of palm or of maguey leaves. Many houses have no windows, and the only light source is the doorway. Seats, table, and altar are made of maguey logs. People sleep either on sleeping mats or on board or branch beds. Kitchens are often outside the house. There are also underground caves 2 meters in depth, where the people weave palm-leaf hats, the major source of income for the Chocho; weaving takes place underground so as to keep the palm leaves moist and supple.

Men wear trousers, a shirt, a palm hat, and sandals; women wear a cotton dress, a blouse, and an apron.

Men perform all agricultural work, whereas women perform domestic work and educate the children. Agriculture is primarily performed through the use of the plow, either Egyptian or moldboard, but in either case yields are poor. As a result, palm weaving is an important economic activity in most families. In addition to palm weavers, there are also wool weavers, carpenters, masons, butchers, hairdressers, shopkeepers, and curers.

The most important social relationships are among the patrilocal extended family and between godchildren and godfathers. Marriages are arranged; they take place when the prospective bride and groom are 18 to 20 years of age. The best man and best woman are the godparents of the couple. Newlyweds live with the groom's parents. Later, the couple build their own house, which they own themselves. Women bear children with the aid of a midwife.

Following death, the corpse is dressed in his or her best clothes, and a wake is held the first night. The next day, the handwritten obituary is distributed. Many mourners attend the wake on the second night, and there is a band; mourners consume coffee, mescal, and bread and smoke cigarettes. The corpse is buried in a box or sleeping mat, along with all clothes and personal possessions.

Bibliography

Acevedo, María Luisa, et al. (1993). "Chochos." In _Etnografía y Educación en el Estado de Oaxaca_, 41–48. Mexico City: Instituto Nacional de Antropología e Historia, Colección Científica, no. 268.

Hoppe, Walter A., and Roberto Weitlaner (1969). "The Chocho." In _Handbook of Middle American Indians_, edited by Robert Wauchope. Vol. 7, _Ethnology, Part One_, edited by Evon Z. Vogt, 506–515. Austin: University of Texas Press.

Jäcklein, Klaus (1974). _Un pueblo popoloca_. Mexico City: Instituto Nacional Indigenista; Secretaría de Educación Pública.

Ch'ol

ETHNONYM: Chol

Orientation

Identification. "Ch'ol" is a term that applies to the speakers of an American Indian language spoken in southern Mexico; they refer to it simply as _lak t'an_ ("our language"). In colonial documents, the Ch'ol were also called "Palencanos," "Pochutlas," "Topiltepeques," and "Lacandones."

Location. The Ch'ol occupy a continuous area in the southern Mexican state of Chiapas. Population is concentrated in the _municipios_ of Tila, Tumbala, Salto de Agua, Yajalon, Palenque, and Sabanilla but has expanded in modern times to jungle areas in Ocosingo.

Demography. The great majority of Ch'ol live in small rural settlements, but a few urban centers are dominated by Ch'ol populations, notably Tila, Tumbala, and Salto de Agua. Allowing for some undercounting, the Ch'ol-speaking population numbers about 100,000.

Linguistic Affiliation. Ch'ol is a member of the Western Branch of the Maya Family of languages, and within Western Mayan, Ch'ol belongs to a subdivision composed of Tzeltalan (Tzeltal and Tzotzil) and Cholan proper. Cholan proper includes Western Cholan (Chontal and Ch'ol) and Eastern Cholan (Ch'orti' and its colonial ancestor, Cholti). Within Ch'ol itself, there are two major dialect areas, the Tila (or Western) dialect and the Tumbala (or Eastern) dialect. There is a high degree of intelligibility between the varieties. Ch'ol has been shown to be closely related to the language transcribed in the Classic period (A.D. 300–900) Maya hieroglyphic inscriptions.

History and Cultural Relations

The Cholan, the historical predecessors of the Ch'ol, once occupied most of the lowland areas from the Río Grijalva on the west to the Río Motagua on the east, including the southern (riverine) half of the Yucatán Peninsula. The urban centers of this civilization were abandoned with the fall of the Classic Maya around the tenth century; the Cholan survived in small agricultural settlements until the sixteenth century, when they were decimated by diseases and other repercussions of Spanish colonialism.

At the end of the sixteenth century, Ch'ol settlements were located along the Río Usumacinta and its lowland tributaries, from northern Guatemala to the Gulf coast. The Ch'ol resisted Spanish incursions, including missionary activity, and carried out raids on highland areas that were pacified and controlled by the Spanish Crown. As a consequence, the Ch'ol were subjected to a 100-year military effort (1590–1690). Conquest and resettlement of the Ch'ol, area by area, resulted, beginning with the lower Río Usumacinta and Río Tulija area and proceeding upriver in successive campaigns that concluded with the subjugation of the Mopán and the Itza' Maya, to the east of the Ch'ol. Ch'ol populations that survived pacification were resettled in Palenque, Tila, Tumbala, and Bachajon, in Chiapas, and in Retalhuleu, Guatemala, but only those in the Tila and Tumbala areas survived into the twentieth century.

John Loyd Stephens, a U.S. explorer who traveled through the Tumbala area in 1840, remarked that the Indians there lived in essentially aboriginal conditions, with little sign of Spanish influence. After mid-century, however, German and North American interests founded coffee plantations and incorporated the Ch'ol in a system of debt peonage. This system disappeared after the Mexican Revolution, and, in the 1930s, Ch'ol gained control of many coffee plantations through land reform.

About 1960, the federal government authorized expansion of highland populations into lowland jungle areas left virtually unpopulated since the seventeenth century. As groups organized and petitioned for lands under the *ejido* system, hundreds of new settlements evolved, and the population expansion has taken Ch'ol into almost all of the Mexican territory their ancestors occupied in the sixteenth century.

Settlements

The major urban settlements occupied by Ch'ol speakers are Tila, Tumbala, Salto de Agua, and Palenque; however, these are to some extent dominated by their non-Indian (Ladino) populations. The great majority of Ch'ol live outside these urban centers, in smaller agricultural settlements, the result of land reform under the ejido system.

Ejido settlements tend to be small because the laws governing land reform specify how many heads of family will have land rights and restrict inheritance to one son; land-poor younger sons are the major factor in the formation of newer ejidos. Consequently, these settlements also tend to be peculiar demographically, as they are founded by young generation mates and initially have few elders. By the same token, they are innovative socially; little traditional life survives in the ejidos. A great majority are dominated by Protestant sects, in contrast to the well-entrenched Catholicism of the highlands.

Economy

Subsistence and Commercial Activities. There is considerable diversity to the economy of Ch'ol settlements, although there is a strong component of subsistence agriculture based on maize, beans, and squashes, with the addition of manioc, chili peppers, tomatoes, and other vegetables, as well as tropical fruits. Cacao was produced in early colonial times but was replaced by coffee. Nine-

teenth- and early twentieth-century plantations also produced cattle, mahogany and other tropical hardwoods, rubber, and vanilla.

The economy of the ejidos varies widely, as each settlement struggles independently to develop its own locale. Some ejidos are strictly limited to subsistence; others have developed a variety of cash crops, including not only coffee but cacao and fruit trees. Farming of produce for local markets is poorly developed. Government support of cattle production often results in lands cleared for farming being converted to pasturage.

Industrial Arts. The Ch'ol are overwhelmingly agricultural, with little development of other industries. Weaving and embroidery, once essential crafts for women, have now disappeared almost entirely, replaced by sewing. Western-style dresses of brightly decorated satinlike cloth, worn with rows of beads and numerous hair clips, are a hallmark of ejido Ch'ol women.

Trade. The major regional product for outside trade is coffee, produced both on large commercial plantations and by family enterprise on smaller plots.

Division of Labor. Males do most of the agricultural work, women perform domestic chores (i.e., men produce food, and women process it, as in other Mayan communities).

Land Tenure. Most land is held through the ejido system, as prescribed by law: groups of heads of households petition for use of unoccupied lands (or lands held in excess of legal limits) and are granted an ejido. Shares can neither be bought nor sold, and are inherited by only one son. Other sons traditionally emigrate to form other ejidos—the process by which the lowland rain forest has been repopulated since about 1960.

Kinship

Kinship terminology and kin-based organization are rapidly acculturating to regional Hispanic norms, but reconstructions based on internal Ch'ol and external Mayan comparisons indicate an earlier stage with patrilineal clans, and this hypothesis is supported by evidence from Classic-period hieroglyphic inscriptions.

Kin Groups and Descent. Various forms of evidence indicate the former existence of patrilineal exogamous clans (Villa Rojas 1969, 236), but these currently survive mainly in a feeling of implied kinship and reciprocal obligation between persons of the same surname. Ethnohistorical records in Classic-period hieroglyphic inscriptions indicate rule normally passed to a child of the preceding (male or female) ruler. Because most rulers were male, dynasties of patrilineally related kings resulted, and the data suggest patrilineal descent groups were important elements in Classic political organization.

Kinship Terminology. Kinship terminology of the Omaha type is attested, but in most communities a degree of acculturation is noted. Unacculturated terminology is structurally identical to the working Omaha system attested in the nearby Tzotzil community of Chalchihuitan (i.e., patrilineages with sibling marriage exchange between neighboring families).

Marriage and Family

Family units are important and positively valued. Relations between brothers are said to be strained and competitive, whereas relations with cousins are friendly. Uncles are counselors and helpers; grandparents are treated with respect and are sought out for advice.

Marriage. Marriage is expected to take place when both parties are about 21. Accompanied by an older male family member, the prospective groom calls on the bride's parents in a series of informal visits, during which gifts of food are delivered. After tacit agreement is reached, courtship lasts six months or more. Marriage is accomplished by both civil registration and religious ceremonies. Postmarital residence is usually patrilocal, but the possibilities include the groom residing matrilocally and working with his father-in-law, ultimately inheriting as if he were a son.

Domestic Unit. Residential units are nuclear-family or extended-family households with elder parents or recently married children added to the nuclear family.

Inheritance. Inheritance goes to the last child, especially if this child is male. If the last child is female, she must be unmarried so that the goods remain in the same patrilineal family.

Socialization. Socialization of young children is by a combination of good role models, discipline, and instruction, with the expectation that positive early formation prevents problems from occurring later.

Sociopolitical Organization

Ejido settlements are governed by prescribed structures (an ejido commissioner and councils) but often function more democratically, with men meeting daily for public discussions and weekly more formal public assemblies, decisions being made by consensus. Religious authorities exercise considerable influence over community members. Highland and urban settlements have legally prescribed systems of governance under federal law, balanced against a traditional _cargo_ system. The latter now has mainly religious functions but nonetheless constitutes a political power base capable of opposing civil authority.

Social Organization. The traditional cargo system (_ch'ujulbä e'tel_, "holy work") survives best in Tila. There, more than fifty citizens at a time hold ritual offices for one-year terms, organizing festivals, caring for sacred images, and receiving and interceding on petitions from supplicants, including pilgrims from outside the community. Marriage is a prerequisite for these offices, and cargo holders' wives have ritual obligations.

In Tila, each saint represented in the central cathedral has a _mayordomo_, and ritual advisors and assistants fill out the ranks of the cargo holders. Men who have passed through various offices gain the status of respected elders (local Spanish: _tatuches_; Ch'ol: _lak tatnabb_, literally "our ancestors"). In Tumbala, religious cargos are partially merged with political offices.

Political Organization. Outside the ejidos, the political organization prescribed by federal law is the _ayuntamiento_, headed by the _presidente municipal_. In Tila, this organization is balanced against the cargo holders and the official church hierarchy (bishop, priests, etc.), who mediate problems informally. In Tumbala, the state-sanctioned offices have largely replaced the political roles of cargo holders.

Conflict and Social Control. Social control is accomplished through socialization. Individuals believe they are responsible for their acts, not only to others but to the supernatural world. Consequently, bad actions will result in illness and other forms of supernatural discipline.

Religion and Expressive Culture

Religious Beliefs. There is great diversity in current religious practices and beliefs among ethnic Ch'ol, ranging from traditional Maya-Christian syncretism of various degrees, to mainstream Catholicism, to fundamentalist evangelical Protestantism.

Traditional syncretic Maya-Catholic beliefs, as manifested in the Ch'ol area, have merged the Sun with Christ and the Moon with the Virgin Mary, in accordance with pre-Columbian mythology, in which the Moon is the mother of the Sun. Tila is the center of a syncretic tradition featuring a Black Christ, the Señor de Tila (Lord of Tila), whose image is preserved in a cave, a center of worship, as an anthropomorphic stalagmite. Worshipers come to annual festivals in great numbers, making Tila a major pilgrimage site in southern Mexico.

The name "Tila" derives from the Gulf Coast Nahuatl _tillan_, "place of (the) black (one)," and Black men who live in caves figure prominently in highland folklore. Caves are also the domain of the principal earth deity (the Earth Owner of the Tzotzil and other Mayan groups), owner of earthly goods who must be petitioned for reasonable use of his plants and animals. Two elements of the overriding Ch'ol philosophy are that gifts must be repaid and that evil will turn back against its agent. Offerings in caves for success in hunting and other pursuits continue to be made.

Religious Practitioners. Apart from priests and pastors serving mainstream Christian churches, shamanistic curers are the principal religious practitioners. Summoned to their responsibility in dreams, curers visit caves to solidify their powers. Curing practices involve invoking supernatural powers; petitions to supernaturals are accompanied by offerings of candles, incense, and liquor. An essential element is the "promise" made by the interlocutor—a pledge of offerings and good behavior in return for divine assistance. Most shamans are male, but a similar position is held by female midwives, who likewise draw their powers from the supernatural and are destined to serve from birth.

Ceremonies. Tila is the site of a major round of religious ceremonies tied to the Christian calendar but retaining elements of pre-Columbian and colonial beliefs and practices. The festival honoring the Señor de Tila occurs in mid-January and features masses and processions of images of the Lord. Carnaval (from the weekend to Ash Wednesday) is the occasion for replacing cargo holders in office, public dance performances (Black Men and Marias), and ritual combat between bulls and jaguars (symbolizing Hispanic versus indigenous cultures). All Saints' is mainly a family occasion, with house altars prepared to receive the family dead. Tumbala, whose patron saint is Saint Michael, celebrates a similar series of festivals, on a smaller scale.

Arts. Verbal arts are respected, and the Ch'ol have a rich body of traditional folktales and sacred myths; they are skillful at joking and narrating ordinary events. Creation stories involve the Moon and her sons, who account for the origin of the animals as well as agricultural practices, and symbolize conflict between male siblings. Other common topics are pursuit by underworld beings, transformation (people changing into animals, and vice versa), and encounters with Earth Owner, who sometimes appears in the guise of a man named Don Juan.

Medicine. Major illness results from souls being imprisoned by earth powers (caves, rivers, and the like). Shamans cure with a combination of herbal and spiritual treatments (prayers, offerings, and threats). Some illness may result from witchcraft, which is accomplished through pacts with earth powers. Principal illnesses are caused by fright, envy, and wrong thoughts, all of which involve disharmony with the spirit world. Curing techniques include ritual bathing, herbal remedies and diets, and prayers and offerings. Midwives care for pregnant women and assist in deliveries.

Death and Afterlife. Death is considered to be a natural process; people must die to make room for others. Burial is with Christian rites. A wake features prayers and offerings on behalf of the soul of the departed. Gifts of food and candles are received by a designated family member of the same sex as the departed, and money, candles, and incense are ritually presented to the cadaver.

Bibliography

Alejos García, José (1988). *Wajalix bä t'an: Narrativa tradicional ch'ol de Tumbalá, Chiapas.* Centro de Estudios Mayas, Cuaderno 20. Mexico City: Universidad Nacional Autónoma de México.

de Vos, Jan (1980). *La paz de dios y del rey: La conquista de la selva lacandona, 1525–1821.* Colección Ceiba, Ensayo 10. Tuxtla Gutiérrez: Gobierno del Estado. 2nd ed. 1988. Mexico City: Fondo de Cultura Económica.

Meneses López, Miguel (1986). *K'uk' witz, Cerro de los Quetzales: Tradición oral del Municipio de Tumbalá.* Dirección de Fortalecimiento y Fomento a las Culturas de la Sub-Secretaría de Asuntos Indígenas, Secretaría de Desarrollo Rural. Tuxtla Gutiérrez, Chiapas: Gobierno del Estado.

Pérez Chacón, José L. (1988). *Los choles de Tila y su mundo: Tradición oral.* Dirección de Fortalecimiento y Fomento a las Culturas de la Sub-Secretaría de Asuntos Indígenas, Secretaría de Desarrollo Rural. San Cristóbal de las Casas, Chiapas.

Stephens, John Lloyd (1841). *Incidents of Travel in Central America, Chiapas, and Yucatan.* 2 vols. New York: Harper & Brothers.

Thompson, J. Eric S. (1938). "Sixteenth and Seventeenth Century Reports on the Chol Mayas." *American Anthropologist* 40(4): 584–604.

Valdez, Luz María, and María Teresa Menéndez (1987). *Dinámica de la población de habla indígena (1900–1980).* Colección Científica, Serie Demografía Etnica. Mexico City: Instituto Nacional de Antropología e Historia.

Villa Rojas, Alfonso (1969). "Maya Lowlands: The Chontal, Chol, and Kekchi." In *Handbook of Middle American Indians,* edited by Robert Wauchope. Vol. 7, *Ethnology, Part One,* edited by Evon Z. Vogt, 230–243. Austin: University of Texas Press.

Whittaker, Arabelle, and Viola Warkentin (1965). *Chol Texts on the Supernatural.* Summer Institute of Linguistics Publications in Linguistics and Related Fields, 13. Norman: Summer Institute of Linguistics of the University of Oklahoma.

NICHOLAS A. HOPKINS

Chontal of Tabasco

ETHNONYMS: Chontales, Chontal Maya, Chontal Mayan, Yocotan, Yokot'an

Orientation

Identification. The word "Chontal" is derived from the Nahuatl word for "foreigner" or "stranger," *chontalli*. This term was originally applied to the Tabascan Maya by the Aztec, whose language, Nahuatl, was used as a lingua franca in many parts of Mesoamerica before and after the Spanish Conquest. The Spanish adopted this term in spite of the fact that it was also applied to different peoples in southern Oaxaca, Mexico, and in Nicaragua whose languages and cultures were unrelated to that of the Chontal of Tabasco. In this article, the word "Chontal" is used to refer only to the Chontal of Tabasco.

Location. The Chontal-Mayan-speaking area of Mexico has shrunk since the pre-Columbian period from an area that included most of the state of Tabasco and western Campeche to just the central part of Tabasco.

Demography. The first Spanish chroniclers, such as Juan de Grijalva and Hernán Cortés, left us with only a vague idea of the population of the Chontal Maya; however, by extrapolating from the data that are available, scholars have estimated that between 135,000 and 240,000 Chontal Mayan speakers lived in Mexico at the time of the Spanish Conquest. In examining tribute lists of the sixteenth and early seventeenth centuries, scholars have discovered that Tabasco and Campeche suffered a rapid population decline during that period. Like other indigenous populations in the New World, the Chontal Maya were not resistant to European diseases such as smallpox and measles. Tabasco's population had fallen to only 8,500 by 1579, and by 1639 amounted to just 4,630. After this severe decline, the population of Tabasco began to recover slowly: by 1794, Tabasco had a population of 35,805 (55 percent Indian, 38 percent mestizo, and 7 percent European).

It was not until the twentieth century, however, that the population of Tabasco began to grow rapidly. Mexican census data from 1960 and 1970 indicated a Chontal-speaking population of approximately 20,000. In the 1990 census, Chontal Mayan speakers older than 5 years of age numbered 30,143 in Tabasco.

Linguistic Affiliation. Chontal is one of the approximately thirty related languages that form the Mayan Language Family. The parent language of all Mayan languages, Proto-Mayan, was last spoken approximately forty-one centuries ago. As time passed, two major language branches appeared: Western and Eastern Mayan. About nineteen centuries ago, Western Mayan split up into Greater Tzeltalan and Greater Kanjobalan. Greater Tzeltalan further divided into Proto-Cholan and Tzeltalan Proper. Chontal, together with Ch'ol, Ch'orti', and Cholti, descended from Proto-Cholan. These four languages form the Cholan Subgroup of the Mayan Language Family.

Chontal, or Yokot'an, as it is called by those who speak it, plays an important role in the sociocultural life of the Chontal community. Unlike many other Maya groups, the modern Chontal Maya cannot be distinguished from Ladinos (non-Indian Spanish speakers) in appearance, occupation, economic level, or place of origin. Knowledge of the Chontal language is therefore the most important social indicator of Chontal ethnic identity.

Chontal Mayan has many dialects. The oldest known dialect of Chontal is exemplified in the Maldonado-Paxbolon Papers (Scholes and Roys 1968; Smailus 1975), which were written between 1610 and 1612. Today, each Chontal-speaking community has its own variety of Chontal; these dialects are mutually intelligible.

Since 93.2 percent of Chontal speakers also speak Spanish, the relationship between Chontal and Spanish is an important one. Spanish, as the more prestigious language, is used in the domains of established religion and education and in the workplace. Chontal is spoken primarily with friends and at home.

Although almost all Chontal speakers are bilingual, the level of fluency varies among the population, based on age and gender. In general, the men and the younger generation (men and women under 50 years of age) speak better Spanish than the women and the older generation (men and women over 50). Just as knowledge of Spanish varies within the Chontal community, so does knowledge of the Chontal language—the children in many communities speak less Chontal and more Spanish than the adults do. As more children are taught Spanish rather than Chontal, Spanish is assuming a greater role in Chontal communities, replacing Chontal even at home and among friends. Chontal Mayan is a dying language.

History, Trade, and Cultural Relations

In the century prior to the Spanish Conquest, the Chontal Maya were prosperous, and the area was well populated. The Chontal occupied a strategic economic position, playing an important part in the trade carried on between the Gulf coast and the Caribbean, across the base of the Yucatán Peninsula. Yucatan traded salt, cotton cloth, and slaves. In exchange, cacao, obsidian, precious metals, feathers, and other luxury items were imported by the Yukateko from Tabasco and the Caribbean coast to the southeast. Tabasco's population included not only native Chontal Maya but also representatives from other Mesoamerican cultures. For example, Nahuatl speakers from central Mexico established several commercial centers in Tabasco, and many Chontal speakers were bilingual. Zoque- and Yucatec Maya-speaking towns were also present in Tabasco.

After the Spanish Conquest, Tabasco lost its strategic economic position. Instead of being prosperous traders, the Chontal became peons, paying cacao, maize, and chickens as tribute to their Spanish overlords. As the Tabascan population declined, so did tribute income, agricultural production, the labor supply, and trade. Tabasco's economy suffered an economic depression that lasted through most of the colonial period and well into the nineteenth century.

The nineteenth and twentieth centuries have been a period of continuous growth in population, territorial expansion, settlement, and economic activity in Tabasco. Economic prosperity returned to Tabasco with the exploitation of petroleum in the twentieth century. The ratio of Chontal speakers to the total population in Tabasco is steadily declining, however, and areas inhabited by the Chontal Maya in Tabasco have shrunk considerably in the last hundred years.

Settlements

The first descriptions of Chontal settlements were recorded by Spanish chroniclers. As early as 1579, Tabasco was described in two reports written by Alfaro Santa Cruz and other officials of the Villa de Tabasco. Their reports included a detailed map of the province. At the time of the Conquest, the most heavily populated part of Tabasco was the Chontalpa, a region that included a group of twenty-three Chontal-speaking towns. Other Chontal towns were located by the coast and along rivers, grouped together in provinces. Each province had a center surrounded by subordinate hamlets.

Another key region of Chontal speakers was the province of Acalan, located on the Río Candelaria where it flows into the Laguna de Términos, in the modern state of Campeche, Mexico. With its seventy-six towns and villages, the province of Acalan was well populated. The late pre-Columbian and early colonial history of Acalan is described in the Maldonado-Paxbolon Papers.

The colonial period produced not only a population decline but also a change in population distribution. Most of the coastal areas were abandoned during the seventeenth and eighteenth centuries, because of raids and looting by pirates. During the height of the pirates' power, most of the people in Tabasco lived in the sierra region and in the Chontalpa. As pirate incursions ceased in the second half of the eighteenth century, many inhabitants of the sierra region returned to the coastal areas.

Today, Chontal speakers are clustered in the Tabascan _municipios_ of Centla, Macuspana, Nacajuca, and Tacotalpa, and the indigenous language that is spoken in western Campeche is Yucatec Maya.

Economy

Subsistence and Commercial Activities. Prior to the Spanish Conquest, Tabasco was a major agricultural and commercial area. Farmers raised not only subsistence crops (maize, beans, squashes, sweet potatoes, and manioc) but also commercial crops, such as cacao. The majority of Chontal subsistence farmers still till their land in the same slash-and-burn manner as their pre-Columbian ancestors. They grow most of the same subsistence crops, as well as plantains and rice. Raising household animals, hunting, and fishing help to supplement the Chontal diet.

Modern commercial farming is limited largely to the production of tropical and subtropical crops, such as cacao, sugarcane, bananas, and coconuts. Cattle raising is also an important commercial enterprise. From 1625 to 1925, the exploitation of tropical-forest products was next in importance to farming and cattle raising. Today the lumber industry is of minor importance, because of overcutting. Commercial fishing, particularly of shrimp, has increased in importance since 1950. Beginning in the 1950s, Tabasco's economy grew astronomically, based on the exploitation of petroleum and natural gas. Consequently, the Chontal are prosperous, compared to most Mayan groups in Mexico and Guatemala, primarily owing to the petroleum industry. The modern economy of Tabasco and the Chontal is tied to the economy of Mexico and the world.

Industrial Arts. For many years, the hat industry was the most important enterprise of the Chontalpa; Chontal Maya men, women, and children used their free time to weave long strips of palm leaf. As the demand for these hats has diminished, and as opportunities for wage labor have increased, the hat industry has lost its importance. Many traditional arts—such as hat weaving, gourd carving, embroidering, and some types of pottery making—continue to be of primary importance because of the tourist market.

Division of Labor and Land Tenure. Traditionally, the Chontal Maya have been subsistence farmers or ranchers. Chontal communities are surrounded by farmland owned or rented by Chontal Maya. Some communities were established as *ejidos*, settlements formed around the new lands that were created by land reform. As the Tabascan economy has boomed, however, so has the number of wage jobs increased.

Chontal men are the traditional breadwinners of the family, either as subsistence farmers or as wage earners. The women are responsible for domestic chores and child rearing. More and more Chontal women are becoming wage earners, however, as Chontal communities become part of mainstream Mexico.

Kinship

The Chontal Maya kinship system is now bilateral, and Spanish kin terms are often used. Chontal kin terms differ from their Spanish counterparts in that they often stress age relative to Ego. Ritual kinship, *compadrazgo* (coparenthood), is widely practiced in baptisms, weddings, and other key events in the life of the Chontal Maya.

Marriage and Family

Marriage, Domestic Unit, and Inheritance. In the past, it was the custom for parents to arrange the marriages of their children. The young man's parents would visit the young woman's parents several times to discuss the marriage. If the marriage was agreed upon, a date was fixed, and a more formal ceremony was held with the young woman's relatives. The groom would bring gifts—candles, maize, beans, cacao, and turkey—to make a large meal to celebrate the wedding announcement. A civil wedding ceremony, occasionally followed by a religious ceremony, would take place several weeks later. Often, the couple would remain at the young man's parents' house until they were able to build their own.

Modern weddings are less formal. The couple, often after a furtive relationship, decide to get married. If the parents do not agree to the marriage, the couple may run away and live together. Common-law marriages are accepted by the community. Most households consist of nuclear families.

Land and property are usually transferred from parents to children in accordance with Mexican law and parental wishes.

Socialization. Chontal-speaking communities are in a state of rapid change. Traditional values and rituals are being replaced with working-class Ladino values. Children are being exposed to mainstream Mexican and Catholic-church values and culture through priests, nuns, missionaries, schoolteachers, radio, and television. In many communities, children are being taught Spanish instead of Chontal.

Sociopolitical Organization

Social Organization. Within Tabascan society, the Chontal Maya (as well as all other Indians) are at the bottom of the social scale. The desire for higher status is a major reason for the assimilation of Chontal Maya into Ladino society. Among the Chontal Maya, status depends on economic success, particularly in communities in which political, religious, and traditional avenues to advancement no longer exist.

Political Organization. The formal government is run by officials of the municipio, who are periodically elected according to Mexican federal laws. For the most part, elected officials are Ladinos. In some Chontal communities, traditional officials—elderly men who have held religious posts—are still being elected.

Social Control and Conflict. Social control is maintained through familial constraints and by Church officials and the Mexican legal systems; however, the 1990s have been characterized as a period of increasing social unrest among the Chontal Maya. The economic crisis in Mexico, the civil war in Guatemala, and the rebellion of the Mayan Indians in the neighboring state of Chiapas are all contributing factors.

Religion and Expressive Culture

Religious Beliefs. The Chontal Maya are very religious. In most Chontal communities, the Catholic church is the most important building. Each town has its own patron saint and some secondary saints. Many Chontal Maya make pilgrimages to visit the saints in other towns, particularly, El Señor de Tila, the patron saint of Tila, in Chiapas. Each patron saint has an annual festival, with a lavish display of music, food, and prayers.

Religious Practitioners. Since the 1940s, however, a growing number of Chontal Maya have converted to Protestantism and no longer participate in the religious festivals for saints. As the religious competition between Catholics and Protestants increases, more Catholic priests and nuns and Protestant missionaries are visiting Chontal communities. The net result is that more adults and children are learning modern Catholic and Protestant doctrine and are being taught to reject traditional rituals. The traditional *recomendores* (religious petitioners) and *patrones* (church officials) are losing influence.

Arts. Among the Chontal Maya, expressive culture is focused primarily on religion. Music, drama, and art are part of all religious and ritual events. Churches and saints are decorated during the festivals, which culminate in elaborate processions, often with music and dancing.

Medicine. Traditional folk practices coexist with Western medicine in most Chontal communities. Most Chontal Maya seek medical help for serious injuries and illness. *Curanderos* (folk healers) are frequently consulted, however, particularly by older, more traditional Chontal Maya.

Death and Afterlife. The Chontal Maya believe in an afterlife in which one is rewarded or punished for having led a good or evil life. Traditional Catholic Chontal Maya believe that communication with the dead is possible and that dead friends and relatives can function as intermediaries between the living and the saints. Consequently, formal petitions to the dead are an important part of traditional Chontal ritual. Such petitions are offered during novenas (nine-day mourning periods) for the dead and during the month of October, climaxing on the second day of November. The petitions are usually offered by a Chontal recomendor, a ritual specialist who is hired to pray and petition the dead and the saints, although laymen occasionally offer the petitions. During these rituals, food, beverages, incense, candles, and skyrockets are offered to the dead and/or the saints, together with requests for aid.

Bibliography

Becerra, Marcos (1934). "Las chontales de Tabasco: Estudio etnográfico y lingüístico." *Investigaciones Lingüísticas* 2:29-36.

Brinton, Daniel (1892). "Chontales and Popolucas, a Contribution to Mexican Ethnography." *Proceedings of the VIII International Congress of Americanists*, 556-564.

Horcasitas de Barros, M. L., and Ana María Crespo (1979). *Hablantes de lengua indígena en México*. Colección Científica, Lenguas, no. 81. Mexico City: Secretaría de Educación Pública, Instituto Nacional de Antropología e Historia.

Knowles, Susan M. (1984). *A Descriptive Grammar of Chontal Maya (San Carlos Dialect)*. Ann Arbor, Mich.: University Microfilms International.

Knowles-Berry, Susan M. (1987) "Linguistic Decay in Chontal Mayan: The Speech of Semi-Speakers." *Anthropological Linguistics* 29(4): 332-341.

Mora, Teresa, and Yolotl González (1981). "La celebración de los muertos entre los chontales." In *Dos ceremonias para los muertos: En Cholula, Puebla y entre los chontales de Tabasco*, edited by Teresa Mora, Yolotl González, and Silvia Ortiz Echaniz, 1-15. Mexico City: Instituto Nacional de Antropología e Historia, Departamento de Etnología y Antropología Social.

Scholes, France V., and Ralph L. Roys (1968). *The Maya Chontal Indians of Acalan-Tixchel*. Norman: University of Oklahoma Press.

Schumann, Otto (1978). "Consideraciones sobre el idioma chontal de Tabasco." In *Estudios preliminares sobre los mayas de las tierras bajas nonoccidentales*, edited by Lorenzo Ochoa, 93-105. Mexico City: Universidad Nacional Autónoma de México.

Smailus, Ortwin (1975). *El maya-chontal de Acalan: Análisis lingüístico de un documento de los años 1610-12*. Cuaderno 9. Mexico City: Universidad Nacional Autónoma de México, Centro de Estudios Mayas.

Villa Rojas, Alfonso (1969). "Maya Lowlands: The Chontal, Chol, and Kekchi." In *Handbook of Middle American Indians*, edited by Robert Wauchope. Vol. 7, *Ethnology, Part One*, edited by Evon Z. Vogt, 230-243. Austin: University of Texas Press.

West, Robert C., Norbert P. Psuty, and Bruce G. Thom (1969). *The Tabasco Lowlands of Southeastern Mexico*. Technical Report no. 70. Baton Rouge: Louisiana State University, Coastal Studies Institute.

SUSAN M. KNOWLES-BERRY

Ch'orti'

ETHNONYMS: Cholotí, Chorté, Chortí

The overwhelming majority of the Ch'orti' (52,000), a highland Maya Indian people, live in the Chiquimula Department of Guatemala. The remaining 4,000 or so live in the department of Copán in Honduras. They have traditionally depended on maize and beans for subsistence. The K'iche' Maya had dominated the Ch'orti' since the early fifteenth century, but by the 1520s the Spanish had become the primary regional power. Warfare and disease killed many Ch'orti' during the sixteenth and early seventeenth centuries, and in the nineteenth century the Ch'orti' lost much of their land to the Guatemalan government. During the 1980s, 25 percent of the Guatemalan Ch'orti' came to the United States to escape political persecution.

Bibliography

Olson, James S. (1991). *The Indians of Central and South America*. New York: Greenwood Press.

Chuj

ETHNONYMS: ajNenton, ajSan Matéyo, ajSan Sabastyán

Orientation

Identification. The Chuj are a Mayan people living in northwestern Guatemala, in the department of Huehuetenango. They prefer and use names based on the name of their municipality: "ajSan Matéyo" (San Mateo Ixtatán), "ajSan Sabastyán" (San Sebastián Coatán), "ajNenton" (Nentón). In 1993 the Chuj Committee of the National Academy of the Mayan Languages of Guatemala was established and began looking for a new name. The term "Chuj," in folk tradition, was first applied to the group by the Spanish on the advice of Tzeltal conscripts for whom "*chuj*" meant *capixay*, the loose wool overgarment worn by Chuj men. In modern Tzeltal, "chuj" refers to brightly printed cotton cloth. In Chuj, "chuj" means "sweat bath."

Location. The municipalities of San Mateo Ixtatán and San Sebastián Coatán, which straddle the backbone of the Cuchumatán Mountains, are Chuj. Nentón, which is the coffee-planting piedmont area of Guatemala, is about one-third Chuj. Some Chuj also live in neighboring areas of Mexico. Political violence in Guatemala, particularly during the early 1980s, forced many Chuj to abandon town centers and established villages and to live in isolation in mountainous holds or leave the country altogether. The Chuj population of Los Angeles now rivals that of San Sebastián.

Demography. The population of San Mateo Ixtatán is about 16,000; that of San Sebastián Coatán is about 9,000; and the Chuj-speaking inhabitants of Nentón number nearly 4,000. Counts of the Chuj population in Los Angeles are hampered by their irregular immigration status.

Linguistic Affiliation. Chuj is a Mayan language of the Q'anjob'alan Branch. It is most closely related to Tojolab'al, spoken in Mexico. These two languages constitute the Chujean Subgroup of the Q'anjob'alan Branch. Most Chuj men are multilingual. Almost all are bilingual in Spanish and Chuj; many can carry on basic commercial transactions and conversations in Q'anjob'al and make some further adjustments for interacting with Jakalteko as well. Since about the 1970s, Chuj women have been bilingual in Spanish and Chuj.

History and Cultural Relations

The Chuj in Guatemala have occupied their territory for millennia. According to the ethnolinguistic and glottochronological calculations of Kaufman (1976) and McQuown (1971), the Chuj occupy an area that is roughly that of the Proto-Maya language homeland. The Chuj have lived in northwestern Guatemala since Proto-Maya began its differentiation into modern Mayan languages about four thousand years ago.

Settlements

Modern San Mateo Ixtatán is superimposed on pre-Columbian mounds and plazas. The structure immediately underlying the modern town dates from the Late Classic period (A.D. 600–900). A major "temple" complex and platform/courtyard lie below the city, which sits astride a rich salt deposit. Chuj salt was traded north through Tzeltal and Tzotzil regions of Mexico. The salt dome is accessible through a series of four wells. During the period of civil strife called the *violencia* (ca. 1979–1982), Guatemalan troops cut forests along the roadways; the deforestation lowered the water table to such a degree that only a single salt well remains in full production. A large temple mound overlooks the main well.

In the pre-Hispanic period, San Sebastián Coatán was a focal point of trade and ritual pilgrimages centering on its natural features, particularly its springs. According to local belief, Saint Sebastian and Saint Michael were walking the hills of the area, looking for a place to settle and to form towns for their followers. Saint Sebastian found a mountain ledge that he liked and called to Saint Michael, in Chuj, "Kotanh!" (come here!). But Saint Michael had also found a place that he liked; so he replied in Akateko/Q'anjob'al, "Aa Katan!" (oh, come here!). Eventually, each saint settled, with his following, on opposite sides of a ravine. The people in San Miguel Acatán share this traditional history.

The place names "Coatán" and "Acatán" are Nahuatl terms. "Coatán" (from *coa:*, "snake," and *tlan/tan*, "place") means "place of the snakes." "Acatán" (from *a:ca*, "reed," and *tlan/tan*, "place") would mean "reed place." Although there are reeds in the Acatán area, residents of San Sebastián deny the presence at any time in their history of large numbers of snakes. The Ixil, however, neighbors south and east of the Q'anjob'alan group, conserve in their oral histories an account of how San Sebastián came to be infested with snakes: a woman who had been converted into a half-human, half-snake, because of her laziness, was dropped on the plaza from a great height, and she shattered into hundreds of pieces, each of which become a serpent.

Nentón is a new settlement, dating from the early 1900s, when coffee was developed as an export crop.

In most of Guatemala, townships have characteristic trade "garb" for both men and women, but men tend to reserve this traditional wear for feast days. In San Mateo, the woman's trade garment is a cotton broadcloth overblouse

(Chuj: _nip;_ Spanish from Nahuatl: _huipil_) elaborately embroidered in red, yellow, green, and black. Before the 1960s the design was one of concentric multicolored circles (the colors arranged roughly as on the coral snake), with birds and flowers adorning the bottom edge, below the outer circle. The overblouse was long, reaching nearly to the knees, and was typically worn over a wrapped skirt. Women wore their hair braided and wrapped with brightly colored woven ribbons. The men wore and still wear cotton pants and shirts, unembroidered, and a wool short-sleeved tunic, (Chuj: _lopil;_ Spanish: _capixay_). The tunic is lightly embroidered at the neck and arms. The arms are not closed, but open at the bottom, and the side seam is left open for several inches below the arms to allow freedom of movement while working and to facilitate pulling the arms inside while resting. In the 1960s the women's overblouse design changed. The concentric rings were rearranged as stars, three in front (one over each breast, one over the stomach), three symmetrically placed in the back. The blouse got shorter and was often worn tucked into the skirt. Since the early 1980s, many women have reserved their overblouses for festival use, and use cotton blouses, sewn in a short, puff-sleeve, square-neck pattern, for daily wear. A short "mini"-length apron, with two zippered pockets has been added. Married women now cover their braids on formal occasions with square scarves of polished cotton. The men's trade garb has remained relatively stable, although the shirt and pants may now be manufactured items. Men in San Sebastián and Nentón dress in basically the same manner, although they tend to wear the wool tunic less as the weather is warmer than in San Mateo. Women in San Sebastián wear a white cotton (often polished) overblouse with internal paisley patterning or lacelike netting, the neckline adorned with concentric rings of colored rickrack and white lace. When traveling, they often wear an overblouse inverted over their heads, as a headcloth. The headcloth overblouse and the one worn on the body can be interchanged, if one gets worn or dirty. The pattern of the women's overblouse in San Sebastián is shared with the Jakaltek, Akatek, and Q'anjob'alan towns of the region. Most women of Nentón wear occidental clothing, though some conserve the wrapped cloth shirt.

Economy

Subsistence and Commercial Activities.   The Chuj conceive of themselves as maize agriculturists. Traditionally, families have had lands in three climactic niches: cold, temperate, and hot country. In cold country they pasture animals, collect plants and firewood, and occasionally plant crops; in the temperate areas they plant corn, beans, squashes, and chilies; and in hot country they plant sugarcane, henequen, reeds, and bananas. Hunting is a marginal dietary supplement because game has become scarce. In the spring, there are migrations of birds and moths. At night, families build mountaintop bonfires to attract the flocks of birds, which they then club, roast, and consume. Households keep chickens, and some have other livestock. Red meat must be eaten to prevent soul loss during the "five bad days" at year's end, after the eighteen lunar months; all families therefore procure animals at that time.

Prior to the opening of the road through the Cuchu-

matanes in 1960, the San Mateo economy relied heavily on the trade of salt. Families of the political leaders controlled collection and sale of the salt. Many planted only symbolic maize fields; they hired laborers to work their fields and imported maize from tributary towns. With the road, commercial salt became easily available, and the salt trade faltered. San Mateños reverted to subsistence maize farming; the median income went from the highest in the department of Huehuetenango to the bottom tier (Hayden and Cannon 1984). Owing to this economic collapse and to the disorder of the _violencia,_ many San Mateños left the town center and now live in lowland villages. These emigrants typically have only hot-country lands, on which they cultivate both the traditional hot-country crops and the maize-beans-squash trilogy. Residents of Nentón, being laborers on the coffee plantations that gave birth to the town, farm relatively less land. Their pay is both in cash and in kind (maize, coffee, and beans).

Chuj women do not weave, but the traditional overblouse of San Mateo is elaborately embroidered on cotton broadcloth. Since the early 1970s, a women's cooperative has marketed their embroideries, overblouses, and tourist items in the departmental capital of Huehuetenango.

Trade.   The Chuj traditionally held markets every five days; under Spanish influence, a second market day was added on a seven-day cycle. San Mateo has gradually meshed these two systems into a fixed seven-day schedule. San Sebastián celebrates a regular five-day market and a seven-day market; when they coincide, Sebastianecos declare it a festival day. Nentón has a small market on the seven-day schedule, but most Nentonecos travel to San Antonio Huista, a Jakaltek town, for weekly trade.

Division of Labor.   Chuj men traditionally work outside the home, especially in agriculture. Children are often sent to the fields to scare off birds and vermin just after planting and as the first sprouts come up. The whole family is usually involved in the harvest, especially that of maize. Men engage in trade outside the community, although women buy and sell in the local markets. Women are responsible for the home. In San Sebastián, women retain a working knowledge of the 260-day Mayan calendar and determine dates for household rituals accordingly.

From the 1930s through the 1960s, debt peonage was prevalent in the Chuj area. Men sometimes went to the coast alone, as laborers, but, more commonly, whole families migrated and worked the fields.

Land Tenure.   Most Chuj families have title to several small parcels of land, at varying distances from the town center. San Mateo and San Sebastián also have communal lands. Proceeds from the usufruct of the land go to town coffers. A few communal lots are rotated among needy families for agriculture. In all the highland Chuj area, there is a severe land shortage. Land passes from parents to children, resulting in the scattered patchwork of modern holdings. The land shortage has motivated some Chuj families to move to the jungle areas of the lowlands, both in Guatemala and in Mexico. Those in Guatemala can apply for title through homesteading procedures; those in Mexico hold their land by squatting.

Kinship

Kin Groups and Descent. The Chuj reckon descent bilaterally. Each child has two surnames; traditionally, the first surname is the father's first name, the second surname is the mother's first name. In San Mateo, some families have adopted Hispanic surnames for men. Thus, a child would have an Hispanic surname from the father and a Chuj-style surname from the mother (i.e., her first name). The first male child is named after the paternal grandfather; the first female child is named for the maternal grandmother. The second male child is named for the maternal grandfather, the second female for the paternal grandmother, and subsequent children may be named for the parents. In large families, the names of the grandparents may be recycled, and, as a result, full siblings may have exactly the same names.

Kinship Terminology. Kin terms follow a bilateral pattern. Both sets of grandparents receive the same address forms and are equally "related." First-cousin marriage is discouraged; marriage with other cousins is permitted, although none is especially preferred. Grandparents and grandchildren use reciprocal address and namesake terms for each other. Women and men share the terms for parents and their siblings, grandparents, grandchildren, and distant relatives. The terms for children, brothers, sisters, cousins, spouses, and in-laws are gender specific. Men have separate terms for sons and daughters; women use a generic "offspring" label. Siblings are distinguished by relative age as well as by gender of the speaker. Twins are sacred and have special powers, but, even among twins, birth order ranks the pair; the younger always addresses the elder as superior.

Marriage and Family

Marriage. Traditionally, Chuj marriages are arranged. In the ideal courtship pattern, a youth finds a girl whom he might like; he contrives to speak with her, usually at communal water sources or along paths to washing places. If she agrees to see him, she finagles opportunities to meet him briefly by asking her parents for legitimate tasks that will take her out of the home (i.e., fetching water, going to market, washing clothes, going to school). When the young man feels he can start a household, he approaches his parents. If they approve of the girl, they take over the negotiations for the marriage. They find spokespersons to go with them to the girl's family; the girl's family may receive the visitors or not. If they reject the first visit, emissaries may set up a second visit. In subsequent visits (ideally there are three in all), the parents discuss what each spouse will bring to the marriage and what compensation will be given the bride's parents. If the groom is poor, he may work for the parents a stipulated amount of time, before or after the marriage. In extreme cases, the groom may join the uxoral compound. After the third visit, the groom's family brings the stipulated gifts to the bride's family and provides a feast for the two families and guests. There are public instructions given to the bride and groom, and they then take up their new residence. These proceedings may also include a civil service in the municipal building and/or a religious service in the church. Church weddings are relatively rare, owing to the cost of paying for the priest and the infrequency of his visits.

A second major marriage mechanism is bride-theft. Once a young man has selected a bride, he may try to carry her off rather than formally petition for her hand. He is especially likely to try this if he cannot afford a bride-price, if he suspects her family will not receive his family's visits, or if the girl seems reluctant to wed. If the girl really is opposed, bride-theft is difficult, given that the man would have to physically carry her away from public space. When such thefts are attempted, neighbors typically come out and scold the couple, until someone from the girl's family comes to escort her home. In cases where the girl allows herself to be carried off, or when the young man has friends who help with the abduction, the couple goes to a hut in the hills. The young man, leaving the girl "locked" in, then goes to his parents and enlists their aid in regularizing the relationship. They enlist a spokescouple to approach the girl's family. Sometimes they are successful in arranging a low bride-price or a short work stint, given the de facto union already realized; sometimes the girl's family refuses to bargain, and the male members of the family try to bring her back; at other times, the de facto unions continue with no financial arrangements negotiated.

Domestic Unit. The nuclear family is the smallest domestic unit. The members typically share a patio with the husband's brothers and parents. In this compound, child-care duties are shared; the women sometimes work together. Planting and harvesting are often shared among members of a compound, or by other siblings living beyond the pale. Farm work can also be shared outside the family unit, on a reciprocal-work basis.

Inheritance. Inheritance is bilateral. Land and material goods should be bequeathed to all siblings; however, there is a tendency to favor the first son. He and some older siblings may be given land and goods before the death of the parents and may then also share in the posthumous redistribution.

Socialization. In the child's first year of life, a "leg-spreading" ceremony is held, which prepares the child ritually for her or his gender role. At the hearth, the mother sets the child across her hip, with one leg over her stomach, one across her back, "legs spread." At the same time, the parents place a small hoe or planting stick in the hands of a boy child, while instructing him on his future occupation as a farmer. They give a little girl a small spindle or a mortar and instruct her on her life as a housewife. Children play in the house compound with their siblings and cousins; older children watch over the younger children as they play with them and are often called upon by the adults to help with chores. Young boys go out to the fields with their fathers once they can walk the distance on their own.

There are now government schools in each town. San Mateo has six grades; San Sebastián and Nentón have three. For education beyond that available locally, children must leave their homes. Even though many students in these boarding schools are Indians, the schools punish native language use and consciously try to shame students into dressing and acting like non-Indians. The schoolbooks, which are standardized nationally, depict the Indian culture as a hindrance to modernity, and the Classic Mayan florescence is passed over lightly. Emphasis is placed on the supposed nudity of the Indian populace at contact and the alleged stupidity of the K'iche' war leader, Tekun Umán, for believing Pedro de Alvarado's horse to be part of the man, and being killed before he could strike at the actual Spanish chieftain. Sistema Integral de Mejoramiento y Adecuación Curricular (Integral System for Curricular Improvement and Adaptation, SIMAC) is a Ministry of Education agency charged with the responsibility of developing educational programs that reflect Indian culture and history positively. Teachers are to be provided manuals for each of twenty-one Mayan topics such as astronomy, social structure, sports and games, and mathematics from the earliest Mayan records through modern vigesimal systems now in use, and are to find ways to incorporate these topics into the curriculum in the absence of texts for the students to read. These programs have not yet been introduced. Indian children leave the government schools with low self-esteem and low expectations for career opportunities as long as they retain their ethnic identity.

Sociopolitical Organization

Social Organization. Much of indigenous Guatemala is—or was until the late twentieth century involved with the *cargo* system, a ladder of alternating political and syncretic Catholic religious offices, through which participants earn esteem and contribute to the public life of the communities. This system was never fully developed in the Chuj region. The political offices exist, being set by Spanish rule, but the Catholic offices are undeveloped; the Chuj have no corresponding lexical items.

Factors involved in the weakening of the cargo system include the spread of Protestantism; Catholic Action's drive in the 1960s and 1970s (since reversed) opposing syncretism as impure; economic opportunities in some Guatemalan towns that made possible capital accumulation, and hence rewards outside the towns' cargo structures; and the revitalization of indigenous religious practices.

Political Organization. The municipal political offices are mayor, four bailiffs, and messengers. In San Sebastián, a council of elders meets to decide town policy, to adjudicate disputes, and to plan festivals. The elected officials serve as their executives. National political parties have a low profile in the communities, but suffrage is mandatory.

Social Control. Women are guardians of the social norm. When someone misbehaves in public, women scold them. When scolding and social ridicule cannot control actions or when disputes arise, the matter is taken to court. Each litigant pleads his or her own case. The judge delivers a harangue as his judgment; sometimes the process suffices to resolve the disputes; at other times, fines, jail terms, or services are demanded.

Since the 1970s, particularly the late 1970s, in response to increased guerrilla activity, the national military has made numerous incursions. Although there is no permanent garrison in Chuj territory, frequent field exercises are held and troops move through town centers, camping in marketplaces. The army has deforested areas along roads and major trails to monitor the transfer of people and goods. The local justice system can be circumvented by denouncing someone to the military.

Conflict. The mayor in San Mateo has control over the communal lands. Since the 1970s, mayors have been embroiled in scandals over their administration of these resources. Two mayors were removed from office after having signed contracts with lumber companies to harvest trees from communal lands. A certain amount of profit taking, with preferential assignment of arable land and firewood rights, is expected of mayors, but mayors have overstepped their bounds. People point to the lack of expenditure for the public weal and for the town festival as the cause of social deterioration, decreased rainfall, unhealthy and/or infertile livestock and bad harvests.

Religion and Expressive Culture

Religious Beliefs. A few families in San Mateo and Nentón have become Protestant. In San Sebastián, the town is split between traditional religious beliefs and the robust doctrinalism of Catholic Action. The traditionalists in San Sebastián maintain the 260-day calendar and celebrate the rituals of planting and harvest, new fire, and new year. The Catholic Action sect refers to all these beliefs as "lies" and to the practitioners as sorcerers.

In San Mateo, Catholicism is much more syncretic. There is a thoroughgoing identification of Meb'a' (Orphan), a culture hero, with Jesus. Mary is both Meb'a''s mother and the moon. God incarnates the sun.

Most natural features—hills, rock outcrops, streams, and caves—have spirits. The spirits in caves, who are often ancestors of the townspeople, may be approached for aid and advice. A petitioner brings an offering, usually candles and liquor, and writes his or her question or request on a small piece of paper, leaving this at the cave entrance. The following day she or he returns and picks up the written answer.

Religious Practitioners. There are several religious specialists. Prayer-makers can petition for health, sobriety, good crops, and strong animals. Each town should have a principal prayer-maker who sets the ritual calendar for the year, does global petitioning for crops, and assigns dates for agricultural and town maintenance tasks. There are also diviners, herbalists, bonesetters, masseurs, midwives, curers, and sorcerers. When a sorcerer becomes too strong or too rich, the community may decide to immolate him or her.

Ceremonies. The life-cycle ceremonies are: at birth, purification of mother and child in a sauna, burial of the afterbirth, and burial of the belly-button stub; in the first year, "leg-spreading," in which gender roles are assigned; in the first three years, baptism/naming, whereby children acquire godparents, and first communion, which is seldom celebrated; at first menses, hair washing and purification by sweat bath; boys' passage to youth, which is less noted than that of girls; marriage; deathbed instructions; burial; postburial purification; and death anniversaries and communion with ancestors.

Annual-cycle ceremonies are: beating of fruit trees and children; blessing of seed and fields; harvest; thanksgiving;

warding off evil during the five "bad" year-end days; and new fire (annual housecleaning).

Ceremonies are held to inaugurate any structure or any major acquisition (e.g., a truck, stereo, or raised hearth), and to open and close public events. Each town has an annual festival for its patron saint.

Medicine. Illness is a function of balance between the spiritual and physical worlds. Western medicine, especially patent remedies such as aspirin, antihistamines, and antacids, accompanied by herbal tonics, are used to treat microbiotic disorders, allergic reactions, and indigestion. A lesion or break will be cleaned, disinfected, set, bandaged, and later massaged. A spiritual disorder (*susto*) may accompany an illness or result from the shock of an injury or near-. "Fright" is cured by a ritual specialist. Envy, anger, alcohol, holiness, and light skin, hair, or eyes make a person "hot." When someone "hot" looks at a child or a pregnant woman, they may cause the child to lose its soul or the woman to become ill and possibly abort. Elders or diviners can perform the necessary curing ritual. Illness may also be sent by ancestors or witches and must be cured by other religious healers. Minor illnesses are classified as "generic, non-human"; major diseases, such as whooping cough, smallpox, and cancer, are classified as "adult males."

Death and Afterlife. Traditional Chuj belief holds that death is the transition to "ancestorhood." Deathbed instructions are binding obligations, and spirits enforce them with sanctions of illness and misfortune. The spirits maintain an interest in the affairs of their families and can be approached for advice and aid, either at family altars, cave entrances, hilltops, or, in San Mateo, at cross-sites and accesses to the Classic Maya structures underlying the modern city. On All Saints' Day graves are cleaned and bedecked with flowers. Families bring feasts to the graveyard and picnic on the graves, leaving portions for the deceased. Marimbas play, and children fly kites. The kites' tails often have the names of dead relatives written on them, together with prayers or petitions.

Life after death is much like life before death. Grave goods typically include clothes, food, dishes, and implements that served the deceased in daily activities. One special task of the dead is to keep volcanic necks clear of debris; many spirits from San Mateo go to work in the Santa María volcano, overlooking Quetzaltenango. They have a market day on Sunday, when they go to a special plaza in Quetzaltenango and sell their wares. Living relatives may visit the dead there but may talk to them only via interpreters. Evangelical and Catholic Action Chuj affirm the doctrine of their faiths regarding death and the afterlife.

Bibliography

Cojtí Marcario, Narciso (1988). *Mapa de los idiomas de Guatemala y Belice.* Guatemala: Piedra Santa.

Hayden, Brian, and Aubrey Cannon (1984). *The Structure of Material Systems: Ethnoarchaeology in the Maya Highlands.* SAA Papers, no. 3. Burnaby, Canada: Society for American Archaeology.

Kaufman, Terrence (1976). "Archaeological and Linguistic Correlations in Mayaland and Associated Areas of Meso-America." *World Archaeology* 8:101–118.

McQuown, Norman (1971). "Los orígenes y la diferenciación de los mayas según se infiere del estudio comparativo de las lenguas mayanas." *Desarrollo Cultural de los Mayas.* 2nd ed., edited by Evon Z. Vogt and Alberto Ruz, 49–80. Mexico: Centro de Estudios Mayas.

JUDITH M. MAXWELL

Cora

ETHNONYMS: Coras-nayaritas, Nayares, Nayaritas

Orientation

Identification.   The Cora are an ethnic group who live almost exclusively in the state of Nayarit, Mexico. The terms "Nayares," "Nayaritas," and "Coras-nayaritas" are derived from the name of an ancient political-religious leader. In 1722, when the Cora were conquered by the Spaniards, the mummy of the Great Nayar was discovered on the Mesa del Nayar. He was at one time the principal Cora oracle, through which the Sun responded to Cora queries. The mummy was taken to Mexico City to be judged by the Holy Inquisition. In 1723 the Inquisition condemned it to the flames "*por ser falsos y prohibidos los cultos y sacrificios con que le solemnizaban . . . los nayaritas . . .*" ("because the rites and sacrifices which they, the Nayaritas, believe in are false"). It is interesting to note that the state was named "Nayarit," after this legendary personage, despite the inquisitorial condemnation.

Location.   The present territory of the Cora is bounded on the north by the state of Durango; on the east by the mestizo communities of San Juan Peyotán, Santa Rosa, Ejido de Higuera Gorda, and Huaynamota, and the Huichol community of San Andrés Cohamiata; on the south by the right bank of the river formed by the rivers Jesús María and Chapalanga as they join before they discharging into the Río Santiago; and on the west by the coastal plain of Nayarit. The region that the Cora occupy has an area of 4,912 square kilometers. The majority of their territory is within the Sierra of Nayarit, a place that is mountainous and without level ground except for the Valley of Huajimic and regions around Camotlán and Santa Teresa. The Sierra of Nayarit is a mountain complex that runs from 21°30' to 23°00' N. The Cora inhabit lands with elevations ranging from 460 to 2,500 meters above sea level. Their territory is made hospitable in the south by the waters of the Río Santiago, in the east by those of the Río Jesús María, and in the north by those of the Río San Pedro.

The Cora live primarily in ten communities located in

three *municipios:* El Nayar, Rosa Morada, and Acaponeta, all in the state of Nayarit. Four of these communities—Jesús María, Mesa del Nayar, Santa Teresa, and San Francisco—are the most important. The other six—San Lucas, Saycota, San Blasito, Rosarito, San Juan Corapan, and San Pedro Ixcatán—are of lesser importance and surround the primary communities.

Demography. When the Spanish arrived, small groups of Cora were scattered throughout the mountains. How many Cora there were at that time is unknown. At the end of the fourteenth century, there were between 2,500 and 3,000. The population rose to 6,242 in 1960 and to 7,043 in 1970. The 1990 census registered 11,434 Cora living in Nayarit and 489 living in other states.

Linguistic Affiliation. Cora is a member of the Uto-Aztecan Language Family. When the Spanish arrived in Nayarit, the following languages were being spoken: Zayahueco, Totorame, Tecual, Tecualme, Tecoxquin (also spelled Tecosquin), Coano, Cora, Huichol, and Tepehuán. Most of these languages have since disappeared; only the Cora, Huichol, and Tepehua, mountain people who entrenched themselves in the highlands, have retained their indigenous languages.

History and Cultural Relations

Along the coastal plain of Nayarit in the sixteenth century, the Spanish conquerors encountered a series of petty domains of greater or lesser influence, among which Aztátlan, Centícpac, and Tzapotzingo were the most prominent. The ruling town of these domains was on the coast and was in the hands the Totorame. Nevertheless, the domain of Aztátlan had incorporated some of the villages belonging to the Cora and the Zayahueco. The domain of Centícpac had also succeeded in dominating several Cora and Zayahueco villages and turning them into tributaries.

The people of the mountains, who needed to obtain salt from the coast, came down from time to time to trade for salt, fish, and meat. They brought with them maize, beans, *sotol* wine, honey, wax, deer and wild-pig skins, precious feathers, and caged birds.

Because of the need for salt, the Cora fell under the power of the Spanish, who set up garrisons at the points where the salt routes descended from the mountains. Among the salt fields were those of Olita (near the present town of Acaponeta), where the Cora provisioned themselves with this valued commodity. Under the pressure of Spanish control of the trade routes, the Cora decided in 1721 to appeal to the viceroy of New Spain, Baltasar de Zúñiga, Marquis of Valero. Led by Chief Tonati of the Mesa del Nayar, a delegation proposed to the viceroy that the Indians would accept the rule of the Spanish Crown if the following conditions were met: Cora rights to their lands and their native government would be respected from then on; the Spanish would also respect equivalent rights among the other natives of the Sierra; the Cora would not have to pay any more tribute; they would have free access to the towns of Acaponeta and Mexcaltitán to obtain salt, free of taxes; and all disputes and problems would be resolved by the viceroy alone.

After the return of the delegation, the Spanish seized Mesa del Nayar on 17 February 1722, and a new series of events unfolded. The Spanish established missions and forts at Santa Teresa in Cuaimaruzi and Santísima Trinidad on the Mesa. They also founded a string of villages along what was then called the "Frontier of San Luis Colotlan," within what is now the state of Jalisco. These villages were designed to support mining centers, such as Los Bolaños, from the attacks by the Coras-nayaritas, who still continued to oppose the Conquest. Included in this frontier were San Sebastián, San Andrés Cohamiata, and Santa Catarina, whose economic base was the salt trade. The Sierra was then fully incorporated into the colonial empire and became part of the Nuevo Reino de Toledo.

From the beginning, Jesuits spread Christianity among the Cora. The Jesuits were banished from New Spain by Charles III in 1767. After they left, the Franciscans were put in charge of evangelizing the Cora. The Franciscans retired from the region a hundred years later to escape the fighting set off by the War of Independence.

The mining centers of Bolaños and Zacatecas declined during the mid-nineteenth century. Mestizos from these regions moved into the Sierra to seize agricultural lands occupied by the Tepecano, Huichol, and Cora. In 1857 these seizures provoked an armed reaction by the Indians. Under the command of Manuel Lozada, Indians fought for their independence during the governments of Benito Juárez and Sebastián Lerdo de Tejada. Lozada was eventually defeated, and the Cora, Huichol, and Tepehuan returned to living in their closed Indian worlds.

In 1895 the ethnologist Carl Lumholtz surveyed the Sierra Madre Occidental and noted the land conflicts set off by the mestizo land grabbing.

On 25 August 1939 the municipio of El Nayar, containing a large majority of Cora, was created, with its capital at Jesús María. In 1962 the Franciscans returned to continue the work of evangelization. Led by a missionary bishop over the Cora, Huichol, and Tepehuan area, they worked at rebuilding the eighteenth-century churches. The Instituto Nacional Indigenista entered the region in 1967. They set up the first medical service among the Cora, organized bilingual assistant extension workers, and implemented national action programs to aid the Indians.

Current relations between the Cora and their Huichol and Tepehuan neighbors are cordial up to a point, generally the point at which land claims are disputed. On the other hand, land claims are a constant problem between Cora and mestizos.

Settlements

The Cora settlement pattern is generally dispersed. Only in the principal towns of San Francisco, Jesús María, Mesa del Nayar, Santa Rosa, Santa Teresa, Presidio de los Reyes, San Juan Corapan, El Rosarito, Dolores, San Blasito, and Santa Cruz can one find a concentration of houses. These towns are actual civil-ceremonial centers, whose inhabitants also have residences in the countryside. The most important buildings in these centers are a court house (*juzgado*), a *casa real* (an administrative building), schools, a church, and a *ramada* (a covered area where religious dances and ceremonies are held).

The most permanent town is Jesús María, the capital of the municipio of El Nayar. It hosts municipio and native governments, and a number of mestizo families live there. Jesús María is divided into four barrios, in which membership is inherited patrilinealy. The inhabitants of each barrio have a collective name.

Economy

Subsistence and Commercial Activities. The bases of the Cora economy are agriculture and cattle raising. In the lower lands, maize is the main crop. In much smaller proportions, black beans, squashes, watermelons, cucumbers, melons, sugarcane, sweet potatoes, peanuts, tomatoes, and chili peppers are also grown. The higher elevations support only maize and small quantities of black beans and squashes. Among the fruit crops are pears, apples, and figs.

Some plants—such as nopal (an edible cactus), mesquite, huamúchil (Pithecollobium dulce, a tree with edible seeds), tuna (the fruit of the nopal), gourds, and wild plums—are gathered wild. Cora also use wood from the forests.

The abundant pastures in the mountains have permitted the development of livestock raising. Historical accounts of the Cora since the eighteenth century allude to mules, horses, cows, donkeys, sheep, and goats. There has been an increase in animal husbandry since 1975 because of the availability of credit to farmers. Mestizo buyers from the surrounding areas have encouraged the Cora to turn to livestock raising.

Fishing is a secondary economic activity and source of food. Fish are trapped in rivers and gullies. Among the species caught are robalo, bagre, trout, mojarra, enterrador, pescado cuchara, and "burrito," as well as shrimp and turtles.

Today hunting is solely a ritual activity. Deer, wild pigs, and iguanas are hunted with bows and arrows.

Cora also leave their homes temporarily for farms on the coast, the highlands of Nayarit, Jalisco, or Zacatecas in order to work as day laborers in planting and harvesting various crops.

Industrial Arts. Today handicrafts provide a sizable income. Objects that once had a purely ritual or household use are being made for sale. Cora artisans produce woolen blankets and woolen or cotton bags embroidered with geometrical animal, plant, flower, or ritual designs. They also make items from woven maguey fiber, fashion pottery, and make fine products from deer and wild-pig pelts.

The Cora prefer to sell their handicrafts outside the Sierra in order to take advantage of better prices. For this reason, they journey to Tepic, the capital of the state of Nayarit; in many cases, however, the cost of the travel uses up the increased revenue gained from the better prices.

Trade. Commercial transactions are carried out with cash, on account, or in anticipation of future deliveries. Mestizos like to bring mules to the Cora, who value them highly, and trade them for cattle. The trade is usually two cows for one mule; a single large cow, however, may be traded for a mule. Cattle are also traded for bolts of muslin, metates (grinding stones), saddles, plastic ware, and other manufactured items. Simply put, most of the trading is to the advantage of the outsider.

Agricultural production is primarily for home consumption; part of the harvest is sold, not only when there is a surplus, but also in times of scarcity, if the family needs money for medicines or clothes.

Division of Labor. The labor of an entire family is needed for agriculture and cattle raising. At 7 or 8 years of age, boys begin to work at planting and harvesting. Girls help their mothers with household tasks. Some Cora families are polygynous. In these cases, one wife takes care of the household while the other works with the husband in the fields.

Land Tenure. Land is held communally. It cannot be bought or sold. A family has rights over the land that it works. Land can be rented to outsiders, but this is viewed with suspicion. Orchards can be inherited. The house and its furnishings are private property belonging to adults.

Kinship, Marriage, and Family

Kinship Terminology. The Cora have a Hawaiian type of kinship nomenclature.

Marriage. Marriage is forbidden with lineal kin, with persons who have the same last name, with godparents, and with the family of godparents. Marriage between first cousins is rare and looked down upon. The predominant form of marriage is monogamy, although sororal polygyny does occur from time to time.

Domestic Unit. The basis of the household is the nuclear family. It is extended by including the wives of recently married sons and grandchildren, with or without their parents.

Socialization. Informal education begins at an early age. Girls learn domestic duties from their mother or grandmother. From the age of 7 or 8, boys learn adult skills by helping their fathers in the fields. Boys who are 5 years old are initiated during the Holy Week celebrations.

Sociopolitical Organization

Social Organization. High status is accorded shamans, elders, and officials. During most of the year, the small settlements (rancherías), formed of extended-family households, operate independently. At special ritual times, they meet in the municipio capital, which functions as a governmental and ceremonial center. These gatherings take place at New Year, the time of the Changing of the Staffs (symbols of authority); during Carnival; during Holy Week; and for the mitotes (see "Ceremonies").

Political Organization. The four largest communities are governed by their own native authorities—generally called principales—who are elected locally by the community. For example, in Jesús María the principales are the gobernador, the teniente, the alcalde, centuriones, the tenanche mayor, the primer mayordomo, the mayordomo grande, two judges, fiscales, alguaciles, justicias or ministros, and topiles. The Cora gobernador has both civil and religious duties. In performing the latter, he is advised by the bástaʼa (Cora: "old man") and the tenanche mayor, who also directs the mayordomos. For each saint, there are two mayordomos. Each mayordomo is assisted by a tenanche. The pasoniles coordinate the work of the tenanches. The offices in this traditional civil-religious hierarchy are unpaid. Jesús María, being the capital of the municipio of El Nayar, also has a municipio president.

Social Control. The Cora have a system of common law. When the infraction is not serious, it is judged by the traditional Indian authorities; when it is serious, it is judged in the municipio capital or in Tepic, the capital of Nayarit.

Conflict. The greatest conflict is with the mestizos in the surrounding areas. Rich mestizo ranchers displace and exploit Indians. They invade Indian pastures and fields by taking advantage of poorly defined deeds. Mestizos pasture their animals on Indian communal land and go as far as planting crops on them without paying rent to the Indians. The Cora forests are also cut by _"rapamontes"_ ("forest rapists"), without compensation to the legitimate Cora owners.

Religion and Expressive Culture

Religious Beliefs. All Cora life revolves around religion. Humans must cooperate with the gods in order to maintain the order of the cosmos. One seeks the gifts of nature from the water, the wind, the sun, the moon, and the fire, in order to survive, as the Cora have always done, by eating the sacred plant, maize.

There are many places of worship, primarily caves, mountains, promontories, glades, lakes, springs, and rivers. One could describe Cora religion as a pre-Hispanic cult with an overlay of eighteenth-century Catholicism, including baptism, the worship of saints, and a ritual calendar.

The Indians feel that the gods are directly related to them. Cora gods are typically equated with Catholic sacred figures. For example Taya'u, "Father," is at the same time God, Jesus Christ, the Holy Burial, the Sun, and Fire. The great celebration of this god is Easter.

Tatí, "Mother" is the earth goddess of fertility. She lives in the Pacific Ocean, to the west, from where she sends the rains. She is equated with the Virgin of the Rosary and the Virgin of Candelmas. Tahás Suravéh, "Big Brother," is the morning star and is equated with Saint Michael. Other gods are Grandmother Moon and Grandfather Fire.

The major shine of the Cora, Thoakamota, is located on the Mesa del Nayar. For centuries the rituals of the Sun have been held there. The first fruits of harvest are also offered there.

Religious Practitioners. Shamans are religious specialists and religious leaders. They communicate with the gods through songs.

Ceremonies. Except for curing, Cora religious rituals involve the whole community and are led by special authorities. There are both Catholic and indigenous rituals. The latter, called mitotes, have a pre-Hispanic origin and are carefully separated from the Catholic rituals. Indigenous rituals are performed to ask for the fertility of the fields. On other occasions, the Cora give thanks for the gifts received. The mitotes are closely tied to the cycle of maize cultivation. Although the most important mitotes are held in the communities, they may also be held in rancherías.

The most important Catholic ceremonies are New Year, Carnival, Easter, and Christmas. During New Year, the Cora hold the ritual of Changing the Staffs, which was introduced by the Spanish as a means of rotating the individuals in authority each year.

Easter is a very important festival. The Christian concept of Easter, introduced by Spanish missionaries during the eighteenth century, was reinterpreted by the Cora and put into a format that was purely indigenous. In order to teach the Passion of Christ to the Cora, the missionaries made use of dances and music that were originally part of puberty initiation and fertility ceremonies associated with spring. In the two centuries that have passed since then, Christian and indigenous concepts have been blended to form the modern Easter ritual. In other cases, indigenous ideas were hidden by expressing them with Christian symbols.

Medicine. Curers treat those suffering from illness, whether the cause is natural or supernatural. Supernatural illnesses are sent by the gods when they feel neglected or when a ritual has not been performed properly for them. Illness may also be sent by dead kin lonely for the company of their living relatives. Sorcery can also produce supernatural illness. The curer diagnoses the cause of a supernatural illness through dreams or songs. The treatments consist of cleansing the sufferer with sacred feathers, sucking small objects from the affected areas, massages, or blowing tobacco smoke on the patient from a clay-and-cane pipe. Natural illnesses are cured with herbs and occasionally in combination with the aforementioned methods.

Death and Afterlife. After death, the body is laid on a blanket or sleeping mat facing the door of the house. Four candles are lit and placed at the four corners of the body. The feet face the door to indicate that the deceased will be leaving permanently. A shaman is sought to pray to the dead person and seek his or her well-being in the other life. A vigil is kept for five days, during which prayers are said. The body is buried with various personal possessions: clothes, hat, sandals, poncho, and drinking gourd.

On the fifth day, a ceremony literally called Chasing the Dead is held. The aim of this ritual is to get rid of the dead soul. An altar is erected, on which foods such as tortillas, tamales, cheese, and fruits are placed. A change of clothing and a poncho are placed at the side of this altar. The shaman prays for several hours, calling to the spirit of the dead person. The spirit is slow to arrive. Finally, in the middle of the night, it arrives in the form of a flying insect. It enters the house, lights on the shaman's sacred feathers, and then flies toward the altar with the food and clothing. The gathered friends and family rise and accompany the soul as it leaves the house. They say good-bye to it outside the house and express the idea that it will never return.

It is believed that the soul ordinarily goes to a round mountain covered with caves, to the northwest of the Cora territory. On the other hand, the souls of mestizos and badly behaved Cora go directly to a hell below the earth or sea.

Bibliography

Anguiano, Marina (1972). "Semana Santa entre los coras de Jesús María." In _Religión en Mesoamérica_, 559–565. XII Mesa Redonda de la Sociedad Mexicana de Antropología. Mexico City: Sociedad Mexicana de Antropología.

Anguiano, Marina (1992). *Nayarit: Costa y altiplanicie en el momento del contacto.* Mexico City: Universidad Nacional Autónoma de México (UNAM), Instituto de Investigaciones Antropológicas.

González Ramos, Gildardo (1972). *Los coras.* Mexico City: Instituto Nacional Indigenista.

Grimes, Joseph E., and Thomas B. Hinton (1969). "The Huichol and Cora." In *Handbook of Middle American Indians,* edited by Robert Wauchope. Vol. 8, *Ethnology, Part Two,* edited by Evon Z. Vogt, 792–813. Austin: University of Texas Press.

Hinton, Thomas B. (1964). "The Cora Village: A Civil-Religious Hierarchy in Northern Mexico." In *Culture Change and Stability: Essays in Memory of Olive Ruth Barker and George C. Barker, Jr.,* edited by Ralph C. Beals, 44–62. Los Angeles: University of California, Los Angeles, Department of Anthropology.

Hinton, Thomas B. (1972). *Coras, huicholes y tepehuanes.* Mexico City: Instituto Nacional Indigenista.

MARINA ANGUIANO AND ENRIQUETA M. OLGUIN

(Translated by James W. Dow)

Costa Ricans

ETHNONYM: Tico (after a diminutive suffix Costa Ricans often add to Spanish adjectives and nouns)

Orientation

Identification. The country's name is attributed to Columbus's visit in 1502 and that of Gil González in 1522. "Rich Coast" (Costa Rica) was suggested by the abundant gold ornaments the Indians were wearing. By 1539, the territory had become officially known as Costa Rica. It borders with Nicaragua on the north and with Panama in the southeast, with the Atlantic Ocean on the north and east and the Pacific Ocean on the south and west. Tico culture is identified with that of the dominant Hispanic majority. There are social-class and regional variations as well as the influences of other distinctive cultural traditions of the country.

Location. The country lies 10 degrees north of the equator. The land area is 51,100 square kilometers. There is great diversity of elevations. The volcanic mountain ranges Guanacaste, Tilarán, and Central rise, in that order, from the northwest to the center. From the center to the southeast lies the higher, Talamanca range whose highest peak is Chirripó, 3,820 meters above sea level. Fifty-two percent of Costa Ricans live in the central part (3.83 per-

cent of the country's surface), now called Central Valley (formerly Central Plateau), at elevations between 800 and 1,500 meters. At lower elevations, there are plains in the Caribbean lowlands to the north (Alajuela and Limón provinces) and the Pacific lowlands to the west (Guanacaste Province), whereas valleys characterize the south Pacific region. The main rivers are the Tempisque, the Grande de Tárcoles, the Reventazón, the San Juan, the Diquís, and the Sixaola, but smaller rivers and creeks are plentiful. Plant and animal life is diverse and abundant. The main cities are the provincial capitals: San José (also the country's capital), Heredia, Alajuela, Cartago, Liberia, Puerto Puntarenas, and Puerto Limón.

Demography. In 1991 the population was 3,087,700; it is projected to rise to 3,710,656 by the year 2000, and to 5,250,122 by the year 2025. In 1992 population density was 62.0 persons per square kilometer, and life expectancy at birth was 75 for men and 79 for women. The birthrate from 1985 to 1990 was 29.7 and general death rate was 3.9 per thousand; annual growth was 2.6 percent. The infant-mortality rate per 1,000 was 12 in 1992, and household average size 4.4. The literacy rate is 93 percent. In 1992 one out of every four Costa Rican households was classified as being below the poverty line. In genetic terms, Costa Rica has a trihybrid population. The three racial stocks from which this hybrid is derived are the Mongoloid Amerindian, the African Negroid, and the European and Near Eastern Caucasoid. The gene flow for this fusion has taken place over the course of the past 500 years. A study of genetic markers has shown that the Caucasoid component varies between 40 and 60 percent, the Negroid component varies between 10 and 20 percent, and the Amerindian component varies between 15 and 35 percent. In specific samples, the variations of these percentages are explained by regional and socioeconomic conditions.

Linguistic Affiliation. Spanish is the official language. The national dialect is non-Castillian. It uses the pronoun *vos* rather than *tú* and particular verb endings for this second-person singular form of address. There are regional and urban-rural variations. English is the foreign language most widely known.

History and Cultural Relations

The Indian chiefdoms found by the Spaniards had achieved considerable skill in government, trade, agriculture, gold- and stonework, pottery, and weaving cotton textiles. After 18 September 1502, when Columbus landed in Limón, Spanish expeditions stayed close to the shoreline. Then, in 1562, Juan Vázquez de Coronado founded the first capital in Cartago. The Central Valley slowly became the nucleus of the nation. The Costa Rican political elite, to a great extent, has been proven to be descendants of Vázquez de Coronado and his companions. From 1569 to the end of the seventeenth century, the *encomienda* system was in place, and it had at least two major effects on Costa Rican society. First, it divided the Spanish into two main classes: an elite of wealthy, dominant merchants and a larger class of poor *campesino criollos* (Central Valley peasantry of Spanish descent). Second, the Indian population, already diminished by the epidemics, battles, and various slavery policies of the early sixteenth century, grew even smaller under the encomienda system. Mestizos were not supposed to pay tribute, and intermarriage with Indians was not encouraged. For this reason, among others, there was not an important process of *mestizaje* (mestizoization) at the time Indians were living in the Central Valley.

Throughout the colonial period, Costa Rica was a poor, neglected, and isolated province of small farmers. The Spanish Crown decreed that no colony was allowed to trade with any country, except Spain. Foreigners were not permitted to enter. Restrictions on commerce were greatly responsible for this poverty. Costa Rica became independent from Spain in 1821. In 1829, the first newspaper appeared. By 1844, a university had been established, and, in the 1840s, a coffee-export and marketing structure built upon British shipping and credit was organized. From that time forward, the coffee economy has influenced all aspects of daily life from personal routines to government regimes, involving all aspects of international relations. The republican type of government and a sense of nationalism developed in the nineteenth century. In spite of national unity, class divisions were marked, from the oligarchy (the coffee-exporting elite) to the rural peasantry. A railroad to the Caribbean coast, built from 1876 to 1883, made commercial growing of bananas feasible. Bananas, like coffee, were dependent on foreign investment and markets. This crop increased economic dependence on the United States, as coffee had done with respect to England.

In the 1880s there began to predominate an ideology of government called *democracia liberal*. Its leaders were conservatives who stood for individual liberties, the separation of church and state, and the spread of formal secular education to all sectors. Many institutions and laws date from that time, such as the National Civil Registry, the National Museum, the National Theater, and the Civil Code. The full achievement of electoral democracy is attributed to the events of 1889. The election held that year had not been rigged by the government, and candidates had sought the popular vote. The president, however, tried to impose his candidate. Peasants angrily marched on the capital, demanding respect for their choice. The 1930s and 1940s brought the decline of the liberales and the new trends of *democracia social*, which meant activist government and the welfare state, especially after the armed revolt in 1948, when new institutions marked a break with the past. The banking system was nationalized, taxes were imposed on wealth, the army was abolished, the civil service was institutionalized, an impartial electoral system was crafted, the franchise was extended to women, and autonomous institutions (public corporations) were created to perform basic services. From the 1960s to the 1990s, the country has experienced different development schemes that have stressed diversified agriculture, industrialization, and state socioeconomic planning. The late 1980s and the 1990s have been characterized by policies of *economía neoliberal* and *democracia participativa;* these are attempts to reduce the role of government in the economy, limit state social programs, expand the free-market economy, join global markets, and obtain more citizen participation in decisions on public issues and solutions to national problems.

Settlements

Costa Rica's seven provinces are divided into *cantones* (townships), and the townships into districts. Each provincial capital is the largest city in the province. The townships' seats are smaller cities or towns in the central districts. The outlying districts had been more rural than urban; in the 1990s this pattern may be observed in the peripheral areas of the country, but it is uncommon in the Central Valley. Urbanization of the whole country has proceeded very rapidly. Even remote areas have electricity, piped water, bus service, telephones, and television. Some may even have computers in public facilities or in some homes. In rural areas as well as in urban ones, however, great differences in levels of income show in the homes and general life-style of the residents. In urbanized areas the neighborhoods are identified as barrios; in sparsely populated rural areas, the neighborhoods are called *caseríos*. The sense of community is associated more with these smaller units than with the larger towns or cities. San José dominates the rest of the country in politics, economic pursuits, and services. The city has grown haphazardly. Planning and zoning have not been very effective against crowded motor and pedestrian traffic, pollution, and constant razing and rebuilding. Most Ticos live in painted wooden or cement-block houses that have metal roofs and wood or tile floors. People prefer to own, rather than rent, their homes; a shortage of adequate housing is one of the problems addressed by government projects.

Economy

Subsistence and Commercial Activities. Ticos have mainly depended on agriculture, whether as a subsistence activity or as a large export business. Maize, beans, plantains, garden vegetables, cocoa, coffee, bananas, and flowers are examples of the crops. In addition, there is animal husbandry: beef and milk cattle, horses, pigs, goats, and birds (chickens, turkeys and, at present, even ostriches) are examples. Fishing has evolved into a major industry. In 1992 the gross national product showed the following percentage structure: primary sector (agriculture, forestry, mining, and fishing) 25.5; secondary sector (industrial) 19.3, and tertiary sector (services) 55.2. Agriculture generates over 28 percent of employment and accounts for close to 70 percent of exports. Tourism was the third source of income in 1989 and first in 1994.

Industrial Arts. Industry was mostly artisanal until the 1950s. One of its products, the painted wooden oxcart, became a symbol of the country. In 1957, 64.7 percent of industrial production and 68.5 percent of employment came from foods, shoemaking, clothing, and lumber products, with an average of three to ten employees per shop or factory. Larger industrial concerns were involved in printing and publishing, rubber products, and brewing plants. By 1963, Costa Rica had become fully integrated into the Central American Common Market. Industrial production became more mechanized in the 1960s and 1970s and grew rapidly. Chemical products, rubber, paper, and metal and electric items gained in importance. Foreign investment also influenced change; in the late 1950s it was 0.6 percent of total investment. By 1969 it was 21.1 percent of that total. By 1978 industry accounted for 24 percent of the gross national product, in contrast to 1 percent in 1950. By 1992, however, it accounted for only 19.3 percent. Costa Rica's Chamber of Industry was founded in July 1943. It had 700 affiliates in 1994, including business associations of the following industries: plastics, metals, vehicles, transportation, pharmaceuticals, shoes, textiles, foods, cosmetics, clothing, and graphic arts.

Trade.   In the 1960s Costa Rica greatly increased the exportation of "traditional" products such as coffee, bananas, sugar, and beef, plus some manufactured products. By 1970, however, industry demanded the importation of 76.9 percent of the value of raw materials and 98.6 of the value of capital goods. The rise of oil prices after 1973 increased the country's trade deficit. Economic growth was reduced in 1974 and afterward. Inflation and public debt increased greatly. The 1980s were marked by a severe economic crisis. The search for new markets became more imperative than in the seventies. By 1975 over half of manufactured goods came from abroad (10 percent from Central America and 43 percent from outside the Isthmus), whereas only 20 percent of industrial production was exported. In 1980 manufactured goods exported to Central America totaled U.S.$255 million but diminished to U.S.$160 million by 1982. Even in 1992, the 1980 value had not been recovered. Exports to markets outside the Isthmus, however, have increased. From 1984 to 1989, the main exported manufactured goods were clothing, jewelry and similar items, machinery and electrical appliances, canned fruits and vegetables, leather, tires, and seafood. In 1990, 25 percent of these "nontraditional" exports went to Central America, and 75 percent went to the rest of the world. The challenge faced in the nineties is to increase production and access to foreign markets, especially those of Mexico, the Caribbean, the United States, and Canada.

Division of Labor.   In the generally prevailing pattern, women devote their time and training to their homes, husband, and children, and men to jobs outside the home. Specific variations of this pattern are numerous, however, for several reasons. Costa Rican laws are considered among the most advanced regarding equality of men and women. The gender movement toward making these laws apply in daily life is strong. Women increasingly combine wife-mother roles with student and work roles outside the home. They have entered practically all the trades, businesses, professions, and careers besides the traditional ones of jobs at home, teaching, social work, nursing, and office work. They have been appointed or elected to high political office; however, at this upper level men greatly outnumber women. Increasingly, men are helping with domestic chores, especially among young, well-educated couples.

Land Tenure.   Private ownership is the norm. Arable land is unequally and inefficiently distributed, although programs for the redistribution of farmlands have been implemented since about the mid-twentieth century. The importance of small landholdings held by independent farmers is often mentioned as a main cause of the Tico cultural distinctiveness; about half the farmers are in the smallholder category. The greatest amount of land surface, however, is taken up by large holdings in the hands of less than 10 percent of all owners. A pattern of large landholdings is known as *latifundismo*. The trend continues toward land concentration and toward tinier plots for the greatest number of owners (*minifundismo*). Wage laborers with miniplots or no land at all are many. Land invasions by "squatters" occur in rural and urban areas. For instance, in 1985 there were 936 cases of invasion.

Kinship

Kin Groups and Descent.   Nuclear-family households are predominant, but extended households are also widespread, and extended-family groups act as units in politics, business, and social affairs. Separate but related nuclear families attend christenings, weddings and, above all, funerals. The descent system is bilateral; people use both the paternal and maternal surnames.

Kinship Terminology.   Tico Spanish sibling-cousin terminology is of the Eskimo type: the same terms are used for cousins on the father's and the mother's side, and cousins are differentiated from siblings.

Marriage and Family

Marriage.   Legal marriages are civil or religious. Free unions comprise roughly one-quarter of the couples living together. The proportion of children born outside legal marriage is close to 40 percent. Ideals of mutual aid expected of family members (spouses, children, parents, grandparents, great-grandparents) are formally required by the Family Code of the country. Some forms of family behavior are attributed to machismo and to *marianismo* (moral and spiritual superiority of women), as well as to vestiges of the Spanish traditional sex roles. Modernity has brought changes in authority patterns. Divorce is no longer the scandal it once was; separation and desertion are common. For the most part, families take care of the aged, but a trend of placing them in homes for the elderly has arisen. The churches and the government have programs addressed to family life.

Inheritance.   The law requires that a surviving spouse inherit half of the possessions of the couple and the other half be divided among the offspring; other relatives may inherit if there are no spouses or children. There is a strong tendency toward equal inheritance.

Socialization.   Most Costa Ricans love and desire children. A child's first birthday is a great occasion. Besides parents, other relatives participate in the care of children. There may also be helpers for this task. The services of nursery schools and kindergartens are increasingly sought. In rural areas, 5- and 6-year-olds are given duties such as running errands or picking coffee. Eight- to 10-year-old girls may perform all the household chores. Young girls are expected to help around the house more than boys are. Punishments are less harsh in the late twentieth century than they were in mid-century. The Family Code obliges parents to be moderate. Upper-class parents emphasize responsibility, honor, loyalty, and self-esteem. The middle class stresses the values of occupational success, personal realization, individual independence, honesty, and generosity. Working-class parents expect obedience, respect, self-discipline, and honesty. Girls' fifteenth birthdays (*quinceañeras*) are well-defined rites of passage, celebrated with a religious ceremony and a party. School graduations of both sexes are likewise celebrated. Legal maturity is at age 18. Young men and women usually stay with their families until they get married. If they remain single, they are not asked to leave but may do so.

Sociopolitical Organization

Social Organization. Ticos are oriented primarily to family, village, and neighborhood. Their community activities center around church, school, and sports. Informal groups for solving immediate problems are common, but Costa Ricans also cooperate through boards and committees, clubs, charity organizations, and community-development organizations. Registered associations for different purposes numbered more than 8,000 in 1991. Costa Ricans, however, are not characterized as joiners; individualism is said to be a trait of their national character, as is localism. Other values attributed to Tico culture are formal education, equality, democracy, freedom, peace, moderation, compromise, conformity, conservatism, caution, amiability, and courtesy.

Political Organization. Presidents are elected by direct popular vote every four years, as are fifty-seven congressional representatives. Citizens of both sexes over eighteen are required to vote. The president appoints the ministers. Each of the provinces has a governor, also appointed by the president. The eighty townships elect their municipal councils. The constitution is highly respected. Reelection of presidents is not allowed. The Supreme Court of Justice is composed of seventeen magistrates chosen by the legislature for eight-year terms. The fourth power is the Supreme Electoral Tribunal. Government is characterized by a well-developed system of checks and balances.

Social Control. Informally, the strongest social control is fear of what others will say. Gossip and _choteo_ (mockery) keep people in line without violence. Choteo ranges from friendly to prejudicial statements. It may be done with humor or with unpleasant ridicule. The importance of making a good impression is another check on behavior. Religion is also widely regarded as such a check. Rates of crime, theft, burglary, narcotics offenses, and corruption have increased with cosmopolitanism. Police corps and the courts handle these problems.

Conflict. Ticos tend strongly to avoid overt conflict in interpersonal relations. Decision making implies constant bargaining in an effort to avoid conflict. When inevitable, domestic conflict (e.g., abandonment of children, alcoholism, child abuse, battering of women) is referred to special agencies that cope with the situation at family and community levels. Communities take collective action against immoral teachers or priests; they may set up road blocks to protest government inefficiency or lack of response to their needs. Everywhere in the country, some moderate political and religious rivalry may be observed. There is a free press in which problems and policies are discussed. Conflict is handled formally, through the judicial system. The _defensoría de los habitantes_ (office for the defense of the inhabitants) controls or checks the exercise of public power. Its basic task is the defense of fundamental human rights. An administrative organization whose recommendations may be taken into account by the judiciary or other branches of government, it has access to all official files except state secrets.

Religion and Expressive Culture

Religious Beliefs. Costa Ricans take pride in religious tolerance, and support of ecumenism is widespread. The constitution guarantees freedom for all faiths. Catholicism is the dominant and official religion. Different Protestant denominations have relatively large memberships. There are all degrees of belief and practice among Catholics, but, nevertheless, it may be said that their religion permeates Tico culture. Some people become deeply faithful and committed to the church. Others simply express faith in God. The "will of God" is a guiding and explanatory concept. The cult of the saints, as intermediaries between supplicants and God, is a feature of the country's Catholicism. Villages and towns are named for saints, and major celebrations are conducted for each patron saint. Pilgrimages to some of the sanctuaries of the Virgin Mary and Christ on the cross are major events. Religious education is required in the public schools. Women are considered more devout than men. A minority believes in the efficacy of witchcraft in matters relating to love, illness, and misfortune. Clients and practitioners may be accused before the courts, however, because witchcraft is forbidden by law. In this matter, as in established religion, there are degrees of belief and practice.

Religious Practitioners. Costa Rica is organized into four Catholic dioceses, each with a bishop; the bishop of San José is the archbishop. There are diocesan priests and religious orders. Priests are scarce—probably one for about every 6,000 Catholics. In 1979 the first lay deacons were authorized to preach sermons, baptize, and give Communion to the sick in the absence of a priest. There are twenty-six congregations of nuns. In the late twentieth century, training for priests, nuns, and the laity emphasized that religion is concerned not only with prayer, ritual, and salvation but also with social justice, community service, and awareness of—and solutions to—social problems.

Death and Afterlife. When a death occurs, friends and relatives are notified by telephone, by announcements in the newspapers, or by radio stations. Mourners attend a wake at the home of the deceased or at a funeral parlor. Funerals are usually held the day following the death. After the church service, mourners accompany the hearse or pallbearers to the cemetery. Someone may say a few words in praise of the deceased or lead a last prayer just before the coffin is placed in a niche or lowered into the grave. When the coffin is covered, the mourners leave. Religious and memorial ceremonies follow for nine days at home and at church, then every month, and again when a year has passed. Some families make public announcements of memorial masses for a few years after the first one. Black is the color of mourning. On 2 November, the Day of the Dead, flowers are placed on graves. Most people believe the life of the soul is eternal.

Bibliography

Biesanz, Richard, Karen Zubris Biesanz, and Mavis Hilt-unen Biesanz (1982). *The Costa Ricans*. Englewood Cliffs, N.J.: Prentice-Hall.

Fondo de Población de las Naciones Unidas (1993). *Situación demográfica y políticas de población en Costa Rica*. Informe para la Conferencia Internacional sobre la Población y el Desarrollo. El Cairo, Egipto, setiembre 1994. San José: Ministerio de Planificación y Política Económca (MIDEPLAN).

Morera-Brenes B., and Ramiro Barrantes (1994). "Estimación de la mezcla racial en la población de Costa Rica mediante marcadores genéticos." *Memorias del Onceavo Congreso Latinoamericano de Genética*, Puerto Vallarta, Mexico.

Sibaja, Luis F., Jorge Rovira, Anabelle Ulate, and Carlos Araya (1993). *La industria: Su evolución histórica y su aporte a la sociedad costarricense*. Cámara de Industrias. San José: Litografía e Imprenta Lil.

MARÍA EUGENIA BOZZOLI DE WILLE

Creoles

The label "Creole" is used in the Caribbean and Middle America with considerable imprecision. Today it usually means a person or group of African or African and some other—such as Indian or European—ancestry. Such groupings include Creoles of Belize, Costa Rica, Dominíca, the Grenadines, and the Miskito Coast. Other groups, such as Haitians, Puerto Ricans, Cubans, and Katicians, also fit this definition of "Creole" but are not referred to as such. Thus, the label "Creole" serves to distinguish those of African ancestry from those of European, Indian, or mixed European and Indian ancestry in multiethnic nations.

Creoles of Nicaragua

ETHNONYMS: Criollos, Miskito Coast Creoles, Morenos, Negros

Orientation

Identification.   The Creoles of Nicaragua are an Afro-Caribbean population of mixed African, Amerindian, and European ancestry, most of whom live in Nicaragua. The Nicaraguan Creoles' distinctive culture is strongly influenced by its West African and British roots, as well as by prolonged interaction with North Americans, Nicaraguan mestizos, and the Miskito (a Nicaraguan Afro-Amerindian group). "Mosquito" is the name given to the region and the latter people by early European visitors to the area. The name "Miskito," currently used to designate this people and their language, is apparently a twentieth-century ethnographic innovation that more closely approximates the Miskito people's name for themselves, in accordance with the phonetics of their own language.

Location.   The bulk of the Creole population is concentrated in the market/port town of Bluefields, located at 12°00′ N and 83°50′ W, and in a number of small communities scattered north and south of that town along Nicaragua's southern Caribbean coast, part of a region known as the Mosquito Coast (or Mosquitia). The terrain is low-lying tropical rain forest, with an average annual rainfall of 448 centimeters and a mean temperature of 26.4° C. This coastal plateau is crossed by large rivers and fringed by brackish lagoons, on the banks of which most Creole settlements are located. Smaller numbers of Creoles reside in the large towns of the northern Caribbean coast, and a substantial number live in Managua (Nicaragua's capital), in other Central American countries, and in the United States.

Demography.   In the early 1990s the approximately 25,000 Creoles who resided in Nicaragua represented less than 1 percent of that country's total population. The national census does not enumerate Creoles separately; during the 1980s, however, estimates of the size of the Creole population were made by an array of government institutions and in the course of various ethnographic studies. These estimates vary substantially. The most reliable approximations place 10,000 Creoles in Bluefields, 11,400 elsewhere on the Caribbean coast, and perhaps 5,000 in other areas of Nicaragua.

Linguistic Affiliation.   Most Creoles speak, as their first language, Miskito Coast Creole (MC Creole), an English-based creole closely related to other creoles spoken in the Anglophone Caribbean, particularly in Belize and Jamaica. By the 1990s, all but the oldest Creoles were fluent Spanish speakers as well. MC Creole is described by Holm (1982, 3) as characterized by a ". . . very African syntax organizing sentences out of words from a variety of sources: most . . . from English . . . but . . . [also] from Miskito, African languages, and . . . New World Spanish." There is evidence that MC Creole is being influenced at the syntactic and the lexical levels by Central American Spanish.

History and Cultural Relations

Many of the Creoles' ancestors arrived on the Nicaraguan/Honduran Caribbean coast (the Mosquitia) from Africa as slaves in the period between the mid-seventeenth and the late eighteenth centuries. They were brought there by the

British to labor in forestry, plantation agriculture, and the transisthmus trade with the Spanish colonies. Over time this African population transformed its cultural and physical traits by combining elements of its African culture with those of its European masters and those of local Amerindian peoples, to create a new culture; simultaneously, miscegenation among these three peoples was common.

In 1787 the British settlers were forced by treaty obligations to evacuate the Mosquito Coast. Many slaves who revolted against, ran away from, or were abandoned by their masters stayed on the Coast, where they created African American communities at Bluefields and at Pearl Lagoon. Subsequently, free Black merchants, turtle fishers, adventurers from Jamaica and the Cayman Islands, escaped slaves from throughout the western Caribbean, and, after Emancipation (1833), freed slaves from the Anglophone Caribbean augmented this population. In 1860 Great Britain signed the Treaty of Managua, under the terms of which Nicaragua recognized Britain's nominal sovereignty over Mosquitia. The treaty also designated a portion of the area as a self-governing "Mosquito Reserve." In the absence of direct colonial control during the first three-quarters of the nineteenth century, this African American community flourished. Their culture solidified and the community began to consolidate economic, political, and social control over the Mosquito Coast. They began referring to themselves as "Creoles," signifying the emergence of a specific racial/cultural group identity.

In the 1880s North American capitalist interests became active in lumber, mining, and bananas and transformed Nicaraguan Mosquitia into an enclave of the U.S. economy. This transformation initiated crucial changes in the Creole political economy. North Americans and other Whites now assumed the top positions in the Coast's socioeconomic hierarchy. A significant portion of the Creole population was transformed into an urban wage-labor force. Creoles went to work for the new companies as laborers, growers, contractors, and clerks.

The enclave's increasing labor requirements were also met by Blacks from other areas of the Caribbean. Although distinctions of color, religion, and class initially served to separate these immigrants from the Creoles, they eventually blended into the Creole group through a process of intermarriage and cultural assimilation. The Creole group was also augmented by the assimilation of Miskito and Garifuna populations with whom they were living in the small biethnic villages of the Pearl Lagoon area.

In 1894 the Nicaraguan national government militarily seized and "Reincorporated" the Mosquito Coast. Mestizos from the Pacific replaced Creoles in the top political positions in the region. Very bitter feelings emerged between Mosquitian Blacks and Nicaraguan mestizos. One response of the Black population to the mounting racial conflict was vigorous participation in the local branches of Marcus Garvey's Universal Negro Improvement Association. Important sectors of the Creole community also actively fomented regional separation from the Pacific portion of the nation.

North American capital began to withdraw from the Coast during the world depression of the 1930s. In search of better economic opportunities, many Blacks abandoned the hinterland for the Coast's urban areas, Managua, and the United States.

During the second half of the twentieth century, the Coast was increasingly integrated, economically and socially, into the rest of Nicaragua. Commerce with western Nicaragua increased, especially after the completion of a road connecting the two halves of the country, and many Pacific-coast mestizos migrated to the Mosquito Coast. The Creole population became a minority in many of the areas in which it had previously been demographically dominant, and it experienced further erosion in its increasingly tenuous political and economic position. As a result, Creoles have been increasingly drawn into the Pacific mestizo social and cultural orbit. Most Creoles now speak Spanish as well as Creole and consider themselves to be Nicaraguan. Many have even intermarried with mestizos. Intermittently, however, they continue to protest their loss of political and economic power to mestizos.

Settlements

By the 1990s, the majority of Creoles were urbanized. In Bluefields, most live in the four predominantly Creole barrios on the banks of Bluefields Lagoon. As these barrios have become increasingly crowded, individual families have taken up residence away from the waterside, in the expanding, predominantly mestizo, barrios of the town. Rural settlement patterns are of two types. Most rural Creoles live in small villages of fewer than 2,000 persons. In these villages, houses are strung out in files, two or three deep, along the water's edge, with missionary churches at their centers. In the Pearl Lagoon area, 36 kilometers north of Bluefields, where most of the small villages are located, settlements are either predominantly Creole or Creole mixed with either Miskito or Garifuna. Other rural Creoles are located on small freehold farmsteads on the Corn Islands and in the Kukra Hill area, which lie 68 kilometers northeast and 30 kilometers north of Bluefields, respectively.

Creoles live primarily in "West Indian cottages"— wood-framed clapboard structures, painted in white or pastel colors, with wooden floors raised from the ground by posts, steep corrugated galvanized "zinc" roofs, and verandas in front. The basic structure of such a cottage is modified according to the economic means of its occupants. In the outlying rural areas, a typical house may be smaller, with only two interior rooms. The zinc roof may be replaced by palm thatch, and the clapboards may remain unpainted. In these areas, the kitchen and bathhouses are usually in separate structures just off the house, as is the outdoor latrine if there is one. In the urban areas, the basic model might be elaborated into a two-story structure with the kitchen and bathroom built in. Even in the urban areas, however, running water is a comparative rarity, and a well and an outhouse are necessities. In the 1980s affluent Creoles began building cement houses that were patterned after those built by mestizos in the Pacific portion of Nicaragua.

Economy

Subsistence and Commercial Activities. The Creoles who live in small rural villages and on farmsteads are predominantly agriculturists. Some are engaged in shifting agriculture, but in many cases soils are of high enough quality to sustain cultivation on a permanent basis. A wide variety of crops are grown, including rice; red beans; a number of edible tubers such as cassava (manioc), *coco* (Spanish: *quequisque*), and dasheen (taro; Spanish: *malanga*); sugarcane; maize; and tree crops such as bananas and plantains, avocados, cacao, coconuts, citrus fruits, pineapples, mangoes, and other tropical fruits. Creole farmers also raise domestic animals such as dogs, cats, chickens, turkeys, ducks, guinea fowl, pigs, horses, and sometimes cattle. Agricultural production is primarily a subsistence activity, but surpluses are marketed through local traders or regional market centers. Some rural Creoles are able to meet their cash needs entirely through their agricultural activities, and some have reached a level of relative affluence through the cultivation of cash crops like coconuts, cocoa, rice, and sugarcane and the raising of cattle. A few of these farmers even hire seasonal labor to assist them.

Most rural Creoles fish as well as farm. Fishing in the coastal lagoons and inshore areas is an important source of cash and subsistence. Fishermen utilize 5.8- to 7.6-meter dugout canoes (*duris*), which are propelled by paddles and sails. A few prosperous fishers use small outboard or inboard motors. Fishing for scale fish is done with hand lines and gill nets. Shrimp fishing is done seasonally with cast nets. The shrimp are generally boiled in salt water and sun dried. Periodically, local fishing companies and traders buy the excess shrimp and scale-fish catch. A few rural Creole communities are also involved in lucrative commercial lobster fishing. This activity is undertaken in open outboard speedboats (*pangas*) or larger (6- to 21-meter), diesel-powered wooden boats, with traps. The catch is sold to processing plants located in Bluefields and on Corn Island. Turtle fishing, which was once an important activity in Creole communities, is now restricted to two Creole villages.

Domestic productive activities such as baking bread, making coconut oil, or raising chickens for sale, which are usually undertaken by women, are also important sources of currency for some families. Many rural Creole men migrate for prolonged periods to other areas of Nicaragua or to the United States to engage in wage labor. They typically work in maritime-related occupations. Remittances from these activities are an important component of the Creole economy.

Many urban Creoles are engaged in independent subsistence and petty-commodity production relating to either farming or fishing activities, which are similar to those in the rural areas. Most of these families also engage in a variety of other economic activities, such as domestic petty-commodity production (e.g., baking) and some form of wage labor; however, urban Creoles typically strive to be employed as professionals (teachers, lawyers, nurses), office workers, administrators, civil servants, and self-employed artisans (mechanics, shipwrights, furniture makers, and carpenters). As in the rural areas, labor migration and remittances are important parts of the urban Creole economy.

Industrial Arts. Creoles are skillful carpenters and woodworkers. They construct and repair wooden boats of

up to 21 meters. They build their own houses, and some are engaged in furniture- and cabinetmaking. Creoles also make much of their fishing equipment, tying a variety of net types. They manufacture some of their domestic utensils, furnishings, and clothes; however, the bulk of the Creoles' manufactured needs are purchased. A large portion of Creole material culture is based on consumer goods imported from the United States.

Trade. In the rural villages, reciprocity governs the exchange of subsistence goods, particularly among extended families. Creoles have been involved in market relations for over two hundred years, however, and these currently dominate Creole trade relations. Although some Creoles have become successful traders and shopkeepers, in Creole communities such positions have historically been held by Chinese and mestizo merchants.

Division of Labor. Creole women work at domestic tasks an average of three to four times longer each week than do Creole men. Women are exclusively responsible for the central domestic tasks of cooking, washing, ironing, household cleaning, child care, and the care of small domestic animals. Both men and women fetch household water and engage in daily marketing; men engage in cleaning the yards and gathering firewood. Men do most of the fishing, but women help process and prepare the catch for sale. Both men and women are involved in agricultural activities. In general, men have central responsibility for such crops as rice and beans, which have commercial as well as subsistence significance, whereas women are more centrally involved in subsistence crops such as cassava and coco. Men usually undertake the clearing and burning of plots. Both adults and children engage in planting, weeding, and harvesting; women are more responsible for the former two, and men for the latter. Marketing outside the community is usually undertaken by men. In the urban areas, both men and women work in a variety of white-collar occupations. Creole women formerly made up the bulk of the unskilled labor force in local fish-processing plants, but, with increased remittances from the United States in the 1980s, this activity has slackened.

There has traditionally been a degree of economic differentiation within Creole communities. The older, better economically connected, and better educated members of the Creole elite tend to occupy professional, administrative, and civil-service positions, whereas most Creoles are small producers or self-employed skilled laborers.

Land Tenure. Each Creole village has extensive communal lands that have been deeded to it. Each villager has use rights to such land. In practice, individuals are able to stake a lasting claim to particular plots of communal land by making permanent improvements to it, which is usually accomplished by planting tree crops such as coconuts or mangoes. The rights to particular parcels that are claimed in this manner are inherited and can be sold to other villagers. It is even possible to sell to outsiders such improvements and, hence, the rights to exclusive use, although this is not commonly done. In areas of shifting cultivation, a villager who wishes to utilize land usually asks permission of villagers who have previously farmed the area. In areas of dispersed farmsteads, like Corn Island and around Bluefields, land tenure is freehold. Family ownership of land is common. Household dwellings are usually owned by the female head of the household or by the wife of the male head of the household.

Kinship

Kin Groups and Descent. Women, their children, and their daughters' children are the basic members of Creole kin groups. The independent nuclear family is the ideal, but extended families constructed around mother, daughter, and daughter's children are common. Creoles reckon kinship bilaterally. Descent is recognized only to the depth of three or four generations, although particularly important ancestors (usually European or Amerindian) are remembered. The lateral extension of Creole kinship reckoning is shifted toward the female side and generally extends to second cousins. There are no formal kin groups above the level of the nuclear family; however, Creoles see themselves as members of related but distinct, loosely structured kindreds based on common family names and consanguineal ties.

Kinship Terminology. Kinship terminology is of the Eskimo type, with a strong tendency not to extend consanguineal terms to affines.

Marriage and Family

Marriage. Marriages sanctioned by church and state are the ideal, but common-law relationships are widespread and may even be prevalent. Creoles generally marry Creoles from their own communities; in the rural areas, however, there has traditionally been significant intermarriage between Creoles and Garifuna and Miskito. Creole/ mestizo marriages are more common in the urban areas. Creole unions are relatively unstable, especially among young adults. An individual may have children with a number of partners and may even establish domestic relations with them before settling into a more permanent relationship in middle age.

Domestic Unit. The independent nuclear-family household under the nominal control of the husband/father is the ideal; however, extended families constructed around the mother–daughter–daughter's children triad are quite common. There is a cyclical relationship between these two household types. Young adult women and their young children often live in their mothers' extended-family households. These daughters may subsequently establish separate nuclear-family households with their male partners and their own children. Often, when these women are no longer of childbearing age, they themselves become the heads of extended-family households, in which some of their adult children and their daughters' children reside. It is very rare to find more than one nuclear family living in the same household.

Inheritance. Inheritance is bilateral; sons and daughters inherit equally. Land may be inherited by siblings as a group, although this often leads to disputes.

Socialization. Grandparents, parents, and older siblings—especially females—raise the children. All Creole children attend school: the curriculum is regulated by the Nicaraguan state, but the missionary churches are very influential socializing agents, through their religious instruction and their control and staffing of many schools.

Sociopolitical Organization

Social Organization. Creole social relations are structured by a complex mix of factors, including kinship, age, gender, class, color, and educational level. Rural Creole communities, although stratified by age and gender, are otherwise relatively egalitarian. In urban areas, however, color, class, and educational level influence many forms of social interaction. Historically, Creoles have been active in a variety of social groupings. These include male social clubs and secret societies (segregated by class), clubs formed around barrio baseball teams, burial societies, men's and women's social-service clubs, barrio-improvement organizations, and church organizations. Urban Creoles consider themselves superior to those living in rural communities. Creoles generally feel superior to the indigenous and mestizo inhabitants of the Coast. Interaction with members of these other groups is often limited to the public sphere in the urban areas.

Political Organization. During much of the nineteenth century, Creole men occupied most of the top positions in the Mosquito Reserve. Although Creoles have periodically protested their political marginalization, since that time their participation in the regional and national political process has in general been through the established, mestizo-dominated national parties and not in organizations that were established on the basis of racial/ethnic or regional identity. There have been some exceptions: many Creoles joined the Garvey movement in the early 1920s; in the 1970s a number of quasi-political civic-action groups sprang up. Since the Reincorporation, there have always been a few Creole men among the top political leadership on the southern Coast. The number of such leaders has increased since the 1960s, but mestizos remain the dominant political force in the area. In the rural communities, elder males from influential families have held the principal positions of leadership. In the twentieth century the Nicaraguan state took advantage of this structure by appointing leading males as local representatives of the executive and judiciary.

Social Control. The principal mechanisms of social control among Creoles are the overlapping structures of family, church, and state. The Protestant missionary churches play an important role not only in establishing the norms of everyday conduct but also, to a certain extent, in enforcing them. The police and the judiciary are the major coercive forces that compel proper conduct.

Conflict. Interfamilial conflict—especially between women—is a constant in Creole society. Creoles traditionally have been antagonistic toward the national government. This animosity has translated into conflictive relationships with mestizos, particularly those from the Pacific. One illustration of this tendency was the Creole opposition to the Sandinista Revolution during the 1980s.

Religion and Expressive Culture

Religious Beliefs and Practitioners. Religion plays a central role in Creole social life and identity. Creoles are mostly Protestant, and the Creole church leaders are the leaders of the Creole community. The largest number of Creoles belong to the Moravian church, but others belong to Anglican, Baptist, Seventh Day Adventist, or "Tabernacle" (Pentecostal) churches. Still others are Catholics or members of the new evangelical sects that were established in the late 1980s. Most of these churches were founded by North American missionaries. As a result, for many years the principal religious practitioners were Anglo pastors. Since the mid-twentieth century, however, Creole men have gradually taken over most of these positions. The majority of these churches remain as they were introduced by the missionaries, with little or no syncretism.

Nonetheless, African features of Creole religious expression lie hidden just beneath the surface in the Creole community. In the 1980s the Creole churches that included in their worship such elements as spirit possession, call-and-response preaching, religious music featuring African rhythms, and clapping and dancing all grew in popularity. Other vestiges of what historical sources indicate was once a well-developed, African-based belief system are still evident in Creole culture. These vestiges include participation in secret semireligious societies and widespread belief in and practice of obeah and necromancy, as well as a number of beliefs and ceremonies surrounding death.

Ceremonies.   The most important Creole religious ceremonies are those commemorating death, marriage, harvest, the end of slavery, the new year, and Christian holidays (Christmas, Easter).

Arts.   Creoles dress in clothing styles that are inspired by North American Black fashion. Their cuisine is based on local and Afro-Caribbean elements such as coconut oil, *eddo* (taro root), and cassava (manioc) and on Anglo elements such as wheat flour and imported processed foods. Creoles have developed their own musical style, which is closely related to West Indian calypso, and a "May Pole" dance style that is associated with it. They also enjoy performing, listening, and dancing to Afro-Caribbean reggae, soca, and calypso and to Afro-American soul music. The U.S. form of country-and-western music is likewise popular. Afro-Caribbean oral traditions, such as stories about Anancy (the West African spider-trickster figure), remain extant, although they are diminishing in importance to the Creole community.

Medicine.   Most Creoles believe in and utilize medical care based on Western science. Nevertheless, herbal medicine is widely practiced in the community, and there are a few herbal experts who are the respected repositories of traditional practices in this area.

Death and Afterlife.   Many Creoles believe in spirits; malevolent spirits of the dead are known as *duppys*. African-influenced Creole ritual surrounding death features participation in wakes and nine-night observations, during which spirits are appeased, call-and-response singing is performed, and, occasionally, stories are told about Anancy. Nevertheless, the Christian belief in heaven and hell is central to Creole ideas about the afterlife.

Bibliography

Gordon, Edmund T. (1987). "History, Identity, Consciousness, and Revolution: Afro-Nicaraguans and the Nicaraguan Revolution." In *Ethnic Groups and the Nation State,* edited by CIDCA (Centro de Investigaciones y Documentación de la Costa Atlantica, Instituto Nicaragüense de la Costa Atlantica)/Development Study Group, 135–168. Stockholm: Development Study Unit.

Holm, John (1982). *The Creole English of Nicaragua's Miskito Coast: Its Sociolinguistic History and a Comparative Study of Its Lexicon and Syntax.* Ann Arbor, Mich.: University Microfilms International.

EDMUND T. GORDON

Cubans

ETHNONYMS: none

Orientation

Identification and Location.   Cuba is the largest of the Caribbean islands in the West Indies. Situated between 19°40′ and 23°30′ N and 74° to 85° W, the Antillean nation of Cuba comprises approximately 120,000 square kilometers of land, including over 1,500 islets and keys and the Isle of Pines southwest of the Gulf of Batabanó. Cuba measures 200 kilometers at its widest, southernmost point and under 35 kilometers at its narrowest point. Natural harbors and ports dot the northern coast's low marshlands, swamps, and bluffs, and mountain ranges define the southern coast.

Elevations of the Maestra, Escambray, and Guaniguanico mountain ranges—located in southeast Santiago de Cuba, south-central Villa Clara, and Pinar del Río provinces respectively—vary from 2,000 meters in the Sierra Maestra to 600 meters in Guaniguanico. Between these chains, which cover 35 percent of the island land mass, are hills and sea-level plains suitable for a wide variety of tropical agricultural cultivation, ranching, and forestry. The stable climate, with temperatures that seldom drop below 21° C and average rainfall of 137 centimeters a year, contributes to the production of tropical crops. Cuba has often been in the path of devastating tropical storms and hurricanes that negatively affect production.

Linguistic Affiliation.   Cuba's earliest inhabitants were the seminomadic Ciboney, and little information on their language remains. Their successors, the Arawak, dominated the island at the time of Spanish exploration and occupation. Terms taken from the Arawak language became incorporated into the major language of Cuba, which continues to be Spanish. By the end of the sixteenth century, most of the native population had ceased to exist, further homogenizing language, but African slaves from Bantu-language groups of West Africa have contributed many terms to Spanish as spoken in Cuba.

Other permanent immigrants from China, Germany, Great Britain, and the United States tended to adopt the Spanish language. After Cuba's separation from Spain in 1898, the English language was incorporated into school curricula and North American terms and commodity trademarks infiltrated Cuban speech. Beginning in 1961, as a consequence of closer ties with the Soviet Union, the government promoted learning Russian and Eastern European languages to facilitate business and diplomatic communication.

Before the 1959 Revolution, the urban literacy rate was high by Latin American standards, but the literacy rate in the countryside was particularly low. An intensive literacy campaign focused first on teaching the rural population the fundamentals of reading and writing Spanish, then on gradually improving levels of literacy. Cuba's accomplishment in this regard has gained universal recognition.

Demography. In 1991 more than half of the Cuban population of 10.7 million was under the age of 30. This pattern is related in part to the emigration of over 1 million Cubans to other countries following the 1959 Revolution. The Cuban population is 51 percent mulatto, 37 percent White, 11 percent Black, and 1 percent Chinese. Forty percent of the population resides in the western provinces and the major urban areas of Havana, Matanzas, and Pinar del Río. Another 20 percent of the population resides in the provinces of Villa Clara and part of western Camagüey. Twenty percent resides in northwestern Santiago de Cuba and Camagüey, and the final 20 percent in the easternmost area of Santiago de Cuba. The eastern naval base of Guantánamo, leased to the United States in 1903, houses 6,000 U.S. military personnel and their families and is effectively separated from Cuba.

Since the late Spanish colonial period, the rural population has migrated to the major cities of Havana, Matanzas, and Santiago de Cuba. Following the 1959 Revolution, efforts have been made to emphasize services to the countryside and slow down the migration to cities. Although population growth has declined in Havana, the trend toward urbanization has continued: in the late twentieth century 62 percent of women and 58 percent of men reside in cities. In contrast to pre-1959 conditions, however, the rural population has enjoyed improved provision of health care, education, housing, and other basic needs.

History and Cultural Relations

The earliest known settlers in Cuba, the Ciboney (1000 B.C.) were joined by Arawaks from A.D. 1100 to 1450. From Christopher Columbus's first landing in 1492 to U.S. troop landings in 1898 during the final stages of the war for Cuban independence, the island was integrated into the Spanish colonial structure, producing as major export crops sugarcane, coffee, and tobacco. The island also served as an administrative center for Spanish political and economic control of the region and was therefore a significant arena of international rivalry over Spanish control of the Western Hemisphere. Population growth and economic and political activity centered on the Havana environs,

marginalizing authority and economic growth in the eastern regions and restraining opportunities there even in the postcolonial period. In the second half of the nineteenth century, the Spanish government proved incapable of resolving conflicts over its policies, resulting in the Ten Years War (1868–1878) and the war for Cuban independence, which began in 1895.

Between 1899 and 1902 the United States occupied Cuba and appointed military governors as administrators; the republic was not formally established until a president was elected in 1902. The Cuban constitutional convention reluctantly incorporated the Platt Amendment (to a U.S. army appropriation bill of March 1901), which became the legal justification for U.S. control of the naval base at Guantánamo, ownership of Cuban land, and intervention in Cuba's internal affairs until the abrogation of the amendment in 1934. Between 1934 and 1959 the Cuban economy strengthened its economic and political ties with the United States. Persistent national conflicts generated the formation of various opposition movements. After the success of the July 26th movement in 1959, Cuba built a socialist system; even after the collapse of socialism in Eastern Europe and the Soviet Union, Cuba's government continued to be a rather stalwart adherent.

Revolutionary Cuban society has attempted to eliminate traditional vestiges of both racism and sexism. With a heritage combining descendants of Spaniards and other western Europeans, African slaves, and Chinese indentured laborers and immigrants, Cuba's Latin African mulatto culture manifests fewer racial tensions than more racially separated societies. The revolutionary government continues to make structural attempts to fully integrate and empower women and Afro-Cubans and to publicly address the foundations of bias.

Settlements

During the colonial period and prior to 1959, the major urban centers of Havana, Matanzas, Cárdenas, and Santiago de Cuba displayed patterns of growth associated with emphasis on the agro-export economy. Towns and villages organized around production of sugar, coffee, and tobacco exports expanded with markets. Migration of seasonal workers and subsistence farmers exerted strong pressures on urban centers as the concentration of landownership proceeded. Since 1959, the revolutionary government has attempted to reduce this migration in keeping with its agenda of providing more social services to rural areas and small cities and towns, radically reforming land-tenure patterns, and diversifying the economy.

As before the Revolution, rural dwellings of the poor, particularly in the mountainous regions, are constructed from palm thatch, cane, and mud with dirt floors. These _bohios_ traditionally dominated the countryside around sugarcane fields and areas where family subsistence plots persisted; they are only gradually being replaced with dweller-constructed, partially prefabricated cement multifamily housing. Cycles of increased construction have occurred from 1959 to 1963, in the mid-1970s, in 1980, and from 1988 to 1989 but have not kept pace with housing needs. In urban centers, housing combines single-family Spanish-style architecture, low-rise apartment units, single-story apartments joined in rows, and, in the oldest cities, some former single-family homes converted into multiple units. The Spanish patio arrangement is more predominant in the older dwellings. Construction of single-family housing has received less priority from the revolutionary government.

Economy

Subsistence and Commercial Activities. Since 1959, the Cuban government has endeavored to provide food security to its population and increase access to basic needs in housing, education, and medical care. Programs have been implemented to diversify and decentralize agricultural production, exploit nickel reserves, develop light industries, expand the fishing and tourist industries, and increase export earnings to provide for other development needs.

Before the collapse of the socialist bloc, over 40 percent of Cuba's food supply was imported. The National Rationing Board attempted to assure distribution of minimum basic food needs based on demographics. The island suffered severe food shortages in 1993 and 1994, following climatic disasters and the loss of most of its oil imports and 30 percent of its agrochemical, machinery, and parts imports. Attempts to address the crisis included the transformation of state farms into worker-owned enterprises or cooperatives, the reintroduction of farmers' markets, and new trade arrangements for food imports from other countries. The government also legalized private markets and private vendors and suppliers of services in many industries.

Industrial Arts. Cuba is well known for its production of handcrafted wood and cane furniture as well as folk-music instruments.

Trade. Until the 1990s, government-owned food stores set uniform prices for rationed foods. Prices remained fixed from the early 1960s to 1981, when they were increased slightly. Government nonrationed food markets were expanded in 1983 and 1994 to provide greater supplies and varieties of foods and to end black marketeering. Consumer goods remained under government ownership and control until 1994, when the government legalized the taxable, direct sale, without price controls, of crafts and surplus industrial goods by licensed private vendors. Price increases on services and some products followed the 1994 decriminalization of the dollar. Taxes were introduced in select areas.

Division of Labor. The traditional division of labor by gender—*casa* (home) and *calle* (street)—ascribed to urban, upper-class Latin American societies began to change significantly during World War II, as more middle-class women entered professional fields. In the postrevolutionary period, transference between gender-traditional occupations has made limited strides. Although women have become more educated, have entered new job fields, and play a greater role in political organizations, they continue to be concentrated in the traditional fields of education and public health and remain underrepresented in politics. The labor force of 3 million presently includes 30 percent engaged exclusively in agriculture, 20 percent in industry, 20 percent in services, 11 percent in construction, 10 percent in commerce, and 5 percent in government.

Land Tenure. Since eliminating foreign ownership and large private estates, which were legacies of the colonial system, agrarian reform has gone through several stages. By the mid-1980s, 80 percent of land had come under state ownership, 11 percent was organized into cooperatives, and 9 percent was held by private owners. Food crises forced alteration of this system in 1994. State farms were replaced by Basic Units of Cooperative Production, which are allowed to sell in farmers' markets any food they produce in excess of government requirements. To diversify the economy further and earn foreign exchange, the government entered into investment contracts with foreign enterprises in the fields of construction technology, consumer goods, mining, biotechnology, oil, sugar, and tourism.

Kinship, Marriage, and Family

Kinship. Prerevolutionary kinship ties and social ties of the Cuban upper class were based in part on patrilineal descent from the Spanish colonial aristocracy. The ability to trace family backgrounds sharing common names and patron saints became somewhat less significant in the decades following establishment of the republic and declined even more significantly after the 1959 Revolution and the exodus of large numbers of the upper class. Lower-class Cubans demonstrated much less regard for lineage than had the middle class but continued the Latin tradition of godparenting and maintaining close relationships with and responsibility for the extended family.

Marriage. In the prerevolutionary period, within the framework of a Catholic-Latin society and rural/urban economic polarization, church-sanctioned marriage and baptisms assumed more importance in the cities than in the countryside. A relatively low marriage rate, cited as less than 5 per 1,000 in the late colonial period, reflected emphasis on common-law marriages in the countryside. Since the 1959 Revolution, rates of both marriage and divorce have tended to increase and become more similar for rural and urban areas. The marriage rate declined somewhat in the late 1970s, however, as the housing shortage limited the establishment of separate households. Postmarital residence tends to be patrilocal and has at times required doubling up of families. In 1979 extended families resided in 40 percent of Cuban households. Various types of birth control, including abortion, are available.

Domestic Unit. Efforts to strengthen family solidarity, stability, and female equality include the enactment of the 1975 Family Code, which identifies the nuclear family as the essential social unit responsible for improving the health and welfare of society. The code calls for equal sharing of responsibilities in household work, maintenance, and child rearing, as well as equal commitment to respect and loyalty in marriage. Legally mandated child-care centers and maternity leaves are among the projects and policies intended to reduce gender inequality and modify traditional gender-defined roles.

Inheritance. The Rent Reform and Agrarian Reform Laws of 1959 and subsequent legislation aimed at redistribution of wealth focused on limiting rent charges, foreign ownership of property, and private landownership, as well as nationalizing rural property, establishing cooperatives, and transferring land to sharecroppers and tenants. Legislation enacted with the objective of progressing toward abolition of private property has restricted the sale, mortgaging, and inheritance of land and has successfully increased state purchases of land. Other personal property assets may be inherited with some restrictions.

Socialization.   In addition to social conformity reinforced by traditional family relationships, Cubans find both overt and subtle pressures to conform to the values of revolutionary socialist ideology.

Sociopolitical Organization

Cuba is organized politically into fourteen provinces and 169 municipalities. Its socialist system is hierarchical and bureaucratic. The 525,000-member vanguard or cadre party, the Cuban Communist party (PCC) is led by Fidel Castro, the first party secretary, and his brother Raúl Castro, the second party secretary. The Political Bureau has responsibility for supervising economic, political, and military activities. In 1991 the 1,667 delegates to the Fourth Party Congress, acting on recommendations at local meetings attended by some 3.5 million people throughout the island, cut the staff of the 225-member Central Committee by one-half and reduced the number of departments by more than one-half. Alternates in the Political Bureau were abolished, and the Secretariat was terminated. The congress also called for increased review and recall of party officials and special sessions to deal with the economic crises at the provincial and municipal levels.

Secret-ballot elections to the municipal assemblies in 1992 and elections to the provincial and national assemblies in 1993 significantly reduced the number of incumbents who had been part of the decision-making bodies for decades. Membership in the Communist party was no longer a requirement in selecting delegates. By 1993, half of the members of the National Assembly were directly elected municipal-assembly delegates; more and younger delegates represented the trades, medicine, and culture.

Social Organization.   In contrast to the prerevolutionary years, Cuba is attempting to create a society in which neither class nor circumstances of occupation, income, race, or sex define social opportunities and rewards. The most significant challenges for the Revolution since the collapse of the Eastern bloc are providing equal access to political and economic opportunities without creating a privileged group in society or loss of conscious socialist goals, and simultaneously moving the economy toward diversification and industrialization.

Political Organization.   Prior to 1959, participation in the national and local political processes was limited. Between 1959 and 1970, the revolutionary government largely centralized authority and provided limited representative or direct access to decision making. Reorganization of the political system in 1970 was designed to allow greater input into policy formation at all levels. Legislative reforms in 1976 and again in 1992 and 1993 were illustrative of a trend toward increasing participation in economic decision making at all levels. To ensure wider input and greater understanding of the potential effects of change

prior to policy formation, it was required that meetings be held with mass organizations and constituencies.

Most citizens belong to at least one of the mass organizations (committees for the defense of the Revolution, the Confederation of Cuban Workers, the Federation of Cuban Women, the National Association of Small Farmers) or to specific professional or student associations. Several human-rights organizations, founded outside the established political process, are not recognized by the government. In 1994 the government announced the visit of the United Nations High Commissioner for Human Rights and the creation of an ad hoc committee within the National Assembly to review and report on political, social, economic, cultural, and individual rights.

Conflict.   From 1898 to 1959, Cuba experienced several political and economic crises that resulted in armed revolts against government officials and in military and political intervention by the United States. Between 1953 and 1959, armed struggle in the cities and countryside culminated in a successful revolution. Subsequently, more than 200,000 mainly upper- and middle-class Cubans left the island. A small percentage of the exiles in the United States has established organizations that have actively sought the overthrow and/or destabilization of the Cuban government and have resisted U.S. rapproachment with Cuba.

U.S. opposition to Cuban expropriation of U.S. businesses, implementation of a socialist agenda, and relations with the Soviet Union strained U.S.-Cuban relations early in the revolutionary struggle. Immediate consequences included U.S. training and equipping of Cuban exiles in the Playa Girón (Bay of Pigs) invasion of 1961, attempts to isolate Cuba economically and diplomatically in the Western Hemisphere, and a U.S. trade embargo. The 1962 Cuban missile crisis and Cuban support of revolutions and anticolonial movements in Latin America and Africa contributed to further tensions between the United States and Cuba.

Dependence on Soviet support and trade with Eastern Europe complicated Cuban–Eastern bloc relations in the late 1980s as those nations disavowed socialism. Cuba has made substantive efforts to rebuild diplomatic and trade relations with Latin America and increase trade with other nonsocialist nations. Despite three separate votes in the United Nations condemning the U.S. embargo of Cuba as a violation of international law, the United States has determinedly continued the embargo.

Within Cuba, the most significant political conflicts center around perceptions of counterrevolutionary activity. Although criticism is encouraged within the socialist-revolutionary framework, individuals and organizations attempting to operate actively outside this framework or perceived as opponents of the socialist system are subject to legal proceedings that typically result in incarceration. Internal conflict in the 1980s was exemplified by the exodus of more than 125,000 Cubans to the United States from Mariel, the growth of various human-rights organizations, and the trials of high-echelon political and military leaders on drug-trafficking and other counterrevolutionary charges. The collapse of the Soviet bloc contributed to shortages of consumer goods, food, and medicine, as well as to blackouts and transportation and production problems resulting from fuel shortages. Emphasis on tourism to earn necessary foreign exchange and the decriminalization of the dollar were increasingly criticized for creating a dual standard of living and social problems such as prostitution. The economic decline resulted in heretofore rare public demonstrations against the government.

U.S. determination to see the Cuban government overthrown was reflected in the tightening of the embargo in 1992. An immigration policy that denied Cubans legal visas while allowing them entry through illegal means created an immigration crisis in the summer of 1994. Ultimately, the United States reversed its policy of preferential treatment for Cubans and sent those attempting to enter the United States illegally to camps at Guantanamo Naval Base and elsewhere. It also entered into new discussions with the Cuban government on immigration but rescinded many travel opportunities and tightened controls on dollar transfers.

Religion and Expressive Culture

Religious Beliefs and Practices. Catholicism has been the principal religion of Cuba, although Methodist, Baptist, and Presbyterian schools, churches, and missions and a number of other religious groups also thrived in the pre-revolutionary period. Researchers contend that the Catholic church had less influence and significance in Cuban society than in many other Latin American countries, which in part accounts for reduced hostilities during the period of strong separation between religion and the revolutionary government (1959–1983). The emergence of liberation theology and Cuban government recognition of a role for religion in revolutionary society resulted in improved relations between the churches and the Cuban government in the latter part of the 1980s.

Afro-Cuban Santería, a syncretic religion that draws on both the Yoruba and Catholic cultural heritages, is deeply engrained in Cuban culture and has at least the tacit respect of practitioners of other religions.

Arts. Under the revolutionary government, Cuba has expanded the number of libraries from 100 to 2,000 and of museums from 6 to 250. Workshops and institutes in music, dance, theater, art, ceramics, lithography, photography, and film are available to amateurs and professionals in the 200 casas de cultura. A new film industry and film school have produced internationally acclaimed works, and several publishing houses, of which the Casa de las Américas is the best known, have produced and reproduced an unprecedented number of publications. Political poster art, street theater, and experimental workplace theaters have been distinctive contributions of the revolutionary period. The rich Afro-Hispanic culture, including the traditional guajiro (folk) songs and dances, have been emphasized with new vigor since 1959.

Medicine. Between 1959 and 1964, almost one-half of Cuba's 6,300 physicians left the island, and the United States imposed a trade embargo that cut off essential medicines. As part of its campaign to increase the availability of medical care, Cuba has since trained more than 16,000 doctors. Medical care is completely free and available to all; Cuba has also sent many physicians and other health-care workers to more than twenty-six countries to provide care, training, and biomedical research. Using the medical-team approach and emphasizing preventative health care, the government expanded the former mutualistas (health-maintenance organizations) to include urban and rural polyclinics, more rural hospitals, and extensive neighborhood health-education and disease-prevention programs. Modern techniques and equipment available from the socialist bloc improved health-care delivery dramatically.

The rapid decline in the importation of medicine, equipment, and pharmaceutical-industry supplies from the former socialist bloc, and the limited availability of hard currency for purchases created a medical crisis in 1993–1994. Shortages of food and chemicals for water treatment led to outbreaks of diseases, including an optic and paralytic epidemic that was stemmed only with the help of the international community. Emphasis on herbal and traditionalist methods of treatment has increased with the loss of manufactured medications.

Death and Afterlife. Funeral rituals and beliefs regarding death and afterlife continue to reflect the combined Santería and Roman Catholic heritage.

Bibliography

Bremer, Philip, William LeoGrande, Donna Rich, and Daniel Siegel, eds. (1989). *The Cuba Reader: The Making of a Revolutionary Society*. New York: Grove Press.

Halebsky, Sandor, and John Kirk, eds. (1985). *Cuba: Twenty-Five Years of Revolution, 1959–1984*. New York: Praeger Special Studies.

Perez, Louis A. (1988). *Cuba: Between Reform and Revolution*. New York: Oxford University Press.

Thomas, Hugh (1971). *Cuba: The Pursuit of Freedom*. New York: Harper & Row.

SUSAN J. FERNÁNDEZ

Cuicatec

ETHNONYMS: none

Orientation

Aside from a few brief and superficial treatments, published ethnographic material on the Cuicatec is based on field studies made prior to 1970. Unless otherwise indicated, the information presented here is based on ethnographic work that was done in the 1950s and 1960s, during which period the most thorough research was conducted.

Identification and Location. The region occupied by the Cuicatec is located in the ex-distrito of Cuicatlán in northeastern Oaxaca, Mexico. It is bounded by the canyon of the Río Santo Domingo to the north, the Chinatec lowlands to the east, the Almoloyas Mountains to the south, and the canyon of the Río Grande (the Cañada de Cuicatlán) to the west. From the Cañada, at an elevation of 500 meters above sea level, the land to the east ascends to the uninhabited Llano Español plateau, at 3,200 meters, and then descends to the Chinatec lowlands. Rainfall varies from 50 centimeters in the Cañada to 150 centimeters in the mountains, and reaches 300 centimeters at the Chinatec border. The Cuicatec region is approximately equidistant between the Tehuacán-Puebla Valley, 100 kilometers to the north, and the Valley of Oaxaca, 100 kilometers to the south.

Before the arrival of the Spanish, both the Cañada and the highlands were occupied by speakers of Cuicateco. Today, however, settlements in the more accessible and agriculturally productive Cañada are dominated by mestizos. Contemporary speakers of Cuicateco are confined largely to the more remote highlands. They retain many elements of Cuicatec culture, including language, cosmology, and decorative arts. They also retain a relative degree of political and economic equality and an economy that emphasizes production for subsistence. In contrast, mestizos are more fully integrated into the national economy, more highly motivated by profit, and more tolerant of inequality.

Much of the contact that occurs between the highland Indians and the Mexican nation state is through mestizo culture-brokers—for example, educators and political administrators—who represent the Indians to the larger society. These culture-brokers draw Indians into the Mexican political economy while, paradoxically, contributing to the maintenance of traditional Indian cultural forms. The boundary between the mestizo and Indian segments, however, is permeable. Mestizos move to the Cuicatec highlands to establish plantations or to assume administrative positions. Indians migrate to the Cañada, the mestizo-dominated area, to engage in wage labor. This movement may or may not be accompanied by the adoption of some or all of the cultural markers of the mestizo segment.

Demography.   According to census figures, the number of speakers of Cuicateco has increased over the past sixty years (9,218 in 1930; 8,771 in 1950; 10,192 in 1970; 13,338 in 1980; and 11,846 in 1990).

Linguistic Affiliation.   Cuicateco and the languages spoken in the regions bordering that of the Cuicatec (Mazateco, Chinateco, Zapoteco, Mixteco, and Ixcateco) belong to the Otomanguean Language Family. It is proposed through glottochronology that diversification of Otomanguean began around 3,500 B.C. and that speakers of proto-Otomanguean occupied the Valley of Tehuacán, Puebla. Cuicateco diverged from its closest relative, Mixteco, around 500 B.C. Dialectal divergence of Cuicateco dates to the sixteenth century.

History and Cultural Relations

From 20,000 to 5,500 B.C., the area from the Valley of Tehuacán to the Valley of Oaxaca was occupied by hunter-gatherers, after which time reliance on agriculture increased gradually. The earliest remains of permanent

villages in the Cuicatec region, near large alluvial fans in the Cañada, date to the Middle Formative period (500 B.C.). Because the type of agriculture that is dependent on rainfall alone is scant in the Cañada, permanent settlement is presumed to have been accompanied by the development of simple methods of irrigation.

The Cañada has long been a corridor between the Valley of Oaxaca to the south and Tehuacán and the Basin of Mexico to the north. The Cañada has been conquered from both directions, by invading Zapotec from the south in the Formative period and by the Aztec coming from the north in the late Postclassic period. Glyphic and archaeological evidence reveals subjugation of the Cañada by Zapotec invaders from the Valley of Oaxaca from A.D. 1 to A.D. 200. Early colonial accounts attest to recurrent antagonistic relations between Cañada settlements and Zapotec, Mixtec, and southern Chinatec groups.

Conflicts with these groups were suppressed by the rise of the Aztec, to whom the Cuicatec paid tribute from as early as 1486. The Aztec did not directly occupy Cuicatec territories, but they exacted tribute indirectly, thus preserving the existing political structure. At the time of Spanish contact, the Cuicatec were organized into discrete political units, designated *señoríos* by the Spanish and numbering three to five thousand in population. These small, moderately stratified units, consisting of headtowns and subject settlements, were bounded geographically by noncultivable land.

The earliest records of the exaction of tribute by the Spanish date to 1530. Like the Aztec, the Spanish imposed a system of indirect rule, incorporating the existing elite into the Spanish bureaucracy. Missionization began in 1528, with the establishment of a Dominican convent in Teutila. A parish church was built in Concepción Pápalo in 1630. By the mid-seventeenth century, the power of the Cuicatec elite had been diminished by the installation of Spanish civil servants.

Settlements

Settlements in the Cuicatec area are organized into *municipios,* the smallest division of state executive authority. Each municipio has a capital or headtown, and most contain one or more additional settlements, called "dependencies." Typically, each settlement has a native Cuicatec name, a Nahuatl name given by the Aztec conquerors, and a saint's name given by the Spanish. Settlement locations are marked by historical continuity. Most of today's municipio capitals were pre-Hispanic señorío capitals, and most of today's dependencies were señorío dependencies.

Economy

Subsistence and Commercial Activities.   In the highlands, seasonal-rainfall agriculture is supplemented with irrigation. Most land, of poor quality relative to the Cañada, is cultivated for subsistence crops. A few crops are grown for export, however, including peaches, walnuts, and coffee, all of which were introduced by the Spanish. Above 2,000 meters, agave plantations are cultivated, and mixed forests are exploited for lumber.

The zone between the Cañada and the highlands is unsuitable for either rainfall agriculture or irrigation. This uninhabited area is sometimes used by the poor for hunting and gathering small game and edible varieties of wild plants and for grazing domesticated goats.

Industrial Arts. According to a 1982 report (*Los cuicatecos*) by the Instituto Nacional Indigenista, wool and cotton textiles continue to be manufactured in Santa María Pápalo, Tlalixtac, Santa Cruz Teutila, and San Andrés Teotilapan. Pottery is important in Santos Reyes Pápalo and San Andrés Pápalo. Baskets of reed grass are made in Concepción and San Lorenzo, and items of woven palm are fashioned in Santa María Tecaxtitlán and San Pedro Nodón. Most of these activities, however, are declining in importance.

Trade and Division of Labor. There are three semipermanent markets in the district of Cuicatlán. Commodities may also be acquired from small local stores, through private exchange, and at the temporary markets that are associated with holy days. Each Cuicatec settlement is characterized by a unique roster of saints, whose corresponding holy days rarely coincide. Traders come from other Cuicatec and non-Cuicatec Indian villages and from mestizo towns within and outside the district. In general, Indians from the highlands provide agricultural goods and handmade crafts, whereas mestizo traders sell agricultural products that are not grown locally, processed foods, and manufactured goods, such as huaraches, shoes, clothing, cigars, and liquor.

Regional trade is dominated by the members of a few elite mestizo families in the Cañada, who export to distant markets the fruit and other products that are grown in the Cañada, as well as the coffee, walnuts, and peaches grown in the highlands. They import such products as hardware, canned goods, clothing, beer, and soft drinks.

Historically, there has been, and there continues to be, economic symbiosis between the highlands and the lowlands. Because irrigation allows greater security than rainfall agriculture, the highlands have depended on the Cañada for staples during times of shortage. In turn, highland communities export wood, charcoal, and other crops to the Cañada and serve as a source of labor for its export agriculture.

Land Tenure. Three major forms of landownership exist in the highlands: communal property, privately owned land, and *ejido* lands. Communal property is land "owned" by the settlement and cultivated by peasant households. Mestizos own coffee plantations and cattle ranches, but Indians also own private land. Ejido lands are communal holdings that are officially not for rent or for sale. Unofficially, however, land in all three categories is sold, rented, leased, and inherited. In addition, fruit trees may be sold, rented, leased, or inherited independently of the land, a continuation of pre-Hispanic practice.

Cultivable land in the highlands is in short supply. Population pressure is the basis of intrasettlement conflict that occasionally leads to the fissioning of settlements and migration to the Cañada and elsewhere for wage labor.

Kinship

Kin Groups and Descent. Most highland settlements are organized into localized or semilocalized extended families (kindreds), with the exception of San Andrés, which is organized into ambilateral descent groups. The mestizo elite form large corporate families that cut across municipal and settlement boundaries.

Marriage and Family

Marriage. Among the nonelite, spouses are expected to be from the same settlement and to be of equal wealth and in the same age range. One should not marry bilateral kin up to the second degree of collaterality; spouses beyond the fourth degree of collaterality are preferred. Where there are Spanish surnames, one should not marry someone with the same surname or the surname of one's mother's father. Indian customary law recognizes common-law marriages and, in rare cases, polygyny. Among the mestizo elite, marriage is preferentially class endogamous.

Domestic Unit. Data gathered in San Andrés indicate a strong tendency for households to be nuclear. Households are organized into clusters, usually linked by siblings of the same sex, preferably females.

Inheritance. In groups with kindred, property tends to be controlled by men. A woman is incorporated into her husband's household at marriage, and she loses her attachment to her natal group and her claim on its property.

Socialization. Cuicatec children are subjected to the conflicting goals of the local community and the Mexican nation-state. At home, they are given lots of time for play, and antisocial behavior is tolerated through adolescence. The assumption of household tasks is gradual and informal, suited to the individual development of the child. By contrast, classroom learning is rigid and highly formalized. Children are taught Spanish, Mexican national history, and modern methods of farming, often by a mestizo or an upwardly mobile Indian who is intolerant of local Indian culture. Such a teacher, who represents Mexican national culture, is not someone with whom most Indian children can identify.

As children become an economic asset to the household, their primary responsibilities are to fulfill the demands of the agricultural cycle. And because classroom learning is irrelevant to these demands, children are not pressured by their parents to attend school. This lack of interest in formal education reinforces the teacher's negative appraisal of Indian culture. Thus, far from promoting integration, the Mexican school system ultimately reinforces the boundaries between Indians and mestizos.

Sociopolitical Organization

Each highland municipio is internally organized into a civil-religious hierarchy, with four to eight levels of offices, ranked in prestige. Officeholders rotate annually. The secular side of the hierarchy is recognized by the Mexican government as the official administration of the municipio.

In the more traditional municipios, participation requires a significant expenditure of resources. Because each adult man of sufficient means is expected to assume a post, the system serves to reduce differences in wealth. In the more acculturated municipios, however, the burden is shared by all taxpayers, lessening the system's redistributive effect.

Social Control and Conflict. If possible, disputes are handled outside the official court system by family elders and shamans. More serious cases are taken to the municipal court or to the district court in Cuicatlán, which handles cases from nineteen municipios. If residents remain dissatisfied, they may take their claims to a neighboring district.

Officially, three offices of the civil hierarchy (*presidente*, *síndico*, and *regidor*) control the municipal court. This court is used in cases of elopement, to ensure that a formal marriage will take place and that the bride will be supported. Spousal conflict, which may lead to the granting of a divorce, and cases involving witchcraft are also handled by the municipal court.

The Cuicatec are discouraged from using the district court by its limited hours of operation (it is open only during the day, when they are working in their fields), its unwillingness to accept nonmonetary payment of fines, and its failure to recognize Indian customary law (for example, common-law marriage and the transgression of local endogamy laws). Witchcraft accusations, when taken to the district level, are either treated as "libel" or dismissed as frivolous. At best, cases against incompetent shamans (who have, for example, failed to bring rain) are treated as "fraud."

Although municipal judicial officials are supposed to adhere to national and state law, in reality they recognize local customary law. This disjunction between the local and district courts serves to conserve Cuicatec culture, since traditional law remains immune to external challenges.

Religion and Expressive Culture

Religious Beliefs. The Cuicatec participate in a ritual and belief system that is not wholly reducible either to Catholicism or to indigenous Cuicatec cosmology. The only Cuicatec deity that is not worshiped in the Catholic church is the spirit of the mountains, Cheve, which is identified with the devil. Other deities that were originally related to the Cuicatec agricultural cycle are now linked to the Christian liturgical calendar and its associated personages.

The agricultural cycle begins after Easter, as the lengthening of daylight anticipates the first rains. The image of Jesus Christ is identified with the emerging sun and rain, and his resurrection with the rebirth of maize as a new plant. During the summer phase, the sun and maize are seen as prime adults. The principal holy days are devoted to Saint Anthony and Saint John the Baptist, both of whom are identified with water. The fall/harvest phase is associated with the death of the sun and the maize. The dominant image is of the Virgin Mary, identified with the moon, who is mourning the death of her son. The winter phase, celebrating the Immaculate Conception and the Nativity, is also dominated by the Virgin.

Religious Practitioners. The public rituals that are associated with holy days are controlled by members of the civil-religious hierarchy. Shamans, trained ritual specialists, tend to control private rituals, including those related to individual health and the annual renewing of the household tools of production. Families that cannot afford shamans may carry out their own rituals. When a Catholic priest visits the settlement, he performs Masses, baptisms, and weddings.

Ceremonies. There are a series of rituals, both private (household) and public (settlement), that are associated with the agricultural cycle. The former are more variable in content. Spring rituals, devoted to Jesus Christ and to the supernatural controllers of the weather, petition for the arrival of the first rains. Summer rituals, devoted to Saint John the Baptist and Saint Anthony, offer thanks for the first rains and petition for the second rains. Rituals of the fall demonstrate gratitude to all supernatural beings for the summer rains and request permission to harvest. In communities with irrigation, a winter crop, believed to be under control of the now-dominant moon, is planted. Rituals are devoted to petitioning the Virgin, who is identified with the moon and with surface waters (water holes, springs, and irrigation canals), to protect the second crop.

Ideally, rites of passage are timed to coincide with the life-cycle phases that are associated with the agricultural calendar. Thus, baptisms and the installation of new members of the civil-religious hierarchy (who are viewed as newborns and are identified with the infant Jesus, the reemerging sun, and maize) occur in the winter, confirmations and first communions in the spring, marriages in the summer, and funerals and ancestral rites in the fall.

Medicine. Traditional explanations for illness include soul loss—resulting from fright and from falling—and witchcraft. A shaman is usually contracted for diagnosis and treatment, which may involve offerings to the mountain spirit, Cheve. In addition, practitioners of Western medicine are sometimes consulted.

Death and Afterlife. After death, one's soul goes west, like the setting sun. On the Day of All Souls and the Day of All the Dead, the principal harvest rituals, the village ancestors return to receive offerings of thanks.

Bibliography

Adán, Elfego (1922). "Los Cuicatecos Actuales." *Anales del Museo Nacional*, 4a época, 1:137–154.

Anderson, E. Richard (1958). "Dr. Swadesh's LISTA DIAGNOSTICA in the San Andrés Teotilalpan Dialect of Cuicateco." Manuscript.

Anderson, E. Richard (1962). "Teutila Cuicatec Kinship." Manuscript.

Anderson, E. Richard, and Hilario Concepción Roque (1983). *Diccionario Cuicateco: Español-Cuicateco, Cuicateco-Español*. Serie de Vocabularios y Diccionarios Indígenas "Mariano Silva y Aceves," no. 26. Mexico City: Instituto Lingüístico de Verano.

Basauri, Carlos (1928). *La situación actual de la población indígena de México*. Publicaciones de la Secretaría de Educación Pública, vol. 16, no. 8. Mexico City: SEP.

Basauri, Carlos (1940). "Familia 'Mixteco-Zapotecana': Cuicatecos." *Población Indígena* 2:527–542.

Beals, Ralph L. (1969). "Southern Mexican Highlands and Adjacent Coastal Regions." In *Handbook of Middle American Indians*, edited by Robert Wauchope. Vol. 7, *Ethnology, Part One*, edited by Evon Z. Vogt, 315-328. Austin: University of Texas Press.

Belmar, Francisco (1902). *El Cuicateco*. Idiomas del Estado de Oaxaca. Oaxaca: Imprenta del Comercio.

Cerda Silva, Roberto de la (1942). "Los cuicatecos." *Revista Mexicana de Sociología* 4:99-127.

Los cuicatecos (1982). Monografías de Grupos Étnicos. Mexico City: Instituto Nacional Indigenista.

Davis, Marjorie (1952). "Translating Nouns into the Cuicateco Language." *Bible Translator* 3:34-38.

Davis, Marjorie (1954). "Translating from FL Cuicateco to TL English." *International Journal of American Linguistics* 20:302-312.

Davis, Marjorie (1962). "Cuicatec Tales about Witchcraft." *Tlalocan* 4:197-202.

Davis, Marjorie, and Margaret Walker (1955). "Cuicateco: Morphemics and Morphophonemics." *International Journal of American Linguistics* 21:46-51.

Fryxell, Paul A. (1993). *Flora del Valle de Tehuacán— Cuicatlán*. Mexico City: Universidad Nacional Autónoma de México, Instituto de Biología.

Gallego, Juan ([1580] 1905). "Relación de Cuicatlán." In *Papeles de Nueva España: Segunda Serie, Geografía y Estadística*. Vol. 4, edited by Francisco del Paso y Troncoso, 183-189. Madrid: Sucesores de Rivadeneyra.

Hernández Díaz, Gilberto (1982). *Nuevos estudios sobre la Cañada: Etnografía moderna de dos pueblos cuicatecos*. [Oaxaca]: Centro Regional de Oaxaca, Instituto Nacional de Antropología e Historia.

Holland, William R. (1959). "Dialect Variations of the Mixtec and Cuicatec Areas of Oaxaca, Mexico." *Anthropological Linguistics* 1(8): 25-31.

Holland, William R., and Robert J. Weitlaner (1960). "Modern Cuicatec Use of Sacrificial Knives." *American Antiquity* 25(3): 392-396.

Hopkins, Joseph W., III (1977). "Irrigation and the Cuicatecs: Environmental Manipulation and Ecosystems. *Western Canadian Journal of Anthropology* 7:129-150.

Hopkins, Joseph W., III (1983). The Tomellín Cañada and the Postclassic Cuicatec. In *The Cloud People: Divergent Evolution of the Zapotec and Mixtec Civilizations*, edited by Kent V. Flannery and Joyce Marcus, 266-270. New York: Academic Press.

Hopkins, Joseph W., III (1984). *Irrigation and the Cuicatec Ecosystem: A Study of Agriculture and Civilization in North Central Oaxaca*. University of Michigan Museum of Anthropology, Studies in Latin American Ethnohistory and Archaeology, vol. 2. Ann Arbor.

Hunt, Eva (1969). "The Meaning of Kinship in San Juan: Genealogical and Social Models." *Ethnology* 8:35-53.

Hunt, Eva (1972). "Irrigation and the Socio-Political Organization of Cuicatec Cacicazgos." In *Chronology and Irrigation*, edited by Frederick Johnson. Tehuacan Archaeological-Botanical Project. *The Prehistory of the Tehuacan Valley*, vol. 4. Austin: University of Texas Press, for the Robert S. Peabody Foundation, Phillips Academy, Andover, Mass.

Hunt, Eva (1976). "Kinship and Territorial Fission in the Cuicatec Highlands." In *Essays on Mexican Kinship*, edited by Hugo G. Nutini, Pedro Carrasco, and James M. Taggart, 97-136. Pitt Latin American Series. Pittsburgh: University of Pittsburgh Press.

Hunt, Eva, and Robert C. Hunt (1969). "The Role of Local Courts in Rural Mexico." In *Peasants in the Modern World*, edited by Philip K. Bock, 109-139. Albuquerque: University of New Mexico Press.

Hunt, Eva, and Robert C. Hunt (1974). "Irrigation, Conflict, and Politics: A Mexican Case." In *Irrigation's Impact on Society*, edited by Theodore Downing and McGuire Gibson. Tucson: University of Arizona Press.

Hunt, Robert C. (1965). "The Developmental Cycle of the Family Business in Rural Mexico." In *Essays in Economic Anthropology*, edited by June Helm, 54-79. Proceedings of the Annual Meeting of the American Ethnological Society. Seattle: University of Washington Press.

Hunt, Robert C. (1968). "Agentes culturales mestizos: Estabilidad y cambio en Oaxaca." *América Indígena* 28:595-609.

Hunt, Robert C. (1971). "Components of Relationships in the Family: A Mexican Village." In *Kinship and Culture*, edited by F.L.K. Hsu, 106-143. Chicago: Aldine Publishing Co.

Hunt, Robert C. (in press) "Irrigation in Cuicatlan: The Question of the Rio Grande." In *Festschrift for Ronald Spores*, edited by Marcus Zeitlin and J. Zeitlin. Publications of the Museum of Anthropology, University of Michigan. Ann Arbor.

Hunt, Robert C., Eva Hunt, and Roberto J. Weitlaner (1966). "From Parallel-Nominal to Patrinominal: Changing Cuicatec Personal Names." *Anales del Instituto Nacional de Antropología e Historia* 19:191-223.

Jaso Vega, Margarita [after 1983]. "Mazatecos, Cuicatecos, Chinatecos." Tesis de la Cátedra de Etnografía de la Universidad Nacional; copia mecanoescrita en la biblioteca del Museo Nacional, México.

Josserand, J. Kathryn, Marcus Winter, and Nicholas Hopkins (1984). *Essays in Otomanguean Culture History.* Vanderbilt University Publications in Anthropology, no. 31. Nashville.

López Hernández, Eusebio Ramón (1987). *Narraciones fantásticas de la Chinantla.* Colección Siete Venado. Oaxaca: Gobierno del Estado de Oaxaca, Casa de la Cultura Oaxaquena, Dirección General de Culturas Populares, Unidad Regional Oaxaca.

Needham, Doris, and Marjorie Davis (1946). "Cuicatec Phonology." *International Journal of American Linguistics* 12:139–146.

Redmond, Elsa (1983). *A fuego y sangre: Early Zapotec Imperialism in the Cuicatlán Cañada Oaxaca.* Memoirs of the Museum of Anthropology, University of Michigan, no. 16. Ann Arbor.

Redmond, Elsa, and Charles Spencer (1983). "The Cuicatlán Cañada and the Period II Frontier Zapotec State." In *The Cloud People: Divergent Evolution of the Zapotec and Mixtec Civilizations,* edited by Kent V. Flannery and Joyce Marcus, 117–120. New York: Academic Press.

Relatos, mitos, y leyendas de la Chinantla (1981). 2nd ed. Colección INI; Serie de Antropología Social, no. 53. Mexico City: Instituto Nacional Indigenista.

Sanchez, Policarpo T. (1911). *El municipio de Cuicatlán: Apuntes ligeros.* Escuela rural (Oaxaca de Juárez, México), vol. 2, no. 7 (1 de Mayo de 1911).

Spencer, Charles S. (1982). *The Cuicatlán Cañada and Monte Alban: A Study of Primary State Formation.* New York: Academic Press.

Spencer, Charles S., and Elsa Redmond (1979). Formative and Classic Developments in the Cuicatlán Cañada: A Preliminary Report. In *Prehistoric Social, Political, and Economic Development in the Area of the Tehuacán Valley,* edited by Robert D. Drennan, 201–212. Technical Report no. 11, University of Michigan Museum of Anthropology. Ann Arbor.

Summer Institute of Linguistics (1958). *Alfabeto en el idioma Cuicateco de Tepeuxila.* SOLINET/ASERL Cooperative Microfilming Project (NEH PS-20317); SOL MN02083.01 LRU.

Summer Institute of Linguistics (1961). *'Iti s'een chi vee 'in'yeendi 'cuu. Idioma cuicateco de Tepeuxila, Oax.* Publicado por el Instituto Lingüístico de Verano en cooperación con la Dirección General de Asuntos Indígenas de la Secretaria de Educación Pública. Mexico City.

Weitlaner, Robert J. (1969). "The Cuicatec." In *Handbook of Middle American Indians,* edited by Robert Wauchope,

Vol. 7, *Ethnology, Part One*, edited by Evon Z. Vogt, 434–437. Austin: University of Texas Press.

AMY TODD AND ROBERT C. HUNT

Curaçao

ETHNONYMS: Curaçaoënaar (Dutch: an islander by birth), Korsou (Papiamento), Kurasoleño (Papiamento), Yu di Korsou (Papiamento: child of Curaçao).

Orientation

Identification. Curaçao is the largest of the six islands comprising the Netherlands Antilles (Curaçao, Bonaire, Saint Martin, Saba, Saint Eustatius) and Aruba. Several theories exist as to the origin of the name "Curaçao," none of which can be proven conclusively. It may have been derived from the Indian Caiquetío language, or it may have evolved from the Spanish *corazón* or the Portuguese *curazon* (heart). After 1525, Spanish maps refer to the island as "Curaçote," "Curasaote," and "Curasaore." By the seventeenth century the island was generally known as "Curaçao" or "Curazao."

Location. The island of Curaçao has a land area of 448 square kilometers. It is located in the Caribbean Sea within view of the Venezuelan coast, between the islands of Aruba and Bonaire. Its landscape is arid and mostly flat, except in the northwest, where hills rise to 375 meters. Deep bays are found along the southern coast, the largest of which, Schottegat, provides the capital, Willemstad, with one of the most important harbors in the Caribbean. The flora is very similar to the flora of the neighboring islands. Its best-known specimens are the divi-divi tree, the *campech* or brazilwood tree, the aloe, and a variety of cactuses. Coconut palms and tamarind, *guyaba* (guava), mango, and papaya trees are found in cultivated areas.

Besides the *biná*, a small deer, there are no large native animals. Goats, horses, and cattle were imported by the Spanish conquerors. There are no poisonous snakes but many varieties of lizards, of which the largest is the iguana. Among the best known of the more than one hundred types of birds are the *palabrua* (barn owl), the *trupial* (a songbird; both the orange *Icterus icterus* and the yellow *I. migrogularis* are present), and the *tortolica* (a small pigeon); pelicans roam the coast in great numbers.

Demography. The population in 1990 was about 148,000. Migration is the primary factor that determines population development in the Netherlands Antilles. In 1947, 20 percent of the population consisted of foreigners, in particular Europeans and Surinamese. During the 1950s, the number of emigrants surpassed the number of immigrants, yet the population continued to grow because of an excess of births over deaths. Since then, however, the population of Curaçao has barely increased. Beginning in 1965, the birthrate steadily decreased from 35 to 20 children born per 1,000 inhabitants, virtually reaching the same level as in industrialized countries. After 1965, the number of Antillean emigrants to the Netherlands gradually increased. In 1981 only 10 percent of the population was foreign born. Life expectancy is 72 years for males and 76 years for females. The death rate, in 1987, was about 5 deaths per 1,000 inhabitants, but the rate is increasing again as the population ages, a development partly owing to the emigration of a large percentage of the younger population.

Linguistic Affiliation. The official language of Curaçao, as throughout the Netherlands Antilles, is Dutch, but the mother tongue of most of the islanders is Papiamento, an Iberian-based creole. Papiamento is also the colloquial language of Aruba and Bonaire. English is the spoken language on Saint Martin, Saba, and Saint Eustatius. Papiamento is a relatively new language that formerly existed only in spoken form. Originally a slave lingo, Papiamento was eventually adopted by the Dutch rulers.

History and Cultural Relations

When the Spanish conqueror Alonso de Ojeda discovered Curaçao in 1499, he found it to be inhabited by the Caiquetío, a coastal tribe of Arawak Indians occupying the nearby mainland. The insular Caiquetío were primarily fishers, but they also did some cultivating, and they collected salt from the Charoma salt pan for barter trade with the coast dwellers. In 1513 many Indians were evacuated by the Spaniards and were forced to work in the copper mines of Hispaniola. During the Spanish period, cattle raising was the principal means of subsistence, along with trading Indian slaves.

In 1634 the Dutch conquered Curaçao after defeating the Spaniards. The Dutch West India Company (WIC) mounted an expedition under Johan van Walbeeck, establishing a maritime base in the heart of the Spanish colonies. With the occupation of the Dutch, most of the remaining Indians scattered to the mainland. Those who stayed were gradually absorbed into the new population of Dutch traders, Spanish and Portuguese refugees, Sephardic Jews, and African slaves.

After 1648, Curaçao became an important base for smuggling, privateering, and the slave trade. The Dutch, venturing with their ships to the coast of Spanish America with slaves, cloth, and spices, soon established regular contact between Curaçao and the South American mainland. From 1662 until the end of the century, most of the African slaves entering the Spanish colonies were shipped by the WIC via Curaçao.

Alongside the slave trade there bloomed a contraband trade among the Spanish colonists in every sort of desired merchandise. Dutch Sephardic Jews played a central role in this lucrative traffic, holding probably more than a 20-percent share of the Dutch trade with Spain. By 1702 the Dutch Sephardic community accounted for 34.5 percent of Curaçao's wealth. Most of these Jews were agents, factors, and brokers.

When the slave trade had begun to prosper, the WIC established several small plantations to produce food for the many slaves in the island's warehouse awaiting shipment to the Spanish colonies. Curaçao, however, remained mainly a trade island. It was never a real plantation colony in the typical Caribbean sense. Climatological factors and soil conditions did not permit the development of large-scale agriculture. Consequently, the Euro-Antillean upper class, composed of merchants and high-ranking Dutch authorities, did not merge into a class of plantation owners (as in Suriname, for example).

The absence of a genuine plantation economy might account for the fact that relations between the White European rulers and the Black African slaves on Curaçao were less strained than elsewhere in the Caribbean. Although social distance was maintained, contact was usually on a much more personal basis than on the plantation. Nevertheless, the division between the Afro-Antilleans and the Euro-Antilleans is still of significance today.

The Black people belonged to the weakest economic sector of the population both before and after the abolition of slavery in 1863. The same can be said of the Mulattoes. Although sexual relations between White, Mulatto, and Black people were not uncommon, marriage was commonly reserved for members of the same group. There did exist, however, a notable cultural exchange between Europeans and Africans.

In 1918, when the Shell company established a large oil refinery on the island, dramatic changes occurred. The immigration of thousands of laborers and an increasing number of births caused rapid population growth. Moreover, the great variety of national and ethnic groups resulted in a complex system of social stratification.

Settlements

Willemstad is the capital of the Netherlands Antilles as well as of Curaçao. The center of Willemstad is divided by the Sint Annebaai. This bay connects the Caribbean Sea with the natural harbor, Schottegat. After the establishment of the oil refinery, the city grew rapidly. New residential areas were built at Schottegat to accommodate a growing labor force. The countryside is sparsely inhabited.

Economy

Subsistence and Commercial Activities. Curaçao's economy centers on the oil refinery, shipbuilding and repair, construction, small local industries, tourism, financial services, and the transit trade. Agricultural production is decidedly modest, and almost all consumer goods have to be imported. There is an extensive informal economic sector in which people who have no access to formal jobs earn a living by selling foodstuffs and illegal lottery tickets. The island has a very open and dependent economy based heavily on imports. As a result, exports and Dutch development aid are essential to pay for the inflow of goods and for public expenditures.

Industrial Arts. With the exception of straw hats, which were manufactured in the first half of the twentieth century, industrial arts were not of great significance on Curaçao.

Division of Labor.   In the eighteenth and nineteenth centuries, Afro-Antillean women were engaged in various spheres of paid domestic work, petty production, and home industry for the local market. Before industrialization came to Curaçao, women performed many of the agricultural tasks, engaged in crafts such as weaving straw hats for export, and sold agricultural products, fish, homemade foodstuffs, and handicrafts. Industrialization brought the end of agriculture and craft. More and more articles that were formerly homemade were replaced by machine-made substitutes. Even the traditional female domain of small trade was taken over by males of foreign minority groups that had settled on the island, and the oil refinery, with its highly mechanized production techniques, provided no alternative employment for Afro-Antillean women.

Marriage and Family

Until the 1920s, the island economy was based on large-scale international trade and shipping, operated by a small group of Euro-Antillean elite families. Within this group there was a highly patriarchal family system. Women were completely subordinate to their husbands and fathers; their primary biological and social role was that of wife and mother of legitimate heirs. In the Afro-Antillean population, however, many households had a female head, who was often the chief provider for herself and her children. Men, in various roles (father, husband, son, brother, lover) might make material contributions to one or more households. The sexual alliances between men and women were often not enduring, and marriage was the exception rather than the rule. The prestige and authority of women in the kinship network is still celebrated in a great variety of songs, proverbs, sayings, and expressions in Papiamento. Women held the family together both during slavery and afterwards. The emotional bond between mother and child was intense and permanent. In order to promote legal marriage, the Catholic church introduced and maintained a number of punitive measures against the offspring of those "living in sin."

Marriage and the nuclear family have since become the most common relationships in the lower Afro-Antillean strata. Economic and social progress enables men to fulfill their roles as husbands and fathers, thus undermining such traditional institutions as matrifocal household groups, visiting relationships (_bibá_), and extramarital liaisons. Marriage in Antillean society, however, still differs from that institution as known in the Western world. Family ties, including mutual responsibility, are much stronger in the Caribbean, whereas monogamy is not as institutionalized as in Europe and Latin America.

Socialization.   During adolescence, Afro-Antillean males are generally very mobile. Peer groups provide a meaningful social context by which males achieve an identity as a person. Peer groups are not centered on the household; for many males the house is little more than a dormitory. For females, more then for males, kinship networks and the household are the principal social environments.

Sociopolitical Organization

Social Organization.   It is often said that, in the Caribbean, there is a weak sense of community cohesion and that local communities are loosely organized. Indeed, the same can be asserted of Curaçao. Nowadays, although Curaçao is a highly urbanized and individualized society, informal networks play an important role in the daily lives of men and women.

Political Organization.   Constitutional structure is complex. There are three levels of government, namely, the Kingdom (the Netherlands, the Netherlands Antilles, and Aruba), the Land (the Netherlands Antilles-of-five), and that of each island. The Kingdom administers foreign affairs and defense; the government is appointed by, and represents, the Dutch Crown. Aruba now has its own governor. The governments of the Antilles and Aruba appoint ministers who represent them in The Hague. These ministers enjoy a special and powerful position and, when called upon, partake in discussions in the Kingdom cabinet.

Theoretically, the Land governs judicial, postal, and monetary matters, whereas the islands take care of education and economic development; however, the tasks of the Land and the islands are not specifically outlined, and duplication often occurs. The population is represented in the Staten (parliament of the Land) and the _eilandsraden_ (insular councils). Both legislative bodies are elected by universal vote for a four-year term.

Political parties are organized island by island; Antilleans have a wide range from which to choose. This diversity prevents any one party from gaining an absolute majority. Consequently, coalitions are necessary in order to form a government. These coalitions are often forged on a shaky basis: machine politics and the so-called patronage system lead to instability. Therefore, a coalition seldom manages to serve a full four-year term, a condition that is not conducive to efficient government.

Conflict.   Serious riots took place on Curaçao on 30 May 1969. According to an investigatory commission, the direct cause of the riots was a labor dispute between the company Wescar (Caribbean Rail) and the Curaçao Workers' Federation (CFW). The commission determined that the riots were not part of a larger plan to overthrow the government of the Antilles, nor was the conflict primarily along racial lines. Antilleans raised strong opposition to the fact that Dutch marines were brought in to restore law and order.

Religion and Expressive Culture

Religious Beliefs.   Even though the Dutch colonizers were Protestant, Catholicism was—and remains—the prevalent religion. Catholic missionary activities, mainly by Spanish priests from Venezuela, were directed toward Afro-Antilleans, and the Franciscans even preached in Papiamento to establish closer ties with potential converts. After Abolition, Catholic friars, nuns, and priests from the Netherlands came as missionaries to Curaçao and the other Dutch islands. The predominance of Catholicism has led to the foundation of a far greater number of Catholic schools than of state schools. Since around 1970, nonmainstream Christian sects have become increasingly widespread. Most of these movements are based in the United States.

Religious Practitioners. Brua is an agglomeration of non-Christian spiritual practices, similar to the obeah of the West Indies. These practices include preparing and using lucky charms, eliminating purported and declared enemies, ensnaring spouses, divining, making amulets, spirit possession, and consultation with the dead. By manipulating supernatural powers, a practitioner attempts to restore the health of his patients and heal disturbed social relationships (which are often considered the cause of certain illnesses). Today most Brua specialists combine their practice with other jobs, such as selling groceries or other small-scale ventures.

Arts. Both music and dance are important facets of Antillean culture. The *tambu* and *tumba* are probably the most popular dances. "Tambu" is the local name for an African drum, the main instrument in the tambu dance music. In contrast to the tambu, the tumba is a more intimate dance. "Tumba" is also the name of an African drum, yet in this music it is not the main instrument.

In contrast to music and dance, interest in literature is largely confined to the educated class. Although the literature of the Netherlands Antilles is multilingual (English, Spanish, Papiamento, and Dutch), most authors from Curaçao have preferred to write in Papiamento or Dutch. Colá Debrot, one of the well-known writers of the Netherlands Antilles, once suggested a distinction between "popular literature" and "art literature." The former—in Papiamento—is realistic, and contains strong Afro-Caribbean elements. The so-called art literature is mainly written in Dutch.

Bibliography

Abraham-Van der Mark, E. E. (1984). "The Impact of Industrialization on Women: A Caribbean Case." In *Women, Men, and the International Division of Labor,* edited by J. Nash and M. P. Fernándes-Kelly, 374–386. Albany: State University of New York Press.

Ansano, Richenel (1990). "Balia ku Almsola or Dance with the Lone Soul." In *Op de bres voor eigenheid: Afhankelijkheid en dominantie in de Antillen* (In place of identity: Dependency and domination in the Antilles), edited by Rose Mary Allen, Paul van Gelder, Mike Jacobs, and Ieteke Witteveen, 165–189. Amsterdam: Caraïbische Werkgroep AWIC, Universiteit van Amsterdam.

Goslinga, Cornelis Ch. (1979). *A Short History of the Netherlands Antilles and Suriname.* The Hague: Martinus Nijhof.

Huisman, Piet (1992). *Sephardim: The Spirit that Has Withstood the Times.* Son, The Netherlands: Huisman Editions.

Koulen, Ingrid, and Gert Oostindie (1987). *The Netherlands Antilles and Aruba: A Research Guide.* Dordrecht: Foris Publications.

PAUL GRIFHORST

Dominicans

ETHNONYMS: none

Orientation

Identification. "Dominicans" is the term used to describe the people of the Dominican Republic. The native population of Taino Indians was decimated during the Spanish Conquest, which began in 1492 and came to be characterized by forced labor and newly introduced diseases. Africans were imported as slaves to replace the Indians on the plantations and in the mines. Today Dominicans physically reflect the ancestry of Europe and Africa; over 70 percent of Dominicans are now officially considered mulatto. Even though the majority of the Dominican people are classified by the government as mulattoes, social status and skin color are correlated, with lighter-skinned Dominicans dominating business, government, and society. Mulattoes constitute most of the Dominican middle class; the working classes are mostly Black or dark mulatto. Other ethnic groups in the Dominican Republic are Lebanese, Chinese, Italians, French, Jews, Japanese, Haitians, and West Indians.

Location. The island of Hispaniola, one of the Greater Antilles, lies between Cuba and Puerto Rico in the Caribbean Sea. The Dominican Republic occupies the eastern two-thirds (i.e., 48,464 square kilometers) of Hispaniola and is strikingly diverse geographically. The Dominican Republic contains mountain ranges interspersed with fertile valleys, lush rain forests, semiarid deserts, rich farmlands, and spectacular beaches. The western third of the island of Hispaniola is the nation of Haiti.

Many Dominicans have migrated to other countries in search of employment and increased opportunity. Between 5 and 8 percent of the population of the Dominican Republic live and work in the United States—most of them in New York City, but substantial numbers have also settled in New Jersey and Florida. Migration between the Dominican Republic and other islands of the Caribbean is less well documented.

Demography. There were about 7,915,000 Dominicans in 1993. About half of them lived in the *campo* (countryside) and worked mainly as peasant farmers. Because of the relative poverty in the countryside, more and more Dominicans have migrated to cities such as Santo Domingo (the capital city), Santiago de los Caballeros, La Vega, San Francisco de Macorís, La Romana, and Puerto Plata on the north coast.

During the period of Rafael Trujillo's rule, from 1930 to 1961, Dominican immigration to the United States was severely limited, given Trujillo's domestic agenda, which depended on a steady supply of an expendable labor source. Dominicans did migrate however, even with Trujillo's restrictive policies. Between 1950 and 1960, almost 10,000 Dominicans emigrated to the United States and became legal residents. Following the overthrow of Trujillo in 1961 and the lifting of his restrictive policies, migration to the United States increased substantially. Between 1961 and 1981, 255,578 legal immigrants entered the United States from the Dominican Republic. It is much more difficult to estimate the number of undocumented Dominicans in the United States. Reports suggest that Dominicans are third among immigrant groups from Latin America admitted into the United States. The economic crisis of the early 1980s has further increased the number of Dominicans seeking to emigrate to the United States. Research suggests that those Dominicans who succeed in doing so are most often young, predominantly urban in origin, often skilled and semiprofessional, and better educated than Dominican nonmigrants.

In 1993 the crude birthrate in the Dominican Republic was 25.2 per thousand, the crude death rate was 5.8 per thousand, the infant mortality rate was 49.3 per thousand, and total life expectancy at birth was 69 years.

Linguistic Affiliation. Spanish is the language spoken by Dominicans. Although there are some regional dialects of Spanish in the Dominican Republic, Dominicans pride themselves on the "purity" of their Spanish. Dominican Spanish is considered by some to be perhaps the clearest, most classical Spanish spoken in Latin America. According to some authors, this may be the result of the virtual elimination of the native population and the fact that the Dominican Republic was the first Spanish-settled colony in the New World.

History, Politics, and Cultural Relations

The history of the Dominican Republic, both colonial and postcolonial, is marked by continued interference by international forces and a Dominican ambivalence toward its own leadership. Between the fifteenth and nineteenth centuries, the Dominican Republic was ruled both by Spain and France and occupied both by the United States and Haiti. Three political leaders influenced Dominican politics from the 1930s to the 1990s. The dictator Rafael Trujillo ran the country for thirty-one years, until 1961. In the years following Trujillo's murder, two aging caudillos, Juan Bosch and Joaquín Balaguer, vied for control of the Dominican government.

In 1492, when Columbus first landed in what is now the Dominican Republic, he named the island "Española," which means "Little Spain." The spelling of the name was later changed to Hispaniola. The city of Santo Domingo, on the southern coast of Hispaniola, was established as the Spanish capital in the New World. Santo Domingo became a walled city, modeled after those of medieval Spain, and a center of transplanted Spanish culture. The Spanish built churches, hospitals, and schools and established commerce, mining, and agriculture.

In the process of settling and exploiting Hispaniola, the native Taino Indians were eradicated by the harsh forced-labor practices of the Spanish and the diseases the Spanish brought with them, to which indigenous peoples had no immunity. Because the rapid decimation of the Taino left the Spanish in need of laborers in the mines and on the plantations, Africans were imported as a slave labor force. During this time, the Spanish established a strict two-class social system based on race, a political system based on authoritarianism and hierarchy, and an economic system based on state domination. After about fifty years, the Spanish abandoned Hispaniola for more economically promising areas such as Cuba, Mexico, and other new colonies in Latin America. The institutions of government, economy, and society that were established, however, have persisted in the Dominican Republic throughout its history.

After its virtual abandonment, once-prosperous Hispaniola fell into a state of disorganization and depression lasting almost two hundred years. In 1697 Spain handed over the western third of Hispaniola to the French, and in 1795 gave the French the eastern two-thirds as well. By that time, the western third of Hispaniola (then called Hayti) was prosperous, producing sugar and cotton in an economic system based on slavery. The formerly Spanish-controlled eastern two-thirds was economically impoverished, with most people surviving on subsistence farming. After the Haitian slave rebellion, which resulted in Haitian independence in 1804, the Black armies of Haiti attempted to take control of the former Spanish colony, but the French, Spanish, and British fought off the Haitians. The eastern part of Hispaniola reverted to Spanish rule in 1809. The Haitian armies once again invaded in 1821, and in 1822 gained control of the entire island, which they maintained until 1844.

In 1844 Juan Pablo Duarte, the leader of the Dominican independence movement, entered Santo Domingo and declared the eastern two-thirds of Hispaniola an independent nation, naming it the Dominican Republic. Duarte was unable to hold power, however, which soon passed to two generals, Buenaventura Báez and Pedro Santana. These men looked to the "greatness" of the sixteenth-century colonial period as a model and sought out the protection of a large foreign power. As a result of corrupt and inept leadership, the country was bankrupt by 1861, and power was handed over to the Spanish again until 1865. Báez continued as president until 1874; Ulises Espaillat then took control until 1879.

In 1882 a modernizing dictator, Ulises Heureaux, took control of the Dominican Republic. Under Heureaux's regime, roads and railways were constructed, telephone lines were installed, and irrigation systems were dug. During this period, economic modernization and political order were established, but only through extensive foreign loans and autocratic, corrupt, and brutal rule. In 1899 Heureaux was assassinated, and the Dominican government fell into disarray and factionalism. By 1907, the economic situation had deteriorated, and the government was unable to pay the foreign debt engendered during the reign of Heureaux. In response to the perceived economic crisis, the United States moved to place the Dominican Republic into receivership. Ramón Cáceres, the man who assassinated Heureaux, became president until 1912, when he was in turn assassinated, by a member of one of the feuding political factions.

The ensuing domestic political warfare left the Dominican Republic once again in political and economic chaos. European and U.S. bankers expressed concern over the possible lack of repayment of loans. Using the Monroe Doctrine to counter what the United States considered potential European "intervention" in the Americas, the United States invaded the Dominican Republic in 1916, occupying the country until 1924.

During the period of U.S. occupation, political stability was restored. Roads, hospitals, and water and sewerage systems were constructed in the capital city and elsewhere in the country, and land-tenure changes that benefited a new class of large landowners were instituted. To act as a counterinsurgency force, a new military security force, the Guardia Nacional, was trained by U.S. marines. In 1930 Rafael Trujillo, who had risen to a position of leadership in the Guardia, used it to acquire and consolidate power.

From 1930 to 1961, Trujillo ran the Dominican Republic as his own personal possession, in what has been called the first truly totalitarian state in the hemisphere. He established a system of private capitalism in which he, his family members, and his friends held nearly 60 percent of the country's assets and controlled its labor force. Under the guise of economic recovery and national security, Trujillo and his associates demanded the abolishment of all personal and political freedoms. Although the economy flourished, the benefits went toward personal—not public—gain. The Dominican Republic became a ruthless police state in which torture and murder ensured obedience. Trujillo was assassinated on 30 May 1961, ending a long and difficult period in Dominican history. At the time of his death, few Dominicans could remember life without Trujillo in power, and with his death came a period of domestic and international turmoil.

During Trujillo's reign, political institutions had been eviscerated, leaving no functional political infrastructure. Factions that had been forced underground emerged, new political parties were created, and the remnants of the previous regime—in the form of Trujillo's son Ramfis and one of Trujillo's former puppet presidents, Joaquín Balaguer—vied for control. Because of pressure from the United States to democratize, Trujillo's son and Balaguer agreed to hold elections. Balaguer quickly moved to distance himself from the Trujillo family in the realignment for power.

In November 1961 Ramfis Trujillo and his family fled the country after emptying the Dominican treasury of $90 million. Joaquín Balaguer became part of a seven-person Council of State, but two weeks and two military coups later, Balaguer was forced to leave the country. In December 1962 Juan Bosch of the Dominican Revolutionary

party (PRD), promising social reform, won the presidency by a 2-1 margin, the first time that Dominicans had been able to choose their leadership in relatively free and fair elections. The traditional ruling elite and the military, however, with the support of the United States, organized against Bosch under the guise of anticommunism. Claiming that the government was infiltrated by communists, the military staged a coup that overthrew Bosch in September 1963; he had been president for only seven months.

In April 1965 the PRD and other pro-Bosch civilians and "constitutionalist" military took back the presidential palace. José Molina Ureña, next in line for the presidency according to the constitution, was sworn in as interim president. Remembering Cuba, the United States encouraged the military to counterattack. The military used jets and tanks in its attempt to crush the rebellion, but the pro-Bosch constitutionalists were able to repel them. The Dominican military was moving toward a defeat at the hands of the constitutionalist rebels when, on 28 April 1965, President Lyndon Johnson sent 23,000 U.S. troops to occupy the country.

The Dominican economic elite, having been reinstalled by the U.S. military, sought Balaguer's election in 1966. Although the PRD was allowed to contest the presidency, with Bosch as its candidate, the Dominican military and police used threats, intimidation, and terrorist attacks to keep him from campaigning. The final outcome of the vote was tabulated as 57 percent for Balaguer and 39 percent for Bosch.

Throughout the late 1960s and the first part of the 1970s, the Dominican Republic went through a period of economic growth and development arising mainly from public-works projects, foreign investments, increased tourism, and skyrocketing sugar prices. During this same period, however, the Dominican unemployment rate remained between 30 and 40 percent, and illiteracy, malnutrition, and infant mortality rates were dangerously high. Most of the benefits of the improving Dominican economy went to the already wealthy. The sudden increase in oil prices by the Organization of Petroleum Exporting Countries (OPEC) in the mid-1970s, a crash in the price of sugar on the world market, and increases in unemployment and inflation destabilized the Balaguer government. The PRD, under a new leader, Antonio Guzmán, once more prepared for presidential elections.

Since Guzmán was a moderate, he was seen as acceptable by the Dominican business community and by the United States. The Dominican economic elite and military, however, saw Guzmán and the PRD as a threat to their dominance. When the early returns from the 1978 election showed Guzmán leading, the military moved in, seized the ballot boxes, and annulled the election. Because of pressure from the Carter administration and threats of a massive general strike among Dominicans, Balaguer ordered the military to return the ballot boxes, and Guzmán won the election.

Guzmán promised better observance of human rights and more political freedom, more action in health care and rural development, and more control over the military; however, the high oil costs and the rapid decline in sugar prices caused the economic situation in the Dominican Republic to remain bleak. Even though Guzmán achieved much in terms of political and social reform, the faltering economy made people recall the days of relative prosperity under Balaguer.

The PRD chose Salvador Jorge Blanco as its 1982 presidential candidate, Juan Bosch returned with a new political party called the Dominican Liberation party (PLD), and Joaquín Balaguer also entered the race, under the auspices of his Reformist Party. Jorge Blanco won the election with 47 percent of the vote; however, one month before the new president's inauguration, Guzmán committed suicide over reports of corruption. Jacobo Majluta, the vice president, was named interim president until the inauguration.

When Jorge Blanco assumed the presidency, the country was faced with an enormous foreign debt and a balance-of-trade crisis. President Blanco sought a loan from the International Monetary Fund (IMF). The IMF, in turn, required drastic austerity measures: the Blanco government was forced to freeze wages, cut funding to the public sector, increase prices on staple goods, and restrict credit. When these policies resulted in social unrest, Blanco sent in the military, resulting in the deaths of more than one hundred people.

Joaquín Balaguer, nearly eighty years old and legally blind, ran against Juan Bosch and former interim president Jacobo Majluta in the 1986 election. In a highly contentious race, Balaguer won by a narrow margin and regained control of the country. He once more turned to massive public-works projects in an attempt to revitalize the Dominican economy but this time was unsuccessful. By 1988 he was no longer seen as an economic miracle worker, and in the 1990 election he was again strongly challenged by Bosch. In the campaign, Bosch was portrayed as divisive and unstable in contrast to the elder statesman Balaguer. With this strategy, Balaguer again won in 1990, although by a narrow margin.

In the 1994 presidential election, Balaguer and his Social Christian Reformist party (PRSC) were challenged by José Francisco Peña Gómez, the candidate of the PRD. Peña Gómez, a Black man who was born in the Dominican Republic of Haitian parents, was depicted as a covert Haitian agent who planned to destroy Dominican sovereignty and merge the Dominican Republic with Haiti. Pro-Balaguer television commercials showed Peña Gómez as drums beat wildly in the background, and a map of Hispaniola with a dark brown Haiti spreading over and covering a bright green Dominican Republic. Peña Gómez was likened to a witch doctor in pro-Balaguer campaign pamphlets, and videos linked him with the practice of Vodun. Election-day exit polls indicated an overwhelming victory for Peña Gómez; on the following day, however, the Central Electoral Junta (JCE), the independent electoral board, presented preliminary results that placed Balaguer in the lead. Allegations of fraud on the part of the JCE were widespread. More than eleven weeks later, on 2 August, the JCE finally pronounced Balaguer the winner by 22,281 votes, less than 1 percent of the total vote. The PRD claimed that at least 200,000 PRD voters had been turned away from polling places, on the grounds that their names were not on the voters list. The JCE established a "revision committee," which investigated 1,500 polling stations (about 16 percent of the total) and found that the names of more than 28,000 voters had been removed from electoral lists, making plausible the figure of 200,000 voters turned away nationally. The JCE ignored the findings of the committee and declared Balaguer the winner. In a concession, Balaguer agreed to limit his term in office to two years instead of four, and not to run for president again. Bosch received only 15 percent of the total vote.

Economy

Subsistence and Commercial Activities. Throughout most of its history, the Dominican economy has been based largely on the production and export of sugarcane. Sugarcane is still the biggest cash crop grown in the Dominican Republic, with coffee and cocoa being the other most important export crops. Agriculture continues to be the largest source of employment in the Dominican Republic, but mining has recently surpassed sugar as the biggest source of export earnings. Tourism is the most rapidly growing sector of the Dominican economy, with receipts in 1990 of U.S.$944 million. With the relative stability of Dominican democracy since the 1970s, tax incentives for building tourist facilities, the most hotel rooms of any country in the Caribbean, and beautiful uncluttered beaches, tourism is now the largest source of foreign exchange. Manufacturing, especially in the Free Trade Zones (FTZ), is also a rapidly growing sector of the Dominican economy.

Industrial Arts. The three main industrial activities in the Dominican Republic are mining, manufacturing, and utilities. In 1991 mining accounted for 33.5 percent of the total earnings from exports. Ferro-nickel is the major mineral mined in the country; bauxite, gold, and silver are also extracted. Manufacturing accounted for 16.1 percent of the Dominican gross domestic product in 1991. A rapidly growing part of the Dominican manufacturing sector are the FTZ being established by foreign multinational corporations. In these FTZ, the main activity is the assembly of products (mainly textiles, garments, and light electronic goods) intended for sale in nations such as the United States. Assembly industries locate in these zones because there they are permitted to pay low wages for labor-intensive activities and because the Dominican government grants exemptions from duties and taxes on exports from FTZ. Sixteen FTZ had been established in the Dominican Republic by 1991, comprising more than 300 companies, which employed around 120,000 workers.

Trade. In 1991 the Dominican Republic had a trade deficit of U.S.$1,070.5 million, with the United States receiving 56 percent of Dominican exports. The other major trading partners of the Dominican Republic are Venezuela and Mexico. The main exports from the Dominican Republic in 1991 were raw sugar and ferro-nickel.

Division of Labor. In 1991 an estimated 34.9 percent of Dominicans worked in the agricultural sector, 28.1 percent were employed in industry, and many others worked in the service sector, which caters mainly to tourism. Labor is divided along the lines of ethnicity, class, and gender. Light-skinned individuals control most of business, finance, government, and other high-status professions, whereas darker-skinned individuals are predominant in the military officer corps and constitute much of the new middle class.

More than three-quarters of the workers in the free trade zones are women; employers can pay them low wages and keep them from forming strong labor unions.

Land Tenure.   Land-tenure patterns reflect both Dominican and international politics. Sugar and cattle are significant products for the Dominican economy, and land-tenure patterns associated with sugar production and cattle raising have changed over time. The 1916 U.S. invasion is often conceptualized an action under the Monroe Doctrine to protect regional security and counter European "interference" in the Americas, especially to stop German expansion in the region; however, the invasion was also a means to protect U.S. sugar producers in the Dominican Republic. World War I destroyed the European sugar-beet industry, allowing for the rapid expansion of Dominican sugar production. During the U.S. occupation, U.S. military authorities enacted legislation to facilitate the takeover of Dominican land by U.S. sugar growers. The 1920 Law Registration Act was designed to break up the communal lands and transfer them into private ownership. In 1925, one year following the withdrawal of U.S. troops, eleven of the twenty-one sugar mills in the Dominican Republic belonged to U.S. corporations, and 98 percent of the sugar exports went to the United States.

Cattle raising, an important source and symbol of wealth in the Dominican countryside, was feasible for many people because the animals were branded and then left to graze freely on open land. In the 1930s Trujillo expropriated large portions of land, reducing the amount available for free grazing. Those lands became further reduced in the 1950s when Trujillo established "La Zona," a law requiring the enclosure of large livestock that effectively prohibited free grazing. In the 1960s and 1970s the Balaguer government tried to increase cattle production for meat exports and, in so doing, created state-subsidized credits for cattle production. Some of these credits made it easier and more rewarding for people to buy parcels of land on which to graze their cattle.

Kinship

Kin Groups and Descent.   Kinship in the upper classes of Dominican society is patrilineal, based on the Spanish model. The eldest man is the ultimate authority; brothers and unmarried sisters stay very close, and sons give their allegiance to their father and mother. Brothers and sons help to support their unmarried sisters and mother, whereas married sisters are expected to become part of their husbands' families. The extended family is also the locus of social activity among the Dominican upper class.

Kinship among the Dominican lower class, on the other hand, is more matrilineal. The eldest woman is the head of the family, with very close ties with her daughters and their children. Because of the practice of consensual unions among lower-class Dominicans, men are not as integral a part of the kin grouping.

Marriage and Family

Marriage.   Three different types of marital union can be found among Dominicans: church marriage, civil marriage, and consensual or common-law union. Church and civil marriage are most prevalent among the upper classes of Dominican society, whereas consensual unions predominate among the poor. These patterns of marriage in Dominican society can be traced back to the Spanish-colonial and slave periods. Among the Spanish settlers that came to Hispaniola, there was a strong ethic of family solidarity, and the father was the dominant figure in the family structure. Among the slaves, however, families were frequently broken up, and marriages were often not allowed. There was also an established pattern of informal unions between Spanish-colonial settlers and African slave women. Reflections of these practices are present today in the range of skin tones and marriage practices among Dominicans.

There are also contemporary reasons for the strong class and racial basis of the different types of marital union. One reason is the high cost of church and civil-marriage ceremonies in the Dominican Republic. Another is that, as throughout the Caribbean, early pregnancies result from consensual relationships. Both sexes initially tend to form a series of consensual unions, each resulting in more children.

Domestic Unit.   The extended family, composed of three or more generations, is the predominant domestic unit among the Dominican elite. Within this extended-family structure, the oldest man holds authority, makes public decisions on all family matters, and is responsible for the welfare of the rest of the family. The eldest married woman commands her household, delivers the decisions in the private sphere, and is a source of love and moral support for the family. The family unit often includes grandparents, parents, and unmarried siblings, along with married brothers and their wives and children; married daughters become part of their husbands' families.

The practice of consensual unions, more prevalent among the Dominican lower classes, creates a much more loosely structured domestic unit. Given that the father often does not live in the household, parental authority and responsibility fall to the mother. In this situation, the eldest woman becomes the center of both public and private authority and the main breadwinner, in contrast to the patriarchal public authority among the elite. The result of this pattern is that a lower-class household often becomes a kind of extended matrilineal family, with the matriarch at the head and her unmarried children, married daughters, and grandchildren constituting the household.

Sociopolitical Organization

Social Organization.   Dominican society is organized strongly on the basis of class and race. Dominicans of the more powerful classes, who control the economic and political processes of the country, have historically been of European ancestry. The poorest of Dominicans are most often Black, descendants of the original African slave population or migrant workers from Haiti. Mulattoes make up the majority of the Dominican population and have created a burgeoning middle class. In the twentieth century the military and lower levels of government have provided avenues of advancement for darker-skinned men, and some have reached the level of general, and even president (i.e., Trujillo).

Political Organization. The Dominican Republic consists of twenty-six provinces, each run by an appointed governor, and the Distrito Nacional (DN), where the capital is located. The 1966 constitution established a bicameral National Congress (Congreso Nacional), which is split into the 30-member Senate (Senado) and the 120-member Chamber of Deputies (Camara de Diputados). Members of Congress are elected for four-year terms. There is an executive branch with a president who is elected by popular vote every four years, a vice president, and a cabinet. There is also a Supreme Court (Corte Suprema).

Although the Dominican political system has long been modeled after that of the United States, with a constitution and tripartite separation of power, the political reality is different. Dominican politics has been based on a system of presidential control since colonial times. Developed to its extreme under the totalitarian dictatorship of Trujillo, this system, even in its most liberal periods, has not strayed very far from its historical model.

In the 1990s the major political parties in the Dominican Republic were the Social Christian Reformist Party (PRSC), led by Joaquín Balaguer; the Dominican Liberation Party (PLD), led by Juan Bosch; the Dominican Revolutionary Party (PRD), led by José Francisco Peña Gómez; and the Independent Revolutionary Party (PRI), led by Jacobo Majluta.

Religion and Expressive Culture

Religious Beliefs. The Catholic church and Catholic beliefs are nominally central to Dominican culture. It is estimated that 98 percent of Dominicans are Catholic, even if not all of these people attend church regularly. Catholicism was introduced to the Dominican Republic by Columbus and the Spanish missionaries and has remained a force in Dominican society ever since. Toward the end of the twentieth century, the dominance of the Catholic church diminished because of a decrease in funding, a shortage of new priests, and a lack of social programs for the people. As a result, Protestant evangelical movements, with their emphasis on personal responsibility and family rejuvenation, economic entrepreneurship, and biblical fundamentalism, have been gaining support among some Dominicans. An unknown number of Dominicans practice synchronistic religions combining Catholicism and Vodun. Santería is also found among Dominicans.

Medicine. The Dominican Republic, like many other countries in Latin America and the Caribbean, has three parallel public health-care delivery systems. The largest is the government-funded Secretaria de Estado de Salud Publica y Asistencia Social (SESPAS), which serves the general population. Because of structural and economic constraints, SESPAS is concentrated in urban areas, has a focus on curative rather than preventive care, often has inoperative medical equipment, and is known for high absenteeism among physicians. These factors severely limit access to health care for the majority of Dominicans in the rural areas. This system, which is inadequate for the needs of the majority of Dominicans, is a result of the Spanish-colonial tradition and the biomedical system put into place by the United States during its occupation from 1916 to 1924. The other health-care delivery systems in the Dominican Republic are the Instituto Dominicano de Sequros Sociales (IDSS), which is a social-security health system, and the Instituto de Seguridad Social de las Fuerzas Armadas (ISSFAPOL), which provides health care to members of the armed forces. Private health care is also available, primarily in the urban centers.

Bibliography

Ferguson, James (1992). *The Dominican Republic: Beyond the Lighthouse.* London: Latin America Bureau.

Georges, Eugenia (1990). *The Making of a Transnational Community: Migration, Development, and Cultural Change in the Dominican Republic.* New York: Columbia University Press.

Whiteford, Linda M. (1990). "A Question of Adequacy: Primary Health Care in the Dominican Republic." *Social Science and Medicine* 30(2): 221–226.

Whiteford, Linda M. (1992). "Contemporary Health Care and the Colonial and Neo-Colonial Experience: The Case of the Dominican Republic." *Social Science and Medicine* 35(10): 1215–1223.

Whiteford, Linda M. (1993). "Child and Maternal Health and International Economic Policies." *Social Science and Medicine* 37(11): 1391–1400.

Whiteford, Linda M., and Donna Romeo (1991). "The High Cost of Free Trade: Women, Work, and Health in Dominican Free Trade Zones." Manuscript.

Wiarda, Howard J., and Michael J. Kryzanek. (1992). *The Dominican Republic: A Caribbean Crucible.* 2nd ed. Boulder, Colo.: Westview Press.

World Health Organization (1993). *Demographic Data for Health Situation Assessment and Projections.* Geneva: World Health Organization, Division of Epidemiological Surveillance and Health Situation and Trend Assessment.

LINDA M. WHITEFORD AND KENNETH J. GOODMAN

East Indians in Trinidad

ETHNONYMS: "Coolies" (now considered offensive; unacceptable in public discourse), Indo-Trinidadians, Overseas Indians (Trinidad)

Orientation

Identification. The East Indians of Trinidad are descendants of indentured laborers who were brought to this island in the West Indies from the South Asian subcontinent during the second half of the nineteenth century. They were called "East Indians" by Europeans to distinguish them from Native Americans.

Location. Trinidad (now part of the West Indian nation of Trinidad and Tobago) is about 10 kilometers east of the coast of Venezuela, encompassing some 4,385 square kilometers between 10°03′ and 10°50′ N and 60°39′ and 62° W. The climate is equable throughout the year, with a wet season from May to January and a dry season from the end of January to the middle of May. Sugar and other crops for export have been grown predominantly on plantations situated in the central county of Caroni and in the southern counties of Victoria and Saint Patrick. The majority of the original East Indians were brought to these areas and their descendants have continued to reside there. The major sources of revenue have been sugar and oil.

Demography. The first 225 "Coolies" (as they were then called) arrived in Trinidad on 30 May 1845. Mostly male, they were brought from Calcutta, India, to work for five to ten years as indentured laborers on the Trinidad sugar estates, replacing the former slaves of African ancestry who began to leave the estates after the passage of the Emancipation Act in 1833. The practice of indenture came to an end in Trinidad in 1920, by which time approximately 143,900 men and women had been brought from South Asia. The majority were recruited in the north, primarily from Bihar, the United Provinces, and Bengal. By 1985, the total population of Trinidad and Tobago exceeded half a million people. Those who considered themselves (or were considered by census takers) to be of solely African or solely Indian descent were approximately equal in numbers: 215,132 "Negroes" and 215,613 "East Indians."

Linguistic Affiliation. The immigrant indentured laborers spoke a number of Indic languages, and a few spoke Tamil, a Dravidian language. By the middle of the twentieth century, English was in common use, although Bhojpuri, a language of northern Bihar, was still understood by many. At that time, too, Standard Hindi began to be taught in Hindu schools. Sanskrit continues to be used in Hindu religious services. Muslim Indo-Trinidadians learn and use Arabic for religious purposes.

History and Cultural Relations

From the mid-seventeenth century on, the cultivation of sugarcane by slaves brought from Africa was a major source of prosperity for European owners of plantations in the West Indies. When slavery ended, the sugar cultivators attempted to continue the system by utilizing indentured laborers. Muslims as well as Hindus—deriving from a wide range of castes—were brought to Trinidad from South Asia. All were initially housed on the estates in the wooden barracks vacated by the emancipated former slaves. The estate owners and their resident managers and overseers had no interest in maintaining the customs and practices of the East Indians and in fact discouraged and tried to eliminate any Indian social or political structure.

A minority of East Indians were able to achieve repatriation; most stayed on in Trinidad, bound to the sugar estates for a source of income, just as they had been under indenture. In the final decades of the nineteenth century, however, East Indians settled on Crown Land, frequently in swampy areas not especially suitable for the growing of sugarcane but capable of supporting other crops—most particularly rice and other subsistence foods. Cutting cane was the only source of cash for many villages. By the mid-twentieth century, therefore, the majority of East Indians resided in rural communities in the sugar-growing regions of central and southern Trinidad.

Life in Trinidad, for all inhabitants, was much affected by a series of events that occurred during the middle decades of the twentieth century. First, during World War II, large numbers of U.S. soldiers and sailors were posted to the island to build and maintain military bases, introducing the "Yankee dollar" along with new perspectives on social relationships, as well as new dimensions of social, familial, political, and religious stress. Better roads were built, transportation improved, and isolation decreased as people in rural areas went in search of employment. Many rural East Indians found, for the first time, sources of income other than work in the cane fields. Bhadase Sagan Maraj, a Brahman and an early sugar-union leader, acquired considerable wealth through his dealings with Americans and became a leader in East Indian political and religious affairs. As head of the Sanatan Dharma Maha Sabha, the most influential Hindu religious organization, he fostered construction of schools and temples throughout the island. Political struggles in the early 1950s resulted in greater popular participation in government.

The achievement of independence by India and Pakistan in 1948 caused great excitement among both Muslims and Hindus in Trinidad. Indian movies began to arrive and became very popular. Extended visits in the early 1950s by Indian missionaries (known as the "Swamis") resulted in an increased interest in Hinduism on the part of many young men; at the same time, the new schools built by the Maha Sabha introduced the teaching of Hindi and Sanskrit along with customary Western secular subjects.

In addition, by mid-century, indentured immigration had become a thing of the past: most of the East Indian population was now Trinidad-born. Some were attracted to West Indian, even European, values and interests, but others sought to hold on to elements of their Indian tradition. As Indo-Trinidadians became increasingly "European" or "cosmopolitan" in lifestyle, their newly acquired wealth made it possible for some to seek out their South Asian heritage. Many young people, however, began to express dissatisfaction at what were seen as "old-fashioned" practices such as arranged marriage, virilocality, and caste restrictions on diet and intermarriage.

The West Indian nation of Trinidad and Tobago achieved independence in 1962. The oil industrry was nationalized in 1974—just before an enormous worldwide increase in the price of oil. The ensuing "oil boom" prosperity affected all ethnic groups. For Indo-Trinidadians in particular, it precipitated a rapid shift from agriculture to the burgeoning fields of construction, commerce (especially in hardware, foodstuffs, and dry goods), and transportation.

Settlements

The first houses constructed by East Indians in their new settlements were small, mud-walled huts with thatched roofs, essentially similar to those of their northern Indian home villages. In many cases a settlement pattern emerged that was also reminiscent of that of northern India: the more prosperous villagers—often of castes considered higher in rank—clustered together in what came to be considered the more prestigious neighborhood, whereas poorer people (particularly those of castes considered in India to be "low" or "untouchable") resided in more peripheral neighborhoods.

Economy

Subsistence and Commercial Activities. Until the time of the oil boom, the most desired economic activity was rice cultivation: with a piece of rice land (rented or owned), a man could provide basic subsistence food for his family and feel reasonably secure. Land on which sugarcane could be grown could provide cash income but was rarely available. Most rural East Indians worked on the sugar estates; a few found work on estates producing other crops, such as cocoa. Those who became "drivers" (gang foremen) became men of power and influence in their home communities.

Apart from agriculture, East Indian men sought work as taxi drivers, on road gangs, and as laborers in the oil fields. In the communities near the Caroni Swamp, some men fished or supported themselves by "crab-catching"; they sold their catch in the weekly markets or daily in the villages. Education was prized, but, until the establishment of Hindu-sponsored schools, few men and fewer women had access to it. Christian-sponsored schools educated a small percentage of East Indians, and those who became doctors, lawyers, and schoolteachers were held in great respect. In most East Indian communities, a few enterprising women (and an occasional man) opened "parlors" (small grocery stores), usually under their houses. Most rural general stores, however, were owned by Chinese storekeepers.

Industrial Arts and Trade. A small number of East Indians made crude, undecorated pottery of red clay—mostly to provide items (e.g., bowls, shallow cups) needed for Hindu ceremonies. Few other industrial arts were known or practiced; most goods—cloth, housewares, tools, and so on—were purchased in the shops or from itinerant peddlers.

Division of Labor. Although women worked alongside men on the sugar estates, most Indian men felt uncomfortable about this practice, and those who could afford to kept their wives—and, particularly, their daughters—away from cane cutting. Rice cultivation was also primarily a male activity, but women often participated in the transplanting process. East Indian taxi drivers and road-gang workers were exclusively male, as were the cooks and musicians who worked at weddings and religious ceremonies. All Hindu priests and religious functionaries were male, but midwifery was a female occupation.

The emergence and spread of Hindu schools in the 1950s fostered a greater willingness on the part of East Indians to send their daughters to school, and the prosperity of the oil boom accelerated this trend: by the 1980s Indo-Trinidadian women teachers were equal in number to their male counterparts, and large numbers of young women had gained employment in the Civil Service.

Land Tenure. From the time Crown Land became available, purchase and ownership was by individuals. Some land was suitable for sugarcane and was worked by the owner with the aid of his sons and whatever hired labor he could afford. Land suitable only for rice, on the other hand, was usually rented out in small parcels (the owner keeping only enough for his family's needs). Those who rented rice land assisted one another, particularly at harvesttime: those with contiguous fields formed communal groups, and together they harvested one another's fields in agreed-upon succession.

Kinship

Kin Groups and Descent. Indentured laborers began to form new kinship networks even before they arrived in Trinidad. Close relationships formed on shipboard were maintained for years, even generations. Considering themselves too intimately related to allow their children to marry each other, _jihaji bhai,_ as they were known, helped one another find spouses for their children, as relatives in separate villages did in India. Over time and generations, bilateral kin networks developed; some were islandwide. Most East Indians, at least until the mid-twentieth century, preferred to seek spouses for their children in communities other than their own. There was much variation from community to community, from caste to caste, and from individual to individual: some discarded all Indian practices of kin ties and marriage, whereas others tried to maintain and enforce traditional practices, even forbidding marriages between children born in the same community.

There is disagreement among scholars over the question "What happened to 'Caste'?" Few men were able to follow traditional caste occupations, and the economic relationships between castes were never reconstructed; nor were marriage-circles or other forms of caste networks. Nevertheless, the majority of East Indians maintained some degree of caste identification over generations, and this sense of affiliation affected marriage and association patterns. Ideally, one inherited caste membership from both parents, but when parents were of different castes, membership was claimed in that of the father. Values and attitudes reflective of Indian caste hierarchy and separation persisted, although in increasingly attenuated form. After the mid-twentieth century, however, caste identification and whatever degree of marriage restriction had been imposed clearly began to disappear throughout Trinidad.

Kinship Terminology.   Although in northern India there is considerable regional and caste variation in kinship terminology, Trinidad East Indian practice reflected the predominance of Hawaiian cousin and bifurcate-collateral uncle terminological systems. The practice of calling all cousins of whatever degree of separation by the terms for "brother" and "sister" particularly separated East Indians from their African- and European-descended neighbors. Muslim East Indians permitted—in fact preferred—marriages between parallel cousins; among Hindus, such marriages were considered incestuous.

Marriage and Family

Marriage.   Marriages were for the most part arranged; dating or other association between unmarried and unrelated boys and girls was condemned by almost all East Indians as late as the mid-twentieth century. Increasingly, however, young people were demanding their right to "free choice" (which meant, in practice, the right to see the prospective spouse at least once before the marriage, along with a right of refusal). Throughout Trinidad, instances of young people marrying without parental permission and ignoring caste and other restrictions increased, and by the 1980s dating had become acceptable throughout the island. Today caste identification has become irrelevant (except for some Brahmans), and marriage with Europeans has become acceptable, but many Indo-Trinidadians, particularly in the rural areas, still disapprove of marriage with Afro-Trinidadians.

Domestic Unit.   For many of the higher-ranked castes, the patrilineal joint family (i.e., married brothers and their families sharing the same household) was the ideal social unit; others preferred the nuclear-family household. Both were present in the new settlements, but by the second half of the twentieth century the nuclear-family household had become the predominant pattern among Indo-Trinidadians.

Inheritance.   Traditionally, male children expected—and indeed, for the most part, still expect—to inherit most of the parental property, dividing it equally among themselves. The biggest problem concerning inheritance derived from the fact that until 1945 marriages performed by Hindu priests were not legally recognized. An unscrupulous brother of a deceased East Indian could therefore claim to be the only "legal" heir, thus disinheriting the "illegitimate" children.

Socialization.   Both mothers and fathers invariably preferred sons to daughters. In the event of divorce or other family breakup, children were often claimed by the parents of the father. Weaning was late, often delayed until the children were almost of school age, and all members of the family contributed to the warmth and easy discipline of the early years. Physical punishment, particularly of small children, was rarely resorted to by East Indians. Girls stayed close to home, discouraged even from going alone to a nearby shop, and restrictions increased as they reached puberty. Boys had much more freedom. Although some families encouraged education for sons and even daughters, for most East Indian children before the oil boom, adolescence meant early marriage for girls and an introduction to cane cutting or other employment for boys.

Sociopolitical Organization

Social Organization.   Few of the traditional Indian social-structural elements received any recognition or support within the Trinidad legal or social system, and few survived for long. Nevertheless, in the newly emerging East Indian settlements, powerful—if informal—sentiments maintained such practices as caste endogamy and neighborhood exogamy for decades. Leaders—called "big men"—emerged in most areas, maintaining peace in their communities by settling disputes and by punishing (sometimes by beatings, more often often by the imposition of fines or ostracism) those who violated tradition.

Political Organization.   By 1956, the People's National Movement (PNM), under the leadership of Dr. Eric Williams and supported by most Afro-Trinidadians (and many Christian and Muslim Indo-Trinidadians), began to dominate the political scene. Hindu East Indians, however, preferred to support "Indian" parties over the years, beginning withn the Democratic Labour party (DLP) led by Bhadase Sagan Maraj. The death of Williams in 1981 and a continuing economic recession precipitated by falling oil revenues led to a realignment of voting blocs and to the fall of the PNM in 1986. After considerable turmoil, including, in 1990, a violent effort to topple the government by Black Muslims (during which the prime minister and half the cabinet were taken hostage), the PNM regained power in 1992, an outcome largely attributable to the widely detested austerity program imposed by the then-governing National Alliance for Reconciliation. Party fragmentation and realignment along ethnic and interest-group lines continues.

Social Control and Conflict.   Bhadase Sagan Maraj and the Sanatan Dharma Maha Sabha received and maintained widespread loyalty because the Maha Sabha, with Maraj's financial support, had provided East Indians with non-Christian-controlled schools. By the 1980s, however, opposition to the Maha Sabha (and Brahmanical control) was developing among the educated youth and the wealthier and more cosmopolitan elite within the Indian community. New and independent political bodies and religious organizations appeared on the scene, although the Maha Sabha maintained support among the less educated, poorer, and more rural Indo-Trinidadians.

Religion and Expressive Culture

Religious Beliefs.   The overwhelming majority of Indian indentured laborers considered themselves Hindus, but most of them were from rural, unsophisticated backgrounds; they left theological questions to the priesthood, which had, in fact, relatively few representatives with real knowledge. Furthermore, Trinidad East Indians were cut off from communication with India until well into the twentieth century, and so had little knowledge of the changes taking place in Indian Hinduism. For most Hindu East Indians, therefore, the practice of their religion entailed making offerings (in some cases, animal sacrifices) to guardian spirits and to divinities at shrines and small temples, along with observing calendrical holidays and events such as Diwali (a festival of lights) and Holi (also known as Phagwa; a springtime festival of play and singing). In addition, *pujas* (ceremonies involving prayers, offerings, and a celebratory feast) were sponsored by families on birthdays or to give thanks for good fortune.

Almost from the day the first immigrants arrived in Trinidad, Christian missionaries sought them out. Some East Indians were converted to Catholicism and some to evangelical sects, but the Presbyterians of the Canadian Mission were most successful, particularly because they alone, among Christian groups, built schools in some of the new Indian settlements. Nonetheless, the majority of Hindu (and Muslim) East Indians did not turn away from ancestral religious practices.

There has been a great resurgence in interest in religion among both Hindu and Muslim Indo-Trinidadians. Trinidad-born disciples of the Swamis who came in the 1950s have become influential in the Sanatan Dharma Maha Sabha and have risen to leadership in India-derived sects, such as the Divine Life Society, and in the movement that accepts Sathya Sai Baba, a holy man of Bangalore, as an incarnation of divinity. Muslim organizations, such as the Sunaat-ul-Jamaat, have fostered stricter religious observance and the building of mosques. Hindus have contributed to the construction of new temples throughout Trinidad, and the ornate and costly *yagna*—seven days of readings from sacred Hindu texts and celebration—has become extremely popular.

Religious Practitioners. Few of the Brahman priests had much training beyond what was imparted by their fathers. Non-Brahman East Indian attitudes ranged from full pious acceptance of Brahmanical authority through reluctant acceptance for want of alternatives. By the 1980s, new movements had emerged that permitted individuals (usually men) other than Brahmans to serve as religious officiants.

Even in the early years of Indian presence in Trinidad, there had been religious officiants other than Brahmans among castes considered (in India) too "low" or "polluted" to be served by Brahmans. To protect their communities from illness and other misfortune, these men annually sacrificed goats or pigs to deities such as Kali. Despite Western education and Hindu reform movements, animal sacrifice continues, particularly among the poorer Indo-Trinidadians, and some of their beliefs and traditional practices have emerged in the form of new religious movements.

Ceremonies. Most Indo-Trinidadian Hindus observe life-cycle rites at birth, marriage, and death and sponsor pujas at special occasions such as the building of a house or the celebration of a recovery from a life-threatening illness. There are calendrical events in which most members of the community participate and, for some, weekly services at the temples.

Observant Muslim Indo-Trinidadians attend weekly services at one of the many mosques to be found on the island; many mark yearly calendrical events and adhere to traditional Muslim practices such as daily prayer and fasting during the month of Ramadan. One Muslim calendrical event—known in Trinidad as "Hosein" or, more popularly, as "Hosay"—has been co-opted by non-Muslims and even non-Indians into a version of Carnival, much to the resentment of pious Muslims.

Arts and Medicine. The indentured Indians brought with them many of the folk arts of rural India, for instance the making of simple pottery for domestic and religious needs and of crude, painted-clay religious statuary. A number of simple musical instruments are still in use, and accompany, along with the ubiquitous harmonium, traditional hymns. Indian cinema has influenced music, wedding costumes, and much else in Indo-Trinidadian life. In more recent decades, because of increased travel and the influence of television, East Indian young people, like their their Afro-Trinidadian counterparts, are greatly attracted to contemporary Caribbean, European, and U.S. popular music. A number of Indo-Trinidadian writers, most particularly V. S. Naipaul, have achieved world renown.

Few traditional Indian medical practices survived for very long in Trinidad (midwifery being the only significant exception). By the middle of the twentieth century, most East Indians chose to go to a Western-educated doctor when ill.

Death and Afterlife. Most Hindus—although they believed in reincarnation—tended to leave theology to the priests, preferring to concentrate on observing the appropriate rites at the death of a family member. Until the mid-twentieth century, this desire was impeded by laws in Trinidad requiring burial in cemeteries and prohibiting cremation. Few Hindu East Indians, however, erected gravestones or revisited the graves. Muslim and Christian Indians observed the mortuary, burial, and commemorative practices of their respective faiths.

See also Trinidad and Tobago

Bibliography

Klass, Morton (1961). *East Indians in Trinidad: A Study of Cultural Persistence.* New York: Columbia University Press. Reprint. 1988. Prospect Heights, Ill.: Waveland Press.

Klass, Morton (1991). *Singing with Sai Baba: The Politics of Revitalization in Trinidad.* Boulder, Colo.: Westview Press.

LaGuerre, John G., ed. (1974). *Calcutta to Caroni: The East Indians of Trinidad.* [Port-of-Spain]: Longman Caribbean.

Malik, Yogendra K. (1971). *East Indians in Trinidad: A Study in Minority Politics.* London: Oxford University Press.

Vertovec, Steven (1992). *Hindu Trinidad: Religion, Ethnicity, and Socio-Economic Change.* Warwick University Caribbean Studies. London: Macmillan.

MORTON KLASS

Emberá and Wounaan

ETHNONYMS: Baudó, Catío, Catru, Chamí, Chocama, Chocó, Choko, Citará, Dabeiba, Embená, Emberá, Empená, Emperá, Epera, Himberá, Humberá, Katío, Noanabs, Noanamá, Noanes, Nonamá, Nonameño, Río Verde, Saija, San Jorge, Tadó, Waunama, Waunan, Waunana, Wounan

Orientation

Identification. The Emberá and the Wounaan form a cultural group residing in eastern Panama and adjacent areas of Colombia. "Chocó"—the common geographic misnomer for the Emberá and the Wounaan Indians—has been used to refer to both the lands and peoples of the Pacific lowlands of Colombia and Panama since the mid-sixteenth century (Ortega Ricaurte and Rueda Briceno 1954). Many other names (e.g., Sambú, Nonama, Baudó) derive from words designating local rivers or other geographic features. Today, although the Indians recognize these terms, they identify themselves as "Emberá" and "Wounaan," both of which indicate the individual or the broader group. This article is concerned primarily with the Emberá and the Wounaan who live in Panama.

The Emberá and the Wounaan have similar material cultures, including post-and-pole dwellings, spoked kitchen fires, and the use of dart poisons that characterize Amazonian tribes. Traditionally, women wear a short wraparound skirt (*paruma*), formerly of bark cloth and now of brightly colored yard cloth, and men wear a slender loincloth (*guayuco*). Both sexes paint geometric designs and color their skin with indigo-hued *jagua* (*Genipa americana*) or red-hued *achiote*. Silver coins are fashioned into necklaces or pounded into bracelets, necklaces, and earrings. Today men wear Western clothes, but women maintain traditional dress. Plantains, bananas, yams, and rice are the staple foods of the Emberá and the Wounaan. Drinks, often fermented, are made from maize, sugarcane, and fruits.

Location. Eight Emberá groups and the Wounaan live in the Colombian Chocó. Their population in the early 1980s was estimated to be 20,000 (Botero 1982): the Katío (pop. 4,500) and Citará (pop. 3,500) live along the Río Atrato; the San Jorge (pop. 1,000) and Río Verde (pop. 1,000) live northeast; the Baudó (pop. 2,000) are named after their Pacific-slope river; the Tadó (pop. 1,000) are along headwaters of the Atrato and San Juan; the Chamí (pop. 2,000) are east on the Río Marmato; the Saija (pop. 1,500) are along the south coast; and the Wounaan (pop. 3,500) occupy San Juan Basin. Another 10,000 Emberá and 2,000 Wounaan lived in Panama, also in the early 1980s, most along the Jaqué, Sambú, Balsas, Tuira, Chucunaque, Sabanas, and Congo rivers of Darién Province the easternmost province of Panama, with smaller numbers west along the Pacific slope and in the Bayano and Panama Canal basins.

Demography. Fifteen thousand to 20,000 Emberá and Wounaan lived in Panama in 1993, 13,000 of them in nearly eighty villages in Darién Province, which borders Colombia. Of those in Darién, 82 percent were Emberá and 18 percent Wounaan (Congreso Emberá/Wounaan 1993, unpublished data). Probably over 50,000 live in Columbia. The Colombian census recorded over 40,000 (94 percent Emberá, 6 percent Wounaan) in 1985.

Linguistic Affiliation. Emberá and Wounaan are classified as either Carib or Paezan languages, but contain loanwords from Chibcha, Arawak, Quechua, and Spanish. Loewen (1963) divided the Emberá language into nine Colombian dialects plus the "Sambú" dialect in Panama, where no Wounaan dialects are recognized.

History and Cultural Relations

It is uncertain whether Emberá and Wounaan speakers lived in Central America during pre-Hispanic times. The Darién region of eastern Panama was Kuna territory between the late sixteenth century and eighteenth century. It was there that the Spaniards established El Real in 1600 to protect the upriver route from the Cana gold mines, once reportedly the richest in the Americas. Another fort was built near the mouth of the Río Sabanas and small placer-mining settlements developed elsewhere. In 1638 the missionary Fray Adrián de Santo Tomás helped agglomerate dispersed Kuna families into villages at Pinogana, Capetí, and Yaviza. The Kuna resisted Spanish demands that they work in mining operations and fought, sometimes alongside pirates, to destroy mission settlements during the 1700s. The Spaniards enlisted "Chocó" (with their feared blowguns) and Black mercenaries in the counteroffensive; the Kuna were pushed into Darién backlands and began their historic migration across the continental divide to the San Blas coast. As a result, the colonization effort failed, and the Spaniards dismantled their forts and left the region in the late eighteenth century.

Emberá began settling Darién during the late eighteenth century, and by the early 1900s had occupied most of the river basins. Some Europeans eventually resettled there, forming new towns, which are now dominated by Spanish-speaking Blacks. The Emberá settled away from these towns and the two remnant Kuna areas. Emberá were found as far west as the canal drainage by the 1950s. Wounaan families had entered Panama during the 1940s.

Emberá and Wounaan life changed dramatically in Panama during the mid-twentieth century. Desire for Western products brought them into cash economies. They traded with Black, Spanish-speaking businessmen, exchanging crops and forest products for cash. Among the hundreds of manufactured goods now important are machetes, ax heads, pots and pans, rifles, bullets, and cloth. Village organization sprang from the need to speak Spanish with these outsiders. Emberá elders petitioned the national government to provide teachers for their riverine sectors, and schools were established at Pulida, Río Tupisa, in 1953 and at Naranjal, Río Chico, in 1956. Initially, "villages" were simply a few households clustered around thatch-roofed schoolhouses. Sustained missionary activity began about the same time. Mennonites, sponsored by Panama's Ministry of Education, began a literacy program designed to record the Emberá and Wounaan languages so as to produce translations of religious materials with which to teach the Indians. Indian families grouped around missionary homes at Lucas in 1954 and El Mamey on the Río

Jaqué in 1956. Three "school villages" and three "mission villages" existed in 1960.

A philanthropic adventurer, Harold Baker Fernandez (nicknamed "Peru"), who began living with the Emberá in 1963, adopted Emberá and Wounaan ways, learned their culture from an insider's perspective, and taught them about securing land rights. He advised them that, by forming villages, they could petition the government for teachers, schools, and medical supplies. Through more effective territorial control, he told them, they might obtain a *comarca*, or semiautonomous political district, like the Kuna had, guaranteeing indigenous rights to land and resources. A "village model," with a schoolhouse, teacher's dorm, meeting hall, and village store amid thatch-roofed houses, diffused across Darién; by 1968, there were twelve Emberá villages. The government of General Omar Torrijos supported these initiatives, which encouraged the Indians to define their own political structure. An appointed Kuna chief (*cacique*) introduced the Kuna political model (*caciquismo*) as the first chiefs were selected. An additional eighteen villages were formed over the next two years, and in 1970 the Darién Emberá and Wounaan formally adopted a new political organization that featured chiefs, congresses, and village leaders, patterned after the Kuna system. By 1980, fifty villages had been formed in Darién and others developed in the direction of central Panama.

The Emberá and Wounaan received comarca status in 1983. The Comarca Emberá—locally called "Emberá Drua"—consists of two separate districts in Darién, Sambú, and Cemaco that cover 4,180 square kilometers of the Sambú and Chucunaque-Tuira basins. Some Spanish-speaking Blacks remain, but only one small non-Indian town is within the district. Today Emberá Drua has forty villages and over 8,000 indigenous inhabitants (83 percent Emberá, 16 percent Wounaan, and 1 percent other).

Settlements

The Emberá and the Wounaan historically lived in household settlements of one or more extended families. Houses were circular, unwalled, thatched-roof, post-and-pole structures, some as large as 15 to 20 meters in diameter, with split-palm floors elevated 1.5 meters or more above the ground. The houses were scattered along the levees and high alluvial terraces of clear water streams; intervening forests shielded neighbors from each others' view, thus forming loose clusters or "sectors" of closely related families along a river.

Today villages dominate the Emberá and Wounaan cultural landscape. Houses are smaller, commonly with board floors and partially divided interiors, and households usually consist of only one extended family. Most villages have a school, meeting hall, and a store or cooperative; many have a church, health center, and basketball court. Most villages have several hundred residents; the largest village, Unión Chocó—the comarca capital—has ninety households and about 600 inhabitants. Rain forest around the settlement has been replaced by cultivated fields and fallow.

Economy

Subsistence and Commercial Activities. The Emberá and Wounaan economy is largely a closed system united by family ties. Subsistence requires cooperation between households, and many tasks are performed communally. The historic previllage economy reflected the settlement pattern: one zone of levee lands contained the house site, animal pens, plantain and banana groves, and orchards and gardens of fruit trees and other useful plants; a forested barricade confined dooryard animals; and amid fallow lands and uncut forest patches was a patchwork of slash-and-burn plots on which grains and tubers, such as maize, rice, and yams, were cultivated. Gathering traditionally occurred close to home. Village organization caused spatial reorganization of subsistence activities. It may now take several hours to walk to fields; preferred hunting, fishing, and gathering spots are even farther. The concentration of people into villages has caused the overexploitation of forest nearby resources.

Spears, bows and arrows, blowguns, and darts were the Emberá and Wounaan hunting weapons until the shotgun and the .22-caliber rifle replaced them in the early twentieth century. Easier access to firearms attracted Indians from Colombia to Darién. The Indians are crack shots; in the previllage era, game depletion brought about settlement relocation. Fishing is done with nets, spears, arrows, traps, hooks; formerly, poisons were also used. Underwater spear fishing developed when diving masks became available in the mid-twentieth century. Freshwater shrimp and crabs are speared from river banks. Prehistoric animal husbandry was limited to the Muscovy duck and tamed forest animals. Today chickens and pigs have been introduced and they fit well into the economy; turkeys and Peking ducks are less prevalent. Dogs have been traditional domesticates; cats are more rare. The extraction of forest resources continues to provide fruits, nuts, roots, construction materials, weapons, dugouts, medicines, and ornaments.

Commercialism developed commensurately with the desire for Western products. The Indians have extracted rubber and other forest products, panned gold, and cut lumber for cash over the past 150 years. Pig husbandry also formerly provided cash. Banana and plantain cropping afforded them the first opportunity for sustained market production.

Industrial Arts. Indian women once fashioned beautiful ceramics, including huge vessels with anthropomorphic designs, in which *chicha* (beer) was stored. They still weave useful items from palms, including the carrying and storage baskets found in all households. Today beautiful palm-leaf baskets with intricate designs are made for the tourist trade. Men made spear shafts and points from palm wood. They fashion beautiful dugout canoes with distinctive bow platforms and carve hardwood into household benches, stools, and kitchen utensils. Some specialize in carving intricate figurines and shafts (*bastones*) for ritual use by shamans and for sale to tourists.

Trade. Bananas became a commercial crop during the 1930s, bringing Indians into the cash economy, but "Panama Disease" reduced production around 1960. Since then, plantains have been the most important cash crop sold to boat merchants who work between the capital and Darién's historic river towns—Sambú, Río Congo, La Palma, Chepigana, and Yaviza. The Pan-American Highway, which reached Darién during the 1970s, has become a focus of economic activity. The Indians have diversified their cash crops to include yams, maize, rice, avocados, oranges, and beans that they sell to truck merchants. The village economy centers on stores and cooperatives that sell merchandise that has become basic to the local inhabitants, including packaged foods, dry goods, tools, and toiletries.

Division of Labor. Men clear and plant the agricultural fields; women help with weeding and harvesting. Men cut and fashion trees and forest products for dugouts and house construction. A system of communal labor (*cambio de mano*) organizes kin for demanding tasks such as house construction. Hunting is a solitary male activity. Women fish with hooks and spear shrimp and crawfish near the village; Boys fish with nets, and also spearfish wearing diving masks. Men normally make cash transactions with outsiders. Women apply themselves to the domestic activities of cooking, sewing, basketry, pottery, and child care.

Land Tenure. Landownership develops with usufructuary rights; both men and women own land. Men normally prepare fields before marriage, but, because they often have traveled some distance to marry, fathers-in-law frequently give them land (Torres de Araúz 1966, 75). Today, with open farmland increasingly scarce and agricultural colonists pushing onto Indian lands, Indian families have begun to mark boundaries and want legal titles. The Comarca law (Ley #22 of 1983) recognizes indigenous land-tenure systems. The comarca's regulating document (Carta Orgánica, 1993) recognizes family, community, and "comarcal" landholdings and prohibits sale or lease of comarca lands to outsiders.

Kinship

Kin Groups and Descent. The exogamous group includes one's cousins. Historic Embará and Wounaan kinship was patrilineal.

Kinship Terminology. Embará kinship terms include *z'aware* (grandfather), *pa˜kore* (grandmother), *dádha* (father), *pápha* (mother), *dr'oa* (uncle), *apíphi* (aunt), *ahavha* or *shavha* (brother), *shavhawera* (sister), *oarra* (son), *káu* (daughter or cousin of the same sex), *wiuzake* (grandson), *ai-zake* (granddaughter), *kimá* (spouse), *wigú* (son-in-law), *aingú* (daughter-in-law), *waú* (brother-in-law), and *anyore* (sister-in-law) (Torres de Araúz 1966, 64-65; Cansarí et al. 1993, 15).

Marriage and Family

Marriage. Marriages were once largely segregated between Embará and Wounaan, but mixed marriages now occur. Marriages with outsiders, Blacks, or mestizos are still not common. Group endogamy provides cultural identity and solidarity. The incest-avoidance group includes one's children, brothers, sisters, cousins, and their offspring. Formerly, men sometimes had more than one wife, but monogamy is encouraged today. Approval by the girl's father is still a requisite for a marriage, which is consummated

when the suitor sleeps with his bride in the in-laws' house. Playful wrestling occurred between the bride's father or brothers and the groom (Torres de Araúz 1980, 178; Faron 1962). Patrilocal residence and patrilineal clans formerly assembled relatives along riverine sectors. Today there are many different postmarital residence patterns. Patrilocal or matrilocal residence is usually limited to the time that a new house is being constructed for the couple. The new Carta Orgánica institutionalizes marriages under the authority of village leaders and requires one to be 18 years old and to marry another Embará or Wounaan no closer than "one-fourth degree of blood relations." When divorce occurs, children normally stay with the mother.

Domestic Unit. The household, today averaging six or seven individuals, serves as the basic domestic group in Embará and Wounaan society. It usually includes one or more couples and their offspring. The household is traditionally directed by the male family head. Subsistence requires group cooperation, and the household continues as the economic, food-sharing unit.

Inheritance. Transfer and inheritance of land and property take place, as traditionally, along kin lines, mostly between males of the same household.

Socialization. Children learn traditions and economic skills through apprenticeship alongside their parents and grandparents. Young children accompany parents during daily chores; by the time they reach 10 years of age, they are contributing their work. Most villages now have elementary schools where children receive primary education. Embará or Wounaan teachers now account for 35 percent of the comarca's teachers, and bilingual instruction is developing. No villages have high schools, but many students attend high schools in non-Indian towns. University education still lies beyond the economic reach of most people.

Sociopolitical Organization

Social Organization. Traditional Embará and Wounaan social structure was egalitarian. The highest authority was the head of the family, who allocated household resources and settled disputes. Both shamans and elders were respected for their knowledge but held no special status.

Political Organization. Historically, no formal tribal leaders, chiefs, councils, or organizations of elders existed. Kin groups along riverine sectors were sometimes guided by a small group of esteemed elders. The Embará and Wounaan were not territorial, those of Panama now have developed a ranked, chief-congress (*cacique congreso*) type of political organization, similar to that of the Kuna, which centers on the semiautonomous comarca and its elected traditional leaders and government officials. Comarca authorities, as defined in the Carta Organica, include village leaders (nokoes in Embará/chi pör in Wounaan) and community police (zarra/papan). Each comarca district has an advisory panel (consejo de nokorã/chi pörnaan) and chief (dadyirã boro/maach pör). A general chief (jumara boro/t'umaam k'n pör) is elected for a term of five years. A general congress meets every other year with delegates from each community. This democratic body is the maximum decision-making body. Regional congresses are held annually in each district, local congresses more frequently at the village level. The comarca also elects government officials, including the governor and national legislators.

Other federations have formed to address territorial, political, economic, and cultural concerns outside the comarca. The Indigenous Organization of Collective Emberá and Wounan Lands (OITCEW) fights for territorial control in the Río Balsas and along the Pan-American Highway. Other groups form in defense of Indians in the Congo and Bayano basins. Indian lands are also circumscribed by the Darién Biosphere Reserve and Mogue Forest Reserve, where Emberá and Wounaan groups struggle for land rights while confronted with state conservation goals.

Social Control. The family head normally settles domestic disputes, but crimes, land conflict, and other issues are increasingly regulated by comarca and state authorities, laws, and regulations.

Conflict. The Emberá and Wounaan were once the bitter enemies of the Kuna but now align with them for indigenous self-determination. Perhaps the most serious threat to Indian life comes from the advance of agricultural colonists and from profiteers invading Indian lands via the extension of the Pan-American Highway.

Religious and Expressive Culture

Religious Beliefs. According to Mennonite missionary Jacob Loewen (1975, 129–132), the Emberá and Wounaan make no distinction between the physical and the metaphysical or between the material and the spiritual, believing that humans, animals, plants, and even natural phenomena have _jai_—generally sexless, amorphous spirits or souls that may or may not be harmful. They are the carriers of witchcraft but also the shaman's tools for both good and evil. Two personified spirit powers stand in an antithetical relationship to each other: Ewandama is the good, the creator god; Tiauru is the mischievous or evil opponent. Missionary activity, from Baptists, Mennonites, and Catholics, has greatly changed religious beliefs since the 1950s. Most Indians acknowledge Christian concepts of sin, heaven, and hell but maintain past beliefs and traditions.

Religious Practitioners. Certain religious beliefs center on the shaman (_jaibaná_ in Emberá/_bënk'ʌʌn_ in Wounaan), who, with knowledge of the medicinal, toxic, and hallucinogenic properties of plants and animals, cures with herbal remedies and by exorcising spirits. The intervention of _jai_ is decisive for determining the causal agent of sickness. Shamans can contact these spirits to improve, alter, or worsen life's conditions. Their powers are sought to "open" rivers for settlement by "cleansing" them of evil spirits and dangers. They are not full-time specialists, and only men apprentice as shamans.

Ceremonies. Girls were formerly secluded within the house during their first menstruation; their hair was cut short, and they followed dietary restrictions. Afterward, they were bathed, painted with jagua, and honored with a chicha celebration. No formal marriage ceremonies existed. Today simple celebrations accompany life-cycle events, including baptisms, marriages, deaths, harvests, or the completion of communal work. The villagers play music, dance, and drink large quantities of maize or sugarcane chicha.

Before the dead are buried in village cemeteries, they are wrapped in parumas and placed in small dugouts or wooden caskets for visitation.

Arts. Men play flutes and small drums to accompany women in dances and songs named after and mimicking rain-forest animals.

Medicine. The Emberá and Wounaan continue to use botanical remedies from garden and forest plants for insecticides, purgatives, sedatives, diuretics, and disinfectants (Torres de Araúz 1980, 185). Today health centers with trained health assistants are increasingly common. The comarca had fourteen communities with health centers and twelve Indian health assistants in 1987. Most centers, however, lacked medical supplies, and doctors rarely visit.

Death and Afterlife. The Emberá and Wounaan believe that human souls become spirits in the land "where Ewandama is," but should a soul fail to turn right after death, it will end up in a dark and treacherous place. Incest, sex with Blacks, and child beating are three unpardonable "sins" that cause one's spirit to become harmful (Loewen 1975, 129–132).

Bibliography

Botero, Livia Correa (1982). _Aprendamos embará._ Medellín: Misineras de Santa Teresita.

Cansarí, Rogelio, Daniel Castañeda, and William Harp (1993). _Estudio socio-cultural en tres regiones del Darién: Río Balsas, Sambú y Garachiné: Un análisis cultural de las comunidades al margen de la Reserva de la Biosfera Darién._ Panama City: N.p.

Faron, Louis C. (1962). "Marriage, Residence, and Domestic Group among the Panamanian Chocó." _Ethnology_ 1:13–38.

Herlihy, Peter H. (1986). "A Cultural Geography of the Emberá and Wounan (Chocó) Indians of Darién, Panama, with Emphasis on Recent Village Formation and Economic Diversification." Ph.D. dissertation, Louisiana State University.

Kane, Stephanie (1986). "Emberá (Chocó) Village Formation: The Politics and Magic of Everyday Life in the Darién Forest." Ph.D. dissertation, University of Texas.

Loewen, Jacob A. (1963). "Chocó I: Introduction and Bibliography." _International Journal of American Linguistics_ 29(3): 239–263.

Loewen, Jacob A. (1975). _Culture and Human Values: Christian Intervention in Anthropological Perspective._ Pasadena, Calif.: William Carey Library.

Ortega Ricaurte, Enrique, and Ana Rueda Briceño (1954). Publicaciones del Departamento de Biblioteca y Archivos Nacionales, vol. 24. _Historia documental de Chocó._ Bogotá: Editorial Kelly.

Pinto Garcia, Constancio (1978). _Lo indios katios: Su_

cultura—su lengua. Vol. 1, *La cultura katia*. Medellín: Pedro Grau Arola, C.M.F.

Reichel-Dolmatoff, Geraldo (1960). "Notas etnográficas sobre los indios del Chocó." *Revista Colombiana de Antropología* 9:73–158.

Reichel-Dolmatoff, Geraldo (1963). "Contribuciones a la etnografía de los indios del Chocó." *Revista Colombiana de Antropología* 11:169–188.

Romoli, Kathleen (1987). *Los de la lengua de Cueva: Los grupos indígenas del istmo oriental en la época de la conquista española*. Bogotá: Instituto Colombiano de Cultura.

Torres de Araúz, Reina (1966). *Estudio etnológico e histórico de la cultura chocó*. Centro de Investigaciones Antropológicas de la Universidad de Panamá. Publicación especial no. 1. Panama City: Universidad de Panamá.

Torres de Araúz, Reina (1980). *Panamá indígena*. Panama City: Instituto Nacional de Cultura/Patrimonio Histórico.

Vargas Sarmiento, Patricia (1993). *Los emberá y los cuna: Impacto y reacción ante la ocupación española siglos XVI y XVII*. Bogotá: Editorial Presencia.

Vasco, Luis Guillermo (1985). *Jaibanás los verdaderos hombres*. Bogotá: Talleres Gráficos Banco Popular.

Wali, Alaka (1989). *Kilowatts and Crisis: Hydroelectric Power and Social Dislocation in Eastern Panama*. Boulder, Colo.: Westview Press.

Wassén, Henry (1935). "Notes on Southern Groups of Chocó Indians in Colombia." *Etnologiska Studier* 1:35–182.

PETER H. HERLIHY

French Antillians

ETHNONYMS: none

The French Antilles is a group of islands (total area, 1,880 square kilometers) in the Caribbean that are governed by two separate *French départments d'outremer*. The department of Guadeloupe governs the islands of Guadeloupe (16°15′ N, 61°30′ W), Saint Barthélemy (17°55′ N, 63°50′ W), Marie Galante (15°57′ N, 61°20′ W), the French part of Saint Martin (Sint Maarten) and the nearby smaller islands of Les Saintes and La Désirade through a prefect appointed in Paris; the total 1994 population in this department is 428,000. The department of Martinique governs the island of Martinique (14°36′ N, 61°05′ W), also through a prefect appointed in France; the total population is over 340,000. Both departments have popularly elected legislatures of thirty-six members, as well as locally elected senators and deputies to the French Parliament. The judicial and monetary systems are French. The official language is French, but most everyday conversation takes place in a local creole that has some African grammatical structures but much French vocabulary. The racial/ethnic makeup of the islands reflects the importance of earlier African slavery: the population is 90 percent Black, 5 percent White, and 5 percent Lebanese, Chinese, or East Indian.

The islands did not attract much early attention from the Spanish because they were defended by the Carib Indians. The French later colonized them, imported slaves, and turned them into important sugar producers. Britain sought them for their sugar, but France managed to keep these islands, although they lost several others to Britain in the Napoleonic wars. The islands' slaves were freed in 1848. The status of the islands was changed in 1946 from that of colonies to that of departments. The major sources of income are construction, cement, and rum and oil refining. Tourism is becoming more important, although the facts that few people speak English and that prices are higher than on other Carribean islands hinders this development.

Bibliography

Burton, Richard D. E., and Fred Reno, eds. (1995). *French and West Indian: Martinique, Guadeloupe, and French Guiana Today*. Charlottesville: University Press of Virginia.

Dauty, Denise, and Monique Potier (1975). *Guadeloupe et Martinique: Bibliographie: Tendences des recherches en sciences humaines et en médecine, 1945–1975*. Paris: École des Hautes Études en Sciences Sociale, Centre Charles Richet.

Garifuna

ETHNONYMS: Black Carib, Island Carib, Garinagu, Karaphuna

Orientation

Identification. The term "Garifuna," or on Dominica, "Karaphuna," is a modern adaptation of the name applied to some Amerindians of the Caribbean and South America at the time of Columbus. That term—"Garif," and its alternate, "Carib"—are derivatives of the same root. The label "Black" derives from the fact that during the sixteenth to eighteenth centuries considerable admixture occurred with Africans whom they captured, or who otherwise escaped being enslaved by Europeans.

Location. Modern-day Garifuna live mostly in Central America, in a series of villages and towns along the Caribbean coastline of Belize, Guatemala, Honduras, and Nicaragua. Many have emigrated to the United States, where they live in large colonies in New York, Chicago, Los Angeles, and several other cities. Small groups survive in Trinidad, Dominica, and Saint Vincent. Although all of them recognize a distant kinship, the Central American and Caribbean groups are virtually distinct today.

Linguistic Affiliation. In spite of their name, their language is basically of the Arawakan Family, although there is a heavy overlay of Cariban, which may once have been a pidgin trading language for them. Linguists term their language Island Carib to distinguish it from Carib as it is spoken among groups ancestral to them still living in the Amazon area of South America.

Demography. Historical sources indicate that only about 2,000 Carib survived warfare with the British to become established in Central America in 1797. Because they reside in so many different countries, and because they are not counted as a distinct ethnic group except in Belize, it is difficult to state how many there may be today. Estimates vary from 200,000 to 500,000; high fertility rates and the absorption into their communities of many other Blacks in the Americas helped boost their population over the last 200 years.

History and Cultural Relations

Archaeologists have still not been able to sort out with precision the cultural history of the various Caribbean groups, except to note that all of them apparently derived from the tropical forests of South America, coming into the Caribbean in at least three waves, dating from about 5000 B.C. to about A.D. 1400. At the time of Columbus, the ancestors of the Garifuna occupied most of the habitable islands of the Lesser Antilles, but by the eighteenth century they were primarily found on Saint Vincent, Dominica, Saint Lucia, and Grenada. For Europeans, the term "Carib" became synonymous with "cannibal," and allegations about such activities formed the justification for killing or enslaving them in the fifteenth and sixteenth centuries. Once agricultural plantations had been established by the various Europeans, Africans were brought in

large numbers as laborers. On Saint Vincent, from the time of the first major British occupation in 1763, the Garifuna sided with the previously resident French colonists in a protracted conflict that ultimately ended in defeat for both of them. In 1797 those with the darkest skin color, (termed "Black Carib") mostly resident on Saint Vincent, were forcibly removed from that island and sent to Spanish Honduras. Many of the lighter-skinned individuals remained in the islands; most were absorbed into the local Creole populations. In Central America the Garifuna joined the Spaniards and at first fought against, but later temporarily joined, the Miskito Indians, who were firmly aligned with the British in opposition to the dominant Spanish colonization. They were quick to adopt whatever innovations they admired in other groups, so that today their culture is a new synthesis, unlike any of its immediate forbears.

Settlements

In aboriginal and early contact times, settlements were on the windward sides of the various islands, whereas gardens were inland on more fertile soil. The earliest houses were circular, and each was inhabited by a woman, her unmarried daughters, and her small sons. Teenage boys and men spent most of their time in centrally located communal houses, where they ate; slept; debated political decisions; made and repaired weapons, tools and utensils; and entertained guests. In Central America they have repeated this settlement pattern, except that they have favored locations close to European settlements and enterprises in which the men could find wage labor and the women could sell their agricultural produce. Today they live in some sixty settlements on the coastline between Gracias a Dios in Nicaragua and Dangriga, Belize. Some of these still harbor only Garifuna, but others are multiethnic towns and cities. In the United States the Garifuna do not necessarily cluster in the same city neighborhoods, although they remain in close contact with their fellows, especially Garifuna coming from the same country.

Economy

Subsistence and Commercial Activities. The Island Carib were fishers, hunters of small land animals, collectors of shellfish, and horticulturists; both sexes participated equally in food production. Only men engaged in offshore fishing and hunting, whereas the women were largely in charge of the fields after the initial clearing. Bitter manioc was the primary staple, of which the Garifuna made a flat, unleavened bread that, when properly stored, would keep for weeks and could be carried on the long sea voyages the men frequently made to other islands and to the South American mainland. Trading and raiding were important activities that often kept the men away for long periods of time. After the arrival of Europeans, the Carib began to trade with them and to sell their labor. They also turned increasingly to plantation agriculture of commercial crops, such as cotton, and, by the time they were deported from Saint Vincent, they seemed well on their way to dependence upon a cash economy. In Central America they were at first in great demand as mercenary soldiers for both the Royalists and the revolutionary Creole forces.

They also worked in the mahogany camps in Belize, Honduras, and Nicaragua, both before and after independence in those areas.

After 1900, when the fruit industry had become the major employer along the coast, they worked as stevedores and in various semiskilled occupations in the major banana ports. During World War II many men worked in the U.S. merchant marine, which led them to seek continued employment in this sector later. This started what has become a migratory stream, with some individuals returning periodically to their home villages until final retirement there and others settling permanently in the United States. The second generation has produced many teachers, physicians, and engineers—professions they follow both in the United States and in their home countries. The largest part of the population, however, remains in the underemployed working-class sector. Women joined the men as migrants during the 1960s, most working as seamstresses, factory workers, or domestics in the large cities of the United States and Central America. The village economies have been bolstered by the remittances sent home to relatives, but little capital has been invested there. Many communities are largely made up of older folk and young children living on irregular and inadequate checks sent by the absent intervening generation.

Industrial Arts. Aboriginal craft products included baskets, cotton cloth, sleeping mats, pottery, and a variety of wooden utensils, including graters for manioc, drums, and dugout canoes. All of these have survived in Central America except pottery, which was replaced by European earthenware and porcelain, probably during the eighteenth century in Saint Vincent. Most of the crafts have been forgotten today, and only a handful of persons in the more remote villages still manufacture the other items.

Trade. Although most scholars believe the Carib engaged in extensive trade in aboriginal times, it is not clear what products they exchanged. During the eighteenth century they were known among European residents in the Caribbean for their silk-grass woven bags, baskets, tobacco, fruits and vegetables, and various forest products. In Central America the women regularly appeared in town markets with superior agricultural produce, and the men sold fish, both fresh and dried. Their reputation as smugglers of arms, liquor, bullion, and consumer goods has survived to the present day.

Division of Labor. Women in aboriginal times were the primary farmers, dependent upon the men only for clearing the land. Women also caught land crabs and other shellfish, cared for pigs and chickens (known only after the arrival of Europeans), prepared the food, cared for the children, and wove cotton cloth and fiber mats on hanging looms. Men fished and hunted, made canoes, and engaged in trading and raiding excursions. They were also largely in charge of the ceremonial life, including public ritual and curing. After the middle of the twentieth century, women left behind while the men migrated took on more and more of the men's responsibilities. Today they are dominant in religious and curing rituals and ceremonies. Women have long enjoyed considerable independence of word and action. They are, in general, as well or better educated than the men and have begun to enter political life and some of the professions in their countries of origin.

Land Tenure. Because their agriculture was largely of a shifting nature, land tenure has not been a major issue for the Island Carib or the Garifuna. So long as there was sufficient land and a small population, tenure was determined by "first come." The very concept of landownership was problematic for them aboriginally, which no doubt worked against them in making treaties with the Europeans. Not until the twentieth century did land scarcity become an issue in Central America, and by then most of the Garifuna were adapted to an economy supported by male wage labor.

Kinship

Kin Groups and Descent. Both kinship terminology and early accounts suggest the former existence of a matrilineally oriented system, but it is not clear whether there were clans or sibs. Early European contacts seem to have altered the aboriginal system. Today they have informal nonunilineal kin associations, active primarily in religious activities and in mutual aid for domestic purposes.

Kinship Terminology. Modern usage is Hawaiian when using the native language, but the Eskimo system of their neighbors is more prevalent.

Marriage and Family

Marriage. The Island Carib may have preferred marriage between cross cousins, and men of higher rank were polygynous. Chiefs excepted, residence was uxorilocal. Today marriage is informal and brittle. Women commonly bear children before a permanent union is established, with or without a legal or religious ceremony. In both aboriginal and modern times, male travelers frequently had wives in more than one location.

Domestic Unit. What has been called the matrifocal household has been typical since at least the 1940s. This formerly was extended through at least three generations of women, but since the 1970s, probably owing to the massive emigration of both men and women, has often been reduced to a grandmother and her grandchildren under the age of puberty. Among more highly educated and affluent Garifuna, monogamy and the nuclear family are highly valued.

Inheritance. Modern Garifuna tend to dispose of their private movable property in the form of gifts to favored persons if and when they feel death is imminent. They favor children or grandchildren who have remained at home to care for them or who have sent back larger sums of money. To control the behavior of their descendants, older people commonly threaten to withhold an inheritance or to dispose of all their property before death.

Socialization. Boys are raised permissively until early manhood, when they are suddenly shoved out of the maternal fold and expected to earn their own living as well as to support their mothers and sisters. Girls are required to "grow up" more quickly—to work at domestic tasks at an early age—and are more severely reprimanded when they transgress. In the absence of the men, women seem to have more difficulty disciplining their sons.

Sociopolitical Organization

Political Organization. Prior to contact with Europeans, there may have been incipient chiefdoms. Leaders were men who excelled in warfare or in supernatural affairs—the older ones usually having greater prestige. In European-colonized Saint Vincent and Central America, these leaders were endowed with greater derivative authority than they may have had aboriginally. Presently, the Garifuna engage in political action within their own countries but do not yet vote as an ethnic block. Few have achieved either elective or appointive office at any level, but recent revitalization efforts may change this.

Social Control. Persons who act in socially deviant ways may be subjected to public criticism, frequently in song or proverb. More serious infringements may be referred to the ancestors in religious rituals. The ancestors, when they assume human form by possessing a descendant, may loudly chastise the culprit and even call him or her to a face-to-face confrontation. Withcraft, which is most often directed toward outsiders, is a force to be feared.

Conflict. The Island Carib were in an almost constant state of war against each other, against Arawakan groups in the Greater Antilles, and, later, against Africans and Europeans. After deportation to Central America, they hired themselves out as mercenaries and also engaged in isolated conflicts with Miskito Indians. Since the middle of the nineteenth century, however, they have largely eschewed violence in both their public and private lives.

Religion and Expressive Culture

Religious Beliefs. Both Island Carib and modern Garifuna believe that human affairs are governed by a higher god, but also by the spirits of their deceased ancestors, whom they both love and fear. Since the nineteenth century, most have also been Roman Catholic. In addition to the ancestors, the shamans call upon "spirit helpers," who assist them in curing and locating lost objects. There may have been a belief in nature spirits in previous times, but today these have been replaced by a faith in Catholic saints and angels.

Religious Practitioners. Called _buwiyes_, shamans are born to their calling, receiving training through dreams and apprenticeships. A very few have become Roman Catholic priests and nuns.

Ceremonies. In addition to the usual Catholic rites, Garifuna have included some prayers and other rituals in their ceremonies in honor of their ancestors. They also sacrifice pigs and roosters, dance, sing, beat drums, and ritually drink alcohol in an effort to get the ancestors to pay attention to them and to assist them in their human trials and tribulations. Several other ritual occasions are celebrated during the year, but these are all taken from either the Catholic calendar or British secular observances. "John Canoe" is an important dance performance during Christmas and the New Year.

Arts. Dancing and singing are the primary means of artistic expression, as they were aboriginally.

Medicine. A wide range of bush medicines is known and used by most Garifuna today, both at home and in their U.S. urban homes. They also respect and use modern Western medicine when they deem it appropriate, but when all else fails, they refer their illnesses to the ancestors, who can either save or doom them.

Death and Afterlife. All Garifuna anticipate a continuing interaction with their loved ones after death. They believe that if not properly propitiated, the dead ancestors can wreak great harm upon them, and they look forward to having such power in their own hands.

Bibliography

Gonzalez, Nancie L. (1988). _Sojourners of the Caribbean: Ethnogenesis and Ethnohistory of the Garifuna_. Urbana: University of Illinois Press.

Gullick, C. J. M. R. (1985). _Myths of a Minority_. Assen: Van Gorcum Press.

Kerns, Virginia (1983). _Women and the Ancestors: Black Carib Kinship and Ritual_. Urbana: University of Illinois Press.

Whitehead, Neil L. (1988). _Lords of the Tiger Spirit_. Leiden: Foris Publications Holland.

NANCIE L. GONZALEZ

Grenadians

ETHNONYMS: none

Grenada is an island nation of 84,000 people (1992) located at 12°10′ N and 61°40′ W, making it the most southerly of the Windward Islands. It maintains a nearly constant average temperature of 29° C year-round, and precipitation is generally plentiful (150 centimeters in the lowlands to more than 350 centimeters on the windward mountainsides).

Besides the island of Grenada itself, there are several hundred small islands belonging to the country, although only two, Carriacou and Petit Martinique, have significant populations; the nation's total land area is 344 square kilometers. The population has remained stable since 1980 because although the birthrate is high, many people emigrate to other Caribbean islands, Canada, Britain, and the United States in search of employment. All but 9 percent of the population is Black, descendants of African slaves brought by the French and the British to work on plantations. Sixty-five percent of the population is Catholic, and the remaining 35 percent is Anglican, Presbyterian, and Methodist. Political and economic power has long rested with an elite group of White and light-skinned people who constitute no more than 5 percent of the population. In 1992 infant mortality was 28 per thousand, and life expectancy was 69 years for females and 74 years for males.

Grenada was originally populated by the Carib Indians. It was briefly in the hands of the Spanish, who gave it its name. Later, it was settled by the French, who conquered the Carib and who grew indigo and sugar. The British conquered the island in 1762. As a result of the Seven Years' War, Grenada became French from 1779 to 1783, at which time the Treaty of Versailles returned it to Britain. Many people remained loyal to the French, however, and some of them attacked the British settlers in what came to be designated the Rebellion of 1795. English is presently the official language, but some people still speak a French patois. Universal adult franchise was instituted in 1950 and led to the election of Eric Matthew Gairy, who appealed to the interests of the peasantry. With the exception of one brief period, Gairy held power until 1979, when Maurice Bishop came to power in a coup. He promised employment, food, housing, education, and free elections, although he quickly suspended the constitution and instituted laws designed to suppress free expression of political ideas. His socialist polices largely failed owing to the inability of Grenada to attract foreign investment. An internal government power struggle in 1983 cost Bishop his life and allowed more radical Marxists to take control. Popular resentment of the new government led to popular uprisings and, on 25 October 1983, U.S. military intervention. The constitution and popular elections were restored; Herbert Blaize served as prime minister from 1984 to 1990, and Nicholas Braithwaite assumed the post in 1990. Although politically independent, Grenada maintains the British monarch as head of state.

The gross domestic product has been rising since 1984. Since the removal of the Marxists, emphasis has been placed upon privatization of wealth and industry, with the aim of attracting foreign investors and increased production for export. A new airport has also been opened in the capital city of Saint George's, which has increased tourism and exports. The traditional base of the economy has long been the export of mace and nutmeg, which has earned Grenada the nickname "the Spice Isle." The buyers of most of Grenada's products are the United States, Britain, and the Caribbean and European economic communities.

Bibliography

Brizan, George I. (1984). *Grenada, Island of Conflict: From Amerindians to People's Revolution, 1498–1979*. London: Zed Books.

Smith, M. G. (1965). *Stratification in Grenada*. Berkeley and Los Angeles: University of California Press.

Steele, Beverley A. (1983). *Grenada Bibliography*. Marryshow House Publications, no. 2. St. George's: University of the West Indies, Grenada, Extra Mural Dept.

Guadeloupians

ETHNONYMS: none

"Guadeloupe" is the name given to a group of four islands, which together are administered by the French government as the department of Guadeloupe. The main island of Guadeloupe is situated at 16°15′ N and 61°30′ W, and the other three islands—Saint Barthélemy, Marie Galante, and Les Saintes—are located to the south and east. Geologically, Guadeloupe is a low-lying limestone formation with a total land area of 1,780 square kilometers.

The 1990 population of 342,175 was 90 percent Black, 5 percent White, and 5 percent East Indian, Lebanese, or Chinese. The languages spoken are French and a creole patois. Ninety-five percent of the population are members of the Catholic church, and the remaining five percent are Hindus or adhere to an African faith.

Guadeloupe was originally inhabited by Carib Indians, who called it "Karukera," or "island of beautiful waters." Columbus was the first European to see the island group, and it was he who gave it its modern name, after the Spanish Virgin of Guadalupe. The French settled the island beginning in 1635 and began to import slaves to work in the sugar industry in 1650. Following the French Revolution, there were riots leading to the killing of landowners and the abolition of slavery. The French reimposed slavery in 1802 to improve sugar production, and when slavery was permanently abolished in 1848, the island's economy faltered for lack of labor.

Today the economy is dependent on tourists, most of whom are French. The islands produce sugarcane, rum, flowers, and bananas, primarily for the French market.

The government is led by a prefect appointed by the federal government in Paris. There is also a popularly elected legislature of thirty-six members. Guadeloupe sends deputies and senators to the French parliament. The judicial system is French.

Bibliography

Bebel-Gisler, Dany, and Laennec Hurbon (1987). *Cultures et pouvoir dans la Caraïbe: Langue creole, vaudou, secte religieuse en Guadeloupe et en Haïti*. 3rd ed. Paris: L'Harmattan.

Bonniol, Jean-Luc (1980). *Terre-de-haut des saintes: Contraintes insulaires et particularisme ethnique dans la Caraïbe*. Paris: Editions Caribéennes.

Leiris, Michel (1987). *Contacts de civilizations en Martinique et en Guadeloupe*. Paris: Gallimard; UNESCO.

Moutoussamy, Ernest (1987). *La Guadeloupe et son indienité*. Paris: Editions Caribéennes.

Guarijío

ETHNONYMS: Guarijio, Guarogíos, Huarijio, Varohío, Varohíos, Varojíos, Warijío, Warijíos

Orientation

Identification. The Guarijío are a semidispersed group of Indians living in the mountains of the state of Sonora, Mexico. They are subsistence farmers with a native political organization based primarily on religious festivals. They are located between the Mayo to the west and the Tarahumara to east.

Location. The Guarijío live in the _municipios_ of Quiriego and Alamos Sonora in the state of Sonora. They inhabit mountainous areas, ravines, and the Valley of the Alto Río Mayo. The Guarijío communities are Guajaray, San Bernardo, Sejaqui, Burapaco, Mochibampo, Mesa Colorada, and Bavícora. Their lands extend from 26°31' to 28°20' N and from 107°00' to 108°37' W.

According to Köppen's classification, the area's climate is of the BSHW type, that is, dry with moderate rainfall in the summer and a mean annual temperature greater than 18° C. The highest recorded temperature is 40.5° C, indicating high thermal instability and extreme variation.

Demography. In such eroded terrain, without natural or cultural resources to attract people, isolated from communication routes, and at great distances from important production and distribution centers, population growth is slow. The 1990 census recorded 1,190 Guarijío in Sonora.

Linguistic Affiliation. The Guarijío language belongs to the Taracahitan Branch of the Uto-Aztecan Language Family. Their language is most closely related to Tarahumaran.

History and Cultural Relations

During the colonization and evangelization of northwestern Mexico, Guarijío lands bordered the Mayo territory, to the west, and the Tarahumara territory, to the south and east. The evangelization process, begun in the 1620s, was laborious; it took some time before the Guarijío accepted the Jesuits, and a mission was established at Chínipas under the direction of Father Juan Castini. He was aware that although the Guarijío had accepted the mission, they had not given up their "pagan" rites.

In 1632, dissatisfied with the missionaries, the Guarijío belonging to the Chínipas group allied themselves with the Guazapares and rebelled against the Jesuits. Many missionaries were massacred, and mission property was burned or otherwise destroyed. As a result, repressive measures were put into effect by the viceroy, who sent military forces into the region to punish the rebels.

Thereupon, the Jesuits decided to incorporate the Chínipas Indians into the missions of the Pueblos Sinaloas, leaving the Guarijío in their own area. Later the Guarijío dispersed, taking different directions; some joined the Sinaloans, others joined unconverted groups, and the great majority went up into the nearby Sierra Tarahumara. It may be concluded that there was a west-east displacement of the "Guarijío tribe," that is to say, from the slopes of the Sierra de Alamos and Quiriego toward the Sierra Alta of the municipios of Sonora and parts of the state of Chihuahua.

It is because of that displacement that the Guarijío are divided into two groups, the Sonoran and the Chihuahua. The latter has merged with the Tarahumara and has adopted their customs. Despite the common cultural heritage, there are no relations between the two Guarijío groups today, and they have developed dialectal variations; the Guarijío of Sonora can now communicate better in their maternal language with the Mayo than with the Guarijío of Chihuahua. Those of Sonora now call themselves "the real Guarijío."

Another explanation of the current distribution of the Guarijío is that they split off from the Tarahumara, moved from east to west, and mingled with the Mayo. These theories can be confirmed or rejected only after further detailed archaeological investigations in the area.

Settlements

Guarijío settlements are dispersed, with the exception of the capitals of the municipios and Bavícora, Mesa Colorada, and Mochibampo. In the municipio of Alamos, the majority of the tribe lives in small hamlets of two or three houses.

Traditional Guarijío living quarters are rectangular, with a single room made of adobe, an earthen floor, and a flat roof. Another style of dwelling has a roof made of palm fronds and walls made of saguaro trunks daubed with mud. An open kitchen is generally built to one side of the living quarters. Cooking is done on a raised surface. Most dwellings have a porch that is used as a place where people rest and breathe in the fresh air. Not infrequently, the porches are used as places to sleep.

Economy

Subsistence and Commercial Activities. The Guarijío raise crops on unirrigated land, care for cattle, gather wild fruit, hunt, fish, and trade. Important crops are maize, beans, and sesame. As a whole, the soil is typical for mountainous areas, characterized by clayey, crumbly earth (_migajones_) and sandy clay. The uneven topography and the soil's structure and composition make extensive irrigation impossible, and mechanization is of little use in agriculture. Moreover, the sloping terrain has led to soil erosion, caused mainly by water runoff from the slopes, creating numerous deep gullies and making the land more uneven.

A traditional form of slash-and-burn agriculture continues to be practiced. Most fields are located on the lower slopes of hills. To open a field, the Guarijío cut the vegetation, let it dry, and burn it; the ashes serve as fertilizer.

Fields appropriate for planting are called _magüeches_. On terrain where it is not possible to use oxen for opening a furrow, a metal rod is used for planting. With it a small hole is made in the earth, into which the seeds are dropped; the hole is then covered with a small amount of earth so as not to slow germination. Magüeches are used only for three years because, at the end of that time, the land is exhausted; another plot is chosen.

Industrial Arts. Manufacturing plays an important role in the Guarijío economy; it is considered a subsistence activity. The Guarijío produce sleeping mats, hats, rawhide shoulder bags, small boxes or cases, harps, and violins. The Guarijío also make a simple kind of pottery that lacks patterns or designs. The more common kind of wares are large water-storage pots, griddles for making tortillas, and dishes; all are handmade and fired in underground ovens. Generally produced solely for personal use, these items are rarely sold.

Trade. Owing to the geographical location of Guarijío territory, regional commerce is light. In the 1990s, under the auspices of government programs, the Guarijío have been able to market some of their products (honey, sesame seeds, and *chiltepín* peppers) and to raise cattle, the latter being their main source of income. Each family owns a number of animals, either cattle or mules.

Division of Labor. Activities are divided on the basis of sex. Among activities falling within men's domain are preparing plots for cultivation, herding, tending cattle, working outside the community as migrant laborers in the Yaqui and Mayo valleys, and mule driving. Men's work also includes gathering firewood, collecting food, planting, and harvesting. Women prepare food, fetch water, care for their children, weave mats, and sew. They also make tortillas and cook. Women procure palm fronds for weaving and build the huts. Many women help their husbands with agricultural work. Girls and boys carry water, do chores, and, when they are older, help in caring for their smaller siblings. They feed domestic animals and help with work in the milpa (maize field).

Land Tenure. Today the Guarijío possess 25,000 hectares of land granted to them on 3 February 1981 in the form of the ejidos of Guarijío, Los Conejos, and Burapaco.

Kinship

The Guarijío have a system of *compadrazgo*, which is considered to be as close a relationship as actual kinship. There are various kinds of compadrazgo: "water compadrazgo" (sponsoring a child's baptism), "political compadrazgo" (sponsoring the first cutting of a child's hair), (3) "blanket compadrazgo" (helping to cure a child's illness).

To create "water" *compadres*, the parents of a child seek godparents for its baptism. The godparents become the compadres of the parents and take upon themselves both moral and material obligations toward the godchild. They try to fulfill these obligations as well as their means permit. The godparents of the firstborn are usually their grandparents.

Others chosen to become compadres are highly esteemed relatives and friends or people who are financially well off. Godparents may be White, mestizo, or indigenous. Compadres treat each other with a great deal of courtesy and respect, and children think of their godparents as relatives who deserve their esteem.

When this type of relationship of trust is established, the polite form of Spanish address, *usted,* is used. Compadres visit frequently and call each other by kinship terms.

Marriage and Family

Marriage. Men usually marry between the ages of 16 and 20, women, between ages 14 and 16—that is to say, earlier among the Guarijío than among mestizos. When a daughter marries or goes to live with a man, her parents, depending on their financial situation, will give her a dowry, which generally consists of cattle or beasts of burden. This is done so she will not be poor. The custom of "bride theft"—especially when there is not enough money for a proper marriage—is widespread. The couple agree to a particular night on which the young woman will leave her paternal home and go off with her future husband.

Marriages are ideally endogamous, but nowadays there are exogamous marriages as well. Women marry basically out of moral and social considerations. Men marry to find a partner—a wife whose help will leave them free to pursue the economic activities required to maintain an independent family unit. Second marriages and adultery are common and more easily accepted than in modern, Westernized Mexican society.

Domestic Unit. Residence patterns and family structure are nuclear and patriarchal. Within the family, the father is an authority figure, and on him rests all the responsibility for making family decisions. The average number of children per family is around seven.

Inheritance. The family does not act as an economic collectivity, but, because of its patriarchal structure, control over certain means of production does rest with the head of the family. Upon his death, this control and concomitant authority pass to the son he has chosen to succeed him.

Socialization. Guarijío women breast-feed their children as long as they demand it or until another child is born. As infants grow older they are given more solid food in conjunction with breast-feeding. When a child begins to sit up, he or she is left on the ground to learn to sit, stand, and crawl alone. Mothers, fathers, or siblings guide children; women are in charge of educating them. Children of school age are needed to perform agricultural chores.

Sociopolitical Organization

Social Organization. Guarijío social structure is still guided by rules reflecting a spirit of communality. There is little status or social stratification, and Guarijío isolation and disposition have given them the self-assurance to safeguard their cultural identity and values.

Political Organization. A governor is the main political authority. He supports the ejido commissioner and the *consejo de vigilancia*, a group in charge of organizing cooperative work groups. These political authorities have their origin in Mexican agrarian law, not in traditional culture.

The religious organization of the community is in the hands of the *alaguisin*, the chief ceremonial leader; the *maynate*, the singer; and the prayer maker. Even though religious *cargos* are formally defined, individuals must become involved as actors in the roles, which have either a propitiating, initiatory, or ancestral character. For example, to stay up all night and into the day, as part of a system of vows or promises, is a rite of passage initiating the participant into a new identity. The symbolism of the rituals equates the musical harp with women and fertility, the Cross and the patron saints with good, and the Pascola dancers with filth and vulgarity. The rituals have the power to link the vulgar and profane to the sacred universe and to create a new vision of human existence.

Social Control and Conflict. There is no external social control, since Guarijío social organization and community spirit preclude conflict among Guarijío. The main conflicts are with White ranchers over the land that they bought from the original Guarijío owners.

Religion and Expressive Culture

Religious Beliefs. Guarijío beliefs reflect the influence of sixteenth- and seventeenth-century Jesuit missionaries. Life is regarded as vital breath. Death is seen as natural or as unnatural (caused by witchcraft, accident, or illness).

Religious Practitioners. When an illness fits into a native category, the Guarijío do not seek a doctor but turn to a shaman, who can divine the source of the illness by looking into smoke. Shamans perform cleansing rituals and cure with natural remedies.

Ceremonies. Among the most important Guarijío ceremonies are Cabapizca, Tugurada, and Cabos de Año. The feast of Cabapizca is performed after the harvest as a sign of gratitude. The Tugurada can be performed at any time of year to ask for rain or to fulfill a promise. Cabos de Años, also called Velaciones (Vigils), is held to honor a deceased member of the community. For a man, it commemorates the anniversary of his death each year for the three following years. Four anniversaries are celebrated for a woman.

Arts. The Tugurada is a dance performed by two lines of women who take several steps forward and, at certain intervals, turn around. Music is performed on the harp and violin, instruments the Guarijío make and use in ceremonies and festivals. Fiestas always include harp and violin music or gourd-rattle rhythm percussion. The native rhythms have a sonority that translates easily into movement.

Dance is the central event of a fiesta. Through dance, musical sounds are given bodily expression, as the dancer tries to represent physically or reinterpret the meaning of the musical forms.

The dance performances establish an imitative harmony between bodily and verbal forms of expression. It is a symbolic form portraying dramatic events that hold the attention of the audience. The mood of the dances is lighthearted. There is a constant attempt at comedy. Characters appear in one or another dance session until a full inventory has been attained: the faithful horse, the wheel, the turkey, the crow, the owl, the cow, the *mapurapi,* the wolf, the bull, the wasp, the priest, the donkey, the watchman, the dawn, and the saints.

Tuburi and Pascola are two styles of dance that are danced together in the Cabapizca fiesta. A singer (maynate), accompanied by a gourd rattle, directs the Tuburi. A group of women dance before the singer. When there are moments of silence, the women turn toward a wooden cross. The maynate narrates stories about people, animals, and things (which are alive in the Indian worldview).

The dance called the Song of the Iguana, or the Canary, opens all fiestas. Suddenly five Pascola dancers (*pascolas*) appear straddling a pole, performing all kinds of clownish pranks, especially of a lewd nature. They genuflect and cavort behind the head *fiestero,* antics that do not fail to make the public laugh. The musician's harp becomes a lewd object equated with woman, fertility, the iguana, and so forth.

One of the pascolas puts his hand into the hollow of the instrument and then licks his fingers and says:

"Oh, darn, this's good."

"What is it, brother, what does it taste like?"

"Tastes like biscuits. . . ."

"Hohoho, mus' be good."

"Yes, like biscuits and chocolate!" (laughter)

Insistently the pascola repeats this remark, and then the iguana bites him—that is to say, a musician burns his hand with a cigarette. The play continues in this fashion until the dancers have made a complete round.

In the Turkey and the Crow, before an improvised altar occupied by the images of the village saints, the pascolas arrange a pile of earth in which they plant a "milpa." The pascolas again surprise the public, this time carrying between their legs a handful of blue woolen cloth with which they simulate a turkey's tail. The imitation is well done and is accompanied by the typical sound made by this bird. The wild turkey goes through a transformation as his song changes into a kind of caw. Later in the play, a watchman is contracted by a landlord to watch over the "crops," but (how unusual!) he likes beer. Some of the crow's accomplices take advantage of this circumstance: they distract and deceive him and get him drunk; then they steal the maize. The watchman has to be dismissed.

Medicine. Three specific types of medicine are practiced: popular medicine, which makes use of patent remedies; traditional medicine, which includes traditional treatments and herbal remedies; and scientific medicine. Sorcery continues to be seen as causing illness and death. The traditional concepts of health and illness have a magico-religious component that is not addressed by the newly introduced Western medicine. People go first to a native curer, then to a doctor if that does not work. Western ideas of organic illness have been introduced through the health programs of the Instituto Nacional Indigenista and the Seguro Social.

Death and Afterlife. When a Guarijío dies, a vigil is held before the burial, and, eight days later, a fiesta is organized by his or her relatives. It is usually a Tugurada. After a year, within a complex ceremonial and religious framework, a Pascola is organized in order for the deceased to ascend into the skies. Some believe that the soul will enter the body of a bird or will roam places it used to visit, which can bring illness and misfortune. The Guarijío do not dress in mourning garb because wearing black clothing will keep the deceased from going up into the sky.

Bibliography

Centro Coordinador Indigenista, Guarijío, San Bernardo, Alamos, Sonora (1987). "Diagnosticó regional de la tribu guarijía." Mimeograph. Hermosillo, Sonora: Instituto Nacional Indigenista.

Haro Encinas, Jesús Armando (1981). "Estudio de comunidad." Unidad Médica Regional no. 3 IMSS-COPLAMAR, Burapaco, Álamos, Sonora. Mimeograph. Biblioteca Centro Regional de Noroeste, Instituto Nacional de Antropología e Historia.

Moctezuma, José Luis (1990). *Las lenguas indígenas del noroeste de México: Pasado y presente*. Memorias del Seminario sobre el Noroeste de México, Sus Culturas Étnicas.

Mexico City: Instituto Nacional de Antropología e Historia.

Muñoz Orozco, Maximiliano (1991). *Cultura festivio-religiosa guarijío, suplemento unísono*. Hermosillo: Universidad de Sonora.

JOSÉ ABRAHAM FRANCO OZUNA

(Translated by James W. Dow)

Haitians

ETHNONYMS: Ayisyens, Haïtiens, Haytians

Orientation

Identification. The Republic of Haiti is the second-oldest independent nation in the Western Hemisphere, and it is the only one with a French-Creole background and an overwhelmingly African culture. Large communities of Haitians exist outside Haiti, especially in the Dominican Republic, on other Caribbean islands, in Central America and northern South America, and in North America. The second-largest Haitian community, after Port-au-Prince, the Haitian capital, is in New York City, with about 500,000 members.

Location. Occupying 27,750 square kilometers on the western third of the Caribbean island of Hispaniola, which it shares with the Dominican Republic, Haiti lies between 18° and 20° N and 72° and 74° W. It is 90 kilometers southeast of Cuba, 187 kilometers northeast of Jamaica, and about 1,000 kilometers from Florida. Its topography ranges from flat, semiarid valleys to densely forested mountains; about one-third of its area lies 200 to 500 meters above sea level, and the remaining two-thirds is covered by three mountain ranges. The highest point of elevation is La Selle Peak (2,680 meters). The mean temperature is somewhere between 24° C and 27° C; averages for the hottest and coolest months differ by perhaps 5° C, although temperature variations on any given day may be as great as 12° C. Temperature decreases three-quarters of a degree per 100 meters of elevation. Port-au-Prince, with an elevation of 40 meters, has a mean temperature of 26.3° C, but Pétionville, at 400 meters, records 24.7° C, and Kenscoff, at 1,450 meters, enjoys 18.5° C.

Demography. Demographic information is at once scarce and unreliable. According to educated estimates, the total population of Haiti is about 6.5 million. Port-au-Prince has a population of about 740,000, and the second-largest city,

Cap Haitien, has about 70,000 inhabitants. Regional cities that can boast populations of 10,000 to 50,000 are Les Cayes, Gonaïves, Port-de-Paix, Jacmel, Jérémie, Saint Marc, and Hinche. The single recent census for which information is generally available was conducted only in urban centers in 1971; a 10 percent sample survey was used to estimate the population in rural areas. The total population calculated from that census was 4,314,628, 79.6 percent of it rural.

Linguistic Affiliation. The language spoken by all Haitians is usually referred to as Haitian Creole. For most of modern history, however, the official language of government, business, and education has been French. At best, only about 8 percent of the population, the educated elite, speaks French well—and then only as a second language. Another 2 to 7 percent uses French with a lesser degree of competence. Traditionally, the elite has used the requirement of fluency in French to exclude the general population from competing for positions in government and business. Haitian Creole, which has often been seen as a nonlanguage in which sophisticated thoughts cannot be expressed or, at best, as a poor imitation of French, is coming into its own, and the prestige of French is rapidly declining in Haiti. In the early 1990s both Creole and French were the country's official languages.

History

At the time of European contact, anywhere from 60,000 to 4 million Indians inhabited the island of Hispaniola. The indigenous population rapidly succumbed to the ravages of disease, slavery, and brutality, and the Europeans soon had to look to Africa for the labor they needed to work their plantations. In the colonial period (1492–1804) sugarcane plantations were established and slavery instituted in Saint Domingue, as the French called their territory on Hispaniola.

A series of minor uprisings culminated in the slave revolt of August 1791. By 1796, White supremacy was at an end, and within the framework of the French Republic, Black rule was established under the leadership of a former slave, the charismatic Toussaint Louverture. In 1800 Napoleon sent 28,000 troops under his brother-in-law, Gen. Charles Leclerc, to retake the colony and reenslave the Blacks. By 1803, however, Haitians had defeated Napoleon's troops, and on 1 January 1804 Jean-Jacques Dessalines, Toussain's successor, proclaimed the independence of Haiti.

In the postindependence period (1820–1915) Haiti became a focal point of debates about the effect of emancipation and the capacity of Blacks for self-government. Many slave insurrections in the southern United States were consciously modeled after the Haitian example.

The U.S. military occupied Haiti from 1915 to 1934 for pressing economic and strategic reasons. The major, though certainly unintended, results of the occupation were the increasing Black consciousness of the elite, the suppression of peasant movements, the training of the army, and the concentration of sociopolitical power in Port-au-Prince.

The postoccupation period (1934–1957) was characterized by a succession of undistinguished administrations, with one notable exception: the government led by President Dumarsais Estimé (1946–1950), which many view as a highly progressive era in Haitian politics that probably spelled the end of mulatto political domination. Important developments during his presidency were the entrance of Blacks into the civil service, increased pride in the African heritage, greater interaction with other Caribbean nations, the beginning of peasant integration into the national polity, and, especially, the rise of the new Black middle class.

François "Papa Doc" Duvalier, president from 1957 to 1971, established his power base largely among this middle class. Duvalier carried out a brutal campaign of oppression against his opponents, and Haiti was increasingly isolated from the international community. When Duvalier's 19-year-old son, Jean-Claude ("Baby Doc"), became president in 1971, a new economic program guided by the U.S. government was put in place; U.S. private investment was wooed with such incentives as no customs taxes, a minimum wage kept very low, the suppression of labor unions, and the right of U.S. companies to repatriate their profits.

With little gain from fourteen years of rule by a second Duvalier, Haitians finally reached the end of their patience and overwhelming public protests led to the ouster of Jean-Claude on 7 February 1986. An interim government, the Conseil National de Gouvernement (CNG) headed by Lieut. Gen. Henri Namphy, took charge. Elections for president and for seats in the national assembly, set for 29 November 1987, were aborted by army-sponsored violence. In January 1988 the CNG held sham elections and announced that Leslie Manigat had won the presidency. About four months later, Manigat's attempt to play off one segment of the army against another led to his own ouster, and Namphy declared himself president. On 17 September 1988 Namphy was forced out of the National Palace and leadership was handed over to Lieut. Gen. Prosper Avril. Jean-Bertrand Aristide of the National Front for Change and Democracy (FNCD) was elected president on 16 December 1990 and assumed office on 7 February 1991 but was deposed on 30 September 1991. The military ousted him a little more than seven months later, but no state (except the Vatican) recognized the military government. After considerable vacillation, the admin-

istration of U.S. president Bill Clinton forced the military leaders to leave Haiti, and in October 1994 Aristide was reinstated under heavy U.S. military sponsorship.

Settlements

With 75 to 85 percent of the population living in a rural setting, the majority of Haitians can be classified as peasants: they live in dispersed villages loosely connected by trade routes. Scattered within these villages are huts of wattle and daub surrounded by gardens, fields, and outbuildings. Regional centers once had considerable cultural and commercial importance, but since the first U.S. occupation, Port-au-Prince has become disproportionately dominant.

Economy

Subsistence and Commercial Activities. About 65 percent of the labor force are small landowners engaged in agriculture (one of the highest proportions of peasants in any country); only about 7 percent are in manufacturing. One percent of workers are involved in construction and 27 percent in other sectors. Agriculture is precarious because the countryside is 95 percent deforested, and 25 percent of the soil is undergoing rapid erosion. Haiti's primary products are coffee, sugar, rice, and cocoa. Its light manufacturing enterprises produce shoes, soap, flour, cement, and domestic oils. Its export industries produce garments, toys, baseballs, and electronic goods for the U.S. market. Despite this small-scale industrialization, the annual per capita income is estimated at $380. The current instability of the government is having deleterious effects on the national economy.

Industrial Arts. Many people engage in part-time craft work, particularly in the manufacture of wood utensils, tools, and furniture. Formerly, many of these items were destined for the tourist trade.

Trade. Most commercial exchange is carried out in open-air markets. The market women are justly famous both for carrying heavy loads of merchandise and for bargaining with great skill. Haiti's economy is closely tied to that of the United States; a sizable portion of its exports go to North America, and it is dependent on governmental and nongovernmental U.S. aid.

Division of Labor. In rural areas, men generally handle agricultural production, and women take charge of the produce. The women depend on the men to provide a product to sell, and the men depend on the women for domestic labor.

Land Tenure. A crucial problem facing the newly independent Haiti was access to land. Having failed in its attempt to reinstate the plantation system of colonial Saint Domingue, the government distributed much of the land among the former slaves. Currently, from 60 to 80 percent of the farmers own their own land, although few have clear title, and the plots are fragmented and small. Fairly large plantations do exist but not nearly to the same extent as in Latin American countries. The state owns land, but the government has rarely shown a sustained interest in agriculture.

Kinship, Marriage, and Family

Marriage. The plantation system and the institution of slavery had a profound influence on domestic entities. Additionally, the laws of the early republic reinforced the tendency of the rural population to avoid legal and church marriages. The most recognizable kinship pattern in rural Haiti is the somewhat patrilineal extended family living in a cluster of households linked through legal, ritual, consanguineal, and affinal ties and headed by the oldest male member.

In addition to conventional church weddings, long-term monogamous unions, and neolocal nuclear-family households, there are socially accepted unions without formal sanction, couples who do not coreside, fathers who do not participate actively in rearing their children, and households without a nuclear family at their core.

In writing about Haiti, anthropologists often avoid the word "family"; instead they use "household," which embraces the wide range of relatives—direct and collateral, on the sides of both parents—that the Haitian "family" typically includes.

Inheritance. The complexity of the domestic unit and the varieties of household types do create inheritance problems. In general, all children from all the varieties of conjugal unions have equal rights of inheritance, but, in practice, residents, contacts, and personal feelings are important determinants of who inherits.

Socialization. Because both adults and children may change residential affiliation with relative ease and frequency and enjoy a variety of temporary residential rights, children often come into contact with a relatively large number of adults who may discipline and train them. In general, a great deal of emphasis is placed on respect for adults, and adults are quick to use corporal punishment to ensure that they receive it. Fewer than half of the rural children attend school, and only about 20 percent of those complete the primary grades.

Sociopolitical Organization

In 1995 Haiti was in the process of reestablishing its political and social institutions under a democratic administration. Agreements with the U.S. government and international finance agencies had created a difficult set of parameters within which a move toward more social equality and justice was being attempted.

Social Organization. One result of the land reform in the early 1800 was that the largely mulatto elite fled to the cities and, with no land of their own, made their living from taxing peasant markets and the nation's imports and exports. This elite also practiced the religion of the slave owners, Roman Catholicism. Driven by fear of a renewed French occupation, the bulk of the population retreated into the mountainous interior, inside a ring of magnificent forts. What emerged from these displacements was a nation with a very small European-oriented, Roman Catholic, mulatto elite residing in several coastal urban centers and a large, scattered Black population that farmed the interior and worshiped in the ancient African manner.

Political Organization. The largely Black peasantry has always regarded the government as having little relevance to their lives. Haiti's regional political units, called *départements*, are further divided into several *arrondissements*, each with an administrative center. Arrondissements consist of several *communes*, which usually coincide with church parishes. Each commune is divided into *sections rurales*, each of which is headed by an appointed *chef de section*, who reports to the *commandant* of the commune, who in turn reports to the *préfet* of the arrondissement. The limited contact rural Haitians normally have with the government is, for the most part, with the chef de section.

Social Control. Criminality is rare, and, for the most part, the rural population, in deference to village elders, polices itself. The urban areas have police and courts, mainly modeled after the French system.

Conflict. Governments in Haiti have been run primarily by members of the elite, and despite the early and heroic independence of Haiti from France and the elimination of slavery, the attitude of the elite classes of Haiti has traditionally been a neocolonial one. Nativism, negritude, and the increasing use of Creole have made all Haitians more aware of their Haitianness, but tensions exist between the affluent city dwellers and the poor peasants and shantytown residents. Aside from a very small but moderately influential group of Middle Eastern merchants, the population of Haiti is exceptionally homogeneous, both culturally and linguistically.

Religion and Expressive Culture

Religious Beliefs. Although the majority of the population is nominally Roman Catholic and although Protestant missionaries have won a number of converts in the poorer rural areas, the religion of Haiti is still Vodun, an ancient religion that focuses on contacting and appeasing ancestral spirits (*lwa*), which include both distant, stereotyped ancestors and more immediate relatives, such as dead parents and grandparents.

Religious Practitioners. Vodun is a particularly egalitarian religion; both men and women serve as priests (*ougan-yo* and *manbo-yo*, respectively; sing. *ougan* and *manbo*).

Ceremonies. As many of its rituals are performed in the context of sickness and death, Vodun is primarily a system of folk medicine that attributes illnesses to angry ancestors; it consists of appeasement ceremonies, including divination rites, which are used to find the cause of illnesses; healing rites, in which a Vodun priest interacts directly with sick people to cure them; propitiatory rites, in which food and drink are offered to specific spirits to make them stop their aggression; and preventive rites, in which ancestors are offered sacrifices to help head off any possible future trouble.

Arts. In the 1940s Haiti burst into the consciousness of the art world with an astonishing display of paintings, and its artists received worldwide attention for their so-called primitive or naive art. In 1944 the Centre d'Art was founded in Port-au-Prince.

Haiti is also renowned for its literature, despite its high rate of illiteracy (85 percent). Major themes include concepts of negritude, which foreshadowed the Black

Power and post-World War II anticolonial movements, and Vodun. The most famous novel in Haitian Creole, Franké-tinne's _Dézafi_, is about the revolt of a colony of zombies.

Medicine. Although Western medicine has been available to the urban elite since the early 1960s, there were only 887 physicians in Haiti in 1988 (Wilke 1993, Table 804). In the rural areas, curing depends on a rich body of folk knowledge that includes herbal medicine and Vodun. The peasants nevertheless suffer from malnutrition and many diseases. Measles, diarrhea, and tetanus kill many children, and the daily per capita caloric intake for 1988 has been estimated at 2,011 (Wilke 1993, Table 824). Only about 38 percent of the population has access to potable water. Tuberculosis is the most devastating disease, followed closely by dysentery, influenza, malaria, measles, tetanus, and whooping cough. Eye problems are endemic in Haiti; the chief causes of blindness are cataracts, glaucoma, pterygium (a growth over the cornea), and scarring of the cornea.

Bibliography

Courlander, Harold (1960). _The Drum and the Hoe: Life and Lore of the Haitian People._ Berkeley and Los Angeles: University of California Press.

Ferguson, James (1987). _Papa Doc, Baby Doc: Haiti and the Duvaliers._ Oxford: Basil Blackwell.

Laguerre, Michel S. (1982a). _The Complete Haitiana: A Bibliographic Guide to the Scholarly Literature, 1900–1980._ 2 vols. Millwood, N.Y.: Kraus.

Laguerre, Michel S. (1982b). _Urban Life in the Caribbean: A Study of a Haitian Urban Community._ Cambridge, Mass.: Schenkman.

Laguerre, Michel S. (1993). _The Military and Society in Haiti._ Knoxville: University of Tennessee Press.

Lawless, Robert (1986). "Haitian Migrants and Haitian-Americans: From Invisibility into the Spotlight." _Journal of Ethnic Studies_ 14(2): 29–70.

Lawless, Robert (1988). "Creole Speaks, Creole Understands." _The World and I_ 3(1): 474–483; 3(2): 510–521.

Mintz, Sidney W. (1995). "Can Haiti Change?" _Foreign Affairs_ 74:73–86.

Nicholls, David (1979). _From Dessalines to Duvalier: Race, Colour, and National Independence in Haiti._ Cambridge: Cambridge University Press.

Weinstein, Brian, and Aaron Segal (1984). _Haiti: Political Failures, Cultural Successes._ New York: Praeger.

Wilkie, James, ed. (1993). _Statistical Abstract of Latin America._ Vol. 30, Part 1. Los Angeles: UCLA.

ROBERT LAWLESS

Huave

ETHNONYMS: Guabi, Huabi, Huavi, Huazontecos, Juave, Mareños, Wabi

The Huave are a peasant people who occupy five villages and dozens of hamlets on the Pacific coast of the Isthmus of Tehuantepec, Mexico (approximately 16°30' N, 95° W). The speakers of the Huave language numbered 11,955 in 1990. The language has five main dialects, each associated with one of the five villages. The language has been significantly altered by contact with Spanish.

There are three ecological zones within Huave territory: a thorn forest, which has animal life; a savanna used for pasture and farming; and a mangrove swamp, which supplies fish.

One significant feature of Huave history is their loss of large portions of their lands to Zapotec people, losses that were legalized following the Mexican Revolution. The Huave joined the Zapotec and Spanish trading system in the seventeenth century, about the same time that missionaries and the Catholic church became long-term presences of the Huave community. The Huave, although they retain many Indian cultural traits, are nevertheless socioeconomically very similar to other rural peasants.

In the forest, the Huave hunt for deer, rabbits, and iguanas. Except when it is converted to private farm lands, the savanna is used as a communal pasture, and the Huave graze their goats, sheep, horses, oxen, and donkeys there. Some forest land is also being converted into agricultural or horticultural land. The chief crop is maize; crops of secondary importance include beans, sweet potatoes and chilies. From the ocean, the Huave obtain a variety of species of fish for their own use, and sea perch, mullet, shrimp, and turtle eggs for sale. They fish by the use of dragnets pulled by canoes. People keep swine, chickens, and turkeys in their house yards; chicken eggs are sold. Fish and maize dishes are eaten daily, whereas meat and eggs are eaten only during festivals.

Each endogamous Huave village is made up of several barrios and outlying smaller hamlets. The _escalafón_ is the basis for town political structure. Each male adult in the town holds the various unpaid political offices in the town administration in a serial fashion. Young people acquire political status by age and ascription, whereas older people acquire it by achievement.

The household usually has as its members a patrilocal extended family, and kinship terminology is bilateral. Fictive kinship is important primarily in the case of god-siblings, who often act as godparents to each other's children.

The Huave are, in large measure, part of the national cash economy. They purchase from merchants dugout canoes, metal tools (shovels and machetes), cotton thread for nets, and much of their maize.

Religious activity is often a household matter. Many observances are directed by the head of household at the house's own altar. There are also barrio chapels and visits to villages by missionaries and priests. Other practitioners of the supernatural are the curers and the witches, both of whom are hired for their respective services.

Bibliography

Diebold, Richard A., Jr. (1969). "The Huave." In *Handbook of Middle American Indians*, edited by Robert Wauchope. Vol. 7, *Ethnology, Part One*, edited by Evon Z. Vogt, 478–488. Austin: University of Texas Press.

Signorini, Italo (1979). *Los huaves de San Mateo del Mar, Oaxaca*. Mexico City: Instituto Nacional Indigenista.

Huichol

ETHNONYMS: Huichole, Tevi, Wizarika

Orientation

Identification. The Huichol are a Mexican Indian group located in the states of Jalisco, Nayarit, Zacatecas, and Durango. The name "Huichol" is the term Spaniards used when referring to this group and is possibly a corruption of the name for either the Guachichil or the Wizarika. Some scholars believe the Huichol were originally the desert-dwelling culture known as the "Guachichil," who, in turn were one of the many people collectively called "Chichimec." "Wizarika" is the term the Huichol use to identify themselves. Its meaning is unclear, but scholars have proposed various interpretations: "the healers," "the sandal wearers," and "the ones." The Huichol use the term "Tevi," meaning one of "the people" when making distinctions between Huichol and non-Huichol individuals.

Location. The majority of the Huichol live in the Sierra Madre Occidental in the states of Jalisco, Nayarit, Zacatecas, and Durango. This area covers the span of 21°30' to 22°35' N and 104°00' to 104°30' W. The rugged sierra was formed in the Tertiary period with the lava flows from active volcanoes. The Huichol occupy some of the most rugged terrain in the mountain chain, characterized by high mesas, sheer cliffs, and deep river valleys ranging in elevation from approximately 600 meters to over 1,800 meters. The geography of the sierra consists of extremes, creating natural barriers that have served to insulate the Huichol from the outside world. The tops of the mesa are covered with oak and pine forest. In the lower elevations are subtropical scrub vegetation and thorn forests, which include such genera as *Acacia, Ficus, Lysiloma, Ceiba, Bombax, Bursera, Opuntia,* and *Agave*. The herbaceous vegetation is predominantly grasses and geophytes.

The major river running through the Huichol territory, the Chapalagana, divides the land into two sections. The Huichol who inhabit the land west of the river have experienced more acculturative pressures. They live in small groups in or around Cora Indian or mestizo settlements, or in urban centers. Those who live to the east have maintained more of their traditions. In this sierra environment, there are two major seasons—rainy and dry. The driest months are December through May. Eighty percent of the annual precipitation of 80 centimeters falls in the rainy season, from June to October. During the rainy season, the canyons at lower elevations are hotter and more humid than the mesas. In the dry seasons, the mesas are subject to colder weather, sometimes with frost and strong winds.

Demography. The number of Huichol at the time of Spanish contact is unknown. Rampant epidemics of measles and smallpox greatly reduced the population. Franciscan missionary documents from the 1780s report a population of 2,000 in the more assimilated communities of Tenzompa, San Nicolás, Soledad, and Huajuquilla. In the three most traditional Huichol communities (San Andrés, Santa Catarina, and San Sebastián), the population totaled 1,000 inhabitants. In 1894 a Mexican government census placed the Huichol population at 4,000. From 1910 to 1940 numerous Huichol fled the sierra because of the turmoil created by the Mexican Revolution and the Cristero revolt (see "History and Cultural Relations") and settled in several areas of Nayarit. Larger numbers of Huichol began to migrate to the Nayarit coast as seasonal laborers, and, beginning in the 1960s, some Huichol began to live in urban centers such as Tepic, Guadalajara, Zacatecas, and Mexico City. In 1981 the total number of Huichol was estimated to be around 10,000, with the greatest concentration, 6,000, living in rural Jalisco, and approximately 2,000 residing in urban centers. The 1990 Mexican census placed the Huichol population over the age of 5 at 20,000.

Linguistic Affiliation. Huichol, the native language, is classified with languages of the Aztecoiden Branch of the Uto-Aztecan Family. It is most closely related to the Cora language. Some Nahuatl terms have been borrowed from Tlaxcalan Indians and incorporated into Huichol.

History and Cultural Relations

Little is known about the origins of the Huichol. Some scholars propose that in pre-Columbian times the Huichol were originally Guachichil from the desert around Zacatecas and San Luis Potosí and were part of the Chichimec culture. According to this theory, ancestors of contemporary Huichol sought refuge in the sierra shortly before or after the arrival of the Spaniards. Others believe that the Huichol had been longtime residents in the sierra, with a strong orientation to the Pacific coast. Regardless of their origins, it is likely that the Huichol culture consisted of four or five tribes, each with distinct regional traditions.

Because of the rugged terrain of the sierra and physical resistance on the part of the Indians, the Huichol held out against direct Spanish domination until the 1720s. By this time their territory and population had been drastically reduced. The Franciscans established centers that served as missions and frontier posts in the area. Some of the first Franciscan missionaries established communities in Tenzompa, Soledad, and San Nicolás, all of which eventually assimilated with the mestizo population. San Andrés, Santa Catarina, and San Sebastián were the most remote of these Franciscan centers, and the Huichol there maintained more of their native beliefs and practices. Since the Huichol area was located along the fringe of Spanish-controlled lands within the frontier of San Luis Colotlán, the centers became outposts to protect the region from Indian attacks. The Huichol received a more privileged status in which they were allowed to have their own tribal government and were exempt from paying tribute.

Intensive missionary influences in the sierra declined after Mexican independence, and by 1860 virtually all clergy left the sierra because of increasing tension among the Indians over land rights. Independence from Spain also meant the end of Spanish-chartered Indian communities in the sierra, which consequently opened Huichol communal lands to mestizo cattlemen and colonists. A ten-year revolution ensued in which Huichol and Cora joined forces under the Indian leader Lozada to protect the sierra from further foreign encroachment. Until the arrival of several ethnographers at the end of the nineteenth century and at the beginning of the twentieth, little was actually known about the Huichol and their cultural traditions. The best known of these ethnographers was the Norwegian Carl Lumholtz, who, under the sponsorship of the Museum of Natural History in New York, documented much of Huichol culture through journals and photographs and assembled an extensive collection of Huichol material culture for the museum.

Shortly thereafter, the Mexican Revolution began, and by 1913 had reached the sierra. The neighboring mestizos, who had been trying to invade Huichol land, sided with Pancho Villa. In response, the Huichol fought under their chief, General Mezquite, who allied himself with Carranza. Mezquite received help from Guadalajara, and he and his Huichol troops were successful in driving the mestizos from their territory. The tranquility in the sierra was to be short-lived. Christian rebels known as Cristeros were campaigning against the recently imposed government policy separating the Catholic church from the state. Those who escaped government troops fled to the protection of the sierra. The Huichol were experiencing strife between their own communities. Members of the community of San Sebastián joined the Cristeros under the leadership of a Huichol named Juan Bautista, taking this opportunity to invade and ransack the ranches and ceremonial centers of Santa Catarina. Juan Bautista was eventually ambushed and killed by Huichol from Tuxpan de Bolaños. During this period, many Huichol fled the sierra to regional towns, cities, and the coast or went to live among the Cora. Some never returned to the sierra. Most Huichol remained neutral or progovernment, depending upon the security of each one's communal lands. Land-reform issues originating with the Mexican Revolution had still not been resolved, and, with the disruption caused by the Cristero rebels, mestizos seized this opportunity to move onto Huichol lands.

In the 1950s the Catholic church again began to make inroads into Huichol communities, constructing airstrips and several missions nearby. Even greater changes occurred in the 1960s when, under then President Luis Echeverría, the National Indian Institute (INI) sponsored a regional development program known as Plan HUICOT (for Huichol-Cora-Tepehuan). This government agency developed projects designed to integrate Huichol into the mainstream of Mexican national culture. Airstrips and roads were built linking the isolated communities to the outside world. Agricultural projects were begun that introduced tractors, fertilizers, and different strains of crops.

Additional projects focused on improving cattle and livestock in the communities. Medical clinics and schools were also created, the latter run by bilingual Huichol teachers.

The Huichol are now tied into the national economy and seek ways of generating cash income, usually as artisans or migrant wage laborers in the cities or on mestizo-owned lands. They are in contact with an increasing number of outsiders, both Mexican nationals and foreigners from such diverse places as the United States, Canada, Europe, Central and South America, and Japan. Huichol lands are still being invaded by mestizos seeking land on which to build homes and graze cattle and forests to exploit for timber. The Huichol, represented by INI officials and other nonprofit development organizations, are still trying to gain legal title to their lands.

Settlements

The Huichol sierra is divided into four major community districts. In the state of Jalisco and bordering on Durango and Zacatecas are the communities of San Andrés Cohamiata (including Banco de Calítique), San Sebastián Teponahuaztlán along with the annexed Tuxpan de Bolaños, and Santa Catarina Cuexcomatitlán. The area in Nayarit includes Guadalupe Ocotán and various small communities in which Cora Indians also live, such as Jesús María and Santa Bárbara. In each district there is a ceremonial center where the governing officials reside and where communitywide political and ceremonial activities take place. Within the community district are temple districts made up of family lineages. Most Huichol live in dispersed family ranchos within the vicinity of the temple district corresponding to the lineage of the elder of the rancho. Rancho settlements consist of individual houses belonging to the eldest couple, to their adult children and grandchildren, and to extended-family members who have received permission from the elder to construct their homes in the rancho. There is usually a communal kitchen and a house that is the family's _xiriki_ (shrine). The xiriki is dedicated to the ancestors of the elders of the rancho. In some instances, there is more than one xiriki, to honor the ancestors of other, more distantly related kin members. All of these buildings encircle a main patio, which features an outdoor fireplace and sacred stone disk where family ceremonies take place. Huichol houses have dirt floors, stone or adobe walls, and grass-thatched roofs. In each rancho there is usually at least one house made of bamboo that is built on stilts above the ground, where maize and other crops are stored after the harvest. Some Huichol are replacing grass roofs with cement or store-bought prefabricated shingles. The walls of some houses are now made of oven-fired bricks.

Economy

Subsistence and Commercial Activities. The Huichol economy is based on hunting, gathering, and fishing along with slash-and-burn subsistence agriculture. Wild animals such as deer, rabbits, peccaries, iguanas, and assorted birds were originally hunted by men with traps, bows and arrows, and a kind of slingshot. Now guns have largely supplanted these devices. Fish and crayfish are caught with handmade nets. Wild greens, roots and tubers, mesquite beans, mushrooms, avocados, nopal cactus and fruits, *huamuchili* fruits, berries, and plums are collected. Animal-pulled wooden plows and digging sticks are used for cultivation, the primary crops being maize, beans, squashes and chilies. Families also own cattle, mules, donkeys, horses, goats, sheep, pigs, chickens, and turkeys. Cheese is made from cows' milk. Various Huichol migrate seasonally to the west coast to work as wage laborers in the harvest of tobacco and commercial food crops. Others are artisans who sell their artwork in the sierra, in the Mexican cities and resorts, and along the U.S.-Mexico border. Much of the money earned in these ventures is earmarked for expenses incurred in sponsoring ceremonies. Some Huichol move to the cities to work as manual laborers. A select group pursues such occupations as bilingual teacher, engineer, economist, and health professional.

Industrial Arts.   Huichol men weave baskets, hats, and baby cradles from plant fibers. They also manufacture chairs, musical instruments, bows and arrows, loom tools, and spindles. Women embroider, weave on backstrap looms, and make some pottery. The multitude of ritual offerings made are divided into male objects, such as prayer arrows, and female ones, which include votive bowls. Both men and women make beaded jewelry, gourd bowls, masks, and other figures for commercial ventures. Woven and embroidered belts, bags, and clothes are made for sale, as well as yarn paintings and other commercially developed art forms.

Division of Labor.   Women gather wild foods, help in horticultural activities, milk cows, prepare food, carry water, sew, weave and embroider, make clothing and accessories, and care for children. Men hunt, fish, perform the heavy manual labor in cultivation, gather firewood, construct buildings, and help with child care. Young boys herd animals and help the men hunt; girls care for younger siblings, make tortillas, and help in household chores. Most shamans are male; those women who are shamans tend to be more discreet about their specialized training. Men are the political leaders and musicians. Women can specialize as midwives and master artisans. Ritual traditions emphasize the importance of male and female counterparts in ceremonial roles.

Land Tenure.   The sierra is divided into districts of community lands. Local Huichol governing officials allocate land to family members of the community. Many families occupy several plots of land, where they reside on a seasonal basis in conjunction with their subsistence activities. A community member can petition for a parcel of unoccupied land. Land is passed down through the family, and inheritance rules place special importance on the oldest and youngest children. Huichol are constantly under pressure from neighboring mestizos encroaching upon their land. There is a great deal of uncertainty among the Huichol about the effect that the 1992 amendment of Article 27 of the Mexican constitution will have on agrarian law.

Kinship

Kin Groups and Descent.   The extended family constitutes the core Huichol social structure. Family lineages are organized within temple districts based on bilineal descent.

Disruption of these districts makes it difficult to reconstruct the original social organization. In some temple districts, the group is organized into moieties of dry- and rainy-season lineages. Each half is united under an ancestor deity. Members of surrounding temple districts are linked to their ritual *cargo*-holding counterparts in each temple group.

Kinship Terminology.   Huichol kinship terminology is Hawaiian. Terms of address distinguish kin one generation from Ego, but in the second generation and beyond, the terms are reciprocal.

Marriage and Family

Marriage.   Traditional marriages are bilateral, between first cousins, and arranged by parents when children are very young. When they reach puberty, they are wed. Women generally share equally in this decision making. Presently marriages frequently occur between more distant kin; however, it is preferred that the spouse be from the same temple district, or at least from the same community. The union of the couple does not include the joining of economic assets; women and men maintain their own property separately, especially cattle and other livestock. Polygynous marriages are more common in some communities; however, this practice appears to be gaining popularity in others as well. Postmarital residence for the first year is at the rancho of the wife's family. Afterwards, the couple decide in which family rancho they will eventually build their own house. If either one of the couple is the oldest or youngest of the family, they will reside in his or her family's rancho. Divorce, although discouraged, is permissible, especially in cases of excessive cruelty. If family members cannot reconcile the couple through mediation, the matter will go before the governor of the community for his decision. Remarriage is less formal: the two families involved are consulted and if they are in agreement the couple starts living together.

Domestic Unit.   The rancho consists of a number of nuclear-family households that usually form an extended family spanning three to four generations, along with sons-in-law, grandchildren, and widowed or divorced adults, who are most likely women. The elder is the decision maker of the group and also represents the family at the community-wide level. Although the elder is usually male, an older female can also hold this position. The family's shrine (xiriki) is located in the rancho of its oldest living elder. Occasionally aunts, uncles, cousins, or godchildren visit and even live at the rancho for extended periods.

Inheritance.   Parents begin to pass on their inheritance to children while they are still living. From an early age, offspring start receiving gifts of cattle, horses, mules, donkeys, pigs, sheep, goats, chickens, and turkeys. In some communities, inheritance may be patrilateral. The eldest and youngest usually receive the largest amount of the wealth and property of the deceased parent. They also inherit the primary responsibilty for fulfilling the temple, government, and church cargos previously held by their parents.

Socialization.   Children are the center of attention, and all family members help in caring for them. Both the mother and father are major figures in child rearing; however, grandparents have a special relationship with their children's offspring. Shortly after birth, children are named by a grandparent or shaman. If a child falls seriously ill, he or she will receive an additional name. Every year for the first five years, children, with the help of their parents, are the major participants in the harvest ceremony, Tatei Neixra. Upon reaching 5 years of age, they are considered complete human beings. Education is informal and nonformal, most of it taking place in the rancho setting among adults and older children, as well as in the ceremonies, deer hunts, and pilgrimages. Children who follow the path of becoming a shaman, master musician, or artist learn from family members proficient in these areas. Some Huichol children attend bilingual government schools in their communities or Catholic missionary schools. When a girl reaches puberty, she has usually mastered the basic embroidery and backstrap-weaving techniques, which she visually displays to mark her intitiation into womanhood. With her first menses, a lock of hair is cut to symbolize this passage.

Sociopolitical Organization

Social Organization. Huichol society was traditionally based on hunting, gathering, and horticulture. Participation in the larger economic market has created some inequality in access to wealth and advantages. Nevertheless, many Huichol rituals involve redistribution of wealth among community members. Huichol ideology retains strong elements of egalitarianism. Social status is based on age (the elders having the highest position) and participation in government, temple, and church cargo roles. Specialists, such as shamans, musicians, or master artists receive higher status and recognition.

Political Organization. The community is led by a council of *kawiteros*, wise elder men who are usually shamans. Through the consensus of their dreams, they annually select the new governor, tribal council, and church cargos. Much of the political organization was structured from eighteenth-century Franciscan missionary teachings. The governor is the major decision maker and serves as arbitrator for the community. Council members include commissioners for each temple-group area, a constable, a judge, a bilingual secretary, and community representatives. The governor, who redistributes goods and services in the community, is a religious figurehead. The governor's wife, who shares the position with him, has much influence in decision making.

Social Control. The most common conflicts involve land disputes, cattle and livestock thefts and transactions, domestic family problems, neglected cargo responsibilities, sorcery, and relations with outsiders. The governor and council members present serve as arbitrators between the parties involved. Punishment varies from fines, service rendered, jail (sometimes in the stocks), and ousting from the community. Matters of murder are settled by the mestizo authorities in the cities.

Conflict. Most conflicts with other groups involve land and property disputes arising, for instance, from mestizo land encroachment and exploitation of natural resources. International outsiders who arrive to make movies, take photographs, write books, and seek messianic experiences can also cause disruptions.

Religion and Expressive Culture

Religious Beliefs. Religion permeates all aspects of life, and most Huichol make no real distinction between the sacred and everyday worlds. For the Huichol, religion is life itself. Following these beliefs and rituals, they petition the deities for sun and rain for the crops, successful deer hunts, fertility, good health, and protection from the dangers of the natural and supernatural worlds. The gods in the Huichol pantheon embody and personify nature in all of its manifestations, with the oldest being Takutsi Nakawé, Grandmother of Growth and Germination, who created the world, and Tatewari, Grandfather Fire. The large company of deities includes the sun, rain, wind, ocean, earth, and deer. Votive offerings, artistically rendered, are made as visual prayers to the deities and communicate innermost Huichol needs and desires. Peyote (*Lophophora williamsii*) has a strong presence in Huichol culture. The Huichol make annual pilgrimages to the sacred peyote land, Wirikuta, in the San Luis Potosí desert. Peyote's psychoactive properties enable participants to see bright, colorful visions that are interpreted as personal communications from their gods. Huichol look upon peyote, which is identified with the deer, as a sacred gift; its consumption is highly ritualized and serves as a unifying force among community members. Some Christian elements have entered into Huichol religious beliefs, and certain Christian ceremonies are observed. The amount of Christian influence varies. In some communities, there is a relatively minor degree of syncretism between the two religions.

Religious Practitioners. The core of Huichol existence lies in the hands of the shamans, known as *mara' akames*. Through five to ten years of intensive training, these men (and sometimes women) acquire knowledge as healers, priests, and diviners. In their dreams, they perceive the causes of illness and environmental instability and the actions to be taken in such cases. Their dreams also instruct them in the performance of major ceremonial functions. They summon souls into the bodies of newborn babies and follow the souls of the dead to send them off to the other world. Shamans who sing travel with their animal messengers to the many worlds in order to communicate with the gods on behalf of the family and community.

Ceremonies. The annual cycle is divided into wet- and dry-season temple ceremonies and activities. Ceremonies for rain and planting of crops take place around the summer solstice. Harvest ceremonies occur close to the fall equinox. Deer hunting and the peyote pilgrimage ensue, completing the cycle. Ceremonies usually last at least two days and nights, during which shamans sing extensive myth cycles with the help of two assistants. When the gods' presence is known, animals are sacrificed to provide them blood, which embodies the life force, and ritual food. Ceremonies also take place in the center of the community and at family ranchos.

Arts. Art is an important part of the traditional Huichol way of life. Through art they express materially their innermost feelings. The designs, which are meticulously embroidered on a shirt or brightly colored bag, or woven into a wide wool belt, are symbols representing their gods and the sacredness of nature. Peyote visions are the source of many of these designs, which are used to decorate ceremonial objects, guitars and violins, gourd bowls, and feathered arrows and for face painting. The contemporary yarn paintings are a relatively new development and are intended for outside consumption. They are unmistakably a form of storytelling, and many designs incorporate elements from Huichol folklore, mythology, beliefs, and rituals. Other kinds of commerical art include beaded earrings, necklaces, gourd bowls, masks, and embroidered and woven textiles.

Medicine.   Illnesses and diseases can result from various causes: not completing ritual vows, dissatisfaction on the part of the gods, revenge taken by the souls of animals or plants for poor and reckless treatment when alive, sorcery, soul loss (especially among children), evil winds, and the return of ancestors who have not been properly propitiated. To diagnose an illness, a shaman undergoes a period of dietary restrictions and he or she dreams for several nights, during which time the patient is treated daily. The shaman sweeps the patient with feathered wands, sucks out foreign objects from the patient's body, and sprays holy water from his or her mouth onto the patient. When the cause of the illness is known, the shaman instructs the patient's family in the appropriate rituals and offerings that must be carried out. If the patient is extremely ill, a shaman will perform a ceremony in which he or she sings through the night to discover the reason for the patient's poor health. Herbs are still used extensively; however, knowledge of these medicinal plants and their lore is not as widesread as it once was. Owing to the introduction of numerous foreign diseases, most Huichol have adopted Western medicine into their traditional practices. Shamans will bless the medicine before it is administered and may work their healings in conjunction with Western doctors.

Death and Afterlife.   Upon death, the soul of the individual retraces its life, following a path into the underworld, where it is faced with trials and tribulations that are a consequence of the actions of the individual while living. If a person has had sexual relations with a non-Huichol, his or her soul is banished to a corral around which stampeding mules or horses eternally run in circles. If the soul has lived a more pure life, it eventually reaches a temple of the dead in the west, where it dances to unwind itself from the thread of life. Five days after the death, the shaman and family hold a ceremony to bid farewell to the soul. The shaman then helps the soul reach the other world in the sky to join the souls of the previously deceased. Five years later, a special ceremony is performed in which the shaman captures the soul in the form of a rock crystal, which is cared for upon the altar in the family shrine. It is anointed with sacrifical animal blood and offered food during family ceremonies.

Bibliography

Berrin, Kathleen, ed. (1978). *Art of the Huichol Indians.* New York: Fine Arts Museums of San Francisco; Harry N. Abrams.

Furst, Peter T. (1967). "Huichol Conception of the Soul." *Folklore Americas* 27(2): 39–106.

Lumholtz, Carl (1902). *Unknown Mexico.* Vol. 2. New York: Scribner's.

Myerhoff, Barbara (1974). *Peyote Hunt: The Sacred Journey of the Huichol Indians.* Ithaca, N.Y.: Cornell University Press.

Weigand, Phil C. (1981). "Differential Acculturation among the Huichol Indians." In *Themes of Indigenous Acculturation in Northwest Mexico,* edited by Phil C. Weigand and Thomas B. Hinton, 9–21. Tucson: University of Arizona Press.

Zingg, Robert (1938). *The Huichols: Primitive Artists.* New York: G. E. Stechert & Co.

STACY B. SCHAEFER

Indians of Baja California

ETHNONYMS: none

The native peoples of Baja California are found today above the 30th parallel in Baja California, Mexico, and southern California in the United States. The five distinct groups, with population estimates for the 1980s, are the Cocopa (Cocopá, Cocopah, Cucapá, Kikima, Kokwapá, Kwikapa), about 800; the Digueño (Diagueño, Diegueño, Digueno, Kumeyaay, Tipai-Ipai), 350 to 400 in Baja California; the Kiliwi (Kaliwa, Kiliwa, Quiligua), about 60; the Paipai (Akwa'ala), about 250; and the Tipai (Campo), about 185. All of these groups were heavily influenced by early and continuous missionary activity in the area.

See also Cocopa; Kumeyaay in Vol. 1, North America

Bibliography

Almstedt, Ruth (1974). _Bibliography of the Diegueno Indians._ Ramona, Calif.: Ballena Press.

Aschmann, Homer (1967). _The Central Desert of Baja California: Demography and Ecology._ Riverside, Calif.: Manessier.

Kelly, William Henderson (1977). _Cocopa Ethnography._ Tucson: University of Arizona Press.

Italian Mexicans

ETHNONYMS: none

Orientation

Identification. People of Italian descent living in Mexico have, since the late nineteenth century, become generally assimilated into mainstream society. Their identity rests on the common experience of migration from Italy in the late 1800s (a period characterized by a more general Italian diaspora to the Americas under the pressures of economic transformation and the process of unification into a nation-state in 1871) and the establishment of communities, primarily in central and eastern Mexico. Most of these immigrants were from northern Italy, with a majority coming from the rural proletariat and farming sector in Italy. Once in Mexico, they attempted to establish themselves in similar economic pursuits, especially dairy farming. Italian Mexicans share the migration experience, speak a dialect of Italian, eat foods that they consciously identify as "Italian" (e.g., polenta, minestrone, pastas, and endive), play games that are Italian in origin (e.g., boccie ball, a form of lawn bowling), and are devoutly Catholic. Although many Italians now live in urban Mexico, many more live in and

strongly identify with one of the original or spin-off communities that are almost entirely Italian in composition. These individuals still stridently claim an Italian ethnic identity (at least to a non-Mexican outsider) but are also quick to note that they are Mexican citizens as well.

Location. Italians in Mexico reside primarily in one of the rural or semiurban original communities or their spin-offs. Members of these communities tend to live in residential isolation from surrounding Mexican society (see "History and Cultural Relations"). It is important to distinguish among three types of Italian Mexican communities. First, there are the larger, original communities, or _colonias_ (i.e., Chipilo, Puebla; Huatusco, Veracruz; Ciudad del Maíz, San Luis Potosí; La Aldana, Federal District—the four remaining communities of the original eight), populated by the descendants of poor, working-class Italian immigrants. Italian Mexicans still form tight-knit ethnic collectivities within their original communities, but population pressure and a circumscribed land base in these "home" communities have resulted in fissioning—the establishment of a second category of newer, spin-off or satellite communities composed of people from one of the original colonias. These include communities in and around San Miguel de Allende, Valle de Santiago, San José Iturbide, Celaya, Salamanca, Silao, and Irapuato in the state of Guanajuato; Cuautitlán, México; and Apatzingan, Michoacán. Third, there are a small number of anomalous communities, such as Nueva Italia and Lombardía, Michoacán, that were established by wealthy Italians who emigrated to Mexico after the 1880 diaspora and established large agricultural estates known as haciendas.

Demography. Only about 3,000 Italians emigrated to Mexico, primarily during the 1880s. At least half of them subsequently returned to Italy or went on to the United States. Most Italians coming to Mexico were farmers or farm workers from the northern districts. In comparison, between 1876 and 1930, 80 percent of the Italian immigrants to the United States were unskilled day laborers from southern districts. Of Italian immigrants to Argentina, 47 percent were northern and agriculturists.

The largest surviving colonia in Mexico—Chipilo, Puebla—has approximately 4,000 inhabitants, almost a tenfold increase over its starting population of 452 people. Indeed, each of the original eight Italian communities was inhabited by around 400 individuals. If the expansion of Chipilo, Puebla, is representative of the Italian Mexican population as a whole, we might infer that in the late twentieth century there are as many as 30,000 people of Italian descent in Mexico—a small number in comparison with the immigrant Italian population in the United States, Argentina, and Brazil. It is estimated that 1,583,741 Italians emigrated to the Americas between 1876 and 1914: 370,254 arrived in Argentina, 249,504 in Brazil, 871,221 in the United States, and 92,762 in other New World destinations. Italian emigration policies from the 1880s through the 1960s favored labor migration as a safety valve against class conflict.

Linguistic Affiliation. The vast majority of Italian Mexicans are bilingual in Italian and Spanish. They use a mixture of Spanish and Italian to communicate among themselves but only Spanish with non-Italian Mexicans (unless they wish not to be understood by, for example, a vendor in the market). The ability to speak *el dialecto* (the dialect), as they refer to it, is an important marker of ethnic identity and in-group membership. MacKay (1984) reports that in all of the original and satellite communities, an archaic (late nineteenth-century) and truncated version of the highland Venetian dialect (as distinct from standard Italian) is spoken.

History and Cultural Relations

In the late 1800s Italy was undergoing considerable political and economic change and upheaval. The northern part of the country was controlled by an industrial bourgeoisie. Rural sharecroppers were pushed off their land and forced into urban industrial centers as poorly paid and erratically employed wage laborers. This political and economic turbulence resulted in large numbers of poor Italians seeking what they perceived as refuge through migration to the Americas. Hence, the period beginning in the late nineteenth century and continuing into the early twentieth century was marked by heavy Italian emigration to the United States, numerous South American countries (especially Argentina and Brazil), and, to a far lesser extent, Mexico and Central America.

Italians were contracted in Italy in the 1880s by agents representing the administration of General Manuel González, a puppet president appointed by Porfirio Díaz; the majority arrived in Mexico between 1881 and 1883. The Mexican government sold them land and provided them with some other resources, including seed, farming implements, and one year's living subsidy to support them before the harvest of their first crop. Their communities were disbursed throughout Mexico in the central and eastern states of Puebla, Morelos, the Federal District, and Veracruz. After 1884, the final year of González's presidency, the official policy of contracting with foreign immigrants was halted in practice and left to the control of private contracting companies, although the actual immigrant legislation was not reversed until 1897. These companies helped establish other Italian communities in Michoacán—the Cusi and Brioschi families, for example, established haciendas in Nueva Italia and Lombardía—and also brought over immigrants to work on railroad construction and other economic activities, including 525 Italians employed in agricultural wage labor on the coffee and sugar plantation of Motzorongo in Veracruz.

The Mexican government's motive for contracting with foreign immigrants to populate rural Mexico was related to Porfirio Díaz's desire to provide a model to help modernize the Mexican peasantry. He opted to do this through the infusion of European immigrants with agrarian backgrounds but who were also oriented toward capitalist market relations and who sought to develop their own agricultural enterprises. Italians were particularly sought after because they were Catholic and had a Mediterranean cultural background that would, it was thought, help them relate to Mexican society and eventually become assimilated into it. The immigration project, however, was a failure. Its result was the

formation of a number of socially isolated communities of Italians in Mexico.

Since the 1930s, the original Italian communities in Mexico have been going through a fissioning process because of population pressure and a small, circumscribed land base. This has resulted in an interesting contrast between old and new communities, especially in terms of their differential constructions of ethnic identity. Chipilo, Puebla, established in 1882, is a largely self-contained community in terms of basic resources and infrastructure (e.g., it has schools, banks, markets, a church, etc.), in which there exists a collective ethnic solidarity marked by the importance of group action to obtain or defend benefits beyond the reach of individuals.

One benefit of Italian Mexican ethnicity is economic: the people of Chipilo can be considered a middleman minority because they controlled the local dairy industry, from direct milk production through processing and marketing, through two community-based dairy cooperatives. In the 1980s these cooperatives were bought out by large dairies in Mexico City. A Chipilo dairymen's association, however, still thrives and supports the interests of the community's farmers. Another type of benefit is political. The community is attempting to become designated as a municipal seat, primarily on the basis of its unique economic and cultural composition.

This contrasts markedly with the construction of identity in the satellite community of La Perla de Chipilo, Guanajuato, established in 1963, where there is no evidence of ethnically based political or economic alliances. La Perla is a small community of twenty-seven dairy-farming households and is far from being self-contained. Initially physically isolated from other Mexican communities by dirt roads and a lack of transportation, La Perla became connected to the outside world in 1972 through the construction of a paved highway into nearby San Miguel de Allende. People must drive to town to go to the market or the bank or to attend church, their children must attend Mexican schools, and, in general, most of a household's important economic and social ties are with non-Italian Mexicans outside the community. Italian identity does, however, have economic implications in that it provides a rationale to justify the existing inequality between Italian Mexican farmers and the Mexican wage laborers working for them.

This construction of a highly individualized ethnic identity and outward focus in satellite communities such as La Perla forces the question of assimilation—the transformation of identity toward decreasing perceptions of distinction from the larger Mexican population. Individuals who live outside of Italian Mexican communities rarely teach their children Italian, prepare Italian foods, or engage in other "ethnic" activities. Satellite communities such as La Perla may be transitory places that have been just isolated enough to maintain a distinct Italian identity. This level of identity maintenance may become increasingly problematic as more children go to Mexican schools and spend the majority of their time in Mexican society and as young men marry Mexican women (although this is not considered the ideal, at least by the parental generation) because of a lack of marriageable Italian women in their satellite communities.

Economy

The Italian Mexicans are primarily known for their participation in the dairy industry. In fact, a well-known line of dairy products—Chipilo Brand—was once produced exclusively by one of the dairy cooperatives owned and operated by farmers in Chipilo, Puebla. These farmers have been small-scale capitalist producers since their arrival in Mexico, producing primarily for a market but always retaining some production for household consumption. In the late twentieth century over 75 percent of the households in Chipilo, Puebla, receive all or part of their income through dairy farming, and virtually all of the inhabitants of La Perla de Chipilo, Guanajuato, gain their income through some aspect of dairying. Farms have herds ranging between 10 and 125 head of cattle (an average of between 25 and 50 head) that are supported by the intensive (often irrigated) cultivation of alfalfa and maize. Many farms use mechanized milking techniques and other forms of technology in their enterprises. Most households are involved in dairying, but they also tend to have multiple income streams; many of their members are considerably educated and are employed in various types of jobs. Nevertheless, the identity of Italian Mexican communities is still anchored to dairying as a way of life. In fact, many of the satellite communities established since the 1930s formed so that community members who could not farm in Chipilo, Puebla, owing to a lack of available land, could pursue a dairy-farming career elsewhere. Although the Chipilo, Puebla, community might be considered to have been, at least in the past, a type of middleman minority, satellite communities tend to be made up of independent farmers who do not participate in ethnic economic or political networks either within or outside the community.

Kinship

Italian Mexican marriage, residential practices, and kinship system generally conform to those of the larger Mexican society: they are characterized by serial monogamy, bilateral descent, a mixture of patrilocal and neolocal nuclear and extended families, and partible inheritance.

Marriage. Serial monogamy is the common form of marriage among Italian Mexicans. The Catholic church has strong sanctions discouraging divorce. Should a couple divorce, neither individual can remarry with the benediction of the church. Should a spouse die, however, individuals are free to remarry. Among the parental generation of Italian Mexicans, group endogamy is strongly viewed as preferable to exogamous arrangements. In original communities, such as Chipilo, Puebla, the great majority of marriages are endogamous. In the satellite community of La Perla de Chipilo, Guanajuato, on the other hand, of seventy-five marriages between 1963 and 1988, 52 percent were exogamous and 48 percent endogamous. Typically, when a woman marries a non-Italian Mexican, the couple resides outside of the community, but an Italian Mexican man is likely to bring his non-Italian bride to live in the Italian Mexican community.

Domestic Unit and Inheritance. The Italian Mexican household is a locus for the reproduction of a rather widely cited Latin American and Mediterranean household ideology that emphasizes hierarchical, patriarchal authority. Gender is a major form of inequality within households, and there is a visible gap in status between sons and daughters that is created and maintained by differential access to farm resources and inheritance. Although ideally inheritance is partible, the reality is that sons but not daughters, who are expected to marry and be supported by their husbands, compete for the inheritance of all or part of the farm (i.e., de facto patrilineal partible inheritance). Sons' bargaining power within the household for resources, and ultimately inheritance, is conditioned by their age and location within the domestic cycle. As sons get older, they start their own petty businesses raising pigs or goats for sale, generating extra spending money for themselves but also demonstrating their entrepreneurial skill to their father. Those with the most skill are likely to enhance their bargaining power and receive the favor of their father—an especially important factor in determining who will inherit the family farm.

There is a second aspect to understanding households that is generational. Through the 1960s, households tended to be large and extended, often with ten to twelve children and multiple generations. This has created problems of inheritance and succession. In the 1970s mechanization began to be adopted by many of these large households, effectively "squeezing out" older sons (especially those who were married and had started their own families and who were, consequently, costly for their father to support), whose labor was replaced by that of younger sons and machinery. Younger sons were more likely to be working on the farm when the father reached retirement age (around the age of 60 to 65) and thus to inherit the estate (these conditions therefore favored a type of ultimogeniture).

The youngest generation of married sons has smaller families (two to five children) and can now rely on machinery as well as the increasing use of wage labor to replace household labor.

Socialization. Early socialization takes place within the home. Parents tend to be strict with their children, often disciplining them physically. Children are taught to speak Italian as well as Spanish. In original communities such as Chipilo, Puebla, schools are staffed by Italian Mexicans, and classes are often conducted in Spanish and Italian. In satellite communities such as La Perla de Chipilo, Guanajuato, children must go to nearby Mexican towns to attend school. Formal education is attaining increasing value. Many Italian Mexicans go well past the mandatory six years of education, and a large percentage attend high schools and universities.

From an early age, children are socialized to accept an occasionally blurred division of labor: boys do farm chores, and girls learn domestic tasks. Older adults report, however, that prior to the adoption of mechanization in farming, women frequently did the milking and field work during critical stages of planting and harvesting.

An important rite of passage for boys and girls around 10 years of age is their first communion in the Catholic church. Another rite, the *quinceañera*, is celebrated on a girl's fifteenth birthday. It introduces her to the community as a marriageable woman and displays her family's wealth.

The main ritual is a lavish feast hosted by her relatives. This modern custom is gaining popularity in mestizo areas of Mexico where the standard of living is improving. Both of these rites have religious dimensions and serve as opportunities for establishing broader kinship ties through *compadrazgo*; they are also social occasions marked by a fiesta, or festival.

Sociopolitical Organization

Social and Political Organization.   Although there is considerable diversity within Italian Mexican communities, Italian Mexicans are generally recognized as being successful and affluent farmers. Many are leaving their rural, homogeneous communities and moving to larger urban centers. Some continue to farm, but others have entered an array of jobs. In large Italian Mexican population centers, such as Chipilo, Puebla, there are community centers that provide a venue for social activities such as wedding receptions, baptismal and quinceañera celebrations, and the like.

Italian Mexicans have no formal social or political organization, although there is a concerted effort in Chipilo, Puebla, to obtain designation as a municipality, a move that would provide money and other state resources. Additionally, the farmers of Chipilo are organized into a community-based dairymen's association.

Social Control and Conflict.   Italian-Mexicans participate in the Mexican legal system to resolve disputes and conflicts.

Religion and Expressive Culture

Italian-Mexicans follow Catholic doctrine. A number of important rites of passage center on the Catholic church: baptisms, first communions, quinceañeras, weddings, and funerals. Larger Italian communities also celebrate the holy day of their patron saint, a festival that is likewise marked in Mexican communities.

Burial in a local *campo santo* (graveyard) is the common mortuary practice of Italian Mexicans. Unlike their Mexican counterparts, Italian Mexicans do not observe the annual Día de los Muertos (Day of the Dead) on 1 November. They do, however, hold novenas (a series of prayers) to commemorate the first anniversary of the death of an individual, and occasionally in subsequent years as well. This ceremony is led by a close female relative of the deceased who "prays the rosary," a call/response prayer ritual that is primarily attended by other women, with men participating at the margins or standing nearby socializing.

Bibliography

Glantz, Susana (1974). *El ejido colectivo de Nueva Italia.* Mexico City: Secretaría de Educación Público; Instituto Nacional de Antropología e Historia.

Klein, Herbert S. (1983). "The Integration of Italian Immigrants into the United States and Argentina: A Comparative Analysis." *American Historical Review* 88(2): 306–329.

McDonald, James H. (1991a). "Small-Scale Irrigation and the Emergence of Inequality among Farmers in Central Mexico." *Research in Economic Anthropology* 13:161–189.

McDonald, James H. (1991b). *The Emergence of Inequality among Capitalizing Family Farmers in Mexico.* Ann Arbor, Mich.: University Microfilms International.

MacKay, Carolyn J. (1984). "The Veneto Dialect in Chipilo, Mexico." *Texas Linguistic Forum* 23:123–133.

Schmitter, Barbara (1984). "Sending States and Immigrant Minorities—The Case of Italy." *Comparative Studies in Society and History* 26:325–334.

Vadala, Titta, and Piera Rella (1984). "Sociological Literature on Migration in Italy." *Current Sociology* 32:143–174.

Zago, José Augustín (1982). *Breve historia de la fundación de Chipilo.* Mexico City: Imprenta Venecia.

Zilli, José B. (1981). *Italianos en México.* Jalapa, Veracruz: Editorial San José.

Zilli, José B. (1986). *Braceros Italianos para México.* Jalapa, Veracruz: Editorial San José.

JAMES H. McDONALD

Itza'

ETHNONYMS: Itzá, Itzá Maya, Itzaj Maya, Maya, Mayeros, Petén Maya, San Joseños

Orientation

Identification.   The Itza' Maya identify themselves as descendants of speakers of the Itza' Maya language and are centered in the town of San José, Petén, Guatemala. Spaniards and scholars have always referred to the San Joseños as "Itzas" but until quite recently they usually referred to themselves as "Mayas" ("Mayeros"). Children stopped learning the language in the 1930s because of the government's repressive language policy. As a result, only about two dozen older adults are fluent in Itza'. Beginning about the mid-1980s, as a consequence of the influx of rainforest activists, the Itza' have become aware of themselves as an important group on the international scene. Many of the townspeople in San José have displayed a revived interest in their traditional culture and language and have adopted "Itzaj" as their self-designation.

Location.   San José is a town on the northern shore of Lake Petén Itza', in the heart of the Mayan lowlands of subtropical northern Guatemala. The town is the administrative center of a *municipio* of the same name. The 2,252-

square-kilometer township falls within the northern subtropical region of Petén.

Demography. Between 1978 and 1993 the population of the town of San José, almost all of Itza' descent, grew rapidly, to approximately 2,000 residents. There are perhaps another 2,000 Itza' in the region, suggesting a total population of about 4,000; however, no accurate census figures are available.

Linguistic Affiliation. Itza' Maya belongs to the Yucatecan Mayan Branch of the Mayan Language Family. Linguistic evidence suggests that Itza' separated from its sister languages—Yukateko, Lakantun, and Mopan Maya—approximately one millennium ago.

History and Cultural Relations

Little is known about the pre-Hispanic Itza'. Legend has it that the Itza' migrated to Yucatán from elsewhere in Mexico or were a remnant Classic Petén Maya group that moved north to Yucatán. After competing with the Xiu clan for control of the Yucatán Peninsula, the Itza' settled in Petén, perhaps in the 1450s (however, some scholars believe they may have settled there around 1200). According to some interpretations of indigenous history recorded in colonial-era Yucatecan Mayan documents called _Books of the Chilam Balam_ (derived from the name of the famous prophet—_chilam_—who was known as _balam_, jaguar), the Itza' fled the region of Chichén Itza' in northern Yucatán to found their island capital of Tayasal in Lake Petén Itza'. There they formed a confederacy composed of four loosely allied political groups. They resisted the Spanish until 1697, about a century and a half after most Mayan groups were conquered. The Itza' maintained contact with other Mayans in Yucatán and in Belize throughout the colonial period, and there probably were waves of migrants from the north who fled the Spanish to settle in Petén. They also had intermittent contact with the Mopan Maya in southern Petén, the Lakantun to the west, and Q'eqchi' immigrants from the Verapaces, Guatemala. Until the 1970s, large stands of tropical forest and the absence of good roads made travel to Petén difficult and helped maintain its relative isolation.

Hernán Cortés passed through the region in 1524 on his way from Mexico City to Honduras, where he planned to punish a subordinate lieutenant, Cristóbal de Olid. He reported being well received by the Itza' "king" Kanek' at Tayasal, present-day Flores. During the colonial era, the Itza' periodically received Spanish emissaries but steadfastly resisted conversion to Catholicism and submission to Spanish authority. Tayasal remained a center of Itza' culture, including the Mayan hieroglyphic scribal tradition, and also inspired Mayan resistance to Spanish domination in Yucatán and Belize, until it was conquered during a Spanish military campaign in March 1697. Warfare and European diseases decimated the Itza' population, which has remained small since the seventeenth century. Indians in the region were forced to live in mission towns or to flee into the forest. San José was one of these mission towns and the only one in which an Itza' ethnic identity has survived to the present.

After 1697, the Itza' of San José were primarily traditional swidden farmers cultivating staples—maize, beans and squash—as well as many supplemental crops. They sold surplus agricultural products as well as clay water jugs, canoes, firewood, construction materials, and other forest products. Since the Conquest, San José and all of Petén have been politically and economically dominated by a mixed Creole and Ladino elite residing in Flores.

In the 1890s, demand for chicle, a tree-resin base for chewing gum, transformed the regional economy of Petén. The chicle boom lasted until about 1970. During the chicle harvest season, from July to February, men formed base camps in the forests, from which they fanned out daily to tap chicle from sapodilla trees. Almost all Itza' men participated in the chicle harvest, as did many other Peteneros. Chicleros (chicle workers) and their families were dependent on a patron, who often supported them until the men returned home from the forest. Chicleros were renowned for pre- and postharvest extravagant and exuberant celebrations. Since the 1960s and 1970s, tourism and extraction of timber and other forest products have become primary industries in the region.

In the 1960s the Guatemalan government sponsored settlement of Petén and, in 1970, completed a road from the more densely populated highlands. Since then, large numbers of immigrants have come to Petén. The Itza' have resisted allowing newcomers to settle in San José, forcing them to found new villages nearby.

In the 1980s the civil war in Guatemala affected Petén, where the military maintain a strong presence. Guerrilla groups have been active in Petén since the 1970s but decreasingly so since the peak of the violence in the mid-1980s. San José was was not occupied or attacked by either side; however, San Joseños, like other Peteneros, were terrified by the violence.

The interest in conservation and ecotourism has brought many foreigners to the region, and the Itza' have become involved in conservation efforts. They are in constant contact with outsiders but so far have generally succeeded in keeping them out of San José.

Settlements

After the Conquest by the Spanish in 1697, many Indians in Petén fled to the forest. Others, including non-Itza', were congregated in mission towns. By the twentieth century, San José and nearby San Andrés were the only towns in northern Petén with significant numbers of residents who spoke a Mayan language. Early in the twentieth century, a group of Itza' fleeing political repression settled in the town of Soccotz, just across the border in Belize. There were a number of Mayan-speaking people living in villages and ranches surrounding Lake Petén Itza'. Almost all these groups, however, have assimilated to Hispanic-Ladino culture. Today, San José is the only town in Petén that maintains its Itza' identity.

San José is a crowded, nucleated town climbing up the steep hillsides from the shores of Lake Petén Itza'. Traditional houses are rectangular, made of wattle and daub with thatched roofs. Houses are internally divided by framed cloth partitions into a central living area with sleeping quarters on the sides. External kitchens are smaller buildings of the same construction. Cement-block, tin-roofed construction is increasingly common.

Economy

Subsistence and Commercial Activities. The traditional economy, based on swidden (milpa) horticulture has undergone radical change in the twentieth century. The chicle industry was the principal employer of men in the region from about 1890 until 1970; since 1990 it has had a mild resurgence owing to Japanese demand for a natural base for chewing gum. Since 1970, the timber industry, which is focused on the extraction of fine woods, has been a major employer, but fine woods are becoming increasingly scarce. Peteneros collect other forest products for overseas export, primarily honey, allspice, and a small palm called *xate* used by florists. Illegal traffic in Mayan antiquities and drugs is also significant in Petén.

Tourism is an increasingly important industry. Tikal and other archaeological ruins of the Classic Maya (A.D. 250 to A.D. 900) attract tourists from all over the world. A number of Itza' men are employed by the national park system as workers or guards. Since 1989, development and conservation groups have been promoting ecotourism as a way to provide alternative employment to the local inhabitants and to preserve the natural ecology of the Petén forest. The Itza' have established a 36-square-kilometer reserve dedicated to the conservation of the forest and of their culture.

Industrial Arts. Many San José men work in traditional and modern construction as carpenters and masons. There are also a half-dozen furniture workshops in town. Several men occasionally make dugout canoes, but these are in decreasing demand.

Trade. San Joseños sell furniture to other Peteneros and forest products destined for overseas export. There are a number of small food shops and saloons in town, mostly run by women. Most food, clothing, and modern goods are purchased in San Benito, on the south side of Lake Petén Itza'.

Division of Labor. Men are swidden farmers, cowboys, masons and carpenters, national park employees, and collectors of nontimber forest products such as chicle. Women manage the household, tend small gardens, and raise chickens and pigs. Some women are shopkeepers, and others prepare food for sale.

Land Tenure. Traditionally, all inhabitants of the township (municipio) had usufruct rights (without charge) to land for their milpas and ranches and ownership rights to improvements. One could sell rights to land previously worked. Population pressure is putting stress on the system, and land that was formerly communal has been sold to outside developers, several of whom plan to build hotels on the beaches of Lake Petén Itza'.

Kinship

Kin Groups and Descent. Descent is reckoned bilaterally. There are no lineages or corporate kin groups.

Kinship Terminology. Spanish kinship terminology is used by all, but Itza' speakers also use Itza' Maya kin terms. The Itza' kinship system is similar to the Spanish, but distinguishes relative age of siblings, with *itz'in* for younger sibling, *kik* for older sister, and *suku'un* for older brother.

Marriage and Family

Marriage. Ideally, marriage is monogamous and virilocal. Men and women are said to marry for love, preferring to select a partner from within the community. Women were previously eligible for marriage at age 15 and now may marry at 18. The prospective groom asks several older men to accompany his parents to petition the parents of the bride for their permission to marry. If the woman's parents agree, the man joins them several hours later. If the woman's parents refuse, the couple will probably elope. The groom must buy the bride's wedding dress and another fine dress and pay all wedding costs. After the wedding, the bride remains in her parents' house for eight days and then joins the groom. She either moves to their new house or to the groom's parents' house. Less often, the groom moves in with the bride's family.

Domestic Unit. Newlyweds ideally establish their own household but may stay with the parents of either spouse until they can afford their own house. Children stay with their parents until they marry. The youngest son is expected to remain with and care for aged parents, but this duty may fall to another child.

Inheritance. Spouses hold property rights jointly and are free to bequeath property as they wish. Ideally, children share equally in inheritance from parents; the youngest child, however, may inherit the parental house.

Socialization. Women and older siblings are the primary caretakers of young children. Infants are held or laid in bed or hammocks until they are 10 months old, when they are seated on the floor. When at home, men also care for and supervise children. Breast and/or bottle demand feeding continues for about two years. Babies are in diapers until they are 2 years old, when they are toilet trained. Physical punishment is used, sparingly, after a child reaches 4 or 5 years of age. Children are trained primarily to obey and respect parents. By between ages 10 and 12, children can execute most adult tasks, which they learn mainly by imitating elders.

Sociopolitical Organization

Social Organization. The elementary family in its own household is the basic unit of social, economic, and religious life. Although cross-household alliances are weak, San Joseños identify with their community, which in this case coincides with Itza' ethnic identity. Rather than joining impersonal, formal groups, San Joseños build personal networks based on kinship, ritual kinship (*compadrazgo*), privileged friendship, and patronage. These networks cut across community lines and serve practical purposes. San Joseños have a reputation for honoring ritual-kinship obligations more faithfully than other Peteneros. San Joseños use formal courtesy to get along with others without becoming embroiled in their affairs. Adults who treat others with courtesy, defend community interests, and manage their own households without interfering with others are esteemed.

Political Organization. The town of San José is the center of an administrative-territorial unit, the township. The township is governed by an elected council headed by a mayor. The council is responsible for the welfare of the township, and although it has a good deal of autonomy, its actions are supervised by the central government. The council is responsible to a provincial governor, who is appointed by the national president. Almost all the new settlers reside in villages that are administratively subordinate to the township center. In 1990, for the first time in San José's history, an immigrant was elected mayor.

Within the town, politics is organized around faction leaders—usually older men esteemed for their managerial skills and concern for community welfare.

The Itza' revitalization movement is not fully integrated with the Maya revitalization movement in Guatemala. The Itza' are developing a separate ethnic identity as lowland Petén Indians and do not identify with the highland Maya. Both movements have political overtones.

Social Control. San Joseños are reluctant to interfere with one another and tolerant of deviance from norms of behavior, so long as it does not directly affect their own households. When it does, they resort to gossip and avoidance. They may also ask the mayor to intervene informally to correct someone's behavior. Serious misdemeanors and crimes are referred to the formal court system.

Conflict. Until 1944, a system of debt peonage prevailed in Guatemala, and outstanding debts were frequently a source of conflict between chicle collectors from San José and other towns in Petén and their patrons. Thereafter, aside from interpersonal antagonisms, the most serious conflicts among San Joseños centered on factions fighting for control of the town council, especially for the post of mayor. The town has also had and still has conflicts with neighboring townships over tax payments for timber and nontimber (e.g., those from which chicle is extracted) forests within the township jurisdiction. Settlers are beginning to compete with San Joseños for control of the township council. The presence of outsiders promoting competing development and conservation strategies has intensified factional and personal disputes within the town and will have an impact on the ability of the Itza' of San José to maintain their traditions and language.

Religion and Expressive Culture

Religious Beliefs. Until the 1980s, all inhabitants of San José were Catholic. Women are more actively involved in worship services than men. Mass was said weekly by a visiting priest until the violence of the 1970s and 1980s, and less regularly since then. In the 1980s about half the town converted to evangelical Protestantism, which stresses moral rectitude and abstinence. Belief in forest spirits or goblins (_duendes_) is common.

Religious Practitioners. The visiting priests are the chief practitioners, but local men may become church stewards, who are responsible for festivals, and sextons, who take care of the church. Both men and women may be catechists.

Ceremonies. Baptisms, girls' 15th birthdays, weddings, deaths, one-year anniversaries of death, All Souls' Day, and the town's saint's day are celebrated with masses.

San José is known for an annual ceremony performed on All Souls' Eve. A skull is carried in procession from the church around the town and is returned to the church at dawn. Three skulls, said to be of former church stewards (_priostes_), are housed on an altar in the church and are brought out in three-year rotations.

Formerly, 3 May, the Day of the Cross and planting time, was observed with a procession that included masked celebrants dancing with a pig's head. A feast followed the procession. There also were Mayan ceremonies in the fields, in which food was offered to the winds at planting time.

Arts. Traditional women's arts include embroidery, crocheting, and pottery making. Men made henequen hammocks and worked wood. Traditional musical instruments included marimbas, drums, flutes, mandolins, and harps. The marimbas and flutes are still played. Modern musical groups playing guitars and drums are now popular.

Medicine. Folk medicine is increasingly limited. Most medical services are provided at a local clinic or at the hospital in San Benito. Some midwives (_parteras_), native curers (_curanderos_), herbalists (_yerbateros_), bone setters, and massagers (_talladores de hueso_) continue to practice; yerbateros are especially recommended for treating snakebite. Itza' suspect that sorcerers (_brujos_) practice in neighboring towns.

Death and Afterlife. Family members typically mourn for six months to a year, during which time they abstain from fiestas. A mass is celebrated one year after death.

Bibliography

Hofling, Charles Andrew (1991). _Itzá Maya Texts, with a Grammatical Overview._ Salt Lake City: University of Utah Press.

Jones, Grant D. (1992). "The Canek Manuscript in Ethnohistorical Perspective." _Ancient Mesoamerica_ 3:243–268.

Reina, Ruben E. (1965). "Town, Community, and Multicommunity." _Estudios de Cultura Maya_ 5:361–390.

Reina, Ruben E. (1967). "Milpas and Milperos: Implications for Prehistoric Times." _American Anthropologist_ 69(1): 1–20.

Schwartz, Norman B. (1990). _Forest Society: A Social History of Petén, Guatemala._ Philadelphia: University of Pennsylvania Press.

Villagutierre Soto-Mayor, Juan de [1701] (1983). _History of the Conquest of the Province of the Itza._ Translated by Robert De. Wood. Edited by Frank E. Comparato. Culver City, Calif.: Labyrinthos.

CHARLES ANDREW HOFLING
AND NORMAN B. SCHWARTZ

Ixil

ETHNONYMS: none

The 55,000 to 80,000 Ixil Indians are a highland Maya tribe living in the mountains of the Quiché and Huehuetenango departments of Guatemala. They inhabit the northern slopes of the Altos Cuchumatanes range and a middle area between it and the Chama Mountains at the edge of the tropical rain forest to the north. Their territory varies in elevation from 700 to 3,000 meters. They live in the three *municipios* of Nebaj, Cotzal, and Chajul in the department of Quiché.

The K'iche' Maya conquered the Ixil in the fifteenth century. Although a sixteenth-century revolution won them independence, by 1540 they had been reconquered, this time by the Spanish. Many were herded into *congregaciones,* where missionaries converted them to Christianity and where they worked for labor contractors. The Ixil population fell to one-tenth of its previous size owing to disease and war with the Lakandon Maya between 1540 and the early seventeenth century. Many Ixil went with labor contractors to plantations on the Pacific coast during the late eighteenth and nineteenth centuries. Guatemalan government land reform following 1871 ended Indian tribal landownership and implemented individual private ownership of land; as a consequence, the Ixil retained less than half of their earlier lands. As many as 20,000 Ixil fled from political persecution in Guatemala to the United States during the 1980s.

The Ixil are primarily maize farmers practicing slash-and-burn farming methods. There is only one maize harvest per year. Other crops are beans, coffee, apples, *guisquiles* (vegetable pears), and potatoes. They also grow vegetables as cash crops.

Bibliography

Colby, Benjamin, and Pierre L. Van den Berghe (1969). *Ixil Country: A Plural Society in Highland Guatemala.* Berkeley and Los Angeles: University of California Press.

Olson, James S. (1991). *The Indians of Central and South America.* New York: Greenwood Press.

Stoll, David (1993). *Between Two Armies in the Ixil Towns of Guatemala.* New York: Columbia University Press.

Jakalteko

ETHNONYM: Jacalteco

The Jakalteko are a western Maya Indian group. Estimates of their population vary from 16,000 to more than 32,000. Nearly all of them live in the Huehuetenango Department of Guatemala, but approximately 1,000 live nearby, across the border in Mexico. Much of their land has been taken in the Guatemalan federal government's land-privatization program, and, as a result, many Jakalteko have become migrant laborers. In the 1980s many of the Guatemalan Jakalteko relocated to the United States to escape government persecution.

Bibliography

Olson, James S. (1991). *The Indians of Central and South America.* New York: Greenwood Press.

Jamaicans

ETHNONYMS: none

Orientation

Identification. The name of the island of Jamaica is derived from the Arawak word "Xaymaca," which may have meant "land of springs," "land of wood and water," or "land of cotton."

Location. Jamaica is located in the Greater Antilles group of the West Indies, 144 kilometers south of Cuba and 160 kilometers west of Haiti. It has an area of 11,034 square kilometers and is the third-largest island in the Caribbean. The interior is very hilly and mountainous, with deep valleys and 120 unnavigable rivers, and the coastal plain is flat and narrow. The climate is generally hot and humid (tropical) but cooler and more temperate in the highlands.

Demography. The population was 2,506,701 in July 1992, with an average annual growth rate of 0.09 percent and a density of 228 people per square kilometer. The ethnic composition of Jamaica is 76.3 percent Black, 15.1 percent Afro-European, 3.2 percent White, 3 percent East Indian and Afro–East Indian, 1.2 percent Chinese and Afro-Chinese, and 1.2 percent other. Approximately 22,000 Jamaicans emigrate every year, and roughly a million now live in the United States, Canada, and Great Britain.

Linguistic Affiliation. Jamaica is officially English speaking, but it actually has what linguists call a postcreole linguistic continuum. An indigenous language, referred to as "patois" by Jamaicans and "Jamaican Creole" by linguists, evolved from contact between African slaves and English planters. Jamaican speech varies, by class, from Creole to Standard English, with many intermediate grades of variation.

History and Cultural Relations

About 60,000 Arawak Indians were living in Jamaica when Columbus landed in 1494, but they were exterminated by disease and enslavement during the Spanish occupation, which lasted from 1509 to 1655, when the island was seized by Great Britain. The British tried to populate the island with convicts and indentured servants from England, Scotland, and Ireland; they also persuaded buccaneers like Henry Morgan to establish their base at Port Royal, which became the center of trade for loot captured in raids on Spanish ships. Yeoman farming, with cocoa as the principal crop, soon gave way to cattle ranching and sugar, coffee, cotton, and pimento (allspice) estates and plantations. About 750,000 Africans were brought in to work the estates, but resistance to slavery was strong, and the society was in an almost constant state of revolt; a permanent population of runaway slaves (Maroons) established communities in the mountains. Production of sugar cane, the principal crop, peaked in the mid-eighteenth century, when Jamaica was regarded as England's richest and most valuable colony, but it began to fall in 1774. The declining economy and an increasingly influential antislavery movement in England led to the abolition of the slave trade by an act of parliament in 1807. A serious slave revolt, the "Baptist War" of 1831, and shocking reprisals against missionaries for their alleged involvement in it, encouraged passage of an emancipation act in 1833, but full freedom did not come until 1838, after a period of "apprenticeship." Many of the freed slaves left the estates, moving to the towns or becoming small farmers, and indentured servants from India (and later China) were brought in to replace them. After 1866, some abandoned sugar estates were turned over to the production of bananas, which rapidly replaced sugar as the leading export. The process of decolonization was set in motion by serious and widespread labor disturbances in 1938 that inspired nationalistic sentiments and led to the formation of the island's first trade union and political party. Large deposits of bauxite ore (the basis for aluminum) were discovered in the 1940s, and by 1960 Jamaica had become the world's leading producer of bauxite and aluminum. Many factories were built in the 1950s, and the value of manufacturing reached that of agriculture by 1960. The tourist industry also began to grow at a tremendous rate in the 1950s. Jamaica received its independence in 1962.

The island was a British colony for over 300 years, and many of its institutions (particularly legal, governmental, and educational) and ideals (for example, monogamy and the patriarchal nuclear family) are essentially English. Jamaican society was initially "pluralistic," embracing the African cultures of the slave majority and the English culture of their masters, but "creolization"—the gradual reshaping of English traditions by African traditions, and vice-versa—led to the emergence of a syncretic, indigenous culture. The African influence is particularly evident in language, cuisine, folklore, folk medicine, religion, and the arts, but rarely does it survive in true form.

Settlements

Urban centers are growing rapidly as a result of migration from rural areas. About 40 percent of the population is in the Kingston–Spanish Town conurbation in the southeast, where most of the factories are located. Another 15 percent live in forty-eight small towns, and the remaining 45 percent live in over one thousand rural settlements. Sugar estates are located in low-lying areas, generally along the coast. Bauxite mining and alumina processing are concentrated in the center of the island. The tourist industry is situated largely along the north coast, from Negril in the west to Port Antonio in the east. Small farms are dispersed throughout the rugged interior.

Economy

Subsistence and Commercial Activities. The gross domestic product was U.S. $1,400 per capita in 1991, up from $960 in 1987. The economy grew rapidly in the 1960s, declined steadily from 1973 to 1980, and recovered slowly in the 1980s. Sugar was the main industry until the slaves were emancipated, whereupon a peasantry and a dual economy came into being. Small farmers produce a variety of crops, such as yams and sweet potatoes, for local consumption. Bananas replaced sugar as the main export at the beginning of the twentieth century, but the peak production level attained in 1937 has never been surpassed. The primary cash crop today is marijuana (ganja), which is largely exported to the United States and had an estimated value of U.S. $3.5 billion in 1984. Marijuana cultivation is illegal (as is its use), but the economy is very dependent on it. The most valuable sector of the formal economy is bauxite mining and alumina processing. Light manufacturing grew rapidly in the 1960s, and in 1984 there were 1,202 small factories (768 of them in the Kingston metropolitan area). The number of tourists fell sharply in the 1970s but rebounded in the 1980s; the island had over a million visitors in 1987. There was a marked decline in the number of tourists and in the rate of economic growth in 1991, as a result of the recession in the United States.

Industrial Arts. Owing to its long history of plantation monoculture, the island has developed few industrial crafts, with the notable exception of basket making. Industrialization has been hampered by a shortage of skilled workers, due in part to emigration.

Trade. There are many small shops in the countryside and a few large grocery and department stores in urban areas. Agricultural products are distributed largely through a system created by slaves; about 20,000 higgler women buy produce from small farmers and sell it at some ninety marketplaces. The economy has always been export oriented and dependent on a few basic commodities. Guided by the philosophy of Mercantilism, the British developed the island for sugar production and as a market for their industrial exports. Jamaica was an important part of the infamous "triangular trade," which brought firearms and manufactured goods from Europe to Africa, slaves from Africa to the Caribbean, and sugar from the Caribbean to Europe. England was Jamaica's main trading partner until the development of the bauxite industry in the 1950s, when the focus of trade shifted to the United States.

Division of Labor. In 1989, 22.5 percent of the labor force was employed in agriculture, 41 percent in the service sector, and 19 percent in industry. The unemployment rate was high, at 17.5 percent, and highest among 20- to 24-year-olds. The proportion of women in the labor force is about 46 percent, one of the highest in the world; women work mainly in the service sector, as higglers, domestics, teachers, and office workers.

Land Tenure. Slave plantations were generally located in flat and fertile areas, such as valleys and the coastal plains. The hilly and less fertile interior was sparsely inhabited until Emancipation; seeking land as a symbol of freedom, former slaves settled there and became peasant farmers. These historical patterns still prevail to some extent. There are about 1,000 farms of over 40 hectares and 151,000 of under 2 hectares. Large farms occupy the best land and produce a single crop, principally for export. Small farms are generally located in hilly areas and produce a variety of crops, mostly for the domestic market. Ownership of land is greatly preferred to renting; some land is held in common by kindreds. All heirs to this "family land" have an equal right to live on and use a portion of it but cannot alienate it. Family land is an important symbol of security and family unity; it usually has little or no agricultural value, but kin are often buried on it.

Kinship

Kin Groups and Descent. There are no corporate kin groups, but kindreds are very important. Jamaicans maintain strong ties with consanguines that include regular exchanges of gifts such as produce. Descent is bilateral, although matrilateral ties are often stronger than patrilateral ones.

Kinship Terminology. Jamaicans have an Eskimo system, using basically the same kin terms as the English and the Americans, but they emphasize consanguines and often ignore affinal or conjugal relationships.

Marriage and Family

Marriage. Legal marriage, monogamy, and the nuclear family are cultural ideals more often attained by the mid-

dle and upper classes than by the lower classes. Sexual relations generally begins during early adolescence among the lower-class majority. Extraresidential or "visiting" relationships are usually followed by several coresidential and neolocal "common-law" or consensual unions. Legal marriage occurs relatively late, after the birth of several children and the attainment of some degree of economic security. Marriage is monogamous; divorce is rare but extramarital relationships are common.

Domestic Unit. The composition of Jamaican households varies greatly. Matrifocal units are common, particularly in urban areas. Nuclear families are the norm among the middle and upper classes. Lower-class households often include children of previous relationships, children of poorer relatives, informally adopted children, and children of daughters who have migrated to urban areas or abroad.

Inheritance. Children generally receive equal shares of their parents' property, which, in the case of land, may be held in common.

Socialization. Men are affectionate toward children but are not usually involved in child care. Child rearing is the mother's responsibility, but it is often delegated to an older sister or, increasingly, to the maternal grandmother. Respect and obedience are very important to parents, who threaten or physically punish children when they are "rude." Girls and, to a lesser extent, boys are given many household chores. The emotional bond between a mother and her children, particularly her sons, is very strong and enduring.

Sociopolitical Organization

Social Organization. Slave society was stratified into three castes: a small number of Whites, a smaller number of "free people of color" (generally mulattoes), and a huge Black slave population. White-minority rule led to the development of a "white bias": European phenotypic and cultural traits were more highly valued than their African or Creole counterparts. With Emancipation, the castes were transformed into classes, but the White bias persisted, resulting in a "color-class pyramid": a White upper class, a "Brown" middle class, and a Black lower-class majority. The addition of Chinese, East Indian, and Lebanese immigrants, who did not have a clear place in the color-class pyramid, made stratification more complex. Color and ethnicity still influence social interactions, but the White bias and the color-class pyramid have become less evident since the mid-twentieth century. Nevertheless, Jamaica is still highly stratified by wealth; it has a very small, prosperous upper class, a small middle class, and a huge, impoverished lower class. In the mid-1960s Jamaica had the highest rate of income inequality in the world.

Political Organization. Jamaica was ruled by a governor appointed by the Crown and an elected House of Assembly until the peasant uprising at Morant Bay in 1865. This event ignited fear among the White oligarchy that democracy would lead to Black rule; so the British abolished the assembly in 1866 and imposed a Crown Colony government, run by the governor and an imperial bureaucracy. Democracy was not restored until 1944, when an elected House of Representatives was created by a new constitution, and full internal self-government was granted in 1957. Jamaica joined the short-lived Federation of the West Indies in 1959 but left it in 1961; the following year Jamaica became an independent nation in the British Commonwealth. The present system of government is a constitutional monarchy with two houses of Parliament. The ceremonial head of state is the governor-general, who is appointed by and represents the British monarch. The sixty members of the House of Representatives are elected for a term of five years—or less, if an early election is called. The leader of the majority party in the House becomes prime minister and selects a cabinet. The twenty-one members of the Senate are appointed by the governor-general on the advice of the prime minister and the leader of the opposition. The two major political parties are the People's National Party (PNP) and the Jamaican Labour Party (JLP). The National Workers Union (NWU) is affiliated with the PNP, and the Bustamante Industrial Trade Union (BITU) is affiliated with the JLP, giving each party a solid core of supporters. Jamaicans are fervently partisan and strongly identify with political leaders, but the political system is remarkably stable. Party support is not clearly related to racial, ethnic, class, or regional divisions; both the PNP and the JLP have governed at various times since the 1940s. Michael Manley, the leader of the PNP, succeeded Edward Seaga, the leader of the JLP, as prime minister after the 1989 elections. Percival J. Patterson became prime minister on 30 March 1992, and his PNP won a 52-to-8 majority in the lower house of Parliament in the March 1993 election. The PNP and the JLP agree that a president should replace the British Crown as constitutional head of state but disagree as to the precise role and scope of the presidency.

Social Control. Ostracism, gossip, derision, and sorcery are the main sanctions in rural communities, where crime (with the exception of theft of crops) is relatively infrequent. In urban areas, however, crime has become a very serious problem. A rapidly escalating rate of violent attacks with firearms led to the passage, in 1974, of legislation providing severe penalties for gun offenders and creating a special Gun Court. The main function of the army (the Jamaica Defense Force) has been to augment the police (the Jamaica Constabulary Force), particularly in efforts to control unrest and suppress the drug trade.

Conflict. Jamaica has a history of organized violence, including many slave revolts, some peasant uprisings, and labor and urban unrest. Individual acts of violence were at one time relatively uncommon; the recent increase in urban violence can largely be attributed to the gangs that protect ghetto neighborhoods and control the drug trade. During the 1970s, gangs also supported politicians and political parties. Over 700 people died in politically related violence during the election of 1980, but there were few fatalities in the 1989 election. The 1993 election was also marred by violence.

Religion and Expressive Culture

Religious Beliefs. Jamaica is a profoundly religious society, with a wide range of cults, sects, denominations, and movements. The religion of the slaves was based on African beliefs and practices, such as ceremonial spirit possession, spiritual healing, sorcery, and drumming and dance as forms of worship. An ancestor cult called Kumina and belief in obeah (sorcery) are living survivals of the African heritage. Missionization of slaves by Moravians, Baptists, Methodists, and Presbyterians began in 1754 and stimulated the development of syncretic, Afro-Christian cults, among them Zion Revival and Pocomania, or Pukkumina, which still exist. The Rastafarian movement, which reveres Haile Selassie as a messiah and regards marijuana as a sacrament, first appeared in 1933 but did not become widespread until the 1960s. American Pentecostalism has grown rapidly since World War II and is perhaps the most popular religion today. "Science," or "De Laurence," a form of magic based on a mail-order catalog from Chicago, developed during the same period. Jamaicans believe strongly in supernatural influence. Zion Revival incorporates such African notions as a supreme but distant creator who is generally uninvolved in human affairs and a polytheistic pantheon of angels who guide and protect people. Obeah is based on the belief that obeah men capture and use ghosts ("duppies") for malicious ends. Pentecostals seek the inspiration and power of the Holy Ghost, which protects them from Satan and demons. "Fallen angels" are said to be in league with De Laurence. Rastafarians worship Jah, a god who is within them.

Religious Practitioners. Ministers of Christian churches are highly respected and influential. The leaders of Zion Revival cults are known as "daddies," "captains," or "mothers," and their authority is based on the "spiritual gifts" of possession, prophecy, healing, dream interpretation, and the like. Obeah men and "scientists" or "professors" are nearly always men, but many if not most traditional healers are women.

Ceremonies. Zion Revival cults perform a circular, hyperventilative dance called "shouting" or "laboring" at feast ceremonies called "Tables," which resemble the "Altar" ceremonies of Pocomania cults. A meeting of Rastafarians is called a _grounation_ or _nyabinghi_.

Arts. Music and dance are very popular. Jonkonnu (or John Canoe) is a secular festival that began in the early 1700s, when masked and costumed dancers paraded in the streets during the Christmas season and gave performances at the houses of prominent citizens. Today, however, it is performed mainly on special occasions, such as the annual national Festival. Jamaica is the home of reggae music and its foremost exponent, the late Bob Marley. Jamaican contributions to literature, dance, drama, painting, and sculpture have won international recognition.

Medicine. Jamaican folk medicine is largely derived from African traditional medicine. Zion Revivalists operate healing centers called "balm yards" and often attribute illnesses to duppies and obeah. Balm practitioners are shamanic in that they use spiritual means to diagnose and treat illnesses, but they also use herbs ("bush"), candles, prayers, and tonics. Healing by the laying on of hands is very common in Pentecostal churches.

Death and Afterlife.   Funerals are important events in Jamaica, and ghosts of the deceased are widely feared. The slaves believed in a good soul that went to Africa after death and a bad one that lingered as a duppy, particularly around cotton trees. A festive wake was held to pacify the deceased and render the ghost harmless, and this "set-up" or "Nine-Night" is still practiced in rural areas.

See also Rastafarians

Bibliography

Hurwitz, Samuel J., and Edith F. Hurwitz (1971). *Jamaica: A Historical Portrait*. New York: Praeger.

Kaplan, Irving, et al. (1976). *Area Handbook for Jamaica*. Washington, D.C.: U.S. Government Printing Office.

Kuper, Adam (1976). *Changing Jamaica*. Boston: Routledge & Kegan Paul.

WILLIAM WEDENOJA

Kaqchikel

ETHNONYMS: Cakchiquel, Kakchiquel

The 445,000 or more Kaqchikel are a Quichean Maya people who live in the Guatemala departments of Chimaltenango, Quiché, Guatemala, Sololá, Escuintla, and Sacatepéquez. Following are the names and locations of the ten major subgroups of the Kaqchikel, each of which speaks a separate sister language: Central (Chimaltenango Department), Eastern (near Guatemala City), Northern (central highlands), Santa María de Jesus (southeast of Antigua Guatemala), Santo Domingo Xenacoj (west of Guatemala City), South Central (west of Guatemala City), Southern (south of Antigua Guatemala), Acatenango Southwestern (municipio of Acatenango), Yepocapa Southwestern (municipio of Yepocapa), and Western (San José Chacaya and Santa Cruz La Laguna).

Conquered by the K'iche' Maya in the fifteenth century, the Kaqchikel allied themselves with the Spanish in the 1520s to retaliate against them. In 1526 they attacked their new masters, the Spanish, but were defeated and fled to the hills. In the seventeenth century, they lived as farmers under control of Spanish missionaries and government. The Kaqchikel lost much of their lands, and many became agricultural laborers. Political repression caused many to leave Guatemala for Mexico and the United States in the 1970s and 1980s.

Jicaque

ETHNONYMS: Cicaque, Hicaque, Ikake, Taguaca, Taupane, Tol, Tolpan, Torrupan, Xicaque

The 8,600 or more Jicaque Indians live in Honduras. Their social and cultural situation today is the result of events that took place in the nineteenth century. At that time, the Catholic priest Manuel Jesús de Subiriana took many of the Jicaque to live in villages and taught them to grow maize; most of them became acculturated and eventually assimilated into the general society. Others, who did not go with the priest, became subsistence horticulturists in the Montaña de la Flor area and retained much of their traditional culture. Later, the federal government granted them a 760-hectare reservation.

Bibliography

Olson, James S. (1991). *The Indians of Central and South America*. New York: Greenwood Press.

Bibliography

Olson, James S. (1991). *The Indians of Central and South America*. New York: Greenwood Press.

Tax, Sol, and Robert Hinshaw (1969). "The Maya of the Midwestern Highlands." In *Handbook of Middle American Indians*, edited by Robert Wauchope. Vol. 7, *Ethnology, Part One*, edited by Evon Z. Vogt, 69–100. Austin: University of Texas Press.

K'iche'

ETHNONYMS: Quiché

Orientation

The K'iche' are one of the largest surviving Maya groups. They live in the midwestern highlands of Guatemala. Specifically, they inhabit the departments of Huehuetenango, Chimaltenango, Quezaltenango, Totonicapán, Quiché, Baja Verapaz, Retalhuleu, Suchitepéquez, Sololá, and Escuintla. The cities of Chichicastenango and Momostenango are especially well known because of ethnographic studies conducted by Ruth Bunzel (1952) and Barbara Tedlock (1982).

There are about 750,000 K'iche' Indians living in Guatemala today. The K'iche' language is still widely used among contemporary Indian populations. It is classified within the Kichean Branch of the Macro-Mayan Language Family.

The geography of the region is unusually rugged. The terrain is marked by a multitude of volcanoes and rocky formations. The largest inland body of water in the region is Lake Atitlán.

History

Soon after the fall of Tula in Mexico, the Toltec moved south and invaded the K'iche' region. Around A.D. 1250, the Toltec gained control over the region and began to diffuse elements of their own culture into K'iche' culture. These cultural features include superior military technology, human sacrifice, monumental buildings, ball courts, and urban life. Although Toltec domination changed the K'iche' way of life, the Toltec were unable to force the K'iche' to change their language. Instead, the Toltec learned the K'iche' language.

Between A.D. 1250 and the early 1500s, K'iche' civilization grew and expanded. One of their accomplishments was an advanced form of hieroglyphic writing, which has been preserved in their holy book, the Popol Vuh. The K'iche' also attempted to conquer surrounding peoples during this period. By the eve of the Spanish Conquest, the K'iche' were fighting wars with the Kaqchikel, the Tz'utujil, the Ixil, and the Uspanteko. The Spanish later made use of this pre-existing conflict by forming alliances with the Kaqchikel and the Tz'utujil.

In 1524 Spanish troops under Pedro de Alvarado marched on the K'iche' nation. At this time, it was known as the state of Utatlán. It was named after the strongest of the three cities that made up the confederacy of the K'iche' nation. Although the K'iche' heavily resisted, de Alvarado was able to conquer them. The city of Utatlán was burned but later rebuilt as the city of Santa Cruz de Quiché.

During the colonial period, the Spaniards attempted to pacify the K'iche' through both missionary and military activity. Another factor in the pacification of the K'iche' was the deaths of large portions of the population from European diseases.

During the nineteenth century, there was increasing pressure from *hacendados,* owners of the large haciendas or plantations, who wanted to usurp communal lands. The Guatemalan government supported private landownership and stripped many K'iche' of their lands, reducing the K'iche' to peasants and migrant laborers.

Since World War II, the K'iche' have become more and more dissatisfied with their treatment by the government and have turned toward left-wing revolutionary causes. Because of reprisals by the government against resistance fighters, many K'iche' have migrated to Mexico or the United States.

Settlements

The settlement pattern of the K'iche' consists of centralized ceremonial and administrative centers surrounded by dispersed villages or hamlets. Each region has its own administrative center. Often these centers are relatively uninhabited for most of the year. For this reason, they have been called "vacant towns." This phenomenon occurs when many individuals maintain two residences, one in the country and one in the town. The rural residence is usually near agricultural lands and is used by the family for most of the year. The town dwelling is utilized during markets and fiestas, or at special times of the year.

Traditional houses consist of rectangular structures with double-pitched, tiled roofs. One of the long walls is often set back into the structure to allow for a covered porch along the front. The walls themselves can be constructed of adobe, cane-daub, rubble, stones and cane, and thatch over boards or poles. As a result of increasing Westernization, Western-style houses incorporating bricks, lumber, and corrugated tin are also common.

Economy

The majority of K'iche' are agricultural workers who combine traditional maize production (milpa farming) with cash cropping and wage labor. Milpa plots have not changed much since the pre-Hispanic period. Land is cleared by burning off the existing vegetation, then the soil is turned with large-bladed hoes. Maize, beans, and squashes are grown together on the milpa plot to ensure a variety of crops for dietary consumption.

Within the region, a number of other crops are cultivated to supplement the K'iche' diet. These include wheat, potatoes, chilies, apples, pears, peaches, plums, avocados, lemons, limes, and oranges.

Certain regions do not participate as heavily in agricultural production but are known for pottery making, blanket manufacture, lumbering, and woodworking. Increasing numbers of K'iche' are beginning to practice carpentry, tailoring, and butchery, professions that have historically been Ladino occupations.

The largest indigenous craft is that of weaving. There are three types of weavers: blanket weavers, napkin or handkerchief weavers, and blouse weavers. Both men and women weave fabric, but the majority of women are spinners, and the majority of men are weavers. In this way, men and women are dependent on each other for economic subsistence.

Markets are held in the regional centers, and merchants travel long distances to attend markets in other communities. Some even travel outside of Guatemala in order to trade their wares. Most traders are men, and they deal largely in commodities such as clothing, blankets, unprocessed foods, and livestock.

Kinship

Historically the K'iche' were patrilineally organized into clans and lineages. The missionaries and governors of the Spanish colonial period, however, stressed the importance of the nuclear family. For this reason, present kinship relations are generally bilateral. Remnants of the patrilineal system include a prohibition against marriage with members of one's mother's patriclan. In some cases, though, patrilineal relatives are unimportant. Kinship terminology is of the Eskimo type.

Fictive kinship (*compadrazgo*) is prevalent in the region. Compadrazgo is the system of ritual relations between godchild and godparent and between godparent and parent. These relations form the basis of much ritual social interaction at events such as births, baptisms, and graduations.

Marriage and Family

In the past, all marriages were arranged by the parents of the bride and groom. The father would pick a bride for his son, then he would visit the parents of the bride to build rapport with them. Since the 1950s, more and more people have been choosing their own partners.

There are two main types of households. The most prevalent is the nuclear household consisting of a husband, his wife, and their children. There are instances, however, when an extended family resides patrilocally. This occurs because newly married couples usually reside with the groom's parents until the birth of their first child. The young married couple then forms an independent residence after the birth of their child, if this is financially feasible. If they are unable to leave the household of the groom's parents, then the household ceases to be a nuclear household and becomes a three-generation patrilocal extended family.

Among the K'iche', authority is emphasized in all areas of life. Children are taught to submit to those above them in authority, including their parents. This emphasis can lead to intense intrafamilial tensions.

Inheritance flows from fathers to sons, with the oldest son receiving the largest portion of land. In most cases, the oldest son lives with or near the father and takes ownership of his father's lands after his father's death.

Sociopolitical Organization

Organization within the villages is subject to the prevailing civil-religious hierarchy. Municipal government offices are filled by the members of the community. Individuals are able to build status within the community based on the positions they have been able to fill.

Social and religious life are organized in the same manner. In every community, there are a number of religious brotherhoods, called *cofradías*. Each of these has its own set of offices, and these are filled on a rotational basis by members of the cofradía. Those serving in the office of *mayordomo* are responsible for sponsoring the various fiestas and religious events that occur during the period of their office.

Religion and Expressive Culture

K'iche' religion is a combination of traditional and Catholic elements. At present, there is a certain amount of conflict between the K'iche' belief system and the Catholic belief system. The Catholic priests argue for a more orthodox Catholicism, whereas the K'iche' priest-shamans subscribe to a syncretic version of traditional and Catholic

beliefs. For example, the K'iche' have accepted the concept of a trinity, but it differs markedly from the Catholic Trinity of God, Jesus, and the Holy Spirit. The K'iche' believe in Dios, Mundo, and Nantat. Dios is a category that consists of all the Christian gods and powers such as God, Jesus, angels, and saints. Mundo refers to nature and the earthly world. Nantat includes all of the ancestors and the spirits involved with them. In this way, K'iche' priest-shamans are able to place traditional views within a Catholic framework.

There are a number of religious functions to be performed in the community, and these are accomplished by a number of different people. Leaders such as the mayordomos are responsible for the success of fiestas, church events, and the care of the saints. Others, such as the *ajk'ij*, or day keeper, fulfill the roles of calendar diviners, dream interpreters, and curers. The calendar diviner uses his knowledge of the 260-day Mayan calendar to tell whether a person's fortune will be positive or negative. Dream interpreters give explanations of people's dreams in light of K'iche' cosmology. Although individuals trained in Western medicine do exist in medical clinics in the K'iche' region, few people use their services. Most prefer to go to traditional curers, who are believed to have a better understanding of the spirituality of healing.

There are a host of ceremonial occasions stemming from traditional culture and Catholic ritual. The most important of these are the ceremonies linked with events in the life cycle. Birth, baptism, and death are important points in the lives of K'iche', and appropriate ceremonies are conducted to commemorate them. At each of the aforementioned occasions, liquor plays an important social and ritual role.

Bibliography

Bunzel, Ruth (1952). *Chichicastenango: A Guatemalan Village.* Seattle: University of Washington Press.

Carmack, Robert M. (1973). *Quichean Civilization: The Ethnohistoric, Ethnographic, and Archaeological Sources.* Berkeley and Los Angeles: University of California Press.

Carmack, Robert M. (1980) *The Quiche Mayas of Utatlán: The Evolution of a Highland Guatemala Kingdom.* Norman: University of Oklahoma Press.

Carmack, Robert M. (1982). *The Historical Demography of Highland Guatemala.* Albany: State University of New York at Albany, Institute for Mesoamerican Studies.

Carmack, Robert M. (1983). "Indians and the Guatemalan Revolution." *Cultural Survival Quarterly* 7(2): 52–54

Fox, John W. (1978). *Quiche Conquest: Centralism and Regionalism in Highland Guatemalan State Development.* Albuquerque: University of New Mexico Press.

Mayer, Karl Herbert (1993). "A K'iche' Diviner in Zunil." *Mexicon* 15(4): 66.

Schultze Jena, Leonhard (1954). *La vida y las creencias de los indígenas K'iche's de Guatemala.* Biblioteca de Cultura Popular, vol. 49. Guatemala: Editorial del Ministerio de Educación Pública.

Tax, Sol, and Robert Hinshaw (1969). "The Maya of the Midwestern Highlands." In *Handbook of Middle American Indians,* edited by Robert Wauchope. Vol. 7, *Ethnology, Part One,* edited by Evon Z. Vogt. Austin: University of Texas Press.

Tedlock, Barbara (1982). *Time and the Highland Maya.* Albuquerque: University of New Mexico Press.

Tedlock, Dennis, trans. (1985). *Popol Vuh: The Definitive Edition of the Mayan Book of the Dawn of Life and the Glories of Gods and Kings.* New York: Simon & Schuster.

IAN MAST

Kikapu

ETHNONYMS: Chikapu, Kickapoo

Orientation

Identification. The Mexican Kikapu originated in the regional frontier that divided the United States from Canada. They began to migrate to Coahuila, Mexico, in the middle of the nineteenth century, and in the 1980s they were provided a locale in Texas. In Mexico they are recognized as Mexican citizens, although their status has not been well defined. Since 1983, they have been recognized by the U.S. government as members of the Kikapu band of Texas and granted citizenship.

Location. The Kikapu have migrated to many U.S. locales as well as to Mexican states such as Coahuila and Sonora. In Coahuila there exists a very traditional Kikapu group situated in a place named by them, El Nacimiento de la Tribu Kikapu, about 32 kilometers northeast of the city of Múzquiz, covering an area of 7,000 hectares. The terrain is semiarid, with the Río Sabinas contributing a needed supply of water.

Demography. Throughout its history, the Kikapu population has changed little in number, varying between 1,500 and 2,500. In Mexico, the 1990 population estimation enumerated 700 Kikapu. The constant movement between Mexico and the United States has made it difficult to establish an exact count of the group.

Linguistic Affiliation. Kikapu, a language of the Algonquian Family, is directly related to Sauk and Fox. Because there is a close relationship between the Oklahoma and Texas/Coahuila Kikapu groups, it is not surprising that there is no dialectal variation between the two different regions where Kikapu is spoken.

History and Cultural Relations

Historically, the Kikapu can be characterized as a highly mobile group that traveled within their territories in the United States. Owing to the arrival of White settlers into these territories, the Kikapu were displaced and began migrating south toward Mexico. To keep their territories and culture, the Kikapu strongly resisted the incursion of settlers. Owing to their strong loyalty to their traditional culture, the Kikapu were able to retain their internal cohesion in spite of two centuries of wars with the Whites.

In the middle of the nineteenth century, a small group of Kikapu asked the Mexican government for permission to settle in Mexico. The government agreed, in exchange for Kikapu assistance in the Mexican army's efforts to subjugate other indigenous groups. It is important to note that in the formal agreement the Kikapu negotiated with the Mexican government, they stipulated that they be allowed to preserve their culture.

In 1912 another group of Kikapu from Oklahoma and Texas/Coahuila migrated to Sonora, Mexico. In 1920 a major portion of this same group returned to Oklahoma, however, when the problems that initially prompted the migration were resolved. In the 1950s the Kikapu who had settled in Coahuila began to migrate throughout the United States, finding work as itinerant farm workers during part of the spring and the entire summer season; for the remainder of the year, they return to Mexico and involve themselves in their cultural traditions. These temporary migrations to the United States, a pattern that still persists, began because of the droughts that plagued the region that the Kikapu occupied in the 1940s and 1950s and the ease of crossing the U.S.-Mexico border to find work. Even though they received land near Eagle Pass, Texas, from the U.S. government, the Kikapu prefer to live in Mexico because in Texas they are physically and socially separated from Mexican society.

Settlements

Historians have noted that before the White colonizers arrived, the Kikapu inhabited what is presently known as the state of Wisconsin. In the middle of the seventeenth century, the Kikapu were located in what is now Michigan and Ohio, where they first encountered White settlers—the French. A short time later, White colonizers began moving southwest to Wisconsin, Indiana, Illinois, Missouri, Kansas, Arkansas, Louisiana, Oklahoma, and then Texas. Presently, the largest group of Kikapu resides on a reservation in Oklahoma, and another smaller group resides in Kansas.

After their arrival in Mexico in the nineteenth century, the Kikapu established their first community, in El Nacimiento, Coahuila. The small Kikapuan community in Texas serves as a stopover for those from Coahuila traveling to U.S. northern states. In 1912 the group of Kikapu that migrated to Sonora purchased land in Tamichopa, Sonora. The descendants of the original Kikapu group still inhabit Tamichopa, although they have lost the traditional Kikapu cultural features.

The Kikapu build two kinds of traditional seasonal houses, the winter house and the summer house, which serve a religious function. The winter house consists of an oval-shaped frame of cedar sticks almost completely covered with tule mats. The frame of the summer house is also of cedar sticks, but in a rectangular shape; the walls are made from reeds and the roof cover of tule mats. The summer house has an open-sided arbor of poles at the entrance.

A third traditional house is built to shelter women during their menstrual periods, when they are not allowed to remain in the seasonal houses. This house is very small; it is constructed of the same materials as the seasonal houses, but the workmanship is less elaborate.

Economy

Subsistence and Commercial Activities. The Kikapu economy has undergone radical changes: from the time of their residence in the United States through their migration to Mexico, the Kikapu relied on hunting and gathering, but in the early twentieth century an incipient agricultural system rapidly emerged alongside hunting and gathering, and in the 1930s the Kikapu developed a modern system of agriculture.

During the 1950s, they abandoned agricultural labor on their own lands and became temporary migrant farm workers in the United States, mostly in the states of Utah, Colorado, Texas, Wisconsin, Wyoming, Oklahoma, Montana, and Florida. At the same time, they abandoned their taboo against breeding cattle and transformed their farm lands in El Nacimiento into grazing lands.

Industrial Arts. Elements of traditional dress such as *teguas* (moccasins) were made from deerskin by Kikapu women; they also did ornamental beadwork on deerskin. Because few women continue to do this kind of work, these crafts are disappearing.

Trade. The Kikapu are not active traders. For a short time in the first half of the twentieth century, they traded the excess of their harvests, wild fruits, and deerskin items to Mexicans who lived nearby. Some Kikapu continue to trade cattle to Mexicans and handicrafts to the Kikapu of Oklahoma.

Division of Labor. Kikapu men and women who are able to work as migrant farm laborers enter the work force that travels to the United States seeking these jobs. Women do housework and handcrafting; they also gather the materials for the construction of their traditional housing. Men, when in El Nacimiento, are involved only in the small commercial trade of cattle and in discussions of permanent land tenure. Young adults and children are not responsible for any productive activity while in El Nacimiento.

Land Tenure. Following the model of *ejido* tenure, a collective use of land, the occupation of Kikapu land in El Nacimiento is communal. During the early years of the settlement, each family was allotted a parcel of land for cultivation. The land is passed down to the next generation in order of oldest to youngest, with males having preference over females.

Kinship

Kin Groups and Descent. The Kikapu kinship system is based on patrilineal clans. These clans underlie a system in which name-groups are not unilineal. Clan affiliation is determined through the affiliation of the donor who provides the personal name for an individual.

Kinship Terminology. Cousin terms are of the Omaha type. Kin solidarity is more important to the Kikapu than genealogical relationship. The Kikapu have three names. One is given by the donor to determine specific clan affiliation. Another name is given during baptism and used only after death, and the last is a Spanish name—the surname of the individual's father.

Marriage and Family

Marriage. The Kikapu marital relationship is formed through the decision of two individuals to establish a family. The union of the couple does not occur through a formal ritual, either religious or civil, but rather through the clan system, which regulates the marriage possibilities of each individual. The relationships are defined through emotional affections and are not arranged, as they were in the past. Marriages are now monogamous, whereas in the past some were polygynous.

Domestic Unit. Postmarital residence is patrilocal. The nuclear family is the most common form of domestic integration, and it is very common to find members of the extended family occupying the same land.

Inheritance. The rights to the land in the community are passed down from father to son. Until the late twentieth century, the political leader of the group bequested his leadership to his sons. A group composed of the heads of the families now chooses the community leader.

Socialization. Parents, along with the elders, are responsible for teaching Kikapu values to their children. Within the community, there is no formal educational institution. The Mexican government has attempted on several occasions to establish a school in the community; Kikapu resistance has contributed to the maintenance of their culture. Girls, during the first menstrual cycle, are isolated in a special house and are taught and advised by older adult women about the menstrual taboo and their future responsibilities as women.

Sociopolitical Organization

Social Organization. There is no class differentiation in Kikapu culture; however, some social differentiation is beginning to develop, causing conflicts among certain group members. It appears that the only individual held in esteem by all group members is the religious leader. In general, the social organization of the Kikapu falls under the leadership and guidance of the elders of the group.

Political Organization. In the past, the Kikapu had a leader who was assisted by a council of elders in making political decisions. Today the president of the ejido provides the political leadership, even though the assembly consisting of the heads of families makes the most important political decisions. Only internal Kikapu matters are within the purview of these political leaders; they have no influence in regional, state, or federal politics in Mexico. In these larger arenas, the Kikapu can only participate as individuals.

Social Control. In earlier times, social control was exerted by group leaders, especially the elders. This control has begun to dissipate, adversely affecting younger members of the group.

Conflict. Conflicts, first with White settlers in their northern territories and later with Texans, forced the Kikapu to migrate to Mexico. In their Coahuilan settlement, one of their major problems has been the loss of hunting grounds—deer are crucial to Kikapu religious ceremonies. Surrounding ranchers have not allowed the Kikapu to hunt on their properties. Furthermore, recent conflicts over power have emerged within the Kikapu group itself, leading to strong divisions in the community. Alcoholism and drug addiction are the severest problems the Kikapu face today.

Religion and Expressive Culture

Religious Beliefs. Kikapu religion is fundamentally animistic, centering on a superior spirit considered to be the creator called Kisiaata. The central element in this religion is the possession and veneration of sacred packs, which are believed to be manitous. The Kikapu religion is one of the fundamental features of the group and has been crucial, along with the language, in sustaining the culture group. Catholicism and Protestantism have not influenced the Kikapu in any way.

Religious Practitioners. A major figure for the Kikapu is the religious leader, who celebrates religious ceremonies and marks the important dates in the Kikapu calendar. The religious leader selects as his successor a qualified member of his family or of the group at large.

Ceremonies. The Kikapu have a number of religious ceremonies, including ceremonies that involve the whole community, even kin from Oklahoma, as well as ceremonies that only involve clans or the nuclear family. The most important ceremonies are those that involve the whole community, such as the ceremonies for the dead, which take place in March and April. In these ceremonies, dances and ritual plays are performed by men and women. There are two traditional religious teams, the Blacks and the Whites. Foreigners are excluded from ceremonies that take place in individual homes. Other ceremonies take place during the change of seasonal homes, when a child is named, and in February, when the Kikapu mark the new year.

Medicine. The traditional Kikapu had a traditional medical system, which included the practices of the herbal societies. At present, they have abandoned their traditional practices and have begun to rely on Western medical services provided in Mexico and the United States—even in regard to childbearing, which in earlier times the woman performed alone.

Death and Afterlife. When someone in the Kikapu culture dies, the corpse is removed through a hole located in the back of the traditional house and buried in a community cemetery. After the corpse is removed, the house is destroyed, and the family builds a new one. Various ceremonies are performed after the death until the ceremonies of the dead take place in March and April. During these ceremonies, the spirits of the deceased meet their creator, Kisiaata. The Kikapu believe in a heaven, where those who have lived good lives go to hunt deer. Those who have lived bad lives are bound to a tree, where they can see the hunters who have been rewarded for their good lives.

Bibliography

Fabila, Alfonso (1945). *La tribu kikapoo de Coahuila.* Biblioteca Enciclopédica Popular, no. 50. Mexico City: Secretaría de Educación Pública.

Gibson, A. M. (1963). *The Kickapoos: Lords of the Middle Border.* Norman: University of Oklahoma Press.

Latorre, Felipe A., and Dolores L. Latorre (1976). *The Mexican Kickapoo Indians.* Austin and London: University of Texas Press.

Ritzenthaler, Robert, E., and Frederick A. Peterson (1956). *The Mexican Kickapoo Indians.* Publications in Anthropology, 2. Milwaukee: Milwaukee Public Museum.

JOSÉ LUIS MOCTEZUMA ZAMARRON

Kittsians and Nevisians

ETHNONYMS: People of Saint Kitts, People of Nevis, Kittitians

The Federation of Saint Kitts and Nevis is an independent nation formed by two islands in the Leeward Islands of the Lesser Antilles; its population was 40,923 in 1991. Saint Kitts (originally, Saint Christopher's island) is located at 17°17′ N and 62°43′ W; Nevis is at 17°8′ N and 62°37′ W. The two islands, separated by a stretch of water only 3.2 kilometers wide, have a total area of 269 square kilometers. Their geologic origin is volcanic. The climate is tropical, with temperatures varying between 18°C and 32°C, and precipitation ranging from 100 to 300 centimeters yearly. There is no rainy season, but there is a hurricane season from July to September. There is an abundance of water, to a degree that irrigation is unnecessary; however, erosion, caused by poor agricultural practices and the overgrazing of livestock, has damaged the naturally fertile soils in parts of Saint Kitts and in wide areas of Nevis.

All but 10 percent of the population is Black, descendants of African slaves. The small number of Whites have a disproportionately large influence on the economy by virtue of their great influence in trading and banking. There are also some people with ancestry in both races. Most people are Anglicans, with the rest adhering to the Catholic, Church of God, Methodist, and Baptist faiths.

These islands were inhabited by the Carib Indians. After landing in 1493, Christopher Columbus named Saint Kitts after his patron saint Saint Christopher, the name eventually being shortened to the English nickname "Kitt." In 1623 the British settled a portion of Saint Kitts, and the French settled the rest of the island in 1624. In 1628 some of the British on Saint Kitts settled Nevis. Together, the French and British eliminated the Carib presence. The Treaty of Utrecht in 1713 gave Saint Kitts to the British, but the French later made several attempts to gain control there. The Treaty of Paris restated British dominion in 1783. The British subsequently established sugarcane plantations worked by African slaves. Soil erosion on Nevis caused the plantation owners there to leave, relinquishing the land to peasant farmers.

Saint Kitts and Nevis adopted their constitution and gained independence from Britain on 19 September 1983, although the British monarch still stands as their head of state. The country is officially a constitutional monarchy within the British Commonwealth, and the Crown is represented by a governor general. The legislature has eleven popularly elected members, eight from Saint Kitts and three from Nevis. There is also a cabinet and a prime minister. Further, there is a Nevis Island Legislature and Nevis Island Assembly with a premier.

The economy remains heavily dependent on the government-owned sugar industry, which—given declining world prices and intermittent hurricane damage—often runs at a loss. Because this industry pays such low wages, most citizens of the country will not work in it; laborers must be imported from Saint Vincent and Guyana. Nevis depends primarily on Sea Island cotton raised on small farms. In the late twentieth century the tourism industry has been strong, and owing to a government policy encouraging foreign investment, there are also some small manufacturers of clothing and electronics components. The United States is the nation's most important trading partner, followed by the United Kingdom.

Bibliography

Aronoff, Joel (1967). *The Inter-Relationship of Psychological and Cultural Systems: A Case Study of a Rural West Indian Village.* Ann Arbor, Mich.: University Microfilms.

Aronoff, Marilyn (1973). *Community in Industrial Society: A Study of a West Indian Labor Movement.* Ann Arbor, Mich.: University Microfilms.

Richardson, Bonham C. (1983). *Caribbean Migrants: Environment and Human Survival on St. Kitts and Nevis.* Knoxville: University of Tennessee Press.

Kuna

ETHNONYMS: Cuna, Tule, Tulemala

Orientation

Identification.   The Kuna are one of Panama's three major groups of indigenous peoples. Most of the Kuna live in the *comarca* (district) of San Blas, or Kuna Yala, along Panama's northern coast. Literally "Kuna Yala" means Kuna Land. The comarca of San Blas is the legal name of the region, but the Congreso General Kuna has petitioned the Panamanian government to have the name of the region officially changed to Kuna Yala. "Cuna" and "Kuna" are Spanish designations; the ethnonyms "Tule" and "Tulemala" are in the Kuna language.

Location.   The comarca of San Blas lies along the northeastern coast of Panama. It is comprised of a long, narrow strip of mainland jungle extending 200 kilometers along the coast and 15 to 20 kilometers inland and an archipelago of 365 small islands. A single road links San Blas to the Pan-American Highway and to the rest of Panama. The road is only passable in a four-wheel drive vehicle and, as of 1985, had not been used for regular transport of people or agricultural produce. Because of road conditions, most travel in and out of the region is by plane or boat.

Demography.   According to the 1980 Panamanian national census, the total population of San Blas was 28,567. There are fifty-four communities ranging in size from 70 to over 2,000 inhabitants each. Forty-two of these communities are located on small islands, ten are situated on the mainland coast, and two are inland, on the riverbanks. All the inhabited islands are no farther than about 1.5 kilometers from the mainland coast and the mouth of a freshwater river. Proximity to the coast makes daily travel possible from the islands to the Kuna's agricultural field on the mainland. Freshwater mainland rivers provide an easily accessible source of water for drinking, bathing, and washing clothes.

In addition to the San Blas Kuna, or the Island Kuna, as they are called, there are Kuna who live outside the comarca. Approximately 10,000 Kuna live in Panama City and Colón, the two largest cities in Panama. Many of these individuals retain close ties with San Blas and consider the region their home. About ten other small villages, with a combined population of fewer than 2,000, are located in the Darién jungle.

Linguistic Affiliation.   Kuna, or Tule Kaya, is the primary language spoken in San Blas. Many Kuna also speak Spanish, Panama's official language. A considerable number of Kuna speak some English, especially those who have traveled internationally on trade boats in the Canal Zone. A few individuals know other languages such as French, Russian, or Chocó (spoken by the Chocó Indians who inhabit the Darién).

History and Cultural Relations

When the Spaniards arrived, the Kuna lived primarily near the Gulf of Urabá in what is today Colombia. Contact with the Spanish, which began in the 1600s, was violent, and trade was limited. Fleeing from the Spaniards, the Kuna traveled up the jungle rivers and settled in the Darién region of what is now Panama. As early as the mid-1800s, entire Kuna villages started to relocate gradually to the sandy islands near the mouths of freshwater rivers. Moving to the islands gave the Kuna easier access to trade vessels plying coastal routes and freedom from disease-carrying insects.

When Panama became an independent nation in 1903, the new government attempted to impose by force a "national culture" on the Kuna. In 1925 the Kuna staged a rebellion (La Revolución Tule, or the Kuna Revolution), and with the backing of the U.S. government were able to negotiate a semiautonomous status for their region. In 1938 the region was officially recognized as a Kuna reserve, and their new constitution, known as _la carta orgánica de San Blas_, was approved in 1945. Legal recognition of San Blas as a territory collectively owned by the Kuna people had implications for the economic organization of the region. The carta orgánica prohibited non-Kuna from purchasing, renting, or otherwise using land within Kuna territory. This law has been used by the Kuna to try to ensure that all enterprise within the San Blas region is owned and operated by Kuna rather than by outsiders. A subsequent law (Ley 16), passed by the Panamanian government in 1953, further delineated the reserve's boundaries, as well as political and economic relations between the Kuna and the national government. Political and economic relationships between San Blas and the rest of Panama continue to be the subject of negotiation.

Settlements

Today most Kuna villages are located in four distinct areas. Most are situated in the comarca of San Blas. Three others are near the headwaters of the Río Bayano, and seven are located along the Río Chucunaque near a hydroelectric dam; all ten are in the Darién jungle. A few small communities can be found in Colombia. Kuna also live in Panama City and Colón and a few live abroad.

In San Blas, island communities are crowded; there is scant space between the houses, which are constructed of locally produced materials. The Kuna live in large matrilocal households composed of senior couples, their married daughters, grandchildren, great-grandchildren, and in-married, subordinate sons-in-law. Households usually span three or four generations. Generally, the compound includes a kitchen and one or more sleeping houses. Most Kuna sleep in hammocks, which are strung from the supporting beams of the house. Clothes are draped over bamboo poles suspended from the rafters or are stored in wooden or cardboard boxes. Most houses have bamboo walls and thatched roofs, but some Kuna have built two-story cement houses with corrugated-metal roofs. These structures often house a store, in addition to providing living space.

Economy

Subsistence and Commercial Activities. The Kuna practice slash-and-burn agriculture and use intercropping techniques. Although plantains are now their primary subsistence crop, they also grow rice, maize, _yucca_ (manioc), sugarcane, coconuts, fruits (such as mangoes, pineapples, lemons, limes, and oranges), and hot peppers. Fishing, hunting, and gathering supplement the Kunal diet. Some households keep a pig to slaughter for a special occasion.

The most common source of cash income is the export of coconuts to Colombia and _molas_ (multilayered panels of cloth cut away to reveal intricate patterns and then carefully hand stitched) to the United States, Europe, and Japan. Coconuts have been exchanged with Colombian traders for goods or cash since the late 1800s. Molas were commercialized in a major way starting in the 1960s. Kuna women sew mola panels into their blouses (also called molas), and sew panels and other items (e.g., small mola patches, animal pillows, pockets, purses, Christmas-tree ornaments) specifically for sale. Mola commercialization occurred concurrently with an increase in Kuna male migration in search of wage labor and a consequent decrease in subsistence-agriculture production. Lobsters and, to a lesser extent, crabs and octopuses began to be harvested for export starting in the 1960s; however, because diving for and preserving the catch require special equipment, and because only young men dive, the impact of this commercial activity has not been as widespread as that of the production of molas.

Kuna men seek wage labor opportunities especially in the Canal Zone, Panama City, Colón, and on Changuinola—a banana plantation. Outside San Blas, few job opportunities are available for Kuna women, but within the region, wage-labor opportunities are equally accessible to Kuna men and women. Such salaried government positions as those of teacher and health worker are filled by both sexes. A few positions, such as air-traffic controller, national guardsman, and agricultural-extension worker, are occupied only by men, but either men or women can be airport attendants, accountants, or store clerks within the community.

Tourism, primarily concentrated in the western third of San Blas, increased dramatically during the 1960s. Most tourists visit the region in luxury cruise ships. Some visit one of several Kuna- or foreign-owned small hotel resorts.

Industrial Arts. Sewing molas is the primary art form for Kuna women and for _omekits_ (Kuna men who are socially defined as women). Some women have special gifts for creating and cutting mola designs and for fashioning _wini_, strings of tiny colored beads worn wrapped around the forearms and lower legs of Kuna women to form geometric designs. Wini, mola blouses, wraparound skirts, head scarves made from imported cloth, and a gold nose ring are considered "traditional dress" for women. Most women in San Blas dress "traditionally." A few elderly women still make hammocks and ceramic vessels, but these traditional crafts are rapidly disappearing as commercial goods become increasingly available. Kuna men make baskets, ladles, wooden stools, and fans that women use to keep the fires burning. Some men make their own clothing: a solid-colored shirt with pleats in the front and a pair of pants, also without designs. Most Kuna men, however, wear Western clothing. Men who live in the area frequented by tourists carve small model boats and balsawood Kuna doll heads to sell to visitors. Dugout wooden canoes are handcrafted by men who have learned this special skill.

Trade. Starting in the 1600s, the Kuna engaged in lucrative trade with the Scots, the French, and with the British colony of Jamaica. Kuna chiefs learned European languages and traveled throughout the Caribbean. The Kuna also traded with pirates as early as the 1600s. A Scottish colony was established in the area in 1698. Alliances and trade relations with Kuna communities were developed and maintained until the 1700s, when the Spanish expelled the Scots.

In the 1700s the French began to trade with the Kuna and to forge military alliances that protected both parties from the Spanish and British. Relations were sufficiently amicable to allow intermarriage. In the 1740s, however, the French began to cultivate cacao for export and, soon thereafter, to use Kuna labor. Relations between the two groups deteriorated; the Kuna rebelled, attacking the French settlers and driving them from the region. Taking over the production of cacao (about 100,000 trees on an estimated seventy-three properties), the Kuna began to trade with the British for guns, ammunition, tools, and cloth. By the 1850s, maritime trade with pirates and merchants was well developed, and trade continues to provide the Kuna with a steady source of goods.

Nowadays the Kuna are actively engaged in commerce with Colombians on boats; they trade coconuts for sugar, rice, cocoa, or cash. Trade boats, most of which are collectively owned by Kuna villages, travel to Colón (an international trade zone), returning to San Blas with a wide range of goods. Kuna storekeepers and itinerant traders acquire their merchandise either directly from Panama City or from the trade boats. Interregional trading of agricultural produce is minimal; plantains and roof thatch, abundant in the east, are mostly sold to communities in the west, where they are needed. Molas, coconuts, and lobsters are the region's primary exports. Although the Kuna still produce much of the goods they consume, they import a wide range of consumer goods including boat motors, cookware, clothing, shoes, certain staples (cocoa, rice, sugar), cement, guns, harpoons, lanterns, tape decks, and radios.

Division of Labor. Concurrent with commercialization of coconuts and relocation of many mainland villages to the islands, Kuna men increasingly took over subsistence-agricultural production as women turned their attention to the coconut trade. This shift did not occur in all Kuna communities, nor did it happen all at once. Despite the variations, however, men generally took increased responsibility for plantain, maize, rice, yucca, fruit, and sugarcane production. Both men and women still planted, weeded, and harvested coconuts, but the women from each household were usually the ones to exchange them for goods or cash.

Women continue to be responsible for child care; food gathering, preparation, and preservation; hauling water; and other tasks related to household maintenance. They also sew molas for themselves, their daughters, and elderly mothers. Men continue to engage in agricultural production and to hunt, fish, build houses, and craft many necessary household items. Women in the eastern region of San Blas and older women throughout the region are active in agricultural production. Women who spend most of their time sewing molas for sale are the least involved in agricultural and household-maintenance activities. Omekids usually work alongside women but may also participate in men's activities. Many omekids in the region are known as outstanding sewers of molas.

Land Tenure. Private property did not exist among the Kuna until the mid- to late nineteenth century. Increased population pressure and the cash cropping of coconuts are factors that precipitated this change. Since 1938, all lands located within the comarca of San Blas have been owned collectively by the San Blas Kuna, although they do not own subsoil rights. The Kuna recognize individuals' rights to land. According to Kuna law, whoever first clears a plot may pass the land to his heirs. Because only men clear land, women generally inherit easily accessible, already producing fields. Women's brothers are expected to clear unclaimed land and often inherit fallow plots. Heirs retain their rights to land even if it has not been cultivated for many years.

Kinship

The Kuna kinship system is bilateral. Age and sex are reflected in kin terms. Cross and parallel cousins are not terminologically distinguished. Kinship terms are often used in place of personal names.

Marriage and Family

Marriage. In the past, young people did not choose their own partners. A girl's father and mother chose a young man, based on his ability to work, and made arrangements for the marriage, usually without the knowledge of either young person. Today young people usually choose their own partners. Couples may "marry in the hammock"—a short ritual that is considered the "traditional" form of marriage. Alternatively, they may present themselves to the *congreso* (a politico-religious community gathering) and state their intention to marry. Unmarried men who move in with women are considered "married," and such couples are expected to notify the congreso. Some of the younger women who meet their future husbands in Panama City marry there according to civil law. Religious ceremonies either in San Blas or in Panama City are another possibility. Children take their biological father's surname unless he refuses to recognize his baby, in which case the child uses the mother's name. No apparent stigma is attached to the mother or to children bearing her name. Women retain their own names. No money, food, land, or other goods are exchanged between households before, during, or after the marriage. Island endogamy prevails, and interracial marriages are frowned upon.

Once married, a man is expected to reside in his mother-in-law's household and to work under the direction of his father-in-law. Any fish caught, game hunted, or produce harvested (even from fields to which he owns the rights) must be given to his mother-in-law to distribute.

Domestic Unit. The prototypical Kuna household is comprised of a senior couple, one or more married daughters with their husbands and children, and any unmarried children. Households may reorganize any number of times within the life span of any given generation. For example, a woman may return to her mother's household each time her husband goes to Panama City to work. Kin, unrelated children, visitors, teachers, or other government-paid employees working in the village—even an anthropologist—may join any given household for several days, months, or even years.

Inheritance. Inheritance of land is bilateral. Although Kuna sons and daughters inherit approximately equal amounts of land, men have greater possibilites for acquiring land than do women. Women inherit but do not lay claim to new plots of land. Only men clear uncultivated land. For example, virgin jungle may be claimed by clearing and cultivating a plot. Whoever clears the land retains usufruct rights, which are passed to his children. Spouses do not inherit land from one another. Husband and wife each retain rights to his or her own property and other resources. If one spouse dies, his or her property is distributed among his or her offspring.

Coconut groves, located on the mainland coast or on uninhabited islands, may be inherited by an individual or by groups (descended from a male or female ancestor) that collectively own and exploit coconut groves and, sometimes, agricultural lands.

Socialization. Infants are raised primarily by their mothers and grandmothers with the help of other female relatives. At around the age of 5, boys start accompanying their fathers and other male relatives to the fields and on hunting and fishing trips. Girls stay with their female relatives. Adolescent girls help with the care of their younger siblings. Since about the 1960s, Kuna boys and girls have been required to attend primary school. Many youths go on to secondary school and high school; a few attend the university.

Sociopolitical Organization

Social Organization. The Kuna are known for their egalitarian forms of social organization. Most agricultural labor in San Blas is organized at the community and household levels or through small collective entrepreneurial groups called _sociedades_ (voluntary associations). All males and females of appropriate age are required to participate in community work projects and are fined if they do not. The senior male and female of each household are responsible for the organization of its labor. Sociedades, which are prevalent, consist of aggregates of friends, relatives, and neighbors. They are organized around specific activities such as selling gasoline, operating a retail store, or engaging in subsistence-agricultural production or coconut cultivation.

Kuna households and/or individuals may have different amounts of land or money. Factors affecting socioeconomic differentiation include the amount of land a household controls, ancestors' level of industriousness in planting coconuts, the extent to which current household members have planted coconuts, opportunities for paid employment, and income from mola sales. Age is another key variable in determining differences in wealth. Older men and women hold most of the land, whereas young migrant laborers obtain consumer goods and cash. Wealthier households in San Blas do not automatically accrue politi-

cal power, nor do they usually appropriate the labor of poorer ones. Inheritance patterns tend to prevent the accumulation of wealth and ensure the redistribution of rights to land and to coconut trees among households across the generations.

Political Organization. Each Kuna village has a local congreso (community meeting house). Every village in San Blas has four to six traditional or administrative _saklas._ Traditional saklas are considered political as well as religious leaders. Ranks and strata are absent, and very little social distance separates leaders and followers. Leaders are chosen for their wisdom and morality; leadership is not hereditary. After the 1925 Kuna uprising known as "La Revolución Tule," a Congreso General Kuna, comprised of local authorities representing each village, was established. The Congreso General Kuna created a unified political entity that can negotiate with the Panamanian government. Today it meets approximately every six months; emergency sessions are called if a crisis occurs. The region has three caciques (chiefs), each responsible for a particular subregion, and a regionwide _intendente_ (administrator). Caciques are selected from Kuna leaders at the local level, whereas the intendente, until the 1990s always a non-Kuna, is named by Panama's president.

In 1968 new political boundaries were drawn throughout Panama. San Blas became politically and administratively separate from the province of Colón. Government ministries, previously administered through Colón, opened regional offices in San Blas. The comarca of San Blas was divided into four subareas called _corregimientos._ Each area elects one representative to the Asamblea Nacional de Representantes de Corregimientos. Local chapters of a wide range of political parties were organized within their communities. In most villages, women organized their own chapters and activities separately from the men's, even within the same political party. Women have become increasingly active in politics at the national level. In 1980 the Kuna elected a Kuna representative to the national legislature.

Social Control. Within a household, the eldest man and woman exercise the most authority. He is responsible for organizing the labor of the men, she that of the women. At the village level, the local congresos are the loci for social control. In the past, public shamings were sufficient control mechanisms. Today congresos levy fines and require community labor in addition to public shaming. The region has several jails. Serious cases are referred to the Panamanian judicial system.

Conflict. Disputes that cannot be resolved within a household are taken to the local congreso. There is ongoing conflict both with the Panamanian national government and with outsiders (non-Kuna Panamanians or U.S. citizens) trying to establish businesses (usually hotels, tourist resorts, or stores) in the region or to convert the Kuna to a particular religion. There are also occasional confrontations with _colonos_ (settlers) from the interior who encroach upon Kuna land. The Kuna have developed the Project for the Study of the Management of Wildland Areas of Kuna Yala (PEMASKY) to help firmly establish the comarca's borders and to stop the deforestation of their rain forest. This project has received substantial support from international funding sources.

Religion and Expressive Culture

Religious Beliefs and Practitioners.   The Kuna creation myth includes references to both Pab Dummat (Big Father) and Nan Dummat (Big Mother). The Kuna religion is now called the "Father's Way." Communities alternate political meetings in the local congresos with singing gatherings where saklas and caciques chant religious and historical songs full of symbolism and myth, and the *arkar* (*vocero*, or chief's spokesman) interprets the meaning of the chants. Many Kuna attend Catholic and Protestant churches, in addition to the singing gatherings.

Ceremonies.   Kuna ceremonies include an *ikko inna* (needle ceremony), in which a baby girl's nose is pierced for a gold nose ring; an *inna tunsikkalet* (short ceremony), a puberty rite that usually lasts one or two days; and an *inna suit* (long ceremony), a ritual cutting of the hair that usually lasts three or more days. Once a young girl's hair is ritually cut short, she becomes available for marriage. Sometimes an inna suit is held for a very young girl even though she will not be ready for marriage for many years. There are no similar ceremonies for Kuna boys. Special chants exist for birth, death, and the healing of the sick.

Arts.   The Kuna are known internationally for their molas. Kuna verbal arts include three different types of chants: *pab ikar*, historical, religious and political material sung by Kuna leaders; songs sung by *kantules* (ritualists) during female puberty rites; chants used in curing ceremonies. Kuna women sing lullabies. Kuna dance groups are becoming increasingly popular among Kuna youth. Rattles and reed panpipes are used by the dancers.

Medicine.   Kuna medicinal healers are called *inatulets* or *neles* (a nele is a seer). They use a combination of herbs and chants to heal their patients. Family, friends, and elderly women play an important role by sitting with patients while healers chant. Beginning in the 1970s, health centers staffed by a nurse or a Western-trained health paraprofessional were established on many islands. The region has one hospital. Many Kuna combine Western and Kuna approaches to healing when they are ill.

Death and Afterlife.   Kuna women and children prepare the body for burial. Women are responsible for wailing and mourning; they review the deceased's life and character and refer to punishments or rewards that will be his or hers in the afterworld. To guide the deceased, a death chanter (*masartulet*) may be employed to sing a long narrative song describing the soul's journey through the underworld to heaven. Kuna cemeteries are located on the mainland. Small houses, many furnished with a table, dishes, and other everyday objects, are often constructed over the graves. These articles are for the deceased to use in the afterworld and to take as gifts to previously departed relatives. Kuna women (usually the elders) are responsible for visiting the dead, bringing them food, and keeping their houses clean.

Bibliography

Chapin, Mac (1990). "The Silent Jungle: Ecotourism among the Kuna Indians of Panama." *Cultural Survival Quarterly* 14(1): 42–45.

Herrera, Francisco (1972). "Aspectos del desarollo economico y social de los indios kunas de San Blas." *América Indígena* 32(1): 113–138.

Holloman, Regina (1976). "Cuna Household Types and the Domestic Cycle." In *Frontier Adaptation in Lower South America*, edited by Mary Helms and Franklin Loveland, 131–149. Philadelphia: Institute for the Study of Human Issues.

Howe, James (1986). *The Kuna Gathering: Contemporary Village Politics in Panama.* Austin: University of Texas Press.

Sherzer, Joel (1983). *Kuna Ways of Speaking.* Austin: University of Texas Press.

Stier, Frances Rhoda (1982). "Domestic Economy: Land, Labor, and Wealth in a San Blas Community." *American Ethnologist* 9(3): 519–537.

Stout, David (1947). *San Blas Cuna Acculturation: An Introduction.* New York: Viking Fund.

Tice, Karin E. (1994). *Kuna Crafts, Gender, and the Global Economy.* Austin: University of Texas Press.

KARIN E. TICE

Ladinos

ETHNONYMS: none

"Ladino" is a term that was applied to the Old Castilian or Romance language to differentiate it from Latin, from which it was derived and of which it was considered to be a degenerate form. During the time that Muslims were in Spain, the term was applied to Muslims who spoke Castilian. In Mexico during the sixteenth century, Indians who had been educated by the friars and who knew the necessary Latin for the Catholic liturgy were sometimes called "Latinos" and, more generally, "Ladinos" or "Ladinizados." Later the term began to be applied to those Indians who learned Spanish. In a distorted sense, because of the cultural values attributed to the term "Ladino," the word came to be used to describe someone who was deceptive or malicious.

Orientation

Identification. Despite the connotations of "Ladino" during the colonial period, the term took root; it persists only in Central American usage, with two distinct meanings. According to some authors who specialize in this area, the term "Ladino" is applied to any non-Indian. So, for example, the populations of Guatemala, and Honduras, and the Mexican state of Chiapas would be divided between Indians and Ladinos. North of the Isthmus of Tehuantepec, the term "mestizo" is now often used to refer to rural non-Indian people. According to other researchers, the classification is more complex: it is necessary to employ the more traditional colonial vocabulary and speak of Indians, criollos, mestizos, and Ladinos—including in the Ladino group those who have deliberately rejected any cultural link to Indian culture. "Criollo" is a term usually reserved for Whites born in the New World without any admixture of Indian. Mestizos are people with mixed Indian-Hispanic ancestry. Whatever their contact with Indian culture has been, Ladinos try to prove that they have no connection with it. Ladino identity is fragile because it is defined in negative terms—by what one is not; it is acquired by maintaining contact with the culture of more urban areas. In this article, we adopt the more restricted, but more complex, definition of "Ladino," as the culture of persons who have some degree of Indian culture in their background and who have turned away from it to seek a new, non-Indian, national, and urban cultural identity.

Location. Ladinos are found intermixed with indigenous, mestizo, or criollo groups and with mestizos or criollos in the areas of Chiapas, Guatemala, and Honduras, mainly in the cities and larger villages of the region. They do not form communities identifying themselves as Ladino; rather they try to imitate or blend in with criollos or mestizos. Under the other definition of "Ladino," however, as "anyone with a non-Indian culture," many rural villages are characterized as "Ladino" by social scientists because they have no obvious indigenous cultural characteristics and, in particular, no indigenous language.

Demography. According to the Guatemalan censuses of 1970 through 1990, 45 percent of the total population of

the country is classified as "Ladino," amounting to approximately 4,500,000 people. In Chiapas, the category of "Ladino" is not registered in the census; in 1990, 240,429 non-Indian people resided in that state, constituting 19 percent of the population, but this is not a measure of the number of Ladinos in the cultural terms outlined here.

In the case of Honduras, the non-Indian population consists of around 4,200,000 people—that is, about 70 percent of the total population of the country; of these, only a few hundred thousand people on the urban periphery are Ladinos.

Linguistic Affiliation. Ladinos are by definition speakers of Spanish, the language they use habitually. Spanish gives them a sense of identity, despite the fact that many learned it as a second language and can also speak an indigenous language. They try, however, to deny that they know their mother tongue—and try to forget it—and, of course, they will not teach it to their children. Yet their Spanish is filled with terms and words that have their origin in Indian languages spoken in the area.

History and Cultural Relations

Under the more restricted definition of the term, Ladinos emerged in the sixteenth century, when Spanish domination was consolidated. The first Ladinos were Indians who were faced with the dissolution of their communities because of loss of their lands, because of congregation into towns (a policy that the Spaniards carried out coercively and from which some Indians tried to escape), or because the community disappeared as a result of an epidemic. Later, some Indians abandoned their communities to look for a better way of life; they established themselves in cities and tried to assimilate to the culture and values of the conquerors. During the colonial period, Ladinos were members of the Indian community, experts in matters pertaining to criollo culture. They could continue being Indians in racial terms, but they were treated differently.

Ladinos who adopted the values of Spanish culture—and in this way ameliorated their social position—were not well regarded. Rather, they were feared and distrusted because they had rejected their own people, and they were never totally accepted by groups of purely European origin. In the colonial cities of Chiapas and Guatemala, distinct groups of criollos and Ladinos formed, although miscegenation, which is prevalent in the area, blurred the distinction and made it more difficult to define the borderline between one group and the other.

With no definite criteria for identifying their group, Ladinos began to relate to the nascent "national state" on an individual basis and adopted state institutions. Although they established relations with Spanish and criollo groups and, subsequently, with mestizos, and attempted to assimilate their cultural practices, Ladinos generally remained in a subordinate position. Relations were reestablished with Indian communities years after the initial rupture.

Settlements

There are no settlements that one might consider specifically Ladino, unless we adopt Adams's (1956, 1964,

1970) criterion and classify as "Ladino" every non-Indian city or town in Guatemala, Chiapas, and Honduras. There are family groups or individuals who live in the middle- or lower-class areas of cities and larger towns in the area, having adopted models of urbanization and settlement typical of these urban milieus. One frequently finds two- and three-generation families whose houses are located on the same land or on adjacent lands, but, in contrast to those who revindicate their Indian origin, Ladinos do not form migrant colonies originating from a single place.

Economy

Subsistence and Commercial Activities.   Since precolonial times, the right to the usufruct of the land was linked to membership in a community. Ladinos originally gave up their agricultural rights in order to work at various occupations within urban areas, mainly in manufacture and commerce. In the nineteenth century Ladino laborers began to be employed in haciendas and, later, on coffee plantations, although only when there was a scarcity of indigenous labor. Nowadays it is unusual to find them performing agricultural labor; their presence is more noticeable in small-scale commerce and in the service sector. Some hold jobs as low- and middle-level public functionaries.

Industrial Arts.   There is no handicraft production that might be considered typically Ladino; however, Ladinos are associated with agro-industrial and local industries; they participate as wage earners within mestizo establishments. In the highlands of Chiapas and isolated villages of Guatemala, Ladinos work in the production of *aguardiente* (a cane liquor), which they monopolize in a kind of clandestine emporium that illegally introduces the product to Indian communities.

Trade.   Most Ladinos are employed in commerce. They incorporate themselves within the system established by the urban majority, operating small stores or stalls in local markets or working as traveling salesmen in cities. Often they are also intermediaries between suppliers of agricultural products (especially rural Indian communities) and large-scale urban merchants. Some are small private entrepreneurs who transport cargo in their own trucks or vans, or drive passenger vehicles.

Division of Labor.   Ladinos have adopted models of division of labor that are predominant among mestizo groups: a father must provide for his family and a mother must dedicate herself to domestic work and the care of her children. Nevertheless, compelled by economic need, women are now increasingly having to find employment outside the home. They run family businesses or sell food or other items from ambulatory stalls. Increasingly, sons and daughters of better-off Ladino families study at universities to become elementary-school teachers or occupy positions as public functionaries.

Land Tenure.   Neither members of indigenous communities nor well established in mestizo farming communities, Ladinos can own land only as private proprietors. Given their commercial orientation, however, their primary interest is not in working the land. If they do own property, it is more likely to be land in the city that they use for business

ventures, as investments, to build and rent housing, or to leave to their children.

Kinship

Kin Groups and Descent.   Ladino families are isolated groups that can trace their descent back two or three generations but rarely maintain solid relationships with collateral kin. Their relationships tend to be extended through *compadrazgo*, which provides an opportunity for betterment, if not in economic terms, at least in terms of status.

Children of nuclear families, if both of their parents are living, carry the paternal name, and when they form their own families they frequently maintain their patrilocal residence. There are cases of single mothers, and among them a lack of continuity in family names is more frequent. Some children take the name of the putative father, others that of their mother.

Kinship Terminology.   Ladino kinship terminology is the same as that used by other Spanish-speaking groups in the area. That is, one speaks of grandparents, parents, aunts and uncles, sons and daughters, brothers and sisters, cousins, brothers- and sisters-in-law, fathers- and mothers-in-law, and sons- and daughters-in-law in the same way in which these terms are used within Hispanic culture. The only unusual characteristic is the rather frequent incorporation of an *entenado*—a child given into someone's care by its parents, or semiadopted by another family for various reasons. The child may have been orphaned, been mistreated at home, or come from a family in dire economic straits. A child facing such circumstances may be sent to another family to be cared for in exchange for doing some work. The entenado is almost always a relative by marriage or a more remote family member—perhaps a godson or goddaughter.

Marriage and Family

Marriage.   Mixed marriages, either between Ladinos and mestizos of other groups or between Ladinos and Indians, are the most common form of marriage. In urban marriages with mestizos, the Christian ceremony is performed in the church of which both bride and groom are members, and, in many cases, there is also a civil ceremony. In the case of marriage to an Indian woman, the indigenous tradition of asking for the woman's hand must be followed, and traditional ceremonies must be performed in each community, including a Christian religious ceremony.

With increasing frequency, lack of money to pay the cost of any type of ceremony leads to "stealing" the bride, which also obviates the need for gifts. As a rule, however, even though it might be several years later and the couple may already have had children, they will attempt to formalize the relationship and reestablish relations with the wife's family.

Domestic Unit.   For people who have only recently become Ladinos, or first-generation Ladinos, neolocal domestic units and simple nuclear families are typical. With succeeding generations, however, extended families that include the husband's mother and some of the sons and their wives become more common. Sons take their spouses to their paternal home, but daughters do not. Sometimes the youngest daughter of the family remains in the home and does not marry so as to attend to the needs of her parents in their old age, but, more frequently, an entenada or an older granddaughter takes on this obligation.

Inheritance. There are no clear rules regarding inheritance; however, it is expected that the oldest son or several of the sons will continue working in their father's occupation and will inherit his business. Nevertheless, if a daughter or younger son takes care of the business, she or he will be the one to inherit it, albeit with an obligation to help one's brothers. Families who are in a position to do so try to leave houses, lands, and some kind of small business to each of their children, including married daughters.

Socialization. Socialization of children—just as in the case of mestizos—takes place in schools, neighborhoods, and churches. Sometimes it occurs within the workplace, given that some of these children work from a very early age.

Sociopolitical Organization

Social Organization. Ladinos are groups that consolidated and developed from the second half of the nineteenth century onward. Because of this short history, Ladino families have no extensive network of social relations. They have abandoned their communities of origin and the institutions that would have permitted them to build up a collective identity.

Political Organization. Ladinos participate in the political system of the society as a whole. In Honduras, they do not take an active part in politics, but simply accept what the dominant system expects of them in terms of respect toward national institutions. They do not appear to be linked to any Indian organizations. In Guatemala and Chiapas, their political participation is mixed; some have opted for supporting the governing classes, actively setting themselves off from subversive indigenous organizations. In the Chiapas Indian mobilizations of 1994, however, Ladino groups supported the Indian movement in its demands, perhaps in opposition to the _coletos_ (inhabitants of San Cristóbal de las Casas who consider themselves direct descendants of the old colonial aristocratic families).

Social Control. Because the group does not identify itself as such, there are almost no mechanisms for social control beyond those established by the society at large.

Religion and Expressive Culture

Religious Beliefs. Ladinos are people whose syncretic processes have been deeply internalized. They come from Indian communities in which the customs of their grandparents persists; because the mainstream society holds these traditions in contempt, Ladinos reject them, yet, simultaneously, they are ashamed of the extent to which the costumbre still influences them. All of them are members of some Christian church—formerly it was only the Catholic church, but increasingly Ladinos have joined various Protestant churches or fundamentalist sects.

Medicine. Although Ladinos pride themselves on using only conventional allopathic medicine, in cases they consider to be serious, almost all will go to an herbalist, bone-setter, shaman, midwife, or curer in their community of origin or of some indigenous group in the city.

Bibliography

Adams, Richard N. (1956). _Encuesta sobre la cultura de los ladinos en Guatemala._ Guatemala City: Ministerio de Educación Pública, Seminario de Integración Social Guatemalteca.

Adams, Richard N. (1964). "La mestización cultural en centroamérica." _Revista de Indias_ (Madrid) 95–96:153–176.

Adams, Richard N. (1970). _Crucifixion by Power: Essays on Guatemalan National Social Structure, 1944–1966._ Austin: University of Texas Press.

Casaus Arzú, Marta (1992). _Guatemala: Linaje y racismo._ San José, Costa Rica: Facultad Latinoamericana de Ciencias Sociales.

Glittenberg, Joann Elizabeth Kropp (1976). "A Comparative Study of Fertility in Highland Guatemala: A Ladino and an Indian Town." Ph.D. dissertation, University of Colorado at Boulder.

Pitt-Rivers, Julian (1970). "Palabras y hechos: Los ladinos." In _Ensayos de antropología en la zona central de Chiapas_, edited by Norman McQuown and Julian Pitt-Rivers, 21–42. Mexico City: Instituto Nacional Indigenista.

Spielberg, Joseph (1965). "San Miguel Milpas Altas: An Ethnographic Analysis of Interpersonal Relations in a Peasant-Ladino Community of Guatemala." Ph.D. dissertation, Michigan State University.

MARÍA DE LA PALOMA ESCALANTE GONZALBO

(Translated by Ruth Gubler)

Lakandon

ETHNONYMS: Lacandon, Lacandone

Some 300 Lakandon Maya live in Chiapas, Mexico, at 16°00′ to 17°15′ N and 91°36′ to 92°05′ W. The two main subgroups, the Northern and Southern Lakandon, live in tropical rain forests at an elevation of 900 meters and in jungle at an elevation of about 100 meters, respectively. The Southern group differs linguistically and culturally from the Northern, and is composed of two smaller groups, the Cedro-Lacanha and the Jatate. The Northern Lakandon actively resist acculturation, but the Southern Lakandon have been more open to assimilation into Mexican society. This difference came about as a result of a yellow-fever epidemic and the later influx of chicle gatherers in World War II. The chicle workers exposed the Southern Lakandon to a number of European diseases, which killed many people. These diseases disrupted the practice of the native religion, which was more centralized and hierarchical among the Southern Lakandon. The diseases killed some of the high priests, and at the same time the ill Lakandon were helped not by their own gods but by Western medicine. Missionaries were thus able to convert the Southern group to Protestant Christianity, after having failed for several decades to convert the Northern group.

The region has two seasons, wet and dry. The dry season begins in January and lasts until April. Because of this, the Lakandon begin to clear and burn their fields in January and to plant in April and May. The first maize crop is harvested from July through October, and the second in December. They also grow tomatoes, beans, squashes, root vegetables, onions, and chayotes and gather other fruits and vegetables from the forest and jungle year-round. Hunting, with bows and arrows as well as with firearms, takes place in all months, but different animals are hunted at different times. Game animals include coatis, toucans, monkeys, boars, squirrels, and other rodents such as the tepescuintle (or paca), and parrots and other birds such as the chachalaca. In addition, pumas, crocodiles, nutrias, ocelots, and jaguars are hunted for their skins, which are sold. Fish are caught most of the year with hooks or spears.

Dogs are kept for hunting and security, cats to keep rats and mice away. In the 1940s or 1950s, the Lakandon acquired chickens and turkeys from workers brought to the area to harvest rubber and chicle. Poultry are owned by women, who sell the meat and eggs for money to buy dress materials.

The patrilineal, patrilocal Lakandon belong to clans; the oldest male member of the clan is its leader. Clans were exogamous at the beginning of the twentieth century, but now only a preference for marriage to members of other clans is observed. Kinship terminology is unilateral, and parallel cousins (who may not be married) are classed with siblings, whereas cross cousins (who may be married) are classed with mother's father and daughter's child. Lakandon may not marry non-Lakandon people. Polygyny is accepted, although no man has more than three wives. Divorce occurs when either spouse wishes it. If a man wishes to divorce his wife, she may keep her children and whatever he has given her, and he must find her a new husband. A woman who wishes divorce leaves with only her own possessions. Beating and refusing to feed and clothe one's wife are the most common causes of divorce.

Much of the traditional religion has been lost, especially detailed knowledge of formal ceremonies and rituals, whereas taboos and the practice of praying for good weather, fertility, and health persist. The ceremonies that were formerly of great importance include the pilgrimmage to Yaxchilan, home of the most important deities, and the offering of *balché* (an alcoholic drink) to the gods.

The Lakandon believe that Kakoch, the middle-level heaven, created the god Hachakyum, who in turn created the world. There are two other heavens, one associated with great goodness and the god Chembeku, and another linked to the god Hachakyum (also called Yumbrikan), where all Lakandon go after death. The underworld is dominated by Kisin, who tries to demolish the world at night, only to be fought by Sukukyum, older brother of Hachakyum, who brings the sun back. Sinners go to the underworld, where they become animals and work forever. Kisin's anger is the source of earthquakes.

The people now on earth are believed to be the product of a union between the first people (who were made of clay) and the second people (descendants of the Yaxté, or silk-cotton tree). These early forms of human life are now extinct.

Pregnant women are believed to possess the power to heal. Men pray for them during their pregnancies and during delivery. Childbirth takes place in the forest or, if at night, inside a house. Children are weaned and toilet trained at or before 2 years of age. Parents raise their children without much use of corporal punishment or raised voices. The puberty ritual in which a boy's nose was pierced for the insertion of a feather is no longer practiced. Young men usually marry old widows as their first wives, and young women as their second wives. The older women are able to help their husbands acquire food; young men rarely have the ability to make a large farm. The second and third wives are often very young girls, who move into their new husband's house as soon as they are able to make tortillas. The husbands of these young girls behave toward them as if they were daughters until the girls reach maturity. The bride-price demanded by a girl's parents is large and increasing.

The deceased are buried, wrapped in a tunic and a hammock, facing the sun. Several grave goods are included so that certain obstacles encountered on the trip to the afterlife can be overcome and so that the necessary payments can be made. Some Lakondon believe they all spend time in the underworld prior to reaching heaven. Others think that all who commit serious offenses such as stealing or homicide will spend eternity in the underworld.

Bibliography

Baer, Phillip, and William R. Merrifield (1971). *Two Studies on the Lacandones of Mexico*. Norman: Summer Institute of Linguistics of the University of Oklahoma.

Blom, Gertrude Duby (1944). *Los lacandones: Su passado y su presente*. Mexico City: Secretería de Educación Pública.

Bruce, Robert D. (1975). *Lacandon Dream Symbolism*. Perugino, Mexico: Ediciones Euroamericanas Klaus Thiele.

Davis, Virginia Dale (1978). "Ritual of the Northern Lacandon." Ph.D. dissertation, Tulane University.

Duby, Gertrude, and Frans Blom (1969). "The Lacandon." In *Handbook of Middle American Indians*, edited by Robert Wauchope. Vol. 7, *Ethnology, Part One*, edited by Evon Z. Vogt, 276–297. Austin: University of Texas Press.

McGee, R. Jon (1990). *Life, Ritual, and Religion among the Lacandon Maya*. Belmont, Calif.: Wadsworth.

Nations, James Dale (1979). "Population Ecology of the

Lacandon Maya." Ph.D. dissertation, Southern Methodist University.

Perera, Victor, and Robert D. Bruce (1982). *The Last Lords of Palenque: The Lacandon Mayas of the Mexican Rain Forest.* Berkeley and Los Angeles: University of California Press.

Soustelle, Jacques (1937). *La culture matérielle des indiens lacandons.* Paris: Societé des Américanistes.

Villa Rojas, Alfonso (1967a). "Los lacandones: Su origen, costumbres y problemas vitales." *América Indígena* 27:25–54.

Villa Rojas, Alfonso (1967b). "Los lacandones: Sus dioses, ritos y creencias." *América Indígena* 28:81–138.

Lenca

ETHNONYMS: Opatoro

Orientation

The contemporary Lenca are descendants of South American Chibchan peoples who migrated to El Salvador and Honduras during the eleventh century. They live in the forests of the volcanic mountains of western Honduras, predominantly in the departments of Intibucá, La Paz, and Lempira. A smaller number of Lenca Indians live in eastern El Salvador. Present estimates of the Lenca population vary from 50,000 to 95,000. They currently occupy about 10,000 square kilometers.

It is almost impossible to locate speakers of the Lenca language, which is generally considered to be extinct. Adding to the ambiguity surrounding the Lenca language is that it has eluded clear linguistic classification. Scholars disagree about whether it is more closely related to the Macro-Chibchan Family or the Macro-Mayan Family.

History and Cultural Relations

The pre-Conquest Lenca Empire consisted of four interrelated regions. These were the Care, Cerquin, and Lenca in Honduras and the Potón in El Salvador. The Lenca were not originally indigenous to this area; they emigrated to the region from South America. Their contact with the various Mayan groups and the Aztecan Pipil contributed much to their culture. It is estimated that, at the time of the Conquest, the Lenca numbered between three and six hundred thousand and occupied around 26,000 square kilometers.

In the 1520s Spanish forces under Cortés entered the Lenca region and attempted to conquer them. The Lenca tried to defend themselves but were unable to resist. In the years immediately following, European diseases and forced labor took their toll on the Lenca. By 1550, there were only 25,000 Lenca Indians left. This population level remained relatively stable throughout the colonial period.

In contrast to many other groups in the area who lost their communal lands during the colonial period, many Lenca communities were able to retain their communal lands and to continue their agricultural way of life into the present. Others migrated for wage-labor jobs on the coffee and banana plantations or in the mines. Because the Lenca have been heavily involved in Honduran society, much of traditional Lenca culture has been lost through the process of acculturation.

Settlements

The most common settlement pattern is a regional center surrounded by small conglomerations of people. Most Lenca live in the surrounding countryside, where they can be close to their fields. They make trips to town on special occasions such as fiestas or going to market.

Traditional houses have walls constructed of adobe and thatched roofs of straw or grass. These dwellings have one main room, and one wall is set back into the structure to allow for a covered porch. Not all houses are built in the traditional manner, however; it is not uncommon for a house to be built of bricks or wood and to have a tile or galvanized-tin roof.

Economy

The central component of subsistence is the production of maize, beans, and squashes. These crops are raised together on small plots (milpas). Traditional implements such as the hoe, machete, and digging stick are utilized to cultivate crops in the milpa. Other crops that are grown to supplement the Lenca diet include, wheat, bananas, sugarcane, yucca, chilies, and oranges. These crops are raised on *ejido* lands: officially, the land is owned by the community, but plots are assigned to individuals, who farm the land as if it were their own.

A smaller portion of time is devoted to hunting and fishing. Men hunt for deer or jaguars with their bows and arrows. The Lenca have a unique way of fishing. They first dam up a stream or river with stones, leaving an opening where water can still flow through. They then place a net over the opening and place poisonous *barbasco* vines in the river upstream. The poison from the vine kills the fish, and they are then caught in the net.

The Lenca also make use of a number of domesticated animals. Dogs, chickens, pigs, ducks, and turkeys are commonly owned. Horses, mules, and cows are rarer possessions but are valued very highly. Horses and mules are important for transportation, and cows are prized for their milk, which is given to infants.

The Lenca make a number of objects for their own use. Basketry and pottery are important industries at the village level. Using pine needles or a type of cane, they make many types of baskets. By employing various organic dyes they decorate the baskets with colorful patterns. Pottery is made by coiling strands of clay into jugs and bowls. These are then fired in kilns that are built into the ground.

Another important manufactured good is cordage. Fibers from the maguey plant are spun into long strands of cord by two individuals standing 9 to 27 meters apart.

These cords are used for construction purposes and are often traded for other goods.

Also, the Lenca produce candles for use in their homes and in the churches. The berries of the weed *Myrica cerifera* are picked, crushed, and boiled. The residue from this process is then placed into candle molds and left to cool.

Marriage and Family

Marriage usually occurs between the ages of 12 and 14 for females and between the ages of 14 and 18 for males. Although marriage is often prearranged by the parents of the children, this is not always the case. Often, the bride goes to live with the parents of the groom and the groom goes to live with the parents of the bride for a trial period before the marriage is finalized. In most cases, newly married couples move in with the parents of the bride until it is possible for them to maintain their own household. For this reason, nuclear households are the most common form of household, with some instances of matrifocal extended-family households.

Because land is held communally, there are few substantial possessions to be passed on to children; however, houses and farming implements are often inherited by the oldest son.

Sociopolitical Organization

The sociopolitical organization of the Lenca is that of a Latin American civil-religious hierarchy. Historically, each town was an autonomous unit, and, for this reason, each town presently has its own complement of governing officials. The most important function of the civil side of the hierarchy, beyond the day-to-day governance of the town, is the allotment of ejido lands. This is done by either the mayor or the group of governing elders.

The most important position to be held on the religious side of the hierarchy is that of *mayordomo*. This office is held by a married couple. The husband is called the mayordomo, but his wife must carry out her obligations as well. They are responsible for taking care of church affairs for a period of one year. Their most important duty is to sponsor the festivals that are held annually to venerate the patron saint of the town. Mayordomos finance these festivals with their own personal funds. Much status and prestige is conferred upon those who fill this office.

Religion and Expressive Culture

The religious beliefs of the Lenca are a combination of traditional beliefs and the teachings of the Catholic church. Traditionally, the Lenca believe in a direct link between the spiritual and the natural. Spirits and *dioses* (gods) abound in the Lenca cosmology and must be carefully dealt with.

From the Catholic church, the Lenca have taken the concepts of an overarching creator God, the Virgin Mary, and the saints. The Catholic saints have been combined with the traditional spirits and are worshiped as household deities.

As the Catholic church has moved closer and closer to orthodoxy in Latin America, traditional Lenca beliefs have been harder and harder to find. This is a function of both a small-scale return to orthodoxy and an attempt to take traditional beliefs underground.

The Lenca maintain a multitude of ceremonies and rituals derived from both Catholic and traditional practices. The most sacred day of the year is the day on which the patron saint of the town is carried through the streets. This day is marked by a great festival and worship of the saints in the streets.

There are no trained medical personnel in rural areas. In those areas where medical professionals do exist, many people distrust them and remain under the care of traditional healers. Curing is carried out by pharmacists, *curanderos* (traditional curers), and midwives. A popular method of treatment is traditional herbal therapy.

When a person dies, mourners hold a feast during which large amounts of *chicha*, a fermented maize beverage, are consumed. The drinking and mourning often go on for nine days.

Bibliography

Chapin, Mac (1991). "Población indígena de El Salvador." *Mesoamerica* 21:1–40.

Chapman, Anne (1985). *Los hijos del Copal y la Candela: Ritos agraria y tradición oral de los lencas de Honduras.* Mexico City: Universidad Nacional Autónoma de México.

Chapman, Anne (1986). *Los hijos del Copal y la Candela: Tradición católica de los lencas de Honduras.* Mexico City: Universidad Nacional Autónoma de México.

Herranz Herranz, Atanasio (1987). "El lenca de Honduras: Una lengua moribunda." *Mesoamerica* 14:429–444.

Stone, Doris (1948). "The Northern Highland Tribes: The Lenca." In *Handbook of South American Indians.* Vol 4, edited by Julian H. Steward. Washington D.C.: United States Government Printing Office.

Weeks, John M., and Nancy J. Black (1992). "Notes on the Ethnopharmacology of the Lenca Indians of Western Honduras and Eastern El Salvador." *Mexicon* 14(4): 71–74.

IAN MAST

Maleku

ETHNONYMS: Guatuso, Guatuzo, Jaika

The Maleku are a group of fewer than 200 Indians living in the middle of Costa Rica, near the border with Nicaragua. They have little sense of tribal identity, are very acculturated, and speak Spanish as their mother tongue. Their traditional territory was once much larger than it is today.

Bibliography

Bozzoli de Wille, María et al. (1973). *Costa Rica: Patrones culturales de comunidades indígenas.* San José: Biblioteca del CEDAL.

Leiva, Imelda, and María Bozzoli (1987). *Bibliografía antropológica de Costa Rica.* San José: Universidad de Costa Rica, Departamento de Antropología, Laboratorio de Etnología.

Mam

ETHNONYMS: Mames (in Spanish), Mam Maya

Orientation

Identification. The Mam are contemporary Maya Indians who speak the Mam language, which is, after K'iche' (Quiché), the secondmost widely spoken of the twenty-one Maya languages currently spoken in Guatemala. Not since the Spanish Conquest, and perhaps never, have the Mam constituted a unified polity or society. They share many cultural traits with other Maya of Guatemala but remain divided into local communities and linguistically distinct subgroups with no pan-Mam or pan-Maya identity.

Location. The Mam live in southwestern Guatemala and, across the Mexican border, in extreme southeastern Chiapas. The region varies from hot tropical lowlands along the Pacific Ocean to more temperate highlands in the interior. These highlands, located mostly between 1,500 and 2,700 meters in elevation, once sustained oak and pine forests, much of which Mam have cleared for farming. There are marked rainy and dry seasons: the heaviest rains fall between April and November, and the driest days are in February and March. To the north, Mam towns in the Cuchumatán Highlands border Jakalteko, Q'anjob'al, Ixil, and Awakateko Maya. To the east, Mam have contested K'iche' Maya intrusions since pre-Hispanic times.

Demography. Estimates from the 1981 Guatemalan census suggest well over 500,000 Mam currently occupy fifty-six administratively autonomous and culturally distinctive *municipios* in the departments of Huehuetenango, San Marcos, and Quezaltenango. The Mam share their municipios with Ladinos (Spanish-speaking mestizos disavowing any Indian identity), who comprise about 40 percent of the region's total population. The number of Ladinos generally varies with elevation: Mam outnumber Ladinos three to one in municipios above 2,700 meters, where subsistence maize agriculture prevails and about four-fifths of the Mam population lives; Ladinos dominate three to two in townships under 2,700 meters, more suitable for commercial coffee and cotton production.

Linguistic Affiliation. Mam belongs to the Mamean Branch of Eastern Mayan languages; it is most closely related to Ixil, Awakateko, and Tektiteko; Mamean separated from the K'ichean languages perhaps 3,400 years ago. Today Mam consists of some fifteen dialects grouped into three divisions: northern Mam is spoken in nineteen municipios in southern Huehuetenango and northern San Marcos, southern Mam in thirty-four municipios in San Marcos and Quezaltenango, and western Mam in three municipios in northwestern San Marcos, near the Mexican border. Considerable differences reduce intelligibility between divisions, and minor variations mark the dialects within each. Each municipio also has a distinctive style of speech, sufficient to identify speakers by their accent.

History and Cultural Relations

Mam speakers have occupied western Guatemala for perhaps 2,600 years. Some historical linguists suggest that the precursor of all Mayan languages may have diversified from a homeland just north of contemporary Mam territory beginning some four thousand years ago. During pre-Hispanic times, Mam vied for control of their lands with more powerful K'iche' lords to the east. In February 1524 Spanish forces under Pedro de Alvarado passed through the southern Mam region en route to subjugating the K'iche' and Kaqchikel. They subdued the northern Mam in late 1525, but the southern Mam evidently escaped military conquest, perhaps by initially allying with the Spaniards against their K'iche' enemies. Following the Conquest, the rugged inaccessibility of the Mam region attracted few Spanish colonists. Dominican and, later, Mercedarian friars sought to convert the Mam to Catholicism; although the friars resettled them into mission *congregaciones* (nucleated Spanish-style towns), aside from demands for tribute and labor and the periodic ravages of Old World epidemic diseases, the Mam remained relatively autonomous. Not until the late nineteenth century, with the expansion of commercial coffee plantations along Guatemala's southern Pacific coast, did Mam become directly incorporated into Guatemala's export economy. Mam nearest the coast lost lands to the expanding coffee plantations, whereas highland Mam were forced into migratory wage labor to harvest the crop. Only in the 1940s, as population growth outstripped available farmland in the highlands, did Mam begin migrating to the plantations of their own accord. In the mid-twentieth century short-lived agrarian and political reforms in Guatemala, and then increasingly repressive military regimes, further disrupted Mam communities. In the 1950s Mam converts to more orthodox Catholicism challenged traditional Mam "folk" religion and community organization. Missionary health, education, and technical programs eventually fostered new leadership and a renewed sense of self-determination in Mam communities. Growing political violence between leftist guerrillas and the Guatemalan government, however, subjected Mam to brutal counterinsurgency warfare during the 1980s. Although they escaped the worst of the massacres, forced resettlement, and militarization suffered by other Maya, the Mam felt caught between two antagonists who demanded their support but cared little about their problems or priorities. In the 1990s the Mam remain second-class citizens in Guatemala—mostly poor subsistence farmers and rural wage laborers—but they have yet to succumb to the dominant Ladino society and seek a better place within it.

Settlements

Traditionally swidden cultivators, the Mam favor dispersed settlements. Municipal *cabeceras* or "head towns" often consist of little more than a cluster of houses surrounding the church, town hall, and marketplace; the few streets usually radiate out from a central square in a grid pattern, an artifact of colonial town planning. All cabeceras now have electricity and potable water, but most lack urban amenities such as paved streets, shops, or diversions beyond the ubiquitous cantinas. Some 90 percent of Mam still live in scattered hamlets of less than 500 people. Although dispersed, hamlets maintain formal administrative ties to the cabecera of their municipio and share patterns of traditional dress and speech unique to the municipio as a whole. A high degree of endogamy also helps to maintain municipio cohesion. Mam houses typically consist of a hard-packed dirt floor, adobe walls, and a tile or corrugated metal roof. Small, usually shuttered windows leave the interiors dark and often smoky from cooking fires. Most houses have a sweatbath, and Mam bathe as often as the availability of firewood allows.

Economy

Subsistence and Commercial Activities.   Since pre-Hispanic times, Mam have been primarily subsistence farmers, cultivating the typical Mesoamerican crops of maize, beans, and squashes. Until the 1960s, Mam cleared fields with machete and hoe, planted them for several years, then fallowed them to work other plots. Yields ranged from 570 to 1,000 kilograms of shelled maize per acre. Land was under nearly continuous cultivation in richer valley bottoms, but less promising terrain required five to ten years or more of fallow for at most two years of use. Since the 1960s, chemical fertilizers have extended periods of use and raised yields, but population growth offsets any real gains. Most clearing, planting, and weeding is done between April and August; harvests are between November and January, depending on the elevation. To generate needed income, Mam with suitable lands now also cash-crop in coffee on a small scale. Those without coffee land or enough maize land to feed themselves must migrate seasonally to lowland plantations, where coffee and cotton harvests fall mostly between July and January.

Industrial Arts.   During slack periods in the agricultural cycle, many Mam traditionally engaged in artisanal production of cloth, pottery, furniture, and basic necessities such as salt, lime, and stone metates for grinding maize. Almost all Mam women still weave on traditional backstrap looms. Using commercially manufactured thread, they make their own blouses, skirts, belts, and whatever handwoven articles of clothing men in their towns still wear.

Trade.   During the late nineteenth century, Guatemala's coffee economy stimulated the growth of rural marketplaces to supply Ladino towns and plantations. Mam traders still work these markets today, peddling local goods from different Mam communities and the few consumer goods that rural Mam need and can afford—coffee, salt, lime, unrefined sugar, soap, kerosene, thread for weaving, clothing, tools, and pots for cooking and for fetching, storing, and heating water; occasional luxuries include cigarettes, sweets, jewelry, radios or tape recorders, and sugarcane rum. Better roads and transportation have eased Mam access to major market centers, but the inflow of cheap imported goods has also undermined local artisanal production.

Division of Labor.   Mam men work the fields, engage in trade, and construct and repair buildings; women cook, weave, wash clothes, and provide primary child care. Both men and women work for wages, and, during the harvest season, entire families migrate to the plantations, many for months at a time. Truck and bus transport and commercial weaving on foot looms are prominent among the few nonagricultural Mam professions. Younger Mam also work as schoolteachers, usually in rural posts eschewed by Ladino teachers.

Land Tenure.   Until the twentieth century, most Mam municipios held land communally, granting usufruct rights to individuals for specific plots. Because use rights could be sold, sublet, or passed on to heirs, renters often came to consider these parcels private property, although they were forbidden by law actually to sell the land. As competition for land intensified and the Guatemalan government sought to sustain communal land tenure, Mam turned increasingly to individual legal titles to secure access to land. By the 1950s, private landholding predominated in most Mam communities.

Kinship

Kin Groups and Descent.   The basic Mam kin group is the patrilineal, patrilocal extended family of two to four generations. It serves as the primary locus for shared resources and socioeconomic cooperation between fathers, sons, their spouses, and unmarried children. Although families with the same surname avoid intermarrying, they currently serve no other role as kin groups. Mam also practice *compadrazgo*, or ritual kinship, which establishes a bond of mutual support and respect between parents and the couples who sponsor their children's baptisms; *compadres* are usually nonkin neighbors who extend the parent's social network.

Kinship Terminology.   Kinship terminology is bilateral and Iroquoian but with sibling terms for younger sibling of either sex, older sibling of the same sex, older sister of a male, and older brother of a female; terms for cousins, nieces, and nephews are presently descriptive. Fathers have separate terms for son/child and daughter; mothers use a single term for children of either sex. The term for grand-father and grandchild of a man is reciprocal, whereas those for grandmother and grandchild of a woman are not. Reciprocal terms exist for affines of the same sex and generation, parents-in-law and sons-in-law, and parents-in-law and daughters-in-law; other affinal terms are presently descriptive. Descriptive terms may reflect the long influence of Spanish terminology.

Marriage and Family

Marriage. Traditionally, the groom's father initiated marriage negotiations with the prospective bride's father, but Mam children have long had latitude in choosing a spouse. Ideally, the groom, his father, and witnesses to his good character petition the bride's father and present her family with gifts of sweet breads, cigarettes, rum, and at least a nominal—in some towns substantial—payment to compensate for "raising the girl." After sometimes protracted negotiations, the bride moves into her new father-in-law's house. Within a year or so, the marriage will be formalized in the local civil registry, and, if the families are religious, in a church ceremony. Mam men usually marry in their late teens, once they can provide for a family; women marry a year or two younger, once they have mastered weaving and making tortillas. Mam gauge a potential spouse in terms of practical skills and proper character, not physical attractiveness or romantic love.

Domestic Unit. The Mam domestic unit ideally follows a cycle from newly independent nuclear family to an extended family of parents, sons, and their families, then back to a nuclear family as the sons move out, the parents die, and the remaining son inherits the house. Although ideally cooperative and collective, the extended family manifests tensions between fathers and sons over land and between mothers-in-law and daughters-in-law over allocation of household resources. The extended family usually, but not always, shares a single hearth and larder.

Inheritance. By Guatemalan law, inheritance is bilateral, although sons often receive more and better land than daughters, whose husbands are expected to provide for them. Formerly, Mam fathers sought to delay inheritance of family lands as long as possible to control their sons' labor, but shrinking landholdings and increasing involvement in the cash economy have weakened patriarchal authority. Today Mam men buy, rather than inherit, much of what land they own.

Socialization. Mam children learn largely by observing and imitating others in the intimacy of one-room houses and close-knit communities. Even intricate tasks such as weaving entail little explicit instruction. Sons begin working in the fields alongside their fathers as soon as they can handle a hoe; young girls assist their mothers at an even earlier age. Although children should attend school through the sixth grade, work at home and in the fields comes first, and few Mam continue beyond primary school.

Sociopolitical Organization

Social Organization. Mam social organization centers on the patrilineal, patrilocal extended family and the territorial, largely endogamous municipio. Between these two units lie exogamous, patrilineal surname groups that in the past may have constituted lineages or clans, and residential hamlets ideally made up of clusters of patrilineally related households that form as fathers build houses for their married sons. Hamlets can become the nucleus of new municipios, as has happened with at least eight Mam municipios since the Conquest. Class distinction within Mam communities continues to grow, yet the line between rich and poor, landed and landless, subsistence farmer and petty commodity producer, remains relative and permeable. Racial prejudice and hostility between Indians and Ladinos can also mitigate such divisions within Mam communities.

Political Organization. Mam political organization consists of municipio-based hierarchies of administrative and ritual offices of four or more levels with progressively fewer, more burdensome, positions at each level. Ideally, all men in the municipio take turns carrying these year-long *cargos* (burdens), beginning as youths in the lowest positions, then advancing from one office to the next in life-long public careers. In the past, heavy ritual expenses meant cargoholders had to "rest" after their year in office to recoup debts and to save for the even greater expenses of their next cargo. Those who completed service on all levels of the hierarchy became the town elders who chose new cargoholders each year and made all important decisions affecting the town. After the advent of nominally popular elections in Mam municipios during the 1940s, party politics slowly replaced the ritual obligations of traditional cargos with the bureaucratic legalities of the Guatemalan state. Despite the changes, cargo hierarchies persist as a way of defining membership in the community and of gaining local recognition. Political ideology or party loyalty still matters less to Mam than struggles for local advantage because, however factionalized, the municipio remains the focus of Mam politics and the basis for Mam negotiations with a national government they have long considered an instrument of Ladino domination.

Social Control. In larger towns with detachments of the National Police, social control lies formally with legal authorities, but in most municipios and hamlets, local Mam officials and elders exercise great latitude in resolving conflicts and punishing offenders as long as the parties involved agree to abide by their judgments. In serious crimes or intractable conflicts where such consensus is impossible, cases go to the national courts.

Conflict. Conflicts commonly involve jurisdictional disputes between municipios and between town centers and their outlying hamlets; political feuds between different factions; religious disputes between Catholics, Protestants, and traditionalists; and personal quarrels over land and sexual indiscretions. Resentments, especially personal ones, often smolder until drunken quarrels on market days or fiestas bring them out into the open.

Religion and Expressive Culture

Religious Beliefs. Most Mam consider themselves nominally Catholic, although local heterodoxies abound. Traditional Mam religion focused on Catholic saints in the local church and spirit "owners" of nearby mountain peaks. Mam saints embody powers in their own right, not Christian exemplars, which Mam domesticated by dressing their images in local Mam attire and "feeding" them candles, rum, and pine-pitch incense. Conversely, mountain spirits appeared as greedy Ladinos who enslaved Mam souls after death. Both saints and mountain spirits could send misfortune or illness to punish ritual neglect or offense; ritual specialists would then have to divine the cause and determine the restitution. Cosmologically, the paths of "Our Father Sun" and "Our Grandmother Moon" encircled "Our Mother Earth," and the twenty day-names of the Maya calendar held divinatory significance. Since the 1950s, Catholic missionaries, mostly of the North American Maryknoll order, and fundamentalists of the Central American Mission have won sizable, if shifting, Mam congregations. Not all ex-traditionalists, however, accept formal baptism into a church, and many say they now live "without religion."

Religious Practitioners. In the past, all Mam men knew the rudiments of *costumbre*, literally "custom" in Spanish, but used by Mam to refer to their prayers and offerings to God, the saints, and mountain spirits. Religious specialists called *chmaan*, "grandfathers"—a reference to their status as elders—contributed both a greater eloquence to their costumbre and esoteric knowledge of the twenty-day Maya calendar to divine and protect Mam health, crops, and destiny. Particularly powerful chmaan could even bargain directly with mountain spirits in matters of illness and sorcery. Mam men also gained ritual knowledge through rotating service in the *cofradías*, or religious brotherhoods, dedicated to care of the saints in the local church, which often constituted an integral part of the municipio's cargo hierarchy. Religious specialists today include Mam catechists who preside over Catholic congregations in towns without a resident priest and Mam preachers in local evangelical churches.

Ceremonies. Mam celebrate Holy Week (Easter), All Saints' Day, Christmas, and the feast days of local patron saints. Celebrations generally include a holiday market, Catholic Mass, and processions of local saints' images through the streets of the town. Some Mam municipios still practice reciprocal saint exchange, in which local religious officials carry their saint to "visit" neighboring saints on their feast days.

Arts. In addition to weaving, Mam enjoy the marimba—a large xylophonelike instrument with wooden bars suspended over resonators, which is played by three or four musicians with small wooden mallets; its complex, liquid rhythms pervade all public celebrations.

Medicine. Herbal cures are often administered by female herbalists who double as midwives. Since the late 1960s, an almost magical faith in Western pills and injections has augmented the Mam pharmacopoeia. Health normally depends on the blood, which Mam view as the seat of physical strength and sensory perceptions. Curing restores the requisite "heat" to the blood through "hot" medicines and sweatbaths.

Death and Afterlife. At death, Mam hold a wake for the deceased, then bury the body in the local cemetery. During All Saints' Day (1 November), Mam remember the dead by decorating their graves, offering them food and drink, and having a marimba played at the graveside. Con-

cepts of the afterlife remain unelaborated: Mam formerly said that the dead worked for Ladino spirits inside nearby peaks and distant volcanoes; today they speak of being with God in heaven or burning in hell, or perhaps of wandering the earth as a ghost.

Bibliography

Ebel, Roland H. (1969). "Political Modernization in Three Guatemalan Communities." In *Community Culture and National Change*, edited by Margaret A. L. Harrison and Robert Wauchope. 131–206. Middle American Research Institute Publication 24. New Orleans: Tulane University.

England, Nora (1983). *A Grammar of Mam, A Mayan Language*. Austin: University of Texan Press.

Hawkins, John (1984). *Inverse Images: The Meaning of Culture, Ethnicity, and Family in Postcolonial Guatemala*. Albuquerque: University of New Mexico Press.

Oakes, Maud (1951). *The Two Crosses of Todos Santos: Survivals of Mayan Religious Ritual*. Bolligen Series, no 27. Princeton, N.J.: Princeton University Press.

Scotchmer, David G. (1986). "Convergence of the Gods: Comparing Traditional Maya and Christian Maya Cosmologies." In *Symbol and Meaning Beyond the Closed Community: Essays in Mesoamerican Ideas*, edited by Gary H. Gossen, 197–226. Studies on Culture and Society, vol. 1. Albany: State University of New York at Albany, Institute of Mesoamerican Studies.

Smith, Waldemar R. (1977). *The Fiesta System and Economic Change*. New York: Columbia University Press.

Valladares, León A. (1957). *El hombre y el maíz: Etnografía y etnopsicología de Colotenango*. Mexico City: Editorial B. Costa-Amic.

Wagley, Charles (1941). *Economics of a Guatemalan Village*. Memoirs of the American Anthropological Association, no. 58. Menasha, Wis.: American Anthropological Association.

Wagley, Charles (1949). *The Social and Religious Life of a Guatemalan Village*. Memoirs of the American Anthropological Association, no. 71. Menasha, Wis.: American Anthropological Association.

Watanabe, John M. (1992). *Maya Saints and Souls in a Changing World*. Austin: University of Texas Press.

JOHN M. WATANABE

Martiniquais

ETHNONYMS: Béké (the elite White minority descended from slave owners); Creoles (refers to both the non-White, mixed-heritage local population and to the local language); Metropolitans (refers to people of European descent who live in French-speaking former colonies)

Orientation

Identification. In many ways, Martinique is a unique island culture: it is part of a major industrial world power (France) but set in a third-world geographic region. With its neighbors, Martinique shares an important social history of slavery and a monocrop economy based on sugar. Like other Caribbean islands whose sugar production has dwindled since the late 1950s, Martinique also lacks the mineral and natural resources to support its own economic growth. Because of Martinique's political assimilation to France, however, the islanders' standard of living remains well above that of most Caribbean countries. Incorporation translates into French import subsidies, social transfer payments, and provisions for a large, highly paid local government sector.

Location. Part of the eastern Caribbean chain of islands known as the Lesser Antilles, the French islands of Martinique and Guadeloupe constitute the French Antilles. Martinique is situated south of Dominica, and north of Saint Lucia, encompassing a total land mass of 1,100 square kilometers.

Demography. The French, who first arrived in Martinique and Guadeloupe in 1635, found only a sparse population of native Carib Indians. At the hands of the colonists, these Indians were a short-lived labor source. Realizing the need for a cheap, abundant source of hardy laborers to work the sugar plantations, the settlers looked to Africa. Thus began more than two centuries of the Atlantic slave trade. By 1680, African slaves in Martinique outnumbered White planters two to one.

The forced migration of Africans to the New World, and specifically to Martinique, transformed the social order and composition of the local population. By the mid-1700s, all non-Spanish island populations were overwhelmingly Black but included a small number of mulatto Browns and an even smaller number of Whites. By 1770, 85 percent of Martinique's population were slaves, 12 percent masters, and 3 percent freed. The number of slaves imported to the island grew from 258,000 in 1810 to 365,000 in 1848, the year slavery was abolished in France.

Abolition created pressures to find a new source of plantation labor. Colonists turned to contract laborers, primarily from India, but also from China and Africa. Again, the composition of the population changed.

A demographic boom in Martinique occurred between 1930 and 1965 as a declining death rate and an increasing birthrate combined to double the population of the island. By the mid-1960s, the steady out-migration of Martiniquais to the Metropole (continental France) had reduced the impact of these changes on population growth. Once the birthrate began to decline in the late 1960s, net population growth began to lose momentum; a decade later, by the end of the 1970s, the growth of the island's population had slowed drastically.

Out-migration to France from Martinique peaked in the early 1970s and has continued to decline since 1980 as job prospects in the Metropole have become increasingly bleak. In fact, from 1982 to 1990, more people immigrated to the island than emigrated from it; some were return migrants, others were Metropolitan French coming to Martinique to live.

According to the 1990 census, there are approximately 360,000 residents of Martinique, an increase of almost 31,000 (or 10 percent) since 1982. As in Latin America and the neighboring Caribbean islands, rural-to-urban migration continues in Martinique. Today, more than half of all island households are situated in the general urban area of the capital city, Fort-de-France.

Linguistic Affiliation. The official language is French, and most people take pride in their facility with the language. A French-based Creole, not intelligible to French speakers, is the historical mother tongue of Martiniquais, however. One is likely to hear more Creole than French in rural areas, at cockfights and storytelling events, and in informal and intimate settings of family and friends. In recent years, local linguists created a written French Creole grammar. Since then, a number of novelists and poets have published works in Creole.

History and Cultural Relations

Both the long-term continuity of a plantation economy and the Martiniquais assimilation to French culture have produced unique social as well as economic realities. Together, these forces of history forged new ideological and cultural foundations for a transplanted African people and generated a complicated sense of self-identity. Therefore, although the history of Martinique is the story of Caribbean colonization, of sugar plantations, and of slavery, it is also the story of how the French treated their Caribbean colonies: how they prized the riches they represented and how they assumed a proprietary interest in the people they claimed as their own.

The French colonization of the Caribbean began in the late sixteenth century as a way to break up Spanish dominance of the waterways from gold-rich Mexico to the Atlantic route home. The political strategy of Caribbean settlement took a decidedly economic turn in the early 1600s, however, when it became feasible to cultivate sugar on a large but labor-intensive scale. The need for laborers stimulated the Atlantic slave trade, which supplied African slaves to French, British, and Dutch Caribbean planters.

The other historic legacy that has shaped contemporary Martiniquais life was the assimilation-oriented nature of French colonization. Certainly, French colonists instituted a system of slavery no less brutal than other Europeans; unlike the British or Dutch, however, the French came to identify their own strength and international power with their colonies and the populations there.

In keeping with its colonial "mission," France declared Martinique, Guadeloupe, and the South American coastal area of French Guiana _départements outre-mers_ (overseas departments, DOMs) of France in 1946. This status guaranteed the population of the French Caribbean the same rights and privileges that the citizens of France enjoy. The new status granted DOM residents representation in both the French National Assembly and Senate and made the three départements eligible for the extensive social-security-system allocations.

The legacies of the French assimilation ethic are easily visible today in Martinique and Guadeloupe. Following departmentalization, schools, hospitals and clinics, libraries, social-service and welfare agencies, and government bureaus were built to make the French feel at home and to provide continuing evidence to the Martiniquais of the value of being French. A system of excellent roadways and an administrative infrastructure were designed to replicate Continental standards and are the envy of other Caribbean islanders.

Appearances suggest that the Martiniquais have indeed welcomed the assimilation to French life. They have incorporated the status markers of all things European: language, table manners, religion, fashion, cuisine, and education. Local advocates of independence from France have only gained credibility since about 1980, and they do not represent the prevailing view. Understandably, people of the French West Indies do not wish to be independent when their standard of living is kept artificially high through French subsidies and allocations.

Settlements

Because Martinique's three mountain ranges account for a considerable portion of the island's area, 90 percent of the population lives on one-quarter of the land. The island population is dispersed among thirty-four communes, most of which are coastal. The administrative capital is Fort-de-France.

Fort-de-France became the capital of Martinique when picturesque Saint Pierre was destroyed by the eruption of Montagne Pelée in 1902. Fort-de-France is situated at the edge of Caribbean waters and benefits from a calm, deepwater port that supports the island's import-driven economy. The urban center is comprised of several square kilometers of boutiques and offices, a large park, the cathedral, and government offices, banks, restaurants, and rented residences located on upper floors of the street-level storefronts.

Two classes of people were the first to populate the port town: the emerging group of *mulatre* merchants and a number of younger Békés whose families had invested their plantation fortunes in the import-export trade. By the 1950s, when agricultural workers began to stream into the city in search of wage labor, working-class neighborhoods sprouted up in the hills around the flat town center, eventually surrounding it on three sides. Today, the residents of Fort-de-France span all socioeconomic groups and ethnic identities.

The greater Fort-de-France area extends almost without interruption north to Schoelcher, a town of 20,000, and south to Lamentin, the industrial center of the island where 30,000 people live and where the international airport is located. Compared to the size and density of this urban sprawl, which continues to lead island growth, other settlements are quite small, most under 10,000 people.

The population residing in the lush, mountainous northern area is thinning, but the island's southern end, with its agricultural possibilities, fine beaches, and tourist economy, attracts an increasing number of residents.

Economy

In slightly less than thirty years following departmentalization of Martinique in 1946, the entire basis of the economy had shifted. Where once agriculture had dominated the lives of islanders, tertiary production, including services and commerce, had come to employ nearly 70 percent of the active population.

Since World War II, there have been no new sectors of productive growth to accommodate the increased population of workers resulting from the demographic boom. Instead, growth has been centered on the public sector: in 1954 it accounted for 2 percent of employment, by 1974, 18 percent, and by 1986, 32 percent. Still, increases in the number of jobs in government and commerce have only served to offset the fall in agricultural and craft-related production.

Since the early 1970s, unemployment in Martinique has hovered around 30 percent. There is a thriving underground economy, however, that is not accounted for in official statistics. In addition, French social-transfer payments have helped offset the economic hardships of irregular work or lack of work.

These transfer payments have meant that in spite of dramatic declines in self-sufficiency beginning in the 1950s, Martiniquais have enjoyed a constant rise in income, life expectancy, and overall living standards. For instance, whereas only half of all households had both water and electricity in the mid-1970s, by the early 1990s, 90 percent did. Most also have a refrigerator, a television, and a telephone, and more than half own a car. Between 1970 and 1985, the minimum wage guaranteed to full-time workers multiplied more than 7 times. As consumption has soared, dependency on credit purchases has also increased. Thus, economic dependency on France is deep and wide, and despite the fact that Martinique cannot sustain its own standard of living, Martiniquais live relatively affluent, consumer-oriented lives.

Kinship, Marriage, and Family

Kin Groups and Descent. On Martinique, the system of kinship is bilateral, and informal adoption of children by relatives or close friends is fairly common. The only social group with rigid rules of kinship, marriage, and social affiliation is the Béké population; however, many East Indians also prefer to marry endogamously.

Marriage. Traditionally, marriage was reserved for later in life, after the couple had successfully raised children, but today the situation is changing. The elite, for whom marriage prior to having children was the norm, have become the current model, leading a trend to marry early. In contrast to the commonly mixed marriages among other population segments in Martinique, Békés still carefully guard their aristocratic origins by continuing to practice endogamy. Their insistence on marrying only members of other Béké families has helped them maintain control of most arable land and economic power in Martinique.

Domestic Unit.   In Martinique, household units may involve one-, two-, or three-generation family members, with or without a conjugal couple at the center of the group. The membership of a household is variable according to the group's resources and needs at the time. Neither nuclear families nor extended-family arrangements are the norm, but these represent possible units among a range of other, equally suitable groupings. Approximately one in three households is "female-headed," a pattern occurring mostly among lower-income and younger people.

Socialization.   Martiniquais children are considered a cultural treasure and represent an important source of status for parents, irrespective of socioeconomic level. Thus, children are indulged, and even parents with the most meager resources find it important to dress their children in smart, modern clothes.

Fewer than 40 percent of the population over 15 years of age holds any kind of school degree. As jobs become even scarcer, however, there is an increasing recognition that education is the key to social mobility and professional success. Enrollment in the island's only university remains modest because only programs in law and economics are offered. Those wishing to study other subjects generally attend college in France.

Sociopolitical Organization

Social Organization.   The complex social structure of urban Martinique involves a combination of the following factors: income, occupation, education, skin color, language, family organization, and religion. Distinctions of social class are primarily a matter of one's income/ occupation and one's skin color. Refinements in the hierarchy are often determined by education, the success of one's children, the degree to which one can freely associate with lighter-skinned people, and the number of socially important parties one can host and attend.

Martiniquais informants describe the local color hierarchy in a precise system involving distinct linguistic terms, which identify a particular combination of skin color, cheekbone features, lip size, and hair consistency. In brief, the most common distinctions include the following: Mulatre, the offspring of a White and Black parent, generally with very light skin, smooth hair, and Caucasian facial features; Chabin/Chabine, the offspring of a mulatto and a Black parent, generally with light skin, broader features and light brown, kinky hair; Chappe cooli, pure East Indian parent and Black parent, generally with wavy hair, well-defined cheekbones, narrow nose, and small lips; Câpre/Câpresse, offspring of a Black parent and a mixed-race parent, such as Chappe cooli and Chabin, or Chabin and Brune, generally with kinkier hair and less well-defined cheekbones than the Chappe cooli; Brun/Brune, brown-skinned, of mixed-race parentage, generally with kinky hair and African facial features; Rouge/Marron, of Chabin ancestry and therefore with lighter skin but stronger African features; Noir/Negre, pure Black parentage with very dark skin, kinky hair, and broad, African facial features.

Some color terms are used for political reasons. "Noir" may be used as the term "Black" is used by English speak-

ers in the United States: for example, a Chabin man might refer to himself as "Noir." "Negre" is considered old-fashioned, and derivatives of it are used perjoratively in Creole, whereas "Metis," a deliberately nondescriptive term, is typically used by people who, for social or political reasons, prefer not to refer to their specific mix of parentage.

Skin color generally darkens as one follows the occupational ladder down to the least-skilled workers and the unemployed. Because of the early economic benefits accorded the mulatto offspring of unions between masters and slaves, the tradition of prestige associated with lighter-colored skin continues to exist today. Along with White Metropolitans from France, light-skinned blacks tend to dominate the professions and highest offices of government.

The small group of endogamous Békés, representing about 1 percent of the population, remains a dominant minority in terms of economic power and social status. In addition to their large-scale retail and import/export concerns, Béké families continue to hold the bulk of productive land and employ the vast majority of agricultural workers in production of bananas, rum, and tropical flowers.

Political Organization.   Political power in Martinique is in the hands of the Creole population, irrespective of the economic prominence of the Békés. Since the island's designation as a département outre-mers, its political pyramids have been effectively inverted so that the mixed-race, Creole majority of the population controls the local affairs of government and represents island interests in the French legislative bodies.

Conflict.   The price of full French citizenship and economic dependency is high and takes a psychological toll on the Martiniquais. Underneath the overlay of aspirations to be European lies a recognition of a Creole reality made of truths that are neither wholly French nor African. These truths live in the native tongue of French Creole, are told by the old group of _conteurs_ at traditional funeral rites, and are felt swelling up from a collective consciousness during the Chanté Noël songfest at Christmas.

This resilient Martiniquais culture offers the mixed-race majority both hope of self-understanding and despair of ever becoming completely French. The distinctly non-French or only French-in-part traditions and attitudes of the Martiniquais recall hostilities and struggles for dignity born in a time of slavery.

Religion and Expressive Culture

Religious Beliefs.   The vast majority of Martiniquais, both in Fort-de-France and throughout the island, consider themselves Catholic, although a rapidly declining proportion consider themselves "practicing" Catholics. Since the early 1970s, a small but increasing number of people have been shifting their religious affiliation to become Evangelists, Adventists, and Jehovah's Witnesses. In addition, there is a Muslim following among the minority population of Middle Easterners from Syria and Lebanon.

Martiniquais of all social classes also embrace many non-Christian beliefs, for example, in the power of sorcery. In contrast to sorcerers who are hired to inflict harm, shamans and folk healers generally are recruited to help people solve a variety of health and psychological problems.

Ceremonies. Catholic holy days are observed in Martinique, as are numerous locally distinct ritual events and traditional ceremonies including funeral rites, Chanté Noël at Christmas, and Mardi Gras.

Arts. Martiniquais society has a strong artistic tradition that has produced gifted, internationally recognized literary talents. Other creative and popular traditions include public storytelling, music and dance, costumes, and cuisine.

Medicine. Most urban dwellers prefer to treat serious illnesses and injuries at local clinics or hospitals, although herbal medicines and shaman healers are also recognized as effective sources of treatment for many health and personal problems.

Bibliography

Aldrich, Robert, and John Connell (1992). *France's Overseas Frontier: Départements et Territoires d'Outre-Mer.* Cambridge: Cambridge University Press.

Browne, Katherine E. (1993). *Factors Underlying Differential Participation in the Informal Economy.* Ann Arbor, Mich.: University Microfilms International.

Horowitz, Michael M. (1967). *Morne-Paysan: Peasant Village in Martinique.* New York: Holt, Rinehart & Winston.

Lirus, Julie (1979) *Identité antillaise.* Paris: Éditions Caribéennes.

Lowenthal, David (1972). *West Indian Societies.* London: Oxford University Press.

Massé, Raymond (1978). *Les adventistes du septième jour aux Antilles Françaises: Anthropologie d'une espérance miléneariste.* Ste. Marie, Martinique: Université de Montréal.

Mintz, Sidney, and Sally Price (1985). *Caribbean Contours.* Baltimore: Johns Hopkins University Press.

Slater, Miriam (1977) *The Caribbean Family: Legitimacy in Martinique.* New York: St. Martin's Press.

KATHERINE E. BROWNE

Mazahua

ETHNONYMS: Mazahuas

Orientation

Identification. There is no agreement about the origin of the name "Mazahua" ("deer people"). Some historians say that it derives from *mazatl*, the Aztec word for "deer," or from the name of the group's first leader, Mazatl Tecutli ("Lord Deer"). Others say it comes from Nahuatl. The term does not exist in the Mazahua language; but there is the designation "Teetho ñaatho jñaatho." "Teetho" means "real people," and "*ñaatho jñaatho*" means "those who speak the language."

Location. The Mazahua area is located to the north of the state of México. Its boundaries are with the municipality of Acambay to the north, the Valle de Bravo to the south, and the state of Michoacán to the west. It encompasses approximately eleven municipalities with an area of 3,723 square kilometers, equivalent to 17 percent of the total area of the state. Mazahua also live in some villages in the state of Michoacán, near Ciudad Hidalgo. In the Mazahua area there are also nonindigenous populations, and Otomí Indians live in some municipalities.

Owing to migration, it is now possible to find Mazahua living in the cities of other states, for example in Ciudad Juárez, Chihuahua, and Mexico City.

Demography. According to the 1990 census, there are 127,826 Mazahua speakers over the age of 5; 68,070 are women, and 59,756 are men. Of the total, 114,294 live in the state of México, 3,007 in Michoacán, 7,864 in the Federal District, and 444 in the state of Chihuahua; the rest are dispersed over the remaining areas of the country.

Linguistic Affiliation. The Mazahua language is classified within the Otomanguean Language Group and is most closely related to Otomí.

History and Cultural Relations

There are only scant historical references to the Mazahua, relating mainly to their subordinate relationships to other groups. In one hypothesis about their background, they are believed to have formed part of the five tribes that made up Chichimec migrations to the Valley of Mexico. It is thought that they, together with the Matlazincas and Tlahuicas, were the founders of the cities of Culhuacan, Otompan, and Tula. According to another version, the Mazahua were one of the Acolhua groups that arrived in the Valley of Mexico around the twelfth century, along with the Otomí, their linguistic relatives. The Mazahua were soon subjugated by the Tecpanecs; nonetheless, their numerical superiority increased. Once Aztec rule was consolidated, the Mazahua came under their control, and their villages marked the borders with Michoacán. Among the most important cities of the Mazahua province of Mazahuacán were Azcapotzalco, Tenayocan (Tenayuca), Temazcalcingo, Atlacomulco, Chiapan, Xiquipilco, Xocotitlán, Malacatepec, and Ixtlahuaca. During the colonial period, the Mazahua occupied more or less the same habitat, but their subjugation was even more onerous than before. The system of tribute and slavery continued: the *encomienda* and later the *repartimiento* provided the colonists access to forced indigenous labor. The concentration of land in haciendas, the development of mining, and the establishment of manufacturing workshops were colonial means of economic subjugation. After the independence of Mexico in 1810, the situation of the Mazahua did not improve because this was a period when large haciendas were consolidated, and many Indians worked on them as peons. During the later Juárez reforms, the remaining communal lands belonging to indigenous communities were expropriated. They passed from the communal property system, which had protected them since colonial times, into the hands of large estate owners. It was only after the Mexican Revolution of 1910 that land was returned to indigenous peoples, in the form of _ejidos._ The small amount of land apportioned to each Mazahua family during the agrarian reforms of the 1930s set the stage for a mixed economy in which they were simultaneously producers of basic subsistence foodstuffs, consumers of industrially produced products, and sources of low-paid seasonal labor in the cities and on farms and cattle ranches.

Economy

Subsistence and Commercial Activities. A large percentage of the Mazahua population performs agricultural labor, mainly planting maize, beans, and chilies. Because they inhabit an interethnic area with great economic diversity, they also work at other jobs, as wage earners. Work opportunities in the major Mazahua _municipios_ are in agriculture and cattle herding, or in factories and shops that produce clothing, chemicals, paper products, packaged foods, and electrical appliances. They also work at wood and lumber production and in gold and silver mines. Temporary migration is another work option. In the cities, Mazahua men are often employed in the construction industry, and women in domestic service.

Handicrafts. Handicrafts are yet another Mazahua activity, especially the production of woolen textiles, pottery, and basketry. In some areas, brooms and brushes are made from zacatón roots (_Muhlenbergia macroura_).

Commerce. Zacatón-root products, as well as handicrafts in general, are intended mainly for the market. Many Mazahua products are marketed by intermediaries; generally nonindigenous, these middlemen make most of the profit. In view of this situation, the Mazahua have looked for other options: one alternative is to organize cooperatives, among which women's cooperatives are the most prominent. Some Mazahua choose to become traders themselves, first trading local handicrafts and later industrially produced products, which Mazahua families transport throughout Mexico. They learn trading skills from the nonindigenous peoples for whom they work as helpers. Among the inhabitants of the municipality of Temascalcingo, this is an increasingly important option. Many of the Mazahua who trade on the northern and southeastern frontiers of Mexico come from that area.

Division of Labor. Every member of a Mazahua family works. Besides caring for their children, women tend to their homes and collaborate with their husbands on some agricultural tasks—harvesting, for example. In the production of pottery, women paint or adorn the pots; men prepare the clay, take charge of the ovens, and oversee the firing. Children help the parent of the same sex. In the fabrication of textiles, women tend the sheep, card the wool, and weave; men perform other related tasks.

All members of a family participate when it is involved in trading. In the cities, Mazahua saleswomen ply the streets in traditional costumes, offering their handicrafts. Others, accompanied by their children, sell sweets and chewing gum on street corners. Men dress less distinctively; they sell auto parts, ceramics, and domestic utensils (china, pots and pans, plastic utensils, etc.) from ambulatory stalls or sell fruit or ice-cream sticks from small carts.

Land Tenure. Land tenure among the Mazahua is mainly through an ejido. The amount of land available for each family varies: it may be less than one hectare or more than six hectares. It is usually unirrigated land, dependent on seasonal rainfall. Ejidos consist of land divided into plots and lands for common use. Mazahua families cultivate their crops on the plots; the common lands are used for grazing, gathering wood, collecting medicinal and edible plants, and, sometimes, exploiting the timber.

Kinship

Kin Groups and Descent. Mazahua group association is by place of birth, community membership, and right to land. Descent is through the paternal line, although kinship is recognized bilaterally to the third degree. Another form of social relationship not necessarily based on consanguinity is _compadrazgo_ (ritual coparenthood).

Kinship Terminology. Native kinship terms have not been retained; Spanish terms for father, mother, son and daughter, sibling, grandparent, cousin, and aunt and uncle are used. Incest prohibitions proscribe marriage with anyone sharing common descent—Mazhua cannot marry either parallel or matrilateral cross cousins, or the children of the father's _compadres_, who are considered to be in the same category as Ego's grandparents or father's siblings.

Marriage and Family

Marriage. Marriage is monogamous, preferentially endogamous by ethnic group, and preferentially exogamous by locality. Owing to migration, however, marriage with nonindigenous partners is increasingly frequent, especially among women. Elopement and later reconciliation between families is the preferred form of marriage; nevertheless, negotiated marriages have not been abandoned, and they more frequently lead to proper church weddings.

Domestic Unit. Among the Mazahua, there are both nuclear and extended families because, during the first four or five years of marriage, a young couple lives with the groom's parents. Family units are also the basis of economic organization, whether productive or nonproductive. Kin networks are a support system facilitating migration.

Inheritance. Property passes from father to son because a woman becomes part of her husband's family. Agrarian laws legalize this procedure where land is concerned, despite the increasing struggle of some indigenous women for recognition of their right to own land.

Socialization. Socialization begins in childhood with constant participation in daily tasks within the household and with early participation in religious rituals that involve social obligations. Primary-school education, which is bilingual in some places, is a formal means of socialization.

Sociopolitical Organization

Social Organization.   Cooperation within extended families, cooperation within the household, compadrazgo, mutual help, and community service create a sense of belonging that unites the community and gives people a sense of obligation to it.

Political Organization.   The Mazahua do not have their own native system of government, so each village falls under a municipal administration. Each village has its delegate or subdelegate, who is named by the municipal president. Where there are both an indigenous and a nonindigenous population, presidential appointments fall to the latter. In some places there are also a *tata-bisca* and a *tata-pale*, survivals of a native council of elders.

A strong religious organization may provide a village with a respected authority not recognized officially by the municipal government. Villages with ejido lands have an ejido commission with a president, secretaries, a treasurer, and an oversight council. Some Mazahua belong to a political party and/or a peasant organization involving production, marketing, or credit. The Mazahua Supreme Council is an ethnic organization, but, initially sponsored by the federal government, it is not particularly representative of Mazahua concerns.

Social Control.   Municipal and ejido authorities are officially responsible for problem solving. There are, however, mechanisms of coercion and sanction for correcting those who do not act according to tradition or who do not fulfill community obligations. For example, those who have emigrated and changed their religion can not be buried in the same graveyard as their ancestors.

Conflict.   The most frequent conflicts are over the control of local government (municipio delegates and ejido posts), and, in some cases, they are of an interethnic nature (between indigenous and nonindigenous members). At certain times, there may be conflicts between sympathizers of rival political parties or craft organizations. With changes occurring in the religious affiliation of some Mazahua, religious conflicts have also become noticeable.

Religion and Expressive Culture

Religious Beliefs.   Folk Catholicism predominates, and, in some places, religious and political organization are parts of a single system. *Juntas*, assemblies led by influential men in the community, assemble people with political and religious *cargos* and are responsible for new appointments in both the civil and religious branches of the organization.

There are three locations for religious expression: the village church, *oratorios*, and domestic altars. Each corresponds to a level of social organization: the village, the extended family and its allied members through compadrazgo, and the domestic family. A system of religious cargos (*fiscales, mayordomos, topiles,* prayer makers, sacristans, and "companions") favors community integration through family ties and compadrazgo, which unite the constituents of *mayordomías*. Compadrazgo is established between parents and godparents at the time of baptism, confirmation, first communion, and marriage. Compadrazgo also results from seeking godparental sponsors for a funeral, a girl's fifteenth birthday, a Bible, a priest's new habit, a house, an oratorio, or clothing for a religious image. Lay compadrazgo results from secular ritual events related to primary- or secondary-school graduation and the sponsorship of football and basketball teams. Religious fiestas are accompanied by prayers, music, floral arrangements, and dances and, in general, are complemented with a feast.

Ceremonies.   Each village/town holds its main fiesta on the day of its patron saint; there are also two sanctuaries, shared by the Mazahua and the Otomí, to which pilgrimages are made. The shrine of the Holy Cross of Tepexpan celebrates the day of the Holy Cross in May and the day of Saint Theresa in October. The other sanctuary is Chalma, a famous mountain shrine to the southwest of Mexico City, on the edge of the Mazahua area. During rituals in which a community participates in the religious fiestas of a nearby pueblo, the patron saints "visit" one another. Among the most important ritual dances are the "Moors and Christians," the "Arrow Shooters" ("Huehueches"), and the "Shepherdesses." There are also dialogues (stagings) called "Charles the Great" and "The Shepherds."

Medicine.   There are several traditional specialists, among them midwives, curers, bonesetters, and sorcerers. On different levels, they are knowledgeable about medicinal plants, the human body, the world in general, and the supernatural world. Illness may be caused by sorcery. As is the case with the majority of indigenous peoples of the area, the Mazahua have recourse to three types of medicine in case of illness: biomedical, traditional, and domestic. The last involves folk and herbal remedies and is mainly the domain of women and elders in treating their families. Migrants have recourse to health centers in the cities where they live, that is to say, when it is not a matter of culturally defined illness, in which case they return to their place of origin to be cured.

Death and Afterlife.   Death, like birth, is an important ritual moment in which ties of compadrazgo and group solidarity are reaffirmed. For the Mazahua, the supernatural world is the origin of many illnesses and of death. When someone becomes ill, a curer must be consulted for a "cleansing" and to determine the origin of the illness. The illness may be caused by the "masters of the earth," some deceased person, the *animas solas* (lonely souls), the envy of a still-living person, or the failure to comply with some social or ritual norm. The dead can cause illness when their relatives forget them or when they enjoy the benefits of an inheritance that was not rightfully theirs. In order for the dead to rest, they must receive prayers, and a mass and offering must be given them. The dead must be remembered on the Day of the Dead (Todos Santos); offerings of flowers, fruit, drink, and breads are placed on domestic altars.

Bibliography

Arizpe, Lourdes (1985). *Campesinado y migración.* Mexico City: Secretaría de Educación.

Cortés Ruíz, Efraín (1972). *San Simón de la Laguna.* Mexico City: Instituto Nacional Indigenista.

García Collino, Ana (1986). "Los mazahuas: Trabajo migratorio y cambio lingüístico." Licenciatura thesis in linguistics, Escuela Nacional de Antropología, Mexico City.

Nolasco, Margarita (1963). *Los mazahuas del estado de México*. Mexico City: Instituto Nacional de Antropología e Historia.

Pérez Ruíz, Maya Lorena (1993). "La identidad entre fronteras: Los mazahuas en Ciudad Juárez." In *Nuevas identidades culturales en México*, edited by Guillermo Bonfil Batalla. Mexico City: Consejo Nacional para la Cultura y las Artes.

Ruíz Chavez, Glafira (1981). *Acerca de los mazahuas del estado de México*. Toluca: Gobierno de Estado de México.

Segundo Romero, Bartolomé, and Alfonso Gutiérrez García (1988). "Los discursos orales de identidad teetho ñaatho jñaatho en Potla, Temascalcingo." Licenciatura thesis in social anthropology, Universidad Autónoma del Estado de México.

MAYA LORENA PÉREZ RUÍZ

(Translated by Ruth Gubler)

Mazatec

ETHNONYM: Shuta enima ("those who work in the forest")

Orientation

Identification. The Mazatec, together with other ethnic groups, inhabit the Sierra Madre Occidental in central Mexico. They took their name from their ancient capital, called Maza-apatl or Mazatlan, founded around A.D. 890.

Location. Until around the 1950s, the Mazatec were concentrated in the northern part of the state of Oaxaca. In 1954 the construction of a system of dams over the effluents of the Río Papaloapan (Río de las Mariposas) had a serious effect on some of the Mazatec and Chinantec communities. Consequently, they were relocated elsewhere in Oaxaca and in the southern part of the state of Veracruz.

Mazatec territory consists of two areas that have distinct environments and cultures. In the highlands, or the sierra, elevations vary from 1,800 to 3,200 meters, and the climate ranges from temperate to cold. It is humid, and there is cloud cover almost year-round. There is abundant rainfall in summer. The natural vegetation consists of forests of pine, oak, and *madroño* (*Arbustus*).

The lowlands lie in both tropical and temperate zones, at elevations from sea level to 1,800 meters. Irrigated by the four effluents of the Río Papaloapan—the Santo Domingo, the Río Tonto, the Qiuotepec, and the Usila—the lowland area has a great variety of ecosystems within

humid mountain-tropical forests at 400 to 1,700 meters above sea level, which contain woods like balsam (*Myroxylon*), *primavera* (*Tabebuia*), and *guanacaste* (*Enterolobium*).

Demography. The 1990 general census reported a population of 168,374 Mazatec, most of them in an area of approximately 2,400 square kilometers, within the states of Oaxaca, which has the largest population (146,928), and Veracruz. The remainder are distributed principally in the state of Puebla and in Mexico City. Population density in some zones approaches 60 inhabitants per square kilometer. Approximately 70 percent of the Mazatec live in the highlands, 30 percent in the lowlands. The *municipios* with the largest indigenous populations are Huautla de Jiménez, San José Tenango, and San Cristóbal Mazatlán (in the highlands) and Santa María Chilchotla, San Miguel Soyaltepec, and San Lucas Ojitlan (in the lowlands).

Linguistic Affiliation. Morris Swadesh (1960) classified Mazatec as belonging to the Popoloca-Zapoteca Language Group, a subgroup of the Macro-Mixtecan Family. Other linguists place it within the Mazatec-Popoluca Family, of the Savizaa Trunk of the Otomanguean Group. Mazatec is a tonal language: the meaning of a word depends on the tone in which it is pronounced. There are at least four different dialects that are mutually intelligible.

History and Cultural Relations

The origins and history of the Mazatec are little known. They are possibly descendants of the Nonoalca-Chichimeca who emigrated from Tula at the beginning of the twelfth century, settling in the highlands in the villages of Teotitlán, Eloxochitlán, Mazatlán, and Chinchotla. According to other scholars, the Mazatec already inhabited the area before the arrival of the Nonoalca-Chichimeca, who subdued them around the year 1170. In 1300 the Mazatec freed themselves, founding two kingdoms: one in the highlands, or the East, and another in the lowlands, or West.

Before the arrival of the Spaniards, these kingdoms were invaded and subordinate by the Mexica (Aztec) Empire between 1455 and 1456, during the reign of Montezuma Ilhuicamina. Military posts were established in Teotitlán and Tuxtepec, and there tribute was collected. The first Spanish conquerors arrived in Mazatec territory in 1520, at which time the process of evangelization was begun by the Franciscans, who founded the first church in Teotitlán in 1542.

The Mazatec have participated actively in two major social movements in Mexico during the last two centuries, the War of Independence and the Revolution of 1910.

In 1954 a gigantic development project was begun in the area, of which the Papaloapan Commission (dependent on the federal government) was in charge. This brought about momentous changes for the Mazatec. Hydroelectric dams were built, which, besides helping to control the great cyclical floods of the Río Papaloapan, provided the basic infrastructure for the area's economic development. This scheme focused on the lowlands and favored the development of cattle raising and commercial agriculture for export. Large tracts of the jungle were cut down, the monoculture of sugarcane was promoted, and private banks supported the development of pasture for cattle. In the process, the territorial and cultural unity of the Mazatec was severed: approximately 22,000 villagers who inhabited the basin of the Miguel Aleman dam were moved and relocated to five areas in the states of Oaxaca and Veracruz, some 250 kilometers away from their traditional habitat. With the construction of the dam, the lowland Mazatec lost 500 square kilometers, equivalent to 50 percent of their cultivable land.

In the highlands, on the other hand, where the emphasis was on coffee production, the infrastructure and services were left relatively undeveloped.

Settlements

The Mazatec population is distributed over twenty-three municipios. Small towns and hamlets of less than 500 inhabitants that are dispersed within the territory are subordinate to the capitals of the municipios. The houses in the towns are built from a variety of materials, depending on the area and the natural resources at hand. In the tropical climate of the lowlands, cane and wood are used for the walls, and roofs are constructed of palm and banana leaves. In the highlands, the most frequently used materials are adobe, plaited cane and mud, and wood; roofs are of hay and batten. As roads increasingly penetrate the area, however, other types of construction material have become available: roofs made of asphalt-impregnated cardboard sheets and, in some cases, houses made of brick and mortar.

The houses are usually quadrangular, built on a floor of packed-down earth; they have a single large room, with a wood-burning hearth for cooking. This multifunctional room serves as a kitchen, a place to eat, a setting where family members get together, and, at night, as a family room in which hammocks are hung or cots are set up.

Houses are surrounded by a patio or plot of land on which some domestic animals (e.g., chickens, pigs) are generally kept for household consumption. Frequently, there is a steam bath of pre-Hispanic origin, called a temascal, with walls made of mud and a straw roof. In many communities houses are still built collectively through tequio, a type of exchange of work and mutual help in which an individual who wants to build a house gathers the necessary materials and invites his friends and relatives to help him, offering them abundant food and drink. Whoever receives such help is socially obliged to repay in like manner all those who participated in the construction of the house.

Economy

Subsistence and Commercial Activities. Mazatec life revolves around the production of maize, beans, chilies, and squashes. Any surplus of these staple foods is sold in local markets. Various noncultivated foods are also gathered to complement the diet. Mamey (Calocarpum sapota, a member of the Zapote family), sapodilla, mango, banana, papaya, tamarind, citrus, and avocado trees are planted for their fruits.

The cultivation of maize is not only an economic activity, but is the foundation of the group's social organization and symbolic interaction. Generally, in the cultivation of maize and that of the group's other subsistence culti-

gens, cooperative forms of food production are the rule. Two maize crops are grown annually: that of the tonamil (the dry season, extending from November to May) and that of the rainy season, harvested in October.

Besides providing subsistence, there is also an important commercial aspect to Mazatec agriculture. In the highlands of the sierra, coffee is cultivated extensively, but because of the infrequent use of fertilizers, productivity per hectare is far below the national average. Sesame is grown in the lowlands, as is sugarcane (which is sold directly to the area's sugar mills), and large tracts of land are set apart for pasture for cattle. On a lesser scale, tobacco, cacao, and achiote (which is used as a spice) are harvested and sold in the local market. In the area of Ayautla and Jalapa de Díaz, great mullein, a tuber from which certain hormones are obtained, is collected and sold to both national and international pharmaceutical companies.

The Mazatec have organized their commerce along two levels: national and international commerce for commercial products and, parallel to that, local commerce, wherein people of the sierra deal with people from the lowlands, exchanging products of regional specialization like clay pots, chairs, clay griddles, paper made from the bark of amate trees, leather sandals, bread, salt, fruit, eggs, candles, chilies, and so forth. This local commercial network is very important because it is a mechanism for integrating the more isolated producers. Exchange is by cash or barter. Handicrafts include the embroidering of textiles for the manufacture of huipiles. These traditional Mazatec women's garments are shifts with round necks and short sleeves; they are richly embroidered with floral or faunal motifs, depending on the village. Some artisans create ceramic objects or weave basketry from cane or palm leaves.

Land Tenure.   Land is held communally, privately, and by ejidos. Until shortly before the Papaloapan Commission development project, private landownership was rare. Since then, as a result of the influx of capital and the movement and relocation of large contingents of the population, the dispossession of land has been facilitated, especially in the lowlands, and land has been redistributed into private hands. As of 1992, with the modification of Article 27 of the Mexican constitution, the judicial status of the ejido system was altered, and, as a result, problems regarding landownership are becoming more acute in the area.

Kinship

Kin Groups and Descent.   The kinship system is based on nuclear and extended patrilineal and patrilocal families. Within this system, relationships of reciprocity and family alliances are sustained by the Council of Elders, the traditional Mazatec form of government.

Marriage and Family

Marriage.   Marriage is generally monogamous, although polygamy and concubinage are tolerated. There are communities in which approximately 20 percent of families are polygamous.

Marriage is normally between young people of the same village and the same neighborhood. Villages are subdivided into districts, on the basis of which marriage is regulated. This is arranged by the parents and is a time for establishing alliances between extended families. Marriage prohibitions extend to second cousins of both sides, although the father's side is emphasized.

Domestic Unit. The basic domestic unit is the nuclear family integrated within an extended family, entailing reciprocal obligations for collective labor and other forms of social solidarity.

Inheritance. Because the Mazatec have a patrilineal society, it is generally the older son who inherits his father's land and other property, although sometimes land is divided among the children, causing increasing fragmentation of property and lessening the opportunity for productive gain.

Socialization. Mazatec children are taught the tenets of their indigenous worldview as they are cared for by the women in the household. Their symbolic world is organized on the basis of the Mazatec language. When they enter school, however, they are inculcated with the basic strategies for getting along in the mestizo world that surrounds them, usually by a bilingual teacher.

Sociopolitical Organization

Social Organization. The profound inequalities relating to landownership and the resources to make land productive, as well as differentiated access to services, characterize the Mazatec as a highly stratified ethnic group. This stratification is especially marked in the lowlands. Large and medium-sized landholders (with more than 100 hectares under cultivation) and wholesale merchants, called _shuta nya_ (_principales_), are linked to the regional and national middle class and have large amounts of money. It is generally the members of this group who hold the government posts in town and borough councils and the more important religious _cargos_. The _shuta yuna_ ("those who own something") include small businessmen and smallholders who grow commercial products on 3 to 5 hectares of land. The _shuta shun'da_ (poor people) own no land and are hired as day workers on coffee and sugar plantations. They generally live as "settlers" in the communities, that is, on land that has been lent or given them by the community.

Political Organization. The largest political organizational unit is the municipio, which is generally in the hands of mestizos or, in some cases, wealthy Indians. There is no government that could be called typically indigenous, but the most honest and capable elders meet around the town hall; they have served their communities in public or religious posts, and it is they who constitute the Council of Elders, or Chotj Chinka. This council, together with the president of the municipio, can designate the alcaldes and other members of the town hall. Elders on the council are generally men who head patrilocal extended families. Only rarely does one find two elders who are members of the same family on the Council of Elders. Any problem that affects the community or the municipio must be dealt with by the council.

Social Control. The norms established by religion in the form of myths and ritual practices are important forms of social control. It is through them that a great portion of daily life is ruled.

Conflict. The main conflicts in the area are over the demarcation of boundaries of the community's landed property. The chief authority with the power to resolve such conflicts is the Council of Elders.

Religion and Cultural Expression

Religious Beliefs. The predominant religion is Catholicism, although pre-Hispanic concepts of understanding and ordering life persist—for example, the cult of the spirits, the veneration of mountains, and the sacred relationship with nature. Sorcerers, witches, and shamans, together with prayer makers and singers, are present in the most important moments in the life of an individual or of the community.

Religious Practices. _Mayordomos_ are in charge of the entire process of arranging religious festivals to honor the patron saint of each community. Besides the patronal festivities, Holy Week, the Day of the Dead, Palm Sunday, and New Year are observed.

Medicine. Medicinal practice is linked to the pre-Hispanic concepts of the body, life, death, health, and sickness. The shaman is an intermediary between the deities and humans. The most common illnesses are _mal aire_ (evil wind), _mal de ojo_ (evil eye), _susto_ (sudden fright), and soul loss. There is also a belief—present in all Mesoamerican belief systems—in _tonales_ (animal protectors) and _nahuales_ (the evil tonales of sorcerers, into which they have the power to change). Knowledge of herbal medicine is widely held. The most frequently used therapeutic methods are the extraction of objects through suction, _limpias_ (cleansing) with bird's eggs, exorcisms, and divination with maize kernels.

Bibliography

Barabas, Alicia (1973). _Hydraulic Development and Ethnocide: The Mazatec and Chinantec People of Oaxaca, Mexico_. Copenhagen: International Work Group for Indigenous Affairs.

Boege, Eckart (1988). _Los mazatecos ante la nación: Contradicciones de la identidad étnica en el México actual_. Mexico City: Siglo XXI Editores.

Estrada, Álvaro (1977). _Vida de María Sabina, la sabia de los honglos_. Mexico City: Siglo XXI Editores.

MacMahon, David (1973). _Antropología de una presa: Los mazatecos y el proyecto del Papaloapan_. Mexico City: Instituto Nacional de Antropología e Historia; Secretaría de Educación Pública.

Nieburg, Frederico (1984). _Identidad y conflicto en la sierra mazateca: El caso de Consejo de Ancianos de San José Tenango_. Mexico City: Instituto Nacional de Antropología e Historia; Secretaría de Educación Pública.

Portal Ariosa, María Ana (1986). _Cuentos y mitos en una zona mazateca_. Mexico City: Instituto Nacional de Antropología e Historia; Secretaría de Educación Pública.

Swadesh, Morris (1960). "The Oto-Manguean Hypothesis and Macro-Mixtecan." *International Journal of American Linguistics* 26:79-111.

Vázquez Mendoza, Heriberto (1881). *Los mazatecos.* Mexico City: Instituto Nacional Indigenista.

Villa Rojas, Alfonso (1955). "Los mazatecos y el problema indígena de la Cuenca de Papalopan." In *Memorias del Instituto Nacional Indigenista.* Mexico City: Instituto Nacional Indigenista.

Wasson, R. Gordon et al., comps. (1974). *María Sabina and Her Mazatec Mushroom Velada.* Ethno-Mycological Studies, no. 3. New York: Harcourt Brace Jovanovich.

Weitlaner, Roberto J., and Walter A. Hoppe (1969). "The Mazatec." In *The Handbook of Middle American Indians,* edited by Robert Wauchope. Vol. 7, *Ethnology, Part One,* edited by Evon Z. Vogt. Austin: University of Texas Press.

MARIA ANA PORTAL ARIOSA

(Translated by Ruth Gubler)

Miskito

ETHNONYMS: Miskitu, Moskito, Mosqueto, Mosquito, Moustique

Orientation

Identification. The name "Miskito" is of foreign origin. It may be derived from various European spellings for "musket," because the population in question was originally distinguished from its neighbors as a literally musket-bearing group. "Miskitu" emerged as an ethnonym for the ethnic identity of the Miskito people following the Sandinista Revolution. The other terms are no longer commonly used but are found in historical literature by English, North American, and Spanish writers of the eighteenth and nineteenth centuries.

Location. The Miskito inhabit the eastern regions of the Central American republics of Nicaragua and Honduras, a territory bordering the Caribbean coast and known historically as the Miskito (or Mosquito) Coast, La Mosquitia, or La Costa Atlántica. Much of this region is hot, low-lying savanna, crossed by numerous rivers and lined with gallery forests that extend from the interior mountains to the Caribbean. The heartland of the Miskito territory is the Río Coco or Wangks River, which today delineates the border between Nicaragua and Honduras.

Demography. The population has expanded more or less constantly over the last 300 years and numbered at least 75,000 as of 1985.

Linguistic Affiliation. The Miskito language is related to the Macro-Chibchan Language Family of northern South America. As a result of over three hundred years of continued European contact, many foreign words have been added, and significant grammatical changes have occurred. Historically, three major linguistic divisions have been recognized, all mutually intelligible but differing somewhat in vocabulary and pronunciation; one is characteristic of the Miskito living along the coast of eastern Nicaragua, another of the Miskito living along the Río Coco, the third of the Miskito of eastern Honduras.

History and Cultural Relations

Prior to European contact, this territory was populated by numerous native tribes, each resident along one of the many rivers. Although Spain colonized western Nicaragua and Honduras during the sixteenth century, the eastern regions were not contacted until approximately 1700. At this time the population of the Miskito Coast began its long affiliation with English-speaking peoples, first buccaneers and later traders and settlers. In the late seventeenth century a small Indian population near the mouth of the Río Coco obtained guns and ammunition and other trade goods. This population also began to accept Black slaves fleeing from various Caribbean and Central American locales, who quickly intermixed with the local Indian population. This mixed native-Black society became the Miskito people—that is, the Miskito did not exist in pre-Columbian times but developed as a result of European-African–Native American contact and admixture.

This native–Black Miskito society had access to European guns and thereby expanded their territory at the expense of other Indian groups. Some of these Indian groups were assimilated into the Miskito, who expanded from the mouth of the Río Coco north along the coast of eastern Honduras, south along the coast of eastern Nicaragua, and upriver along the banks of the Río Coco. Those indigenous natives who were not assimilated were pushed farther into the interior. Today, their survivors are known collectively as "Sumu." Their population has declined steadily, whereas that of the Miskito, who are frequently identified as "Zambos," meaning a mixed Indian-Black population, increased, making them the dominant coastal group. Miskito success derived from their peaceful relations with the small groups of English-speaking traders and settlers who came to the coast and from their role as middlemen between English traders and Sumu. The Miskito also developed a strong hatred for the Spanish-speaking peoples of western Nicaragua and Honduras. These attitudes persist to this day.

After Nicaragua and Honduras became independent republics, the dominant anglophone foreign influence on the Miskito Coast was the United States. By the late nineteenth century, various U.S. business concerns found the area attractive, including those interested in banana production. Banana-plantation managers imported dark-skinned, English-speaking laborers from the West Indies. Descendants of this new West Indian population, called "Creoles," became identified as the dominant "Black" population of the coast; they lived predominantly in the port towns that developed in the early twentieth century. The

Miskito, who spoke a distinctive non-European language and lived in rural villages, now became known as "Indians," although they continued to intermarry with many types of foreigners. After centuries of de facto isolation from western, Hispanic Nicaragua, Miskito life has been strongly affected by the Sandinista Revolution, which began in 1979 and which will almost certainly draw the Miskito Coast closer to the Hispanic cultural pattern and national political organization of the Republic of Nicaragua. The description of Miskito culture that follows refers to conditions prior to the Revolution.

Settlements

Prior to European contact, the indigenous native tribes lived in small camps along the riverbanks. After contact, some Miskito settled in small coastal villages close to lagoons in which fish were abundant and in the vicinity of English trading posts located near the river mouths. The Río Coco Miskito, however, established interior villages along the banks of the river below the rapids that impeded travel toward the interior. After the mid-nineteenth century, Moravian mission stations replaced trading posts as foci for Miskito village development. The Moravian missionaries encouraged strong community organization, and mission church activities provided a new focal point for Miskito community identity and cooperation. Miskito villages have varied in size from a few houses to 600 or more persons. Villages are kept cleared of grass; homes are built on pilings. They may be constructed of split bamboo or of sawed lumber; roofs are either thatched or of corrugated metal. There may be a separate kitchen. Houses were traditionally large, thatched, open lean-tos but now are partitioned into several interior rooms and a porch and contain doors and windows.

Economy

Subsistence and Commercial Activities. The indigenous tribes combined cultivation of manioc and other root crops, plantains, and maize with hunting and fishing. Pigs, cattle, horses, chickens, and various agricultural foods, especially rice, beans, and bananas, were introduced after European contact. The Miskito also worked for Europeans for barter or wages. The coastal economy in general has been characterized by boom-and-bust cycles; foreign entrepreneurs have periodically invested in rubber, timber, gold, or bananas. When foreign companies were hiring, the Miskito sought labor opportunities; when depressions struck, the Miskito relied on their continuing subsistence agriculture and fishing for support.

Industrial Arts. Aboriginal pottery is no longer produced, but many other traditional household utensils and furniture are still woven of strips of tree fibers or carved of wood. Traditional dugout canoes are still made, as is bark cloth, formerly used for clothing but now used as bed covering. European-style clothing has been worn since contact.

Trade. During the eighteenth and nineteenth centuries, the Miskito flourished as middlemen between interior Sumu and English traders. The Miskito also became feared slave raiders throughout much of eastern and interior Central America during the period when Indian slaves were bought by English plantation owners in Jamaica. The Miskito have always eagerly participated in trade with Europeans, exchanging coastal raw materials for manufactured goods. They have readily adopted English styles of clothing, home furnishings, foods, tools, and weapons.

Division of Labor. Miskito women have always tended agricultural plots, though men clear plots and help with planting and harvesting seed crops (rice, beans). Men have traditionally fished and hunted and taken jobs with Europeans. Within the family, women and men share childrearing responsibilites, although most of the day-to-day domestic work falls to women. When men are away performing wage-labor, perhaps for several months, women ably conduct all necessary household, agricultural, and fishing activities.

Land Tenure. The Miskito have never had a concept of landownership, but they do recognize family use of agricultural plots. During the latter half of the twentieth century, the intrusion from the west of Hispanic frontier farmers has begun to threaten the availability of land to Miskito in some areas. Miskito claims to territory as an essential future resource have become a critical issue in relations between the Miskito and the Nicaraguan government.

Kinship

Kin Groups and Descent. Nothing is known about the composition of precontact indigenous kin groups. There is no evidence of descent groups or lineages. Three types of kin groups are recognized today: the _taya_, the _kiamp_, and the nuclear family. The taya is a loose kindred including all living persons considered to be Ego's relatives, regardless of where they live. Descendants of Ego's great-grandparents of both mother's and father's families are included. The kiamp includes only part of the taya—all living descendants of a pair identified by the surname of the male. Ego is a member of his father's kiamp. Neither taya nor kiamp serves any corporate function, but both afford oases of hospitality for traveling Miskito. The nuclear family or the household is the usual cooperative domestic group.

Kinship Terminology. Kin terms have undergone changes following contact. The modern kinship system is characterized by Hawaiian cousin terms with bifurcate-collateral terms in the parental generation. Before the twentieth century, cross and parallel cousins were distinguished. Generational depth has declined on both sides of the family.

Marriage and Family

Marriage. Couples traditionally were monogamous, but polygyny was allowed. Marriage residence was ideally matrilocal, although population growth and increased village size has encouraged village endogamy in the twentieth century. Matrilocal residence was favored because of the frequent and lengthy absences of men seeking wage labor. Matrilocal residence also encouraged solidarity among core groups of related women, which are important socialization agents. A couple will postpone church marriage until they are sure the marriage is stable. Formal divorce is absent; a couple simply separates.

Domestic Unit. The domestic unit is generally the nuclear family. One or several related nuclear families with additional single relatives may compose a household.

Inheritance. Traditionally, all property was either destroyed upon the death of the owner or buried with him or her. Today, property is inherited by the surviving spouse or by children of the union, but lack of firm guidelines leads to much conflict.

Socialization. The core group of matrilocally resident or village-endogamous related women (mother, sisters, daughters) is the most important socialization unit. These conservative women, who do not mingle with foreigners, continue to inculcate children with traditional Miskito customs and language. Children are raised permissively and are strongly individualistic (especially the boys) yet cooperative village members.

Sociopolitical Organization

Social Organization. Miskito society has always been egalitarian, with status based on age, parenthood, and kinship categories.

Political Organization. Each Miskito village is politically autonomous, although linked by relatively weak ties to the Nicaraguan state by a village headman. Regulations of the Moravian church (or other mission churches)—effected by church elders, pastors, and lay pastors—direct village life to some extent. During the colonial era the Miskito were said to compose a "kingdom" with a "king." There is little solid evidence for such a kingdom, and the Miskito kings recognized by the English had limited power within Miskito society. The traditional political format emphasized regional strongmen involved in external affairs but held in check locally by community elders.

Social Control. Communities control individuals informally through gossip but tolerate a high degree of forceful expression of personality, especially in men. Women's behavior is more closely monitored.

Conflict. Intervillage feuds and mistrust are common, as are personal quarrels within a village. The Sandinista Revolution involved the entire Miskito region in large-scale military action, leading to severe population dislocation, the destruction of villages, and refugee conditions for many. In colonial times the Miskito were widely feared by all neighboring groups as ferocious slave raiders. Today, many have fought against the Sandinista intrusions.

Religion and Expressive Culture

Religious Beliefs. Little is known of traditional religion beyond beliefs in various harmful spirits and in spirits inhabiting natural phenomena. The Miskito readily adopted Christianity; the Moravian church is by far the dominant mission group. The Catholic church and several fundamentalist Protestant churches also proselytize. Belief in dreams, in strange and inexplicable omens and occurrences, and in the power of the moon persists. Specific native deities are unknown, but an impersonal "Father" spirit may have been recognized. Evil spirits were more important. The Christian trinity is now accepted, although belief in evil spirits, frequently associated with the Christian Satan, continues.

Religious Practitioners. Native shamans acted as curers, diviners, and exorcisers. During the twentieth century, village lay pastors and fully ordained native pastors have worked with foreign missionaries.

Ceremonies. Prior to Christianization the Miskito conducted group ceremonies, particularly funeral rites, characterized by dancing and extensive drinking of locally made intoxicants. They now celebrate the Christian ceremonies of the mission churches.

Arts. Traditional Miskito songs are popular, and simple round dances may be performed on holidays. Theatricals concerning a legendary Miskito "king," now an important ethnic symbol, are performed in some communities. Decorative arts are not developed, although wooden masks were traditionally carved for funeral ceremonies.

Medicine. Traditional herbal cures are combined with Western medical care. Illness was traditionally thought to be caused by evil spirits, and remnants of that belief persist, but God's will and the weather are more commonly blamed today.

Death and Afterlife. Death can be foretold by dreams or other types of omens. Traditional funeral rites were relatively elaborate. Today, Christian rites are followed. The spirit of the deceased is thought to continue to associate with the living for a while.

Bibliography

Dennis, Philip A. (1981). "The Costeños and the Revolution in Nicaragua." *Journal of Interamerican Studies and World Affairs* 23:271–296.

Helms, Mary W. (1971). *Asang: Adaptations to Culture Contact in a Miskito Community*. Gainesville: University Presses of Florida.

Nietschmann, Bernard (1973). *Between Land and Water*. New York: Seminar Press.

MARY W. HELMS

Mixe

ETHNONYMS: Ayuuk, Mije

Orientation

Identification. The Mixe are one of the major Middle American Indian groups in the southern Mexican state of Oaxaca. They were usually referred to as "Mije" in the early literature, but the standardized spelling is currently "Mixe." This name was probably given to them by Indian auxiliaries arriving with the Spaniards; it is derived either from the Nahuatl term for "death" or the term for "datura." The Mixe use the word "Ayuuk," meaning "language" or "word" to designate themselves. This word is etymologically closely related to their term for "people of the mountains."

Location. The Mixe occupy an area of 5,829 square kilometers in the Sierra Madre of northeastern Oaxaca. Elevations range from 400 meters to more than 3,300 meters. Their habitat is characterized by pine-oak and tropical mountain forests, and open grasslands. Much of the area is under cultivation and in various states of reforestation by secondary vegetation. There are several lowland, riverine communities, situated in a wet, tropical-forest zone in the northeastern portion of the Mixe region. The average annual rainfall is from 150 to 250 centimeters, with the greatest portion occurring from June to October. The climate is a moderately warm, pluvial one with cold winters and hot summers.

Demography. In 1872 the Mixe population was 31,736. By 1950 it had increased to 52,754, and in 1991 it was estimated to be about 76,000, distributed among fifty villages and numerous small hamlets. Some reside in Isthmus of Tehuantepec towns and Mexico City, but the vast majority of the population have remained in the Mixe region.

Linguistic Affiliation. Comprising three major dialects, the Mixe language is a subgroup of the Mixe-Zoque Language Phylum, which includes Zoque, Sierra Popoluca, and Tapachultec; the latter is now extinct.

History and Cultural Relations

Mixe territory originally extended from the Río Nexapa to Coatzacoalcos and from Villa Alta to the Isthmus of Tehuantepec. At the beginning of the fourteenth century, Mixe continuity on the Gulf Coast was disrupted by a series of Central Mexican (Pipil) and Maya invasions. They were also forced to cede the western isthmus region to the Huave, and Nexapa to the Zapotec. Under a succession of kings, the Mixe waged war against the Zapotec, the Mixtec, and their allies. Despite their numerical superiority, these groups, seeking tribute and territory, were unable to defeat the Mixe. By 1522, however, the Mixe had become tributary subjects of the Zapotec lord of Tehuantepec. The Spaniards and their Indian allies were unable to defeat the Mixe in several expeditions launched against them. Although the Spaniards were able to subdue a few settlements in 1531, by 1560 the Mixe had not been conquered. The final pacification of the Mixe nation was carried out by Dominican friars, who established parishes and centers of evangelization throughout the region. Cruel treatment and excessive tribute resulted in serious insurrections in 1570, 1660, and 1661. Following the initial expeditions of the Conquest, there were no large movements of Spanish settlers into the region. In 1660 a decree ordering the consolidation of the dispersed settlements into larger nucleated towns, in order to administer and missionize the Mixe more effectively, resulted in the decimation of the population from typhoid, smallpox, and influenza epidemics.

Although forced labor drafts had been discontinued by 1650, tribute in goods was drawn from the Mixe region as late as 1789. In 1780 the Dominicans were replaced by Spanish secular priests, who were expelled after the War of Independence. Thereafter, the region was served by only one priest, who came to the villages for the annual religious feast. In the latter part of the twentieth century, the Mixe region has undergone marked economic, political, and religious change brought about by the construction of roads, the advent of state development agencies, and renewed Catholic missionary activity.

Contemporary Mixe culture is an amalgam of indigenous, Spanish-colonial, and regional Oaxaca traits. The retention of the Mixe language and territory was instrumental in preserving many native religious beliefs and practices. Spanish influence is most evident in village layout and housing construction, religion, livestock, and the use of metal tools. Slash-and-burn agriculture and digging-stick technology is complemented, in some villages, by European plow agriculture. Regional influence, such as the presence of the dress and music of the Isthmus in eastern Mixe villages, is also a factor. The construction of roads in the region has greatly facilitated the introduction of new foods, industrial goods, and the replacement of thatched roofs with corrugated-metal ones.

Settlements

Prior to the conquest, the Mixe lived in nucleated settlements and small farms dispersed along mountain crests and slopes, and concentrated in valleys. Contemporary settlements consist of nucleated, compact communities or single homesteads and hamlet clusters centripetally dispersed from the community center. People may live in the village except for a three-month period, when they reside and work in their coffee plantations. In communities where good agricultural lands are distant from the village, families reside on small farms during the planting, weeding, and harvesting periods. Since community members are required to serve in the civil-religious organization and participate in communal labor each year, homestead families must carry heavy household goods and food back and forth over the mountains to and from the community center, fomenting discord between centers and outlying farms. Population growth and consequent use-pressure on land resources has resulted in diminished yields of maize. The necessity of modifying their settlement pattern, by moving to distant land better suited to agriculture, has been checked by the cash cropping of coffee and by intervillage trade.

Economy

Subsistence and Commercial Activities. Maize as well as beans, chilies, and squashes are grown by means of slash-and-burn agriculture. Bananas, potatoes, root crops, and a variety of tropical fruits are also cultivated to a certain extent. Turkeys and chickens are kept around the household, and, in some villages, sheep, goats, pigs, and cattle are raised. Fishing and hunting constitute a significant, but not major, means of obtaining provisions. The Mixe also take on part-time occupations as merchants, traders, and craft specialists. In various villages, coffee is grown and sold as a cash crop. Because many villages are inaccessible to motorized transport, supplies such as maize, sugar, salt, and beer are brought in by pack animals. Store owners in larger villages sell dry goods to the local and surrounding population. Many store owners also sell maize and beer in large quantities to muleteers who then transport this merchandise to surrounding villages, where it is exchanged for coffee or cash. The Mixe region participates in the national and world economy by exporting large amounts of coffee. The profit from the cash crop, coffee, and the price paid for commercial maize and other imported merchandise depend on how far a village is from motorized transport facilities.

Industrial Arts.   Pottery, baskets, and woven wool and cotton cloth for ponchos, women's blouses, sashes, belts, and headdresses are produced in a few villages for the local market. Each village has one or more specialists in sandal- and leatherworking, carpentry, butchering, bread baking, masonry, and the construction of clay griddles for heating maize-meal cakes. Most male adults are able to construct habitations with adobe, wattle and daub, or logs, and furniture such as wooden stools.

Trade.   The Mixe region has a number of village markets, where a wide variety of foodstuff products and merchandise, such as clothing, is sold. Village marketplaces operate on different weekdays to form a mutually interdependent regional market system. Itinerant traders carrying fish, rope, sandals, hats, and other merchandise ply their wares from house to house. These items are usually exchanged for coffee, which serves as an all-purpose exchange medium. The traders bring the coffee to the lowlands to be sold, and return with more merchandise.

Division of Labor.   Men do most of the agricultural work, but they are assisted by women in the weeding, harvesting, shelling, and storing of the maize. The two sexes also share in the harvesting and preparation of coffee beans and in attending to the pigs and poultry, gathering firewood, sewing, housekeeping, marketing, and carrying loads. Men are responsible for the pasturing of livestock and beasts of burden, house building, hunting and fishing, distant marketing, and the repair of tools. Politics, government, and the administration of village feasts are also in the hands of the men. Women care for the children, prepare and cook the food, do laundry, and clean the house.

Land Tenure.   In villages that annually shift plots, cultivated fields are held in usufruct by a family for one season, after which it reverts back to the community. In villages with longer intervals between fallow periods and annual cultivation, the land is held by a family as long as it is worked continuously. Since the land is legally owned by the community, only usufruct rights and capital improvements made on the land may be transferred to another individual by cash payment. Only coffee trees can be sold, not the soil on which the trees are grown. Lands unsuitable for agriculture are used as a communal source of firewood and grazing.

Kinship

Kin Groups and Descent.   Mixe kin groups are comprised of nuclear and extended families in one household and of nonlocalized, Ego-oriented, bilateral kin networks, or kindreds. Although kinship is reckoned bilaterally, virilocal residence and the predominant control of land and inheritance by males place emphasis on the patriline.

Kinship Terminology.   The Mixe kinship system follows the generational or Hawaiian scheme, except for terms of reference for aunts, which are lineal: there is one term for mother, another for mother's sister and father's sister. Moreover, in several villages, cousins are terminologically differentiated from sisters. Ritual-kinship terms are extensions of the consanguineal terminology.

Marriage and Family

Marriage.   Marriage is regulated by the parents as an alliance between kin groups, formalized by gift exchange. Although the nuclear family is the predominant type, limited polygamy occurs in several villages. Marriages are village endogamous and prohibited with individuals whose ancestors are separated less than four generations from Ego. Couple- and father-dominated households vary according to residence location and differential wealth. The residence pattern is virilocal after marriage, with subsequent shift to neolocal residence, once such a move is economically feasible. Divorce is rare and informal.

Domestic Unit.   The nuclear family is the dominant form of household composition. Extended families typically consist of two families of procreation from adjacent generations, as well as the offspring of siblings and affines. Stem families consist of two- and three-generational families and married siblings living jointly in one household.

Inheritance.   Property is ideally distributed to all children, irrespective of age or sex. In some cases, the father will give more to his sons and less to his daughters or, if there is insufficient land, all will go to the son. A woman retains the rights over her lands and other property after she becomes married. In case of divorce, she retains her property. Offspring who are faring poorly are given more consideration than siblings in a better economic position. The expenses for a son's marriage or education may be considered his inheritance, and the house lot and lands divided among the other siblings. Inheritance from husband to wife is rare.

Socialization.   Obedience is stressed in late childhood but is seldom enforced. Older children learn gender-related domestic and economic tasks by observing and imitating their parents. Siblings and nonkin playmates obey each other on the basis of age. Children are scolded and restrained from displaying aggression toward siblings and playmates, and begin to perform public service at early adolescence.

Sociopolitical Organization

Social Organization.   Families extend solidarity and economic reciprocity by establishing fictive- or ritual-kinship ties, often at life-cycle celebrations. Reciprocal ritual-kinship relations may be between two families or extended into highly elaborate, interwoven networks within the community and beyond it. Mixe age sets involve an array of roles and obligations related to the politico-religious organization. Kinship terms are used to address nonkin on the basis of age relative to the speaker. Except for that of the elders, Mixe age sets are noncorporate and serve to underscore the status of villagers as equals, juniors, and seniors.

Dancers and musicians are organized into formal groupings. There are also communal work groups and informal groups for agricultural production and other daily activities. The construction of new roads linking the Mixe region with the national economy has led to incipient class formation in the form of large retail enterprises and a truck-owning elite.

Political Organization. The Mixe region is composed of territorial districts, divided into a number of *municipios* and an administrative head town. Each municipio administers its own affairs and those of smaller villages and farms within its territorial boundaries. Villages are divided typically into two landowning divisions or wards. Civil officials are chosen from each ward in alternating years; kin groups tend to be ward localized. Except for the secretary, elected town officials receive no salary and work as a community service. Refusal leads to banishment. Positions are ranked in a hierarchy and prestige is largely related to the kinds of positions a man has held in the political and religious organizations. A formal, corporate organization that owns land or cattle provides for the administration, upkeep, and religious services of the village church. In addition, there is a complex hierarchy of religious officials appointed by the civil officials and village elders. Each of these religious officials or "stewards" is required to provide work, goods, and funds for a village feast lasting from one to several days.

Social Control. Grievances resulting from theft, inheritance, debts, and drunkenness are handled by town courts; major crimes, such as homicide, by the district court. Informal mechanisms of social control include fear of gossip, threats of sorcery, and ostracism from social life. A strong deterrent is the belief that anger and aggression cause illness and death.

Conflict. Quarrels arising from village boundary disputes and religious factionalism are adjudicated by the state government. In conflicts within the kin group, lineal relatives or in-laws will often act as mediators. In nonkin conflicts, apart from self-help and recourse to sorcery, the case proceeds to the court.

Religion and Expressive Culture

Religious Beliefs. Mixe religious belief consists of diverse elements of Spanish Catholic and indigenous origin. In some villages, Protestant groups have had significant success in converting the villagers. Devotion to God and the Catholic saints is expressed by the maintenance of household altars and a cycle of religious feasts. Native deities include Thunder, a rain and crop deity; Earth, a source of sustenance and the repository of wisdom; Great Lady Life, the deity of conception, childbirth, and medicine; and the Lord of the Underworld, a source of illness and wealth. There are also a number of lesser spirits, demonic beings, and supernatural serpents related to heavy rains and wealth. Along with body souls, an individual possesses one or more guardian spirits. Typically in animal form, these alter egos reside in forests and fields. Mixe mythology revolves around the sacred twins, a boy and girl, who after a series of episodic adventures, ascend to the sky to become the Sun and Moon.

Religious Practitioners. Each community has a lay organization responsible for the care and functioning of the church. There are also shaman-curers, who vary in the extent of their healing knowledge and skills. Curers obtain the knowledge to cure through dreams, plant-induced visions, apprenticeship, and by means of cash payments to other shamans or the exchange of information with them. Divination with maize and the interpretation of the pulse are the primary means of diagnosis; curing is done primarily by means of medicinal plants and ritual sacrifices. The propitious days for rituals or any major undertaking, the meaning of dreams and omens, and the causes of social disequilibrium and affliction are ascertained by a class of calendar priests.

Ceremonies. Mixe culture commands a large corpus of ceremonies, including rites of passage, rituals related to agriculture, hunting, and other economic pursuits, rituals for civil-religious authorities, and rituals for the well-being of the family and the community. These ceremonies include offerings of bundles of split wood, eggs, maize meal, agave brandy, candles, tobacco, and sacrificial offerings of fowl.

Arts. Preoccupied with subsistence activities, the Mixe are perforce restricted in their concern for arts and crafts. A few communities engage in textile weaving, basketwork, and ceramics. Women's blouses are woven for the tourist trade. Great artistic attention is given to music, dance, and costume, which are exhibited primarily during community feasts. Aesthetic sentiment is also expressed in festive household altars and in the elegant arrangement of candles, pine needles, and other objects for nocturnal ceremonies.

Medicine. Dispensaries and practitioners of cosmopolitan biomedicine are limited to towns accessible by motorized transport. Some illnesses are recognized as owing to natural agencies, such as sudden shifts in body temperature, anger, and overexertion. Diarrhea, skin infections, and many other illnesses are treated with medicinal plants and sweat baths. Superhuman causes of illness include nonfulfillment of ritual obligations, social conflict, soul loss, witchcraft, and sorcery. Shamanic curing rituals of sacrificial burned and blood offerings are carried out to expiate a moral offense, retrieve a soul, or remove an injury caused by malevolent human forces. There are also specialists for childbirthing, setting broken bones, massaging body ailments, and healing snake bites.

Death and Afterlife. Prior to the Spanish Conquest, the dead were buried in fields; the bones were later hung in baskets from trees or placed in temple charnel houses. Although burial within cemeteries was instituted by the Catholic missionaries, until the nineteenth century, the dead were also buried inside churches. Prior to interment, a wake and feast are held, and some communities have elaborate ceremonies to insure that the ghost does not harm or frighten its living relatives. The spirits of the dead are believed to dwell in the vicinity in which they had previously lived. Another belief is that the errant soul is purified in an underworld flame prior to its journey to heaven.

During a yearly feast for the dead, food is given to household visitors who are said to represent the ancestral spirits.

Bibliography

Beals, Ralph K. (1945). *Ethnology of the Western Mixe.* University of California Publications in American Archaeology and Ethnology, vol. 42, no. 1. Berkeley.

Kuroda, Etsuko (1984). *Under Mt. Zempoaltépetl: Highland Mixe Society and Ritual.* Senri Ethnological Studies, no. 12. Osaka.

Lipp, Frank J. (1991). *The Mixe of Oaxaca: Religion, Ritual, and Healing.* Austin: University of Texas Press.

Nahmad Sittón, Salomón (1965). *Los Mixes.* Memorias del Instituto Nacional Indigenista, vol. 6. Mexico City.

FRANK J. LIPP

Mixtec

ETHNONYMS: Cloud People, Ñuu Savi

Orientation

Identification. Speakers of Mixtec live in the southern Mexican states of Oaxaca, Guerrero, and Puebla. Mixtec speakers usually refer to themselves as "Ñuu Savi" (people of the rain).

Location. The Mixteca, the homeland of the Mixtec people, has traditionally been divided into three broad geographical zones: the Mixteca Alta, a mountainous, forested region; the Mixteca Baja, a high, dry area northwest of the Alta; and the Mixteca de la Costa, a low-lying tropical area bordering the Pacific Ocean. Within each of these zones, the sharply faulted topography has created a great deal of environmental diversity. A lack of economic opportunity has caused many Mixtec speakers to migrate from this area, and there are now substantial colonies of Mixtec speakers located in the Isthmus of Tehuantepec region, in Oaxaca City, in Mexico City, in Baja California, and in various places in the United States. Groups of Mixtec labor migrants have been reported to be working as far north as Alaska.

Demography. Prior to the Spanish Conquest, the population of the Mixteca (which included non-Mixtec-speaking groups) was over 500,000. The plagues of the sixteenth century reduced the population by 90 percent. After reaching a nadir in the early seventeenth century, the population has steadily recovered, to the point where by 1980 there were 323,137 speakers of Mixtec in Mexico, making them the fourth-largest indigenous group in the country.

Linguistic Affiliation. Mixtec is classified as an Otomanguean language, although sharp dialectal differences mean that the Mixtec spoken in one area is often not intelligible to speakers of Mixtec in other areas. The Summer Institute of Linguistics has identified twenty-nine "dialects" of Mixtec that fall below the 70-percent intelligibility level with one another.

History and Cultural Relations

In the early sixteenth century the Mixteca was divided into numerous small kingdoms, or *cacicazgos,* ruled over by a hereditary elite. The Mixtec elite also ruled over non-Mixtec-speaking peoples, and some Mixtec kingdoms had, in turn, been conquered by the Central Mexican Triple Alliance. The Mixtec elite, related to one another by marriage and descent, patronized one of the finest artistic traditions in the New World. The area was conquered by the Spanish between 1522 and 1524. Owing to severe population decline in the wake of the sixteenth-century plagues, as well as to the region's lack of major mineral and agricultural resources, relatively few Spaniards settled in the area, however, and the pressures for change, although substantial, were not as great as in other areas in Mesoamerica. In the nineteenth and twentieth centuries outsiders began to move into the Mixteca in increasing numbers, and commercial agriculture was expanded. At the same time, the region became a center for several armed political movements, and Mixtec-speaking peoples actively participated in the struggle for independence, as well as in the Wars of the Reform and the Mexican Revolution of 1910–1920. Today, most Mixtec speakers are what anthropologists call peasants, but there is a growing Mixtec middle class, made up of teachers, government workers, technicians, politicians, health officials, and other professionals.

Settlements

Rural Mixtec speakers reside in village communities. Some of these communities form municipalities (the basic unit of political organization within Mexico), and some are hamlets within municipalities. In physical terms, most village communities have at their centers a main plaza surrounded by a church, a schoolhouse, and government buildings. Domestic dwellings are traditionally built of locally available materials. In higher, colder areas, most people tend to live in log cabins, but in the warmer, lower-lying areas, houses are usually made of cane and thatch. Adobe bricks are used throughout the region, and in some areas the waterproof husk of the banana is used as a roofing material. Today, many people construct their homes of cement cinder blocks and corrugated iron roofs.

Economy

Subsistence and Commercial Activities. Most rural Mixtec people are peasants who subsist chiefly on maize, beans, squash, chilies, local fruits, and other vegetables. In some areas, swidden, or slash-and-burn, agriculture is widely practiced; in other areas oxen-drawn plows are used. In favored areas, irrigation works have been developed. The *lama-bordo* technique of building hillside terraces to control erosion and bring fertile soil off the mountains onto agricultural plots appears to be unique to the Mixteca. In some areas, where virgin forests still exist, wild game (deer, squirrels, coati, iguanas, and birds) supplements the diet. Principal cash crops include coffee, wheat and other grains, tobacco, sugarcane, and fruits. In most areas, significant numbers of goats and sheep are raised, and the coastal area is known for the large number of cattle bred there.

Industrial Arts. In traditional Mixtec villages, there are adept weavers, candle makers, and house builders. In addition, many communities specialize in particular crafts such as pottery making, sugar and liquor production, baking, the manufacture of straw hats and mats, firework production, the manufacture of agricultural tools, leatherworking, and furniture making.

Trade. Much of the trade within the Mixteca is carried out at weekly markets. Local trade involves the exchange of the crafts of different communities and the products of complementary ecozones. Long-distance trade between the Coastal Mixteca and other regions has traditionally focused on salt. Cotton, cacao, chilies, fish, and coconuts are also traded from the coast into highland areas, in exchange for pulque, squashes, herbs such as oregano, and temperate fruits. Pilgrimage centers also function as trading points in the Mixteca, as do sites of religious festivals. Some regions lack weekly markets, and traders simply go from house to house with their wares.

Division of Labor. For rural peasants, the division of labor is by gender and age. Men are responsible for agricultural tasks and house building, whereas women cook and process food, maintain the house, and care for children. In some places, this division of labor is defined by taboos, such as the one arising from the belief that husbands become ill if their wives perform agricultural chores. Both sexes gather firewood; only men hunt. Children and older people are often assigned the task of caring for goats and sheep.

Land Tenure. Patterns of land tenure vary greatly from place to place within the Mixteca, the result of Mexico's complicated agrarian history and local ecological factors. In some areas, land is held privately by individuals and can be freely bought and sold. Elsewhere, land is held privately but cannot be sold to outsiders. In still other places, no individual titles exist, although the same plots may stay within families for generations. In places where swidden agriculture is practiced and there is abundant land, fields are abandoned after a year or two, and the family that worked a plot may never again return to it. Most Mixtec communities maintain at least some communal lands, which are used by community members for pasturage, cutting timber, collecting wild plants, and gathering fuel.

Kinship

Kin Groups and Descent. In the pre-Hispanic period, many local groups were organized as demes, a practice that continues in at least some communities in the area today. For purposes of inheritance, descent is reckoned bilaterally. _Compadrazgo,_ or ritual kinship, is extremely important in all areas. There are several different kinds of compadrazgo relationships, but those deriving from baptism and marriage are considered the most significant. The compadrazgo tie extends beyond the immediate partners and the godchild to embrace a range of lineal and collateral relatives, who may then refer to one another by kinship terms.

Kinship Terminology. Mixtec is characterized by Hawaiian cousin terminology. Three separate terms for siblings and cousins are used, depending on whether the persons are of the same or the opposite sex.

Marriage and Family

Marriage. Parents traditionally selected mates for their children. Often people married before they were sexually mature. Today, marriage occurs much later, and the young people involved have much more influence over the decision about who and when to marry, although the older pattern can still be found in some areas. Bride-wealth payments are made, and in some places can amount to the equivalent of several years' wages. Bride-service, with residence by the groom in the father-in-law's house, is also required in some areas. Community endogamy is the predominant pattern, although members of the growing Mixtec middle class are as likely to marry someone outside their community as they are to marry an insider. Polygyny is practiced by wealthy individuals. Residence is usually virilocal. When divorce occurs, the woman returns to her parents' or brothers' households. If it occurs relatively soon after marriage, a portion of the bride-wealth must be repaid.

Domestic Unit. The ideal domestic unit for most Mixtec peasants is a husband and wife, their unmarried children, and their adult married sons, who bring their wives to live with them in their father's house. Often separate houses are erected, forming a residential compound, for each of the different nuclear families. There is, however, much variation in the composition of Mixtec households, depending on the phase of the developmental cycle, selective mortality, divorce, and other factors.

Inheritance. Traditionally, all sons inherited equally. Daughters inherited land only when a man died without any sons. In many places today, women are given the same rights to their parent's estate as their brothers.

Socialization. All members of the household help raise children. Females with nursing infants may breast-feed one another's children, and older children often spend as much time caring for their younger siblings as do the parents. Once children reach the age of 4 or 5, they begin to leave the compound to play with other children. Boys are encouraged to roam freely with their peers, but girls are expected to stay near the household. Both sexes are given productive tasks to perform from a very early age. Marriage is often a difficult time for young girls, who are suddenly separated from their home and kin.

Sociopolitical Organization

Social Organization. The basic social unit of Mixtec peasant communities today is the household. Households are linked to one another through reciprocal exchange of goods and labor, marriage, ritual kinship, and corporate interest. The municipal subunits of _rancheria_ and _agencia,_ as well as the barrio, often form intermediate organizations between household and community.

Political Organization. In settlements where Mixtec speakers predominate, leadership and decision making rest in the hands of officers of the civil-religious hierarchy. It is often the case in these areas that ultimate authority rests with a group of *tañuu* and *ñañuu*, men and women who have passed through all the offices of the hierarchy and are now respected elders. Elsewhere, a single individual, or cacique, may control local government, often by being a broker between the state bureaucracy and the local village. In rural areas with mestizo populations, the power of Mixtec speakers in local government is usually limited.

Social Control. Gossip, public ridicule, the threat of evil spells, and fear of being accused of witchcraft are important mechanisms of social control in village life. The assignment of offices in the civil-religious hierarchy to those who violate community norms is another very effective form of punishment, since work in these offices requires a substantial expenditure of time and money. In the case of serious infractions, such as the theft of property, local authorities may decide that incarceration and the payment of fines is necessary. Habitual criminals may be subjected to banishment or some form of corporal punishment. In most areas, murderers are sent to the district capital for trial and punishment.

Conflict. Intervillage conflict is widespread throughout southern Mexico, but it is particularly intense in Oaxaca, where disputes between neighboring communities over land boundaries have continued for hundreds of years. These disputes have sometimes degenerated into open warfare, resulting in deaths and the destruction of property. Within communities, conflicts frequently take place between community members over land, with drunkenness and witchcraft accusations often playing precipitating roles. Some Mixtec communities have homicide rates that exceed those recorded in the most violent cities in the United States.

Religion and Expressive Culture

Religious Beliefs. There are several basic elements to contemporary Mixtec peasant religious beliefs. These include a cosmology divided between the Earth and the Sky; a monistic pantheon, wherein the distinction between a particular deity, such as the image of the rain god, and its manifestations in rain and water, is unimportant; a focus on the renewal and fertility of the world through acts of self-sacrifice; and a modeling of contemporary social interactions on those that occurred between humans and the gods in mythic times. At the center of many Mixtec rituals are the saints introduced by the Spanish during the colonial period, and almost every Mixtec town has a Catholic church at its center. Protestant missionaries have made inroads in some Mixtec communities since the 1930s, often dividing the community into factions based on religious affiliation.

Religious Practitioners. Native religious practitioners are only rarely full-time specialists; they usually function as a combination of curer, diviner, and shaman, with individuals specializing in particular divinatory and curing techniques. Both men and women play these roles.

Ceremonies. Ceremonial life in Mixtec communities is very rich and centers around the fiesta complex. Fiestas, held to celebrate the feast days of major saints, are often sponsored by a *mayordomo*. On these occasions, hundreds of people may be involved in the rituals, which include gift exchange, sacrifices, processions, a mass, and much eating and drinking. Fiestas are also held to commemorate the life crises of baptism, marriage, and death and may involve hundreds of participants in rituals, the exchange of gifts, and feasting. Other major events include Carnival, just before Lent, which often involves the performances of dance troupes, and rituals to bring rain and celebrate the return of the dead (the latter occurring at harvest time in late October and early November). Pilgrimage sites are scattered throughout the Mixteca, and Mixtecs often make pilgrimages to important places outside their region, such as Juquila, and to the Shrine of the Virgin of Guadalupe in Mexico City.

Medicine. Most people are familiar with a wide range of plant and animal products that have curative properties. Specialists are called to cure illnesses such as soul loss, evil eye, and those believed to be caused by witchcraft. Many sicknesses are attributed to moral failings by the sufferer or by the sufferer's immediate kin. The Mexican government has established free rural clinics throughout the Mixteca, staffed by trained nurses and doctors. These have been especially effective at reducing the mortality rate of young children and women of childbearing age who develop complications during pregnancy.

Death and Afterlife. Death is commemorated by elaborate mourning rituals, which involve gift exchange and feasting and seven or nine nights of prayer, depending on whether the deceased was a child or an adult. The world of the dead is the mirror image of the world of the living. Thus, one year for the living is one day for the dead; when it is night for the living, it is day in the land of the dead. In some places, the dead are said to reside on certain mountaintops. Many people subscribe to the ancient Mesoamerican belief that one's final resting place is determined by the manner in which one died. Thus, those who drown serve the rain deity; those who die in the forest serve the demon. Most of the dead are believed to return during the All Saints' observance to visit with the living.

Bibliography

Butterworth, Douglas (1975). *Tilantongo*. Mexico City: Instituto Nacional Indigenista.

Jansen, Maarten (1982). *Huisi Tacu*. Amsterdam: Centrus voor Studie en Documentatie van Latijns Amerika.

Monaghan, John (1990). "Reciprocity, Redistribution, and the Transaction of Value in the Mesoamerican Fiesta." *American Ethnologist* 17:758–774.

Ravicz, Robert, and A. Kimball Romney (1969). "The Mixtec." In *Handbook of Middle American Indians*, edited by Robert Wauchope. Vol. 7, *Ethnology, Part One*, edited by Evon Z. Vogt, 367–399. Austin: University of Texas Press.

Smith, Mary Elizabeth (1973). *Picture Writing of Ancient Southern Mexico*. Norman: University of Oklahoma Press.

Spores, Ronald (1984). *The Mixtec in Ancient and Colonial Times.* Norman: University of Oklahoma Press.

JOHN MONAGHAN

Montserratians

ETHNONYMS: Alliouagana (said to be the pre-Conquest aboriginal name)

Orientation

Identification. Geographically, Montserrat is a small island of the Lesser Antilles; politically, it was part of the former British Leeward Islands colony and is now one of the few remaining British colonies and a Commonwealth member. It was and remains part of the historical, economic, and cultural sphere created by the slave plantations of the Americas.

Location. Montserrat lies in the eastern Caribbean at 17° N. Its 99 square kilometers include a variety of environments and plant communities correlated with rainfall and elevation. The terrain is dissected by streams that flow in deep guts created by volcanic activity. The south and central volcanic peaks bear tropical deciduous and evergreen forest, whereas the lower, drier region of the north bears grasses and cactus scrub encouraged by grazing. Erosion, deforestation, subsistence cultivation, plantation agriculture, and alien plants and animals from Europe, Africa, and Asia have transformed Montserrat, as they have all the Caribbean islands.

Demography. About 12,000 people inhabit Montserrat, a decline of 2,000 since 1960. This drop is a consequence of emigration, a significant demographic process that began in 1838, as freed slaves sought opportunity elsewhere. In 1850, for example, half the people were under the age of sixteen and the annual birthrate was about 36 per thousand, yet the population had dwindled from what it was in 1834. Emigration is a problem because youth and talent leave the island; it is a solution because the economy and available resources cannot sustain everyone born there, and many households are partly or wholly supported by money sent by family members living abroad, especially in England, the United States, and Canada.

The great majority of people are native-born Afro-Caribbeans, although there is a small foreign colony. Life expectancy at birth in 1992 was 74 years for males and 78 for females, but the morbidity rate is high. Skin and intestinal parasites are widespread, with schistosomiasis increasing alarmingly. Many pregnant women suffer from anemia, and about 25 percent of children younger than age 5 are underweight. As in other Caribbean islands, there is a high incidence of diabetes and hypertension, and AIDS is spreading.

Linguistic Affiliation. Montserratians are diglossic, speaking both Standard English learned in school and Montserrat Creole, the local variation on the Creole mother tongue spoken everywhere in the Commonwealth Caribbean. Montserrat Creole uses an English-based lexicon in a Creole structural framework. Although casual observers sometimes mistake it for an Irish brogue, linguistic research on native speakers has shown that there is nothing Irish in the Creole rhythm, intonation, or syntax, and only one word of Irish origin in the lexicon, although there are many Irish place-names. Creoles based on English do share a few phonological features with Southern Irish English, most likely artifacts of the common experience of British colonization.

History and Cultural Relations

Montserrat's history can be organized into five periods: that of Amerindian habitation; the early colonial period, 1632–1705; the sugar- and slave-plantation period, 1705–1834; post-Emancipation, 1834–1895; and the period from 1895 to the present. Before 2,000 years ago, small groups of archaic peoples with pottery and ground-stone tools were scattered in the Lesser Antilles. They were followed by Saladoid people, entering from South America with a new ceramic style and represented in Montserrat by sites dating from 1,800 years ago. Montserratian post-Saladoid sites, identified by a thick, rough-surfaced pottery without polychrome decoration and situated near streams, the coast, and cultivatable land, are less than 1,000 years old. After 1492, the people whom Europeans called Caribs were almost wiped out by invasion, slavery, disease, and demoralization. Nevertheless, Caribs raided Montserrat well into the seventeenth century.

European settlement of Montserrat began in 1632 with Irish indentured servants from nearby Saint Christopher (Saint Kitts), who raised tobacco on smallholdings. By 1670 their economy and culture were overwhelmed by large capitalized landholdings, a developing sugar economy, and slaves imported from Africa, all under the control of a dominant British oligarchy of merchants and planters. By 1705 Montserrat's plantation society was fully developed, and the island, like others in the region, had become a social and physical arrangement for the production of sugar. An important cultural process that accompanied the plantation was the fusing of Amerindian, African, and European elements into a regional, creolized Afro-Caribbean culture.

Expanding slavery and environmental degradation subsidized Montserrat's thriving sugar economy in the eighteenth century, but shortly after 1800 the island underwent a period of instability and change. The White plantocracy was threatened by a faltering economy, the end of the slave trade in 1807, a growing class of free persons of color demanding rights, and the mandated amelioration of slave conditions. The governing minority grew corrupt, inept, and recalcitrant. By Emancipation in 1834, the island was in financial and sociopolitical disarray.

After 1834, the newly freed people struggled to find land and establish livelihoods in the face of depressed wages and continued economic exploitation in a dying sugar economy. By 1895 their descendants had managed to gain land and work out a peasant productive economy that finally received recognition by and assistance from the colonial authorities.

After 1905 commercial cotton production surged briefly, but the nineteenth-century legacy of unemployment, poverty, and an inadequate economy, educational system, and infrastructure persist to this day. Peasant production and emigration cushion these problems in a colonial economy that still suffers from its history of monocrop plantations and provides neither land nor wage work to everyone. Necessity has become culture, making emigration a desired experience. Émigrés send back money that is important both to household and island economies.

Settlements

Plymouth is the capital and port for the island, as it has been since the seventeenth century, rivaled then, but not now, by Kinsale. Otherwise, the first Europeans occupied dispersed small plots, later replaced by settlements conterminous with sugar estates, each with its plantation house, agricultural buildings, and slave quarters. After the end of slavery, free rural villages developed slowly even as settlements associated with estates persisted.

Today Montserrat is dotted with line and cluster villages, all with access to electricity, piped water, public education, and buses.

Economy

Commerce, Industry, and Trade. From the end of the small-plot tobacco economy in 1670 to the official colonial encouragement of peasant production in the 1890s, Montserrat's was a plantation economy, dependent on large-scale production of a single tropical commodity for a world market. Attempts at diversification failed in the nineteenth century. In the twentieth, commercial cotton production had some success through the 1950s. Montserratian cotton was a superior long staple sea-island variety for which the world market collapsed in the 1960s. Since 1968, Montserrat has had no staple export commodity. Montserrat joined a cooperative cotton-production scheme in 1990, with a central ginnery in Barbados, but its success is not yet clear.

Montserrat has now developed its tourist industry, which accounts for a quarter of the gross domestic product. In the 1960s the island was successfully promoted as an ideal place for retired and vacationing foreign residents. New communities for foreign residents were built under restrictive zoning laws that prevented land prices from rising throughout the island. Many of the prosperous North American and British residents have a genuine interest in the island but, with those who cater to them, constitute a core of resistance to independence from the United Kingdom. An offshore medical school, again catering to foreigners, has been boosting the economy since the early 1980s. Montserrat also began to lure short-term tourists, even though it is not clear that the one-tenth of each short-term tourist dollar that remains in the local economy compensates for the added cost of infrastructure, the environmental and resource burden, or the resentment of the local people.

In addition to tourism, some light industry, Radio An-

tilles, and recording studios enhance the economy. Nevertheless, large trade deficits are normal. Remittances sent by emigrants mitigate them, as does the economic activity of the expatriate segment on the island.

Subsistence Activities. The other side of the economy—the side that could benefit from bottom-up development—is small-plot production of food and market crops, known to have been practiced by slaves since at least 1690. There is also a small amount of charcoal production, mainly for home use, and livestock production. This subsistence complex was the foundation of the postslavery peasant adaptation. A lively market persists in Montserrat to supply food internally, and an interisland trade on small vessels carries market crops to neighboring islands. The volume, value, and functions of food production, marketing, and food trade are still important research questions.

Division of Labor and Land Tenure. Land tenure and gender-determined labor are important aspects of subsistence and small cash production in rural Montserrat. Women are the principal producers and internal marketers of food, whereas men predominate in interisland trade, cash cropping, and the raising of livestock, including cattle, sheep, and goats. Small plots may be freeholds, leaseholds, or squattage; cash-crop small farming may involve *métayér*, or sharecropping. Some freeholds are family land, a Caribbean form of customary tenure in which undivided parcels are inherited by a group of siblings in common ownership, although not all of them cultivate it.

Kinship

Kin Groups and Descent. Kinship is bilateral and descent cognatic, even though such simple descriptions do not do justice to behavioral and ideological complexity. Since the Caribbean was the first part of the world to be modernized by a rigid industrial labor regime and a land and economic system dedicated wholly to capitalized commodity production, the development and morphology of kinship, family, and marriage are relevant to a general anthropological understanding of kin processes in the modern world. Kinship practices and ideologies in Montserrat and throughout the Caribbean are linked with labor and land systems, class, gender, and law, but these connections are yet to be investigated in Montserrat.

Kinship Terminology. Kinship terminology separates the elementary family from other kin. Outside of the elementary family it is generational, without distinguishing matrilateral and patrilateral relatives. It would be a serious error, however, to draw any conclusions about family organization from the kinship terminology.

Marriage and Family

Marriage. Montserratian mating follows the same patterns that prevail elsewhere in the Caribbean, although the incidence of different forms may vary. There are visiting relationships between partners who live in their mother's or parents' households, long-term neolocal cohabitation without legal marriage, legal marriage, and legal marriages in which husbands keep "outside" mates and children. Women often have incentives not to marry, especially if they have a house, rights to land, or a central role in a consanguineal matrifocal household. Nevertheless, the dominant ideology values legal marriage, even when many people by choice or necessity live in other arrangements.

Domestic Unit and Socialization. As elsewhere in the Caribbean, households are the locus of early socialization and may be elementary family units with or without legal marriage; woman- and couple-headed households of two or more generations; or single-person households. Except for the last, they may include short- or long-term foster children or may be augmented for a while by other temporary residents, for instance a sibling or child of a sibling. Although classes may differ in ideologies about household composition and behavior, research on middle-class women has shown that ideologies of male dominance prevail, even among educated, salaried women who contribute significantly to household income.

Inheritance. Houses, land, and chattels may all be bequeathed within the legal system. There is also customary transmission of undivided "family land" in common to all the owner's or owners' legitimate children.

Sociopolitical Organization

Social Organization. Various informal networks integrate people and households into larger, loosely structured social complexes. There are networks that employ the ties of bilateral and affinal kinship, loose associations of women based on their residence around house yards and in villages, ties between women and the patrilateral kin of their children, clusters of men who socialize and work together, and reciprocal links focused on marketing and the market. Outside of these supportive networks, visible disparities in income, housing, skin color, employment, nationality, and access to resources stratify Montserratian society. These disparities, legacies of the colonial plantation past, are sharpened in Montserrat by the expatriate and tourist presence. Corporate groups include churches and religious societies and urban voluntary associations.

Political Organization. One of the principal issues that Montserratians struggle with today is their dependent status as a British colony. As a legislative colony, the island has long had a locally elected government, with a mainly decorative British-appointed governor in residence. Montserrat has received many benefits from its status as a colony: it is included in Britain's national health plan, it receives budget allocations, and emigrants to Britain have not had immigration problems. Understandably, then, many Montserratians prefer to remain a safely dependent territory. Others strongly advocate independence and autonomy despite the risks of small size and economic uncertainty. In February 1989 the island's political status declined when the United Kingdom suspended internal self-government and unilaterally revised the constitution to grant more genuine power to the resident governor. Local government and the Organization of Eastern Caribbean States protested, but this step backward to colonial control was a consequence of fraud and money laundering in Montserrat's uncontrolled offshore banking industry, which is now defunct.

Both of Montserrat's effective political parties, the Progressive Democratic Party (PDP) and the Peoples' Lib-

eration Movement (PLM), agree in their commitment to agricultural development, education, and infrastructural improvements that will, it is hoped, open the way for other forms of economic development, but only the PLM advocates independence. That issue suddenly lost salience, however, in September 1989, when Hurricane Hugo devastated the island and destroyed 98 percent of all buildings. Since then, the only issue has been recovery, for which assistance from the United Kingdom has been essential.

Social Control and Conflict. Officially, forms of social control are those of a British colony. The legal, court, police, and criminal-justice systems that operate islandwide are the heirs of the British legal system. Other, informal methods of social control function at village, social-network, household, and interpersonal levels. Peer pressure, obligations of reciprocity, kinship bonds, gossip, and pungent public harangues all exert control over individual behavior, containing conflict and contributing to social leveling.

Religion and Expressive Culture

Religious Beliefs and Practices. Christian denominations have deep roots in postaboriginal Montserratian history, and most Montserratians claim some Christian identity. The Catholic church has been present since the first Europeans arrived, although its adherents suffered legal discrimination until the early nineteenth century. The Anglican church was the favored and established church of the English colonizers. Toward the end of the eighteenth century, Methodist missionaries began to work assiduously in Montserrat, as they did elsewhere in the Caribbean. For a century they taught Christianity, literacy, and English middle-class morality, first to slaves and then to freed people and their descendants, wherever they were able to establish schools and congregations. These three denominations, along with the Pentecostal sects that began to penetrate Montserrat in the 1940s, are still strong.

Alongside and underneath Christianity, however, a strain of folk religion persists. The local variant on Afro-Caribbean obeah and possession religion is the Jombee or Jumbie religion, although this is said to be disappearing. Jumbies are spirits of the dead that influence and can help living persons. Montserrat's Jombee dance is (or was) the feast of food, music, and dance that reinforces bonds with living and ancestral kin, sets the scene for spirit possession, and often functions as a healing ritual. Folk spirit healers continue to practice, even without an institutionalized Jombee dance, and the practice of obeah today is an important research question. Another folk-religious movement that may be gaining in Montserrat is Rastafarianism.

Arts. The decline of folk music and dance forms and traditional festival arts parallels the decline of the Jombee religion. Most music and dance in Montserrat today are commoditized products, and indeed a major commercial recording studio is located on the island. There is a small but active cadre of poetry and fiction writers.

Medicine. Montserratians have access to national health care, a central hospital, contraceptive and family-planning services, village nursing services, and folk herbalists and healing practitioners.

Death and Afterlife. Conventional Christian beliefs coexist with folk beliefs in jumbies, or ancestral spirits, although not all individuals or classes hold either or both sets of beliefs.

Bibliography

Berleant-Schiller, Riva (1989). "Free Labor and the Economy in Seventeenth-Century Montserrat." *William and Mary Quarterly* 66:539–564.

Berleant-Schiller, Riva (1991). *Montserrat: A Critical Bibliography*. Oxford: Clio Press.

Berleant-Schiller, Riva, and Lydia M. Pulsipher (1986). "Subsistence Cultivation in the Caribbean." *Nieuwe West-Indische Gids/New West Guide* 60:1–40.

Dobbin, Jay D. (1986). *The Jombee Dance of Montserrat*. Columbus: Ohio State University Press.

Fergus, Howard A. (1994). *Montserrat: History of a Caribbean Colony*. London and Basingstoke: Macmillan Caribbean.

Moses, Yolanda T. (1977). "Female Status, the Family, and Male Dominance in a West Indian Community." *Signs: Journal of Women in Culture and Society* 3:142–153.

Philpott, Stuart B. (1973). *West Indian Migration: The Montserrat Case*. London School of Economics Monographs on Social Anthropology, no. 47. London: Athlone Press; New York: Humanities Press.

Skelton, Tracey (1989). "Women, Men, and Power: Gender Relations in Montserrat." Ph.D. dissertation, University of Newcastle upon Tyne, U.K.

Watters, David Robert (1980). "Transect Surveying and Prehistoric Site Locations on Barbuda and Montserrat, Leeward Islands, West Indies." Ph.D. dissertation, University of Pittsburgh.

Wells, J. C. (1980). "The Brogue That Isn't." *Journal of the International Phonetics Association* 10:74–79.

RIVA BERLEANT-SCHILLER

Mopan

ETHNONYMS: Mopane, Mopanero, Mopán Maya

The 10,000 Mopan Indians live in approximately equal numbers in Guatemala and Belize. This Yucatec Maya people lived in Mexico at the time of contact. During the large-scale political unrest and violence of the late 1840s and early 1850s, the Mopan left Mexico to live in west-central Guatemala and the Cayo District of Belize. The political repression in Guatemala since the mid-twentieth century has caused many to leave Guatemala and move to Belize. The Mopan live close to the Q'eqchi' Indians, and many now speak Q'eqchi' as well as Mopan.

Bibliography

Gregory, James R. (1984). *The Mopan: Culture and Ethnicity in a Changing Belizean Community*. Columbia: University of Missouri—Columbia, Museum of Anthropology.

Howard, Michael C. (1975). *Ethnicity in Southern Belize: The Kekchi and the Mopan*. Columbia: University of Missouri—Columbia, Museum of Anthropology.

Wilk, Richard R. (1990). *Ethnic Minorities in Belize: Mopan, Kekchi, and Garifuna*. Belize City: SPEAR.

Nahua Peoples

ETHNONYMS: none

Numbering 1,197,328 in the census of 1990, the Nahuatl-speaking peoples are the largest Indian group in Mexico, forming 22.67 percent of the native population of that country. "Nahua" or "Nahuatl" is a generic label for the peoples located mainly in central Mexico who speak dialects of the Aztec language. The Nahua usually refer to themselves and their language as "Mexicano." Today the Nahua are located around the periphery of what was once the core of the Aztec Empire. The Nahua live in four major regions: the Huasteca, the northern Sierra de Puebla, the southern Sierra de Puebla, and Morelos and Guerrero.

The Nahua of the Huasteca live to the north of Mexico City in thirty-three contiguous municipios, the populations of which are 30 percent or more indigenous. These municipios are located in the southeastern tip of the state of San Luis Potosí, in the northern part of Hidalgo, and in adjoining areas of Veracruz. The number of Nahua speakers age 5 or older in the Huasteca area was 385,032 in 1990. More Nahua live dispersed in other municipios of the Huasteca.

The Nahua of the northern Sierra de Puebla live in the northern part of the state of Puebla with the exception of one municipio, Acaxochitlán, in Hidalgo. In 1990, the speakers of Nahua over 5 years of age in the northern Sierra de Puebla numbered 194,739 in thirty-four municipios, each with an indigenous population of more than 30 percent. There is also a small group of Nahua, consisting of only 316 speakers over 5 years of age, living in the Jalapa area of Veracruz.

The Nahua of the southern Sierra de Puebla live in the mountains of west-central Veracruz, south of the municipio of Coatepec, in some adjoining municipios of Puebla, in the mountains of the southeastern tip of Puebla, and in a few municipios of Oaxaca, where they adjoin the Mazatec. A population of 203,785 speakers over 5 years of age lived in the region in fifty-six municipios in 1990, each with an indigenous population of more than 30 percent. The densest population of Nahua of the southern Sierra de Puebla is in the border region between Veracruz and Puebla around the Río Tonto and the Sierra de Zongolico, south of Orizaba and Córdoba.

The Nahua of Morelos and Guerrero are a more dispersed group, which numbered 98,254 speakers of 5 years of age or older in 1990. They are located in municipios extending east to west across southern Puebla into Morelos and from there south into the state of Guerrero, where the Nahua region borders the Tlapanec and Mixtec regions.

Bibliography

Arizpe S., Lourdes (1973). *Parentesco y economía en una sociedad Nahua: Nican pehua Zacatipan.* Mexico City: Instituto Nacional Indigenista.

Chamoux, Marie-Nöelle (1981). *Indiens de la Sierra: La communauté paysanne au Mexique.* Paris: L'Harmattan.

Chamoux, Marie-Nöelle (1987) *Nahuas de Huachinango: Transformaciones sociales en una comunidad campesina.* Serie de Antropología Social, no. 73. Mexico City: Instituto Nacional Indigenista.

Dehouve, Daniele (1974). *Corvée des saints & luttes de marchands.* Paris: Klincksieck.

Friedlander, Judith (1975). *Being Indian in Hueyapan: A Study of Forced Identity in Contemporary Mexico.* New York: St. Martin's Press.

Instituto Nacional de Estadística Geografía e Informática (1991). *XI° censo general de población y vivienda, 1990. Resultados definitivos. Tablados básicos.* Mexico City: INEGI.

Instituto Nacional Indigenista (1993). *Indicadores socioeconómicos de los pueblos indígenas de México.* Mexico City: INI.

Lewis, Oscar (1960). *Tepoztlan: Village in Mexico.* New York: Holt.

Lockhart, James (1992). *The Nahuas after the Conquest: A Social and Cultural History of the Indians of Central Mexico, Sixteenth through Eighteenth Centuries.* Stanford, Calif.: Stanford University Press.

Madsen, William (1960). *The Virgin's Children: Life in an Aztec Village Today.* Austin: University of Texas Press.

Madsen, William (1969). "The Nahua." In *Handbook of Middle American Indians,* edited by Robert Wauchope. Vol. 8, *Ethnology, Part Two,* edited by Evon Z. Vogt, 602–607. Austin: University of Texas Press.

Montoya Briones, José de Jesús (1964). *Atla: Etnografía de un pueblo nahuatl.* Mexico City: Instituto Nacional de Antropología e Historia.

Nutini, Hugo G. (1968). *San Bernardino Contla.* Pittsburgh: University of Pittsburgh Press.

Nutini, Hugo G., and Barry L. Isaac (1974). *Los pueblos de habla nahuatl de la región de Tlaxcala y Puebla.* Mexico City: Instituto Nacional Indigenista.

Reck, Gregory G. (1978). *In the Shadow of Tlaloc: Life in a Mexican Village.* Harmondsworth and New York: Penguin Books.

Redfield, Robert (1941). *Tepoztlan, a Mexican Village: A Study of Folk Life.* Chicago: University of Chicago Press.

Sandstrom, Alan R. (1991). *Corn Is Our Blood: Culture and Ethnic Identity in a Contemporary Aztec Indian Village.* Norman: University of Oklahoma Press.

Soustelle, Georgette (1958). *Tequila: Un village nahuatl du Mexique oriental.* Paris: Institut d'Ethnologie.

Taggart, James M. (1975). *Estructura de los grupos domésticos de una comunidad nahuat de Puebla, México.* Colección SEP-INI, no. 41. Mexico City: Instituto Nacional Indigenista y Secretaria de Educación Publica.

Taggart, James M. (1983). *Nahuat Myth and Social Structure.* Austin: University of Texas Press.

Van Zantwijk, Rudolf A. M. (1969). *Los indígenas de Milpa Alta: Herederos de los aztecas.* Amsterdam: Instituto Real de los Trópicos.

Nahua of the Huasteca

ETHNONYMS: Aztec, Mexicano, Mexijcatl (pl., Mexijcaj), Nahuatl

Orientation

Identification.   The Nahua are the most populous Native American group living in Mexico. The name "Nahua" is used by scholars to designate people who speak the Nahuatl language. The appellation derives from Nahuatl and appears to mean "intelligible," "clear," or "audible." Nahuatl speakers recognize the name "Nahua," but rarely employ it themselves. More commonly, they use the word "Mexicano" to refer to the Nahuatl language and as a general name for their ethnic group. "Mexicano" also derives from Nahuatl but has been Hispanicized and is pronounced and pluralized as in Spanish. Some writers use "Nahuatl" to refer both to the people and the language. Older-generation Nahua in the Huasteca sometimes refer to a member of their ethnic group as a "Mexijcatl," recalling the term of self-reference used by the ancient Aztecs. The name "Aztec" is properly used to refer only to the short-lived Mexica Empire that was forged by certain highland groups of Nahua before the Spanish Conquest. Scholars commonly divide contemporary Nahua into subgroups based on the geographical area they inhabit. The Nahua described here live in the Huasteca region in east-central Mexico. William Madsen (1969) noted the relative lack of ethnographic studies of Huastecan Nahua culture at that time.

Location.   The Huasteca is a cultural-geographic region composed of portions of six states on the Gulf Coast of Mexico—Veracruz, San Luis Potosí, Tamaulipas, Hidalgo, Querétaro, and Puebla. The precise boundaries of the Huasteca are disputed by local inhabitants and experts alike. The region is bordered on the east by the Gulf of Mexico and on the west by the great Sierra Madre Oriental range. Many authorities agree that the Río Cazones defines the southern limit, and the Sierra de Tamaulipas forms the northernmost boundary. The Nahua generally occupy the hilly southern and western portions of this vast region; they are concentrated in northern Veracruz and northern Puebla, northeastern portions of Hidalgo, and southeastern San Luis Potosí. At lower elevations the climate is tropical and the territory well watered, with numerous rivers and arroyos flowing from the mountains and emptying into the Gulf. At higher elevations the climate becomes dryer and colder, supporting pine forests. There are distinct wet and dry seasons corresponding to summer and winter, respectively.

Demography.   It is impossible to determine the precise population of the Nahua of the Huasteca. Official counts are suspect because census takers usually do not have access to all members of the population. The Nahua live in communities scattered widely throughout hilly or mountainous terrain penetrated by few roads. Furthermore, when census takers determine linguistic affiliation, they count only people 5 years of age and older. Finally, there is the problem of deliminiting the boundaries of the Huasteca. Defining the Huasteca as consisting of ninety-two *municipios*, the 1990 census recorded 431,805 speakers of Nahuatl 5 years of age or older who live in the region.

Linguistic Affiliation.   Nahuatl belongs to the Uto-Aztecan Family and is related to several languages spoken in Mexico and North America. It was the language spoken by the Aztecs (Mexica-Tenochca), Toltecs, Tlaxcalans, and many other pre-Hispanic and contact-era peoples. Speakers are generally concentrated in the highland region of central Mexico. Linguists divide Nahuatl spoken in the Huasteca into eastern, western, and T dialects, although these are probably 95 percent mutually intelligible. The western dialect is spoken mainly in San Luis Potosí, Hidalgo, and a small area of Veracruz. Eastern Huastecan Nahuatl is spoken in extreme eastern Hidalgo, Veracruz, and the northern tip of Puebla. The T dialect (called Nahuat, as opposed to Nahuatl) is represented by an island of speakers located in and around the town of Huejutla de Reyes in Hidalgo.

History and Cultural Relations

Neither the prehistory nor the history of the Huasteca is well known. A number of archaeological sites have been explored, and from these it appears that the earliest identifiable people to occupy the region were Huastec speakers. At the time of the Spanish invasion, the Huastec were struggling against Mexica expansion in their region.

Sometime probably during the late pre-Hispanic era, groups of Nahua, along with Otomí and Tepehua, migrated into the Huasteca. Ethnohistorical sources indicate that the first Nahua to settle on the Gulf Coast may have been refugees from the highlands escaping a great famine during the mid-1450s. Other sources mention that Motecuhtzoma II sent colonists to the coast to repopulate the area following a series of epidemics there. Documents record a number of military invasions launched by the Mexica and their allies. Archaeological evidence confirms a Mexica presence in the southern Huasteca; the best-known site is Castillo de Teayo. This ruin has not been excavated, nor even surveyed. It features a pyramid, ceramics, and at least fifty-two sculptures, all purportedly of Mexica origin. Dates for the site are uncertain, but the late fifteenth century seems reasonable. Based upon the few ethnographic studies conducted among the Nahua of the Huasteca, Nahua culture is linked to that of the highland peoples. Many rituals, deities, and beliefs, for example, are similar to those reported by sixteenth-century chroniclers of the Mexica. Nahua from more western regions of the Huasteca may originally have been part of the Aculhuacán Empire; they have remained largely independent of the Mexica.

During the colonial period, the Nahua of the Huasteca, along with most Native Americans in Mexico, experienced a cataclysmic decline in population owing to social disruption, forced labor, and disease. The scattered remnants of the population caused difficulties for Spanish administrators, who instituted a policy of establishing *reducciones* (areas where indigenous peoples were forced to settle) as early as 1592 in the southern Huasteca. These centralized locales were also known as *congregaciones* (congregations). Many contemporary Nahua communities are products of these colonial programs. Spanish missionary work began in the Huasteca prior to 1630, spearheaded by the Franciscans. Despite long exposure to missionaries, the southern Huasteca remains a conservative stronghold of pre-Hispanic religious beliefs and practices.

The Nahua areas of the Huasteca played an active part in the Mexican War of Independence in the early nineteenth century. Many people, probably including the Nahua, also participated in the war against France in the late 1860s and in the Mexican Revolution in the early part of the twentieth century. The Revolution brought land reform and the establishment of the _ejido_ system, which effectively redistributed private land to many Native American communities, including some Nahua.

In 1901 the first government concessions were granted to oil companies to exploit reserves in the southern Huasteca. This development and other factors led to the building of roads into the interior and subsequent changes entailed by increased contact with urban Mexico. Prior to World War I, sugarcane was the major cash crop grown by people in the Huasteca. Following the war, people in the higher elevations, including many Nahua, began to grow coffee for the international market. Also during this time, cattle ranching became a lucrative business for people of the region. Most cattle ranches were owned by mestizos, but Nahua participated in production by acting as temporary laborers on ranches and, among the more affluent, by owning a few head of cattle that they raised in conjunction with their farming activities.

Population increases following World War II, along with economic and political instability, have caused a crisis for many Nahua farmers. Economic exploitation of small-scale village farmers and competition with cattle ranchers for arable land have led to a series of sometimes violent confrontations. Land invasions and military repression have given the Huasteca a reputation among urban Mexicans as being a lawless and dangerous region. Political crises, violence, and lack of economic opportunity have led increasing numbers of Nahua to leave the region and migrate to cities in search of employment. In 1992 the government of Mexico amended the land-reform laws established after the Revolution. It remains to be seen what effect this fundamental change in land tenure will have on Nahua of the Huasteca.

Settlements

In general, the Nahua live in villages that range in population from 200 to 800. Larger, more acculturated communities may be organized according to the Spanish model, with a church and plaza at the center. Smaller villages are often scattered groupings of houses belonging to kin. Dwellings of less acculturated people usually consist of a single room with a thatched roof. The floor plan is rectangular, although sometimes one of the short ends of the rectangle is curved. The walls are made from vertical poles tied to a framework with vines, and mud mixed with dried grass is sometimes applied to form a solid wall. Floors are of packed earth, kept clean by women who sprinkle them with water and sweep them daily. An architectural cycle is evident in which people use a newer house for sleeping and other activities while using the older habitation as a kitchen. Interiors are sparsely furnished with few manufactured items. Increasingly, houses have tar-paper or corrugated-iron roofs and may be constructed from cement block. Such houses frequently have cement floors as well. More acculturated villages may have electricity.

Economy

Subsistence and Commercial Activities.   The Nahua of the Huasteca practice a mixed form of agriculture based upon the subsistence farming of maize. Members of some communities use a horse- or mule-drawn plow to turn the soil, whereas people in other communities, sometimes constrained by hilly terrain, use the slash-and-burn method with a dibble stick for seeding. Besides maize, the Nahua grow beans, chili peppers, squashes, onions, tomatoes, papayas, citrus fruits, tobacco, and condiments such as cilantro. Major cash crops include maize, sugarcane, and coffee. Animals raised include turkeys, chickens, pigs, bees, and, in well-to-do households, cattle. Virtually all Nahua families supplement their farming activities with secondary occupations.

Industrial Arts.   The only widespread industrial production entails the manufacture of sugarloaf. A wooden, or, in the late twentieth century, a metal _trapiche_ (cane press) is used to squeeze the cane stalks and extract the juice. This liquid is boiled until a thick syrup is rendered, then poured into molds and cooled, with the resulting loaf wrapped in cane leaves and sold in the market.

Trade.   Major trading takes place in weekly markets organized throughout the region. Many Nahua attend one or more markets, often at considerable distances from their home base.

Division of Labor.   The major division of labor is by sex. Women prepare food, make and repair clothing, attend to domestic chores, help with the harvest, and provide major care for children. They may also engage in one of a number of secondary occupations to help increase family income. These activities include baking bread, embroidering, gathering and selling firewood, pottery making, bonesetting, curing, midwifery, or operating a stall in a regional market. Men clear and plant fields, care for animals, build and maintain houses, weave fishing nets, hunt and fish, carry produce to the market for sale, and make sugarloaf. They may also engage in clearing forest and brush for regional cattle ranchers, picking coffee beans, temporarily working as a laborer in an urban area, playing music, curing, raising bees, or selling produce or animals at the regional market. Both men and women may choose to run a small one-room shop in their community as a means of earning extra money.

Land Tenure.   The land-tenure situation in the Huasteca is exceedingly complex. Many Nahua have rights to ejido land. Many others had invaded private ranch land and were in the process of applying for ejido status. Still others sharecrop or farm as tenants, and many families combine several such approaches in order to gain access to farmland.

Kinship

Kin Groups and Descent.   The nuclear family is the most important kin group in Huastecan Nahua communities, but these units are often linked through male and sometimes female ties to form functioning extended families. Descent is determined bilaterally.

Kinship Terminology.   Huastecan Nahua kinship terminology has characteristics of both the Hawaiian and Eskimo systems. Parents are distinguished from parents' siblings, and grandparents are distinguished from their siblings, although not according the side of the family to which they belong. Cousins and those married to cousins are in some instances equated with Ego's siblings and their spouses.

Marriage and Family

Marriage.   Marriage customs vary according to degree of acculturation. In more remote communities, a couple may elope without the permission of the bride's parents, usually following a villagewide ritual or social occasion held for other reasons. Sometimes the bride's father feigns anger upon learning of the elopement, but he is eventually reconciled to the inevitable union. In some communities, marriage is a more formal affair in which an older kinsman of the husband-to-be acts as a go-between with the family of the potential wife. Gifts are exchanged, feasts may be held, and the two families enter into ritual kinship with each other. Weddings derived from Catholic or Protestant traditions are increasingly common in Nahua communities throughout the Huasteca. Postmarital residence is ideally patrilocal, but actual practice is in fact more flexible.

Domestic Unit.   A majority of the domestic units in Huastecan Nahua communities are nuclear families. Related household heads often build their dwellings near one another, thus forming nonresidential patrilocal extended families. After marriage, young couples may live in the household of the groom's parents until they are able to build their own place of residence. This creates a temporary extended family living in the same household.

Inheritance.   In theory, property is passed equally to male and female descendants; however, family lands usually pass to male heirs under the assumption that it is they who will farm them. Daughters acquire access to land through their husbands. In the absence of male heirs, daughters inherit land rights. In cases where arable land is scarce, the eldest son or daughter inherits the bulk of the estate, leaving younger siblings to face the problem of gaining access to additional fields. The house usually reverts to the youngest son with the expectation that he will care for his surviving aged parents.

Socialization.   Nahua children are provided much attention, love, and support by both their fathers and mothers. Often an older sister cares for her younger siblings during the day, freeing parents to pursue their work unhindered. A child is normally surrounded by many relatives who are nearly the same age, and children have the run of the community and surrounding areas. Parents usually value education for their children and support local schools.

Sociopolitical Organization

Social Organization.   Nahua social organization can be conceived of as a series of concentric rings surrounding the individual nuclear- or extended-family household. One step removed from the household is the nonresidential extended family. The next largest subdivision is a toponymic group composed of residents of a named subarea in a community. These subareas are based on residence, may entail shared ritual obligations, and usually include nonkin. In some cases, the toponym functions as a type of surname for residents. Smaller Nahua communities are often divided into upper and lower halves, which constitute an extension of the social circle beyond named subareas. Larger communities may be divided into two or more barrios, and these can be important extrakin groupings as well. The entire village or town constitutes the next encompassing circle. Daughter communities, usually established by families in search of land, extend the social circle outside of the local community. These may serve as a buffer between individual communities and the municipio and state levels of government.

Political Organization.   Larger towns are invariably led by mestizo elites, with Nahua occupying lesser positions in the hierarchy. A *cargo* system or civil-religious hierarchy often characterizes larger communities. In this system, individuals work their way up a series of unpaid political offices and sponsorships of saints' celebrations. In traditional villages, an informal council of male elders may be looked to for leadership, particularly in times of crisis. Ejidos are run by elected political officials as mandated by federal and state law.

Social Control.   Most social control is effectively handled within the community by means of gossip, accusations of sorcery, and the threat of ostracism. More serious offenses often result in the person having to leave the community for indefinite periods. In the severest cases, local authorities may bring an offender to officials of the municipio for trial and punishment.

Conflict.   Disputes over access to scarce land resources are a common feature of many Nahua communities. Community members may band together in the face of external threats, but unsettled internal conflicts inevitably surface. Factions form along kinship lines and, if violence erupts, entire extended families may be forced to leave the community.

Religion and Expressive Culture

Religious Beliefs.   Nahua religious beliefs are generally a syncretic mix of Native American traditions and Spanish Catholicism; however, even in areas where Catholicism appears to prevail, beliefs tracing to pre-Hispanic practices often remain strong. The sun has been syncretized with Jesus Christ and is seen as a remote creator deity. The moon-related Virgin of Guadalupe, a manifestation of the pre-Hispanic earth and fertility deity Tonantsin, is widely venerated. The pantheon incorporates a complex array of spirits representing manifestations of a unified sacred universe: earth spirits associated with death and fertility, water spirits that distribute rain and provide fish, and celestial spirits that watch over people and also provide rain. A complex sacred geography is associated with mountains, springs, caves, lakes, arroyos, and the Gulf of Mexico. More acculturated communities may have a cult surrounding the saints. A significant religious development in the 1970s and 1980s was the conversion of increasing numbers of Nahua by U.S.-based Protestant-fundamentalist missionaries.

Religious Practitioners. In more traditional Nahua communities, the primary religious specialist is the shaman, called *tlamatiquetl* ("person of knowledge"). These shamans may be either male or female, and they undergo an apprenticeship under an established master before practicing on their own. Other specialists include midwives, and, in more acculturated communities reflecting Catholic influence, catechists and prayer leaders. Few Nahua communities have a resident priest. During the 1980s, under the influence of North American missionaries, some Nahua have become lay Protestant pastors.

Ceremonies. The Nahua have a rich ceremonial life that is partially synchronized with the Catholic liturgical calendar. Major occasions include a winter-solstice ritual devoted to Tonantsin, planting and harvest ceremonies, and important commemorations of underworld spirits at Carnival in the early spring and on the Day of the Dead in the fall. In more Hispanicized communities, celebrations of saints' days may be part of a civil-religious hierarchy. Noncalendrical observations include curing and disease-prevention rituals, ceremonies to control rain, pilgrimages to sacred places, ceremonial washing of newborn infants, the creation of ritual kinship ties, house blessings, divinations, and funerals.

Arts. Nahua of the Huasteca generally do not recognize artistic expression as a separate sphere of activity. Women take pride in creating beautiful, colorful embroidery on their blouses and in constructing well-made clothing for their families. Men fashion headdresses from mirrors, folded paper, and ribbons and perform dances during important ritual occasions. Men also play musical instruments and are the ones most likely to engage in storytelling. Both male and female shamans engage in the practice of cutting intricate and aesthetically powerful images of spirits from paper; as part of their religious observations, they also construct complex altars designed to be beautiful places.

Medicine. Medical practices include the use of herbs to treat symptoms of disease, bonesetting through massage, and attendance by midwives at births. These pragmatic measures are supplemented by elaborate symbolic healing procedures orchestrated by shamans. The use of cut-paper figures to represent various spirits is characteristic of curing rituals held by the Nahua of the southern Huasteca. These rituals, which vary in complexity and length according to the seriousness of the symptoms, are usually preceded by a divination to determine the cause of the malady. In extreme or chronic cases, individuals may visit a regional clinic to seek help from a Western-trained medical specialist.

Death and Afterlife. Beliefs concerning the afterlife are in transition under influence from both the Hispanic dominant culture and late-twentieth-century Protestant proselytizing efforts. The fate of the soul is linked to the circumstances of death rather than being a reward or punishment for behavior. The *yolotl* soul, representing a person's life force, generally travels to an underworld place of the dead called *mictlan*, where it eventually dissipates. The *tonali* soul, linked to the personality, disappears at death. There is a widespread belief that the souls of those who die from water-related causes go to a kind of watery paradise. People who die prematurely are thought to become disease-causing wind spirits.

Bibliography

Beller, Ricardo N., and Patricia Cowan de Beller (1984–1985). *Curso del Náhuatl moderno: Náhuatl de la Huasteca.* 2 vols. Mexico City: Instituto Lingüístico de Verano.

Madsen, William (1969). "The Nahua." In *Handbook of Middle American Indians,* edited by Robert Wauchope. Vol. 8, *Ethnology, Part Two,* edited by Evon Z. Vogt, 602–637. Austin: University of Texas Press.

Medellin Zenil, Alfonso (1982). *Exploraciones en la región de Chicontepec o Huaxteca meridional.* Jalapa, Veracruz: Editora del Gobierno de Veracruz.

Ochoa, Lorenzo (1984). *Historia prehispánica de la Huaxteca.* Instituto de Investigaciones Antropológicas, Serie Antropológica, no. 26. Mexico City: Universidad Nacional Autónoma de México.

Reyes García, Luis (1960). *Pasión y muerte del Cristo Sol: Carnival y Cuaresma en Ichcatepec.* Cuadernos de la Facultad de Filosofía y Letras, no. 9. Jalapa, Veracruz: Universidad Veracruzana.

Reyes García, Luis, and Dieter Christensen, eds. (1976). *Das Ring aus Tlalocan: Mythen und Gabete, Lieder und Erzählungen der heutigen Nahua in Veracruz und Puebla, Mexiko; El Anillo de Tlalocan = Mitos, oraciones, cantos y cuentos de los Nawas actuales de los Estados de Veracruz y Puebla, México.* Berlin: Gebr. Mann Verlag.

Sandstrom, Alan R. (1991). *Corn is Our Blood: Culture and Ethnic Identity in a Contemporary Aztec Indian Village.* Civilization of the American Indian Series, vol. 206. Norman: University of Oklahoma Press.

Schryer, Frans J. (1990). *Ethnicity and Class Conflict in Rural Mexico.* Princeton, N.J.: Princeton University Press.

Williams García, Roberto (1957). "Ichcacuatitla." *La Palabra y el Hombre* 3:51–63.

ALAN R. SANDSTROM

Nahua of the State of Mexico

ETHNONYMS: none

Orientation

Identification. Most of the communities in the state of Mexico in which Nahuatl is still spoken are located in three areas within the neovolcanic axis: on the western slope of the Sierra de Tlaloc to the northeast of the basin of the Valley of Mexico, on the western slopes of the volcanoes Iztaccihuatl and Popocatépetl to the southeast of the Valley of Mexico, and on the spurs of Montes de Ocuilan in the western part of the Valley of Toluca. Thus, these Nahua live in high mountain valleys and on slopes, where conifers are the most common type of vegetation. Although no *municipios* in the state of Mexico are registered as more than 30 percent Nahua speaking, in 1990 the total population of Nahua speakers stood at 26,927, or 8.6 percent of the Indian population of the state.

History and Cultural Relations

These communities can be considered highly modified remnants of Aztec civilization. Because the current Nahua settlements are a result of Spanish Conquest and colonization, it would be imprecise to maintain that they are a direct legacy of Aztec culture. In the first place, most are products of colonial policies of resettling pre-Hispanic populations after the demographic collapse of the sixteenth and seventeenth centuries. Furthermore, during the nineteenth century, when laws freeing communal lands were decreed by liberal governments, the resources of these communities were seriously affected. In many cases, they lost a large share of their lands as a result of the impressive growth of the haciendas during the nineteenth century. Only in some instances, in the first half of the twentieth century, through agrarian reform laws, were they able to recuperate a portion of the lands granted them by the Spanish Crown.

The recovery of Nahua lands was mainly attributable to strong agrarian consciousness and the fact that they joined the Zapatistas during the Mexican Revolution. At the end of the armed conflict, and after decades of bureaucratic proceedings, the Nahua were able to recover the farm and forest lands that belonged to them before the nineteenth-century laws abolishing communal property led to their loss. Now, in the form of *ejidos*, or communal property, the Nahua control a good portion of the resources that had previously belonged to the haciendas.

To a certain degree, these communities remained isolated until the first decades of the twentieth century. In the area of the Sierra Nevada, they share some cultural traits with Nahua communities in the states of Puebla and Tlaxcala, on the other side of the Sierra Nevada. In the Valley of Toluca, they are totally surrounded by Matlantzinca and Otomí groups. By the beginning of the twentieth century, there was evidence of a high degree of sharing between Nahua and Hispanic-colonial cultures. During the middle of the twentieth century, with accelerated urbanization and industrialization, cultural patterns in these communities, which were shaped during the colonial and independence periods, began to change considerably. Nowadays one can observe an accelerated process of homogenization toward forms of national culture.

Settlements

There is great variety in settlement patterns among Nahua communities in the state of Mexico, which range from highly dispersed, formless agglomerates of houses to the lattice pattern characteristic of the colonial period. The former are found in the area of Texcoco, where the settlement pattern is closely linked to the irrigation system; this network determines the way streets and paths are laid out within the community. Here houses are next to cultivated terraces.

In the southern part of the Valley of Toluca, the settlement pattern is in the form of an aggregation of houses around a church. The villages are generally located in small valleys near a source of water and are surrounded by broad extensions of agricultural land dependent on seasonal rainfall. *Pueblos* (towns) laid out in the Spanish rectangular form are also found in the Valley of Toluca, especially in areas near the plains. This same rectangular settlement pattern is found in the lower part of the slopes of Popocatépetl and Iztaccihuatl.

Economy

Owing to their location on the slopes of mountains on the neovolcanic axis, most Nahua communities have access to a great variety of natural resources, for example, forests of oak, *oyamel* (*Abies religiosa*), and pine and various types of pastureland. Besides, all these communities have access to unirrigated lands dependent on seasonal rainfall. Access to irrigated arable land is the exception and only occurs in the area of Texcoco and, in isolated cases, toward Ozumba, on the slope of Popocatépetl.

In the majority of these towns, landownership is in the form of ejido property. The form of land tenure is closely related to the necessity of proving to the agrarian authorities that the original titles granted by the viceregal authorities during the colonial period contain the requisite elements to make them legally valid communal titles.

Among the most common cultigens are maize, beans, broad beans, wheat, and barley, all destined for household use. The most important for commercial purposes are fruit trees, flowers, and medicinal plants. Several kinds of livestock are kept: cattle (for investment), horses and mules (for transportation) sheep (for meat and wool) and, among penned animals, mostly hens and turkeys.

Many nonagricultural resources are obtained from the mountain ecosystem. Forests provide lumber, firewood, charcoal, cane (used for the construction of pens), and pine boughs (for decorations). The mountain bushes provide wood for handcrafted animal figurines and handmade brooms. They are also the source of medicines, as are some smaller plants. The Nahua also gather numerous varieties of edible mushrooms, another widely used resource.

Cattle and sheep raising and the use of oxen for plowing are increasingly important, mainly because of the availability of various kinds of pastureland for grazing, especially during the rainy season. During the dry season, animals are fed mostly maize, wheat, and barley stalks.

An important factor in the economic development of Nahua communities in the state of Mexico is their proximity to large market centers. For communities in the Texcoco and the Amecameca-Ozumba regions, the commercial center is Mexico City, especially the markets of la Merced, Jamaica, and Central de Abastos. For communities located in the Valley of Toluca, the market center is the city of Toluca.

Besides the direct link to markets in urban centers, the communities of the Amecameca-Ozumba region enjoy a system of weekly traditional rotating markets. The main open market is in Ozumba. The Valley of Toluca has another system of rotating markets; their main open market center is in Santiago Tianguistengo.

Throughout the twentieth century, the Nahua communities have responded to the demands of urban markets. At the beginning of the century, commerce was based mainly on the sale of forest products (lumber, firewood, and charcoal) and handmade crates. In the 1940s, with the ban on the use of forest resources (decreed to accelerate the production of natural gas from the recently expropriated petroleum industry), the communities' strategy became to diversify the range of products for sale. In Nahua towns located in the Valley of Mexico, this strategy translated into the cultivation of flowers and medicinal plants, the collection of edible mushrooms, and the collection of wild medicinal plants. In the Valley of Toluca, besides gathering mushrooms, people began to raise sheep and goats in order to sell the meat. In addition, in some cases, people began to sell ornaments made from pine branches.

Nonagricultural occupations within these communities consist of work in the construction trades, as gardeners, as maids, and in other service occupations. In certain highland towns in the area of Texcoco, local bands of musicians are formed, from which, in earlier times, musicians were recruited by important musical groups in Mexico City, such as the military band of the Secretaría de la Defensa Nacional (Department of National Defense).

New small commercial businesses that sell flower arrangements, medicinal plants, juices, and handmade Christmas decorations were added to these occupations in the 1990s. Furthermore, an emphasis on formal education by the state has increased entry into nonagricultural occupations. These educational opportunities have resulted in more Nahua obtaining white-collar jobs in industry and government.

Kinship, Marriage, and Family

The most common family unit is the nuclear family; the extended family can be considered only a temporary phase before the formation of a nuclear family. Generally, when a son marries, he lives in his parents' home for two or three years, during which time he will build his own home on land given him by his father. A married daughter generally lives in the home of her in-laws, if her husband is of the community. In any case, the bride always leaves her paternal home—it is said that she "*se ajena*" (becomes separated from the community). Only in isolated cases—for example, when there are no male siblings—will a woman

remain in her parents' home with her husband and stand to inherit a piece of land from her parents.

In the 1970s there was still a tendency toward endogamy within the communities, or at least there were matrimonial relations only between members of neighboring communities. Nowadays there are indications that women are marrying men from outside the local region.

The custom of sponsoring as godparent the most important ritual events in a family's life—marriage and baptism—creates the bond of ritual coparenthood (*compadrazgo*). In fact, compadrazgo derives not only from these rituals, but also from other, less intimate, sponsorship, such as confirmation, the celebration of a girl's fifteenth birthday, and school graduation.

The community is in essence a collection of nuclear-family households. The social or political participation of an individual in community life is based on his or her membership in a household, in this sense representing the special interest of a family.

The nuclear family is the fundamental unit of production and consumption. Within the family, there is a clear sexual division of labor. Men devote themselves to agricultural activities, the collection of mushrooms, the extraction of forest products, and the sale of flowers, mushrooms, cattle, and handicrafts. For their part, women attend to domestic chores, the care of their children, raising penned animals, and the cultivation, harvesting, and sale of medicinal plants. Among the family-unit activities in which both sexes cooperate are the making of handicrafts and floral arrangements.

Sociopolitical Organization

The structure of local political offices is established by state law. In this structure, each community is a *delegación* (delegation) belonging to a municipio. The highest local official in a community is the *delegado* (delegate). In addition, there is a series of subordinate officials to assist the delegate; these offices are held by people of the community for three years. The main functions of the delegate are to represent the community's interests before the municipal and state authorities and to seek help in providing for the community's most pressing public needs, which include roads and schools, government-operated electrical and telephone services, a safe public water supply, a functioning sewer system, and a bus-company franchise.

As these Nahua communities are not strategic groups in state and federal economic and political thinking, in most cases their petitions for help are delayed for several years, sometimes for decades. Governmental authorities thus make rendering these services contingent on unconditional community support of the government party (Institutional Revolutionary Party [PRI]), for example at political rallies and, above all, during elections.

Within each delegación, there are several sources of friction. Members of the communities accuse their local officials of not working sufficiently hard to satisfy their needs. When support is finally obtained to implement some type of public works, the state government contributes only the materials essential to its implementation; the community must contribute the necessary labor. The ability of the delegate to mobilize community members is made evident when he calls on them to provide the required labor.

Although local officials traditionally judged cases of petty crime (e.g., fights, thefts), nowadays problems of this type are referred to the municipio capital, where formal legal resources are available for resolving them. Presently, local authorities only function as advocates.

There are also officials in charge of the agricultural affairs of a community who are totally independent of the delegate's authority. The natural resources and the agricultural and wooded lands of all the communities within the Nahua area of the state of Mexico are under communal and/or ejido control. These forms of land tenure are regulated by the federal agrarian-reform laws, which stipulate that local ejido and communal property must be administered locally by the community. The most important function of the agricultural officials is to resolve conflicts related to use of community resources.

The election of local authorities, civil as well as agricultural, is done with full independence from the government authorities themselves. Generally, it is through the system of religious *cargos* that the community evaluates a potential candidate's capacity for occupying one of the offices, basing their judgment on how he has moved through the system. Important criteria are honesty, an interest in community affairs, and an ability to speak and read Spanish.

These communities are not exempt from the problem of having corrupt officials. When their dishonesty is not serious enough to threaten the economic and social stability of the community, the officials become the butt of jokes and ridicule throughout the community. On the other hand, should their corrupt acts seriously threaten the stability of the community, for example putting at risk the community's agricultural and forest resources, the people will not hesitate to use violence to remove them.

Religion

Like the majority of Mesoamerican indigenous communities since the Conquest, the Nahua in the state of Mexico have developed an elaborate system of religious cargos centered on Catholic religious practices.

The objective of the system is to carry out the festivals honoring the patron saint of each community and to perform other religious celebrations in the Catholic ritual calendar. A committee is formed for each festival and placed in charge of organizing the event, collecting funds from the town's inhabitants, and mounting the celebration. In most cases committees are reconstituted annually, creating a general understanding that everyone will eventually be involved in organizing these religious rituals. One consequence of this system of religious duties is that it produces a deep feeling of unity and identification with the community.

Nevertheless, the cargo system is deteriorating because of the high cost of organizing festivities and the influence of Protestant sects that are beginning to change how people think about religious matters. In addition to these factors, the impact of the the modern national culture on the traditions of these communities is posing an enormous challenge to those who want to maintain their culture.

Bibliography

Bataillon, Claude (1978). *El Valle de Toluca, raíces indígenas, luchas campesinas y suburbanización.* Toulouse: Université de Touluse.

Fabilla, Gilberto (1958). *Los ejidos del Estado de México.* Toluca: Gobierno del Estado de México.

García, Carlos (1981). *Naturaleza y sociedad en Chalco-Amecameca.* Mexico City: Biblioteca Enciclopédica de Estado de México.

Giménez, Carlos (1985). "El régimen comunal agrario: Estudio comparativo de los bienes comunales en España y México." Ph.D. dissertation, Universidad Complutense (Madrid).

Huitron, Arturo (1972). *Bienes comunales en el Estado de México.* Toluca: Dirección General de Hacienda.

Sokolovsky, Jay (1978). "Local Roots of Community Transformation in a Nahuatl Village." *Anthropological Quarterly* 50(3): 163–173.

JOSÉ GONZÁLEZ RODRIGO

(translated by Ruth Gubler)

Nahuat of the Sierra de Puebla

ETHNONYMS: Mācēhualmeh (commoners), Mexica, Mexicanos, Sierra Nahuat

Orientation

The Nahuat of the Sierra de Puebla, also known as the "Sierra Nahuat," are speakers of an Aztec language who live on the eastern edge of the central Mexican highlands in the northern Sierra de Puebla. Their language is commonly referred to as "Mexicano," which derives from the term "Mexica," an ethnic label applied to Aztec speakers.

Location. The Sierra Nahuat live in nineteen *municipios* between the Nahuatl speakers of the high plateau and the Totonac on the coastal lowlands. These nineteen municipios, at elevations between 800 and 1,200 meters, are within a triangle marked by Teziutlán, Cuetzalan del Progreso, and Tetela de Ocampo. The municipios occupy a range of ecological niches, all of which have plentiful rainfall supporting luxuriant vegetation and abundant crops. At lower elevations, where there are no winter frosts, maize can be grown throughout the year, as well as coffee, sugarcane, and citrus fruits. At higher elevations, in the winter frost zone, summer maize, apples, plums, avocados, and flowers are grown.

Demography. Approximately 100,000 adults and children —about 40 percent of the region's population—speak Sierra Nahuat as their first language in the home. The other 60 percent are Spanish-speaking Mexicans, who sometimes describe themselves as *gente de razón* ("people of reason").

Linguistic Affiliation. Sierra Nahuat is the Zacapoaxtla variant (Key and Key 1953) that is close to the Nahuatl spoken by the ancient Aztec of the central Mexican highlands. Karttunen (1983, xxi) defines Sierra Nahuat as "a T-dialect" that, although it has "lost the characteristic lateral release" of the *tl* sound, "lexically is very similar to Colonial Period Nahuatl."

History and Cultural Relations

The earliest mentions of Sierra Nahuat settlements appear in post-Conquest reconstructions of Aztec history referring to the extension of the tribute empire of Moctezuma I (1440–1468) into what is now known as the northern Sierra de Puebla. The Sierra Nahuat contributed maize, beans, and cotton and provided men for Aztec armies fighting the Nahuatl of Tlaxcala. Hernán Cortéz apparently passed through the region on his way to the Valley of Mexico early in the sixteenth century, but Spaniards did not settle in the region until late in the next century. The first settlers, who opened mines in Tetela de Ocampo, Tlatlauquitepec, and Teziutlán, were followed by cattle ranchers and farmers. With the development of railroads in the last decades of the nineteenth century, many Spanish-speaking Mexicans moved into lower-elevation Sierra Nahuat communities to grow sugarcane and coffee. Spanish and mestizo settlement created a number of biethnic communities with clearly defined Sierra Nahuat and Spanish-speaking populations organized into systems of ethnic stratification. Spanish-speaking Mexicans have taken the bulk of the land, with help from the Colonization laws of 1883 and 1894, which forced the Sierra Nahuat, who held land corporately, to adopt fee-simple tenure (ownership with unrestricted rights to dispose of the land) and register their land in the district capitals. Many could not prove ownership and lost their land in public sales or pawned it to Spanish-speaking merchants. Some regained less productive land as *ejidos* during the Agrarian Land Reform of the 1930s and 1940s, but changes made in Mexican law in 1992 create the possibility of converting ejidos into private property. Spanish-speaking Mexicans export the vast majority of cash crops (coffee, sugarcane, plums, apples, and avocados); occupy the most important state, regional, and municipio offices; and run many of the schools. Sierra Nahuat in the few monoethnic communities retain their land and run their municipio government.

Settlements

The policy of *congregación*, by which the colonial government relocated indigenous families in planned settlements of perpendicular and parallel streets that were organized around a central plaza, affected the settlement pattern of some areas more than that of others. Municipios in the vicinity of Teziutlán are more congregated than those in the vicinity of Cuetzalán. The Sierra Nahuat live in the rural areas, and the Spanish-speaking Mexicans occupy the centers of most major towns and villages. Railroads, automobiles, trucks, and buses provide transportation among the communities in the northern Sierra de Puebla. Highway construction was uneven, however, until an ambitious *interserrana* project, initiated during the regime of Luís Echeverría (1970–1976), created roads passable by car, truck, and bus; roads reached the municipios between Cuetzalán and Tetela de Ocampo for the first time. Interserrana highways facilitated the transportation of people and goods from the northern Sierra de Puebla to the main market centers on the central Mexican highlands.

Sierra Nahuat dwellings vary in their construction materials but conform to a similar plan. Most are set off from roads and footpaths by a well-marked or well-understood space, which a visitor should not enter without announcing his or her presence. The dwelling itself usually consists of a single room, at one end of which stands a family altar decorated with flowers and candles and displaying images of saints. Family members sleep on mats (*petatmeh*) laid down at night on the earthen floor or on boards raised above the ground. A number of houses, particularly in the area around Teziutlán, have beds with box springs and mattresses. The kitchen occupies a corner of the main room or is a separate room. The traditional Sierra Nahuat kitchen is a hearth (a ceramic pot buried in the ground) for a wood fire surrounded by three stones supporting a flat ceramic or metal griddle (*comāl*), around which are placed a variety of ceramic cooking pots. Near the hearth are a grinding-stone base and stone pin (*metat* and *metlapīl*) for grinding dried maize boiled in lime water (*nixtamal*), a large ceramic vessel for storing water, and small containers for spices, coffee, and sugar. Harvested maize may be stacked in neat rows inside the dwelling, and dried maize, beans, processed sugarcane, and chilies are placed in the attic above the hearth. The attic is demarcated by reeds placed sufficiently apart to permit smoke from the hearth to rise into the food-storage area and drive away pests. A number of Sierra Nahuat families have kerosene or propane-gas stoves, and many now have electric lights.

Economy

Subsistence and Commercial Activities. The Sierra Nahuat have traditionally cultivated milpas, plots planted with rows of maize interspersed with beans and squashes. Small chili and tomato gardens, avocado trees, and herbs gathered in the forest provide the ingredients for a variety of sauces. Domesticated turkeys and small game (deer and armadillos) are important sources of meat. Spaniards introduced chickens, domesticated pigs, sheep, cattle, goats, sugarcane, oranges, wheat, and coffee. A number of villages specialize in the production of baskets and pottery. Women weave cloth on backstrap looms in some communities, and men weave on European looms in others.

Trade. The northern Sierra de Puebla is a region with many villages occupying diverse ecological niches and specializing in different crops and crafts. A complex system of periodic markets for exchanging goods was developed during the pre-Hispanic era. Patterns of trade changed after the construction of railroads and highways and the introduction of cash crops intended for the domestic and, particularly, the international market. Coffee orchards replaced many milpas, and the subsistence cultivation of maize and beans decreased dramatically in lower-elevation communities. Higher-elevation communities send plums, peaches, apples, avocados, and flowers to the regional market centers and Mexico City.

Division of Labor. Traditionally, women have brought water from springs; simmered maize in lime to make nixtamal; ground maize on metates; made tortillas, bean soups, and sauces; fed domesticated turkeys; cared for small children; and washed and mended clothes. Men have hunted, cultivated their milpas, and collected and split firewood for the kitchen. Women and men gathered crayfish in rivers, harvested and transported milpa crops, shelled maize, and bought and sold in local markets. Changes in the economy have modified the division of labor: many Sierra Nahuat now work on the coffee plantations, where men transplant coffee trees and cultivate orchards, and women and children harvest the crop. Men migrate to coastal sugar and maize plantations and work on construction projects in the central Mexican highlands (particularly in Mexico City). Women work as domestic servants or prepare food for workers in migratory labor groups.

Land Tenure. Most arable land is held in fee simple and as ejidos, which will become private property because of changes in agrarian law.

Kinship

The Sierra Nahuat have cognatic descent and do not form descent groups. Kinship terminology in the first ascending generation is Eskimo; father (*taht*) and mother (*nān*) are differentiated from father's and mother's brother (*tahitzin*) and father's and mother's sister (*āhui*). Terms in Ego's generation are either Hawaiian, with one term (*icnīuh*) applied to all cognatic blood kin in the speaker's generation. The Nahua of the sixteenth century used different terms for siblings, depending on the gender of the speaker, and terminologically distinguished siblings by their gender and their age relative to the speaker. Male and female Sierra Nahuat speakers of today generally use the same sibling terms and specify gender and relative age by adding qualifying words to the general term for sibling/cousin (*icnīuh*). *Nocnīuh tācat* ("my sibling/cousin who is a man") and *nocnīuh cihuāt* ("my sibling/cousin who is a woman") denote gender. *Nocnīuh tayacāna* ("my sibling/cousin who is ahead") and *nocnīuh tacuitapan* ("my sibling/cousin who is behind") specify relative age. Many speakers use the abbreviated terms *tayacānqueh* ("he who is ahead") for oldest or firstborn sibling and *taxocōyot* ("spoiled one") for youngest or lastborn sibling. *Tayacānqueh* sometimes refers to the eldest brother who succeeds the father as head of the household. Men and women still use different affinal terms for spouse's siblings.

Marriage and Family

Marriage. One may not marry anyone who is a blood relative or ritual coparent, but most communities are highly endogamous. A boy customarily begins marriage negotiations by asking an old and respected woman (*cihuātanqueh*) to convey his intentions to a girl's parents. The

boy and his family deliver to the girl's family a bride-gift, usually consisting of turkeys, spices, alcohol, cigarettes, and some money. The cihuatanqueh directs the couple to embrace in front of the family altar and surrounds them with a cloud of incense. A second celebration takes place several months later in honor of the godparents of the marriage, who often become the godparents of the baptisms of the couple's children.

Domestic Unit. The most important kin group is the household, identified by the expression *cē coza tequiti* ("work for one thing"), referring to the communal organization of labor to fill a common granary and purse. The majority (80 percent) of couples begin married life in the household of the groom's parents, but a substantial number (20 percent) live matrilocally. Many young couples move several times between the two parental domestic groups. The men of a household work together on a common milpa; women cook either at a common hearth or at separate hearths.

Inheritance. Most privately owned land passes patrilineally from parents to sons, but Sierra Nahuat inheritance exhibits a wide range of variations. Bilateral bequests are more frequent in families and communities where land is abundant and when the mother has acquired property from her own parents.

Socialization. Parents teach their children to work. Children develop very strong filial loyalties because of weaning practices and sleeping arrangements. A mother weans her nursing infant during the sixth month of her next pregnancy by applying a bitter herb (*chichicxihuit*) to her nipples. The weaned infant, who is usually about 18 months old, is moved to the sleeping mat of the father, who provides the child with warmth and comfort at night for several years. The father-weaned infant sleeping arrangements help form strong father-son loyalties, which reinforce the bonds of the patrilineally extended household.

Sociopolitical Organization

Social and Political Organization. The pre-Hispanic social and political organization of the Sierra Nahuat is unclear. Today communities throughout the northern Sierra de Puebla have a political and administrative organization that may have developed from a pre-Hispanic structure, according to the process Lockhart (1992) described for the Nahua of central Mexico. The pre-Hispanic Nahua had a cellular corporate organization consisting of the ethnic state (*āltepētl*), its *cālpolli* (localized kin group) or *tlaxilacālli* (house of lords), and member households. The Spanish introduced the town council (*cabildo*) as the governing body of the ethnic state, which eventually broke into cellular units now called municipios and barrios. Rank became less marked among Nahua families, and the term for "commoner" (*mācēhualli*) came to mean "Indian." Contemporary Sierra Nahuat call themselves "Mācēhualmeh," they are governed by a town council, and organized into municipios and barrios, which only remotely resemble the pre-Hispanic altepetl and calpolli.

Social Control and Conflict. The formal agents of social control are municipio judges, who listen to disputes and handle cases of petty crime. Those accused of more serious offenses appear before judges in the regional capitals. Spanish-speaking Mexicans generally control the regional and local town councils and use their power to maintain their economic and social position. Some parts of the northern Sierra de Puebla have experienced extensive peasant insurgency. In 1978 the Unión Campesina Independiente (U.C.I.) organized Sierra Nahuat in Huitzilan de Serdán. To control insurgency, the ruling Institutional Revolutionary party (PRI) sponsored a second peasant group called the Antorcha Campesina (Peasant Torch). The U.C.I. and Antorcha fought bloody battles from which the latter emerged victorious and took over the town council and school. Both groups have appeared in other parts of Mexico.

Religion and Expressive Culture

Religious Beliefs. The Sierra Nahuat identify themselves as Christians, but their mythology expresses a mixture of Spanish Catholicism and pre-Hispanic beliefs (Taggart 1983). Myths depict a geocentric conception of the universe, according to which the masculine sun revolves around the feminine earth. Creation of the universe resulted from the interaction of masculine and feminine forces in a process on the same order as, or analogous to, human reproduction and agricultural production. Anthropomorphic supernaturalism mixes with Christian symbolism; the sun is Christ, and the moon is the Virgin Mary. Humans have animal companions, and some humans, considered to be lightning-bolt diviners, have animal companions that are serpents. Diviners support the moral order by punishing thieves, adulterers, and Spanish-speaking Mexicans bent on taking Sierra Nahuat land. Some Sierra Nahuat have abandoned Catholicism and joined Protestant sects. Missionaries representing many different Protestant denominations—particularly Methodists, evangelicals, and Pentecostals—have operated small churches in the northern Sierra de Puebla for many years. Mass conversions took place in the 1970s in communities like Huitzilan, where peasant insurgency also has been rife.

Religious Practitioners and Ceremonies. The efficacy of ritual is extremely important for the Sierra Nahuat who remain within the Catholic church. Their ceremonies mark major life stages and honor important saints. Individual sponsors (_mayordomos_) of saints support communitywide celebrations arranged according to a ceremonial calendar that is a fusion of pre-Hispanic and Catholic tradition. Ritual offices (_cargos_) are generally separate from civil ones, but elders, who have had many years of civil-religious ceremonial service, are the governing group in some smaller Sierra Nahuat communities.

Arts. The northern Sierra de Puebla is particularly well known for beautiful textiles. Women in villages near Teziutlán weave and embroider very colorful shawls with animal and flower designs that may derive from pre-Hispanic themes.

Medicine. Women are midwives, and men and women cure disease with herbal remedies and rituals designed to remove impurities sometimes introduced into the bodies of victims by means of witchcraft.

Death and Afterlife. Destiny after death depends on the sacraments and on moral conduct in life. Infants who die before being baptized cannot see God, and sinners become the slaves of the Devil, who appears as an animal (often a goat) and lives in the underworld (Mictān). The baptized who have committed few sins go to paradise (Tālocan), where milpas grow tall, and animals graze on rich pastures.

Bibliography

Karttunen, Frances (1983). _An Analytical Dictionary of Nahuatl._ Austin: University of Texas Press.

Key, Harold, and Mary Ritchie Key (1953). _Vocabulario de la Sierra de Zacapoaxtla, Puebla._ Mexico City: Instituto Lingüístico de Verano.

Lockhart, James (1992). _The Nahuas after the Conquest: A Social and Cultural History of the Indians of Central Mexico, Sixteenth through Eighteenth Centuries._ Mexico City: Instituto Macional Indigenista.

Taggart, James M. (1983). _Nahuat Myth and Social Structure._ Austin: University of Texas Press.

JAMES M. TAGGART

Netherlands Antillians

ETHNONYMS: none

The Netherlands Antilles is made up of two groups of islands separated by 800 kilometers; it is an autonomous unit of the Netherlands and has political equality with the Netherlands homeland under the constitution. The southern group, consisting of Curaçao and Bonaire, are known informally, together with Aruba, as "the ABCs." (Aruba is a self-governing part of the Netherlands and is not part of the Netherlands Antilles; however, it shares much of its culture with the other islands.) The northern group, consisting of Saint Eustatius (Sint Eustatius; Statia), Saint Martin (Sint Maarten), and Saba, are known informally as the "Three S's." Curaçao (home of the capital city, Willemstad) is located at 12°12′ N and 68°56′ W; Saint Martin at 18°03′ N and 63°05′ W. Although the official language is Dutch, most people also speak English, and many speak Spanish; the lingua franca, however, is Papiamento, a language based on Portuguese but with infusions of Dutch, Spanish, and English as well as of African and Indian languages. Racially and ethnically, the population of 183,500 is mixed. Most of the people (85 percent) are of mixed Black African descent, and the rest are Carib Indian, Oriental, European, and Latin.

Each island has had a somewhat different history, but

common to all was conflict among European powers over ownership and at least one change of hands, and in the case of Saint Martin sixteen changes of ownership. Generally speaking, the Spanish lost interest in these islands because they found little of economic value and, in particular, no gold.

The islands have been autonomous since 1948, even though the Dutch Crown appoints the governor, who, since the 1960s, has been Antillian. Crown influence is further limited in that the governor's power is used only by the Council of Ministers. The legislature is the Parliament, which consists of fourteen members from Curaçao, three from Bonaire, three from Saint Martin, one from Saba, and one from Saint Eustatius. In addition, each island has its own council and lieutenant governor. The Netherlands Antilles has its own independent court system.

Economic development is greatest on Curaçao, which has a tourist industry, petroleum refining and shipment, and manufacturing, primarily of electronics components. Saint Martin has a developed tourist industry as well, and Bonaire has petroleum-shipment facilities.

See also Arubans; Curaçao

Bibliography

Bor, Wout van den (1981). *Island Adrift: The Social Organization of a Small Caribbean Community, the Case of St. Eustatius.* Leiden: Royal Institute of Linguistics and Anthropology, Department of Caribbean Studies.

Juliana, Elis (1988). *Matrimonio i parto.* Report no. 5. Willemstad: Institute of Archeology and Anthropology of the Netherlands Antilles.

Koulen, Ingrid, and Gert Oostindie (1987). *The Netherlands Antilles and Aruba: A Research Guide.* Providence, R.I.: Foris Publications.

Ngawbe

ETHNONYMS: Guaymí, Move, Movere, Ngäbe, Ngawbére, Ngóbe

Orientation

Identification. The Ngawbe are the most numerous indigenous population in the Republic of Panama. They are often referred to in the literature as "Guaymí" and are reported to refer to themselves as "Guaymí" when working for wages on banana plantations, but in their own communities they refer to themselves as "Ngawbe" (the people). The term "Guaymí" is said to mean "people" in Muoi, the language of a now-extinct group that was closely related, possibly ancestral, to the present-day Ngawbe.

Location. In contact times (the early sixteenth century), the Ngawbe and other related (now-extinct) groups occupied much of western Panama, extending east into Coclé Province and south into portions of the Azuero Peninsula. During the centuries since contact, the Ngawbe have gradually lost much of their land because of encroachment and illegal occupation by nonindigenous peoples. They now occupy the rugged mountains and portions of the lower slopes of the three westernmost provinces of Panama: Bocas del Toro, Chiriquí, and Veraguas. (About 1,800 to 2,000 Ngawbe live on three small reserves in Costa Rica, having emigrated from Chiriquí, beginning in the 1940s, because of a land shortage.) Their Panamanian territory is estimated to encompass about 6,000 square kilometers. The boundaries have never been surveyed, and the government of Panama has not granted the Ngawbe any official title to their land.

Demography. The 1990 census of Panama reports a total of 124,513 Ngawbe in Panama: 63,712 in Chiriquí; 51,086 in Bocas del Toro; 6,971 in Veraguas; and 2,744 in other provinces. Of those counted as Ngawbe in Veraguas Province, perhaps 1,200 to 1,500 identify themselves as "Bugle." These numbers are very high compared to those of earlier censuses, especially for the provinces of Bocas del Toro and Chiriquí, and they indicate an average annual population growth rate of over 3.5 percent since 1960.

Linguistic Affiliation. Most of the Ngawbe speak Ngawbére; a few thousand, principally in Veraguas, speak Murire. Mutually unintelligible but closely related, both are languages of the Central American Branch of the Chibchan Family. Several dialects of both Ngawbére and Murire are recognized.

History and Cultural Relations

Little is known about the Ngawbe of precontact times. It is likely that the present population consists of an amalgamation of peoples who are descended from the original inhabitants of the territory that is currently occupied by the Ngawbe and by remnants of other groups who fled from Spanish oppression in the more accessible coastal areas of western Panama. Descriptions of Ngawbe culture, beginning with the account of Fray Adrián de Ufeldre (1682) attest to the considerable cultural continuity between many contemporary features of Ngawbe society and their traditional culture and social organization. Their closest cultural affiliations are with the Bugle and Teribe in Panama and the Bribri and Cabécar in Costa Rica. Early contact led to mestizoization of some segments of the population and isolation of other segments. For the isolated Ngawbe, contact with the outside world was sporadic and infrequent until the 1930s, when it dramatically increased in frequency and intensity. Influences in the late nineteenth and early twentieth centuries came mainly through the Ngawbe who engage in wage labor on the cattle ranches and the coffee and banana plantations in western Panama and through their contacts with Panamanians in the villages and towns while buying and selling goods. Additional contact has come about through schooling, mining exploration in their territory at Cerro Colorado, and the construction of penetration roads. Prior to the 1970s, there were no roads anywhere in Ngawbe territory. The Ngawbe of Veraguas have been more strongly influenced as a group by outside contact than those of Chiriquí and Bocas del Toro. This differentiation is reflected in their clothing, the degrees to which traditional practices are continued, and the rates of literacy and bilingualism.

Settlements

The Ngawbe live in highly dispersed small hamlets (_caseríos_), which traditionally consisted of about two to eight houses occupied by families related through kinship ties. The distance between one hamlet and another is usually a kilometer or more. This pattern of dispersed hamlets existed prehistorically. Rapid population increase has led to many larger hamlets, often occupied by members of two or more distinct kin groups. Because postmarital residence is ideally virilocal, Ngawbe hamlets tend to be composed largely of patrilineally related males, their wives, and their children. The traditional house type was round, with a conical thatched roof, low walls of sticks tied together, an earthen floor, a single entrance, and no interior partitions. This house type was widespread among the indigenous peoples of western Panama and eastern Costa Rica. It is now rare among the Ngawbe; the round houses have been largely replaced by rectangular houses with hip roofs, made of the same construction materials. Each of these two types of house has an interior platform under the roof, which is accessed by a log ladder and is used for storage of agricultural produce and personal belongings. A few houses now have corrugated metal roofs. The largest Ngawbe houses have a long dimension of about 12 meters. Some houses in Bocas del Toro are elevated on poles, and these dwellings occasionally have interior partitions.

Economy

Subsistence and Commercial Activities. One characteristic of the Ngawbe in the twentieth century has been a shift from a predominantly self-sufficient economy, based on sharing, barter, and reciprocity, to a mixed subsistence and cash economy (although swidden-based agriculture remains the main source of livelihood for most Ngawbe families). Crops raised by the Ngawbe include maize, millet, bananas, plantains, beans, rice, sweet manioc, _otoe_ (taro/ _Xanthosoma_ spp.), _ñampi_ (yams/ _Dioscorea_ spp.), sweet potatoes, squashes, sugarcane, pigeon peas (_Cajanus indicus_), chili peppers, coffee, and pineapples, as well as tree fruits such as peach palms (_Guilielma gasipaes_), avocados, papayas, mangoes, soursops (_Anona muricata_), guavas (_Psidium guajaba_), oranges, lemons, grapefruits, and cacao. The Ngawbe also cultivate tobacco, century plant (for its fiber), and gourds and calabashes (for use as containers). The crops that make up the bulk of the diet differ from one part of the Ngawbe territory to another, depending on environmental conditions. In Chiriquí and southern Veraguas, where a true dry season exists, maize, beans, bananas (harvested green and then usually boiled), and rice are of major importance. In Bocas del Toro and the Caribbean side of Veraguas, where there is no dry season, the Ngawbe depend heavily on various root crops, bananas, and peach-palm fruits during a part of the year. The livelihood derived from agriculture is supplemented by the raising of a few cattle, chickens, or pigs and, to a lesser extent today

than in the past, by hunting, fishing, and gathering. The Ngawbe traditionally hunted deer, tapir, wild pigs, and a number of small forest animals for food, but game of any kind has become scarce throughout much of Ngawbe territory. Most hunting is done with shotguns or .22-caliber rifles; few men today are skilled in the use of the bow and arrow. Fishing is done traditionally, using dams, weirs, nets, spears, bows and arrows, and fish poison; the use of hook and line has caught on only in a minor way. Foodstuffs are occasionally purchased on trips to town or from Ngawbe who have established small stores in the area. Some Ngawbe have formed small cooperatives, to reap the advantage of wholesale purchasing. Temporary wage labor outside their territory on cattle ranches and on banana, coffee, and sugarcane plantations is currently the major source of cash income for many Ngawbe families. Wages are very low and have not kept pace with the rate of inflation in Panama; working conditions are unhealthy in the extreme.

Industrial Arts.   The Ngawbe manufacture crude baskets for utilitarian purposes, large wooden trays, net bags of various sizes (some of extremely fine quality), stone pipes, grinding stones, wooden mortars, woven hats, hammocks, fiber string and rope, horsehair rope and bridles, and broad, beaded collars known as _chaquiras_. Except for net bags, baskets, and string, which all girls and women (and a few men) know how to make, items are made by part-time specialists and are obtained by others through trade. Ceramic vessels have been replaced by metal pots, and all knowledge of pottery manufacture has been lost. Although bark cloth is no longer worn as clothing, it is still made by some women for use as saddle blankets, bed coverings, and sanitary napkins.

Trade.   Among themselves, the Ngawbe traditionally bartered manufactured goods for other goods or foodstuffs and exchanged food among kin on a reciprocal basis. Since the early 1970s, cash purchases have become more frequent, even among kin, which is an indication of the strong penetration of the cash-based economy into Ngawbe culture. Since contact times, the Ngawbe have engaged in trade with nonindigenous peoples. Dependence on such trade has increased dramatically during the latter half of the twentieth century and is now largely cash based. Maize, beans, rice, coffee, domestic animals, and net bags are sold to Panamanian merchants in small quantities, especially by those families with no wage-labor income, in order to purchase items of Western manufacture that have become necessities—for example, cloth, clothing, machetes, salt, medicines, metal pots, blankets, and the shotguns, rifles, and ammunition that are used in hunting. Panamanian buyers occasionally travel into Ngawbe territory to purchase cattle. The Ngawbe raise horses for riding and for use as pack animals, and these, too, are sometimes sold to outsiders.

Division of Labor.   Men hunt, clear land for planting, weed fields, organize cooperative labor parties called _juntas_, tend cattle and horses, collect firewood during the rainy season, chop firewood, and engage in wage labor. Women cook, care for children, clean house, fetch water, collect firewood during the dry season, make clothing for women and children (male clothing is now almost entirely purchased), make net bags, harvest cultivated foodstuffs on a daily basis, gather some wild foods, and occasionally work for wages as domestics or as pickers during the coffee harvest, when they may accompany their husbands to the plantations. Both women and men (and sometimes children) plant crops, participate in major harvest activities, and fish. There is some evidence that women have become responsible for an increasing number of agricultural tasks, as men have become more occupied with cattle and wage labor. The division of labor among the Ngawbe is not rigid, however, and both women and men will do whatever needs doing, albeit sometimes reluctantly. Ritual and political activities are primarily organized and led by men, but women do attend these activities and have participatory roles in traditional rituals. Mainly spectators at nontraditional political gatherings in the 1960s, women have come to play an increasing role on such occasions.

Land Tenure.   Land is owned collectively by cognatic kin groups, and use rights are generally regulated by the senior male members. Use rights are inherited equally by women and men. In the past, when a man cleared climax forest, the land became his property, and his descendants had use rights. Today, however, climax forest is virtually nonexistent. Although the actual right to use land is complicated by several factors, use rights to land are generally lost if the lineal descendants of a person fail to exercise such rights for two generations and if the person is not living in a hamlet located on the land in question.

Kinship

Kin Groups and Descent.   Descent among the Ngawbe is cognatic. No clans or lineages exist, and there is no strong evidence for the existence of unilineal descent groups in the past. As a general rule, a person's kin group consists of all individuals known to be related through the second ascending generation. Residence in the same hamlet, as well as geographic distance and personal acquaintance, may alter this basic equation.

Kinship Terminology.   Ngawbe kinship terms generally distinguish sex and generation. Terms are bifurcate-merging in the first ascending generation, meaning that father and father's brother are referred to by a single term and mother's brother by a distinct term, and mother and mother's sister are referred to by a single term and father's sister by a distinct term. Cousin terms are Hawaiian, that is, all individuals recognized as cousins are referred to by terms for siblings. Sibling terms refer to siblings of the same sex and siblings of the opposite sex.

Marriage and Family

Marriage.   In Ngawbe society, traditional marriage is not simply a union of man and woman; it is the basis of a sociopolitical and economic alliance between two kin groups. Ideally, a symmetrical exchange of women occurs between two kin groups after a series of negotiations between the parents of the respective brides and grooms. Such arranged marriages are less common than in the past, but they still occur. There is no formal wedding ceremony. After a period of time during which the groom visits his wife in her parents' hamlet and provides gifts and labor for his father-in-law, the woman will move to her husband's hamlet. Virilocal residence is the ideal. In cases of nonexchange marriage or when the husband's group is experiencing a shortage of land, the young couple may reside uxorilocally. Polygyny is a male ideal and is quite common. Both sororal and nonsororal forms of polygyny occur. Betrothal of female infants to adult males, said to be common in the past, is now rare. It is often the case, however, that women marry shortly after first menses—at age 12 to 14—whereas men are normally in their twenties before they marry for the first time. First marriages tend to be quite stable, as are polygynous unions in which the women are in the kinship category of "sibling of the same sex" to one another. Nonsororal polygynous unions are less stable, with younger women often leaving their husbands in favor of unions with men closer to their own ages. Both the sororate and the levirate are acknowledged practices but are said to be no longer common. Cousin marriage is prohibited. All first cousins and parallel second cousins are excluded by this proscription; second cross cousins and others may also be excluded, depending on the way kinship terms are applied in particular instances. Members of the older generation claim that traditional forms of marriage are becoming less common, as many young people now marry for love. A quantitative sample taken in the 1960s did not support this claim (Young 1971, chap. 7).

Domestic Unit.   The household is the basic unit of production and consumption and may consist of a nuclear family (most common); a polygynous family of a man, his wives, and their children; a laterally extended family, usually consisting of two brothers with their respective wives and children; or a lineally extended family, containing members of three or more generations. Larger groups, usually consisting of individuals related either by blood or by marriage, often cooperate in subsistence activities.

Inheritance.   Although some personal property is buried with an individual, and the house is abandoned if a person dies in it, houses are generally inherited by the eldest married child who remains in the household. Other personal belongings, including domestic animals, are inherited by the children of the same sex as the deceased. To avoid conflict, cattle are likely to be given to children by elderly parents in anticipation of death.

Socialization.   Ngawbe children are normally given considerable freedom during their early childhood years, under the watchful eyes of parents and older siblings. Seldom are they harshly disciplined. At an early age, children of both sexes begin to assist their parents in daily tasks, learning by observation and imitation. Although such assistance is voluntary for boys into their adolescent years, it is generally compulsory for girls from the age of 4 or 5. Most play activities of young children also are imitations of adult activities of the appropriate sex. By late adolescence, children of both sexes are expected to do their parents' bidding without question. At puberty, girls are the focus of a ritual during which older women instruct them in appropriate behavior as wives and daughters-in-law. They are then eligible to marry if they have not already been betrothed. In former times, young males underwent a physically taxing puberty ritual that served to mark their transition from childhood to full adulthood and marriageable status. This ritual apparently has not been performed since the early decades of the twentieth century.

Sociopolitical Organization

Social Organization. There are no social or economic classes. Women and men cooperate in household decision making. Men dominate in the public arena, occupying most leadership positions in political and ritual affairs, but elderly women are listened to with respect. The cognatic kin group is the locus of socioeconomic power and authority. Cooperation in work activities beyond the household level is accomplished by reciprocal labor groups (juntas), organized by men. These labor groups, a major aspect of the structure of production, are normally made up mostly of consanguineally related men living in the same hamlet. Additional participants are recruited from among consanguines and affines in nearby communities. When a man organizes a junta, he owes equivalent labor to each man who helps him. The distribution of food to kin is a major feature of the structure of consumption. Formal patterns of sharing serve to distribute food on a large scale among near and distant kin during periods of localized scarcity. Men who are able to provide regularly for needy kin gain prestige, which can also be gained through sponsorship of rituals.

Political Organization. Ngawbe oral history is rich with descriptions of great caciques (chiefs) of the past, who supposedly exercised authority over regions within Ngawbe territory. During the nineteenth and early twentieth centuries, a system of appointed native governors existed. The actual power of the governors was directly related to their personal prestige. Throughout the twentieth century, men have been appointed by outside officials as _corregidores_ (magistrates), with responsibility for keeping the civil registry and serving as judges within their _corregimientos_ (municipalities). Since 1972, the Ngawbe have elected their own representatives to the National Assembly. In addition, there are currently three individuals who are recognized by the Panamanian government as provincial chiefs. Each has personally appointed several assistants, who represent the chief at the local level. Each of these chiefs has a personal following, but their authority is not recognized by all Ngawbe. In fact, the locus of Ngawbe political decision making remains predominantly the kin group, despite the current overlay of other political structures. Since the first Ngawbe General Congress in 1979, the provincial chiefs have organized several general, regional, and special congresses to discuss the problems that face the Ngawbe and to decide on courses of action. Legal title to their land has continued to be their greatest concern. Despite years of negotiation, the Panamanian government has refused to grant title.

Social Control. The kin group regulates the behavior of its members and provides moral and sometimes economic support in the disputes that individuals may have with members of other kin groups. Disputes over land rights and crop destruction by cattle are common. When disputes or crimes of any kind occur, the usual procedure is to select as arbitrator a man of acknowledged prestige and ability who is acceptable to both sides, whether or not he holds the official office of corregidor. The case is then dis-cussed at a nightlong meeting by all present, after which the arbitrator renders his judgment. Arbitrators are chosen for their acknowledged ability to render judgments that are deemed fair and equitable by both sides. If the accused and his or her kin do not agree with the judgment, however, they may attempt to reopen the case at a later date with a different arbitrator. The Ngawbe seldom seek outside authorities to settle either civil or criminal cases.

Conflict. Internal conflicts may occur over land, cattle, crops, women, or unpaid debts; arbitration is usually sufficient to resolve them (see "Social Control"). Most violence involves the use of alcohol. Current relations with the outside world have produced divisiveness, which sometimes threatens kin group solidarity: traditionalists wish to minimize contact with the outside world, liberals argue for greater involvement, and moderates prefer a middle course. Conflict between the Ngawbe and outside agencies has resulted in strikes on the banana plantations over wages and working conditions, public protests over government refusal to grant reserve status to Ngawbe lands and over other human-rights violations, and confrontations with government officials over the proposed open-pit copper mine at Cerro Colorado, in the heart of Ngawbe territory.

Religion and Expressive Culture

Religious Beliefs. Despite almost five hundred years of Christian—mainly Catholic—influence, the Ngawbe still retain certain traditional religious beliefs, which are manifest in their oral traditions and in certain rituals. Included are beliefs in a protector god, a god of lightning, various spirits of good and evil, and a number of culture heroes to whom the Ngawbe attribute godlike qualities. Wooden crosses placed on rooftops and on trails at the entrances to hamlets ward off evil spirits when someone is ill. The use of such crosses appears to be non-Christian in origin.

In 1961 a nativistic religious movement, known as the religion of Mama Chi (Little Mother) emerged among the Ngawbe as a result of the visionary experience of a young Ngawbe woman. This movement, at once transformative, revitalistic, and innovative, discouraged all contact with the outside world, prohibited the consumption of alcohol and the principal Ngawbe rituals at which alcohol is consumed (_balserías_ and _chicherías_), instituted periodic prayer meetings, and prophesied doom and destruction if the Ngawbe did not comply with the tenets of the new religion and great good fortune at the end of five years if they did. Throughout the 1960s, the Mama Chi religion had a profound social impact on Ngawbe culture. Today it has only a small following.

Religious Practitioners. Traditional religious practitioners are called _sukias_. They make predictions, interpret dreams, and effect cures for certain types of illness through communication with the deities and the spirits. Sukias were also included among the priests of the Mama Chi religion, and many remain among its adherents today.

Ceremonies. The major Ngawbe ritual is called _krun_ in Ngawbére, "_balsería_" in Spanish. Prohibited for a time during the heyday of the Mama Chi religion, it is once again being practiced. Krun rituals are grand events, with attendance numbering in the hundreds, and sometimes in the thousands. A man who serves as the host of a krun ritual achieves the pinnacle of renown and prestige in his region. Central to this ritual is the *etdabali*, the ritual-sibling relationship that exists between the host and his principal guest, who must also be a man of renown in his region. The ritual lasts for four days, with the central event, the throwing of 1.8-meter-long balsa sticks at opponents, taking place on the third day. Stick-throwing contests occur between teams from the host's and the guest's side, as well as between individuals. Only males participate in the stick throwing. Sponsorship of a krun ceremony requires provision of enormous quantities of food and drink, so a man must be able to call in obligations from a large number of kin. "Chicheria" is the Spanish term for several different Ngawbe rituals of lesser scale than the krun, all of which involve consumption of large quantities of *chicha* (maize beer), as well as singing, dancing, and music. The etdabali relationship is also central to these rituals.

Arts. Several rituals involve stylized singing and dancing and the music of flutes, rattles, and conch shells. The songs or chants are not sung in Ngawbére, but in what is reported to be a dialect of Murire. Face painting, usually featuring geometric designs in black, red, white, or a combination thereof, is seen most often at rituals, although the more traditional Ngawbe say that they paint their faces whenever they are happy. Of the plastic arts, beaded collars and finely made, colorfully decorated net bags are most notable. Some collars and bags are now made expressly for sale.

Medicine. Traditional curers (commonly referred to by the Spanish term *curandero*) have extensive knowledge of plant medicines and can cure illnesses that are not deemed to be the result of supernatural causes. Both men and women may be curers. Sukias are often curanderos as well. Most adults have some minimal knowledge of plant medicines. Nowadays, individuals with serious illnesses are often taken to clinics in Panamanian towns for treatment, especially if treatment by a curandero or sukia has proved ineffective.

Death and Afterlife. When death occurs in a house, the dwelling must be abandoned. For this reason, an individual on the verge of death will be moved to a temporary shelter near the house, if possible. An initial period of mourning begins immediately after death. Some personal belongings are buried with the deceased, some of her or his clothing is placed on top of the grave, and the head of the grave is marked by the planting of wild ginger and sometimes a small wooden cross. Dietary restrictions are imposed upon the close relatives of the deceased and are strictly observed. Both salt and meat are prohibited. Another ceremony is held at the end of about one month, at which time the eating restrictions are removed, all guests are given a meal that includes meat, and the day is spent in reminiscing about the deceased. It is not known whether any aspects of belief in an afterlife are non-Christian in origin.

See also Bugle

Bibliography

Bort, John R., and Philip D. Young (1982). "New Roles for Males in Guaymí Society." In *Sex Roles and Social Change in Native Lower Central American Societies*, edited by Christine A. Loveland and Franklin O. Loveland, 88–102. Urbana: University of Illinois Press.

Bort, John R., and Philip D. Young (1985). "Economic and Political Adaptations to National Development among the Guaymí." *Anthropological Quarterly* 58(1): 1–12.

Bourgois, Philippe I. (1985). *Ethnic Diversity on a Corporate Plantation: Guaymí Labor on a United Brands Subsidiary in Bocas del Toro, Panama, and Talamanca, Costa Rica.* Cultural Survival Occasional Papers, no. 19. Cambridge, Mass.: Cultural Survival.

Bourgois, Philippe I. (1989). *Ethnicity at Work: Divided Labor on a Central American Banana Plantation.* Baltimore: Johns Hopkins University Press.

Gjording, Chris N. (1991). *Conditions Not of Their Choosing: The Guaymí Indians and Mining Multinationals in Panama.* Washington, D.C.: Smithsonian Institution Press.

Johnson, Frederick (1948). "Caribbean Lowland Tribes: The Talamanca Division." In *Handbook of South American Indians*, edited by Julian H. Steward, Vol. 4, *The Circum-Caribbean Tribes*, 231–252. Bureau of American Ethnology Bulletin 143. Washington, D.C.: Smithsonian Institution.

Sarsanedas, Jorge (1978). *Tierra para el guaymí: La expoliación de las tierras guaymíes en Chiriquí.* Serie El Indio Panameño, no. 3. Panama City: Centro de Capacitación Social.

Séptimo, Roger A., and Luz Graciela Joly (1986). *Kugüe kira nie ngäbere* (Guaymí ethnohistory). Asociación Panameña de Antropología. David, Chiriquí, República de Panamá: Multi-Mipresos.

Torres de Araúz, Reina (1980). "Guaymíes (Movere)." In *Panamá indígena*, 215–268. Panama City: Instituto Nacional de Cultura, Patrimonio Histórico.

Ufeldre, Fray Adrián de (1682). "Conquista de la provincia del guaymí." In *Tesoros verdaderos de las Indias*, edited by Fray Juan Melendez. Vol. 3, Book 1, Chapter 1. Rome: N. A. Tunassio.

Young, Philip D. (1970). "A Structural Model of Ngawbe Marriage." *Ethnology* 9: 85–95.

Young, Philip D. (1971). *Ngawbe: Tradition and Change among the Western Guaymí of Panama.* Illinois Studies in Anthropology, no. 7. Urbana: University of Illinois Press.

Young, Philip D. (1975). "Guaymí Nativism: Its Rise and Demise." *Proceedings of the XLI International Congress of Americanists.* Vol. 3, 93–101. Mexico City.

Young, Philip D. (1976). "The Expression of Harmony and Discord in a Guaymí Ritual: The Symbolic Meaning of Some Aspects of the Balsería." In *Frontier Adaptations in Lower Central America*, edited by Mary Helms and Frank Loveland, 37–53. Philadelphia: Institute for the Study of Human Issues.

Young, Philip D. (1978a). "La trayectoria de una religión: El Movimiento de Mama Chi entre los guaymíes y sus consecuencias sociales." *La Antigua* (Panama: Universidad Santa María La Antigua) 11:45–75.

Young, Philip D. (1978b). "Los rituales guaymíes: Perspectivas simbólicos y culturales." *Revista Patrimonio Histórico* 2(1): 7–38. Panama City: Instituto Nacional de Cultura, Dirección Nacional del Patrimonio Histórico.

Young, Philip D. (1980a). "Marañon: A Report of Ethnographic Research among the Bocas Guaymí." In *Adaptive Radiations in Prehistoric Panama*, edited by Olga F. Linares and Anthony J. Ranere, 491–498. Peabody Museum Monographs, no. 5. Cambridge, Mass.

Young, Philip D. (1980b). "Notes on Guaymí Traditional Culture." In *Adaptive Radiations in Prehistoric Panama*, edited by Olga F. Linares and Anthony J. Ranere, 224–232. Peabody Museum Monographs, no. 5. Cambridge, Mass.

Young, Philip D. (1985). "Guaymí Socionatural Adaptations." In *The Botany and Natural History of Panama/La Botánica e Historia Natural de Panamá*, edited by W. G. D'Arcy and Mireya D. Correa A., 357–365. St. Louis: Missouri Botanical Garden.

Young, Philip D., and John R. Bort (1976). "Edabali: The Ritual Sibling Relationship among the Western Guaymí." In *Ritual and Symbol in Native Central America*, edited by Philip D. Young and James Howe, 77–90. University of Oregon Anthropological Papers, no. 9. Eugene: University of Oregon Press.

Young, Philip D., and John R. Bort (1979). "The Politicization of the Guaymí." *Journal of the Steward Anthropological Society* 11(1): 73–110.

PHILIP D. YOUNG AND JOHN R. BORT

Opata

ETHNONYMS: Ópata

The Opata today are a distinct ethnic entity, but their culture is similar to that of the non-Indian people of the area. The Opata live in the western foothills of the Sierra Madre Occidental, in the Mexican state of Sonora, between Hermosillo and the Chihuahua border. The villages that can trace direct Opata ancestry are Pívipa, Terapa, Tépupe, Guayacora, Turuachi, and Wachierieno. There are also remnants of a smaller Indian group, the Jova, scattered within the Opata region. The land that the Opata occupy is variegated and ranges from semiarid plains at 400 to 500 meters to higher regions reaching about 2,000 meters in elevation. Travel is difficult.

The Indians of Sonora numbered around 60,000 at the time of Conquest. The Opata were reduced to around 5,000 by 1750 because of epidemics and warfare with the Apache. Hinton estimated in 1959 that the Opata numbered between 500 and 600. The Opata language belongs to the Cahita Branch of the Uto-Aztecan Language Family. It is virtually extinct: only twelve speakers were registered in the 1990 census.

The Opata were sedentary agriculturists at the time of the first intrusion of the Spaniards in 1540. The Jova, on the other hand, were primarily gatherers. Missions were established by the Jesuits in 1614. The Opata rebelled against oppressive Spanish overlords in 1820 and were defeated. In 1825 they joined the Yaqui and Mayo in battles against the forces of the newly formed republic.

Archaeological evidence has revealed that at the beginning of the sixteenth century the Opata lived in two types of houses: large circular or rectangular semisubterranean dwellings and rectangular adobe houses. Today the Opata build two types of houses: one is rectangular with a stone foundation, adobe walls, and a flat roof; the other is made of sticks packed with clay. The houses serve as dwellings; there is often a separate kitchen house. Furnishings consist mainly of tables, chairs, benches, cupboards, wooden chests, beds, cots, and sleeping mats. Fenced flower gardens and animal corrals are commonly set up near the houses.

Most agricultural land is held privately. There are also some *ejidos*. Most Opata grow maize, beans, and wheat. Some grow onions, chilies, garlic, tobacco, watermelons, and citrus fruits. A few foods—such as *quelites* (edible leafy ground plants such as amaranths), watercress, nopal leaves, and nopal fruit—are gathered. In the 1970s cotton was introduced as a cash crop to add to the other cash crop, wheat. Men in land-poor families work for richer ranchers. Various crafts are practiced in Opata communities. Men make trays and wood and leather products.

Women weave baskets and hats from palm leaves. Pottery is also manufactured locally.

The primary kinship group is the nuclear family. Extended households are formed by coresidence with both maternal and paternal kin. Men have the highest authority within the family, but women also have a say in family affairs and have control over children. The Opata are monogamous. Marriage outside the ethnic group is permitted. Unmarried women with children live with their parents, and their children are accepted without question by the family and the community.

The political organization of the villages follows the legal structure set up by the state. There is no special indigenous form of government. Opata religion has been greatly influenced by Spanish Catholic missionaries; however, many of the festival dances seem to have a pre-Hispanic origin. The Opata perform a Pascola ritual during Easter, as do the Yaqui, the Mayo, and other Indians of Sonora. Besides celebrating Easter and Palm Sunday, each village celebrates the feast of its patron saint.

Bibliography

Basauri, Carlos. (1940) "Los Opatas." In *La población indígena de México*. Mexico City: Secretaria de Educación Pública.

Braniff C., Beatriz (1992). *La frontera protohistorica Pima-Opata en Sonora, México: Proposiciones arqueológicas preliminares*. Mexico City: Instituto Nacional de Antropología e Historia.

Hinton, Thomas B. (1959). *A Survey of Indian Assimilation in Eastern Sonora*. University of Arizona, Anthropological Papers, no. 4.

Hinton, Thomas B. (1969). "Remnant Tribes in Sonora: Opata, Pima, Papago, and Seri." In *Handbook of Middle American Indians*, edited by Robert Wauchope. Vol. 8, *Ethnology, Part Two*, edited by Evon Z. Vogt, 879–888. Austin: University of Texas Press.

Johnson, Jean Bassett (1950). *The Opata: An Inland Tribe of Sonora*. University of New Mexico Publications in Anthropology, no.6. Albuquerque: University of New Mexico Press.

Wence Angel, Jorge (1982). *Los opatas y los jovas*. Mexico City: Instituto Nacional Indigenista.

Otomí of the Sierra

ETHNONYMS: Hñãhñų, Ñạñ̃ų, Ñ̥ųhų, N'yũhũ, Otomí of the Eastern Sierra of Hidalgo, Otomí of the Sierra Norte de Puebla, Otomí of the Southern Huasteca

Orientation

Identification.   The Otomí could have been the original inhabitants of the Valley of Mexico, before the Nahua speakers arrived. Today they are split into two main groups: the Highland Otomí, living mainly to the north of the Valley of Mexico, and a smaller group, the Sierra Otomí, who live in the mountains of eastern Hidalgo and in adjoining parts of the states of Veracruz and Puebla. The Otomí of the Sierra refer to themselves as "Ñạñ̃ų," meaning "speakers of the Otomí language," or, more formally, as "Ñ̥ųhų," meaning "Otomí people."

The subgroup of Sierra Otomí who live in and around the village of Santa Ana Hueytlalpan, Hidalgo, are considered by some to be a separate cultural group. Their culture is adapted to the highland environment of the Tulancingo Basin; however, their commercial and social contacts are with the other Sierra Otomí to the east in the mountains, rather than with the Highland Otomí.

Location.   In 1990 the Sierra Otomí occupied the area within 20°7' to 20°46' N and 97°56' to 98°27' W. The environment in which the Sierra Otomí live is varied. Ninety-four percent of the population live in mountains ranging from 160 to 2,000 meters in elevation. The mountains are steep and folded. Monthly rainfall ranges from 0.5 centimeters in February to 50 centimeters in September at the lower elevations and from 0.6 centimeters to 44 centimeters during the same months at the higher elevations. Temperatures vary from a monthly average of 18° C in December to 28° C in June at the lowest elevations and from 14° C in December to 19° C in March at the highest inhabited elevations. The mountain climate has been classified as (A)C(fm)a(e) in the Köppen system. Natural vegetation ranges from tropical rain forest at the lower elevations to tropical cloud forest at the higher elevations. The natural vegetation has been cut back to make room for villages, fields, and pastures. The remaining 6 percent of the population live in the intermontane plain around the village of Santa Ana Hueytlalpan, Hidalgo, at 2,150 meters, where the rainfall and temperature patterns are quite different.

Demography.   In 1990 the Sierra Otomí population (as defined by language) was approximately 40,000. Their populations in the three states where they were located was: Hidalgo, 22,500; Puebla, 6,500; and Veracruz, 11,000.

Linguistic Affiliation.   Otomí is a member of the Otopamean Language Family, which is a subfamily of the Otomanguean Language Group. Among the Sierra Otomí there are many dialects, not all of which are mutually intelligible.

History and Cultural Relations

The Sierra Otomí culture arose from the complex civilizing influences that began in the Preclassic period in central Mexico. The legendary Toltec traversed the Sierra Otomí region, which was probably part of their empire. The Otomí were known to the Aztec, who regarded them as one of the important races in central Mexico. Between the fall of the Toltec Empire at Tula, in 1168, and the rise of the Aztec in 1400, the Sierra Otomí were isolated from the Highland Otomí.

At the time of the Conquest, the Sierra Otomí region was governed as a principality from Tutotepec, Hidalgo. The Indians rebelled against the Spanish but were put down several times in the sixteenth century. During the colonial period, the Sierra Otomí remained isolated and resisted the control of secular and ecclesiastical authorities.

Settlements

The Sierra Otomí live in Indian villages ranging in population from 500 to 1,500 persons, in smaller Indian hamlets, and in towns often politically controlled by a non-Indian elite. The villages and hamlets are dispersed, irregularly organized settlements with fields between the houses. Traditional dwellings are small, averaging 5 by 9 meters. The construction varies with climate: at the higher elevations, vertical or horizontal wooden walls and wood-shingled roofs prevail; at the lower elevations, vertical pole walls with thatched roofs are common. Stone masonry is often used for public or religious buildings. Modern houses are being built of concrete blocks, manufactured roofing, and reinforced concrete. The main agricultural structure is a crib for storing dried maize on the cob.

Economy

Subsistence and Commercial Activities. The Sierra Otomí are primarily subsistence farmers. They are smallholders who farm 1 to 3 hectares per nuclear family. Many own goats or cows. The crops grown depend on elevation. The main subsistence crops are maize, beans, chili peppers, *tomates,* and squashes. One seasonal crop of maize is grown above 1,500 meters. At lower elevations, two crops can be grown. Forests are exploited for timber and fuel. The people of Santa Ana also grow barley and alfalfa.

Public works are performed by work groups (*faenas*). Men are expected to work a prescribed number of days each year. The other costs of public works are paid by monetary assessments.

Industrial Arts. The peasant way of life includes the production of traditional manufactures such as pottery, cloth, clothing, agricultural tools, and furniture. At the higher elevations, the traditional female garb is a barrel skirt and heavy blouse, whereas at the warmer, lower altitudes, pleated cotton skirts and cotton dresses are worn. Manufactured cloth has replaced most handwoven cloth, and Indian garb for men is being replaced by modern manufactured clothing.

Trade. The region has many weekly markets. The main cash crops are coffee, peaches, and sugarcane. Subsistence crops are also sold. Some families specialize in trading. Traders may make trips lasting several weeks during which they buy, sell, and transport products to take advantage of market-price differentials between the highlands and the lowlands.

Division of Labor. Men do most of the cultivation. Women do most of the domestic work such as gathering water and preparing food. Both sexes share the work of harvesting. Women may work in the fields when and if men migrate to find well-paying jobs. The following occupations are often practiced in conjunction with peasant agriculture: shaman, mason, potter, woodworker, trader, store owner, bonesetter, herbalist, and musician.

Land Tenure. Land may be held privately, communally, or as an *ejido*. Forest land tends to be communal and belong to a village. Private land is purchased or inherited. Ejido land may be agricultural or forested and is allocated by a local ejido commission under national law. It is in the process of being privatized. There is a strong tendency toward keeping private landownership in the hands of local families. As a nuclear family matures, it receives parental land on which to farm independently.

Kinship

Kin Groups and Descent. The nuclear family is the most important kin group, but extended families are also common.

Kinship Terminology. Kin terms are bilateral. Sibling terms are extended to first and second cousins. In Ego's generation, sibling-cousin and affinal terms depend on the sex of the speaker. There are dialectal differences in the kinship terminology.

Marriage and Family

Marriage. There are three validations of marriage: native custom, marriage by Mexican civil law, and marriage by the Catholic church. The native custom is the most important. The groom's family petitions the bride's family. Later, if the negotiations are successful, the bride is escorted to the groom's house during a native ceremony called the "delivery (*däpi*) of the bride." The ceremony includes formal counsel, a procession to the groom's house, and a feast. If the parents do not agree, elopement is possible. Postmarital residence is virilocal and then neolocal.

Domestic Unit. The household is either a nuclear family or an extended family made up of parents, married children, and their offspring. In the extended-family household, each nuclear family usually has its own house within a residential complex.

Inheritance. Land is inherited by both sons and daughters but not necessarily in equal amounts. Parents determine who receives what. The amount of land inherited depends on the needs of the offspring and their ability to work the land. *Oratorios,* religious buildings housing family religious images, are inherited patrilineally.

Socialization. Newborn infants are secluded. Infants are swaddled until they are a year old. Mothers play with nursing children and tease them with their breasts. Complete weaning may not take place until 4 years of age. Infant play is relatively unrestricted. On the peasant farm, children perform traditional gender roles as soon as they are able. Schooling is encouraged for both sexes up to the third grade—and beyond, if there are facilities. Government-run secondary schools are available in the towns and some villages. Children from more remote communities who desire more education live with another family in a town and go to school there.

Sociopolitical Organization

Social Organization.   Kinship, residence, and religion are the primary forces organizing the society. Family-to-family *compadrazgo* (ritual coparenthood) knits the society together. Neighborhoods are organized in a peaceful manner by local oratory groups. A core family owning an oratory with images will select another person to be the ritual godfather. Supporters of the owning family and the supporters of the godfather regard themselves and refer to each other as *compadres* during the annual fiesta of the image.

Political Organization.   The vast majority of the population are Otomí Indians, but they share political power with a small mestizo elite. Profits to be made from trade, cattle ranching, and coffee production have attracted such elites into the sierra. *Municipio* government may represent Indian interests, but it more often reflects the interests of a town-dwelling mestizo elite.

The Indian villages are the seats of Indian political power. The political organization of the Otomí villages has changed in modern times. After the Revolution, powerful armed caciques ruled the villages and exploited the people. The caciques were driven out, and the villages set up governments supported by religious *cargo* systems. The cargo system allowed men to exchange wealth for political power through the sponsorship of religious rituals. The religious redistributive philosophy of the cargo systems is being challenged by Protestantism and other reforms. The power of the elders who gained authority from cargo systems is waning; civil officers are now often elected by the citizens of the village rather than appointed by the elders.

In a village, the maximal authorities are a group of elders and a judge (*juez*). The hamlets have "judges" who are executive officers with limited judicial powers; they take serious cases to the municipio president or to authorities in a nearby village or town.

Social Control.   Age is the primary source of authority. Older persons are often called "grandfather" or "grandmother" as a sign of respect. Although codes of conduct are unwritten, issues of proper behavior are constantly discussed, and young people receive counsel from their parents and others. Assisted by elders as necessary, the judge of a village hears a wide variety of cases, including breach of contract, domestic disputes, assault, abandonment, and failure to perform civic duty. Persons may be jailed or fined if they do not obey the village authorities.

Conflict.   The major source of conflict is land: neighbors may quarrel over the boundaries between their fields, and families may split apart over land inheritances. Other sources of conflict are breaches of commercial contracts, elopements, and adultery.

Interfamily feuding is maintained by a cycle of revenge. Sorcery is considered the equivalent of physical assault, so death from disease may be avenged by murder.

Conflicts are most easily resolved if they take place in a village, where the authorities can intervene. In the hamlets, conflicts can go on for generations without resolution. The effectiveness of municipio authorities in resolving conflicts varies with the degree of corruption of the judicial system. It is common for state-appointed judges to take bribes.

Religion and Expressive Culture

Religious Beliefs.   Religious beliefs have been affected by three major philosophies: Mesoamerican Indian, Catholic, and evangelical Protestant. The Mesoamerican Indian beliefs are influential and are undergoing a revival in some areas. Tradition has it that a life force, *zaki*, animates all beings—plants, animals, humans, and superhumans. The world of beings is arranged in a hierarchy. A benevolent god, Sacred Father, and Sacred Mother are at the top. Below them are more approachable beings, all of whom influence the lives of humans: Lord Sun (Maka Hyadi), the Lady of the Waters (Maka Xumpø Dehe), Grandfather Fire (Maka Xita Sibi), and Lord Earth (Maka Häi). A pantheon of lesser lords (*zidąhmų*), which includes Catholic saints, are beneath these "principal" lords. The life force of humans is weaker and vulnerable to sorcery. Rą Zudapi is an intercessor god to whom humans can appeal for influence with the higher gods. The lives of lesser beings—animals and plants—must be cared for by humans. The Sierra Otomí also believe in companion animal spirits, a special order of higher beings.

Most people believe that sorcery is possible. Evil airs are believed to cause sickness. The Sierra Otomí use the term *nagual* to refer to superhuman vampires and the companion animal spirits of sorcerers. Evil lords, such as Rainbow, Santa Catarina, and the Queen of the Earth, cause harm to humans. Some lords have a dual character, working evil at some times and good at others.

Sierra Otomí people who live near the towns that have priests often subscribe to Catholic doctrine. Many villages have been influenced by evangelical Protestantism, which rejects all other beliefs and provides an ideology for rejecting cargo service.

Religious Practitioners.   Shamans are religious specialists who deal with personal and familial problems with other beings—superhuman, human, plant, and animal. They are called *vądi* or *bądi*, meaning "sage" or "one who knows." Besides providing personal consultations and cures, they also participate in and preside over public ceremonies for pagan deities. Thus, they have priestly functions as well, but they are not organized in a bureaucratic hierarchy.

Advised by elders, village cargo holders carry out the ritual duties specified by their offices. These vary with local tradition. "Godfather" is the most prestigious ritual office. Lesser titles, not as prestigious because they involve fewer expenses, are "first *mayordomo*" (*tąbɛtoni*) and "second *mayordomo*" (*tedabɛtoni*). Even lesser titles are *tąmbekhą, dądaju,* and *dągwenda.*

Ceremonies.   The ritual flower ceremony (*costumbre*) is a model for the majority of the rituals. Carefully prepared flower offerings are delivered to a cross. This creates sacred space and time through a symbolic reference to the sun, the cross, giver of life. Sacred music and sacred dances are performed in an oratory. Offerings of food are left for whatever supernaturals are being summoned. The flower offerings are lowered from the cross, and the participants eat together. Flower ceremonies usually, but not always, take place during the night. Offerings may be left for the

Lady of the Waters, Lord Sun, Rą Zudapi, or Lord Earth at other times and in other places.

Ceremonies include rites of passage, calendrical ceremonies, cargo rituals, cleanings (_limpias_), and curing. The primary rites of passage are for birth, marriage, and death. Grammar and secondary-school graduations are also important ceremonies. Calendrical rituals are both pagan and Christian. An important traditional ritual is the Fiesta of the Cross, during which seeds are taken to the top of a sacred mountain to be blessed by shamans and imbued with the life force of the sun god. Cargo rituals are performed for images in public churches and public oratories. A village usually has two fiesta seasons, one during the growing period and one at the end of the year. All the cargo holders perform rituals at these times. Every oratory has an annual religious fiesta.

Curing rituals are performed by shamans. They practically always make use of paper figures that represent the life forces of the beings that the shaman manipulates. Typical rituals cleanse a house and occupants of evil winds, restore the life force of a sick person, counter sorcery sent against a client, control envy, and restore love between couples.

Arts. Art is not practiced for art's sake but appears in the various crafts that the Sierra Otomí practice. One of the most colorful and popular art forms is embroidery, which originated as decoration on women's blouses.

Medicine. Diseases are classified into infectious diseases sent by God, for which there is a medicinal cure, and evil diseases, in which there is a supernatural element. In the latter case, a shaman is consulted to neutralize the supernatural element. Whenever supernatural elements are involved, there is the ever-present possibility that the evil is manipulated by a sorcerer working with enemies of the patient.

Minor aliments are treated in the home, either with commercial pharmaceuticals or with a wide variety of herbal cures. Poultices, teas, and purgatives are the most common forms of herbal treatment. Because of federal and private programs, modern biomedicine has reached most of the Sierra Otomí; however, this alternative is sought only after less expensive native remedies have been tried.

Death and Afterlife. After a person has died, the body is washed and a vigil is kept for a day, during which friends gather and make offerings of food, liquor, and cigarettes to the departing soul. The body is buried at dawn the next day in the village graveyard. Godparents of death are sought. A nine-day vigil is kept during which a prayer maker (_rezandero_) sings prayers. The godparents deliver the cross on the ninth day, and it is taken to the graveyard at dawn. In the Tutotepec area, an altar called a "tomb" is erected in the house during the nine days.

Dead children receive the light-hearted music of "the little angels" played by a guitar and violin. Their souls go directly to heaven.

The souls of women who die in childbirth, people who drown, people who are killed by snakes, or people who die violently go to live with Thunder. The souls of persons who have died a natural death ordained by God journey across a river to find rest in heaven. Some souls who have been set loose by a particularly violent death may wander the earth like rabid dogs and bring sickness to the living. They are often conceived of as evil winds.

The souls return to their homes during the annual celebration of the Days of the Dead, first the little angels, then, on the following day, the adults. Altars are erected in the homes and sometimes in the graveyards. In Tutotepec during the Days of the Dead, a special ceremony recognizing the twelve months of the year is held in the graveyard of the ruined Augustinian monastery.

Bibliography

Dow, James (1974). _Santos y supervivencias: Funciones de la religión en una comunidad otomí, México._ Mexico City: Instituto Nacional Indigenista; Secretaría de Educación Pública.

Dow, James (1975). _The Otomí of the Northern Sierra de Puebla, Mexico: An Ethnographic Outline._ Monograph Series, no. 12. East Lansing: Michigan State University, Latin American Studies Center.

Dow, James (1986). _The Shaman's Touch: Otomí Indian Symbolic Healing._ Salt Lake City: University of Utah Press.

Galinier, Jacques (1979). _N'yũhũ, les indiens otomis: Hiérarchie sociale et tradition dans le sud de la Huasteca._ Mexico City: Mission Archéologique et Ethnologique Française au Mexique.

Galinier, Jacques (1990). _La mitad del mundo: Cuerpo y cosmos en los rituales otomíes._ Mexico City: Universidad Nacional Autónoma de México, Centro de Estudios Mexicanos y Centroamericanos; Instituto Nacional Indigenista.

JAMES W. DOW

Otomí of the Valley of Mezquital

ETHNONYMS: Hñahñu, Otomi, Otomíes

Identification

The term "Otomí" comes from _otomitl_ and, by inference, from _totomitl_ ("one who hunts birds with [bow and] arrow"). Sources on pre-Hispanic culture refer to "Totomihuatzin," who represents birds shot with arrows, and "Totomihuacan," which means "place where those who hunt birds with [bow and] arrow live." The Otomí in the Valley of Mezquital call themselves "Hñahñu," a term made up of the words _hña_ (to speak) and _hñu_ (nose) and signifying "those who speak a nasal language."

Location. The Valley of Mezquital is located in the Mexican state of Hidalgo between 20°11′ and 20°41′ N and 98°50′ and 99°20′ W. The area abuts with Queretaro on the west, with San Luis Potosí on the north, and with Tlaxcala and parts of the states of Mexico and Puebla on the south. The Valley of Mezquital is made up of twenty-eight *municipios*. Those with the highest density of Otomí speakers are Actopan, Alfajayucan, El Cardonal, Chilcuautla, Ixmiquilpan, Nicolás Flores, San Salvador, Santiago de Anaya, Tasquillo, and Zimapan.

Demography. The Mexican census of 1990 registered a total of 313,838 people in the state of Hidalgo, 5 years of age or older, who spoke an indigenous language. Of these, 117,393 were Otomí speakers. In the ten municipios in the Valley of Mezquital that show the highest density of Otomí speakers, the census indicated a total of 80,775 people aged 5 years or more.

Linguistic Affiliation. The Otomí language belongs to the Otopamean Branch of the Otomanguean Language Family. Other languages also forming part of this branch can be grouped into three subbranches: Otomí Mazahua, Matlazinca-Ocuilteca, and Pame-Chichimeca-Jonaz. Among the Otopamean speakers there are two distinct cultural traditions: the Otomí, Mazahua, Matlazinca, and Ocuilteca influenced by the highly developed Mesoamerican culture and the Pame and Chichimeca-Jonaz influenced by hunters-gatherers from northern Mexico. In the Valley of Mezquital there are fourteen variants of spoken Otomí.

History and Cultural Relations

The Otomí were firmly established in the valleys of Toluca, Tula, and Mexico before the first Nahua invasions. Theirs was a sedentary life-style, and they lived in peaceful coexistence with the Olmec and other peoples of the area. The first Nahua who arrived were the Toltec who established themselves by force toward the year 800, founding the city of Tula. The Otomí were incorporated into the Toltec Empire as a subject people. In the twelfth century hunting peoples (generally known as Chichimec) invaded the highlands; they destroyed the Toltec capital of Tula around the year 1200.

After the fall of Tula, the Otomí settled in Xillotepec and Chiapan in the Valley of Toluca. In 1220 they moved east and founded the city-state of Xaltocan to the north of the Valley of Mexico. In 1395 their territory was conquered by the Tepanec. From then on, many Otomí emigrated northeast and east, settling in the provinces of Meztitlan, Tutotepec, Cempoala, and Tlaxcala.

Under Aztec rule, the Otomí became tributaries. The Aztecs did not interfere very much in the affairs of the Valley of Mezquital because it was desertlike and unproductive, and therefore of little interest to them.

When the Spaniards arrived, the Otomí of the Mezquital allied themselves with them, envisoning the possibility of freeing themselves from Aztec rule. During the colonial period, the Otomí played an intermediary role between the Spaniards and the nomadic tribes of the north, thus avoiding serious conflicts and confrontations, especially during the sixteenth and seventeenth centuries. At the beginning of the eighteenth century, silver mining induced the Spaniards to colonize the area and to begin frontal attacks and open warfare against the Chichimec, a war that turned into one of extermination. The Otomí were made to work in the mines, and many fled toward the more arid areas.

Although they were not able to free themselves from servitude under the *encomienda* (labor-tribute system), the Mezquital Otomí nevertheless benefited from the fact that theirs was not a rich area and so did not attract a large number of White migrants; low population density allowed the Otomí to have extensive landholdings.

The Otomí were involved in the armed conflicts of the nineteenth century, including the War of Independence. Independence did not ameliorate their economic condition, however. Large landed estates were divided into small landholdings that became the property of criollos and mestizos, but the Indians remained laborers.

As a result of the agrarian reform of the 1930s, the Otomí of the Valley of Mezquital were given lands of very bad quality and low productivity, in the form of *ejidos*. Beginning in 1975, the semiarid lands began to receive drainage and sewage waters for irrigation from Mexico City, thereby becoming productive.

Economy

Subsistence and Commercial Activities. Each family group can count on an average of two hectares of land, either ejido land or their own small property. The economy is based on small-scale agriculture and wage labor. Cattle ranching is practiced on a small scale, and the production of handicrafts brings in supplementary income.

On unirrigated land the Otomí raise maize, beans, *nopal* (an edible cactus), squashes, and chickpeas, which form the basis of their diet, together with a juice (*aguamiel*) extracted from the maguey plant. Their diet is complemented with vegetables, fruits, the meat of wild animals, and products purchased with the scant income they obtain from selling their handicrafts and their wage labor.

It is quite usual for the Otomí to rent out irrigated land to the area's mestizo agrobusinessmen, who plant it with alfalfa and vegetables and hire indigenous people as day laborers or peons. Although the sewage waters used for irrigation are a grave health hazard, they are one of the few means by which the Otomí of the Valley of Mezquital can earn a minimal income.

Limited production and the small size of their plots have led the Otomí to emigrate. The migratory flow is directed mainly toward Mexico City and the conurban municipios of the state of Mexico, where the men are hired as day laborers in construction work and the women as domestic servants. Since the mid-1970s, the migratory flow—especially that of men—has also been directed toward the United States, where they are hired as agricultural day laborers in the state of Florida. In both cases, the Otomí make an effort to return to their communities of origin when village fiestas are held.

Industrial Arts. In Ixmiquilpan and surrounding areas, the Otomí make baskets, flowerpots, and a number of ornaments out of reeds. They make pot scrubbers and mats from maguey fiber, tortilla baskets from willow switches, and hats from palm leaves; the hats are woven and sewn by hand. They also produce dove-shaped rattles. In Alfajayucan, they make pottery water pitchers that are used to store water or *pulque* (beer made from maguey juice).

Trade. Commercial networks are controlled by mestizo intermediaries who buy products from the Otomí at very low prices. Since the beginning of the 1980s, the Otomí have struggled to take over the commercialization of their products. For example, women have turned their efforts to the organization of cooperatives for selling their handicrafts, and now have a store in Ixmiquilpan. Other organizational efforts—pertaining to the production and commercialization of cheeses and to the sale of birds and other products—have also been undertaken mainly by women, who have received the support and advice of government institutions and civil associations.

Division of Labor. The entire family participates in agricultural labor, and children begin to help from the age of 5 or 6. Young people, men as well as women, emigrate from the area, looking for wage labor; old men and the children are left to tend the fields. During planting and harvesting, the men return to their communities to take part in agricultural labor. Women are left in charge of small children and apply themselves to making handicrafts. They are assisted by their older daughters, who later will also form part of the migratory flow.

Land Tenure. Frequently, the same family will have a small plot within the ejido and another as their own small property, the latter obtained through purchase. In general, the total amount of land they hold does not exceed two hectares.

Kinship

Kin Groups and Descent. Families are nuclear, and residence is patrilocal. When an Otomí man marries, he takes his wife to live in his paternal home until their first child is born. At that point the couple will build their own house on land that has either been purchased or given them by the husband's father. Descent is reckoned bilaterally, although the paternal line is predominant, and the father's family name is inherited.

Family ties through consanguinity and affinity tend to be reinforced by *compadrazgo*, an institution that is of vital importance to the Mezquital Otomí because it creates a network of relationships and obligations of great permanence, which unite families during an entire lifetime. Compadrazgo is associated with Catholic sacraments, particularly baptism. The two baptismal godparents become the child's new spiritual relatives, who will guide him or her and be a substitute for the father, should this become necessary. The Otomí term for godparenthood is *shatsi*.

The *compadre*, the godparent of one's child, is a central figure in situations of mutual help; in family matters, he or she acts as an adviser, offering moral support, settling controversies, and participating in the solution of diverse problems.

Kinship Terminology. In several of the Otomí communities in the Valley of Mezquital, native kinship terms are still used. There are terms for mother, father, son, daughter, brother, sister, grandfather and grandmother, grandson and granddaughter, compadre and baptismal godfather. In several of these terms there is a marked recognition of sex as a referent, including the sex of the speaker, which is recognized in terms for brother, sister, father-in-law, mother-in-law, sister-in-law, and brother-in-law. The word for cousin (*primo*) has been adopted from the Spanish. There is no differentiation among cousins. No distinction is made between parallel and cross cousins, whether from the maternal or paternal side.

Marriage and Family

Marriage. Marriage is monogamous. Owing to migration, marriage of Otomí to nonindigenous partners is common, especially the marriage of Otomí women to mestizo men. Marriage generally takes place between 17 and 20 years of age in the case of men, and 15 and 17 years of age in the case of women. The marriage proposal is made by the man to his future in-laws. If the bride's parents approve, the betrothal period lasts between six months and a year. During this time, the young man will help his bride's family in agricultural work and will give presents to his future father-in-law.

Inheritance. Inheritance of land is through the paternal line. Women do not inherit land from their parents because they are incorporated into their husband's family; therefore they frequently inherit their husband's lands when they are widowed.

The oldest son receives part of the paternal landholdings when his first son is born; the same occurs with the other sons, except for the lastborn, who lives in his parents' home and will not inherit until his father dies. Migration diminishes the number of heirs and thereby reduces tension and intrafamily conflicts over landholdings.

Socialization. Socialization begins within the family nucleus and continues through early participation in work. With the declining importance of religious *cargos*, socialization is being transferred from the tutelage of elders to government primary school and, in some cases, to school hostels administered by the Instituto Nacional Indigenista. Children often drop out of school because they are needed to help with agricultural labor.

Sociopolitical Organization

Social Organization. Social organization among the Otomí is based on family relations and the network of mutual help that is interwoven through compadrazgo. The political solidarity created by the system of religious cargos has weakened, whereas the civil organizations linked to the national state have begun to take on greater importance. The religious festivals create cohesion and social identity. Migrants return to their communities at fiesta time and participate in social conviviality. Community work groups (*faenas*) and community service are still important in the construction of public works.

Political Organization. Otomí political organization is set by state and federal law. As a result of agrarian land reform, ejidos were created and, with them, organizational structures that link the community to municipio, state, and federal institutions.

Each ejido has an ejido commission that is the community's maximum authority dealing with problems having to do with landholding and agricultural work. In addition, there is a judge (*juez auxiliar*), and, in several cases, he is also the president of the ejido commission.

Social Control. Social control is exerted through the judge and, in some cases, a councilor (*juez conciliador*), named by the municipio authorities to solve minor conflicts, that is to say, those not involving bloodshed. Homicide is dealt with directly by institutions in charge of administering justice on a national level. The capital of the municipio is the regional political center; the highest political authority is the municipio president.

Conflict. In the 1980s primary and secondary school teachers in the state of Hidalgo, many of Otomí origin, mobilized to increase their salaries and gain control of their union. This struggle influenced other democratic movements in the municipios, generating electoral conflicts between political parties. Another source of conflict has been entrenched power holders, called caciques, who continue to dominate commerce and control the area's land and water resources. Finally, there are frequent conflicts over land boundaries.

Religion and Expressive Culture

Religious Beliefs. Catholicism is the predominant religion in the Valley of Mezquital. In the more isolated and traditional communities, practices and beliefs that are probably of pre-Hispanic origin persist, linking native and Christian deities, the cult of the dead, nahualism (the capacity of witches to turn into animals), and beliefs relating to the causality of illness. In separating itself from the civil arm, the religious system has suffered an appreciable loss of authority. Protestantism has spread out over the area since the mid-twentieth century.

Ceremonies. Religious festivals are the main type of community celebrations, but they have lost their relationship to the agricultural cycle. The times for the festivals are now dictated by the Catholic calendar; among the most important are the festivities for the patron saint of the local town or village. Another important ceremony is the celebration of the Day of the Dead.

Religious Practices. The Otomí perform private religious rituals in their homes. The houses have small oratories where images of Catholic saints are venerated. There are small niches in a corner of the home, where candles are kept lit in honor of the saints and of the dead. Failure to perform religious services can make the saints and the dead angry, bringing misfortune on the family or the milpa.

Medicine. Among the Otomí, folk medicine is one of the most important means of dealing with illness and death. Herbs are used on a daily basis for maladies such as headaches, stomachaches, sprains, the general feeling of being unwell, emotional tension, and so forth. They are used to prepare teas, infusions, creams for massages, and balms. There are few traditional medical specialists in the communities, except for midwives.

Death and Afterlife. Because they believe in life after death, the Otomí feel an obligation to venerate the dead at their family oratories, together with the saints. The dead can become angry and send misfortune when proper rules of conduct are not observed. On the Day of the Dead, their souls come down to earth for a time of conviviality with the living, so offerings—food, sweets, pulque, and everything the dead liked to eat when they were alive—are set out for them.

Bibliography

Basauri, Carlos (1990). *La población indígena de México.* Vol. 3. 2nd ed. Instituto Nacional Indigenista; Conaculta.

Bernard, H. Russell, and Jesús Salinas Pedraza (1989). *Native Ethnography: A Mexican Indian Describes His Culture.* Newbury Park, Calif.: Sage Publications.

Carrasco, Pedro. (1950) *Los otomíes: Cultura e historia prehispánica de los pueblos mesoamericanos de habla otomíana.* Mexico City: Universidad Nacional Autónoma de México, Instituto de Historia en colaboración con el Instituto Nacional de Antropología e Historia.

Kenny, Michael, and H. Russell Bernard, eds. (1973). *Ethnological Field Training in the Mezquital Valley, Mexico.* Washington, D.C.: Catholic University of America, Department of Anthropology.

Muñoz, Héctor. (1982). *El sistema de vida de los otomíes del Valle del Mezquital.* Cuadernos de la Casa Chata, no. 59. Mexico City: Cuadernos de la Casa Chata.

Nolasco Armas, Margarita (1966). *Los otomíes del Mezquital: Época postrevolucionaria.* Mexico City: Instituto Nacional de Antropología e Historia.

Tranfo, Luigi (1974). *Vida y magia de un pueblo otomí.* Serie Antropología Social, no. 34. Mexico City: Secretaría de Educación Pública; Instituto Nacional Indigenista.

Vázquez Valdivia, Héctor (1992). *Los otomíes del Valle del Mezquital, versión preliminar.* Mexico City: Instituto Nacional Indigenista.

CRISTINA OEHMICHEN BAZÁN

(Translated by Ruth Gubler)

Pame

ETHNONYMS: none

Orientation

As speakers of a language in the Otopamean Family, the Pame are linguistically related to the Otomí and the Mazahua. Present-day Pame are the descendants of the nomadic Chichimec, who lived to the north of the Aztec Empire, in central Mexico. The Pame Indians are divided into the Northern Pame and the Southern Pame. They live in the Mexican states of San Luis Potosí, Querétaro, and Hidalgo. The heart of the Pame region is the Sierra Gorda in San Luis Potosí. The terrain in this region is semiarid to temperate and ranges from 1,000 to 2,000 meters in elevation.

Assessing the total number of Pame is difficult because of varying Mexican government policies, which led to attempts, at differing times, both to maximize and minimize census counts of indigenous groups. The 1980 census recorded 5,649 Pame speakers; of these, 4,670 lived in San Luis Potosí. There are two dialects of the Pame language. The 1990 census listed 5,732 speakers of Pame, of which 5,669 lived in San Luis Potosí.

History and Cultural Relations

Since there is no archaeological evidence concerning the Pame, most of what is known about their history has been written since the Conquest. It is believed, though, that the Pame were part of the larger Chichimec, a group of nomadic hunters, in northeastern Mexico. The Chichimec formed a cultural boundary between the sedentary agriculturists of Mesoamerica and the nomadic Indians of the Mesa del Norte. That the Pame exist today can be largely attributed to the fact that they were able to accept a sedentary life-style under Spanish colonial rule much more easily than other Chichimec groups.

Neither the missionaries nor the military forces were ever fully capable of colonizing the Pame, primarily because the Pame lived in dispersed groups in the mountains and in the desert. The Spanish found it both difficult and undesirable to conquer peoples living in a land of such rough terrain.

The missionaries attempted to move the Pame into centralized towns, where missions could be established; however, in most cases, the Pame returned to their own homes. In this way, missionary attempts to establish communities in which to socialize and evangelize the Pame failed.

One of the most prolonged attempts at military pacification in Latin America occurred between 1550 and 1590. This conflict was known as the Chichimec wars. All of the various groups of Chichimec Indians banded together to defend themselves against the Spanish. The conflict centered on land; the Spanish wanted to mine deposits of ore that had been discovered on Chichimec land.

The Pame remained relatively uninvolved in this war. It is difficult to tell if this was because the lands they inhabited were marginal and thus not so greatly threatened, or if the Pame simply sought to stay out of the war. In any case, the Pame, unlike many of the neighboring tribes, were not destroyed.

During the colonial period, private landowners used their political power to usurp lands held by Pame Indians. This process, which continued until the Mexican Revolution, reduced many of the Pame to migrant laborers and landless peasants. The revolutionaries who gained power in the wake of the Mexican Revolution desired, among other things, to bring about agrarian reform. Many Pame were granted parcels of land that their ancestors had held; however, most of the land that was returned to the Pame was inadequate to provide economic subsistence to the Pame landholder.

At present, the Pame continue to live as migrant laborers and peasants on marginal lands. Throughout their history, the Pame ability to live on the periphery of more densely populated Mesoamerica has enabled them to continue to exist, while at the same time limiting Pame ability to succeed within the dominant community.

Settlements

The Pame do not generally congregate in communities; they prefer to disperse themselves over the region. Congregations of Pame are generally functions of either the necessity of living close to water, or of historical forces (e.g., the missionaries who were able to establish a few settlements).

Houses are constructed by young men, usually near their fathers' houses, of wooden-pole walls and palm roofs. The structures are usually one-roomed buildings; they can be rectangular, rectangular with one circular side, or two parallel walls with two circular sides. Some Pame can afford to use galvanized tin for roofing material. This is considered a symbol of higher status. Also, many households construct separate rooms for kitchens or bedrooms.

Economy

The base of the Pame economy is subsistence agriculture. Their staple crops are maize, beans, and squashes. They also raise goats. Fishing is carried out in rivers and lagoons at the lower elevations but is a relatively insignificant component of the Pame subsistence strategy. Additional crops grown to supplement income include sugarcane, peanuts, and coffee. Because of the difficulties of subsistence, many Pame have turned to temporary emigration to other areas, to earn cash wages.

The two main crafts practiced within Pame villages are _petate_ and _ixtle_ production. Petates are mats made by weaving straw or wicker together. Ixtle is a cord that is spun from the fibers of the maguey plant.

That men and women perform differing activities is a fundamental component of Pame culture. Male labor usually consists of agricultural work, carpentry, curing, trading, and performing duties as political and religious officials. The female sphere consists generally of household duties, raising children, cooking, making clothing, and the care of chickens and pigs.

On the weekends, many males journey to other villages to trade. Petates, chickens, and pigs are traded for needed items such as rope, shoes, food, and coffee. Very little trade occurs within villages.

Kinship

The Pame have bilateral descent, and kinship terms emphasize generational differences. Children obey their parents and consider it important to help their brothers and sisters when needed. Cousins are referred to by the same terms as brothers and sisters and are considered to be almost the same as siblings.

The most outstanding characteristic of Pame kinship is the system of ritual fictive kinship known as *compadrazgo*. The role of godparent confers respect on the individual. Compadrazgo also serves to create strong familial ties beyond biologically related kin. These relations become relevant during births, baptisms, weddings, and other social activities.

Marriage and Family

Children have close relations with their mothers, because it is they who take care of the home. As the sons grow, however, they start to form stronger relationships with their fathers. At the age of 6 or 7, a son accompanies his father to the milpa plot and helps with the agricultural duties. Fathers also begin to initiate their sons into the male world at this time. A daughter stays close to her mother until she marries, at which time she goes to live with her husband and her husband's family.

Marriage takes place early for both males and females: most women marry between the ages of 12 and 13, and most men marry between the ages of 15 and 17. When a young man has decided upon a marriage partner, he tells his father. His father, in turn, goes to the father of the potential bride to ask for the other man's daughter. During the next few weeks, the father of the groom will visit the family of the potential bride and bring gifts. If the potential bride accepts, the two are married.

Marriage entails two separate ceremonies. A civil ceremony is conducted to legalize the marriage; a religious ceremony legitimizes the marriage in the eyes of the church.

Although couples reside with the parents of the groom for a short period of time after marriage, the nuclear family is the basic household unit. When it is financially possible to start their own home, they move and create a new and independent household. Thus, both nuclear households and patrilocal extended-family households exist among the Pame.

Within the family, the husband makes decisions regarding family affairs; however, if a grandparent lives within the household, he or she will often acquire the status of *jefe* (head).

Sociopolitical Organization

The civil government of a village consists of a central governing officer and a hierarchy of lesser offices that are filled by members of the community. It is important to note that most of these offices are filled by mestizos and not by Pame Indians.

The religious organization involves the Indian population more closely. There are a number of important religious offices that are filled by members of the community, the most important of which is that of *mayordomo*. Individuals hold the office of mayordomo for a period of one year, during which time they are responsible for cleaning the chapel and furnishing money for the fiestas during which the saints are celebrated. Both a man and his wife have duties to perform, and this office confers upon them a high degree of status and prestige.

Religion and Expressive Culture

Pame beliefs are a combination of traditional forms of religion and the Catholic religion, which was brought to them during the colonial period. That Pame beliefs are syncretic is demonstrated by the fact that the Pame use the same term for the Sun and the Catholic God, and the same term for the Moon and the Virgin Mary.

Pame beliefs are dominated by a belief in *muertos* (spirits of the dead), *brujas* (witches), and *dioses* (gods). The Pame also believe that there are a number of spirits, called *nahuales*, which take the form of animals. These spirits are believed to be the cause of many illnesses and evil in general. Within the Pame cosmology, the central religious actors are the *curanderos*, or curers. Some illnesses are considered to be caused by natural conditions, but most are believed to be caused supernaturally.

Besides the general ceremonies of birth, baptism, and funerals, the Pame conduct many other rituals. These include the annual fiestas of the patron saints and the ritual veneration of saints and ancestors on altars within their homes.

Upon death, the deceased is dressed in fine clothes and laid out for observation by relatives. The family gathers together. They all eat, and the men drink *aguardiente*. The next morning the corpse is buried with items that may be needed in the afterlife, such as tools, food, water, and money.

Bibliography

Chemin, Dominique (1980). "Rituales relacionadas con la Venida de la lluvia, la cosecha y la manifestaciones atmosféricas y telúricas maléficas en la región Pame de Santa Maria Acapulco, San Luis Potosí." *Anales de Antropología* 17(2): 67–97.

Chemin Bässler, Heidi (1984). *Los pames septentrionales de San Luis Potosí.* Mexico City: Instituto Nacional Indigenista.

Friedlander, Judith (1986). "The National Indigenist Institute of Mexico Reinvents the Indian: The Pame Example." *American Ethnologist* 13(2): 363–367.

Manrique C., Leonardo (1969). "The Otomí." In *Handbook of Middle American Indians,* edited by Robert Wauchope. Vol. 8, Ethnology, Part Two, edited by Evon Z. Vogt, 682–722. Austin: University of Texas Press.

Soustelle, Jacques (1937). *La famille otomi-pame du Mexique central.* Travaux et Mémoires de l'Institut d'Ethnologie. Paris: Université de Paris.

Soustelle, Jacques (1967). *The Four Suns.* London: Ebenezer Baylis & Son.

IAN MAST

Paya

ETHNONYMS: Pahaya, Pawyer, Pech, Pesch, Popya, Poya, Poyai, Poyer, Seco, Taia, Tawka, Taya

The Paya live in and around eleven villages in northeastern Honduras. The terrain in this area consists of pine- and savanna-covered upland valley. The greatest concentration of Paya Indians is in the towns of Dulce Nombre de Culmí and Santa María del Carbón in the department of Olancho; nevertheless, the Paya language is nearly extinct in the latter town. The language itself is difficult to classify. It is hypothesized that it is most closely related to the Chibchan and Cariban languages of South America. The size of the Paya population has been drastically reduced by assimilation and colonial pressures. In 1990 there were only 1,800 Paya Indians, and, of these, only a few hundred were able to speak the Payan language. Even more striking is a report in 1982 that documented only 17 "racially pure" Paya Indians.

Before the Conquest, there were thousands of Paya inhabiting up to 26,000 square kilometers. They were a seminomadic people that hunted, fished, and cultivated various crops. On his third trip to the New World in 1498, Christopher Columbus encountered the Paya and called them the Taia. During the colonial period, the Paya were ravaged by European diseases and military attacks by their neighbors, the Miskito Indians.

In 1864 the Paya were awarded legal title to their communal lands; however, the Honduran frontier continued to move eastward and eventually enveloped the Paya. Because of this, the Paya presently inhabit separate villages rather than a specific region. By the 1920s, only 600 Paya were left. Since the 1950s, loggers and immigrants have continued to exert pressure on the lands of the Paya. This pressure has resulted in erasing almost all vestiges of traditional culture.

There are, however, groups of Paya living in Las Marías that still maintain much of the traditional life-style. Although they have traded bark breechcloths for Latino clothing and blowguns for shotguns, they continue to catch iguanas by hand, to catch fish with handmade harpoons, and to navigate the waters of the local rivers in dugout canoes. Likewise, they adhere to traditional swidden agricultural practices. They raise maize, beans, and cassava with simple implements such as hoes, digging sticks, and machetes.

Many also continue to raise *Opuntia*, a *nopal* cactus plant on which the cochineal insect feeds. Cochineal is still used as a food and cosmetic dye. Where animals have not been overhunted, the Paya make use of deer, monkeys, wild pigs, wild turkeys, iguanas, and tapir.

Bibliography

Carranza, Sucelinda Zelaya (1984). "Santa Maria del Carbon: Un expediente de tierras payas." *América Indígena* 44(3): 461–466.

Kolankiewicz, Leon (1989). "The Pesch of Honduras Face Uncertain Prospects." *Cultural Survival Quarterly* 13(3): 34–36.

Miller, Marc S. (1993). *State of the Peoples: A Global Human Rights Report on Societies in Danger*. Boston: Beacon Press.

Olson, James Stuart (1991). *The Indians of Central and South America: An Ethnohistorical Dictionary*. Westport, Conn.: Greenwood Press.

Pima Bajo

ETHNONYMS: Lower Pima, Óob, 'O'odham, Ó Odham

Orientation

Identification. The Pima Bajo, or Lower Pima of northern Mexico, are related to other Piman-speaking groups living in southern Arizona. These latter groups were referred to by Spaniards as the "Pimeria Alta" and today consist of various groups in southern Arizona and a small group living across the border in northern Mexico. The lowland Pima identify themselves as 'O'Odham (people, tribesman, person, human) and the highland, or Mountain Pima as Taramil 'O'Odham (Tarahumara-like people). The highland Pima refer to themselves as Óob and to the lowland groups as Ó Odham. Spanish missionaries called them all "Pima," after the indigenous term for "nothing" or "I don't know."

Location. The Pima Bajo were situated aboriginally in their current location, and in a larger territory in east-central Sonora and the adjacent areas in western Chihuahua. They were split into two groups: the lowland, desert branch of central Sonora, consisting of the Névomes living on both sides of the middle Río Yaqui and the Ures located near the confluence of the Sonora and San Miguel rivers, and the highland branch, the Yécora of the Sierra Madre Occidental in and around the towns of Yécora and the Tutuaca between the headwaters of the Papagochi, Tutuaca, and Mayo rivers near the Sonora-Chihuahua border. Today the Névome may be extinct, whereas the Ures group is rapidly acquiring the social and material traits of the local non-Indian population.

Demography. At the end of the seventeenth century, the Pima Bajo population was estimated at less than 6,000 and that of the Mountain Pima at less than 2,000. During the nineteenth century, the Pima Bajo experienced an abrupt decline in numbers. Disease and warfare did not decrease their numbers as they had in other cases of Spanish contact, but an ever-increasing number of Spaniards and mestizos displaced them from their native soil. In the early 1990s the best estimates of the lowland Pima Bajo population were about 200 and, of the highland Pima Bajo, between 1,500 and 2,000 persons, with some estimates ranging as high as 4,000. Population size is difficult to estimate accurately because the Pima Bajo live in small scattered clusters and migrate in search of temporary work in surrounding mines, mills, and lowland towns for work in agriculture.

Linguistic Affiliation.   The Pima Bajo language is part of the Northern Branch, or Tepiman, of the Uto-Aztecan languages; thus, the Pima Bajo are grouped linguistically with the Tepehuan of Durango and southern Chihuahua and the Northern Piman speakers in Arizona. Lowland and Highland Piman are related languages, and each is characterized by two dialects. One of the lowland dialects is now extinct. The other lowland dialect is similar to the Pima Alta language spoken by the Papago, now called the Tohono O'Otam.

History and Cultural Relations

All Piman-speaking people probably originated near the present Arizona-Sonora border. After the Pima Bajo had moved south, an intrusion of the Opata and, later, other groups such as the Apaches, split the Upper from the Lower Pima. Spanish explorers visited the Pima in the lower reaches of the Río Yaqui in 1533 and took slaves. The early main route to the north, pioneered by Álvar Núñez Cabeza de Vaca's retreat from the Texas Gulf (1536), passed through Pima Bajo and Opata country, up the Sonora and other rivers into the Sierra Madre. Some explorers using this route included Marcos de Niza (1539), Francisco Vásquez de Coronado (1540), and Francisco de Ibarra (1565). Spanish miners penetrated the region of the upper Río Sonora in search of minerals in the late sixteenth century, but missionaries and settlers had a greater impact on the Pima Bajo in the seventeenth.

Jesuit priests contacted the first Pima in the lower Río Sinaloa in 1591 and established missions. Father Eusebio Francisco Kino arrived in the region in 1697, and soon thereafter Jesuits established a system of missions among the Pima Alto, protected by a line of presidios. The Franciscans worked with the Opata to the north. Except when the Pima rebelled against the Spaniards with the neighboring Tarahumara in 1697, with the Yaqui and Mayo in 1740, and with the Seri in 1751, the relationship between priests and Indians was largely peaceful, although paternalistic and exploitative.

During this period of early exploration and Spanish settlement, the Mountain Pima accepted elements of western European culture—particularly social and political organization, agricultural products and technology, and Catholicism. At the same time, the Jesuits tried to administer the Pima Bajo more effectively by gathering them into centrally located villages, where they could be converted and taught the principles of Christianity as well as Spanish social and political customs. This process was called *reducción.* Many Pima preferred their traditional *ranchería* life-style, which gave them freedom and arable lands for agriculture. The little resettlement that did occur was mitigated by a high death rate from diseases contracted through closer contact with Europeans. At this time, the Pima worked both Jesuit farmlands and Spanish mines, as

well as their own farms. Sometimes mine officials removed Pima from the mission without consulting the missionaries and made the Pima work for goods and clothing assessed at inordinately higher prices, creating a form of debt peonage. In addition, Spanish settlers invaded Indian property for more land for cattle grazing.

In 1767 the Jesuits were expelled from the New World by order of the king of Spain. The Jesuits had faced conflicts with cattlemen and miners and had been unable to maintain the production of food and livestock because of constant attacks by raiding Seri and unrest among the Pima Bajo, particularly those in Névome country. After a brief hiatus following the Jesuits' departure, Franciscans replaced them and enlarged the mission fields and herds. Apache raiding after the early 1700s reduced mining activity and forced the Spaniards out of Pima Bajo territory by the end of the century. At first, the attacks were only against small groups of Pima caught unawares while cultivating or traveling. Residents of outlying *ranchos* moved into Maycoba for protection and only returned to their fields under armed escort. Even Yécora lay ruined and deserted in the 1790s. At one point, the Maycoba Pima purchased the church santos (statues of patron saints) from the Spanish to help them defeat the Apache. Raids increased after the mid-1850s as pressures from U.S. cavalry troops made life difficult for the Apache in the north.

After the 1910 Revolutionary War, according to Pima accounts, the new Mexican government acknowledged the help of the Pima in Maycoba in combating the Apache raiders by presenting them with *ejido* land. The war led to a large migration of Mexicans into northern Sonora, especially in the 1930s; these migrants took over Pima lands and watering places. Some Pima Bajo, such as those in Yécora and Sahuaripa, migrated into deeper recesses in the Sierra Madre rather than face open conflict. Like many of the Sierra Indian groups, the Pima Bajo have been gradually displaced by non-Indians and absorbed into the larger Mexican society. Ceremonial rituals and other cultural practices are more intensely observed by the highland than by lowland groups, and there is more separation—and conflict—between highland Pima and neighboring town-dwelling mestizos than is the case with the lowland groups.

Settlements

The Pima Bajo live in isolated homesteads called ranchos, in rock shelters, and in dwellings on the outskirts of mestizo towns or cities. Each rancho is made up of one or more households linked by kinship ties and surrounded by small farms. The word *paraje* is used by Dunnigan (1981a) to refer to a group of ranchos (similar to what the Spaniards called a ranchería) as well as to a neighborhood found in towns. Pima also live in the traditional Indian town of Maycoba, the ranching town of Yécora, two sawmill towns, in lowland towns and cities, and in a *colonia* in Cuidad Obregón. A *campo* is a small camp of agricultural workers similar to the migrant labor camps inhabited by undocumented workers in the United States. A few Mountain Pima use caves. Most Pima dwellings are constructed of adobe, wattle and daub, or pine boards or shingles nailed over a one-room pole framework. Most dwellings have an enclosed porch attached for cooking. *Ramadas,* or brush-roofed habitations with no walls or low walls of piled stones, are used as temporary structures in warmer seasons, when Pima work away from home. Occasionally a _huki_, a semisubterranean one-room structure with a slanted roof, is still used as a place for keeping weaving fibers moist and as a cool place for women to make baskets, mats, and hats.

Economy

Subsistence and Commercial Activities. Pima Bajo cash income is derived from agricultural wage labor for mestizos (who are called "Blancos" by the Pima), or in large agribusinesses near Ciudad Obregón, and from labor in the mining and timber industries. Mine wages exceed those from rancho farming, but such work is rarely permanent; miners face frequent layoffs and long periods of unemployment. Sawmills likewise tend to offer only temporary employment.

Pima Bajo have traditionally depended on agriculture. Many Pima, even while working in the mines or sawmills, maintain an economic partnership with family members who remain at the rancho. Working sons may send money home or return to help with the harvest or other agricultural work. In the highlands, the average Pima usually farms 0.4 hectares of arable land intensively along a river and keeps 1.6 hectares for grazing or hoe cultivation on hillsides. The basic crops are beans and maize; these are supplemented with squashes, wheat, potatoes, watermelons, and legumes. Flowers, tomatoes, green beans, chilies, onions, garlic, and other vegetables are grown in small fenced gardens. Pima Bajo maintain pear, peach, and, occasionally, apple trees; they also raise a few chickens and turkeys. Cattle are rare, and horses, mules, and oxen even more rare. The gathering of food plants, hunting, and fish trapping with narcotic plants are still very important during periods of drought and food shortage.

Economic exchange includes reciprocal relations with brothers, brothers-in-law, nephews, and paternal uncles, as well as other affinally and consanguineally related persons or _compadres_. The exchange may involve the loan of a draft animal or a labor partnership known as a _medias_, in which one partner provides seed and labor and the second land and labor. In times of crisis, such as death, childbirth, drought, or conflicting obligations, a type of generalized reciprocity exists: assistance will be given without expectation of immediate or near-future return. When persons not of the nuclear family or of a different ethnic group are involved, the reciprocal relationship will be more temporary and quid pro quo; a Pima farmer might exchange with a Blanco store owner wild honey for cheese, venison for nonperishable goods, or palm fiber for a share in the profits of hat and mat making. In a situation in which many Pima are unable to become economically self-sufficient because of an inadequate supply of good land or a lack of draft animals, plows, or seeds, the pooling of resources and the striking of bargains with Pima and non-Pima alike make economic survival more likely. In addition, this arrangement can strengthen family relationships, provide a greater variety of foods, and act as an insurance policy against the failure of a part or all of one's crops.

Despite the potential effectiveness of economic exchange in keeping Pima families and culture intact, an in-creasing number of Mountain Pima become migrant laborers by necessity. Many move because of conflicts over the use or ownership of land and poor prospects for employment in the local mining and lumber industries. With their families or alone, they leave home in small groups for destinations in Ciudad Obregón, Hermosillo, or Navajoa to perform unskilled labor such as tending irrigating ditches, chopping cotton, and harvesting crops. The more experienced Pima may even travel a circuit of Sonoran towns and cities where peak work seasons occur at different times. Most of those who move away from the mountains frequently maintain home ties through economic and social reciprocity during visits and by receiving visitors from the mountains. Some individuals who remain at the workplace for many years lose their ties with Pima culture and become absorbed into the larger Mexican society.

Division of Labor. Within the core nuclear family, women usually are in charge of the domestic work such as cooking, washing, housekeeping, weaving, pottery making, and child care. Adult males are responsible for heavy labor such as farming and house building, and the young children are expected to watch the crops after seeding to protect them from birds and other scavengers. Older children assist their parents.

Land Tenure. The Pima were found living in what the Spaniards called rancherías, small groups of households surrounded by cultivated fields. The surrounding lands were used in common for small slash-and-burn cultivation, hunting, fishing, and gathering of medicinal plants. Over time, the Pima have lost possession of most of their land to intrusive Spaniards and mestizos. Outsiders considered the land open, unused, and therefore free to be settled. They characterized as grossly inefficient the land-tenure practices of the Pima, who used shifting cultivation of small tracts of land and communal lands for hunting and other purposes. The outsiders reasoned that, because the land was not being used appropriately from their point of view, they could assume ownership. Blanco ranchers today believe that only the farming of large tracts of land is efficient and good for the state's economy. The Pima continue to believe that the land has been theirs for centuries and that the mestizos are intruders who have gained possession through dubious means. The Pima also have ejidal lands, which are cultivated in individual plots and held in common.

Kinship

Kin Groups and Descent. The bilateral kindred of the Pima Bajo typically consists of nuclear families that have increasingly intermarried so that affinal and consanguineal connections have produced a pattern of endogamy. The latent function may be to retain possession within the kin group of sufficient land to assure subsistence production. The pattern may also result from the small size of the intermarrying group. Among the Mountain Pima, nuclear families frequently live on ranchos or small farms, often with extended family in the household or in the parajes. The unification of family groupings through the association of siblings allows for the greatest reciprocity in economic and social terms.

Kinship Terminology.   Kinship usage varies considerably among the different segments of Pima society. Generally persons under age 40 and those living in Blanco communities tend to use terminology modeled on the Spanish use. Modification of Pima kinship terminology has occurred in two ways: reduction in the number of kin categories recognized in speech, and extensive substitution of Spanish words for Pima terms. In particular, the bifurcate collateral classification for parents' siblings has been collapsed into a lineal system by applying the same term for relatives previously designated by different words; both mother's and father's sister came to be addressed as *tía* (Spanish: aunt) rather than by the separate terms indicating age (younger or older) and designating father's or mother's side of family. The same changes hold true for the father's side of the family, with use of the Spanish term *tío*. Similar changes occur in designations of the child's and grandparental generations.

Fictive Kinship.   The custom of selecting cosponsors for various ceremonies, called *compadrazgo* (ritual coparenthood), has been adopted from Spanish conventions. This institution takes on the manifestations of fictive kinship, replete with all the reciprocal social and economic relationships that characterize kin ties. The most important aspect surrounds the Catholic ritual of baptism, with those for marriage and confirmation generally missing among the Pima. Compadres, as the cosponsors and parents of the sponsored are called, may on occasion be Blancos, but they are more frequently Pima and are usually selected from close blood relatives and affines of the parents. The presence of Pima terms for the male and female compadres may indicate that it overlays an ancient Pima practice, or it may mean that Pima terms have been applied to this institution. The child being sponsored (Pima: *vak már*; Spanish: *ahijado*), calls his or her sponsors *padrino* and *madrina*. The parents of the child and the sponsors establish a lifelong relationship involving gift giving and respect; they refer to each other as *vak 'dog* and *vak dáad* (in Pima, the reciprocal terms in Spanish being compadre and *comadre*). As with their mestizo neighbors, the most important relationship between nuclear families is with compadres.

Marriage and Family

Marriage.   Young Pima men and women enter into a conjugal relationship without a church or indigenous ritual, and the first household is usually neolocal within the same paraje as the husband's parents. Common residence for centuries in a restricted environment has led to a high rate of local endogamy between persons within the same or nearby communities. If a Pima woman has a conjugal relationship with a non-Indian, a situation which is rare (a male Pima marrying a non-Indian being even rarer), she usually lives with Pima relatives and raises any offspring as Pima. The non-Indian husband visits occasionally, but eventually deserts the union.

Domestic Unit.   The basic unit of the Pima Bajo society is the nuclear family, with widowed parents or other consanguineal or affinal kin living in a one-room household with attached cooking shelter. The landholding unit, the rancho, sometimes includes an unmarried brother and sister or other combination of relatives. Mobile wage earners frequently attach themselves to the households of relatives at the place where they are seeking work, although this residency is not usually long-term. Male relatives will frequently return during planting or harvesting as part of the economic reciprocity established between both consanguineal and affinal relatives to ensure mutual survival.

Inheritance.   Land and sometimes livestock are inherited equally among married sons and daughters. The land, however, tends to be held as a cooperative working unit among siblings. The larger tracts of land thus made available with joint tenancy permit more efficient production and the setting aside of fallow lands. If land and cattle are scarce, daughters defer usufruct rights to their brothers. If a man only has daughters, sons-in law can inherit the land after a period of working it. Wage earners must return to help during planting and harvesting to retain the rights of inheritance.

Socialization.   Although little is known about the socialization process for Pima living in the lowlands or for females in general, young Yécora males working on the Maycoba ranchos of their immediate family or other relatives undergo socialization experiences quite different from those living in the towns. They learn to farm, hunt, fish, and collect wild plants and acquire knowledge of Pima subsistence techniques. During this time, they learn the importance of reciprocity and strong kinship relationships. They also learn good working habits and important cultural lore, such as mythology.

Sociopolitical Organization

Political Organization and Social Control.   When first encountered, the Pima appear to have had an elected headman. Early Spanish influences resulting in the involvement of Pima in military forays perhaps imposed military leaders called captain, general, corporal, and others. The names have been translated into Pima at times, so that it is difficult to discern original from later political structure. The leadership structure seems to have been more like that of the Mayo and Cora, even more like the pre-Hispanic Gila River Pima and the Mesoamerican pattern than that of the neighboring Tarahumara. Today political control involves ejidal, municipio, and Indian leaders. Indigenous political organization consists of an Hispanic-colonial imposed system of elected governors and assistant governors. A governor controls the affairs of the Pima residents in the town of Maycoba and the nearby ranchos. The governor represents the tribe in matters involving municipio and state governments and, with the aid of his assistant, keeps official census records, is responsible for health matters and the schools, and arbitrates domestic and other disputes. As one of the few literate Indians, he deals with outsiders, is used as an intermediary by mestizos in assembling community work groups for local public projects such as road building, and acts as a hiring agent for mestizos.

Beyond this indigenous domain, political control is handled by ejido officers, mostly mestizos. This involves dealing with municipio, state, and federal authorities; protecting landholdings; collecting taxes; and registering land. The chief ejido official, called the *presidente* or *comisario*, is responsible for acting as liaison among local citizens, including in matters affecting Indians, and brings before the municipio leaders any Pima who commits a serious crime such as murder, rape, or theft. The tribe does not have its own court, and members complain that problems of crime, except for petty matters handled by the governor and his assistant, are ignored by the Blanco authorities. Other ejidal officers include a treasurer, one charged with maintaining law and order and his assistant, and a range marshal and his assistant. The native and mestizo land-tenure and political systems are overlaid by another layer, that of the municipio, a wardlike system. The Yécora municipio administrative seat is in the town of Yécora. The *presidente municipal* and other officers take responsibility for law and order and other functions. Municipal officers are the main contacts with outside state and other political and legal entities, and hence have the greatest power in that they dispense federal and state services and funds, such as those for building and maintaining roads.

Despite holding civil offices in towns such as Maycoba, Pima responsibility and authority are severely limited by the Blanco power structure. Fourteen families have large landholdings in the area, with a member of one of them acting as the presidente municipal. Five of these families live in Maycoba, a supposed "Indian" town. Three of these families own stores where Pima must shop because there are no other facilities available. Other ranching families hire Pima for work. Pima dependence on the Blancos for store goods and wages ensures that Indian officials will not have power to implement decisions not favored by the non-Indians. In fact, the chief Pima political leader, the governor, must have approval of the mestizo power structure before standing for election.

Conflict. Initial relations between the Blancos and the Pima were friendly, or at least without marked conflict. In the beginning, the outsiders who settled in the region did not exploit the land being used, and the Pima earned wages as herders, drovers, plowmen, and laborers. Blancos also provided a small market for Pima crafts such as baskets, sleeping mats, and ceramic containers. After the 1910 Revolutionary War, the influx of Blancos increased steadily, and conflict over land use became widespread. For many reasons, the Pima are politically, socially, and economically powerless compared to their mestizo neighbors. They lack fluency in Spanish, literacy, money, and the influence needed to defend their rights. Power lies totally in the hands of the Blancos. The Pima say that lands the mestizos claim they purchased were acquired illegally; those who sold lands were duped or had no legal right to sell because communally owned properties can not be sold by individuals in the case of ejido lands. In other cases, the Pima maintain that the property had been temporarily rented or placed as collateral for loans, or that usufruct rather than sale of land had been intended. With more power and access to the institutions of power in Mexican society, the Blancos have developed effective strategies for the continued domination and exploitation of the indigenous people. They create economic dependency on store credit and wages, influence the election of Indian officials, and deny them representation at ejido, municipio, and state levels.

Religion and Expressive Culture

Religious Beliefs and Ceremonies. As the Jesuits established themselves in Mexico in the mid-seventeenth century, the Pima Bajo became nominal Catholics. Little is now known about early Pima religious beliefs except for references to fertility rites practiced at planting time to assure that seeds would grow. According to some accounts, this ceremony was performed among the lowland Pima in the 1920s. Women danced on a plank-covered *olla* (jar) buried in the ground, containing maize, squash, and beans. The dancers disrobed as they ran to the Río Yaqui between lines formed by men. Sunday meetings were held in the central pueblos by members of surrounding rancherías. Local disputes were settled, matters of mutual interest were discussed, and news exchanged. This was accompanied by eating and drinking maize beer, *húun váki*, the *tesguino* of the Tarahumara. Similar Sunday meetings are still held by the Tarahumara today.

Although nothing has been written about the religious ceremonies of the lowlands, the highland group celebrates two main fiestas attended by many in Maycoba, the feast days of San Francisco (4 October) and Easter. Minor celebrations are held to honor the Virgin of Guadalupe (12 December) and the Day of the Cross (3 May). The feast day of San Juan, 24 June, celebrates the coming of the summer rains at each rancho. Ritual bathing, visiting, and the drinking of húun váki accompanies this celebration. Every year on the feast day of San Francisco, parents bring their unbaptized children to Maycoba to be christened by a priest and formally registered as members of the ejido. Special masses are held, and the saint is paraded in procession around the town square. This baptismal ceremony becomes legal proof of an individual's community of origin.

Easter week, with its more elaborate rituals, revolves around an organization of *fariseos* (Pharisees) consisting of young men installed by the Pima governor to run the community during Holy Week. The young men either volunteer or join through capture by other fariseos. They paint their faces white and bind bandannas around their heads. Their duties are to protect the holy relics (a crucifix and a picture of the Virgin Mary), which are placed on litters for daily processions. They enforce a prohibition on bathing and unnecessary work through patrols during the week, organize the Good Friday processional along with members of the Blanco church, and carry out the ritual creation and destruction of a Judas effigy. At times they act like clowns or tricksters, especially when they go from house to house during the week asking for food and when they try to douse all the hearth fires in town with water on Holy Saturday. After the hearth fires have been doused, the fariseos perform rituals involving dancing, parading, and wrestling with each other and with Blanco boys. Another group called the *judíos*, organized by mestizo young men, holds similar fiestas in Maycoba. Both organizations exist in Yepachi under the control of Pima. Here they also still have the Pascola dancer and the more traditional and sacred rituals called *yumaris*, which are similar to the practices of the neighboring Guarijío and Tarahumara.

Although many of the activities of Easter week involve cooperation and coordination with the Blancos on the use of the church and religious artifacts, the fiesta also contains symbolic and real undertones of the rivalry that exists between the Mountain Pima and the Blancos. The Pima church, which originally held the town santos, deteriorated, and the Blancos built a new church in which they placed the santos from the old church. The conflict between Pima fariseos and mestizo judíos is a significant symbolization of the hostility between Blancos and the Pima. In other places where both group roles are played by members of the same ethnicity, hostility and conflict between the two groups is still symbolized. Blanco youths costumed as judíos wear grotesque costumes with devil-faced paper-bag masks. They, too, cause mischief and even clown with the Pima fariseos and challenge them to wrestling matches. After the Holy Saturday parade of the santos, the fariseos dance to music supplied by Pima and Blanco guitars, then return to the church and hurl broken pottery shards into the air so that they fall on everyone. Another snakelike line dance moves before the statue of San Francisco. When the Pima governor signals the end of the dance, the fariseos fall to the ground and are beaten by some of the Pima women. Subsequently, the fariseos engage in friendly physical combat with each other and with some of the Blanco males. The fariseos dance with the Judas effigy, which is ritually shot and burned later that Saturday afternoon.

Arts. Pima Bajo women provide additional family income by weaving baskets, mats, and hats, although in some places only a few women do so. Ceramic production is still an important industry among many Pima as well. Woodworking—in the form of stools, bowls, wooden plows, bottle stoppers, and husking pegs—can be found among both the Maycoba and the Onavas Pima. Most of the pottery is plainware, but a subtle blending of clays and mineral pigments and an eye for form have produced fine examples of indigenous crafts. They use the coil and scrape technique. Making baskets was once one of the major occupations of Pima women, who utilized palm and bear-grass fibers in their construction. Although both Pima basketry and ceramic pottery are made for utilitarian purposes, they also merit artistic praise. Some pottery and baskets are so well crafted that they are displayed at folk-art exhibits and, with mats and hats, are traded or sold in Mexican markets. Elaborate body painting and scarification, adopted in Spanish colonial times, were applied on chest, arms, lips, or chin at baptism by a medicine man.

Medicine. Earlier reports exist of *curanderos*, or curers using massage, herbs, and songs to treat a patient, but little is known about what curanderos do today. Seventeenth-century references suggest that they took typical shamanic roles such as *chupadore* (sucker) and *sopladore* (blower), who would try to cure a patient by removal of foreign objects or evil elements from the body. Today older women serve as midwives, and certain persons are known for their ability to cure specific maladies. There is scant knowledge about Pima etiology of disease, but in general they make extensive use of medicinal plants for medical problems. For example, a poultice of *Agave bovicornuta* or a lotion from *Hymenocallis sonorensis* is used for wounds, whereas stomach and kidney disorders are treated with the boiled roots of *Aristolochia brevipes*. The bark of the *palo piojo* is mashed and soaked in water for use as a flea dip, and

whooping cough is treated with an iguana grease (the iguana is also eaten). Malaria, however, remains a constant problem. The Mexican government has at times issued malaria pills, but few doctors are available in this rural, isolated region.

Death and Afterlife. Little is known about early Pima beliefs regarding death and afterlife, but the practice of providing food and drink after the burial has been maintained. Cattle were formerly slaughtered on such occasions, presumably as a sacrifice, but few Pima now raise cattle. Likewise, few can afford a casket. There is a tendency to avoid a church funeral, perhaps for economic reasons as well.

Bibliography

Dunnigan, Timothy (1970). "Subsistence and Reciprocity Patterns among the Mountain Pima of Sonora, Mexico." Ph.D. dissertation. Tucson: University of Arizona.

Dunnigan, Timothy (1981a). "Adaptive Strategies of Peasant Indians in a Biethnic Mexican Community: A Study of Mountain Pima Acculturation." In *Themes of Indigenous Acculturation in Northwest Mexico*, 36–49. Anthropological Papers of the University of Arizona, no. 38. Tucson: University of Arizona.

Dunnigan, Timothy (1981b). "Ritual as Interethnic Competition: Indito Versus Blanco in Mountain Pima Easter Ceremonies." In *Persistent Peoples: Cultural Enclaves in Perspective*, edited by George Pierre Castille and Gilbert Kushner, 132–150. Tucson: University of Arizona Press.

Dunnigan, Timothy (1983). "Lower Pima." In *Handbook of North American Indians*, edited by William C. Sturtevant. Vol. 10, *Southwest*, edited by Alfonso Ortiz, 217–229. Washington, D.C: Smithsonian Institution.

Hinton, Thomas B. (1969). "Remnant Tribes of Sonora: Opata, Papago, and Seri." In *Handbook of Middle American Indians*, edited by Robert Wauchope. Vol. 8, *Ethnology, Part Two*, edited by Evon Z. Vogt, 879–888. Austin: University of Texas Press.

Mason, J. Alden, and David M. Brugge (1991). "Notes on the Lower Pima." In *Ethnology of Northwest Mexico: A Sourcebook*, edited by Randall H. McGuire, 211–297. New York: Garland Publishing Co. Originally published in 1958.

Pennington, Campbell W. (1980). *The Pima Bajo of Central Sonora, Mexico*. Vol. 1, *The Material Culture*; vol. 2, *Vocabulario en la lengua nevome*. Salt Lake City: University of Utah Press.

Spicer, Edward H. (1962). *Cycles of Conquest: The Impact of Spain, Mexico, and the United States on the Indians of the Southwest, 1533–1960*. Tucson: University of Arizona Press.

Weaver, Thomas (1992). *Los indios del gran suroeste de los*

Estados Unidos: Viente siglos de adaptaciones culturales. Madrid: Editorial Mapfre.

THOMAS WEAVER AND ANNE BROWNING

Pipil

ETHNONYMS: none

Orientation

The Pipil are a contemporary Indian group living along the southern coast of western El Salvador. They are the descendants of the Aztec-related Pipil who migrated from central Mexico to El Salvador, Guatemala, and Honduras. Presently, there are an estimated 2,000 Pipil Indians living in El Salvador, with the greatest concentrations in the cities of Cuisnahuat and Santo Domingo de Guzmán. Linguistically, Pipil is an Aztecoidan language of the Uto-Aztecan Family; this sets them apart from many neighboring Indian groups that speak Mayan languages.

History and Cultural Relations

During a series of migrations that started in the eighth century and ended in the fourteenth century, the Pipil established a strong presence in El Salvador and Honduras. In the eleventh century the Pipil swept into El Salvador, displaced the Poqomam Indians and established the capital of their kingdom, Cuzcatlán.

Originally, the Pipil successfully resisted attempts at conquest by the Spanish. The Pipil were able to defeat forces led by Pedro de Alvarado in the Battle of Acajutla in June of 1524; however, de Alvarado returned in 1525 and this time succeeded in defeating them.

The history of the Pipil in El Salvador is much different from the history of Indians living in the mountains of Guatemala. Whereas many Maya were able to live in relative isolation through much of the colonial period, the terrain of El Salvador offered little protection. As a result, the Pipil were assimilated into the colonial economy of El Salvador much more than the Maya.

Although the Salvadoran government was sympathetic to Indian affairs in many ways, the Pipil eventually lost their communal lands in 1881, when the government abolished titles on all communal lands. In the wake of this event, many private landholders swept in to usurp lands that had traditionally been worked by Pipil. In the century since land privatization, most Pipil have become landless peasants and wage laborers.

Bibliography

Armas Molinas, Miguel (1974). _La cultura pipil de Centro América._ San Salvador: Ministerio de Educación.

Campbell, Lyle (1985). _The Pipil Language of El Salvador._ Berlin: Mouton.

Castaneda Paganini, Ricardo (1959). _La cultura tolteca-pipil de Guatemala._ Guatemala City: Editorial del Ministerio de Educación Publica.

Chapin, Mac (1989). "The 500,000 Invisible Indians of El Salvador." _Cultural Survival Quarterly_ 13(3): 11–16.

Fowler, William R., Jr. (1983). "La distribución prehistórica e histórica de los pipiles." _Mesoamerica_ 4(6): 348–372.

Fowler, William R., Jr. (1985). "Ethnohistoric Sources on the Pipil-Nicarao of Central America: A Critical Analysis." _Ethnohistory_ 32(1): 37–62.

Fowler, William R., Jr. (1989a). _The Cultural Evolution of Ancient Nahua Civilizations: The Pipil-Nicarao of Central America._ Norman: University of Oklahoma Press.

Fowler, William R., Jr. (1989b). "Pipil of Pacific Guatemala and El Salvador." In _New Frontiers in the Archaeology of the Pacific Coast of Southern Mesoamerica,_ edited by Frederick Bove and Lynette Heller. Anthropological Research Papers, no. 39. Tempe: Arizona State University.

Popoloca

ETHNONYMS: none

The approximately 26,000 speakers of Popolocan live in twenty towns and hamlets in southern Puebla, Mexico, between 18°00′ and 19°00′ N and 97°00′ and 98°30′ W, where they are almost completely surrounded by Mixtec and Nahua Indians. They are linguistically and culturally related to the Chocho of Oaxaca. There are five Popoloca languages. Many Popoloca also speak Spanish, and a number speak Nahuatl for economic purposes. Some people have moved from the area to work in factories. The 1990 census regarded Chocho and Popoloca as the same language and listed 9,658 speakers of this language in the state of Puebla. These are undoubtedly the native Popoloca whom Hoppe, Medina, and Weitlaner (1969) and Jäcklein (1970) regard as a separate cultural group. A branch of the Popoluca of southern Veracruz are also called Popoloca and should not be confused with the Popoloca of Puebla.

The region is arid: only about 65 centimeters of precipitation fall annually; hence, despite the rich soil, farming is a risky pursuit. The Popoloca subsist on maize and black beans, as well as other grains, citrus fruits, avocados, and papayas. They consume several kinds of alcoholic beverages, including pulque, mescal, and _aguardiente_ (a white rum distilled from fermented raw sugar). Crops are cultivated through the use of the Mediterranean and moldboard plows, shovels, and iron hoes. Men perform all of the field chores.

There is some local manufacturing as well. People make pottery and items of woven cloth and woven palm. The palm weavers' products include sleeping mats, several types of baskets, and hanging cribs. In general, men procure the raw materials and sell the final product, whereas women do the actual manufacturing.

The Popoloca live either in traditional wooden houses with thatched roofs or in more Mexican-style houses made of hardpan (*tepetate*) blocks with tile roofs. Towns are constructed around a square, which has public buildings and is the site of markets and fiestas. Furniture is sparse. People sleep on mats or bamboo beds, sit on pole benches, eat at wooden tables, and hang their clothes from ropes. There is also usually an altar in each home. The kitchen is located within the house.

The basis of social organization is the residential group of the monogamous patrilineal family. Town organization is based on barrios. The people elect seven *regidores* to govern them, as well as seven alternate regidores, one of whom is chosen as president. The regidores select several other people to fill a number of municipal and religious offices.

Women deliver their babies in a crouching position with the aid of both husband and midwife. The parents seek a wealthy godfather for their child; it is he who bears the expense of the baptism, which takes place within six days after birth. Mothers educate their young children. When children reach the age of 6 or 7, they receive training in adult tasks. The Popoloca harshly punish children who behave poorly; they may force children to breathe the smoke of burning chili peppers or hang them by their thumbs. Adolescents marry between their fourteenth and sixteenth years. The groom's parents pay a bride-price of cash or animals. The couple live with the groom's parents until they have their first child, and subsequently build their own house. Wakes are held for the deceased, and prayers are said as the body is taken by the church to the cemetery.

The world of the supernatural is a syncretic mix of mostly traditional and some Christian beliefs. Witchcraft is pervasive, and most curing is done by traditional curers who use herbs; bad air, soul loss, and fright are the most common complaints. The folklore bespeaks a non-Christian worldview. Fowl are sacrificed to improve crop yields, although much more emphasis was placed on sacrifice in earlier times. The Popoloca believe that humans are composed of three parts: upon death, the body perishes; the heart goes to the places that the soul goes, according to Catholic belief (heaven, hell, or purgatory); and feeling goes into the air.

Bibliography

Hoppe, Walter A., Andrés Medina, and Roberto Weitlaner (1969). "The Popoloca." In *Handbook of Middle American Indians*, edited by Robert Wauchope. Vol. 7, *Ethnology, Part One*, edited by Robert Wauchope and Evon Z. Vogt, 489–498. Austin: University of Texas Press.

Jäcklein, Klaus (1970). *San Felipe Otlaltepec: Beiträge Ethnoanalyse der Popoloca de Puebla, Mexico.* Göppingen: Verlag Alfred Kümmerle.

Popoluca

ETHNONYMS: none

The 1990 Mexican census tallied 29,203 Popoluca speakers living in southern Veracruz. They are culturally and linguistically similar to the Mixe and Zoque Indians of nearby Chiapas and Oaxaca. There are four separate social groups, which have distinctive cultures and languages. The largest of these groups, the Sierra or Highland Popoluca, is dispersed in twenty-five towns and hamlets. The other four groups live in the towns of Oluta, Sayula, and Texistepec.

The various Popoluca groups inhabit two greatly different environments. The Sierra Popoluca live at elevations of 100 to 800 meters; precipitation there is abundant, and there are oak and pine forests at higher elevations, savanna at lower elevations. In contrast, the villages of Oluta, Sayula, and Texistepec are located very close to sea level and are very dry, as well as dusty in the spring; the terrain is covered by savanna.

Despite their earlier conquests by the Nahua and by the Spanish, the Popoluca had little contact with non-Popoluca until the twentieth century, when the social agitation caused by the Mexican Revolution brought them into contact with other groups.

The Popoluca subsist through the cultivation of maize, beans, and squashes, although they also raise tomatoes, pineapples, chayotes, *camotes* (yams), manioc, and other fruits and vegetables. They grow coffee to sell for cash. Swidden agriculture (in the milpa pattern) is practiced, and two crops are planted annually. Fields are usually planted with digging sticks, although a few people use plows. Small numbers of poultry and pigs are kept. Some men hunt with featherless arrows, taking deer, boars, rabbits, and some birds. Fish are caught with the aid of nets and poisons.

Houses are simple structures. Four posts at the corners hold up the roof, which is woven of *zacate* grass and lasts as long as twenty-five years. The walls are made of vertical sticks, which do not exclude wind and rain. Lofts are constructed for the storage of maize and domestic goods. People sit on a unique type of bench made from a log, or on hammocks, and sleep on beds made of cane splints.

The Spanish had very limited success in urging the Popoluca to live in dense villages, and no success whatsoever in influencing them to line up streets in a grid pattern, although terrain limitations were at least partly responsible for the latter failure.

Men wear clothing of a type sold in most parts of Mexico—muslin pants and shirts. Women wear precontact-style wrap skirts and no garments above the waist.

Women tend to domestic chores and raising children, take care of the domestic animals, and weave. Men do the agricultural work, construct houses, and hunt and fish. Unmarried women also work in the fields. The Popoluca have no markets, but instead buy and sell to itinerant traders from outside their society. Some towns have resident Zapotec traders, and there are a few Popoluca stores that sell alcoholic beverages and, occasionally, household goods. There is usually very little wealth left when the expenses of living have been met, and this little is spent on fiestas.

Social and economic organization is based upon the nuclear family—or, sometimes, upon polygynous families. Kinship reckoning is bilateral.

Town political organization is by _municipio_, but because this scheme is of foreign origin, the people themselves find little meaning in it. The municipal president is elected. A few villages have barrios, although, like the municipios, they hold no significance for the people.

The supernatural world is largely pre-Columbian and very similar to the conceptions of the Aztec, Zapotec, and Maya. Figures similar to those present in the _Popol Vuh_, a sacred Mayan text that has been preserved from versions recorded just after the Conquest, are common, including the hurricane god, who can either help or can destroy agricultural fields. The Popoluca also have maize gods and _chanekos_, small spirits who live in caves and take care of game animals. There are in addition dangerous spirits, who live in specific places and who can kill people. The _nagual_, or witch, may be either a supernatural being or a human, and can transform himself or herself into an animal. The Popoluca take great care in making offerings to supernatural beings so that their maize will grow well or their hunting and fishing expeditions will be successful. Illness is believed to be caused by the supernatural intrusion of objects into the body and by loss of soul, the latter indicated by a weak pulse.

Women deliver their children while either kneeling or sitting at the end of a bench. Children are given Spanish names. Education and socialization consist primarily of teaching adult tasks. A prospective groom enlists an aide to ask the family of a prospective bride for her hand in marriage. Once the prospective groom's offer has been accepted, he must perform bride-service; later the marriage is finalized by a feast. Marriages tend, however, toward easy dissolution. The dead are buried with grave goods believed necessary for the long journey to their final destinations, as well as a coin to pay for admittance to the afterworld.

Bibliography

Baez-Jorge, Felix (1973). _Los zoque-popolucas, estructura social_. Mexico City: Instituto Nacional Indigenista; Secretaria de Educación Publica.

Foster, George M. (1982). _A Primitive Mexican Economy_. Westport, Conn.: Greenwood Press.

Foster, George M. (1969). "The Mixe, Zoque, Popoluca." In _Handbook of Middle American Indians_, edited by Robert Wauchope. Vol. 7, _Ethnology, Part One_, edited by Evon Z. Vogt, 448–477. Austin: University of Texas Press.

Munch Galindo, Guido (1983). _Etnología del istmo veracruzano_. Mexico City: Universidad Nacional Autónoma de México, Instituto de Investigaciones Antropológicas.

Poqomam

ETHNONYMS: Pokomám, Pokomán, Pocomám, Pocomán

Orientation

The Poqomam are a member of the Poqom group, which includes the Poqomchi' Indians in northern Guatemala. The Poqomam language belongs to the Poqom Language Group, which is part of the greater Quichean Maya Group. The Poqomam live in the Guatemalan departments of Jalapa, Guatemala, Escuintla, and Chiquimula. A small number of Poqomam have emigrated to El Salvador. In the late 1980s the Poqomam numbered forty-five to fifty thousand.

History and Cultural Relations

The Poqom group, including the Poqomchi' and the Poqomam, originally inhabited a region stretching from the highlands of Guatemala to the coast of El Salvador. The Poqom group eventually grew into two distinct ethnic groups. Present-day Poqomchi' live in the northern part of this region in Guatemala, and the Poqomam live in the central part, in southeastern Guatemala. Those Poqomam who lived in El Salvador were largely displaced by the immigration of the Pipil in the eleventh century. Later, in the fifteenth century, the Poqomam fell under the control of the expanding K'iche' Empire.

They were eventually able to reestablish political autonomy, but it was short-lived. In the early sixteenth century the Spanish moved into the region and conquered the Poqomam. During the colonial period, the European diseases to which the Poqomam were exposed and warfare reduced the Poqomam population. Relocation to missionary settlements and Guatemalan policies that outlawed communal lands forced the Poqomam onto ever-decreasing parcels of land.

During the twentieth century, the Poqomam population and their landholdings have remained stable; however, increasing attempts by Guatemalan leftist political groups to restore traditional lands to the Poqomam have met with repression and military reprisals. As a result, many Poqomam have emigrated to the United States.

Settlements

The Poqomam generally live in small settlements that surround large urban centers. For example, the *municipio* of Chinautla is a central urban area surrounded by many rural *aldeas* (hamlets). Officially, the urban centers have the authority to govern the hamlets that surround them. In practice, however, most inhabitants of the hamlets like to retain a certain degree of local autonomy.

Within the hamlets, people often live in extended family compounds so they can be close to their immediate kin. Whereas the ideal household form is the nuclear family, it can be said that the traditional ideal of the extended family is preserved through the practice of clustering immediate family households into a single household compound. The process of clustering often occurs across generations, and familial lands remain in the hands of the eldest male of the compound.

Houses are constructed either in the traditional way or in the Ladino way. In the case of traditional structures, the walls are made of cane or adobe, and the roofs are thatched with long grasses. The walls of Ladino houses are generally built of brick, and the roofs are made of either tile or galvanized tin.

Economy

The local economy of the Poqomam rests on the tripartite foundation of milpa, charcoal making, and pottery production. Milpa, or plot agriculture furnishes much of a family's subsistence needs. The staple crops are maize and beans. Milpa plots average about 0.08 hectares in size and are cultivated using traditional implements such as machetes, hoes, and digging sticks. Ideally, farmers hope to raise a surplus of maize, which they can then sell for cash; however, this goal is rarely realized.

For this reason, during the part of the year when there is no agricultural work, many men produce charcoal to sell in the markets in Guatemala City. To produce charcoal, oak is purchased, or cut from one's own groves, and then burned in a covered pit in the ground. For three days, the men control the heat in the pit, making sure not to completely burn the wood. At the end of the three days, the wood is uncovered and bundled together to take to market.

Thus, men's work consists largely of agricultural and heavy-labor jobs. Women's work consists of household work such as cooking, maintaining a garden, and washing clothing. To help supplement family income, many women sell the pottery they produce. The most common product is the tinaja (water jar). These are made by building a vessel out of thick coils of clay. After the pottery dries, it is polished and then fired.

Kinship

Traditionally, families were organized patrilineally into lineages and clans. Also, extended families were common and highly valued. As a result of Spanish-colonial influences, however, the family structure of the Poqomam has been altered. Presently, the nuclear family is the most common form of organization. Nevertheless, extended-family households do exist for reasons of economic and emotional interdependence. Kinship terms are of the Eskimo type, placing emphasis on generational differences.

Kinship is traced through both the mother and the father, producing a bilateral rather than a patrilineal system; however, there are vestiges of the traditional family apparent in some current practices. Although villagers believe that they are all related to each other, marriage partners are limited by surname. That is to say, individuals with the same patrilineal surnames are not to marry. In this way, the village as a whole can be thought to loosely represent a clan, and all those with the same patrilineal surname can be thought to loosely represent the members of a patrilineal lineage.

Marriage and Family

Marriage among the Poqomam involves large expenditures and a long period of negotiations between families. Ideally, a wedding proposal begins when the parents of the prospective bride and groom enter into a long period of economic bargaining. During this period, the parents exchange gifts at their many visits until one set of parents is unable to match the gifts of the other. At this time, the family with the lesser gift offers their child in marriage to the child of the other family. After this period of negotiations, both a civil ceremony and a religious ceremony are held during a three-day period of celebration.

Because of the expense accrued by following the traditional marriage pattern, many individuals have opted for alternative forms of marriage. *Juntados*, are those who simply live together without a civil or religious ceremony. Often, couples who have lived together for a period of time and who have children will go ahead and be married in a formal ceremony. This is called an *unión de hecho*.

Children are socialized into their gender roles from an early age. Female children are taught by their mothers to cook and to make clothing and pottery. Male children are taken to the milpa plot and are expected to help their fathers in making charcoal. They are also allowed to carry machetes and to smoke.

Inheritance patterns provide a means for parents to ensure their care in old age: the children who take care of their parents inherit their material possessions.

Sociopolitical Organization

The social organization of Poqomam culture is affected by a civil-religious hierarchy and by the ritual relations of *compadrazgo* and *camaradería*. Village organization, similar to that of other Latin American indigenous groups, centers around the civil-religious hierarchy. The civil hierarchy consists of an alcalde (mayor) who presides over a council, who in turn preside over a number of other lesser officials, such as police. The alcalde conducts the formal business of the town and represents his village both to other villages and to regional government.

Within the religious hierarchy, there is a system of *cofradías* (religious brotherhoods) that conduct the business of the church and help to cement social ties between members of the village. The most important office within the religious hierarchy is that of *mayordomo*, which is held jointly by a husband and wife. For a period of one year, they are responsible for cleaning the church and sponsoring the annual celebration held in honor of the patron saint of the village.

Compadrazgo also helps to organize social life among the Poqomam. Compadrazgo is the system of fictive-kin relations that is created between godparents and the families of their godchildren. These relations are often the basis of social interaction and mobility.

Camaradería functions on a lesser scale than compadrazgo in organizing social interaction. Young unmarried men may enter into special bonds of friendship, known as camaradería, with other men. These individuals usually spend much time together drinking and dancing. These friendships provide bonds of loyalty before marriage but are often dissolved abruptly after marriage.

Religion and Expressive Culture

Present-day Poqomam religion consists of a traditional framework into which Catholicism has been assimilated. Although they accept elements of Catholicism, it is clear that the Poqomam tailor Catholic beliefs to reinforce local beliefs and practices. For instance, the Catholic stories about creation and Jesus are interpreted from their perspective to mean that God taught the original Poqomam the secret of milpa and that Jesus came into the world to distribute land.

Creencias, secretos, and luck are other integral components of Poqomam religious life. Creencias are the myths that explain the unknown. Central to many of these stories is a belief in charmed places where it is possible to pass into the underworld. In the underworld, it is possible to find wealth and knowledge. Secretos are carefully guarded formulas that can be used to solve both physical and spiritual problems. It is believed that luck comes to individuals either through birth or as a gift from the underworld.

Disease is thought to be largely caused by supernatural forces. Since Poqomam believe that _brujos_ (witches) cast spells that cause illnesses, many people search out other brujos to counteract the effects of a spell; however, if God has decided that it is a person's time, no cure will succeed in making the patient well again.

Numerous rituals and ceremonies maintain the balance between the realm of the supernatural and the earthly. In fact, there are sixty-eight days during the year when formal rituals are conducted. These rituals include fertility rites, veneration of saints, and the Day of the Dead.

At death, the family gathers together and holds a feast. The descendants of the departed are obligated to pray for the soul of the deceased for nine days, after which time they must pray for the soul of the deceased during each Day of the Dead for the next seven years. It is thought that these prayers will help the soul to pass into heaven. Other services offered to the departed include the placement of food, drink, and candles at the grave and the placement of water at the home altar.

Bibliography

Feldman, Laurence H. (1981). "Definiendo un estado pokom." _Anales de la Academia de Geografía e Historia de Guatemala_ 55:7–22.

Fox, John W. (1978). "Chinautla Viejo: Un sito estratégico en la frontera pokoman-cakchiquel." _Anales de la Sociedad de Geografía e Historia de Guatemala_ 51:13–25.

Ghidinelli, Azzo (1984). "Traje de los pocomames orientales en Guatemala." _Tradiciones de Guatemala_ 21–22:66–72.

Ghidinelli, Azzo, and Rosalba Terranova (1974). "The Tree Test and the Study of Acculturation among the Pokomam." _Current Anthropology_ 15(3): 338–342.

Muñoz, Jorge Luján (1985). "Cambios en la estructura familiar de los indígenas pokomames de Petapa (Guatemala) en la primera mitad del siglo XVI." _Mesoamerica_ 6(10): 355–369.

Reina, Ruben E. (1966). _The Law of the Saints: A Pokomam Pueblo and Its Community Culture._ New York: Bobbs-Merrill.

Reina, Ruben E. (1969). "Eastern Guatemalan Highlands: The Pokomames and Chortí." In _Handbook of Middle American Indians,_ edited by Robert Wauchope. Vol. 7, _Ethnology, Part One,_ edited by Evon Z. Vogt, 101–120. London: University of Texas Press.

IAN MAST

Poqomchi'

ETHNONYMS: Poconchí, Pokomchí, Pokonchi

The Poqomchi' are a Mayan group living south of the Q'eqchi' in the Guatemalan departments of Alta Verapaz and Baja Verapaz. Their language is closely related to that of the Poqomam, and they share many cultural traits with the Q'eqchi'. They are bordered by such Mayan groups as the Q'eqchi', the Ixil, the Uspanteko, and the K'iche'. At present, there are about 60,000 Poqomchi' living in Guatemala.

The history of the Poqomchi' is one of domination. During the pre-Hispanic period the Poqomchi' were under the control of the K'iche'. Although they were able to break away from the K'iche', during the 1530s they came under the rule of the Spanish. Throughout the colonial period, Poqomchi' lands were privatized as a result of Guatemalan governmental policies that sought to reward rich private landholders. In the second half of the twentieth century, the Poqomchi' have been renewing their efforts to regain their communal lands. Politically, they have turned to left-wing groups that promise agrarian reform. The Guatemalan governmental response has consisted of violence and repression. As a result, during the 1980s, many Poqomchi' emigrated from Guatemala.

Bibliography

Davidson, William V., and Melanie A. Counce (1989). "Mapping the Distribution of Indians in Central America." *Cultural Survival Quarterly* 13(3): 37–40.

Puerto Ricans

ETHNONYM: Puertorriqueños

Orientation

Identification. The people of Puerto Rico weave their distinctive ethnic identity from three historical traditions: Spanish colonial, Afro-Caribbean, and North American. Puerto Rican cuisine, religious beliefs, and other identifying components of their expressive culture draw heavily upon Spanish and Afro-Caribbean traditions. Puerto Ricans share rituals and practices with their neighbors throughout Latin America as well as with English- and French-speaking peoples of the Caribbean; yet Puerto Rican educational, political, and economic systems have had to incorporate many North American features owing to U.S. domination since 1898. Puerto Ricans identify strongly with their homeland, their history, and their place in the Caribbean. Although Puerto Ricans have a legal claim to U.S. citizenship, they rarely refer to themselves as "Americans," even while residing on the U.S. mainland. Puerto Rican attachment to their islands has endured despite large-scale emigration to the mainland since 1917, the year they were granted citizenship status (largely because the War Department wanted legal grounds to enlist Puerto Ricans into the World War I endeavor).

One segment of the population, derogatorily referred to as "Nuyoricans," are children born to Puerto Ricans living in New York City. The often impoverished condition and ambivalent cultural status of mainland Puerto Ricans adds yet another dimension to Puerto Rican identity, with some segments of the population incorporating urban street-survival methods and outlooks into their ways of life.

Location. Lying on the eastern end of the Greater Antilles in the Caribbean, between Hispaniola and the U.S. Virgin Islands, Puerto Rico is so well situated in the sea-lanes that it was a prize territory of the Spanish from the earliest years of the Conquest. The main island is around 169 kilometers long and 56 kilometers wide, although the territory includes a number of smaller outer islands, the largest of which, Vieques, rivals Saint Croix (U.S. Virgin Islands) in size and serves, in part, as a base for the U.S. Navy. Puerto Rico has a land mass of 8,874.6 square kilometers, and its climate is subtropical.

Three overlapping mountain ranges—Cordillera Cen-

tral, Sierra de Cayey, and Sierra de Luquillo—extend in an east-west direction along its interior. North of the chain of mountains, as with most Caribbean islands, the island is generally wetter and lusher; the southern slopes and plains tend to receive less rain and have a drier, savanna appearance. Its surrounding waters include the Mona Passage (just west of the main island)—a highly productive fishing ground and often treacherous channel for illegal immigrants crossing from the Dominican Republic—and the extremely deep Puerto Rican Trench, renowned in the tourist industry for its sportfishing.

Demography. Puerto Rico is the homeland of between 6 and 7 million people, although only slightly more than half the population actually resides on the island. The 1990 census counted 3,522,037 Puerto Ricans living on the island, and estimates of those living in the continental United States range between 2.5 and 3 million. The Puerto Rican people thus constitute a diaspora—a dispersed people —residing in areas of New York City, such as the South Bronx, as well as in the Caribbean. Migration, a common demographic feature of the population at least since 1917, has been a means to escape domestic problems, seek education and fortune, and deal with economic woes. The Puerto Rican fertility rate—perceived to be high in relation to natural and economic resources—has been a matter of much social planning and dispute, leading to spotty and largely ineffective sterilization and other family-planning programs. Population density on the island is high, with 369.9 persons per square kilometer.

Linguistic Affiliation. Puerto Ricans speak Spanish, although it is distinctly different from the Spanish spoken in other Latin American or Caribbean regions. The ability to speak English is widespread, owing to the high rates of migration between Puerto Rico and the U.S. mainland and to the practice of teaching English in many of the private and public schools. At the university level, much of the instruction is in English, and the exchange of faculty and students between U.S. mainland and Puerto Rican universities is quite common.

The teaching of English in the primary and secondary public schools has been a subject of much debate in Puerto Rico, since many regard the teaching of English instruction as an infringement upon Puerto Rican cultural autonomy. Others view the lack of English instruction in school as a barrier to statehood; still others view it as a mechanism for maintaining the island's status quo.

Settlements

Because Puerto Ricans constitute a diaspora, it is difficult to locate them in terms of defined territory. Their "settlement" patterns include New York City and other major metropolitan areas off the islands, and the dispersed households of Puerto Ricans may include members living in as many as three to five locations on the islands and the mainland.

The main island of Puerto Rico is most densely populated along its coastal fringe. The four major metropolitan centers are San Juan, Ponce (south-central coast), Mayagüez (west-central coast), and Arecibo (north coast). The San Juan metropolitan area, which includes several cities and districts, extends in all directions except north (the seaward side). Old San Juan retains its prominent position at the mouth of San Juan harbor. Bayamón and Cataño ajoin the western limit of the metropolis. The business and financial center of Hato Rey, along the Río Piedras, home of the main campus of the University of Puerto Rico, lie along the south end of the city, and the tourist districts stretch out along the ocean to the east.

Most of the settlements depart from the usual grid pattern of Spanish settlement and instead extend outward from town squares that might have once been centrally located. The development of public housing and land-annexation schemes to accommodate the growing population have undermined the centrality of town squares. Government housing-development schemes have been implemented islandwide.

Economy

Subsistence and Commercial Activities. Puerto Rico emerged from a Spanish colonial past of haciendas and peasant farming to become dominated by large-scale farming of sugarcane, coffee, and tobacco following the U.S. annexation of the island, in 1898, during the Spanish-American War. During the first part of the twentieth century, the sugar industry in particular stimulated migrations of the small peasant farmers from the inland highlands to create a rural proletariat to work on the sugar plantations. Until after World War II, agriculture in general and sugar in particular dominated the economy, lending a seasonal dimension to the island's work that was common throughout much of the Caribbean. It became usual to work on the island during the later fall and winter months, when sugarcane and other crops needed their heaviest labor inputs, and then to migrate to the mainland during the summer months. This regime succeeded in converting much of the smallholding peasant population into wage laborers.

Puerto Rico retains the vestiges of a peasantry today, but few Puerto Ricans conform to the *jíbaro* stereotype of the strong, hardworking, independent farmer, which today serves as a Puerto Rican national symbol. For part of their subsistence, many of the island's inhabitants still rely on combinations of fishing, farming, and gardening with casual wage work. The Caribbean practice of "occupational multiplicity"—combining a number of odd jobs—is common enough in Puerto Rico that short-term, irregular jobs have been given their own term—*chiripas*. Puerto Ricans are eligible for some social assistance from the U.S. government. Although they receive fewer transfer payments per capita annually than the general population of the United States, transfer payments make up proportionately more of the incomes of Puerto Rican households that receive them.

Industrial Arts. Since the 1950s, agriculture as a cornerstone of the Puerto Rican economy has yielded ground to service industries, tourism, and manufacturing. A development program known as "Operation Bootstrap" was designed to industrialize the island following the decline of sugar production. Much of the growth in manufacturing has been the result of special provisions in the U.S. tax code that make it desirable for U.S. firms to operate assembly plants on the island. Most of the products of these plants are produced solely for export. They include optical equipment, pharmaceuticals, chemicals, shoes and clothing, and electronics.

Attracting industry to the island is also facilitated by a labor force perceived to be docile and generally antiunion. Owing to similarities between Cuban and Puerto Rican histories and the fear of a revolution like Cuba's, since the late 1950s there has been a subtle yet comprehensive suppression of socialist thought in Puerto Rico. The antiunion sentiments thus derive in part from the association of unionism with socialism.

Puerto Rico's tourist industry is centered around San Juan, which serves as a port for cruise ships. Old San Juan, with its Spanish-colonial cathedrals, fortifications, customs and merchant houses, and other impressive architecture, is a well-known shopping and historical district for tourists. San Juan is also known for its luxury resort hotels and casinos, which grew in favor after restrictions on travel between the United States and Havana. The promotion of other parts of the island, especially its beaches and two national parks—El Yunque (a tropical rainforest), and Bosque Seco (a dry forest on the southwest coast)—has intensified since the early 1980s.

Trade. Puerto Rico's position in the sea-lanes established San Juan as an important port early in the island's European history. Today Puerto Rico competes with Miami as an international center of banking and commerce for many Latin American and Caribbean nations. Its political status as a U.S. territory, combined with the bilingual capabilities of most of its businesspeople, gives it an advantage over other Caribbean nations in acting as a liaison between Latin American and North American business interests. Its commerce is constrained, however, in that the same restrictions that apply to trade between the United States and other nations also apply to Puerto Rico. Puerto Rican politicians cannot negotiate trading and other international arrangements independently of the U.S. federal government.

Division of Labor. Unskilled and semiskilled labor has been one of Puerto Rico's principal exports since late in the nineteenth century. Migration between the mainland and the island, whether spontaneous or encouraged by the insular government, served the needs of low-wage industry and agriculture much more than it encouraged or facilitated upward mobility across generations or entrepreneurial behavior. The working histories of Puerto Ricans reveal cycles of work and rest, or employment and unemployment, owing to the hazardous or monotonous nature of many of the jobs Puerto Ricans obtain. Most civilian Puerto Ricans work either in the public sector or at low-wage jobs. Since 1917, the U.S. military has drawn upon Puerto Ricans as soldiers and civilian workers; the large number of Puerto Ricans involved in the Vietnam War is reflected in the fact that some neighborhoods bear Southeast Asian names.

Although much of the population remains a low-income proletariat, partially dependent on government transfer payments, the labor force includes a substantial professional and managerial class because of the growth of the island's prominence in banking, insurance, and commerce. Many of these individuals have found work in Sunbelt cities such as Miami and Houston, where their bilingual skills are in demand because of growing Latino business transactions.

The island's labor force also includes those who occupy positions in the informal economy of petty commerce, small-scale manufacturing, food processing, fishing, and farming. Historically, within peasant farming and fishing families, there has been a division of labor by sex, although men and women tend to be capable of most of the same tasks required to pursue small-scale fishing and farming. Often these "informal sector" jobs are combined with government jobs, which tend to be allocated through political patronage.

Land Tenure. The agrarian past and jíbaro identity make landownership a desirable goal for Puerto Ricans. In accordance with U.S. law, land in Puerto Rico is privately owned and available for sale or purchase on the open market. Yet there have been variations owing to Puerto Rico's special political status and circumstances. The state has owned and operated sugar plantations, for example, but more common have been government schemes designed to make land available to the poor for house construction. These schemes emerged as the sugar industry began to decline in importance, leaving many sugar workers unemployed or displaced from company housing. Called *parcelas,* the program consisted of providing plots of land to families with low incomes and then providing a number of contiguous plots with public services such as water, sewer, garbage collection, and electricity. The growth of squatters' settlements is not unknown to Puerto Rico; sometimes these precede parcelas development.

Kinship

Puerto Ricans trace their ancestry through both sexes, but have nothing corresponding to corporate lineal descent groups. Their kinship terminology conforms to the Eskimo system, with some local variations for the expression of deference, affection, respect, and fictive-kinship ties based on the common Latin tradition of *compadrazgo.* Compadrazgo, acknowledged as ritual coparenthood at the baptism of a child, is one of the principal institutions for establishing interhousehold relations.

Marriage and Family

Marriage. Marriages in Puerto Rico are usually recognized by the Catholic church. Common-law or consensual unions, once typical in peasant regions, have become less common. Marriage takes place at a young age, usually in the teens, and most Puerto Ricans desire children shortly after marriage. Both marriage and the birth of children are important events in terms of forming bonds between families and households, with well-established visiting patterns among related households and compadrazgo relations formed between households at the baptisms of children.

Domestic Unit. The Puerto Rican diaspora has had a strong influence on the character of the domestic unit. Households may or may not be units bounded by dwellings, plots of land, or even the boundaries of the commonwealth. The 1990 census reports 3.31 persons per household in Puerto Rico, a figure that is probably an underestimate because of the dispersed nature of Puerto Rican households. Interdependent groups of individuals residing in a number of different locations characterize most Puerto Ricans' domestic units. Individuals come together and part over the course of seasons, years, and phases of the life cycle. In Puerto Rico, the typical unit consists of a woman and man and their unmarried children, yet it is not uncommon for unmarried or widowed parents to live with their children, and visiting patterns among households and dwellings are such that the lines between households often become blurred. On the mainland, there is a much higher incidence of households headed by women with small children than there is on the island.

Inheritance. In principle, all possessions of the deceased are to be divided into three equal parts: the *legitimá* (legitimate), which is divided equally among the children; the *mejora* (best), which is divided among the children according to the decisions of the deceased; and the *libre disposición* (freely disposable), which is given to the spouse. In real terms, possessions are divided among surviving kin and heirs based on access and residence. Specifically, heirs who have direct access to family land or fishing equipment because they farm or fish nearby plots or waters are likely to benefit from the inheritance more than heirs who have migrated to an urban area in Puerto Rico or emigrated to the U.S. mainland. The extent to which inheritance causes legal disputes among surviving family members varies with the size of the inheritance. A small inheritance generates few disputes, whereas great wealth is likely to be transferred from the dead to the living by careful legal documentation.

Socialization. The socialization and enculturation of Puerto Rico's young occurs in the home and neighborhood, public and private schools, the Catholic church, and in the fluid social realms of the diaspora. In these varied social fields, Puerto Ricans are affectionate and loving toward their own and others' children. Much of the teaching is by example; corporal punishment is rare.

In the ghettos of the South Bronx, these ideals are difficult to uphold under the stress of poverty. Puerto Rican children on the mainland are as susceptible as any ghetto youth to the influences of the street: gangs, drugs, crime, the reification of sports as an escape, and pressures to leave school. Witnessing their children coming under these influences, many household heads choose to return to the island with their families or, failing that, send their children back to families still on the island once those children have reached adolescence. On the island, children from lower-class families who work in the informal sector, from fishing households, or from small farming households tend to learn the crafts of the household between the ages of 8 and 10.

Sociopolitical Organization

Political Organization. Puerto Rico is a highly politicized society, with three main political parties that compete with one another in elections. For the first five decades of U.S. domination of the island, island politics were overseen by a series of U.S. government officials similar to colonial administrators. Just before, during, and after World War II, the Partido Popular Democrático (Popular Democratic Party, PPD) gained the strength necessary for Puerto Ricans to demand greater autonomy from Washington.

Early in Puerto Rican party politics, the issue of the island's political status was at the forefront of its relationship with Washington. Prior to 1952, the political debate dealt with whether the island should become a state or become independent, but in 1952 the compromise status of commonwealth was granted, which allowed the islanders to continue receiving tax benefits and limited assistance from the United States yet elect their own governor. Luis Muñoz Marín oversaw the declaration of the new status; his legacy remains in Puerto Rican politics to this day. Today three political parties, differentiated from one another primarily over the issue of the island's status relative to the United States, compete for power in Puerto Rico. The most powerful party since 1952, the PPD, still prefers commonwealth status, and two others, the Partido Nuevo Progresista (New Progressive Party), and Partido Independentisa Puertorriqueño (Puerto Rican Independence Party), are prostatehood and proindependence, respectively. Elections often affect one's job prospects, as changing local and regional politics determine the distribution of jobs in the public sector.

Social Control. Puerto Rico has its own civilian police force, along with a National Guard. The U.S. military maintains bases on the island as well. All this force is insufficient to control crime, which ranges from petty theft, larceny, and carjacking to murder and terrorism. The high crime rate has been linked to the island's poverty, high unemployment, high fertility levels (which have resulted in large proportions of juveniles), and the influence of New York City street culture on Puerto Rican youth. Many programs designed to alleviate poverty and unemployment are seen as social-control mechanisms, particularly the housing-development programs. The Catholic church has had a moderating influence on the island's crime rate.

Conflict. Conflict and conflict resolution occur on formal and informal levels. Formal conflicts involve crimes against people and property and are dealt with through police, judicial, and penal methods common throughout the United States. Informal conflicts arise within and between Puerto Rican households over moral and ethical behaviors, inheritance, courtship, and other issues important to Puerto Rican values. These types of conflicts often involve families, as opposed to individuals, in their resolution. Conflicts among groups quite often are resolved through combinations of negotiation, publicity, and civil disobedience.

Religion and Expressive Culture

Religious Beliefs. Puerto Ricans are predominantly Catholic, yet their beliefs, rituals, and practices often stray outside the orthodox boundaries of Catholicism. Puerto Ricans do not generally differentiate between official Catholicism and their rituals and beliefs and give little credit to African and Latin American influence on their religion. In addition to the rich homage paid to saints, as is common throughout Latin America, parts of the island still host beliefs in the evil eye, saints' miracles, faith healing, and witchcraft. Catholic icons are common in Puerto Rican households, often intermingled with photographs of family members and clusters of ceramic and porcelain figures. Protestant sects—particularly the Pentecostal church—have converted a small portion of the population.

Ceremonies. Baptisms, marriages, weddings, vigils, processions, and funerals all come within the scope of Catholic ceremonies. In addition to these, Puerto Ricans celebrate religious and political holidays with great enthusiasm —singing, playing music, drinking, and feasting in recognition of a sacred day, an historical event or figure, or a time of year. Often called "home fiestas," these observances tend to be private affairs that bring together close friends and family members. Public fiestas include those that honor patron saints and occasional folk-music festivals. Some towns, for commercial reasons, have invented festivals, for example, the seafood festival in Puerto Real, a fishing community on the west coast. Cockfights, which can assume as ritualist and ceremonial a flavor as other sporting events, bring large numbers of people together.

Arts. Puerto Rican theater, dance, and other arts benefit from the culture's association with New York City yet combine with these influences more local cultural elements considered unique to the island. Puerto Rico has a rich history of folk music, which incorporates Caribbean and Spanish influences and often involves public storytelling, social critique, and joking. As in other Caribbean countries, there exist wood carving, doll making, and weaving traditions on the island, although many of these have come to be oriented toward the tourist trade.

The distinctive literary tradition of Puerto Ricans negotiates among Spanish, Latin American, and Nuyorican influences. Critics all too easily dismiss much of Puerto Rican literature and drama as overly political, obsessed with U.S. domination and the colonial past. For example, René Marqués uses rebellious and critical protagonists to illustrate the complex effects that imposed economic and political structures have on dislocated folk, but his work goes beyond a simple indictment of the status quo, tracing subtle and overt influences of social conditions on individual character. In personal essays, he acknowledges without apology his kinship with social critics throughout Western history.

In their poetry, Puerto Ricans have labored to free themselves from the formal qualities that characterized their verse during the years after U.S. occupation, when many poets withdrew into Spanish traditions in search of a defining cultural identity. Julia de Burgos internalized this struggle in her poems and marshaled it to confront the difficulties of romantic love and desire in a society dominated by Catholicism and machismo. Since the 1960s, growing attention has been given to the poetry originating from New York's Nuyorican Poets' Cafe: violent images in the work of Miguel Piñero, pride in the Puerto Rican heritage overcoming despair in that of Pedro Pietri, or the strength that poverty and bitterness inspire in that of Jorge Lopez.

Medicine. Western medicinal practice is as firmly established in Puerto Rico as it is throughout much of the United States, yet the Latin American and Caribbean traditions continue to provide solutions where Western medicine is weak, especially in the realm of prevention. *Curanderos* (native curers) and *brujas* (witches) are still prevalent throughout the island; these individuals often mix herbal remedies with religious ritual and Western medicines in their cures.

Death and Afterlife.   In Puerto Rico, death and the passage into afterlife are commonly marked by vigils, or wakes, and novenas, which are days of prayer for the dead. During the vigils, which occur between death and burial, the close friends and relatives of the dead gather around the body, which lies in state, and pray for the soul's passage into heaven. Throughout the night of the vigil, people who knew the deceased come and go while a small group of women and men who were particularly close to the dead say the rosary. Candles burn, and the prayers last until dawn of the day the person is to be buried. Following the funeral, the novenas begin. These nine consecutive days of prayer take place in the house of the deceased and constitute a means by which God's favor is solicited on behalf of the deceased's surviving kin and friends, as well as a means of reaffirming ties among households and community solidarity.

Bibliography

Bonilla, Frank, and Ricardo Campos (1981). "A Wealth of Poor: Puerto Ricans in the New Economic Order." *Daedalus* 110:133–176.

Buitrago Ortiz, Carlos (1973). *Esperanza: An Ethnographic Study of a Peasant Community in Puerto Rico.* Tucson: University of Arizona Press.

Griffith, David, Manuel Valdés Pizzini, and Jeffrey C. Johnson (1992). "Injury and Therapy: Proletarianization in Puerto Rico's Fisheries." *American Ethnologist* 19:53–74.

Koss-Chioino, Joan (1992). *Women as Healers, Women as Patients: Mental Health Care and Traditional Healing in Puerto Rico.* Boulder, Colo.: Westview Press.

Lewis, Oscar (1977). *La Vida; A Puerto Rican Family in the Culture of Poverty: San Juan and New York.* New York: Random House.

Mintz, Sidney W. (1974). *Worker in the Cane: A Puerto Rican Life History.* New York: W. W. Norton & Co.

Picó, Fernando (1986). *Historia general de Puerto Rico.* Río Piedras, P.R.: Ediciones Huracán.

Steward, Julian, Robert A. Manners, Eric R. Wolf, Elena Padilla Seda, Sidney W. Mintz, and Raymond L. Scheele (1956). *The People of Puerto Rico.* Urbana: University of Illinois Press.

DAVID GRIFFITH

Q'anjob'al

ETHNONYMS: Kanhobal, Kanjobal

Orientation

The Q'anjob'al are one of a number of Mayan groups living in Guatemala. Specifically, they inhabit the Cuchumatan Mountains in the department of Huehuetenango. The terrain in this isolated region is filled with high ridges and deep gorges. Because of differences in elevation, the climate ranges from very warm (27–32° C) in the valleys to very cool (10–16° C) in the mountains.

At present, there are about 70,000 Q'anjob'al Indians living in the northwestern highlands of Guatemala. They speak the Q'anjob'al language, which belongs to the Macro-Mayan Language Family. It is part of the Q'anjob'al Language Branch, which also includes Chuj, Tojolab'al and Jakalteko.

History and Cultural Relations

The Spanish Conquest of the Q'anjob'al began in the 1520s, when Pedro de Alvarado led soldiers through present-day Guatemala with the purpose of conquering the various Indian groups who lived there. Many forces contributed to the conquest of the Q'anjob'al by the Spaniards. European disease, military attacks, and missionary settlements all served to weaken and deplete the Q'anjob'al population.

During the colonial period, private landholders exerted their political power to subsume indigenous lands into their own personal estates. The private landholders used these lands to grow coffee, which was a lucrative cash crop during the colonial period. Because of government policies, Q'anjob'al Indians lost more than 70 per cent of their lands to Ladinos between 1880 and 1920. As a result of three centuries of colonial policy that rewarded large private landholders over the indigenous Q'anjob'al, the latter were reduced to peasant farmers and migrant laborers.

Q'anjob'al lands have been under continued pressure, and, as a result, many individuals have turned to left-wing political causes, which promise land reform. The government of Guatemala's response has been to repress the Q'anjob'al violently. Because of this policy, many Q'anjob'al began emigrating to the United States during the mid-1980s.

Settlements

Q'anjob'al villages reflect the agricultural character of the people. Settlements usually consist of a central urban center that is utilized for trade and regional government; however, most Indians live in dispersed households near their fields. Houses generally consist of one-room dwellings made of pole walls and thatch roofs. Many Q'anjob'al construct sweat baths adjacent to the main structure.

Economy

Agriculture is the central component of Q'anjob'al economic life. The staple crops, maize, beans, and squashes, are grown on milpa plots according to swidden agricultural practices. The Q'anjob'al are unique because they have not only cultivated maize as a subsistence crop, but they have also been able to grow surpluses, which they sell for cash. They farm on the sides of mountains and slopes that are often as steep as 45°. Because of the slopes, they are unable to use heavy plows or animals. They utilize the traditional hoe, machete, and digging stick. Opportunities are severely limited outside of agriculture; those unable to farm because of a lack of land are forced to become migrant laborers.

Weaving is the main economic activity for women. They utilize traditional looms to create intricately designed clothes and blouses. Clothing is not only produced as an economic good, but also as a symbol of municipal identity. Because each town has its own particular design, it is possible to tell which villages individuals come from by simply looking at their clothing.

Kinship

Q'anjob'al descent is traced patrilineally. There is also evidence that vestiges of traditional clans and lineages are still recognized. Children are given their father's surname. All of those people who have the same surname are considered to be members of the same clan. It is prescribed that one should marry someone with a different last name, that is, someone who does not belong to the same patrilineal clan. One is, however, expected to marry another member of the village.

Fictive kinship, or _compadrazgo_ is also an important element of Q'anjob'al kinship. Compadrazgo is the system of ritual relations created between godparents and children and between godparents and the parents of the children. These relations serve religious and social purposes and are most often called into action during births and baptisms.

Marriage and Family

From the age of 3 or 4, children are dressed in miniature copies of the clothes their parents wear. Female children work with their mothers around the home, and male children accompany their fathers to the milpa plot.

Marriage involves much ritual social interaction, and it is necessary for the groom's parents to pay a bride-price to the family of the bride. Marriages are arranged by the parents of the bride and groom. Most often marriage occurs between the ages of 12 and 16 for females and 15 and 18 for males. Upon marrying, the couple moves into the compound of the groom's father. Households are generally nuclear units; however, because sons build their houses close to their father's dwelling, it is possible to describe Q'anjob'al households as patrilocal extended-family compounds.

Sociopolitical Organization

The sociopolitical organization of the Q'anjob'al follows the traditional model of a Latin American civil-religious hierarchy. It is important to note that each town has its own complement of offices within its own hierarchy. The civil sector consists of a hierarchy of offices consisting of mayor, police, and assistants. The most prestigious and wise individuals who have held office can become a _principal_. Each town has a council of principales, which directs the affairs of the town. They also appoint individuals to civil offices.

The religious sector is similar in that it consists of a hierarchical system of offices. The most important position to be held is that of _mayordomo_. This office is held by a married couple; their responsibilities include taking care of church affairs and maintaining the physical condition of the saints. The most prestigious aspect of this office is sponsorship of the festivals that are held annually to celebrate the patron saint of the town. Mayordomos sponsor these festivals with their time, effort, and money. Much status and prestige is conferred to those who have filled the office.

Religion and Expressive Culture

Q'anjob'al religion is a combination of elements of traditional beliefs with Catholicism. Although they recognize the Catholic God, Jesus, and the Virgin Mary, they place them within the context of their own traditional religious perspectives. God is believed to have appeared on earth during the creation and Jesus is believed to have been crucified in each local village. The Virgin Mary and the saints are spiritual beings that protect local villages from evil. The Q'anjob'al believe that evil exists in many forms and that it may exist simultaneously with good in the same deity.

A central symbol within the Q'anjob'al cosmology is the cross. Crosses stand in front of the churches in the villages. These crosses vary in height from 4.5 to 21.2 meters high. Whereas Catholics identify the cross with the Crucifixion, the cross also represents traditional conceptions of the heavens and the earth. In addition, it is an integral part of the Maya calendar, which is the basis for much of Q'anjob'al cosmology.

Bibliography

Burns, Allan F. (1988). "Resettlement in the US: Kanjobal Maya in Indiantown, Florida." _Cultural Survival Quarterly_ 12(4): 41–45.

Burns, Allan F. (1993). _Maya in Exile: Guatemalans in Florida_. Philadelphia: Temple University Press.

Wagley, Charles (1969). "The Maya of Northwestern Guatemala." In _Handbook of Middle American Indians_, edited by Robert Wauchope. Vol. 7, _Ethnology, Part One_, edited by Evon Z. Vogt, 46–68. Austin: University of Texas Press.

Q'eqchi'

ETHNONYMS: Kekchí, K'ekchí

Orientation

The Q'eqchi' are a Central American Mayan group who speak a number of different dialects of the Q'eqchi' language. Located largely within the department of Alta Verapaz, Guatemala, there are also lesser populations of Q'eqchi' Indians in the departments of Petén, Izabal, and Baja Verapaz, as well as parts of the Toledo District of southern Belize.

In the late 1980s the number of Q'eqchi' speakers was estimated at 350,000 in Guatemala and 4,000 in Belize. The Q'eqchi' inhabit a combined total land area of 12,000 square kilometers.

The Q'eqchi' language is a descendant of Proto-Mayan; it belongs to the Quichean Branch of the Macro-Mayan languages and is closely related to the Poqomam and Poqomchi' languages spoken today.

History and Cultural Relations

The Q'eqchi' have a long history of political conflict. Even before the Spanish Conquest, which began in earnest in 1529, Guatemala was known as Tezulutlan, or "the land of war." The combined factors of military resistance and the dispersal of the Q'eqchi' population for agricultural reasons made centralized governmental control by the Spanish highly difficult. For this reason, Friar Bartolomé de las Casas was given permission to attempt to pacify the Q'eqchi' through religious conversion. Although the church was never able to gain complete control, its actions did have a strong influence on the Q'eqchi' people. The church's attempts to protect the Q'eqchi' led to an isolated Q'eqchi' enclave that was not part of the economic growth of Spanish-colonial Guatemala. Once the church lost its ability to govern the Q'eqchi', the Indians were open to exploitation from outside sources.

During the nineteenth century, plantation agriculture, which was supported by government policies, had two marked negative effects on the indigenous population. First, communal tribal lands were privatized by the plantation owners, and second, it became increasingly necessary for the Q'eqchi' to work on the plantations as wage laborers for their economic subsistence. By 1877, all communal landownership was abolished by government decree. Because of the ensuing land pressures, in 1889 many Q'eqchi' began to emigrate east to Belize.

Because of the poverty created by these historical developments, there has been much political unrest during the twentieth century. The Guatemalan government has responded to indigenous activism with military repression which has often proved devastating to the Q'eqchi'. During the 1980s, as much as 25 percent of the Q'eqchi' population in Guatemala emigrated to the United States.

Settlements

The Q'eqchi' live in relatively dispersed villages. Because they are an agricultural people, they locate their houses at the center of their maize fields rather than in dense communities; however, it is not uncommon for closely linked kin to cluster into groups of up to five households. Traditional houses consist of single-room dwellings with pole walls and a palm roof. Additional rooms are occasionally constructed for food storage.

Economy

Maize, otherwise known as milpa, is central to the lives of the Q'eqchi'. It is produced through swidden agriculture: at the beginning of each growing season, the farmer chooses his field, marks it with stones, burns the vegetation on the growing area, and plants his crop. Coffee and cardamom are also cultivated as cash crops.

The staples of the Q'eqchi' diet are maize, beans, and chilies. Other crops supplementing the diet are squashes, sweet potatoes, and tomatoes. Fish caught in mountain streams are also consumed.

There is a certain degree of flexibility within the division of labor between men and women, but most agricultural production is performed by males, and most food-processing and household maintenance is completed by females. Many Q'eqchi' women are also skilled in textile production. On their looms they create intricately woven and brocaded blouses.

Differing policies by the Guatemalan and Belizean governments have shaped Q'eqchi' land tenure in these respective countries. Privatization of tribal lands in Guatemala has forced many to become day and migrant laborers. In Belize, the government has allowed the Q'eqchi' to live on reservations. In both countries, individuals lease government lands or simply squat on government lands unofficially.

Kinship

Although the patrilineal bond is important, there are no formal patrilineal descent groups. Kinship is traced bilaterally. Kinship terms emphasize generational differences, and cousins are considered marriageable.

Marriage and Family

At the age of 6 or 7, male children begin to go to the fields with their fathers, and female children stay at home with their mothers. Between the ages of 12 to 15 for females and 15 to 18 for males, children are considered adults. At this time, they are able to marry and become independent.

Marriage is arranged by the parents of the children and most often includes a form of bride-price. The parents of the male form a relationship with the parents of the female over time, and if all is satisfactory the children are married. After marriage, the children usually form an independent household.

Households usually consist of only the nuclear family, but it is not uncommon for households to cluster, creating a form of multidwelling extended-family household.

Given the degree of mobility in Q'eqchi' society, there is often little to transmit; however, parents often grant the inheritance of property to the children who offer labor or care giving to the parent during his or her lifetime.

Sociopolitical Organization

The Q'eqchi' have strong beliefs in egalitarianism. Within the nation of Guatemala, however, they are considered secondary citizens. For this reason, Q'eqchi' social and political power is limited to the community level, at which a civil-religious hierarchy prevails. There are three main officers within the civil hierarchy—the alcalde, the _concejal_, and the _sindico_; they are elected by a popular assembly.

The religious hierarchy shows less of a Spanish influence. It is here that Q'eqchi' are able to build status for themselves. The role of mayordomo consists of organizing and funding fiestas and church festivals. Sponsorship of these events translates into prestige and status.

Religion and Expressive Culture

Traditional beliefs in the Tzuultaq'a (gods of the mountains and valleys) have been influenced by the Catholic church. The Q'eqchi' have accepted the Christian God, and they hold fiestas to celebrate the patron saint of each village. Within the Q'eqchi' cosmology, the Tzuultaq'a preside over nature. It is believed that the Tzuultaq'a live in caves in the mountains, from which they are able to maintain the natural order.

Other than the priest of each local Catholic church, there are three types of traditional religious specialists: _ilonel_, curers who use ceremonies and herbs; _aj ke_, diviners who advise and predict; and _aj tul_, sorcerers who cast spells. Although these are three separate roles, it is possible for one person to fulfill all three.

Before planting his crops each year, the farmer and his wife perform a fertility ritual. They simulate intercourse in three corners of their dwelling and then consummate the act in the fourth corner. Other ceremonies include both the veneration of saints and idols at altars within the homes and observance of the Day of the Dead.

At death the body is wrapped in a _petate_ (a straw sleeping mat) and buried with all the things that will be needed for the journey to the afterlife. These items include a hat, sandals, and a net.

Bibliography

Bert, Nancy A. (1988). "K'ekchi' Horticultural Labor Exchange: Productive and Reproductive Implications." In _Human Reproductive Behavior_, edited by L. Betzig, M. Borgerhoff Mulder, and P. Turke, 83–96. Cambridge: Cambridge University Press.

Carter, William E. (1969). _New Lands and Old Traditions: Kekchi Cultivators in the Guatemalan Lowlands_. Gainesville: University of Florida Press.

International Work Group for Indigenous Affairs (1978). _Guatemala 1978: The Massacre at Panzos_. IWGIA Document 33. Copenhagen: International Work Group for Indigenous Affairs.

Schackt, Jon (1986). _One God, Two Temples: Schismatic Process in a Kekchi Village_. Oslo: University of Oslo, Department of Social Anthropology; Universitetsbokhandelen.

Wilk, Richard R. (1991) _Household Ecology: Economic Change and Domestic Life among the Kekchi Maya in Belize_. Tucson: University of Arizona Press.

Wilk, Richard, and Mac Chapin (1989). "Belize: Land Tenure and Ethnicity." _Cultural Survival Quarterly_ 13(3): 41–46.

Wilson, Richard (1991). "Machine Guns and Mountain Spirits: The Cultural Effects of State Repression among the Q'eqchi' of Guatemala." _Critique of Anthropology_ 11(1): 33–62.

Wilson, Richard (1993). "Anchored Communities: Identity and History of the Maya-Q'eqchi'." _Man_ 28:121–138.

Wilson, Richard (1995). _Maya Resurgence in Guatemala: Q'eqchi' Experiences_. Norman: University of Oklahoma Press.

Rama

ETHNONYMS: none

The nearly 700 Rama Indians live in the Atlantic-coast region of Nicaragua, in the departments of Zelaya Norte, Zelaya Sur, and Río San Juan. Only 15 or 20 people now speak the Rama language, although many more speak Rama Cay Creole.

The social dislocations caused by the wars of Spanish Conquest produced a mixed group of Voto, Suerre, and Guetar Indians, and out of this mixed group was formed the modern Rama people. The Miskito Indians, allies of the English, conquered and then dominated the Rama in the seventeenth and eighteenth centuries. The Rama were among the many victims of the Nicaraguan military and political fighting of the 1980s. They have lived in an autonomous political zone since 1987.

Bibliography

Centro de Investigaciones y Documentación de la Costa Atlántica, ed. (1987). *Ethnic Groups and the Nation State: The Case of the Atlantic Coast in Nicaragua.* Edited by CIDCA/Development Study Unit. Stockholm: University of Stockholm, Department of Social Anthropology.

Vilas, Carlos Maria (1989). *State, Class, and Ethnicity in Nicaragua: Capitalist Modernization and Revolutionary Change on the Atlantic Coast.* Translated by Susan Norwood. Boulder, Colo.: L. Rienner Publishers.

Rastafarians

ETHNONYMS: Dreadlocks, Dreads, Nati Dread, Rastafari, Rastas

Orientation

Identification.   Rastafarianism is a Black-nationalist religious movement, founded in Jamaica, which affirms that the late emperor of Ethiopia, Haile Selassie, is the returned messiah, Jesus Christ; that God is Black; and that like the children of Israel, all people of African descent in Jamaica and throughout the Americas, live in enforced exile. Repatriation to the ancestral home will bring redemption and freedom from the system of White oppression, which Rastafari identify as "Babylon." The majority of Rastas are highly visible owing to their matted hair, or dreadlocks, which they hold to be sacred and which they sometimes cover under woolen caps colored red, gold, and green (representing blood, gold, and land). They regard the herb ganja (*Cannabis sativa*) as a special gift of God—first found on the grave of King Solomon—and smoke it as part of their sacred ritual discussion, using a hookah, or "chalice."

Location.   Although it maintains its highest concentration of adherents in Jamaica, Rastafarianism has spread to all islands of the Caribbean and to Black populations throughout the hemisphere and in Europe. Rastafarians are also found in many African countries, including South Africa, and in Australia and New Zealand. It would appear, however, that the belief in Haile Selassie is not as pronounced in countries outside Jamaica, although the focus on an African identity remains.

Demography.   There are no reliable estimates of the number of Rastafarians in Jamaica or elsewhere. Official Jamaican censuses so far do not recognize Rastafari as a legitimate religion. Even if they did, however, the results would still be uncertain, owing to Rastafari hostility toward cooperation with Babylon. Nevertheless, rough estimates put adherents in Jamaica at between seventy thousand and a hundred thousand, or 3 percent to 4 percent of the population.

Linguistic Affiliation.   Dread talk, an argot of neologisms, homonyms, and inversions, is used to express certain basic philosophical concepts, the most prominent example being the use of the pronomial *I* to express oneness and divine immanence.

History and Cultural Relations

The Rastafari movement began shortly after the coronation, in November 1930, of Ras (Prince) Tafari Makonnen as Emperor Haile Selassie. Claiming descent from King Solomon of Jerusalem and the Queen of Sheba, Selassie took the imperial titles "King of Kings, Lord of Lords, Conquering Lion of the Tribe of Judah," which a few Jamaicans saw as proof that the messiah had returned to redeem the Black race. The new doctrine, however, has to be understood against the background of Garveyism, which focused on a positive Black self-image and Black ethnicity and thus predisposed early adherents to interpret the coronation event the way they did. The doctrine appealed mainly to Jamaica's urban poor—the rural migrants and the unemployed living in the slums of Kingston. Relations with the state, which were at all times generally bad—Rastafarians were subject to arbitrary victimization and harassment—reached their lowest ebb in 1960, when Claudius Henry and a small group of his followers were cited for treason. Out of that crisis came a study by a team of university scholars and an unofficial government mission to investigate the possibility of migrations to several African countries; both activities contributed to a more positive evaluation of the Rastafari. A state visit by Emperor Haile Selassie himself in 1966 also served to enhance the legitimacy of the movement. By the end of the 1960s, nearly all the major popular artistes were Dreadlocks, and by 1975 the majority of urban youths and a growing section of the middle classes were either adherents or sympathizers. During this period, reggae artistes became, through their recordings and tours, the main missionaries of the Rastafari movement in other parts of the Caribbean and Europe, particularly the United Kingdom, where the cult provided the descendants of immigrants from the Caribbean with a sense of Black identity.

Sociopolitical Organization

Organizational Structure.   As a whole, Rastafarianism is an acephalous religious movement, resistant to centralization and control. Most Dreadlocks belong to the House of Nyabinghi, a quasi group led by elders whose status derives from a combination of age, experience in the faith, and oral skills. The affairs of the house are run democratically, and all, including elders, are subject to the challenge of every Dread. Other Dreadlocks belong to one of two groups organized around a charismatic leader: the Twelve Tribes of Israel, led by Prophet Gad; and the Ethiopia Africa Black International Congress, or Bobo, led by Prince Emmanuel. The Bobo are the only Rastafarians who physically separate themselves by living in a commune. They also distinguish themselves from other Dreadlocks by wearing a white or black turban.

Political Organization.   Rastafarians eschew involvement in local politics, although since the mid-1960s there have been isolated examples of individual Rastafarians who have sought to mobilize a Rastafari vote in Jamaica, the better, so they argue, to bring about repatriation. On a number of Caribbean islands, however, Rastafarians have identified with political movements against the established political order. Rastafarians are proud of the tradition of resistance that has attended the rise and spread of their movement; in their view, resistance is the continuation of struggles against slavery. One of the founders, Leonard Howell, was imprisoned for preaching sedition; others were imprisoned for defiance of colonial authority. Today the Rastafari critique of society finds symbolic expression in dreadlocks, the Babylon metaphor, the use of ganja, and adoption of an African or Ethiopian identity. In Jamaica Rastafarians were among the foremost local supporters of the antiapartheid movement of South Africa.

Religion and Expressive Culture

Religious Beliefs and Practices. Rastafarians believe in the existence of one supernatural spirit, whom they call Jah and associate with Haile Selassie. They hold that Jah exists in every Rastafarian, who thereby shares in his divinity. They eschew salt, pork, and processed foods, a practice called *ital,* and many exclude all meats and fish from their diet. Rituals are of two kinds, the reasoning and the *binghi.* In the reasoning, small groups gather to take part in informal discussions of matters of faith, and the ceremonial smoking of the sacred herb. Participants sit in a circle, uncover their heads, pray before the chalice is lit and passed in a clockwise direction. The binghi is a celebration of a liturgical event that lasts several days; it involves reasoning by day and drumming, singing, and dancing by night. Binghis are held to commemorate the coronation of Haile Selassie, Ethiopian Christmas, Haile Selassie's birthday, and Haile Selassie's state visit to Jamaica.

Religious Practitioners. Unlike other forms of religion in Jamaica, Rastafarianism does not have a priesthood.

Arts. Rastafarians have been closely associated with Jamaican folk and popular art, particularly reggae music, which rose to prominence nationally in the 1960s and internationally in the 1970s, and intuitive painting and wood carving.

Death and Afterlife. In keeping with a philosophy that celebrates life, many Rastafarians deny the possibility of death, except as a consequence of sin, and believe that the doctrine of the existence of, and reward in, the afterlife is the White man's teaching aimed at deflecting Blacks from the pursuit of their just rewards in this life.

See also Jamaicans.

Bibliography

Barrett, Leonard (1977). *The Rastafarians: The Dreadlocks of Jamaica.* London: Heinemann.

Nettleford, Rex (1972). *Identity, Race, and Protest in Jamaica.* New York: William Morrow. Originally published as *Mirror, Mirror: Identity, Race, and Protest in Jamaica.* Kingston, Jamaica: Collins Sangster, 1970.

Owens, Joseph (1976). *Dread: The Rastafarians of Jamaica.* Kingston, Jamaica: Sangster.

BARRY CHEVANNES

Saint Lucians

ETHNONYM: Lucians (colloquial)

Orientation

Identification. Although Saint Lucians regard themselves as West Indians, their Saint Lucian identity is primary.

Location. Saint Lucia is one of the Windward Islands, which constitute the southern chain of the Lesser Antilles, in the eastern Caribbean. The island is located 40 kilometers south of Martinique and 48 kilometers north of Saint Vincent. Its proximity to these two islands—a former French colony and a former British colony—reflects and reveals Saint Lucia's dual European history and culture.

Demography. The population of Saint Lucia was estimated to be 151,774 in 1992. In contrast to other West Indian societies, Saint Lucia is and always has been ethnically homogeneous. People of African descent constitute 90.3 percent of the population; of these, some are Melates (a combination of African and European lines), others are Doglas (African and East Indian), and still others Chabeans (African, East Indian, and Amerindian). East Indians, descendants of contract workers recruited from India in the 1850s, account for 3.2 percent of the population. Less than 1 percent of Saint Lucians are Caucasians.

Linguistic Affiliation. Saint Lucians are largely bilingual. Although English is the island's official language and about 45 percent of the population is literate in English, Patwah, the nonwritten language that developed between French-speaking planters and African slaves, is widely spoken. Whereas French and Patwah had at one time been the island's sole languages, a linguistic transition to English occurred in the early 1800s, after Saint Lucia became a British colony.

History and Cultural Relations

Saint Lucia was first occupied by Amerindians. Around A.D. 200, the Arawak, who are thought to have emigrated from the coast of South America, arrived in Saint Lucia. By 1300, the Arawak were displaced by the Carib, who probably also originated on the South American mainland. Although Amerindian communities are no longer found on the island, their cultural contributions are still apparent. In particular, many of their craft skills, such as pottery making and boat building, are still practiced on a small scale.

Although Columbus is generally credited with discovering the island on 13 December 1502 (the feast day of Saint Lucy), its actual European discoverer remains unknown. The English were the first Europeans to attempt to colonize Saint Lucia, but their 1605 settlement had to be abandoned following a Carib ambush in which most of the main party of sixty-seven men were killed. The French, who had a more amicable relationship with the Carib, are credited with establishing the first successful colony on the island in 1650.

By 1674, as the French continued to settle the island, Saint Lucia was claimed by the French Crown and made a dependency of Martinique. Ten years later, however, because France and Great Britain contested its ownership, Saint Lucia was declared neutral, but the dispute continued for 150 years. During this period, the "Helen of the West"—as Saint Lucia was known because of its beauty and strategic harbor—passed back and forth some fourteen times between Great Britain and France. Even though the island was finally ceded to Great Britain in 1814, the French exerted a tremendous influence over Saint Lucia, today most evident in the realms of religion (i.e., Catholicism), language (i.e., Patwah), and culture (particularly the Flower Society revels, described under "Ceremonies," and Carnival).

Once the British gained control of the island and political stability was restored, a plantation economy was established, based on the cultivation of sugarcane. Adjusting to the vicissitudes of the nineteenth-century sugar market and compensating for a shortage of African laborers, the British introduced the *meytage* (sharecropping) system in the 1840s. Devised as a means to supply planters with a cheap labor force while providing the recently freed slaves with an incentive to remain on the estates, the meytage system created a dual plantation and peasant economy.

In spite of its remote location, Saint Lucia was affected both politically and economically by World War I and World War II. As a British colony, Saint Lucia sent troops to Europe and allowed the United States to establish an air base near Vieux Fort. The global depression of the 1930s also adversely affected Saint Lucia. Owing to perennial slumps in sugar prices, the islanders began to divert land from sugar to banana production, and by 1964 sugar was no longer a commercial crop.

In February 1967 Saint Lucia was granted the status of a state associated with the United Kingdom, with full internal self-government. Great Britain remained responsible for external affairs and defense. On 22 February 1979 Santa Lucia achieved full independence.

Settlements

On the basis of French ecclesiastical principles of organization, Saint Lucia is divided into eleven geo-demographic districts for purposes of administration: Ansye-la Raye, Canaries, Castries, Choiseul, Dennery, Gros Islet, Laborie, Michoud, Soufrière, and Vieux Fort. Approximately three-fifths of the population is concentrated in Castries, the island's capital, in the north, and Vieux Fort, a semi-industrial zone in the south. The rest of the population is dispersed along the coastline, in the other nine administrative zones. Thickly forested mountains in the interior of the island preclude either cultivation or habitation.

Parallel to this pattern is the Saint Lucian notion of spatial zoning. The island is divided into two discrete geo-social zones—"town" and "country." "Town" almost always refers to Castries, whereas "country" is generically applied to all other inhabited regions, including those areas that contain relatively large pockets of settlement and industry.

Economy

Subsistence and Commercial Activities. Despite efforts to promote the development of industry and tourism, Saint Lucia's economy is still primarily dependent on agriculture. The cultivation and export of bananas account for nearly 80 percent of the island's revenue. Saint Lucia is wholly dependent on the banana industry, the future of which is uncertain. Until 1992, when Europe became a single market, Geest, a British-based transshipment corporation, transported, distributed, and retailed all the bananas Saint Lucia produced. The European union resulted in the loss of Saint Lucia's ready-made market because Britain is no longer in a position to give preferential treatment to its former colonies. Saint Lucia's exceedingly low productivity level for the cultivation of bananas was not a concern prior to 1992, but now the island's chief export must compete on the world market. The government has been seeking to diversify the island's agricultural activities.

Tourism, the second-largest earner of foreign exchange, is an enclave industry that is still evolving. Although revenues from tourism have continued to increase, it, too, is a precarious industry. The vast majority of hotels and restaurants are foreign owned. Hurricane Allen caused heavy damage to the tourist infrastructure in 1980.

Ranking third in contribution to the island's economy is the industrial sector. Small in scale, it includes about 200 enterprises that produce furniture, clothing, paper products, electronic appliances, beverages, and textiles.

Industrial Arts. In 1971 the Saint Lucian government established the Craft Centre at Choiseul. Its purpose was to provide jobs for villagers and to preserve such traditional craft skills as pottery making, wood carving, and weaving.

Trade. The chief exports include bananas, cardboard boxes, clothing, and coconut products. Approximately 40 percent of Saint Lucia's exports are to Great Britain, the remainder to neighboring islands and the United States. Food, live animals, and electronic parts are imported.

Division of Labor. The division of labor is based on precepts of reciprocity, interdependency, and cooperation. At the village level, this ethos is best exemplified in the *coup-de-main*, a type of organized work party into which an individual gathers friends and relatives to accomplish a labor-intensive task such as building a house or preparing a baptismal party. All members of the work party are fed by the host in exchange for their labor. At the household level, each member of the family, including children, is expected to work. Men and women toil side by side in the banana fields, but women are responsible for the bulk of domestic and child-care chores.

Land Tenure. The land-tenure system is a legacy of colonialism. Almost 47 percent of Saint Lucia's agricultural holdings, or 13,074 hectares, are owned in estate by seventeen families, whereas about 4,700 smallholders till plots of land that average less than 0.4 hectares. Unless there is a specific arrangement regarding inheritance of land, all offspring are entitled to an equal share. Because there rarely is a prearranged agreement and because multiple offspring often have claim to land, fragmentation of landholdings has occurred.

Kinship

Saint Lucians trace descent through both parents. The extended family, including fictive kin such as godparents and informal adoptive parents, also assumes an important role in social and economic interpersonal relations.

Marriage and Family

Marriage. Three types of heterosexual unions are common in Saint Lucia, as is true for the West Indies in general: visiting unions, in which a couple engages in sexual/economic relations but does not share a residence; common-law unions, in which in addition to having a sexual/economic relationship, the couple also shares a domicile; and marital unions, in which the couple engages in sexual/economic relations, is legally wed, and shares a common residence. Each union entails different degrees of stability, typically correlating with differing levels of economic obligation and commitment. Moreover, union types vary with the life cycle: visiting unions are most common during early adulthood, marital unions later on.

Domestic Unit. Like the vast majority of West Indian societies, Saint Lucia is matrifocal; households are not only largely composed of women and their offspring, but women also assume a dominant role in the domestic domain. Although individuals in the upper stratum of society are likely to be found in households that approximate the European ideal of a nuclear family, for those in the lower stratum of society, the nuclear-family pattern is exceptional.

Socialization. Women are the primary socializing agents, although children are greatly valued by both men and women in Saint Lucian society. Children provide labor while they are young, and as adults they are expected to care for their aging parents. The concept of familial reciprocity is instilled in children at a very early age.

Sociopolitical Organization

Social Organization. Saint Lucia has long had a dual class structure: an elite class that controls the economic and political scene, and a poor, laboring class. A popularly expressed differentiation, analogous to the geo-spatial distinction between "town" people and "country" people (see "Settlements"), is drawn between "high" people and "low" people. The former are typically associated with urbanity, a light skin hue, the English language, and "high" occupations—attorney, landowner, teacher—whereas the latter pertains to rural residence, darker skin hues, the Patwah language, and "low" occupations—manual labor and domestic service.

In Lucian society, particularly among "low" people, there is a strong sense of community and sharing, which is achieved by cultivating an extensive social network. This ethos is perhaps best exemplified by "friendly societies"—voluntary associations established for extending mutual aid to members in times of financial need caused by illness or death in the family. Each member contributes monthly dues, and officers are expected to oversee the funds. In times of distress, members apply to the association for benefits. Operating at the individual level is the *su-su*, another type of revolving-credit association, in which individuals merge into small groups of about six. Every month, members of the su-su give one individual in the group a fixed amount of money to be disposed of as he or she chooses.

Political Organization. Saint Lucia is a constitutional monarchy and a member of the Commonwealth of Nations. A prime minister governs the island with the aid of a ten-member cabinet. The legislature consists of a seventeen-seat elected House of Assembly and an eleven-seat Senate, whose members are appointed by the governor general, the prime minister, and the leader of the opposition. The constitution also provides for a parliamentary commissioner and an integrity commissioner, both appointed by the governor general.

Social Control and Conflict. Major deviant behavior is handled through the judicial system, which consists of the Magistrates Court, the High Court, the Court of Appeal, and the Privy Council in Britain. Minor deviance is controlled at the community level through gossip, obeah, and familial intervention.

Religion and Expressive Culture

Religious Beliefs. Owing to the legacy of French influence, 90 percent of Saint Lucians are Catholics. In conjunction with their Catholic beliefs and practices, however, Saint Lucians also adhere to obeah. Although not as formalized as other African-based West Indian religions, obeah, like Catholicism, influences the way Saint Lucians construct and conduct their lives.

A type of sorcery, obeah is predicated on the belief that the world is a dangerous place—evil lurks in spirits, demons, and human agents who are capable of inflicting injury on others. Saint Lucians thus believe that one must be prepared to thwart these harmful agents before they can realize their malignant intentions, while simultaneously being prepared to combat them. Outlawed in 1954 and long castigated by the church, obeah is still commonly practiced in Saint Lucia, albeit covertly.

Religious Practitioners. In addition to the Catholic clergy, obeah practitioners assume a role in the spiritual life of Saint Lucians. The *jagajey*, who obtains power directly from Satan, is an obeah practitioner; the *gade*, who gains knowledge through divination, uses power to counteract obeah.

Ceremonies. The vast majority of holidays and ceremonies center around the church's liturgical calendar. Others are either sponsored by the government under the auspices of the Ministry of Culture, or they transpire at the community level, among individual families. Three events are unique to Saint Lucia: the pageantry of Flower Societies, A-Bwe, and Kele. The Flower Societies hold an annual round of revels that effectively divide Saint Lucian society into the Roses (*lawozes*) and the Marguerites (*lamagwites*). Beginning with Mass at dawn, each group, on its respective feast day (30 August for the Roses and 17 October for the Marguerites) stages a parade, complete with a court of Kings and Queens. The day and evening are spent feasting, dancing, and playacting. A-Bwe, a singing ceremony, transpires in Dennery during the months of November and December. Kele, like A-Bwe, is limited to only a few communities on the island. It is a ceremony in which homage is paid to the ancestors.

Medicine. Medical services are delivered through a network of health-care centers and hospitals under the direction of the Ministry of Health. The island has three hospitals: Victoria, which is located in Castries and operated by the government; Golden Hope, which is also in Castries and is a treatment center for mental illness and alcohol/drug addiction; and St. Jude's, situated in Vieux Fort and administered by the Order of Sorrowful Sisters of Mary.

Saint Lucians also have recourse to "bush medicine." Illnesses caused by forces of nature such as cold air and dampness are treated with teas made from local plants, popularly known as "bush tea."

Death and Afterlife. Upon hearing that a friend or family member has died, mourners convene a small wake in the home of the deceased, bringing coffee, sugar, rum, and juices. The next day, a Catholic Mass is held and the deceased is buried in a cemetery. Following the funeral, the wake continues. In rural areas, a *raconteur* (storyteller) is summoned, and the evening is spent riddling, singing, playing games, drinking, and eating. It is not unusual for the wake to last nine consecutive nights. The dead are remembered on 1 November, All Saints' Day. At this time, graves are cleaned and adorned with paper wreaths, fresh flowers, and lighted candles.

Bibliography

Auberteen, Michael (1987). "Patterns of Gender Socialization in St. Lucia." M.A. thesis, University of Manchester.

Breen, Henry (1970). *St. Lucia: Historical, Statistical, and Descriptive.* London: Frank Cass & Co.

Dressler, William (1982). *Hypertension and Culture Change: Acculturation and Disease in the West Indies.* New York: Redgrave.

Jones, Rose (1994). "Songs from the Village: An Ethnography of Gender, Reproduction, and Sexuality in St. Lucia, West Indies." Ph.D. thesis, Southern Methodist University.

Koester, Stephen (1986). "From Plantation Agriculture to Oil Storage: Economic Development and Social Transformation." Ph.D. thesis, University of Colorado.

ROSE JONES

Seri

ETHNONYMS: Cere, Ceri, Comcaac, Guayma, Heri, Sadi, Salineros, Sori, Tastioteños, Tepoca, Tiburone, Upanguayma

Orientation

Identification. The name "Seri" is of unknown origin and meaning. It was first applied as "Heri" in 1645. The Seri call themselves "Comcaac" (the people).

Location. In aboriginal times the Seri lived along a 208-kilometer strip of the central Sonoran coast between about 28° and 30° N, and on adjacent Tiburón and San Esteban islands in the Gulf of California. This region is one of the hottest and most arid portions of North America. At present, the Seri reside in two villages, El Desemboque de Los Seris and Punta Chueca.

Linguistic Affiliation. Serian is a Hokan language. Only one dialect is still spoken, but two other mutually intelligible dialects are recalled. They are considered isolates.

Demography. Population estimates for the early historic period vary from around 1,000 to 4,000. Severe population decline began with the onset of full-scale war with the Spaniards in 1750. Of some 500 Seri remaining in 1855, about one-half were killed in the next dozen years. By the 1930s Seri numbers had dropped to about 175. Since then, the population has rebounded, reaching 516 in 1990 and over 700 in 1994.

History and Cultural Relations

Archaeological evidence indicates that Seri occupation of their traditional territory extends well back into prehistoric times. The Seri were in contact with the neighboring Papago, Pima, Yaqui, and Cochimí, and some cultural borrowing occurred. After contact with Europeans, the southernmost band (Guayma) was absorbed fairly quickly into mission life. The island Seri and some coastal people rarely saw Europeans and retained a peaceable and traditional life well into the nineteenth century. The Seri the Europeans came to know were opportunistic groups that migrated into the interior of Sonora and took to raiding and stealing livestock. The mission of Nuestra Señora del Pópulo was founded in 1679 to deal with these trouble-makers, but the Seri had little interest in sedentary life, and the mission was never a success. Seri-European relations worsened and in 1750 erupted in open warfare that raged unabated for twenty years. The nominal peace that followed was soon punctuated by sporadic raids and reprisal campaigns.

After Mexican independence, the pace of hostile encounters quickened, leading to an abortive campaign to exterminate the Seri in 1844. That same year Pascual Encinas established a ranch deep within the Seri range, intending to pacify the Seri with jobs and good treatment. His efforts failed, and in the dozen years of the "Encinas War" beginning in 1855, about one-half of the Seri were killed in skirmishes with Encinas's cowboys. By the late nineteenth century the remaining Seri were shifting between a foraging existence along the coast and islands and eking out a precarious existence on the encroaching ranches. During the 1920s the emerging Mexican fishing industry at Bahía Kino encouraged the Seri to try commercial fishing. A fish cooperative was established in 1938, transforming El Desemboque into the first permanent Seri community. Increasing numbers of North American tourists arriving in the 1960s stimulated a revival of traditional crafts for sale. Although the Seri communities now include a school, a clinic, and an evangelical church, core aspects of Seri culture and social life persist.

Settlements

Aboriginally, the Seri were nomadic. Their movements reflected both seasonal and fortuitous changes in the food supply and in the most critical commodity, fresh water. People moved among temporary camps as resources shifted. Camps were occupied for up to several weeks and might be composed of a single nuclear family or as many as fifteen families. Although the Seri now reside in two permanent villages, the population of each fluctuates greatly as people move freely between them. Some traditional camps are still used during fishing or foraging expeditions.

Most activities were conducted outdoors, and shelters served primarily as windbreaks and for storage. Houses were fabricated of ocotillo branches and resembled a Quonset hut or a simple rectangular box. They were covered with brush, seaweed, or anything handy. Housing today in the two villages is more substantial. Here the Seri have built both Mexican-style _jacales_ of wattle and daub, and small wood-frame structures. During the 1960s and 1970s the Mexican government constructed cinder-block bungalows for the Seri.

Economy

Subsistence and Commercial Activities. The aboriginal Seri economy was based on hunting, gathering, and fishing. The relative contribution of each of these activities may have been quite different for the different bands, and surely varied with the season. Many species of plants were gathered, notably mesquite seeds, amaranth, cactus fruits, agave, and a marine seed-bearing eelgrass (_Zostera marina_). The most important game animals were mule deer and jackrabbits. Slow game included chuckwallas, iguanas, and desert tortoises. Some Seri groups relied heavily on sea products. By far the most important were sea turtles, hunted with a barbed harpoon (_balsas_) made from cane. Fish, including sea bass, mullet, groupers, snappers, and triggerfish, were speared with balsas or from shore. Shellfish and other littoral and intertidal creatures were sometimes gathered in quantity. Several types of large seabirds were stalked at night as they roosted. Gull eggs were collected in the spring. For coastal and island Seri, the diet probably changed little with the coming of the Spaniards. Those Seri who moved inland added cattle, horses, and other livestock to their roster of fair game during raiding, and thievery and soliciting handouts expanded their inventory of subsistence techniques. Farming was tried by some Seri at the mission of Nuestra Señora del Pópulo and later at the presidio of Pitic (now Hermosillo) but without lasting success. Nor did they adapt to wage labor on ranches in the late 1800s. By the early 1900s nearly all Seri had resumed a foraging existence on Tiburón Island and the adjacent coast. Commercial fishing, beginning in the 1930s, introduced cash, which the Seri began to use to buy commercial food imported by Mexican entrepreneurs. Some commercial fishing continues. In the 1960s the focus of economic life shifted to craft production for sale to tourists. Most food consumed by the Seri is now purchased in Mexican-owned stores. Although the new staples include wheat flour, canned meat, rice, beans, canned fruits, coffee, and soft drinks, some fishing and even gathering occasionally supplement the packaged diet. Dogs, cats, chickens, and some goats are kept as pets. They are not eaten.

Industrial Arts. The most important indigenous crafts were pottery making and basketry. Aboriginal pottery was seldom decorated but its thinness, hardness, and symmetry attest to consummate skill. Its quality declined as metal containers became common in the late 1800s. Today an occasional piece is made for the tourist market. Baskets, made by close coiling on a bundle foundation, were regarded as a woman's most important domestic item. Although baskets had been replaced by commercial containers, the recent tourist market has stimulated a renaissance of basket making. New forms and designs, along with refinements in technique, have won Seri baskets major prizes at North American tribal fairs. An entirely new craft, ironwood carving, appeared around 1960. The carved figurines, made strictly for sale, are representations of animals familiar to the Seri. The sale of these superb items has proved so lucrative that ironwood carving has become a near-universal cottage industry and the foundation of the modern Seri economy.

Trade. Some Seri may have traded salt and hides for maize. European goods were obtained by Seri who roamed inland, but the island people may have had almost no contact with the outside world.

Division of Labor. Hunting and fishing is exclusively men's work, whereas basket making, pottery making, and sewing are the prerogative of women. Otherwise the division of labor is not rigid. A man might sometimes gather plant foods, fetch water, and cook, but these are normally women's tasks. Ironwood carving is undertaken by both sexes, although men usually rough out the basic form. The few positions of temporary leadership recognized in the past went to men, but either men or women could become shamans.

Land Tenure. Seri oral tradition associates each of the former bands and their subunits (*ihizitim*) with a specific geographic region. Although sometimes construed as "territories," they probably did not confer exclusive rights of passage or use, for there was much movement and shifting residence throughout the entire region. More likely, band and ihizitim territories served as theoretical reference points that helped objectify the social identity of individuals. By the mid-nineteenth century the Mexican government had declared the Seri coast to be public land, and the Seri increasingly found themselves hemmed in by Mexican ranching and fishing operations. In 1965 they were evicted from Tiburón Island, which had been declared a wildlife preserve. In 1975, however, a 56-kilometer strip of mainland coast was designated a Seri *ejido*. The Seri were also given formal title to Tiburón Island, although their use of it is still restricted.

Kinship

Kin Groups and Descent. Today, Seri descent is reckoned bilaterally, and residence is neolocal with a slight patrilocal preference. The nuclear family is the core residential and economic unit. The "tribe" is recognized as a valid concept, although it functions mainly as a unit of ethnic identity. There are no formal groupings between the level of nuclear family and tribe. In the past, the Seri were divided into several geographically separate, politically independent units (bands), which differed in dialect and culture. Spanish recognition of "nations" only partly coincides with bands as recalled in Seri oral history. The Seri maintain that bands were further subdivided into geographical groupings called ihizitim, which they believe were well-integrated patrilineal, patrilocal, and exogamous units of everyday life. To what extent Seri social structure differed in the past has been a subject of intense debate. Different sources—Seri oral history, colonial documents, ecological considerations, and anthropological theory—have led investigators to an astonishing array of reconstructions. These include matrilineal, patrilineal, and bilateral descent; clans; subclans; patrilocal bands; composite bands; and *rancherías* (groups of huts). The data on which reconstructions must be based are so ambiguous that it is doubtful that aboriginal Seri sociopolitical structure and descent will ever be well understood.

Kinship Terminology. Kinship terminology is bifurcate collateral, with sibling terms extended to both parallel and cross cousins. Numerous terminological distinctions are made. One quasi-kinship system that still operates is the *hamac* relationship of reciprocal obligations for sponsorship of burials and the girls' puberty fiesta.

Marriage and Family

Marriage. Marriages are usually negotiated by parents. A boy may initiate the process, after which his parents take over if they approve his choice. If the girl's parents also approve they begin negotiating bride-price, which since the 1960s has become considerable. When bride-price transactions are completed, the bride moves in with the husband without ceremony. Ideally, some bride-service obligations continue indefinitely. All close kin are excluded as potential marriage partners, including parallel and cross cousins who are terminologically equated with siblings. Some polygyny existed in the past, but all present marriages are monogamous. European-style weddings, encouraged by the local evangelical church, have become common. Since the 1960s, intermarriage with Mexican fishermen who are willing to live in El Desemboque and Punta Chueca has been increasing. Divorce is not common. It may be initiated by either partner, usually amid accusations of laziness or ill-tempered behavior. The bride-price is not returned.

Residence. Residence is neolocal, although the couple may reside briefly with the boy's parents.

Domestic Unit. The normal household is a simple nuclear family.

Inheritance. A few personal items were traditionally interred with the body. Nearly all the remaining property of the deceased and his household were exchanged for equivalent possessions of the hamac that performed the burial. This system is breaking down as the Seri acquire large amounts of consumer goods.

Socialization. Children, including twins, are welcomed. Girls are preferred for the bride-price they will bring. Children are raised in a permissive atmosphere with little or no physical punishment.

Sociopolitical Organization

Social Organization. Seri society is fundamentally egalitarian. Husbands have limited status as heads of households. In the past, older males may have held some authority. A war leader was accorded temporary status during military action. Especially powerful shamans have commanded both respect and fear. The authority of twentieth-century tribal "chiefs" has been restricted to external matters.

Political Organization. The Seri say that band and ihizitim structure collapsed when their population was decimated in the mid-nineteenth century. The resulting "tribe" emerged as a de facto grouping consisting of all surviving Seri; today it has little formal structure and few political functions. An informal council of elder men occasionally deliberates on matters involving external relations. The current "chief," however, has been an effective advocate for Seri interests with both the state and federal governments.

Social Control. The Seri value individualism. They are willing to tolerate considerable latitude in behavior, but are equally willing to express themselves if behavior exceeds acceptable bounds. Minor excesses are sometimes controlled by gossip, but angry diatribes directed squarely at the offender are not uncommon.

Conflict. Conflict is generated mostly at the interpersonal rather than the group or tribal level. Most disputes are resolved with little more than loud quarreling. Occasional fights have erupted, and rare instances of homicide are recalled. It is said that shamans were formerly capable of killing by witchcraft. Today a constable is charged with keeping the peace.

Religion and Expressive Culture

Religious Beliefs. Seri religion entailed belief in a large number of malevolent spirits who were placated by appropriate ritual. Most ritual is individual and often private. Seri religion as an integrated system no longer functions, although many rituals are followed out of custom. Spanish missionary efforts had no lasting effect on the Seri. Mexican evangelical Protestants, who arrived in 1953, have had some influence on most Seri and have won a number of genuine converts.

Religious Practitioners. Shamans controlled forces of both good and evil. Although they could place curses, their primary role was healing and the prevention of sickness and misfortune. Healing was accomplished solely through their influence over the spirits; any medicinal cures were administered by ordinary individuals. Anthropomorphic figurines were carved by shamans and rented to clients as fetishes. Some influence over the spirits was thought to come naturally with age. Individuals aspiring to shamanism, however, sought direct contact with the spirits during a four-day vision quest. Shamans were paid for their services.

Supernaturals. In addition to individual spirits, the Seri recognize certain more general supernatural forces. One, called Icor, controls the spirit of each plant, and its power can be tapped by shamans. Another is Hant caai, responsible for creating much of the world. He is thought to be male and is vaguely associated with the sun. Although Hant caai seems to be indigenous, the Seri say he is the same deity the Mexicans call Dios.

Ceremonies. The festive tone of Seri group ceremonies is intended to placate potentially malevolent spirits. Today the only regularly performed ceremony is the four-day girls' puberty fiesta. While the girl is secluded and subject to several taboos, the community engages in festive singing, Pascola dancing on a foot drum, betting games, and feasting. A puberty fiesta for boys was last held about 1923. The rare capture of a leatherback turtle prompts a similar ceremony. Completion of a giant basket also necessitated a fiesta to pacify the basket's spirit. The scalp dance has not been performed since warfare with the Europeans ended.

Arts. Face painting, especially of females, was a major art form but is rarely evident today. Much visual art now takes the form of basketry design and ironwood carving. The only dancing that survives today is the solo Pascola. Neither men's nor women's circle dances have been performed since the early 1900s. Music, especially singing, is still important. Despite exposure to Mexican popular music, many people prefer traditional Seri music; it is commonplace to record and listen to traditional songs on battery-powered tape recorders.

Medicine. Shamans cured serious illness supernaturally, but ordinary Seri treated lesser maladies with medicinal preparations. These were often simple teas, but the pharmacopoeia included more than 100 species of plants and animals. Clinics and commercial medicines have largely replaced traditional remedies.

Death and Afterlife. Traditional burials were performed by a hamac of the deceased, without public ceremony.

Today, funerals are increasingly common. The name of the deceased is not spoken. Ideally, the person is forgotten fairly quickly, although female relatives may wail for as long as a year. The afterlife, which transpires in the sky near the setting sun, is a replica of the present world but contains only good things. Virtuous Seri arrive there after four days, whereas evildoers are permanently stranded in one of several hells along the way.

Bibliography

Bowen, Thomas (1983). "The Seri." In _Handbook of North American Indians_, edited by William C. Sturtevant. Vol. 10, _Southwest_, edited by Alfonso Ortiz, 230–249. Washington, D.C.: Smithsonian Institution.

Felger, Richard Stephen, and Mary Beck Moser (1985). _People of the Desert and Sea._ Tucson: University of Arizona Press.

Grifffen, William B. (1959). _Notes on Seri Indian Culture, Sonora, Mexico._ School of Inter-American Studies Latin-American Monograph Series, 10, Gainesville: University of Florida Press.

Kroeber, Alfred L. (1931). _The Seri._ Southwest Museum Papers, 6. Los Angeles.

Nolasco Armas, Margarita (1967). "Los seris, desierto y mar." _Anales del Instituto Nacional de Antropología e Historia_ (Mexico City) 18:125–194.

THOMAS BOWEN AND MARY BECK MOSER

Sipakapense

ETHNONYMS: Sipacapa Quiché, Sipacapeño, Sipacapense

The 4,000 to 5,000 Sipakapense Indians are a Maya Indian group who live in the vicinity of Sipacapa, San Marcos Department, Guatemala. Most speak Spanish as well as the Sipakapense language. They subsist primarily on maize, beans, and avocados, but also grow citrus fruits for sale. They live in an isolated region and have difficulty bringing their produce to market.

Bibliography

Lovell, W. George (1992). _Conquest and Survival in Colonial Guatemala: A Historical Geography of the Cuchumatan Highlands, 1500–1821._ Rev. ed. Montreal and Buffalo: McGill–Queen's University Press.

Sumu

ETHNONYMS: Mayangna, Ohlwa, Olua, Panamaka, Smoo, Smu, Somoo, Summoo, Sumo, Sumoo, Taguaca, Tahuajca, Taoajka, Tawahka, Towcka, Twahka, Twaka, Twanka, Twaxha, Ulúa, Ulwa, Woolwa, Woowa, Wulwa, Zumo

Orientation

Identification. "Sumu" is the common name used since the mid-1800s to refer to a group of related peoples of eastern Nicaragua and Honduras. The Miskito, the traditional enemies of the Sumu, also called them "Albatuina" (slaves) or "Ialtanta" (flat heads); the Spaniards labeled them "Caribes" (savages) and "Chatos" (flat heads). Von Houwald (1975; 1990) claims sixty different names have been used to refer to them, many (Batuca, Patuca, Bocayes) corrupted from a particular river or region they inhabited. The Sumu call themselves "Mayangna," meaning "we" (*yagna*) of the "sun" (*ma*), referring to their origin myth (Rizo 1993, 31), or they identify themselves by their linguistic affiliation.

Location. Three Sumu groups now occupy the rain forests of the Mosquitia region of eastern Nicaragua and Honduras. The Tawahka, about 20 percent of the Sumu, live in northern Nicaragua along the Río Bambana where Wasakin, the largest Tawahka village, has 900 residents; other villages are along the Río Coco (between its Waspuk and Lakus tributaries) and farther north in Honduras on the middle Río Patuca. The Panamaka, about 70 percent of all Sumu, center on the Bosawás (Río *Bocay-Saslaya-Waspuk*) region, especially along the Bocay and Umbra rivers and along the headwater streams of the Bambana and Waspuk; others are southward along the upper reaches of the Prinzapolca, Matagalpa, and Escondido rivers and in the village of Awastingni, farther east along the Río Wawa. Musawás, on the Río Waspuk, has 1,700 inhabitants and is the largest Sumu village. The Ulwa, 10 percent of the Sumu, live in Karawala (with a population of 770) and Kara, near the mouth of the Río Grande de Matagalpa; others are along the Río Sikia, a tributary of the Río Escondido. Some families choose to live in coastal Miskito settlements (Hale 1991, 27; Herlihy 1993; Williamson et al. 1993).

Demography. Eduard Conzemius (1932, 14) estimated from fieldwork in the 1920s that a mere 3,000 to 3,500 Sumu survived, remarking that the "day of their complete disappearance or absorption by the Miskito does not seem far off." The Tawahka, Panamaka, and Ulwa each numbered about 1,000 at the time. In 1990, 13,000 to 15,000 Sumu lived in Nicaragua and fewer than 1,000 in Honduras.

Linguistic Affiliation. Sumu languages are considered variants of a common family called Misumalpa, which includes the languages of the Miskito, Sumu, and Matagalpa who inhabited the prehistoric frontier between Mesoamerican and South American influences. The family apparently fissioned off its Chibchan trunk thousands of years ago and may have remained united until a century or two before Spanish contact, when Sumu languages separated. Of the remaining three, Tawahka and Panamaka are very similar, whereas Ulwa is more distinct; all contain loanwords from Miskito, English, and Spanish.

Sumu parlance declined with missionaries and government programs of the twentieth century, and a large part of the population is now trilingual. Children learn Spanish in school, speak Miskito in the village, and converse in Tawahka, Panamaka, or Ulwa with their families. Few Indians can read and write Sumu languages, but bilingual education programs may awaken new interest.

History and Cultural Relations

The Sumu were once the most widespread populations on the Caribbean slope of Central America. According to folklorists, they were nomadic bands of hunters, fishers, and collectors, but early accounts indicate they were farmers. Reports of cannibalism probably stem from ceremonial vengeance rites. European contact brought dramatic population decline and dislocation owing to Old World diseases, warfare, and the slave trade, but little evidence exists to estimate the magnitude of change.

The first images of Sumu life come from colonial times. Men wore loincloths, and women short skirts. Probably ten or more groups existed, including the Tawahka, Panamaka, Silam, Kum, Bawihka, Prinsu, Yusku, Boa, Ulwa, and Kukra. They occupied a territory inland from the Río Patuca in Honduras south to the Río Escondido in Nicaragua, bordered by Pearl Lagoon to the east and the savannas/uplands to the west, largely coincident with the limits of Spanish influence. Men had long straight hair, sometimes shoulder length, whereas women wore their hair down their backs with cut bangs in front; both wore decorative necklaces and bracelets. Infanticide controlled birth defects. Wooden slats were applied to flatten an infant's head.

Spanish authorities never effectively controlled the Mosquitia region. Some frontier missions evangelized western Sumu settlements during the seventeenth century, but most Spanish campaigns into the region found no wealth, and some ended in disaster. Concurrently, the east coast attracted British privateers from Jamaica who entered into commercial relations with the Miskito. To exert control over the area, the privateers, whose aim was to exploit forest resources, recognized a succession of Miskito kings. The British enlisted Miskito war parties in their campaigns against the Spaniards, giving them firearms and a degree of sovereignty. Firearms gave Miskito warriors the advantage over the Sumu, whom they conquered, enslaved, or commercially incorporated into the "kingdom." The Sumu were obliged to pay tribute to Miskito kings and governors in the form of dugouts, deerskins, maize, cacao, rubber, and more. In the face of this situation, Sumu families retreated inland. Miskito reign declined and the British withdrew by 1860, wi en Mosquitia became part of Honduras and received "Reserve" status in Nicaragua. The Miskito Reserve was incorporated as a Nicaraguan department, Zelaya, in 1894. Surviving Sumu groups lived relatively isolated from outsiders and maintained cultural traditions.

Since colonial times, most Sumu groups—including the Yusku, Prinsu, Boa, Silam, Ku, and Bawihkas—have disappeared or assimilated into the expansive Miskito or Spanish-Indian (Ladino) cultures. The Ulwa, for example, once the most widespread group, were reduced by diseases and conflicts to only a few headwaters areas by the late 1700s. Conzemius (1932) found only about 150 Bawihka, and the Kukra were practically extinct by the 1920s.

Moravian missionaries, who began work on the Miskito Coast in 1849, launched evangelization efforts among the Sumu in 1910 (Oertzen et al. 1990, 41). Missionaries encouraged families to resettle around prayer-house sites or their homes. Musawás had eight lodges and a prayer house in 1922 (Oertzen et al. 1990, 308). A Honduran state education program agglomerated the Tawahka into a school-site settlement in 1916, but an epidemic forced its abandonment (Landero 1980). Despite good intentions, missionaries and educators were insensitive to indigenous identity, grouping Sumu with Miskito families in the same settlements and teaching them in English, Spanish, or the Miskito language.

The Marxist government of Nicaragua tried to bring about the political integration of the indigenous peoples after the Sandinista Revolution of 1979. Indian resistance forces demanded self-government and respect for their own traditions, fighting bloody battles against government troops during the 1980s. The Sandinistas occupied Musawás in 1982, killing and forcibly conscripting Sumu men, and began a mass evacuation of Sumu villagers from the Río Coco war zone. Some 3,000 moved to Honduran refugee camps; others stayed, living under threats of being killed, kidnapped, or forced into military service by one side or the other. The war destroyed Sumu community life in Nicaragua. Since 1985, most Sumu have been repatriated and have been resettling and rebuilding their former villages.

Though formerly integrationist, Nicaragua and Honduras have now begun to recognize the rights, identity, and political institutions of indigenous peoples. Nicaragua adopted the Autonomy Statute of 1987, establishing a regime of self-government, and Honduras is considering territorial status for its Sumu populations. Sumu identity and political clout are increasing because of international recognition of their role in conserving regional natural and cultural heritage. Nevertheless, road penetrations and agricultural colonization continually bring new conflicts, economies, and politics to Sumu territory.

Settlements

The Sumu, riverine rain-forest people, build their settlements along clear-water streams, above tidal influence. They formerly lived in large (20 meters by 10 meters) multifamily lodges, dispersed, or in small clusters on high levee banks. In the early 1900s missionary and government programs began to agglomerate them into villages. Today there are about forty villages in Nicaragua and five in Honduras. Most have between 100 and 500 people, fewer than fifty houses, a church, school, and store. Houses are now smaller thatch- or tin-roofed, post-and-pole framed structures with board, split-bamboo, or palm floors elevated about a meter above the ground. Normally a house is sided with a door and windows; sometimes it has a divided interior.

Economy

Subsistence and Commercial Activities. Sumu subsistence has changed very little over time. The household is the self-contained economic unit. Farmers use slash-and-burn cultivation to grow root crops (sweet manioc, yams, and *Xanthosoma*), plus maize. Plantains and bananas, which are grown in groves along the natural levee, are the staple foods. Eaten fresh, boiled, and baked, these fruits, when ripe, are also mashed, along with maize, palm fruits (especially *supa, Bactris gasipaes*), manioc, and sweet potatoes and mixed with water to produce *chicha* drinks (*wakisá*) that ferment into a "beer" (*mishla* or *wasak*). Three types of gourds, cacao, avocados, and other native palm and fruit trees are grown in dooryard and outfield orchard gardens, along with medicinal herbs, dyes, spices, cotton, tobacco, and ornamentals. Old World fruit trees—citrus, breadfruit, mango—and rice, beans, and sugarcane are also grown for food and sale, as are tomatoes, green peppers, and cabbage.

Bows and arrows, spears, and blowguns were the primary aboriginal weapons for hunting a diversity of forest game. Hunters now choose .22-caliber rifles and shotguns. The importance of wild game in Sumu diets depends on local ecological and economic conditions. Fishing is done with hooks, spears, nets, and, less commonly, bows and arrows; piscicides are uncommon. Animal husbandry is limited to raising wild forest "pets" in addition to some chickens, ducks, turkeys, pigs, cows, and horses. Dogs are used for hunting, but cats are rare. Villagers still depend greatly on foods, materials, and medicines collected from forest and regrowth fallow.

Sumu men have worked for foreign enterprises extracting roots, saps, resins, and gums for dyes, medicines, and other uses since the seventeenth century. Native woodsmen collected sarsaparilla and cut mahogany in the eighteenth century, bled latex from rubber trees in the nineteenth and early twentieth centuries, and more recently tapped chewing-gum latex from chicle trees. Individuals have also worked as turtlers, shrimpers, and, most recently, divers for lobsters in the coastal fishing industry. Gold panning is an important cash-earning activity in some areas, and cash cropping increases with improved market access.

The Sumu cash-involved subsistence economy requires broad territories for agriculture, hunting, fishing, and collecting resources. The approximately 650 Tawahka Sumu living along the middle Río Patuca in 1990 used about 770 square kilometers, with only 5 percent under agriculture.

Industrial Arts. Sumu men craft dugouts, a trade and tribute item since colonial times. Men still cut *tuno* (*Poulsenia armata*) tree bark that women pound into cloth (*tikam*), formerly fashioned into loincloths and skirts, now into blankets and mosquito netting. Twine, used to weave carrying bags and hammocks, comes from the pounded bark of the *majao* (*Heliocarpus Donell-Smithii*) tree. Silk grass formerly provided a durable fiber for nets, bowstrings, and fishing lines. Tree gourds still serve as bowls, and other kitchen utensils are made of carved wood. Women previously made pottery and dyed, spun, and wove cotton for clothes, hammocks, and bedsheets, but no longer do so.

Trade.   No formal marketplaces existed among aboriginal Sumu populations, but evidence of gold ornaments links them to broad Central American trade networks (Newson 1987, 78). They traded dugouts, bark cloth, hammocks, woven bags, and pottery with the Miskito. Europeans exchanged commercial products for hides, dyes, feathers, resins, and timber. Today the Sumu use cash to buy tools, kitchenware, clothes, and many manufactured products, including foods. They fashion majao bags, decorative tree gourds, and cloth tapestries made from tuno bark for an expanding indigenous crafts market.

Division of Labor.   Hunting and cutting forest are exclusively male activities. Women do household chores and help in planting, weeding, harvesting, and collecting forest-plant and animal materials. Few men still fish with spears or bows and arrows; using a line and hook, both sexes catch river crustaceans. Villagers have a labor-exchange system (*biribiri*), commonly organized along kin lines, for more physically demanding work. Nowadays payments of meat, grains, bullets, or cash substitute for labor exchange, as wage labor has become embedded in Sumu life. Sumu men now specialize as boatmen, teachers, ministers, nurses, and storeowners.

Land Tenure.   Landownership develops as former usufructuary rights and planted fields become the private property of the farmer who prepares them. Villagers share use of hunting, fishing, and collecting territories. Sumu land use exhibits communal attitudes toward resource use, and land has not historically been a commodity exchanged for profit.

Kinship

Kin Groups and Descent.   Little information is recorded about the kin-based features of Sumu life. Conzemius (1932, 146) observed that the children of two brothers or of two sisters are considered real brothers and sisters and are not allowed to marry each other. The children of brothers and sisters, however, are not considered blood relatives, and union of such cousins is common.

Kinship Terminology.   Some studies and dictionaries list certain Sumu kin terms, but apparently no study of their kinship terminology exists.

Marriage and Family

Marriage.   Sumu men often took more than one wife, but it is unclear if polygamy was an aboriginal practice. Conzemius (1932) reported that non-Sumu marriages were forbidden, and offspring from such unions would be killed. Girls were betrothed at an early age, when a suitor asked the girl's parents directly. Even today the suitor must show his capacity to provide for his intended wife and bring her parents firewood, meat, produce, or other esteemed items. The Sumu may have once practiced patrilocal residence, but now newlyweds live with either in-laws until their own house is completed. The new groom avoided contact with his mother-in-law, who stayed secluded when he was at home. Divorce simply meant the separation of the couple and apparently was unaccompanied by any ritual. During the twentieth century, mixed marriages with Miskito, Pech, Blacks, and mestizos have become common. Today, perhaps due to missionary influence, most Sumu men have only one wife.

Domestic Unit.   The extended family is the most common domestic arrangement. Lodges once contained three or more families under the same roof, but today each family normally has its own house.

Inheritance.   Transfer and inheritance of land and property occur traditionally along kin lines, usually between males.

Socialization.   Children learn traditions and subsistence lessons through daily apprenticeship alongside their parents. Boys sharpen hunting skills by playing with scaled-down spears and bows and arrows, and they accompany fathers on hunting, fishing, and farming trips. Girls learn domestic chores while helping their mothers. The grandmother cares for infants when the mother is gone, and grandparents and other elders enjoy relating tales and traditions to youngsters.

Sociopolitical Organization

Social Organization.   Sumu social structure was egalitarian. The head of the extended family—the eldest able-bodied male—was the highest authority figure. Shamans and elders were respected for their knowledge and wisdom but held no special status. Sometimes shamans or others with special skill or bravery rose to ephemeral leadership in times of turmoil or warfare. Missionary and government influence have brought new political positions into Sumu village life.

Political Organization.   There were no chiefs, village leaders, or broad tribal organizations in traditional Sumu society. A loosely structured council of elders sometimes convened to resolve community relations. The Sumu did not traditionally delimit tribal lands.

Today Sumu villagers elect community leaders and establish political institutions. The Nicaraguan Sumu organized the Sumu Kalpapakna Wahaini Lani (SUKAWALA) or Sumu Brotherhood in 1974, and the Honduran populations set up the Federación Indígena Tawahka de Honduras (FITH) in 1987 to address political, cultural, economic, and territorial concerns. These entities have become the de facto Sumu governments. In 1990 FITH solicited recognition of a 2,300-square-kilometer reserve. SUKAWALA is struggling for legal title to Sumu lands in the Bosawás Reserve established in 1991. Their lands are not part of a proposed binational reserve system covering the rain forests north to the Caribbean Sea. The federations struggle to assure legal title to their lands within these protected areas.

Social Control.   Crimes, land disputes, and other social issues were formerly resolved by the head of the extended family. Peer pressure was also a powerful leveling force. Offenders must now answer to community and federation leaders, and state laws and regulations are applicable.

Conflict.   Since the seventeenth century, the Sumu have faced outside aggressions by other indigenous populations and Europeans and, later, by the postcolonial national governments of Honduras and Nicaragua, seeking to control them, their territories, and their resources. These clashes with outsiders greatly reduced both Sumu population and their territory. Recent solidarity against outside aggressions has strengthened Sumu identity and resolve toward their own cultural practices.

Religion and Expressive Culture

Religious Beliefs. Little systematic study exists of the original Sumu beliefs. In 1915 Moravian missionary George Heath was told that long ago the Sun was looked upon as creator and supreme lord, and the Moon was also a god, but this worship ceased suddenly thirty or forty years earlier with the spread of the gospel among the Miskito (Oertzen et al. 1990, 302–303). Landero (1980, 16) recorded that this sun god, Mapapak (from Ma, "Sun," and Papak, "my Father") lives in the heavens (*mapikidiká*), distributing life and happiness. Rizo (1993, 37) adds that "Father Sun," Moon, and Wind are represented in one image called Uwawau, the "Heart of the gods" and notes that the earthly world is submissive to the influence of other tiers inhabited by good and evil spirits. Nature was animated by all sorts of spirits (*walasá, nawah, lilkadutni,* or *dimalah*) that punished humans when they violated the laws of nature, or were benevolent if humans were so.

Most Nicaraguan Sumu now follow Moravian beliefs, whereas the Honduran Tawahka are mostly Catholics. Most Sumu acknowledge the Christian design of the universe, along with the concepts of sin, heaven and hell, and private property, but retain some traditional beliefs.

Religious Practitioners. The *sukia* is the Sumu shaman whose knowledge cures the sick, divines the hidden, and helps individuals communicate with gods, demons, and spirits. Shamans are advisors, conjurers, counselors, diviners, exorcists, folklorists, herbalists, priests, and teachers. The position was not hereditary; rather, it was acquired through apprenticeship. The *ditalyang* was reportedly another botanical healer, but the sukia possessed greater spiritual knowledge and had the ability to communicate with the supernatural. Indeed, a successful hunt may be attributed to the just and generous actions of the sukia (Rizo 1993, 38). Sumu pastors now teach Moravian and Catholic beliefs, and many hold political power.

Ceremonies. Sumu formerly held a "festival" (*asang lawana*) at which men secluded themselves in sacred places deep in the forest to prepare young men to endure warfare. Other ceremonies proved the skills and fortitude of young boys. Menstrual seclusion sequestered the "impure" women in makeshift huts, where they were unable to "contaminate" food or forest. Today's simple ceremonies focus on life-cycle events, such as marriages and burials, or mark the end of communal-work efforts. These, as well as Christmas, Easter, and other Christian and state celebrations are normally accompanied by feasts with *mishla* (or other alcoholic beverage) drinking, singing, and dancing.

Arts. The arts, per se, were never highly developed in Sumu society. Pottery, figurines, and masks found on abandoned sites and in burials may indicate greater skill in the past. They had no writing aside from some crude pictographs etched into boulders, and stonework was probably restricted to the manufacture of grinding stones and grinders. Landero (1980, 18) described Sumu music as simple; the instruments were drums, rattles, and flutes, the latter often melodically imitating bird songs.

Medicine. The use of household remedies made from the bark, roots, leaves, and seeds of native plants is declining as manufactured medicines become widely available. Herbalists still use plant concoctions to cure deadly snake bites and other ailments. The sukia could also effect a cure by exorcising the evil spirit from the patient. Today medical assistants work in some villages.

Death and Afterlife. Even before accepting contemporary Christian beliefs, the Sumu probably believed in an afterlife (Newson 1987, 82). Death was formerly believed to be caused by sorcery or evil spirits. Mourning their dead husbands, widows cut their hair short and endured self-inflicted pain. Some of these practices still occur. The dead are now buried in coffins in graveyards near each settlement.

Bibliography

Americas Watch Committee (1987). *The Sumus in Nicaragua and Honduras: An Endangered People.* New York and Washington, D.C.: Americas Watch.

Conzemius, Eduard (1932). *Ethnographical Survey of the Miskito and Sumu Indians of Honduras and Nicaragua.* Bureau of American Ethnology Bulletin 106. Washington, D.C.: Smithsonian Institution.

Hale, Ken (1991). "El Ulwa (Sumo Meridional): ¿Un idioma distinto?" *Wani,* no. 11 (August–December), 27–50.

Helms, Mary W. (1971). *Asang: Adaptations to Culture Contact in a Miskito Community.* Gainesville: University of Florida Press.

Herlihy, Peter H. (1993). "Securing a Homeland: The Tawahka Sumu of Mosquitia's Rain Forest." In *State of the Peoples: A Global Human Rights Report on Societies in Danger,* edited by Marc S. Miller, 54–62. Boston: Beacon Press.

Houwald, Götz Freiherr von (1990). *Mayangna = Wir: Zur Geschichte der Sumu-Indianer in Mittelamerika.* Hohenschäftlarn bei München: Kommissionsverlag Klaus Renner.

Houwald, Götz Freiherr von, and Jorge Jenkins M. (1975). "Distribución y vivienda sumu en Nicaragua." *Encuentro, Revista de la Universidad Centroamericana* (Managua) 7:63–92.

Landero, Francisco Martínez (1980). *La lengua y cultura de los sumos de Honduras.* Estudios Antropologicos e Historicos, 3. Tegucigalpa: Instituto Hondureño de Antropología e Historia.

Mangus, Richard Werner (1978). "The Prehistoric and Modern Subsistence Patterns of the Atlantic Coast of Nicaragua: A Comparison." In *Prehistoric Costal Adaptations: The Economy and Ecology of Maritime Middle America,* edited by Barbara L. Stark and Barbara Voorhies, 61–80. New York and London: Academic Press.

Newson, Linda A. (1987). *Indian Survival in Colonial Nicaragua*. Norman and London: University of Oklahoma Press.

Oertzen, Eleonore von, Lioba Rossbach, and Volder Wündreich, eds. (1990). *The Nicaraguan Mosquitia in Historical Documents, 1944–1927: The Dynamica of Ethnic and Regional History*. Berlin: Dietrich Reimer Verlag.

Ortega, Marvin (1991). *Nicaraguan Repatriation to Mosquitia*. Washington, D.C.: Hemispheric Migration Project/Center for Immigration Policy and Refugee Assistance.

Rizo, Mario (1993). "Mito y tradición oral entre los sumus del Río Bambana." *Wani*, no. 14 (June): 28–44.

Williamson, Dennis, Janette Avilés, and Melba McLean (1993). "Aspectos generales de las communidades sumus de la RAAN." *Wani*, no. 14 (June): 18–27.

PETER H. HERLIHY

Tarahumara

ETHNONYMS: Ralámuli, Rarámuri, Tarahumar, Tarahumari, Taraumar

Orientation

Identification. In Spanish colonial records the Tarahumara are usually designated as "Tarahumaes" and "Tarahumaras," the names that non-Tarahumara continue to apply to them. The Tarahumara today refer to themselves as "Rarámuri," which means—on increasingly specific levels—"human beings," "Indians" (as opposed to non-Indians), "the Rarámuri proper" (as opposed to other Indian groups), and "men" (as opposed to women). The term "Rarámuri" first appeared in print in 1826 (but spelled "Rarámari" and translated as "Tarahumares"). The etymologies of "Tarahumara" and "Rarámuri" and the relation between the two terms remain unclear. "Ralámuli" is becoming the standard spelling in writings by Rarámuri people. Around 3 percent of contemporary Tarahumara reject a formal affiliation with the Catholic church and are called *gentiles* and *cimarrones*. The rest of the Tarahumara identify themselves as "Pagótame" or "Pagótuame" (Baptized ones).

Location. At Spanish contact, the Tarahumara lived across much of what is now central and western Chihuahua, Mexico, from 106° to 108° W and 26° to 30° N. During the colonial period, some Tarahumara entered Spanish economic centers to the south and east of their aboriginal territory, whereas others retreated to the west. The incursions of non-Indian settlers and the integration of the Tarahumara into the emerging mestizo society have reduced their territory to the mountains and canyons of western Chihuahua. In the mountains, summers are cool and winters mild, but the climate of the canyon floors is semitropical.

Demography. The 1980 Mexican census recorded 62,419 speakers of the Rarámuri language over 5 years of age, of which 56,400 resided in Chihuahua and 3,916 in the adjacent states of Sinaloa, Sonora, and Durango. Sixty percent of the Tarahumara in Chihuahua live in the mountains and canyons of the Sierra Madre Occidental, and the remainder around urban centers outside the sierra.

Linguistic Affiliation. The Rarámuri language, of which there are three dialects, belongs to the Uto-Aztecan Language Family. Of extant languages, it is most closely related to Guarijío and Yaqui-Mayo.

History and Cultural Relations

The meager archaeological evidence available suggests that the Tarahumara have lived in Chihuahua for at least two thousand years. At Spanish contact (around 1600), they were bordered on the south by the Tepehuan, on the east and north by the Concho, on the northwest by the Mountain Pima, on the southwest by the Tubar, and on the west by the Guarijía and a number of other small groups closely related culturally and linguistically to the Tarahumara. Spanish settlement in and around Tarahumara country was motivated primarily by the discovery of rich silver and gold deposits; the settlers carried Old World diseases that decimated local Indian populations. The Tarahumara served as both forced and free laborers in the colonial economy; they adopted Old World livestock and agricultural technology. Between 1639 and 1767, Jesuits established missions across the Tarahumara region, but most Tarahumara maintained only a loose affiliation with the Catholic church. Although there were Tarahumara who integrated into Spanish colonial society, many resisted Spanish expansion: several revolts erupted throughout the seventeenth century, Spanish settlements were raided during the eighteenth century, and some Indians sought refuge by establishing communities in inaccessible areas. Franciscan and secular priests replaced the Jesuits in 1767.

By the mid-nineteenth century, social and economic disruptions following Mexican independence in 1821 led to the abandonment of the mission system, but the Jesuits reestablished it in 1900. Since the late nineteenth century, expanded mining, agriculture, and lumbering have displaced the Tarahumara from many areas outside the Sierra and have attracted non-Indian settlers into the Sierra. Tarahumara relations with these non-Indians vary from community to community, but generally each ethnic group views the other negatively and intermarriage between them is rare. The Mexican government and the Catholic mission provide the Tarahumara schools and medical services. In the late twentieth century Protestant missionaries have been active in several Tarahumara communities, where they also offer some social services.

Settlements

The Tarahumara in the Sierra Madre continue their traditional pattern of living near their fields in hundreds of hamlets and isolated homesteads scattered along streams and canyons. Catholic missionary efforts to congregate the Tarahumara into compact villages have largely failed, but their churches have become the foci of community religious and political activities. In the second half of the twentieth century, notched log houses have replaced more traditional stone and mixed stone and handhewn-plank houses over much of Tarahumara country. In many areas, residents move during the growing season to cultivate dispersed fields; some shift to rock shelters or winter houses during the colder months of the year.

Economy

Subsistence and Commercial Activities. As in the past, the Tarahumara economy is based on the cultivation of maize, beans, and squash. The European introduction of plows, axes, livestock, fruit trees, and Old World crops such as wheat enhanced rather than transformed traditional agricultural practices. Wild plants continue to provide an important component of the diet, but wild-plant fibers used for weaving have been supplanted by wool and commercial yarn. The destruction of much of the larger fauna, especially deer, once a crucial source of meat and raw materials, has increased the importance of introduced livestock, in particular sheep, goats, and cattle, which provide manure, wool, and hides in addition to meat. Many Tarahumara supplement their agricultural activities by working in the local Mexican economy, typically in lumbering and road construction, and by performing chores for their non-Indian neighbors. They also acquire cash by selling their agricultural products and by producing items for sale to tourists. Since the colonial period, the Tarahumara have migrated to work in economic centers outside their territory; in the second half of the twentieth century such out-migration, both temporary and permanent, has been increasing.

Industrial Arts. The Tarahumara make most of their basic household and agricultural implements and ritual paraphernalia from locally available raw materials, but they purchase manufactured goods such as cloth, metal tools, and plastic and metal containers. They also produce textiles, pottery, musical instruments, and wood carvings for the outside, mostly tourist, market.

Trade. In the colonial period, the Tarahumara traded maize and other agricultural products for European manufactured goods, providing a significant proportion of the food for some Spanish mining towns. A similar exchange continues, but goods are now more frequently bought and sold rather than bartered. Items found locally in the canyons of southwestern Chihuahua, especially medicinal plants, are traded and sold in the uplands and in areas outside the Sierra.

Division of Labor. The Tarahumara divide most work into male or female tasks, but when the need arises both men and women perform basic household chores associated with the opposite gender. Women tend to prepare the food, care for the children and livestock, weave, and make pottery; men undertake most of the horticultural work, construct houses, cut and haul firewood, and carve. Men are the principal political officials and are also more prominent than women in wage labor for non-Indians and in ritual activities, including curing.

Land Tenure. Most Tarahumara live in _ejidos_, communal landholding units created as part of the agrarian-reform program of the Mexican Revolution. Land tenure is ultimately subject to ejido rules but tends to conform to traditional practices. Both men and women own fields individually, which they exchange, sell, lend, and transmit to their heirs. Usufruct applies to abandoned fields and uncultivated lands. Reforms to the Mexican constitution in 1992 allow ejido holdings to be converted to private property and sold to non-ejido members, potentially jeopardizing Tarahumara control of their lands.

Kinship

Kin Groups and Descent. The Tarahumara reckon descent bilaterally and have no corporate kin groups. Their kin terminology is classified as Neo-Hawaiian.

Marriage and Family

Marriage. People who share a lineal ancestor theoretically cannot marry, but in practice this prohibition usually extends only to second cousins because genealogical connections seldom are remembered beyond three generations. Many marriages are arranged, often by special marriage officials; only the Tarahumara most influenced by Jesuit missionaries are married by Catholic priests. Because interaction between unrelated men and women is discouraged, young people often marry several times, until they find compatible spouses, after which their marriages are stable. Polygyny occurs but is rare. Young newlyweds usually move between their natal households until they are economically independent.

Domestic Unit. Households are composed of nuclear families, frequently extended to include relatives of either spouse but seldom of both. Closely related nuclear families often live near one another, sharing food and working cooperatively.

Inheritance. Children inherit equally from both parents. Spouses do not inherit from one another, but surviving spouses often retain some property if there are no surviving children or serve as trustees for property inherited by their small children. During life, parents often give their children livestock and (especially at marriage) fields so they can begin forming separate economic bases.

Socialization. Children enjoy considerable independence and are scolded but seldom struck when they misbehave. A child's older siblings and grandparents share child-rearing duties with the parents. Industriousness, sharing, cooperation, and nonaggression are encouraged. The Tarahumara have no initiation rites or formal educational institutions; children are educated informally by participating in household and community activities. Most children also attend government or Jesuit primary schools, which somewhat disrupt traditional patterns of cultural transmission.

Sociopolitical Organization

Social Organization. The basic unit of social organization is the household. Neighboring households cooperate in the performance of rituals and in work projects such as planting and harvesting maize. Sponsoring households usually serve maize beer in conjunction with such activities. Households also share an affiliation with a pueblo, an organizational unit established by Catholic missionaries in the Spanish colonial period. Tarahumara society is egalitarian. There are variations in the amount of land and livestock individuals own, but wealth does not translate into political power, and redistributive mechanisms preclude the development of class divisions. Men and women are regarded as complementary equals.

Political Organization. At Spanish contact, local elders directed the political affairs of their communities but apparently exercised little real power. Today, a hierarchical political organization introduced by the Spanish is found in each Tarahumara pueblo, but no overarching tribal organization links the different pueblos. All officials are men, who choose their successors subject to the approval of the other men of the pueblo. The Tarahumara also participate with their non-Indian neighbors in the local political organizations of the ejido and the Mexican government.

Social Control. Social control is achieved informally through shunning, gossip, and scolding. The pueblo's political officials, sometimes joined by local ejido and Mexican-government authorities, hold formal trials in cases of assault, theft, failure to pay debts, and spouse desertion, punishing offenders by scolding, fining, or jailing them. People who commit more serious crimes (e.g., murder) are turned over to government officials for trial and punishment.

Conflict. Overt violence occurs almost exclusively in drinking contexts, most frequently between spouses. Such conflicts are often forgotten, but if they persist the pueblo political officials sometimes intervene. Although tensions exist between the Tarahumara and their non-Indian neighbors, few violent confrontations have occurred in the twentieth century.

Religion and Expressive Culture

Religious Beliefs. Catholicism has affected Tarahumara ritual more than it has their religious beliefs. Contemporary Tarahumara religion is oriented toward maintaining proper relations with their deities, who tend to be either benevolently or malevolently inclined toward them. Through dances, offerings, and other acts, the Tarahumara attempt to promote the benevolence or deflect the malevolence of these deities.

Religious Practitioners. Indigenous ritual specialists include chanters and curers; of the latter, raspers who direct peyote ceremonies are considered by many to be the most powerful. Curers are compensated for their services, but few are full-time specialists. Catholic missionaries have introduced additional ritual roles, principally *matachine* dancers and the musicians who accompany them on violins and guitars; the sodalities that direct the Easter ceremonies; and male and female officials who recite prayers, offer incense, and care for the church.

Supernaturals. The principal deities are "Our Father" and "Our Mother," associated with the sun and moon respectively. In many communities, the Christian God (often conflated with Jesus Christ) and the Virgin Mary have been assimilated to these deities. The Devil, considered the elder brother but implacable opponent of "Our Father," has been incorporated as the father of non-Indians. He controls the levels of the universe below the earth, whereas "Our Father" and "Our Mother" control those above. Minor deities and spirits also help or harm people but do not serve as intermediaries between humans and the supreme deities; Catholic saints are almost entirely absent.

Ceremonies. The Tarahumara perform rituals at their homes to cure ailments, to promote good health in people, livestock and maize, and to send offerings to their deities and the dead. They stage their most elaborate ceremonies at the pueblo churches during the Christmas and Easter seasons.

Arts. The Easter pageantry and the matachine dance, with its costumed performers and extensive musical repertoire, are the most highly developed examples of Tarahumara expressive culture.

Medicine. The Tarahumara consider illnesses to be of two types: those that afflict people's bodies and those that afflict their souls. The former usually are cured with plant or commercial medicines and increasingly are treated by physicians in Mexican government or Catholic facilities; the latter, which are usually produced by spirits, deities, or sorcerers, require the intervention of curing specialists who rely on their dreams to discover the causes of illness.

Death and Afterlife. Death occurs when people's souls permanently abandon their bodies. Tarahumara souls ascend to spend eternity with their heavenly parents, whereas those of non-Indians descend to live with the Devil. The souls of the Tarahumara who have committed offenses are punished—with destruction if their crimes are especially serious—but there is no eternal punishment or suffering. Surviving relatives sponsor a series of rituals to provide the dead food and goods and to encourage them to sever their relations with the living. Visitations from the dead, which usually occur in dreams, are feared as potential causes of illness and death.

Bibliography

Bennett, Wendell C., and Robert M. Zingg (1935). *The Tarahumara: An Indian Tribe of Northern Mexico.* Chicago: University of Chicago Press.

González Rodríguez, Luis (1984). *Crónicas de la Sierra Tarahumara.* Mexico City: Secretaría de Educación Pública.

Kennedy, John G. (1978). *Tarahumara of the Sierra Madre:*

Beer, Ecology, and Social Organization. Arlington Heights, Ill.: AHM Publishing Corp.

Lumholtz, Carl (1902). _Unknown Mexico._ 2 vols. New York: Charles Scribner's Sons.

Merrill, William L. (1988). _Rarámuri Souls: Knowledge and Social Process in Northern Mexico._ Washington, D.C.: Smithsonian Institution Press.

Pennington, Campbell W. (1963). _The Tarahumar of Mexico: Their Environment and Material Culture._ Salt Lake City: University of Utah Press.

Sheridan, Thomas E., and Thomas H. Naylor, eds. (1979). _Rarámuri: A Tarahumara Colonial Chronicle, 1607–1791._ Flagstaff, Ariz.: Northland Press.

Velasco Rivero, Pedro de (1983). _Danzar o morir: Religión y resistencia a la dominación en la cultura tarahumar._ Mexico City: Centro de Reflexión Teológica.

WILLIAM L. MERRILL

Tarascans

ETHNONYMS: Michuguaca, Phorhépicha, Phurhépecha, Purepecha, Purépecha, Tarascos

Orientation

During the past seven centuries, the Phurhépecha or Tarascans have inhabited and defined a territorial homeland that territory corresponds roughly to the physiographic region known as the Tarascan Subprovince in the Neovolcanic Axis of west-central Mexico. It is now a cultural mosaic of Tarascan-Mexican and Hispano-Mexican (mestizo) towns, but the Tarascan ethnic core is still predominant in three contiguous subareas of the zone—the island and shoreline communities of Lake Pátzcuaro, the highland forests to the west of Lake Pátzcuaro (called the Sierra Phurhépecha or Meseta Tarasca) and a small valley of the Río Duero to the north of the Sierra Phurhépecha (called "La Cañada de los Once Pueblos" in Spanish and "Eráxamani" in Phurhépecha).

The term "Phurhépecha" referred to "the commoners" in ancient Tarascan society and is a counterpart to the Aztec term _macehualli._ The term "Tarascan," in contrast, probably entered into use during contact with the first Spanish soldiers in the sixteenth century, displacing the Aztec term, _michoaque_ (possessors of fish, sing. _michua_), which in the locative form was the Aztec name for the ancient Tarascan empire. Michoacán (Aztec: _michi_, "fish,"

plus _atl_, "water," plus _kan_, locative) is still the name of the state where the Tarascan homeland is situated.

It remains commonplace for older-adult generations, especially in peasant villages, to refer to themselves as "Tarasco" or "Tarasca" (Tarascan) or forego any identification beyond the name of the central Tarascan town of their township. In contrast, the younger-adult generations, especially young professionals who live—or have resided—in regional or national urban centers, use the term "Phurhépecha." The entire population shares a common reference for significant others (especially their mestizo neighbors), who are called "Turísicha."

The Tarascan Subprovince of the Neovolcanic Axis is located in the area demarcated by the coordinates 19°20′ to 19°55′ N and 101°00′ and 103°00′ W. The Neovolcanic Axis is a unique east-west range of volcanoes in central Mexico. It forms a central to west-central belt of highland plateaus and forests of great climatological and ecological diversity that drain precious water into a stairway of lake basins branching to the northwest along the Lerma-Santiago riverway and due west to the Balsas River Basin. This belt is often referred to as the "Tarascan-Aztec System," a label that refers to the two pre-Hispanic state empires that controlled the Central Volcanic belt and surrounding areas during the two centuries prior to the Spanish Conquest.

The inhabited areas of Tarascan Subprovince are between 1,700 and 2,400 meters in elevation. During the rainy season (May or June to October or November), moist air rising from the Pacific precipitates on this volcanic mountain range and filters through the porous rock into the Duero River Basin in the north and northwest, Lake Pátzcuaro in the east, and into the region of Uruapan and the Tecaltecatepec River Basin in the south.

The Tarascans are for the most part highlanders. Approximately 70 percent of the Tarascan-speaking population lives between 1,700 and 2,300 meters above sea level. The rest of the homeland population occupies the valleys and slopes on the perimeter of Tarascan Subprovince approximately 1,500 meters in elevation.

The Mexican national census of 1990 reported 87,088 Phurhépecha speakers above the age of 5 years in the state of Michoacán. This figure is approximately 50 percent lower than a 1994 estimate (which includes children under age 5 as well as emigrants) by the Mexican Institute of Indigenous Affairs. Accordingly, Tarascan speakers probably number between 125,000 and 185,000. Contemporary Tarascan speakers are overwhelmingly bilingual, with Spanish as their second language. Defined in terms of ethnic identity rather than language use, the Tarascan population is certainly larger and, perhaps, growing in response to increasing local awareness and pride in the Tarascan heritage.

The linguistic affiliation of Tarascans has not been established. Affiliation with Macro-Mixtecan has been proposed, but convincing comparative evidence is lacking. Although considerable phonological and lexical variation exists, all dialects of Tarascan are mutually intelligible.

History and Cultural Relations

Among the groups that constituted the pre-Hispanic culture of the Mexican highlands, the Tarascans were unique in their skill in metallurgy, as well as in the use of rounded monumental structures (*yácatas*, or pyramids, which are common in western Mexico) on rectangular platforms in ceremonial centers. Equally distinctive is the evidence of complex social differentiation without corresponding social distinctions based on access to, and use of, alienable lands. It is probable that the Tarascan system of tribute depended on the labor of commoners on public lands. Similarly, bondage involved the exclusive obligation to perform specific services for an individual. This practice probably formed the basis of a complex system of labor appropriation in which forms of mutual servitude may have existed, thus distinguishing the Tarascan system from both the Aztec *mayeque* system of slavery and from European systems of slavery and serfdom. Both the division between noble and priestly groups and the more flexible forms of Tarascan political succession—based on personal leadership qualities and organized by a form of ambilateral kin reckoning still imperfectly understood by scholars—were typical of Aztec and other Middle American groups of highland Mexico.

At the time of the arrival of the Spaniards, the Tarascan state was controlled from three main centers: Tzintzuntzan (the seat of the supreme leader, or *caltzontzin*), Ihuatzio, and Pátzcuaro. Between the first major intervention in the area by the Spanish in 1522 and the arrival of Bishop Vasco de Quiroga in 1538, the Tarascan state, as well as Tarascan society and culture, suffered severely both from Spanish conscription for the Conquest of western Mexico and from forced labor. Even before the Spanish forces arrived, smallpox and measles introduced by the Europeans radically reduced the Tarascan population, with tragic consequences for the prevailing social order.

Vasco de Quiroga, supported by a group of European humanist friars, instituted a major program of social reform in the Tarascan homeland between the years of 1538 and 1565. The widely settled Tarascans were congregated in towns organized around religious-communal institutions. Local specialization in crafts was established in different towns, as were markets and a series of norms concerning dress, communal work and property, and even nuptiality.

A problem for Tarascan cultural history is raised both by the brutal disruption of Tarascan culture and society through epidemics and violent oppression during the first two decades of Spanish occupation and by the successful social reforms of noted priest-humanists like Vasco de Quiroga, Juan de San Miguel, and Jacobo Daciano in the following decades. Some scholars have argued that although the Tarascans have maintained their language, as well as such objective cultural elements as the Middle American nutritional and culinary system based on beans, squashes, chilies, and maize, they have adopted the basic complex of Spanish peasant culture in regard to religion, economy, and traditional forms of empirical or "folk" knowledge. In contrast to this "Hispanist" point of view, some Mexicanists argue that the Tarascans continue to represent major continuities in Middle American culture, especially in the relation between language and culture and in such diverse domains as gender relations, socialization, cosmology, and ethnoscience.

Given their importance as a pre-Hispanic state, present knowledge of the Tarascan situation during the Mexican colonial period is amazingly limited. Only at the end of the nineteenth century did systematic study of Tarascan ethnohistory and linguistics begin. In that period, the Tarascan homeland was being significantly altered. In the Sierra Phurhépecha, forest was cut by foreign companies to provide the railroad ties needed for the modernization program initiated during the dictatorship of Porfirio Díaz. Similarly, in the Zacapu Valley region, the draining of the shallow Zacapu and its replacement by a major maize plantation altered radically the traditional lifeways of the Tarascan population in that area. Both environmental alterations were associated with a significant immigration of the Hispano-Mexican population. In the twentieth century, revolution, agrarian reform, and resistance to state policies of social reform wrought major changes in the demography, economy, and local political and moral order of the Tarascan homeland.

Settlements

Most Tarascan towns were formed during the social reforms of the sixteenth century. To this day, the central plaza in each town contains a church whose patron saint represents the local indigenous community and a building site dedicated to the Virgin of the Immaculate Conception (called the *yurhixu* in Tarascan or *hospital* in Spanish). Towns are organized into barrios leading out from the central plaza and typically grouped together to divide the settlement in two halves. Barrios are composed of household compounds, each of which traditionally features wooden structures for storing goods in the front facing the street and leading to a packed-earth courtyard (called *ek'ukutiniarhu* in Tarascan). Typically, at the end of a compound's courtyard is a wooden kitchen house (which also serves as sleeping quarters), a granary, and a small, roofed corral. Behind the cooking house is a large area (*inchákutini*) for cultivating maize, fruit trees, and medicinal and ornamental plants for family consumption. Bilingual Tarascans often use the Spanish term *solar* to describe this compound garden plot and orchard, whereas local Hispano-Mexicans use the Tarascan borrowing *ecuaro*, which also refers to areas of cultivation in lands suitable only to hoe farming.

Tarascan towns range in population from 1,000 to 7,000 inhabitants. The pattern of town settlements varies in the different subregions of the Tarascan homeland. Most distinctive are the settlements in the small Duero River Valley, or Cañada de las Once Pueblos, which form an almost continuous line along the original colonial road connecting Morelia with Guadalajara. All Tarascan towns are associated with a constellation of small hamlets, or *ranchos*, ranging from as few as 30 to as many as 500 inhabitants. Generally these hamlets were formed over generations when sites for seasonal cultivation and pasturage gradually became permanent residences.

The traditional texture of Tarascan settlements has changed significantly in the last half of the twentieth century. The movable wooden cabin, or *troje*, with its fir shingles, and the stacked-stone walls of the family compounds are rapidly being replaced by constructions of brick and concrete. Migrants to Mexican cities and to the United States have returned with new house plans and a taste for concrete floors and two-story structures with windows. These changes are especially visible in the towns along the shores of Lake Pátzcuaro.

Economy

The Tarascan homeland is characterized by local and regional specialization in the production, extraction, and control of both natural and social resources. Tarascan towns and barrios are identified by their distinctive pottery, woodworking, weaving of cloth and straw, and embroidery. Although the region is dominated by small-scale agricultural activities, there are also some communities of fishers with exclusive commercial rights to Lake Pátzcuaro. Other communities specialize in certain forest-based activities (ranging from the extraction of turpentine to the splitting of shingles), and still others have developed unions of tour guides, rental services (boats and horses), and souvenir shops to accommodate tourists.

The regional economy is marked by central wholesale-retail markets in large mestizo towns, as well as by special markets that operate during religious festivals in individual Tarascan towns. Money is the basic medium of exchange, although bartering is still common and, on certain days in certain markets, the expected practice.

In general, the Tarascan economy has a peasant substrate that combines food production (maize, beans, squashes, fruit, hogs, chickens, turkeys) and collection for consumption with cash cropping, share cropping, day labor, and handicrafting. Legally, land in Tarascan townships is collectively held. In those areas of the Tarascan homeland once controlled by large agricultural estates (haciendas), collective land rights were established through federal appropriation of the former estate's lands to create *ejidos*. In other areas, the collective landholding unit is the Indian community, recognized by law as a communal property-holding body. Often, both forms of collective land tenure overlap in a single town. By law, each individual's right to land is established either by membership in the collective unit or by kinship with a legitimate landholding member. The cultivator is referred to as a *comunero* when the holding is through family membership in the Indian community or as an *ejidatario* if family membership is in the ejido assembly. In practice, these collective lands were, for the most part, divided into de facto private holdings, with varying degrees of collective constraint over the right to purchase individual titles, especially as regards persons not recognized as community members. A 1992 constitutional reform allows commercial title to the land—that is, permits each individual holder to sell his or her land freely. Local Tarascan political groups, however, produced and cosigned a declaration rejecting this reform and forbidding the individual alienation of any collective land in the Tarascan homeland. This declaration was reaffirmed by cosigners and additional Tarascan groups in February 1994.

The Tarascan population is characterized by a clear sexual division of labor. Women prepare food, wash clothes, care for infants and toddlers with the help of older children,

cultivate the solar in the household compound, and, when necessary, help men prepare, plant, and harvest field crops or orchards. Carpentry, construction, net fishing, and lumber work are exclusively men's activities. Certain phases of ceramic work and straw weaving are organized by sex. For example, women typically paint designs on clay objects, but men fire the pottery. Both men and women enter into commercial activities. It is common for women to control the commerce in products of exclusively feminine activities such as embroidery and hand weaving shawls and blankets.

Since World War II, the Tarascans have left their homeland to find jobs in other parts of Mexico and in the United States and have been the recipients of government programs of formal schooling. Since the late 1960s, professionalization through formal education, new strategies of economic accumulation, and new consumption practices associated with migration have combined to bring significant changes to the traditional peasant substrate of the Tarascan economy.

Kinship, Marriage, and Family

Tarascan kinship reckoning is bilateral to such a degree that each nuclear family must be seen as the union of the respective kindreds of mother and father. The major kin-term distinction is between highly familiar terms for members of the nuclear family and more formal bilateral terms for the extended kindred. There is, however, a degree of patrilineal bias. Ideally, postmarital residence is virilocal; daughters-in-law are clearly subordinate to their respective in-laws, especially the husband's mother. Similarly, the order of preferred namesakes for children reflects a flexible ambilateral kin hierarchy with patrilineal bias. The first-born is named by, or after, the parents' marriage godparents, who, as ritual kin, bring together the respective kindreds of husband and wife. The paternal grandparents are the next preferred namesakes, and the maternal grandparents follow in priority. Newlyweds are called *achâti* or *warhíti sapichu* ("little mister and misses") until the birth of their first child, when they usually will establish neolocal residence. Thus, at different moments in the domestic life cycle, a Tarascan will live in an extended-family compound composed of several separate family houses and in a single household compound cofounded by husband and wife.

Both rights of primogeniture and ultimogeniture are loosely recognized in inheritance. The lastborn often inherits the family compound, along with the obligation to provide daily care for parents in their old age. Inheritance is a major source of conflict, given the relative independence of a husband's and wife's property rights, the general and overlapping expectations of all offspring, and the tremendous irregularities in the written titles to the lands of the Tarascan homeland.

Tarascan adulthood is traditionally established by marriage and parenthood. Baptismal godparents are the preferred go-betweens in marriage negotiations, especially in cases of marriage by elopement. Sixteenth-century accounts of Tarascan marriages, as well as excellent ethnographic descriptions in the twentieth century, indicate striking continuities in the ritual process. Marriage leads to the establishment of new ritual-kin relations. It is common for the marriage godparents to name, or approve of, the baptismal godparents of each child. Baptismal godparents will, in turn, approve or name the marriage godparents of their godchild.

By tradition, a child is baptized after the *patsákuni*, the forty-day postpartum period of rest and isolation of mother and child. Prior to baptism, reference to the child is made in terms of the marriage godparents, *painu pitántskata* or *maína pitántskata* (godfather's or godmother's namesake). Children are swaddled for the first six weeks of life and usually remain in constant bodily contact with the mother or with an elder sister, cousin, or aunt during the first year. Nursing is prolonged, often lasting until the third or fourth year. Gender-differentiated imitation of adult activities results from prolonged periods of parallel play while accompanying adults engaged in everyday tasks. This is the most common mode of socialization in Tarascan towns and hamlets. In contrast to children socialized in urban environments, Tarascan children enjoy constant physical and emotional contact with care givers.

Sociopolitical Organization and Ritual

Tarascan sociopolitical organization and ritual reflect the complex and intertwining power relations of mestizo and Tarascan coexistence over the centuries. With the Mexican constitution of 1917, rural, regional, and local social institutions had to contend with a nationalist postrevolutionary socialism and a policy of agrarian reform. This constitutional affirmation of an exclusively secular basis for community properties and their government (ejidos and Indian communities) conflicted with the traditional religious-communal organization of the Tarascan homelands.

Traditionally, each town's *cabildo* was composed of the members of the community who had carried out a series of costly ritual obligations organized around the annual calendar of religious celebrations. With the exception of the Catholic sacraments, the cabildo designated or ratified all local civil and religious functions and served as the supreme community-level body for adjudication. In the first half of the twentieth century, a purely civil institutional order was implemented and the cabildo lost all real political authority. In this context, asymmetrical relations between Tarascans and mestizos became politically explicit by rejecting the political legitimacy of native religious authority. By 1950, with the exception of the *municipio* of Cherán, all Tarascan villages and hamlets came under the control of mestizo townships or municipios. Most communities were divided by prolonged local conflicts depicted in Purhépecha oral tradition as a struggle between the conservative followers of Tarascan Catholic tradition and its institutions, on the one hand, and radical agrarian "atheists," on the other.

Currently this political-religious dichotomy is fading. Now, different groups of Tarascan professionals seek both to consolidate a general pan-Tarascan regional identification among Tarascan towns and to achieve institutional recognition of this unity through electoral redistricting. These aims have inspired a revisionist revitalization of the Tarascan heritage. The cabildo, now seen as a council of elders, is being actively promoted in several communities, and a pan-Tarascan version of the cabildo and *cargo* system is present in the celebration of the Phurhépecha New Year (P'urhépecherhi Jimpanhi Wéxurhini). Since 1982, this event has been organized both to revitalize Tarascan custom and ethnic pride and to promote local consciousness of the homeland. The celebration is organized at the regional level along lines similar to the local religious cargo systems. The celebration rotates annually among the Tarascan towns of the subregions of the homeland. The representatives of the host town are responsible for the recently created pan-Tarascan national symbols, the Phurhépecha flag and the *ta'rhésï* (a stone on which is engraved the emblem of each town that hosts the New Year's celebration). After the celebration, each town's representatives become part of a council of elders, a pattern that is reminiscent of the former cabildo system.

Religion and Expressive Culture

The Tarascans have developed their own distinctive form of Native Mesoamerican Catholicism, often described as a "folk" or "popular" version of Catholic doctrines and religious ritual. These practices include community-based devotion to saints and virgins, organized by the system of religious cargos and festivals, and a complex calendar of pilgrimages to local, regional, and national shrines. There is also a rich oral tradition that includes supplications and songs for the perpetuation of harvests, as well as stories centered on the figure of the Pingua or devil-patron. Local orators, *tiósïrhi wantárhicha* ("those who speak of God"; sing. *tiósïrhi wantárhi*), officiate at burials, intercede during marriage negotiations (especially those involving elopement), and at wedding celebrations. They possibly represent continuity with the role of the *petamuti*, a pre-Hispanic religious orator responsible for preserving the collective memory of Tarascan cosmology. Specialization in magical ritual and curing with herbs and oral incantations is widespread and associated with certain towns such as Cherán in the Sierra Phurhépecha. The dual concept of soul and body is the source of many practices, for example, the *matsïp'ini* ("twisting" of body and soul) of a firstborn son is intended to make him resistant to the danger of *espanto* (the separation of body and soul) and to the harmful effects of the *mal de ojo* ("evil eye," the malicious interest of others who might endanger body-soul harmony). Tarascans typically believe in an afterlife and in a complex Catholic conception of heaven, including purgatory and limbo, as well as notions of bondage in life to the devil. They have specialists to aid the soul's struggle to leave the body during the agony of death and to accept its eternal destiny.

Tarascan singers and composers, *pirericha*, are recognized through out the Tarascan homeland. Many are regionally and nationally famous, their songs performed by numerous local groups and their recordings purchased and enjoyed throughout the Tarascan homeland and beyond. In the ceramic arts, the Tarascans have received international recognition in many categories, whether for the fantastic creations of Ocumicho, the giant green pineapples of Patamban, or the white ware of Tzintzuntzan.

Bibliography

Alcalá, Fray Jerónimo de (1980). _La relación de Michoacán._ Morelia, Mexico: FIMAX. Originally issued in 1541.

Beals, Ralph L. (1946). _Cherán: A Sierra Tarascan Village._ Washington, D.C.: Smithsonian Institution, Institute of Social Anthropology.

Beals, Ralph L. (1969). "The Tarascans." In _Handbook of Middle American Indians,_ edited by Robert Wauchope. Vol. 8, _Ethnology, Part Two,_ edited by Evon Z. Vogt, 725–773. Austin: University of Texas Press.

Brandes, Stanley (1988). _Power and Persuasion: Fiestas and Social Control in Rural Mexico._ Philadelphia: University of Pennsylvania Press.

Carrasco, Pedro (1952). _Tarascan Folk Religion._ Publication 17. New Orleans: Tulane University, Middle American Research Institute.

Carrasco, Pedro (1986). "Economía y política en el reino tarasco." In _La sociedad indígena en el centro y occidente de México,_ edited by P. Carrasco et al., 63–102. Zamora: El Colegio de Michoacán.

Foster, George M. (with the assistance of Gabriel Ospina) (1948). _Empire's Children: The People of Tzintzuntzan._ Washington, D.C.: Smithsonian Institution, Institute of Social Anthropology.

Friedrich, Paul (1984). "Tarascan: From Meaning to Sound." In _Supplement to the Handbook of Middle American Indians,_ edited by Victoria Reifler Bricker. Vol. 2, _Linguistics,_ edited by Munro S. Edmonson, 56–83. Austin: University of Texas Press.

Kemper, Robert V. (1981). "Urbanization and Development in the Tarascan Region since 1940." _Urban Anthropology_ 10(1): 89–110.

Pollard, Helen Perlstein (1993). _Tariacuri's Legacy: The Prehispanic Tarascan State._ Norman: University of Oklahoma Press.

Swadesh, Morris (1969). _Elementos del tarasco antiguo._ Mexico City: Universidad Nacional Autónoma de México.

West, Robert C. (1948). _Cultural Geography of the Modern Tarascan Area._ Washington, D.C.: Smithsonian Institution, Institute of Social Anthropology.

ANDREW ROTH-SENEFF AND ROBERT V. KEMPER

Tepehua

ETHNONYMS: none

Orientation

Identification. The Tepehua are a farming people occupying mountainous regions of eastern Hidalgo and northern Veracruz in Mexico. They are most closely related linguistically to the Totonac, who inhabit nearby lower regions to the east, in the state of Veracruz. The name "Tepehua" may be derived from either of the Nahua words _tepetl_ (mountain) or _ueialtepetl_ (town dweller).

Location. There are two regions of Tepehua settlement: a band stretching from Huehuetla, Hidalgo, northwestward through Tlachichilco, Veracruz, where the Tepehua are surrounded by Otomí and mestizo settlements; and a U-shaped area at lower elevations to the northeast of Pantepec, Veracruz, where they are surrounded by Totonac and Otomí settlements. These regions are at the southern boundary of a region generally known as the "Huasteca." All Tepehua settlements are found between 20°25' and 20°40' N and 97°40' and 97°15' W. They extend over a wide range of elevations between 150 and 1,700 meters, but most are at the lower levels.

Demography and Language. The total number of Tepehua speakers in the 1990 census was 8,702. Out of these, 2,001 were in Hidalgo and 5,742 in Veracruz. The Tepehua language is in the Totonacan Subfamily of the Macromayan (Mexican Penutian) Family.

History and Cultural Relations

Little is known about the pre-Columbian history of the Tepehua. One theory is that for a long time they occupied the region in which they are now found and have been reduced in numbers as the Otomí moved in from the south. During the colonial period, Tepehua lands were turned over to Spanish owners without proper authority. At various times, some of their lands were placed under the control of the Catholic church. After independence, Tepehua communal lands were divided, and the titles were gradually acquired by mestizos. The Mexican Revolution provided some redress of the land imbalance. For example, before the Revolution, only 2 lots among the lands of San Pedro Tzilzacuapan, Veracruz, were legally in the hands of Indians. In 1926, after the Revolution, 56 were registered to Indians, as opposed to 172 to mestizos (Williams García 1963, 90). Struggles with mestizos unwilling to have lands classified as _ejidos_ led to armed conflict in the early 1930s. "White guards," armed bands of mestizo ranchers, terrorized Indians at that time. The southern Huasteca was still an area of agrarian conflict in the 1990s.

Settlements

A typical Tepehua village has a central plaza around which are arranged shops, public offices, and a school. There may be a covered area for meetings and religious rituals. The streets radiate outward and end in paths leading to homesteads and hamlets (_rancherías_).

The typical house is a rectangular structure with a thatched roof rounded at the ends. There is only one room, with two doors and no windows. The walls are made of vertical poles, sometimes plastered with mud-and-straw mortar. Tepehua utilize small wooden chairs and tables as furnishings. Houses near a source of water will have a washing stand on the patio. Normally there is a separate kitchen. In the kitchen a ceramic griddle (*comal*) laid on three hearth stones on the floor is used to cook tortillas.

Economy

Subsistence and Commercial Activities. Tepehua agriculture uses a slash-and-burn method. Fields (milpas) are abandoned and allowed to accumulate natural cover; this *monte* is later cut and burned to reopen the field. Each farmer cultivates his own land, but neighbors also provide mutual aid. Two crops of corn are sown, one in December and the other in June. Beans, squash, and some chili peppers are planted in the milpas. *Tomates* and an edible leafy plant called *misis* grow wild in the fields without requiring cultivation. The following fruits are grown in small quantities: *pagua*, mangoes, avocados, melons, papayas, and bananas. In the twentieth century, new vegetable crops such as lentils, onions, garlic, peas, and sesame have been introduced.

Many farmers cultivate sugarcane as a cash crop. The cane is pressed in local wooden presses (*trapiches*) powered by oxen. It is boiled and made into raw sugar cakes (*piloncillos* in Spanish, *za'as* in Tepehua) for sale. Another important cash crop is coffee.

Industrial Arts. Women weave sashes and *quexquémetl* (an ancient style of small poncho) from cotton and wool, on belt looms. They also sew and embroider blouses. As with the various other ethnic groups, the traditional female garb (*liado*) immediately identifies the ethnicity of the wearer. The Tepehua liado consists of a barrel skirt gathered by a sash, a blouse, and a quexquémetl. It is gradually being replaced by cotton dresses. Weaving and sewing by the women provide clothing for the family and products that can later be exchanged or sold. The Tepehua also manufacture pottery griddles, harvesting baskets (*chiquihuites*), fishing nets, and candles.

Weekly open-air markets are held throughout the region. The traditional market centers are in the capitals of the *municipios*, but other market centers appear wherever there is a need and some motivation to open one. At the markets, the various ethnic groups from this region—Tepehua, Totonac, Nahua, Otomí, and mestizo—interact. Merchants who travel from market to market are often accomplished linguists. Some Tepehua have established stores in the larger villages. These stores stock the basic necessities between markets. Often the store owners become mule drivers, traveling afar to bring new items to their establishments. As a consequence of dealing with mestizos, they tend to replace elements of their Indian culture by more commercially acceptable mestizo ones. In the smaller rancherías, small stores offer only a meager selection of soap, rum, cigarettes, and soft drinks.

Land Tenure. Land is held as private property or as an ejido. Whether or not a community has an ejido depends on the outcome of various agrarian struggles with the land grabbers of pre- and postrevolutionary Mexico. The Huasteca—because of its valuable potential for cattle raising—has been a zone of agrarian conflict throughout the twentieth century.

Marriage and Family

A proper marriage requires that the groom's family formally petition the bride's family. The two families meet weekly at the house of the potential bride. The petitioning family brings gifts of rum. At the last meeting, quantities of beer and rum are given to the future in-laws to distribute to their kin. The date of the delivery of the bride to the groom's house, the formal culmination of the marriage, is agreed upon. This will often be delayed for a year. There is a feast in honor of the bride and her family when the bride is delivered. Turkey *mole* (a sauce made from many ingredients including cacao) is served. The bride's family dresses her in new clothes. The couple then lives with the groom's family (patrilocal residence) until a new house can be built on the groom's family land.

This traditional marriage usually takes a year to complete. Reluctant to wait, many young men take their brides without the formal ceremonies. Seductions and rapes also occur. In these cases, the woman is taken to the man's home and the tension between the families is resolved through quiet diplomacy. A shaman may be called in to perform a ritual that assures that the children born of such a union do not suffer supernatural consequences because of the aggressive acts leading to their conception.

Sociopolitical Organization

An *agente municipal* is the maximal authority in Tepehua villages located in the state of Veracruz. He is elected every three years by a public assembly in the village, and his election is certified by the president of the municipio. Other offices make up the civil government of the village. In the Tepehua village of Pisaflores, for example, four *tupiles* are appointed to assist the agente, and a village judge (*juez auxiliar*) is also chosen by the assembly. The judge is aided by police (*alwásil*) selected from the young men of the community. The police have the responsibility of collecting levies, guarding public areas when necessary, apprehending wrongdoers, and notifying people to appear before the village authorities. Pisaflores recognizes another respected councilor called the *jefe de la comunidad*, who is not formally recognized by the municipio authorities. This post derives from an earlier period of agrarian conflict when strong autonomous leadership was needed. The jefe de la comunidad does not interfere with the normal workings of the other authorities in the village but does oversee their activities.

Public work groups (*faenas*) are organized to repair trails and roads, to construct needed public facilities, and to cultivate the public lands supporting the school. Public oratory (*lacachínchin*) is the responsibility of an official called the *mayordomo*, who is aided by four other appointees (*vocales*), who collect assessments from all the villagers to pay for the major ritual at the lacachínchin. The mayordomo remains in office as long as he carries out his ritual duties properly.

The agente names an older man to serve as a *fiscal*, an

official who has ritual duties related to the New Year's celebration. The fiscal is aided by three *pixcales mayores*, also named by the agente. According to custom, the pixcales mayores should be either sickly or feebleminded, as the Tepehua define these categories. The fiscal keeps the village's images of Catholic saints in his own house and takes them to the covered area in the center of the village for the rituals when the time arrives.

Women are also appointed as *cantantes*. Their duty is to sing Spanish songs during the Christmas celebrations. Four *campaneros*, one of whom is a leader called the *mapaulán*, are appointed by the authorities to take charge of the festivities during the Days of the Dead.

Religion and Expressive Culture

Religious Beliefs. Christian religions have made only moderate impressions on Tepehua culture. Tepehua villages generally did not have Catholic churches until after the 1950s. The native religion is the most important. It is part of a religious complex that is found also among the Otomí and Nahua people of the same region. It involves the worship of nature gods, ceremonies that address soul forces represented by paper figures, and musical flower rituals carried out in homes, at shrines, and in native oratories.

The supreme Tepehua deity is the Sun (Wítcháan). When he sets at night, he leaves the stars to guard over the world. The Moon (Maɫkuyú) is a troublesome character associated with the Devil (Tlakakikuru, derived from the Nahua word *tlacatecólotl*, meaning were-owl). The Lord of the Earth (Xalapanlakat'un) is offended by urination and buried afterbirth and so must receive periodic offerings of appeasement. He is nasty and eats the bodies of humans after they have died. Earth is the father of fire because cooking fires are made on the ground.

The Lord of the Water (Xalapána·k Xkán) has a male and a female guardian, the sirens (Sereno and Serena). Both are dressed in green. The first is the Lord of the Animals, and the second has duck's feet and lives in a hidden place of human pilgrimage from whence the wind and rain are sent. The Lord of the Air is called Xalapanakún.

The gods and beings worshiped by the Tepehua are all called *antiguas*. They live in a mythical place called the Golden Mountain. At a great table on the Golden Mountain sit the Sun and the Stars. At other tables sit lesser deities. There they judge the activities of humans.

The Tepehua believe in a life force called by outside observers, at various times, the spirit (*espíritu*), soul (*alma*), or shade (*sombra*). The spirit can separate itself from a living person for a short time. Such a separation places the person in danger, and, if it goes on for too long, the spirit must be restored by a shaman to keep the person from dying. When the person does die, the spirit remains on the earth, normally for a short time. The spirits of humans, and of other beings, are represented by paper figures cut by shamans.

Religious Practitioners. Midwives and shamans are the main religious practitioners. Other religious officials, such as the mayordomo, are in charge of rituals; however, the Tepehua do not regard these religious officials as specialists, like shamans and midwives, who have an understanding of the superhuman world.

Shamans are usually people who have suffered in life and who have received visions directing them toward a curing profession. Novice shamans are encouraged by—and trained by—other shamans. Shamanic visions teach them how to cure. The shaman cuts magical paper figures, places them on a paper mat, and wraps them up to use in curing rituals. These figures symbolize the spirits of beings involved in the rituals. Shamans also acquire pottery figurines and other pieces taken from the earth to keep on their altars. Such spiritual objects are also called antiguas. They are images of the tutelary beings who appear to the shaman in dreams and visions. A shaman and his wife often work as a couple.

Midwives and shamanesses are all considered to be a single type of female religious curer called *hat'aku·nu'*. Great semidivine shamanesses and are called *lak'ainananín*. Midwives are usually widows. They may work alone or in conjunction with a shaman.

Ceremonies. *Costumbre* is the name given to the general ritual form through which the antiguas are worshiped. Costumbres are led by shamans, whose role in this context must be seen as a leader of public worship rather than as a magical healer. During a costumbre, musicians play sacred music on a guitar and violin. The shaman (or shamans) cuts paper figures representing the spirits of various beings. A sacred time opens as the actual superhuman invisible beings arrive to attend the costumbre in the evening. Offerings are made. As dawn approaches the beings leave.

Agricultural plants are important beings. Their spirits are attended by shamans in a major annual costumbre held at the public oratory (lacachínchin). The figures of the seeds are cut by shamans on mountaintops. Afterwards they are returned to the village and placed in chests in the lacachínchin. Music, dance, and a ritual meal are part of the lacachínchin celebration.

A planting ceremony is also held in family homes. During this ritual, turkey blood is sprinkled on a basket of maize seeds containing flower decorations, bottles of rum, and palm leaves.

Arts. Religious dances are performed during village fiestas. These are learned and maintained by groups of villagers who dedicate themselves to this sacred art. Among the dances are: Los Viejos de Todos Santos, Los Santiagos, Los Tambulanes (23 and 24 December), Palo Volador, and Los Pastores. Storytelling is a popular form of entertainment, particularly while men are performing routine tasks in the fields. The Tepehua have their own set of classic folktales.

Medicine. Medical treatment is given by shamans and midwives. Costumbres are held for curing as well as for public worship. The Tepehua believe that illness can be caused by anger or negative feelings toward a victim. The cure in these cases is for a shaman to restore the spirit of the victim. "Fright," a childhood illness that is caused by sudden falls or scares, is also cured by restoration of the spirit.

Death and the Afterlife. After death, a Tepehua goes to the Golden Mountain where he or she is judged before the tables of the gods. Those who have been faithful to the gods remain there on the Golden Mountain, whereas the rest are sent to La'nín, where they remain under the power of the Lord of the Earth. La'nín is not a place of punishment, however. Priests, midwives, musicians who play sacred music, and dancers of the sacred dances always remain on the Golden Mountain. Women who die in childbirth go to live with the Lord of the Water, who also has his residence on the Golden Mountain. The spirits of people who die tragically are condemned to wander the world of the living with evil spirits commanded by the Devil.

The body of the deceased is dressed in new clothes. A procession with musicians carries the body in a coffin to the graveyard. Men and women take different roles in the funeral rituals. The godmother of burial adorns the graves of children and adolescents with paper decorations. Adult graves are left plain. It is believed that the spirits of the dead remain in their homes for a week. At dawn on the seventh day after the death, a cross is erected over the grave.

Bibliography

Gessain, Robert (1953). "Les indiens tepehuas de Huehuetla." In *Huastecos, totonacos, y sus vecinos*. Mexico City: Sociedad Mexicana de Antropología.

Williams García, Roberto (1963). *Los tepehuas*. Jalapa: Universidad Veracruzana.

Williams García, Roberto (1972). *Mitos tepehuas*. Mexico City: Secretaría de Educación Pública.

JAMES W. DOW

Tepehuan of Chihuahua

ETHNONYMS: Northern Tepehuan, Òdami

Orientation

Identification and Location. Both Northern and Southern Tepehuan refer to themselves as "Òdami." Although the etymology of the name "Tepehuan" is still a matter of contention, the word almost certainly stems from *tepetl*, the Nahuatl word for "mountain." The Northern Tepehuan are scattered over sparsely settled high woodlands and canyons in the southwestern corner of the northern Mexican state of Chihuahua. The Southern Tepehuan are separated from the Northern by several hundred kilometers, and are found in the rugged country of southern Durango.

The upper perimeter of Northern Tepehuan land is the Río Verde, flowing westward into Sinaloa and carving deep gorges into this remote part of the Sierra Madre Occidental. The average elevation is around 2,350 meters, but widely varying elevations make for a craggy terrain that is strikingly harsh and isolating. Travel into and within the coarsely contoured region is arduous; the few roads provide only limited accessibility. At the higher elevations are the pine-covered uplands referred to locally as the *tierra templada* (the temperate zone). Downslope is the *tierra caliente* (the warm country), the canyon expanses of poorer soil covered with shrubs and grasses.

Aside from linguistic similarity and some sharing of a type of communal organization, the Northern and Southern Tepehuan now differ remarkably in sociocultural attributes. This separation of two groups bearing the same name and sharing a parallel and arguably liminal position in the threshold between the Mesoamerican and the Southwestern cultural areas has propagated a mystique that has yet to be cleared up by definitive research. As of this writing, these groups, whose homeland is rugged and remote, remain little known and studied.

Demography. There are approximately 10,000 Tepehuan presently living in Chihuahua. (The 1990 census recorded 2,980 speakers of Tepehuan aged 5 years or older in Chihuahua.) Because of the difficulties of travel and the insufficiency of government services, an accurate count is hard to come by in this poor and isolated region of Mexico. As is common in other parts of the country, the elusiveness of numbers is also attributable to the elusiveness of definitions of ethnicity, about which Indians, mestizos, and the census takers hold conflicting views. Various aspects of affiliation, connection, and identity may be denied, embraced or overlooked by both the counters and the counted. In the past, inexperienced or ill-informed observation, mistaking subtle complexity for assimilation, has often misrepresented the Northern Tepehuan as completely mestizoized or simply lumped them with the Tarahumara, another local group. More recent work, however, has established that they remain a discrete culture with a distinct language, living as an indigenous group, separate from—and coexisting—several thousand Tarahumara and tens of thousands of mestizo neighbors.

Linguistic Affiliation. The Tepehuan speak an Uto-Aztecan language. The languages of the Uto-Aztecan Family are more widely spoken than those of the five other major language families in the southwestern United States and northwestern Mexico. The language of the Northern Tepehuan is most closely related to that of the Southern Tepehuan, although their point of divergence has not been determined by linguists. Along with Pima and Papago (which are spoken in Arizona and northern Sonora), these languages comprise the Tepiman or Piman Group of the Sonoran Branch of the Uto-Aztecan Language Family.

History and Cultural Relations

Today's relative obscurity belies an apparently long and once prominent Tepehuan regional presence. The Tepehuan of Chihuahua are the northern descendants of an aboriginal group whose broad territory ranged from north of the Río Verde in Chihuahua southward through Durango into the contemporary states of Nayarit and Jalisco. Archival evidence suggests that at the time of the arrival of the Spanish conquerors, the Tepehuan were probably the largest and most important tribe in the Sierra Madre Occidental. About half a millennium before the Conquest, their ancestors hunted and gathered in the desert region near the border between Arizona and Sonora before migrating, along with other Southern Uto-Aztecan groups, southward into the mountainous regions of northwestern Mexico, where they began to rely on farming.

After the Conquest of central Mexico, Spaniards moved northward, mining and establishing haciendas and missions in Zacatecas and Durango. In Durango, they ruptured the unity of Northern and Southern Tepehuan by eliminating the central Durango groups northward to Chihuahua. By the end of the sixteenth century, a few miners, missionaries, and soldiers had penetrated southern Chihuahua. The Franciscans, in 1560, were the first order to work with the Tepehuan in the Santa Barbara region of southern Chihuahua. The Jesuits previously ministered to the Tepehuan in central and southern Durango. They entered the northern territory in 1610 and began congregating the Tepehuan into mission towns, and, by 1708, had established missions at Baborigame, Nabogame, and Guadalupe y Calvo. Over a hundred years of isolation followed the expulsion of the Jesuits in 1767. The overextended Franciscans, now responsible for the whole region, maintained modest sway. The Jesuits returned at the beginning of the twentieth century. The Tepehuan are usually described as "nominally Catholic," given that the religion practiced is an amalgamation of Hispanic and indigenous elements. Some indigenous groups do not practice any form of Catholicism. Perhaps the most important consequence of Tepehuan relations with the Church is the local acquisition of European plants, livestock, and technology.

The convergence of Indian and mestizo culture was a process driven by the economic exploitation of resources. Chihuahua's first mine and first hacienda were established by thirty Spanish families in 1575, initiating mining and grazing as the future primary industries of the region. Sometimes Indians worked in mines and farms out of choice, but more often they were forced laborers or slaves. At first, wool clothing was a great attraction to volunteer laborers, but impressed labor and harsh treatment soon became unbearable. Beginning in the first decade of the seventeenth century, uprisings led by the Tepehuan resulted in severe repression by the Spaniards. Soon, Santa Barbara, with 7,000 inhabitants, became the largest town in the province of Nueva Vizcaya, even larger than the city of Durango, to the south. From this outpost, the subjugation of the northern territory continued over the next century. The whole of the seventeenth century was one of revolt across the northern frontier by practically every Indian group living north of Durango. Spaniards retreated to protected outposts. Priests met martyrdom. Soon these rebellions were put down, and in the nineteenth century northward expansion continued. Mines, new towns, and presidios, were created, the Jesuits were expelled, and all indigenous peoples—except for a few remote groups—were generally pacified.

Excluding a few settlements such as those at Baborigame and Guadalupe y Calvo, the region of the northern Tepehuan remained mostly isolated and little settled, which allowed the indigenous people to follow a simple subsistence pattern of life relatively unmolested. Even during the turbulent nineteenth century, when revolution and independence consumed most of Mexico, the indigenous people were left very much alone by a Mexico otherwise occupied. Independence from Spain in 1821 resulted in much infighting in the central government, as opposing parties competed for control. Lack of funds meant that soldiers on the far northern frontier were not paid, and it was difficult to influence politics in such remote regions without providing the minimum of services. For Mexico, the nineteenth century culminated in the loss of more than one-third of its territory to the United States. During the nineteenth century, Apache invaders began to drive a wedge between the people living in the high Sierra and the Pima Alta cultures in the north. As mountain dwellers, the Northern Tepehuan, like the Tarahumara, were able to defend themselves against displacement by these Apache raiders. Mostly, however, they were far removed from the major centers of Apache raiding in northern Chihuahua.

The twentieth century has been even less auspicious. The Tepehuan have remained isolated, except for recent decades. In 1952 there was an attempt to bring the Tepehuan into the fold of mainstream culture and economy when the federal government installed an Indian Coordinating Center at Guachochi, across the Río Verde from the Tepehuan homeland. Through the Center, the National Indian Institute has followed a policy of assimilation. It administers various social and welfare services but is hampered by the remoteness of the region. In southwestern Chihuahua, Indians are outnumbered by mestizos by as much as three to one and this ratio increased as economic enterprises grew in the 1970 and 1980s. Logging in this densely forested area has become particularly important as an alternative to the heavily exploited Tarahumara woodlands north of the Río Verde. Forest roads and a paved highway from Parral to Guadalupe y Calvo have also opened the region to the negative impacts of illegal drug harvesting and transportation. Drug traffickers are having a profound impact on local indigenous groups, and many Indians are fleeing to more remote regions to follow a hunting-and-gathering mode of life.

Settlements

Today the Northern Tepehuan are closer to the Tarahumara cultural pattern than to that of the Southern Tepehuan, and relations with the Tarahumara are plainly evident. In a few communities, the two groups live together in bicultural and bilingual situations, but the precise relationship between them is unclear. The Northern Tepehuan are found in the municipios of Guadalupe y Calvo, Morelos, and Balleza on the southern edge of the Tarahumara country, across the Río Verde. Land is communally held in _ejidos_ or _comunidades_, with Tepehuan holding title separately, or sometimes with mestizos. They live in groups of small named settlements, called _rancherías_, surrounding pueblos, or small towns that act as social and political centers. Rancherías are small and widely dispersed, consisting of the separate dwellings of four or five families. Houses in the tierra templada are constructed of timber in small clusters on the great mesas. In the tierra caliente they are made of stone-and-mud mortar and are usually located along the streams that lead down into the canyons.

Economy

Subsistence and Commercial Activities. Practically every household grows food for its own consumption on small plots. Maize, squashes, and beans are the staple crops whereas wheat, barley, potatoes, oats, and peas are also commonly grown. Tobacco and chilies are grown in the lowlands. The dibble stick and wooden plows drawn by oxen are adjuncts to farming. A dibble stick is a sharpened pole used to punch a hole in the plowed earth or a slash-and-burn plot for planting seeds. One season for cultivating is available in the highlands compared to two in the hotter lowlands. Maize fields are cultivated separately from garden plots dedicated to the other vegetables. Old World fruit trees, introduced by the missionaries, are also tended near the settlements. In the highlands, there are small groves of fig, pomegranate, peach, and apple trees, and, in the hot canyon lands, there are orange and lemon trees. Gathering wild foods is still an important activity as well. Seasonal wild fruits, piñon nuts, walnuts, and edible species of acorns are collected, as is crude honey. Certain insects, reptiles, grubs, and the occasional rattlesnake round out the choices of consumable undomesticated resources. Hunting and trapping also supplement the diet, and deer and wild turkeys are the most highly prized game.

The raising of chickens and, to a lesser extent, turkeys and pigs provides additional sustenance. Livestock are a source of wealth and prestige. Horses—ridden for transportation—and burros and mules—used as pack animals—are much valued. There are many sheep and goats, which are prized for their wool and as food during fiestas. For the most part, the family is the unit of production and consumption, but this configuration is changing. One frequent pattern is an unfortunate circle of need. During hard times, some of the maize harvest is sold, but because most families only grow enough in their gardens to feed themselves, the maize is bought back at an inflated price before the next harvest. Off-farm income usually consists of low pay for unskilled labor. Those who take jobs in the mines receive a slightly better wage. Forestry is an increasingly important economic factor in the region.

Industrial Arts. Crafts and industry include basket and mat weaving and the making of rope and hats. There is also the manufacture of small violins, an art learned from the Jesuits. Skilled carvers make bowls, utensils, and bows and arrows, used mainly for costume and ceremony, and many other wooden articles. Skins of various animals are utilized for the manufacture of sandals, sleeping mats, carrying baskets, and other items useful in everyday activities. Canteens, bowls, and dippers are made from common gourds. Cooking pots are expertly made from clay. A wide variety of clothing, adornments, and other household items, such as blankets, are woven from domestic wool or sewn from purchased cloth.

Trade. There is little evidence of much trade and commercial exchange. Between Indians and mestizos, there was some petty trading of subsistence commodities. The household is the basic production unit, but exchange of labor (e.g., for house building or harvesting activities) accompanies beer-drinking festivals similar to the *tesguinadas* of the Tarahumara.

Division of Labor. The household division of labor by sex and age is generally egalitarian, with the exception that Tepehuan women have more numerous and diverse responsibilities, laboring both in and around the house and in the fields. Along with the usual household and family-related chores, women also weave, make pottery and baskets, milk cows and goats, and participate in the harvesting of maize. Most of the heavy work—such as cutting and preparing logs, house building, and preparing the fields—is by men. Hat making, basket weaving, and rope making are also generally men's activities. Women weave blankets and sash-belts on a horizontal loom.

Land Tenure. Ejidos are communal properties established by the Mexican constitution after the 1917 Revolution. Large estates were broken up and either indigenous or peasant residents took possession. Neighbors or interested others could apply for membership. Membership is not hereditary—continued membership depends upon residence and continued use of the land—but the rules are bent for absent friends or relatives. Land may stay within a family for an extended period of time, but because a long fallow period is required for most plots, land frequently changes hands between families.

Comunidades are an older type of communal organization found in both Durango and Chihuahua. Membership is entirely indigenous, unlike that of ejidos. Members, usually males, are approved for membership by the *asamblea*, which is the governing body. Occasionally mestizos are allowed membership because of intermarriage into—and long-standing loyalty to—the community. Membership in the comunidad is preserved, and passed on to the widow, also in contrast to ejido membership.

Land-tenure law promulgated in 1992 (Article 27 of the Mexican constitution) includes changes that will affect the future of rural and indigenous people. Communal lands have now become rentable, can be divided and owned individually, and sold or pledged as collateral for loans. Each ejido or comunidad will be able to make a decision among its members whether to hold title to their lands individually or collectively. Indigenous comunidades and ejidos appear to favor the option of adopting comunidad status in lieu of privatization.

Kinship

Kin Groups and Descent. Descent and inheritance are reported as patrilateral, with exceptions made in the passing of property to daughters at times. This may not be the case, since the indigenous pattern for neighboring groups is bilateral and gender egalitarian, with male and female inheriting land bilaterally and with the spouses making homes in either or both pieces of inherited land. The reported patrilaterality, and certainly patronymy, may be influenced by the dominant mestizo pattern and sampling bias. Kinship is probably reckoned bilaterally, which means that relatives on father's and mother's side of the family are counted as relatives. There are no lineages, clans, moieties, or other such descent groups.

Kinship Terminology. Kinship terminology is descriptive (tends to combine elementary terms) with distinctions made among each of Ego's four grandparents, mother, mother's sister, mother's brother, father, father's sister, and father's brother. These relatives are also categorized by age and sex, but in Ego's generation, cousins and siblings are not distinguished by sex or in any other manner. Except in Ego's generation, in which brother-in-law and sister-in-law are designated by the same term, affinal kinship terms are descriptive. Ego's children are distinguished by sex but not by relative age. Terms of reference and terms of address differ. Elder brother, for example, is addressed with a special term of respect. In other cases, Spanish personal names are used. Kinship terms are not affected by the sex of the speaker. Godparents (_padrinos_) are selected when children are baptized in the church, but since there are no church weddings or confirmations, there are no other godparents.

Marriage and Family

Marriage. Neither church nor state influences marriages except where rancherías are located close to active missions. Marriage is generally a matter of mutual consent and results in a fragile alliance. Some ethnologists report that marriages are not arranged by the families but are usually enacted through the custom of "robbing," an old Hispanic practice common throughout rural Mexico, in which the groom surreptitiously brings the bride to the home of his father and keeps her there until the anger of her family subsides. Except for acculturated families, the Tepehuan pattern much resembles that of surrounding groups: marriages are matters of consensual cohabitation, followed by social acknowledgment by the immediate social group, and at any time afterwards, easily severed by either party.

Domestic Unit. The household unit consists of the nuclear family of parents and children, with the occasional addition of other extended relatives such as a widowed parent. The rancherías comprised of adjacent households may include relatives of either parent. The married couple lives with the husband's parents for about a year until the groom receives land from his father, upon which a separate dwelling is erected. The ideal model of patrilocality, however, is often modified by the acquisition of land from another part of the ejido or from the parents of the girl.

Inheritance. Inheritance is reported by some ethnologists as patrilineal, but land and property may be passed on to daughters in the absence of male inheritors. The actual pattern is probably bilateral, in consonance with surrounding aboriginal patterns, and coinciding with the choice of bilateral residence by the couple after marriage.

Socialization

Sociopolitical Organization and Social Control. The best way to depict Tepehuan sociopolitical organization is to visualize it as nested in hierarchical strata of national, state, local, and cultural sociopolitical systems. The matter is further complicated by the presence of mixed populations of Tepehuan, Tarahumara, and mestizos wherein officeholders represent the dominant group in any single community. There are national and state representatives of various agencies, ranging from those who control Indian affairs to those who maintain roads and members of the state judiciary. Locally, the complexity of organization be-

gins with the municipio. Elected leaders include the president of the municipio and those in charge of policing and other services. Land-tenure organizations such as ejidos and comunidades have leadership structures and responsibility for—and control of—land; the comunidad is more likely to have total Indian autonomy. Ejidos are governed by a president of the ejido commission, a secretary, a treasurer, and a president of the oversight council (_consejo de vigilancia_). Comunidades have a governor (_gobernador_), a vice governor (_segundo gobernador_), auxiliary secretary (_secretario auxiliar_), and a police commissioner (_comisario de policía_). They make decisions in group meetings (_asambleas_), at which all male and some female members vote.

Pueblos are townships that act as centers of governance for surrounding rancherías. The pueblo hierarchy combines elements of ancient and colonial ritual and bureaucracy. Each _gobernancia_ (pueblo) elects a gobernador, an assistant for a two-year term, and other officials dealing with policing. The _capitán-general_, appointed by the gobernadores, oversees all six regions, and along with an assistant and seven _justicias_, is the guardian of order and justice. Traditionally, punishment for serious offenses was public whipping in the churchyard, clearly another European custom learned from the Spanish missionaries. Meetings are held every other Sunday when the gobernador calls together the justicias to hear and resolve complaints. A lower tier of officials serves shorter terms and carries out ceremonial duties dealing with the maintenance of the church and the organizing of fiestas. The residential units, the rancherías, do not have a governing structure. The only person with quasi-authority and influence is the native curer.

Some towns are divided into subsections by common references to "the people of _arriba_" (those who live upstream) and "the people of _abajo_" (those who live downstream). This division is most apparent in the loyalties and rivalries that are expressed during ceremonies, the popular foot races and ball games that take place during fiestas, and in the elaborate political hierarchy. Arriba-abajo distinctions are common throughout Latin American small towns and are not moiety divisions in the strict ethnological sense; however, they may be utilized in this manner by some indigenous groups.

Religion and Expressive Culture

Religious Beliefs. The amalgam of Tepehuan and Catholic beliefs, ceremonies, practices, and myth is a kind of "folk Catholicism" with strong aboriginal components. A single creator, called "God Our Father," is accompanied by a number of other deities of ancient origin. The Lord of the Deer is named Kukúduli and is responsible for success in hunting. When someone dies, Úgai is a spirit that appears as a light in the sky, and another god, in the mountains, takes the form of an owl as a herald of death. There is also a spirit that is the master of the wind. Mythology includes tales of the Cocoyomes, a group of giants who ate children. The church and churchyard are the center of Sunday meetings, which are important for the dispensation of justice and the sharing of information and tradition.

Religious Practitioners. As a spiritual intermediary, the shaman-curer is called _bajadios_, "he who brings God down." The term is derived from Spanish. The Tarahumara refer to this specialist as *overúame*; there must be a similar term in the language of the Tepehuan, but it is not recorded in the literature. Not only a diagnostician and healer of illness, the shaman is reputed to see the unseen and is called upon in many instances, such as when a valuable object has been lost. The shaman makes entreaties to the supernatural through the performance of a kind of séance. Courses of action are often revealed to him afterward in a dream. *Tesguino* (maize beer) is used in curing and blessing, in addition to its communal functions.

Ceremonies. Like the mestizo communities in the region, the Tepehuan observe and perform the customary Catholic pastoral dramas, introduced by the Jesuits in colonial times, during Christmas, Holy Week, and the October fiestas of San Francisco. The fiestas have an urban, mestizo phase and a Tepehuan phase, with the two groups working together on occasion. The fiestas consist of ritual activities surrounding defense and ultimate destruction of the figure of Judas and groups of participants called *fariseos* who engage in sham battles. There are also ceremonies led by the shaman to ask for good crops, to show reverence for the dead, and to petition for the physical well-being of both people and animals. The festivities are lively affairs with much dancing, the placing of offerings of food in front of a cross, and an ample supply of tesguino, an alcoholic beverage of fermented maize sprouts. Some ceremonies are held in secret with all outsiders excluded.

Arts. Music is important in Tepehuan life. Old Spanish *matachines* tunes, songs with Tepehuan themes sung in Tepehuan, and popular Spanish-Mexican songs are played at dances and fiestas on homemade violins, gourd rattles, reed flutes, rasping sticks, and drums. Oral tradition is carried on by some adult members of the communities in the spirited performance of folklore. Stories include animal tales of regional origin, as well as local renderings of familiar tales of Old World derivation.

Medicine, Death, and Afterlife. Sickness and death are blamed on spirits and witchcraft, revealed by—or made manifest in—the singing of one of three birds in the mountains. The three birds are called Tukurai, Kukuvuri, and Tokovi. There is a wide array of medicinal treatment using indigenous plants. Various poultices, solutions, and teas are made from an extraordinary number of roots, leaves, seeds, and stems of at least fifty-six plant families and a good many others that are still unidentified by outsiders.

The soul exists in the heart, but leaves the body when a person is asleep or unconscious. Upon death, the soul lingers around the house of the dead person for a month until a fiesta is held as a way of saying good-bye. After this, the house may be abandoned in fearful respect for the vicious ill will of a returned soul. If all goes well, the soul departs to live in the sky. The church cemetery is the usual place of burial. A coherent description of the Tepehuan conception of the afterlife has not yet been recorded.

Bibliography

Hedrick, Basil C., J. Charles Kelley, and Carroll L. Riley, eds. (1971). *The North Mexican Frontier: Readings in Ar-chaeology, Ethnohistory, and Ethnography.* Carbondale: Southern Illinois University Press.

Mason, J. Alden (1952). "Notes and Observations on the Tepehuan." *América Indígena* 12(1): 33–53.

Pennington, Campbell W. (1969). *The Tepehuan of Chihuahua: Their Material Culture.* Salt Lake City: University of Utah Press.

Pennington, Campbell W. (1983). "Northern Tepehuan." In *Handbook of North American Indians.* Vol. 10, *Southwest*, edited by Alfonso Ortiz, 306–314. Washington, D.C.: Smithsonian Institution.

Pequeño-Rossie, Pedro A. (1974). "The Tepehuan Indians of Northern Mexico: An Ethnohistorical Study." Ph.D. dissertation, University of Southern Illinois.

Service, Elman R. (1969). "The Northern Tepehuan." In *Handbook of Middle American Indians*, edited by Robert Wauchope. Vol. 8, *Ethnology, Part 2*, edited by Evon Z. Vogt, 822–829. Austin: University of Texas Press.

THOMAS WEAVER AND WILLIAM LEE ALEXANDER

Tepehuan of Durango

ETHNONYMS: none

Orientation

Identification and Location. The Sierra Madre Occidental range cuts a north-south swath through northern Mexico, splitting the states of Chihuahua and Durango into eastern and western parts. In extreme southwestern Durango, several hundred kilometers south of the land of the Northern Tepehuan of Chihuahua and across this mountainous rupture live the Southern Tepehuan. The sublime variance of the peaks and canyons rent from the earth by two rivers, the Mezquital and the Huazamota, and their tributaries, renders the discordant beauty of some of the roughest and most wondrous land in Mexico. This terrain makes communication possible only by unmaintained dirt roads and trails. Like the Northern Tepehuan, members of the Southern group call themselves "Dami" ("We the People" or "those who live in this place"). The name "Tepehuan" comes from the Nahuatl word *tepetl* (hill). Ethnographic work in this remote area is sparse, and although they have probably lived here for about a thousand years, the Tepehuan are relatively unknown to outsiders.

There are seven *comunidades* in Southern Tepehuan territory. Santa María Ocotán, San Francisco Ocotán, Santiago Teneraca, and Santa María Magdalena de Taxicaringa are in the *municipio* of Mezquital, Durango. San Bernardino de Milpillas Chico and San Francisco de Lajas are in the municipio of Pueblo Nuevo, Durango. Farthest to the south, in the municipio of Huajicori, Nayarit, is the comunidad of San Andrés de Milpillas Grande. Santa María Ocotán was established as an *ejido*. Each comunidad is a town that acts as the central political and religious center for several *anexos* (small settlements) and a multitude of *rancherías*.

Demography. A small proportion of the 1.3 million people living in the thinly populated state of Durango are Indians—about 24,000, of whom some 16,000 are Tepehuan. The other indigenous groups in the area are the Huichol and the Nahuatl-speaking Mexicanero Indians. A small number of Tepehuan live across the border in the states of Nayarit and Zacatecas. As in the case of the Tepehuan of Chihuahua, narrow-sighted suppositions of assimilation and acculturation often led early researchers to write them out of the ethnographic present and wrongly to assume that a viable Tepehuan culture no longer existed in Durango. The region is poorly served by federal and state agencies, and seasonal population movement in search of wage labor is a further impediment to accurate assessment.

Linguistic Affiliation. The language of the Southern Tepehuan is probably more closely related to the extinct Tepecano language that was spoken in the northern part of the state of Jalisco than to the three other languages (Northern Tepehuan, its closest living relative; Pima; and Papago of Sonora and southern Arizona) that make up the Tepiman or Piman Branch of the Sonoran Division of the Uto-Aztecan Family. There are at least two mutually intelligible dialects. Southeastern Tepehuan, spoken chiefly in the municipio of El Mezquital, is the most studied and best understood by linguists. Another dialect is in the southwestern municipio of Pueblo Nuevo.

History and Cultural Relations

The Tepehuan were hunters and gatherers who came from near the present border between the modern states of Sonora and Arizona, the originating place for all Tepiman speakers. In their present location, they were influenced by Mesoamerican culture, the culture of the more urbanized people to the south, especially in their acceptance of farming, ceramics, platform architecture, and religion. At the time of the arrival of Spaniards in the Durango region in the mid-sixteenth century, the Tepehuan were horticulturists who supplemented their subsistence with hunting and gathering during certain times of the year.

The Spaniards introduced the use of oxen in farming; the raising of cattle, sheep, and goats; the use of animal fertilizer; and new religious and political forms and clothing styles. Spanish occupation and control of the central part of present-day Durango state, around the city of Durango and immediately to the north, created a split between the Southern and Northern Tepehuan. Although there is no lucid setting apart of the two Tepehuan in the early Spanish records, there is no real evidence to confirm that they were much closer culturally at the time of the Conquest than they are now. The distance of several hundred kilometers between the two divisions may have been sufficient to create the cultural and linguistic differences that

now exist. Interestingly, considered separately, it is apparent that a long period of isolation was necessary to produce the remarkable language dissimilarity. Although it is generally observed that the Northern Tepehuan are closer to the culture pattern of the Indians of the Greater Southwest and the Southern Tepehuan are closer to that of Mesoamerica, appraised as a whole, the Tepehuan emerge as a kind of bridge between the two. Today the Southern Tepehuan seem particularly close to the Cora and the Huichol in the neighboring states of Nayarit and Jalisco.

Upon their arrival, the Spaniards immediately subjugated the Indians, forcing them to labor in mines and on farms, imposing virtual slavery, brutality, and rape, and confiscating their goods and lands. Following the era of the gold seekers, the missionizing process became a concerted and intense effort in Durango between 1607 and 1615. After the establishment of missions and the settlement of Indians in towns, the Spaniards built garrisons to protect their settlements and haciendas to farm and tend cattle. This encroachment was not passively received. Continuous trouble culminated in a bloody uprising from 1616 to 1618, the first large—and possibly the most devastating—Indian rebellion in the border regions in the seventeenth century. The Spanish settlement that is now Durango city came under siege, and there was fighting at Mezquital in the south and at Canatlán in the north. By early 1621, pacification was well enough under way to allow the Spanish appointment of forty-six Tepehuan political officers to govern the Indian communities. Although sporadic insurgency continued (raids on Spanish farms and ranches were common around Mezquital), the two decades that followed are seen as the time of conclusive efforts to quell significant resistance.

Drought and widespread epidemics in Southern Tepehuan towns in the late seventeenth century decreased the population and pushed many Tepehuan away from their native homes and closer toward Spanish settlements and influences, or further into the southern mountains. After the Spanish colonial administration expelled the Jesuits in 1767, a period of relative isolation allowed the Southern Tepehuan to produce an amalgamated, distinct culture. Continued inroads by mestizo culture, the seizing of lands, and continued poverty, as well as isolation in a rugged country, have ensured that this distinct culture would develop without interference from outside governmental agencies. The greatest threats to cultural integrity and survival today are changes in national land-tenure laws, the exploitation of forests, continued labor migration, and—most devastating—the invasion of Tepehuan lands by drug lords, who impose a regime of forced labor.

Settlements

Each comunidad is a territorial and political unit. At the center of a comunidad is a main town that is the religious-political center for the surrounding anexos (named villages) and isolated rancherías belonging to the comunidad. A ranchería consists of clustered houses surrounded by widely scattered small farm plots. The towns act as central foci for government, social, and religious rituals and are official headquarters for holding elections and discussing matters affecting the comunidad. In addition to a town's public and administrative buildings, there are also a church or chapel, a school, and a community kitchen. Elected officials live in these centers during their terms of office.

A typical Southern Tepehuan dwelling is a rectangular two-room construction built on a platform of earth that has been prepared by continual watering, sweeping, and hollowing out. The walls are made of stone and adobe and the roof is thatched with grass. One room is used for cooking and the other for sleeping. There are variations in the construction of homes in different villages, depending on available materials. Where sawmills are accessible, lumber is used in the construction of community and residential buildings.

Economy

Subsistence and Commercial Activities.   The great variation in elevation (from 600 meters at the deepest point in the vast Mezquital Canyon to 3,250 meters at the crown of Cerro Gordo) produces a great variation in plants and wildlife. The choices of cultivable crops are extremely limited because of the lack of water and topsoil; another determinent is the rugged terrain cut by two deep rivers, which flow southward through Nayarit into the Pacific. Deep canyons create different ecosystems and dictate the types of crops that can be grown. Pine and hardwood forests cover high plateaus. Deep valleys, with hot, dry climates and tropical flora and fauna in the lowlands alternate with the higher, temperate zones that experience heavy rainfall in the summer and frost in winter.

Agriculture and pastoralism are the main economic resources, although the lumber industry has made a minor contribution since about 1980. Maize, beans, and two kinds of squash are the traditionally cultivated crops and remain the dietary staples, given that the rocky mountains and the scarcity of water leave only a trifling amount of arable land and permit little diversification. Despite the importance of maize as a dietary staple, the Southern Tepehuan do not grow sufficient quantities to feed themselves. Around the beginning of the twentieth century, it was reported that cotton was grown for ceremonial purposes, but this practice has been abandoned. Heavy on tortillas, beans, cheese, and other farm products that need no irrigation, the Tepehuan diet is fortified by a good deal of gathered foods. These include roots, wild tubers, fruits, greens, and mushrooms. The constraints of the land greatly impinge both on the economy and on patterns of settlement and migration.

Along with the pines that support the lumber industry are banana, plum, and avocado trees that are native to the area, as well as the introduced apple and peach species. Also in the more tropical areas are found mangos and *guayabo* fruits. Most families keep chickens. Cattle and goats are fairly common, and an accumulation of them is a mark of wealth. Other domesticated animals include sheep, turkeys, pigs, horses, and donkeys. Hunting and fishing are less important today than in the past. Firearms for hunting are luxuries that not many can afford. Cattle and most available wild game, such as deer, are saved for ceremonial use.

Trade.   The Southern Tepehuan engage in a modest amount of trade and commerce. Fruits, livestock, maize, and mescal are brought to Mexican markets for sale or trade. Household goods such as cloth, cooking utensils, and tools are procured at occasional market outings.

Division of Labor.   These trading ventures and most other economic matters are the exclusive domain of males. For the most part, the division of labor by gender falls along the same lines as that of the Northern Tepehuan. Men perform the heavy farm and forestry work, and women maintain the home, weaving clothing and household items from wool, cotton, and maguey fiber and participating in the harvest. At a very young age, children begin to herd goats and cattle. Labor exchange occurs within extended families, and communal labor is required for certain tasks, especially during communal rituals.

Kinship

The household is the main unit of production and consumption—with the occasional addition of others from what appears to be an extended patrilineal family, often localized in the same ranchería, neighborhood, or village. Along with the offices and loyalties of the towns and anexos are the *apellido* group alliances, which crosscut village boundaries. These are associations (sometimes three or four in a village) of individuals sharing the same Spanish surname. Children of the same parents often have different surnames. Apellido groups may be the remaining shells of nonlocalized patrilineal clans of antiquity.

Marriage and Family

Marriage.   Few, if any, marriage restrictions have been recorded. Marriages are usually arranged by the parents of the couple and take place before either the bride or the groom reaches the age of 20 and, often, at a younger age. The parents of the prospective groom pay ceremonial visits to the family of the chosen bride for five consecutive nights, and on the fifth night the girl's parents decide whether to accept or reject the offer of marriage. Formerly, the newly married husband went to work for his wife's relatives for five months. After this, the couple either went to live with his family or set up their own household. This is not the only pattern of marriage; other variations may involve the groom appearing before a native official called an *ixkai* with his hands tied. After a brief invocation the man is untied, and the couple go to live at the groom's paternal home. As soon as possible, the couple construct their own home near the groom's paternal residence.

Domestic Unit and Inheritance.   People live as either nuclear or patrilineal extended families, with members added who are related through either descent or marriage. Houses and privately owned land property are ordinarily passed down from father to son.

Land Tenure, Sociopolitical Organization, and Social Control

Sociopolitical organization is complicated by the presence of sometimes conflicting forms of land tenure and systems introduced at different times by the Spaniards and Mexicans that crosscut traditional organization. There are two forms of communal land tenure present in the region. The comunidad is an older, indigenous form, in which land is held patrilineally and inherited by sons or widows. The ejido is a form of communal land-tenure system provided for in the constitution of 1917, following the Mexican Revolution. It allocated communal lands to applicants—whether Indian, mestizo, or together—to be held as long as the land is used economically. Under the ejidal system, land is not officially or legally inheritable, but actual practice often violates this proviso. An elected body of officials governs the ejido and its economic business. Residential units found within ejidos and comunidades include towns and rancherías.

Comunidades are governed by a popularly elected *asamblea* (assembly of voting members), who decide upon matters presented and select minor political and economic officials. The asamblea officers include the traditional *gobernador*, representatives from each of the anexos, and others who act as police and church assistants, as well as those who announce and conduct religious ceremonies and similar activities. Overlapping this group—and conflicting with them—are ejidal officers, in those instances where the ejido controls the land-tenure system. A *comisario* is elected for a three-year term to transact business with lumber companies (where sawmills exploiting ejidal forest land are present); other officials supervise sawmills, work in the forest, watch over forest exploitation according to established rules, and deal with officials of the Secretaría de la Reforma Agraria, the federal agency that oversees and adjudicates matters regarding ejidos.

The traditional gobernador (ixkai) is responsibile for public works, supervision of communal work, maintaining public order, and ceremonies honoring the community's patron saint. In some communities he is also in charge of the *xiotahl* ritual (see "Religion and Expressive Culture"), judges minor cases of crime and family disputes, and imposes punishment as necessary. The *gobernador segundo* acts in the place of the former in his absence. *Regidores* act as the gobernador's messengers. *Alguaciles* are in charge of keeping order and dispensing punishment (such as whippings) in some cases. The *topil* is an assistant. The position of *teportado* is filled by a youth who accompanies the governor during fiestas and calls the community by beating a drum. The *kapchin* is charged with matters dealing with boundaries. The *alférez* and others are assistants in communal religious and political matters, for instance, keeping order during Holy Week.

Religious festivals are held on days designated by the Catholic church (e.g., Holy Week) and to celebrate the patron saint's day. *Mayordomías*, officers within a *cargo*-system hierarchy, are in charge of this important festival. *Mayordomos* are in control, with assistants called *priostas; pasioneros* accompany the image of the saint, and a *fiscal* is the sacristan in charge of the images of the saints. The numbers and duties of these officials vary from community to community. Generally, they are in charge of the appropriate traditional performance of the ceremonies, the operation of communal kitchens, and keeping order during the ritual.

The political system is overlaid with systems of personal influence, municipal jurisdictions and officials, and political activities dealing with national, state, and municipal elections. Unofficial governance, influence, and power is also imposed by caciques, local bosses who enforce their rule through violence and torture. The municipio is divided into *manzanas*, or *cuarteles*, each with an appointed chief who may act as a parallel authority and often displaces the traditional ixkai. A Supreme Council of the Tepehuan has been created to provide a single voice for the whole of the Southern Tepehuan, but it seems to have little authority. Political parties such as the Partido del Pueblo Mexicano (PPM) and others are making their appearance in some communities to oppose the ruling state party, the Partido Revolucionario Institucional (PRI).

Religion and Expressive Culture

Religious Beliefs, Ceremonies, and Religious Practitioners. The Tepehuan have accepted Catholicism while maintaining aspects of their original religious precepts, an example of what anthropologists call "compartmentalism." This means that the two religions are practiced separately at different times of the year, with different rituals, and for different purposes. Catholics are served by a resident priest at San Bernardino, who also serves the surrounding areas. Other communities are served by visiting missionaries who arrive before Easter Sunday and stay several weeks. The archbishop comes yearly from Durango to baptize and confirm children. No other priests or members of Protestant religions missionize or visit the region.

A traditional pantheon of gods is syncretized in name and ritual with Catholic religious figures. Dios Padre (God the Father) is associated with the sun, whereas Jesús Nazareno (Jesus the Nazarene) is identified with the moon. Madre María (the Holy Mother) is represented by several figures, one of which is the Virgin of Guadalupe. The Morning Star is referred to as "our elder brother." There is a local figure named Ixaitiung whose heroic story of a fall from grace through the human failings of drunkenness and fornication, absolvement by performing the first sacred dance, and ultimate passage into heaven recounts a conventional religious theme. He also provided the xiotahl ritual.

Like other Indians in Mexico, the Southern Tepehuan celebrate the Christian holy days of Easter, the Feast of the Virgin of Guadalupe (12 December), Christmas, and village saints' days with spirited fiestas that are predominantly Mexican in character, during which the standard *matachines* are danced. The *elote* (tender maize) first-fruits festival is a non-Christian celebration that takes place in early October; fresh maize cannot be eaten until this festival is held.

The ceremonies that set the Tepehuan apart from mestizo culture in Durango are the ceremonies of fertility and thanksgiving called *mitotes* (Spanish) or *xiotahl* (Tepehuan). Shamans function as directors of these sacred ceremonies during the fiestas and as curers. For five days there is fasting and much prayer. On the fifth night there is a grand display of ritual dancing, and, when the sun rises, the celebrants break their fast by eating food that has been set as offerings at the east end of the dance platform, on an altar dedicated to the rising sun. Mitotes are not as frequent nor as extravagant as they were in the past. Today they are held, on average, three times a year, in accordance with the agricultural cycle (to appeal for protection against the harsh dry winter, to bless the spring sowing, to give thanks for the fall harvest) and on other occasions, including the blessing of newly elected officers. During times of drought a special mitote may be given to ask for rain. Traditional native mitotes are more reverent occasions of abstinence and prayer, whereas mestizo-influenced fiestas are opportunities for revelry and mescal drinking.

Each family and community has a patio where ceremonies are conducted. At both the village and the apellido-group level, there is an officer called the *jefe del patio* who organizes and leads the mitotes. The jefe of the apellido group—almost always an elderly male shaman—is in charge of special apellido festivals, which are celebrated by the production of a xiotahl in May and October. At these times, recently born children are ritually inducted into the apellido group, and young adults of 15 years of age are recognized as adults of the group. Some feel that the shamans held ruling power in ancient Tepehuan culture. It is traditional that there be a female jefe del patio in both apellidos groups and territorial villages to preside over the affairs of female members.

Arts and Industrial Arts. By Jesuit accounts, precolonial musical instruments that were played during dances and ceremonies included rasping sticks, rattles, and reed or ceramic flutes. These instruments along with the musical bow played on a gourd sounder, are still used to provide music during the ceremonial mitote. The drum and the violin, an instrument of Spanish origin, are added when playing *corridos* and other popular Mexican songs at the fiestas. Clay pipes and incense burners similar to pre-Spanish objects that have been unearthed are sometimes used by curers for their healing rituals. Although some pottery is still made, it is, for the most part, strictly functional and undecorated, and weaving has all but vanished.

Illness and Death. When illness strikes, anyone in the family of the afflicted may petition the supernatural through prayer, but more serious conditions require the efforts of shaman curers. These individuals are endowed with the gift of healing, may be of either sex but are usually male, and specialize in the treatment of specific infirmities. Well-known curers are often consulted by mestizo neighbors. A young person who is called to be a shaman will train for five years as an apprentice to an older shaman. During this time he learns ritual prayers and makes an ascetic retreat of seclusion for one month each year, nourished only by plain tortillas, water, meditation, and prayer.

Treatment entails a long, elaborate ceremony that normally lasts for five days. The curer fasts, prays, and chants long routinized orations. The sick person is massaged and has smoke from the curer's pipe blown over his or her body. Typical of shamanistic healing in this part of the world, the ritual involves sucking the material object that caused the disease from the body of the patient, the use of eagle feathers for sweeping the patient, incantations including invocation of Catholic saints, the symbolic use of the cross and images of saints, and the use of various herbs. Ritualized confession of the patient, the participation of other family members as beneficiaries of healing, and special healing mitotes, in which a large number of people are cured en masse by the spiritually charged aura of the ceremony, are some of the curing practices with wider social dimensions.

The malady that brings death is believed to be both spiritual and physical in nature, a result of sickness and sorcery. Throughout the life cycle, intervals of five are of significant symbolic importance: note the lengths of the premarriage visits of the parents (five successive days), the shaman's training period (five years), and mitotes (five days). A special five-day ceremony, which is conducted by the shaman and closely involves the surviving family members, marks the end of a life on earth and concludes with the driving of the soul out from the body and into heaven. In this capacity as funeral director, the shaman's role has been interpreted as that of a practitioner whose principal responsibility is to prevent the soul from coming back to its corporeal home. The usual place of interment of the dead is the village burial ground, which is commonly located in the churchyard.

Bibliography

Gonzalez Elizondo, Martha (1991). "Ethnobotany of the Southern Tepehuan of Durango, Mexico: Edible Mushrooms." *Journal of Ethnobiology* 11(2): 165–173.

Hedrick, Basil C., J. Charles Kelley, and Carroll L. Riley, eds. (1971). *The North Mexican Frontier: Readings in Archaeology, Ethnohistory and Ethnography.* Carbondale: Southern Illinois University Press.

Mason, J. Alden (1948). "The Tepehuan, and the Other Aborigines of the Mexican Sierra Madre Occidental." *América Indígena* 8(4): 289–300.

Pequeño-Rossie, Pedro A. (1974). "The Tepehuan Indians of Northern Mexico: An Ethnohistorical Study." Ph.D. dissertation, University of Southern Illinois.

Riley, Carroll L. (1969). "The Southern Tepehuan and Tepecano." In *Handbook of Middle American Indians*, edited by Robert Wauchope. Vol. 8, *Ethnology, Part 2*, edited by Evon Z. Vogt, 814–821. Austin: University of Texas Press.

Sánchez Olmedo, José Guadalupe (1980). *Etnografía de la Sierra Madre Occidental: Tepehuanes y Mexicaneros.* Colección Científica, 92. Mexico City: Secretaria de Educación Pública; Instituto Nacional de Antropología e Historia (SEP-INAH).

Willett, Thomas L. (1991). *A Reference Grammar of Southeastern Tepehuan.* Arlington: Summer Institute of Linguistics; University of Texas at Arlington.

WILLIAM LEE ALEXANDER AND THOMAS WEAVER

Tequistlatec

ETHNONYMS: Chontal, Chontalpa, Tequistlateco

The Tequistlatec are the largest ethnic group in the _municipios_ of Asunción Tlacolulita, San Miguel Tenango, San Pedro Huamelula, Santa María Ecatepec, and Santiago Astata in southeastern Oaxaca, Mexico. The Instituto Nacional Indigenista estimates that there were 13,880 Tequistlatec in these municipios in 1990. They are relatively acculturated; only 14.7 percent of the population speaks the native language. They are often referred to as the "Chontal," an Aztec word meaning "foreigner."

Two related languages divide the Tequistlatec into separate cultural groups, the Highland Chontal living in the mountains away from the coast at elevations of 1,200 to 2,400 meters, and the Lowland Chontal living in the coastal municipios of San Pedro Huamelula and Santiago Astata at an elevation of 300 meters. The Tequistlatec were probably subjects of the Aztecs and were subjugated by the Spanish. Contact was more intensive with the lowlanders.

The economy is based on subsistence agriculture practiced with the aid of animal-drawn plows. Maize and sugarcane are grown as cash crops. Highland Chontal produce mescal for sale. Land is owned privately or by the village.

Bibliography

Carrasco Pizana, Pedro (1960). _Pagan Rituals and Beliefs among the Chontal Indians of Oaxaca, Mexico._ Berkeley and Los Angeles: University of California Press.

Turner, Paul R. (1972). _The Highland Chontal._ New York: Holt, Rinehart & Winston.

Teribe

ETHNONYM: Terraba

The slightly more than 1,000 Teribe Indians live along the Teribe, San Juan, and Changuinola rivers in the western Panamanian province of Bocas del Toro. Nearly all of them speak the Teribe language, which belongs to the Chibchan Family. They are linguistically and culturally related to the Térraba (who also are known as Teribe) Indians of Costa Rica. The majority of Teribe of Panama live as farmers or laborers.

Bibliography

Reverte Coma, José Manuel (1967). _Los indios teribes de Panamá: Trabajo presentado al XXXVII Congreso Internacional de Americanistas, septiembre, 1966._ Panama: N.p.

Von Chong S., Nilka, and Myrna Ortiz (1982). _Estudio etnográfico sobre el grupo Teribe._ Panama: N.p.

Tlapanec

ETHONYMS: none

The Tlapanec live southeast of Chilpancingo, in the Mexican state of Guerrero. The 1990 census listed 68,483 speakers of the Tlapanec language. They form about 21 percent of the Indian population of Guerrero, living primarily in the _municipios_ of Atlixtac, Malinaltepec, Tlacoapa, and Zapotitlán Tablas. Their language belongs to the Hokaltecan Stock and is most closely related to the language once spoken by the Subtiaba of Nicaragua.

The Tlapanec people subsist primarily upon maize, beans, and chili peppers, crops they grow themselves. The poorer people of this society cannot afford to eat beans as frequently as do others of the region. Meat is usually eaten only during fiestas. They also grow bananas, sugarcane, and coffee for cash.

The Tlapanec men do most of the agricultural, construction, and carpentry work. They are well known for the high quality of their carpentry, despite their rudimentary tools, which include only machetes, wedges, and chisels. Women produce most of the cotton and wool cloth. Tlapanec people also produce for sale hats, fans, saddles, and _petates_ (straw mats). Many also work in the fields of their mestizo neighbors, where they enjoy a reputation as good day laborers.

Little is known about Tlapanec social and political organization. Families are patriarchal. Political and religious leaders work together in governing. The highest level of government is a council of chiefs. This council, however, is able to do little that is not permitted them by the Mexican government and Catholic church authorities of the region.

The Tlapanec pantheon of gods is dominated by a male god and a female god; in addition, there are so called "impersonal" gods. These gods have lost much of their former importance owing to the introduction of Catholicism. Also of reduced influence are beliefs in witchcraft and traditional sacred places. Fiestas are now held on Catholic holy days and assume the pattern of those held by mestizos. During the fiestas, people drink the alcoholic beverages pulque and _aguardiente._

No knowledge survives concerning traditional indigenous music, musical instruments, or dances.

Bibliography

Dehouve, Daniele (1990). *Quand les banquiers étaient des saints: 450 ans de l'histoire économique et sociale d'une province indienne du Mexique*. Paris: Éditions du Centre National de la Recherche Scientifique.

Oettinger, Marion (1980). *Una comunidad tlapaneca: Sus linderos sociales y territoriales*. Mexico City: Instituto Nacional Indigenista.

Olmsted, D. L. (1969). "The Tequistlatec and Tlapanec." In *Handbook of Middle American Indians*. Vol. 8, *Ethnology, Part Two*, edited by Evon Z. Vogt, 553–564. Austin: University of Texas Press.

Suárez, Jorge A. (1988). *Tlapaneco de Malinaltepec*. Mexico City: El Colegio de México.

Tojolab'al

ETHNONYMS: Chanabal, Chañabal, Chaneabal, Jocolabal, Jojolabal, Tojolabal

Orientation

Identification. The Tojolab'al take their name from their language: Tojolab'al (*tojol*: legitimate/true; *ab'al*: word/language). They call themselves "Tojolwinik'otik" (legitimate or real men).

Location. Today the Tojolab'al live mainly in the *municipio* of Las Margaritas, in Chiapas, Mexico, on the frontier with Guatemala, although there are residential groups in the neighboring municipios of Altamirano, Comitan, Independencia, and La Trinitaria. This was not always so. Their present location is a result of processes of miscegenation, of cultural Ladinization, and—above all—of land expropriation, from which they have suffered at least since the arrival of the Spaniards in their territory in 1528 (a time when they ruled over the area of the valleys of Comitan).

Demography. There is enormous divergence regarding the numerical count of the Tojolab'al. The highest reckonings, which generally duplicate those given in censuses, are those of anthropologists and other scholars who have worked in the area. Based on these, the number of Tojolab'al should be calculated at between 35,000 and 40,000.

Linguistic Affiliation. Tojolab'al belongs to the Maya Language Family; it is closely related to Chuj and more distantly related to Tzeltal, Tzotzil, and Q'anjob'al.

History and Cultural Relations

After the Spanish Conquest, the Tojolwinit'otik suffered from unprecedented exploitation, which continues to this day. As a result of it, they have seen a drastic reduction in the extension of their best lands, the product of their labor going to others, and the irrevocable loss of many elements of their culture.

Early on, the fertile area around Comitan attracted the Spanish invaders. Although, in the beginning, Comitan was no more than one of the "large villages" of what was called the province of Los Llanos, it soon became the economic axis of this region, which can aptly be described as a mosaic. Within it can be found dense forests of conifers and oak groves in the northern triangle; the high jungle of the western plains; the wide plains of the southern triangle, irrigated by the Río Grijalva and its affluents; and riverbeds and small fertile valleys in the east, where minor rivers and lagoons dot the landscape. The scene changed from conifers to subhumid forests of aromatic balsams and oaks before descending into the high green Lakandon jungle, now cut down mercilessly.

The multizoned ecology eventually supported a complex of farming and animal husbandry including the raising of maize, wheat, sugarcane, cotton, and cattle, and the collection of salt. A fair portion of the commerce between Guatemala and New Spain passed through this area.

The province was, at the same time, an ethnic mosaic, where Tojolab'al, Cabil, Tzeltal, and Totique (Tzotzil) settled, and where these people met the Mocho', Lakandon, Chuj, Q'anjob'al, Mam, and Jakalteko. These different peoples had differing levels of social organization, but all eventually became a source of available and exploitable labor.

To the south of Comitan there were also a series of pueblos that colonial chronicles call "Coxoh." The general tendency had been to consider them Tzeltal, but nowadays it is believed that they were probably Tojolab'al (Lenkersdorf 1986).

At first, the conquerors and their descendants who had settled in Ciudad Real seem to have been satisfied with collecting tribute from the villages in the region of Llanos. The Dominican friars, however, taking advantage of the legislation that allowed them to live in the Indian towns and their ascendancy over the population as a result of their increasing familiarity with local languages and their roles as spiritual leaders, began accumulating property, especially in the warmer areas, from around the second half of the sixteenth century.

When the Crown disallowed the *encomiendas*, the loss of these tributaries made direct spoliation an insufficient mechanism to ensure the economic well-being of the Spanish civilians of Ciudad Real, so they began to turn their attention toward the Indian settlements in Comitan and the surrounding area.

As cattle ranches, sugar mills, and other types of businesses proliferated, there was an increase in miscegenation and indigenous acculturation. It also gave many Indians the possibility of escaping heavy fiscal, ecclesiastical, and communal taxes as well as a precarious existence in villages that were periodically afflicted with epidemics. In 1795 some Indians themselves mentioned this human crucible, noting that their village was made up of Spaniards, mestizos, and Ladinos, as well as themselves.

The increase in the mestizo population and the greater integration of local economies into the regional market, as well as the reorganization undertaken by the Bourbon regimes in modifying tributary and labor policies, led to a movement of the Indian working force to cattle ranches and haciendas. Indirectly it encouraged Ladinization of many of the indigenous peoples and, in the process, altered the level of regional mobilization.

The struggle for independence did not in any way mean the end of indigenous oppression. Various republican regimes took advantage of the rationale of judicial equality for exploiting the little remaining communal land that the indigenous peoples had managed to keep. Then began a period of veritable slavery for the Indians employed in haciendas, which indentured them for generations.

In 1931, after the Mexican Revolution, the first timid land distribution began. The peons in the *fincas* (commercial farms) were freed from their debts and given land. From each finca one, two, and even three *ejidos* were formed out of hacienda land.

Settlements

The settlement pattern generally corresponds to what is termed "compact low density" and has a rectangular layout. Each block is occupied by four to six families, almost always linked by family ties. Around the settlement are the cultivated lands; farther out are pastures and communal forests, if these exist.

Houses are built following a rectangular plan, and, although construction materials vary according to the ecological zone, almost without exception they have earthen floors. There is almost no furniture in the houses. Only seldom are there latrines or piped water. Other common constructions in the block compound are chicken coops, pigsties, granaries, sheep corrals and sweat baths (*ik'a*).

Economy

Land distribution is very irregular. Some settlements have over 3,000 hectares of cultivable land, whereas others have no more than 300. The main difference lies in the quality of the land. Depending on the ecological niche, the kind of crop will vary according to soil type, climate, rainfall, and so forth. In all cases, mountainous lands are communal.

In the highlands, the Tojolab'al cultivate mainly the classic Mesoamerican triad (maize, beans, and squashes), in an effort to be self-sufficient. Those living in the valleys and riverbeds can diversify their cultigens with vegetables, sugarcane, coffee, and citric and other fruits, but those living in the jungle concentrate on the cultivation of coffee and, in some cases, on raising cattle. Forest products (cedar, mahogany, and others) are sold to private and state companies, at risibly low prices.

Tojolab'al living in the highlands, riverbeds, and valleys are obliged to find other ways of boosting their meager family income. They sell their seasonal agricultural surplus in local markets; raise chickens, pigs, and sheep; sometimes sell their handicrafts (embroidered blouses, ceramics, cordage); and—above all—work for wages on coffee plantations, in construction businesses, on maize farms, on cattle ranches, or in sugar mills in the basin of the Río Grijalva. Periods of wage-labor migration can be as long as eight months out of the year (the average is between four and five), and during this time the women are left in charge of all agricultural labor at home, except plowing.

Kinship

Consanguineous kinship terminology shows a clear cognatic orientation, in which the only indicated differences between collateral kin are by relative age and sex. The following terminology would be used by a male speaker: *tatjun* (male relative older than father or mother), *me'jun* (female relative older than father or mother), *b'ankil* (male relative older than Ego but younger than his father or mother), *watz* (female relative older than Ego but younger than his father or mother), and *ijtz'in* (male or female relative younger than Ego). The only variant for a female speaker is to replace the term b'ankil by *nu'*.

The idea of contrasting older with younger is not limited to kinship terms; almost all objects, beings (including supernaturals), and even *cargos* are conceptualized within a relationship of older/younger (*b'ankilal/ijtz'inal*). Hierarchy, determined by the criterion of relative age, is reflected in the humble and respectful conduct of minors toward their elders, and even in how work groups are structured.

In contrast to consanguineous kinship, affinal kinship is rather poorly delineated. Relatives by marriage are integrated into the consanguineous kinship system.

Marriage and Family

Marriage. There are six types of marriage: traditional marriage (*chak'abal*); a series of long marriage petitions accompanied by continuous gift giving; elopement (*yiaj'nel*); "dragging off" (*sjoko'ajnel*, wherein the bridegroom forces his bride to follow him, interrupting the process of "petitions"); abduction (*elk'anel*), which is frequent among young couples who are not betrothed; and marriage either according to the Catholic rite (*nupanel ba iglesya*) or before the civil registry, which is becoming ever more frequent among those converting to some of the Protestant rites or sects. The choice of one or the other method is influenced greatly by the economic situation of the bridegroom. The chak'abal is becoming ever less frequent, especially in the jungle, but questions of prestige also play a role in choosing a marriage type.

Domestic Unit. Daily life is structured around extended-family groups, which in communities in the highlands, valleys, and riverbeds continue to live together virilocally. The mother acts as the domestic authority and is the jealous guardian of traditional values, whereas the father is the primary authority within the family and the community.

The kind of family unit that predominates shows important variations: in Agua Azul, in the jungle, nuclear families make up 62.80 percent of the total, compared with 36.70 percent in Veracruz, in the higher lands, where extended patrilocal families predominate (40.80 percent versus 8.57 percent in Agua Azul).

The variation in the percentage of these family types apparently stems from economic differences. Oriented toward the cultivation of maize and in great measure dependent on men's wage labor, the Veracruzan family requires group work. On the other hand, the cultivation of coffee in the jungle, which requires labor beyond that which it is possible for the family to offer, has accelerated a reduction in family size in Agua Azul.

Variations are also observed in the type of postmarital residential pattern: in 1981 in Veracruz 54.7 percent of the male population had lived with their parents for over seven years; 61.8 percent for over 5 years, and 97.4 percent for over one year. In Agua Azul, however, 72.5 percent of the married *ejidatarios* had built their own houses before spending three years in patrilocal residence, and 100 percent had left the paternal home before five years of marriage. Of the present-day inhabitants of Agua Azul who formerly lived in Veracruz, 89.20 percent lived with the husband's parents; 3.57 percent with those of the wife, and barely 7.14 percent lived in their own homes. Among them all only 11.80 percent owned land in Veracruz.

Sociopolitical Organization

Community structure is rather lax; individuals identify themselves as members of a community and show this even in the small variations in typical female dress. Although it is said that local authority was formerly vested in a council of elders, today the political offices in each colony are limited to those of the ejido commissioner, *agente municipal,* church president, and their respective helpers, secretary-treasurer, policemen, and *alféreces.*

The significance of such posts is rather limited. The church president, for example, limits himself to opening the church on Saturdays, making sure that prayer services are performed (led by a chatechist), and serving the priest when he visits the community. Although *cofradías* were common in the area until the nineteenth century, there is no record of any today.

The agente municipal is elected in an assembly and holds his post for a year, during which he plays the difficult role of intermediary between the community and the municipal authorities.

The most important post is that of the ejido commissioner, elected in the assembly and ratified by the municipio (which is controlled by mestizos). His main areas of activity are the organization of agricultural labor and the resolution of local problems, situations in which he acts as a mere regulator and represents the group's decisions, because, in the last analysis, decisions are always taken by the community assembly. This does not mean, however, that the Tojolab'al practice pure democracy. There are fragmentary power units focused on family nuclei, each of which tries to carry water to its own mill. Nonetheless, anyone can express his opinion and defend his point of view, and final decisions are always made by consensus; an assembly can consequently last an entire day.

Community cohesion is faced with increasingly adverse conditions. It is being threatened by the divisionary tactics of the political parties (Institutional Revolutionary party, Revolutionary Democratic party) and the cult of individualism encouraged by the new churches and sects, which multiply vertiginously in the area. Intracommunity confrontations, including armed conflicts, are ever more frequent.

Economic activities and rituals also reflect community structures, for example, in obligatory community work; in *jelanel*, lending grain in times of scarcity; in *k'otak'in*, sacrificing cattle that are hopelessly hurt, cutting up the carcass, and selling the meat within the community to help

the animal's owner recuperate from the loss; and finally, when a neighbor needs more manual labor than his family can supply. Such a person can appeal to the community assembly for help. The assembly then names those who are to help him and fixes the wages to be paid, which are always lower than those demanded when working outside the community.

Community efforts to keep its members immersed in a climate of cooperation and friendship are not always successful. Conflicts are frequent, and, at times, a great deal of energy and wisdom is required on the part of the authorities and the community to keep them from ending up in fights that, given the network of extensive kinship relations, could involve the entire population.

In the highlands and in the poorer riverbed communities, where land disputes have led to occupations by the landless Indians and have been brutally put down by the military and paramilitary, ejido unions tend to achieve a greater ethnic unity as an effective defense against the interests of the dominant mestizo group.

In the early 1990s some Tojolab'al groups nominated Indians for municipio posts. Although they did not win, the Tojolab'al are conscious of their rights and have been strengthening their position in successive elections; the consciousness of being an oppressed people crystallizes with increasing frequency in revindicatory agrarian, economic, political, and ethnic demands.

Religion and Expressive Culture

Religious Beliefs. The universe is conceived of as being composed of three levels: Satk'inal or sky, Lumk'inal or terrestrial space (divided into three concentric levels: sea, hot land, and cold land), and K'ik'inal or underworld. Each is inhabited by different beings whose intervention can effect changes in both community as well as individual harmony.

Satk'inal is inhabited by K'ajwaltik Dios (Our Lord God), Nantik Santa Maria (Our Lady Mary), and two stars that direct the cycle of daily life: K'ak'u (Sun) and Ixaw (Moon).

In Lumk'inal there reside, besides men, the "gods" or saints, representatives of God, who ordered them to found and protect the villages, and their counterparts, the allies of the Lord of the Underworld, who punishes behavior that is considered unacceptable, including that directed against the environment.

Pukuj or Niwan Winik (Great Man) is the Lord of the Underworld, of the forest, and of its inhabitants. He also holds the secrets of witchcraft, which on occasion he may communicate to some men.

Throughout his existence the individual tries to maintain an equilibrium between the various forces that populate the universe; if any of them were to dominate, this could result in drought, epidemic, flood, plague or, on a personal level, illness, defined as the loss of the harmonious equilibrium between biological and sociocultural factors, that is, between the natural and supernatural worlds.

On the individual level, this equilibrium resides, to a great degree, in the *sk'ujol*, an entity located in the region of the heart, but which has many of the functions often attributed to the brain; in it reside sensibleness, spirit, character, memory, confidence, goodness, happiness, sadness, genius, soul force, judgment, and the conscience.

Ceremonies. One way to maintain equilibrium is through traditional rituals that mix Christian elements with others of clear pre-Hispanic origin, for example, the cult of the dead and the community carnival (Ta an k'ou).

Myths and tales in the oral tradition speak of how the abandonment of rituals (*costumbre*) can cause trouble to the individual or the community. If equilibrium is destroyed, it can be restored by performing personal rites, such as those performed by *pitachik'* and sorcerers, or by family and community rituals.

According to Tojolab'al concepts, there are certain men, designated as *vivos* (living ones), who have received a special grace from God. Whereas some vivos—such as lightning-strike-men (*hombres-rayo*), rainbow-men, and sheet-lightning-men (*hombres-relámpagos*)—use their power for doing good or simply to entertain themselves, others seek further power from alliances with the beings of the underworld and then cause harm. These vivos possess a *nahual* (*wayjel*), with whom they share their good and bad fortune.

Of the four pilgrimages that were of prime importance for all Tojolab'al but are nevertheless declining in significance, three are performed before the rainy season, with the objective of asking the saints to bring rain.

Conversion to Protestantism or certain sects is a phenomenon that is on the rise among the Tojolab'al, especially among those living in the jungle, and has resulted in a loss of traditional values. Some communities have even given up using their native language because the priests say that "God does not understand Tojolab'al." These religions encourage individualism and break up community solidarity.

Medicine. Local curers are also considered vivos; they have an animal companion and the gift of curing. Among them are the *ajnanum*, herbalist; the *pitachik'*, a curer capable of hearing messages that the blood transmits through the pulse beat (*pita* = *hear*, *chik'* = *blood*); and the *me'xep*, midwife (lit., grandmother).

Music. As befits a culture with an oral tradition, it is music, together with language, that occupies a privileged place in all these ceremonies. Not surprisingly, the Tojolab'al are splendid performers on the drums (*wajabal*) and the flute (*aj-may*), as well as on the guitar, violin, and harmonica. The latter are used on festive, but not ritual, occasions, and they never accompany rites in which flutes and drums are used. Besides the aforementioned, other elements in ritual activities are the use of copal (*pom*), certain flowers, fireworks, and *aguardiente* (*snichim Dyos*: flower of God), a spirituous liquor.

Just as Tojolab'al values are expressed in their language, social organization, and the continuance of attitudes, concepts, and common beliefs, there is also an auto-perception that reflects the uniqueness of this people, expressed in their interaction with other ethnic groups and the society at large, in which they are immersed and which determines their daily life as well as their transformations and their permanence.

Bibliography

Brody, Jill, and John S. Thomas, eds. (1988). *Tojolabal Maya Ethnographic and Linguistic Approaches*. Baton Rouge: Louisiana State University.

Furbee-Loose, Louanna (1976). *The Correct Language, Tojolabal: A Grammar with Ethnographic Notes*. New York: Garland.

Gomez Hernández, Antonio, and Mario Humberto Ruz (1992). *La memoria baldía: Los tojolabales y las fincas*. Testimonios Bilingües. Mexico City: Universidad Nacional Autónoma de México; Universidad Nacional Autónoma de Chiapas.

Lenkersdorf, Carlos (1979–1981). *B'omak'umal* (Dictionary). Vol. 1, *Tojolab'al-kastiya* (Tojolab'al-Spanish); Vol. 2, *Kastaiya-tojolab'al* (Spanish-Tojolab'al). Mexico City: Editorial Nuestro Tiempo.

Lenkersdorf, Gudrun (1986). "Contribuciones a la historia colonial de los tojolabales." In *Los legítimos hombres*. Vol. 4, 13–102. Mexico City: Universidad Nacional Autónoma de México, Instituto de Investigaciones Filológicas, Centro de Estudios Mayas.

Ruz, Mario Humberto (1982). *Los legítimos hombres*. Vol. 2, *Aproximación antropológica al grupo tojolabal*. Mexico City: Universidad Nacional Autónoma de México, Instituto de Investigaciones Filológicas. 2nd ed. 1990.

Ruz, Mario Humberto (1983). "Médicos y loktores: Enfermedad y cultura den dos comunidades tojolobales." In *Los legítimos hombres*. Vol. 3, 13–102. Mexico City: Universidad Nacional Autónoma de México, Instituto de Investigaciones Filológicas. 2nd ed. 1991.

Ruz, Mario Humberto (1992). *Savia india, floración ladina: Apuntes para una historia de las fincas comitecas (siglos XVIII y XIX)*. Mexico City: Consejo Nacional para la Cultura y las Artes.

MARIO HUMBERTO RUZ

Totonac

ETHNONYMS: Totonaca, Totonaco

Orientation

Identification. The word "Totonaco" is recognized as the name of this Amerindian ethnic group by its own members. According to oral tradition, "Totonaco" is derived from two words in their language: *tutu* (three) and *naku* (heart). The interpretation most frequently given, which is also noted by Kelly and Palerm (1952), is that the name refers to the three historical centers of the Totonac population. The exact locations of these three centers vary according to historical references and regional traditions. The area inhabited by the Totonac has been known as the Totonacapan since at least the sixteenth century.

Location.   The Totonacapan includes portions of the Mexican states of Puebla and Veracruz. In the former, the Totonac lived in the mountainous region known as the northern Sierra de Puebla. In Veracruz, the Totonac were found from the mountain highlands to the coastal plains, between the Río Cazones and the Río Tecolutla. Currently, this area continues to have the highest concentration of the Totonac population; however, a growing number have migrated to cities in search of higher wages. There are Totonac living in urban areas such as Mexico City, Poza Rica, Jalapa, Cholula, and Puebla de Zaragoza.

Demography.   According to the 1990 census, there were 207,876 speakers of the Totonac language who were 5 years of age or older. The state of Puebla had 86,788 speakers of Totonac, and the state of Veracruz had 111,305; 3,056 Totonac speakers resided in Mexico City. There are also Totonac migrants in the states of Tlaxcala and México.

Linguistic Affiliation.   The Mesoamerican language closest to that of the Totonac is Tepehua, the language of their nearby neighbors. Together they form a linguistic group known as Totonacan, which is related to the Huastec and Mayan linguistic groups, although the nature of this relationship is under discussion. Totonac has some dialectal variations, but these can be understood without difficulty by native speakers.

History and Cultural Relations

According to Totonac oral tradition, their ancestors helped build the ancient city of Teotihuacán, located 42 kilometers northeast of Mexico City; however, there is no archaeological evidence to support this claim. After the decline of the city, Totonac legend maintains, they migrated to the area that became known as Totonacapan. They established important centers of population at Cempoala and Tajin, in coastal Veracruz. Traditional deities are still worshiped at the temple complex at Tajin. Aztec warfare and domination weakened the Totonac rulers. Archaeologists have developed a different, more objective view of the early history of the people of this area, but this is the history the Totonac accept.

Eager to defeat the Aztec, the Totonac helped the Spanish invaders, as was noted by the chronicler Bernal Díaz del Castillo. Nevertheless, they fared no better than any other Indian group under Spanish colonial rule. In areas where the Spanish colonists resided, newly introduced diseases ravaged the Amerindian population, and forced labor occasioned a soaring mortality rate. The Franciscan clergy evangelized Totonacapan, building churches with Indian labor and converting the communities to a somewhat superficial Catholicism.

Fortunately for the Totonac, the region's hot, wet climate and uneven terrain made it unattractive to most of the Spanish colonizers, thus affording a certain amount of

political and cultural autonomy for the indigenous people during the colonial period. Essentially self-governing, Totonac communities experienced limited external influence.

Following Mexican independence in 1821, the Totonac of Veracruz became enmeshed in conflict with mestizos over land and over interference with Totonac ritual life. In 1836 the bishop of Puebla, Francisco Pablo Vázquez, prohibited the Indians from celebrating their Holy Week rituals. The ensuing rebellion (1836–1838), led by Mariano Olarte, began at Papantla. Eventually, the establishment of *conduenazgos* (the legal term for the recognition of communal lands by the state) permitted the Indian communities of Veracruz to defend their lands for the remainder of the nineteenth century.

The Totonac of the northern Sierra de Puebla were able to maintain a greater autonomy. They proved to be valuable allies to the regional leaders, usually mestizos. The Totonac supported these strongmen as long as Totonac villages were left alone. They also contributed to the triumph of liberal forces at Puebla in the Batalla del Cinco de Mayo in 1863.

During the Mexican Revolution, Totonac villages were attacked and burned by different factions. People from remote areas entered Totonacapan, and growing numbers of mestizos entered Totonac villages. The situation of social unrest allowed mestizos to establish themselves and find economic opportunities in villages in which mestizos had been previously unwelcome, and conflict over landownership became acute.

A few Indian strongmen (*caudillos*) arose after the Revolution, but mestizos obtained political control with the help of regional leaders who were able to obtain power on a national level. The most notable case is that of Manuel Avila Camacho, who was president of Mexico in the 1930s and was from the northern Sierra de Puebla, where his wealthy family was prominent in mestizo society.

Economy

Subsistence and Commercial Activities.   The principal crop, maize, is considered a basic part of every Totonac's diet. In the highlands, there is only one season for the cultivation of maize (March to September or October). In the lowlands, two crops per year are possible; however, land erosion and overuse of the soil have made double cropping more difficult. Agriculture is labor intensive. Other subsistence crops are beans, chilies, and, on a lesser scale, other vegetables that are grown on small family plots near the houses.

Sugarcane became an important commercial crop in Totonacapan during the colonial period, although production could not rival that of the great sugar plantations. Coffee began to be cultivated on a large scale around 1950. The ecological conditions in many communities are favorable for this plant, and production boomed in the following decades. Prices, however, are dependent on the international market for coffee beans, and cultivators suffer great losses when they go down.

In Veracruz, vanilla has traditionally been an important commercial crop. Because of a growing consumer rejection of artificial chemical substitutes for vanilla, the cultivation of this crop has expanded and may offer an alternative to dependence on coffee as the only cash crop.

The oil industry has created new jobs for many Totonac men living on the coastal plains of Veracruz, but it has damaged the marine environment and some agricultural lands.

Industrial Arts. Tools, household items, and clothing are made by family members. There is no external market for these goods.

Trade. The Totonac rely on middlemen to take their agricultural produce to distant markets. Aware that these individuals were monopolizing the transport and distribution of produce to the detriment of the growers, the Mexican government created agencies to replace the middlemen, who had become local caciques, but corruption and mismanagement proved difficult to eradicate. The Instituto Mexicano del Cafe, a government agency for the purchase and marketing of coffee beans, was terminated in 1989. Attempts to create nonprofit marketing agencies that aid the small growers of cash crops continue, with varied results.

Division of Labor. For many years, men were in charge of the maize fields and women took care of the household and the family vegetable plots. Coffee cultivation, which requires a great deal of labor, has altered these patterns; women, children—in fact, entire families—work together to harvest the delicate beans. Migration in search of wage labor has led to further changes: when the men are absent, women must work the fields themselves or find someone else to carry out the household agricultural labor.

Land Tenure. Small private holdings are predominant in Totonac communities. There are few _ejidos_ in the northern Sierra de Puebla. Communal lands, which do not fall within the category of government-granted ejidos, are also scarce. The distribution of land is unequal; mestizo cattlemen own large ranches, whereas many Indian families are landless rural laborers. Many owners of small plots of land have formed cooperatives, often with government aid, to obtain mutual benefits. Along the coast of Veracruz, Totonac fishers are also organized into cooperatives.

Kinship

Kin Groups and Descent. Some Totonac communities in the northern Sierra de Puebla had patrilineal systems of descent that were based on residence in a specific location and on a common surname. Conflicts over land, a consequence of the Mexican Revolution, destroyed these systems, although they are still remembered by aged persons. Great importance is given to the relationship of _compadrazgo_ (ritual coparenthood).

Kinship Terminology. Few kinship terms in Totonac remain—only those for uncles, aunts, grandchildren, cousins, and members of the nuclear family. No distinction is made between maternal and paternal relatives.

Marriage and Family

Marriage was traditionally arranged by both families. Preferably, a high "price" was paid for the bride, in goods or the groom's labor. When this was not possible, couples eloped and negotiation of payment followed. A church-sanctioned marriage is an ideal today, but the cost of a wedding feast deters many couples.

Domestic Unit. The ideal domestic arrangement is a nuclear family living near the relatives of the husband. Extended families spanning at least three generations are also common. The practice of polygamy, which is considered a symbol of wealth, is diminishing because of the efforts of both Catholic priests and Protestant preachers.

Inheritance. Customarily, among the Totonac of the northern Sierra de Puebla, upon a man's death, his land is inherited by his eldest son. Among coastal Totonac, a father bequeaths land to all sons equally. Direct inheritance from father to daughter is highly exceptional.

Socialization. From infancy, a child is educated by the extended family. All children must go to elementary school, but what is taught there is not always adequate to meet the needs of the communities. Bilingual education has rarely been fully implemented.

Sociopolitical Organization

Social Organization. Community identity is not always related to ethnic identity because various locations have multiethnic populations. The most important obligation to the community is communal labor, but this tradition has been weakened in some areas owing to religious conflict between Catholics and Protestants.

Political Organization. All Totonac communities have elected political authorities, but the political process itself is subject to outside control. Indian participation varies greatly from one location to another. Those who are elected to office tend to speak Spanish and to have migratory experience and at least a grade-school education. Religious and civil hierarchies were once united in all the communities; they are now separate, but this development is more recent in some areas than in others.

Social Control. Municipal authorities are responsible for maintaining peace in the communities. Officials rely not only on their limited knowledge of the Mexican penal code but also base decisions on local customs that establish the parameters of socially acceptable conduct. The influence of elders was once important but has been greatly weakened. When offenders commit major crimes, they are now judged and sentenced by higher authorities outside the community.

Conflict. Unequal distribution of land remains a principal cause of conflict. Agrarian struggles continue, and political parties have become involved in them. Peasant movements are widespread. Elections are highly contested, and factionalism is prevalent. The federal government all too often resorts to force to end conflicts. Violence is commonplace; the charge on which Totonac are most frequently incarcerated is homicide.

Religion and Expressive Culture

Religious Beliefs. Totonac popular Catholicism is a complex reelaboration of elements of both Iberian and Amerindian religion. The concepts of the deities and their relations to humans are not those of institutional Catholicism. According to the Totonac view, there are sacred beings that have power over aspects and places of the world. These include not only the images of saints in churches but beings with Amerindian attributes, such as the Dueño del Monte, a mountain god. Many Totonac have been converted to Protestantism, especially that of the Pentecostals, who are highly critical of popular Catholic beliefs. In some communities, this has created conflict.

Religious Practitioners.   Prestige was traditionally accrued by those who sponsored religious festivals honoring the saints and their images. Participation by all families was obligatory. Those persons who had held official positions in a *cargo* system (which governs sponsorship of festivals) received the important status of *principales*. The cargo systems were independent of the Catholic clergy.

Pentecostalism offered an opportunity for young people to obtain status outside the cargo system by becoming charismatic preachers. To counter the growth of Protestantism, the Catholic church also created pastoral programs for laypersons. Such programs often characterize traditional Indian religion with its Catholic borrowings as "superstitious."

Ceremonies.   Rising costs have affected the system of individual-family sponsorship of religious festivals. An alternative to individual-family sponsorship has been the establishment of collective groups to finance the ceremonies.

Arts.   The Totonac consider the Dance of the Voladores, in which the performers unwind from ropes attached to the top of a pole, to be an important symbol of their ethnic identity. Although other indigenous peoples of the region perform this dance, the Totonac regard themselves as the best performers. The dance is rich in symbolism; it represents birds descending from the sky. Professional troupes of Volador dancers travel to large cities within Mexico and abroad.

Medicine.   There are various native health specialists. *Parteras* (midwives) are elderly women who attend pregnant women and supervise natural births, for which they enjoy high status. *Curanderos* heal through the use of medicinal plants and ritualized ceremonies. *Brujos* have knowledge of sorcery and can cast and break magic spells through contact with the supernatural. In the past, persons accused of sorcery often were murdered. Medical care is also given by doctors at government clinics that exist in most communities. The Totonac tend to consult either traditional or institutional medical practitioners, or both, depending on the circumstances.

Death and Afterlife.   There are specific godparents (*compadres*) of death, who help pay the cost of burial. The Day of the Dead, on which spirits are said to return to the village, is an important feast. Protestants, like Catholics, arrange flowers on the tombs of the dead, although they do not celebrate with alcohol or incur excessive expenditures.

See also Tepehua

Bibliography

Garma Navarro, Carlos (1987). *Protestantismo en una comunidad totonaca de Puebla*. Mexico City: Instituto Nacional Indigenista.

Harvey, H., and Isabel Kelly (1969). "The Totonac." In *Handbook of Middle American Indians*, edited by Robert Wauchope. Vol. 8, *Ethnology, Part Two*, edited by Evon Z. Vogt, 638–681. Austin: University of Texas Press.

Kelly, Isabel, and Angel Palerm (1952). *The Tajin Totonac*. Washington, D.C.: Smithsonian Institution.

Masferrer, Elio (1986). "Las condiciones históricas de la etnicidad entre los totonacos." *América Indígena* 46(4).

CARLOS GARMA NAVARRO

Trinidadians and Tobagonians

ETHNONYM: Trinidadians

Orientation

Identification.   The name "Trinidad and Tobago" is a conjunction of the names of the two islands that comprise this independent state. "Trinidad" is often used alone to refer to the two islands as a political unit. Columbus, on his third voyage, in 1498, sighted three points of an island; in appropriating it for Spain, he called it "Trinidad," in honor of the Holy Trinity. This etymological history has subsequently been commemorated by various Christian authorities, including John Paul II during a 1986 papal visit. The name "Tobago" apparently derives from the Carib word for a smoking receptacle for tobacco, the plant that was reportedly the first item from Tobago to be exported to Europe.

Location.   The island of Trinidad is located in the Caribbean Sea at 10°30′ N and 6°30′ W, and 11 kilometers (at the nearest point) from the Venezuelan coast. It has an area of 4,950 square kilometers. The island of Tobago lies 32 kilometers northeast of Trinidad and has an area of 290 square kilometers.

Demography.   The population of the two islands was 1,299,301 in 1992, with an average of 214 people per square kilometer. Life expectancy at birth is 70 years. The average annual growth rate from 1965 to 1980 was 1.3 percent, although the rate fluctuated with net annual migration, which reached a high of 17,370 in 1970 and a low of 2,200 in 1976. Brooklyn, London, and Toronto are the most common destinations for Trinidadians. Because many return after many years, and many move back and forth a number of times in a lifetime, the process is better described as one of transmigration rather than emigration.

Linguistic Affiliation.   Although Trinidad and Tobago is an English-speaking country, its speech forms are diverse. They vary with class and social context, from a local "dialect" that is substantially opaque to foreign English speakers to a Global Hegemonic English (G.H.E.) articulated by television newscasters and prescribed in schoolrooms. Moreover, almost all Trinidadians hear a substantial portion of the range of English used on U.S. television programs and in contemporary popular music by U.S. artists. In general, writing is in G.H.E., and there have been few efforts to establish a written form of the local dialect.

History and Cultural Relations

The pre-Columbian population of Trinidad has been estimated at nearly 30,000 to 40,000. Almost a century passed after Columbus's landing on Trinidad before the Castilian Crown attempted, in 1592, to establish a permanent European settlement. By then, intermittent contact had probably reduced the indigenous population by one-half. For the next two centuries, the island remained an insignificant and sparsely colonized outpost of Castile's empire in the Americas. In 1725 Trinidad's settler population included only 162 adult males. In the last three decades of the eighteenth century, during a period of alliance between Paris and Madrid, the Castilian government sought to fortify and increase profits from its colonies. Catholic planters from elsewhere in the Caribbean—largely from French colonies rocked by the Haitian Revolution, other slave uprisings, and the French Revolution—were encouraged to settle with their slaves in Trinidad. By 1797, the population of the island had reached nearly 18,000 persons, of whom 10,000 were slaves and just over 1,000 were Amerindians. It was during this period of French settlement, specifically in 1787, that the first sugar mill was built on Trinidad. Ten years later, however, approximately 130 mills were in operation. British forces took control of the island in 1797, and Trinidad, along with nearby Tobago, was formally ceded to Britain in 1802. Tobago had been largely ignored by Europeans until the early seventeenth century; thereafter, it was regarded as a strategic military site and shifted hands some twenty-two times between 1626 and 1802.

The British slave trade was abolished in 1807, and Emancipation was initiated in 1834, with a planned six-year period of "apprenticeship." At the time of Emancipation, the colonial state recorded a population of some 20,000 slaves; 3,200 Whites; 16,300 Coloreds; and only 750 Amerindians. Apprenticeship ended in 1836, some two years before the date scheduled by the British state, owing to resistance by the enslaved population. During the 1840s, the colonial state acted both to anglicize Trinidad (establishing the Church of England, for instance) and to ensure a continued supply of abundant, exploitable labor for plantation agriculture. Beginning in 1845, indentured laborers were brought to Trinidad from India, and, when such immigration ended in 1917, just under 144,000 indentured laborers had entered the colony. Beginning in 1868, these primarily Hindu and Islamic settlers—together termed East Indians—were missionized by Canadian Presbyterians.

In 1889 Tobago and Trinidad were for the first time joined as a unit of colonial administration. Commercial production of oil began in Trinidad in 1902, and by 1911 Trinidad's first refinery was in operation. Following labor protests in 1925, Trinidad's Legislative Council was reformed to include a small number of elected members, although suffrage was limited to approximately 6 percent of the population. Beginning in 1935, laborers struck the sugar plantations, and in 1937, the oil fields. The primary leaders of this working-class uprising were Adrien Rienzi and Tubal Uriah Butler. By the time of these strikes, petroleum had become the colony's most valuable export: in 1932 oil accounted for 50 percent of Trinidad's export earnings, and by 1943, 80 percent. Trinidad's petroleum was, moreover, a significant fraction of the British Empire's total production as Britain fought World War II: 44 percent in 1938, rising to 65 percent by 1946. The petroleum industry was not, however, significant in terms of direct employment—only 8,000 persons were so engaged in 1939, whereas some 40,000 were involved in farming and refining sugarcane in 1930, even though Trinidad's sugar industry was increasingly unprofitable. In 1941 Britain ceded land for two military bases to the United States. Over the next four years, Trinidad's economy was driven by the construction of the U.S. bases. Following a wartime ban on Carnival, victory in Europe was celebrated in Port-of-Spain by a V-E Carnival, at which bands of tuned petroleum drums—steelbands—were first seen in public performance.

In 1946 universal adult suffrage was introduced, and in 1956 the People's National Movement (PNM) led by Eric Williams, formed Trinidad's first home-rule government. In 1957, in the midst of negotiations to establish the Federation of the West Indies, Williams and Norman Manley of Jamaica each announced that they would not stand for election to the federal parliament, thereby foreshadowing their states' withdrawals from the federation. A year later, a structurally weak federation was established, comprised of all the British West Indian colonies except Guyana and Belize. In 1960, after leading nationalist demonstrations against the U.S. military bases, Williams negotiated leases for the bases. Within a decade, however, the United States concluded that the bases were of little importance and returned them to Trinidad. Following Jamaica's withdrawal from the federation at the end of 1961, Williams and the British made plans for Trinidad and Tobago to be established as an independent state. In January 1962 the British Parliament passed the acts granting independence to both Jamaica and Trinidad, and, in the same month, it passed the new Commonwealth Immigration Bill, which restricted entry from independent former colonies. Trinidad and Tobago became independent on 31 August 1962. In 1970, following a period of rising unemployment, Black Power demonstrators focused attention on continued racial discrimination in employment and on Trinidad's economic dependence. As a result of price increases instituted by the Organization of Petroleum Exporting Countries (OPEC), state revenues increased by 1,100 percent between 1973 and 1978. In the 1980s, however, the decline in the world oil price produced a severe recession. There has yet to be a sustained economic recovery, primarily because the Trinidadian economy remains largely tied to world petroleum prices. After thirty years of continuous rule by the PNM (1956–1986), Trinidad has had two changes of government during this recession: the 1986 elections were won by the National Alliance for Reconstruction (NAR); in 1992, the electorate returned the PNM to power.

Counting persons by "ethnic origin," the 1990 census

reported that 43 percent of the population was African, 40 percent East Indian, 14 percent mixed, 1 percent White, 1 percent Chinese, and 1 percent other. In Trinidad, however, race and color identities are, to a great extent, shifters, which vary with observer and context. Thus, counts of ethnic groups give them a false concreteness: distinctions between "mixed" persons and others are particularly ambiguous and contested. Historically, African, East Indian, and European cultures interacted and were re-shaped in colonial society. Today these labels of ethnic origin are used for lifeways, worldviews, and values that are decidedly West Indian. Trinidadian culture has also been shaped by the society's historic porosity vis-à-vis the North Atlantic metropolises.

Settlements

Approximately 50 percent of the population lives in the east-west corridor that includes both Port-of-Spain and Arima. As much as 20 percent of the population lives in a second densely populated area around San Fernando, in the southeast. Oil refineries are located in the south of the island, oil rigs off the southern coast. Sugar fields are concentrated in low-lying areas on the western coast.

Economy

Subsistence and Commercial Activities.   Since independence, per capita gross domestic product (GDP) has fluctuated with international oil prices. In 1973 per capita GDP was estimated at U.S.$1,180; the figure peaked in 1982 at $6,800 (using official exchange rates) but has declined since then, reportedly to $4,210 in 1987. Trinidad has a large middle class, but there are also extremes of wealth: the wealthiest quintile of the population has 50 percent of GDP, and the poorest, 4 percent. During the oil-boom years, the government sought to end the economy's dependence on the world oil market by establishing state-owned energy-based industries, including a steel mill and a fertilizer plant. The economy's performance in the 1980s indicates, however, that this diversification did not meet its goal. The costly steel mill is now owned and operated by Nucor, a U.S. company. Since the end of World War II, both commercial and subsistence agriculture have declined steadily, although there is evidence of increased food production during the continuing recession; most food, however, continues to be imported.

Industrial Arts.   In 1980 Trinidad had a reported literacy rate of 96 percent, and three-quarters of the secondary-school-age population were enrolled in schools in 1986. As a consequence of state educational policies and employment in the petroleum industry, Trinidadians have become a highly skilled industrial labor force. Transemigration has, however, removed a disproportionate number of skilled laborers and professionals. Trinidadians have also developed important organizational, manufacturing, and design skills through the production of the annual Carnival.

Trade.   Two local conglomerates import most consumer and commercial goods. Trinidad has some half-dozen large shopping malls, each with its own supermarket. Until the recession of the mid-1980s, the government restricted the importation of many items and levied large tariffs on oth-

ers, for the purpose of promoting local production. Only in a very few cases did these policies lead to the development of alternatives to foreign imports. Moreover, large import companies were often able to obtain exemptions from trade restrictions. A "suitcase trade" in light goods—notably clothing—thrived, although such trade was largely outside the official economy. After the elections of 1986, the NAR government adopted a policy of increased trade liberalization, which has largely been continued under the PNM government since 1992. Throughout the postindependence era, the United States has been Trinidad's main trading partner.

Division of Labor.   In 1982 some 21 percent of the population was employed in services (including public administration), 19 percent in commerce, 19 percent in construction, 16 percent in mining and manufacturing, and 8 percent in agriculture. Women constituted 33 percent of the labor force in 1982.

Kinship

Although Trinidadians follow the Euro-American pattern of reckoning genealogical relatedness, such relatedness is not, in social practice, a distinct principle of association or group formation: kinship and friendship merge in daily life. Descent is bilateral. Trinidadians use basically the same kin terms as the English and Americans.

Marriage and Family

Marriage.   Euro-American ideals of religiously sanctioned weddings and monogamy were avowed by colonial elites as signs of "respectability." For some, these ideals remain guides for conduct; for others, they are the basis for stigmatizing and stereotyping certain segments of society; and for still others, they are foreign values, largely irrelevant to local circumstances. In contrast to their espoused ideals, colonial elites practiced a system of dual marriages or sexual unions. Upper-class males characteristically married a status equal but had extralegal unions—some of long duration, some acts of rape—with women of lower status. The cultural distinction between "inside" and "outside" partners remains important.

Domestic Unit.   There is great variation in the composition of Trinidadian households. Households of monogamous couples and their children are not culturally aberrant, but neither is one comprised of a middle-aged woman, her (transmigrant) son's former girlfriend, and the latter's child by a subsequent boyfriend. Such an example illustrates the open rather than distinctive character of "kinship." Attributional aspects of sexual difference are culturally emphasized: men and women are deemed fundamentally different. Concomitantly, husbands and wives generally have separate household roles and responsibilities.

Inheritance.   Property generally passes from parents to children. Historically, the distinction between "inside" and "outside" children has been manifest in patterns of inheritance.

Socialization.   Women are regarded as more suited to the care of young children, although both men and women display great affection for children. It is not unusual for grandmothers and aunts, as well as mothers, to raise children. Formal education in schools, generally beginning by age 5, is highly valued.

Sociopolitical Organization

Social Organization. Colonial society was organized hierarchically by the valorization of things European. The hierarchy of race and color was not, however, scalar: it did not rank all non-Europeans on a single social ladder. Rather, the discourse of race inscribed two very different principles of subordination to Europeans. Africans, deemed lacking an ancestral civilization, could, through both education and sexual "mixing" with Whites, become at least partially Europeanized; paradoxically, they could also be seen as becoming "West Indian" or "Creole" through this mixing. By contrast, East Indians were considered saturated with an (inferior) ancestral civilization of their own and therefore not amenable to "mixing," "Europeanizing," or becoming "West Indian"—even when they adopted and developed lifeways that reflected their presence in Trinidad. This ideological image prevailed, notwithstanding substantial social and sexual "mixing" of Indians with both Whites and Afro-Trinidadians. Historically, this complex system of racial distinctions and identities has shaped class relations. This system of racial typifications has served to naturalize the value placed on being "White" or "European," to divide subordinated classes by masking the social entanglements of East Indians in the West Indies, and to define Trinidad as a "mixed" and/or "plural" society, in contrast to the imagined purity and homogeneity of European nation-states. These racial typifications and their consequences have been contested throughout Trinidadian history, and, since independence, racial stratification has been substantially attenuated.

Political Organization. Trinidad is a parliamentary democracy with a bicameral parliament comprised of an elected House of Representatives and an appointed Senate. Peaceful elections have taken place regularly since independence. The head of government is the prime minister; the presidency is a largely ceremonial position. For the first thirty years after independence, Trinidad had a single stable political party, the People's National Movement, and a frequently reorganized and renamed opposition alliance. During this time, political support broke roughly along racial lines, between Afro-Trinidians (in support of the PNM) and East Indian Trinidadians (in support of the opposition). Until his death in 1981, Eric Williams, an Oxford-trained historian, led the PNM. In 1986 opposition groups formed the National Alliance for Reconstruction. Under the leadership of A. N. R. Robinson, the NAR that year drew electoral support from nearly all classes and ethnicities. Once in power, however, the alliance and its wide support quickly eroded. In 1992 the PNN returned to power, with Patrick Manning serving as the new prime minister.

Social Control and Conflict. In 1965 new legislation limited the right to strike, and since then the government has intervened, with substantial success, to impose labor stability. High unemployment in the late 1960s led to widespread unrest by the urban proletariat and lumpenproletariat in 1970. The resulting demonstrations, supported by a segment of the small military force, posed a serious threat to the government and were dispersed by police and military intervention. The unrelated rise in oil revenues that began in 1972 led to a decrease in unemployment, a dramatic increase in government patronage for the urban underclasses, and, consequently, a substantial increase in mass support for the state. This patronage, however, declined dramatically during the recession of the 1980s. In July 1990 an attempted coup by about a hundred members of the Jamaat-al-Muslimeen, a relatively small group of Afro-Trinidadian Muslims, led to four days of unrest and considerable loss of state control. Although the coup had little mass support, it was symptomatic of widespread disaffection from the state among workers and the urban unemployed.

Religion and Expressive Culture

Religious Beliefs. The 1980 census counted Catholics (32 percent), Hindus (25 percent), Anglicans (15 percent), Muslims (6 percent), Presbyterians (4 percent), Pentacostals (3 percent), as well as other religious groups. What these figures fail to reveal, however, is the prevalent belief that these (and other) religions all worship the same God in largely valid ways. Most Trinidadians have attended, and to a greater or lesser extent participated in, services outside their own religion. For many in Trinidad, religious differences are understood as stylistically different routes to a shared divinity rather than as incompatible systems of values.

Ceremonies. The world religious traditions present in Trinidad conduct their characteristic ceremonies in globally recognizable ways. With some exceptions, however, there is a modulation of religious piety. For example, although the pre-Lenten Carnival is intensely celebrated, Lent is not a time of dramatic self-denial, and neither is Ramadan.

Arts. The most popularly practiced arts are associated with the annual Carnival. For each Carnival, topical calypsos are composed and performed, and costumes for new masquerade bands—some with as many as 2,500 persons—are designed and crafted. Steelbands, or *pan*, require meticulous tuning and rehearsal, activities which are aesthetically and socially complex. A number of other important musical forms and traditions—notably *tassa* drumming—are associated specifically with Indo-Trinidadians, although this ethnic identification is oversimplistic. Peter Minshall, who has designed masquerade bands and worked in other performance genres, has achieved wide renown within Trinidad, as well as among avant-garde elements of the international art world. Novelist and essayist V. S. Naipaul and political theorist C. L. R. James are internationally acclaimed writers. Saint Lucia-born Nobel laureate Derek Walcott has worked in Trinidad for much of his adult life, while maintaining an academic appointment in the United States.

Medicine. Medical care is provided primarily by physicians, dentists, and registered nurses. There is a mixed system of private and public financing of health care.

Death and Afterlife. Christians and Muslims are generally interred in cemeteries, as are some Hindus, although cremation is more common for Hindus. Ideas about the afterlife are highly diverse.

See also East Indians in Trinidad

Bibliography

Brereton, Bridget (1981). *A History of Modern Trinidad.* London: Heinemann.

James, C. L. R. ([1963] 1983). *Beyond a Boundary.* New York: Pantheon.

Naipaul, V. S. (1962). *The Middle Passage.* New York: Vintage.

Segal, Daniel (1989). "Nationalism in a Colonial State." Ph.D. dissertation, University of Chicago.

Singh, Kelvin (1994). *Race and Class Struggles in a Colonial State: Trinidad, 1917–1945.* Calgary: University of Calgary Press.

Yelvington, Kevin, ed. (1992). *Trinidad Ethnicity.* London: Macmillan.

DANIEL A. SEGAL

Triqui

ETHNONYMS: Triques, Triquis

Orientation

Identification. The Triqui are an indigenous Mexican group who live in the southwestern part of the state of Oaxaca. The term "Triqui" comes from the word *driqui.* *Dri* derives from *dre,* "father," and *qui,* "great" or "superior"; consequently, "driqui" means "supreme father" or "supreme lord," alluding to the clan "representative" who was consulted on government matters.

Location. The Triqui live in an enclave of the Mixteca Alta and Mixteca Baja in the state of Oaxaca, in a vertex between the districts of Juxtlahuaca, Tlaxiaco, and Putla. The area lies between 17°10′ and 17°15′ N and 97°45′ and 97°50′ W.

Demography. In the sixteenth century the Triqui population did not exceed 2,000. In 1900 the number barely reached 3,000, but in 1980 it exceeded 15,000. The 1990 census registered 14,981 speakers of Triqui.

Linguistic Affiliation. The Triqui language is in the Mixtecan Branch of the Otomanguean Family.

History and Cultural Relations

During the middle of the fifteenth century, the Triqui, together with the Mixtec, were subjugated by the fifth Aztec monarch, who built a fortress on their lands. They witnessed the wars between the Mixtec kings of Achiutla and Tuxtepec and probably took part in the conflicts on the side of the former, the territory of which lay nearer the Triqui area.

During the Spanish Conquest, the social and cultural situation of the Triqui must have been similar to that of the agrarian communities subordinate to the Mixtec ceremonial centers. Triqui communities, which were autonomous up to a point, did not suffer drastic changes in their sociopolitical organization. There were existing agreements according to which a powerful Mixtec cacique would pledge to defend them in exchange for their tribute and, in case of war, a supply of warriors.

During the early period of colonization in the state of Oaxaca, the Spaniards took over the best lands in the valleys and fertile lowland riverine areas, but did not bother with the mountainous, less fertile terrain, which was perhaps one of the reasons Triqui agrarian communities maintained their descent groups and held on to many cultural values. The Triqui constituted a "cultural island" within a wide Mixtec area. They occupied high, cold, misty mountains that were not inviting to the visitor; however, the lowlands, with a temperate climate and mountains of lesser elevation, proved appropriate, at the beginning of the twentieth century, for the cultivation of coffee. The export of the beans outside the Triqui area furthered the process of acculturation of the low-lying area to neighboring mestizo populations. In the latter, commercial demands favored the penetration of private property side by side with communal property, leading to a gradual deterioration of the communal social organization. In contrast, the traditional organization of the mountainous region suffered lesser modifications.

Settlements

Triqui territory encompasses 26,030 hectares, with two main centers: San Andrés Chicahuaxtla, in the highlands, and San Juan Copala, in the lowlands. The former, with a semicompact settlement pattern, is located to the south of the mestizo city of Tlaxiaco, at an elevation of 2,300 meters. It is located on one of the spurs of the cordillera, which begins at the so-called Mixtec Knot. San Juan Copala, which has a more compact settlement pattern, is situated to the north of the mestizo city of Putla, at an elevation of 1,300 meters. It rests in a depression surrounded by several mountains. Other Triqui towns include Santo Domingo del Estado, San Martín Itunyoso, San José Xochistlan, and San Miguel Copala. The remainder of the settlements are small hamlets with a dispersed settlement pattern. Houses have log walls and roofs covered with wood shingles or straw.

Economy

Subsistence and Commercial Activities. Variations in patterns of cultivation are determined by differences in soil, climate, and irrigation in the cold and temperate zones.

The main cultivated crops in the cool highland zone are maize, beans, chilies, and squashes, whereas in the lowland zone the preferred crop for cultivation is coffee, and in still lower-lying regions, sugarcane, bananas, pineapples, oranges, and mangoes. On a lesser scale, maize, chilies, beans, and squashes are also grown there.

One of the factors leading to low agricultural production is the unevenness of the terrain; the Egyptian plow, in common use on the plains, cannot be used. Another factor is the scarcity of water for irrigation and the lack of financial and informational resources for the use of chemical fertilizers.

Industrial Arts. Family industry is geared to the manufacture, for sale, of women's dresses, called _huipiles,_ on the _malacate_ (a horizontal strap loom, with four stakes). Shirts and belts are also made, and palm hats and baskets are woven for personal use.

Commerce. The exchange of agricultural produce, products of the hunt, and domestic animals for manufactured goods from nearby mestizo cities takes place mainly in local markets twice a week. The markets provide the indigenous population with industrial manufactured goods and with grain for local consumption when the supply has run out.

Division of Labor. Men cultivate the land, and women do the domestic work. With the approach of the harvest, men go to tend their fields, remaining there for several days until the work is finished. Women help in clearing the field of weeds, but planting is done only by men.

Land Tenure. Economic life rests on the communal property—both lineage and clan—and private property held by nuclear families. The use of communal property requires customs for cooperation and solidarity, and use of private land leads to competition between nuclear families. Communal land belongs to the entitled population, which has rights of common usufruct of the pasturelands and forest. Property rights are inalienable, and the indigenous community can increase landholdings by requesting it of the "lineage head" and the Comisariato de Bienes Comunes, an institution that is attached to the Ministry of Agrarian Reform.

Kinship

Kin Groups and Descent. The Triqui have endogamous patrilineal clans and exogamous lineages within the clans. The latter are corporate, and lineages hold land scattered within clan territory. Clan endogamy promotes alliances between lineages through marriage, joining kin outside the third degree of consanguinity. Within the elite/noble group belonging to a lineage head's ascendant line, a man may take a wife from the head of another clan. Breaking the pattern of endogamy and hypergamy is one of their prerogatives.

This specific type of lineage is a consequence of the contradictions resulting from the relationship between the heads of descent groups and the common people. Lines of descent do not conform to a totally patrilineal pattern, owing to the establishment of two lines of ascendancy, one for the nobility and one for the commoners. The nobility, which is in the minority, has bilateral ascent, that is to say, their lineage is traced through the father's and the mother's father's lineage. The commoners, who are in the majority, trace their lineage solely through the patrilineal line. The intertwining of both types of ascendancy hinders the imposition of unilineality and produces a global type of descent, which, for lack of a better term, can be called "quasi-patrilineal," as George P. Murdock did for a society in southeast Asia.

Kinship Terminology. The basic kinship terminology is generational; terms for brother and sister extend to sons and daughters of the father's and mother's brothers and sisters, which is typical of the Hawaiian type. The norm for Ego's parents' generation is nonfusion among collaterals. Criteria of sex and the speaker's sex are recognized, but no distinction is made between cross and parallel cousins.

Marriage and Family

Marriage. Marriage within three degrees of consanguinity between cousins is forbidden, no differentiation being made between cross and parallel cousins. There are other guidelines: Ego may not marry a woman who belongs to his lineage or that of his mother's father. When a pair that is courting realize that they belong to the same lineage territory, they scrutinize the degree of kinship that exists between them. If they discover that they both live on their ancestor's lands, they abstain from marrying. Said in another way, knowing up to four or five degrees of ascendant consanguinity in the father's and the mother's father's line, these two patrilineal ascendancies are used to determine rules governing marriage, prohibiting it in cases where the territory of the father's and mother's father's lineage coincides. This has resulted in a kinship category of "land brothers."

Domestic Unit. There are different phases in family development. Initially, a family is nuclear; it becomes an extended family when the children grow up and procreate; later, the family splits into nuclear units which, in their turn, initiate a new cycle. A married daughter abandons the extended family milieu and moves to her new home in the house of the groom's parents or the house he built next to that of his parents.

Inheritance. Commoners inherit land patrilineally; those belonging to the nobility inherit bilaterally land belonging to their father and their mother's father. Women of the noble group inherit lands patrilineally, but the women of the common folk do not inherit land.

Socialization. Boys and girls learn how to perform various tasks from an early age: girls wash their own clothes and help in the kitchen. At the age of 6, boys help with farmwork and, when there are cattle, in tending them. No puberty rites are held. Inculcated values agree with Triqui perception of a world in which life is austere and frugal, with a lack of opportunity produced by the harsh agricultural milieu in which they subsist.

Sociopolitical Organization

Social Organization. The sanctioned unequal access to wealth is the structure on which the Triqui society is based; nobles have greater access to scarce goods than do the common people, but lineage heads try to demonstrate their capacity and disposition for generosity toward people of their own lineage. There are oscillations in the breach between the two strata—sometimes expanding, sometimes contracting—but the egalitarian conscience has not totally died out within the nobility, so long as the common people contribute to maintaining the existing social structure.

Political Organization. The main unit of the modern political apparatus, the *municipio*, coincides with the structures of descent groups. The apparatus of traditional government, made up of lineage heads, has not been assimilated by the modern government apparatus. It is kept in force, even in weakened form, and imposes many of its criteria on the latter. Because it reinforces clan cohesion, the modern apparatus contributes to the maintenance of the traditional institutions.

Social Control. There is a noticeable disparity between the norms of the local and national society. In the more local society, where descent groups prevail, internal community laws govern behavior. In the wider society, where national interest prevails, laws of an external nature have been brought in by the modern political apparatus.

Conflict. If disputes over land boundaries involve homicide, a normative principle of revenge is followed. The killer is not sanctioned by the community but the victim's relatives will be out to avenge themselves on him. That is why such a killer does not capitulate before the judicial apparatus of the modern government. Knowing that he will be sent to jail in a mestizo city, he protests. His act falls within an implicit consensus of the members of his community regarding acts of vengeance; the victim's relatives are the only ones who should take reprisals, not the state.

Religion and Expressive Culture

Religious Beliefs. In the indigenous belief system there are nine major gods: seven good and two evil. There is another god whom everyone venerates, but who does not belong to the aforementioned Triqui pantheon, the God of Lightning, who resembles the classic Feathered Serpent. In addition to the major gods, there are minor divinities, like the *naguals* (individual totems).

Each person receives a nagual shortly after birth. Lineage chiefs have two different naguals (e.g., the eagle and the jaguar). There is a cult to the dead, which emphasizes important lineage ancestors. Religious activities are carried out on two levels: those of the Catholic church and belief system and those related to the traditional belief system.

Religious Practitioners. *Principales* are men who have occupied various *cargos* within the religious cargo system. One of the principales, a man of advanced age and wisdom, gives a traditional invocation when the authorities representing the modern governmental apparatus are sworn in. He describes how the universe was created, relates Triqui theogony, and tells how the organization of the "chiefs who take care of the land," that is to say, the organization of lineage heads, took place. This orator knows and conducts all the community rituals.

Ceremonies. The main Triqui ceremony is the festival for the God of Lightning on 25 April. It is held within caves called the House of Lightning. It joins many symbols around the figure of the Feathered Serpent, that is to say Quezalcoatl, who introduced the cultivation of maize. A live goat is brought into the cave by one of the principales. Uttering prayers in Mixtec, he offers the goat to the God of Lightening at the same time that he makes a deep cut in the animal's neck, from which a stream of blood gushes out, bathing the place in blood. They say that "blood is a petition for water," alluding to the rains they are asking for. Later the goat's meat is distributed among the participants, observing a hierarchical order: first, to the principales and authorities, and afterward to the public participants, all eating together.

Arts. The most important handicraft is the manufacture of women's dresses (huipiles). A huipil is made of a wide, long piece of cloth, with horizontal borders, woven by the women from varicolored cotton thread. The huipil is adorned with two wide vertical borders, with zigzag designs in yellow and purple thread.

Death and Afterlife. After being washed, a corpse is wrapped in a blanket. If it is a man, next to him are placed his wife's wedding gift, the clothing he wore when he died, a mat, a belt, sandals, and a woven bag. Some money is placed on one side of the body, intended for "traveling expenses" and fourteen beans, with which cattle will be fed during the deceased's last voyage. The seven pairs of beans are repayment for the eyes of animals he killed while he lived, and which they demand in the course of his trip.

Prayers asking for a better afterlife for the dead in the underworld are said on nine days after a person dies. These days are distributed as follows: eight consecutive days of prayer, after which twenty days (the sacred Precolumbian month) for receiving visitors who live far away are intercalated. On the twenty-ninth day, the last prayer is said.

Bibliography

Dahlgren de Jordán, Barbro (1954). *La mixteca, su cultura e historia prehispánica*. Mexico City: Imprenta Universitaria.

Durand, Carlos A. (1989). "Algunas consideraciones acerca de la etnia de Oaxaca, República Mexicana." *Revista Geográfica* (Mérida, Venezuela: Instituto de Geografía) 30:37–60.

Gay, José Antonio (1881). *Historia de Oaxaca*. Vol. 1. Mexico City: Biblioteca de Autores y Asuntos Oaxaqueños.

Huerta Ríos, César (1981). *Organización socio-política de una minoría nacional (los triqui de Oaxaca)*." Mexico City: Instituto Nacional Indigenista.

CESAR HUERTA RIOS

Turks and Caicos Islanders

ETHNONYMS: none

The Turks and Caicos Islands are a British dependency consisting of forty islands—only eight of which are inhabited—located at the southern end of the Bahamas and north of Hispaniola. The total land area of these low coral and limestone islands is 430 square kilometers; only 2 percent of the land is arable. The Turks Islands are all much smaller than each of the five largest Caicos Islands. Early salt producers had deforested much of Grand Turk, Salt Cay, and South Caicos in the belief that trees bring rain. Precipitation ranges from 100 to 150 centimeters annually, most of it falling in the wet season (May through October). The temperature ranges between 16° C and 32° C.

Most of the 9,761 (1990) residents of the colony, who call themselves "Belongers," are descendants of African slaves. There is also a large population of illegal immigrants who work in the tourist industry; many illegal immigrants were deported in 1985 because of their social-welfare costs to the government. Forty-two percent of the Turks and Caicos islanders are Baptists, 19 percent are Methodist, and the rest are Anglican, Catholic, Church of God, and Seventh Day Adventist. The birthrate is 25.5 per thousand, infant mortality is 24 per thousand, and life expectancy is just over 70 years.

The islands were populated by Indians at the time of contact, but because of disease and slavery none survived past the mid-sixteenth century. The first Europeans to live on the islands were pirates, who used them as a base from which to attack Spanish shipping as it passed by. The first settlers were Bermudans who collected salt. They fought off invaders from the Bahamas, Spain, and France, although a second French attack in 1764 was successful, and the Bermudans were sent to Haiti. The British later gained control and have held it ever since. A governor was installed in 1972, and a constitution was approved in 1976. The Turks and Caicos legislature has two houses, and there is also a Supreme Court. In 1985 the chief minister, the minister of commerce and development, and another official were arrested in Miami on drug-related charges, an event that reduced investor confidence in the colony.

The economy of the islands has long been weak, owing in large part to poor infrastructure, the collapse of the salt industry in 1964, and the closure of a U.S. Navy base in 1983. Almost all consumer goods are imported, and even water is in short supply. There is some fishing, primarily for lobsters and conchs, which are exported to the United States and the United Kingdom. During the 1960s and 1970s, many people left the islands to find employment in the United States or the Bahamas. Offshore companies, particularly banks and other financial institutions, arrived in force in the 1980s, attracted by the absence of taxes on income, capital gains, and business; by 1990 there were more than 9,000 offshore companies registered in the Turks and Caicos Islands. This development, along with the growth of the tourist industry spurred by the construction of a new airport and hotels, brought back most of those who had left in the 1960s and 1970s, as well as laborers from Haiti and the Dominican Republic. Nevertheless, the colony has yet to become financially self-supporting; it still receives moneys from London, the European Community, the European Investment Bank, and the Caribbean Development Bank. The U.K. government has tried to improve economic productivity by privatizing industry.

Bibliography

Boultbee, Paul G. (1991). _Turks and Caicos Islands_. Santa Barbara, Calif.: ABC-Clio.

McElroy, Jerome L., and Klaus de Albuquerque (1988). "Migration Transition in Small Northern and Eastern Caribbean States." _International Migration Review_ 22(3): 30–57.

Tzeltal

ETHNONYMS: none

The Tzeltal are an American Indian group concentrated in the central highlands of the Mexican state of Chiapas. Contiguous Indian groups are the Tzotzil to the west, the Ch'ol to the north and northeast, and the Tojolab'al to the southeast. The Tzeltal and Tzotzil languages form the Tzeltalan Subdivision of the Mayan Language Family. Lexicostatistic studies indicate that these two languages probably became differentiated around A.D. 1200. The Tzeltal-speaking population numbers approximately 50,000 and is distributed through twelve _municipios_, with thirteen main communities. Of the latter, nine are mainly Tzeltal: Aguacatenango, Amatenango, Cancuc, Chanal, Chilon, Oxchuc, Tenejapa, Petalcingo, and Sitalá. The other four communities are about 65 to 80 percent Tzeltal speaking: Altamirano, Ocosingo, Villa de las Rosas, and Yajalón.

Ecologically, the Tzeltal region divides into three zones: north, central, and south. Some demographic and cultural variations are associated with these zones. More fundamentally, however, each Tzeltal community constitutes a distinct social and cultural unit, with its own lands, dialect forms, clothing style, kinship system, politico-religious organization, and crafts.

The Tzeltal are farmers. Traditional Mesoamerican crops—maize, beans, squashes, and chilies—are the most important, but a variety of other crops, including wheat, manioc, sweet potatoes, cotton, chayote, and some fruits and vegetables, are also grown. Regional variations in ecological conditions lead to a certain amount of regional differentiation in agriculture. Domestic animals include poultry, pigs, burros, and cattle, but these animals are seldom eaten. Tzeltal villages are noted for particular craft specialties. Surplus produce and craft products are traded throughout the region through a system of regional periodic markets, and these markets link the Tzeltal to the wider Mexican economic system. Finally, many Tzeltal are dependent to some extent on working for wages in order to provision their households.

All of the Tzeltal communities have a similar structural pattern, with a town center, which may be heavily or thinly populated, and a number of communities, called parajes, which are scattered over the municipio. The town is the political, religious, and commercial center of the entire community. The town centers are divided into two sections, called barrios or calpules, each with its own local authorities and sometimes its own patron saint. In addition to its political and religious functions, each barrio traditionally was endogamous. Some of the other major aspects of traditional Tzeltal social organization that persist today in the more conservative communities are exogamous patrilineal sibs, patrilineal lineages within which land is inherited, and an Omaha type of kinship terminology. In the more acculturated communities, the sib-lineage system tends to disappear and to be replaced by a bilateral system similar to that characterizing Ladino society. Although there are some extended families, the nuclear family is the basic pattern.

The Tzeltal religious system is a blend of Catholic and indigenous elements. Annual community ceremonies are held in honor of particular saints. As in most Mesoamerican Indian communities, officeholders in the civil-religious hierarchy are in charge of these celebrations as well as the more secular village affairs. Shamanism and witchcraft are also found among the Tzeltal.

Bibliography

Berlin, Brent (1974). Principles of Tzeltal Plant Classification: An Introduction to the Botanical Ethnography of a Mayan-Speaking People of Highland Chiapas. New York: Academic Press.

Breton, Alain (1984). Bachajon: Organización socioterritorial de una comunidad tzeltal. Mexico City: Instituto Nacional Indigenista.

Cámara Barbachano, Fernando (1966). Persistencia y cambio cultural entre tzeltales de los altos de Chiapas: Estudio comparativo de las instituciones religiosas y políticas de'los municipios de Tenejapa y Oxchuc. Mexico City: Escuela Nacional de Antropología e Historia, Sociedad de Alumnos.

Collier, George (1994). Basta! Land and the Zapatista Rebellion in Chiapas. Monroe, Oreg.: Food First Books.

Esponda Jimeno, Víctor Manuel (1994). La organización social de los tzeltales. Tuxtla Gutiérrez: Gobierno del Estado de Chiapas, Consejo Estatal de Fomento a la Investigación y Difusión de la Cultura (DIF-Chiapas); Instituto Chiapaneco de Cultura.

Guiteras Holmes, Calixta (1992). Cancuc: Etnografía de un pueblo tzeltal de los altos de Chiapas, 1944. Tuxtla Gutiérrez: Gobierno del Estado de Chiapas, Consejo Estatal de Fomento a la Investigación y Difusión de la Cultura (DIF-Chiapas); Instituto Chiapaneco de Cultura.

Harman, Robert Charles (1974). Cambios médicos y sociales en una comunidad maya-tzeltal. Mexico City: Instituto Nacional Indigenista; Secretaría de Educación Pública.

Hermitte, M. Esther (1970). Poder sobrenatural y control social en un pueblo maya contemporáneo. Mexico City: Instituto Indigenista Interamericano.

Hunn, Eugene S. (1977). Tzeltal Folk Zoology: The Classification of Discontinuities in Nature. New York: Academic Press.

Medina, Andrés. (1991). Tenejapa: Familia y tradición de un pueblo tzeltal. Tuxtla Gutiérrez: Gobierno del Estado de Chiapas, Consejo Estatal de Fomento a la Investigación y Difusión de la Cultura (DIF-Chiapas); Instituto Chiapaneco de Cultura.

Nash, June C. (1970). In the Eyes of the Ancestors: Belief and Behavior in a Maya Community. New Haven and London: Yale University Press.

Nash, Manning (1960). "Witchcraft as Social Process in a Tzeltal Community." América Indígena 20(2): 121–126.

Redfield, Robert, and Alfonso Villa Rojas. (1939). Notes on the Ethnography of Tzeltal Communities of Chiapas. Washington, D.C.: Carnegie Institution of Washington.

Siverts, Henning (1969). Oxchuc. Mexico City: Instituto Indigenista Interamericano.

Villa Rojas, Alfonso (1969). "The Tzeltal." In Handbook of Middle American Indians, edited by Robert Wauchope. Vol. 7, Ethnology, Part One, edited by Evon Z. Vogt, 195–225. Austin: University of Texas Press.

Villa Rojas, Alfonso (1990). Etnografía tzeltal de Chiapas: Modalidades de una cosmovision prehispanica. Tuxtla Gutiérrez: Gobierno del Estado de Chiapas, Consejo Estatal para el Fomento a la Investigación y Difusión de la Cultura.

Vogt, Evon Z. (1969). "Chiapas Highlands." In Handbook of Middle American Indians, edited by Robert Wauchope. Vol. 7, Ethnology, Part One, edited by Evon Z. Vogt, 133–151. Austin: University of Texas Press.

Tzotzil and Tzeltal of Pantelhó

ETHNONYMS: Catarineros, Santa Catarina Pantelhó, Tzotzil and Tzeltal Maya

Orientation

Identification. The indigenous Tzotzil- and Tzeltal-speaking highland Maya Indians share the municipio of Pantelhó—which means "bridge over water" in Tzotzil—

with an equal number of Tzeltal Maya and a small group of Ladinos; the latter two groups include both recent immigrants and long-term residents.

Migrations, shifting municipio boundaries, and political considerations make identity a matter of social construction rather than immutable fact. The Ladinos of Pantelhó define themselves in opposition to the indigenous population and identify with the larger Mexican culture. The indigenous population defines itself as "Catarinero" (from Santa Catarina Pantelhó) in opposition to other highland Indian groups, as Tzotzil or Tzeltal Indians in certain contexts both within and outside the municipio, and as indigenous people in opposition to local Ladinos and in larger pan-Indian contexts.

Location. The municipio of Pantelhó is located on the northern edge of the highlands, 48 kilometers north of San Cristóbal de las Casas, a commercial and administrative center. Surrounded by Indian municipios, Pantelhó circumscribes 137 square kilometers, extending from 17°00′ to 17°07′ N and 92°31′ to 92°25′ W.

Steep hillsides and deep valleys make up most of the land area of Pantelhó. Pantelhó's hillsides range up to 1,400 meters, into what the people of Pantelhó call *tierra fría* (cold country), where there are occasional frosts. The valley of the Río Grande, at the other extreme, descends to 500 meters. This is *tierra caliente* (hot country). Much of the land area of Pantelhó falls into the category of *tierra templada* (temperate climate), at an elevation of around 1,000 meters. Annual temperatures range from 4° C to 32° C. The warmest months are April and May, the coldest December and January. The greater portion of the 150 centimeters of annual precipitation falls between May and December.

Demography. Historical documents indicate Pantelhó was abandoned between 1713 and 1796. In 1809 the parish priest reported a thriving community of 602 souls, but epidemics of measles and cholera ravaged Pantelhó throughout the eighteenth century. For example, between January and March of 1843, 186 people died of cholera. Nevertheless, the community's population continued to grow, reaching 721 in 1825; 871 in 1850; 2,860 in 1900; and 3,953 in 1950. In 1990, 13,949 people lived in Pantelhó.

Tzotzil and Tzeltal Maya, in roughly equal numbers, constitute the majority of Pantelhó's population. In 1990 only 7 percent of the residents of Pantelhó were Ladinos, a decline from 14 percent in 1980. The Tzotzil are concentrated in the *cabecera*, or "headtown," and a few other hamlets on the south side of the river. The Tzeltal predominate in hamlets on the north side of the river and in some more recently established hamlets on the south side. Despite this general tendency, Tzotzil and Tzeltal live together in several communities.

Linguistic Affiliation. The indigenous populations of Pantelhó speak Tzotzil and Tzeltal, two closely related Mayan languages from the Maya-Quiché Family. Pantelhó's dialects of these two languages are, to some extent, mutually intelligible, and municipio business may be conducted in either. The indigenous languages are spoken at home and in bilingual classrooms. Whereas the older generations are often monolingual Tzotzil or Tzeltal speakers, the younger generation is becoming more competent in Spanish.

History and Cultural Relations

The highlands of Chiapas were conquered in 1524 by the Spaniard Luis Marín. The administrators of Spanish-imposed institutions, such as *encomienda* and *repartimiento*, forced the indigenous populations to provide labor and tribute. In 1712 Indians in the Chiapan highlands revolted, marking the beginning of Indian militancy in Pantelhó. The uprising was quickly suppressed, but, because of their participation, the Indians of Pantelhó were exiled for eighty-four years. Chiapas became part of Mexico in 1824, and, as Mexico liberalized agrarian legislation over the course of the nineteenth century, the indigenous population became landless agricultural workers (peons) on newly established Ladino ranches (haciendas). In their terms, they had become the "slaves" of the Ladinos.

The Mexican Revolution (1910–1920) ushered in a new era. The constitution of 1917 established the possibility of obtaining land (*ejidos*; see "Land Tenure") expropriated from large Ladino ranches; however, the Indians' struggle for land was long and bitter. Ladino ranchers resisted expropriation through legal actions and by force of arms. Deaths occurred on both sides, and ethnic antagonisms were reinforced. The first ejidos were not granted until the 1940s, and Ladinos managed to maintain control of the majority of the land until the 1980s. Throughout most of the twentieth century, the Indians remained poor and landless, but in the 1980s a combination of political and economic factors changed landholding patterns. The first Indian mayor was elected in 1982. Indians gained control of the land through land reform and through sales made by Ladinos under the threat of increasing Indian militancy. By 1990, Indians controlled 90 percent of the land.

Many other changes occurred in the 1980s as well: Indians from nearby municipios immigrated in large numbers, new communities were created on former Ladino ranches, and Protestant groups entered the area and gained converts.

Settlements

About one-third of the population (4,700 individuals) is concentrated in the headtown, also named Pantelhó. The headtown is divided into five sections: a Ladino-dominated center and four largely Indian barrios. The remaining two-thirds live in many small homesteads and in thirty-seven recognized hamlets (*agencias*) ranging in size from 50 to 1,000 inhabitants. Generally, households in the ejido communities tend to be densely concentrated, whereas the small property owners are more likely to live dispersed on individual parcels, although late-twentieth-century improvements in public services (e.g., water, schools) have increased residential concentration.

A typical household complex consists of from one to three small buildings: a cooking/eating building, a sleeping building, and a storage building. Cooking is done over a wood fire on the floor, and beds consist of either a raised wooden platform or a straw mat (*petate*) on the floor. If there are fewer than three buildings (which is often the case), the structures tend to serve multiple functions. Buildings are framed with poles, and the walls are made of either vertical wooden planks tied in place or mud plastered into a cornstalk lattice. Roofs are of either thatch or *lamina* (corrugated metal sheeting). A few Indians have constructed houses of concrete block.

Economy

Subsistence and Commercial Activities.   Agriculture is the basis of the economy. The Indians of Pantelhó use a slash-and-burn technique: fields (milpas) ranging from 0.5 to 3 hectares are cleared with machetes and axes in March and April and burned in early May, in anticipation of the coming rains. Maize (in several varieties) is planted with a digging stick (*abonte'*) later that month. Milpas are weeded twice, and, when mature, the maize plant is doubled over and left to dry. Then, in September, beans (principally black beans) are sown among the corn plants. In hot country, a second crop of maize is planted in January. Depending on the climatic zone, bananas, chilies, pineapples, squashes, and tomatoes are cultivated. Citrus trees are also common.

In the nineteenth century Ladinos introduced coffee, along with cattle, tobacco, and sugarcane to the area. After obtaining land, Indians continued the cultivation of coffee, and it has become the dominant cash crop: in 1990 Pantelhó produced more than 450 metric tons. The production and marketing of coffee represent an important source of revenue and a continuing source of conflict between largely Indian producers and Ladino traders.

Throughout most of the last two centuries, Indians labored on Ladino ranches in Pantelhó or migrated to work on the coffee plantations of the southern coastal highlands (Soconusco). Once they obtained land of their own, however, they ceased to work for wages. Wage labor is now a pursuit of young men and those who remain landless.

Industrial Arts.   The people of Pantelhó rely heavily on imported goods, given that indigenous crafts are limited. A few Tzeltal women continue to make clay cooking pots and *comals* (large griddles on which tortillas are cooked). The Tzotzil women of the headtown maintain an age-old tradition of textile manufacture. Blouses for women and shirts for men are woven of imported cotton on backstrap looms and brocaded in the unique style of Pantelhó. Women have begun to manufacture napkins and tablecloths for the tourist market in San Cristóbal.

Trade.   Commercial activity centers on agricultural products (primarily coffee), the revenue from the sale of which is used to purchase manufactured goods, food, medicine, and transportation. The headtown, where a weekly regional market is held on Friday and Saturday, is a major commercial center. In addition, Ladinos operate several stores that sell a variety of items ranging from machetes to cheap rum (*pox*), and they also supply smaller stores in Indian hamlets. The headtown is a transportation hub connecting Pantelhó to San Cristóbal by bus and truck.

Division of Labor.   A pronounced division of labor by gender characterizes Pantelhó, as does segregation in other aspects of life. Men's work revolves around agriculture, wage labor, construction (e.g., house building), and com-

munity work projects. Men and boys clear fields and—with occasional help from women and girls—burn the fields, plant, weed, and harvest. Men also raise cattle and horses. Women maintain the household: their work includes cooking (the processing of maize into tortillas alone is a time-consuming task), cleaning, child care, textile production, and, to varying degrees, helping in the fields. They also raise chickens, turkeys, ducks, and pigs but rarely engage in wage labor.

The gender division of labor is more pronounced among the Tzotzil than among the Tzeltal. Tzotzil women are less likely to work in the fields and more likely to spend time on textile manufacture; they also collect firewood, whereas Tzeltal men and women share this task.

Land Tenure.   The pattern of land tenure in Pantelhó has fluctuated repeatedly over the centuries between communal and private. As recently as 1993, there were still two forms—ejido and private. According to the Mexican constitution, qualified rural landless agriculturists could petition the government for grants of land, ejidos. The eight ejidos in Pantelhó offered their members the right to inherit (but not to own) land. In the early 1990s there were two local variations of private property: ranches and *copropiedades*. Ranches were owned by individual families, usually Ladino. Copropiedades consisted of former ranches purchased by collective groups of Indians who assigned individual ownership but often maintained an association with some control over the use and distribution of the land. Ejidos make up about 60 percent of landholdings. Most landholdings in Pantelhó, with the exception of individually owned ranches, range between 2 and 10 hectares.

In 1992, led by President Carlos Salinas de Gortari, Mexico changed its constitution, allowing for the privatization of the ejido, in effect ending the ejido system. The ramifications are unclear, but a comparison of ejido and non-ejido members in Pantelhó suggests that increased inequalities and greater poverty are likely outcomes.

Kinship

Kin Groups and Descent.   The nuclear family is the fundamental kin group in Pantelhó. Frequently, the nuclear family becomes an extended family, when it is expanded to include the spouses of married children and their children. They may live in the same household area and work land cooperatively. This group, however, has no permanence; it will likely dissolve as soon as financial independence is achieved, although the youngest son will often remain to care for the aging parents and inherit the house and remaining property. Relations may continue, but it is a matter of individual choice. Dyadic relations (i.e., *compadrázgo*) often replace kin ties. Descent is patrilineal, and the Spanish double surname (father's last name followed by mother's father's last name) is used throughout Pantelhó.

Kinship Terminology.   Traditional kinship is bilateral, distinguishing lineal from collateral relatives. Relative age is also distinguished, marking younger and older siblings. Terms for older siblings are often extended to nonkin as respectful modes of address.

Marriage and Family

Marriage. Marriage practices are changing. Traditional marriages were arranged by the parents, and the groom was required to provide maize, beans, pigs, and alcohol to the bride's father. This bride-wealth payment was substantial—the equivalent of 400 to 600 days' wage labor—but it could be spread out over a period of two years or so. Today young people often meet at public events. Some couples decide to elope; then, after they are married, they will ask to be pardoned, and the groom will provide some small gifts (amounting to about 10 days' wage labor) to the bride's father. Men are often married by the age of 18, women by 16.

Postmarital residence is variable, being determined largely by access to land. Because fathers usually pass on land to their sons, there is a tendency for couples to live in the hamlet of the groom's family. If a couple lacks access to land, however, they may decide to live with the bride's family or to migrate and establish a new household.

Domestic Unit. A married man usually heads the household. Female-headed households are rare. A typical household consists of a husband, a wife, and their several children (on average, more than four), but other family members—such as an aged single parent, children's spouses, and grandchildren—may join these households. Each household works collectively in the fields, cooks and eats together, and provides money and labor for community projects.

Inheritance. Inheritance is bilateral, as prescribed by Mexican law; however, there is a marked tendency for sons to inherit productive resources such as land, coffee trees, and large domestic animals. Resources are divided equitably among the sons. Daughters usually receive a minor cash settlement or other compensation, but occasionally they inherit animals or coffee trees.

Socialization. Children are socialized in the household. They are rarely apart from their mothers, who carry their children in large shawls tied on their backs as they work during the day and sleep next to them at night. Older siblings, especially girls, also play a large caretaking role. As children grow, they learn by watching and working with their parents and siblings. Young boys work with their fathers, girls with their mothers. Parents are generally tolerant, and children are usually respectful, although excessive drinking does, on occasion, produce abusive behavior in adult men. Schools, which are now found in most communities, are beginning to play a larger role; they are acquainting Indian children with Mexican national culture, history, and identity. Pupils rarely attend beyond the fourth grade because, to do so, they would need to migrate to the headtown or outside the municipio. The impact of formal education thus remains limited.

Sociopolitical Organization

Social Organization. During the nineteenth century, the Indians, as a class, were impoverished peons with little control over their lives. Marriage, residence, and other aspects of their existence were subject to control by Ladino ranchers. A strong sense of shared poverty persists. High status among Indians was traditionally achieved through community service, both civil and religious. Although these patterns remain evident, class differences are becoming more salient. Three classes are widely recognized: the landless, the subsistence farmers, and those who grow coffee and/or raise cattle.

Political Organization. Political organization closely follows the overall Mexican pattern. A *presidente municipal* (mayor of the municipio) is elected every three years and, together with a *síndico* (vice-mayor), a treasurer, and six *regidores* (aldermen), controls municipio finances, dispenses justice, and represents the municipio to the outside world. These are paid political offices. In monthly meetings, representatives from each hamlet discuss issues with municipio leaders. Within their hamlets, these *agentes*, who are chosen yearly, settle disputes and, with the help of secretaries and various public-works directors, plan hamlet activities. These are all voluntary positions.

Social Control. Social control is effected at one of three hierarchical levels: hamlet, municipio, and state. Although hamlet agentes can impose no sanctions, they are often successful at mediating internal disputes. Minor crimes and disputes within municipio boundaries are adjudicated by the municipio mayor or judge, who can impose fines and/or brief jail sentences. Serious crimes are often referred directly to the state judiciary or the legal section of the Indian-affairs agency. Land disputes that cannot be mediated locally go to the judiciary or to the land-reform office. There is a general desire among Indians to resolve their problems locally, but major conflicts, especially those crossing ethnic lines, are usually taken to outside authorities.

Conflict. Most conflicts involve land, and most of these conflicts, at least through the 1980s, pitted Indian against Ladino. The Indian strategy to obtain land was to invade, en masse, a Ladino ranch, harvest the coffee, kill and eat the cattle, plant milpas, and build houses. Then they would either offer to purchase the land or petition the government to grant it as an ejido. Ladinos, in response and sometimes in anticipation, would destroy Indian milpas and even whole communities. Recently, land disputes between Indians have increased.

Other sources of conflict are marital infidelity and accusations of witchcraft. The former are usually settled between the households involved; the latter frequently involve the assassination of the suspected witch. Theft is very rare.

Religion and Expressive Culture

Religious Beliefs. Religious beliefs and practices vary widely. Ceremonies range from the dedication of a new water system (to the earth god) to the singing of Baptist hymns on Saturday night. About 70 percent of the people are Catholic, and around 25 percent are Protestant; some profess no religious beliefs.

Local Catholic religious practices involve various saints, to whom certain aspects of Mayan gods are ascribed. The faithful pray to the saints and care for their images. In addition, many Catholics and a few others continue to believe in animal-spirit counterparts (*chulel*).

Religious Practitioners. A Catholic priest holds regular church services and performs other ceremonies, such as baptisms and marriages, in the headtown for Indians and Ladinos. Catechists, lay people who read and discuss the Bible, lead Catholic services in many of the hamlets. Protestant speakers (*predicadores*) lead church services in Pantelhó's several Protestant churches. Few traditional curers live in Pantelhó; most come from neighboring municipios.

The Tzotzil of Pantelhó have an active religious *cargo* system. Individual men, supported by their families, serve voluntarily in one of two sets of socially ranked cargos. There are fourteen year-long positions (six *alguaciles,* four *mayores,* and four *regidores*). These cargo holders are responsible for the care of the saints as well as the performance of other religious duties. Other individuals take responsibility for major celebrations. *Alfereces* sponsor the events, often at great personal expense; they are assisted by *capitanes.*

Ceremonies. The most important communitywide ceremonies occur on important Catholic holidays and saints' days. Carnaval is the largest celebration, followed by the feast days of Santa Catarina (the patron saint of Pantelhó), San Sebastián, San Martín, and Jesus of Good Hope. During these ceremonies, food, drink, and music are provided for all. Holy Week and All Saints' Day (Todos Santos) are also celebrated. Local residents believe their participation shows respect for God and will bring good fortune. Ceremonies devoted to Mayan gods are held in some hamlets before planting. Ceremonies are also held at the inauguration of new public works, on New Year's Eve, and on Independence Day. Curing ceremonies, which involve prayer and the ritual sacrifice of a chicken, are held in individual households.

Arts. Women's richly brocaded textiles are the traditional form of artistic expression. Men play the flute, guitar, and violin during religious celebrations. Peonage, poverty, and hard work have left little time for the development of diverse artistic traditions.

Medicine. A wide variety of medicinal practices can be found in Pantelhó. Doctors are available in the headtown, and antibiotics are widely used. Trained health workers administer Western medicine in the hamlets, and Indian midwives assist childbirth. In addition to Western medicine, herbal cures are widely used to treat digestive and respiratory disorders.

Death and Afterlife. Death may be attributed to natural or supernatural causes. Untimely death is suspect, especially in the case of healthy adults or children, and is often attributed to sorcery.

The dead are buried in unmarked graves in community cemeteries as soon as possible. Funeral celebrations are common and may involve considerable expense. During Todos Santos, the graves are covered with marigold petals, and candles are burned. Women ritually wail over the graves of family members. The dead are thought to return to visit their living relatives on Todos Santos and may bring good fortune if treated well, or bad fortune if neglected.

Bibliography

Benjamin, Thomas (1989). *A Rich Land, A Poor People.* Albuquerque: University of New Mexico Press.

Brown, Pete (1993). "The Creation of Community: Class and Ethnic Struggle in Pantelhó, Chiapas, Mexico." Ph.D. dissertation, University of California, Irvine.

Cancian, Frank (1992). *The Decline of Community in Zinacantán.* Stanford, Calif.: Stanford University Press.

Collier, George (1975). *Fields of the Tzotzil.* Austin: University of Texas Press.

Eber, Christine (1995). *Women and Alcohol in a Highland Maya Town.* Austin: University of Texas Press.

Garcia de León, Antonio (1985). *Resistencia y utopía.* Mexico City: Ediciones Era.

Gutierrez-Holmes, Calixta (1961). *Perils of the Soul.* New York: Free Press of Glencoe.

MacLeod, Murdo J., and Robert Wasserstrom, eds. (1983). *Spaniards and Indians in Southern Mesoamerica.* Lincoln: University of Nebraska Press.

Marion Singer, Maria Odile (1984). *El movimiento campesino en Chiapas, 1983.* Mexico City: Centro de Estudios Históricos del Agrarismo en México.

Moscoso Pastrana, Prudencio (1972). *Pajarito, el ultimo lider chamula.* Tuxtla Gutiérrez: Gobierno del Estado.

Pérez Castro, Ana Bella (1989). *Entre montañas y cafetales.* Mexico City: Universidad Autonoma de México.

Wasserstrom, Robert (1983). *Class and Society in Central Chiapas.* Berkeley and Los Angeles: University of California Press.

PETE BROWN

Tzotzil of Chamula

ETHNONYMS: Batz'i Krisanoetike ("true people" in Chamula), Chamula, Chamo' (Chamula's civil-ceremonial center), San Juan Chamula

Orientation

Identification. San Juan Chamula is a Maya township located in the highlands of central Chiapas, the southernmost state of Mexico. Chamula's Tzotzil name is "Chamo'," or "[where] the water died." According to a myth, Chamula's civil-ceremonial center was built on the site of a lake that San Juan (the patron saint) had dried up in order to make it habitable. Chamula is the largest and most densely populated of more than thirty Maya-speaking communities in the Chiapas highlands.

Location. Chamula occupies an area of 364 square kilometers and the average elevation of its lands is 2,300 meters. Most people live close to the lands they plant, in hamlets scattered along hills and basins across Chamula's eroded terrain. As a consequence of erosion, water holes, the main sources of water, tend to dry up before the rainy season. When this happens, the Chamula abandon their hamlets, temporarily or permanently, and find other places to live. The highest mountain in the region, the Tzontevitz, lies within Chamula and is sacred to the Chamula and neighboring indigenous groups.

Demography. The Chamula number around 100,000, of which about one-half live in the township, and the rest have emigrated to establish new communities both within and outside the highlands. The emigration process began more than a century ago and continues today as land shortages and political and religious conflicts force people to leave.

Linguistic Affiliation. The Chamula speak Tzotzil, a language belonging to the Tzeltalan Group (Tzotzil, Tzeltal, and Tojolab'al) of Mayan languages.

History and Cultural Relations

Recent archaeological studies place the arrival of Maya speakers into Chiapas around 100 B.C. Theories suggesting that the immigrants may have come from the Chuj region in Guatemala are not yet supported by archaeological findings. Dispersion over the area appears to have been relatively rapid. Highland Tzotzil and Tzeltal lived in proximity with Zoque groups to the west and other Maya groups to the north (Chontal and Ch'ol) and east (Tojolab'al and Chuj). Aggressive Chiapanec groups entered the region about A.D. 900, settling to the south and constantly pressuring Tzeltal and Tzotzil towns. During the late Postclassic period (A.D. 900 to 1250), central Mexico strongly influenced highland Chiapas's political ideology, organization, religion, and other aspects of its culture. The area functioned as regional intermediary of an extensive network of trade between Guatemala, Tabasco, and central Mexico.

Upon the arrival of the Spanish, highland Chiapas was divided into small, warring petty states. Chamula was a large population center. The Chamula built a fort to confront the invaders, whom they attacked with bows and arrows, slingshots, stone-tipped spears, boiling water, and boiling resin. Aided by Zinacantec warriors, Bernal Díaz del Castillo besieged the town and finally succeeded in entering the fort and overwhelming its defenders. In order to control the indigenous population, the Spanish founded Ciudad Real (now San Cristóbal de las Casas) in 1528.

Since that time, the city has been a center of Ladino (non-Indian) political and commercial domination in the highlands. The defiant attitude of the Chamula toward the dominant society has remained constant for five centuries. Exploited and oppressed through exaggerated tribute and taxes and forced-labor arrangements, the Chamula managed to keep alive central elements of their culture and identity that have helped them resist invasive forces. When

the abuses of Spanish-colonial, and later, Mexican societies became intolerable, the Chamula joined other indigenous groups to rebel openly against their oppressors. Major rebellions took place in 1712 and 1867, when the insurgents struggled for the right to their own religion and better living conditions. The rebellions were quelled, but the insurgents were able to secure a measure of religious freedom. The Zapatista rebellion of 1994 focused international attention on the plight of indigenous peoples in Chiapas. Although the Chamula did not participate directly in this uprising (in view of the alliance of the Chamula oligarchy with the ruling Mexican Institutional Revolutionary party), many Chamula sympathize with the movement and recognize that their situation will be deeply affected by the aftermath of this struggle.

The Chamula maintain friendly relations with people from nearby indigenous communities such as Zinacantan, Chenalhó, and Tenejapa, with whom they share many cultural traits. They visit these and other communities to trade and attend their celebrations. Most of their interaction with other indigenous people and with Ladinos takes place in San Cristóbal de las Casas, where they go to sell their produce or woven goods, buy necessities, and worship. Ladinos despise indigenous people and usually mistreat and humiliate them, making them feel unwelcome in the city. To combat this situation, the Chamula utilize quiet resistance, forbidding Ladinos to take up residence within their *municipio* and making their own presence in San Cristóbal felt in ever larger numbers, as more of them seek economic opportunities there.

Settlements

Chamula's contemporary settlement pattern represents a continuation of ancient Maya ones. Most of the people live close to their land, in about one hundred hamlets of varying size. The civil-ceremonial center, or *jteklum* as the Chamula call it, contains a small permanent population. Civil officials move into Chamula Center for one to three years to carry out their duties, whereas religious officials rent a house for a few weeks to celebrate the saint under their care. The Chamula flock into town for market days (Saturdays and Sundays) and for religious celebrations (several times a year). Before 1960, the Chamula built wattle-and-daub homes with thatched roofs. At present, only the poorest people live in such houses. Most Chamula eventually build homes with cement blocks and tile roofs. Dirt floors are the rule. The fact that emigrants found new colonies that reproduce fundamental cultural traits of the original community reveals the vitality of Chamula culture and society.

Economy

Subsistence and Commercial Activities. The Chamula still define themselves as independent agriculturists who plant their small milpas with the sacred trilogy of maize, beans, and squashes. Planting one's own land is still the most respected occupation for men, as it stresses independence and commitment to traditional values. This, however, has increasingly become an unreachable dream since the end of the nineteenth century, when large coffee farms in Chiapas started recruiting a cheap labor force from highland indigenous groups. The high elevation of lands in Chamula, the fact that they have been intensively planted for hundreds of years, and the fractionalization of land bestowed upon both male and female children have reduced the size of landholdings and their productivity. On average, the Chamula can produce only about 20 percent of their yearly food requirements on their own lands. Most Chamula depend upon wage labor on farms and plantations to support their families or to supplement their plots' production. Many rent lands at lower elevations to plant their foodstuffs—and move there during several months each year to care for their crops. The majority of households own sheep, an important economic asset, since they are the source of wool to weave the family's clothing. Most households also raise chickens, which are eaten occasionally during celebrations and as ritual food. Some households tend pigs to sell to Ladinos.

Industrial Arts. Some households produce utilitarian pottery, furniture, and candles, but weaving is a universal activity for Chamula women and is considered the quintessential female occupation. In the late 1970s many women learned to embroider and to produce more modern-looking garments for tourists.

Trade. From Pre-Hispanic times, periodic local markets have been of central importance in the area. Everything is sold in these markets, from ritual objects, fresh produce, and cooked food to clothes, furniture, and other household needs. People attend the market with enthusiasm, for it is not only a place to buy and sell but also to exchange the latest gossip and visit with relatives and friends. Many Chamula peddle goods on the streets in some of southern Mexico's large cities.

Division of Labor. A traditional, complementary division of labor between men and women existed in the past and still holds as the contemporary ideal; men are independent agriculturists, and women are weavers; they complement each other in household tasks. At present, men leave for wage labor, and women take charge of the household, domestic animals, and children, and plant their small plots.

Land Tenure. Most lands within the township are individually owned, but forests and water holes are community property. Many Chamula have received *ejido* lands (i.e., lands granted by the government under agrarian reform laws) outside of the community.

Kinship

Kin Groups and Descent. Patrilineages are constituted by two or more virilocal domestic units living in adjacent lands inherited from their ancestors. Strong in the past, patrilineages are rapidly losing ground because of a shrinking land base. Although there is still some preference for virilocality, the system now tends more toward bilocality. Young couples choose their residence near the groom's or bride's family, according to which family can offer them more land or space in the house; or, they establish residence close to either but manage their economy independently.

Kinship Terminology. Kin terms reflect the principles of age, gender, and generation, central organizing axes among the Chamula. People of a generation older than the

speaker are addressed respectfully as "uncle" and "aunt." A Chamula couple establishes a fictive-kinship tie, or *compadrazgo*, with the godparents of their children. These ties are very important; they create or reinforce life-long friendships and foster respect and mutual aid among the people involved.

Marriage and Family

Marriage. Although the Chamula consider monogamy to be the moral way of life, many Chamula men have more than one wife. Polygyny has always been an option in this community. To contract marriage, a young man, assisted by his family and especially selected petitioners, goes to a woman's house to request her hand. Ideally, bride and groom have never spoken to one another, although they may have exchanged looks or words that signal their mutual interest. The young woman has a say in the decision, but parents may pressure her into accepting. Three weeks to a month go by from the beginning of the petition to the actual marriage (the "house-entering" ceremony), the process taking place according to Chamula tradition. Church weddings, in accordance with Catholic sacraments, are rare.

Domestic Unit. A household compound consists of several domestic units. The primary domestic unit consists of a couple, their unmarried children, their married sons, their sons' wives, and their son's children, all sharing a single maize supply and a house altar. This situation is changing because of the lack of land and other resources that supported the father's claim to his sons' and their families' labor; domestic units often manage their economy in an independent manner. The relationship of a woman to her in-laws may be strained; she tries to get her husband to build a new house for her and move out of his parents' house as soon as possible. Separation and divorce are common, especially during the first years of marriage. Major causes cited are the husband's drinking and domestic violence, his quest to acquire a second wife, the husband's or wife's laziness, or either spouse's conflict with in-laws.

Inheritance. Houses, land, and personal property are bequeathed in equal measure to male and female children.

Socialization. Children are viewed as sources of joy and important economic assets. Socialization takes place mainly within the domestic unit and extended family, with mothers, sisters, grandmothers, and aunts being the main socializing figures, given that men leave for months at a time for wage work. Fathers take their young male children with them to the fields in Chamula and to the farms or rented fields in the lowlands when the children are around 10 years old. Although more children are attending school now than were in the 1970s, children still participate actively, from a very tender age, in the household economy. They fetch water and wood, tend the sheep, help their parents at home and in the fields, grind maize, cook, spin, and weave. They start earning money from about age 15, when girls start selling their woven and embroidered goods, and boys begin wage work.

Sociopolitical Organization

Social Organization. The extended family, compadrazgo, and the *cargo* system constitute the backbone of sociopolitical organization in Chamula. The cargo system in Chamula is a variant of civil-religious hierarchies in indigenous Mesoamerica, a system through which individuals alternate between civil and religious positions, thus climbing the ladder of prestige and power in their communities. The Chamula express their strong feeling of community by serving in this traditional hierarchy. Assisting the deities, they bring blessings upon their families and all the Chamula people.

Political Organization. The regional town council, the traditional form of government, consists of several civil officials selected by a group of respected community elders. Its function is to uphold traditional Chamula values, arbitrate disputes over lands, and resolve intrafamilial problems. The regional town council also includes the religious hierarchy, a body of officials who sponsor public and private celebrations in honor of the saints. The regional town council represents a survival of the system of government that prevailed before the direct intervention of national and state controls in local affairs. Although Spanish and Mexican authorities had always encroached upon the affairs of Chamula, the government has intervened directly in its political life since the 1930s. Through the creation of the constitutional town council mandated by law, the government effectively manipulates the Chamula governing elite. A native elite has benefited from these ties, becoming rich and powerful while acting against their own people. This new imposed system has diminished the influence of the traditional system of government in which community and religion were central guiding forces.

Social Control. Shame is a powerful deterrent both for children who are learning Chamula ways and for adults who stray from the community's mores; hence, gossip acts as a central control mechanism. Minor offenses are punished by the regional council: the offender is shamed before a large audience at the town hall and is required to spend a few days in jail in Chamula. Rape and murder cases are adjudicated by the state authorities outside Chamula and punished by terms in state prisons.

Conflict. Since the early 1970s, political opposition against the ruling oligarchy in Chamula has taken the form of religious conversion to several evangelical sects. Converts oppose the authority of *ilols* (shamans), object to paying taxes for celebrations they consider pagan, and stop buying liquor. The ruling elite claims this behavior imperils the unity and cultural continuity of the Chamula people and, consequently, expels the converts. More than 15,000 people have been ousted in this way. The converts usually establish residence in colonies close to Chamula, on the outskirts of the Ladino town of San Cristóbal de las Casas. Conflict between traditional Chamula and expelled converts periodically erupts in violence and has become a major source of instability in Chamula.

Religion and Expressive Culture

Religious Beliefs. The Chamula transformed imposed Christian beliefs to suit their central Maya ideas. They merged Christ and Sun into the figure of Our Father, the Sun/Christ, and they merged the Virgin Mary, the Moon, and the Earth into a single female entity, Our Mother, the Earth-Moon/Virgin. Catholic saints, imbued with Maya characteristics, are viewed as helpers of Sun and Moon. Nature and topographic features of the landscape, such as mountains, caves, and water holes are infused with a sense of sacredness: they represent sources of life and places where human beings and deities come into contact. The Earthlord, who lives inside mountains and "owns" all wild animals and water sources, must be propitiated before one partakes of his possessions. From birth, all human beings share a part of their soul with an animal. The Chamula interpret sudden death as the death of one's animal soul-companion.

Religious Practitioners. Women or men ilols (i.e., "seers") conduct private healing rituals for individuals. Ilols obtain their gift for healing in dreams, directly from Our Father and Our Mother. They also preside over annual ceremonies at the water holes to ensure the water supply. Midwives conduct several ceremonies during a woman's pregnancy and labor to safeguard her soul and that of her baby.

Ceremonies. Private curing rituals occur frequently and are held by the hearth in the patient's home or in the church in Chamula's civil-ceremonial center. Ilols entreat the deities, offering prayers, liquor, candles, and food to release their patients' souls from the hold of evil powers. Major and minor public ceremonies take place almost monthly to celebrate the day of a specific deity. Hundreds, sometimes thousands, of Chamula attend these long and complicated rituals, which include processions, dance, prayers inside and outside the church, and distribution of ceremonial foods at the religious official's home.

Medicine. The Chamula interpret illness as the result of the actions of an envious or ill-willed person who appeals to evil beings to seize his or her enemy's soul. The person targeted becomes "colder," loses his or her life force, becomes increasingly weak, and finally dies. "Heat," the essential component of life and health, must be restored through prayer (defined by the Chamula as "heated words"), liquor, nutritious foods such as chicken, ritual sweat baths, and coming under the life-giving influences of Our Father and Our Mother.

Arts. Most Chamula women weave their own and their family's clothing on the backstrap loom; this ancient weaving technique has deep cultural and religious associations. The gift of weaving, like that of healing, is granted in dreams by Our Mother, the Earth-Moon/Virgin, to young women.

Death and Afterlife. Like illness, death is viewed as the result of the loss of one's soul through the schemes of malevolent individuals. The souls of dead people come back to visit their relatives and partake of their food offerings once a year, during the Festival of the Dead (K'in Santo), from 30 October to 1 November. Men and women intone special prayers beseeching the deities to release the souls of their dead relatives and inviting them to come to earth and enter their home.

Bibliography

Calnek, Edward (1988). "Highland Chiapas before the Spanish Conquest." In *Archaeology, Ethnohistory, and Ethno-archaeology in the Maya Highlands of Chiapas, Mexico*. Papers of the New World Archaeological Foundation, nos. 54–56. Provo: Brigham Young.

Eber, Christine, and Brenda Rosenbaum (1993). "'That We May Serve beneath Your Hands and Feet': Women Weavers in Highland Chiapas, Mexico." In *Crafts in the World Market*, edited by June Nash, 103–112. Albany: State University of New York Press.

Gossen, Gary H. (1974). *Chamulas in the World of the Sun*. Cambridge: Harvard University Press.

Gossen, Gary H. (1986). "The Chamula Festival of Games: Native Macroanalysis and Social Commentary in a Maya Carnival." In *Symbol and Meaning beyond the Closed Community: Essays in Mesoamerican Ideas*, edited by Gary H. Gossen, 227–254. Albany: State University of New York at Albany, Institute for Mesoamerican Studies.

Posas, Ricardo (1959). *Chamula: Un pueblo indio de los altos de Chiapas*. Mexico City: Instituto Nacional Indigenista.

Rosenbaum, Brenda (1993). *With Our Heads Bowed: The Dynamics of Gender in a Maya Community*. Albany: State University of New York at Albany, Institute for Mesoamerican Studies.

Wasserstrom, Robert (1983). *Class and Society in Central Chiapas*. Berkeley and Los Angeles: University of California Press.

BRENDA ROSENBAUM

Tzotzil of San Andrés Larraínzar

ETHNONYMS: Andresero, Batz'i vinik, Yahval lum

Orientation

Identification. "Batz'i vinik"—"real men" or "real people"—is the label Andreseros use to distinguish themselves from Ladinos, the Spanish-speaking Mexicans of the area. Although they also refer to other Tzotzil-speaking Indians as "Batz'i vinik," the Andreseros use "Yahval lum"—"owner of the land" or "owner of the village"—only for people belonging to their community, San Andrés Larraínzar. Today these labels are often replaced by the term "Andreseros," which refers to the colonial name of the village, "San Andrés Ista-

costoc," or, since 1933, "Larraínzar" or "San Andrés Larraínzar." Unofficially, the name "San Andrés Chamula" was also used for a long time, but today only "San Andrés Larraínzar"—or among the Andreseros themselves simply "San Andrés"—is used. "Tzotzil," which can be freely translated as "the people of the bat," refers to their language group, and it is spoken in other villages as well. Today the most common term used by the people of San Andrés is "Andreseros," which is also the label used in the anthropological literature.

Location. San Andrés Larraínzar is one of several *municipios* in the highlands of Chiapas, the southernmost state of Mexico. San Andrés Larraínzar, like most other communities in highland Chiapas, consists of a central village and several hamlets. Altogether, the municipio comprises an area of 22,517 hectares. The central village is located at 16°53′ N and 92°43′ E. It is situated at an elevation of 2,100 meters in *sikil osil* ("cold land"), but some hamlets also have access to *k'ixin osil* ("hot land"), where coffee as well as bananas and citrus fruits can be cultivated. In *tierra fría*, the Spanish term for the cold area, mainly maize is grown in the milpa, a field where maize, beans, and squash are usually cultivated together. In the late twentieth century maize has often been produced in monoculture; cabbage and flowers are planted, both as cash crops to be sold in San Cristóbal de las Casas, the nearest city. This is a response to enhanced marketing possibilities but also to growing land scarcity. There is essentially one rainy season from around June to November. The annual rainfall ranges from 100 to 120 centimeters per year. The temperature during the dry season can range from 3°C to 23°C, but can go as high as 40°C during the day. The highlands of Chiapas are a botanically unique area. Various plant species are found only in this area throughout the Americas. Common problems of the area include increasing population density, unequal distribution of land, and, as a result, deforestation, land erosion, and a reduction of the biodiversity. Larger mammals such as deer, which the Andreseros used to hunt, have become very rare; their hunting stories now focus on raccoons, rabbits, and opossums. Larger carnivores such as jaguars are also extinct.

Demography. William Holland (1963) reported that there were 7,285 inhabitants of San Andrés in 1960. Of these, 608 were Ladinos, living in the main village. For the entire Tzotzil population, gives a figure of 182,815 people. According to the 1990 government census, the population of San Andrés Larraínzar was 15,303, including approximately 30 Ladinos. The population density increased from around 0.3 persons to almost 0.7 persons per hectare.

Linguistic Affiliation. Tzotzil is a Maya language and belongs to the Tzeltalan Group, which includes Tzotzil, Tzeltal, and Tojolab'al. Tzotzil has a number of mutually understandable dialects. Each village uses a different dialect, but there are also several dialects spoken within larger villages. The Andreseros are well aware of the fact that the Tzotzil spoken in their village differs from that spoken in other villages, and local dialects are often the target of jokes. Differences are not only in pronunciation or intonation, but also in vocabulary, grammar, word choice, and entire interaction schemes. Nowadays only older people are monolingual; most Tzotzil know at least some Spanish, and some also know some Tzeltal, the most closely related Maya language. Tzotzil is the predominant language in the main village, however, and is also dominant in the hamlets.

History and Cultural Relations

There is no evidence that the different Tzotzil groups formed one unit at any time in history. According to the oral history of the Andreseros, in former times the main village was located approximately 2 kilometers to the south. Until 1591, San Andrés had the Tzotzil name "Sacamch'en" (white cave/cliff), translated by the Aztecs as "Istacostoc." Indeed, the place designated in the accounts of the Andreseros is close to a huge white cliff with a cave. Although the spot is located in the municipio of San Juan Chamula, the land there is still cultivated by Andreseros.

The Spaniards first arrived in Chiapas in 1524 but were not able to colonize the area until the arrival of Diego Mazariegos, four years later. During the colonial time, the village was known as "San Andrés Istacostoc" or "San Andrés Chamula." The latter name derives from the fact that San Andrés belonged to the parish of San Juan Chamula. In 1933, during the anticlerical campaign, the name of the village was changed to "Manuel Larraínzar," to honor an important Ladino diplomat of Chiapas. Nowadays the village is known as "San Andrés Larraínzar," "San Andrés," or, among Ladinos in San Cristóbal, as "Larraínzar." Changes in the village name alone show that it is not possible to understand the history and culture of San Andrés without taking into account the broader context of its interactions. It also shows that San Andrés was already an established community before the time of the Spaniards. San Andrés, as any other community in this area, experienced huge transformations during the colonial period, as well as after the independence of Mexico in 1821.

During colonial times, the Indians of highland Chiapas were forced to live in villages, rather than maintain the former pattern of dispersed settlements. These villages were largely constructed after the Spanish model, in which the center of the village was occupied by a town plaza and the church. Diseases, brought from the "Old World," high taxes, tribute, and forced labor led to the economic and physical exhaustion of the Indians and resulted in a decline of their population. The Indians were very often forced to give up subsistence maize farming to produce cash crops such as cacao, sugar, or cochineal in the lowland areas for the *encomendero*, who held the Spanish royal grant for the land and was therefore allowed to collect tribute from the Indians living there. The Conquest not only had an impact on the Indian economy but also on their social and cultural environment. *Cofradías*, brotherhoods responsible for organizing saints' day celebrations and collecting money for the church, were introduced. These brotherhoods increasingly gained power at the local level. In the nineteenth century these cofradías were almost entirely dissolved, and today individuals called *alféreces* (sing., *alférez*) are responsible for these celebrations. They, together with the other religious officeholders and the *ayuntamiento regional* (town council), form the civil-religious hierarchy of San Andrés.

To assess the impact of the colonial period on the highland villages is almost impossible because there are few descriptions of individual villages. Spanish chronicles, official letters, royal orders, and letters of complaint are the main sources available. In addition, these are only sufficient to give an impression of the atrocities that took place and to indicate that royal orders from Spain were not enacted very often on a local level.

Most colonial laws were abolished with Mexico's independence, after which non-Indians were allowed to settle in Indian communities. Around 1848, four Ladinos lived in San Andrés but apparently left during the Tzotzil uprising in 1869–1870. In the early twentieth century other Ladinos, some of them *enganchadores* (hiring agents for coffee or sugar plantations), settled in San Andrés. Through purchase and through land titles granted by the government, but also through fraudulent contracts, coercion, and the indebtedness of some Indians, the enganchadores managed to gain control over most of the land around the main village. They created several cattle ranches and coffee plantations in more distant areas. Because of their connections and their superior economic situation, some of them also gained control of trade within, as well as outside, the village, mainly with San Cristóbal de las Casas, the main trading center of the highlands of Chiapas. These Ladinos' estates often contained gardens of 1 hectare of land, which is more than many Andreseros currently have for subsistence.

Owing to their economic power, the Ladinos also dominated the politics within San Andrés, and the Indians were consistently ill-treated by some Ladinos. Although the *presidente* of San Andrés was an Indian, the Indians had little access to the state government and the legal system because of their lack of knowledge of the Spanish language. Therefore the Ladinos held most of the power in the village, and were able to treat the Indians as they wanted. As a product of the exploitation, inequality, and injustice of their colonial past, which persisted even after the independence of Mexico, the Andreseros formed a strong identity based on the Indian-Ladino dichotomy. Separate religious festivals were held by Indians and Ladinos. In fact, given that the Ladino community could not exist without the Indians, one could argue that there were two communities in one. At the same time, through the accounts of their parents' and grandparents' experiences, the Indians knew that they were the true "owners of the land," the *yahval lum*, and that the Ladinos had only recently arrived. Between 1974 and 1976, after several appeals to the government for reconciliation failed, the Indians chased almost all the Ladinos out of San Andrés. Although they threatened and frightened the Ladinos, there was only one serious incident—a landowner who had shot at the Indians, and his son, were subsequently killed.

Today there are approximately thirty Ladinos left in San Andrés, most of whom never left the village during the local uprising. They no longer have large amounts of land, and their main economic activities are running small-scale businesses and shops. They participate as regular community members in the political meetings, but they do not act as alfereces or as authorities in the *cabildo*. Although the Indians of San Andrés clearly see themselves as being closer to other Indian communities than to Ladinos living in their own village, their ethnic identity is nevertheless bound up with their village. On the other hand, this does not prevent some villagers from organizing at supra-community levels, even including non-Indians, as was the case during the Zapatista rebellion of 1994.

The Spanish imposed Catholicism on the Indians of highland Chiapas in the sixteenth century. Nowadays most of the Indians of San Andrés are nominally Catholic, but this Catholicism is actually a synthesis of a pre-Spanish religion, of Catholic belief, and also of their own invention over the last 450 years. Since the late 1970s, many Protestant sects have established their churches in the *cabecera*, the main village, as well as in different hamlets of San Andrés.

Settlements

There exist no clear data about the precolonial settlement pattern in San Andrés, but it seems that the Andreseros lived in compounds and hamlets based on patrilineages. Today the land is normally inherited by the sons of the family head, and women move into the compounds of their husbands. With the exception of some marginal plots, forests, and pastureland that are still communally held, the landholding pattern has been transformed into one resembling private property—at least insofar as Andreseros now build fences around their plots. Nevertheless, most of the land in San Andrés remains *terreno comunal*: there are no private land titles, and the land cannot be sold. The scarcity of land was already evident in 1960, when the average amount of land per proprietor was 3.82 hectares. It must be remembered that Ladino landowners often held titles to large plots, frequently divided among their family members. San Andrés never faced the problem of huge fincas, such as those found in Pantelhó and other highland villages.

Houses are usually rectangular constructions with a roof made of tile, fiber cement, sheet metal, or grass. Walls are generally wooden or of various types of mud construction. Cement-block or brick constructions were introduced to the more accessible hamlets in the late twentieth century. Use of the latter is widely favored by the Indians but depends heavily on income. The traditional grass roof is rarely built because it is now very difficult to obtain sufficient grass. The normal compound contains one or more multifunctional houses, which include a kitchen, a sleeping room, and, more often than not, a granary. Sometimes separate kitchen houses or granaries are constructed.

The plan of the house symbolizes the shape of the earth, a rectangle. Its four main posts (*yoyal na*), which support the roof, symbolize the four pillars of the sky (*yoyal vinahel*); the four pillars are located at the four corners of the earth to support the sky. The center of the world, which—according to the oral tradition of the village—is San Andrés itself, has its counterpart in the center of the house, where the fireplace is usually located. Here, during the opening ceremony of the new house, the Andreseros bury bones of animals as offerings to the gods.

Economy

Subsistence and Commercial Activities. The Andreseros still depend heavily on their milpas, which they normally cultivate in a slash-and-burn manner. Because of the lack of land and forest, fallow periods are very short, and fertilizer is often used to maintain the yield of the field.

The machete, the hoe, and the planting stick remain the most important tools in agriculture. Maize is the main crop and, together with beans, constitutes the staple food of the Andreseros. Some richer families also have cattle, and almost every household raises some poultry, but sheep are rarely found in San Andrés. Adding to the diet, different vegetables are collected by women, or raised in house gardens. In the early 1980s cabbage was introduced as a cash crop. Cut flowers and apples are also becoming more and more important. In lowland areas, different kinds of fruits and coffee are grown and sold. Whereas most fruits are produced for the local market in San Andrés, coffee is sold outside the village.

Industrial Arts. Surely the most impressive craft in San Andrés is weaving. Weaving is a woman's task, accomplished with a backstrap loom. Carpentry and clay-brick and tile manufacturing are other village crafts. Wooden equipment and furniture were traditionally made by each individual or obtained in trade from the neighboring village of San Juan Chamula, but there are now four carpenters in San Andrés. There are also some men who make musical instruments, such as harps and guitars. Today San Andrés has bakeries, a butcher, a *tortillería*, several maize mills, a car-repair shop, and even a hostel. Other sources of income include government jobs, transport service to San Cristóbal de las Casas, various shops and restaurants, and wage labor, particularly in construction or agriculture. Besides the shops, there is a weekly (Sunday) market in San Andrés, where people from different villages and Ladinos from San Cristóbal come to sell their products. Most of the Andreseros also have access to different markets and shops in surrounding villages and cities. Seasonal labor migration to plantations is still an additional source of income.

Division of Labor. Most of the heavy field work is done by men, who also take care of the larger animals and are responsible for house construction. The political and religious offices are held by men, but women expend a considerable amount of effort while their husbands hold an office. Sheep, pigs, and poultry are raised by women, who also carry firewood, weave, cook, and cultivate house gardens. Marketing is done by both women and men, but trade outside the village and the transport of goods are mainly men's work. Other agricultural tasks are shared by members of the household—the parents with their unmarried children, and sometimes also the husband's parents. Workers from the village are hired occasionally, because of the intensification of agriculture.

Kinship

The two most important features of kinship relations are age and generation. Men of more or less the same age traditionally refer to each other as "brother," distinguishing only between *itz'inal* (younger brother) and *bankilal* (older brother). Older men are addressed as *htot* (my father) or *tata*, a term to address very old men. In a similar way, women are addressed as *hme'* (my mother) or *yaya*, for a very old woman. People are also addressed by their personal first names and titles.

Residence patterns following marriages are traditionally viri-patrilocal, and although there are some cases of polygyny, the majority of the marriages are monogamous. Bride-price is paid, consisting of food and liquor, and sometimes soft drinks. The groom also has to work for a designated period of time at the house of his father-in-law.

Sociopolitical Organization

Most of the political system was created—or at least strongly influenced—by outside forces during the past 450 years. Today stratification is evident among the Andreseros: there are the landless, those with land for subsistence, cash-crop farmers, and others who no longer depend on their land. Aside from this, San Andrés is clearly male dominated. Women usually do not own land, and political and religious offices are held exclusively by men. There are two political and administrative bodies in San Andrés, the _ayuntamiento constitucional_ and the ayuntamiento regional. The former consists of thirteen men who govern the municipio. These men, led by the _presidente municipal_, are elected for three years and receive a salary from the state government. Until the mid-1980s, it was necessary to be a member of the Institutional Revolutionary party to be elected president of a municipio anywhere in Chiapas. The ayuntamiento regional consists of twenty-nine men, and its main concern is with the ritual organization of the village. Men are appointed for one year for these offices and receive no salary. Crimes, misdeeds, land disputes, and the like were originally adjudicated by the local authorities, and some still are. Because of the distance to the nearest city, many cases are never filed. Among the Andreseros, local resolution of legal matters depends on consensus, reached between the authorities of the village and the parties involved. Consequently, power relations and authority have a great impact on these decisions. Nowadays the situation is much more complicated because younger men speak Spanish and, if they have enough money, have access to legal advice in the city.

It seems that when most of the Ladinos were chased out of the village (see "History and Cultural Relations"), the Indians lost their opposition group, against which a common identity was formed. After the liberation from most of the Ladinos, the Catholic part of the village tried unsuccessfully to chase out the Protestant Indians, too, as the Indians of other highland villages had done. Conflicts within the Indian community have been intensifying. Partly because of these conflicts, but also because of the steep expenses incurred by officeholders, many people refuse to fill religious offices, and an increasing number of Protestant churches are gaining supporters. Even among the supporters of the Catholic church, there are religious and political struggles.

Religion

There is no easy way to disentangle contemporary and precolonial belief. Contemporary religion is a product of a constant shaping and reshaping, ordering and reordering of the world. The main source drawn upon in this process is colonial Catholicism. San Andrés, the patron of the village, is the highest god of the village, as well as its founder. His feast is the most important ceremony of the year. Andreseros say that saints, with their supporters from other villages, come to visit, and the two alfereces of the patron saint San Andrés spend a huge amount of money on the celebration. They act as hosts to local authorities, to visiting authorities from other communities, and to several other attendees. Assisted by a _nakanvaneh_ (ritual advisor) they give offerings such as fireworks, incense, and _pox_ (liquor), in order to please the gods. Every saint in the church has his or her own ceremony conducted once a year by an alférez, who takes this office for one year, borrowing money from other villagers to fulfill all his duties. Besides the alférez, who is in charge of the ceremony to honor the saint, every saint has at least one _martoma_, a man who oversees the care of the saint and the church. The martoma's office in San Andrés, is filled annually, giving young married men the chance to enter the _cargo_ system, a variant of a system of civil and religious offices known all over Mesoamerica. There is one group of gods in the church (the saints), but another group dwells in the various mountains and caves in San Andrés. These _anheletik_, spirits who own the land, must grant permission for new house construction, planting of a field, and so forth. For example, if people do not ask for permission from these spirits, they may send illness and death to the persons living in a newly constructed house.

People can also be harmed through the animal companion of another person. Each person has at least one of these animal companions, the destiny of which is closely related to the destiny of the human being. If an animal companion of a person dies, the person normally gets sick and might also die. Another source of illness is the loss of parts of the soul, which can be caused by fright or induced by malevolent forces. Healing the sick most often consists of appealing for help from different spirits, or even offering them a substitute for a lost soul or animal companion. This tradition has changed through the years. In former times, the death of the highest animal companion (there can be as many as thirteen per person) meant death to the person. Today this kind of illness can be healed by paying a considerable amount of money as an offering to the spirits involved. The animal companions are normally kept in a corral in one of the sacred mountains of San Andrés, where they are fed.

Most healers and practitioners are men; certainly the most important healers of the community are men. Nevertheless, there are also women who are healers. As in other highland villages, the role of the healers, _ilvaneh_, is very ambiguous. Just as they can heal, they can also bring illness through witchcraft. Many of these beliefs no longer exist, however, and knowledge of this sort is often preserved only through stories and histories.

Bibliography

Calnek, Edward (1961). _Distribution and Location of the Tzeltal and Tzotzil Pueblos of the Highlands of Chiapas of the Present._ Chicago: University of Chicago Man-Land Project. Microfilm.

Holland, William (1961). "Tonalismo y nagualismo entre los indios tzotziles de Larráinzar, Chiapas, México." _Estudios de Cultura Maya_ 1:167–182.

Holland, William (1963). *Medicina maya en los Altos de Chiapas.* Mexico City: Instituto Nacional Indigenista.

Instituto Nacional de Estadística Geografía e Informática (1993). *Anuario estadístico del estado de Chiapas, Ed. 1993.* Aguascalientes: INEGI.

Laughlin, Robert (1969). "The Tzotzil." In *Handbook of Middle American Indians,* edited by Robert Wauchope. Vol. 7, *Ethnology, Part One,* edited by Evon Z. Vogt, 152–194. Austin: University of Texas Press.

Ochiai, Kazuyasu (1985). *Cuando los santos vienen marchando.* San Cristóbal de las Casas: Universidad Autónoma de Chiapas.

Ochiai, Kazuyasu (1989). *Meanings Performed, Symbols Read: Anthropological Studies on Latin America.* Tokyo: Tokyo University of Foreign Studies.

Roβ, Norbert (In press). "Der traditionelle Hausbau von San Andrés Larraínzar." *Jahrbuch des Museums für Völkerkunde* (Leipzig).

Vogt, Evon Z. (1969). "Chiapas Highlands." In *Handbook of Middle American Indians,* edited by Robert Wauchope. Vol. 7, *Ethnology, Part One,* edited by Evon Z. Vogt, 133–151. Austin: University of Texas Press.

Wasserstrom, Robert F. (1983). *Class and Society in Central Chiapas.* Berkeley and Los Angeles: University of California Press.

NORBERT ROβ

Tzotzil of San Bartolomé de los Llanos

ETHNONYMS: Indians of Venustiano Carranza, San Bartoleños, Totiketik, Totiques, Tzotziles

Orientation

Identification and Location.   San Bartolomé de los Llanos is the capital of the *municipio* of Venustiano Carranza, near the center of the Mexican state of Chiapas. The population of the town, which is also called San Bartolomé Venustiano Carranza, is half Tzotzil and half Ladino (Spanish speakers of mixed Indian, Spanish, and African ancestry). More than half the remainder of the population of the municipio is non-Indian. The Tzeltal-speaking Indian community of Aguacatenango occupies a corner of the municipio lands, but maintains a separate identity. The municipio also includes a large sugar-mill community at Pujiltic, and several Ladino towns.

The town is built on a side ridge of an extinct volcano, about 800 meters in elevation; the lower end of the town is in the temperate climatic zone. Most of the other lands of the municipio are in the plains (*los llanos*)—hence the community name—immediately north of the Río Grijalva. The average elevation in the plains is less than 500 meters, fully within the hot tropical climatic zone.

Demography.   There were approximately 7,500 Tzotzil in the municipio in 1960, about 5,000 of whom had their principal residence in the town center. In 1990 there were between 8,000 and 10,000 Tzotzil living in the town center and in a new settlement next to it, and perhaps another 8,000 to 10,000 living in the rest of the municipio. Official census figures are not reliable, and numbers cited here are estimates by anthropological field workers and knowledgeable residents.

Linguistic Affiliation.   Tzotzil is a major language of the Maya Family, which is spoken by more than 150,000 Indians in Chiapas. Its closest linguistic relative is Tzeltal, spoken by about the same number of people in adjacent parts of Chiapas. San Bartolomé Tzotzil is unique among Highland Chiapas dialects in possessing phonemic tones. It is the language of the home and the first language learned by the Indians of San Bartolomé, but all adults can also speak Spanish. Indian women are usually more at ease speaking Spanish than are Indian men, contrasting sharply with the pattern in most Chiapas Indian communities.

History and Cultural Relations

Tzotzil speakers entered the Chiapas Highlands around A.D. 1000. After the Conquest, the Spanish implemented a policy of *reducción,* moving the scattered population into towns built on a standard model. San Bartolomé appears in historical records of the late 1500s. It has been continuously occupied ever since. All regional censuses, beginning in 1572, have listed substantial numbers of both Ladinos and Indians in the town center. Colonial censuses also list "mulattos" and "Negroes" as residents, but the terms are not used in post-1821 census records. The basic relations between Ladinos and Indians were those of dominance and subordination from the town's founding until the 1970s.

From Mexican independence from Spain in 1821 through 1932, the town of San Bartolomé had two parallel governing bodies: the official town council and municipal officers, who were all Ladinos, and a separate, officially tolerated Indian government. The Indian political system was intimately linked with a structure of religious offices connected with the celebration of religious fiestas.

The Indian governing structure was suppressed by the state government in 1932. At the same time, public celebrations of religious fiestas were prohibited, and new names were given to all towns formerly named after Catholic saints. Both the town and the municipio of San Bartolomé de los Llanos were renamed Venustiano Carranza; however, when speaking Spanish, Indians continued to call themselves San Bartoleños. The separate Indian political system was maintained but not publicly or legally recognized. Lay prayer leaders continued religious services, and saints' days were commemorated, but churches were padlocked and there were no public celebrations of religious fiestas.

Churches were reopened and fiesta celebration recommenced with the change of government in 1940, but there was no resident priest between 1932 and 1954. National emphasis on agrarian reform led to the creation of a series of *ejido* communities within the municipio in the 1930s. Most members of these new communities were Indians of San Bartolomé, but they also included some landless, poor Ladinos. The land base of the new ejidos was taken from lands claimed by the traditional Indian community. Ejido members moved away from the town center to new towns in their newly granted lands, but their Indian majorities recognized a spiritual connection to their former home. When town fiestas were reinstated, Indian ejido members participated and held religious offices.

Completion of a hydroelectric dam across the Río Grijalva in the early 1970s displaced several of the major ejido communities. Resettlement was undertaken by several agencies of government, with little coordination among them. The allocation of lands to the resettled communities was confused, and neighboring towns often made competing claims to the same lands. Ominously, some of the monetary compensation to the displaced communities went to purchasing weapons from international sources.

Disputes over access to land led to repeated armed conflict between opposing Indian groups beginning in 1976 and continuing ever since. As these groups gained armed strength, they also began taking back lands from Ladino ranchers. The largest group, successors to the traditional Indian community of the town center, took credit for the assassination of a well-known, politically powerful Ladino rancher in 1976. Others received death threats, and several Ladino leaders fled the town.

Traditionally, the Indian community looked inward, and Indians of other communities were not seen as having common interests. In the 1970s internal factions began to seek outside allies among other Indians. At the urging of political activists from Mexico City in the mid-1970s, three militant peasant organizations founded in Venustiano Carranza expanded to other towns. This led to increasing solidarity among Indian communities across Chiapas. Intracommunity relationships in recent years are also reflected in greater political participation at the national level.

The January 1994 uprising of the Zapatista Army of National Liberation (EZLN) intensified pan-Indian interaction both in support of official national policy and in opposition to it. Political openings arising from the Zapatista rebellion have been exploited by multicommunity peasant organizations, and San Bartoleños have played a prominent role. Ladinos have openly organized in resistance to Indian demands, and they have been raising private armies to intimidate Indian communities. The presence of about half of the entire Mexican army in Chiapas has complicated all of these conflicts.

By 1995 large areas within the municipio had gone out of production because of uncertainties about who would end up controlling them. Thousands of hectares of arable land changed hands in 1994, often because of extralegal seizures. Every month during 1994 groups of Indians occupied land as squatters, locally called "invaders." For a time, government agencies responded by paying landowners for the occupied lands, and then granting them to landless peasants, not necessarily the squatters who began the process. After the August 1994 elections, this program stopped. Private armies, organized by Ladino landholders, frequently were used to eject squatters. Just before planting time in 1995, a large group representing the San Bartolomé community attempted to occupy communal lands to which legal title had recently been reconfirmed. They were met by the army and state police. There were five deaths.

Settlements

San Bartolomé was founded as a nucleated town center that was the year-round place of residence for its inhabitants. By around 1900, most Indians resided on scattered estates held by Ladinos, returning to town for fiestas and other ceremonies. During the active phases of the Mexican Revolution (1915–1922 in this area), nearly all Indians returned to living in the town center. In the 1920s illegal land seizures by Ladinos forced most Indians into reliance on communal lands 16 kilometers or farther away from the town center.

The response was a new and unusual residence pattern. Women and children maintained the family's primary residence in the town, while men typically walked out to their distant maize fields on Mondays, slept there in rude shelters, and did not return to the town until Friday or Saturday. Most of the town-based Indians followed this pattern of periodic male absence until the 1980s, when improved roads and increasing Indian truck ownership made daily commuting feasible.

Two mid-sized colonies and a number of smaller settlements near the Río Grijalva were abandoned in the 1970s because of rising waters behind the new hydroelectric dam. Elsewhere in the municipio, rising population since the 1960s has led to the establishment of many new settlements.

Economy

Subsistence and Commercial Activities. The primary source of economic support in San Bartolomé is shifting cultivation of maize, beans, and squashes. Other cash crops are planted to a lesser degree. Most men with access to land produce much more than is consumed by their immediate families; the excess is sold for cash. In the late twentieth century, however, population pressure on land resources has left many younger men with nowhere to plant their own crops. Some work as agricultural laborers; their employers may be other Indians of the community, local Ladinos, or distant plantations. The Chiapas oil boom provided the opportunity for highly paid laboring jobs in the 1970s. Some of those who worked in the oil fields used their earnings to buy cargo trucks, either as individuals or as members of cooperatives. Indian truck owners began to displace Ladino middlemen in the purchase, transport, and resale of surplus Indian crops. They now provide alternative employment to drivers, loaders, and maintenance workers. Since the start of the Zapatista uprising, numbers of government programs have provided new job opportunities throughout the municipio. Nonetheless, unemployment and underemployment are increasing problems.

Although women do very hard work for very long hours in San Bartolomé, their work usually consists of unpaid household tasks. Women add to family cash income by planting gardens at their house sites, weaving for hire, selling in the market or door to door, or by paid domestic service in Ladino homes. Some are part-time curers and midwives, occupations that have been declining in importance since the establishment of a large public hospital at the edge of town. Except for those in domestic service, women usually are not fully self-supporting. Exceptions include small clusters of related women working in weavers' cooperatives and a small number of full-time tortilla makers.

Industrial Arts.   The only traditional craft recently practiced by men was the weaving of straw hats in a shape and pattern unique to the community. Only four or five men continue to make hats today. Although Indian men work as laborers in craft shops managed by Ladinos, custom and discrimination exclude them from the practice of skilled crafts. A few men work part-time as adobe brick makers; this is seen as more of a laborer's job than as a valued skill. Until the latter half of the twentieth century, most San Bartolomé women learned to be skilled weavers on the backstrap loom. They were also expected to be good at embroidery. The materials produced once were used to make shirts, blouses, men's trousers, and belts of the distinctive local costume. Since the mid-1960s, most men and many women of the community have begun to wear mass-produced clothing, except on special occasions. Women who continue to weave and embroider produce primarily for the national and tourist craft market.

Land Tenure.   Individuals may legally own private plots of arable land, and houses and house lots are individually owned. Most of the agricultural land base of the community is communally owned. Title to the core of this land is traceable to land grants of the fifteenth and sixteenth centuries. Ejidos that were formed in the 1930s received land carved from original holdings of the Indian community. New ejidos established since 1970 usually received land that was purchased by the government from private holdings, or lands of disputed ownership. Until 1992, ownership of both traditional communal lands and the land base of ejido communities was regarded as inalienable. Nonetheless, large areas of communal lands were effectively transferred into private holdings continuously from the 1920s onward. The seized lands were taken illegally and held by private armed force. Much of this force was applied on behalf of Ladino cattle ranchers, but armed groups of Indians also seized land for themselves out of lands belonging either to the traditional community or to various ejidos.

Kinship

Kin Groups and Descent.   Kinship in San Bartolomé is formally bilateral, but there is a slight bias toward patrilineality in practice. Family names are transmitted patrilineally; they take a binomial form in which the first surname is in Spanish, the second in Tzotzil. Each Tzotzil surname is linked to one and only one Spanish surname, but most Spanish surnames in local use are tied to more than one Tzotzil surname. There are no corporate social groups based on family names, but rules of exogamy prohibit marriage between two individuals with the same Tzotzil patronymic. Codescendants of the same grandparents may not marry.

Ritual kinship (*compadrazgo*) is established by the sponsorship of ceremonies, particularly child baptism. Primary relatives do not become *compadres*. After the ceremony, all the ancestors of a child being baptized and the current spouses of those ancestors still alive are regarded as compadres of the ritual sponsor and all of the sponsor's ancestors. Compadrazgo thus establishes an explicitly bounded corporate group, and the living members of the group have social functions as a group.

Kinship Terminology.   The cross-generational principle of age relative to Ego affects all terms for consanguineal relatives. For example, father's brother, brother, and brother's son are all called by the same term if they are older than Ego. Another term is used for younger brother and other collateral relatives younger than Ego, even if those relatives are in an ascending generation. Kinship terms and accompanying behavior emphasize the inequality between elder and younger consanguineal relatives. Affinal terms, on the other hand, are reciprocal and reflect status equality for those of the same generation relative to the couple whose marriage established the affinal relationship. Kinship is recognized bilaterally. Lineal relatives older than Ego are distinguished from collateral relatives. The line blurs among relatives younger than Ego, particularly in the second descending generation.

Although most terms are shared, the terminological system used by men is not the same as that used by women; differences include both the delineation of classes of relatives and individual lexical items. For example, men's terms for collateral relatives distinguish males from females when these are younger than Ego, whereas women use a single term for younger collaterals of both sexes. The women's term is not phonetically similar to either of the terms used by men.

In the case of ritual kinship, only the terms for ritual kin are used, even though compadres might also be related by birth or by marriage. Where there is neither ritual, nor consanguineal, nor affinal kinship, kinship terms for collateral relatives are extended to all members of the community on the basis of relative age. Kinship terminology used in this extended sense marks senior/junior status inequality. Only compadres and same-generation affinals are seen as equals.

Marriage and Family

Marriage.   Marriages are strictly monogamous, but marriage is not regarded as a permanent, lifelong relationship. Separation or divorce followed by a long-term relationship with a new partner is extremely common. For first marriages, marriage in San Bartolomé traditionally was arranged by a ritual exchange of visits and gifts between the parents of the bride and the groom. Girls usually were 14 or 15 at the time of an arranged marriage; boys married at 18 or later. Traditional arranged marriage is now rare, and marriages occur later. Marriage today includes civil marriage before municipal authorities, and church marriage, which by law requires civil marriage first. The relationship of a man and a woman who live together openly without any marriage ceremony is legally and socially equivalent to marriage with regard to the property and inheritance rights of both the couple and their children, as well as in the establishment of affinal links. If such a couple later separates, the rights of their children to support and inheritance from both biological parents continue. Despite Catholic doctrine, divorce and remarriage are as common for couples married in church as for anyone else.

At first marriage, newlyweds move in with an established domestic group, almost always that of a close relative of the bride or the groom. Preference is given to virilocal residence, but other arrangements are possible. Residence with relatives usually is for a limited time only, and most couples move to their own separate residence after the birth of their second child. For second and succeeding marriages, residence is usually neolocal.

Domestic Unit. The basic domestic and economic unit in San Bartolomé society is the household. A household usually contains a married couple at its center, together with their never-married children. Other spouseless adult relatives of the central couple may also function as members. Some households do not include adult men, but every man belongs to a household that includes an adult or nearly adult woman. When more than one married couple resides in a single house, they form separate households. Two coresident households under the same roof cook and eat separately and control their own funds and stored maize.

Inheritance. All children, male and female, of a deceased property owner are regarded as being entitled to equal shares in inheriting land, houses, and personal property. The spouse is usually excluded from inheritance as such, but title to jointly owned property remains exclusively with the surviving spouse. The spouse's children by another marriage, even if they were living with or being supported by the deceased at the time of death, are not entitled to a share of the estate. Older individuals may convey real estate or major possessions to individual heirs while alive, but both custom and legal practice hold that other heirs are entitled to equivalent shares of property when the owner dies. The anticipatory heir may keep the property without division if the transfer was in payment for services rendered.

Socialization. At about the age of 3, or when their next younger siblings are born, children are given over to the care of siblings aged 5 or 6 or more. When newlyweds move in with relatives, children of other coresident households are available for child care when the time comes. Neolocal residence is sought when a couple's first child is old enough to care for a younger sibling. Deference to one's elders is fundamental in all social interaction. At all ages, younger people are not supposed to initiate interaction with their elders, or ask questions unless conveying the request of an older person. Discipline usually is by scolding or ridicule, but physical punishment is sometimes used.

Children are expected to learn new tasks by observing others and by following instructions and orders from their elders. Boys are taken to the maize fields beginning at age 10 or 11, where they work under their fathers' direction.

Under virilocal residence, a mother-in-law is a disciplinarian to her coresident daughter-in-law, but also is responsible for teaching her the fine points of weaving and other domestic skills. In the late twentieth century most Indian children have been expected to attend formal school at least through sixth grade. School classes are conducted in Spanish, and most teachers do not speak Tzotzil.

Sociopolitical Organization

Until 1932, Indian San Bartolomé had a typically Mesoamerican system of a civil-religious hierarchy. Political groups were territorially based; recruitment to leadership was through ceremonial organizations.

The significant unit of interaction in the territorial system was the *sitio*, a group composed of all households living on a single bounded house site. The owner of the sitio, if male, or the owner's husband, if the owner was a woman, was effectively the leader of the group. Contiguous sitios formed neighborhoods; the centers of these neighborhoods were known to all, but their peripheries were only vaguely distinguished. Neighborhoods were potential support groups behind individual leaders. Neighborhoods in the Indian areas of the town were divided into five barrios, larger areas with explicit boundaries. Each barrio recognized a legitimated group of leaders. Finally, the Indian community as a whole was divided into two endogamous moieties: the "upper" section, consisting of the barrios of Calvario, San Sebastián, and Convento, and the "lower" section, those of Señor del Pozo and San Pedro. "Upper" and "lower" referred to elevation on the mountainside, not to status.

Ceremonial groups were organized in a single status hierarchy. Each of the five barrios had a ceremonial organization to celebrate its annual fiesta. Similar organizations at the community level were dedicated to saints and the celebration of their fiestas. Each fiesta group had four ranked officers, the *mayordomos*. Higher status groups had additional upper-level officers, *alcaldes* and *alféreces*. Many groups also enlisted temporary participants for their annual fiesta day.

Men accrued status and power through periodic service in named offices at rising levels in the fiesta groups. Officeholding required a man to be joined by his wife or a relative able to provide equivalent services. Officeholders paid all the expenses of monthly public ceremonies and the annual fiesta; their wives prepared food for participants and onlookers. Each successive level of service required larger expenditures; the highest office, *alférez* of San Bartolomé, cost the equivalent of several years' income.

Men were required to serve up to four times as mayordomos as they accumulated enough surplus to pay the cost. Prayer leaders and ritual musicians were permanently exempt from mayordomo service, and those who accepted public ritual roles for the day of a major fiesta were exempt from other service that year. Once a man had been mayordomo four times, he became a *pasado*, one who had passed through. He did not have to serve again. Pasados with certain Tzotzil surnames had hereditary eligibility to take on higher ceremonial offices if they chose, but they could not be required to do so. A pasado who served in three higher offices became a *principal,* a legitimated leader entitled to both decision-making power and ritual deference.

San Bartolomé had a town council of six *regidores* and an alcalde; these named political offices were alternated annually between moieties. These offices conferred no decision-making power; any communitywide decisions were made by the principales. Internal disputes at the community level were adjudicated by principales; they also controlled interchanges with outsiders. They had the power to arrest and jail Indians, to assess fines and penalties, and to expel community members. Each barrio was led by a council consisting of all principales of the barrio. They exercised similar power within the barrio.

Specific portions of communal lands were assigned to each barrio and controlled by barrio principales. Members of other barrios within the same moiety were granted usufruct without payment, but men from the other moiety had to pay for the right to use barrio lands. In rare cases in which a man wanted to marry across moiety lines, he had to get permission of the principales of his potential spouse's moiety.

Traditional recruitment to the rank of principal ended in 1932 when fiestas were banned and the Indian government was suppressed. In the final years of the old system, a young Indian who was literate in Spanish was hired by the Indian government to serve as communal scribe. He used his control of paperwork to insert himself as cultural broker between the Indian community and the outside world. The scribe was not a principal, but the links he set up with principales from all five barrios gave him a unique support base, which he converted into effective political power. His example and his day-to-day political maneuvering encouraged others to seek power by nontraditional means.

New-style leaders accumulated power through multiplying dyadic links of several kinds. The core of their support came from control of a sitio group and from close consanguineal kin. From this base, leaders recruited supporters by managing strategic marriages to gain the support of new affines. They solicited ritual kinship to bind others to the support group. Emerging leaders made special efforts to link up with close neighbors, and with traditional-style principales. Leaders also encouraged possible followers to work fields close to their own. The initial labor investment in clearing a field would only be repaid if the same field were planted several years in a row. Shared tasks and close association in the milpas over the years led to particularly solid relationships. Of course, every man had many individual ties to birth, affinal, and ritual kin, as well as to neighbors both in town and in the fields. What marked the new style of leader was the conscious doubling and tripling of such links by means such as inviting work companions to become compadres, marrying a daughter to a neighbor, and encouraging close kin to join a work group in the fields. Those bound to a rising leader through multiple links became his solid support group and the source of his power.

When open celebrations of fiestas returned in 1940, they were organized by the new-style leaders, and old-style principales took a secondary role. It was no longer possible to jail or fine men for refusing to take ceremonial offices. Instead, expenses of fiestas were paid by public contributions, barrio by barrio.

Organized by the new leaders, all the barrio principales went in a body from house to house collecting payments for the fiestas. Since acting mayordomos no longer faced large cash outlays, men were willing to serve voluntarily. The major barrio fiestas are still celebrated, but some other fiestas are extinct, and the remainder have not had mayordomos for many years.

Gradually, the new-style leaders took over control from the traditional principales in landholding organizations as well as in the fiestas. Indeed, they came to be called principales even though none of them had completed the requisite service. They continued to show ritual deference to the old-style principales, and were not themselves shown the same kind of deference. Still, the new-style principales became the recognized leaders of the community. The five barrios continue as significant political subunits. The barrios of each moiety of the past continue as allies against the barrios of the opposite moiety.

Beginning in the 1970s, competing groups of new-style principales have sought support from competing national organizations. Affiliates of the Confederación Nacional Campesina (CNC), essentially a subunit of the reigning Institutional Revolutionary party (PRI), formed "La Casa del Pueblo." With help from CNC organizers, they seized control of the main communal lands and ejected those who did not accept the leadership of CNC-linked principales. Others broke away, joining established ejido with support from the National Institute of Agrarian Reform in taking over other communal land. Other leaders took their followers into militant statewide peasant groups, "invading" both Indian and Ladino landholdings. These invasions at times led to transfer of land titles to members of the occupying group; sometimes such a group holds control by armed force without legal title. Struggles over land are now the principal arena of San Bartolomé politics.

Religion and Expressive Culture

San Bartoleños are Catholics. Resident priests lead Catholic services, perform church weddings, and teach Catholic doctrine. Folk Catholicism is practiced alongside the Catholicism of the priests, often without their approval. Protestant converts and families who became Jehovah's Witnesses in the 1940s were promptly denied access to communal lands and ejected from their homes in the Indian barrios.

The cult of San Miguel Arcángel illustrates syncretistic folk Catholicism. San Miguel has two feast days, one in early May, the other in late September, bracketing the local rainy season. Each fiesta is marked by a pilgrimage to the top of the mountain above Venustiano Carranza, a climb that takes more than an hour. Three large wooden crosses mark the place of celebration. The mountaintop rituals are led by Indians; priests do not attend. Tojolab'al speakers walk about 100 kilometers to participate, praying to San Miguel for rain. There are frequent explosions of ceremonial mortars and skyrockets, reputedly "to call the thunder." San Miguel clearly represents a rain god. Other saints and holy images also show syncretism, and Tzotzil prayers dedicated to them use the names and attributes of pre-Hispanic Maya deities.

Church-centered fiestas also have syncretistic elements. Riders wearing costumes recalling eighteenth-century Spanish dress run ritual races at three fiestas. The beginning of Lent is marked by a costumed dance-drama reenacting the conquest of Chiapas by Spain. Saints' images are dressed in Indian clothes on their feast days. More private rites, such as the dedication of a new house, may include prayers led by a priest at one point and the sacrifice and ritual burial of a chicken after the priest leaves.

Religio-medical beliefs affect much of what San Bartoleños do. According to those beliefs, every illness and misfortune has two simultaneous causes: those visible in the normal world and those coming from supernatural actions. Visible causes call for mundane remedies, such as treatment in a modern hospital. Supernatural causes (evil eye, witchcraft, magical fright, or soul loss) require supernatural treatment by ritual specialists and traditional healers. Much of ritual behavior is connected to beliefs about supernatural effects of interpersonal relationships.

Envy causes disease directly and is the most common pernicious supernatural force in society. Involuntary evil eye may indirectly bewitch a person. Anyone who has good fortune or who exhibits wealth publicly is a natural target for envy. In consequence, San Bartoleños are reluctant to take political or ceremonial office. Publicly visible individuals who suffer no ill show by that fact that they have strong spirits and enough power to defend themselves against supernatural attack. People believe that defensive power only comes from the power to cause misfortune to others; therefore, the visible person who survives envy must have witchcraft power. Witches who do not correct or legitimate their behavior are shunned and may be killed. Becoming a principal shows great supernatural power, contained by legitimization. Nonetheless, principales are individually feared.

Bibliography

Morales Avendano, Segundo Juan Maria (1977). _Evolución y tenencia de la tierra en San Bartolomé de los Llanos._ Venustiano Carranza: Editorial Fray Bartolomé de las Casas.

Morales Avendano, Segundo Juan Maria (1986). _San Bartolomé de los Llanos en la historia de Chiapas._ Tuxtla Gutiérrez: Universidad Autónoma de Chiapas.

Moscoso Pastrana, Prudencio (1992). _Rebeliones indígenas en los altos de Chiapas._ Mexico City: Universidad Nacional Autónoma de México, Centro de Investigaciones Humanísticas de Mesoamerica y del Estado de Chiapas.

Salovesh, Michael (1971). "The Political System of a Highland Maya Community: A Study in the Methodology of Political Analysis." Ph.D. dissertation, University of Chicago.

Wasserstrom, Robert (1983). _Class and Society in Central Chiapas._ Berkeley and Los Angeles: University of California Press.

MICHAEL SALOVESH

Tzotzil of Zinacantan

ETHNONYMS: Sotz'leb (Tzotzil), Zinacantecos (Spanish), Zinacantecs (English)

Orientation

Identification. Zinacantan is one of twenty-one Tzotzil-speaking _municipios_ in the state of Chiapas in southeastern Mexico. The name "Zinacantan" derives from the pre-Columbian epoch when Aztec traders named the region and its people "Tzinacantlan," meaning "place of bats" in Nahuatl. Zinacantecos refer to themselves as "Sotz'leb," meaning "people of the bat" in Tzotzil.

Location. The municipio of Zinacantan, an area of 117 square kilometers, is located along the north and south sides of the Pan-American Highway approximately 10 kilometers west of the city of San Cristóbal de las Casas in the central highlands of Chiapas. These rugged limestone and volcanic mountains rise to over 2,900 meters. The ceremonial and political center of Zinacantan is located at 16°45′ N and 92°42′ W. Chiapas has marked wet and dry seasons. During the winter dry season, the days are sunny and warm and the nights cold, with occasional frost. During the summer, the heavy rains provide a mean annual rainfall of 129 centimeters, the sky is frequently overcast, and it is generally cool. Magnificent stands of pine and oak cover the higher elevations. At lower elevations, oaks replace the pines, and the oaks in turn give way to tropical broadleaf forest and savanna in the hot lowlands of the Río Grijalva.

Demography. In 1994 Zinacantan had an estimated population of 22,000, a dramatic increase over the 7,650 Zinacantecos reported in the national census of 1960.

Linguistic Affiliation. Tzotzil is one of the twenty-nine Mayan languages spoken by over 5 million Indians—the descendants of the ancient Maya—who live in Chiapas, the Yucatán Peninsula of Mexico, Guatemala, and Belize. Tzotzil is most closely related to the Tzeltal that is spoken in municipios to the east of the Tzotzil area in the Chiapas highlands. Linguists classify the two together as the Tzeltalan languages.

History and Cultural Relations

Linguistic and archaeological data indicate that the Tzeltalan ancestors of the contemporary Tzotzil and Tzeltal moved into their present habitat in Chiapas by A.D. 300, perhaps as early as 100 B.C. Over time, they differentiated into Tzotzil speakers and Tzeltal speakers, and ultimately into the groups that became incorporated into the municipalities that were established by the Spaniards. Spanish chronicles report that Aztec traders came to Zinacantan in the decades before the Conquest to trade for quetzal feathers and amber, which were prized in the Aztec capital of Tenochtitlán.

The Spanish conquerors reached the highlands of Chiapas in 1523. The first Spanish colony, Villa Real, was founded first at Chiapa de Corzo and soon moved to the cooler site of San Cristóbal de las Casas in 1528. Whereas the neighboring Chamula fought ferociously against the Spanish forces led by Diego de Mazariegos, the Zinacantecos appear to have yielded to, and later assisted, the Spanish penetration. Specific mentions of Zinacantan in the early post-Conquest period emphasize their trading activities and religious rituals. The trading of salt from wells near Ixtapa, northwest of Zinacantan Center, which was then resold in markets throughout the Chiapas highlands, was probably pre-Hispanic and continued during colonial and modern times. A Spanish chronicler described Zinacantan as a pueblo with "an infinite number of gods; they worshiped the sun and offered sacrifices to it, and to the full rivers, to the springs, to the trees of heavy foliage, and to the high hills they gave incense and gifts ... their ancestors discovered a stone bat and considered it God and worshiped it" (Ximenez 1929–1931, 360).

During the colonial period, Zinacantan was subject to missionary activity by the Catholic friars, and many Zinacantecos became peons on the large estates that had evolved from the earlier *encomiendas* owned by the descendants of the conquering Spaniards. In 1592 Zinacantan was called "El Pueblo de Santo Domingo," but by 1792 the community was called "San Lorenzo Zinacantan," signaling that Saint Lawrence had replaced Saint Dominic as patron saint. Chiapas was part of Guatemala until (following Mexico's independence from Spain) it seceded and joined Mexico in 1824. When President Benito Juarez came to power in 1863, the Leyes de Reforma stripped both the church and the Indian towns of their corporate lands. Many Zinacantecos lost their ancestral lands and were forced into debt-indentured labor on haciendas owned by the Ladinos in the lowlands. These Ladinos, who were descendants of the Spanish conquerors interbred with Indians over the centuries, speak Spanish, live mainly in the towns and cities, and control the economic and political system of Chiapas.

The three most important recent historical events in their impact on Zinacantan have been: the *ejido* program stemming from the Mexican Revolution (1910–1921) which provided long-delayed additional farming lands for the Zinacantecos beginning in 1940; the construction of the Pan-American Highway (completed in 1954), which passes through the municipio of Zinacantan and provides access to markets by truck and bus; and the establishment of the Instituto Nacional Indigenista (National Indian Institute) center in 1950 in San Cristóbal de las Casas, which was followed by various federal programs to improve the quality of Indian life in the highlands of Chiapas. Zinacantecos are aware of the 1992 provisions allowing the privatization of ejidos; there has been no immediate move to change the status of their landholdings.

Settlements

Zinacantan has a dispersed settlement pattern, with a ceremonial and political center and twenty-six outlying hamlets. The ceremonial center, usually called "Zinacantan" in Spanish or "Htek-lum" (meaning literally "the land of a group from one set of ancestors") in Tzotzil, is located in a well-watered mountain valley at 2,252 meters, with the hamlets at elevations ranging from 2,580 meters down to 1,600 meters. The 1982 population of the center was 2,269. Hamlets varied in population from the largest—Nachih (2,221), Paste' (2,093), and Navenchauk (1,122)—to the smallest—Icalum (152), Comlum (113), and Tzum El (99). Some hamlets are compact in settlement, others more dispersed, the crucial variables being the terrain and availability of household water in the dry season. Even in compact hamlets, houses are never wall-to-wall. Each extended family constructs a cluster of houses in a compound surrounded by a maize field and separated from neighboring families. House plots are normally inherited by the sons of the family head, and women move into the compounds of their husbands. Houses are usually rectangular, one-room constructions. The traditional house had wattle-and-daub walls and a steep, four-sided roof, thatched with grass. Modern houses are of adobe brick or cinder block roofed with tile. The fire—burning within the area enclosed by the three hearthstones that hold the griddle for cooking maize tortillas and support the pots of boiling beans or squashes—is located on the floor, normally toward the setting-sun side of the house, the domain of the women. The men's domain, which is toward the rising sun, is where they keep their belongings and sometimes set up an altar containing images or pictures of saints. Since these one-room houses normally have only one or two doors and no windows, they are often smoky. Men sit on small wooden chairs or benches, women on the ground. The members of the family sleep on reed mats placed on platform beds or on the floor.

Economy

Subsistence and Commercial Activities.   Until recently the Zinacantecos were almost all agriculturists, growing crops of maize, beans, and squashes, which were cultivated by swidden agriculture using axes, machetes, planting sticks, and hoes. Sheep are owned and herded by women to provide wool for weaving ponchos and shawls. Chickens are kept both for their eggs (to sell) and to eat, especially on ritual occasions. Although families who own sufficient land continue to farm maize, an increasing number of Zinacantecos have gone into a variety of alternative enterprises, such as wage work on highways and in construction, driving trucks and buses, and cultivating flowers and fruit for urban markets. Many Zinacantecos have also become merchants, buying and selling maize, beans, fruit, and flowers. Most households have a mix of off-farm and on-farm production.

Industrial Arts.   The most notable craft is weaving, which is performed by women on backstrap looms on which they weave both the cotton and the wool clothing that is worn by both sexes. Zinacanteco clothing is distinctive in the Chiapas highlands, instantly recognizable from the abundant use of red cotton threads and wool dyed bright red. Men weave their hats from white and black strips of palm or plastic, adorning them with long, flowing red ribbons reminiscent of the feathered headdresses worn by the ancient Maya. Women traditionally go barefoot, whereas men wear sandals purchased in San Cristóbal and, on ceremonial occasions, high-backed sandals manufactured by Chamula artisans. In the 1960s many men began to wear purchased, European-style clothing, especially when away from their homes.

Division of Labor. In the Zinacanteco view, men are the maize growers, women the tortilla makers. Men do all of the field work, tend large animals (e.g., the horses or mules used as pack animals), build the houses, hold all of the political offices and most of the religious posts. Women cook, fetch water and wood, herd sheep, weave, hold a few of the ritual offices—some shamans and all of the "incense-bearers" are women—and assist their husbands in their _cargo_ duties. Children are cared for by the women, but men assist when they are at home.

Land Tenure. In theory, all land is owned by the ancestors and transmitted to descendants within patrilineages each generation. Although Mexican law stipulates that daughters must also receive shares of the land inheritance, the choice lands for houses and farming are in fact transmitted to sons, whereas daughters (who will be supported by their husbands) are given plots on steep hillsides.

Kinship

Kin Groups and Descent. The basic unit of the social structure is the domestic group composed of kin who live together in a house compound and share a single maize supply. Each of these domestic groups is symbolized by the "house cross" that is erected outside the principal house in the compound and serves as the ritual entrance to the house. The exact composition of the domestic group varies as the unit moves through developmental cycles and responds to economic and social pressures. The nuclear family has become increasingly prevalent as Zinacantecos have become involved more in outside wage labor and less in traditional farming at home, a trend that began in the 1960s and accelerated in the 1980s.

The domestic groups are embedded in two other crucial social units—the localized lineage and the water-hole group—which are in turn grouped into hamlets. The localized lineage is composed of one or more patrilineages that are extensions of patrilineally extended families. The water-hole groups consist of a series of localized lineages living around a communal water hole, from which they draw water for livestock and for household use. Each of these localized lineages and water-hole groups maintains a number of cross shrines—some on hills and mountains, for praying to their ancestors, and some in caves, for making offerings to the Earth Lord.

Kinship Terminology. Age, gender, and generation are strongly reflected in kin terms. The terms "older brother" (_bankilal_) and "younger brother" (_its'inal_) are of such importance that they are used as a general principle for classifying much of the universe, including sacred mountains, musical instruments, and saints, which are thus placed in pairs—one "older" and the other "younger." Much respect is tendered older people, who are addressed as "father" (_htot_) and "mother" (_hme'_). Affinal terms are proliferated and commonly used. Ritual kinship is universal as "co-father" (_compadre_) and "comother" (_comadre_) terms acquired during Catholic baptisms and confirmations are extended to all of the people who sit together at ritual meals following these ceremonies or weddings. All adults linked by this system of ritual kinship are strongly bonded and may count on one another for political support, loans of money, and assistance in ceremonies.

Marriage and Family

Marriage. The patterns of courtship and marriage are innovative creations deriving from both ancient Tzotzil and sixteenth-century Spanish Catholic practices. A formal petitioning for the bride is followed by a lengthy courtship, during which gifts are presented by the boy's family to the girl's family. On the wedding day, the couple goes through a triple ritual process of registering at the town hall, then having a Catholic priest marry them in the church, and finally attending an elaborate Tzotzil ceremony at the house of the groom. The bride is then left in her new home. Since the 1980s, a majority of Zinacantecos have been eloping, thereby reducing the time and expense for all concerned.

Socialization. All Zinacanteco babies are born at home with the aid of midwives, who attend the mother, assist in the birth (which takes place in a crouching position, over a reed mat), cut the umbilical cord with a machete, and perform the necessary after-birth rituals. Babies are kept constantly with their mothers, nursing, wrapped in shawls and carried on their mothers' backs, or asleep beside their mothers in bed. After a few months, the infants' contacts are expanded to include members of the extended family. By age 7 or 8, girls begin to work for the household; at 9 or 10, boys begin to accompany their fathers to work in the fields.

Sociopolitical Organization

The Mexican municipio structure has been imposed upon the ancient Tzotzil political system. In the town hall in Zinacantan Center, a set of ranked officials (_presidente, sindico_, four _alcalde jueces_, and nine _regidores_) serve three-year terms to carry out their political duties, including collecting funds for and supervising public works and settling disputes among Zinacantecos. In the hamlets there are official representatives of the governing town hall in Zinacantan Center; some hamlets also now have an official _agente_, who can perform many of the duties of the presidente, including holding court and settling disputes.

Religion and Expressive Culture

Religious Beliefs. The mountainous terrain that reaches into the clouds of highland Chiapas is the visible surface of the Zinacanteco world, which is conceived of as a large, flat quincunx in quadrilateral form. The center of this surface is the "navel," a mound of earth located in the ceremonial center. The world rests on the shoulders of the Vashak-Men, the local version of the "Four-Corner Gods" or "Sky-Bearers" of the ancient Maya. Below the visible world is the "Lower World," inhabited by a race of dwarfs who, along with monkeys, were made in the past when the gods unsuccessfully attempted to create real men. In the sky above the earth is the domain of the Sun, the Moon, and the Stars. The Sun, called "Our Father Heat," travels on a path that encircles the earth each day. Preceded by the "Sweeper of the Path" (Venus), the Sun appears in the morning, pauses at high noon to survey the affairs of the Zinacantecos, and disappears in the evening. The Moon, called "Our Holy Mother," travels on a similar path around the world. Under the influence of Spanish Catholicism, the Zinacantecos have come to associate the Sun with God the Father or Jesus Christ and the Moon with the Virgin Mary. The quincuncial model of the cosmos is reflected in the rites performed for houses and fields—the ceremonial circuits proceed counterclockwise around the four corners and end in the center, where offerings are made to the gods. Hills and mountains located near Zinacanteco settlements are the homes of ancestral gods, called "Fathers-Mothers," who are the most important deities of all. It is impossible to pray in Tzotzil to a male or female ancestor; the name for these gods is Totilme'il, literally translated as "Sir Father–Madam Mother," with the father image always linked to the mother image, indicating a unitary concept representing the primordial reproductive pair. These ancestors provide the ideal models for human life. Next to the ancestral gods, the most important deity is the Earth Lord. He is pictured as a large, fat Ladino living under the ground with piles of money, herds of livestock, and flocks of chickens. He owns the water holes and all the earth products used by Zinacantecos—trees and mud to build houses and limestone for lime. A person cannot use land or its products without compensating the Earth Lord with appropriate offerings in a ceremony.

In the centuries since the Conquest, the Zinacantecos have acquired over seventy sacred objects that they call "Saints," including carved wooden or plaster images of Catholic saints and pictures of saints. The images are clothed in long, flowing robes derived from colonial styles, but almost all have some item of Zinacanteco dress. The most important have distinctive personalities, and there are special myths about how they came to be in Zinacantan. Shrines composed of large wooden crosses, including one called a kalvaryo, where the ancestral gods have their weekly meetings, are also sacred.

Interaction between living Zinacantecos and their gods takes place via two types of souls that are possessed by each human being: a ch'ulel and a chanul. The ch'ulel is an inner, personal soul, located in the heart; it is also found in the blood, which is known to be connected with the heart. It is placed in the unborn embryo by the ancestral gods. This Zinacanteco "inner soul" has special attributes. It is composed of thirteen parts, and a person who loses one or more of these parts must have a curing ceremony performed by a shaman to recover them. At death, the inner soul leaves the body and ultimately joins a pool of souls that is kept by the ancestors. It is later utilized for another person. "Soul loss" is caused by fright, which can be engendered by falling down or seeing a demon on a dark night. At a more profound level, soul loss is believed to be due to the ancestral gods, who, in order to punish misbehavior, cause a person to fall down or send a lightning bolt to knock out parts of the soul; it may also be caused by an evil person who performs witchcraft in order to sell the soul to the Earth Lord for use as a servant.

The inner soul of a person, the ch'ulel, is shared with a chanul, a wild animal, which is an animal-spirit companion. Throughout each person's life, whatever happens to the animal spirit also happens to the person and vice versa. These animal-spirit companions, consisting of jaguars, ocelots, coyotes, and smaller animals such as squirrels and opossums, are kept by the ancestral gods in four corrals inside "Senior Large Mountain," east of Zinacantan Center. If the animal spirit is turned out of the corral by the ancestral gods, the person is in mortal danger and must undergo a lengthy ceremony to round up the chanul and return it to its corral.

Religious Practitioners.   The religious rites in Zinacantan Center are performed by a religious hierarchy, or "cargo system," consisting of sixty-one positions at four levels of a ceremonial ladder. To ascend the ladder, men must serve a year at each of the levels—mayordomos and mayores; alfereces; regidores (not to be confused with the civil regidores at the town hall); and alcaldes (again, not the same as the political alcalde jueces). During the year he spends at each level, a man is expected to move from his hamlet into the Ceremonial Center and engage in a complex and expensive round of ceremonies. An increasing number of the first-level cargos are now being served in the hamlets, however, most of which have local chapels. Many of the ceremonies, especially those of the mayordomos, take place in the Catholic churches, two of which are located in the Ceremonial Center—the church of Saint Lawrence and the church of Saint Sebastian; other cargo ceremonies occur in the hamlets. The Center also has a chapel dedicated to Señor Esquipulas (a Christ-on-the-cross image connected to the salt trade in Guatemala and in Zinacantan), in which additional ceremonies, especially office-changing rites, are performed by cargoholders. Other ceremonial practitioners carry out ritual and political duties in the hamlets—these are the h'iloletik, or "shamans." The word h'ilol means "seer," signifying that the shamans have the power to look into the mountains and see the ancestral gods. There are now more than 300 shamans in Zinacantan, all ranked in order of the time that has elapsed since their debuts (following their dreams of being called before the ancestral gods and instructed as to how to perform their ceremonies).

Ceremonies.   Two basic types of ceremonies are performed: the rituals of the cargoholders in Zinacantan Center, which follow the annual Catholic calendar of saints' days, and the rites of the shamans, which include curing illnesses, dedicating new houses, blessing maize fields, making offerings to lineage and water-hole group ancestral deities, renewing the year, and rainmaking.

Death and Afterlife.   At death, the body is washed and placed in a pine coffin with various offerings, including a chicken head, representing the chicken who will guide the inner soul of the deceased to the other world. Burial takes place in a cemetery located near the hamlet. Interaction with the deceased continues for many years, as the descendants light candles and leave offerings at the grave each Sunday and on All Saints' Day.

Bibliography

Borhegyi, Stephan F. (1953). "The Miraculous Shrines of Our Lord of Esquipulas in Guatemala and Chimayo, Mexico." El Palacio 60:83–111.

Borhegyi, Stephan F. (1954). "The Cult of Our Lord of Esquipulas in Middle America and Mexico." El Palacio 61:387–401.

Breedlove, Dennis E., and Robert M. Laughlin (1993). *The Flowering of Man: A Tzotzil Botany of Zinacantan*. Smithsonian Contributions to Anthropology, no. 35. Washington, D.C.: Smithsonian Institution Press.

Bricker, Victoria R. (1973). *Ritual Humor in Highland Chiapas*. Austin: University of Texas Press.

Bricker, Victoria R. (1981). *The Indian Christ and the Indian King: The Historical Substrate of Maya Myth and Ritual*. Austin: University of Texas Press.

Bricker, Victoria R., and Gary H. Gossen, eds. (1989). *Ethnographic Encounters in Southern Mesoamerica: Essays in Honor of Evon Zartman Vogt, Jr.* Austin: University of Texas Press.

Cancian, Francesca M. (1975). *What Are Norms? A Study of Beliefs and Action in a Maya Community*. Cambridge: Cambridge University Press.

Cancian, Frank (1965). *Economics and Prestige in a Maya Community: The Religious Cargo System in Zinacantan*. Stanford, Calif.: Stanford University Press.

Cancian, Frank (1972). *Change and Uncertainty in a Peasant Community: The Maya Corn Farmers of Zinacantan*. Stanford, Calif.: Stanford University Press.

Cancian, Frank (1992). *The Decline of Community in Zinacantan: Economy, Public Life, and Social Stratification, 1960–1987*. Stanford, Calif.: Stanford University Press.

Colby, Benjamin N. (1966). *Ethnic Relations in the Chiapas Highlands*. Santa Fe: Museum of New Mexico Press.

Collier, George A. (1975). *Fields of the Tzotzil: The Ecological Basis of Tradition in Highland Chiapas*. Austin: University of Texas Press.

Collier, Jane F. (1973). *Law and Social Change in Zinacantan*. Stanford, Calif.: Stanford University Press.

Fabrega, Horacio, Jr., and Daniel B. Silver (1973). *Illness and Shamanistic Curing in Zinacantan: An Ethnomedical Analysis*. Stanford, Calif.: Stanford University Press.

Haviland, John B. (1977). *Gossip, Reputation, and Knowledge in Zinacantan*. Chicago: University of Chicago Press.

Haviland, John B. (1981). *Sk'op sotz'leb: El tzotzil de San Lorenzo Zinacantan*. Mexico City: Universidad Nacional Autónoma de México, Instituto de Investigaciones Filologicas.

Laughlin, Robert M. (1975). *The Great Tzotzil Dictionary of San Lorenzo Zinacantan*. Smithsonian Contributions to Anthropology, no. 19. Washington, D.C.: Smithsonian Institution Press.

Laughlin, Robert M. (1976). *Of Wonders Wild and New: Dreams from Zinacantan*. Smithsonian Contributions to Anthropology, no. 22. Washington, D.C.: Smithsonian Institution Press.

Laughlin, Robert M. (1977). *Of Cabbages and Kings: Tales from Zinacantan*. Smithsonian Contributions to Anthropology, no. 23. Washington, D.C.: Smithsonian Institution Press.

Laughlin, Robert M. (1980). *Of Shoes and Ships and Sealing Wax: Sundries from Zinacantan*. Smithsonian Contributions to Anthropology, no. 25. Washington, D.C.: Smithsonian Institution Press.

Laughlin, Robert M. (1988). *The Great Tzotzil Dictionary of Santo Domingo Zinacantan*. Smithsonian Institution Contributions to Anthropology, no. 31. Washington, D.C.: Smithsonian Institution Press.

Vogt, Evon Z. (1969). *Zinacantan: A Maya Community in the Highlands of Chiapas*. Cambridge: Harvard University Press, Belknap Press.

Vogt, Evon Z. (1978). *Bibliography of the Harvard Chiapas Project: The First Twenty Years, 1957–1977*. Cambridge: Harvard University, Peabody Museum of American Archaeology and Ethnology.

Vogt, Evon Z. (1990). *The Zinacantecos of Mexico: A Modern Maya Way of Life*. 2nd ed. Fort Worth, Tex.: Holt, Rinehart & Winston.

Vogt, Evon Z. (1993). *Tortillas for the Gods: A Symbolic Analysis of Zinacanteco Rituals*. Norman: University of Oklahoma Press.

Vogt, Evon Z. (1994). *Fieldwork among the Maya: Reflections on the Harvard Chiapas Project*. Albuquerque: University of New Mexico Press.

Vogt, Evon Z., ed. (1966). *Los zinacantecos: Un pueblo tzotzil de los altos de Chiapas*. Mexico City: Instituto Nacional Indigenista.

Vogt, Evon Z., ed. (1974). *Aerial Photography in Anthropological Field Research*. Cambridge: Harvard University Press.

Wasserstrom, Robert F. (1983). *Class and Society in Central Chiapas*. Berkeley and Los Angeles: University of California Press.

Wood, Elena Uribe (1982). *Compadrazgo en Apas*. Mexico City: Instituto Nacional Indigenista.

Ximenez, Francisco (1929–1931). *Historia de la provincia de San Vicente de Chiapa y Guatemala de la orden de nuestro glorioso padre Santo Domingo*. 3 vols. Guatemala City: Tipografia Nacional.

EVON Z. VOGT

Tz'utujil

ETHNONYMS: Maya, Vinuk

Orientation

Identification. The Tz'utujil are a Mayan population inhabiting Guatemala's central highland region. The various Tz'utujil communities tend to be separated by high volcanoes, precipitous cliffs, and expansive lake surfaces. In part reflecting geographical obstacles to easy interaction, the primary linkage between the communities is linguistic rather than social. Tz'utujil refer to themselves as "Vinuk" (lit., twenty; named being), which can be glossed to mean "the people."

Location. The Tz'utujil communities are clustered along the south and west shores of Lake Atitlán, as well as just to the south of the Lake Atitlán basin in the town of Chicacao. In addition, Tz'utujil speakers constitute minority populations in several nearby non-Mayan coastal communities. Certainly the defining feature of the Tz'utujil territory is Lake Atitlán, which lies at an average elevation of 1,545 meters above sea level. The communities along the shore of the lake occupy a border zone between tropical and mesothermal environments. Rains are monsoonal, with the wet season running from May to November. In its natural state, the vegetation is primarily chaparral and oak-pine forest, although much of the arable land has been diverted to the cultivation of maize and coffee.

Demography. In 1994, following nearly a century of explosive population growth, there were approximately 70,000 Tz'utujil. In contrast, a post-Conquest demographic collapse triggered by the introduction of Old World diseases brought about a decline in population that did not bottom out until around 1780, when the number of Tz'utujil was about 10 percent of its pre-Conquest number. Although the Tz'utujil population would not regain its pre-Conquest level until the mid-1960s, since that time it has more than doubled.

Linguistic Affiliation. The name "Tz'utujil" means "flower of the maize plant." Tz'utujil is a language of the Greater Quichean Branch of the Eastern Division of Mayan languages and is most closely related to Kaqchikel, K'iche', Sakapulteko, and Sipakapense. Even among the various Tz'utujil communities, there is lexical, phonological, morphological, and syntactic variation in the use of the language. Exemplifying that variation, the people of Santiago Atitlán claim that only they speak the true form of the language, what they invariably refer to as "Ktz'oj' bal," *the* language. In contrast, they claim that the people of San Pedro la Laguna speak Pedrano, those of San Juan speak Juanero, and so on. In addition to the indigenous language, more than half of the Tz'utujil are at least conversant in Spanish.

History and Cultural Relations

Although the Lake Atitlán region has been inhabited for at least several thousand years, the Tz'utujil did not enter the area until the Late Postclassic period (A.D. 1200–1524).

According the ancient K'iche' book *Popol Vuh*, the Tz'utujil were the first of a wave of conquering groups to arrive in the area during that period. The point of origin of those migrants remains conjectural, but it was probably the Campeche/Tabasco region of Mexico. Until the subsequent arrival of the Kaqchikel, the entire Lake Atitlán region was under Tz'utujil control. In addition, the Tz'utujil had extensive landholdings in the agriculturally rich coastal and piedmont zones. At the time of the Spanish arrival in 1524, much of the former Tz'utujil territory had been seized by the more numerous Kaqchikel. Led by Pedro de Alvarado, the Spanish force exploited preexisting regional hostility, enlisting the Kaqchikel as allies in his conquest of the Tz'utujil.

In 1547 the Spanish began to congregate formerly autonomous and dispersed Tz'utujil communities into the municipality configuration that continues to characterize local social organization. That process, called *congregación,* was designed to aid in the political administration and religious instruction of the indigenous population. Importantly, the initial disruption of Tz'utujil social existence did not entail the significant loss of land. Rather, exploitation was first in the form of *encomiendas* and later *repartimientos.* Those extractive mechanisms entitled the Spaniards to tribute and/or to force the Tz'utujil to purchase overpriced goods. Two other factors were particularly important in defining the Tz'utujil colonial experience. The first was the catastrophic population decline noted above (see "Demography"). Hardest hit was the coastal zone, where disease contributed to the virtual abandonment of the region by the Tz'utujil. The second factor was Guatemala's chronic economic stagnation and its anemic capacity to engage in the global economy. As a result, the colonizers tended to remain in a few Spanish centers, lessening acculturation pressure in peripheral areas such as that of the Tz'utujil. In the late nineteenth century, however, a whole new dynamic was to be unleashed when Guatemala began the large-scale production of coffee. To meet the requirements of that crop, extensive Tz'utujil lands were expropriated. That loss, combined with a rebounding population, led to the landlessness that characterizes contemporary Tz'utujil existence. This shortage of land has not only undermined agriculture as the primary means of subsistence but has contributed to decades of Guatemalan civil war.

Settlements

The great majority of Tz'utujil live either in one of seven *municipalidades* or in one of the satellite hamlets (*aldeas* and *caseríos*) surrounding those larger centers. Listed in clockwise order, the Tz'utujil municipalidades lining the shore of Lake Atitlán are San Lucas Tolimán, Santiago Atitlán, San Pedro la Laguna, San Juan la Laguna, and San Pablo la Laguna. In addition Santa María Visitación is situated in the mountains to the west of the lake and Chicacao in the piedmont region to the south. Differing from Guatemala's common "vacant center" towns, in which residents tend to return from more permanent habitations in the surrounding mountains and valleys only on market days and fiestas, Tz'utujil towns are of the "town nucleus" configuration, in which residency is characterized by permanent inhabitation. Until the mid-twentieth century dwellings in most Tz'utujil towns were comprised of a rectangular stone wall of about a meter in height upon which rested a secondary lashed-cane wall extending to ceiling height. The roof of this earthquake-resistant structure was constructed of wooden beams and grass thatch. Although these structures are still to be seen, population pressure and the resulting necessity to construct multistoried dwellings, combined with the new earthquake-resistant materials (particularly cement block and reinforcing steel rods) has led to a revolution in construction techniques.

Economy

Subsistence and Commercial Activities. Highland Mayan economics has long been based on the swidden cultivation of maize. In the Tz'utujil area, other traditional crops include avocados, beans, chickpeas, citrus fruits, tomatoes, and chilies. Except in certain small garden plots (*tablones*) situated along the immediate lakeshore, the Tz'utujil utilize little irrigation. Depending on the community, garden-plot irrigation ranges from a primitive process in which hand-carried containers of water are dumped directly on the crops (Santiago) to the use of giant hoses and pumps submerged in the lake (San Pedro). Reflective of underlying social changes, these garden plots are increasingly being used to grow nontraditional cash crops. Similarly, many Tz'utujil have converted their maize fields (*milpas*) to the production of coffee destined for distant markets. Moreover, whereas until the mid-twentieth century maize fields were planted for three to ten years, depending on the elevation, and then left fallow for four to twenty years, population pressure has increasingly made fallow time an unaffordable luxury. Instead, local farmers have become dependent on costly chemical fertilization. Although that fertilization raises crop yields threefold (albeit at a cost to soil quality), because of population growth and loss of land to other crops, the Tz'utujil are now net importers of maize. Even more significant is that increasing landlessness has fueled the move away from farming altogether; fewer than half of the Tz'utujil still engage in agriculture as their primary occupation, many having turned to other traditional activities such as fishing or mercantilism. Others, however, have made the transition to nontraditional occupations such as teaching (particularly in San Pedro) or to tourism-related jobs (San Pedro and Santiago).

Industrial Arts. Concerning their textile-producing capacity, Aldous Huxley once referred to Santiago and San Pedro as being the "Manchester and Bradford" of the highlands. Although the Tz'utujil have traditionally woven fabrics for domestic use, increasingly their skills are being tapped for international fashion markets. Similarly, many Tz'utujil supplement their income by braiding "friendship bracelets" destined for boutiques in Europe and the United States. Other significant industrial arts include canoe making, rope making, and mat making.

Trade. The Tz'utujil, particularly those from Santiago, have long been renowned as traders. Older men from that town still recall the days when they would haul wares on their backs to distant markets in Antigua and Mazatenango. Increasingly, the economies of virtually all Tz'utujil communities are reliant on trade. Although no doubt reflecting the loss of agricultural viability, the Tz'utujil evolution toward mercantilism stems as well from infrastructural

advances, including improved roads, regularly scheduled boat and bus transportation, and improved electronic communication. Most contemporary Tz'utujil merchants conduct virtually all of their trade outside of their respective communities. In other words, such *comerciantes de fuera* buy and sell commodities in distant communities. Importantly, despite the increasing reliance on such mercantilism, the available data on its economic viability are mixed.

Division of Labor. Many daily tasks in Tz'utujil life reveal a sexual division of labor. Typical female tasks include weaving on a backstrap loom, cooking, going to market, and caring for children. In contrast, male tasks include weaving on a treadle loom, farming, fishing, and cutting firewood. Whereas mercantilism outside of the community used to be an exclusively male occupation, some leading Tz'utujil merchants (particularly those dealing in textiles) are now female. There is also a division of labor based on community, with certain towns specializing in specific trades (e.g., rope making in San Juan).

Land Tenure. Since 1877, when it became legal in Guatemala to assign title to and sell communal land, most Tz'utujil land has been privatized. Since that time, huge amounts of land have been transferred to non-Tz'utujil owners, primarily in the form of coffee plantations (*fincas*) and increasingly as sites for the luxury weekend homes that line the shore between Santiago and San Lucas. While the sale of shoreline property has enriched those Tz'utujil fortunate enough to own such land, many more residents have been negatively impacted by the resulting explosive escalation of land prices.

Kinship

Kin Groups and Descent. Tz'utujil kinship is bilateral and lacks clans or any other such affiliation. Although at one time the fictive-kinship pattern known as *compadrazgo* was important, it now exists primarily in vestigial forms.

Kinship Terminology. The Tz'utujil have adopted Spanish naming patterns, according to which children receive the last names of both the mother and the father. Many of those names, however, are those of the lineage-based units of indigenous social organization (*calpul, chinamit*) that at one time dominated Tz'utujil society (e.g., Chavajay). First names tend to conform to the traditional Mayan *k'exel* naming pattern, according to which the firstborn son and daughter take the name of the father's parents, and the secondborn are named after the mother's parents. Depending on the community and the individual, the *k'exel* pattern may carry ancient religious significance.

Marriage and Family

Marriage. Individual Tz'utujil communities tend to be endogamous. In most cases, women who marry into a community continue to wear the style of costume of their natal community. Marriage is by the partners' choice. Although most Tz'utujil marriages were formerly conducted according to so-called Christo-pagan rituals, the great majority of Tz'utujil marriages today include either a Catholic or a Protestant wedding ceremony. This transition began in the 1930s and accelerated after 1950. Further reflecting outside influences, most young Tz'utujil brides now insist on wearing white wedding gowns and veils for their marriage ceremonies. With regard to Tz'utujil marriage, monogamy is the norm and polygyny the exception.

Domestic Unit. The nuclear-family household, or *sitio*, is the basic unit of Tz'utujil social organization. In many cases, there exists an extended family grouping of sitios known as a *vivienda*. Economic and domestic interaction between the component households in the vivienda is limited, but children typically contribute economic assistance to their parents. In most cases, postmarital residence is patrilocal, although for economic or interpersonal reasons, matrilocal residence is common.

Inheritance. Tz'utujil inheritance is bilateral—but not necessarily equally distributed.

Socialization. The socialization of Tz'utujil children takes place primarily in the home, where they are raised by their parents and older siblings alike. In addition, national law mandates that children attend six years of school. Primarily because of economic and domestic demands, however, fewer than half of Tz'utujil children are able to satisfy that mandate.

Sociopolitical Organization

Political Organization. As has been the case in virtually all the region's Mayan communities, until recently political organization in Tz'utujil towns revolved around the civil-religious hierarchy known as the *cofradía* system. Participants in that system ascended a hierarchical ladder of alternating political and religious offices, eventually attaining the status of *principal* (elder). Males and females participated in the system. To weaken the autonomy of rural communities, in 1945 the Guatemalan government declared it illegal for cofradías to have a civil component. That action, combined with religious competition from Protestants and orthodox Catholics alike has gradually eroded the cofradía system. In all Tz'utujil towns, the primary locus of community political organization is now democratic politics, with the office of mayor (alcalde) being the highest elected office in a given municipalidade.

Social Control. Social control in Tz'utujil towns is exercised through formal and informal means. On the one hand, gossip, envy, and ridicule exert considerable potency in routinizing Tz'utujil behavior. On the other hand, all of the towns are subject to the laws and authority of the Guatemalan state. That reality is underscored by the country's militarization owing to its civil war.

Conflict. Certainly the most grievous modern conflict in the Tz'utujil area stems from the civil war and has pitted the forces of the state against guerrillas of the Organization of People in Arms (ORPA), with most of the population caught in the middle. In addition, resentment over earlier land conflicts between San Juan and San Pedro continues to fester. Several Tz'utujil towns are rent by bitter internal religious divisions, particularly between Catholics and Protestants, but also between cofradía members and Catholics who do not belong to cofradías and between members of different Protestant sects.

Religion and Expressive Culture

Religious Beliefs. Until about 1960, Tz'utujil beliefs were closely associated with the cofradía systems in the various towns and revolved around a blending of pre-Conquest elements with the Catholic cult of the saints. Since then, cofradía hegemony has given way to both orthodox Catholicism and Protestantism. The rate of that disappearance has varied: San Pedro, which entirely abandoned the system between about 1955 and 1970, contrasts with Santiago, where it remains vital. Of continuing importance in several Tz'utujil towns is Maximón, a cofradía deity who combines Mayan calendrical and fertility attributes with a persona loosely linked to Judas of the New Testament.

Religious Practitioners. Practitioners of traditional religion in the Tz'utujil area fall into two basic categories: shamans and rank-and-file cofradía members. In contrast to cofradía rituals, which entail highly routinized procedures linked to the individual positions, Tz'utujil shamanism tends to be idiosyncratic. Increasingly, the most important religious practitioners in Tz'utujil life are the Catholic priests or the Protestant pastors.

Ceremonies. Most religious ceremonies in Tz'utujil towns are tied to the saints' calendar of Catholicism, with the fiesta of a given town's patron saint being particularly important. To the participating community, however, the relationship to a Catholic saint may be only nominal. For instance, in Santiago the fiesta of San Martín pays homage to an ancient sacred bundle associated with agricultural fertility.

Arts. The religious arts of the Tz'utujil range from exquisite textiles woven for cofradía use to the ritual dances that are occasionally performed. In some towns, those dances are informed by local variants of the rich corpus of myths and legends for which the Tz'utujil area is noted.

Medicine. There are several types of traditional medical specialists found in the Tz'utujil area, most of which could be classified under the generic category of "shaman." Among the most important are the *iyoma* (midwives), many of whom have a shamanic relationship with the moon, and the *aj'kuna* ("hunters"), who typically have relationships with the deities of certain medicinal plants. Other types of shamans found in the Tz'utujil area include the lsay ruki kumats (snakebite specialists), the *ruki kik 'om* (spider-bite specialists), and the *aj'mes* (mediums). In addition, the *aj'q'umanel* (herbalists) may be shamans, as may by the *rukoy bak* (bonesetters), those of San Pedro being particularly renowned.

Death and Afterlife. Many Tz'utujil have traditionally believed that after death one's life essence (*k'aslimal*) is regenerated in one's descendants. Depending on a person's station in life, another part of the soul (*q'aqal*) may go to the sky and assist the movement of the sun. The people of Santiago believe that those who have drowned inhabit the bottom of Lake Atitlán, and they are particularly feared. Increasingly, the Tz'utujil embrace either Catholic or Protestant views of the afterlife.

Bibliography

Dayley, Jon P. (1985). *Tzutujil Grammar*. University of California Publications in Linguistics, vol. 107. Berkeley and Los Angeles: University of California Press.

McBryde, Felix W. (1947). *Cultural and Historical Geography of Southwest Guatemala*. Smithsonian Institute, Institute of Social Anthropology Publication no. 4. Washington, D.C.

Madigan, D. (1976). "Santiago Atitlán: A Socioeconomic and Demographic History." Ph.D. dissertation, University of Pittsburgh.

Orellana, Sandra L. (1984). *The Tzutujil Mayas: Continuity and Change, 1250–1630*. Norman: University of Oklahoma Press.

Paul, Benajmin, and Lois Paul (1962). *Ethnographic Materials on San Pedro Laguna, Solola, Guatemala*. Chicago: University of Chicago Microfilm Collection of Manuscripts on Cultural Anthropology.

ROBERT S. CARLSEN

Uspantec

ETHNONYM: Uspanteco

The 2,000 Uspantec, of whom 1,000 still speak the Uspantec language, are Quichean Maya Indians who live in the Quiché Department of Guatemala. The K'iche' Maya conquered the Uspantec in the fifteenth century. The Uspantec successfully rebelled in approximately 1500, only to fall under Spanish subjugation in the 1530s. Starting in the latter part of the nineteenth century, the Guatemalan government began to appropriate Indian lands all over Guatemala, including the lands of the Uspantec. This led to increased poverty among the Uspantec, who again rebelled. The Guatemalan government retaliated, with the result that perhaps as many as one-fourth of all Uspantec migrated to the United States. The Uspantec in Guatemala subsist primarily on maize and beans.

Virgin Islanders

ETHNONYMS: none

The Virgin Islands are two groups of islands governed by two separate powers, the United States and the United Kingdom. The British Virgin Islands are known by that name, while the U.S. Virgin Islands are often known simply as the Virgin Islands. The Virgin Islands are an unorganized and unincorporated U.S. territory, and the British Virgin Islands are formally known as a Crown Colony of the U.K. The U.S. Virgin Islands are three large islands and fifty or so smaller islands with a total area of 352 square kilometers, located between Puerto Rico and the Leeward Islands. The British Virgin Islands consist of forty or so mountainous islands to the north of the U.S. Virgin Islands.

The origin of the 101,809 people who lived in the U.S. Virgin Islands in 1990 is predominantly West Indian (74 percent), with most of the rest coming from the U.S. mainland (13 percent) and Puerto Rico (5 percent). Racially and ethnically, the population is mixed. Eighty percent of the people are Black, and 15 percent are White. The Hispanic population is 14 percent of the total. The official language is English, but Spanish and a creole are also spoken. The most prevalent religious denominations are Baptist (42 percent), Catholic (34 percent), and Episcopalian (17 percent); 7 percent adhere to other faiths.

The 12,258 (1990) people of the British Virgin Islands are predominantly Black (more than 90 percent). The people speak English, and most are Methodists.

The Virgin Islands were inhabited by the Carib Indians when Columbus first sighted them during his second voyage in 1493. Columbus named the islands after Saint Ursula and her martyred virgins. Spain claimed ownership of the islands at the time, but it was the Dutch, English, and French who began to settle what are now the U.S. Virgin Islands in the 1600s; the British Virgin Islands were first settled by Dutch farmers. Eventually, the Danish government laid claim to the U.S. Virgin Islands and used the islands for transshipment and to raise sugarcane. Shipping improved, the price of sugar fell, and in 1917 the Danish government sold the islands to the United States, which wanted to locate a naval base there. The U.S. Virgin Islands became tourist destinations early in the twentieth century, with the result that the average income on the islands is among the highest in the Caribbean. The destruction caused by Hurricane Hugo in 1989 led to looting and rioting, which was not effectively restrained by the local government and had to be stopped by the U.S. army. Local political pressure then developed for a more responsive territorial government. Presently, the government consists of an elected governor and unicameral legislature, as well as two U.S. district courts. The economy is centered around tourism, but there is also manufacturing (watches, textiles, electronics, and rum) and oil refining.

The British Virgin Islands came under British control in 1666 and have remained a colony since. Most of their trade is with the U.S. Virgin Islands, not with other British colonies. A constitution came into force in 1967 and was amended in 1977 to grant greater local authority. The government consists of a governor, a cabinet, and a legislature with nine elected members. The colony's monetary unit is the U.S. dollar. Many offshore corporations have located in the British Virgin Islands to escape taxes and the unstable politics of Panama and Hong Kong. The major industries are tourism, construction, and rum, although there is some export of fish, gravel, sand, and fruits. The British Virgin Islands are far less economically developed than the U.S. Virgin Islands.

Bibliography

Boyer, William W. (1983). *America's Virgin Islands: A History of Human Rights and Wrongs*. Durham, N.C.: Carolina Academic Press.

Creque, Darwin D. (1968). *The U.S. Virgins and the Eastern Caribbean*. Philadelphia: Whitmore Publishing Co.

Dookhan, Isaac. (1975). *A History of the British Virgin Islands*. Epping, Essex: Caribbean Universities Press.

Gibson, Margaret A. (1976). *Ethnicity and Schooling: A Caribbean Case Study*. Ann Arbor: University Microfilms International.

Moll, Verna P. (1991). *Virgin Islands*. Santa Barbara, Calif.: ABC-Clio.

Pickering, Vernon W. (1983). *Early History of the British Virgin Islands: From Columbus to Emancipation*. New York: Falcon Publications International.

Pickering, Vernon W. (1987). *A Concise History of the British Virgin Islands: From the Amerindians to 1986*. New York: Falcon Publications International.

Varlack, Pearl I., and Norwell Harrigan (1977). *The Virgins: A Descriptive and Historical Profile*. St. Thomas: Caribbean Research Institute, College of the Virgin Islands.

Wasteko

ETHNONYMS: Cuextecatl, Huastec, Panoteca, Teenek

Orientation

Identification. The Wasteko are Mayan-language speakers who live in San Luis Potosí and Veracruz, Mexico, distant from other Mayan groups in Guatemala, Belize, and southern Mexico. They migrated north from the Mayan heartland in Guatemala around 2200 B.C., but, despite 4,000 years of separation from other Maya, they have maintained their Mayan cultural patterns and beliefs. The Wasteko refer to themselves as "Teenek" (*te'en inik*, "laughing people," or *tehe' inik*, "right-here people"). The name "Wasteko" (Spanish: Huasteco) derives from the Nahuatl *cuextecatl*, a name used by the Aztecs that may be derived from two Wasteko words, *kweech* (coil) and *te'* (tree), in reference to the crown of coiled vines that Wasteko women wore on their heads. Traditional women's garb remains distinctively Wasteko. The costume in San Luis Potosí is a mid-calf to knee-length black sarong skirt and a short, embroidered cape, worn over one or more ruffled blouses. A small embroidered bag is carried over the shoulder.

Through the 1960s, embroidery patterns served to identify the home community of the wearer. Hair is tucked over a thick circle of bright yarn, a replacement for the traditional coil of vines. An embroidered cloth is folded and placed on top of the coronet on special occasions. In Veracruz and in a few San Luis Potosí communities, traditional women's clothing includes a long, flounced skirt instead of the shorter sarong, and the hair is worn in braids. Today men and most women wear factory-made apparel.

Location. According to Laughlin (1969), in the late 1400s the Wasteko occupied a large area of highland desert, mountain jungles, and coastal lowlands that encompassed much of the state of San Luis Potosí, southern Tamaulipas, northern Veracruz, and parts of Queretaro and Hidalgo. In the early 1500s the Spanish invaders forced the Wasteko out of their coastal towns, westward into the foothills and mountains of the Sierra Madre Oriental. Many Wasteko were sent as slaves to the Antilles, large numbers died as a result of the introduction of Old World diseases, and others succumbed to mistreatment by the Spanish conquerors. Today the Wasteko occupy a more limited area, living in small hamlets or isolated farmsteads at elevations from 60 to 500 meters above sea level on the Gulf Coastal slopes of the Sierra Madre Oriental in eastern San Luis Potosí and northern Veracruz. This region, known as the Huasteca, is populated by several other ethnolinguistic groups: Nahua, Totonac, Pame, Otomí, Tepehua, and mestizo. The Huasteca is a diverse area, with forested mountains to the west and drier plains to the east. Average rainfall ranges from 115 centimeters per year in the Gulf Coastal areas of Veracruz up to 315 centimeters per year in the moist tropical forests of San Luis Potosí. The area is drained by many small streams and several major rivers. Temperatures are generally very warm, averaging from 20° C to 24° C, but lows sometimes approach freezing during winter. The Huasteca remained an isolated backwater until the discovery of oil around 1910. The Pan-American Highway opened the area to international traffic in 1935, but even today secondary roads remain relatively few, and footpaths are common.

Demography.   Since 1970, the Wasteko population has nearly doubled, but the absolute number of people reported as monolingual has remained stable. In 1970 the total number of Wasteko speakers in the states of San Luis Potosí and Veracruz was 64,888, of whom 18 percent were monolingual. Wasteko communities in San Luis Potosí are more isolated than those in Veracruz, and they report having almost twice as many monolinguals. In 1990 the total Wasteko population of the two states was 115,630, and 10 percent were monolingual: 14 percent of women and 6 percent of men. (There were only 5,109 Wasteko in the rest of Mexico.) In spite of the decrease in the percentage of monolinguals, Wasteko remains the primary language of most of the Huastec people. In San Luis Potosí in 1980, for example, half the children ages 5 to 9 spoke only Wasteko. Most adults over 40 are illiterate.

Linguistic Affiliation.   Thirty mutually unintelligible living languages form the Mayan Language Family. Of these, nineteen are spoken primarily in Guatemala and Belize and eleven primarily in Mexico. The fifth-largest Mayan language of Mexico, but the most linguistically isolated, is Wasteko. Its two main dialects, Potosino and Veracruzano, are mutually intelligible but differ slightly in vocabulary and in details of pronunciation. A third dialect, Sierra Otontepec, has been reported from an isolated area in northern Veracruz. One colonial grammar and vocabulary of the language survives (Tapia Zenteno 1767). Modern studies of the language include Larsen's (1955) dictionary and Edmonson's (1988) grammar, which has an extensive bibliography of linguistic and other material pertaining to the Wasteko.

The Wasteko are great storytellers, and, in their tales and legends, they employ a parallel-couplet structure that is common to all of the Mayan languages. Successive lines in a story are linked in terms of either their grammatical structure or their content. In effect, the second line of a couplet repeats the information contained in the first line, altered slightly for variety. There are several different genres of Wasteko speech, from ritual incantations pronounced by a shamanic curer, to well-known stories told by an accomplished storyteller, to the conversations of everyday life. Even when explaining so mundane a topic as how to plant a maize field, native speakers slip almost unconsciously into couplets.

History and Cultural Relations

Despite an abundance of house and temple mounds throughout the region, there has been relatively little archaeological exploration in the Huasteca; however, excavations at Tamuin, in San Luis Potosí, and at Teayo, in Veracruz, among others, have produced examples of native architecture, mural paintings, sculpture, and pottery of Wasteko origin. The area near Tampico, particularly the land known as Pánuco, was heavily populated at the time of the Spanish Conquest.

According to the sixteenth-century Franciscan historian Sahagun, the Wasteko were distinguished by their tall, sloping foreheads (the result of head deformation); their tattooed skin; and their blackened, filed teeth. They were notorious for their male nudity, homosexual rituals, and indulgence in alcoholic _pulque,_ which they drank and also administered as enemas. They wore colorful woven cloaks and nose ornaments and bracelets made from feathers, gold, jade, and turquoise. Warriors wore large metal bells and padded-cotton armor, and they were believed to wield powerful sorcery in battle. Their weapons included bows and arrows, throwing sticks, curved clubs, and, possibly, obsidian-edged swords. Aztec tribute lists show that the Wasteko traded cotton textiles, maize, deerskins, tropical fruits, and exotic birds. Other historical records indicate that the sixteenth-century Gulf-coastal forest cultures managed forest orchards as well as swidden agricultural plots and may have drained fields in swampy areas. Archaeological evidence of agriculture from this area has been dated to 1700 B.C.

At the time of the Conquest, the Wasteko were organized into independent territorial groups that engaged in wars under shifting alliances. On the Gulf Coast, Wasteko society included nobles, commoners, and, possibly, slaves. From the seventeenth century to the mid-nineteenth century, the northern and coastal areas of the Huasteca were occupied by expanding haciendas, but small Indian communities also occupied refuges scattered in the forested foothills to the west. On the haciendas, Wasteko served as laborers in return for rights to use plots of land for raising their own food. In foothill settlements, they provided unpaid labor and tribute to the Catholic church.

Under Spanish domination, a major cultural distinction was drawn between mestizos (those who participated in the national, Spanish-derived culture, regardless of their genetic heritage) and _indios_ (a pejorative term for indigenous people). In eighteenth-century censuses, Negroes and mulattoes were grouped with Spaniards, whereas Indians were considered a race apart. Although the Wasteko distinguish themselves from neighboring Nahua, Otomí, and Totonac, they recognize a more fundamental cultural difference between mestizos and indigenous peoples. Mexican government policy has consistently encouraged cultural assimilation of indigenous peoples through promotion of Spanish-language schools, incentives for concentration into townships, and other means.

Settlements

Most Wasteko live in scattered farmsteads, but there is a trend toward the development of hamlets comprised of second homes that are located where electricity is available.

The few roads that exist are in bad condition, and, although bus and taxi service is available in the larger town centers, most outlying hamlets are accessible only on foot. A trip to the weekly market can require a walk of two hours or more.

The typical household cluster on each farmstead includes a one-room apsidal structure and a one-room round structure, both with thatched roofs, walls of unplastered vertical poles, and dirt floors. Furnishings are minimal: a table and a chair or so, a traditional three-stone hearth for boiling dried maize kernels with ash to soften them, a metal grinder for the initial coarse grinding of the softened maize, and a metate (grindstone) to grind it fine for tortilla dough. A raised hearth with an inset pottery griddle for cooking tortillas, a few pots, and a small altar complete the household furnishings. Some households have raised beds made of wooden poles, but most people put their sleeping mats on the dirt floors or outside on their patios. A cleared open space around the house and the area under the wide roof overhang provide additional living space. Households often include extended families, and the house cluster may support several hearths. Households belong to communities that occupy sites that range in size from 500 to several thousand hectares. The communities are integrated into *municipios,* which include blocks of Wasteko settlements scattered on the marginal lands around ranches and small private parcels owned by mestizos. Each municipio is named after the main town center, which is the site of the weekly market and the focus of churchgoing on Sundays. Few Wasteko live in the town center. The population density of municipios with significant Wasteko presence is approximately 100 persons per square kilometer.

Economy

Subsistence and Commercial Activities.   Subsistence is derived indirectly by purchases with cash from seasonal wage labor and from the sale of raw sugar, coffee, or other cash crops, and directly from production of maize, fruits, firewood, plant-derived medicines, and construction materials. The basic diet of tortillas and beans is supplemented by fruits, wild greens, garden foods, and occasional small game. Most of the maize and beans are purchased with cash. The Wasteko agro-ecosystem is a fluid mosaic of several resource zones, including permanent planted fields (primarily sugarcane or henequen), periodically planted fields (for maize production and gardens), fallows in various stages of forest regeneration, orchards, dooryards, permanent forests, and streams. The Wasteko use a short-fallow version of the Mesoamerican swidden system known as "milpa." This system produces sufficient firewood from the regenerating forest in fallows but insufficient maize to meet subsistence needs. Approximately 25 percent of an average San Luis Potosí Wasteko community's land is under forest, 50 percent in fallow-milpa cycled land, and 25 percent in sugarcane. Coffee is grown under native forest.

Industrial Arts and Trade.   Raw sugar is produced as a cottage industry. Cane is harvested by hand and put through an animal-powered press to extract the juice. The juice is then boiled in a large open vat until it reaches the sugaring stage, when it is poured into small pottery molds.

The unmolded raw sugar is sold to mestizo traders or to cooperatives. Other trade is limited to small-scale selling at weekly markets or church-festival events. Women make pocket money by selling piglets, chickens, eggs, fruit, garden produce, cooked food, small amounts of ground coffee, and embroidered cloths. A few men in any given community are specialists in the repair of tools, radios, or tape recorders. Some work as barbers. The Wasteko construct their own houses, weave cloth on backstrap looms, and produce pottery and clay votive figures for personal use.

Division of Labor.   Women are responsible for cooking, cleaning, laundry, child care, caring for domestic livestock, and gathering firewood. They also bear the primary responsibility for carrying water from wells or springs for household use, a task that can become onerous in the dry season, when even the nearest source of stagnant or polluted water may be as far as several kilometers away. In mountainous areas, women often have to climb down into caves to find a source of water. Men clear and plant fields for milpas, cut sugarcane and henequen for processing, and build houses. Both sexes weed and harvest crops, process sugar, and weave henequen bags for sale. Children assist adults from an early age. The division of labor is not rigid; a man may take on household responsibilities if a woman is ill or if he has free time.

Land Tenure.   Wasteko land rights were lost in the late 1800s, when federal laws eliminated indigenous peoples' communal-property rights. After the Mexican Revolution, the 1917 Constitution recognized community ownership of land under Article 27 in the form of *ejidos* and *comunidades.* Ejidos were granted to groups of people who petitioned for access to resources to which they had had no prior claim. Comunidades are preexisting corporate entities, whose rights were recognized if their members could demonstrate prior, longstanding, community-based use of the land and waters. Because it was easier to establish rights to ejidos, the Wasteko claimed property in both ways. In either case, the community is the primary allocator and enforcer of local rights to resources within its boundaries, and it regulates both inheritance and membership. The corporate group's cultural and social integrity reinforces a unified approach to management decisions. Communities can grant to individual households the rights to manage and benefit from long-term, private access to specific community resources. Thus, each household owns, operates, and passes on inheritance rights to its own farmstead within the borders of the comunidad or ejido, but it cannot sell or rent community lands outside the community. Some Wasteko own small plots of individually titled property (*parcelas particulares*). Households share the rights to harvest their crops or use their land with poorer community members and kin to ensure that the subsistence needs of all are met.

Kinship

Kin Groups and Descent.   Modern Wasteko have adopted the Spanish system of reckoning descent through both parents. Surnames are all Spanish, and the Spanish pattern of given name plus father's surname plus mother's surname is followed.

Kinship Terminology. Wasteko words for kin are still in common use. There are separate terms for "father" and "mother" and for "grandfather" and "grandmother," but a single term is used for "grandchild." The word meaning "sibling" can be specified for sex by adding "male" or "female." Cousins are called by the Spanish term _primo._ Traces of an older system remain; for example, in addition to "son" and "daughter," used by both parents, there is a separate word meaning "woman's child," and, whereas there is a single term meaning both "uncle" and "nephew" and another meaning both "aunt" and "niece," there are also separate words for uncles who are "father's brothers," and aunts who are "mother's sisters." A distinction is also made between a "man's brother-in-law" and a "woman's brother-in-law" and between a man's and a woman's sister-in-law. Terms for "step-" and "adoptive" kin are derived by adding the suffix _-le'_ to the basic term. Catholic priests introduced the concept of ritual kinship, such as "godparent" and "godchild," and the relationship between "parent" and "godparent" (Spanish _comadre_ and _compadre_). These ritual kin relationships are described either by Spanish-derived terms or by a combination of Spanish and Wasteko terms.

Marriage and Family

Marriage. The isolation and the sedentary living patterns of Wasteko families ensure that most marriages are contracted locally. They usually take place in the Catholic church, but they are arranged by a traditional broker and require a ritual process.

Domestic Unit and Socialization. The minimum domestic unit consists of father, mother, and unmarried children, but most households also include grandparents, children of deceased relatives, godchildren, other kin, or unrelated individuals. Residence after marriage tends to be patrilocal, but it is not uncommon for a daughter's husband to move onto her family's farmstead, where the married couple usually occupies a separate house. Children learn traditional Wasteko values and behavior in the home. Schools attempt to socialize the children into the national mestizo culture, but few children attend school beyond the sixth grade. Secondary schools exist only in the larger town centers, which are often more than an hour's walk from most of the children's homes.

Sociopolitical Organization

Social and Political Organization. For most Wasteko, life revolves around the local Indian community. Community institutions have developed around the _compadrazgo_ system of fictive kinship, kinship-based reciprocity, the _cargo_ (the ritual obligation, shared by a set of communities, to sponsor the fiestas of saints), other church-based groups, marketing cooperatives, and the organizations that have been created by the state to regulate activities on community lands. The latter organizations include the General Assembly, in which each household is represented by one person, and two important elected three-person committees: the _comisariado,_ which represents the community to outside authorities and settles land disputes, and the _consejo de vigilancia,_ which monitors the activities of the first committee. Community decisions are made in

General Assembly meetings by majority vote. At the municipio level, however, political power is held by mestizos. The Wasteko do not actively participate in pan-Mexican indigenous organizations.

Social Control and Conflict. Peer pressure derived from a shared value system is generally effective in maintaining community standards. Accusations of witchcraft are made against those who attempt to appropriate resources for private gain. Curers reinforce socially appropriate behavior during their interactions with patients by looking for illness caused by the patient's or others' misuse of resources or for other antisocial behavior.

Religion and Expressive Culture

Religious Beliefs and Ceremonies. The Wasteko maintain a strong belief in pre-Hispanic religious traditions and possess a rich repertory of oral history. Although nominally Catholic, most Wasteko interpret the world in a pre-Hispanic cosmological framework. Saints are associated with particular native deities. The elaborate history of Thipaak, the culture hero who brought maize to the Wasteko, is linked to accounts of other supernatural beings. Creation stories include references to human origins in male homosexual relations; to the _lintsi_ ("flat asses"), giants who, lacking orifices for elimination, wasted their food because they only inhaled its aroma; and to people who lost access to special powers because they failed to respect the gods. Major deities include the Earth, Time, the Sun, and rain bringers who are associated with the East, the North, and the West. In addition, minor deities, conceived as male and female pairs, control specific realms of human interest, including sorcery (associated with the South), dance, medicine, pottery, beekeeping, and weaving. They are called fathers, mothers, grandfathers, and grandmothers. The ancestral nature of these deities, their association with the landscape of Wasteko territories, and the powers they control all reflect the integration of social, ecological, and historical elements in Wasteko ontology and epistemology.

Major ritual ceremonies include those that are deemed necessary for marriage, naming a child, and death. There are also special rituals for the New Year, house protection, illness, and agriculture. Details of religious beliefs and curing are found in Alcorn (1984).

Arts. The Wasteko are known for their music and for their traditional dances, which are named for animals and birds. Artistic expression is no longer elaborated in their material culture, although in pre-Hispanic times the Wasteko were famous for weaving and for producing engraved-shell pectorals and stone sculpture.

Medicine. The combination of isolation and poverty has meant that most Wasteko have only minimal access to modern medicine. Malnutrition and lack of sanitation contribute to a high incidence of tuberculosis. Intestinal parasites are endemic, and fungal infections, respiratory ailments, and traumatic injuries are common. Women have scant medical assistance during pregnancy, and they give birth in unsanitary surroundings. Many are so malnourished that they lack adequate milk for their babies and are forced to feed them maize gruel or powdered milk mixed with dirty water. In addition, few children are immunized against the common childhood diseases. As a result, early-childhood mortality is high. The Wasteko response to these conditions is a reliance on a complex system of traditional medicine, which employs over 550 species of medicinal plants. Illness is considered a social and physical phenomenon; one or more of the four essential parts becomes disordered—heart, soul, spirit, and "growing shoot"—Curers participate in a shamanic tradition, learning from their dreams and deriving their legitimacy from their innate ability to speak directly to the gods—a necessary skill for curers, who are described as lawyers who argue the patient's case before the gods. Both men and women may be curers, and their spouses often assist them. The curer's tools include an altar, candles, crystals, pitch-pine sticks, a hollow cane tube for sucking out illness, shoots of special plants, music, copal incense, *aguardiente* liquor, and, most important, language. Curers identify the causes of an illness, remove these causes, and help the body to return to a normal state of order.

Bibliography

Alcorn, Janis B. (1984). *Huastec Mayan Ethnobotany.* Austin: University of Texas Press.

Alcorn, Janis B. (1989). "An Economic Analysis of Huastec Mayan Forest Management." In *Fragile Lands of Latin America: Strategies for Sustainable Development,* edited by J. Browder, 182–206. Boulder: Westview Press.

Barthas, Brigitte. (1993). "Sistemas de producción y conflictos agrarios de la Huasteca potosina (1870–1910)." *Cuadrante* 12–13:30–42.

Cabrera, Antonio J. (1876). *La Huasteca potosina.* San Luis Potosí: Tipografía del Comercio.

Chipman, Donald E. (1966). *Nuño de Guzmán and the Province of Pánuco in New Spain, 1518–1533.* Glendale, Calif.: Arthur H. Clark.

de la Fuente, Beatriz (1978). "Arte huaxteco prehispánico." *Artes de México* 22 (187): 5–96.

Domínguez, Xorge A., and Janis B. Alcorn (1985). "Screening of Medicinal Plants Used by the Huastec Mayans of Northeastern Mexico." *Journal of Ethnopharmacology* 13:139–156.

Edmonson, Barbara (1988). *A Descriptive Grammar of Huastec (Potosino Dialect).* Ann Arbor, Mich.: University Microfilms International.

Estados Unidos Mexicanos (1970, 1980, 1990). *Censo general de población y vivienda.* Mexico City: Instituto Nacional de Estadística, Geografía e Informática.

Larsen, Raymond S. (1955). *Vocabulario huasteco.* Mexico City: Summer Institute of Linguistics.

Laughlin, Robert M. (1969). "The Huastec." In *Handbook of Middle American Indians,* edited by Robert Wauchope. Vol. 7, *Ethnology, Part One,* edited by Robert Wauchope and Evon Z. Vogt, 298–311. Austin: University of Texas Press.

Meade, Joaquín (1942). *La Huasteca, epoca antigua.* Mexico City: Editorial Cassio.

Ochoa Salas, Lorenzo (1979). *Historia prehispánica de la Huaxteca.* Mexico City: Universidad Nacional Autónoma de México.

Sanders, William T. (1978). *The Lowland Huasteca Archaeological Survey and Excavation. 1957 Field Season.* Columbia: University of Missouri Museum of Anthropology.

Stresser-Péan, Guy (1967). "Problèmes agraires de la Huastèque ou région de Tampico (Mexique)." In *Les problèmes agraires des Amériques Latines,* 201–214. Paris: Colloques Internationaux du Centre Nacional de la Récherche Scientifique.

Tapia Zenteno, Carolos de (1767). *Noticia de la lengua huasteca.* Mexico City: Biblioteca Mexicana.

Wilkerson, S. Jeffrey K. (1979). "Huastec Presence and Cultural Continuity in North-Central Veracruz, Mexico." *Actes du XLII Congrés International des Américanistes* 9B:41–55.

JANIS B. ALCORN AND BARBARA EDMONSON

Xinca

ETHNONYMS: none

The 3,500 Xinca Indians live in the communities of Taxisco, Chiquimulilla, and Guazacapan in Santa Rosa Department, in southeastern Guatemala. As a tribal group or social entity, they cannot be said to exist any longer; only individuals who call themselves Xinca still exist. The Xinca language is dead or nearly so. Culturally and linguistically, the Xinca are related to the Lenca Indians. The Xinca have not borne well the stresses of the Spanish Conquest, nor the more recent influences of acculturation.

Bibliography

Campbell, Lyle, et al. (1975). *Papers on the Xinca of Eastern Guatemala.* Columbia: Museum of Anthropology, University of Missouri–Columbia.

Yaqui

ETHNONYMS: Cahita, Yoeme, Yoreme

Orientation

Identification. The Yaqui, an indigenous people of southeast Sonora, Mexico, belong to a larger ethnic group known as the "Cahita." The great majority of the Yaqui nowadays live in the same region, but other Yaqui groups have settled in Arizona owing to the great Yaqui migration at the beginning of the twentieth century. Ethnographic literature has referred to all these people as "Yaqui" since 1645, when Andrés Pérez de Rivas wrote that people said, "Can't you see I'm a Yaqui?" He goes on to explain that this is what they used to say because the term meant "he who speaks in a loud voice" (Pérez de Ribas 1944, 65).

All Yaqui call themselves "Yoreme" (person or human); they also apply this term to Mayo Indians. When European missionaries heard of the similarities between the Yaqui language and that of the Mayo, they decided upon the native Cahita term to refer to both the language and its speakers.

Location. The original Yaqui group resided in a long coastal valley strip opposite the Sea of Cortés. The Jesuits, however, concentrated the population within eight villages from south to north along the Río Yaqui (27° to 31° N and 10.7° to 11° W). Their original territory has diminished considerably, and as of 1937 it has been restricted by presidential decree to an extension of 485,235 hectares, over which irrigation district no. 18 spreads. This semiarid zone consists of sandy clay and humic ground, with temperatures that vary from 0° C to 47° C; it includes a mountainous area, a coastal area, and an irrigated valley.

Demography. In the 1530s a population of 30,000 Indians was registered, a figure that decreased to 12,000 by 1830. After less than sixty years—1830 to 1887, which corresponds to the period of the Yaqui wars—not more than 4,000 Yaqui remained in the valley. In 1905 there were 18,000 inhabitants. Because of the massive deportation and revolutionary wars, however, only 8,500 were left by 1930. According to the 1990 Mexican census, the number of Yaqui inhabitants of the state of Sonora has stabilized at about 10,000.

Linguistic Affiliation. The Yaqui belong to the Cahita Subgroup, which is a Taracahita Group from the Sonoran Branch of the Uto-Aztecan Family. The Cahita Language Group now consists of Mayo and Yaqui, which are mutually intelligible.

History and Cultural Relations

With respect to the pre-Hispanic period, a hypothesis of late Yaqui arrival in the river valleys is generally supported by the limited archaeological record as well as by colonial chroniclers. Approaches by the Spanish have been recorded since 1532. The first confrontations were with the ill-fated expedition of Diego Martínez de Hurdaide in 1607.

Toward 1610, the Yaqui accepted two Jesuit missionaries: friars Andrés Pérez de Rivas and Tomás Basilio. The Yaqui revolted against the missionary regime, however, and in 1741 a treaty was signed by which they acquired the rights to keep their own customs. Government would only be administered by members of their own group, and they would have total possession of their land as well as the right to retain their weapons. In 1767 the expulsion of the Jesuits brought the end of the relative peace the Yaqui had so far enjoyed and placed the communities under Franciscan governance. As a result, the Yaqui lost more territory to the colonists. By 1825, the Yaqui rebellion had begun. It would later mark the course of the relationship between the Yaqui and the subsequent regimes of the Mexican Republic. This period is often referred to as the "Wars of the Yaqui." It resulted in a drastic population loss and political imbalance, conditions that permitted the oligarchy, to continue colonizing the entire valley.

The genocidal offensive was intensified during Porfirio Diaz's rule, and thousands of Yaqui were expelled to Yucatán and Quintana Roo to be sold as slaves. Hundreds looked for refuge in Arizona, in the United States, where they have lived ever since in the towns of Pascua, Guadalupe, and Barrio Libre. The Yaqui participation in the revolutionary conflict was based on the promise by General Alvaro Obregón to return their land. The promise was not fulfilled, and a new revolt started. It lasted until the end of 1929, when President Emilio Portes Gil signed a peace agreement with the Yaqui that forced them to live under supervision by the army until 1936.

Through the agreements reached with President Lázaro Cárdenas, 485,235 hectares of land were ratified and acknowledged as exclusive Yaqui territory. Armed confrontations came to an end, and a period of reintegration began, during which several thousand Yaqui returned to their territories. In 1940 irrigation district no. 18 was created, and new plans for agricultural development arose. Owing to the construction of several dams, the river, a resource indispensable for production, was lost.

Settlements

When the Jesuits arrived, the Yaqui resided in irregularly distributed settlements along the Río Yaqui. Such quarters consisted of wood-and-mud shacks in the form of domes. This pattern was changed by the missionaries when they moved natives into eight towns. Although two of these towns had to be abandoned on account of boundary struggles and floods, their traditional identity was preserved in the new settlements that replaced them. At present there are about one hundred hamlets and villages within the Yaqui territory, assigned for political, religious, and ritual purposes to one of the eight traditional towns. Traditional housing consists of only one or two rooms used for different purposes according to the season. Both walls and roofs are of reeds and mesquite mixed with mud.

Economy

Subsistence and Commercial Activities. Reliable sources indicate that precontact Yaqui were farmers who frequently had to emigrate because of floods. They grew maize, beans, calabashes, amaranth seeds, and cotton. They complemented such activity with hunting, fishing, and gathering, as well as raids on their closest neighbors. During the colonial period, labor was regulated by the missions. New crops were introduced, and production increased to such an extent that it was possible to satisfy local needs. During armed conflicts, the pacified Indians were left in charge of agriculture, whereas the "Broncos" alternated their fighting activities with work as laborers on haciendas. Nowadays the main Yaqui economic activity continues to be agriculture. Since 1940 the collective exploitation of the land has led to the end of subsistence agriculture and to a new need to sell farm products in order to buy food that was formerly produced locally. Other important economic activities are fishing and cattle raising (which are conducted through cooperative societies), wood cutting, coal mining, pitch mining, temporary migration, and the exploitation of salt deposits that have been in use since the time of the Jesuits.

Industrial Arts. The design and manufacture of ceremonial paraphernalia constitutes the main artistic activity of the Yaqui. This has no commercial purpose; the dancers and musicians themselves make the items for personal use. A few families are devoted to the manufacture of *petates* (sleeping mats), baskets, and reed crowns, while others make earthenware cups and saucers that are used exclusively at ceremonies.

Trade. From the time of the Jesuit missions, the farm produce from the eight traditional villages provided for other missions that were situated in less fertile territories. Currently, the crops and the catch are primarily destined for regional and national markets.

Division of Labor. Farm labor is primarily performed by men, but women help with certain activities during those periods requiring a larger labor force. Fishing, cattle raising, and work in the salt mines are almost exclusively done by male workers. Young women take teaching jobs and are employed as social workers and occasionally as home aides.

Land Tenure. Since the presidential acknowledgement of an exclusively Yaqui territory in 1936, the land-tenure regime has been communal. Every head of a family is assigned a piece of land on which to build a home and to work collectively in farming associations.

Kinship

Kin Groups and Descent. Referring to the pre-Jesuit period, some writers, such as Ralph Beals, have suggested the existence of unilineal descent groups among the "Cahita." Currently, however, descent is bilateral and there are no exogamy rules between descent groups.

Kinship Terminology. Kinship terminology is of a Yuman type and similar to the Opata, Tepehuan, and Tarahumara systems from the north of Mexico. The Yaqui system distinguishes relatives on the basis of the speaker's sex and relative age, particularly with respect to the first ascending generation.

Marriage and Family

Marriage. All marriage prohibitions have to do with blood relatives and *compadres*. It is traditional that the bride's and the groom's families reach an agreement and exchange gifts before the actual ceremony takes place. The majority of weddings are performed according to Catholic religious norms; however, this is not an indispensable requirement for the children to be legitimate. Common-law marriages and the separation of spouses occur quite frequently.

Domestic Unit. The basic residence unit is the *ho'akame*, or neighborhood, consisting of a group of relatives who live in one or two lodges. There are no rules for residence, and authority is entrusted to the oldest able-bodied adult male.

Inheritance. When the head of the family dies, the oldest adult is compelled to decide what should happen to the ho'akame in general; there is no individual assignation of the land or property.

Socialization. The domestic group as well as civil, military, and religious societies socialize the young. Adults teach traditions and customs to the young, beginning with the mother tongue. The grandmother helps the parents care for the children. Both boys' and girls' education is complemented by school-sponsored attendance at traditional festivities.

Sociopolitical Organization

Social Organization. The Yaqui "tribe" includes every individual born within Yaqui territory or to Yoreme parents. Every Yaqui residing in a small village or quarter in the territory is assigned to one of the eight traditional towns, each of which is a political, military, and ritual unit. The Yaqui leader resides in Vicam Pueblo. The internal political organization of each of the eight towns is identical, consisting of five governing groups, or _yau'uras_: the civil authorities, the military authorities, the fiesta authorities (_fiesteros_), the church authorities, and the Holy Week customs authorities (_kohtumbre yau'uras_).

Political Organization. The highest political authority in each of the towns is comprised of the five elected governors (_cobanaos_) of the civil authority, who are hierarchically organized and are complemented by a group of elderly men. They are responsible for economic administration, relations with external agents, and relations with the Mexican government. The governors of the eight towns do not assemble except on special occasions requiring decisions with respect to the entire tribe and its allies.

Social Control. The military authority is in charge of keeping order and carrying out punishments when offenses are committed during the ceremonies. When there is a robbery, murder, or assault, justice is in the hands of the state courts. The federal and state government have appointed agents in each town to act as police. The presence of these outside authorities has frequently caused friction.

Conflict. Yaqui history has been an almost uninterrupted series of armed struggles—first against the Spanish conquerors and later against a local oligarchy and the Mexican federal government. Since the presidential decrees of the 1930s, the Yaqui struggle has been directed at defining their southern territorial boundary and controlling adjacent marine resources. The governors of the eight towns keep in touch with the inhabitants at weekly meetings. Because of the success of this political system, other types of government imposed by the state have been rejected.

Religion and Expressive Culture

Religious Beliefs. Five days after the first two Jesuit missionaries set foot on Yaqui territory, they had already christened five thousand Yaqui natives. Today Yaqui religion is a complex syncretism of native and Catholic beliefs. There are no contradictions whatsoever between them, nor any supremacy of one over the other. The Virgin Mary is identified with Itom Aye (Our Mother) and Jesus Christ with Itom Achai (Our Father). Jesus appears in myth as a Yaqui culture hero, to whom the Pascola, Deer, and Coyote ritual dances are attributed; the Matachines ritual dance is attributed to the Virgin.

Religious Practitioners. The church authorities are the trustees of the liturgy and ritual knowledge that underlie the cults of the patron saints of each town. They also preside over rites of transition. The members of a _cofradia_ (religious brotherhood or fraternity) remain under oath and occupy hierarchical ranks. Their maximum authority is the liturgical master, or _yo'owe_. The yo'owe masters and the _temastian_ (liturgist) of every single town once assisted the missionary in his teaching, and they remained in charge of performing religious rites after the deportation of the Jesuits. Today a Catholic priest goes to each town on Sundays to say Mass. The "singers" are lower in the hierarchy. Following them are the women in charge of the altars and temples, then the young girls who carry the banners during rituals, and then the boys who participate in the Holy Week ritual and the Matachines.

Ceremonies. The people responsible for the fulfillment of the ritual cycle in every village are the fiesteros, eight men and eight women who are responsible for the celebrations in honor of patron saints. As in many areas of rural Mexico, there are two groups: Moors (who wear red costumes) and Christians (who wear blue costumes). The celebrations are a ritual contest between the two. The Yaqui ritual cycle follows the liturgical Catholic calendar but puts more emphasis on particular dates and defines two different periods very clearly: Lent and regular time. During Lent, strict prohibitions are imposed on the people and on the kohtumbre yau'ura. During the rest of the year, traditional rites and festivities are classified as follows: organization festivities, religious- and military-fraternity festivities, trade-union festivities, and required Catholic church festivities.

Arts. Yaqui dancing and music go together in their ritual practices. Matachines, Pascola, Deer, and Coyote dancers make a spiritual promise to perform after they are called to their vocation in dreams. The same happens to the musicians who accompany them. Poetry, literature, and plastic arts have evolved in all eight towns.

Medicine. Traditional curative practices coexist with modern ones. Traditional curers, most of whom are female, do not have a superior social status. This occupation is inherited from one of the parents or an ancestor who transmits knowledge of the supernatural, herbs, different types of illness, and curative rites. The main curative techniques are purification, preparation of herbal remedies, and kneading.

Death and Afterlife. Beliefs about death are blended with Catholic elements. Funeral rites, however, have a hallmark of their own. Four godfathers of death are in charge of the funeral rites. At the end of the year in which a person dies, a ritual takes place to commemorate the event.

See also Cahita

Bibliography

Beals, Ralph L. (1943). "The Aboriginal Culture of the Cahita Indians." _Iberoamericana_ (Berkeley, Calif.), no. 19.

Favila, Alfonso (1940). _Las tribus yaquis de Sonora, su cultura y anhelada autodeterminación._ Mexico City: Departamento de Asuntos Indígenas.

McGuire, Thomas R. (1986). _Politics and Ethnicity on the Rio Yaqui: Potam Revisited._ Tucson: University of Arizona Press.

Olavarría, María Eugenia (1989). _Análisis estructural de la mitología yaqui._ Mexico City: Universidad Autónoma Metropolitana, Instituto Nacional de Antropología e Historia.

Pérez de Rivas, Andrés (1944). _Triunfos de Nuestra Santa_

Fé entre gentes las mas bárbaras y fieras del Nuevo Orbe. 3 vols. Mexico City: Layac.

Spicer, Edward H. (1969). "The Yaqui and Mayo." In *Handbook of Middle American Indians*, edited by Robert Wauchope. Vol. 8, *Ethnology, Part Two*, edited by Evon Z. Vogt, 830–844. Austin: University of Texas Press.

Spicer, Edward H. (1980). *The Yaquis: A Cultural History*. Tucson: University of Arizona Press.

MARÍA EUGENIA OLAVARRÍA

Yukateko

ETHNONYMS: Máasehual, Maya, Mayero, mestizos

Orientation

Identification. The term "Maya" is of indeterminable antiquity and today is usually used by the Yukateko to refer only to their language, not to themselves. For self-identification, the terms used are "Mayero," which refers to a speaker of Maya; mestizo, which in Spanish means "mixed people"; or "Máasehual," an adapted Nahuatl word that denotes "poor people."

Location. In pre-Columbian times and today, the Yukateko have inhabited much of the Yucatán Peninsula of Mexico, including the states of Yucatán, Quintana Roo, and Campeche. They live adjacently with other Maya groups such as the Kekchi and Mopan to the south near Belize, Guatemala, and the Mexican state of Tabasco.

Demography. It is difficult to enumerate the Yukateko population because classification criteria used by the Mexican government and those used by anthropologists differ, owing in part to the *mestizaje*, or Spanish/Maya "mixture" process, as well as the isolation of hundreds of communities. The best estimate is about 500,000, which suggests a recovery to near precontact levels.

Linguistic Affiliation. Yukateko belongs to the Maya Language Family and is believed to have separated from other languages about 1000 B.C. Although there are regional Maya dialectal differences identifiable by native speakers, the language used among all Maya is rather homogeneous, the result of frequent population movements during colonial and contemporary times.

History and Cultural Relations

Archaeological evidence indicates that the earliest known settlements in the Yucatán Peninsula were fishing villages on the eastern coast, suggesting a Maya presence in the area for many thousands of years. The earliest Yukateko historical records in the form of hieroglyphic texts date to the fourth century A.D., with earlier texts found to the south. These Maya were probably Ch'ol speakers with a large-scale system of trading and warring city-states, ruled by priest/kings, at centers such as Tikal, Palenque, and Copán, which flourished and then declined during what has come to be known as the Classic period, from A.D. 250 to 900. The Yukateko were also present at Cobá, Ek'Balam, Edzná, Dzibilchaltún, and other centers, although the cataclysmic collapse of this system seems to have resulted in less depopulation in Yucatán than in other Maya centers. In fact, there is some evidence that when the sites in the Guatemala region were abandoned, through some combination of environmental abuse and internal discord, Yukateko people moved south to fill the void.

By A.D. 1000, the emerging central-Mexican Toltec apparently established dominance during what is called the Postclassic period at the previously Classic Maya site of Chichén Itzá, increasing their control of the Mesoamerican trade network. Following the demise of the Toltec, beginning about A.D. 1250, the Yukateko lived in regional chiefdoms until their first contact with the Spanish off the eastern coast in 1511. In 1526 Francisco de Montejo ("El Adelantado") began a military campaign that culminated in the official Spanish aquisition of the Yucatán in 1545, although many groups remained isolated. Thousands of years of indigenous cultural development were superseded by a European colonial system of *encomienda* (Spanish ownership of land inhabited by the Maya); forced religious conversion by Spanish friars, often through torture and Inquisition-style campaigns; and centuries of enslavement to the Spanish speakers.

Yucatán's attempt to secede from Mexico in 1846 and the use of Maya conscripts in the Yucatán militia led to a release of Yukateko resentment in what has come to be called the Caste War. Two years after the beginning of this organized Maya revolt in 1847, all Spanish-speaking Yukateko were driven to take refuge in the state capitals of Mérida and Campeche, but the arrival of the spring rains caused the Maya to return to the cornfields and thus to lose their military advantage. Skirmishes and retribution against the Maya continued until about 1910. During the Mexican Revolution, the Maya made their most recent attempt to "throw off slavery," by joining in local fighting against dominant landlords. Today, the development of tourism on the peninsula has put the Maya in increasing contact with North Americans and Europeans. The Maya generally regard these light-skinned people with respect for their socioeconomic prominence but consider their morality questionable or unclear.

Settlements

There is virtually no running water in the Yucatán Peninsula because of the karst (limestone-cap) topography with its maze of underground caverns; consequently, most settlements are found near naturally occurring sinkhole wells (Maya: *c'ono'ot*; Spanish: *cenotes*). Both the pre-Hispanic city-state and the colonial village or hamlet relied extensively on these cenotes for drinking water, although in the city-states, containment systems for rain water were built as well. Contemporary villages depend on wells dug in the twentieth century or on electronically run potable water systems installed by the Mexican government. The pre-

Columbian village often clustered around a cenote, as did the administrative/ceremonial center of the nobility. Farmers and the general populace lived on the outskirts of such centers. Pre-Columbian centers, like contemporary hamlets, were constructed as quadrilaterals, with their four corners marking points aligned with the imagined four corners of the flat Maya earth. This quadripartate form provided a framework for integrating human living space within cosmological conceptions, through ritual activity that fostered human health and prosperity with supernatural assistance. Today, the thousands of communities, often isolated in the scrub brush of the north or the jungle of the south, can be contrasted with the few quasi-urban centers that also have considerable Maya habitation. In most of these, Maya is a lingua franca that many non-Maya must speak out of necessity.

Economy

Subsistence and Commercial Activities. For most of the thousands of years of occupation of the peninsula, the Yukateko have relied upon slash-and-burn (milpa, or _kòol_) horticulture. Evidence exists that pre-Hispanic Mayas supplemented _kòol_ horticulture with other more intensive techniques such as raised fields. To make _kòol_, quadrilaterals of jungle are felled and burned in the dry spring. Planting occurs after the arrival of the first rains and continues for a total of three consecutive years. The fertilizing ash supplements the shallow soil. The field is then left fallow for fifteen to twenty years. This digging-stick-based system is perfectly adapted to the Yucatán environment, which does not favor mechanized agriculture. Maize, beans, and squashes have long been planted together. The maize tortilla (_wah_) is a dietary staple, and fruits and vegetables are often grown in house gardens. Since pre-Hispanic times, and to a lesser extent today, salt has been produced from coastal lagoons.

Today wage labor supplements subsistence or income-producing agriculture. In the northeast, residual estates producing henequen provide agricultural employment. Tourist resorts provide many low-paying construction jobs. These jobs have great allure for Yukateko men, however, because urban merchants pay below-market prices for their produce simply because they are Maya, a discriminatory practice that limits the potential for economic success through agriculture.

Industrial Arts. Certain communities have a reputation for producing high-quality hammocks (_k'áan_), hats, shoes, pottery, or _huipil_ dresses, but such industry is highly localized.

Trade. Pre-Columbian trade networks were both sea and land based, with the latter depending exclusively on foot transport, owing to the absence of draft animals. Markets as centers for exchange were more common in the past than they are today, with private or government-controlled capitalism requiring Mayas to transport their wares to urban centers. Village-level exchange, often based on Mexican currency, is usually preferred, given the difficulties of transport.

Division of Labor. The Yukateko man is known by his profession of _kòolnàal_, or maize farmer, and is comple-

mented by his wife, who is in charge of the domestic unit, usually venturing forth only to take her daily maize to the local grinder, collect firewood and water, go to market, go to church, or visit friends and family.

Land Tenure. In pre-Columbian times, land use was controlled by political and kin groups. Today, the Maya have access to both private land, if resources allow, or federal _ejido_ lands, which were made available through agricultural reform after the Mexican Revolution.

Kinship

Kin Groups and Descent. Hieroglyphic inscriptions of the elite ruling class suggest that the centers of pre-Hispanic communities were inhabited by patrilineal and patrilocal extended families in which dynastic rulership would most often pass from father to son. Dynastic lineages are represented in great detail in hieroglyphic texts, tracing the right to rule back to cosmological creator deities and thereby linking kings with the supernatural realm and affording them divine authority. Spanish Conquest and subsequent subjugation removed this dynastic level from the social hierarchy, and a patrifocal system remains for the general populace.

Kinship Terminology. Both Maya and Spanish terms are used in a patrifocal bilateral system.

Marriage and Family

Marriage. Marriage is and has been expected of all adults, and in fact almost all Yukateko adults are married; those who are not are considered childlike in a number of contexts. Mexican law requires civil ceremonies for all, with those who can afford it also having a church service. In either, their parents' _compadres_, who are the couple's godparents, play a crucial role as they support and advise the couple, publicly and privately. First-cousin marriages are avoided. Postmarital residence is usually either neolocal or patrilocal, and divorce is uncommon.

Domestic Unit. Extended families are often still important, especially in maize production, but with wage labor at tourist centers increasing as an economic option, nuclear families, with spouses often separated for long periods of time, are becoming increasingly common.

Inheritance. As imposed by Spanish conquerors, Mayas acquire both of their parents' first surnames, with the father's being first. Property is divided only when both parents have died and the children have married.

Socialization. Parents seem quite lenient, and although Maya life is typically very demanding, great tenderness often exists between parents and children. A major paradox for parents is the conflict between maintaining pride in traditional culture and sensing the need for children to pursue economic opportunities outside the village. Toward this end, many parents will speak to their children in whatever little Spanish they know, although a high degree of Maya monolingualism is still evident. There is often great ambivalence for both parent and child if children leave, either to attend high school or to seek wage labor.

Sociopolitical Organization

Social Organization.   The more complex hierarchy of the pre-Columbian period changed to a system of local governance at the community or regional level, which has persisted from colonial times to today, as a result of the social and physical isolation of the Indians by the dominant Hispanics. Local prestige is attainable with age, by being skilled, or by having likable personal characteristics, such as being able to converse well. Formally organized social events center on the church, as during certain fiestas, where *gremios* (religious groups) carry the burden (*kúuc*) of celebrating their saint through the preparation of food and care of the saint's ritual paraphernalia. The *socios,* or those in charge of such groups, enhance their status by bearing this burden well. Organized cooperation is also characteristic of the ejido group, which is managed at the local level by the *comisario ejidal,* who coordinates access to federal ejido farmlands and assigns labor to be performed as service to the community.

Political Organization.   After the encomienda system of landlord rule ended with the Caste War and the Mexican Revolution, the new federal system became the political milieu for the Yukateko. The *municipio* is controlled by its largest community, which is called the *cabecera,* or head, and is governed by the municipal president. At the village level, a *comisario* (commissioner) represents local authority and is subservient to the president. He is elected for a multiyear term and is most effective if he is adept at negotiation and persuasion and refrains from trying to exert his power through coercion. Although mostly isolated in the bush and jungle of the peninsula, the Yukateko are integrated into the national political system, albeit at the bottom of the hierachy of power.

Social Control.   Yukateko communities are noted for hospitality and reserved behavior, with theft and other crimes being almost unknown, except in the larger cities. The only type of village disruption might be an occasional display of drunkenness, which is either handled informally or by the police chief, who heads the community's *guardia* (unarmed police force). The guardia has a rotating membership, through which men fulfill their communal obligations and qualify for use of ejido land. Language also acts as a social-control mechanism: in the majority of bush communities, pressure is great for mestizos and Hispanics to speak Maya in public, strengthening Maya ethnic identity and countering external social domination.

Conflict.   For some Maya and Hispanics, bitter memories linger of the killing that occurred during the Caste War. In general, however, violence across ethnic lines is very rare. Most Maya feel helpless in the face of Hispanic domination.

Religion and Expressive Culture

Religious Beliefs.   The Pre-Columbian symbolic complex representing a worldview of the joined yet distinct realms of sky, earth, and underworld endures despite centuries of forced Christianization. Only recently have the Yukateko begun to call themselves "Catholics," because of the increased presence of various Protestant sects. The Catholic/ Protestant division is a clear schism in the social fabric. Although from an external perspective Maya beliefs and ritual practices can be considered a syncretic mix of indigenous and European symbols, the Maya themselves make no such distinction, as they practice their religion daily.

Many pre-Hispanic deities are still significant today, although there is variation across the total population. The supreme creator deity of the past was probably a double-headed sky serpent representing the astronomical ecliptic. Today, Hahal Dios, or the "true god," is a syncretic combination of Jesus Christ and the sun. His assistants are the *càak* (rain deities) and the *báalam* (guardians), who, like all supernaturals, can punish as well as cure, "lest people forget that they exist." Punishments come to earth as illnesses in the form of "winds" and are expelled or prevented through elaborate ritual offerings.

Religious Practitioners.   In response to the brutal crusades of the first Spanish priests, Maya shamans went "underground" and continued the traditional roles of curer, counselor, and diviner. Today called *hmèen* or *ah k'iin,* this individual occupies a dual social status: mediating between humans and supernatural forces yet being an ordinary farmer.

Ceremonies.   The central ritual has probably always been the rain ceremony, today called *c'a càak,* or "take càak," performed during the period of the summer when the maize fields are most in need of rain. The structure in time and space of this and all ritual activity is dependent on the four-corners concept, reflecting the centrality of the Maya worldview. Whether rain or a cure for an illness is being sought, the setting of the ritual—the maize field, community, house plot, or corral—is always a quadrilateral (i.e., a model of the cosmos). These hmèen-directed functions share this symbolic structure with public fiestas centered on the church.

Arts.   The monumental architecture, carved hieroglyphic texts, pottery, and other aspects of Maya material culture are mainly responsible for the worldwide attention focused on the Yucatán Peninsula. Today, the huipil, or women's garment, with its embroidered floral patterns, is the most visible form of Maya artistry.

Medicine.   A hmèen has a sophisticated awareness of medicinal plants. These treatments, however, are always administered in the context of ritual, and the combination of ritual healing and organic remedy has apparently proven very effective over time. Governmental clinics notwithstanding, the Mayan hmèen continue to gain recognition for their curative capabilities and are sometimes even sought out by Hispanic Yucatecos.

Death and Afterlife.   It is evident from funerary remains that the rulers of the past confirmed their divine qualities through pictographic renditions of their anticipated afterlife. Although the subterranean realm was a part of this spiritual domain, the flat-earth perspective and the constancy of astronomical motion within the earth and back into the sky added a celestial component to the assumed destination of souls. The contemporary hmèen still hold these beliefs, and general mortuary practices symbolically express the cosmological motion of the human soul after death.

Bibliography

Hammond, Norman (1982). *Ancient Maya Civilization.* New Brunswick, N.J.: Rutgers University Press.

Redfield, Robert (1941). *The Folk Culture of the Yucatan.* Chicago: University of Chicago Press.

Redfield, Robert, and Alfonso Villa Rojas (1962). *Chan Kom: A Maya Village.* Chicago: University of Chicago Press.

Sosa, John R. (1989). *Cosmological, Symbolic, and Cultural Complexity among the Contemporary Maya of Yucatán.* World Archaeoastronomy. New York: Cambridge University Press.

Villa Rojas, Alfonso (1945). *The Maya of East Central Quintana Roo.* Washington, D.C.: Carnegie Institution of Washington.

JOHN R. SOSA

Zapotec

ETHNONYMS: Ben 'Zaa, Binii Gula'sa', Tsapotecatl, Za, Zapoteco

Orientation

Identification. The Spanish name "Zapoteco" stems from the Nahuatl name for the Zapotec, "Tsapotecatl," which, in turn, was derived from the name of a fruit, the *zapote,* that was common in the region. Pre-Hispanic Zapotec referred to themselves as the "Ben 'Zaa" (cloud people). On occasion, modern Zapotec refer to themselves as "Za" (the people), but it is more typical of them to identify themselves as being from a particular community or region.

Location. The Zapotec are the largest indigenous group in the Mexican state of Oaxaca. Oaxaca is located between 15° and 19° N and 94° and 99° W. The Zapotec inhabit four main areas of Oaxaca: the central valley, the Isthmus of Tehuantepec, the sierra region in the north, and the southern coastal mountain area called the Sierra de Miahuatlán. The central valley (average elevation 1,550 meters) has a temperate climate, the isthmus and other coastal areas are tropical and semiarid, whereas the sierra regions to the north and south, with variable elevations higher than the central valley, have a cooler climate than the temperate central valley. All regions experience dry and rainy seasons, the latter beginning in May and extending to October. Diverse microclimates exist in all of these regions.

Demography. The indigenous populations of Oaxaca generally, and the Zapotec in particular, underwent a marked depopulation following the Spanish Conquest. For example, the population of the central valley, estimated at about 350,000 when the Spanish arrived, had declined to about 40,000 or 45,000 by the 1630s, and regained its pre-Conquest level only in the mid-1970s. In 1971 the state of Oaxaca had 307,245 Zapotec speakers; in 1960 the figure was 253,438.

Linguistic Affiliation. Zapotec languages belong to the Otomanguean Language Family. There are probably at least nine separate, mutually unintelligible Zapotec languages: one in the central valley, one in the isthmus, four in the northern sierra, and three in the southern Sierra de Miahuatlán. Additionally, dialect differences often exist between communities.

History and Cultural Relations

Today, the impressive ruins of Monte Albán, Mitla, and Yagul (among others) stand as testimony to the accomplishments of the pre-Hispanic Zapotec. Prior to the arrival of the Spanish, the Zapotec developed a powerful state system that flourished and then declined. Long before the rise of the state (ca. 8000 to 1,500 B.C.), the Zapotec and the related Mixtec camped in small groups probably of twenty-five persons or less. Permanent villages appeared during the Formative period (ca. 1,500 to 100 B.C.) as did various new customs and practices, including loom weaving, adobe construction, stone masonry, pottery making, a 260-day calendar, human and animal sacrifice, and redistribution and reciprocal exchange systems. During the Classic period (ca. A.D. 300 to 900), Monte Albán was the metropolis of the Zapotec area, the center of a state organization that exerted its influence throughout southern Mexico. The Postclassic (ca. A.D. 900 to 1520) was the time of competitive Zapotec city-states. During the fifteenth century, the Aztec occupied the central valley and founded a garrison that would later become the state capital, Oaxaca City. When the Spanish arrived in Oaxaca, this garrison served as their colonial headquarters. Compared with the Aztec invasion, the Spanish presence in Oaxaca was exploitative and religious rather than military; compared to many parts of Mexico, most Zapotec communities remained relatively autonomous. Presently, through the market system, the Zapotec have contact with other indigenous groups and mestizos.

Settlements

The Zapotec are primarily town-dwelling peasant farmers. In the central valley, for instance, communities are compact and most villages have fewer than 5,000 inhabitants. The mountain Zapotec also live in compact settlements, although in the southern sierra there are some scattered ranches. In the isthmus, in addition to rural villages, there are two urban centers that are primarily Zapotec in composition—Juchitán and Tehuantepec. A typical Zapotec community has a Catholic church, a central plaza, local governmental buildings, a primary school, perhaps a health clinic, and probably several small dry-goods stores. Depending on its history and size, the community may be divided into barrios or sections. Generally, narrow unpaved streets are lined with adobe house walls, fences of woven cane, or cacti planted in a row. Yards and patios are often only semi-private, being visible from the street and neighboring compounds.

Economy

Subsistence and Commercial Activities. The majority of Zapotec in all regions are peasant farmers, practicing a mixture of subsistence and cash agriculture with some animal husbandry. This is also the case in the isthmus urban centers. The primary subsistence crops are maize, beans, and squashes; various other crops are grown, depending on the climate, the availability of irrigation sources, and soil conditions. The household is the basic production unit but it is linked to the outside through an elaborate, cyclical marketplace system that has operated for centuries. At times, maize may be sold as a cash crop. In the valley region, a limited number of farmers plant garbanzo beans or wheat as off-season crops, whereas maguey, which is used to make the liquor mescal, is widely planted as a cash crop. In the mountain regions, coffee is a cash crop; in the isthmus, cash crops are bananas, mangoes, and coconuts. Crops are sometimes irrigated, although many villages remain totally dependent on rainfall. In all regions, farmers use teams of oxen to plow their fields; however, when mountain slopes are too steep for oxen, planting may be accomplished with a digging stick. Tractor use is gradually increasing.

Industrial Arts. Many Zapotec communities are specialized by craft and industry. In the valley, for instance, village specializations include the production of pottery, wool serapes, grinding stones (metates), woven belts, baskets, and other goods. In the northern sierra, crafts are less prevalent but include leatherworking and cotton weaving. Dress varies both among and within the Zapotec regions, with women's clothing showing greater variety than men's apparel. The Zapotec can often identify a woman's village of origin by her style of dress.

Trade. Oaxaca is known for its highly developed market system, and the Zapotec are renowned for their commercial activities. Since pre-Hispanic times, the Zapotec have maintained trade routes through much of Oaxaca. Products were carried by tumpline, a device that is still used by farmers to transport such loads as firewood. Certain localities, for example, the valley community of Mitla, specialized in trading activities. Presently, the Zapotec play a central role in the indigenous marketplace activities in both Oaxaca City and Tehuantepec.

Division of Labor. In each Zapotec region, men and women engage in different activities, but the specific nature of the division of labor is somewhat variable. Generally, men farm, and women prepare food, perform domestic chores, and perhaps participate in commercial activities. The isthmus Zapotec women are well known for their commercial activities and are almost exclusively the traders in marketplaces. Selling is an activity closed to isthmus men, whereas in other regions both men and women produce and sell various goods. In the valley town of Teotitlán del Valle, only men weave and generally sell serapes. Some men are so successful as weavers (they now sell to an international market) that they hire farmers from neighboring villages to work their fields.

Land Tenure. Prior to changes in the Mexican constitution in 1992, land tenure consisted of a mixture of private land, communal land, and *ejidos*. A farmer's private land usually consists of several small separate parcels, not one continuous holding. Local authorities grant permission to community members to farm or graze livestock on communal lands, which generally are of poor quality. Ejidos do not exist everywhere. They were established under the land reforms following the Mexican Revolution and are portions of communities (sometimes whole communities) that hold land in common under a special local authority structure. The large haciendas, common in other parts of Mexico, were relatively insignificant in Zapotec Oaxaca.

Kinship

Kin Groups and Descent. The aboriginal Zapotec kinship system was bilateral and ambilineal, that is, descent was reckoned in both lines—and still is today. With variation from place to place, the system of ritual coparenthood, *compadrazgo*, is used by the Zapotec.

Kinship Terminology. Zapotec kinship terms, ancient and modern, are closest to the Hawaiian type. Spanish terms are replacing some of the Zapotec designations.

Marriage and Family

Marriage. Most Zapotec communities are endogamous, although this is by custom, not by rule, and there are exceptions in most locations. Monogamy is generally practiced. The Zapotec discuss at least two types of marriage: free union and church marriage. Divorce is not permitted by the Catholic church, but sometimes spouses simply separate and take other spouses. Young couples sometimes live together prior to a formal marriage. Often they are later married by the church, but sometimes they separate. A pregnancy often will prompt a marriage, either through the church or through common law. The most common residence pattern is patrilocal for young couples, but neolocality sometimes follows patrilocality, perhaps after the birth of the first child. Less commonly, residence may be matrilocal; for example, when a bride lacks brothers, her husband may come to live with her and assist his father-in-law in the fields.

Domestic Unit. Depending on his or her stage in the life cycle, a Zapotec may live in a nuclear or an extended family.

Inheritance. The rule is that all children should inherit equally, but in actuality, younger offspring who are still living with parents at the time of death may inherit more. Additionally, sons tend to inherit more land than do daughters. Land may be inherited at the parent's death, at an offspring's marriage, or when a parent becomes too old to work the fields.

Socialization. There is considerable variation in socialization practices even among closely situated Zapotec communities. For instance, parents in two adjoining valley communities may have very different beliefs about the use of physical punishment on children and also have different expectations about their children's conduct. Generally, young children up to the age of 3 years are treated affectionately, but often, corresponding with the arrival of the next sibling, parental affection is curtailed. Parents regularly frighten children by threatening that outsiders will take them away or eat them. Children are rarely instructed in how to accomplish a task or how to behave; rather, children are expected to observe, practice, and consequently learn. Older children are regularly the caretakers of younger children, which allows the adults to tend to their work.

Sociopolitical Organization

Social Organization. From the Postclassic period onward, the local community has been the primary sociopolitical entity in Zapotec society. Post-Classic Zapotec society consisted of three groups: commoners, priests, and the nobility, with each community having a controlling lord. In modern Oaxaca, the community remains the essential unit of organization, bound together by an institutionalized form of exchange called the _guela uetza_, or _gozana_, which has several manifestations. It can involve the exchange of agricultural labor or the exchange of goods during celebrations such as weddings and saint's day fiestas. For example, when a son or daughter is going to marry, the father visits all the households that owe him some form of debt from past occasions (e.g., mescal or turkeys) and asks for repayment at the upcoming wedding.

Political Organization. In most Zapotec communities, citizens are elected to fill positions in a _cargo_ system. Zapotec Cargos are hierarchically arranged, age-graded religious and political posts in which adult men in the community serve terms of office without pay. The cargo system itself is consistently present in Zapotec communities, although variation exists as to details such as how officials are nominated and elected, the number of posts, and the duties of particular positions. Common posts include mayor, judge, and other officials such as treasurer and police captain. It is also noteworthy that the isthmus Zapotec women in particular wield considerable political power.

Social Control. The Zapotec employ a variety of formal and informal social controls. Formally, disputes may be brought before the local or district authorities, who have the ability to fine and imprison wrongdoers. At the informal level, mechanisms such as the avoidance of conflict situations; the denial of hostility and anger; the internalization of ideals such as respect, cooperation, and responsibility; fear of witchcraft; gossip; envy; and the withdrawal of social support operate variably in different locations. One frequently noted Zapotec ideal involves respect for others. The renowned former Mexican president, Benito Juárez, a Zapotec, reflected the importance of respect in Zapotec thinking when he wrote, "respect for the rights of others is peace."

Conflict. Notwithstanding the Zapotec valuation of respect, they have been involved in conflict. For much of the Classic and Post-Classic periods, there is evidence that military conquest, coupled with the enslavement and at times sacrifice of captives, was a prevalent Zapotec institution. During the Mexican Revolution, some Zapotec communities, such as Ixtepeji in the northern sierra, became involved in the conflict, but others did not. Intervillage disputes over community boundaries, sometimes resulting in the loss of life, have periodically arisen in many areas for at least the last several hundred years. Interestingly, the level of intracommunity conflict is extremely variable; some Zapotec communities are very peaceful, whereas others are much more violent. Historical, social-structural, and psychocultural variables appear to be interrelated factors accounting for this pronounced variability.

Religion and Expressive Culture

Religious Beliefs. The pre-Hispanic Zapotec perceived their universe as consisting of the center surrounded by four quarters, each with a certain color and supernatural attributes. Time was viewed as cyclical, not lineal, and the Zapotec believed in gods associated with various natural elements, such as rain. The Zapotec rain god was worshiped in the northern sierra region until the mid-twentieth century. Presently, the Zapotec follow a form of Catholicism wherein saint worship plays a dominant part and pre-Hispanic beliefs have become fused with Catholicism. The Zapotec worldview includes a cast of supernaturals: witches, male and female devils, images of Christ (as a child and as an adult), and animal guardians (_tonos_). At birth, each person acquires his or her tono (e.g., a mountain lion). An unbaptized person risks becoming a _nahual_—an animal form assumed in the state of possession.

Religious Practitioners. Aside from Catholic priests, specialized Zapotec ritual leaders, _hechiceros_, also conduct certain ceremonies, including offerings of flowers, food, poultry blood, mescal, money, cigarettes, and prayers at occasions such as weddings, funerals, and house initiations.

Ceremonies. Traditionally, the Zapotec engaged in numerous rituals associated with their farming activities. Lightning, Cosijo, was seen as alive; the powerful deity was offered human blood, quail, dogs, human infants, and war captives in exchange for rain. Modern Zapotec mark major life-cycle events such as baptism, communion, marriage, and death with ceremonies in the church and in their homes. Important ceremonies occur on Todos Santos (All Saints' Day) and on the patron saints' days in each community.

Arts. Pre-Hispanic Zapotec architectural achievements are especially evident from the temples, compounds, and courts of Monte Albán and Mitla. Some modern Zapotec towns are renowned for serape weavings, pottery, and other crafts.

Medicine. The Zapotec have an impressive repertoire of remedies and cures. Members of both sexes are curers, but only women are midwives, and only men mend bones. Illness may be attributed to improper religious conduct, soul loss, envy, anger, the evil eye, fright (_susto_ or _espanto_), and witchcraft.

Death and Afterlife. The Zapotec distinguish between ordinary death and sudden violent death; in the latter, the deceased's soul does not make the transition to heaven. A distinction is also made in the death ritual for married and unmarried persons.

Bibliography

Chiñas, Beverly L. (1973). *The Isthmus Zapotec: Women's Roles in Cultural Context.* New York: Holt, Rinehart & Winston.

Flannery, Kent, and Joyce Marcus, eds. (1983). *The Cloud People.* New York: Academic Press.

Nader, Laura (1969). "The Zapotec of Oaxaca." In *Handbook of Middle American Indians,* edited by Robert Wauchope. Vol. 7, *Ethnology, Part One,* edited by Evon Z. Vogt, 329-357. Austin: University of Texas Press.

Whitecotton, Joseph W. (1977). *The Zapotecs.* Norman: University of Oklahoma Press.

DOUGLAS P. FRY

Zoque

ETHNONYMS: Soques, Tsoque, Tzoques, Zoc

Orientation

Identification. The name "Zoque" is applied to different groups who today live in the states of Tabasco, Oaxaca, and Chiapas, in southeastern Mexico. They have been called by the name of their language, "Zoque," although they like to call themselves "O' de pot," that is to say, "people who have a language" or "human speech." The origin of this name is uncertain, although it is believed that it comes from the word *zoquitl,* of Nahua origin, meaning "mud" or "humid earth."

Location. The Zoque peoples live in the mountains of the northwestern portion of the state of Chiapas, known as the Sierra de Pantepec, and on the two slopes of the lowlands that originate there: the plains of the Gulf of Mexico in the states of Tabasco and Chiapas and the plains of the Central Depression of Chiapas. Zoque also live in the eastern part of the state of Oaxaca, where the *municipios* of San Miguel and Santa María Chimalapa meet in what is called the Selva de los Chimalapas. Zoque land contains mountain ranges, hilly terrain, plateaus, ravines, and small valleys. Settlements range between elevations of 330 meters in Tecpatán and 1,770 meters in the Selva de los Chimalapas.

The climate is varied, ranging from the hot lowlands to the cold high-mountain regions. The rainy season, be-

tween May and October, is generally extensive, with abundant precipitation, especially in the Sierra de Pantepec and in the Gulf piedmont, places where populations have located in the river flood plains because of their fertility.

The eruption of the Chichonal volcano in 1982 resulted in the disappearance of the municipio of Francisco León and some of the surrounding area. Survivors relocated in other communities of the state of Chiapas, even in such little-known and inhospitable habitats as the Chiapas jungle.

Demography. After the conquest of Chiapas by the Spaniards in 1523, the Zoque population declined, with no increase until after 1877, during the government of the dictator Porfirio Díaz. Census data from 1895 and 1900 show that the Zoque population of Chiapas, Tabasco, and Oaxaca did not exceed 20,000 inhabitants at that time. In 1970 the Zoque population oscillated between 27,000 and 30,000 inhabitants, and in 1980 it reached nearly 40,000. The 1990 census registered 43,160 speakers of Zoque; however, the territorial dispersion of the Zoque, the fact that the census is based only on those who speak the language, and the noninclusion of minors below 5 years of age make it very difficult to establish a reliable count of the Zoque population.

Linguistic Affiliation. Zoque linguistic affiliation is still a subject of discussion, but recent evidence shows the existence of a Mixe-Zoque-Popoluca Language Family. Glottochronological data indicate that these languages may have derived from that spoken by the Olmec. There are several dialectal variations within the modern Zoque language.

History and Cultural Relations

At the time of the Spanish Conquest, the Mixe-Zoque Language Group and speakers of Mayan languages were south of a line running from the coastal plains of the Gulf of Mexico through the present-day city of Tapachula, on the Pacific Coast. Their earliest known ancestors lived on the Pacific coast of Chiapas, some 5,800 years ago. This coastal culture is the first known in Mesoamerica to transform its mode of production from hunting-fishing-gathering to maize cultivation. Migration toward the Gulf of Mexico could have been associated with the rise of the so-called Olmec culture which, according to glottochronological reconstructions, could have shared a language with the inhabitants of the Chiapas coast. This was the vehicle for the transmission of names of cultigens like cacao and beans.

When the Spaniards arrived in 1523, the Zoque were divided into chiefdoms, some independent and others subjects of the Nahua and Chiapas Indians. The disparate geographical distribution of the Zoque led to differentiated economic development; the warm lands were more appropriate for cultivation and better connected commercially by riverine navigation. Regional differences were maintained after the arrival of the conquerors, who imposed new political and economic concepts on the subjugated territories. The policies of evangelization and tributary obligations, first to *encomenderos* and later to the Spanish Crown, affected agricultural labor, which was based on maize for subsistence and on cochineal, cotton, sugar, and livestock raising for trade with the colonists. Mistreatment and the use of the Zoque as beasts of burden—they were even branded to serve as slaves—provoked several uprisings against the ruling Spaniards in 1693 and 1722.

Cofradías (confraternities), a Spanish institution transferred to indigenous communities, were the center of the social and religious life of the Zoque until the establishment of local governments (_ayuntamientos constitucionales_) in the 1920s.

The rapid loss of Zoque culture because of Spanish pressure was especially felt in the Central Chiapas Depression and Gulf piedmont. Zoque culture survived in the Sierra de Pantepec and surrounding countryside. Zoque culture was similar to that of other Mesoamerican peoples; it was based on the cultivation of maize, beans, and squashes, and on religious practices wherein natural elements—the earth, the mountains, the sun, the moon—were objects of worship.

In spite of the breakup of their communities by the Spanish, the Zoque kept up their contacts with their Maya neighbors through commercial and ritual exchange. In the 1990s Zoque often worked temporarily outside their communities. The contacts with Spaniards and various neighboring groups and the variations in their economies and dialects led to the dispersal of, and an eventual variation in, Zoque culture. The unifying mark of "Zoqueness" today may possibly be a common worldview and a common linguistic origin.

Settlements

Beginning in 1549, Spanish conquerors destroyed the dispersed settlement pattern of the Zoque in order to resettle them in communities that were more suitable for evangelization and the collection of tribute. The agricultural pattern that characterized the pre-Hispanic Zoque made it easy to assemble them. Nowadays this settlement pattern continues. The Zoque communities are dependencies of municipios, many of which have no Zoque in their capital towns.

Living quarters have a four- or two-eaved roof made of palm fronds or metal sheets. House construction is done with locally available natural materials, generally cane and adobe. Homes usually have a single room that serves both as a sleeping and eating place. Frequently the kitchen is separate from the main building.

Economy

Subsistence and Commercial Activities. The main agricultural activities, such as cultivation of maize, beans, squashes, or cacao, have been continued from pre-Hispanic times through the twentieth century. In Pre-Hispanic times, the Zoque traded cacao, quetzal feathers, yellow topaz, and cotton cloth with the neighboring Maya and Nahua. They use cochineal dye to decorate cloth and skins. The colonial Spanish disrupted the networks of commerce and oriented the economy toward the production of goods needed by the colonial empire. Plantations were established to increase production of cochineal, cotton, sugarcane, and cattle.

After the annexation of Chiapas by Mexico during the third decade of the nineteenth century, basic cultigens continued to be raised, but the Zoque worked on cattle ranches and on colonial cacao, banana, and coffee plantations established on what was historically Zoque land. In many instances, the Indian peasants began to raise coffee instead of maize and sugarcane on their own land. Zoque seeking wage-labor opportunities have worked in the construction of tourist complexes on the Caribbean and Pacific coasts.

Industry. Textiles were the most important local industry, especially in Chiapas territory; however, already in the 1940s there was a marked decline in handmade textiles because they could not compete with cheaper manufactured goods. The Zoque in Oaxaca produce spun and woven goods from _ixtle,_ especially bags, sacks, hammocks, and nets, which they sell in the Isthmus of Tehuantepec or the lowlands of Chiapas and Tabasco. Both the Oaxaca as well as the Chiapas Zoque make clay cooking pots, casseroles, and jugs, but the tendency has been to substitute industrially produced plastic and metal items for these. In the Sierra de Pantepec some old people still weave baskets, taking them to sell outside their communities.

Trade. Long before the pre-Hispanic period, the Zoque already had an important trade network over land and riverine routes that connected the Pacific coast to the highlands of Chiapas and the piedmont of the Gulf of Mexico. Many of these routes were followed by the Spaniards in their conquest, and today they are highways and roads. The main items of trade were cacao, maize, beans, chilies, fine cloth, grinding stones, straw mats, baskets, and quetzal feathers. With the arrival of the Spaniards, this trade decreased and, in the twentieth century (especially since roads have been made passable), a large number of Zoque have bought industrially manufactured products—specifically, woven goods, shoes, and household appliances—wholesale, in order to sell them in their own and neighboring communities.

Division of Labor. Men are in charge of cultivating the land, tending cattle, and manufacturing items such as pottery and basketry, whereas women take care of the home, the children, and small domestic animals (chickens and turkeys). Often women will also work in ceramics and textiles. Present-day economic needs have caused both men and women to leave their communities to work as wage laborers in the city. Women, generally the single ones, work as domestic servants. Boys help their fathers in the field; it is very unusual for them to go to school after the age of 12. Something similar occurs with young girls, who take care of their younger siblings.

Land Tenure. It can be inferred that during pre-Hispanic times a _calpulli_ system organized kinship and residential relations. During the colonial period, the Spanish Crown granted communities land for subsistence and tribute. The land continued to belong to the Crown and was distributed as usufruct in the form of family plots. The Crown also gave the community pastures and forest lots, known as _ejidos._ Communal lands attracted Spanish colonists, who seized them and established commercial farms and cattle ranches. Where communal land was taken over by the colonists, the Zoque suffered a rapid sociocultural transformation. In the second half of the nineteenth century, the "liberal" policies of the Mexican government destroyed the remaining system of communal land tenure. "Liberalization" led to an increase in the expanse of commercial farms and a loss of land for the Zoque. This was only partially corrected by the postrevolutionary policy under which the modern *ejido* became the foundation of the Indian peasants' right to cultivate their own land. Beginning in the 1930s, ejidos were given to the Zoque.

Kinship

Kin Groups and Descent.   Before the agrarian land distribution that resulted in the ejido, the patrilineal orientation of Zoque nomenclature was more evident; both inheritance and postmarital residence depended on the father, and the family was extended for two to three generations. Family fragmentation typical of a market economy and the arrival of new religious beliefs has led to a system that recognizes both the father's and the mother's side of the family; there is now a tendency for postmarital residence to be ambilocal. At baptism, the child was once named for a relative from the previous generation, in a sense becoming his or her replacement on earth, but this practice has been infrequent since 1970.

Kinship Terminology.   Traditional family terms follow the Omaha kinship pattern.

Marriage and Family

Marriage.   Family-arranged marriage has practically disappeared, giving place to marriage based on individual decision or elopement. Thereby the long and costly marriage negotiations are avoided, which could entail up to ten visits and presents of chocolate, bread, refreshments, and alcoholic drinks—things that the groom's family must take to the prospective bride's family. The ancient division of communities into ceremonial wards and kinship-oriented entities facilitated internal endogamy. Nowadays their almost total disappearance leaves endogamy at the community level as a defensive mechanism to limit the usufruct of community lands to community families. Polygamy is infrequent, and those cases that do occur are condemned by Catholic or Evangelical ecclesiastical authorities.

Domestic Unit.   The basic residential unit is the nuclear family, particularly since the decline in patrilocal residence. Each biological or nuclear family takes meals by itself, independently of the other families, although nuclear families help one another in agricultural labor and in ritual obligations.

Inheritance.   Traditionally, inheritance was in the male line. Patrilineal inheritance has been replaced by bilateral inheritance, although the tendency is for men to receive lands, whereas women inherit domestic animals and utensils. Many inheritances are granted in life, causing tensions and disputes between parents and children and between siblings.

Socialization.   Children are generally treated with respect and are not punished. Their play is relatively unsupervised, and they are very close to their mothers, with whom they live and whom they help in various domestic tasks. School is obligatory, although very few children finish their primary studies. The other medium of socialization is participation in religious rituals, depending on the family's religious orientation.

Sociopolitical Organization

Social Organization.   During the pre-Hispanic period, the social hierarchy was based on wealth and traditional authority. The former was displayed by the chiefs, whereas the latter was divided among chiefs, priests, elders, and shamans, who performed ceremonial rites and preserved the ancient knowledge. The father of each household was recognized as the head of the extended family. After the Spanish Conquest, new social institutions originating in the Iberian Peninsula were incorporated: the Catholic church, *cofradías*, and *compadrazgo* (ritual kinship). The cofradías served to create social prestige through the assumption of *cargos* within them. Elders continued their active participation in ceremonies; this is still evident in traditional ritual practices.

Political Organization.   When the Spaniards arrived in Zoque territory, they found it organized into chiefdoms with subject peoples. There was no centralization of power, and each chiefdom exerted control over a specific area, based on kinship. The status of the chief was extended to his kin; thus social differentiation was created in the chiefdom.

After the Conquest, a system of religious cargos maintained the principles of age and prestige within a civil-religious hierarchy. After the second decade of the twentieth century, the establishment of the local village governments removed political power from the civil-religious hierarchies and recast Zoque political systems within institutions created by the national and state governments.

Social Control.   Territorial dispersion of the Zoque makes it difficult to identify control mechanisms that represent the whole group; however, in the municipio of Tapalapa, Chiapas, a form of social control on the natural and supernatural level has been noted. People believe that a mythical tribunal of I'ps Tojk ("twelve houses" or "twelve places") punishes people who transgress social and moral norms. This tribunal is addressed in dreams by people who possess *kojama* (animal-companion spirits). Illness is an indication that the kojama of the victim may be held prisoner by the tribunal. Only treatment by a *jama yoye* (curer) can lead the victim to health. The jama yoye persuades the victim to abandon his incorrect social behavior and/or involves himself in symbolic combat between various implicated animal-companion spirits. Another mechanism of social control is ritual reciprocity, which communicates trust and good intentions, thus reducing tension between families within the community.

Conflict.   Conflicts are generally generated out of scarcity, such as the need for land. Conflicts between neighbors over land can become serious. Confrontations involve nuclear or extended families and can be started by an illness interpreted as sorcery. Physical violence is generally avoided through the mediation of a curer, who supernaturally protects the victim. The disappearance of curers and the decline of rituals that functioned as mechanisms to calm social tensions between families and neighbors has resulted in the use of legal mechanisms to resolve land disputes and other problems such as adultery, marital conflict, insult, physical aggression, theft, and murder.

Religion and Expressive Culture

Religious Beliefs. The Catholic religion was systematically imposed, beginning in 1564, with the foundation of the convent of Tecpatán, Chiapas. Nevertheless, in the twentieth century, there is an evident religious split between the Catholics linked to the official church and people maintaining traditional ritual forms. In the 1930s groups of Seventh Day Adventists successfully penetrated the communities and now are practically the only Protestant denomination in Zoque municipios.

The Spanish Conquest did not result in the complete acceptance of Catholic beliefs. Traditional gods continued to be worshiped at sacred places. In caves and mountains, gods of nature—the sun, the moon, lightning, the serpent, the jaguar, Jantepusi (Mother of the Earth)—were venerated, as were gods who were apparently a synthesis of pre-Hispanic agricultural cults represented in various images sculpted in stone, clay, and wood. Such deities could appear in various forms, but were almost always associated with the moon and water. Mythical figures among present-day Zoque are Piowacwe ("little old woman" or "burning woman"), a female god of misfortune who lives in the bowels of the earth in the Chichonal volcano, and Nawayomo ("evil woman" or "water woman"), deceiver of men. Both have the capability of transforming themselves, and the latter appears in the form of a woman and a serpent with a dentate vagina.

Religious Practitioners. Native ritual practices aimed at propitiating the gods were performed clandestinely during the colonial period or were syncretized with Catholic institutions. Through cofradías and *mayordomías,* the role of wise elders as ritual specialists was perpetuated. Festivals for the saints, which were institutionalized in mayordomías, maintained the religious life of many communities. Religious fragmentation now has decreased the influence of elders as ritual leaders, making it possible for younger men to hold important posts in official Catholic and Seventh Day Adventist institutions.

Ceremonies. The Catholic ceremonial calendar was superimposed on the pre-Hispanic calendar, and the saints took the place of the ancient deities. This has resulted in a public religious system organized around festivals for the patron saints of communities or barrios. These ceremonies involve processions, the ritual exchange of saints with other communities, the distribution of images among ritual participants, and offerings in the form of dances, music, flowers, food, and drink. Pilgrimages and Carnival festivities expand the ritual repertoire, which also includes marriages, baptisms, communions, deaths, and ritual curing.

Arts. The production of textiles and ceramics is now practically nonexistent among the Zoque. Basketry is still produced, however, and masks and musical instruments (drums and flutes) are designed and made for ritual use. Dance and music are an integral part of ritual. Also, bilin-

gual- and indigenous-language publications have opened an expressive literary field to Zoque narrators and poets.

Medicine. Illness is seen as the result of transgression against the social order or the effect of sorcery. In both cases, the mediation of a curer is required, usually a man knowledgeable in the ancient ways, who by "pulsing"—reading the rhythm of the patient's blood—can determine the causes of illness. By means of various rituals, in which dreaming plays an important part, he will be able to restore the patient's kidnapped *tonal.* This practice is becoming increasingly infrequent, and the knowledge is dying out; recourse to community health centers has become more frequent. Medicinal plants continue to be used, however; men specialize in their collection. Women function as midwives, but only rarely do they engage in ritual mediation.

Death and Afterlife. Zoque believe that the soul separates from the body at the time of death. They do not see death as contaminating members of the family; therefore, when someone dies, relatives and people close to the family offer help and support. Wakes are held; coffee, bread, and, sometimes, alcohol are distributed to attending guests.

The Days of the Dead (Todos Santos) are celebrated on the first two days of November. These are joyful days with ritual exchanges of food and the preparation of altars in honor of the dead. In the graveyard, tombs are cleaned, and offerings of food and drink of the kind that the deceased enjoyed during his or her lifetime are made. Each family enjoys a ritual meal near the remains of their loved ones.

Bibliography

Aramoni Calderón, Dolores (1992). *Los refugios de lo sagrado: Religiosidad, conflicto, y resistencia entre los zoques de Chiapas.* Mexico City: Consejo Nacional para la Cultura y las Artes (CNCA).

Codry, Donald Bush, and Dorothy Codry (1941). *Costumes and Weaving of the Zoque Indians of Chiapas.* Paper 15. Los Angeles: Southwest Museum.

Fábregas Puig, Andrés (1986). "Los estudios sobre zoques de Chiapas: Una lectura desde el olvido y la reiteración." In *Anuario de investigación, 1993,* 78–125. Tuxtla Gutiérrez: Instituto Chiapaneco de Cultura; Gobierno del Estado de Chiapas.

Thomas, Norman D. (1974). *Envidia, brujería, y organización ceremonial: Un pueblo zoque.* Mexico City: Secretaría de Educación Pública.

Villa Rojas, Alfonso, José Velasco, Félix Báez-Jorge, Francisco Córdoba, and Norman Thomas (1975). *Los zoques de Chiapas.* Mexico City: Instituto Nacional Indigenista; Secretaría de Educación Pública.

MIGUEL LISBONA GUILLEN

Glossary

alcalde Mayor of a town. A town in Middle America has considerable political power over the surrounding area.

affine A relative by marriage.

age grade A social category composed of persons who fall within a culturally defined age range.

aguardiente A white rum distilled from fermented raw sugar.

agnatic descent. *See* patrilineal descent

aguacil An agent of town or municipal officials with limited police powers.

ambilineal descent The practice of tracing kinship affiliation through either the male or the female line.

anciano An elder of a village.

animal husbandry. *See* pastoralism

animism A type of religious belief in which the world is made to move and becomes alive because of spiritual (soul) forces in beings and things.

autochthones The indigenous inhabitants of a region. Often used to refer to the native inhabitants encountered by European explorers or settlers.

avunculocal residence The practice of a newly married couple residing in the community or household of the husband's mother's brother.

ayuntamiento The government of a town, the town hall.

barrio A subdivision and residential area of a town.

bilateral descent The practice of tracing kinship affiliation more or less equally through both the male and the female line.

bride-price The practice of a groom or his kin giving substantial property or wealth to the bride's kin before, at the time of, or after marriage.

bride-service The practice of a groom performing work for his wife's kin for a set period of time either before or after marriage.

bride-wealth. *See* bride-price

cabecera The capital or head town of a municipio.

cabildo A village or town council composed of a hierarchy of officeholders in countries that were formerly Spanish colonies; the town hall.

cacao A tropical tree cultivated since pre-Hispanic times for its seeds. The seeds were used by the Aztecs to make a beverage called *chocolatl*, and today they are the key ingredient in modern chocolate.

cacique A local strongman or political boss. The word "cacique" was adopted into Spanish to designate a native chief. Today it is applied variously to Indians and non-Indians to designate a local political boss who leads and controls people through the more or less undemocratic exercise of political power.

campo santo Graveyard.

cargo An obligation to perform and sponsor religious rituals in honor of a public saint. Also it can refer to any official duty. Religious cargos are publicly recognized obligations to the community. Cargo means "burden," which connotes the heavy responsibility to the community felt by the person who has the obligation.

cargo system A formal social structure of religious obligations (cargos) taken on for a defined period, usually a year, with community recognition. These obligations involve the performance of public religious rituals.

cassava A plant of the genus *Manihot* (also known as manihot, manioc, tapioca, and yuca), cultivated by aboriginal farmers for its nutritious starchy roots.

chayote The fruit of cucurbitaceous vine (*Sechium edule*) cultivated by the Middle American Indians from remote times. It has a spiny outer skin and a starchy, tasty interior.

chicha A native beerlike drink made from fermented maize, sugarcane, manioc, sweet potatoes, and/or fruit.

civil-religious hierarchy A system through which individuals alternate between civil and religious offices, thus climbing a ladder of prestige and power in their communities. Civil-religious hierarchies depend on cargo systems.

clan A unilineal descent group in which people claim descent from a common ancestor but cannot demonstrate this descent.

classificatory kin terms Kinship terms such as "aunt" that designate several categories of distinct relatives, such as mother's sister and father's sister.

cochineal A red dye obtained by Middle American natives from an insect that lives on a type of nopal cactus. This cactus is still cultivated today as a source of a natural dye for food and cosmetics. In the colonial period cochineal dye was a source of wealth for the Europeans who exported it.

cofradía A religious organization. Modern cofradías are dedicated to the veneration of the religious images in their charge. The term is often used in the Mayan area to refer to a group of men in charge of the celebrations of a particular saint. These groups are similar to groups called "mayordomías" farther north. In the nineteenth century cofradías had other communal economic functions, such as providing loans.

cognates Words that belong to different languages but have similar sounds and meanings.

collaterals A person's relatives, not related to him or her as ascendants or descendants; one's uncle, aunt, cousin, brother, sister, nephew, niece.

compadrazgo Ritual coparenthood. It involves two married couples. One couple becomes godparents of something—typically but not necessarily a child—belonging to the other couple. Compadrazgo establishes a special bond between the two couples through a ritual of godparenting and engenders a special form of trust and respect between the two couples, each of which refers to the other as "compadres." Compadrazgo goes well beyond the godparenting of children to include godparenting of religious images, objects, and life-cycle events such as graduation, death, and marriage. *See also* fictive kinship

comunero A person who farms communal lands by right.

consanguine A relative by descent from a common ancestor.

cousin, cross Children of one's parent's siblings of the opposite sex—one's father's sisters' and mother's brothers' children.

cousin, parallel Children of one's parent's siblings of the same sex—one's father's brothers' and mother's sisters' children.

creole A general, inconsistently used term usually applied to a spoken language or dialect that is based on grammatical and lexical features combined from two or more natural languages. It is a first language, distinct from a pidgin.

Creole "Creole" is most often used today to refer to the Black populations of the West Indies and Central America. It is derived from the Spanish *criollo* and the French *créole,* meaning a White or Black person descended from immigrants.

criollo Used during the colonial period to describe a White or Black person born in the colonies with no Indian admixture.

Cristero movement A pro-Catholic rebellion in the late 1920s in the Mexican states of Jalisco, Michoacán, and Colima against the federal government repression of the Catholic church.

cross cousin. *See* cousin, cross

cult The beliefs, ideas, and activities associated with the worship of a supernatural force or its representations, such as an ancestor cult or a bear cult.

Día de los Muertos Day of the Dead. *See* Todos Santos

double descent Kinship affiliation by both matrilineal and patrilineal descent.

dowry The practice of a bride's kin giving substantial property or wealth to the groom or to his kin before or at the time of marriage.

Ego In kinship studies, a male or female whom the anthropologist arbitrarily designates as the reference point for a particular kinship diagram or discussion of kinship terminology.

ejidatario A beneficiary of land distributed as an ejido.

ejido Ejido is a form of landholding created by Mexican federal agrarian reform. Land was taken by the federal government and given to a group of subsistence farmers as an ejido with the provision that they could not rent or sell the land. Membership in the ejido group was not legally heritable, and continued membership depended upon residence and use of the land. Many ejido plots nevertheless remained in a single family for generations. A change in Article 27 of the Mexican Constitution in 1992 permitted the ejidatarios, members of the ejido, to obtain title to the land. The titles are restricted by complex laws and do not necessarily split the land into individual privately sellable plots. This change also brought to an end the transformation of large landholdings into ejidos. Land-poor people and ejidatarios have been threatened by the change, and it was an important factor causing Indians in Chiapas to rebel against the Mexican state in 1994 (Collier 1995). The rebels were known as "Zapatistas," after their organization, the Zapatista Army of National Liberation.

encomienda A Crown grant of Indian tribute to a Spaniard during the colonial period. The encomienda system allowed colonists to utilize Indian labor and wealth in setting up agricultural and mining enterprises.

encomendero The person receiving an encomienda grant.

endogamy Marriage within a specific group or social category of which the person is a member, such as one's caste or community.

exogamy Marriage outside a specific group or social category of which the person is a member, such as one's clan or community.

fictive kinship A social relationship, such as blood brotherhood or godparenthood, between individuals who are neither affines nor consanguines but who are referred to or addressed with kin terms and treated as kin. _See also_ compadrazgo

fiesta A celebration and feast held according to ritual traditions.

hacienda A landed estate. Haciendas came into existence during the colonial period in Middle America. In the nineteenth century haciendas expanded as profit-making ventures that exploited the labor of the people whose lands they expropriated.

hacendado The owner of a hacienda.

horticulture Plant cultivation carried out by relatively simple means, usually without permanent fields, artificial fertilizers, or plowing.

initiation rites Ceremonies and related activities that mark the transition from childhood to adulthood or from secular status to being a cult member.

ixtle The rough fiber of the _maguey_ (agave) plant or rope made of it.

jacal A shack, a humble dwelling.

kindred The bilateral kin group of near kin who may be expected to be present and participant on important ceremonial occasions, usually in the absence of unilineal descent.

kinship Family relationship, whether traced through marital ties or through "blood" descent.

kin terms, bifurcate-collateral A system of kinship terminology in which all collaterals in the parental generation are referred to by different kin terms.

kin terms, bifurcate-merging A system of kinship terminology in which members of the two descent groups in the parental generation are referred to by different kin terms.

kin terms, Crow A system of kinship terminology in which matrilateral cross cousins are distinguished from each other and and from parallel cousins and siblings, but

patrilateral cross cousins are referred to by the same terms used for father or father's sister.

kin terms, descriptive Kinship terms that are used to distinguish different categories of relatives, such as _mother_ or _father_.

kin terms, Dravidian. _See_ kin terms, Iroquois

kin terms, Eskimo A system of kinship terminology in which cousins are distinguished from brothers and sisters, but no distinction is made between cross and parallel cousins.

kin terms, generational A system of kinship terminology in which all kin of the same sex in the parental generation are referred to by the same term.

kin terms, Hawaiian A system of kinship terminology in which all male cousins are referred to by the same term used for "brother," and all female cousins are referred to by the same term used for "sister."

kin terms, Iroquois A system of kinship terminology in which parallel cousins are referred to by the same terms used for brothers and sisters, but cross cousins are identified by different terms.

kin terms, lineal A system of kinship terminology in which direct descendants or ascendants are distinguished from collateral kin.

kin terms, Omaha A system of kinship terminology in which female matrilateral cross cousins are referred to by the same term used for one's mother, and female patrilateral cross cousins are referred to by the same term used for one's sister's daughter.

kin terms, Sudanese A system of kinship terminology in which there are distinct terms for each category of cousin and sibling, and for aunts, uncles, nieces, and nephews.

Köppen, Waldimir Peter A German meteorologist and climatologist who introduced a system for classifying climates. His system has been adapted for use in Middle American anthropology. There are four major climatic types in Middle America: "A," warm humid climates in which the average temperature of the coldest month is greater than 18° C; "B," dry climates determined by calculations involving rainfall and temperature; "C," humid temperate climates in which the average temperature of the coldest month is between −3° and 18° C; and "E," cold climates in which the average temperature of the warmest month is less than 6.5° C. Other letters in a climate code indicate the seasonality of the precipitation, seasonal average temperature extremes, and other factors. _See_ García (1964) and Vivió Escoto (1964).

Ladino During the colonial period, "Ladino" referred to an Indian who had acquired Hispanic culture and language. Today it is often used south of the Isthmus of Tehuantepec to refer to people who follow a modern, market-oriented, non-Indian culture pattern of Hispanic origin.

levirate   The practice of requiring a man to marry his brother's widow.

lineage   A unilineal descent group in which all members can reckon their descent from a common ancestor either through males (patrilineage) or females (matrilineage).

magic   Beliefs and ritual practices designed to harness supernatural forces to achieve the goals of the magician.

maíz   maize, New World Indian corn (*Zea mays*). Maize is the most important crop in the native Americas.

matrilineal descent   The practice of tracing kinship affiliation only through the female line.

matrilocal residence   The practice of a newly married couple residing with the wife's kin.

mayordomo   A Spanish word meaning "a servant in charge of something." It is commonly applied by Mesoamerican Indians to higher officials in a religious cargo system. Its original meaning has been changed: whereas it once referred to a person in change of a church, image, or public religious treasury, it now refers to a person who sponsors religious rituals at great personal expense.

mescal   A strong alcoholic beverage distilled from a species of maguey (*Agave*) cactus. When the cactus is mature, the base of the leaves is cut into chunks and baked in a pit oven with heated rocks. Water is added to the sealed oven to produce steam that helps to cook the chunks. When done, the chunks are cooled and taken to the distillery to be beaten into a mash. The mash is squeezed to extract a juice, which is then fermented. An ingenious native still distills the fermented juice in a two-stage process to produce the final product.

messianic movement   A form of social movement in which adherents believe that a particular individual—a messiah—will lead them to a more prosperous and better life.

mestizo   During the colonial period, a mestizo was a person of mixed Indian and other ancestry. Today the term is often used to designate a person who follows a modern, market-oriented, non-Indian culture pattern of Hispanic origin.

milpa   A field cultivated in the traditional Indian way. The primary cereal crop planted in the milpa is maize. This is supplemented by cocropping beans and squashes. A milpa can be a slash-and-burn field with long fallowing or a plowed field with short fallowing.

moiety   A form of social organization in which an entire cultural group is made up of two social groups. Each moiety is often composed of a number of interrelated clans, sibs, or phratries.

monogamy   Marriage between one man and one woman at a time.

municipio   A political/territorial division of the executive power of a Mexican state. Although the municipio is often thought of as a territorial division of a state, it corresponds only to the executive branch of the government, headed by the governor.

nagual/nahual   Because of the idiosyncratic way in which Aztec words were applied by the Aztecs and later by the Spanish, the word "nagual" has been used to describe two different types of animal-spirit companions, an evil one allied with the forces of the underworld and a basically helpful one that is a personal animal-companion spirit for the individual. The latter is also called the "tonal." An article by Foster (1944) clarifies these differences.

neolocal residence   The practice of a newly married couple living apart from the immediate kin of either party.

pacification   The cessation of warfare by indigenous peoples enforced by colonial nations or their agents.

paraje   A village that is a subdivision of a municipio.

parallel cousin.   *See* cousin, parallel

pasado.   *See* anciano

pastoralism   A type of subsistence economy based on the herding of domesticated grazing animals, such as sheep or cattle.

patrilineal descent   The practice of tracing kinship affiliation only through the male line.

patrilocal residence   The practice of a newly married couple residing with the husband's kin.

peasants/peasantry   Small-scale agriculturists producing only subsistence crops, perhaps in combination with some fishing, animal husbandry, or hunting. They live in villages in a larger state but participate little in the state's commerce or cultural activities. Today many peasants rely on mechanized farming and are involved in the national economy and are called *postpeasants* by anthropologists.

peón/peon   In the past, a peon was a person attached to a hacienda and compelled to work for the owner. Today the word refers to any agricultural day laborer.

petate   A mat woven of straw or cane used for sleeping. In the most rudimentary native house, the petates are unrolled each evening on the packed dirt floor to provide sleeping space.

pidgin   A second language, very often composed of words and grammatical features from several languages and used as the medium of communication between speakers of different languages.

polyandry   The marriage of one woman to more than one man at a time.

polygyny   The marriage of one man to more than one woman at a time.

puberty rites. *See* initiation rites

pulque A mildly alcoholic drink made by fermenting the juice of a highland species (*Agave atrovirens*) of maguey cactus. The juice (*aguamiel*) is drawn from the live plant after it flowers and then fermented.

quinceañera The celebration of a girl's fifteenth birthday. It is a celebration of the girl's sexual maturity. In many Latin American countries it has become an occasion for a lavish feast held by the girl's parents.

ranchería A settlement that is smaller and has less political status than a pueblo (village).

repartimiento A system of coerced Indian labor set up by the Spanish in the sixteenth century to supply labor for colonial enterprises. Application for Indians to work on needed services could be made to the Crown authorities. The person receiving the benefit had to pay the Indians' wages.

rezandero A person who says, sings, or chants traditional prayers, usually in Spanish, from a prayer book. These are often at vigils for the dead.

shaman A religious practitioner who receives his or her power directly from supernatural forces.

shifting cultivation A form of horticulture in which plots of land are cleared and planted for a few years and then left to fallow for a number of years while other plots are used. Also called swidden, extensive, or slash-and-burn cultivation.

sib. *See* clan

sierra A mountainous region.

sister exchange A form of arranged marriage in which two men exchange their sisters as wives.

slash-and-burn cultivation A system of food production that involves burning trees and brush to clear and fertilize a garden plot, and then planting crops. The plot is used for a few years and then left to fallow while other plots are similarly used.

sorcery (brujería) Magic practiced for evil and antisocial ends. It may be practiced by a sorcerer, for money paid by a client. In Middle America there is a widespread belief in sorcery, but few will admit to practicing it.

sororal polygyny The marriage of one man to two or more sisters at the same time.

sororate The practice of marrying one's sister's widower.

sucking cure A curing technique often used by shamans that involved sucking out a foreign object from the patient's body through an implement such as a bone tube. The foreign object, a piece of bone or stone, was viewed as the cause of the malady, and the sucking out as the cure.

swidden The field or garden plot resulting from slash-and-burn field preparation.

teknonymy The practice of addressing a person after the name of his wife or his or her child rather than by the individual name. For example, "Bill" is called "Father of John."

topil *See* aguacil

Todos Santos A festival beginning on the evening of 31 October and lasting for several days. It coincides with the Catholic All Saints' Day but has other origins in the Aztec Days of the Dead at the end of the secular Mesoamerican year. It is celebrated by all classes in all parts of Mexico and is one of the most universal Mesoamerican festivals. People believe that the souls of departed family members visit the earth for a day. The souls are welcomed by an altar filled with food offerings. It is an important time for strengthening family bonds.

tona/tonal An animal-companion spirit. Existing in various forms, this native American religious belief can be found in all parts of the Western Hemisphere. The tonal is usually unseen. Shamans can work with it in curing rituals. The tonal is a guardian and a life spirit. Some people believe that people have more than one given to them at birth. The fate of the tonal parallels that of its owner, and its vulnerability reflects the vulnerability of the owner to the vicissitudes of life. The tonal can aid and revive persons who are in need of help.

transhumance Seasonal movement of a society or community. It may involve seasonal shifts in food production between hunting and gathering and horticulture or the movement of herds to more favorable locations.

tribe Although there is some variation in use, the term "tribe" usually applies to a distinct people who view themselves and are recognized by outsiders as a distinct culture. The tribal society has its own name, territory, customs, subsistence activities, and often its own language.

unilineal descent The practice of tracing kinship affiliation through only one line, either the matriline or the patriline.

unilocal residence The general term for matrilocal, patrilocal, or avunculocal postmarital residence.

usufruct The right to use land or property without actually owning it.

uterine descent. *See* matrilineal descent

uxorilocal residence The practice of a newly married couple living at or near the former residence of the wife.

virilocal residence The practice of a newly married couple living at or near the former residence of the husband.

wattle-and-daub A method of house construction whereby a framework (wattle) of poles and twigs is covered (daubed) with mud and plaster.

witchcraft　The use of innate supernatural forces to control or harm another person. Unlike sorcery, witchcraft does not require the use of magical rituals.

Bibliography

Collier, George (1994). *Basta! Land and the Zapatista Rebellion in Chiapas.* Monroe, Oreg.: Food First Books.

Foster, George (1944). "Nagualism in Mexico and Guatemala." *Acta Americana* 2:85–103.

García, E. (1964). *Modificaciones al sistema de clasificación de Köppen para adaptarlo a las condiciones particulares de la República Mexicana.* Mexico City: Offset Larios.

Vivió Escoto, Jorge (1964). "Weather and Climate of Mexico and Central America." In *Handbook of Middle American Indians,* edited by Robert Wauchope. Vol. 1, *Natural Environment and Early Cultures,* edited by Robert C. West. Austin: University of Texas Press.

Filmography

The following is a list of films and videos on Middle American nations and cultures. The list is not meant to be complete; rather, it is a sampling of documentary films available from distributors in North America. Listing a film or video does not constitute an endorsement by the volume editors or any of the contributors, nor does the absence of a film represent any sort of nonendorsement. Names of distributors are provided at the end of each citation. Please consult the National Information Center for Educational Media (NICEM) or the *Educational Film and Video Locator* for current addresses. Some of the films and videos listed here are also available through the Extension Media Center of the University of California at Berkeley (2176 Shattuck Ave., Berkeley, CA 94704) and/or the Penn State Audio-Visual Services (Special Services Building, Pennsylvania State University, University Park, PA 16802), as indicated by (EMC) or (PS) at the end of the citation.

1. *Appeals to Santiago.* (Mexico; Maya) 1968. Produced by the University of California at Irvine. Color, 27 minutes. CRM/McGraw-Hill Films.
2. *Arts and Crafts of Mexico.* Part 1, *Pottery and Weaving.* (Mexican Indians) 1961 (rev. ed.). Color, 14 minutes, 16mm. Encyclopedia Brittanica Educational Corporation. (PS).
3. *Arts and Crafts of Mexico.* Part 2, *Basketry, Stone, Wood, and Metals.* (Mexican Indians). 1961 (rev. ed.). Color, 14 minutes, 16mm. Encyclopedia Brittanica Educational Corporation. (PS).
4. *Before Reggae Hit the Town.* (Jamaica) 1992. Color, 21 minutes, VHS. (EMC).
5. *Bitter Cane.* (Haiti) 1983. Produced by Haiti Films. Color, 75 minutes. Cinema Guild.
6. *Camino Triste: The Hard Journey of the Guatemalan Refugees.* (Guatemala) 1983. Produced by Seventh Day Productions. Color, 30 minutes. First Run Features/Icarus Films.
7. *Capital of Earth: The Maroons of Moore Town.* (Maroons) 1979. Color, 40 minutes, 16mm, U-matic. Pennsylvania State University Psych Cinema Register. (PS).
8. *Chichicastenango.* (Maya) 1987. Produced by Claudia Feldmar for Camara 2. Color, 30 minutes, VHS, U-matic. Pennsylvania State University Psych Cinema Register. (PS).
9. *The Chinamapas.* (Farming; Mexico) 1990. Color, 31 minutes, VHS. (EMC).
10. *Comalapa: Traditions and Textiles.* (Maya) 1987. Color, 26 minutes, VHS, U-matic. Pennsylvania State University Psych Cinema Register. (PS).
11. *Conflict of the Gods,* Program 2. (Mexico) 1991. Color, 59 minutes. Films, Incorporated.
12. *Daughters of Ixchel: Maya Thread of Change.* (Guatemalan Maya) 1993. Color, 29 minutes, VHS. (EMC).
13. *The Devil's Dream.* (Dance of Death; Guatemala) 1991. Color, 58 minutes. Cinema Guild.
14. *Guatemalan Pottery.* (Guatemala) 1987. Produced by Claudia Feldmar, Camara 2. Color, 60 minutes, VHS, U-matic. Pennsylvania State University Psych Cinema Register. (PS).
15. *Hidden Scars.* (K'iche' Maya) 1994. Produced by Grace Barnes. Color, 50 minutes, VHS. (EMC).
16. *Holy Week in Antigua, Guatemala.* (Guatemala) 1987. Produced by Claudia Feldmar, Camara 2. Color, 26 minutes, VHS, U-matic. Pennsylvania State University Psych Cinema Register. (PS).
17. *Huichol Sacred Pilgrimage to Wirikuta.* (Huichol) 1991. Color, 29 minutes, VHS. (EMC).
18. *Invisible Indians: Mixtec Farmworkers in California.* (Mixtec) 1993. Color, 43 minutes, VHS. (EMC).
19. *Kantik'i Maishi: Songs of Sorghum.* (Netherlands Antilles) 1992. Color, 58 minutes, VHS. (EMC).
20. *Kiliwa: Hunters and Gathers of Baja California.* (Kiliwa) 1975. Color, 14 minutes, 16mm. (EMC).
21. *Lancandon Maya Balche Ritual.* (Lakandon) 1988. Color, 40 minutes, VHS. (EMC).
22. *The Living Maya: Part 1.* (Maya) 1982. Directed by Hubert Smith. Color, 58 minutes, VHS. Cinema Guild. (EMC) (PS).
23. *The Living Maya: Part 2.* (Maya) 1982. Directed by Hubert Smith. Color, 58 minutes, VHS. Cinema Guild. (EMC) (PS).
24. *The Living Maya: Part 3.* (Maya) 1982. Directed by Hubert Smith. Color, 58 minutes, VHS. Cinema Guild. (EMC) (PS).
25. *The Living Maya: Part 4.* (Maya) 1982. Directed by Hubert Smith. Color, 58 minutes, VHS. Cinema Guild. (EMC) (PS).
26. *Maya of Ancient and Modern Yucatan.* (Maya) 1949. B&W, 22 minutes, 16mm. Phoenix Films. (PS).
27. *Ollero Yucateco (Yucatan Potter).* (Maya) 1965.

Color, 25 minutes, 16mm. University of Illinois Film Center. (PS).

28. *Popol Vuh: The Creation Myth of the Maya.* (Maya) 1989. Color, 60 minutes, 16mm. (EMC).

29. *Sacred Games.* (Maya) 1989. Color, 59 minutes, 16mm. Cinema Guild. (EMC).

30. *Slash-and-Burn Agriculture.* (Nicaragua) 1975. Color, 16 minutes, VHS. B and C Films. (EMC).

31. *Swidden Horticulture among the Lacandon Maya.* (Lakandon) 1987. Color, 29 minutes, VHS. (EMC).

32. *Todos Santos Cuchumatan.* (Mam) 1982. Color, 41 minutes, 16mm. First Run Features/Icarus Films. (EMC).

33. *Todos Santos: The Survivors.* (Guatemala) 1988. Color, 55 minutes, VHS. First Run Features/Icarus Films.

34. *To Find Our Life: The Peyote Hunt of the Huichols of Mexico.* (Huichol) 1969. Produced by the Latin American Center at UCLA. Color, 60 minutes, 16mm. (PS).

35. *To Make the Balance.* (Oaxaca, Mexico; Law) 1970. Color, 33 minutes, VHS. (EMC).

36. *The Toured: The Other Side of Tourism in Barbados.* (Barbados) 1993. Color, 38 minutes, VHS. (EMC).

37. *Tremors in Guzman.* (Mexico) 1988. Produced by John Hewitt and Sam Wonderly. Color, 30 minutes, VHS. (EMC).

38. *Trique Weaving.* (Mexico; Weaving) 1971. Color, 30 minutes. University Film and Video.

39. *The Turtle People.* (Miskito) 1973. Produced by James Ward. Color, 26 minutes, 16mm. B and C Films. (PS).

40. *Tzintzuntzan in the 1990's: A Lakeside Village in Highland Mexico.* (Mexico) 1992. Color, 126 minutes. Indiana University.

41. *Voices of the Orishas.* (Cubans) 1994. Color, 37 minutes, VHS. Cinema Guild. (EMC).

42. *Voodoo and the Church in Haiti.* (Haiti) 1989. Color, 40 minutes, VHS. (EMC).

43. *Weavers in Ahuiran.* (Michoacán, Mexico) 1990. Color, 54 minutes, VHS. (EMC).

44. *Witch Doctor.* (Hatians) 1952. Story and choreography by Jean Leon Destine. B&W, 10 minutes, 16mm. Films, Incorporated. (PS).

45. *Women in Jamaica.* (Jamaica; Women) 1989. Color, 58 minutes, VHS. Films for Humanities and Sciences.

Index to Filmography

Barbados, 36
Cubans, 41
Dance of Death, 13
Farming, 9
Guatemala, 6, 13, 14, 16, 33
Guatemalan Maya, 12
Haiti, 5, 42
Haitians, 44
Huichol, 17, 34
Jamaica, 4, 45
K'iche' Maya, 15
Kiliwa, 20
Lakandon, 21, 31
Law, 35
Mam, 32
Maroons, 7
Maya, 1, 8, 10, 12, 15, 22–29, 31
Mexican Indians, 2, 3
Mexico, 1, 9, 11, 37, 38, 40
Michoacán, Mexico, 43
Miskito, 39
Mixtec, 18
Netherlands Antilles, 19
Nicaragua, 30
Oaxaca, Mexico, 35
Weaving, 38
Women, 45

Ethnonym Index

This index provides some of the alternative names and the names of major subgroups for cultures covered in this volume. The culture names that are entry titles are in boldface.

African Mexicans
Aguacateco—**Awakateko**
Aguateca—**Awakateko**
ajNenton—**Chuj**
ajSan Matéyo—**Chuj**
ajSan Sabastyán—**Chuj**
Alliouagana—**Montserratians**
Amuzgo
Andresero—**Tzotzil of San Andrés Larraínzar**
Anguillans
Antigua and Barbuda
Arubans
Awaketeco—**Awakateko**
Awakateko
Ayisyens—**Haitians**
Ayuuk—**Mixe**
Aztec—**Nahua of the Huasteca**

Bahamians
Balamiha—**Awakateko**
Barbadians
Batz'i Krisanoetike—**Tzotzil of Chamula**
Batz'i vinik—**Tzotzil of San Andrés Larraínzar**
Baudó—**Emberá and Wounaan**
Béké—**Martiniquais**
Ben 'Zaa—**Zapotec**
Bermudians
Bianco Cabécar—**Boruca, Bribri, and Cabécar**
Binii Gula'sa'—**Zapotec**
Black Carib—**Garifuna**
Blacks of Costa Rica
Bogotá—**Bugle**
Bokotá—**Bugle**
Boruca—**Boruca, Bribri, and Cabécar**
Boruca, Bribri, and Cabécar
Bribri—**Boruca, Bribri, and Cabécar**
Bribriwak Bribri—**Boruca, Bribri, and Cabécar**
Brunca Boruca—**Boruca, Bribri, and Cabécar**
Brunka Boruca—**Boruca, Bribri, and Cabécar**
Bugle
Buglere—**Bugle**
Bukueta—**Bugle**

Cabécar—**Boruca, Bribri, and Cabécar**
Cahita

Cahita—**Yaqui**
Cakchiquel—**Kaqchikel**
los Cantoneses—**Chinese of Costa Rica**
Carib of Dominica
Carifuna—**Carib of Domninica**
Catarinos—**Tzotzil and Tzeltal of Pantelhó**
Catío—**Emberá and Wounaan**
Catru—**Emberá and Wounaan**
Cattle Ranchers of the Huasteca
Cayman Islanders
Cere—**Seri**
Ceri—**Seri**
Chami—**Emberá and Wounaan**
Chamo'—**Tzotzil of Chamula**
Chamula—**Tzotzil of Chamula**
Chanabal—**Tojolab'al**
Chañabal—**Tojolab'al**
Chaneabal—**Tojolab'al**
Chatino
Cha'tno—**Chatino**
Chikapu—**Kikapu**
Chinantec
Chinese in the English-Speaking Caribbean
Chinese of Costa Rica
Chinese Royal—**Chinese in the English-Speaking Caribbean**
los Chinos—**Chinese of Costa Rica**
Chocama—**Emberá and Wounaan**
Chocho
Chochol—**Chocho**
Chocholteca—**Chocho**
Chochón—**Chocho**
Chocho-Popolocan—**Chocho**
Chochoteco—**Chocho**
Chocó—**Emberá and Wounaan**
Choko—**Emberá and Wounaan**
Chol—**Ch'ol**
Ch'ol
Cholotí—**Ch'orti'**
Chono—**Chocho**
Chontal—**Tequistlatec**
Chontales—**Chontal of Tabasco**
Chontal Maya—**Chontal of Tabasco**
Chontal Mayan—**Chontal of Tabasco**

Chontal of Oaxaca—**Tequistlatec**
Chontal of Tabasco
Chontalpa—**Tequistlatec**
Chorté—**Ch'orti'**
Chortí—**Ch'orti'**
Ch'orti'
Chucho—**Chocho**
Chuchón—**Chocho**
Chuj
Cicaque—**Jicaque**
Citará—**Emberá and Wounaan**
Cloud People—**Mixtec**
Cocopa—**Indians of Baja California**
la Colonia China—**Chinese of Costa Rica**
Colored Chinese—**Chinese in the English-Speaking Caribbean**
Comcaac—**Seri**
Cora
Coras-nayaritas—**Cora**
Costa Ricans
Creole Chinese—**Chinese in the English-Speaking Caribbean**
Creoles
Creoles—**Martiniquais**
Creoles of Nicaragua
Criollos—**Creoles of Nicaragua**
Cubans
Cuextecatl—**Wasteko**
Cuicatec
Cuna—**Kuna**
Curaçao
Curaçaoënaar—**Curaçao**

Dabeiba—**Emberá and Wounaan**
Digueño—**Indians of Baja California**
Dominicans
Dreadlocks—**Rastafarians**
Dreads—**Rastafarians**
Dzah-hmi—**Chinantec**

East Indians in Trinidad
Embená—**Emberá and Wounaan**
Emberá and Wounaan
Empená—**Emberá and Wounaan**

Emperá—**Emberá and Wounaan**
Epera—**Emberá and Wounaan**

French Antillians

Garifuna
Garifuna—**Carib of Dominica**
Garinagu—**Garifuna**
Grenadians
Guabi—**Huave**
Guadeloupians
Guarijío—**Guarijío**
Guarijío
Guarogíos—**Guarijío**
Guatuso—**Maleku**
Guatuzo—**Maleku**
Guayma—**Seri**
Guaymí—**Ngawbe**
Guaymí-Sabanero—**Bugle**

Haitians
Haïtiens—**Haitians**
Haqui—**Cahita**
Haytians—**Haitians**
Heri—**Seri**
Hicaque—**Jicaque**
Himberá—**Emberá and Wounaan**
Hñahñu/Hñą hñų —**Otomí of the Sierra;
    Otomí of the Valley of Mezquital**
Hochón—**Chocho**
Huabi—**Huave**
Huarijío—**Guarijío**
Huastec—**Wasteko**
Huave
Huavi—**Huave**
Huazontecos—**Huave**
Huhmei—**Chinantec**
Huichol
Huichole—**Huichol**
Humberá—**Emberá and Wounaan**

Ikake—**Jicaque**
Indians of Baja California
Indians of Venustiano Carranza—**Tzotzil of
    San Bartolomé de los Llanos**
Indo-Trinidadians—**East Indians in Trinidad**
Island Carib—**Carib of Dominica; Garifuna**
Italian Mexicans
Itza'
Itzá—**Itza'**
Itzaj Maya—**Itza'**
Itzá Maya—**Itza'**
Ixcatec-Chocho—**Chocho**
Ixil

Jacalteco—**Jakalteko**
Jaika—**Maleku**
Jakalteko
Jamaicans
Jicaque
Jocolabal—**Tojolab'al**
Jojolabal—**Tojolab'al**
Juave—**Huave**

Kabekirwak Cabécar—**Boruca, Bribri, and
    Cabécar**
Kakchiquel—**Kaqchikel**
Kanhobal—**Q'anjob'al**

Kanjobal—**Q'anjob'al**
Kaqchikel
Karaphuna—**Garifuna**
Katío—**Emberá and Wounaan**
Kekchí—**Q'eqchi'**
K'ekchí—**Q'eqchi'**
K'iche'
Kickapoo—**Kikapu**
Kikapu
Kiliwi—**Indians of Baja California**
Kittitians—**Kittsians and Nevisians**
Kittsians and Nevisians
Korsou—**Curaçao**
Kuna
Kurasoleño—**Curaçao**

Lacandon—**Lakandon**
Lacandone—**Lakandon**
Ladinos
Lakandon
Lenca
Lower Pima—**Pima Bajo**
Lucians—**Saint Lucians**

Máasehual—**Yukateko**
Mācēhualmeh—**Nahuat of the Sierra de
    Puebla**
Maleku
Mam
Mames—**Mam**
Mam Maya—**Mam**
Mareños—**Huave**
Martiniquais
Maya—**Awakateko; Chontal of Tabasco;
    Ch'ol; Cho'rti'; Chuj; Itza'; Ixil;
    Jakalteko; Kaqchikel; Ki'che';
    Lakandon; Mam; Mopan; Poqomam;
    Poqomchi'; Q'anjob'al; Q'eqchi';
    Sipakapense; Tojolab'al; Tzeltal; Tzotzil
    and Tzeltal of Pantelhó; Tzotzil of
    Chamula; Tzotzil of San Andrés
    Larraínzar; Tzotzil of San Bartolomé de
    los Llanos; Tzotzil of Zinacantan;
    Tz'utujil; Uspanteko; Wasteko;
    Yukateko**
Mayangna—**Sumu**
Mayero—**Itza'; Yukateko**
Mayo—**Cahita**
Mazahua
Mazatec
mestizo rancheros—**Cattle Ranchers of the
    Huasteca**
Metropolitans—**Martiniquais**
Mexica—**Nahuat of the Sierra de Peubla**
Mexicano—**Nahua Peoples; Nahua of the
    Huasteca; Nahua of the State of Mexico;
    Nahuat of the Sierra de Puebla**
Mexijcatl—**Nahua of the Huasteca**
Michuguaca—**Tarascans**
Mije—**Mixe**
Miskito
Miskito Coast Creoles—**Creoles of
    Nicaragua**
Miskitu—**Miskito**
Mixe
Mixtec
Montserratians
Mopan

Mopane—**Mopan**
Mopanero—**Mopan**
Mopán Maya—**Mopan**
Morenos—**Creoles of Nicaragua**
Moskito—**Miskito**
Mosqueto—**Miskito**
Mosquito—**Miskito**
Moustique—**Miskito**
Move—**Ngawbe**
Movere—**Ngawbe**
Muri—**Bugle**
Murire—**Bugle**

Nahua of the Huasteca
Nahua of the State of Mexico
Nahua Peoples
Nahuat of the Sierra de Puebla
Ñą ñų —**Otomí of the Sierra**
Nati Dread—**Rastafarians**
Nayares—**Cora**
Nayaritas—**Cora**
Negros—**Creoles of Nicaragua**
Netherlands Antillians
Ngäbe—**Ngawbe**
Ngawbe
Ngawbére—**Ngawbe**
Ngóbe—**Ngawbe**
Noanabs—**Emberá and Wounaan**
Noanamá—**Emberá and Wounaan**
Noanes—**Emberá and Wounaan**
Nonamá—**Emberá and Wounaan**
Nonameño—**Emberá and Wounaan**
Northern Tepehuan—**Tepehuan of
    Chihuahua**
Ñų hų —**Otomí of the Sierra**
Ñuu Savi—**Mixtec**
N'yũhũ—**Otomí of the Sierra**

Ódami—**Tepehuan of Chihuahua**
Ohlwa—**Sumu**
Oirubae—**Arubans**
Olua—**Sumu**
Óob—**Pima Bajo**
ÓOdham—**Pima Bajo**
'O'odham—**Pima Bajo**
Opata
Ópata—**Opata**
Opatoro—**Lenca**
Ora Oubao—**Arubans**
Oro Ubo—**Arubans**
Otomí of the Sierra
Otomí of the Sierra Norte de
    Puebla—**Otomí of the Sierra**
Otomí of the Southern Huasteca—**Otomí
    of the Sierra**
Otomí of the Valley of Mezquital
Overseas Indians—**East Indians in
    Trinidad**

Pahaya—**Paya**
Paipai—**Indians of Baja California**
Pame
Panamaka—**Sumu**
Panoteca—**Wasteko**
Pawyer—**Paya**
Paya
Pech—**Paya**
People of Nevis—**Kittsians and Nevisians**

People of Saint Kitts—**Kittsians and Nevisians**
Pesch—**Paya**
Petén Maya—**Itza'**
Phorhépicha—**Tarascans**
Phurhépecha—**Tarascans**
Pima Bajo
Pipil
Pocomám—**Poqomam**
Pocomán—**Poqomam**
Poconchí—**Poqomchi'**
Pokomám—**Poqomam**
Pokomán—**Poqomam**
Pokomchí—**Poqomchi'**
Pokonchi—**Poqomchi'**
Popoloca
Popoluca
Popya—**Paya**
Poqomam
Poqomchi'
Poya—**Paya**
Poyai—**Paya**
Poyer—**Paya**
Puerto Ricans
Puertorriqueños—**Puerto Ricans**
Purepecha—**Tarascans**
Purépecha—**Tarascans**

Q'anjob'al
Q'eqchi'
Quiché—**K'iche'**

Ralámuli—**Tarahumara**
Rama
rancheros—**Cattle Ranchers of the Huasteca**
Rarámuri—**Tarahumara**
Rastafari—**Rastafarians**
Rastafarians
Rastas—**Rastafarians**
Río Verde—**Emberá and Wounaan**

Sabanero—**Bugle**
Sadi—**Seri**
Saija—**Emberá and Wounaan**
Saint Lucians
Salineros—**Seri**
San Bartoleños—**Tzotzil of San Bartolomé de los Llanos**
San Jorge—**Emberá and Wounaan**
San Joseños—**Itza'**
San Juan Chamula—**Tzotzil of Chamula**
Santa Catarina Pantelhó—**Tzotzil and Tzeltal of Pantelhó**
Seco—**Paya**
Se'ie Bribri—**Boruca, Bribri, and Cabécar**
Seri
Shuta enima—**Mazatec**
Sierra Nahuat—**Nahuat of the Sierra de Puebla**
Sipacapa Quiché—**Sipakapense**
Sipacapeño—**Sipakapense**
Sipacapense—**Sipakapense**
Sipakapense
Smoo—**Sumu**

Smu—**Sumu**
Somoo—**Sumu**
Soques—**Zoque**
Sori—**Seri**
Sotz'leb—**Tzotzil of Zinacantan**
Summoo—**Sumu**
Sumo—**Sumu**
Sumoo—**Sumu**
Sumu

Tadó—**Emberá and Wounaan**
Taguaca—**Jicaque; Sumu**
Tahuajca—**Sumu**
Taia—**Paya**
Talamanca Bribri—**Boruca, Bribri, and Cabécar**
Taoajka—**Sumu**
Tasioteños—**Seri**
Taupane—**Jicaque**
Tarahumar—**Tarahumara**
Tarahumara
Tarahumari—**Tarahumara**
Tarascans
Tarascos—**Tarascans**
Taraumar—**Tarahumara**
Tawahka—**Sumu**
Tawka—**Paya**
Taya—**Paya**
Teenek—**Wasteko**
Tehueco—**Cahita**
Tepehua
Tepehuan of Chihuahua
Tepehuan of Durango
Tepoca—**Seri**
Tequistlatec
Tequistlateco—**Tequistlatec**
Teribe
Terraba—**Teribe**
Tevi—**Huichol**
Tiburone—**Seri**
Tico—**Costa Ricans**
Tipai—**Indians of Baja California**
Tlapanec
Tojolabal—**Tojolab'al**
Tojolab'al
Tol—**Jicaque**
Tolpan—**Jicaque**
Torrupan—**Jicaque**
Totiketik—**Tzotzil of San Bartolomé de los Llanos**
Totiques—**Tzotzil of San Bartolomé de los Llanos**
Totonac
Totonaca—**Totonac**
Totonaco—**Totonac**
Towcka—**Sumu**
Trinidadians and Tobagonians
Triques—**Triqui**
Triqui
Tsapotecatl—**Zapotec**
Tsoque—**Zoque**
Tule—**Kuna**
Tulemala—**Kuna**
Turks and Caicos Islanders
Twahka—**Sumu**
Twaka—**Sumu**

Twanka—**Sumu**
Twaxha—**Sumu**
Tzeltal
Tzoques—**Zoque**
Tzotzil and Tzeltal of Pantelhó
Tzotziles—**Tzotzil of San Bartolomé de, los Llanos**
Tzotzil of Chamula
Tzotzil of San Andrés Larraínzar
Tzotzil of San Bartolomé de los Llanos
Tzotzil of Zinacantan
Tz'utujil

Ulúa—**Sumu**
Ulwa—**Sumu**
Upanguayma—**Seri**
Uspantec—**Uspanteko**
Uspanteco—**Uspanteko**
Uspanteko

Varohío—**Guarijío**
Varohíos—**Guarijío**
Varojíos—**Guarijío**
Viceita Bribri—**Boruca, Bribri, and Cabécar**
Vinuk—**Tz'utujil**
Virgin Islanders

Wabi—**Huave**
Wa-hmi—**Chinantec**
Warijío—**Guarijío**
Warijíos—**Guarijío**
Wasteko
Waunama—**Emberá and Wounaan**
Waunan—**Emberá and Wounaan**
Waunana—**Emberá and Wounaan**
Wizarika—**Huichol**
Woolwa—**Sumu**
Woowa—**Sumu**
Wounaan—**Emberá and Wounaan**
Wounan—**Emberá and Wounaan**
Wulwa—**Sumu**

Xicaque—**Jicaque**
Xinca

Yahval lum—**Tzotzil of San Andrés Larraínzar**
Yaqui
Yaqui—**Cahita**
Yocotan—**Chontal of Tabasco**
Yoeme—**Yaqui**
Yokot'an—**Chontal of Tabasco**
Yoreme—**Yaqui**
Yu di Korsou—**Curaçao**
Yukateko

Za—**Zapotec**
Zapotec
Zapoteco—**Zapotec**
Zinacantecos—**Tzotzil of Zinacantan**
Zinacantecs—**Tzotzil of Zinacantan**
Zoc—**Zoque**
Zoque
Zumo—**Sumu**

The Editors

Editor in Chief

David Levinson (Ph.D., State University of New York at Buffalo) is vice-president of the Human Relations Area Files, in New Haven, Connecticut. He is a cultural anthropologist whose primary research interests are in social issues, worldwide comparative research, and social theory. He has conducted research on homelessness, alcohol abuse, aggression, family relations, and ethnicity. Among his dozens of publications are the award-winning text *Toward Human Culture* (with Martin J. Malone), *The Tribal Living Book* (with David Sherwood), and *Family Violence in Cross-Cultural Perspective*. Dr. Levinson also teaches anthropology at Albertus Magnus College in New Haven, Connecticut.

Volume Editor

James W. Dow (Ph.D., Brandeis University), professor of anthropology at Oakland University, has studied indigenous cultures since 1963. His major fieldwork has been conducted among the Otomí-speaking people of the eastern sierra of Hidalgo, concerning whom he has published three books, *Santos y supervivencias*, *The Otomí of the Northern Sierra de Puebla*, and *The Shaman's Touch*. He has been a Fulbright Scholar and the recipient of a research award from the Society for the Scientific Study of Religion. He is the coeditor of and a contributor to *Peasant Livelihood: Studies in Economic Anthropology and Cultural Ecology* and *Class, Politics, and Popular Religion in Mexico and Central America*. He is also the author of articles appearing in various journals such as *American Anthropologist*, *Human Organization*, *Peasant Studies*, and *Social Science Information*. He is a member of the executive committee of the Central States Anthropological Society and is the treasurer of the Society for Latin American Anthropology. Besides studying the ethnology of Middle America, he has an interest in anthropological methods, both qualitative and quantitative, and is administrator of the ANTHAP computer network that serves the Society for Applied Anthropology and the National Association for the Practice of Anthropology.

Associate Editor

Robert V. Kemper (Ph.D., University of California, Berkeley) is professor of anthropology at Souther Methodist University, Dallas, Texas. He has served as president of the Society for Urban Anthropology and as copresident of the Society for Latin American Anthropology. He has been editor for socio-cultural anthropology of the *American Anthropologist*, associate editor of *Urban Anthropology*, and editor of *Human Organization*. He is a member of the executive board of the Council for the Preservation of Anthropological Records, has been a member of the executive board of the American Anthropological Association, and is the founding chair of the Commission on the Anthropology of Tourism of the International Union of Anthropological and Ethnological Sciences. He has published widely on migration, urban studies, tourism, the history of anthropology, applied anthropology, and education, with a special focus on Mexico and Hispanic populations. His major publications include *Anthroplogists in Cities* (coedited with George M. Foster); *Migration and Adaptation: Tzintzuntzan Peasants in Mexico City*; *The History of Anthropology: A Research Bibliography* (with John F. S. Phinney); *Metropolitan Latin America: The Challenge and the Response* (coedited with Wayne A. Cornelius); *Long-Term Field Research in Social Anthropology* (coedited with George M. Foster, Thayer Scudder, and Elizabeth Colson); and *Migration across Frontiers: Mexico and the United States* (coedited with Fernando Cámara).